Webster's Dictionary for Students

FEDERAL
STREET
PRESS

A Division of Merriam-Webster, Incorporated
Springfield, Massachusetts

This 2003 edition published by
Federal Street Press,
A Division of Merriam-Webster, Incorporated
P.O. Box 281
Springfield, MA 01102

Federal Street Press books are available for bulk purchase for sales promotion and premium use. For details write the manager of special sales, Federal Street Press, P.O. Box 281, Springfield, MA 01102

ISBN 1-892859-55-6

Printed in the United States of America
04 05 06 07   5 4

Preface

This dictionary has been specially written for students in the elementary grades. It is intended as a student's first real dictionary. While it has many of the features of the larger dictionaries meant for adults, the meanings are written in easy-to-understand language. In this dictionary are the meanings and uses of more than 32,000 words and phrases—words that most elementary students need to look up.

While this dictionary is written in simple language, it has the features of much larger dictionaries. There are a number of things that dictionaries must do to save space on the printed page, and it is important to understand these features to allow you to make best use of your dictionary. The rest of this Preface explains these features.

The **bold** word that begins an entry is known as the **main entry word**. All of the material in the entry is related to the main entry word or to derived words or phrases that also appear in the entry.

> **as·pen** *n* : a poplar tree whose leaves move
> easily in the breeze

Centered dots in the bold forms show where the words may be hyphenated at the end of a line on a page and they serve as an aid in sounding out the words.

Other bold forms may appear in this entry, such as **variant spellings** and **inflected forms** of the main entry word. Inflected forms are the plurals of nouns, the principal parts of verbs, or the comparative and superlative forms of adjectives.

> **¹cad·die** *or* **cad·dy** *n, pl* **cad·dies** : a person
> who carries a golfer's clubs
> **¹free** *adj* **fre·er; fre·est 1** : having liberty : not
> being a slave . . .
> **pul·sate** *vb* **pul·sat·ed; pul·sat·ing** : to have
> or show a pulse or beats

Other bold items in the entry may be **defined run-on phrases** that have the main entry word in the phrase and **run-in entries**, that are being explained in the definition itself.

> **¹stand** *vb* . . . — **stand by** : to be or remain
> loyal or true to — **stand for 1** : to be a
> symbol for . . . **2** : to put up with . . .
> **chest·nut** *n* **1** : a sweet edible nut that grows
> in burs on a tree (**chestnut tree**) related to
> the beech . . .

One of the more common bold forms appearing at an entry is the **undefined run-on entry**. This is a word at the end of an entry that is derived from the main entry by the addition of a common word ending (suffix).

> **har·mo·ni·ous** . . . — **har·mo·ni·ous·ly** *adv*
> — **har·mo·ni·ous·ness** *n*

Since you know the meaning of the main entry word and the meaning of the suffix, the meaning of the run-on entry is self-explanatory.

The way a word is used in a sentence, its *function*, sometimes called its *part of speech*, is indicated by any of several *italic* abbreviations: *n* for noun (**cat, dog, mother**), *vb* for verb (**run, jump, cry**), *adj* for adjective (**blue, tall, happy**), *adv* for adverb (**easily, fast, nearby**), *pron* for pronoun (**who, them, none**), *conj* for conjunction (**and, but, if**), *prep* for preposition (**about, for, to**), and *interj* for interjection (**hello, adios**). Others include *helping verb* (**may, can**), *prefix* (**anti-, bio-**), and *suffix* (**-age, -er, -graph**).

When there are two or more words that have the same spelling but are different in their meanings or how they function in a sentence, these are distinguished by a small superscript numeral in front of the spelling. The numeral is not part of the spelling; it is there in this dictionary to distinguish these identically spelled words (call **homographs**).

> ¹**seal** *n* **1** : a sea mammal . . .
> ²**seal** *n* **1** : something (as a pledge) that makes safe or secure
> ³**seal** *vb* **1** : to mark with a seal . . .

One very important way a dictionary saves space when two or more words have the same meaning is by putting the definition at the more common word and linking to that entry by means of a **cross-reference** in SMALL CAPITALS. Look at the following.

> **ductless gland** *n* : ENDOCRINE GLAND

The treatment here tells you to look at the entry **endocrine gland** for a definition of both *ductless gland* and *endocrine gland*. And this treatment tells you also that *ductless gland* and *endocrine gland* are **synonyms**.

Sometimes the synonym cross-reference is used in place of a definition and sometimes following a definition.

> **hare·brained** *adj* : FOOLISH
> **staunch** *adj* **1** : strongly built : SUBSTANTIAL

When the synonym cross-reference has a following sense number or has a superscript homograph number attached, it tells you which specific sense number and which homograph to look to for the shared meaning.

> ¹**dain·ty** *n, pl* **dain·ties** : DELICACY 1
> **mom** *n* : ¹MOTHER 1

Your dictionary also guides you in the way a particular word is used. **Usage notes** may follow a definition or be used in place of a definition

> **air·wave** *n* : the radio waves used in radio and television transmission — usually used in pl.
> **rev·er·end** *adj* . . . **2** — used as a title for a member of the clergy

Guidance on capitalization for entries where the main entry word is not shown capitalized is usually shown by an italic note at the beginning of the definition.

> **brus·sels sprouts** *n pl, often cap B* : green heads like tiny cabbages. . .

As a special added feature, this dictionary has, ahead of the main A-Z section, a separate list of commonly used Abbreviations, and following the main A-Z section a special section of Confused, Misused, or Misspelled Words.

Abbreviations

Most of these abbreviations are shown in one form only. Variation in use of periods, in kind of type, and in capitalization is frequent and widespread (as *mph, MPH, m.p.h., Mph*)

abbr abbreviation
AD in the year of our Lord
adj adjective
adv adverb
AK Alaska
AL, Ala Alabama
alt alternate, altitude
a.m., A.M. before noon
Am, Amer America, American
amt amount
anon anonymous
ans answer
Apr April
AR Arkansas
Ariz Arizona
Ark Arkansas
assn association
asst assistant
atty attorney
Aug August
ave avenue
AZ Arizona

BC before Christ
bet between
bldg building
blvd boulevard
Br, Brit Britain, British
bro brother
bros brothers
bu bushel

c carat, cent, centimeter, century, chapter, cup
C Celsius, centigrade
CA, Cal, Calif California
Can, Canad Canada, Canadian
cap capital, capitalize, capitalized
Capt captain
ch chapter, church
cm centimeter
co company, county
CO Colorado
COD cash on delivery, collect on delivery
col column
Col colonel, Colorado
Colo Colorado
conj conjunction
Conn Connecticut
cpu central processing unit

ct cent, court
CT Connecticut
cu cubic
CZ Canal Zone

d penny
DC District of Columbia
DDS doctor of dental surgery
DE Delaware
Dec December
Del Delaware
dept department
DMD doctor of dental medicine
doz dozen
Dr doctor
DST daylight saving time

E east, eastern, excellent
ea each
e.g. for example
Eng England, English
esp especially
etc et cetera

f false, female, forte
F Fahrenheit
FBI Federal Bureau of Investigation
Feb February
fem feminine
FL, Fla Florida
fr father, from
Fri Friday
ft feet, foot, fort

g gram
G good
Ga, GA Georgia
gal gallon
GB gigabyte
gen general
geog geographic, geographical, geography
gm gram
gov governor
govt government
gt great
GU Guam

HI Hawaii
hr hour
HS high school

ht height

Ia, IA Iowa
ID Idaho
i.e. that is
IL, Ill Illinois
in inch
IN Indiana
inc incorporated
Ind Indian, Indiana
interj interjection
intrans intransitive

Jan January
jr, jun junior

Kan, Kans Kansas
KB kilobyte
kg kilogram
km kilometer
KS Kansas
Ky, KY Kentucky

l left, liter
La, LA Louisiana
lb pound
Lt lieutenant
ltd limited

m male, meter, mile
MA Massachusetts

Maj major
Mar March
masc masculine
Mass Massachusetts
MB megabyte
Md Maryland
MD doctor of medicine, Maryland
Me, ME Maine
Mex Mexican, Mexico
mg milligram
MI, Mich Michigan
min minute
Minn Minnesota
Miss Mississippi
ml milliliter
mm millimeter
MN Minnesota
mo month
Mo, MO Missouri
Mon Monday
Mont Montana

Abbreviations

mpg miles per gallon
mph miles per hour
MS Mississippi
mt mount, mountain
MT Montana

n noun
N north, northern
NC North Carolina
ND, N Dak North Dakota
NE Nebraska, northeast
Neb, Nebr Nebraska
Nev Nevada
NH New Hampshire
NJ New Jersey
NM, N Mex New Mexico
no north, number
Nov November
NV Nevada
NW northwest
NY New York

O Ohio
obj object, objective
Oct October
off office
OH Ohio
OK, Okla Oklahoma
OR, Ore, Oreg Oregon
oz ounce, ounces

p page
Pa, PA Pennsylvania
part participle
pat patent
Penn, Penna Pennsylvania
pg page
pk park, peck
pkg package
pl plural
p.m., P.M. afternoon
PO post office
poss possessive
pp pages
pr pair
PR Puerto Rico
prep preposition

pres present, president
prof professor
pron pronoun
PS postscript, public school
pt pint, point
PTA Parent-Teacher
   Association
PTO Parent-Teacher
   Organization

qt quart

r right
rd road, rod
recd received
reg region, regular
res residence
Rev reverend
RFD rural free delivery
RI Rhode Island
rpm revolutions per minute
RR railroad
RSVP please reply
rt right
rte route

S south, southern
Sat Saturday
SC South Carolina
sci science
Scot Scotland, Scottish
SD, S Dak South Dakota
SE southeast
sec second
Sept September
SI International System of
   Units
sing singular
so south
sq square
sr senior
Sr sister
SS steamship
st state, street
St saint
Sun Sunday
SW southwest

t true
tbs, tbsp tablespoon
TD touchdown
Tenn Tennessee
Tex Texas
Thurs, Thu Thursday
TN Tennessee
trans transitive
tsp teaspoon
Tues, Tue Tuesday
TX Texas

UN United Nations
US United States
USA United States of
   America
USSR Union of Soviet
   Socialist Republics
usu usual, usually
UT Utah

v verb
Va, VA Virginia
var variant
vb verb
VG very good
vi verb intransitive
VI Virgin Islands
vol volume
VP vice president
vs versus
vt verb transitive
Vt, VT Vermont

W west, western
WA, Wash Washington
Wed Wednesday
WI, Wis, Wisc Wisconsin
wk week
wt weight
WV, W Va West Virginia
WWW World Wide Web
WY, Wyo Wyoming

yd yard
yr year

A

¹a *n, pl* **a's** *or* **as** *often cap* **1** : the first letter of the English alphabet **2** : a grade that shows a student's work is excellent

²a *indefinite article* **1** : some one not identified or known **2** : the same **3** : ¹ANY 1 **4** : for or from each

a- *prefix* **1** : on : in : at **2** : in (such) a state, condition, or manner **3** : in the act or process of

aard·vark *n* : an African animal with a long snout and a long sticky tongue that feeds mostly on ants and termites and is active at night

ab- *prefix* : from : differing from

aback *adv* : by surprise

aba·cus *n, pl* **aba·ci** *or* **aba·cus·es** : an instrument for doing arithmetic by sliding counters along rods or in grooves

abaft *adv* : toward or at the back part of a ship

ab·a·lo·ne *n* : a large sea snail that has a flattened shell with a pearly lining

¹aban·don *vb* **1** : to give up completely : FORSAKE **2** : to give (oneself) up to a feeling or emotion — **aban·don·ment** *n*

²abandon *n* : a complete yielding to feelings or wishes

aban·doned *adj* : given up : left empty or unused

abash *vb* : to destroy the self-confidence of

abate *vb* **abat·ed; abat·ing** : to make or become less

ab·bess *n* : the head of an abbey for women

ab·bey *n, pl* **abbeys** **1** : MONASTERY, CONVENT **2** : a church that once belonged to an abbey

ab·bot *n* : the head of an abbey for men

ab·bre·vi·ate *vb* **ab·bre·vi·at·ed; ab·bre·vi·at·ing** : to make briefer : SHORTEN

ab·bre·vi·a·tion *n* **1** : a making shorter **2** : a shortened form of a word or phrase

ab·di·cate *vb* **ab·di·cat·ed; ab·di·cat·ing** : to give up a position of power or authority

ab·di·ca·tion *n* : the giving up of a position of power or authority

ab·do·men *n* **1** : the part of the body between the chest and the hips including the cavity in which the chief digestive organs lie **2** : the hind part of the body of an arthropod (as an insect)

ab·dom·i·nal *adj* : of, relating to, or located in the abdomen

ab·duct *vb* : to take a person away by force : KIDNAP

ab·duc·tion *n* : the act of abducting

abeam *adv or adj* : on a line at right angles to a ship's keel

abed *adv or adj* : in bed

ab·er·ra·tion *n* : a differing from what is normal or usual

ab·hor *vb* **ab·horred; ab·hor·ring** : to shrink from in disgust : LOATHE

ab·hor·rent *adj* : causing or deserving strong dislike

abide *vb* **abode** *or* **abid·ed; abid·ing** **1** : to bear patiently : TOLERATE **2** : ENDURE 1 **3** : to live in a place : DWELL — **abide by** : to accept the terms of : OBEY

abil·i·ty *n, pl* **abil·i·ties** **1** : power to do something **2** : natural talent or acquired skill

-abil·i·ty *also* **-ibil·i·ty** *n suffix, pl* **-abil·i·ties** *also* **-ibil·i·ties** : ability, fitness, or likeliness to act or be acted upon in (such) a way

ab·ject *adj* : low in spirit or hope — **ab·ject·ly** *adv* — **ab·ject·ness** *n*

ablaze *adj* **1** : being on fire **2** : bright with light or color

able *adj* **abler; ablest** **1** : having enough power or skill to do something **2** : having or showing much skill

-able *also* **-ible** *adj suffix* **1** : capable of, fit for, or worthy of being **2** : tending or likely to — **-ably** *also* **-ibly** *adv suffix*

ably *adv* : in an able way

ab·nor·mal *adj* : differing from the normal usually in a noticeable way — **ab·nor·mal·ly** *adv*

¹aboard *adv* : on, onto, or within a ship, train, bus, or airplane

²aboard *prep* : on or into especially for passage

¹abode *past of* ABIDE

²abode *n* : the place where one stays or lives

abol·ish *vb* : to do away with : put an end to

ab·o·li·tion *n* : a complete doing away with

A–bomb *n* : ATOMIC BOMB

abom·i·na·ble *adj* **1** : deserving or causing disgust **2** : very disagreeable or unpleasant — **abom·i·na·bly** *adv*

abominable snow·man *n, often cap A&S* : a mysterious creature with human or apelike characteristics reported to exist in the Himalayas

abom·i·na·tion *n* : something abominable

ab·orig·i·ne *n, pl* **ab·orig·i·nes** : a member of the original race to live in a region : NATIVE

abound *vb* **1** : to be plentiful : TEEM **2** : to be fully supplied

¹about *adv* **1** : ALMOST, NEARLY **2** : on all sides : AROUND **3** : one after another **4** : in the opposite direction

²**about** *prep* **1** : on every side of : AROUND **2** : on the point of **3** : having to do with

¹**above** *adv* : in or to a higher place

²**above** *prep* **1** : higher than : OVER **2** : too good for **3** : more than

³**above** *adj* : said or written earlier

¹**above·board** *adv* : in an honest open way

²**aboveboard** *adj* : free from tricks and secrecy

ab·ra·ca·dab·ra *n* : a magical charm or word

abrade *vb* **abrad·ed; abrad·ing** : to wear away by rubbing

¹**abra·sive** *n* : a substance for grinding, smoothing, or polishing

²**abrasive** *adj* : having the effect of or like that of abrading

abreast *adv or adj* **1** : side by side **2** : up to a certain level of knowledge

abridge *vb* **abridged; abridg·ing** : to shorten by leaving out some parts

abridg·ment *or* **abridge·ment** *n* : a shortened form of a written work

abroad *adv or adj* **1** : over a wide area **2** : in the open : OUTDOORS **3** : in or to a foreign country **4** : known to many people

abrupt *adj* **1** : happening without warning : SUDDEN **2** : ¹STEEP 1 — **abrupt·ly** *adv* — **abrupt·ness** *n*

ab·scess *n* : a collection of pus with swollen and red tissue around it — **ab·scessed** *adj*

ab·sence *n* **1** : a being away **2** : ²LACK 1, WANT

¹**ab·sent** *adj* **1** : not present **2** : not existing **3** : showing that one is not paying attention

²**ab·sent** *vb* : to keep (oneself) away

ab·sen·tee *n* : a person who is absent

ab·sent·mind·ed *adj* : not paying attention to what is going on or to what one is doing — **ab·sent·mind·ed·ly** *adv* — **ab·sent·mind·ed·ness** *n*

ab·so·lute *adj* **1** : free from imperfection : PERFECT, COMPLETE **2** : free from control or conditions **3** : free from doubt : CERTAIN — **ab·so·lute·ly** *adv* — **ab·so·lute·ness** *n*

ab·so·lu·tion *n* : a forgiving of sins

ab·solve *vb* **ab·solved; ab·solv·ing** : to set free from a duty or from blame

ab·sorb *vb* **1** : to take in or swallow up **2** : to hold all of one's interest **3** : to receive without giving back

ab·sor·ben·cy *n* : the quality or state of being absorbent

ab·sor·bent *adj* : able to absorb

ab·sorp·tion *n* **1** : the process of absorbing or being absorbed **2** : complete attention

ab·stain *vb* : to keep oneself from doing something — **ab·stain·er** *n*

ab·sti·nence *n* : an avoiding by choice especially of certain foods or of liquor

¹**ab·stract** *adj* **1** : expressing a quality apart from an actual person or thing that posseses it **2** : hard to understand — **ab·stract·ly** *adv* — **ab·stract·ness** *n*

²**ab·stract** *n* : ²SUMMARY

³**ab·stract** *vb* **1** : to take away : SEPARATE **2** : SUMMARIZE

ab·strac·tion *n* **1** : the act of abstracting : the state of being abstracted **2** : an abstract idea

ab·struse *adj* : hard to understand — **ab·struse·ly** *adv* — **ab·struse·ness** *n*

ab·surd *adj* : completely unreasonable or untrue : RIDICULOUS — **ab·surd·ly** *adv*

ab·sur·di·ty *n, pl* **ab·sur·di·ties** **1** : the fact of being absurd **2** : something that is absurd

abun·dance *n* : a large quantity : PLENTY

abun·dant *adj* : more than enough : PLENTIFUL — **abun·dant·ly** *adv*

¹**abuse** *n* **1** : a dishonest practice **2** : wrong or unfair treatment or use **3** : harsh insulting language

²**abuse** *vb* **abused; abus·ing** **1** : to blame or scold rudely **2** : to use wrongly : MISUSE **3** : to treat cruelly : MISTREAT

abu·sive *adj* : using or characterized by abuse — **abu·sive·ly** *adv* — **abu·sive·ness** *n*

abut *vb* **abut·ted; abut·ting** : to touch along a border or with a part that sticks out

abut·ment *n* : something against which another thing rests its weight or pushes with force

abyss *n* : a gulf so deep or space so great that it cannot be measured

ac·a·dem·ic *adj* **1** : of or relating to schools or colleges **2** : having no practical importance — **ac·a·dem·i·cal·ly** *adv*

acad·e·my *n, pl* **acad·e·mies** **1** : a private high school **2** : a high school or college where special subjects are taught **3** : a society of learned persons

ac·cede *vb* **ac·ced·ed; ac·ced·ing** : to agree to

ac·cel·er·ate *vb* **ac·cel·er·at·ed; ac·cel·er·at·ing** **1** : to bring about earlier : HASTEN **2** : to move or cause to move faster

ac·cel·er·a·tion *n* : a speeding up

ac·cel·er·a·tor *n* : a pedal in an automobile for controlling the speed of the motor

¹**ac·cent** *vb* **1** : to give a greater force or stress **2** : to mark with a written or printed accent

²**ac·cent** *n* **1** : a way of talking shared by a group (as the residents of a country) **2** : greater stress or force given to a syllable of a word in speaking or to a beat in music **3**

: a mark (as **'** or **.**) used in writing or printing to show the place of greater stress on a syllable

ac·cen·tu·ate *vb* **ac·cen·tu·at·ed; ac·cen·tu·at·ing 1** : ¹ACCENT **2** : EMPHASIZE

ac·cept *vb* **1** : to receive or take willingly **2** : to agree to

ac·cept·able *adj* **1** : worthy of being accepted **2** : ADEQUATE — **ac·cept·able·ness** *n* — **ac·cept·ably** *adv*

ac·cep·tance *n* **1** : the act of accepting **2** : the quality or state of being accepted or acceptable

ac·cess *n* **1** : the right or ability to approach, enter, or use **2** : a way or means of approach

ac·ces·si·ble *adj* **1** : capable of being reached **2** : OBTAINABLE — **ac·ces·si·bly** *adv*

ac·ces·sion *n* : a coming to a position of power

¹ac·ces·so·ry *n, pl* **ac·ces·so·ries 1** : a person who helps another in doing wrong **2** : an object or device not necessary in itself but adding to the beauty or usefulness of something else

²accessory *adj* : adding to or helping in a secondary way : SUPPLEMENTARY

ac·ci·dent *n* **1** : something that happens by chance or from unknown causes : MISHAP **2** : lack of intention or necessity : CHANCE

ac·ci·den·tal *adj* **1** : happening by chance or unexpectedly **2** : not happening or done on purpose — **ac·ci·den·tal·ly** *adv*

¹ac·claim *vb* : ¹PRAISE 1

²acclaim *n* : ²PRAISE 1, APPLAUSE

ac·cli·mate *vb* **ac·cli·mat·ed; ac·cli·mat·ing** : to change to fit a new climate or new surroundings

ac·cli·ma·tize *vb* **ac·cli·ma·tized; ac·cli·ma·tiz·ing** : ACCLIMATE

ac·com·mo·date *vb* **ac·com·mo·dat·ed; ac·com·mo·dat·ing 1** : to provide with a place to stay or sleep **2** : to provide with something needed : help out **3** : to have room for

ac·com·mo·dat·ing *adj* : ready to help — **ac·com·mo·dat·ing·ly** *adv*

ac·com·mo·da·tion *n* **1** : something supplied that is useful or handy **2 accommodations** *pl* : lodging and meals or traveling space and related services

ac·com·pa·ni·ment *n* : music played along with a solo part to enrich it

ac·com·pa·nist *n* : a musician who plays an accompaniment

ac·com·pa·ny *vb* **ac·com·pa·nied; ac·com·pa·ny·ing 1** : to go with as a companion

2 : to play a musical accompaniment for **3** : to happen at the same time as

ac·com·plice *n* : a partner in wrongdoing

ac·com·plish *vb* : to succeed in doing : manage to do

ac·com·plished *adj* : skilled through practice or training : EXPERT

ac·com·plish·ment *n* **1** : the act of accomplishing : COMPLETION **2** : something accomplished **3** : an acquired excellence or skill

¹ac·cord *vb* **1** : ¹GIVE 6 **2** : to be in harmony : AGREE

²accord *n* **1** : AGREEMENT 1, HARMONY **2** : willingness to act or to do something

ac·cor·dance *n* : AGREEMENT 1

ac·cord·ing·ly *adv* **1** : in the necessary way : in the way called for **2** : as a result : CONSEQUENTLY, SO

ac·cord·ing to *prep* **1** : in agreement with **2** : as stated by

¹ac·cor·di·on *n* : a portable keyboard musical instrument played by forcing air from a bellows past metal reeds

²accordion *adj* : folding or creased or hinged to fold like an accordion

ac·cost *vb* : to approach and speak to often in a demanding or aggressive way

¹ac·count *n* **1** : a record of money received and money paid out **2** : a statement of explanation or of reasons or causes **3** : a statement of facts or events : REPORT **4** : ²WORTH 1, IMPORTANCE — **on account of** : for the sake of : BECAUSE OF — **on no account** : not ever or for any reason

²account *vb* **1** : to think of as : CONSIDER **2** : to give an explanation **3** : to be the only or chief reason

ac·coun·tant *n* : a person whose job is accounting

ac·count·ing *n* : the work of keeping track of how much money is made and spent in a business

ac·cu·mu·late *vb* **ac·cu·mu·lat·ed; ac·cu·mu·lat·ing 1** : COLLECT 1, GATHER **2** : to increase in quantity or number

ac·cu·mu·la·tion *n* **1** : a collecting together **2** : something accumulated : COLLECTION

ac·cu·ra·cy *n* : freedom from mistakes

ac·cu·rate *adj* : free from mistakes : RIGHT — **ac·cu·rate·ly** *adv* — **ac·cu·rate·ness** *n*

ac·cu·sa·tion *n* : a claim that someone has done something bad or illegal

ac·cuse *vb* **ac·cused; ac·cus·ing** : to blame a fault, wrong, or crime on (a person) — **ac·cus·er** *n*

ac·cus·tom *vb* : to cause (someone) to get used to something

ac·cus·tomed *adj* **1** : CUSTOMARY 2, USUAL **2** : familiar with : USED

¹ace *n* **1** : a playing card with one figure in its center **2** : a person who is expert at something

²ace *adj* : of the very best kind

¹ache *vb* **ached; ach·ing 1** : to suffer a dull continuous pain **2** : YEARN

²ache *n* : a dull continuous pain

achieve *vb* **achieved; achiev·ing 1** : to bring about : ACCOMPLISH **2** : to get by means of one's own efforts : WIN

achieve·ment *n* **1** : the act of achieving **2** : something achieved especially by great effort

¹ac·id *adj* **1** : having a taste that is sour, bitter, or stinging **2** : sour in temper : CROSS **3** : of, relating to, or like an acid — **ac·id·ly** *adv*

²acid *n* : a chemical compound that tastes sour and forms a water solution which turns blue litmus paper red

acid·i·ty *n, pl* **acid·i·ties** : the quality, state, or degree of being acid

ac·knowl·edge *vb* **ac·knowl·edged; ac·knowl·edg·ing 1** : to admit the truth or existence of **2** : to recognize the rights or authority of **3** : to make known that something has been received or noticed

ac·knowl·edged *adj* : generally accepted

ac·knowl·edg·ment *or* **ac·knowl·edge·ment** *n* **1** : an act of acknowledging some deed or achievement **2** : something done or given in return for something done or received

ac·ne *n* : a skin condition in which pimples and blackheads are present

acorn *n* : the nut of the oak tree

acous·tic *or* **acous·ti·cal** *adj* **1** : of or relating to hearing or sound **2** : deadening sound

acous·tics *n sing or pl* **1** : a science dealing with sound **2** : the qualities in a room or hall that make it easy or hard for a person in it to hear clearly

ac·quaint *vb* **1** : to cause to know personally **2** : to make familiar : INFORM

ac·quain·tance *n* **1** : personal knowledge **2** : a person one knows slightly

ac·qui·esce *vb* **ac·qui·esced; ac·qui·esc·ing** : to accept, agree, or give consent by keeping silent or by not making objections

ac·qui·es·cence *n* : the act of acquiescing

ac·quire *vb* **ac·quired; ac·quir·ing** : to get especially by one's own efforts : GAIN

ac·qui·si·tion *n* **1** : the act of acquiring **2** : something acquired

ac·quis·i·tive *adj* : GREEDY **2** — **ac·quis·i·tive·ly** *adv* — **ac·quis·i·tive·ness** *n*

ac·quit *vb* **ac·quit·ted; ac·quit·ting 1** : to declare innocent of a crime or of wrongdo-ing **2** : to conduct (oneself) in a certain way

ac·quit·tal *n* : the act of acquitting someone

acre *n* : a measure of land area equal to 43,560 square feet (about 4047 square meters)

acre·age *n* : area in acres

ac·rid *adj* **1** : sharp or bitter in taste or odor **2** : very harsh or unpleasant

ac·ro·bat *n* : a person (as a circus performer) who is very good at stunts like jumping, balancing, tumbling, and swinging from things

ac·ro·bat·ic *adj* : of or relating to acrobats or acrobatics

ac·ro·bat·ics *n sing or pl* **1** : the art or performance of an acrobat **2** : stunts of or like those of an acrobat

acrop·o·lis *n* : the upper fortified part of an ancient Greek city

¹across *adv* : from one side to the other

²across *prep* **1** : to or on the opposite side of **2** : so as to pass, go over, or intersect at an angle

¹act *n* **1** : something that is done : DEED **2** : a law made by a governing body **3** : the doing of something **4** : a main division of a play

²act *vb* **1** : to perform (a part) on the stage **2** : to behave oneself in a certain way **3** : to do something : MOVE **4** : to have a result : make something happen : WORK

act·ing *adj* : serving for a short time only or in place of another

ac·tion *n* **1** : the working of one thing on another so as to produce a change **2** : the doing of something **3** : something done **4** : the way something runs or works **5** : combat in war

action figure *n* : a small figure usually of a superhero used especially as a toy

ac·ti·vate *vb* **ac·ti·vat·ed; ac·ti·vat·ing** : to make active or more active

ac·tive *adj* **1** : producing or involving action or movement **2** : showing that the subject of a sentence is the doer of the action represented by the verb **3** : quick in physical movement : LIVELY **4** : taking part in an action or activity — **ac·tive·ly** *adv*

ac·tiv·i·ty *n, pl* **ac·tiv·i·ties 1** : energetic action **2** : something done especially for relaxation or fun

ac·tor *n* : a person who acts especially in a play or movie

ac·tress *n* : a woman or girl who acts especially in a play or movie

ac·tu·al *adj* : really existing or happening : not false

ac·tu·al·ly *adv* : in fact : REALLY

acute *adj* **acut·er; acut·est 1 :** measuring less than a right angle **2 :** mentally sharp **3 :** SEVERE **4 :** developing quickly and lasting only a short time **5 :** CRITICAL 4, URGENT — **acute·ly** *adv* — **acute·ness** *n*

ad *n* **:** ADVERTISEMENT

ad·age *n* **:** an old familiar saying **:** PROVERB

ad·a·mant *adj* **:** not giving in

Ad·am's apple *n* **:** the lump formed in the front of a person's neck by cartilage in the throat

adapt *vb* **:** to make or become suitable or able to function — **adapt·er** *n*

adapt·abil·i·ty *n* **:** the quality or state of being adaptable

adapt·able *adj* **:** capable of adapting or being adapted

ad·ap·ta·tion *n* **1 :** the act or process of adapting **2 :** something adapted or helping to adapt

add *vb* **1 :** to join or unite to something **2 :** to say something more **3 :** to combine numbers into a single sum

ad·dend *n* **:** a number that is to be added to another number

ad·den·dum *n, pl* **ad·den·da :** something added (as to a book)

ad·der *n* **1 :** any of several poisonous snakes of Europe or Africa **2 :** any of several harmless North American snakes (as the **puff adder**)

¹ad·dict *vb* **:** to cause to have a need for something

²ad·dict *n* **:** a person who is addicted (as to a drug)

ad·dic·tion *n* **:** the state of being addicted (as to the use of harmful drugs)

ad·di·tion *n* **1 :** the adding of numbers to obtain their sum **2 :** something added — **in addition :** ²BESIDES, ALSO — **in addition to :** over and above **:** ¹BESIDES

ad·di·tion·al *adj* **:** ¹EXTRA — **ad·di·tion·al·ly** *adv*

¹ad·di·tive *adj* **:** relating to or produced by addition

²additive *n* **:** a substance added to another in small amounts

ad·dle *vb* **ad·dled; ad·dling :** to make confused

¹ad·dress *vb* **1 :** to apply (oneself) to something **2 :** to speak or write to **3 :** to put directions for delivery on

²ad·dress *n* **1 :** a rehearsed speech **:** LECTURE **2 :** the place where a person can usually be reached **3 :** the directions for delivery placed on mail **4 :** the symbols (as numerals or letters) that identify the location where particular information (as a home page) is stored on a computer especially on the Internet

ad·dress·ee *n* **:** the person to whom something is addressed

ad·e·noids *n pl* **:** fleshy growths near the opening of the nose into the throat

ad·ept *adj* **:** very good at something — **adept·ly** *adv* — **adept·ness** *n*

ad·e·quate *adj* **1 :** ¹ENOUGH **2 :** good enough — **ad·e·quate·ly** *adv* — **ad·e·quate·ness** *n*

ad·here *vb* **ad·hered; ad·her·ing 1 :** to stay loyal (as to a promise) **2 :** to stick tight **:** CLING

ad·her·ence *n* **:** steady or faithful attachment

ad·her·ent *n* **:** a person who adheres to a belief, an organization, or a leader

ad·he·sion *n* **:** the act or state of adhering

¹ad·he·sive *adj* **:** tending to stick **:** STICKY — **ad·he·sive·ly** *adv* — **ad·he·sive·ness** *n*

²adhesive *n* **:** an adhesive substance

adi·os *interj* — used instead of goodbye

ad·ja·cent *adj* **:** next to or near something — **ad·ja·cent·ly** *adv*

ad·jec·ti·val *adj* **:** of, relating to, or functioning as an adjective — **ad·jec·ti·val·ly** *adv*

ad·jec·tive *n* **:** a word that says something about a noun or pronoun

ad·join *vb* **:** to be next to or in contact with

ad·journ *vb* **:** to bring or come to a close for a period of time — **ad·journ·ment** *n*

ad·junct *n* **:** something joined or added to something else but not a necessary part of it

ad·just *vb* **1 :** to settle or fix by agreement **2 :** to move the parts of an instrument or a machine to make them work better **3 :** to become used to — **ad·just·er** *n*

ad·just·able *adj* **:** possible to adjust

ad·just·ment *n* **1 :** the act or process of adjusting **:** the state of being adjusted **2 :** a deciding about and paying of a claim or debt **3 :** something that is used to adjust one part to another

ad·ju·tant *n* **:** an officer who assists a commanding officer

ad–lib *vb* **ad–libbed; ad–lib·bing :** to improvise something and especially music or spoken lines

ad·min·is·ter *vb* **1 :** to be in charge of **:** MANAGE **2 :** to give out as deserved **3 :** to give or supply as treatment

ad·min·is·tra·tion *n* **1 :** the act or process of administering **2 :** the work involved in managing something **3 :** the persons who direct the business of something (as a city or school)

ad·min·is·tra·tive *adj* **:** of or relating to administration

ad·mi·ra·ble *adj* **:** deserving to be admired — **ad·mi·ra·bly** *adv*

ad·mi·ral *n* : a commissioned officer in the Navy or Coast Guard ranking above a vice admiral

ad·mi·ral·ty *adj* : of or relating to conduct on the sea

ad·mi·ra·tion *n* : great and delighted approval

ad·mire *vb* **ad·mired; ad·mir·ing** : to feel admiration for : think very highly of — **ad·mir·er** *n*

ad·mis·si·ble *adj* : deserving to be admitted or allowed : ALLOWABLE

ad·mis·sion *n* 1 : an admitting of something that has not been proved 2 : the act of admitting 3 : the right or permission to enter 4 : the price of entrance

ad·mit *vb* **ad·mit·ted; ad·mit·ting** 1 : ¹PERMIT 2, ALLOW 2 : to allow to enter : let in 3 : to make known usually with some unwillingness

ad·mit·tance *n* : permission to enter

ad·mon·ish *vb* 1 : to criticize or warn gently but seriously 2 : to give friendly advice or encouragement

ad·mo·ni·tion *n* : a gentle or friendly criticism or warning

ado *n* : fussy excitement or hurrying about

ado·be *n* 1 : brick made of earth or clay dried in the sun 2 : a building made of adobe

ad·o·les·cence *n* : the period of life between childhood and adulthood

ad·o·les·cent *n* : a person who is no longer a child but not yet adult

adopt *vb* 1 : to take (a child of other parents) as one's own 2 : to take up and practice as one's own 3 : to accept and put into action — **adopt·er** *n*

adop·tion *n* : the act of adopting : the state of being adopted

ador·able *adj* : CHARMING, LOVELY — **ador·able·ness** *n* — **ador·ably** *adv*

ad·o·ra·tion *n* : deep love

adore *vb* **adored; ador·ing** 1 : ²WORSHIP 1 2 : to be very fond of — **ador·er** *n*

adorn *vb* : to try to make prettier by adding decorations

adorn·ment *n* 1 : DECORATION 1 2 : ¹ORNAMENT 1

adrift *adv or adj* : in a drifting state

adroit *adj* : having or showing great skill or cleverness — **adroit·ly** *adv* — **adroit·ness** *n*

ad·u·la·tion *n* : very great admiration

¹adult *adj* : fully developed and mature

²adult *n* : an adult person or thing

adul·ter·ate *vb* **adul·ter·at·ed; adul·ter·at·ing** : to make impure or weaker by adding something different or of poorer quality

adult·hood *n* : the period of being an adult

¹ad·vance *vb* **ad·vanced; ad·vanc·ing** 1 : to help the progress of 2 : to move forward 3 : to raise to a higher rank 4 : to give ahead of time 5 : PROPOSE 1

²advance *n* 1 : a forward movement 2 : IMPROVEMENT 1 3 : a rise in price, value, or amount 4 : a first step or approach 5 : a giving (as of money) ahead of time — **in advance** : ¹BEFORE 1 — **in advance of** : ahead of

ad·vanced *adj* 1 : being far along in years or progress 2 : being beyond the elementary or introductory level

ad·vance·ment *n* 1 : the action of advancing : the state of being advanced 2 : a raising or being raised to a higher rank or position

ad·van·tage *n* 1 : the fact of being in a better position or condition 2 : personal benefit or gain 3 : something that benefits the one it belongs to

ad·van·ta·geous *adj* : giving an advantage : HELPFUL — **ad·van·ta·geous·ly** *adv*

ad·vent *n* : the arrival or coming of something

¹ad·ven·ture *n* 1 : an action that involves unknown dangers and risks 2 : an unusual experience

²adventure *vb* **ad·ven·tured; ad·ven·tur·ing** : to expose to or go on in spite of danger or risk — **ad·ven·tur·er** *n*

ad·ven·ture·some *adj* : likely to take risks : DARING

ad·ven·tur·ous *adj* 1 : ready to take risks or to deal with new or unexpected problems 2 : DANGEROUS 1, RISKY — **ad·ven·tur·ous·ly** *adv* — **ad·ven·tur·ous·ness** *n*

ad·verb *n* : a word used to modify a verb, an adjective, or another adverb and often used to show degree, manner, place, or time

ad·ver·bi·al *adj* : of, relating to, or used an an adverb — **ad·ver·bi·al·ly** *adv*

ad·ver·sary *n, pl* **ad·ver·sar·ies** : OPPONENT, ENEMY

ad·verse *adj* 1 : acting against or in an opposite direction 2 : not helping or favoring — **ad·verse·ly** *adv* — **ad·verse·ness** *n*

ad·ver·si·ty *n, pl* **ad·ver·si·ties** : hard times : MISFORTUNE

ad·ver·tise *vb* **ad·ver·tised; ad·ver·tis·ing** 1 : to announce publicly 2 : to call to public attention to persuade to buy 3 : to put out a public notice or request — **ad·ver·tis·er** *n*

ad·ver·tise·ment *n* : a notice or short film advertising something

ad·ver·tis·ing *n* 1 : speech, writing, pictures, or films meant to persuade people to buy something 2 : the business of preparing advertisements

ad·vice *n* : suggestions about a decision or action

ad·vis·able *adj* : reasonable or proper to do : DISCREET — **ad·vis·ably** *adv*

ad·vise *vb* **ad·vised; ad·vis·ing** **1** : to give advice to : COUNSEL **2** : to give information about something — **ad·vis·er** *or* **ad·vi·sor** *n*

ad·vi·so·ry *adj* **1** : having the power or right to advise **2** : containing advice

¹**ad·vo·cate** *n* **1** : a person who argues for another in court **2** : a person who argues for or supports an idea or plan

²**ad·vo·cate** *vb* **ad·vo·cat·ed; ad·vo·cat·ing** : to argue for

adz *or* **adze** *n* : a cutting tool that has a thin curved blade at right angles to the handle and is used for shaping wood

-aemia — see -EMIA

ae·on *or* **eon** *n* : a very long period of time : AGE

aer- *or* **aero-** *prefix* : air : atmosphere : gas

aer·ate *vb* **aer·at·ed; aer·at·ing** **1** : to supply (blood) with oxygen by breathing **2** : to supply or cause to be filled with air **3** : to combine or fill with gas — **aer·a·tor** *n*

aer·a·tion *n* : the process of aerating

¹**ae·ri·al** *adj* **1** : of, relating to, or occurring in the air **2** : running on cables or rails that are raised above the ground **3** : of or relating to aircraft **4** : taken from or used in or against aircraft — **ae·ri·al·ly** *adv*

²**aer·i·al** *n* : ANTENNA 2

ae·rie *n* : the nest of a bird (as an eagle) high on a cliff or a mountaintop

aero·nau·ti·cal *or* **aero·nau·tic** *adj* : of or relating to aeronautics

aero·nau·tics *n* : a science dealing with the building and flying of aircraft

aero·sol *n* **1** : a substance (as an insecticide) that is dispensed from a container as a spray of tiny solid or liquid particles in gas **2** : a container that dispenses an aerosol

aero·space *n* **1** : the earth's atmosphere and the space beyond **2** : a science dealing with aerospace

aes·thet·ic *or* **es·thet·ic** *adj* : of or relating to beauty and what is beautiful — **aes·thet·i·cal·ly** *adv*

¹**afar** *adv* : from, at, or to a great distance

²**afar** *n* : a long way off

af·fa·ble *adj* : polite and friendly in talking to others — **af·fa·bly** *adv*

af·fair *n* **1 affairs** *pl* : BUSINESS 1 **2** : something that relates to or involves one **3** : an action or occasion only partly specified

¹**af·fect** *vb* **1** : to be fond of using or wearing **2** : ASSUME 3

²**affect** *vb* **1** : to attack or act on as a disease does **2** : to have an effect on

af·fect·ed *adj* : not natural or genuine — **af·fect·ed·ly** *adv*

af·fect·ing *adj* : causing pity or sadness

af·fec·tion *n* : a feeling of attachment : liking for someone

af·fec·tion·ate *adj* : feeling or showing a great liking for a person or thing : LOVING — **af·fec·tion·ate·ly** *adv*

af·fi·da·vit *n* : a sworn statement in writing

af·fil·i·ate *vb* **af·fil·i·at·ed; af·fil·i·at·ing** : to associate as a member or branch

af·fin·i·ty *n, pl* **af·fin·i·ties** : a strong liking for or attraction to someone or something

af·firm *vb* **1** : to declare to be true **2** : to say with confidence : ASSERT

af·fir·ma·tion *n* : an act of affirming

¹**af·fir·ma·tive** *adj* **1** : declaring that the fact is so **2** : being positive or helpful

²**affirmative** *n* **1** : an expression (as the word *yes*) of agreement **2** : the affirmative side in a debate or vote

¹**af·fix** *vb* : FASTEN 1, 2, ATTACH

²**af·fix** *n* : a letter or group of letters that comes at the beginning or end of a word and has a meaning of its own

af·flict *vb* : to cause pain or unhappiness to

af·flic·tion *n* **1** : the state of being afflicted **2** : something that causes pain or unhappiness

af·flu·ence *n* : the state of having much money or property

af·flu·ent *adj* : having plenty of money and things that money can buy

af·ford *vb* **1** : to be able to do or bear without serious harm **2** : to be able to pay for **3** : to supply one with

¹**af·front** *vb* : to insult openly

²**affront** *n* : ²INSULT

afield *adv* **1** : to, in, or into the countryside **2** : away from home **3** : outside of one's usual circle or way of doing **4** : ASTRAY 2

afire *adj* : being on fire

aflame *adj* : burning with flames

afloat *adv or adj* : carried on or as if on water

aflut·ter *adj* **1** : flapping quickly **2** : very excited and nervous

afoot *adv or adj* **1** : on foot **2** : happening now : going on

afore·men·tioned *adj* : mentioned before

afore·said *adj* : named before

afraid *adj* : filled with fear

afresh *adv* : again from the beginning : from a new beginning

¹**Af·ri·can** *n* : a person born or living in Africa

²**African** *adj* : of or relating to Africa or the Africans

African–American *n* : AFRO-AMERICAN — **African–American** *adj*

African violet *n* : a tropical African plant grown often for its showy white, pink, or purple flowers and its velvety leaves

Af·ro–Amer·i·can *n* : an American having African and especially black African ancestors — **Afro–American** *adj*

aft *adv* : toward or at the back part of a ship or the tail of an aircraft

¹af·ter *adv* : following in time or place

²after *prep* **1** : behind in time or place **2** : for the reason of catching, seizing, or getting **3** : with the name of

³after *conj* : following the time when

⁴after *adj* **1** : later in time **2** : located toward the back part of a ship or aircraft

af·ter·ef·fect *n* : an effect that follows its cause after some time has passed

af·ter·glow *n* : a glow remaining (as in the sky after sunset) where a light has disappeared

af·ter·life *n* : an existence after death

af·ter·math *n* : a usually bad result

af·ter·noon *n* : the part of the day between noon and evening

af·ter·thought *n* : a later thought about something one has done or said

af·ter·ward *or* **af·ter·wards** *adv* : at a later time

again *adv* **1** : once more : ANEW **2** : on the other hand **3** : in addition

against *prep* **1** : opposed to **2** : as protection from **3** : in or into contact with

agape *adj* : wide open

ag·ate *n* **1** : a mineral that is a quartz with colors arranged in stripes, cloudy masses, or mossy forms **2** : a child's marble of agate or of glass that looks like agate

aga·ve *n* : a plant that has sword-shaped leaves with spiny edges and is sometimes grown for its large stalks of flowers

¹age *n* **1** : the time from birth to a specified date **2** : the time of life when a person receives full legal rights **3** : normal lifetime **4** : the later part of life **5** : a period of time associated with a special person or feature **6** : a long period of time

²age *vb* **aged; ag·ing** *or* **age·ing** **1** : to grow old or cause to grow old **2** : to remain or cause to remain undisturbed until fit for use : MATURE

-age *n suffix* **1** : collection **2** : action : process **3** : result of **4** : rate of **5** : house or place of **6** : state : rank **7** : fee : charge

aged *adj* **1** : very old **2** : of age

age·less *adj* : not growing old or showing the effects of age — **age·less·ly** *adv*

agen·cy *n, pl* **agen·cies** **1** : a person or thing through which power is used or something is achieved **2** : the office or function of an agent **3** : an establishment doing business for another **4** : a part of a government that runs projects in a certain area

agen·da *n* : a list of things to be done or talked about

agent *n* **1** : something that produces an effect **2** : a person who acts or does business for another

ag·gra·vate *vb* **ag·gra·vat·ed; ag·gra·vat·ing** **1** : to make worse or more serious **2** : to make angry by bothering again and again

ag·gra·va·tion *n* **1** : an act or the result of aggravating **2** : something that aggravates

¹ag·gre·gate *adj* : formed by the collection of units or particles into one mass or sum

²ag·gre·gate *vb* **ag·gre·gat·ed; ag·gre·gat·ing** : to collect or gather into a mass or whole

³ag·gre·gate *n* **1** : a mass or body of units or parts **2** : the whole sum or amount

ag·gre·ga·tion *n* **1** : the collecting of units or parts into a mass or whole **2** : a group, body, or mass composed of many distinct parts

ag·gres·sion *n* : an attack made without reasonable cause

ag·gres·sive *adj* **1** : showing a readiness to attack others **2** : practicing aggression **3** : being forceful and sometimes pushy — **ag·gres·sive·ly** *adv* — **ag·gres·sive·ness** *n*

ag·gres·sor *n* : a person or a country that attacks without reasonable cause

ag·grieved *adj* **1** : having a troubled or unhappy mind **2** : having cause for complaint

aghast *adj* : struck with terror or amazement

ag·ile *adj* **1** : able to move quickly and easily **2** : having a quick mind — **ag·ile·ly** *adv*

agil·i·ty *n* : the ability to move quickly and easily

aging *present participle of* AGE

ag·i·tate *vb* **ag·i·tat·ed; ag·i·tat·ing** **1** : to move with an irregular rapid motion **2** : to stir up : EXCITE **3** : to try to stir up public feeling — **ag·i·ta·tor** *n*

ag·i·ta·tion *n* : the act of agitating : the state of being agitated

agleam *adj* : giving off gleams of light

aglow *adj* : glowing with light or color

ago *adv* : before this time

agog *adj* : full of excitement

ag·o·nize *vb* **ag·o·nized; ag·o·niz·ing** : to suffer greatly in body or mind

ag·o·ny *n, pl* **ag·o·nies** : great pain of body or mind

agree *vb* **agreed; agree·ing** **1** : to give

one's approval or permission **2** : to have the same opinion **3** : ADMIT 3 **4** : to be alike **5** : to come to an understanding **6** : to be fitting or healthful

agree·able *adj* **1** : pleasing to the mind or senses **2** : willing to agree — **agree·able·ness** *n* — **agree·ably** *adv*

agree·ment *n* **1** : the act or fact of agreeing **2** : an arrangement made about action to be taken

ag·ri·cul·tur·al *adj* : of, relating to, or used in agriculture

ag·ri·cul·ture *n* : the cultivating of the soil, producing of crops, and raising of livestock

aground *adv or adj* : on or onto the shore or the bottom of a body of water

ah *interj* — used to express delight, relief, disappointment, or scorn

aha *interj* — used to express surprise, triumph, or scorn

ahead *adv or adj* **1** : in or toward the front **2** : into or for the future

ahead of *prep* **1** : in front of **2** : earlier than

ahoy *interj* — used in calling out to a passing ship or boat

¹aid *vb* : ¹HELP 1, ASSIST

²aid *n* **1** : the act of helping **2** : help given **3** : someone or something that is of help or assistance

aide *n* : a person who acts as an assistant

AIDS *n* : a serious disease of the human immune system in which large numbers of the cells that help the body fight infection are destroyed by a virus carried in the blood and other fluids of the body

ail *vb* **1** : to be wrong with **2** : to suffer especially with ill health

ai·le·ron *n* : a movable part of an airplane wing that is used to steer it to one side or the other

ail·ment *n* : SICKNESS 2

¹aim *vb* **1** : to point a weapon toward an object **2** : INTEND **3** : to direct to or toward a specified object or goal

²aim *n* **1** : the directing of a weapon or a missile at a mark **2** : ¹PURPOSE

aim·less *adj* : lacking purpose — **aim·less·ly** *adv* — **aim·less·ness** *n*

¹air *n* **1** : the invisible mixture of odorless tasteless gases that surrounds the earth **2** : air that is compressed **3** : outward appearance **4** : AIRCRAFT **5** : AVIATION **6** : a radio or television system **7 airs** *pl* : an artificial way of acting

²air *vb* **1** : to place in the air for cooling, freshening, or cleaning **2** : to make known in public

air bag *n* : an automobile safety device consisting of a bag that will inflate automatically in front of a rider to act as a cushion in an accident

air base *n* : a base of operations for military aircraft

air–con·di·tion *vb* : to equip with a device for cleaning air and controlling its humidity and temperature — **air con·di·tion·er** *n* — **air–con·di·tion·ing** *n*

air·craft *n, pl* **aircraft** : a vehicle (as a balloon, airplane, or helicopter) that can travel through the air and that is supported either by its own lightness or by the action of the air against its surfaces

air·drome *n* : AIRPORT

air·field *n* **1** : the landing field of an airport **2** : AIRPORT

air force *n* : the military organization of a nation for air warfare

air lane *n* : AIRWAY 2

air·lift *n* : a system of moving people or cargo by aircraft usually to or from an area that cannot be reached otherwise

air·line *n* : a system of transportation by aircraft including its routes, equipment, and workers

air·lin·er *n* : a large passenger airplane flown by an airline

¹air·mail *n* **1** : the system of carrying mail by airplanes **2** : mail carried by airplanes

²airmail *vb* : to send by airmail

air·man *n, pl* **air·men** **1** : an enlisted person in the Air Force in one of the ranks below sergeant **2** : AVIATOR

airman basic *n* : an enlisted person of the lowest rank in the Air Force

airman first class *n* : an enlisted person in the Air Force ranking above an airman second class

airman second class *n* : an enlisted person in the Air Force ranking above an airman basic

air·plane *n* : an aircraft with a fixed wing that is heavier than air, driven by a propeller or jet engine, and supported by the action of the air against its wings

air·port *n* : a place either on land or water that is kept for the landing and takeoff of aircraft and for receiving and sending off passengers and cargo

air·ship *n* : an aircraft lighter than air that is kept in the air by a container filled with gas and has an engine, propeller, and rudder

air·sick *adj* : sick to one's stomach while riding in an airplane because of its motion — **air·sick·ness** *n*

air·strip *n* : a runway without places (as hangars) for the repair of aircraft or shelter of passengers or cargo

air·tight *adj* : so tight that no air can get in or out — **air·tight·ness** *n*

air·wave *n* : the radio waves used in radio and television transmission — usually used in pl.

air·way *n* **1** : a place for a current of air to pass through **2** : a regular route for aircraft **3** : AIRLINE

airy *adj* **air·i·er; air·i·est 1** : of, relating to, or living in the air **2** : open to the air : BREEZY **3** : like air in lightness and delicacy

aisle *n* : a passage between sections of seats (as in a church or theater)

ajar *adv or adj* : slightly open

akim·bo *adv or adj* : with hands on hips

akin *adj* **1** : related by blood **2** : SIMILAR

¹-al *adj suffix* : of, relating to, or showing

²-al *n suffix* : action : process

al·a·bas·ter *n* : a smooth usually white stone used for carving

à la carte *adv or adj* : with a separate price for each item on the menu

alac·ri·ty *n* : a cheerful readiness to do something

¹alarm *n* **1** : a warning of danger **2** : a device (as a bell) that warns or signals people **3** : the fear caused by sudden danger

²alarm *vb* : to cause a sense of danger in : FRIGHTEN

alas *interj* — used to express unhappiness, pity, or worry

al·ba·tross *n* : a very large seabird with webbed feet

al·bi·no *n, pl* **al·bi·nos 1** : a person or an animal that has little or no coloring matter in skin, hair, and eyes **2** : a plant with little or no coloring matter

al·bum *n* **1** : a book with blank pages in which to put a collection (as of photographs, stamps, or autographs) **2** : one or more phonograph records or tape recordings carrying a major musical work or a group of related pieces

al·bu·men *n* **1** : the white of an egg **2** : ALBUMIN

al·bu·min *n* : any of various proteins that are soluble in water and occur in plant and animal tissues

al·co·hol *n* **1** : a colorless flammable liquid that in one form is the substance in fermented and distilled liquors (as beer, wine, or whiskey) that can make one drunk **2** : a drink (as beer, wine, or whiskey) containing alcohol

¹al·co·hol·ic *adj* **1** : of, relating to, or containing alcohol **2** : affected with alcoholism

²alcoholic *n* : a person affected with alcoholism

al·co·hol·ism *n* : a sickness of body and mind caused by too much use of alcoholic drinks

al·cove *n* : a small part of a room set back from the rest of it

al·der *n* : a tree or shrub related to the birches that has toothed leaves and grows in moist soil

al·der·man *n* : a member of a lawmaking body in a city

ale *n* : an alcoholic drink made from malt and flavored with hops that is usually more bitter than beer

¹alert *adj* **1** : watchful and ready to meet danger **2** : quick to understand and act **3** : ACTIVE **3**, BRISK — **alert·ly** *adv* — **alert·ness** *n*

²alert *n* **1** : a signal (as an alarm) of danger **2** : the period during which an alert is in effect — **on the alert** : watchful against danger

³alert *vb* : to call to a state of readiness : WARN

al·fal·fa *n* : a plant with purple flowers that is related to the clovers and is grown as a food for horses and cattle

al·ga *n, pl* **al·gae** : any of a large group of simple plants and plant-like organisms that include the seaweeds and that include the seaweeds and that produce chlorophyll like plants but do not produce seeds and cannot be divided into roots, stems, and leaves

al·ge·bra *n* : a branch of mathematics in which symbols (as letters and numbers) are combined according to the rules of arithmetic

¹alias *adv* : otherwise known as

²alias *n* : a false name

¹al·i·bi *n, pl* **al·i·bis 1** : the explanation given by a person accused of a crime that he or she was somewhere else when the crime was committed **2** : ²EXCUSE 2

²alibi *vb* **al·i·bied; al·i·bi·ing 1** : to offer an excuse **2** : to make an excuse for

¹alien *adj* : FOREIGN 2

²alien *n* : a resident who was born elsewhere and is not a citizen of the country in which he or she now lives

alien·ate *vb* **alien·at·ed; alien·at·ing** : to cause (one who used to be friendly or loyal) to become unfriendly or disloyal

¹alight *vb* **alight·ed** *also* **alit; alight·ing 1** : to get down : DISMOUNT **2** : to come down from the air and settle

²alight *adj* : full of light : lighted up

align *vb* : to bring into line — **align·er** *n* — **align·ment** *n*

¹alike *adv* : in the same way

²alike *adj* : being like each other — **alike·ness** *n*

al·i·men·ta·ry *adj* : of or relating to food and nourishment

alimentary canal *n* : a long tube made up of the esophagus, stomach, and intestine into which food is taken and digested and from which wastes are passed out

al·i·mo·ny *n* : money for living expenses paid regularly by one spouse to another after their legal separation or divorce

alit *past of* ALIGHT

alive *adj* 1 : having life : not dead 2 : being in force, existence, or operation 3 : aware of the existence of — **alive·ness** *n*

al·ka·li *n, pl* **al·ka·lies** *or* **al·ka·lis** 1 : any of numerous substances that have a bitter taste and react with an acid to form a salt 2 : a salt or a mixture of salts sometimes found in large amounts in the soil of dry regions

al·ka·line *adj* : of or relating to an alkali

1all *adj* 1 : the whole of 2 : the greatest possible 3 : every one of

2all *adv* 1 : COMPLETELY 2 : so much 3 : for each side

3all *pron* 1 : the whole number or amount 2 : EVERYTHING

Al·lah *n* : the Supreme Being of the Muslims

all–around *adj* 1 : having ability in many areas 2 : useful in many ways

al·lay *vb* 1 : to make less severe 2 : to put to rest

al·lege *vb* **al·leged; al·leg·ing** : to state as fact but without proof

al·le·giance *n* : loyalty and service to a group, country, or idea

al·le·lu·ia *interj* : HALLELUJAH

al·ler·gen *n* : a substance that causes an allergic reaction

al·ler·gic *adj* : of, relating to, causing, or affected by allergy

al·ler·gist *n* : a medical doctor who specializes in treating allergies

al·ler·gy *n, pl* **al·ler·gies** : a condition in which a person is made sick by something that is harmless to most people

al·le·vi·ate *vb* **al·le·vi·at·ed; al·le·vi·at·ing** : to make easier to put up with

al·ley *n, pl* **al·leys** 1 : a narrow passageway between buildings 2 : a special narrow wooden floor on which balls are rolled in bowling

al·li·ance *n* 1 : connection between families, groups, or individuals 2 : an association formed by two or more nations for assistance and protection 3 : a treaty of alliance

al·lied *adj* 1 : being connected or related in some way 2 : joined in alliance

al·li·ga·tor *n* : a large four-footed water animal related to the snakes and lizards

al·lot *vb* **al·lot·ted; al·lot·ting** : to give out as a share or portion

al·lot·ment *n* 1 : the act of allotting 2 : something that is allotted

al·low *vb* 1 : to assign as a share or suitable amount (as of time or money) 2 : to take into account 3 : to accept as true : CONCEDE 4 : to give permission to 5 : to fail to prevent 6 : to make allowance

al·low·able *adj* : not forbidden — **al·low·ably** *adv*

al·low·ance *n* 1 : a share given out 2 : a sum given as repayment or for expenses 3 : the taking into account of things that could affect a result

al·loy *n* : a substance made of two or more metals melted together

all right *adj or adv* 1 : satisfactory in quality or condition 2 : very well

all–round *adj* : ALL-AROUND

all–star *adj* : made up mainly or entirely of outstanding participants

al·lude *vb* **al·lud·ed; al·lud·ing** : to talk about or hint at without mentioning directly

al·lure *vb* **al·lured; al·lur·ing** : to try to influence by offering what seems to be a benefit or pleasure

al·lu·sion *n* : an act of alluding or of hinting at something

1al·ly *vb* **al·lied; al·ly·ing** : to form a connection : join in an alliance

2al·ly *n, pl* **allies** : one (as a person or a nation) associated or united with another in a common purpose

al·ma·nac *n* : a book containing a calendar of days, weeks, and months and usually facts about the rising and setting of the sun and moon, changes in the tides, and information of general interest

al·mighty *adj, often cap* : having absolute power over all

al·mond *n* : a nut that is the edible kernel of a small tree related to the peach

al·most *adv* : only a little less than : very nearly

alms *n, pl* **alms** : something and especially money given to help the poor : CHARITY

aloft *adv or adj* 1 : at or to a great height 2 : in the air and especially in flight 3 : at, on, or to the top of the mast or the higher rigging of a ship

1alone *adj* 1 : separated from others 2 : not including anyone or anything else

2alone *adv* 1 : and nothing or no one else 2 : without company or help

1along *prep* 1 : on or near in a lengthwise direction 2 : at a point on

2along *adv* 1 : farther forward or on 2 : as a companion or associate 3 : throughout the time

along·shore *adv or adj* : along the shore or coast

¹along·side *adv* : along or by the side

²alongside *prep* : parallel to

¹aloof *adv* : at a distance

²aloof *adj* : RESERVED 1 — **aloof·ly** *adv* — **aloof·ness** *n*

aloud *adv* : using the voice so as to be clearly heard

al·paca *n* : a South American animal related to the camel and llama that is raised for its long woolly hair which is woven into warm strong cloth

al·pha·bet *n* : the letters used in writing a language arranged in their regular order

al·pha·bet·i·cal *or* **al·pha·bet·ic** *adj* : arranged in the order of the letters of the alphabet — **al·pha·bet·i·cal·ly** *adv*

al·pha·bet·ize *vb* **al·pha·bet·ized; al·pha·bet·iz·ing** : to arrange in alphabetical order

al·ready *adv* : before a certain time : by this time

al·so *adv* : in addition : TOO

al·tar *n* 1 : a usually raised place on which sacrifices are offered 2 : a platform or table used as a center of worship

al·ter *vb* : to change partly but not completely

al·ter·ation *n* 1 : a making or becoming different in some respects 2 : the result of altering : MODIFICATION

¹al·ter·nate *adj* 1 : occurring or following by turns 2 : arranged one above, beside, or next to another 3 : every other : every second — **al·ter·nate·ly** *adv*

²al·ter·nate *vb* **al·ter·nat·ed; al·ter·nat·ing** : to take place or cause to take place by turns

³al·ter·nate *n* : a person named to take the place of another whenever necessary

alternating current *n* : an electric current that reverses its direction of flow regularly many times per second

al·ter·na·tion *n* : the act, process, or result of alternating

¹al·ter·na·tive *adj* : offering or expressing a choice — **al·ter·na·tive·ly** *adv*

²alternative *n* 1 : a chance to choose between two things 2 : one of the things between which a choice is to be made

al·though *conj* : in spite of the fact that

al·ti·tude *n* 1 : height above a certain level and especially above sea level 2 : the perpendicular distance from the base of a geometric figure to the vertex or to the side parallel to the base

al·to *n, pl* **altos** 1 : the lowest female singing voice 2 : the second highest part in four-part harmony 3 : a singer or an instrument having an alto range or part

al·to·geth·er *adv* 1 : COMPLETELY 2 : on the whole

al·tru·ism *n* : unselfish interest in others

al·um *n* : either of two aluminum compounds that have a sweetish-sourish taste and puckering effect on the mouth and are used in medicine (as to stop bleeding)

alu·mi·num *n* : a silver-white light metallic chemical element that is easily worked, conducts electricity well, resists weathering, and is the most plentiful metal in the earth's crust

alum·na *n, pl* **alum·nae** : a girl or woman who has attended or has graduated from a school, college, or university

alum·nus *n, pl* **alum·ni** : one who has attended or has graduated from a school, college, or university

al·ways *adv* 1 : at all times 2 : throughout all time : FOREVER

am *present 1st sing of* BE

amal·gam·ation *n* : the combining of different elements into a single body

amass *vb* : to collect or gather together

¹am·a·teur *n* 1 : a person who takes part in sports or occupations for pleasure and not for pay 2 : a person who takes part in something without having experience or skill in it — **am·a·teur·ish** *adj*

²amateur *adj* : of, relating to, or done by amateurs : not professional

amaze *vb* **amazed; amaz·ing** : to surprise or puzzle very much

amaze·ment *n* : great surprise

am·bas·sa·dor *n* : a person sent as the chief representative of his or her government in another country — **am·bas·sa·dor·ship** *n*

am·ber *n* 1 : a hard yellowish to brownish clear substance that is a fossil resin from trees long dead, takes a polish, and is used for ornamental objects (as beads) 2 : a dark orange yellow

ambi- *prefix* : both

am·bi·dex·trous *adj* : using both hands with equal ease — **am·bi·dex·trous·ly** *adv*

am·bi·gu·i·ty *n, pl* **am·bi·gu·i·ties** : the fact or state of being ambiguous

am·big·u·ous *adj* : able to be understood in more than one way — **am·big·u·ous·ly** *adv*

am·bi·tion *n* 1 : a desire for success, honor, or power 2 : the aim or object one tries for

am·bi·tious *adj* 1 : possessing ambition 2 : showing ambition — **am·bi·tious·ly** *adv*

¹am·ble *vb* **am·bled; am·bling** : to go at an amble

²amble *n* : a slow easy way of walking

am·bu·lance *n* : a vehicle meant to carry sick or injured persons

¹am·bush *vb* : to attack from an ambush

²**ambush** *n* : a hidden place from which a surprise attack can be made

amen *interj* — used to express agreement (as after a prayer or a statement of opinion)

ame·na·ble *adj* : readily giving in or agreeing

amend *vb* **1** : to change for the better : IMPROVE **2** : to change the wording or meaning of : ALTER

amend·ment *n* : a change in wording or meaning especially in a law, bill, or motion

amends *n sing or pl* : something done or given by a person to make up for a loss or injury he or she has caused

ame·ni·ty *n*, *pl* **ame·ni·ties** **1** : the quality of being pleasant or agreeable **2** *amenities* *pl* : something (as good manners or household appliances) that makes life easier or more pleasant

¹**Amer·i·can** *n* **1** : a person born or living in North or South America **2** : a citizen of the United States

²**American** *adj* **1** : of or relating to North or South America or their residents **2** : of or relating to the United States or its citizens

American Indian *n* : a member of any of the first peoples to live in North and South America except usually the Eskimos

am·e·thyst *n* : a clear purple or bluish violet quartz used as a gem

ami·a·ble *adj* : having a friendly and pleasant manner — **ami·a·bly** *adv*

am·i·ca·ble *adj* : showing kindness or goodwill — **am·i·ca·bly** *adv*

amid *or* **amidst** *prep* : in or into the middle of

amid·ships *adv* : in or near the middle of a ship

ami·no acid *n* : any of numerous acids that contain carbon and nitrogen, include some which are the building blocks of protein, and are made by living plant or animal cells or obtained from the diet

¹**amiss** *adv* : in the wrong way

²**amiss** *adj* : not right : WRONG

am·i·ty *n*, *pl* **am·i·ties** : FRIENDSHIP

am·me·ter *n* : an instrument for measuring electric current in amperes

am·mo·nia *n* **1** : a colorless gas that is a compound of nitrogen and hydrogen, has a sharp smell and taste, can be easily made liquid by cold and pressure, and is used in making ice, fertilizers, and explosives **2** : a solution of ammonia and water

am·mu·ni·tion *n* **1** : objects (as bullets) fired from guns **2** : explosive objects (as bombs) used in war

am·ne·sia *n* : an abnormal and usually complete loss of one's memory

amoe·ba *n*, *pl* **amoe·bas** *or* **amoe·bae** : a tiny water animal that is a single cell which flows about and takes in food

among *also* **amongst** *prep* **1** : in or through the middle of **2** : in the presence of : WITH **3** : through all or most of **4** : in shares to each of

¹**amount** *vb* **1** : to add up **2** : to be the same in meaning or effect

²**amount** *n* : the total number or quantity

am·pere *n* : a unit for measuring the strength of an electric current

am·per·sand *n* : a character & standing for the word *and*

am·phet·amine *n* : a drug that causes the nervous system to become more active

am·phib·i·an *n* **1** : any of a group of cold-blooded animals (as frogs and toads) that have gills and live in water as larvae but breathe air as adults **2** : an airplane designed to take off from and land on either land or water

am·phib·i·ous *adj* **1** : able to live both on land and in water **2** : meant to be used on both land and water **3** : made by land, sea, and air forces acting together — **am·phib·i·ous·ly** *adv* — **am·phib·i·ous·ness** *n*

am·phi·the·ater *n* : an arena with seats rising in curved rows around an open space

am·ple *adj* : more than enough in amount or size — **am·ply** *adv*

am·pli·fy *vb* **am·pli·fied**; **am·pli·fy·ing** **1** : to add to **2** : to make louder or greater — **am·pli·fi·er** *n*

am·pu·tate *vb* **am·pu·tat·ed**; **am·pu·tat·ing** : to cut off

am·u·let *n* : a small object worn as a charm against evil

amuse *vb* **amused**; **amus·ing** **1** : to entertain with something pleasant **2** : to please the sense of humor

amuse·ment *n* **1** : something that amuses or entertains **2** : the condition of being amused

an *indefinite article* : ²A — used before words beginning with a vowel sound

¹**-an** *or* **-ian** *also* **-ean** *n suffix* **1** : one that belongs to **2** : one skilled in or specializing in

²**-an** *or* **-ian** *also* **-ean** *adj suffix* **1** : of or relating to **2** : like : resembling

an·a·con·da *n* : a large South American snake of the boa family

anal·y·sis *n*, *pl* **anal·y·ses** : an examination of something to find out how it is made or works or what it is

an·a·lyst *n* : a person who analyzes or is skilled in analysis

an·a·lyt·ic *or* **an·a·lyt·i·cal** *adj* : of, relating to, or skilled in analysis — **an·a·lyt·i·cal·ly** *adv*

an·a·lyze *vb* **an·a·lyzed; an·a·lyz·ing** : to examine something to find out what it is or what makes it work

an·ar·chist *n* : a person who believes in or practices anarchy

an·ar·chy *n* **1** : the condition of a country where there is no government or law and order **2** : a state of confused disorder or lawlessness

an·a·tom·i·cal *or* **an·a·tom·ic** *adj* : of or relating to anatomy

anat·o·my *n, pl* **anat·o·mies 1** : a science that has to do with the structure of the body **2** : the structural makeup especially of a person or animal

-ance *n suffix* **1** : action or process **2** : quality or state **3** : amount or degree

an·ces·tor *n* : one from whom an individual is descended

an·ces·tral *adj* : of, relating to, or coming from an ancestor

an·ces·try *n, pl* **an·ces·tries** : one's ancestors

¹an·chor *n* **1** : a heavy iron or steel device attached to a ship by a cable or chain and so made that when thrown overboard it digs into the bottom and holds the ship in place **2** : something that keeps something else fastened or steady

²anchor *vb* **1** : to hold or become held in place with an anchor **2** : to fasten tightly

an·chor·age *n* : a place where boats can be anchored

¹an·cient *adj* **1** : very old **2** : of or relating to a time long past or to those living in such a time

²ancient *n* **1** : a very old person **2** **ancients** *pl* : the civilized peoples of ancient times and especially of Greece and Rome

-an·cy *n suffix, pl* **-an·cies** : quality or state

and *conj* **1** : added to **2** : AS WELL AS, ALSO — **and so forth** : and others or more of the same kind — **and so on** : AND SO FORTH

and·iron *n* : one of a pair of metal supports for firewood in a fireplace

an·ec·dote *n* : a short story about something interesting or funny in a person's life

ane·mia *n* : a sickness in which there is too little blood or too few red blood cells or too little hemoglobin in the blood

an·e·mom·e·ter *n* : an instrument for measuring the speed of the wind

anem·o·ne *n* : a plant related to the buttercup that blooms in spring and is often grown for its large white or colored flowers

an·es·the·sia *n* : loss of feeling or consciousness

¹an·es·thet·ic *adj* : of, relating to, or capable of producing anesthesia

²anesthetic *n* : something that produces anesthesia

anew *adv* **1** : over again **2** : in a new or different form

an·gel *n* **1** : a spiritual being serving God especially as a messenger **2** : a person thought to be like an angel (as in goodness or beauty)

¹an·ger *vb* : to make strongly displeased

²anger *n* : a strong feeling of displeasure and often of active opposition to an insult, injury, or injustice

¹an·gle *n* **1** : a sharp corner **2** : the figure formed by two lines meeting at a point **3** : POINT OF VIEW

²angle *vb* **an·gled; an·gling** : to turn, move, or direct at an angle

³angle *vb* **an·gled; an·gling 1** : to fish with hook and line **2** : to try to get what one wants in a sly way

an·gler *n* : a person who fishes with hook and line especially for pleasure

an·gle·worm *n* : EARTHWORM

an·gling *n* : fishing with hook and line for pleasure

An·glo- *prefix* **1** : English **2** : English and

¹An·glo–Sax·on *n* **1** : a member of the German people who conquered England in the fifth century A.D. **2** : a person whose ancestors were English

²Anglo–Saxon *adj* : of or relating to the Anglo-Saxons

an·go·ra *n* : cloth or yarn made from the soft silky hair of a special usually white domestic rabbit (**Angora rabbit**) or from the long shiny wool of a goat (**Angora goat**)

an·gry *adj* **an·gri·er; an·gri·est** : feeling or showing anger — **an·gri·ly** *adv*

an·guish *n* : great pain or trouble of body or mind

an·guished *adj* : full of anguish

an·gu·lar *adj* **1** : having angles or sharp corners **2** : being lean and bony

an·i·mal *n* **1** : any of the great group of living beings (as jellyfishes, crabs, birds, and people) that differ from plants typically in being able to move about, in not having cell walls made of cellulose, and in depending on plants and other animals as sources of food **2** : any of the animals lower than humans in the natural order **3** : MAMMAL

animal kingdom *n* : a basic group of natural objects that includes all living and extinct animals

¹an·i·mate *adj* : having life

²an·i·mate *vb* **an·i·mat·ed; an·i·mat·ing 1** : to give life or energy to : make alive or lively **2** : to make appear to move

an·i·mat·ed *adj* **1** : full of life and energy

: LIVELY **2** : appearing to be alive or moving

an·i·mos·i·ty *n, pl* **an·i·mos·i·ties** : ¹DISLIKE, HATRED

an·kle *n* **1** : the joint between the foot and the leg **2** : the area containing the ankle joint

an·klet *n* : a sock reaching slightly above the ankle

an·ky·lo·saur *n* : any of several plant-eating dinosaurs with bony plates covering the back

an·nals *n pl* **1** : a record of events arranged in yearly sequence **2** : historical records : HISTORY

an·neal *vb* : to heat (as glass or steel) and then cool so as to toughen and make less brittle

¹an·nex *vb* : to add (something) to something else usually so as to become a part of it

²an·nex *n* : something (as a wing of a building) added on

an·nex·ation *n* : an annexing especially of new territory

an·ni·hi·late *vb* **an·ni·hi·lat·ed; an·ni·hi·lat·ing** : to destroy entirely : put completely out of existence

an·ni·ver·sa·ry *n, pl* **an·ni·ver·sa·ries** : the return every year of the date when something special (as a wedding) happened

an·nounce *vb* **an·nounced; an·nounc·ing** **1** : to make known publicly **2** : to give notice of the arrival, presence, or readiness of

an·nounce·ment *n* **1** : the act of announcing **2** : a public notice announcing something

an·nounc·er *n* : a person who introduces radio or television programs, makes announcements, and gives the news and station identification

an·noy *vb* : to disturb or irritate especially by repeated disagreeable acts

an·noy·ance *n* **1** : the act of annoying **2** : the feeling of being annoyed **3** : a source or cause of being annoyed

an·noy·ing *adj* : causing annoyance — **an·noy·ing·ly** *adv*

¹an·nu·al *adj* **1** : coming, happening, done, made, or given once a year **2** : completing the life cycle in one growing season — **an·nu·al·ly** *adv*

²annual *n* : an annual plant

an·nu·ity *n, pl* **an·nu·ities** : a sum of money paid at regular intervals

an·nul *vb* **an·nulled; an·nul·ling** : to cancel by law : take away the legal force of — **an·nul·ment** *n*

an·ode *n* **1** : the positive electrode of an electrolytic cell **2** : the negative end of a battery that is delivering electric current **3** : the electron-collecting electrode of an electron tube

anoint *vb* **1** : to rub or cover with oil or grease **2** : to put oil on as part of a religious ceremony

anon·y·mous *adj* **1** : not named or identified **2** : made or done by someone unknown — **anon·y·mous·ly** *adv*

¹an·oth·er *adj* **1** : some other **2** : one more

²another *pron* **1** : one more **2** : someone or something different

¹an·swer *n* **1** : something said or written in reply (as to a question) **2** : a solution of a problem

²answer *vb* **1** : to speak or write in reply to **2** : to take responsibility **3** : ¹SERVE 5, DO

an·swer·able *adj* **1** : RESPONSIBLE 1 **2** : possible to answer

answering machine *n* : a machine that receives telephone calls by playing a recorded message and usually also recording messages from callers

ant *n* : a small insect related to the bees and wasps that lives in colonies and forms nests in the ground or in wood in which it stores food and raises its young

ant- *see* ANTI-

¹-ant *n suffix* **1** : one that does or causes a certain thing **2** : thing that is acted upon in a certain way

²-ant *adj suffix* **1** : doing a certain thing or being a certain way **2** : causing a certain action

an·tag·o·nism *n* : a state of not liking and being against something

an·tag·o·nist *n* : a person who is against something or someone else : OPPONENT

an·tag·o·nis·tic *adj* : being against something or someone : HOSTILE, UNFRIENDLY — **an·tag·o·nis·ti·cal·ly** *adv*

an·tag·o·nize *vb* **an·tag·o·nized; an·tag·o·niz·ing** : to stir up dislike or anger in

ant·arc·tic *adj, often cap* : of or relating to the south pole or to the region around it

ante- *prefix* **1** : before in time : earlier **2** : in front of

ant·eat·er *n* : any of several animals that have long noses and long sticky tongues and feed chiefly on ants

an·te·cham·ber *n* : ANTEROOM

an·te·lope *n* : any of a group of cud-chewing animals that have horns that extend upward and backward

an·ten·na *n* **1** *pl* **an·ten·nae** : one of two or four threadlike movable feelers on the head of insects or crustaceans (as lobsters) **2** *pl* **an·ten·nas** : a metallic device (as a rod or wire) for sending or receiving radio waves

an·te·room *n* : a room used as an entrance to another

an·them *n* **1** : a sacred song usually sung by a church choir **2** : a patriotic song of praise and love for one's country

an·ther *n* : the enlargement at the tip of a flower's stamen that contains pollen

ant·hill *n* : a mound of dirt thrown up by ants in digging their nest

an·thol·o·gy *n, pl* **an·thol·o·gies** : a collection of writings (as stories and poems)

an·thra·cite *n* : a hard glossy coal that burns without much smoke

an·thrax *n* : a dangerous bacterial disease of warm-blooded animals that can affect humans

an·thro·poid *adj* : looking somewhat like humans

an·thro·pol·o·gy *n* : a science that studies people and especially their history, development, distribution and culture

anti- *or* **ant-** *prefix* **1** : opposite in kind, position, or action **2** : hostile toward

an·ti·bi·ot·ic *n* : a substance produced by living things and especially by bacteria and fungi that is used to kill or prevent the growth of harmful germs

an·ti·body *n, pl* **an·ti·bod·ies** : a substance produced by the body that counteracts the effects of a disease germ or its poisons

an·tic *n* : a wildly playful or funny act or action

an·tic·i·pate *vb* **an·tic·i·pat·ed; an·tic·i·pat·ing** **1** : to foresee and deal with or provide for beforehand **2** : to look forward to

an·tic·i·pa·tion *n* **1** : an action that takes into account and deals with or prevents a later action **2** : pleasurable expectation **3** : a picturing beforehand of a future event or state

an·ti·cy·clone *n* : a system of winds that is like a cyclone but that rotates about a center of high atmospheric pressure in a clockwise direction north of the equator and a counterclockwise direction south of the equator

an·ti·dote *n* : something used to reverse or prevent the action of a poison

an·ti·freeze *n* : a substance added to the liquid in an automobile radiator to prevent its freezing

an·ti·mo·ny *n* : a silvery white metallic chemical element

an·tip·a·thy *n, pl* **an·tip·a·thies** : a strong feeling of dislike

an·ti·quat·ed *adj* : OLD-FASHIONED 1, OBSOLETE

¹an·tique *n* : an object (as a piece of furniture) made at an earlier time

²antique *adj* : belonging to or like a former style or fashion

an·tiq·ui·ty *n* **1** : ancient times **2** : very great age

¹an·ti·sep·tic *adj* : killing or making harmless the germs that cause decay or sickness

²antiseptic *n* : an antiseptic substance

an·ti·so·cial *adj* **1** : being against or bad for society **2** : UNFRIENDLY

an·tith·e·sis *n, pl* **an·tith·e·ses** : the exact opposite

an·ti·tox·in *n* : a substance that is formed in the blood of one exposed to a disease and that prevents or acts against that disease

ant·ler *n* : the entire horn or a branch of the horn of an animal of the deer family — **ant·lered** *adj*

ant lion *n* : an insect having a larva form with long jaws that digs a cone-shaped hole in which it waits for prey (as ants)

an·to·nym *n* : a word of opposite meaning

an·vil *n* : an iron block on which pieces of metal are hammered into shape

anx·i·ety *n, pl* **anx·i·eties** : fear or nervousness about what might happen

anx·ious *adj* **1** : afraid or nervous about what may happen **2** : wanting very much : EAGER — **anx·ious·ly** *adv*

¹any *adj* **1** : whatever kind of **2** : of whatever number or amount

²any *pron* **1** : any individuals **2** : any amount

³any *adv* : to the least amount or degree

any·body *pron* : ANYONE

any·how *adv* **1** : in any way, manner, or order **2** : at any rate : in any case

any·more *adv* : NOWADAYS

any·one *pron* : any person

any·place *adv* : in any place

any·thing *pron* : a thing of any kind

any·way *adv* : ANYHOW

any·where *adv* : in, at, or to any place

any·wise *adv* : in any way whatever

A1 *adj* : of the very best kind

aor·ta *n* : the main artery that carries blood from the heart for distribution to all parts of the body

apace *adv* : at a quick pace : FAST

apart *adv* **1** : away from each other **2** : as something separated : SEPARATELY **3** : into parts : to pieces **4** : one from another

apart·ment *n* **1** : a room or set of rooms used as a home **2** : a building divided into individual apartments

ap·a·thet·ic *adj* : having or showing little or no feeling or interest — **ap·a·thet·i·cal·ly** *adv*

ap·a·thy *n* : lack of feeling or of interest : INDIFFERENCE

apato·sau·rus *n* : BRONTOSAURUS

¹ape *n* : any of a group of tailless animals (as gorillas or chimpanzees) that are most closely related to humans — **ape·like** *adj*

²ape *vb* **aped; ap·ing** : to imitate (someone) awkwardly

ap·er·ture *n* : an opening or open space : HOLE

apex *n, pl* **apex·es** *or* **api·ces** : the highest point : PEAK

aphid *n* : any of various small insects that suck the juices of plants

apiece *adv* : for each one

aplomb *n* : complete freedom from nervousness or uncertainty

apol·o·get·ic *adj* : sorry for having done something wrong — **apol·o·get·i·cal·ly** *adv*

apol·o·gize *vb* **apol·o·gized; apol·o·giz·ing** : to make an apology

apol·o·gy *n, pl* **apol·o·gies** : an expression of regret (as for a mistake or a rude remark)

apos·tle *n* **1** : one of the twelve close followers of Jesus sent out to teach the gospel **2** : the first Christian missionary to a region **3** : the person who first puts forward an important belief or starts a great reform — **apos·tle·ship** *n*

apos·tro·phe *n* : a mark ' used to show that letters or figures are missing (as in "can't" for "cannot" or " '76" for "1776") or to show the possessive case (as in "James's") or the plural of letters or figures (as in "cross your t's")

apoth·e·cary *n, pl* **apoth·e·car·ies** : DRUGGIST

ap·pall *vb* : to shock or overcome with horror

ap·pall·ing *adj* : being shocking and terrible

ap·pa·ra·tus *n, pl* **apparatus** *or* **ap·pa·ra·tus·es** : the equipment or material for a particular use or job

ap·par·el *n* : things that are worn : WEAR 2

ap·par·ent *adj* **1** : open to view : VISIBLE **2** : clear to the understanding : EVIDENT **3** : appearing to be real or true — **ap·par·ent·ly** *adv* — **ap·par·ent·ness** *n*

ap·pa·ri·tion *n* **1** : an unusual or unexpected sight **2** : GHOST

¹ap·peal *n* **1** : a legal action by which a case is brought to a higher court for review **2** : an asking for something badly needed or wanted : PLEA **3** : the power to cause enjoyment : ATTRACTION

²appeal *vb* **1** : to take action to have a case or decision reviewed by a higher court **2** : to ask for something badly needed or wanted **3** : to be pleasing or attractive

ap·pear *vb* **1** : to come into sight **2** : to present oneself **3** : SEEM 1 **4** : to come before the public **5** : to come into existence

ap·pear·ance *n* **1** : the act or an instance of appearing **2** : way of looking

ap·pease *vb* **ap·peased; ap·peas·ing 1** : to make calm or quiet **2** : to give in to — **ap·pease·ment** *n* — **ap·peas·er** *n*

ap·pend *vb* : to add as something extra

ap·pend·age *n* : something (as a leg) attached to a larger or more important thing

ap·pen·di·ci·tis *n* : inflammation of the intestinal appendix

ap·pen·dix *n, pl* **ap·pen·dix·es** *or* **ap·pen·di·ces 1** : a part of a book giving added and helpful information (as notes or tables) **2** : a small tubelike part growing out from the intestine

ap·pe·tite *n* **1** : a natural desire especially for food **2** : ²TASTE 4

ap·pe·tiz·er *n* : a food or drink usually served before a meal to make one hungrier

ap·pe·tiz·ing *adj* : pleasing to the appetite

ap·plaud *vb* **1** : ¹PRAISE 1 **2** : to show approval especially by clapping the hands

ap·plause *n* : approval shown especially by clapping the hands

ap·ple *n* : the round or oval fruit with red, yellow, or green skin of a spreading tree (**apple tree**) that is related to the rose

ap·pli·ance *n* **1** : a device designed for a certain use **2** : a piece of household or office equipment that runs on gas or electricity

ap·pli·ca·ble *adj* : capable of being put to use or put into practice

ap·pli·cant *n* : a person who applies for something (as a job)

ap·pli·ca·tion *n* **1** : the act or an instance of applying **2** : something put or spread on a surface **3** : ¹REQUEST 1 **4** : ability to be put to practical use

ap·pli·ca·tor *n* : a device for applying a substance (as medicine or polish)

ap·ply *vb* **ap·plied; ap·ply·ing 1** : to put to use **2** : to lay or spread on **3** : to place in contact **4** : to give one's full attention **5** : to have relation or a connection **6** : to request especially in writing

ap·point *vb* **1** : to decide on usually from a position of authority **2** : to choose for some duty, job, or office

ap·poin·tee *n* : a person appointed to an office or position

ap·point·ment *n* **1** : the act or an instance of appointing **2** : a position or office to which a person is named **3** : an agreement to meet at a fixed time **4 appointments** *pl* : FURNISHINGS

ap·po·si·tion *n* : a grammatical construction in which a noun is followed by another that explains it

ap·pos·i·tive *n* : the second of a pair of nouns in apposition

ap·prais·al *n* : an act or instance of appraising

ap·praise *vb* **ap·praised; ap·prais·ing** : to set a value on

ap·pre·cia·ble *adj* : large enough to be noticed or measured — **ap·pre·cia·bly** *adv*

ap·pre·ci·ate *vb* **ap·pre·ci·at·ed; ap·pre·ci·at·ing** 1 : to admire greatly and with understanding 2 : to be fully aware of 3 : to be grateful for 4 : to increase in number or value

ap·pre·ci·a·tion *n* 1 : the act of appreciating 2 : awareness or understanding of worth or value 3 : a rise in value

ap·pre·cia·tive *adj* : having or showing appreciation — **ap·pre·cia·tive·ly** *adv*

ap·pre·hend *vb* 1 : ¹ARREST 2 2 : to look forward to with fear and uncertainty 3 : UNDERSTAND 1

ap·pre·hen·sion *n* 1 : ²ARREST 2 : an understanding of something 3 : fear of or uncertainty about what may be coming

ap·pre·hen·sive *adj* : fearful of what may be coming — **ap·pre·hen·sive·ly** *adv* — **ap·pre·hen·sive·ness** *n*

¹ap·pren·tice *n* : a person who is learning a trade or art by experience under a skilled worker

²apprentice *vb* **ap·pren·ticed; ap·pren·tic·ing** : to set at work as an apprentice

ap·pren·tice·ship *n* 1 : service as an apprentice 2 : the period during which a person serves as an apprentice

¹ap·proach *vb* 1 : to come near or nearer : draw close 2 : to begin to deal with

²approach *n* 1 : an act or instance of approaching 2 : a beginning step 3 : a way (as a path or road) to get to some place

ap·proach·able *adj* : easy to meet or deal with

¹ap·pro·pri·ate *vb* **ap·pro·pri·at·ed; ap·pro·pri·at·ing** 1 : to take possession of 2 : to set apart for a certain purpose or use

²ap·pro·pri·ate *adj* : especially suitable — **ap·pro·pri·ate·ly** *adv* — **ap·pro·pri·ate·ness** *n*

ap·pro·pri·a·tion *n* 1 : an act or instance of appropriating 2 : a sum of money appropriated for a specific use

ap·prov·al *n* : an act or instance of approving

ap·prove *vb* **ap·proved; ap·prov·ing** 1 : to think well of 2 : to accept as satisfactory

¹ap·prox·i·mate *adj* : nearly correct or exact — **ap·prox·i·mate·ly** *adv*

²ap·prox·i·mate *vb* **ap·prox·i·mat·ed; ap·prox·i·mat·ing** 1 : to bring near or close 2 : to come near : APPROACH

ap·prox·i·ma·tion *n* 1 : a coming near or close (as in value) 2 : an estimate or figure that is almost exact

apri·cot *n* : a small oval orange-colored fruit that looks like the related peach and plum

April *n* : the fourth month of the year

apron *n* 1 : a piece of cloth worn on the front of the body to keep the clothing from getting dirty 2 : a paved area for parking or handling airplanes

apt *adj* 1 : just right : SUITABLE 2 : having a tendency : LIKELY 3 : quick to learn — **apt·ly** *adv* — **apt·ness** *n*

ap·ti·tude *n* 1 : ability to learn 2 : natural ability : TALENT

aqua *n* : a light greenish blue

aqua·ma·rine *n* : a transparent gem that is blue, blue-green, or green

aqua·naut *n* : a person who lives for a long while in an underwater shelter used as a base for research

aquar·i·um *n* 1 : a container (as a tank or bowl) in which living water animals or water plants are kept 2 : a building in which water animals or water plants are exhibited

Aquar·i·us *n* 1 : a constellation between Capricorn and Pisces imagined as a man pouring water 2 : the eleventh sign of the zodiac or a person born under this sign

aquat·ic *adj* : growing, living, or done in water

aq·ue·duct *n* : an artificial channel (as a structure that takes the water of a canal across a river or hollow) for carrying flowing water from one place to another

aque·ous *adj* 1 : of, relating to, or like water 2 : made of, by, or with water

-ar *adj suffix* : of or relating to

¹Ar·ab *n* 1 : a person born or living in the Arabian Peninsula 2 : a member of a people that speaks Arabic

²Arab *adj* : of or relating to the Arabs : ARABIAN

¹Ara·bi·an *n* : ¹ARAB 1

²Arabian *adj* : of or relating to the Arabian Peninsula or Arabs

¹Ar·a·bic *n* : a language spoken in the Arabian Peninsula, Iraq, Jordan, Lebanon, Syria, Egypt, and parts of northern Africa

²Arabic *adj* 1 : of or relating to Arabia, the Arabs, or Arabic 2 : expressed in or making use of Arabic numerals

Arabic numeral *n* : one of the number symbols 1, 2, 3, 4, 5, 6, 7, 8, 9, and 0

ar·a·ble *adj* : fit for or cultivated by plowing : suitable for producing crops

Arap·a·ho *or* **Arap·a·hoe** *n, pl* **Arapaho** *or* **Arapahos** *or* **Arapahoe** *or* **Arapahoes** : a member of an Indian people of the plains region of the United States and Canada

ar·bi·ter *n* **1** : ARBITRATOR **2** : a person having the power to decide what is right or proper

ar·bi·trary *adj* **1** : coming from or given to free exercise of the will without thought of fairness or right **2** : seeming to have been chosen by chance — **ar·bi·trari·ly** *adv* — **ar·bi·trar·i·ness** *n*

ar·bi·trate *vb* **ar·bi·trat·ed; ar·bi·trat·ing 1** : to settle a disagreement after hearing the arguments of both sides **2** : to refer a dispute to others for settlement

ar·bi·tra·tion *n* : the settling of a disagreement in which both sides present their arguments to a third person or group for decision

ar·bi·tra·tor *n* : a person chosen to settle differences in a disagreement

ar·bor *n* : a shelter of vines or branches or of a frame covered with growing vines

ar·bo·re·al *adj* **1** : of or relating to a tree **2** : living in or often found in trees

ar·bo·re·tum *n, pl* **ar·bo·re·tums** *or* **ar·bo·re·ta** : a place where trees and plants are grown to be studied

ar·bor·vi·tae *n* : any of several evergreen trees with tiny scalelike leaves on flat branches shaped like fans

ar·bu·tus *n* : a plant that spreads along the ground and in the spring has bunches of small fragrant flowers with five white or pink petals

¹arc *n* **1** : a glowing light across a gap in an electric circuit or between electrodes **2** : a part of a curved line between any two points on it

²arc *vb* **arced; arc·ing 1** : to form an electric arc **2** : to follow an arc-shaped course

ar·cade *n* **1** : a row of arches with the columns that support them **2** : an arched or covered passageway often between two rows of shops

¹arch *n* **1** : a usually curved part of a structure that is over an opening and serves as a support (as for the wall above the opening) **2** : something suggesting an arch — **arched** *adj*

²arch *vb* **1** : to cover with an arch **2** : to form or shape into an arch

³arch *adj* **1** : ²CHIEF 1, PRINCIPAL **2** : being clever and mischievous — **arch·ly** *adv* — **arch·ness** *n*

ar·chae·ol·o·gy *or* **ar·che·ol·o·gy** *n* : a science that deals with past human life and activities as shown by fossils and the monuments and tools left by ancient peoples

ar·cha·ic *adj* **1** : of or relating to an earlier time **2** : surviving from an earlier period

arch·an·gel *n* : a chief angel

arch·bish·op *n* : the bishop of highest rank in a group of dioceses

ar·cher *n* : a person who shoots with a bow and arrow

ar·chery *n* : the sport or practice of shooting with bow and arrows

ar·chi·pel·a·go *n, pl* **ar·chi·pel·a·goes** *or* **ar·chi·pel·a·gos 1** : a body of water (as a sea) with many islands **2** : a group of islands in an archipelago

ar·chi·tect *n* : a person who designs buildings

ar·chi·tec·tur·al *adj* : of or relating to architecture — **ar·chi·tec·tur·al·ly** *adv*

ar·chi·tec·ture *n* **1** : the art of making plans for buildings **2** : a style of building

ar·chive *n* : a place in which public records or historical papers are saved

arch·way *n* **1** : a passage under an arch **2** : an arch over a passage

-archy *n suffix, pl* **-archies** : rule : government

arc·tic *adj* **1** *often cap* : of or relating to the north pole or to the region around it **2** : very cold

ar·dent *adj* : showing or having warmth of feeling : PASSIONATE — **ar·dent·ly** *adv*

ar·dor *n* **1** : warmth of feeling **2** : great eagerness : ZEAL

ar·du·ous *adj* : DIFFICULT 1 — **ar·du·ous·ly** *adv* — **ar·du·ous·ness** *n*

are *present 2d sing or present pl of* BE

ar·ea *n* **1** : a flat surface or space **2** : the amount of surface included within limits **3** : REGION 1 **4** : a field of activity or study

are·na *n* **1** : an enclosed area used for public entertainment **2** : a building containing an arena **3** : a field of activity

aren't : are not

ar·gue *vb* **ar·gued; ar·gu·ing 1** : to give reasons for or against something **2** : to discuss some matter usually with different points of view **3** : to persuade by giving reasons — **ar·gu·er** *n*

ar·gu·ment *n* **1** : a reason for or against something **2** : a discussion in which reasons for and against something are given **3** : an angry disagreement : QUARREL

ar·id *adj* **1** : not having enough rainfall to support agriculture **2** : UNINTERESTING, DULL

Ar·ies *n* **1** : a constellation between Pisces and Taurus imagined as a ram **2** : the first sign of the zodiac or a person born under this sign

aright *adv* : in a correct way

arise *vb* **arose; aris·en; aris·ing 1** : to move upward **2** : to get up from sleep or after lying down **3** : to come into existence

ar·is·toc·ra·cy *n, pl* **ar·is·toc·ra·cies 1 :** a government that is run by a small class of people **2 :** an upper class that is usually based on birth and is richer and more powerful than the rest of a society **3 :** persons thought of as being better than the rest of the community

aris·to·crat *n* : a member of an aristocracy

aris·to·crat·ic *adj* : of or relating to the aristocracy or aristocrats — **aris·to·crat·i·cal·ly** *adv*

¹arith·me·tic *n* **1 :** a science that deals with the addition, subtraction, multiplication, and division of numbers **2 :** an act or method of adding, subtracting, multiplying, or dividing

²ar·ith·met·ic *or* **ar·ith·met·i·cal** *adj* : of or relating to arithmetic

ar·ith·met·ic mean *n* : a quantity formed by adding quantities together and dividing by their number

ark *n* **1 :** the ship in which an ancient Hebrew of the Bible named Noah and his family were saved from a great flood that God sent down on the world because of its wickedness **2 :** a sacred chest in which the ancient Hebrews kept the two tablets of the Law **3 :** a closet in a synagogue for the scrolls of the Law

¹arm *n* **1 :** a human upper limb especially between the shoulder and wrist **2 :** something like an arm in shape or position **3** : ¹POWER 1 **4 :** a foreleg of a four-footed animal — **armed** *adj*

²arm *vb* **1 :** to provide with weapons **2 :** to provide with a way of defense

³arm *n* **1 :** WEAPON, FIREARM **2 :** a branch of an army or of the military forces **3 arms** *pl* : the designs on a shield or flag of a family or government **4 arms** *pl* : actual fighting : WARFARE

ar·ma·da *n* **1 :** a large fleet of warships **2** : a large number of moving things (as planes)

ar·ma·dil·lo *n, pl* **ar·ma·dil·los** : a small burrowing animal of Latin America and Texas whose head and body are protected by a hard bony armor

ar·ma·ment *n* **1 :** the military strength and equipment of a nation **2 :** the supply of materials for war **3 :** the process of preparing for war

ar·ma·ture *n* : the part of an electric motor or generator that turns in a magnetic field

arm·chair *n* : a chair with arms

arm·ful *n, pl* **arm·fuls** *or* **arms·ful** : as much as a person's arm can hold

ar·mi·stice *n* : a pause in fighting brought about by agreement between the two sides

ar·mor *n* **1 :** a covering (as of metal) to pro-

tect the body in battle **2 :** something that protects like metal armor **3 :** armored forces and vehicles (as tanks)

ar·mored *adj* : protected by or equipped with armor

ar·mory *n, pl* **ar·mor·ies 1 :** a supply of arms **2 :** a place where arms are kept and where soldiers are often trained **3 :** a place where arms are made

arm·pit *n* : the hollow under a person's arm where the arm joins the shoulder

arm·rest *n* : a support for the arm

ar·my *n, pl* **armies 1 :** a large body of men and women trained for land warfare **2** *often cap* : the complete military organization of a nation for land warfare **3 :** a great number of people or things **4 :** a body of persons organized to advance an idea

aro·ma *n* : a noticeable and pleasant smell

ar·o·mat·ic *adj* : of, relating to, or having an aroma

arose *past of* ARISE

¹around *adv* **1 :** in circumference **2 :** in or along a curving course **3 :** on all sides **4** : NEARBY **5 :** here and there in various places **6 :** to each in turn **7 :** in an opposite direction **8 :** in the neighborhood of : APPROXIMATELY

²around *prep* **1 :** in a curving path along the outside boundary of **2 :** on every side of **3 :** here and there in **4 :** near in number or amount

arouse *vb* **aroused; arous·ing 1 :** to awaken from sleep **2 :** to excite to action

ar·range *vb* **ar·ranged; ar·rang·ing 1 :** to put in order and especially a particular order **2 :** to make plans for **3 :** to come to an agreement about : SETTLE **4 :** to make a musical arrangement of — **ar·rang·er** *n*

ar·range·ment *n* **1 :** a putting in order : the order in which things are put **2 :** preparation or planning done in advance **3 :** something made by arranging **4 :** a changing of a piece of music to suit voices or instruments for which it was not first written

¹ar·ray *vb* **1 :** to set in order : DRAW UP **2** : to dress especially in fine or beautiful clothing

²array *n* **1 :** regular order or arrangement **2** : a group of persons (as soldiers) drawn up in regular order **3 :** fine or beautiful clothing **4 :** an impressive group **5 :** a group of mathematical elements (as numbers or letters) arranged in rows and columns

ar·rears *n pl* **1 :** the state of being behind in paying debts **2 :** unpaid and overdue debts

¹ar·rest *vb* **1 :** to stop the progress or movement of : CHECK **2 :** to take or keep in one's control by authority of law **3** : to attract and hold the attention of

²arrest *n* : the act of taking or holding in one's control by authority of law

ar·riv·al *n* **1** : the act of arriving **2** : a person or thing that has arrived

ar·rive *vb* **ar·rived; ar·riv·ing 1** : to reach the place one started out for **2** : to gain a goal or object **3** : COME 2 **4** : to gain success

ar·ro·gance *n* : a sense of one's own importance that shows itself in a proud and insulting way

ar·ro·gant *adj* : overly proud of oneself or of one's own opinions — **ar·ro·gant·ly** *adv*

ar·row *n* **1** : a weapon that is made to be shot from a bow and is usually a stick with a point at one end and feathers at the other **2** : a mark to show direction

ar·row·head *n* : the pointed end of an arrow

ar·row·root *n* : a starch obtained from the roots of a tropical plant

ar·se·nal *n* : a place where military equipment is made and stored

ar·se·nic *n* : a solid poisonous chemical element that is usually steel gray and snaps easily

ar·son *n* : the illegal burning of a building or other property

art *n* **1** : skill that comes through experience or study **2** : an activity that requires skill **3** : an activity (as painting, music, or writing) whose purpose is making things that are beautiful to look at, listen to, or read **4** : works (as pictures, poems, or songs) made by artists

ar·tery *n, pl* **ar·ter·ies 1** : one of the branching tubes that carry blood from the heart to all parts of the body **2** : a main road or waterway

ar·te·sian well *n* **1** : a bored well from which water flows up like a fountain **2** : a deep bored well

art·ful *adj* **1** : done with or showing art or skill **2** : clever at taking advantage — **art·ful·ly** *adv* — **art·ful·ness** *n*

ar·thri·tis *n* : a condition in which the joints are painful and swollen

ar·thro·pod *n* : any of a large group of animals (as crabs, insects, and spiders) with jointed limbs and a body made up of segments

ar·ti·choke *n* : a tall plant of the aster family with a flower head cooked and eaten as a vegetable

ar·ti·cle *n* **1** : a separate part of a document **2** : a piece of writing other than fiction or poetry that forms a separate part of a publication (as a magazine) **3** : a word (as *a, an,*

or *the*) used with a noun to limit it or make it clearer **4** : one of a class of things

¹ar·tic·u·late *adj* **1** : clearly understandable **2** : able to express oneself clearly and well — **ar·tic·u·late·ly** *adv* — **ar·tic·u·late·ness** *n*

²ar·tic·u·late *vb* **ar·tic·u·lat·ed; ar·tic·u·lat·ing** : to speak clearly

ar·tic·u·la·tion *n* : the making of articulate sounds (as in speaking)

ar·ti·fice *n* **1** : a clever trick or device **2** : clever skill

ar·ti·fi·cial *adj* **1** : made by humans **2** : not natural in quality **3** : made to look like something natural — **ar·ti·fi·cial·ly** *adv*

artificial respiration *n* : the forcing of air into and out of the lungs of a person whose breathing has stopped

ar·til·lery *n* **1** : large firearms (as cannon or rockets) **2** : a branch of an army armed with artillery

ar·ti·san *n* : a person (as a carpenter) who works at a trade requiring skill with the hands

art·ist *n* **1** : a person skilled in one of the arts (as painting, sculpture, music, or writing) **2** : a person who has much ability in a job requiring skill

ar·tis·tic *adj* **1** : relating to art or artists **2** : showing skill and imagination — **ar·tis·ti·cal·ly** *adv*

¹-ary *n suffix, pl* **-ar·ies** : thing or person belonging to or connected with

²-ary *adj suffix* : of, relating to, or connected with

¹as *adv* **1** : to the same degree or amount **2** : for example

²as *conj* **1** : in equal amount or degree with **2** : in the same way that **3** : at the time that **4** : BECAUSE, SINCE

³as *pron* **1** : THAT, WHO, WHICH **2** : a fact that

⁴as *prep* **1** : ⁴LIKE 1 **2** : in the position or role of

as·bes·tos *n* : a grayish mineral that separates easily into long flexible fibers and is used in making fireproof materials

as·cend *vb* : to go up : RISE

as·cen·sion *n* : the act or process of ascending

as·cent *n* **1** : the act of rising or climbing upward **2** : an upward slope : RISE

as·cer·tain *vb* : to find out with certainty

as·cribe *vb* **as·cribed; as·crib·ing** : to think of as coming from a specified cause, source, or author

asex·u·al *adj* : of, relating to, or being a process of reproduction (as the dividing of one cell into two cells) that does not involve the combining of male and female germ cells — **asex·u·al·ly** *adv*

¹ash *n* : a common shade tree or timber tree that has winged seeds and bark with grooves

²ash *n* **1** : the solid matter left when something is completely burned **2 ashes** *pl* : the last remains of the dead human body

ashamed *adj* **1** : feeling shame, guilt, or disgrace **2** : kept back by fear of shame

ash·en *adj* **1** : of the color of ashes **2** : very pale

ashore *adv* : on or to the shore

ash·tray *n* : a container for tobacco ashes and cigarette and cigar butts

ashy *adj* **ash·i·er; ash·i·est 1** : of or relating to ashes **2** : very pale

¹Asian *adj* : of or relating to Asia or the Asians

²Asian *n* : a person born or living in Asia

aside *adv* **1** : to or toward the side **2** : out of the way : AWAY **3** : away from one's thought

aside from *prep* : with the exception of

as if *conj* **1** : the way it would be if **2** : the way one would if **3** : ²THAT 1

ask *vb* **1** : to seek information **2** : to make a request **3** : to set as a price **4** : INVITE 2 **5** : to behave as if looking

askance *adv* **1** : with a side glance **2** : with distrust or disapproval

askew *adv or adj* : out of line

aslant *adv or adj* : in a slanting direction

¹asleep *adj* **1** : being in a state of sleep **2** : having no feeling

²asleep *adv* : into a state of sleep

as of *prep* : ¹ON 5, AT

as·par·a·gus *n* : a vegetable that is the thick young shoots of a garden plant that is related to the lilies and lives for many years

as·pect *n* **1** : a position facing a certain direction **2** : a certain way in which something appears or may be thought of **3** : the appearance of an individual : LOOK

as·pen *n* : a poplar tree whose leaves move easily in the breeze

as·phalt *n* **1** : a dark-colored substance obtained from natural beds or from petroleum **2** : any of various materials made of asphalt that are used for pavements and as a waterproof cement

as·phyx·i·ate *vb* **as·phyx·i·at·ed; as·phyx·i·at·ing** : to cause (as a person) to become unconscious or die by cutting off the normal taking in of oxygen whether by blocking breathing or by replacing the oxygen of the air with another gas

as·pi·rant *n* : a person who aspires

as·pi·ra·tion *n* : a strong desire to achieve something high or great

as·pire *vb* **as·pired; as·pir·ing** : to very

much want something and especially something high or fine

as·pi·rin *n* : a white drug used to relieve pain and fever

ass *n* **1** : an animal that looks like but is smaller than the related horse and has shorter hair in mane and tail and longer ears : DONKEY **2** : a dull stupid person

as·sail *vb* : to attack violently with blows or words

as·sail·ant *n* : a person who attacks

as·sas·sin *n* : one who kills another person either for pay or from loyalty to a cause

as·sas·si·nate *vb* **as·sas·si·nat·ed; as·sas·si·nat·ing** : to murder a usually important person by a surprise or secret attack

as·sas·si·na·tion *n* : the act of assassinating

¹as·sault *n* **1** : a violent or sudden attack **2** : an unlawful attempt or threat to harm someone

²assault *vb* : to make an assault on

¹as·say *n* : an analyzing (as of an ore or drug) to determine the presence, absence, or amount of one or more substances

²as·say *vb* : to analyze (as an ore) for one or more valuable substances

as·sem·blage *n* : a collection of persons or things

as·sem·ble *vb* **as·sem·bled; as·sem·bling 1** : to collect in one place or group **2** : to fit (parts) together **3** : to meet together — **as·sem·bler** *n*

as·sem·bly *n, pl* **as·sem·blies 1** : a gathering of persons : MEETING **2** *cap* : a lawmaking body **3** : the act of assembling : the state of being assembled **4** : a collection of parts that make up a complete unit

assembly line *n* : an arrangement for assembling a product mechanically in which work passes from one operation to the next in a direct line until the product is finished

¹as·sent *vb* : to agree to something

²assent *n* : an act of assenting : AGREEMENT

as·sert *vb* **1** : to state clearly and strongly **2** : to show the existence of — **assert oneself** : to insist strongly that others respect one's rights

as·ser·tion *n* **1** : the act of asserting **2** : a positive statement

as·sess *vb* **1** : to decide on the rate or amount of **2** : to assign a value to for purposes of taxation **3** : to put a charge or tax on — **as·ses·sor** *n*

as·set *n* **1 assets** *pl* : all the property belonging to a person or an organization **2** : ADVANTAGE 3

as·sid·u·ous *adj* : DILIGENT — **as·sid·u·ous·ly** *adv* — **as·sid·u·ous·ness** *n*

as·sign *vb* **1** : to appoint to a post or duty

2 : to give out with authority **3** : to decide on definitely

as·sign·ment *n* **1** : the act of assigning **2** : something assigned

as·sim·i·late *vb* **as·sim·i·lat·ed; as·sim·i·lat·ing** : to take something in and make it part of the thing it has joined

as·sim·i·la·tion *n* : the act or process of assimilating

1as·sist *vb* : to give aid : HELP

2assist *n* : an act of assisting

as·sis·tance *n* **1** : the act of helping **2** : the help given

1as·sis·tant *adj* : acting as a helper to another

2assistant *n* : a person who assists another

1as·so·ci·ate *vb* **as·so·ci·at·ed; as·so·ci·at·ing** **1** : to join or come together as partners, friends, or companions **2** : to connect in thought

2as·so·ci·ate *adj* **1** : closely joined with another (as in duties or responsibility) **2** : having some but not all rights and privileges

3as·so·ci·ate *n* **1** : a fellow worker : PARTNER **2** : a person who is one's friend or companion

as·so·ci·a·tion *n* **1** : the act of associating : the state of being associated **2** : an organization of persons having a common interest **3** : a feeling, memory, or thought connected with a person, place, or thing

as·so·cia·tive *adj* **1** : serving to associate **2** : being a property of a mathematical operation (as addition or multiplication) in which the result is independent of the original grouping of the elements

as·sort *vb* : to sort into groups

as·sort·ed *adj* **1** : made up of various kinds **2** : suited to one another

as·sort·ment *n* : the act of assorting : the state of being assorted **2** : a collection of assorted things or persons

as·sume *vb* **as·sumed; as·sum·ing** **1** : to take upon oneself : UNDERTAKE **2** : to take over usually by force **3** : to pretend to have or be **4** : to accept as true

as·sump·tion *n* **1** : the act of assuming **2** : something accepted as true

as·sur·ance *n* **1** : the act of assuring **2** : the state of being certain **3** : a being sure and safe : SECURITY **4** : confidence in one's own self

as·sure *vb* **as·sured; as·sur·ing** **1** : to make safe : INSURE **2** : to give confidence to **3** : to make sure or certain **4** : to inform positively

as·sured *adj* **1** : made sure or certain **2** : very confident — **as·sured·ly** *adv* — **as·sured·ness** *n*

as·ter *n* : any of various herbs related to the daisies that have leafy stems and white, pink, purple, or yellow flower heads which bloom in the fall

as·ter·isk *n* : a character * used in printing or in writing as a reference mark or to show that letters or words have been left out

astern *adv* **1** : behind a ship or airplane **2** : at or toward the stern **3** : 1BACKWARD 1

as·ter·oid *n* : one of thousands of small planets that move in orbits mostly between those of Mars and Jupiter and have diameters from a fraction of a kilometer to nearly 800 kilometers

asth·ma *n* : an ailment of which difficult breathing, wheezing, and coughing are symptoms

astir *adj* **1** : showing activity **2** : being out of bed : UP

as to *prep* **1** : with respect to : ABOUT **2** : ACCORDING TO 1

as·ton·ish *vb* : to strike with sudden wonder or surprise

as·ton·ish·ment *n* : great surprise : AMAZEMENT

as·tound *vb* : to fill with puzzled wonder

astray *adv or adj* **1** : off the right path or route **2** : in or into error

1astride *adv* : with one leg on each side

2astride *prep* : with one leg on each side of

as·trin·gent *adj* : able or tending to shrink body tissues — **as·trin·gent·ly** *adv*

astro- *prefix* : star : heavens : astronomical

as·trol·o·gy *n* : the study of the supposed influences of the stars and planets on human affairs by their positions in the sky in relation to each other

as·tro·naut *n* : a traveler in a spacecraft

as·tro·nau·tics *n* : the science of the construction and operation of spacecraft

as·tron·o·mer *n* : a person who is skilled in astronomy

as·tro·nom·i·cal *or* **as·tro·nom·ic** *adj* **1** : of or relating to astronomy **2** : extremely or unbelievably large — **as·tro·nom·i·cal·ly** *adv*

as·tron·o·my *n* : the science of celestial bodies and of their motions and makeup

as·tute *adj* : very alert and aware : CLEVER — **as·tute·ly** *adv* — **as·tute·ness** *n*

asun·der *adv or adj* **1** : into parts **2** : apart from each other in position

as well as *prep or conj* : in addition to : and also

asy·lum *n* **1** : a place of protection and shelter **2** : protection given especially to political refugees **3** : a place for the care of the poor or sick and especially of the insane

at *prep* **1** — used to indicate a particular place or time **2** — used to indicate a goal

3 — used to indicate position or condition

4 — used to tell how or why something is done

ate *past of* EAT

¹-ate *n suffix* : one acted upon in such a way

²-ate *n suffix* : office : rank : group of persons holding such an office or rank

³-ate *adj suffix* : marked by having

⁴-ate *vb suffix* : cause to be changed or influenced by : cause to become : furnish with

athe·ist *n* : a person who believes there is no God

ath·lete *n* : a person who is trained in or good at games and exercises that require physical skill, endurance, and strength

athlete's foot *n* : a fungus infection of the foot marked by blisters, itching, and cracks between and under the toes

ath·let·ic *adj* **1** : of, relating to, or characteristic of athletes or athletics **2** : vigorously active **3** : STURDY 2

ath·let·ics *n sing or pl* : games, sports, and exercises requiring strength, endurance, and skill

-ation *n suffix* : action or process : something connected with an action or process

-ative *adj suffix* **1** : of, relating to, or connected with **2** : tending to

at·las *n* : a book of maps

at·mo·sphere *n* **1** : the gas surrounding a celestial body : AIR **2** : the air in a particular place **3** : a surrounding influence or set of conditions

at·mo·spher·ic *adj* : of or relating to the atmosphere

atoll *n* : a ring-shaped coral island or string of islands consisting of a coral reef surrounding a lagoon

at·om *n* **1** : a tiny particle : BIT **2** : the smallest particle of an element that can exist alone or in combination

atom·ic *adj* **1** : of or relating to atoms **2** : NUCLEAR 3

atomic bomb *n* : a bomb whose great power is due to the sudden release of the energy in the nuclei of atoms

at·om·iz·er *n* : a device for spraying a liquid (as a perfume or disinfectant)

atone *vb* **atoned; aton·ing** : to do something to make up for a wrong that has been done

atone·ment *n* : a making up for an offense or injury

atop *prep* : on top of

atro·cious *adj* **1** : savagely brutal, cruel, or wicked **2** : very bad — **atro·cious·ly** *adv* — **atro·cious·ness** *n*

atroc·i·ty *n, pl* **atroc·i·ties** : an atrocious act, object, or situation

at·tach *vb* **1** : to take (money or property) legally in order to obtain payment of a debt **2** : to fasten one thing to another **3** : to bind by feelings of affection **4** : to assign by authority **5** : to think of as belonging to something

at·tach·ment *n* **1** : connection by feelings of affection or regard **2** : a device that can be attached to a machine or tool **3** : a connection by which one thing is joined to another

¹at·tack *vb* **1** : to take strong action against : ASSAULT **2** : to use unfriendly or bitter words against **3** : to begin to affect or to act upon harmfully **4** : to start to work on — **at·tack·er** *n*

²attack *n* **1** : the act of attacking **2** : beginning to work **3** : a spell of sickness

at·tain *vb* **1** : to reach as a desired goal **2** : to come into possession of **3** : to arrive at — **at·tain·able** *adj*

at·tain·ment *n* **1** : the act of attaining : the state of being attained **2** : ACCOMPLISHMENT 3

at·tar *n* : a sweet-smelling oil from flowers

¹at·tempt *vb* **1** : to try to do or perform **2** : to try to do something

²attempt *n* : the act or an instance of attempting

at·tend *vb* **1** : to pay attention to **2** : to go with especially as a servant or companion **3** : to care for **4** : to go to or be present at **5** : to take charge

at·ten·dance *n* **1** : the act of attending **2** : the number of persons present

¹at·ten·dant *n* : a person who attends something or someone

²attendant *adj* : coming with or following closely as a result

at·ten·tion *n* **1** : the act or the power of fixing one's mind on something : careful listening or watching **2** : a state of being aware **3** : careful thinking about something so as to be able to take action on it **4** : an act of kindness or politeness **5** : a military posture with body stiff and straight, heels together, and arms at the sides

at·ten·tive *adj* **1** : paying attention **2** : being thoughtful and polite — **at·ten·tive·ly** *adv* — **at·ten·tive·ness** *n*

at·test *vb* : to give proof of

at·tic *n* : a room or a space just under the roof of a building

¹at·tire *vb* **at·tired; at·tir·ing** : to put clothes and especially fine clothes on

²attire *n* : clothing meant for a particular occasion

at·ti·tude *n* **1** : the position of the body, or of the parts of the body, or of an object **2** : a feeling or opinion about a certain fact or situation

at·tor·ney *n, pl* **at·tor·neys** : a person who acts as agent for another in dealing with business or legal matters

at·tract *vb* **1** : to draw to or toward oneself **2** : to draw by appealing to interest or feeling

at·trac·tion *n* **1** : the act or power of attracting **2** : something that attracts or pleases

at·trac·tive *adj* : having the power or quality of attracting : PLEASING — **at·trac·tive·ly** *adv* — **at·trac·tive·ness** *n*

¹**at·tri·bute** *n* **1** : a quality belonging to a particular person or thing **2** : a word (as an adjective) indicating a quality

²**at·trib·ute** *vb* **at·trib·ut·ed; at·trib·ut·ing** **1** : to explain as the cause of **2** : to think of as likely to be a quality of a person or thing

at·tri·bu·tion *n* : the act of attributing

at·tune *vb* **at·tuned; at·tun·ing** : to bring into harmony : TUNE

atyp·i·cal *adj* : not typical — **atyp·i·cal·ly** *adv*

au·burn *adj* : of a reddish brown color

¹**auc·tion** *n* : a public sale at which things are sold to those who offer to pay the most

²**auction** *vb* : to sell at auction

auc·tion·eer *n* : a person in charge of auctions

au·da·cious *adj* **1** : very bold and daring : FEARLESS **2** : very rude : INSOLENT — **au·da·cious·ly** *adv* — **au·da·cious·ness** *n*

au·dac·i·ty *n, pl* **au·dac·i·ties** : the fact or an instance of being audacious

au·di·ble *adj* : loud enough to be heard — **au·di·bly** *adv*

au·di·ence *n* **1** : a group that listens or watches (as at a play or concert) **2** : a chance to talk with a person of very high rank **3** : those of the general public who give attention to something said, done, or written

¹**au·dio** *adj* **1** : of or relating to sound or its reproduction **2** : relating to or used in the transmitting or receiving of sound (as in radio or television)

²**audio** *n* **1** : the transmitting, receiving, or reproducing of sound **2** : the section of television equipment that deals with sound

au·dio·tape *n* : a tape recording of sound

au·dio·vi·su·al *adj* : of, relating to, or using both sound and sight

¹**au·dit** *n* : a thorough check of business accounts

²**audit** *vb* : to make an audit of

¹**au·di·tion** *n* : a short performance to test the talents of a singer, dancer, or actor

²**audition** *vb* : to test or try out in an audition

au·di·tor *n* **1** : a person who listens especially as a member of a radio or TV audi-

ence **2** : a person who audits business accounts

au·di·to·ri·um *n* **1** : the part of a public building where an audience sits **2** : a hall used for public gatherings

au·di·to·ry *adj* : of or relating to hearing

au·ger *n* : a tool used for boring holes

aught *n* : ZERO 1

aug·ment *vb* : to increase in size, amount, or degree

au·gust *adj* : being grand and noble : MAJESTIC — **au·gust·ly** *adv* — **au·gust·ness** *n*

Au·gust *n* : the eighth month of the year

auk *n* : a diving seabird of cold parts of the northern hemisphere with a heavy body and small wings

aunt *n* **1** : a sister of one's parent **2** : the wife of one's uncle

au·ra *n* : a feeling that seems to be given off by a person or thing

au·ral *adj* : of or relating to the ear or sense of hearing — **au·ral·ly** *adv*

au·ri·cle *n* : the part of the heart that receives blood from the veins

au·ro·ra bo·re·al·is *n* : broad bands of light that have a magnetic and electrical source and that appear in the sky at night especially in the arctic regions

aus·pic·es *n pl* : support and guidance of a sponsor

aus·pi·cious *adj* **1** : promising success **2** : PROSPEROUS 1 — **aus·pi·cious·ly** *adv*

aus·tere *adj* **1** : seeming or acting harsh and stern **2** : ¹PLAIN 1 — **aus·tere·ly** *adv*

aus·ter·i·ty *n, pl* **aus·ter·i·ties** **1** : an austere act or manner **2** : lack of all luxury

¹**Aus·tra·lian** *adj* : of or relating to Australia or the Australians

²**Australian** *n* : a person born or living in Australia

aut- *or* **au·to-** *prefix* **1** : self : same one **2** : automatic

au·then·tic *adj* : being really what it seems to be : GENUINE — **au·then·ti·cal·ly** *adv*

au·thor *n* **1** : a person who writes something (as a novel) **2** : one that starts or creates

au·thor·i·ta·tive *adj* : having or coming from authority — **au·thor·i·ta·tive·ly** *adv* — **au·thor·i·ta·tive·ness** *n*

au·thor·i·ty *n, pl* **au·thor·i·ties** **1** : a fact or statement used to support a position **2** : a person looked to as an expert **3** : power to influence the behavior of others **4** : persons having powers of government

au·tho·rize *vb* **au·tho·rized; au·tho·riz·ing** **1** : to give authority to : EMPOWER **2** : to give legal or official approval to

au·thor·ship *n* : the profession of writing

au·to *n, pl* **au·tos** : AUTOMOBILE

auto- — see AUT-

au·to·bi·og·ra·phy *n, pl* **au·to·bi·og·ra·phies** : the biography of a person written by that person

¹**au·to·graph** *n* : a person's signature written by hand

²**autograph** *vb* : to write one's signature in or on (as a book)

au·to·mate *vb* **au·to·mat·ed; au·to·mat·ing** : to make automatic

¹**au·to·mat·ic** *adj* **1** : INVOLUNTARY **2** : being a machine or device that acts by or regulates itself — **au·to·mat·i·cal·ly** *adv*

²**automatic** *n* **1** : an automatic machine or device **2** : an automatic firearm

au·to·ma·tion *n* **1** : the method of making a machine, a process, or a system work automatically **2** : automatic working of a machine, process, or system by mechanical or electronic devices that take the place of humans

¹**au·to·mo·bile** *adj* : AUTOMOTIVE

²**automobile** *n* : a usually four-wheeled vehicle that runs on its own power and is designed to carry passengers

au·to·mo·tive *adj* : SELF-PROPELLED

au·tumn *n* : the season between summer and winter that in the northern hemisphere is usually the months of September, October, and November

au·tum·nal *adj* : of or relating to autumn

¹**aux·il·ia·ry** *adj* : available to provide something extra

²**auxiliary** *n, pl* **aux·il·ia·ries** **1** : an auxiliary person, group, or device **2** : HELPING VERB

¹**avail** *vb* : to be of use or help

²**avail** *n* : help toward reaching a goal : USE

avail·able *adj* **1** : SUITABLE, USABLE **2** : possible to get : OBTAINABLE

av·a·lanche *n* : a large mass of snow and ice or of earth or rock sliding down a mountainside or over a cliff

av·a·rice *n* : strong desire for riches : GREED

av·a·ri·cious *adj* : greedy for riches — **av·a·ri·cious·ly** *adv* — **av·a·ri·cious·ness** *n*

avenge *vb* **avenged; aveng·ing** : to take revenge for — **aveng·er** *n*

av·e·nue *n* **1** : a way of reaching a goal **2** : a usually wide street

¹**av·er·age** *n* **1** : ARITHMETIC MEAN **2** : something usual in a group, class, or series

²**average** *adj* **1** : equaling or coming close to an average **2** : being ordinary or usual

³**average** *vb* **av·er·aged; av·er·ag·ing** **1** : to amount to usually **2** : to find the average of

averse *adj* : having a feeling of dislike

aver·sion *n* **1** : a strong dislike **2** : something strongly disliked

avert *vb* **1** : to turn away **2** : to keep from happening

avi·ary *n, pl* **avi·ar·ies** : a place (as a large cage) where birds are kept

avi·a·tion *n* **1** : the flying of aircraft **2** : the designing and making of aircraft

avi·a·tor *n* : the pilot of an aircraft

av·id *adj* : very eager — **av·id·ly** *adv*

av·o·ca·do *n, pl* **av·o·ca·dos** : a usually green fruit that is shaped like a pear or an egg, grows on a tropical American tree, and has a rich oily flesh

av·o·ca·tion *n* : an interest or activity that is not one's regular job : HOBBY

avoid *vb* : to keep away from

avoid·ance *n* : a keeping away from something

avow *vb* : to declare openly and frankly

avow·al *n* : an open declaration

await *vb* **1** : to wait for **2** : to be ready or waiting for

¹**awake** *vb* **awoke; awo·ken** *or* **awaked; awak·ing** **1** : to arouse from sleep : wake up **2** : to become conscious or aware of something

²**awake** *adj* : not asleep

awak·en *vb* : ¹AWAKE

¹**award** *vb* **1** : to give by judicial decision **2** : to give or grant as deserved or needed

²**award** *n* : something (as a prize) that is awarded

aware *adj* : having or showing understanding or knowledge : CONSCIOUS — **aware·ness** *n*

awash *adv or adj* **1** : washed by waves or tide **2** : floating about **3** : flooded or covered with water

¹**away** *adv* **1** : from this or that place **2** : in another place or direction **3** : out of existence **4** : from one's possession **5** : without stopping or slowing down **6** : at or to a great distance in space or time : FAR

²**away** *adj* **1** : ¹ABSENT 1 **2** : DISTANT 1

¹**awe** *n* : a feeling of mixed fear, respect, and wonder

²**awe** *vb* **awed; aw·ing** : to fill with awe

awe·some *adj* : causing a feeling of awe

aw·ful *adj* **1** : causing fear or terror **2** : very disagreeable or unpleasant **3** : very great

aw·ful·ly *adv* **1** : in a disagreeable or unpleasant manner **2** : to a very great degree

awhile *adv* : for a while : for a short time

awk·ward *adj* **1** : not graceful : CLUMSY **2** : likely to embarrass **3** : difficult to use or handle — **awk·ward·ly** *adv* — **awk·ward·ness** *n*

awl *n* : a pointed tool for making small holes (as in leather or wood)

aw·ning *n* : a cover (as of canvas) that shades or shelters like a roof

awoke *past of* AWAKE

awoken *past participle of* AWAKE

awry *adv or adj* **1** : turned or twisted to one side : ASKEW   **2** : out of the right course : AMISS

ax *or* **axe** *n* : a tool that has a heavy head with a sharp edge fixed to a handle and is used for chopping and splitting wood

ax·i·om *n* **1** : MAXIM   **2** : a statement thought to be clearly true

ax·is *n, pl* **ax·es** : a straight line about which a body or a geometric figure rotates or may be supposed to rotate

ax·le *n* : a pin or shaft on or with which a wheel or pair of wheels turns

ax·on *n* : a long fiber that carries impulses away from a nerve cell

¹aye *adv* : ¹YES 1

²aye *n* : an affirmative vote or voter

aza·lea *n* : a usually small rhododendron that sheds its leaves in the fall and has flowers of many colors which are shaped like funnels

azure *n* : the blue color of the clear daytime sky

B

b *n, pl* **b's** *or* **bs** *often cap* **1** : the second letter of the English alphabet   **2** : a grade that shows a student's work is good

¹baa *n* : the cry of a sheep

²baa *vb* : to make the cry of a sheep

¹bab·ble *vb* **bab·bled; bab·bling** **1** : to make meaningless sounds   **2** : to talk foolishly   **3** : to make the sound of a brook — **bab·bler** *n*

²babble *n* **1** : talk that is not clear   **2** : the sound of a brook

babe *n* : ¹BABY 1

ba·boon *n* : a large monkey of Africa and Asia with a doglike face

¹ba·by *n, pl* **babies** **1** : a very young child   **2** : the youngest of a group   **3** : an older person who acts like a baby

²baby *adj* : ¹YOUNG 1

³baby *vb* **ba·bied; ba·by·ing** : to treat as a baby

ba·by·hood *n* **1** : the time in a person's life when he or she is a baby   **2** : the state of being a baby

ba·by·ish *adj* : like a baby

ba·by–sit *vb* **ba·by–sat; ba·by–sit·ting** : to care for children usually during a short absence of the parents

ba·by–sit·ter *n* : a person who baby-sits

bach·e·lor *n* : a man who has not married

ba·cil·lus *n, pl* **ba·cil·li** **1** : a rod-shaped bacterium that forms internal spores   **2** : a bacterium that causes disease : GERM, MICROBE

¹back *n* **1** : the rear part of the human body from the neck to the end of the spine : the upper part of the body of an animal   **2** : the part of something that is opposite or away from the front part   **3** : a player in a team game who plays behind the forward line of players — **backed** *adj*

²back *adv* **1** : to, toward, or at the rear   **2** : in or to a former time, state, or place   **3** : under control   **4** : in return or reply — **back and forth** : backward and forward : from one place to another

³back *adj* **1** : located at the back   **2** : not yet paid : OVERDUE   **3** : no longer current

⁴back *vb* **1** : to give support or help to : UPHOLD   **2** : to move back — **back·er** *n*

back·bone *n* **1** : the column of bones in the back : SPINAL COLUMN   **2** : the strongest part of something   **3** : firmness of character

¹back·fire *n* **1** : a fire that is set to check the spread of a forest fire or a grass fire by burning off a strip of land ahead of it   **2** : a loud engine noise that happens when fuel ignites with a valve open

²backfire *vb* **back·fired; back·fir·ing** **1** : to make a backfire   **2** : to have a result opposite to what was planned

back·ground *n* **1** : the scenery or ground that is behind a main figure or object   **2** : a position that attracts little attention   **3** : the total of a person's experience, knowledge, and education

¹back·hand *n* **1** : a stroke made with the back of the hand turned in the direction in which the hand is moving   **2** : handwriting in which the letters slant to the left

²backhand *adv or adj* : with a backhand

back·hand·ed *adj* **1** : ²BACKHAND   **2** : not sincere

back of *prep* : ²BEHIND 1

back·stage *adv or adj* : in or to the area behind the stage

back·track *vb* : to go back over a course or a path

¹back·ward *or* **back·wards** *adv* **1** : toward the back   **2** : with the back first   **3** : opposite to the usual way

²backward *adj* **1** : turned toward the back

2 : BASHFUL **3** : slow in learning or development

back·wa·ter *n* **1** : water held or turned back from its course **2** : a backward place or condition

back·woods *n pl* **1** : wooded or partly cleared areas away from cities **2** : a place that is backward in culture

ba·con *n* : salted and smoked meat from the sides and the back of a pig

bac·te·ri·um *n, pl* **bac·te·ria** : any of numerous microscopic organisms that are single cells and are important to humans because of their chemical activities and as causes of disease

bad *adj* **worse; worst 1** : not good : POOR **2** : not favorable **3** : not fresh or sound **4** : not good or right : morally evil **5** : not enough **6** : UNPLEASANT **7** : HARMFUL **8** : SEVERE 4 **9** : not correct **10** : ¹ILL 4, SICK **11** : SORRY 1 — **bad·ness** *n*

bade *past of* BID

badge *n* : something worn to show that a person belongs to a certain group or rank

¹bad·ger *n* : a furry burrowing animal with short thick legs and long claws on the front feet

²badger *vb* : to annoy again and again

bad·ly *adv* **worse; worst 1** : in a bad manner **2** : very much

bad·min·ton *n* : a game in which a shuttlecock is hit back and forth over a net by players using light rackets

baf·fle *vb* **baf·fled; baf·fling** : to defeat or check by confusing

¹bag *n* **1** : a container made of flexible material (as paper or plastic) **2** : ¹PURSE 1, HANDBAG **3** : SUITCASE

²bag *vb* **bagged; bag·ging 1** : to swell out **2** : to put into a bag **3** : to kill or capture in hunting

ba·gel *n* : a hard roll shaped like a doughnut

bag·gage *n* : the trunks, suitcases, and personal belongings of travelers

bag·gy *adj* **bag·gi·er; bag·gi·est** : hanging loosely or puffed out like a bag

bag·pipe *n* : a musical instrument played especially in Scotland that consists of a tube, a bag for air, and pipes from which the sound comes

¹bail *vb* : to dip and throw out water from a boat — usually used with *out*

²bail *n* : a promise or a deposit of money needed to free a prisoner until his or her trial

³bail *vb* : to get the release of (a prisoner) by giving bail

bail out *vb* : to jump out of an airplane with a parachute

¹bait *vb* **1** : to torment by mean or unjust attacks **2** : to put bait on or in

²bait *n* : something used in luring especially to a hook or a trap

bake *vb* **baked; bak·ing 1** : to cook or become cooked in a dry heat especially in an oven **2** : to dry or harden by heat

bak·er *n* : a person who bakes and sells bread, cakes, or pastry

baker's dozen *n* : THIRTEEN

bak·ery *n, pl* **bak·er·ies** : a place where bread, cakes, and pastry are made or sold

baking powder *n* : a powder used to make the dough rise in making baked goods (as cakes or muffins)

baking soda *n* : SODIUM BICARBONATE

¹bal·ance *n* **1** : an instrument for weighing **2** : a steady position or condition **3** : equal total sums on the two sides of a bookkeeping account **4** : something left over : REMAINDER **5** : the amount by which one side of an account is greater than the other

²balance *vb* **bal·anced; bal·anc·ing 1** : to make the two sides of (an account) add up to the same total **2** : to make equal in weight or number **3** : to weigh against one another : COMPARE **4** : to put in or as if in balance

bal·co·ny *n, pl* **bal·co·nies 1** : a platform enclosed by a low wall or a railing built out from the side of a building **2** : a platform inside a building extending out over part of a main floor (as of a theater)

bald *adj* **1** : lacking a natural covering (as of hair) **2** : ¹PLAIN 3 — **bald·ness** *n*

bald eagle *n* : the common North American eagle that when full-grown has white head and neck feathers

¹bale *n* : a large bundle of goods tightly tied for storing or shipping

²bale *vb* **baled; bal·ing** : to make up into a bale — **bal·er** *n*

¹balk *n* : HINDRANCE

²balk *vb* **1** : to keep from happening or succeeding **2** : to stop short and refuse to go

balky *adj* **balk·i·er; balk·i·est** : likely to balk

¹ball *n* **1** : something round or roundish **2** : a usually round object used in a game or sport **3** : a game or sport (as baseball) played with a ball **4** : a solid usually round shot for a gun **5** : the rounded bulge at the base of the thumb or big toe **6** : a pitched baseball that is not hit and is not a strike

²ball *vb* : to make or come together into a ball

³ball *n* : a large formal party for dancing

bal·lad *n* **1** : a simple song **2** : a short poem suitable for singing that tells a story in simple language

ball–and–socket joint *n* : a joint (as in the

shoulder) in which a rounded part can move in many directions in a socket

bal·last *n* **1** : heavy material used to make a ship steady or to control the rising of a balloon **2** : gravel, cinders, or crushed stone used in making a roadbed

ball bearing *n* **1** : a bearing in which the revolving part turns on metal balls that roll easily in a groove **2** : one of the balls in a ball bearing

bal·le·ri·na *n* : a female ballet dancer

bal·let *n* **1** : a stage dance that tells a story in movement and pantomime **2** : a group that performs ballets

¹bal·loon *n* **1** : a bag that rises and floats above the ground when filled with heated air or with a gas that is lighter than air **2** : a toy consisting of a rubber bag that can be blown up with air or gas **3** : an outline containing words spoken or thought by a character (as in a cartoon)

²balloon *vb* : to swell or puff out like a balloon

¹bal·lot *n* **1** : an object and especially a printed sheet of paper used in voting **2** : the action or a system of voting **3** : the right to vote **4** : the number of votes cast

²ballot *vb* : to vote or decide by ballot

ball·point *n* : a pen whose writing point is a small metal ball that inks itself from an inner supply

ball·room *n* : a large room for dances

balmy *adj* **balm·i·er; balm·i·est** : gently soothing

bal·sa *n* : the very light but strong wood of a tropical American tree

bal·sam *n* **1** : a material with a strong pleasant smell that oozes from some plants **2** : a plant (as the evergreen **balsam fir** often used as a Christmas tree) that yields balsam

bal·us·ter *n* : a short post that supports the upper part of a railing

bal·us·trade *n* : a row of balusters topped by a rail to serve as an open fence (as along the edge of a terrace or a balcony)

bam·boo *n* : a tall treelike tropical grass with a hard jointed stem that is used in making furniture and in building

¹ban *vb* **banned; ban·ning** : to forbid especially by law or social pressure

²ban *n* : an official order forbidding something

ba·nana *n* : a yellow or red fruit that is shaped somewhat like a finger and grows in bunches on a large treelike tropical plant (**banana plant** or **banana tree**) with very large leaves

¹band *n* **1** : something that holds together or goes around something else **2** : a strip of

material around or across something **3** : a range of frequencies (as of radio waves)

²band *vb* **1** : to put a band on : tie together with a band **2** : to unite in a group

³band *n* **1** : a group of persons or animals **2** : a group of musicians performing together

¹ban·dage *n* : a strip of material used especially to dress and bind up wounds

²bandage *vb* **ban·daged; ban·dag·ing** : to bind or cover with a bandage

ban·dan·na *or* **ban·dana** *n* : a large handkerchief usually with a colorful design printed on it

ban·dit *n* : a lawless person : one who lives outside the law

band·stand *n* : an outdoor platform used for band concerts

band·wag·on *n* **1** : a wagon carrying musicians in a parade **2** : a candidate, side, or movement that attracts growing support

¹bang *vb* : to beat, strike, or shut with a loud noise

²bang *n* **1** : a violent blow **2** : a sudden loud noise **3** : ²THRILL 1

³bang *n* : hair cut short across the forehead — usually used in pl.

⁴bang *vb* : to cut (hair) short and squarely across

ban·ish *vb* **1** : to force to leave a country **2** : to drive away : DISMISS

ban·ish·ment *n* : a banishing from a country

ban·is·ter *n* **1** : one of the slender posts used to support the handrail of a staircase **2** : a handrail and its supporting posts **3** : the handrail of a staircase

ban·jo *n, pl* **banjos** : a musical instrument with four or five strings and a fretted neck

¹bank *n* **1** : a mound or ridge especially of earth **2** : something shaped like a mound **3** : an undersea elevation : SHOAL **4** : the rising ground at the edge of a river, lake, or sea

²bank *vb* **1** : to raise a bank around **2** : to heap up in a bank **3** : to build (a curve) with the road or track sloping upward from the inside edge **4** : to cover with fuel or ashes so as to reduce the speed of burning **5** : to tilt an airplane to one side when turning

³bank *n* **1** : a place of business that lends, exchanges, takes care of, or issues money **2** : a small closed container in which money may be saved **3** : a storage place for a reserve supply

⁴bank *vb* **1** : to have an account in a bank **2** : to deposit in a bank

⁵bank *n* : a group or series of objects arranged together in a row

bank·er *n* : a person who is engaged in the business of a bank

bank·ing *n* : the business of a bank or banker

¹bank·rupt *n* : a person who becomes unable to pay his or her debts and whose property is by court order divided among the creditors

²bankrupt *adj* : unable to pay one's debts

³bankrupt *vb* : to make bankrupt

bank·rupt·cy *n*, *pl* **bank·rupt·cies** : the state of being bankrupt

¹ban·ner *n* **1** : ¹FLAG **2** : a piece of cloth with a design, a picture, or some writing on it

²banner *adj* : unusually good or satisfactory

ban·quet *n* : a formal dinner for many people often in honor of someone

ban·tam *n* : a miniature breed of domestic chicken often raised for exhibiting in shows

¹ban·ter *vb* : to speak to in a friendly but teasing way

²banter *n* : good-natured teasing and joking

bap·tism *n* : the act or ceremony of baptizing

bap·tize *vb* **bap·tized; bap·tiz·ing** **1** : to dip in water or sprinkle water on as a part of the ceremony of receiving into the Christian church **2** : to give a name to as in the ceremony of baptism : CHRISTEN

¹bar *n* **1** : a usually slender rigid piece (as of wood or metal) that has many uses (as for a lever or barrier) **2** : a usually rectangular solid piece or block of something **3** : something that blocks the way **4** : a submerged or partly submerged bank along a shore or in a river **5** : a court of law **6** : the profession of law **7** : a straight stripe, band, or line longer than it is wide **8** : a counter on which liquor is served **9** : a place of business for the sale of alcoholic drinks **10** : a vertical line across a musical staff marking equal measures of time **11** : ¹MEASURE 6

²bar *vb* **barred; bar·ring** **1** : to fasten with a bar **2** : to block off **3** : to shut out

³bar *prep* : with the exception of

barb *n* : a sharp point that sticks out and backward (as from the tip of an arrow or fishhook) — **barbed** *adj*

bar·bar·i·an *n* : an uncivilized person

bar·bar·ic *adj* : of, relating to, or characteristic of barbarians

bar·ba·rous *adj* **1** : not civilized **2** : CRUEL 2, HARSH — **bar·ba·rous·ly** *adv*

¹bar·be·cue *vb* **bar·be·cued; bar·be·cu·ing** **1** : to cook over or before an open source of heat **2** : to cook in a highly seasoned sauce

²barbecue *n* **1** : a large animal roasted whole **2** : an outdoor social gathering at which food is barbecued and eaten

bar·ber *n* : a person whose business is cutting and dressing hair and shaving beards

bard *n* **1** : a person in ancient societies skilled at composing and singing songs about heroes **2** : POET

¹bare *adj* **bar·er; bar·est** **1** : having no covering : NAKED **2** : ¹EMPTY 1 **3** : having nothing left over or added : MERE **4** : ¹PLAIN 3

²bare *vb* **bared; bar·ing** : UNCOVER 1, 2

bare·back *adv or adj* : on the bare back of a horse : without a saddle

bare·foot *adv or adj* : with the feet bare

bare·head·ed *adv or adj* : with the head bare : without a hat

bare·ly *adv* : with nothing to spare

¹bar·gain *n* **1** : an agreement between persons settling what each is to give and receive in a business deal **2** : something bought or offered for sale at a desirable price

²bargain *vb* : to talk over the terms of a purchase or agreement

barge *n* : a broad boat with a flat bottom used chiefly in harbors and on rivers and canals

bar graph *n* : a chart that uses parallel bars whose lengths are in proportion to the numbers represented

bari·tone *n* **1** : a male singing voice between bass and tenor in range **2** : a singer having a baritone voice **3** : a horn used in bands that is lower than the trumpet but higher than the tuba

¹bark *vb* **1** : to make the short loud cry of a dog **2** : to shout or speak sharply

²bark *n* : the sound made by a barking dog

³bark *n* : the outside covering of the trunk, branches, and roots of a tree

⁴bark *vb* : to rub or scrape the skin off

⁵bark *or* **barque** *n* **1** : a small sailing boat **2** : a three-masted ship with foremast and mainmast square-rigged

bark·er *n* : a person who stands at the entrance to a show or a store and tries to attract people to it

bar·ley *n* : a cereal grass with flowers in dense heads that is grown for its grain which is used mostly to feed farm animals or make malt

barn *n* : a building used for storing grain and hay and for housing farm animals

bar·na·cle *n* : a small saltwater shellfish that fastens itself on rocks or on wharves and the bottoms of ships

barn·yard *n* : a usually fenced area next to a barn

ba·rom·e·ter *n* : an instrument that measures air pressure and is used to forecast changes in the weather

bar·on *n* : a member of the lowest rank of the British nobility

bar·on·ess *n* **1** : the wife or widow of a baron **2** : a woman who holds the rank of a baron in her own right

bar·on·et *n* : the holder of a rank of honor below a baron but above a knight

ba·ro·ni·al *adj* : of, relating to, or suitable for a baron

barque *variant of* BARK

bar·racks *n sing or pl* : a building or group of buildings in which soldiers live

bar·rage *n* : a barrier formed by continuous artillery or machine-gun fire directed upon a narrow strip of ground

¹bar·rel *n* **1** : a round bulging container that is longer than it is wide and has flat ends **2** : the amount contained in a full barrel **3** : something shaped like a cylinder

²barrel *vb* **bar·reled** *or* **bar·relled; bar·rel·ing** *or* **bar·rel·ling** : to move at a high speed

¹bar·ren *adj* **1** : unable to produce seed, fruit, or young **2** : growing only poor or few plants

²barren *n* : an area of barren land

bar·rette *n* : a clasp or bar used to hold a girl's or woman's hair in place

¹bar·ri·cade *vb* **bar·ri·cad·ed; bar·ri·cad·ing** : to block off with a barricade

²barricade *n* : a barrier made in a hurry for protection against attack or for blocking the way

bar·ri·er *n* **1** : something (as a fence) that blocks the way **2** : something that keeps apart or makes progress difficult

bar·ring *prep* : aside from the possibility of

¹bar·row *n* : a castrated male hog

²barrow *n* **1** : WHEELBARROW **2** : PUSH-CART

¹bar·ter *vb* : to trade by exchanging one thing for another without the use of money

²barter *n* : the exchange of goods without the use of money

¹base *n* **1** : a thing or a part on which something rests : BOTTOM, FOUNDATION **2** : a line or surface of a geometric figure upon which an altitude is or is thought to be constructed **3** : the main substance in a mixture **4** : a supporting or carrying substance (as in a medicine or paint) **5** : a place where a military force keeps its supplies or from which it starts its operations **6** : a number with reference to which a system of numbers is constructed **7** : a starting place or goal in various games **8** : any of the four stations a runner in baseball must touch in order to score **9** : a chemical substance (as lime or ammonia) that reacts with an acid to form a salt and turns red litmus paper blue

²base *vb* **based; bas·ing** : to provide with a base or basis

³base *adj* **bas·er; bas·est** **1** : of low value and not very good in some ways **2** : not honorable : MEAN — **base·ness** *n*

base·ball *n* **1** : a game played with a bat and ball by two teams of nine players on a field with four bases that mark the course a runner must take to score **2** : the ball used in baseball

base·board *n* : a line of boards or molding extending around the walls of a room and touching the floor

base·ment *n* : the part of a building that is partly or entirely below ground level

bash *vb* : to hit very hard

bash·ful *adj* : uneasy in the presence of others

ba·sic *adj* **1** : of, relating to, or forming the base of something **2** : relating to or characteristic of a chemical base — **ba·si·cal·ly** *adv*

ba·sil *n* : a fragrant mint used in cooking

ba·sin *n* **1** : a wide shallow usually round dish or bowl for holding liquids **2** : the amount that a basin holds **3** : a natural or artificial hollow or enclosure containing water **4** : the land drained by a river and its branches

ba·sis *n, pl* **ba·ses** : FOUNDATION 2, BASE

bask *vb* : to lie or relax in pleasantly warm surroundings

bas·ket *n* **1** : a container made by weaving together materials (as reeds, straw, or strips of wood) **2** : the contents of a basket **3** : something that is like a basket in shape or use **4** : a goal in basketball — **bas·ket·like** *adj*

bas·ket·ball *n* **1** : a game in which each of two teams tries to throw a round inflated ball through a raised basketlike goal **2** : the ball used in basketball

bas·ket·ry *n* **1** : the making of objects (as baskets) by weaving or braiding long slender pieces (as of reed or wood) **2** : objects made of interwoven twigs or reeds

bas-re·lief *n* : a sculpture in which the design is raised very slightly from the background

¹bass *n, pl* **bass** *or* **bass·es** : any of numerous freshwater and sea fishes that are caught for sport and food

²bass *n* **1** : a tone of low pitch **2** : the lowest part in harmony that has four parts **3** : the lower half of the musical pitch range **4** : the lowest male singing voice **5** : a singer or an instrument having a bass range or part

bass drum *n* : a large drum with two heads

that produces a low booming sound when played

bas·soon *n* : a double-reed woodwind instrument with a usual range two octaves lower than an oboe

bass viol *n* : DOUBLE BASS

bass·wood *n* : a pale wood with straight grain from the linden or a related tree

1baste *vb* **bast·ed; bast·ing** : to sew with long loose stitches so as to hold the work temporarily in place

2baste *vb* **bast·ed; bast·ing** : to moisten (as with melted fat or juices) while roasting

1bat *n* 1 : a sharp blow or slap 2 : an implement used for hitting the ball in various games 3 : a turn at batting

2bat *vb* **bat·ted; bat·ting** 1 : to strike with or as if with a bat 2 : to take one's turn at bat

3bat *n* : any of a group of mammals that fly by means of long front limbs modified into wings

batch *n* 1 : a quantity of something baked at one time 2 : a quantity of material for use at one time or produced at one operation 3 : a group of persons or things

bath *n, pl* **baths** 1 : a washing of the body 2 : water for bathing 3 : a place, room, or building where persons may bathe 4 : BATHTUB 5 : a liquid in which objects are placed so that it can act upon them

bathe *vb* **bathed; bath·ing** 1 : to take a bath 2 : to go swimming 3 : to give a bath to 4 : to apply a liquid to 5 : to cover with or as if with a liquid — **bath·er** *n*

bathing suit *n* : SWIMSUIT

bath·room *n* : a room containing a bathtub or shower and usually a washbowl and toilet

bath·tub *n* : a tub in which to take a bath

ba·ton *n* 1 : a stick with which a leader directs an orchestra or band 2 : a rod with a ball on one end carried by a drum major or drum majorette

bat·tal·ion *n* 1 : a part of an army consisting of two or more companies 2 : a large body of persons organized to act together

1bat·ter *vb* 1 : to beat with repeated violent blows 2 : to damage by blows or hard use

2batter *n* : a thin mixture made chiefly of flour and a liquid beaten together and used in making cakes and biscuits

3batter *n* : the player whose turn it is to bat

bat·tered *adj* : worn down or injured by hard use

bat·ter·ing ram *n* 1 : an ancient military machine that consisted of a heavy beam with an iron tip mounted in a frame and swung back and forth in order to batter down walls 2 : a beam or bar with handles used to batter down doors or walls

bat·tery *n, pl* **bat·ter·ies** 1 : two or more big military guns that are controlled as a unit 2 : an electric cell for providing electric current or a group of such cells 3 : a number of machines or devices grouped together

bat·ting *n* : cotton or wool in sheets used mostly for stuffing quilts or packaging goods

1bat·tle *n* 1 : a fight between armies, warships, or airplanes 2 : a fight between two persons or animals 3 : a long or hard struggle or contest 4 : WARFARE

2battle *vb* **bat·tled; bat·tling** : to engage in battle

bat·tle–ax *or* **bat·tle–axe** *n* : an ax with a broad blade formerly used as a weapon

bat·tle·field *n* : a place where a battle is fought or was once fought

bat·tle·ground *n* : BATTLEFIELD

bat·tle·ment *n* : a low wall (as at the top of a castle or tower) with openings to shoot through

bat·tle·ship *n* : a large warship with heavy armor and large guns

1bawl *vb* 1 : to shout or cry loudly 2 : to weep noisily

2bawl *n* : a loud cry

bawl out *vb* : to scold severely

1bay *n* 1 : a reddish-brown horse 2 : a reddish brown

2bay *vb* : to bark with long deep tones

3bay *n* 1 : the baying of dogs 2 : the position of an animal or a person forced to face pursuers when it is impossible to escape 3 : the position of pursuers who are held off

4bay *n* : a part of a large body of water extending into the land

5bay *n* : the laurel or a related tree or shrub

bay·ber·ry *n, pl* **bay·ber·ries** : a shrub with leathery leaves and small bluish white waxy berries used in making candles

1bay·o·net *n* : a weapon like a dagger made to fit on the end of a rifle

2bayonet *vb* **bay·o·net·ed; bay·o·net·ting** : to stab with a bayonet

bay·ou *n* : a creek that flows slowly through marshy land

bay window *n* : a window or a set of windows that sticks out from the wall of a building

ba·zaar *n* 1 : an Oriental marketplace containing rows of small shops 2 : a large building where many kinds of goods are sold 3 : a fair for the sale of goods especially for charity

ba·zoo·ka *n* : a portable shoulder gun consisting of a tube open at both ends that shoots an explosive rocket able to pierce armor

be *vb, past 1st & 3d sing* **was;** *2d sing* **were;** *pl* **were;** *past subjunctive* **were;** *past participle* **been;** *present participle* **be·ing;** *present 1st sing* **am;** *2d sing* **are;** *3d sing* **is;** *pl* **are;** *present subjunctive* **be** **1 :** to equal in meaning or identity **2 :** to have a specified character or quality **3 :** to belong to the class of **4 :** EXIST 1, LIVE **5** — used as a helping verb with other verbs

be- *prefix* **1 :** on : around : over **2 :** provide with or cover with : dress up with **3 :** about : to : upon **4 :** make : cause to be

¹**beach** *n* **:** a sandy or gravelly part of the shore of the sea or of a lake

²**beach** *vb* **:** to run or drive ashore

beach·head *n* **:** an area on an enemy shore held by an advance force of an invading army to protect the later landing of troops or supplies

bea·con *n* **1 :** a guiding or warning light or fire on a high place **2 :** a radio station that sends out signals to guide aircraft

¹**bead** *n* **1 :** a small piece of solid material with a hole through it by which it can be strung on a thread **2 :** a small round mass **3 :** a small knob on a gun used in taking aim

²**bead** *vb* **1 :** to cover with beads **2 :** to string together like beads

beady *adj* **bead·i·er; bead·i·est :** like a bead especially in being small, round, and shiny

bea·gle *n* **:** a small hound with short legs and a smooth coat

beak *n* **1 :** the bill of a bird **2 :** a part shaped like a beak — **beaked** *adj*

bea·ker *n* **:** a deep cup or glass with a wide mouth and usually a lip for pouring

¹**beam** *n* **1 :** a long heavy piece of timber or metal used as a main horizontal support of a building or a ship **2 :** a ray of light **3 :** a constant radio wave sent out from an airport to guide pilots along a course

²**beam** *vb* **1 :** to send out beams of light **2 :** to smile with joy **3 :** to aim a radio broadcast by use of a special antenna

bean *n* **1 :** the edible seed or pod of a bushy or climbing garden plant related to the peas and clovers **2 :** a seed or fruit like a bean

¹**bear** *n, pl* **bears** **1** *or pl* **bear :** a large heavy mammal with long shaggy hair and a very short tail **2 :** a grumpy or glum person

²**bear** *vb* **bore; borne; bear·ing** **1 :** ¹SUPPORT 4 **2 :** to have as a feature or characteristic **3 :** to bring forth : give birth to **4 :** to put up with **5 :** ²PRESS 1 **6 :** to have a relation to the matter at hand

bear·able *adj* **:** possible to bear

beard *n* **1 :** the hair on the face of a man **2 :** a hairy growth or tuft

bear·er *n* **1 :** someone or something that bears, supports, or carries **2 :** a person holding a check or an order for payment

bear·ing *n* **1 :** the manner in which one carries or conducts oneself **2 :** a part of a machine in which another part turns **3 :** the position or direction of one point with respect to another or to the compass **4 bear·ings** *pl* **:** understanding of one's position or situation **5 :** CONNECTION 2

beast *n* **1 :** a mammal with four feet (as a bear, deer, or rabbit) **2 :** a farm animal especially when kept for work **3 :** a mean or horrid person

¹**beat** *vb* **beat; beat·en** *or* **beat; beat·ing** **1 :** to strike again and again **2 :** ¹THROB 2, PULSATE **3 :** to flap against **4 :** to mix by stirring rapidly **5 :** to win against **6 :** to measure or mark off by strokes — **beat·er** *n*

²**beat** *n* **1 :** a blow or a stroke made again and again **2 :** a single pulse (as of the heart) **3 :** a measurement of time or accent in music **4 :** an area or place regularly visited or traveled through

³**beat** *adj* **1 :** being very tired **2 :** having lost one's morale

beat·en *adj* **:** worn smooth by passing feet

be·at·i·tude *n* **:** one of the statements made in the Sermon on the Mount (Matthew 5: 3-12) beginning "Blessed are"

beau *n, pl* **beaux** *or* **beaus :** BOYFRIEND

beau·te·ous *adj* **:** BEAUTIFUL

beau·ti·cian *n* **:** a person who gives beauty treatments (as to skin and hair)

beau·ti·ful *adj* **:** having qualities of beauty : giving pleasure to the mind or senses — **beau·ti·ful·ly** *adv*

beau·ti·fy *vb* **beau·ti·fied; beau·ti·fy·ing** **:** to make beautiful

beau·ty *n, pl* **beauties** **1 :** the qualities of a person or a thing that give pleasure to the senses or to the mind **2 :** a beautiful person or thing

beauty shop *n* **:** a place of business for the care of customers' hair, skin, and nails

bea·ver *n* **:** an animal related to the rats and mice that has webbed hind feet and a broad flat tail, builds dams and houses of sticks and mud in water, and is prized for its soft but strong fur

be·calm *vb* **:** to bring to a stop because of lack of wind

became *past of* BECOME

be·cause *conj* **:** for the reason that

because of *prep* **:** as a result of

beck *n* **:** a beckoning motion

beck·on *vb* **:** to call or signal by a motion (as a wave or nod)

be·come *vb* **be·came; become; be·com·ing** **1 :** to come or grow to be **2 :** to be suitable to : SUIT — **become of** : to happen to

be·com·ing *adj* : having a pleasing effect — **be·com·ing·ly** *adv*

¹bed *n* **1** : a piece of furniture on which one may sleep or rest **2** : a place for sleeping or resting **3** : a level piece of ground prepared for growing plants **4** : the bottom of something **5** : LAYER 2

²bed *vb* **bed·ded; bed·ding 1** : to put or go to bed **2** : to plant in beds

bed·bug *n* : a small wingless insect that sucks blood and is sometimes found in houses and especially in beds

bed·clothes *n pl* : coverings (as sheets and pillowcases) for a bed

bed·ding *n* **1** : BEDCLOTHES **2** : material for a bed

be·dev·il *vb* : to trouble or annoy again and again : PESTER, HARASS

bed·lam *n* : a place or scene of uproar and confusion

be·drag·gled *adj* **1** : limp and often wet as by exposure to rain **2** : soiled from or as if from being dragged in mud

bed·rid·den *adj* : forced to stay in bed by sickness or weakness

bed·rock *n* : the solid rock found under surface materials (as soil)

bed·room *n* : a room to sleep in

bed·side *n* : the place beside a bed

bed·spread *n* : a decorative top covering for a bed

bed·stead *n* : the framework of a bed

bed·time *n* : time to go to bed

bee *n* **1** : an insect with four wings that is related to the wasps, gathers pollen and nectar from flowers from which it makes beebread and honey for food, and usually lives in large colonies **2** : a gathering of people to do something together

bee·bread *n* : a bitter yellowish brown food material prepared by bees from pollen and stored in their honeycomb

beech *n* : a tree with smooth gray bark, deep green leaves, and small triangular nuts

beef *n, pl* **beefs** *or* **beeves 1** : the flesh of a steer, cow, or bull **2** : a steer, cow, or bull especially when fattened for food — **beef-like** *adj*

beef·steak *n* : a slice of beef suitable for broiling or frying

bee·hive *n* : HIVE 1

bee·line *n* : a straight direct course

been *past participle of* BE

beer *n* : an alcoholic drink made from malt and flavored with hops

bees·wax *n* : wax made by bees and used by them in building honeycomb

beet *n* : a leafy plant with a thick juicy root

that is used as a vegetable or as a source of sugar

bee·tle *n* **1** : any of a group of insects with four wings the outer pair of which are stiff cases that cover the others when folded **2** : an insect (as a bug) that looks like a beetle

beeves *pl of* BEEF

be·fall *vb* **be·fell; be·fall·en; be·fall·ing 1** : to take place : HAPPEN **2** : to happen to

be·fit *vb* **be·fit·ted; be·fit·ting** : to be suitable to or proper for

¹be·fore *adv* **1** : in front : AHEAD **2** : in the past **3** : at an earlier time

²before *prep* **1** : in front of **2** : in the presence of **3** : earlier than

³before *conj* **1** : ahead of the time when **2** : more willingly than

be·fore·hand *adv* : ¹BEFORE 1 : ahead of time

be·friend *vb* : to act as a friend to : help in a friendly way

beg *vb* **begged; beg·ging 1** : to ask for money, food, or help as a charity **2** : to ask as a favor in an earnest or polite way

beg·gar *n* **1** : one who lives by begging **2** : PAUPER

be·gin *vb* **be·gan; be·gun; be·gin·ning 1** : to do the first part of an action **2** : to come into existence

be·gin·ner *n* : a young or inexperienced person

be·gin·ning *n* **1** : the point at which something begins **2** : first part

be·gone *vb* : to go away : DEPART — used especially in the imperative mood

be·go·nia *n* : a plant with a juicy stem, ornamental leaves, and bright waxy flowers

be·grudge *vb* **be·grudged; be·grudg·ing** : to give or do reluctantly

begun *past of* BEGIN

be·half *n* : one's interest or support

be·have *vb* **be·haved; be·hav·ing 1** : to conduct oneself **2** : to conduct oneself properly **3** : to act or function in a particular way

be·hav·ior *n* **1** : the way in which one conducts oneself **2** : the whole activity of something and especially a living being

be·head *vb* : to cut off the head of

¹be·hind *adv* **1** : in a place that is being or has been departed from **2** : at, to, or toward the back **3** : not up to the general level

²behind *prep* **1** : at or to the back of **2** : not up to the level of

be·hold *vb* **be·held; be·hold·ing** : to look upon : SEE — **be·hold·er** *n*

beige *n* : a yellowish brown

be·ing *n* **1** : the state of having life or existence **2** : one that exists in fact or thought **3** : a living thing

be·la·bor *vb* : to keep working on to excess

be·lat·ed *adj* : delayed beyond the usual or expected time

¹belch *vb* **1** : to force out gas suddenly from the stomach through the mouth **2** : to throw out or be thrown out violently

²belch *n* : a belching of gas

bel·fry *n*, *pl* **belfries** : a tower or room in a tower for a bell or set of bells

¹Bel·gian *adj* : of or relating to Belgium or the Belgians

²Belgian *n* : a person born or living in Belgium

be·lief *n* **1** : a feeling sure that a person or thing exists or is true or trustworthy **2** : religious faith : CREED **3** : something that one thinks is true

be·liev·able *adj* : possible to believe

be·lieve *vb* **be·lieved; be·liev·ing 1** : to have faith or confidence in the existence or worth of **2** : to accept as true **3** : to accept the word of **4** : THINK 2

be·liev·er *n* : one who has faith (as in a religion)

be·lit·tle *vb* **be·lit·tled; be·lit·tling** : to make (a person or a thing) seem small or unimportant

bell *n* **1** : a hollow metallic device that is shaped somewhat like a cup and makes a ringing sound when struck **2** : the stroke or sound of a bell that tells the hour **3** : the time indicated by the stroke of a bell **4** : a half-hour period of watch on shipboard **5** : something shaped like a bell

bell·boy *n* : BELLHOP

bell·hop *n* : a hotel or club employee who answers calls for service by bell or telephone and assists guests with luggage

¹bel·lig·er·ent *adj* **1** : carrying on war **2** : eager to fight

²belligerent *n* **1** : a nation at war **2** : a person taking part in a fight

bell jar *n* : a usually glass vessel shaped like a bell and used to cover objects or to contain gases or a vacuum

¹bel·low *vb* : to give a loud deep roar like that of a bull

²bellow *n* : a loud deep roar

bel·lows *n sing or pl* **1** : a device that produces a strong current of air when its sides are pressed together **2** : the folding part of some cameras

¹bel·ly *n*, *pl* **bellies 1** : ABDOMEN 1 **2** : the under part of an animal's body **3** : STOMACH 1 **4** : an internal cavity (as of the human body) **5** : the thick part of a muscle

²belly *vb* **bel·lied; bel·ly·ing** : to swell out

belly button *n* : NAVEL

be·long *vb* **1** : to be in a proper place **2** : to be the property of a person or group of persons **3** : to be a part of : be connected with : go with

be·long·ings *n pl* : the things that belong to a person

be·lov·ed *adj* : greatly loved : very dear

¹be·low *adv* : in or to a lower place

²below *prep* : lower than : BENEATH

¹belt *n* **1** : a strip of flexible material (as leather or cloth) worn around a person's body for holding in or supporting clothing or weapons or for ornament **2** : something like a belt : BAND, CIRCLE **3** : a flexible endless band running around wheels or pulleys and used for moving or carrying something **4** : a region suited to or producing something or having some special feature — **belt·ed** *adj*

²belt *vb* **1** : to put a belt on or around **2** : to strike hard

be·moan *vb* : to express grief over

bench *n* **1** : a long seat for two or more persons **2** : a long table for holding work and tools **3** : the position or rank of a judge

¹bend *vb* **bent; bend·ing 1** : to make, be, or become curved or angular rather than straight or flat **2** : to move out of a straight line or position : STOOP **3** : to turn in a certain direction : DIRECT

²bend *n* : something that is bent : CURVE

¹be·neath *adv* : in a lower place

²beneath *prep* **1** : lower than : UNDER **2** : not worthy of

bene·dic·tion *n* **1** : an expression of approval **2** : a short blessing by a minister or priest at the end of a religious service

ben·e·fac·tor *n* : one who helps another especially by giving money

ben·e·fi·cial *adj* : producing good results : HELPFUL — **ben·e·fi·cial·ly** *adv*

ben·e·fi·cia·ry *n*, *pl* **ben·e·fi·cia·ries** : a person who benefits or is expected to benefit from something

¹ben·e·fit *n* **1** : something that does good to a person or thing **2** : money paid in time of death, sickness, or unemployment or in old age (as by an insurance company)

²benefit *vb* **ben·e·fit·ed** *or* **ben·e·fit·ted; ben·e·fit·ing** *or* **ben·e·fit·ting 1** : to be useful or profitable to **2** : to receive benefit

be·nev·o·lence *n* : KINDNESS, GENEROSITY

be·nev·o·lent *adj* : having a desire to do good : KINDLY, CHARITABLE

be·nign *adj* **1** : of a gentle disposition **2** : likely to bring about a good outcome — **be·nign·ly** *adv*

¹bent *adj* **1** : changed by bending : CROOKED **2** : strongly favorable to : quite determined

²bent *n* : a strong or natural liking

be·queath vb 1 : to give or leave by means of a will 2 : to hand down

be·quest n 1 : the act of bequeathing 2 : something given or left by a will

1be·reaved adj : suffering the death of a loved one

2bereaved n, pl **bereaved** : a bereaved person

be·reft adj 1 : not having something needed, wanted, or expected 2 : **1BEREAVED**

be·ret n : a soft round flat cap without a visor

berg n : ICEBERG

beri·beri n : a disease caused by lack of a vitamin in which there is weakness, wasting, and damage to nerves

1ber·ry n, pl **berries** 1 : a small pulpy fruit (as a strawberry) 2 : a simple fruit (as a grape or tomato) in which the ripened ovary wall is fleshy 3 : a dry seed (as of the coffee tree)

2berry vb **ber·ried; ber·ry·ing** : to gather berries

berth n 1 : a place where a ship lies at anchor or at a wharf 2 : a bed on a ship, train, or airplane

be·seech vb **be·sought** or **be·seeched; be·seech·ing** : to ask earnestly

be·set vb **be·set; be·set·ting** 1 : to attack from all sides 2 : SURROUND

be·side prep 1 : by the side of : NEXT TO 2 : compared with 3 : **1BESIDES** 4 : away from : wide of — **beside oneself** : very upset

1be·sides prep 1 : in addition to 2 : other than

2besides adv : in addition : ALSO

be·siege vb **be·sieged; be·sieg·ing** 1 : to surround with armed forces for the purpose of capturing 2 : to crowd around — **be·sieg·er** n

besought past of BESEECH

1best adj superlative of GOOD : good or useful in the highest degree : most excellent — **best part** : **3MOST**

2best adv superlative of WELL 1 : in the best way 2 : **2MOST** 1

3best n 1 : a person or thing or part of a thing that is best 2 : one's greatest effort

4best vb : to get the better of

be·stir vb **be·stirred; be·stir·ring** : to stir up : rouse to action

be·stow vb : to present as a gift

1bet n 1 : an agreement requiring the person who guesses wrong about the result of a contest or the outcome of an event to give something to the person who guesses right 2 : the money or thing risked in a bet

2bet vb **bet** or **bet·ted; bet·ting** 1 : to risk in a bet 2 : to be sure enough to make a bet

be·tray vb 1 : to give over to an enemy by treason or fraud 2 : to be unfaithful to 3 : REVEAL 2, SHOW

be·troth vb : to promise to marry or give in marriage

be·troth·al n : an engagement to be married

1bet·ter adj comparative of GOOD 1 : more satisfactory than another thing 2 : improved in health — **better part** : more than half

2better vb : to make or become better — **bet·ter·ment** n

3better adv comparative of WELL : in a superior or more excellent way

4better n 1 : a better person or thing 2 : ADVANTAGE 1, VICTORY

bet·tor or **bet·ter** n : one that bets

1be·tween prep 1 : by the efforts of each of 2 : in or into the interval separating 3 : functioning to separate or tell apart 4 : by comparing 5 : shared by 6 : in shares to each of

2between adv : in a position between others

1bev·el n : a slant or slope of one surface or line against another

2bevel vb **bev·eled** or **bev·elled; bev·el·ing** or **bev·el·ling** : to cut or shape (an edge or surface) so as to form a bevel

bev·er·age n : a liquid that is drunk for food or pleasure

be·ware vb : to be cautious or careful

be·whis·kered adj : having whiskers

be·wil·der vb : to fill with uncertainty : CONFUSE — **be·wil·der·ment** n

be·witch vb 1 : to gain an influence over by means of magic or witchcraft 2 : to attract or delight as if by magic — **be·witch·ment** n

1be·yond adv : on or to the farther side

2beyond prep 1 : on the other side of 2 : out of the reach or sphere of

bi- prefix 1 : two 2 : coming or occurring every two 3 : into two parts 4 : twice : doubly : on both sides

1bi·as n 1 : a seam, cut, or stitching running in a slant across cloth 2 : a favoring of one way of feeling or acting over another : PREJUDICE

2bias vb **bi·ased** or **bi·assed; bi·as·ing** or **bi·as·sing** : to give a bias to

bib n 1 : a cloth or plastic shield tied under a child's chin to protect the clothes 2 : the upper part of an apron or of overalls

Bi·ble n 1 : the book made up of the writings accepted by Christians as coming from God 2 : a book containing the sacred writings of a religion

bib·li·cal adj : relating to, taken from, or found in the Bible

bib·li·og·ra·phy *n, pl* **bib·li·og·ra·phies :** a list of writings about an author or a subject

bi·car·bon·ate of soda : SODIUM BICARBONATE

bi·ceps *n, pl* **biceps** *also* **bi·ceps·es :** a large muscle of the upper arm

bick·er *vb* **:** to quarrel in a cross or silly way

bi·cus·pid *n* **:** either of the two teeth with double points on each side of each jaw of a person

1bi·cy·cle *n* **:** a light vehicle having two wheels one behind the other, a saddle seat, and pedals by which it is made to move

2bicycle *vb* **bi·cy·cled; bi·cy·cling :** to ride a bicycle

bi·cy·clist *n* **:** a person who rides a bicycle

1bid *vb* **bade** *or* **bid; bid·den** *or* **bid; bid·ding** **1 :** 1ORDER 2, COMMAND **2 :** to express to **3 :** to make an offer for something (as at an auction) — **bid·der** *n*

2bid *n* **1 :** an offer to pay a certain sum for something or to do certain work at a stated fee **2 :** INVITATION 2

bide *vb* **bode** *or* **bid·ed; bid·ed; bid·ing :** to wait or wait for

1bi·en·ni·al *adj* **1 :** occurring every two years **2 :** growing stalks and leaves one year and flowers and fruit the next before dying — **bi·en·ni·al·ly** *adv*

2biennial *n* **:** a biennial plant

bier *n* **:** a stand on which a corpse or coffin is placed

big *adj* **big·ger; big·gest** **1 :** large in size **2 :** IMPORTANT 1 — **big·ness** *n*

Big Dipper *n* **:** a group of seven stars in the northern sky arranged in a form like a dipper with the two stars that form the side opposite the handle pointing to the North Star

big·horn *n* **:** a grayish brown wild sheep of mountainous western North America

big tree *n* **:** a very large California sequoia with light soft brittle wood

bike *n* **1 :** BICYCLE **2 :** MOTORCYCLE

bile *n* **:** a thick bitter yellow or greenish fluid supplied by the liver to aid in digestion

bi·lin·gual *adj* **:** of, expressed in, or using two languages

1bill *n* **1 :** the jaws of a bird together with their horny covering **2 :** a part of an animal (as a turtle) that suggests the bill of a bird — **billed** *adj*

2bill *n* **1 :** a draft of a law presented to a legislature for consideration **2 :** a record of goods sold, services performed, or work done with the cost involved **3 :** a sign or poster advertising something **4 :** a piece of paper money

3bill *vb* **:** to send a bill to

bill·board *n* **:** a flat surface on which outdoor advertisements are displayed

bill·fold *n* **:** a folding pocketbook especially for paper money : WALLET

bil·liards *n* **:** a game played by driving solid balls with a cue into each other or into pockets on a large rectangular table

bil·lion *n* **1 :** a thousand millions **2 :** a very large number

1bil·lionth *adj* **:** being last in a series of a billion

2billionth *n* **:** number 1,000,000,000 in a series

1bil·low *n* **:** a great wave

2billow *vb* **1 :** to roll in great waves **2 :** to swell out

bil·ly club *n* **:** a heavy club (as of wood) carried by a police officer

billy goat *n* **:** a male goat

bin *n* **:** a box or enclosed place used for storage

bi·na·ry *adj* **:** of, relating to, or being a number system with a base of 2

bind *vb* **bound; bind·ing** **1 :** to fasten by tying **2 :** to hold or restrict by force or obligation **3 :** 2BANDAGE **4 :** to finish or decorate with a binding **5 :** to fasten together and enclose in a cover

bind·er *n* **1 :** a person who binds books **2 :** a cover for holding together loose sheets of paper **3 :** a machine that cuts grain and ties it into bundles

bind·ing *n* **1 :** the cover and the fastenings of a book **2 :** a narrow strip of fabric used along the edge of an article of clothing

bin·go *n* **:** a game of chance played by covering a numbered space on a card when the number is matched by one drawn at random and won by the first player to cover five spaces in a row

bin·oc·u·lar *adj* **:** of, using, or suited for the use of both eyes

bin·oc·u·lars *n pl* **:** a hand-held instrument for seeing at a distance that is made up of two telescopes usually having prisms

bio- *prefix* **:** living matter

bio·de·grad·able *adj* **:** possible to break down and make harmless by the action of living things (as bacteria)

bio·di·ver·si·ty *n* **:** biological variety in an environment as shown by numbers of different kinds of plants and animals

bio·graph·i·cal *adj* **:** of or relating to the history of people's lives

bi·og·ra·phy *n, pl* **bi·og·ra·phies :** a written history of a person's life

bi·o·log·i·cal *adj* **:** of or relating to biology

bi·ol·o·gist *n* **:** a specialist in biology

bi·ol·o·gy *n* **:** a science that deals with living things and their relationships, distribution, and behavior

bio·re·gion *n* **:** a region whose limits are

naturally defined by geographic and biological features (as mountains and ecosystems) — bio·re·gion·al *adj*

bio·tech·nol·o·gy *n* : the use of techniques from genetics to combine inherited characteristics selected from different kinds of organisms into one organism in order to produce useful products (as drugs)

bi·ped *n* : an animal (as a person) that has only two feet

bi·plane *n* : an airplane with two wings on each side of the body usually placed one above the other

birch *n* : a tree with hard wood and a smooth bark that can be peeled off in thin layers

bird *n* : an animal that lays eggs and has wings and a body covered with feathers

bird·bath *n* : a basin for birds to bathe in

bird dog *n* : a dog trained to hunt or bring in game birds

bird·house *n* 1 : an artificial nesting place for birds 2 : AVIARY

bird of prey : a bird (as an eagle or owl) that feeds almost entirely on meat taken by hunting

bird·seed *n* : a mixture of small seeds used chiefly for feeding wild or caged birds

bird's–eye *adj* : seen from above as if by a flying bird

birth *n* 1 : the coming of a new individual from the body of its parent 2 : the act of bringing into life 3 : LINEAGE 1 4 : ORIGIN 2

birth·day *n* 1 : the day on which a person is born 2 : a day of beginning 3 : the return each year of the date on which a person was born or something began

birth·mark *n* : an unusual mark or blemish on the skin at birth

birth·place *n* : the place where a person was born or where something began

birth·right *n* : a right belonging to a person because of his or her birth

bis·cuit *n* 1 : CRACKER 2 : a small cake of raised dough baked in an oven

bi·sect *vb* 1 : to divide into two usually equal parts 2 : INTERSECT

bish·op *n* 1 : a member of the clergy of high rank 2 : a piece in the game of chess

bis·muth *n* : a heavy grayish white metallic chemical element that is used in alloys and in medicine

bi·son *n, pl* bison : a large animal with short horns and a shaggy mane that is related to the cows and oxen

¹bit *n* 1 : a part of a bridle that is put in the horse's mouth 2 : the cutting or boring edge or part of a tool

²bit *n* 1 : a small piece or quantity 2 : a short time 3 : ¹SOMEWHAT

³bit *n* : a unit of computer information that represents the selection of one of two possible choices (as *on* or *off*)

bitch *n* : a female dog

¹bite *vb* bit; bit·ten; bit·ing 1 : to seize, grip, or cut into with or as if with teeth 2 : to wound or sting usually with a stinger or fang 3 : to cause to sting 4 : to take a bait

²bite *n* 1 : a seizing of something with the teeth or the mouth 2 : a wound made by biting : STING 3 : the amount of food taken at a bite 4 : a sharp or biting sensation

bit·ing *adj* : producing bodily or mental distress : SHARP

bit·ter *adj* 1 : sharp, biting, and unpleasant to the taste 2 : hard to put up with 3 : very harsh or sharp : BITING 4 : caused by anger, distress, or sorrow — bit·ter·ly *adv* — bit·ter·ness *n*

bit·tern *n* : a brownish marsh bird which has a loud booming cry

¹bit·ter·sweet *n* 1 : a poisonous vine with purple flowers and red berries 2 : a North American woody climbing plant with orange seedcases that open when ripe and show the red-coated seeds

²bittersweet *adj* : being partly bitter or sad and partly sweet or happy

bi·tu·mi·nous coal *n* : a soft coal that gives much smoke when burned

bi·zarre *adj* : very strange or odd

blab *vb* blabbed; blab·bing : to talk too much

¹black *adj* 1 : of the color black 2 : very dark 3 : of or relating to any peoples having dark skin and especially any of the original peoples of Africa south of the Sahara 4 *often cap* : of or relating to Americans having ancestors from Africa south of the Sahara 5 : WICKED 6 : very sad or gloomy 7 : UNFRIENDLY — black·ness *n*

²black *n* 1 : a black pigment or dye 2 : the color of coal : the opposite of white 3 : black clothing 4 : a person belonging to a people having dark skin and especially a black African 5 *often cap* : an American having black African ancestors

³black *vb* : BLACKEN 1

black–and–blue *adj* : darkly discolored (as from a bruise)

black·ber·ry *n, pl* black·ber·ries : the black or dark purple sweet juicy berry of a prickly plant related to the raspberry

black·bird *n* : any of several birds of which the males are mostly black

black·board *n* : a hard smooth usually dark surface used especially in a classroom for writing or drawing on with chalk

black·en *vb* 1 : to make or become black 2 : ²SPOIL 2

black–eyed Su·san *n* : a daisy with yellow or orange petals and a dark center

black·head *n* : a dark plug of hardened oily material blocking the opening of a skin gland

black·ish *adj* : somewhat black

¹black·mail *n* **1** : the forcing of someone to pay money by threatening to reveal a secret that might bring disgrace on him or her **2** : money paid under threat of blackmail

²blackmail *vb* : to threaten with the revealing of a secret unless money is paid — **black·mail·er** *n*

black·out *n* **1** : a period of darkness enforced as a protection against air raids **2** : a period of darkness caused by power failure **3** : a temporary loss of vision or consciousness

black out *vb* : to lose consciousness or the ability to see for a short time

black·smith *n* : a person who makes things out of iron by heating and hammering it

black·snake *n* : either of two harmless snakes of the United States with blackish skins

black·top *n* : a black material used especially to pave roads

black widow *n* : a poisonous spider the female of which is black with a red mark shaped like an hourglass on the underside of the abdomen

blad·der *n* **1** : a pouch into which urine passes from the kidneys **2** : a container that can be filled with air or gas

blade *n* **1** : a leaf of a plant and especially of a grass **2** : the broad flat part of a leaf **3** : something that widens out like the blade of a leaf **4** : the cutting part of a tool or machine **5** : SWORD **6** : the runner of an ice skate — **blad·ed** *adj*

¹blame *vb* **blamed; blam·ing 1** : to find fault with **2** : to hold responsible **3** : to place responsibility for

²blame *n* **1** : expression of disapproval **2** : responsibility for something that fails — **blame·less** *adj*

blame·wor·thy *adj* : deserving blame

blanch *vb* **1** : ¹BLEACH, WHITEN **2** : to scald so as to remove the skin from **3** : to turn pale

¹blank *adj* **1** : seeming to be confused **2** : not having any writing or marks **3** : having empty spaces to be filled in

²blank *n* **1** : an empty space in a line of writing or printing **2** : a paper with empty spaces to be filled in **3** : a cartridge loaded with powder but no bullet

¹blan·ket *n* **1** : a heavy woven covering used for beds **2** : a covering layer

²blanket *vb* : to cover with a blanket

¹blare *vb* **blared; blar·ing 1** : to sound loud and harsh **2** : to present in a harsh noisy manner

²blare *n* : a harsh loud noise

¹blast *n* **1** : a strong gust of wind **2** : a stream of air or gas forced through an opening **3** : the sound made by a wind instrument **4** : EXPLOSION 1

²blast *vb* **1** : ²BLIGHT **2** : to break to pieces by an explosion : SHATTER

blast–off *n* : an instance of blasting off (as of a rocket)

blast off *vb* : to take off — used of vehicles using rockets for power

¹blaze *n* **1** : a bright hot flame **2** : great brightness and heat **3** : OUTBURST 1 **4** : a bright display

²blaze *vb* **blazed; blaz·ing 1** : to burn brightly **2** : to shine as if on fire

³blaze *n* : a mark made on a tree by chipping off a piece of the bark ·

⁴blaze *vb* **blazed; blaz·ing 1** : to make a blaze on **2** : to mark by blazing trees

¹bleach *vb* : to make white by removing the color or stains from

²bleach *n* : a preparation used for bleaching

bleach·er *n* : open seats for people to watch from (as at a game) usually arranged like steps — usually used in pl.

bleak *adj* **1** : open to wind or weather **2** : being cold and cutting **3** : not hopeful or encouraging — **bleak·ly** *adv* — **bleak·ness** *n*

¹bleat *vb* : to make the cry of a sheep, goat, or calf

²bleat *n* : the sound of bleating

bleed *vb* **bled; bleed·ing 1** : to lose or shed blood **2** : to feel pain or pity **3** : to draw fluid from

¹blem·ish *vb* : to spoil by or as if by an ugly mark

²blemish *n* : a mark that makes something imperfect : FLAW

¹blend *vb* **1** : to mix so completely that the separate things mixed cannot be told apart **2** : to shade into each other : HARMONIZE

²blend *n* **1** : a complete mixture : a product made by blending **2** : a word formed by combining parts of two or more other words so that they overlap **3** : a group of two or more consonants (as *gr-* in green) beginning a syllable without a vowel between

bless *vb* **blessed** *or* **blest; bless·ing 1** : to make holy by a religious ceremony or words **2** : to ask the favor or protection of God for **3** : to praise or honor as holy **4** : to give happiness or good fortune to

bless·ed *adj* **1** : HOLY 1 **2** : enjoying happiness — **bless·ed·ness** *n*

bless·ing *n* **1** : the act of one who blesses **2** : APPROVAL **3** : something that makes one happy or content

blew *past of* BLOW

1blight *n* **1** : a plant disease marked by drying up without rotting **2** : an organism (as a germ or insect) that causes a plant blight

2blight *vb* : to injure or destroy by or as if by a blight

blimp *n* : an airship filled with gas like a balloon

1blind *adj* **1** : unable or nearly unable to see **2** : lacking in judgment or understanding **3** : closed at one end **4** : using only the instruments within an airplane and not landmarks as a guide — **blind·ly** *adv* — **blind·ness** *n*

2blind *vb* **1** : to make blind **2** : to make it impossible to see well : DAZZLE

3blind *n* **1** : a device to reduce sight or keep out light **2** : a place of hiding

4blind *adv* : with only instruments as guidance

1blind·fold *vb* : to shut light out of the eyes of with or as if with a bandage

2blindfold *n* : a covering over the eyes

blind·man's buff *n* : a game in which a blindfolded player tries to catch and identify one of the other players

blink *vb* **1** : to look with partly shut eyes **2** : to shut and open the eyes quickly **3** : to shine with a light that goes or seems to go on and off

blink·er *n* : a light that blinks

bliss *n* : great happiness : JOY — **bliss·ful** *adj* — **bliss·ful·ly** *adv*

1blis·ter *n* **1** : a small raised area of the skin filled with a watery liquid **2** : a swelling (as in paint) that looks like a blister

2blister *vb* **1** : to develop a blister or blisters **2** : to cause blisters on

blithe *adj* **blith·er; blith·est** : free from worry : MERRY, CHEERFUL — **blithe·ly** *adv*

bliz·zard *n* : a long heavy snowstorm

bloat *vb* : to make swollen with or as if with fluid

blob *n* : a small lump or drop of something thick

1block *n* **1** : a solid piece of some material (as stone or wood) usually with one or more flat sides **2** : something that stops or makes passage or progress difficult : OBSTRUCTION **3** : a case enclosing one or more pulleys **4** : a number of things thought of as forming a group or unit **5** : a large building divided into separate houses or shops **6** : a space enclosed by streets **7** : the length of one side of a block

2block *vb* **1** : to stop or make passage through difficult : OBSTRUCT **2** : to stop or make the passage of difficult **3** : to make an opponent's movement (as in football) difficult **4** : to mark the chief lines of

1block·ade *vb* **block·ad·ed; block·ad·ing** : to close off a place to prevent the coming in or going out of people or supplies

2blockade *n* : the closing off of a place (as by warships) to prevent the coming in or going out of persons or supplies

block and tackle *n* : an arrangement of pulleys in blocks with rope or cable for lifting or hauling

block·house *n* : a building (as of heavy timbers or of concrete) built with holes in its sides through which persons inside may fire out at an enemy

1blond *adj* **1** : of a light color **2** : having light hair and skin

2blond *or* **blonde** *n* : someone who is blond

blood *n* **1** : the red fluid that circulates in the heart, arteries, capillaries, and veins of persons and animals **2** : relationship through a common ancestor : KINSHIP — **blood·ed** *adj*

blood bank *n* : blood stored for emergency use in transfusion

blood·hound *n* : a large hound with long drooping ears, a wrinkled face, and a very good sense of smell

blood pressure *n* : pressure of the blood on the walls of blood vessels and especially arteries

blood·shed *n* : 1MURDER, SLAUGHTER

blood·shot *adj* : being red and sore

blood·stream *n* : the circulating blood in the living body

blood·suck·er *n* : an animal that sucks blood — **blood·suck·ing** *adj*

blood·thirsty *adj* : eager to kill or hurt — **blood·thirst·i·ly** *adv* — **blood·thirst·i·ness** *n*

blood vessel *n* : an artery, vein, or capillary of the body

bloody *adj* **blood·i·er; blood·i·est** **1** : smeared or stained with blood **2** : causing or accompanied by bloodshed

1bloom *n* **1** : 1FLOWER 1 **2** : the period or state of blooming **3** : a condition or time of beauty, freshness, and strength **4** : the rosy color of the cheek **5** : the delicate powdery coating on some fruits and leaves

2bloom *vb* **1** : to produce blooms : FLOWER **2** : to be in a state of youthful beauty and freshness

1blos·som *n* **1** : 1FLOWER 1 **2** : 1BLOOM 2

2blossom *vb* **1** : 2BLOOM **2** : to unfold like a blossom

1blot *n* **1** : a spot or stain of dirt or ink **2** : STIGMA 1, REPROACH

2blot *vb* **blot·ted; blot·ting** **1** : 2SPOT 1 **2**

: to hide completely **3** : to dry with a blotter

blotch *n* **1** : a blemish on the skin **2** : a large irregular spot of color or ink — **blotched** *adj*

blot·ter *n* : a piece of blotting paper

blot·ting paper *n* : a soft spongy paper used to absorb wet ink

blouse *n* **1** : a loose outer garment like a smock **2** : the jacket of a uniform **3** : a loose garment for women and children covering the body from the neck to the waist

1blow *vb* **blew; blown; blow·ing** **1** : to move or be moved usually with speed and force **2** : to move in or with the wind **3** : to send forth a strong stream of air from the mouth or from a bellows **4** : to make a sound or cause to sound by blowing **5** : to clear by forcing air through **6** : to shape by forcing air into — **blow·er** *n*

2blow *n* : a blowing of wind : GALE

3blow *n* **1** : an act of hitting (as with the fist or a weapon) **2** : a sudden act **3** : a sudden happening that causes suffering or loss

blow·gun *n* : a tube from which a dart may be shot by the force of the breath

blow·out *n* : a bursting of a container (as an automobile tire) by pressure of the contents on a weak spot

blow·pipe *n* **1** : a small round tube for blowing air or gas into a flame so as to make it hotter **2** : BLOWGUN

blow·torch *n* : a small portable burner in which the flame is made hotter by a blast of air or oxygen

blow up *vb* **1** : EXPLODE 1 **2** : to fill with a gas (as air)

1blub·ber *vb* : to weep noisily

2blubber *n* : the fat of various sea mammals (as whales) from which oil can be obtained

1blue *adj* **blu·er; blu·est** **1** : of the color blue **2** : low in spirits : MELANCHOLY

2blue *n* **1** : the color in the rainbow between green and violet : the color of the clear daytime sky **2** : something blue in color — **out of the blue** : suddenly and unexpectedly

blue·bell *n* : a plant with blue flowers shaped like bells

blue·ber·ry *n, pl* **blue·ber·ries** : a sweet blue berry that has small seeds and grows on a bush related to the huckleberry

blue·bird *n* : any of several small North American songbirds more or less blue above

blue·bot·tle *n* : a large blue hairy fly

blue cheese *n* : cheese ripened by and full of greenish blue mold

blue·fish *n* : a bluish saltwater food fish of the eastern coast of the United States

blue·grass *n* : a grass with bluish green stems

blueing *variant of* BLUING

blue jay *n* : any of several crested and mostly blue American birds related to the crows

blue jeans *n pl* : pants usually made of blue denim

1blue·print *n* **1** : a photographic print made with white lines on a blue background and used for copying maps and building plans **2** : a detailed plan of something to be done

2blueprint *vb* : to make a blueprint of

blues *n pl* **1** : low spirits **2** : a sad song in a style that was first used by American blacks

blue whale *n* : a very large whale that is probably the largest living animal

1bluff *adj* **1** : rising steeply with a broad front **2** : frank and outspoken in a rough but good-natured way — **bluff·ly** *adv* — **bluff·ness** *n*

2bluff *n* : a high steep bank : CLIFF

3bluff *vb* : to deceive or frighten by pretending to have more strength or confidence than one really has — **bluff·er** *n*

4bluff *n* **1** : an act or instance of bluffing **2** : a person who bluffs

blu·ing *or* **blue·ing** *n* : something made with blue or violet dyes that is added to the water when washing clothes to prevent yellowing of white fabrics

blu·ish *adj* : somewhat blue

1blun·der *vb* **1** : to move in a clumsy way **2** : to make a mistake — **blun·der·er** *n*

2blunder *n* : a bad or stupid mistake

blun·der·buss *n* : a short gun that has a barrel which is larger at the end and that was used long ago for shooting at close range without taking exact aim

1blunt *adj* **1** : having a thick edge or point : DULL **2** : speaking or spoken in plain language without thought for other people's feelings — **blunt·ly** *adv*

2blunt *vb* : to make or become blunt

1blur *n* : something that cannot be seen clearly

2blur *vb* **blurred; blur·ring** **1** : to make hard to see or read by smearing **2** : to make or become smeared or confused

blurt *vb* : to say or tell suddenly and without thinking

1blush *n* **1** : a reddening of the face from shame, confusion, or embarrassment **2** : a rosy color

2blush *vb* **1** : to become red in the face from shame, confusion, or embarrassment **2** : to feel ashamed or embarrassed

1blus·ter *vb* **1** : to blow hard and noisily **2** : to talk or act in a noisy boastful way

2bluster *n* : noisy violent action or speech

boa *n* : a large snake (as a python) that coils around and crushes its prey

boar *n* **1** : a male pig **2** : a wild pig

¹board *n* **1** : a sawed piece of lumber that is much broader and longer than it is thick **2** : a dining table **3** : meals given at set times for a price **4** : a number of persons having authority to manage or direct something **5** : a usually rectangular piece of rigid material used for some special purpose **6** : BLACKBOARD **7 boards** *pl* : the low wooden wall enclosing a hockey rink **8** : a sheet of insulating material carrying electronic parts (as for a computer) — **on board** : ABOARD

²board *vb* **1** : to go aboard **2** : to cover with boards **3** : to give or get meals at set times for a price

board·er *n* : a person who pays for meals or for meals and lodging at another's house

board·ing·house *n* : a house at which people are given meals and often lodging

boarding school *n* : a school at which most of the students live during the school year

board·walk *n* : a walk made of planks especially along a beach

¹boast *n* **1** : an act of boasting **2** : a cause for boasting or pride

²boast *vb* **1** : to praise what one has or has done **2** : to have and be proud of having

boast·ful *adj* **1** : having the habit of boasting **2** : full of boasts — **boast·ful·ly** *adv* — **boast·ful·ness** *n*

¹boat *n* **1** : a small vessel driven on the water by oars, paddles, sails, or a motor **2** : ¹SHIP 1

²boat *vb* : to use a boat — **boat·er** *n*

boat·house *n* : a house or shelter for boats

boat·man *n, pl* **boat·men** : a person who works on or deals in boats

boat·swain *n* : a warrant officer on a warship or a petty officer on a commercial ship who has charge of the hull, anchors, boats, and rigging

¹bob *vb* **bobbed; bob·bing 1** : to move or cause to move with a short jerky motion **2** : to appear suddenly **3** : to try to seize something with the teeth

²bob *n* : a short jerky up-and-down motion

³bob *n* **1** : a float used to buoy up the baited end of a fishing line **2** : a woman's or child's short haircut

⁴bob *vb* **bobbed; bob·bing** : to cut in the style of a bob

bob·by pin *n* : a flat metal hairpin with the two ends pressed close together

bob·cat *n* : an American wildcat that is a small rusty brown variety of the lynx

bob·o·link *n* : an American songbird related to the blackbirds

bob·sled *n* : a racing sled made with two sets of runners, a hand brake, and often a steering wheel

bob·tail *n* **1** : a short tail : a tail cut short **2** : an animal with a short tail

bob·white *n* : an American quail with gray, white, and reddish coloring

bode *past of* BIDE

bod·ice *n* : the upper part of a dress

bodi·ly *adj* : of or relating to the body

body *n, pl* **bod·ies 1** : the material whole of a live or dead person or animal **2** : the main part of a person, animal, or plant **3** : the main or central part **4** : a group of persons or things united for some purpose **5** : a mass or portion of something distinct from other masses — **bod·ied** *adj*

body·guard *n* : a person or a group of persons whose duty it is to protect someone

¹bog *n* : wet spongy ground that is usually acid and found next to a body of water (as a pond)

²bog *vb* **bogged; bog·ging** : to sink or stick fast in or as if in a bog

bo·gey *or* **bo·gy** *or* **bo·gie** *n, pl* **bogeys** *or* **bogies 1** : GHOST, GOBLIN **2** : something one is afraid of without reason

¹boil *n* : a hot red painful lump in the skin that contains pus and is caused by infection

²boil *vb* **1** : to heat or become heated to the temperature (**boiling point**) at which bubbles rise and break at the surface **2** : to cook or become cooked in boiling water **3** : to become angry or upset

³boil *n* : the state of something that is boiling

boil·er *n* **1** : a container in which something is boiled **2** : a tank heating and holding water **3** : a strong metal container used in making steam (as to heat buildings)

bois·ter·ous *adj* : being rough and noisy — **bois·ter·ous·ly** *adv* — **bois·ter·ous·ness** *n*

bold *adj* **1** : willing to meet danger or take risks : DARING **2** : not polite and modest : FRESH **3** : showing or calling for courage or daring — **bold·ly** *adv* — **bold·ness** *n*

bold·face *n* : a heavy black type — **bold–faced** *adj*

bo·le·ro *n, pl* **bo·le·ros 1** : a Spanish dance or the music for it **2** : a loose short jacket open at the front

boll *n* : the seedpod of a plant (as cotton)

boll weevil *n* : a grayish insect that lays its eggs in cotton bolls

bo·lo·gna *n* : a large smoked sausage usually made of beef, veal, and pork

¹bol·ster *n* : a long pillow or cushion sometimes used to support bed pillows

²bolster *vb* : to support with or as if with a bolster

¹bolt *n* **1** : a stroke of lightning : THUNDER-BOLT **2** : a sliding bar used to fasten a door **3** : the part of a lock worked by a key **4** : a metal pin or rod usually with a head at one end and a screw thread at the other that is used to hold something in place **5** : a roll of cloth or wallpaper

²bolt *vb* **1** : to move suddenly and rapidly **2** : to run away **3** : to fasten with a bolt **4** : to swallow hastily or without chewing

¹bomb *n* **1** : a hollow case or shell filled with explosive material and made to be dropped from an airplane, thrown by hand, or set off by a fuse **2** : a container in which something (as an insecticide) is stored under pressure and from which it is released in a fine spray

²bomb *vb* : to attack with bombs

bom·bard *vb* **1** : to attack with heavy fire from big guns : SHELL **2** : to attack again and again

bomb·er *n* : an airplane specially made for dropping bombs

bon·bon *n* : a candy with a soft coating and a creamy center

¹bond *n* **1** : something that binds **2** : a force or influence that brings or holds together **3** : a legal agreement in which a person agrees to pay a sum of money if he or she fails to do a certain thing **4** : a government or business certificate promising to pay a certain sum by a certain day

²bond *vb* : to stick or cause to stick together

bond·age *n* : SLAVERY

¹bone *n* **1** : the hard material of which the skeleton of most animals is formed **2** : any of the pieces into which the bone of the skeleton is naturally divided — **bone·less** *adj*

²bone *vb* **boned; bon·ing** : to remove the bones from

bon·fire *n* : a large fire built outdoors

bong *n* : a deep sound like that of a large bell

bon·go *n, pl* **bongos** *also* **bongoes** : either of a pair of small drums of different sizes fitted together and played with the fingers

bon·net *n* : a child's or woman's hat usually tied under the chin by ribbons or strings

bon·ny *or* **bon·nie** *adj* **bon·ni·er; bon·ni·est** *chiefly British* : HANDSOME 3, BEAUTI-FUL

bo·nus *n* : something given to somebody (as a worker) in addition to what is usual or owed

bony *adj* **bon·i·er; bon·i·est** **1** : of or relating to bone **2** : like bone especially in hardness **3** : having bones and especially large or noticeable bones

¹boo *interj* — used to express disapproval or to startle or frighten

²boo *n, pl* **boos** : a cry expressing disapproval

³boo *vb* : to express disapproval of with boos

boo·by *n, pl* **boobies** : an awkward foolish person

¹book *n* **1** : a set of sheets of paper bound together **2** : a long written work **3** : a large division of a written work **4** : a pack of small items bound together

²book *vb* : to reserve for future use

book·case *n* : a set of shelves to hold books

book·end *n* : a support at the end of a row of books to keep them standing up

book·keep·er *n* : a person who keeps accounts for a business

book·keep·ing *n* : the work of keeping business accounts

book·let *n* : a little book usually having paper covers and few pages

book·mark *n* : something placed in a book to show the page one wants to return to later

book·mo·bile *n* : a truck with shelves of books that is a traveling library

¹boom *vb* **1** : to make a deep hollow rumbling sound **2** : to increase or develop rapidly

²boom *n* **1** : a booming sound **2** : a rapid increase in activity or popularity

³boom *n* **1** : a long pole used especially to stretch the bottom of a sail **2** : a long beam sticking out from the mast of a derrick to support or guide something that is being lifted

boom box *n* : a large portable radio and often tape player with two attached speakers

boo·mer·ang *n* : a curved club that can be thrown so as to return to the thrower

boon *n* **1** : something asked or granted as a favor **2** : something pleasant or helpful that comes at just the right time

¹boost *vb* **1** : to raise or push up from below **2** : to make bigger or greater — **boost·er** *n*

²boost *n* : an act of boosting : a push up

¹boot *n* : a covering usually of leather or rubber for the foot and part of the leg

²boot *vb* : ¹KICK 1

boo·tee *or* **boo·tie** *n* : an infant's knitted sock

booth *n, pl* **booths** **1** : a covered stall for selling or displaying goods (as at a fair or exhibition) **2** : a small enclosure giving privacy for one person **3** : a section of a restaurant consisting of a table between two backed benches

boo·ty *n* : goods seized from an enemy in war : PLUNDER

bo·rax *n* : a compound of boron used as a cleansing agent and water softener

¹**bor·der** *n* **1** : the outer edge of something **2** : a boundary especially of a country or state **3** : an ornamental strip on or near the edge of a flat object

²**border** *vb* **1** : to put a border on **2** : to be close or next to

bor·der·line *adj* : not quite average, standard, or normal

¹**bore** *vb* **bored; bor·ing 1** : to make a hole in especially with a drill **2** : to make by piercing or drilling — **bor·er** *n*

²**bore** *n* **1** : a hole made by boring **2** : a cavity (as in a gun barrel) shaped like a cylinder **3** : the diameter of a hole or cylinder

³**bore** *past of* BEAR

⁴**bore** *n* : an uninteresting person or thing

⁵**bore** *vb* **bored; bor·ing** : to make weary and restless by being uninteresting

bore·dom *n* : the state of being bored

bo·ric acid *n* : a weak acid containing boron used to kill germs

born *adj* **1** : brought into life by birth : brought forth **2** : having a certain characteristic from or as if from birth

borne *past participle of* BEAR

bo·ron *n* : a powdery or hard solid chemical element that melts at a very high temperature and is found in nature only in combination

bor·ough *n* **1** : a self-governing town or village in some states **2** : one of the five political divisions of New York City

bor·row *vb* **1** : to take or receive something with the promise of returning it **2** : to take for one's own use something begun or thought up by another : ADOPT — **bor·row·er** *n*

¹**bos·om** *n* **1** : the front of the human chest **2** : the breasts of a woman

²**bosom** *adj* : ³CLOSE 8, INTIMATE

¹**boss** *n* **1** : the person (as an employer or foreman) who tells workers what to do **2** : the head of a group (as a political organization)

²**boss** *vb* **1** : to be in charge of **2** : to give orders to

bossy *adj* **boss·i·er; boss·i·est** : liking to order people around

bo·tan·i·cal *adj* : of or relating to botany

bot·a·nist *n* : a specialist in botany

bot·a·ny *n* : a branch of biology dealing with plants

botch *vb* : to do clumsily and unskillfully : SPOIL, BUNGLE

¹**both** *pron* : the one and the other : the two

²**both** *conj* — used before two words or phrases connected with *and* to stress that each is included

³**both** *adj* : the two

¹**both·er** *vb* **1** : to trouble (someone) in body or mind : DISTRACT, ANNOY **2** : to cause to worry **3** : to take the time or trouble

²**bother** *n* **1** : someone or something that bothers in a small way **2** : COMMOTION **3** : the condition of being bothered

¹**bot·tle** *n* **1** : a container (as of glass or plastic) usually having a narrow neck and mouth and no handle **2** : the quantity held by a bottle

²**bottle** *vb* **bot·tled; bot·tling 1** : to put into a bottle **2** : to shut up as if in a bottle

bot·tle·neck *n* : a place or condition where improvement or movement is held up

bot·tom *n* **1** : the under surface of something **2** : a supporting surface or part : BASE **3** : the bed of a body of water **4** : the lowest part of something **5** : low land along a river

bot·tom·less *adj* **1** : having no bottom **2** : very deep

bough *n* : a usually large or main branch of a tree

bought *past of* BUY

bouil·lon *n* : a clear soup made from meat (as beef or chicken)

boul·der *n* : a large detached and rounded or very worn mass of rock

bou·le·vard *n* : a wide avenue often having grass strips with trees along its center or sides

¹**bounce** *vb* **bounced; bounc·ing 1** : to spring back or up after hitting a surface **2** : to leap suddenly **3** : to cause to bounce

²**bounce** *n* **1** : a sudden leap **2** : ²REBOUND 1

¹**bound** *adj* : going or intending to go

²**bound** *past of* BIND

³**bound** *vb* : to form the boundary of

⁴**bound** *adj* **1** : tied or fastened with or as if with bands **2** : required by law or duty **3** : covered with binding **4** : firmly determined **5** : very likely to do something : CERTAIN, SURE

⁵**bound** *n* : a fast easy leap

⁶**bound** *vb* : to make a bound or move in bounds

bound·ary *n, pl* **bound·aries** : something that points out or shows a limit or end : a dividing line

bound·less *adj* : having no limits

bounds *n pl* : a point or a line beyond which a person or thing cannot go

boun·te·ous *adj* **1** : LIBERAL 1 **2** : ABUNDANT

boun·ti·ful *adj* **1** : giving freely or generously **2** : PLENTIFUL 2 — **boun·ti·ful·ly** *adv*

boun·ty *n, pl* **boun·ties 1** : GENEROSITY 1

2 : generous gifts 3 : money given as a reward for killing certain harmful animals

bou·quet n : a bunch of flowers

bout n 1 : a contest of skill or strength between two persons 2 : 2ATTACK 3

1bow vb 1 : 1YIELD 8 2 : to bend the head or body as an act of politeness or respect

2bow n : the act of bending the head or body to express politeness or respect

3bow n 1 : a weapon used for shooting arrows and usually made of a strip of wood bent by a cord connecting the two ends 2 : something shaped in a curve like a bow 3 : a rod with horsehairs stretched from end to end used for playing a stringed instrument (as a violin) 4 : a knot made with one or more loops

4bow vb 1 : to bend into a bow 2 : to play with a bow

5bow n : the forward part of a ship

bow·el n 1 : INTESTINE — usually used in pl. 2 : a part of the intestine

bow·er n : a shelter in a garden made of boughs of trees or vines

1bowl n 1 : a round hollow dish without handles 2 : the contents of a bowl 3 : something in the shape of a bowl (as part of a spoon or pipe)

2bowl n : a rolling of a ball in bowling

3bowl vb 1 : to roll a ball in bowling 2 : to move rapidly and smoothly as if rolling 3 : to hit with or as if with something rolled

bow·legged adj : having the legs bowed outward

bow·line n : a knot used for making a loop that will not slip

bowl·ing n : a game in which balls are rolled so as to knock down pins

bow·man n, pl **bow·men** : ARCHER

bow·sprit n : a large spar sticking out forward from the bow of a ship

bow·string n : the cord connecting the two ends of a bow

1box n : an evergreen shrub or small tree used for hedges

2box n 1 : a container usually having four sides, a bottom, and a cover 2 : the contents of a box 3 : an enclosed place for one or more persons

3box vb : to enclose in or as if in a box

4box vb : to engage in boxing

box·car n : a roofed freight car usually having sliding doors in the sides

box elder n : an American maple with leaves divided into several leaflets

1box·er n : a person who boxes

2boxer n : a compact dog of German origin that is of medium size with a square build and has a short and often tan coat with a black mask

box·ing n : the sport of fighting with the fists

box office n : a place where tickets to public entertainments (as sports or theatrical events) are sold

boy n 1 : a male child from birth to young manhood 2 : a male servant

1boy·cott vb : to join with others in refusing to deal with someone (as a person, organization, or country) usually to show disapproval or to force acceptance of terms

2boycott n : the process or an instance of boycotting

boy·friend n : a regular male companion of a girl or woman

boy·hood n : the time or condition of being a boy

boy·ish adj : of, relating to, or having qualities often felt to be typical of boys — **boy·ish·ly** adv — **boy·ish·ness** n

Boy Scout n : a member of a scouting program (as the Boy Scouts of America)

bra n : a woman's undergarment for breast support

1brace vb **braced; brac·ing** : to make strong, firm, or steady

2brace n 1 : two of a kind 2 : a tool with a U-shaped bend that is used to turn woodboring bits 3 : something that braces 4 : a usually wire device worn on the teeth for changing faulty position 5 : a mark { or } used to connect words or items to be considered together

brace·let n : a decorative band or chain usually worn on the wrist or arm

brack·en n : a large coarse branching fern

1brack·et n 1 : a support for a weight (as a shelf) that is usually attached to a wall 2 : one of a pair of marks [ ] (**square brackets**) used to enclose letters or numbers or in mathematics to enclose items to be treated together 3 : one of a pair of marks ⟨ ⟩ (**angle brackets**) used to enclose letters or numbers

2bracket vb 1 : to place within brackets 2 : to put into the same class : GROUP

brack·ish adj : somewhat salty

brad n : a slender wire nail with a small longish but rounded head

brag vb **bragged; brag·ging** : 2BOAST 1

brag·gart n : a person who brags a lot

1braid vb : to weave together into a braid

2braid n : a length of cord, ribbon, or hair formed of three or more strands woven together

braille n, often cap : a system of printing for the blind in which the letters are represented by raised dots

1brain n 1 : the part of the nervous system that is inside the skull, consists of grayish nerve cells and whitish nerve fibers, and is the organ of thought and the central control point for the nervous system **2 brains** *pl* : a good mind : INTELLIGENCE **3** : someone who is very smart

²brain *vb* : to hurt or kill by a blow on the head

brain·storm *n* : a sudden inspiration or idea

brainy *adj* **brain·i·er; brain·i·est** : very smart

¹brake *n* : a thick growth of shrubs, small trees, or canes

²brake *n* : a device for slowing or stopping motion (as of a wheel) usually by friction

³brake *vb* **braked; brak·ing** : to slow or stop by using a brake

brake·man *n, pl* **brake·men** : a crew member on a train whose duties include inspecting the train and helping the conductor

bram·ble *n* : any of a group of woody plants with prickly stems that include the raspberries and blackberries and are related to the roses

bran *n* : the broken coat of the seed of cereal grain separated (as by sifting) from the flour or meal

¹branch *n* **1** : a part of a tree that grows out from the trunk or from a large bough **2** : something extending from a main line or body like a branch **3** : a division or subordinate part of something — **branched** *adj*

²branch *vb* : to send out a branch : spread or divide into branches

¹brand *n* **1** : a mark of disgrace (as one formerly put on criminals with a hot iron) **2** : a mark made by burning (as on cattle) or by stamping or printing (as on manufactured goods) to show ownership, maker, or quality **3** : TRADEMARK **4** : a class of goods identified by a name as the product of a certain maker

²brand *vb* **1** : to mark with a brand **2** : to show or claim (something) to be bad or wrong

bran·dish *vb* : to wave or shake in a threatening manner

brand–new *adj* : completely new and unused

bran·dy *n, pl* **brandies** : an alcoholic liquor made from wine or fruit juice

brass *n* **1** : an alloy made by combining copper and zinc **2** : the musical instruments of an orchestra or band that are usually made of brass and include the cornets, trumpets, trombones, French horns, and tubas

brat *n* : a naughty annoying child

¹brave *adj* **brav·er; brav·est** : feeling or showing no fear — **brave·ly** *adv*

²brave *vb* **braved; brav·ing** : to face or take bravely

³brave *n* : an American Indian warrior

brav·ery *n* : COURAGE

¹brawl *vb* : to quarrel or fight noisily

²brawl *n* : a noisy quarrel or fight

brawn *n* : muscular strength

brawny *adj* **brawn·i·er; brawn·i·est** : having large strong muscles

¹bray *vb* : to make the loud harsh cry of a donkey

²bray *n* : a sound of braying

bra·zen *adj* **1** : made of brass **2** : sounding harsh and loud **3** : not ashamed of or embarrassed by one's bad behavior : IMPUDENT

Bra·zil nut *n* : a dark three-sided nut with a white kernel

¹breach *n* **1** : a breaking of a law : a failure to do what one should **2** : an opening made by breaking

²breach *vb* : to make a break in

¹bread *n* **1** : a baked food made from flour or meal **2** : FOOD 1

²bread *vb* : to cover with bread crumbs

breadth *n* **1** : distance measured from side to side **2** : SCOPE 2

¹break *vb* **broke; bro·ken; break·ing** **1** : to separate into parts suddenly or forcibly **2** : to fail to keep **3** : to force a way **4** : ²TAME 1 **5** : to reduce the force of **6** : to do better than **7** : to interrupt or put an end to : STOP **8** : to develop or burst out suddenly **9** : to make known **10** : SOLVE **11** : ¹CHANGE 4

²break *n* **1** : an act of breaking **2** : something produced by breaking **3** : an accidental event

break·down *n* : bodily or mental collapse : FAILURE 6

break·er *n* **1** : a person or thing that breaks something **2** : a wave that breaks on shore

¹break·fast *n* : the first meal of the day

²breakfast *vb* : to eat breakfast

break·neck *adj* : very fast or dangerous

break out *vb* **1** : to develop a skin rash **2** : to start up suddenly

break·through *n* : a sudden advance or successful development

break up *vb* **1** : to separate into parts **2** : to bring or come to an end **3** : to end a romance **4** : to go into a fit of laughter

break·wa·ter *n* : an offshore wall to protect a beach or a harbor from the sea

¹breast *n* **1** : a gland that produces milk **2** : the front part of the body between the neck and the abdomen — **breast·ed** *adj*

²breast *vb* : to face or oppose bravely

breast·bone *n* : the bony plate at the front and center of the breast

breast–feed *vb* **breast–fed; breast–feeding** : to feed (a baby) from a mother's breast

breast·plate *n* : a piece of armor for covering the breast

breast·work *n* : a wall thrown together to serve as a defense in battle

breath *n* 1 : a slight breeze 2 : ability to breathe : ease of breathing 3 : air taken in or sent out by the lungs — **out of breath** : breathing very rapidly as a result of hard exercise

breathe *vb* **breathed; breath·ing** 1 : to draw air into and expel it from the lungs 2 : ¹LIVE 1 3 : ¹SAY 1, UTTER

breath·er *n* : a pause for rest

breath·less *adj* 1 : panting from exertion 2 : holding one's breath from excitement or fear — **breath·less·ly** *adv*

breath·tak·ing *adj* : very exciting

breech·es *n pl* 1 : short pants fastening below the knee 2 : PANTS

¹**breed** *vb* **bred; breed·ing** 1 : to produce or increase (plants or animals) by sexual reproduction 2 : to produce offspring by sexual reproduction 3 : to bring up : TRAIN 4 : to bring about : CAUSE — **breed·er** *n*

²**breed** *n* 1 : a kind of plant or animal that is found only under human care and is different from related kinds 2 : ¹CLASS 6, KIND

breed·ing *n* : training especially in manners : UPBRINGING

breeze *n* : a gentle wind

breezy *adj* **breez·i·er; breez·i·est** 1 : somewhat windy 2 : lively and somewhat carefree — **breez·i·ly** *adv* — **breez·i·ness** *n*

breth·ren *pl of* BROTHER — used chiefly in some formal or solemn situations

breve *n* : a mark ˘ placed over a vowel to show that the vowel is short

brev·i·ty *n* : the condition of being short or brief

¹**brew** *vb* 1 : to make (beer) from water, malt, and hops 2 : to prepare by soaking in hot water 3 : ²PLAN 2 4 : to start to form — **brew·er** *n*

²**brew** *n* : a brewed beverage

brew·ery *n, pl* **brew·er·ies** : a place where malt liquors are brewed

bri·ar *variant of* BRIER

¹**bribe** *n* : something given or promised to a person in order to influence a decision or action dishonestly

²**bribe** *vb* **bribed; brib·ing** : to influence or try to influence by a bribe

brib·ery *n, pl* **brib·er·ies** : the act of giving or taking a bribe

¹**brick** *n* 1 : a building or paving material made from clay molded into blocks and baked 2 : a block made of brick

²**brick** *vb* : to close, face, or pave with bricks

brick·lay·er *n* : a person who builds or paves with bricks

brid·al *adj* : of or relating to a bride or a wedding

bride *n* : a woman just married or about to be married

bride·groom *n* : a man just married or about to be married

brides·maid *n* : a woman who attends a bride at her wedding

¹**bridge** *n* 1 : a structure built over something (as water, a low place, or a railroad) so people can cross 2 : a platform above and across the deck of a ship for the captain or officer in charge 3 : something like a bridge

²**bridge** *vb* **bridged; bridg·ing** : to make a bridge over or across

³**bridge** *n* : a card game for four players in two teams

¹**bri·dle** *n* : a device for controlling a horse made up of a set of straps enclosing the head, a bit, and a pair of reins

²**bridle** *vb* **bri·dled; bri·dling** 1 : to put a bridle on 2 : RESTRAIN 1 3 : to hold the head high and draw in the chin as an expression of resentment

¹**brief** *adj* : not very long : SHORT — **brief·ly** *adv*

²**brief** *vb* : to give information or instructions to

brief·case *n* : a flat case for carrying papers or books

briefs *n pl* : short snug underpants

bri·er *or* **bri·ar** *n* : a plant (as the rose or blackberry) with a thorny or prickly woody stem

brig *n* : a square-rigged sailing ship with two masts

bri·gade *n* 1 : a body of soldiers consisting of two or more regiments 2 : a group of persons organized for acting together

brig·a·dier general *n* : a commissioned officer in the Army, Air Force, or Marine Corps ranking above a colonel

bright *adj* 1 : giving off or filled with much light 2 : very clear or vivid in color 3 : INTELLIGENT, CLEVER 4 : CHEERFUL — **bright·ly** *adv* — **bright·ness** *n*

bright·en *vb* : to make or become bright or brighter

bril·liance *n* : great brightness

bril·liant *adj* 1 : flashing with light : very bright 2 : very impressive 3 : very smart or clever — **bril·liant·ly** *adv*

¹**brim** *n* 1 : the edge or rim of something hollow 2 : the part of a hat that sticks out around the lower edge

²**brim** *vb* **brimmed; brim·ming** : to be or become full to overflowing

brin·dled *adj* : having dark streaks or spots on a gray or brownish background

brine *n* **1** : water containing a great deal of salt **2** : OCEAN

bring *vb* **brought; bring·ing** **1** : to cause to come with oneself by carrying or leading : take along **2** : to cause to reach a certain state or take a certain action **3** : to cause to arrive or exist **4** : to sell for — **bring·er** *n*

bring about *vb* : to cause to happen : EFFECT

bring forth *vb* : to give birth to : PRODUCE

bring out *vb* : to produce and offer for sale

bring to *vb* : to bring back from unconsciousness : REVIVE

bring up *vb* : to bring to maturity through care and education

brink *n* **1** : the edge at the top of a steep place **2** : a point of beginning

briny *adj* **brin·i·er; brin·i·est** : of or like salt water : SALTY

brisk *adj* **1** : very active : LIVELY **2** : very refreshing — **brisk·ly** *adv* — **brisk·ness** *n*

¹bris·tle *n* **1** : a short stiff hair **2** : a stiff hair or something like a hair fastened in a brush

²bristle *vb* **bris·tled; bris·tling** **1** : to rise up and stiffen like bristles **2** : to show signs of anger

bris·tly *adj* **bris·tli·er; bris·tli·est** : of, like, or having many bristles

britch·es *n pl* : BREECHES

¹Brit·ish *adj* : of or relating to Great Britain or the British

²British *n pl* : the people of Great Britain

brit·tle *adj* **brit·tler; brit·tlest** : hard but easily broken — **brit·tle·ness** *n*

broach *vb* : to bring up as a subject for discussion

broad *adj* **1** : not narrow : WIDE **2** : extending far and wide : SPACIOUS **3** : ¹COMPLETE 1, FULL **4** : not limited **5** : not covering fine points : GENERAL — **broad·ly** *adv*

¹broad·cast *adj* **1** : scattered in all directions **2** : made public by means of radio or television **3** : of or relating to radio or television broadcasting

²broadcast *vb* **broadcast; broad·cast·ing** **1** : to scatter far and wide **2** : to make widely known **3** : to send out by radio or television from a transmitting station — **broad·cast·er** *n*

³broadcast *n* **1** : an act of broadcasting **2** : the material broadcast by radio or television : a radio or television program

broad·cloth *n* : a fine cloth with a firm smooth surface

broad·en *vb* : to make or become broad or broader : WIDEN

broad–mind·ed *adj* : willing to consider opinions, beliefs, and practices that are un-

usual or different from one's own — **broad–mind·ed·ly** *adv* — **broad–mind·ed·ness** *n*

¹broad·side *n* **1** : the part of a ship's side above the waterline **2** : a firing of all of the guns that are on the same side of a ship

²broadside *adv* **1** : with one side forward **2** : from the side

broad·sword *n* : a sword having a broad blade

bro·cade *n* : a cloth with a raised design woven into it

broc·co·li *n* : an open branching form of cauliflower whose green stalks and clustered flower buds are used as a vegetable

broil *vb* **1** : to cook or be cooked directly over or under a heat source (as a fire or flame) **2** : to make or be extremely hot

broil·er *n* : a young chicken suitable for broiling

¹broke *past of* BREAK

²broke *adj* : having no money

bro·ken *adj* **1** : shattered into pieces **2** : having gaps or breaks **3** : not kept **4** : imperfectly spoken

bro·ken·heart·ed *adj* : overwhelmed by grief : very sad

bro·ker *n* : a person who acts as an agent for others in the buying or selling of property

bro·mine *n* : a chemical element that is a deep red liquid giving off an irritating vapor of disagreeable odor

bron·chi·al *adj* : relating to the branches (bronchial tubes) of the windpipe

bron·chi·tis *n* : a sore raw state of the bronchial tubes

bron·co *n, pl* **bron·cos** : MUSTANG

bron·to·sau·rus *n* : a huge plant-eating dinosaur with a long thin neck and tail and four thick legs

¹bronze *vb* **bronzed; bronz·ing** : to give the appearance or color of bronze to

²bronze *n* **1** : an alloy of copper and tin and sometimes other elements **2** : a yellowish brown color

brooch *n* : an ornamental pin or clasp for the clothing

¹brood *n* **1** : the young of birds hatched at the same time **2** : a group of young children or animals having the same mother

²brood *vb* **1** : to sit on eggs to hatch them **2** : to think long and anxiously about something

brood·er *n* **1** : one that broods **2** : a building or a compartment that can be heated and is used for raising young fowl

brook *n* : a small stream — **brook·let** *n*

broom *n* **1** : a woody plant of the pea family with long slender branches along which grow many drooping yellow flowers **2** : a brush with a long handle used for sweeping

broom·stick *n* : the handle of a broom

broth *n* : the liquid in which a meat, fish, or vegetable has been boiled

broth·er *n, pl* **brothers** *also* **breth·ren** 1 : a boy or man related to another person by having the same parents 2 : a fellow member of an organization

broth·er·hood *n* 1 : the state of being a brother 2 : an association of people for a particular purpose 3 : those who are engaged in the same business or profession

broth·er–in–law *n, pl* **broth·ers–in–law** 1 : the brother of one's husband or wife 2 : the husband of one's sister

broth·er·ly *adj* 1 : of or relating to brothers 2 : ¹KINDLY 2, AFFECTIONATE

brought *past of* BRING

brow *n* 1 : EYEBROW 2 : FOREHEAD 3 : the upper edge of a steep slope

¹brown *adj* 1 : of the color brown 2 : having a dark or tanned complexion

²brown *n* : a color like that of coffee or chocolate

³brown *vb* : to make or become brown

brown·ie *n* 1 : a cheerful elf believed to perform helpful services at night 2 *cap* : a member of a program of the Girl Scouts for girls in the first through third grades in school 3 : a small rectangle of chewy chocolate cake

brown·ish *adj* : somewhat brown

browse *vb* **browsed; brows·ing** 1 : to nibble young shoots and foliage 2 : to read or look over something (as in a book or a store) in a light or careless way

brows·er *n* 1 : one that browses 2 : a computer program providing access to sites on the World Wide Web

bru·in *n* : ¹BEAR 1

¹bruise *vb* **bruised; bruis·ing** : to injure the flesh (as by a blow) without breaking the skin

²bruise *n* : a black-and-blue spot on the body or a dark spot on fruit caused by bruising (as from a blow)

¹bru·net *or* **bru·nette** *n* : someone who is brunet

²brunet *or* **brunette** *adj* : having dark brown or black hair and dark eyes

brunt *n* : the main force or stress (as of an attack)

¹brush *n* : BRUSHWOOD

²brush *n* 1 : a tool made of bristles set in a handle and used for cleaning, smoothing, or painting 2 : a bushy tail 3 : an act of brushing 4 : a light stroke

³brush *vb* 1 : to scrub or smooth with a

brush 2 : to remove with or as if with a brush 3 : to pass lightly across

⁴brush *n* : a brief fight or quarrel

brush·wood *n* 1 : branches and twigs cut from trees 2 : a heavy growth of small trees and bushes

brus·sels sprouts *n pl, often cap B* : green heads like tiny cabbages growing thickly on the stem of a plant of the cabbage family and used as a vegetable

bru·tal *adj* : being cruel and inhuman — **bru·tal·ly** *adv*

bru·tal·i·ty *n, pl* **bru·tal·i·ties** 1 : the quality of being brutal 2 : a brutal act or course of action

¹brute *adj* 1 : of or relating to beasts 2 : typical of beasts : like that of a beast

²brute *n* 1 : a four-footed animal especially when wild 2 : a brutal person

brut·ish *adj* : being unfeeling and stupid

¹bub·ble *n* 1 : a tiny round body of air or gas in a liquid 2 : a round body of air within a solid 3 : a thin film of liquid filled with air or gas

²bubble *vb* **bub·bled; bub·bling** 1 : to form or produce bubbles 2 : to flow with a gurgle

bu·bon·ic plague *n* : a dangerous disease which is spread by rats and in which fever, weakness, and swollen lymph glands are present

buc·ca·neer *n* : PIRATE

¹buck *n* : a male deer or antelope or a male goat, hare, rabbit, or rat

²buck *vb* 1 : to spring or jump upward with head down and back arched 2 : to charge or push against 3 : to act in opposition to : OPPOSE

buck·board *n* : a lightweight carriage with four wheels that has a seat supported by a springy platform

buck·et *n* 1 : a usually round container with a handle for holding or carrying liquids or solids 2 : an object for collecting, scooping, or carrying something (as the scoop of an excavating machine) 3 : BUCKETFUL

buck·et·ful *n, pl* **buck·et·fuls** *or* **buck·ets·ful** 1 : as much as a bucket will hold 2 : a large quantity

buck·eye *n* : a horse chestnut or a closely related tree or shrub

¹buck·le *n* : a fastening device which is attached to one end of a belt or strap and through which the other end is passed and held

²buckle *vb* **buck·led; buck·ling** 1 : to fasten with a buckle 2 : to apply oneself earnestly 3 : to bend, crumple, or give way

buck·shot *n* : coarse lead shot

buck·skin *n* : a soft flexible leather usually having a suede finish

buck·wheat *n* : a plant with pinkish white flowers that is grown for its dark triangular seeds which are used as a cereal grain

¹**bud** *n* 1 : a small growth at the tip or on the side of a stem that later develops into a flower or branch 2 : a flower that has not fully opened 3 : a part that grows out from the body of an organism and develops into a new organism 4 : an early stage of development

²**bud** *vb* **bud·ded; bud·ding** 1 : to form or put forth buds 2 : to grow or reproduce by buds

bud·dy *n, pl* **buddies** : ¹CHUM

budge *vb* **budged; budg·ing** : to move or cause to move from one position to another

¹**bud·get** *n* 1 : a statement of estimated income and expenses for a period of time 2 : a plan for using money

²**budget** *vb* 1 : to include in a budget 2 : to plan as in a budget

¹**buff** *n* 1 : an orange yellow 2 : a stick or wheel with a soft surface for applying polishing material

²**buff** *vb* : to polish with or as if with a buff

buf·fa·lo *n, pl* **buffalo** *or* **buf·fa·loes** : any of several wild oxen and especially the American bison

buffalo wing *n* : a deep-fried chicken wing coated with a spicy sauce and usually served with blue cheese dressing

¹**buf·fet** *vb* : to pound repeatedly : BATTER

²**buf·fet** *n* 1 : a cabinet or set of shelves for the display of dishes and silver : SIDEBOARD 2 : a meal set out on a buffet or table from which people may serve themselves

bug *n* 1 : an insect or other small creeping or crawling animal 2 : any of a large group of insects that have four wings, suck liquid food (as plant juices or blood), and have young which resemble the adults but lack wings 3 : FLAW 4 : a person who is enthusiastic about something

bug·a·boo *n, pl* **bug·a·boos** : BUGBEAR

bug·bear *n* 1 : an imaginary creature used to frighten children 2 : something one is afraid of

bug·gy *n, pl* **buggies** : a light carriage with a single seat that is usually drawn by one horse

bu·gle *n* : an instrument like a simple trumpet used chiefly for giving military signals

bu·gler *n* : a person who plays a bugle

¹**build** *vb* **built; build·ing** 1 : to make by putting together parts or materials 2 : to produce or create gradually by effort 3 : to move toward a peak

²**build** *n* : form or kind of structure : PHYSIQUE

build·er *n* : a person whose business is the construction of buildings

build·ing *n* 1 : a permanent structure built as a dwelling, shelter, or place for human activities or for storage 2 : the art, work, or business of assembling materials into a structure

built–in *adj* : forming a permanent part of a structure

bulb *n* 1 : an underground resting form of a plant which consists of a short stem with one or more buds surrounded by thick leaves and from which a new plant can grow 2 : a plant structure (as a tuber) that is somewhat like a bulb 3 : a rounded object or part shaped more or less like a bulb

bul·bous *adj* 1 : having a bulb 2 : like a bulb in being round and swollen

¹**bulge** *vb* **bulged; bulg·ing** : to swell or curve outward

²**bulge** *n* : a swelling part : a part that sticks out

bulk *n* 1 : greatness of size or volume 2 : the largest or chief part

bulk·head *n* : a wall separating sections in a ship

bulky *adj* **bulk·i·er; bulk·i·est** 1 : having bulk 2 : being large and awkward to handle

bull *n* : the male of an animal of the ox and cow family and of certain other large animals (as the elephant and the whale)

¹**bull·dog** *n* : a dog of English origin with short hair and a stocky powerful build

²**bulldog** *vb* **bull·dogged; bull·dog·ging** : to throw by seizing the horns and twisting the neck

bull·doz·er *n* : a motor vehicle with beltlike tracks that has a broad blade for pushing (as in clearing land of trees)

bul·let *n* : a shaped piece of metal made to be shot from a firearm — **bul·let·proof** *adj*

bul·le·tin *n* : a short public notice usually coming from an informed or official source

bulletin board *n* : a board for posting bulletins and announcements

bull·fight *n* : a public entertainment in which people excite bulls, display daring in escaping their charges, and finally kill them — **bull·fight·er** *n*

bull·finch *n* : a European songbird that has a thick bill and a red breast and is often kept in a cage

bull·frog *n* : a large heavy frog that makes a booming or bellowing sound

bull·head *n* : any of various fishes with large heads

bul·lion *n* : gold or silver metal in bars or blocks

bull·ock *n* **1** : a young bull **2** : ¹STEER, OX

bull's–eye *n* **1** : the center of a target **2** : a shot that hits the center of a target

¹bul·ly *n, pl* **bul·lies** : a person who teases, hurts, or threatens smaller or weaker persons

²bully *vb* **bul·lied; bul·ly·ing** : to act like a bully toward

bul·rush *n* : any of several large rushes or sedges that grow in wet places

bul·wark *n* **1** : a solid structure like a wall built for defense against an enemy **2** : something that defends or protects

bum *n* **1** : a person who avoids work and tries to live off others **2** : ²TRAMP 1, HOBO

bum·ble·bee *n* : a large hairy bee that makes a loud humming sound

¹bump *n* **1** : a sudden heavy blow or shock **2** : a rounded swelling of flesh as from a blow **3** : an unevenness in a road surface

²bump *vb* **1** : to strike or knock against something **2** : to move along unevenly : JOLT

¹bum·per *adj* : larger or finer than usual

²bump·er *n* : a bar across the front or back of a motor vehicle intended to lessen the shock or damage from collision

bun *n* : a sweet or plain round roll

¹bunch *n* **1** : a number of things of the same kind growing together **2** : ¹GROUP

²bunch *vb* : to gather in a bunch

¹bun·dle *n* : a number of things fastened or wrapped together : PACKAGE

²bundle *vb* **bun·dled; bun·dling** : to make into a bundle : WRAP

bung *n* **1** : the stopper in the bunghole of a barrel **2** : BUNGHOLE

bun·ga·low *n* : a house with a single story

bung·hole *n* : a hole for emptying or filling a barrel

bun·gle *vb* **bun·gled; bun·gling** : to act, do, make, or work badly — **bun·gler** *n*

bun·ion *n* : a sore reddened swelling of the first joint of a big toe

¹bunk *n* **1** : a built-in bed **2** : a sleeping place

²bunk *vb* : to share or sleep in a bunk

bunk bed *n* : one of two single beds usually placed one above the other

bun·ny *n, pl* **bunnies** : RABBIT

¹bunt *vb* : to strike or push with the horns or head : BUTT

²bunt *n* : ²BUTT, PUSH

¹bun·ting *n* : any of various birds that are similar to sparrows in size and habits but have stout bills

²bunting *n* **1** : a thin cloth used chiefly for making flags and patriotic decorations **2** : flags or decorations made of bunting

¹buoy *n* **1** : a floating object anchored in a body of water so as to mark a channel or to warn of danger **2** : LIFE BUOY

²buoy *vb* **1** : to keep from sinking : keep afloat **2** : to brighten the mood of

buoy·an·cy *n* **1** : the power of rising and floating (as on water or in air) **2** : the power of a liquid to hold up a floating body

buoy·ant *adj* **1** : able to rise and float in the air or on the top of a liquid **2** : able to keep a body afloat **3** : LIGHT-HEARTED, CHEERFUL

bur *or* **burr** *n* **1** : a rough or prickly covering or shell of a seed or fruit **2** : something that is like a bur (as in sticking)

¹bur·den *n* **1** : something carried : LOAD **2** : something that is hard to take **3** : the carrying of loads **4** : the capacity of a ship for carrying cargo

²burden *vb* : to put a burden on

bur·den·some *adj* : so heavy or hard to take as to be a burden

bur·dock *n* : a tall coarse weed related to the thistles that has prickly purplish heads of flowers

bu·reau *n* **1** : a low chest of drawers for use in a bedroom **2** : a division of a government department **3** : a business office that provides services

bur·glar *n* : a person who is guilty of burglary

bur·glary *n, pl* **bur·glar·ies** : the act of breaking into a building to steal

buri·al *n* : the placing of a dead body in a grave or tomb

bur·lap *n* : a rough cloth made usually from jute or hemp and used mostly for bags and wrappings

bur·ly *adj* **bur·li·er; bur·li·est** : strongly and heavily built — **bur·li·ness** *n*

¹burn *vb* **burned** *or* **burnt; burn·ing** **1** : to be on fire or to set on fire **2** : to destroy or be destroyed by fire or heat **3** : to make or produce by fire or heat **4** : to give light **5** : to injure or affect by or as if by fire or heat **6** : to feel or cause to feel as if on fire

²burn *n* : an injury produced by burning

burn·er *n* : the part of a stove or furnace where the flame or heat is produced

bur·nish *vb* : to make shiny

burr *variant of* BUR

bur·ro *n, pl* **burros** : a small donkey often used as a pack animal

¹bur·row *n* : a hole in the ground made by an animal (as a rabbit or fox) for shelter or protection

²burrow *vb* **1** : to hide in or as if in a burrow

2 : to make a burrow 3 : to make one's way by or as if by digging

1burst *vb* **burst; burst·ing** 1 : to break open or in pieces (as by an explosion from within) 2 : to suddenly show one's feelings 3 : to come or go suddenly 4 : to be filled to the breaking point

2burst *n* : a sudden release or effort

bury *vb* **bur·ied; bury·ing** 1 : to put (a dead body) in a grave or tomb 2 : to place in the ground and cover over for concealment 3 : to cover up : HIDE

bus *n, pl* **bus·es** *or* **bus·ses** : a large motor vehicle for carrying passengers

bush *n* 1 : a usually low shrub with many branches 2 : a stretch of uncleared or lightly settled country

bush·el *n* 1 : a unit of dry capacity equal to four pecks or thirty-two quarts (about thirty-five liters) 2 : a container holding a bushel

bushy *adj* **bush·i·er; bush·i·est** 1 : overgrown with bushes 2 : being thick and spreading

busi·ness *n* 1 : the normal activity of a person or group 2 : a commercial enterprise 3 : the making, buying, and selling of goods or services 4 : personal concerns

busi·ness·man *n, pl* **busi·ness·men** : a man in business especially as an owner or a manager

busi·ness·wom·an *n, pl* **busi·ness·wom·en** : a woman in business especially as an owner or a manager

1bust *n* 1 : a piece of sculpture representing the upper part of the human figure including the head and neck 2 : a woman's bosom

2bust *vb* 1 : to hit with the fist 2 : 1BREAK 1

1bus·tle *vb* **bus·tled; bus·tling** : to move about in a fussy or noisy way

2bustle *n* : fussy or noisy activity

1busy *adj* **busi·er; busi·est** 1 : actively at work 2 : being used 3 : full of activity — **busi·ly** *adv*

2busy *vb* **bus·ied; busy·ing** : to make busy

busy·body *n, pl* **busy·bod·ies** : a person who meddles in the affairs of others

1but *conj* 1 : except that : UNLESS 2 : while just the opposite 3 : yet nevertheless

2but *prep* : other than : EXCEPT

3but *adv* : 2ONLY 1

1butch·er *n* 1 : one whose business is killing animals for sale as food 2 : a dealer in meat 3 : a person who kills in large numbers or in a brutal manner

2butcher *vb* 1 : to kill and dress (an animal) for food 2 : 2MASSACRE 3 : to make a mess of : BOTCH

but·ler *n* : the chief male servant of a household

1butt *vb* : to strike or thrust with the head or horns

2butt *n* : a blow or thrust with the head or horns

3butt *n* : a target of ridicule or hurtful jokes

4butt *n* 1 : the thicker or bottom end of something 2 : an unused remainder

butte *n* : an isolated hill with steep sides

1but·ter *n* 1 : a solid yellowish fatty food obtained from cream or milk by churning 2 : a substance that is like butter in texture and use

2butter *vb* : to spread with or as if with butter

but·ter·cup *n* : a common wildflower with bright yellow blossoms

but·ter·fat *n* : the natural fat of milk that is the chief ingredient of butter

but·ter·fly *n, pl* **but·ter·flies** : an insect that has a slender body and large colored wings covered with tiny overlapping scales and that flies mostly in the daytime

but·ter·milk *n* : the liquid left after churning butter from milk or cream

but·ter·nut *n* : an eastern North American tree that has sweet egg-shaped nuts and is related to the walnuts

but·ter·scotch *n* : a candy made from sugar, corn syrup, and water

but·tock *n* 1 : the back of the hip which forms one of the rounded parts on which a person sits 2 **buttocks** *pl* : RUMP 1

1but·ton *n* 1 : a small ball or disk used for holding parts of a garment together or as an ornament 2 : something that suggests a button

2button *vb* : to close or fasten with buttons

but·ton·hole *n* : a slit or loop for fastening a button

but·ton·wood *n* : SYCAMORE 2

1but·tress *n* 1 : a structure built against a wall or building to give support and strength 2 : something that supports, props, or strengthens

2buttress *vb* : to support with or as if with a buttress

bux·om *adj* : having a healthy plump form

1buy *vb* **bought; buy·ing** : to get by paying for : PURCHASE — **buy·er** *n*

2buy *n* : 1BARGAIN 2

1buzz *vb* 1 : to make a low humming sound like that of bees 2 : to be filled with a low hum or murmur 3 : to fly an airplane low over

2buzz *n* : a sound of buzzing

buz·zard *n* : a usually large bird of prey that flies slowly

buzz·er *n* : an electric signaling device that makes a buzzing sound

¹by *prep* **1** : close to : NEAR **2** : so as to go on **3** : so as to go through **4** : so as to pass **5** : AT **1**, DURING **6** : no later than **7** : with the use or help of **8** : through the action of **9** : ACCORDING TO **10** : with respect to **11** : to the amount of **12** — used to join two or more measurements or to join the numbers in a statement of multiplication or division

²by *adv* **1** : near at hand **2** : ⁴PAST

by–and–by *n* : a future time

by and by *adv* : after a while

by·gone *adj* : gone by : PAST

by·gones *n pl* : events that are over and done with

¹by·pass *n* **1** : a way for passing to one side **2** : a road serving as a substitute route around a crowded area

²bypass *vb* : to make a detour around

by–prod·uct *n* : something produced (as in manufacturing) in addition to the main product

by·stand·er *n* : a person present or standing near but taking no part in what is going on

byte *n* : a group of eight bits that a computer handles as a unit

by·way *n* : a less traveled road off a main highway

C

c *n, pl* **c's** *or* **cs** *often cap* **1** : the third letter of the English alphabet **2** : 100 in Roman numerals **3** : a grade that shows a student's work is fair

cab *n* **1** : a light closed carriage pulled by a horse **2** : TAXICAB **3** : the covered compartment for the engineer and the controls of a locomotive or for the operator of a truck, tractor, or crane

ca·bana *n* : a shelter usually with an open side facing the sea or a swimming pool

cab·bage *n* : a garden plant related to the turnips that has a firm head of leaves used as a vegetable

cab·in *n* **1** : a private room on a ship **2** : a place below deck on a small boat for passengers or crew **3** : a part of an airplane for cargo, crew, or passengers **4** : a small simple dwelling usually having only one story

cab·i·net *n* **1** : a case or cupboard with shelves or drawers for keeping or displaying articles **2** : a group of persons who act as advisers (as to the head of a country)

¹ca·ble *n* **1** : a very strong rope, wire, or chain **2** : a bundle of wires to carry electric current **3** : CABLEGRAM

²cable *vb* **ca·bled; ca·bling** : to telegraph by underwater cable

ca·ble·gram *n* : a message sent by underwater cable

ca·boose *n* : a car usually at the rear of a freight train for the use of the train crew and railroad workers

ca·cao *n, pl* **cacaos** : a South American tree with fleshy yellow pods that contain fatty seeds from which chocolate is made

¹cache *n* **1** : a place for hiding, storing, or preserving treasure or supplies **2** : something hidden or stored in a cache

²cache *vb* **cached; cach·ing** : to place, hide, or store in a cache

¹cack·le *vb* **cack·led; cack·ling 1** : to make the sharp broken noise or cry a hen makes especially after laying an egg **2** : to laugh or chatter noisily

²cackle *n* : a cackling sound

cac·tus *n, pl* **cac·tus·es** *or* **cac·ti** : any of a large group of flowering plants of dry regions that have thick juicy stems and branches with scales or prickles

¹cad·die *or* **cad·dy** *n, pl* **cad·dies** : a person who carries a golfer's clubs

²caddie *or* **caddy** *vb* **cad·died; cad·dy·ing** : to work as a caddie

cad·dis fly *n* : an insect that has four wings and a larva which lives in water in a silk case covered with bits of wood or gravel and is often used for fish bait

ca·dence *n* : the beat of rhythmic motion or sound (as of marching) : RHYTHM

ca·det *n* : a student in a military school or college

ca·fé *also* **ca·fe** *n* **1** : ¹BAR 9 **2** : RESTAURANT **3** : NIGHTCLUB

caf·e·te·ria *n* : a restaurant where the customers serve themselves or are served at a counter but carry their own food to their tables

caf·feine *n* : a stimulating substance in coffee and tea

¹cage *n* **1** : a box or enclosure that has large openings covered usually with wire net or bars and is used to confine or carry birds or animals **2** : an enclosure like a cage in shape or purpose

²cage *vb* **caged; cag·ing** : to put or keep in or as if in a cage

ca·gey *adj* **ca·gi·er; ca·gi·est** : hard to trap or trick

cais·son *n* **1** : a chest for ammunition usually set on two wheels **2** : a watertight box or chamber used for doing construction work under water or used as a foundation

ca·jole *vb* **ca·joled; ca·jol·ing** : to coax or persuade especially by flattery or false promises : WHEEDLE

¹cake *n* **1** : a small piece of food (as dough or batter, meat, or fish) that is baked or fried **2** : a baked food made from a sweet batter or dough **3** : a substance hardened or molded into a solid piece

²cake *vb* **caked; cak·ing 1** : ENCRUST **2** : to form or harden into a cake

ca·lam·i·ty *n, pl* **ca·lam·i·ties 1** : great distress or misfortune **2** : an event that causes great harm

cal·ci·um *n* : a silvery soft metallic chemical element that is an essential for most plants and animals

calcium carbonate *n* : a solid substance that is found as limestone and marble and in plant ashes, bones, and shells

cal·cu·late *vb* **cal·cu·lat·ed; cal·cu·lat·ing 1** : to find by adding, subtracting, multiplying, or dividing : COMPUTE **2** : ¹ESTIMATE 1 **3** : to plan by careful thought

cal·cu·la·tion *n* **1** : the process or an act of calculating **2** : the result obtained by calculating

cal·cu·la·tor *n* **1** : a person who calculates **2** : a usually small electronic device for solving mathematical problems

cal·cu·lus *n* : TARTAR 2

caldron *variant of* CAULDRON

cal·en·dar *n* **1** : a chart showing the days, weeks, and months of the year **2** : a schedule of coming events

¹calf *n, pl* **calves 1** : the young of the cow **2** : the young of various large animals (as the elephant, moose, or whale) **3** *pl* **calfs** : CALFSKIN

²calf *n, pl* **calves** : the muscular back part of the leg below the knee

calf·skin *n* : the skin of a calf or the leather made from it

cal·i·ber *or* **cal·i·bre** *n* **1** : the diameter of a bullet **2** : the diameter of the hole in the barrel of a gun

¹cal·i·co *n, pl* **cal·i·coes** *or* **cal·i·cos** : cotton cloth especially with a colored pattern printed on one side

²calico *adj* : marked with blotches of color

cal·i·per *or* **cal·li·per** *n* : an instrument with two adjustable legs used to measure the thickness of objects or the distance between surfaces — usually used in pl.

ca·liph *or* **ca·lif** *n* : an important official in some Arab countries

cal·is·then·ics *n sing or pl* : exercise to develop strength and grace that is done without special equipment

¹call *vb* **1** : to speak in a loud clear voice so as to be heard at a distance : SHOUT **2** : to say in a loud clear voice **3** : to announce with authority : PROCLAIM **4** : SUMMON 12 **5** : to bring into action or discussion **6** : to make a request or demand **7** : to get in touch with by telephone **8** : to make a short visit **9** : ²NAME 1 **10** : to estimate as —
call for : to require as necessary or suitable

²call *n* **1** : a loud shout or cry **2** : a cry of an animal **3** : a request or command to come or assemble **4** : ¹DEMAND 1, CLAIM **5** : ¹REQUEST 1 **6** : a short visit **7** : a name or thing called **8** : the act of calling on the telephone

call down *vb* : ²REPRIMAND

call·er *n* : one who calls

call·ing *n* : OCCUPATION 1, PROFESSION

cal·li·ope *n* : a keyboard musical instrument consisting of a set of steam whistles

calliper *variant of* CALIPER

cal·lous *adj* **1** : having a callus **2** : feeling no sympathy for others

cal·lus *n* : a hard thickened spot (as of skin)

¹calm *n* **1** : a period or condition of freedom from storm, wind, or rough water **2** : a peaceful state : QUIET

²calm *vb* : to make or become calm

³calm *adj* **1** : not stormy or windy : STILL **2** : not excited or angry — **calm·ly** *adv* — **calm·ness** *n*

cal·o·rie *n* **1** : a unit for measuring heat equal to the heat required to raise the temperature of one gram of water one degree Celsius **2** : a unit equal to 1000 calories — used especially to indicate the value of foods for producing heat and energy in the human body

calve *vb* **calved; calv·ing** : to give birth to a calf

calves *pl of* CALF

ca·lyp·so *n, pl* **calypsos** : a folk song or style of singing of the West Indies

ca·lyx *n, pl* **ca·lyx·es** *or* **ca·ly·ces** : the outer usually green or leafy part of a flower

cam *n* : a device (as a tooth on a wheel) by which circular motion is changed to back-and-forth motion

cam·bi·um *n, pl* **cam·bi·ums** *or* **cam·bia** : soft tissue in woody plants from which new wood and bark grow

came *past of* COME

cam·el *n* : a large hoofed animal that chews the cud and is used in the deserts of Asia and Africa for carrying burdens and for riding

cam·era *n* **1** : a box that has a lens on one side to let the light in and is used for taking pictures **2** : the part of a television sending device in which the image to be sent out is formed

¹cam·ou·flage *n* **1** : the hiding or disguising of something by covering it up or changing the way it looks **2** : the material (as paint or branches) used for camouflage

²camouflage *vb* **cam·ou·flaged; cam·ou·flag·ing** : to hide or disguise by camouflage

¹camp *n* **1** : a place where temporary shelters are erected **2** : a place usually in the country for recreation or instruction during the summer **3** : a group of people in a camp

²camp *vb* **1** : to make or occupy a camp **2** : to live in a camp or outdoors — **camp·er** *n*

¹cam·paign *n* **1** : a series of military operations in a certain area or for a certain purpose **2** : a series of activities meant to get a certain thing done

²campaign *vb* : to take part in a campaign — **campaign·er** *n*

Camp Fire Girl *n* : a member of a national organization for girls from seven to eighteen

cam·phor *n* : a white fragrant solid that comes from the wood and bark of a tall Asian tree (**camphor tree**) and is used mostly in medicine and in making plastics

cam·pus *n* : the grounds and buildings of a university, college, or school

¹can *helping verb, past* **could;** *present sing & pl* **can 1** : know how to **2** : be able to **3** : be permitted by conscience to **4** : have permission to : MAY

²can *n* **1** : a usually cylindrical metal container **2** : the contents of a can

³can *vb* **canned; can·ning** : to keep fit for later use by sealing (as in an airtight jar)

¹Ca·na·di·an *adj* : of or relating to Canada or the Canadians

²Canadian *n* : a person born or living in Canada

ca·nal *n* **1** : an artificial waterway for boats or for irrigation of land **2** : a tubelike passage in the body

ca·nary *n, pl* **ca·nar·ies** : a small usually yellow songbird often kept in a cage

can·cel *vb* **can·celed** *or* **can·celled; can·cel·ing** *or* **can·cel·ling 1** : to cross out or strike out with a line : DELETE **2** : to take back : WITHDRAW **3** : to equal in force or effect : OFFSET **4** : to remove (a common divisor) from numerator and denominator : remove (equivalents) on opposite sides of an equation or account **5** : to mark (as a postage stamp) so as to make impossible to use again

can·cel·la·tion *n* **1** : an act of canceling **2** : a mark made to cancel something

can·cer *n* **1** : a harmful growth on or in the body that may keep spreading and be fatal if not treated **2** : a condition of the body characterized by a cancer or cancers

can·de·la·bra *n* : a candlestick or lamp that has several branches for lights

can·de·la·brum *n, pl* **can·de·la·bra** *also* **can·de·la·brums** : CANDELABRA

can·did *adj* **1** : FRANK, STRAIGHTFORWARD **2** : relating to photography of people acting naturally without being posed — **can·did·ly** *adv* — **can·did·ness** *n*

can·di·da·cy *n, pl* **can·di·da·cies** : the state of being a candidate

can·di·date *n* : a person who runs for or is nominated by others for an office or honor

can·died *adj* : preserved in or coated with sugar

¹can·dle *n* : a stick of tallow or wax containing a wick and burned to give light

²candle *vb* **can·dled; can·dling** : to examine (as eggs) by holding between the eye and a light — **can·dler** *n*

can·dle·light *n* **1** : the light of a candle **2** : a soft artificial light

can·dle·stick *n* : a holder for a candle

can·dor *n* : sincere and honest expression

¹can·dy *n, pl* **can·dies** : a sweet made of sugar often with flavoring and food

²candy *vb* **can·died; can·dy·ing 1** : to coat or become coated with sugar often by cooking **2** : to crystallize into sugar

¹cane *n* **1** : an often hollow, slender, and somewhat flexible plant stem **2** : a tall woody grass or reed (as sugarcane) **3** : WALKING STICK 1 **4** : a rod for beating

²cane *vb* **caned; can·ing 1** : to beat with a cane **2** : to make or repair with cane

¹ca·nine *n* **1** : a pointed tooth next to the incisors **2** : a canine animal

²canine *adj* **1** : of or relating to the dogs or to the group of animals (as wolves) to which the dog belongs **2** : like or typical of a dog

can·is·ter *n* : a small box or can for holding a dry product

can·nery *n, pl* **can·ner·ies** : a factory where foods are canned

can·ni·bal *n* **1** : a human being who eats human flesh **2** : an animal that eats other animals of its own kind

can·non *n, pl* **cannon** *also* **cannons 1** : a heavy gun mounted on a carriage **2** : an automatic gun of heavy caliber on an airplane

can·non·ball *n* : a usually round solid missile for firing from a cannon

can·not : can not

can·ny *adj* **can·ni·er; can·ni·est** : watchful of one's own interest — **can·ni·ly** *adv*

¹ca·noe *n* : a long light narrow boat with sharp ends and curved sides usually driven by paddles

²canoe *vb* **ca·noed; ca·noe·ing** : to travel or carry in a canoe — **ca·noe·ist** *n*

can·on *n* **1** : a rule or law of a church **2** : an accepted rule

can·o·py *n, pl* **can·o·pies 1** : a covering fixed over a bed or throne or carried on poles (as over a person of high rank) **2** : something that hangs over and shades or shelters something else

can't : can not

can·ta·loupe *n* : a muskmelon usually with a hard ridged or rough skin and reddish orange flesh

can·tan·ker·ous *adj* : QUARRELSOME

can·ta·ta *n* : a poem or story set to music to be sung by a chorus and soloists

can·teen *n* **1** : a store (as in a camp or factory) in which food, drinks, and small supplies are sold **2** : a place of recreation for people in military service **3** : a small container for carrying liquid (as drinking water)

can·ter *n* : a horse's gait like but slower than the gallop

can·ti·le·ver *n* **1** : a beam or similar structure fastened (as by being built into a wall) only at one end **2** : either of two structures that extend from piers toward each other and when joined form a span in a bridge (**cantilever bridge**)

can·to *n, pl* **can·tos** : one of the major divisions of a long poem

can·ton *n* : a division of a country (as Switzerland)

can·tor *n* : a synagogue official who sings religious music and leads the congregation in prayer

can·vas *n* **1** : a strong cloth of hemp, flax, or cotton that is used sometimes for making tents and sails and as the material on which oil paintings are made **2** : something made of canvas or on canvas

can·vas·back *n* : a North American wild duck with reddish head and grayish back

¹can·vass *vb* : to go through (a district) or go to (people) to ask for votes, contributions, or orders for goods or to determine public opinion — **can·vass·er** *n*

²canvass *n* : an act of canvassing

can·yon *n* : a deep valley with high steep slopes

¹cap *n* **1** : a head covering that has a visor and no brim **2** : something that serves as a cover or protection for something **3** : a paper or metal container holding an explosive charge

²cap *vb* **capped; cap·ping 1** : to cover or provide with a cap **2** : to match with something equal or better

ca·pa·bil·i·ty *n, pl* **ca·pa·bil·i·ties** : the quality or state of being capable

ca·pa·ble *adj* **1** : having the qualities (as ability, power, or strength) needed to do or accomplish something **2** : able to do one's job well : EFFICIENT — **ca·pa·bly** *adv*

ca·pa·cious *adj* : able to hold a great deal

ca·pac·i·ty *n, pl* **ca·pac·i·ties 1** : ability to contain or deal with something **2** : mental or physical power **3** : VOLUME 3 **4** : ROLE 1, STATUS

¹cape *n* : a point of land that juts out into the sea or into a lake

²cape *n* : a sleeveless garment worn so as to hang over the shoulders, arms, and back

¹ca·per *vb* : to leap about in a lively way

²caper *n* **1** : a gay bounding leap or spring **2** : a playful or mischievous trick **3** : an illegal or questionable act

¹cap·il·lary *adj* **1** : having a long slender form and a small inner diameter **2** : of or relating to capillary action or a capillary

²capillary *n, pl* **cap·il·lar·ies** : one of the slender hairlike tubes that are the smallest blood vessels and connect arteries with veins

capillary action *n* : the action by which the surface of a liquid where it is in contact with a solid (as in a capillary tube) is raised or lowered

¹cap·i·tal *n* : the top part of an architectural column

²capital *adj* **1** : punishable by or resulting in death **2** : being like the letters A, B, C, etc. rather than a, b, c, etc. **3** : being the location of a government **4** : of or relating to capital **5** : EXCELLENT

³capital *n* **1** : accumulated wealth especially as used to produce more wealth **2** : persons holding capital **3** : profitable use **4** : a capital letter **5** : a capital city

cap·i·tal·ism *n* : a system under which the ownership of land and wealth is for the most part in the hands of private individuals

¹cap·i·tal·ist *n* **1** : a person who has capital and especially business capital **2** : a person who favors capitalism

²capitalist *adj* **1** : owning capital **2** : CAPITALISTIC

cap·i·tal·is·tic *adj* **1** : practicing or favoring capitalism **2** : of or relating to capitalism or capitalists — **cap·i·tal·is·ti·cal·ly** *adv*

cap·i·tal·iza·tion *n* **1** : the act or process of capitalizing **2** : the amount of money used as capital in business

cap·i·tal·ize *vb* **cap·i·tal·ized; cap·i·tal·iz·ing 1** : to write with a beginning capital letter or in capital letters **2** : to use as capital (as in a business) : furnish capital for (a business) **3** : to gain by turning something to advantage

cap·i·tol *n* **1** : the building in which a state legislature meets **2** *cap* : the building in

Washington in which the United States Congress meets

ca·po *n, pl* **capos** : a bar that can be fitted on the fingerboard especially of a guitar to raise the pitch of all the strings

ca·pon *n* : a castrated male chicken

ca·price *n* : a sudden change in feeling, opinion, or action : WHIM

ca·pri·cious *adj* : moved or controlled by caprice : likely to change suddenly — **ca·pri·cious·ly** *adv* — **ca·pri·cious·ness** *n*

cap·size *vb* **cap·sized; cap·siz·ing** : to turn over : UPSET

cap·stan *n* : a device that consists of a drum to which a rope is fastened and that is used especially on ships for moving or raising weights

cap·sule *n* **1** : a case enclosing the seeds or spores of a plant **2** : a small case of material that contains medicine to be swallowed **3** : a closed compartment for travel in space

¹cap·tain *n* **1** : a leader of a group : one in command **2** : a commissioned officer in the Navy or Coast Guard ranking above a commander **3** : a commissioned officer in the Army, Air Force, or Marine Corps ranking above a first lieutenant **4** : the commanding officer of a ship

²captain *vb* : to be captain of

cap·tion *n* **1** : the heading especially of an article or document **2** : a comment or title that goes with a picture (as in a book)

cap·ti·vate *vb* **cap·ti·vat·ed; cap·ti·vat·ing** : to fascinate by some special charm

¹cap·tive *adj* **1** : taken and held prisoner especially in war **2** : kept within bounds or under control **3** : of or relating to captivity

²captive *n* : one that is captive : PRISONER

cap·tiv·i·ty *n* : the state of being a captive

cap·tor *n* : one that has captured a person or thing

¹cap·ture *n* : the act of capturing

²capture *vb* **cap·tured; cap·tur·ing** **1** : to take and hold especially by force **2** : to put into a lasting form

car *n* **1** : a vehicle (as an automobile) that moves on wheels **2** : the compartment of an elevator

ca·rafe *n* : a bottle that has a lip and is used to hold water or beverages

car·a·mel *n* **1** : burnt sugar used for coloring and flavoring **2** : a firm chewy candy

car·at *n* : a unit of weight for precious stones equal to 200 milligrams

car·a·van *n* **1** : a group (as of merchants or pilgrims) traveling together on a long journey through desert or in dangerous places **2** : a group of vehicles traveling together one behind the other

car·a·vel *n* : a small sailing ship of the fifteenth and sixteenth centuries with a broad bow and high stern and three or four masts

car·a·way *n* : an herb related to the carrots that is grown for its seeds used especially as a seasoning

car·bine *n* : a short light rifle

car·bo·hy·drate *n* : a nutrient that is rich in energy and is made up of carbon, hydrogen, and oxygen

car·bol·ic acid *n* : a poison present in coal tar and wood tar that is diluted and used as an antiseptic

car·bon *n* : a chemical element occurring as diamond and graphite, in coal and petroleum, and in plant and animal bodies

carbon di·ox·ide *n* : a heavy colorless gas that is formed by burning fuels and by decay and that is the simple raw material from which plants build up compounds for their nourishment

carbon mon·ox·ide *n* : a colorless odorless very poisonous gas formed by incomplete burning of carbon

carbon tet·ra·chlo·ride *n* : a colorless poisonous liquid that does not burn and is used for dissolving grease

car·bu·re·tor *n* : the part of an engine in which liquid fuel (as gasoline) is mixed with air to make it burn easily

car·cass *n* : the body of an animal prepared for use as meat

¹card *vb* : to clean and untangle fibers and especially wool by combing with a card — **card·er** *n*

²card *n* : an instrument usually with bent wire teeth that is used to clean and untangle fibers (as wool)

³card *n* **1** : PLAYING CARD **2** **cards** *pl* : a game played with playing cards **3** : a flat stiff piece of paper or thin pasteboard that can be written on or that contains printed information

card·board *n* : a stiff material made of wood pulp that has been pressed and dried

car·di·ac *adj* : of, relating to, or affecting the heart

¹car·di·nal *n* **1** : a high official of the Roman Catholic Church ranking next below the pope **2** : a bright red songbird with a crest and a whistling call

²cardinal *adj* : of first importance : MAIN, PRINCIPAL

cardinal flower *n* : the bright red flower of a North American plant that blooms in late summer

car·di·nal·i·ty *n, pl* **car·di·nal·i·ties** : the number of elements in a given mathematical set

cardinal number *n* : a number (as 1, 5, 22)

that is used in simple counting and answers the question "how many?"

cardinal point *n* : one of the four chief points of the compass which are north, south, east, west

1care *n* **1** : a heavy sense of responsibility **2** : serious attention **3** : PROTECTION 1, SUPERVISION **4** : an object of one's care

2care *vb* **cared; car·ing** **1** : to feel interest or concern **2** : to give care **3** : to have a liking or desire

ca·reer *n* **1** : the course followed or progress made in one's job or life's work **2** : a job followed as a life's work

care·free *adj* : free from care or worry

care·ful *adj* **1** : using care **2** : made, done, or said with care — **care·ful·ly** *adv* — **care·ful·ness** *n*

care·less *adj* **1** : CAREFREE **2** : not taking proper care **3** : done, made, or said without being careful — **care·less·ly** *adv* — **care·less·ness** *n*

1ca·ress *n* : a tender or loving touch or hug

2caress *vb* : to touch in a tender or loving way

care·tak·er *n* : a person who takes care of property for another person

car·fare *n* : the fare charged for carrying a passenger (as on a bus)

car·go *n, pl* **cargoes** *or* **cargos** : the goods carried by a ship, airplane, or vehicle

car·i·bou *n* : a large deer of northern and arctic North America that is closely related to the Old World reindeer

car·ies *n, pl* **caries** : a decayed condition of a tooth or teeth

car·il·lon *n* : a set of bells sounded by hammers controlled by a keyboard

car·nage *n* : 1SLAUGHTER 3

car·na·tion *n* : a fragrant usually white, pink, or red garden or greenhouse flower that is related to the pinks

car·ne·lian *n* : a hard reddish quartz used as a gem

car·ni·val *n* **1** : a traveling group that puts on a variety of amusements **2** : an organized program of entertainment or exhibition : FESTIVAL

car·ni·vore *n* : an animal that feeds on meat

car·niv·o·rous *adj* **1** : feeding on animal flesh **2** : of or relating to carnivores

1car·ol *n* : a usually religious song of joy

2carol *vb* **car·oled** *or* **car·olled; car·ol·ing** *or* **car·ol·ling** **1** : to sing in a joyful manner **2** : to sing carols and especially Christmas carols — **car·ol·er** *or* **car·ol·ler** *n*

1car·om *n* : a bouncing back especially at an angle

2carom *vb* : to hit and bounce back at an angle

1carp *vb* : to find fault

2carp *n* : a freshwater fish that lives a long time and may weigh as much as eighteen kilograms

car·pel *n* : one of the ring of parts that form the ovary of a flower

car·pen·ter *n* : a worker who builds or repairs things made of wood

car·pen·try *n* : the work or trade of a carpenter

1car·pet *n* **1** : a heavy woven fabric used especially as a floor covering **2** : a covering like a carpet

2carpet *vb* : to cover with or as if with a carpet

car·riage *n* **1** : the manner of holding the body : POSTURE **2** : a vehicle with wheels used for carrying persons **3** : a support with wheels used for carrying a load **4** : a movable part of a machine that carries or supports some other moving part

car·ri·er *n* **1** : a person or thing that carries **2** : a person or business that transports passengers or goods **3** : one that carries disease germs and passes them on to others

car·ri·on *n* : dead and decaying flesh

car·rot *n* : the long orange edible root of a garden plant (**carrot plant**)

car·ry *vb* **car·ried; car·ry·ing** **1** : to take or transfer from one place to another **2** : 1SUPPORT 4, BEAR **3** : WIN 4 **4** : to contain and direct the course of **5** : to wear or have on one's person or have within one **6** : to have as an element, quality, or part **7** : to hold or bear the body or some part of it **8** : to sing in correct pitch **9** : to have for sale **10** : PUBLISH 2 **11** : to go over or travel a distance

car·ry·all *n* : a large bag or carrying case

carry away *vb* : to cause strong feeling in

carry on *vb* **1** : MANAGE 1 **2** : to behave badly **3** : to continue in spite of difficulties

carry out *vb* : to put into action or effect

car seat *n* : a portable seat for a small child that attaches to an automobile seat and holds the child safely

1cart *n* **1** : a heavy vehicle with two wheels usually drawn by horses and used for hauling **2** : a light vehicle pushed or pulled by hand

2cart *vb* : to carry in a cart — **cart·er** *n*

car·ti·lage *n* : an elastic tissue that makes up most of the skeleton of very young animals and is later mostly changed into bone

car·ti·lag·i·nous *adj* : of, relating to, or made of cartilage

car·ton *n* : a cardboard container

car·toon *n* **1** : a drawing (as in a newspaper) making people or objects look funny or foolish **2** : COMIC STRIP **3** : a movie composed of cartoons

car·toon·ist *n* : a person who draws cartoons

car·tridge *n* **1** : a case or shell containing gunpowder and shot or a bullet for use in a firearm **2** : a case containing an explosive for blasting **3** : a container like a cartridge

cart·wheel *n* : a handspring made to the side with arms and legs sticking out

carve *vb* **carved; carv·ing 1** : to cut with care **2** : to make or get by cutting **3** : to slice and serve (meat) — **carv·er** *n*

cas·cade *n* : a steep usually small waterfall

cas·cara *n* : the dried bark of a western North American shrub used as a laxative

¹case *n* **1** : a particular instance, situation, or example **2** : a situation or an object that calls for investigation or action (as by the police) **3** : a question to be settled in a court of law **4** : a form of a noun, pronoun, or adjective showing its grammatical relation to other words **5** : the actual situation **6** : a convincing argument **7** : an instance of disease or injury **8** : ²PATIENT

²case *n* **1** : a container (as a box) for holding something **2** : a box and its contents **3** : an outer covering **4** : the frame of a door or window

ca·sein *n* : a whitish to yellowish material made from milk especially by the action of acid and used in making paints and plastics

case·ment *n* **1** : a window sash opening on hinges **2** : a window with a casement

¹cash *n* **1** : money in the form of coins or bills **2** : money or its equivalent (as a check) paid for goods at the time of purchase or delivery

²cash *vb* : to pay or obtain cash for

cash·ew *n* : an edible nut that is shaped like a kidney and comes from a tropical American tree

¹ca·shier *vb* : to dismiss from service especially in disgrace

²cash·ier *n* : a person who is responsible for money (as in a bank or business)

cash·mere *n* : a soft yarn or fabric once made from the fine wool of an Indian goat but now often from sheep's wool

cas·ing *n* : something that covers or encloses

cask *n* **1** : a container that is shaped like a barrel and is usually used for liquids **2** : the amount contained in a cask

cas·ket *n* **1** : a small box for storage or safekeeping (as for jewels) **2** : COFFIN

cas·se·role *n* **1** : a deep dish in which food can be baked and served **2** : the food cooked and served in a casserole

cas·sette *n* **1** : a container holding photographic film or plates that can be easily loaded into a camera **2** : a container holding magnetic tape with the tape on one reel passing to the other

¹cast *vb* **cast; cast·ing 1** : ¹THROW 1 **2** : to throw out, off, or away : SHED **3** : to direct to or toward something or someone **4** : to put on record **5** : to assign a part or role to **6** : to give shape to liquid material by pouring it into a mold and letting it harden **7** : to make by looping or catching up — **cast lots** : to take or receive an object at random in order to decide something by chance

²cast *n* **1** : an act of casting : THROW, FLING **2** : the form in which a thing is made **3** : the characters or the people acting in a play or story **4** : the distance to which a thing can be thrown **5** : something formed by casting in a mold or form **6** : a stiff surgical dressing of plaster hardened around a part of the body **7** : a hint of color **8** : ²SHAPE 1' **9** : something (as the skin of an insect) thrown out or off

cas·ta·net *n* : a rhythm instrument that consists of two small ivory, wooden, or plastic shells fastened to the thumb and clicked by the fingers in time to dancing and music — usually used in pl.

¹cast·away *adj* **1** : thrown away **2** : cast adrift or ashore

²castaway *n* **1** : something that has been thrown away **2** : a shipwrecked person

caste *n* **1** : one of the classes into which the people of India were formerly divided **2** : a division or class of society based on wealth, rank, or occupation **3** : social rank : PRESTIGE

cast·er *n* **1** : one that casts **2** : a small container (as for salt or pepper) with holes in the top **3** *or* **cas·tor** : a small wheel that turns freely and is used for supporting furniture

cas·ti·gate *vb* **cas·ti·gat·ed; cas·ti·gat·ing** : to punish or correct with words or blows

cast·ing *n* **1** : the act or action of one that casts **2** : something that is cast in a mold **3** : something (as skin or feathers) that is cast out or off

cast iron *n* : a hard and brittle alloy of iron, carbon, and silicon shaped by being poured into a mold while melted

cas·tle *n* **1** : a large building or group of buildings usually having high walls with towers and a surrounding moat for protection **2** : a large or impressive house

cast·off *n* : a cast-off person or thing

cast–off *adj* : thrown away or aside

cas·tor oil *n* : a thick yellowish liquid that comes from the seeds (**castor beans**) of a tropical herb and is used as a lubricant and as a strong laxative

cas·trate *vb* **cas·trat·ed; cas·trat·ing** : to remove the sex glands of

ca·su·al *adj* **1** : happening unexpectedly or by chance : not planned or foreseen **2** : occurring without regularity : OCCASIONAL **3** : showing or feeling little concern : NONCHALANT **4** : meant for informal use — **ca·su·al·ly** *adv*

ca·su·al·ty *n, pl* **ca·su·al·ties 1** : a serious or fatal accident : DISASTER **2** : a military person lost (as by death) during warfare **3** : a person or thing injured, lost, or destroyed

cat *n* **1** : a common furry flesh-eating animal kept as a pet or for catching mice and rats **2** : any of the group of mammals (as lions, tigers, and wildcats) to which the domestic cat belongs

¹cat·a·log *or* **cat·a·logue** *n* **1** : a list of names, titles, or articles arranged by some system **2** : a book or file containing a catalog

²catalog *or* **catalogue** *vb* **cat·a·loged** *or* **cat·a·logued; cat·a·log·ing** *or* **cat·a·logu·ing 1** : to make a catalog of **2** : to enter in a catalog — **cat·a·log·er** *or* **cat·a·logu·er** *n*

ca·tal·pa *n* : a tree of America and Asia with broad leaves, bright flowers, and long pods

¹cat·a·pult *n* **1** : an ancient military machine for hurling stones and arrows **2** : a device for launching an airplane from the deck of a ship

²catapult *vb* **1** : to throw or launch by or as if by a catapult **2** : to become catapulted

ca·tarrh *n* : a red sore state of mucous membrane especially when chronic

ca·tas·tro·phe *n* **1** : a sudden disaster **2** : complete failure : FIASCO

cat·bird *n* : a dark gray songbird that has a call like a cat's mewing

cat·boat *n* : a sailboat with a single mast set far forward and a single large sail with a long boom

cat·call *n* : a sound like the cry of a cat or a noise expressing disapproval (as at a sports event)

¹catch *vb* **caught; catch·ing 1** : to capture or seize something in flight or motion **2** : to discover unexpectedly **3** : to check suddenly **4** : to take hold of **5** : to get tangled **6** : to hold firmly : FASTEN **7** : to become affected by **8** : to take or get briefly or quickly **9** : to be in time for **10** : to grasp by the senses or the mind **11** : to play catcher on a baseball team

²catch *n* **1** : something caught : the amount caught at one time **2** : the act of catching **3** : a pastime in which a ball is thrown and caught **4** : something that checks, fastens, or holds immovable **5** : a hidden difficulty

catch·er *n* **1** : one that catches **2** : a baseball player who plays behind home plate

catch·ing *adj* **1** : INFECTIOUS 1, CONTAGIOUS **2** : likely to spread as if infectious

catchy *adj* **catch·i·er; catch·i·est 1** : likely to attract **2** : TRICKY 2

cat·e·chism *n* **1** : a series of questions and answers used in giving instruction and especially religious instruction **2** : a set of formal questions

cat·e·go·ry *n, pl* **cat·e·go·ries** : a basic division or grouping of things

ca·ter *vb* **1** : to provide a supply of food **2** : to supply what is needed or wanted — **ca·ter·er** *n*

cat·er·pil·lar *n* : a wormlike often hairy larva of an insect (as a moth or butterfly)

cat·fish *n* : any of a group of fishes with large heads and feelers about the mouth

cat·gut *n* : a tough cord made from intestines of animals (as sheep) and used for strings of musical instruments and rackets and for sewing in surgery

ca·the·dral *n* : the principal church of a district headed by a bishop

cath·o·lic *adj* **1** : broad in range **2** *cap* : of or relating to the Roman Catholic Church

Catholic *n* **1** : a member of a Christian church tracing its history back to the apostles **2** : a member of the Roman Catholic Church

cat·kin *n* : a flower cluster (as of the willow and birch) in which the flowers grow in close circular rows along a slender stalk

cat·like *adj* : like a cat (as in grace or slyness)

cat·nap *n* : a very short light nap

cat·nip *n* : a plant of the mint family enjoyed by cats

cat–o'–nine–tails *n, pl* **cat–o'–nine–tails** : a whip made of nine knotted cords fastened to a handle

cat·sup *variant of* KETCHUP

cat·tail *n* : a tall plant with long flat leaves and tall furry stalks that grows in marshy areas

cat·tle *n, pl* **cattle** : domestic animals with four feet and especially cows, bulls, and calves

cat·walk *n* : a narrow walk or way (as along a bridge)

caught *past of* CATCH

caul·dron *or* **cal·dron** *n* : a large kettle or boiler

cau·li·flow·er *n* : a vegetable closely related to the cabbage that is grown for its white head of undeveloped flowers

¹caulk *vb* : to fill up a crack, seam, or joint so as to make it watertight

²**caulk** *also* **caulk·ing** *n* : material used to caulk

¹**cause** *n* 1 : a person or thing that brings about a result 2 : a good or good enough reason for something 3 : something (as a question) to be decided 4 : something supported or deserving support

²**cause** *vb* **caused; caus·ing** : to be the cause of

cause·way *n* : a raised road or way across wet ground or water

caus·tic *adj* 1 : capable of eating away by chemical action : CORROSIVE 2 : ¹SHARP 8, BITING

¹**cau·tion** *n* 1 : ADMONITION 2 : carefulness in regard to danger : PRECAUTION

²**caution** *vb* : to advise caution to : WARN

cau·tious *adj* : showing or using caution — **cau·tious·ly** *adv*

cav·al·cade *n* 1 : a procession especially of riders or carriages 2 : a dramatic series (as of related events)

¹**cav·a·lier** *n* 1 : a mounted soldier 2 : a brave and courteous gentleman

²**cavalier** *adj* 1 : easy and lighthearted in manner 2 : tending to disregard the rights or feelings of others : ARROGANT

cav·al·ry *n, pl* **cav·al·ries** : troops mounted on horseback or moving in motor vehicles

cav·al·ry·man *n, pl* **cav·al·ry·men** : a cavalry soldier

¹**cave** *n* : a hollow underground place with an opening on the surface

²**cave** *vb* **caved; cav·ing** : to fall or cause to fall in or down : COLLAPSE

cave·man *n, pl* **cave·men** : a person living in a cave especially during the Stone Age

cav·ern *n* : a cave often of large or unknown size

cav·ern·ous *adj* 1 : having caverns or hollow places 2 : like a cavern because large and hollow

cav·i·ty *n, pl* **cav·i·ties** : a hollow place

ca·vort *vb* : to move or hop about in a lively way

¹**caw** *vb* : to make a caw

²**caw** *n* : the cry of a crow or a raven

cay·enne pepper *n* : dried ripe hot peppers ground and used to add flavor to food

CD *n* : COMPACT DISC

cease *vb* **ceased; ceas·ing** : to come or bring to an end : STOP

cease·less *adj* : CONSTANT 3

ce·cro·pia moth *n* : a silkworm moth that is the largest moth of the eastern United States

ce·dar *n* : any of a number of trees having cones and a strong wood with a pleasant smell

cede *vb* **ced·ed; ced·ing** : to give up especially by treaty

ceil·ing *n* 1 : the overhead inside surface of a room 2 : the greatest height at which an airplane can fly properly 3 : the height above the ground of the bottom of the lowest layer of clouds 4 : an upper limit

cel·e·brate *vb* **cel·e·brat·ed; cel·e·brat·ing** 1 : to perform publicly and according to certain rules 2 : to observe in some special way (as by merrymaking or by staying away from business) 3 : ¹PRAISE 1

cel·e·brat·ed *adj* : widely known and talked about

cel·e·bra·tion *n* 1 : the act of celebrating 2 : the activities or ceremonies for celebrating a special occasion

ce·leb·ri·ty *n, pl* **ce·leb·ri·ties** 1 : FAME 2 : a celebrated person

cel·ery *n* : a plant related to the carrots whose crisp leafstalks are used for food

ce·les·ta *n* : a keyboard instrument with hammers that strike steel plates to make ringing sounds

ce·les·tial *adj* 1 : of, relating to, or suggesting heaven 2 : of or relating to the sky

cell *n* 1 : a very small room (as in a prison or a monastery) 2 : a small enclosed part or division (as in a honeycomb) 3 : a small mass of living matter that is made of protoplasm, includes a nucleus, is enclosed in a membrane, and is the basic unit of which all plants and animals are made up 4 : a container with substances which can produce an electric current by chemical action — **celled** *adj*

cel·lar *n* : a room or set of rooms below the surface of the ground : BASEMENT

cel·lo *n, pl* **cel·los** : a large stringed instrument of the violin family that plays the bass part

cel·lo·phane *n* : a thin clear material made from cellulose and used as a wrapping

cel·lu·lar *adj* 1 : of, relating to, or made up of cells 2 : of, relating to, or being a telephone that connects to others by radio and is part of a system in which a geographical area is divided into small sections each served by a transmitter of limited range

cel·lu·lose *n* : a substance that is the chief part of the cell walls of plants and is used in making various products (as paper and rayon)

cell wall *n* : the firm outer nonliving boundary of a plant cell

Cel·si·us *adj* : relating to or having a thermometer scale on which the interval between the freezing point and the boiling point of water is divided into 100 degrees with 0 representing the freezing point and 100 the boiling point

¹**ce·ment** n 1 : a powder that is made mainly from compounds of aluminum, calcium, silicon, and iron heated together and then ground, that combines with water and hardens into a mass, and that is used in mortar and concrete 2 : ²CONCRETE, MORTAR 3 : a substance that by hardening sticks things together firmly

²**cement** vb 1 : to join together with or as if with cement 2 : to cover with concrete

ce·men·tum n : a thin bony layer covering the part of a tooth inside the gum

cem·e·tery n, pl **cem·e·ter·ies** : a place where dead people are buried : GRAVEYARD

Ce·no·zo·ic n : an era of geological history lasting from seventy million years ago to the present time in which there has been a rapid evolution of mammals and birds and of flowering plants

¹**cen·sor** n : an official who checks writings or movies to take out things thought to be objectionable

²**censor** vb : to examine (as a book) to take out things thought to be objectionable

¹**cen·sure** n 1 : the act of finding fault with or blaming 2 : an official criticism

²**censure** vb **cen·sured; cen·sur·ing** : to find fault with especially publicly

cen·sus n : a count of the number of people in a country, city, or town

cent n 1 : a hundredth part of the unit of the money system in a number of different countries 2 : a coin, token, or note representing one cent

cen·taur n : a creature in Greek mythology that is part man and part horse

cen·te·nar·i·an n : a person 100 or more years old

¹**cen·ten·ni·al** n : a 100th anniversary or a celebration of this event

²**centennial** adj : relating to a period of 100 years

¹**cen·ter** n 1 : the middle point of a circle or a sphere equally distant from every point on the circumference or surface 2 : one (as a person or area) that is very important to some activity or concern 3 : the middle part of something 4 : a player occupying a middle position on a team

²**center** vb 1 : to place or fix at or around a center or central area 2 : to collect at or around one point

center of gravity : the point at which the entire weight of a body may be thought of as centered so that if supported at this point the body would balance perfectly

cen·ter·piece n : a piece put in the center of

something and especially a decoration (as flowers) for a table

centi- prefix : hundredth part — used in terms of the metric system

cen·ti·grade adj : CELSIUS

cen·ti·gram n : a unit of weight equal to $1/100$ gram

cen·ti·li·ter n : a unit of liquid capacity equal to $1/100$ liter

cen·ti·me·ter n : a unit of length equal to $1/100$ meter

cen·ti·pede n : a small animal that has a long body and many legs and is related to the insects

cen·tral adj 1 : containing or being the center 2 : most important : CHIEF 3 : placed at, in, or near the center — **cen·tral·ly** adv

¹**Central American** adj : of or relating to Central America or the Central Americans

²**Central American** n : a person born or living in Central America

central angle n : an angle with its vertex at the center of a circle and with sides that are radii of the circle

cen·tral·ize vb **cen·tral·ized; cen·tral·iz·ing** : to bring to a central point or under a single control

central processing unit n : PROCESSOR 3

cen·trif·u·gal force n : the force that tends to cause a thing or parts of a thing to go outward from a center of rotation

cen·tu·ry n, pl **cen·tu·ries** : a period of 100 years

ce·ram·ic n 1 ceramics pl : the art of making things (as pottery or tiles) of baked clay 2 : a product made by ceramics

¹**ce·re·al** adj 1 : relating to grain or the plants that it comes from 2 : made of grain

²**cereal** n 1 : a plant (as a grass) that yields grain for food 2 : a food prepared from grain

cer·e·bel·lum n, pl **cer·e·bel·lums** or **cer·e·bel·la** : a part of the brain concerned especially with the coordination of muscles and with keeping the body in proper balance

ce·re·bral adj 1 : of or relating to the brain or mind 2 : of, relating to, or affecting the cerebrum

ce·re·brum n, pl **ce·re·brums** or **ce·re·bra** : the enlarged front and upper part of the brain that is the center of thinking

¹**cer·e·mo·ni·al** adj : of, relating to, or being a ceremony

²**ceremonial** n : a ceremonial act, action, or system

cer·e·mo·ni·ous adj 1 : ¹CEREMONIAL 2 : given to ceremony : FORMAL — **cer·e·mo·ni·ous·ly** adv

cer·e·mo·ny n, pl **cer·e·mo·nies** 1 : an act

or series of acts performed in some regular way according to fixed rules **2** : very polite behavior : FORMALITY

¹cer·tain *adj* **1** : being fixed or settled **2** : known but not named **3** : sure to have an effect **4** : known to be true **5** : bound by the way things are **6** : assured in thought or action

²certain *pron* : certain ones

cer·tain·ly *adv* **1** : with certainty : without fail **2** : without doubt

cer·tain·ty *n, pl* **cer·tain·ties 1** : something that is certain **2** : the quality or state of being certain

cer·tif·i·cate *n* **1** : a written or printed statement that is proof of some fact **2** : a paper showing that a person has met certain requirements (as of a school) **3** : a paper showing ownership

cer·ti·fy *vb* **cer·ti·fied; cer·ti·fy·ing 1** : to show to be true or as claimed by a formal or official statement **2** : to guarantee the quality, fitness, or value of officially **3** : to show to have met certain requirements

ce·ru·le·an *adj* : somewhat like the blue of the sky

ces·sa·tion *n* : a coming to a stop

chafe *vb* **chafed; chaf·ing 1** : IRRITATE 1, VEX **2** : to be bothered : FRET **3** : to warm by rubbing **4** : to rub so as to wear away or make sore

¹chaff *n* **1** : the husks of grains and grasses separated from the seed in threshing **2** : something worthless

²chaff *vb* : to tease in a friendly way

cha·grin *n* : a feeling of being annoyed by failure or disappointment

¹chain *n* **1** : a series of links or rings usually of metal **2** : something that restricts or binds : BOND **3** : a series of things joined together as if by links

²chain *vb* : to fasten, bind, or connect with or as if with a chain

chair *n* **1** : a seat for one person usually having a back and either four legs or a swivel base **2** : an official seat or a seat of authority or honor **3** : an office or position of authority or honor **4** : an official who conducts a meeting

chair·man *n, pl* **chair·men** : CHAIR 4 — **chair·man·ship** *n*

chair·per·son *n* : CHAIR 4

chair·wom·an *n, pl* **chair·wom·en** : a woman who conducts a meeting

chaise longue *n* : a long chair somewhat like a couch

chaise lounge *n* : CHAISE LONGUE

cha·let *n* **1** : a herdsman's hut in the Alps away from a town or village **2** : a Swiss dwelling with a roof that sticks far out past

the walls **3** : a cottage built to look like a chalet

chal·ice *n* : a drinking cup : GOBLET

¹chalk *n* **1** : a soft white, gray, or buff limestone made up mainly of very small seashells **2** : a material like chalk especially when used in the form of a crayon

²chalk *vb* **1** : to rub, mark, write, or draw with chalk **2** : to record or add up with or as if with chalk

chalk·board *n* : BLACKBOARD

chalky *adj* **chalk·i·er; chalk·i·est 1** : made of or like chalk **2** : easily crumbled **3** : very pale

¹chal·lenge *vb* **chal·lenged; chal·leng·ing 1** : to halt and demand a password from **2** : to object to as bad or incorrect : DISPUTE **3** : to demand proof that something is right or legal **4** : to invite or dare to take part in a contest — **chal·leng·er** *n*

²challenge *n* **1** : an objection to something as not being true, genuine, correct, or proper or to a person (as a juror) as not being qualified or approved : PROTEST **2** : a sentry's command to halt and prove identity **3** : a demand that someone take part in a duel **4** : a call or dare for someone to compete in a contest or sport

challenged *adj* : having a disability or deficiency

cham·ber *n* **1** : a room in a house and especially a bedroom **2** : an enclosed space, cavity, or compartment (as in a gun) **3** : a meeting hall of a government body (as an assembly) **4** : a room where a judge conducts business out of court **5** : a group of people organized into a lawmaking body **6** : a board or council of volunteers (as businessmen) — **cham·bered** *adj*

cham·ber·lain *n* **1** : a chief officer in the household of a ruler or noble **2** : TREASURER

cham·ber·maid *n* : a maid who takes care of bedrooms (as in a hotel)

chamber music *n* : instrumental music to be performed in a room or small hall

cha·me·leon *n* : a lizard that has the ability to change the color of its skin

cham·ois *n, pl* **cham·ois 1** : a small antelope living on the highest mountains of Europe and Asia **2** : a soft yellowish leather made from the skin of the chamois or from sheepskin

¹champ *vb* : to bite and chew noisily

²champ *n* : ¹CHAMPION 2, 3

¹cham·pi·on *n* **1** : a person who fights or speaks for another person or in favor of a cause **2** : a person accepted as better than all others in a sport or in a game of skill **3** : the winner of first place in a competition

²**champion** *vb* : to protect or fight for as a champion

cham·pi·on·ship *n* 1 : the act of defending as a champion 2 : the position or title of champion 3 : a contest held to find a champion

¹**chance** *n* 1 : the uncertain course of events 2 : OPPORTUNITY 1 3 : ¹RISK, GAMBLE 4 : PROBABILITY 1 5 : a ticket in a raffle

²**chance** *vb* **chanced; chanc·ing** 1 : to take place by chance 2 : to come unexpectedly 3 : to leave to chance : RISK

³**chance** *adj* : happening by chance

chan·cel·lor *n* 1 : a high state official (as in Germany) 2 : a high officer of some universities 3 : a chief judge in some courts — **chan·cel·lor·ship** *n*

chan·de·lier *n* : a lighting fixture with several branches that usually hangs from the ceiling

¹**change** *vb* **changed; chang·ing** 1 : to make or become different : ALTER 2 : to give a different position, course, or direction to 3 : to put one thing in the place of another : SWITCH, EXCHANGE 4 : to give or receive an equal amount of money in usually smaller units of value or in the money of another country 5 : to put fresh clothes or covering on 6 : to put on different clothes

²**change** *n* 1 : the act, process, or result of changing 2 : a fresh set of clothes 3 : money in small units of value received in exchange for an equal amount in larger units 4 : money returned when a payment is more than the amount due 5 : money in coins

change·able *adj* : able or likely to change

¹**chan·nel** *n* 1 : the bed of a stream 2 : the deeper part of a waterway (as a river or harbor) 3 : a strait or a narrow sea 4 : a closed course (as a tube) through which something flows 5 : a long groove 6 : a means by which something is passed or carried 7 : a range of frequencies used by a single radio or television station in broadcasting

²**channel** *vb* **chan·neled** *or* **chan·nelled; chan·nel·ing** *or* **chan·nel·ling** 1 : to form a channel in 2 : to direct into or through a channel

¹**chant** *vb* 1 : to sing especially in the way a chant is sung 2 : to recite or speak with no change in tone

²**chant** *n* 1 : a melody in which several words or syllables are sung on one tone 2 : something spoken in the style of a chant

cha·os *n* : complete confusion and disorder

cha·ot·ic *adj* : being in a state of chaos

¹**chap** *vb* **chapped; chap·ping** : to open in slits : CRACK

²**chap** *n* : ¹FELLOW 4

chap·el *n* 1 : a building or a room or place for prayer or special religious services 2 : a religious service or assembly held in a school or college

¹**chap·er·on** *or* **chap·er·one** *n* : an older person who goes with and is responsible for a young woman or a group of young people (as at a dance)

²**chaperon** *or* **chaperone** *vb* **chap·er·oned; chap·er·on·ing** : to act as a chaperon

chap·lain *n* 1 : a member of the clergy officially attached to a special group (as the army) 2 : a person chosen to conduct religious services (as for a club)

chaps *n pl* : a set of leather coverings for the legs used especially by western ranch workers

chap·ter *n* 1 : a main division of a book or story 2 : a local branch of a club or organization

char *vb* **charred; char·ring** 1 : to change to charcoal by burning 2 : to burn slightly : SCORCH

char·ac·ter *n* 1 : a mark, sign, or symbol (as a letter or figure) used in writing or printing 2 : ¹CHARACTERISTIC 3 : the group of qualities that make a person, group, or thing different from others 4 : a person who is unusual or peculiar 5 : a person in a story or play 6 : REPUTATION 1 7 : moral excellence

¹**char·ac·ter·is·tic** *n* : a special quality or appearance that makes an individual or a group different from others

²**characteristic** *adj* : serving to stress some special quality of an individual or a group : TYPICAL

char·ac·ter·is·ti·cal·ly *adv* : in a characteristic way

char·ac·ter·ize *vb* **char·ac·ter·ized; char·ac·ter·iz·ing** 1 : to point out the character of an individual or a group : DESCRIBE 2 : to be characteristic of

char·coal *n* : a black or dark absorbent carbon made by heating animal or vegetable material in the absence of air

¹**charge** *n* 1 : the amount (as of ammunition or fuel) needed to load or fill something 2 : an amount of electricity available 3 : a task, duty, or order given to a person : OBLIGATION 4 : the work or duty of managing 5 : a person or thing given to a person to look after 6 : ²COMMAND 2 7 : the price demanded especially for a service 8 : an amount listed as a debt on an account 9 : ACCUSATION 10 : a rushing attack

²**charge** *vb* **charged; charg·ing** 1 : ¹FILL 1

2 : to give an electric charge to **3** : to restore the active materials in a storage battery by passage of an electric current through it **4** : to give a task, duty, or responsibility to **5** : ¹COMMAND 1 **6** : to accuse formally **7** : to rush against : ASSAULT **8** : to take payment from or make responsible for payment **9** : to enter as a debt or responsibility on a record **10** : to ask or set as a price

charg·er n : a cavalry horse

char·i·ot n : a vehicle of ancient times that had two wheels, was pulled by horses, and was used in war and in races and parades

char·i·ta·ble adj **1** : freely giving money or help to needy persons : GENEROUS **2** : given for the needy : of service to the needy **3** : kindly in judging other people

char·i·ty n, pl **char·i·ties** **1** : love for others **2** : kindliness in judging others **3** : the giving of aid to the poor and suffering **4** : public aid for the poor **5** : an institution or fund for helping the needy

char·ley horse n : pain and stiffness in a muscle (as in a leg)

¹charm n **1** : a word, action, or thing believed to have magic powers **2** : something worn or carried to keep away evil and bring good luck **3** : a small decorative object worn on a chain or bracelet **4** : a quality that attracts and pleases

²charm vb **1** : to affect or influence by or as if by a magic spell **2** : FASCINATE 2, DELIGHT **3** : to protect by or as if by a charm **4** : to attract by grace or beauty

charm·ing adj : very pleasing

¹chart n **1** : ¹MAP **2** : a map showing coasts, reefs, currents, and depths of water **3** : a sheet giving information in a table or lists or by means of diagrams

²chart vb **1** : to make a map or chart of **2** : to lay out a plan for

¹char·ter n **1** : an official document granting, guaranteeing, or showing the limits of the rights and duties of the group to which it is given **2** : a contract by which the owners of a ship lease it to others

²charter vb **1** : to grant a charter to **2** : to hire (as a bus or an aircraft) for temporary use

charter school n : a school supported by taxes but run independently to achieve set goals under a charter between an official body (as a state government) and an outside group (as educators and businesses)

¹chase n **1** : the act of chasing : PURSUIT **2** : the hunting of wild animals **3** : something pursued

²chase vb **chased; chas·ing** **1** : to follow in order to catch up with or capture **2** : ¹HUNT 1 **3** : to drive away or out

chasm n : a deep split or gap in the earth

chas·sis n, pl **chas·sis** : a structure that supports the body (as of an automobile or airplane) or the parts (as of a television set)

chaste adj **chast·er; chast·est** **1** : pure in thought and act : MODEST **2** : simple or plain in design

chas·ten vb : to correct by punishment or suffering : DISCIPLINE

chas·tise vb **chas·tised; chas·tis·ing** : to punish severely (as by whipping)

chas·ti·ty n : the quality or state of being chaste

¹chat vb **chat·ted; chat·ting** : to talk in a friendly manner of things that are not serious

²chat n : a light friendly conversation

chat room n : an on-line computer site at which any visitor to the site can send messages that immediately appear on the screen for everyone to read

¹chat·ter vb **1** : to make quick sounds that suggest speech but lack meaning **2** : to talk without thinking, without stopping, or fast : JABBER **3** : to click again and again and without control — **chat·ter·er** n

²chatter n : the act or sound of chattering

chat·ter·box n : a person who talks all the time

chat·ty adj **chat·ti·er; chat·ti·est** **1** : TALKATIVE **2** : having the style and manner of friendly conversation

chauf·feur n : a person hired to drive people around in a car

¹cheap adj **1** : not costing much **2** : worth little : not very good **3** : gained without much effort **4** : lowered in one's own opinion **5** : charging low prices — **cheap·ly** adv

²cheap adv : at low cost

cheap·en vb : to make or become cheap or cheaper

¹cheat vb **1** : to take something away from or keep from having something by dishonest tricks : DEFRAUD **2** : to use unfair or dishonest methods to gain an advantage

²cheat n **1** : an act of cheating : DECEPTION, FRAUD **2** : a dishonest person

¹check n **1** : a sudden stopping of progress : PAUSE **2** : something that delays, stops, or holds back : RESTRAINT **3** : a standard or guide for testing and studying something **4** : EXAMINATION 1, INVESTIGATION **5** : a written order telling a bank to pay out money from a person's account to the one named on the order **6** : a ticket or token showing a person's ownership, identity, or claim to something **7** : a slip of paper showing the amount due : BILL **8** : a pattern in squares **9** : material with a design in squares **10** : a mark typically ✓ placed beside a written or printed item to show that something has been specially noted

2check *vb* **1** : to bring to a sudden stop **2** : to keep from expressing **3** : to make sure that something is correct or satisfactory : VERIFY **4** : to mark with a check **5** : to mark with squares **6** : to leave or accept for safekeeping or for shipment **7** : to be the same on every point : TALLY

check·er·board *n* : a board marked with sixty-four squares in two colors and used for games (as checkers)

check·ers *n* : a game played on a checkerboard by two players each having twelve pieces

check·up *n* **1** : INSPECTION, EXAMINATION **2** : a physical examination

cheek *n* **1** : the side of the face below the eye and above and beside the mouth **2** : IMPUDENCE

1cheep *vb* : 1PEEP, CHIRP

2cheep *n* : 1CHIRP

1cheer *n* **1** : state of mind or heart : SPIRIT **2** : good spirits **3** : something that gladdens **4** : a shout of praise or encouragement

2cheer *vb* **1** : to give hope to : make happier : COMFORT **2** : to urge on especially with shouts or cheers **3** : to shout with joy, approval, or enthusiasm **4** : to grow or be cheerful — usually used with *up*

cheer·ful *adj* : full of good spirits : PLEASANT — **cheer·ful·ly** *adv* — **cheer·ful·ness** *n*

cheer·less *adj* : offering no cheer : GLOOMY

cheery *adj* **cheer·i·er; cheer·i·est** : merry and bright in manner or effect : CHEERFUL — **cheer·i·ly** *adv* — **cheer·i·ness** *n*

cheese *n* : the curd of milk pressed for use as food

cheese·cloth *n* : a thin loosely woven cotton cloth

cheesy *adj* **chees·i·er; chees·i·est** : like or suggesting cheese

chee·tah *n* : a long-legged African and formerly Asian animal of the cat family that has a spotted coat and that is the fastest animal on land

chef *n* **1** : a chief cook **2** : 1COOK

1chem·i·cal *adj* : of or relating to chemistry or chemicals — **chem·i·cal·ly** *adv*

2chemical *n* : a substance (as an acid) that is formed when two or more other substances act upon one another or that is used to produce a change in another substance (as in making plastics)

chem·ist *n* : a person trained or engaged in chemistry

chem·is·try *n* **1** : a science that deals with the composition and properties of substances and of the changes they undergo **2** : chemical composition and properties

cher·ish *vb* **1** : to hold dear **2** : to keep deeply in mind : cling to

Cher·o·kee *n, pl* **Cherokee** *or* **Cherokees** : a member of an Indian people originally from the southern Appalachian Mountains

cher·ry *n, pl* **cherries** **1** : the round red or yellow fruit of a tree (**cherry tree**) that is related to the plum **2** : a medium red

cher·ub *n* **1** : a painting or drawing of a beautiful child usually with wings **2** : a chubby rosy child

chess *n* : a game of capture played on a board by two players each using sixteen pieces that have set moves

chest *n* **1** : a container (as a box or case) for storing, safekeeping, or shipping **2** : a public fund **3** : the part of the body enclosed by the ribs and breastbone — **chest·ed** *adj*

chest·nut *n* **1** : a sweet edible nut that grows in burs on a tree (**chestnut tree**) related to the beech **2** : a reddish brown

chev·ron *n* : a sleeve badge of one or more bars or stripes usually in the shape of an upside down V indicating the wearer's rank (as in the armed forces)

1chew *vb* : to crush or grind with the teeth

2chew *n* **1** : the act of chewing **2** : something for chewing

chew·ing gum *n* : gum usually of sweetened and flavored chicle prepared for chewing

chewy *adj* **chew·i·er; chew·i·est** : requiring chewing

1chic *n* : fashionable style

2chic *adj* : STYLISH, SMART

1Chi·ca·no *n, pl* **Chicanos** : an American of Mexican ancestry

2Chicano *adj* : of or relating to Chicanos

chick *n* **1** : a young chicken **2** : CHILD 2

chick·a·dee *n* : a small bird with fluffy grayish feathers and usually a black cap

1chick·en *n* **1** : the common domestic fowl especially when young : a young hen or rooster **2** : the flesh of a chicken for use as food

2chicken *adj* : CHICKENHEARTED

chick·en·heart·ed *adj* : COWARDLY, TIMID

chicken pox *n* : a contagious disease especially of children in which there is fever and the skin breaks out in watery blisters

chick·weed *n* : a weedy plant related to the pinks that has small pointed leaves and whitish flowers

chi·cle *n* : a gum obtained from the sap of a tropical American tree and used in making chewing gum

chide *vb* **chid** *or* **chid·ed; chid** *or* **chid·den**

or **chided; chid·ing** : to find fault with : SCOLD

¹chief *n* : the head of a group : LEADER — **in chief** : in the chief position or place

²chief *adj* **1** : highest in rank or authority **2** : most important : MAIN

chief·ly *adv* **1** : above all **2** : for the most part

chief master sergeant *n* : a noncommissioned officer in the Air Force ranking above a senior master sergeant

chief petty officer *n* : a petty officer in the Navy or Coast Guard ranking above a petty officer first class

chief·tain *n* : a chief especially of a band, tribe, or clan

chief warrant officer *n* : a warrant officer in any of the three top grades

chig·ger *n* : the larva of some mites that has six legs, clings to the skin, and causes itching

chil·blain *n* : a red swollen itchy condition caused by cold that occurs especially on the hands or feet

child *n, pl* **chil·dren** **1** : an unborn or recently born person **2** : a young person of either sex between infancy and youth **3** : one's son or daughter of any age

child·birth *n* : the act or process of giving birth to a child

child·hood *n* : the period of life between infancy and youth

child·ish *adj* **1** : of, like, or thought to be suitable to children **2** : showing the less pleasing qualities (as silliness) often thought to be those of children

child·like *adj* **1** : of or relating to a child or childhood **2** : showing the more pleasing qualities (as innocence and trustfulness) often thought to be those of children

chili *or* **chile** *n, pl* **chil·ies** *or* **chil·es** **1** : the small very sharply flavored fruit of a pepper plant **2** : a spicy stew of ground beef and chilies usually with beans

¹chill *n* **1** : a feeling of coldness accompanied by shivering **2** : unpleasant coldness

²chill *adj* **1** : unpleasantly cold : RAW **2** : not friendly

³chill *vb* **1** : to make or become cold or chilly **2** : to make cool especially without freezing **3** : to harden the surface of (as metal) by sudden cooling

chilly *adj* **chill·i·er; chill·i·est** : noticeably cold — **chill·i·ness** *n*

¹chime *vb* **chimed; chim·ing** **1** : to make sounds like a bell : ring chimes **2** : to call or indicate by chiming

²chime *n* **1** : a set of bells tuned to play music **2** : the music from a set of bells —

usually used in pl. **3** : a musical sound suggesting bells

chime in *vb* : to break into or join in a discussion

chim·ney *n, pl* **chimneys** **1** : a passage for smoke especially in the form of a vertical structure of brick or stone that reaches above the roof of a building **2** : a glass tube around a lamp flame

chimney sweep *n* : a person who cleans soot from chimneys

chimney swift *n* : a small dark gray bird with long narrow wings that often attaches its nest to chimneys

chimp *n* : CHIMPANZEE

chim·pan·zee *n* : an African ape that lives mostly in trees and is smaller than the related gorilla

¹chin *n* : the part of the face below the mouth and including the point of the lower jaw

²chin *vb* **chinned; chin·ning** : to raise oneself while hanging by the hands until the chin is level with the support

chi·na *n* **1** : porcelain ware **2** : pottery (as dishes) for use in one's home

chin·chil·la *n* : a South American animal that is somewhat like a squirrel and is hunted or raised for its soft silvery gray fur

¹Chi·nese *adj* : of or relating to China, the Chinese people, or Chinese

²Chinese *n, pl* **Chinese** **1** : a person born or living in China **2** : a group of related languages used in China

chink *n* : a narrow slit or crack (as in a wall)

¹chip *n* **1** : a small piece (as of wood, stone, or glass) cut or broken off **2** : POTATO CHIP **3** : a flaw left after a small piece has been broken off **4** : INTEGRATED CIRCUIT **5** : a small slice of silicon containing electronic circuits (as for a computer)

²chip *vb* **chipped; chip·ping** **1** : to cut or break chips from **2** : to break off in small pieces

chip·munk *n* : a small striped animal related to the squirrels

chip·ping sparrow *n* : a small North American sparrow that often nests about houses and has a weak chirp as a call

¹chirp *n* : the short sharp sound made by crickets and some small birds

²chirp *vb* : to make a chirp

¹chis·el *n* : a metal tool with a sharp edge at the end of a usually flat piece used to chip away stone, wood, or metal

²chisel *vb* **chis·eled** *or* **chis·elled; chis·el·ing** *or* **chis·el·ling** : to cut or shape with a chisel

chiv·al·rous *adj* **1** : of or relating to chivalry **2** : having or showing honor, generosity, and courtesy **3** : showing special courtesy and regard to women

chiv·al·ry n **1** : a body of knights **2** : the system, spirit, ways, or customs of knighthood **3** : chivalrous conduct

chlo·rine n : a chemical element that is a greenish yellow irritating gas of strong odor used as a bleach and as a disinfectant to purify water

¹**chlo·ro·form** n : a colorless heavy liquid used especially to dissolve fatty substances and in the past in medicine to deaden the pain of operations but now mostly replaced by less poisonous substances

²**chloroform** vb : to make unconscious or kill with chloroform

chlo·ro·phyll n : the green coloring matter by means of which green plants produce carbohydrates from carbon dioxide and water

chlo·ro·plast n : one of the tiny bodies in which chlorophyll is found

chock–full or **chuck–full** adj : full to the limit

choc·o·late n **1** : a food prepared from ground roasted cacao beans **2** : a beverage of chocolate in water or milk **3** : a candy made or coated with chocolate

¹**choice** n **1** : the act of choosing : SELECTION **2** : the power of choosing : OPTION **3** : a person or thing chosen **4** : the best part **5** : a large enough number and variety to choose among

²**choice** adj **choic·er; choic·est** : of very good quality

choir n **1** : an organized group of singers especially in a church **2** : the part of a church set aside for the singers

¹**choke** vb **choked; chok·ing 1** : to keep from breathing in a normal way by cutting off the supply of air **2** : to have the windpipe blocked entirely or partly **3** : to slow or prevent the growth or action of **4** : to block by clogging

²**choke** n **1** : the act or sound of choking **2** : something that chokes

choke·cher·ry n, pl **choke·cher·ries** : a wild cherry tree with long clusters of reddish black fruits that pucker the mouth

chol·era n : a dangerous infectious disease of Asian origin in which violent vomiting and dysentery are present

choose vb **chose; cho·sen; choos·ing 1** : to select freely and after careful thought **2** : DECIDE 3 **3** : to see fit

choosy adj **choos·i·er; choos·i·est** : careful in making choices

¹**chop** vb **chopped; chop·ping 1** : to cut by striking especially over and over with something sharp **2** : to cut into small

pieces : MINCE **3** : to strike quickly or again and again

²**chop** n **1** : a sharp downward blow or stroke (as with an ax) **2** : a small cut of meat often including a part of a rib **3** : a short quick motion (as of a wave)

chop·per n **1** : someone or something that chops **2** : HELICOPTER

¹**chop·py** adj **chop·pi·er; chop·pi·est** : frequently changing direction

²**choppy** adj **chop·pi·er; chop·pi·est 1** : rough with small waves **2** : JERKY

chops n pl : the fleshy covering of the jaws

chop·stick n : one of two thin sticks used chiefly in Asian countries to lift food to the mouth

cho·ral adj : of, relating to, or sung or recited by a chorus or choir or in chorus

cho·rale n **1** : a hymn sung by the choir or congregation at a church service **2** : CHORUS 1

¹**chord** n : a group of tones sounded together to form harmony

²**chord** n : a straight line joining two points on a curve

chore n **1 chores** pl : the regular light work about a home or farm **2** : an ordinary task **3** : a dull, unpleasant, or difficult task

cho·re·og·ra·phy n : the art of dancing or of arranging dances and especially ballets — **cho·re·og·ra·pher** n

cho·ris·ter n : a singer in a choir

chor·tle vb **chor·tled; chor·tling** : to chuckle especially in satisfaction

¹**cho·rus** n **1** : a group of singers : CHOIR **2** : a group of dancers and singers (as in a musical comedy) **3** : a part of a song or hymn that is repeated every so often : REFRAIN **4** : a song meant to be sung by a group : group singing **5** : sounds uttered by a group of persons or animals together

²**chorus** vb : to speak, sing, or sound at the same time or together

chose past of CHOOSE

cho·sen adj **1** : picked to be given favor or special privilege **2** : picked by God for special protection

chow n : a muscular dog with a blue-black tongue, a short tail curled close to the back, straight legs, and a thick coat

chow·der n : a soup or stew made of fish, clams, or a vegetable usually simmered in milk

Christ n : JESUS

chris·ten vb **1** : BAPTIZE 1 **2** : to give a name to at baptism **3** : to name or dedicate (as a ship) in a ceremony like that of baptism

Chris·ten·dom n **1** : the entire body of Christians **2** : the part of the world in which Christianity is most common

chris·ten·ing *n* : BAPTISM

¹Chris·tian *n* **1** : a person who believes in Jesus and follows his teachings **2** : a member of a Christian church

²Christian *adj* **1** : of or relating to Jesus or the religion based on his teachings **2** : of or relating to Christians **3** : being what a Christian should be or do

Chris·tian·i·ty *n* **1** : CHRISTENDOM 1 **2** : the religion of Christians

Christian name *n* : the personal name given to a person at birth or christening

Christ·mas *n* : December 25 celebrated in honor of the birth of Christ

Christ·mas·tide *n* : the season of Christmas

Christmas tree *n* : a usually evergreen tree decorated at Christmas

chro·mat·ic scale *n* : a musical scale that has all half steps

chrome *n* **1** : CHROMIUM **2** : something plated with an alloy of chromium

chro·mi·um *n* : a bluish white metallic chemical element used especially in alloys

chro·mo·some *n* : one of the rodlike bodies of a cell nucleus that contain genes and divide when the cell divides

chron·ic *adj* **1** : continuing for a long time or returning often **2** : HABITUAL 2 — **chron·i·cal·ly** *adv*

¹chron·i·cle *n* : an account of events in the order of their happening : HISTORY

²chronicle *vb* **chron·i·cled; chron·i·cling** : to record in or as if in a chronicle

chron·o·log·i·cal *adj* : arranged in or according to the order of time — **chron·o·log·i·cal·ly** *adv*

chrys·a·lis *n* : a moth or butterfly pupa that is enclosed in a firm protective case

chry·san·the·mum *n* : a plant related to the daisies that has deeply notched leaves and brightly colored often double flower heads

chub·by *adj* **chub·bi·er; chub·bi·est** : ⁴PLUMP

¹chuck *vb* **1** : to give a pat or tap to **2** : ¹TOSS 2

²chuck *n* **1** : a pat or nudge under the chin **2** : ²TOSS

chuck–full *variant of* CHOCK-FULL

¹chuck·le *vb* **chuck·led; chuck·ling** : to laugh in a quiet way

²chuckle *n* : a low quiet laugh

chuck wagon *n* : a wagon carrying a stove and food for cooking

¹chug *n* : a dull explosive sound

²chug *vb* **chugged; chug·ging** : to move with chugs

¹chum *n* : a close friend : PAL

²chum *vb* **chummed; chum·ming** : to be chums

chum·my *adj* **chum·mi·er; chum·mi·est** : being on close friendly terms : SOCIABLE

chunk *n* : a short thick piece (as of ice)

chunky *adj* **chunk·i·er; chunk·i·est** : STOCKY

church *n* **1** : a building for public worship and especially Christian worship **2** : an organized body of religious believers **3** : public worship

church·yard *n* : a yard that belongs to a church and is often used as a burial ground

¹churn *n* : a container in which milk or cream is stirred or shaken in making butter

²churn *vb* **1** : to stir or shake in a churn (as in making butter) **2** : to stir or shake violently

chute *n* **1** : a sloping plane, trough, or passage down or through which things are slid or dropped **2** : ¹PARACHUTE

ci·ca·da *n* : an insect that has transparent wings and a stout body and is related to the true bugs

-cide *n suffix* **1** : killer **2** : killing

ci·der *n* : the juice pressed out of fruit (as apples) and used especially as a drink and in making vinegar

ci·gar *n* : a small roll of tobacco leaf for smoking

cig·a·rette *n* : a small roll of cut tobacco wrapped in paper for smoking

cil·i·um *n, pl* **cil·ia** : any of the structures on the surface of some cells that look like tiny flexible eyelashes

¹cinch *n* **1** : GIRTH 1 **2** : a sure or an easy thing

²cinch *vb* **1** : to fasten or tighten a girth on **2** : to fasten with or as if with a girth

cin·cho·na *n* : a South American tree whose bark yields quinine

cin·der *n* **1** : SLAG **2** : a piece of partly burned coal or wood that is not burning **3** : EMBER **4 cinders** *pl* : ²ASH 1

cin·e·ma *n* **1** : a movie theater **2** : the movie industry

cin·na·mon *n* : a spice made from the fragrant bark of tropical trees related to the Old World laurel

¹ci·pher *n* **1** : ZERO 1 **2** : an unimportant or worthless person : NONENTITY **3** : a method of secret writing or the alphabet or letters and symbols used in such writing **4** : a message in code

²cipher *vb* : to use figures in doing a problem in arithmetic : CALCULATE

¹cir·cle *n* **1** : a closed curve every point of which is equally distant from a central point within it : the space inside such a closed curve **2** : something in the form of a circle or part of a circle **3** : ¹CYCLE 2, ROUND **4**

: a group of people sharing a common interest

²**circle** *vb* **cir·cled; cir·cling** 1 : to enclose in or as if in a circle 2 : to move or revolve around 3 : to move in or as if in a circle

cir·cuit *n* 1 : a boundary line around an area 2 : an enclosed space 3 : a moving around (as in a circle) 4 : a traveling from place to place in an area (as by a judge) so as to stop in each place at a certain time : a course so traveled 5 : the complete path of an electric current 6 : a group of electronic parts 7 : a chain of theaters at which stage shows are shown in turn

cir·cu·i·tous *adj* 1 : having a circular or winding course 2 : not saying what one means in simple and sincere language

¹**cir·cu·lar** *adj* 1 : having the form of a circle : ROUND 2 : passing or going around in a circle 3 : CIRCUITOUS 2 4 : sent around to a number of persons

²**circular** *n* : a printed notice or advertisement given or sent to many people

cir·cu·late *vb* **cir·cu·lat·ed; cir·cu·lat·ing** 1 : to move around in a course 2 : to pass or be passed from place to place or from person to person

cir·cu·la·tion *n* 1 : motion around in a course 2 : passage from place to place or person to person 3 : the average number of copies (as of a newspaper) sold in a given period

cir·cu·la·to·ry *adj* : of or relating to circulation (as of the blood)

circum- *prefix* : around : about

cir·cum·fer·ence *n* 1 : the line that goes around a circle 2 : a boundary line or circuit enclosing an area 3 : the distance around something

cir·cum·nav·i·gate *vb* **cir·cum·nav·i·gat·ed; cir·cum·nav·i·gat·ing** : to go completely around (as the earth) especially by water

cir·cum·po·lar *adj* 1 : continually visible above the horizon 2 : surrounding or found near the north pole or south pole

cir·cum·stance *n* 1 : a fact or event that must be considered along with another fact or event 2 **circumstances** *pl* : conditions at a certain time or place 3 **circumstances** *pl* : situation with regard to wealth 4 : ¹CHANCE 1, FATE

cir·cum·vent *vb* 1 : to go around : BYPASS 2 : to get the better of or avoid the force or effect of especially by trickery

cir·cus *n* 1 : a show that usually travels from place to place and that has a variety of exhibitions including riding, acrobatic feats, wild animal displays, and the performances of jugglers and clowns 2 : a circus performance 3 : the performers and equipment of a circus

cir·rus *n, pl* **cir·ri** : a thin white cloud of tiny ice crystals that forms at a very high altitude

cis·tern *n* : an artificial reservoir or tank for storing water usually underground

cit·a·del *n* 1 : a fortress that sits high above a city 2 : a strong fortress

ci·ta·tion *n* 1 : an act or instance of quoting 2 : QUOTATION 1 3 : a formal statement of what a person did to be chosen to receive an award

cite *vb* **cit·ed; cit·ing** 1 : to quote as an example, authority, or proof 2 : to refer to especially in praise

cit·i·zen *n* 1 : a person who lives in a city or town 2 : a person who owes loyalty to a government and is protected by it

cit·i·zen·ry *n* : the whole body of citizens

cit·i·zen·ship *n* : the state of being a citizen

cit·ron *n* 1 : a citrus fruit like the smaller lemon and having a thick rind that is preserved for use in cakes and puddings 2 : a small hard watermelon used especially in pickles and preserves

cit·rus *adj* : of or relating to a group of often thorny trees and shrubs of warm regions whose fruits include the lemon, lime, orange, and grapefruit

city *n, pl* **cit·ies** 1 : a place in which people live that is larger or more important than a town 2 : the people of a city

civ·ic *adj* : of or relating to a citizen, a city, or citizenship

civ·ics *n* : a study of the rights and duties of citizens

civ·il *adj* 1 : of or relating to citizens 2 : of or relating to the state 3 : of or relating to ordinary or government affairs rather than to those of the military or the church 4 : polite without being friendly 5 : relating to court action between individuals having to do with private rights rather than criminal action

¹**ci·vil·ian** *n* : a person not on active duty in a military, police, or fire-fighting force

²**civilian** *adj* : of or relating to a civilian

ci·vil·i·ty *n, pl* **ci·vil·i·ties** 1 : civil behavior 2 : COURTESY 1

civ·i·li·za·tion *n* 1 : an advanced stage (as in art, science, and government) of social development 2 : the way of life of a people

civ·i·lize *vb* **civ·i·lized; civ·i·liz·ing** : to cause to develop out of a primitive state

civil service *n* : the branch of a government that takes care of the business of running a state but that does not include the lawmaking branch, the military, or the court system

civil war *n* : a war between opposing groups of citizens of the same country

¹clack *vb* **1 :** PRATTLE **2 :** to make or cause to make a clatter

²clack *n* **1 :** rapid continuous talk : CHATTER **2 :** a sound of clacking

clad *adj* **:** being covered : wearing clothes

¹claim *vb* **1 :** to ask for as rightfully belonging to oneself **2 :** to call for : REQUIRE **3 :** to state as a fact : MAINTAIN **4 :** to make a claim

²claim *n* **1 :** a demand for something due or believed to be due **2 :** a right to something **3 :** a statement that may be doubted **4 :** something (as an area of land) claimed as one's own

¹clam *n* **:** a shellfish with a soft body and a hinged double shell

²clam *vb* **clammed; clam·ming :** to dig or gather clams

clam·bake *n* **:** an outing where food is cooked usually on heated rocks covered by seaweed

clam·ber *vb* **:** to climb in an awkward way (as by scrambling)

clam·my *adj* **clam·mi·er; clam·mi·est :** unpleasantly damp, soft, sticky, and usually cool — **clam·mi·ly** *adv* — **clam·mi·ness** *n*

¹clam·or *n* **1 :** a noisy shouting **2 :** a loud continous noise **3 :** strong and active protest or demand

²clamor *vb* **:** to make a clamor

clam·or·ous *adj* **:** full of clamor : very noisy

¹clamp *n* **:** a device that holds or presses parts together firmly

²clamp *vb* **:** to fasten or to hold together with or as if with a clamp

clan *n* **1 :** a group (as in the Scottish Highlands) made up of households whose heads claim to have a common ancestor **2 :** a group of persons united by some common interest

¹clang *vb* **:** to make or cause to make a loud ringing sound

²clang *n* **:** a loud ringing sound like that made by pieces of metal striking together

¹clank *vb* **1 :** to make or cause to make a clank or series of clanks **2 :** to move with a clank

²clank *n* **:** a sharp short ringing sound

¹clap *vb* **clapped; clap·ping 1 :** to strike noisily : SLAM, BANG **2 :** to strike (one's hands) together again and again in applause **3 :** to strike with the open hand **4 :** to put or place quickly or with force

²clap *n* **1 :** a loud noisy crash made by or as if by the striking together of two hard surfaces **2 :** a hard or a friendly slap

clap·board *n* **:** a narrow board thicker at one edge than at the other used as siding for a building

clap·per *n* **:** one (as the tongue of a bell) that makes a clapping sound

clar·i·fy *vb* **clar·i·fied; clar·i·fy·ing 1 :** to make or to become pure or clear **2 :** to make or become more easily understood

clar·i·net *n* **:** a woodwind instrument in the form of a tube with finger holes and keys

clar·i·on *adj* **:** being loud and clear

clar·i·ty *n* **:** clear quality or state

¹clash *vb* **1 :** to make or cause to make a clash **2 :** to come into conflict **3 :** to not match well

²clash *n* **1 :** a loud sharp sound usually of metal striking metal **2 :** a struggle or strong disagreement

¹clasp *n* **1 :** a device for holding together objects or parts of something **2 :** ²GRASP 1, GRIP **3 :** ²EMBRACE

²clasp *vb* **1 :** to fasten with or as if with a clasp **2 :** ¹EMBRACE 1 **3 :** ¹GRASP 1

¹class *n* **1 :** a group of pupils meeting at set times for study or instruction **2 :** the period during which a study group meets **3 :** a course of instruction **4 :** a body of students who are to graduate at the same time **5 :** a group or rank of society **6 :** a group of plants or animals that ranks above the order and below the phylum or division in scientific classification **7 :** a grouping or standing (as of goods or services) based on quality

²class *vb* **:** CLASSIFY

¹clas·sic *adj* **1 :** serving as a standard of excellence **2 :** fashionable year after year **3 :** of or relating to the ancient Greeks and Romans or their culture **4 :** being very good or typical of its kind

²classic *n* **1 :** a written work or author of ancient Greece or Rome **2 :** a great work of art **3 :** something regarded as outstanding of its kind

clas·si·cal *adj* **1 :** of or relating to the classics of literature or art and especially to the ancient Greek and Roman classics **2 :** of or relating to serious music in the European tradition **3 :** concerned with a general study of the arts and sciences

clas·si·fi·ca·tion *n* **1 :** the act of classifying or arranging in classes **2 :** an arrangement in classes

clas·si·fy *vb* **clas·si·fied; clas·si·fy·ing :** to group in classes

class·mate *n* **:** a member of the same class in a school or college

class·room *n* **:** a room in a school or college in which classes meet

¹clat·ter *vb* **1 :** to make or cause to make a rattling sound **2 :** to move or go with a clatter

²clatter *n* **1 :** a rattling sound (as of hard objects striking together) **2 :** COMMOTION

clause *n* **1** : a separate part of a document (as a will) **2** : a group of words having its own subject and predicate but forming only part of a complete sentence

clav·i·cle *n* : COLLARBONE

¹claw *n* **1** : a sharp usually thin and curved nail on the finger or toe of an animal (as a cat or bird) **2** : the end of a limb of a lower animal (as an insect, scorpion, or lobster) that is pointed or like pincers **3** : something like a claw in shape or use

²claw *vb* : to scratch, seize, or dig with claws

clay *n* **1** : an earthy material that is sticky and easily molded when wet and hard when baked **2** : a plastic substance used like clay for modeling

¹clean *adj* **1** : free of dirt or evil **2** : free of objectionable behavior or language **3** : THOROUGH 1, COMPLETE **4** : having a simple graceful form : TRIM **5** : ¹SMOOTH 1

²clean *adv* **1** : so as to clean **2** : in a clean way **3** : all the way

³clean *vb* : to make or become clean — **clean·er** *n*

clean·li·ness *n* : the condition of being clean : the habit of keeping clean

¹clean·ly *adv* : in a clean way

²clean·ly *adj* **clean·li·er; clean·li·est** **1** : careful to keep clean **2** : kept clean

cleanse *vb* **cleansed; cleans·ing** : to make clean

cleans·er *n* : a substance (as a scouring powder) used for cleaning

¹clear *adj* **1** : BRIGHT 1, LUMINOUS **2** : free of clouds, haze, or mist **3** : UNTROUBLED **4** : free of blemishes **5** : easily seen through **6** : easily heard, seen, or understood **7** : free from doubt : SURE **8** : INNOCENT **9** : not blocked or limited — **clear·ly** *adv* — **clear·ness** *n*

²clear *adv* **1** : in a clear manner **2** : all the way

³clear *vb* **1** : to make or become clear **2** : to go away : DISPERSE **3** : to free from blame **4** : to approve or be approved by **5** : EXPLAIN 1 **6** : to free of things blocking **7** : to get rid of : REMOVE **8** : ⁴NET **9** : to go over or by without touching

⁴clear *n* : a clear space or part — **in the clear** : free from guilt or suspicion

clear·ance *n* **1** : the act or process of clearing **2** : the distance by which one object avoids hitting or touching another

clear·ing *n* : an area of land from which trees and bushes have all been removed

cleat *n* **1** : a wooden or metal device used to fasten a line or a rope **2** : a strip or projection fastened on or across something to give strength or a place to hold or to prevent slipping

cleav·age *n* **1** : the tendency of a rock or mineral to split readily in one or more directions **2** : the action of cleaving **3** : the state of being cleft

¹cleave *vb* **cleaved** *or* **clove; cleav·ing** : to cling to a person or thing closely

²cleave *vb* **cleaved** *or* **cleft** *or* **clove; cleaved** *or* **cleft** *or* **clo·ven; cleav·ing** : to divide by or as if by a cutting blow : SPLIT

cleav·er *n* : a heavy knife used for cutting up meat

clef *n* : a sign placed on the staff in writing music to show what pitch is represented by each line and space

¹cleft *n* **1** : a space or opening made by splitting or cracking : CREVICE **2** : ¹NOTCH 1

²cleft *adj* : partly split or divided

clem·en·cy *n, pl* **clemencies 1** : MERCY 1 **2** : an act of mercy

clench *vb* **1** : to hold tightly : CLUTCH **2** : to set or close tightly

cler·gy *n, pl* **clergies** : the group of religious officials (as priests, ministers, and rabbis) specially prepared and authorized to lead religious services

cler·gy·man *n, pl* **cler·gy·men** : a member of the clergy

cler·i·cal *adj* **1** : of or relating to the clergy **2** : of or relating to a clerk or office worker

¹clerk *n* **1** : a person whose job is to keep records or accounts **2** : a salesperson in a store

²clerk *vb* : to act or work as a clerk

clev·er *adj* **1** : showing skill especially in using one's hands **2** : having a quick inventive mind **3** : showing wit or imagination — **clev·er·ly** *adv* — **clev·er·ness** *n*

¹click *vb* **1** : to make or cause to make a click **2** : to fit in or work together smoothly **3** : to select or make a selection especially on a computer by pressing a button on a control device (as a mouse)

²click *n* : a slight sharp noise

click·er *n* : REMOTE CONTROL 2

cli·ent *n* : a person who uses the professional advice or services of another

cli·en·tele *n* : a group of clients

cliff *n* : a high steep surface of rock

cli·mate *n* : the average weather conditions of a place over a period of years

cli·max *n* : the time or part of something that is of greatest interest, excitement, or importance

¹climb *vb* **1** : to rise little by little to a higher point **2** : to go up or down often with the help of the hands in holding or pulling **3** : to go upward in growing (as by winding around something) — **climb·er** *n*

²climb *n* **1** : a place where climbing is necessary **2** : the act of climbing

clime *n* : CLIMATE

¹clinch *vb* **1** : to turn over or flatten the end of (as a nail sticking out of a board) **2** : to fasten by clinching **3** : to show to be certain or true

²clinch *n* : a fastening with a clinched nail, bolt, or rivet : the clinched part of a nail, bolt, or rivet

cling *vb* **clung; cling·ing 1** : to hold fast or stick closely to a surface **2** : to hold fast by grasping or winding around **3** : to remain close

clin·ic *n* **1** : a group meeting for teaching a certain skill and working on individual problems **2** : a place where people can receive medical examinations and usually treatment for minor ailments

¹clink *vb* : to make or cause to make a slight short sound like that of metal being struck

²clink *n* : a clinking sound

¹clip *vb* **clipped; clip·ping** : to fasten with a clip

²clip *n* : a device that holds or hooks

³clip *vb* **clipped; clip·ping 1** : to shorten or remove by cutting (as with shears or scissors) **2** : to cut off or trim the hair or wool of

⁴clip *n* **1** : an instrument with two blades for cutting the nails **2** : a sharp blow **3** : a rapid pace

clip art *n* : ready-made illustrations sold in books or as software from which they may be taken for use in a printed work

clip·board *n* : a small board with a clip at the top for holding papers

clip·per *n* **1** : a person who clips **2** **clippers** *pl* : a device used for clipping especially hair or nails **3** : a fast sailing ship with usually three tall masts and large square sails

clip·ping *n* : something cut out or off

clique *n* : a small group of people that keep out outsiders

¹cloak *n* **1** : a long loose outer garment **2** : something that hides or covers

²cloak *vb* : to cover or hide with a cloak

cloak·room *n* : a room (as in a school) in which coats and hats may be kept

¹clock *n* : a device for measuring or telling the time and especially one not meant to be worn or carried by a person

²clock *vb* **1** : to time (as a person or a piece of work) by a timing device **2** : to show (as time or speed) on a recording device

clock·wise *adv or adj* : in the direction in which the hands of a clock turn

clock·work *n* : machinery (as in mechanical toys) like that which makes clocks go

clod *n* **1** : a lump or mass especially of earth or clay **2** : a clumsy or stupid person

¹clog *n* **1** : something that hinders or holds back **2** : a shoe having a thick usually wooden sole

²clog *vb* **clogged; clog·ging** : to make passage through difficult or impossible : PLUG

¹clois·ter *n* **1** : MONASTERY, CONVENT **2** : a covered usually arched passage along or around the walls of a court

²cloister *vb* **1** : to shut away from the world **2** : to surround with a cloister

clop *n* : a sound like that of a hoof against pavement

¹close *vb* **closed; clos·ing 1** : to stop up : prevent passage through **2** : to fill or cause to fill an opening **3** : to bring or come to an end **4** : to end the operation of **5** : to bring the parts or edges of together **6** : ¹APPROACH 1

²close *n* : the point at which something ends

³close *adj* **clos·er; clos·est 1** : having little space in which to move **2** : SECRETIVE **3** : lacking fresh or moving air **4** : not generous **5** : not far apart in space, time, degree, or effect **6** : ¹SHORT 1 **7** : very like **8** : having a strong liking each one for the other **9** : strict and careful in attention to details **10** : decided by a narrow margin — **close·ly** *adv* — **close·ness** *n*

⁴close *adv* : ¹NEAR 1

close call *n* : a barely successful escape from a difficult or dangerous situation

closed *adj* **1** : not open **2** : having mathematical elements that when subjected to an operation produce only elements of the same set

¹clos·et *n* **1** : a small room for privacy **2** : a small room for clothing or for supplies for the house

²closet *vb* **1** : to shut up in or as if in a closet **2** : to take into a private room for an interview

close–up *n* : a photograph taken at close range

clo·sure *n* **1** : an act of closing **2** : the condition of being closed

¹clot *n* : a lump made by some substance getting thicker and sticking together

²clot *vb* **clot·ted; clot·ting** : to thicken into a clot

cloth *n, pl* **cloths 1** : a woven or knitted material (as of cotton or nylon) **2** : a piece of cloth for a certain use **3** : TABLECLOTH

clothe *vb* **clothed** *or* **clad; cloth·ing 1** : to cover with or as if with clothing : DRESS **2** : to provide with clothes **3** : to express in a certain way

clothes *n pl* : CLOTHING 1

clothes moth *n* : a small yellowish moth whose larvae feed on wool, fur, and feathers

clothes·pin *n* : a peg (as of wood) with the

lower part slit or a clamp for holding clothes in place on a line

cloth·ing *n* **1** : covering for the human body **2** : COVERING

1cloud *n* **1** : a visible mass of tiny bits of water or ice hanging in the air usually high above the earth **2** : a visible mass of small particles in the air **3** : something thought to be like a cloud — **cloud·less** *adj*

2cloud *vb* **1** : to make or become cloudy **2** : to darken or hide as if by a cloud

cloud·burst *n* : a sudden heavy rainfall

cloudy *adj* **cloud·i·er; cloud·i·est** **1** : overspread with clouds **2** : showing confusion **3** : not clear — **cloud·i·ness** *n*

1clout *n* : a blow especially with the hand

2clout *vb* : to hit hard

1clove *n* : the dried flower bud of a tropical tree used as a spice

2clove *past of* CLEAVE

clo·ven *past participle of* 2CLEAVE

cloven hoof *n* : a hoof (as of a cow) with the front part divided into two sections

clo·ver *n* : any of various plants grown for hay and pasture that have leaves with three leaflets and usually roundish red, white, yellow, or purple flower heads

1clown *n* **1** : a rude and often stupid person **2** : a performer (as in a play or circus) who entertains by playing tricks and who usually wears comical clothes and makeup

2clown *vb* : to act like a clown : SHOW OFF

1club *n* **1** : a heavy usually wooden stick used as a weapon **2** : a stick or bat used to hit a ball in various games **3** : a group of people associated because of a shared interest **4** : the meeting place of a club

2club *vb* **clubbed; club·bing** : to beat or strike with or as if with a club

club·house *n* **1** : a house used by a club **2** : locker rooms used by an athletic team

club moss *n* : a low often trailing evergreen plant that forms spores instead of seeds

1cluck *vb* : to make or call with a cluck

2cluck *n* : the call of a hen especially to her chicks

clue *n* : something that helps a person to find something or to solve a mystery

1clump *n* **1** : a group of things clustered together **2** : a cluster or lump of something **3** : a heavy tramping sound

2clump *vb* **1** : to walk clumsily and noisily **2** : to form or cause to form clumps

clum·sy *adj* **clum·si·er; clum·si·est** **1** : lacking skill or grace in movement **2** : not knowing how to get along with others **3** : badly or awkwardly made or done — **clum·si·ly** *adv* — **clum·si·ness** *n*

clung *past of* CLING

1clus·ter *n* : a number of similar things growing, collected, or grouped closely together : BUNCH

2cluster *vb* : to grow, collect, or assemble in a cluster

1clutch *vb* **1** : to grasp or hold tightly with or as if with the hands or claws **2** : to make a grab

2clutch *n* **1** : the state of being clutched **2** : a device for gripping an object **3** : a coupling for connecting and disconnecting a driving and a driven part in machinery **4** : a lever or pedal operating a clutch

1clut·ter *vb* : to throw into disorder : fill or cover with scattered things

2clutter *n* : a crowded or confused collection : DISORDER

co- *prefix* **1** : with : together : joint : jointly **2** : in or to the same degree **3** : fellow : partner

1coach *n* **1** : a large carriage that has four wheels and a raised seat outside in front for the driver and is drawn by horses **2** : a railroad passenger car without berths **3** : a class of passenger transportation in an airplane at a lower fare than first class **4** : a person who teaches students individually **5** : a person who instructs or trains a performer or team

2coach *vb* : to act as coach

coach·man *n, pl* **coach·men** : a person whose business is driving a coach or carriage

co·ag·u·late *vb* **co·ag·u·lat·ed; co·ag·u·lat·ing** : to gather into a thick compact mass : CLOT

coal *n* **1** : a piece of glowing or charred wood : EMBER **2** : a black solid mineral substance that is formed by the partial decay of vegetable matter under the influence of moisture and often increased pressure and temperature within the earth and is mined for use as a fuel

coarse *adj* **1** : of poor or ordinary quality **2** : made up of large particles **3** : being harsh or rough **4** : crude in taste, manners, or language — **coarse·ly** *adv* — **coarse·ness** *n*

coars·en *vb* : to make or become coarse

1coast *n* : the land near a shore

2coast *vb* **1** : to slide downhill by the force of gravity over snow or ice **2** : to move along (as on a bicycle when not pedaling) without applying power

coast·al *adj* : of, relating to, or located on, near, or along a coast

coast·er *n* **1** : someone or something that coasts **2** : a sled or small wagon used in coasting

coast guard *n* : a military force that guards a coast

¹coat *n* **1** : an outer garment that differs in length and style according to fashion or use **2** : the outer covering (as fur or feathers) of an animal **3** : a layer of material covering a surface — **coat·ed** *adj*

²coat *vb* : to cover with a coat or covering

coat·ing *n* : ¹COAT 3, COVERING

coat of arms : the heraldic arms belonging to a person, family, or group or a representation of these (as on a shield)

coat of mail : a garment of metal scales or rings worn long ago as armor

co·au·thor *n* : an author who works with another author

coax *vb* **1** : to influence by gentle urging, special attention, or flattering **2** : to get or win by means of gentle urging or flattery

cob *n* : CORNCOB

co·balt *n* : a tough shiny silvery white metallic chemical element found with iron and nickel

cob·bled *adj* : paved or covered with cobblestones

cob·bler *n* **1** : a person who mends or makes shoes **2** : a fruit pie with a thick upper crust and no bottom crust that is baked in a deep dish

cob·ble·stone *n* : a naturally rounded stone larger than a pebble and smaller than a boulder once used in paving streets

co·bra *n* : a very poisonous snake of Asia and Africa that puffs out the skin around its neck into a hood when excited

cob·web *n* **1** : the network spread by a spider : SPIDERWEB **2** : tangles of threads of a cobweb

co·caine *n* : a habit-forming drug obtained from the leaves of a South American shrub and sometimes used as a medicine to deaden pain

coc·cus *n*, *pl* **coc·ci** : a bacterium shaped like a ball

¹cock *n* **1** : a male bird : ROOSTER **2** : a faucet or valve for controlling the flow of a liquid or a gas **3** : a cocked position of the hammer of a gun

²cock *vb* **1** : to draw back the hammer of (a gun) in readiness for firing **2** : to set or draw back in readiness for some action **3** : to turn or tip upward or to one side

³cock *n* : the act of tipping at an angle : TILT

cock·a·too *n*, *pl* **cock·a·toos** : any of several large, noisy, and usually brightly colored crested parrots mostly of Australia

cock·eyed *adj* **1** : tilted to one side **2** : FOOLISH

cock·le *n* : an edible shellfish with a shell that has two parts and is shaped like a heart

cock·le·bur *n* : a plant with prickly fruit that is related to the thistles

cock·le·shell *n* : a shell of a cockle

cock·pit *n* **1** : an open space in the deck from which a small boat (as a yacht) is steered **2** : a space in an airplane for the pilot or pilot and passengers or pilot and crew

cock·roach *n* : a troublesome insect found in houses and ships and active chiefly at night

cocky *adj* **cock·i·er**; **cock·i·est** : very sure of oneself : boldly self-confident

co·coa *n* **1** : chocolate ground to a powder after some of its fat is removed **2** : a drink made from cocoa powder

co·co·nut *n* : a large nutlike fruit that has a thick husk and grows on a tall tropical palm (**coconut palm**)

co·coon *n* : the silky covering which caterpillars make around themselves and in which they are protected while changing into butterflies or moths

cod *n*, *pl* **cod** : a large food fish found in the deep colder parts of the northern Atlantic Ocean

cod·dle *vb* **cod·dled**; **cod·dling** **1** : to cook slowly in water below the boiling point **2** : to treat with very much and usually too much care : PAMPER

¹code *n* **1** : a collection of laws arranged in some orderly way **2** : a system of rules or principles **3** : a system of signals or letters and symbols with special meanings used for sending messages **4** : GENETIC CODE

²code *vb* **cod·ed**; **cod·ing** : to put in the form of a code

cod·fish *n*, *pl* **codfish** *or* **cod·fish·es** : COD

cod·ger *n* : an odd or cranky man

co·erce *vb* **co·erced**; **co·erc·ing** : ²FORCE 1, COMPEL

cof·fee *n* **1** : a drink made from the roasted and ground seeds of a tropical plant **2** : the seeds of the coffee plant

cof·fee·pot *n* : a covered utensil for preparing or serving coffee

coffee table *n* : a low table usually placed in front of a sofa

cof·fer *n* : a box used especially for holding money and valuables

cof·fin *n* : a box or case to hold a dead body

cog *n* : a tooth on the rim of a wheel or gear

cog·i·tate *vb* **cog·i·tat·ed**; **cog·i·tat·ing** : to think over : PONDER

cog·i·ta·tion *n* : MEDITATION

cog·wheel *n* : a wheel with cogs on the rim

co·he·sion *n* **1** : the action of sticking together **2** : the force of attraction between the molecules in a mass

¹coil *vb* **1** : to wind into rings or a spiral **2** : to form or lie in a coil

²coil *n* **1** : a circle, a series of circles, or a

spiral made by coiling **2** : something coiled

¹coin n **1** : a piece of metal put out by government authority as money **2** : metal money

²coin vb **1** : to make coins especially by stamping pieces of metal : MINT **2** : to make metal (as gold or silver) into coins **3** : to make up (a new word or phrase)

coin·age n **1** : the act or process of coining **2** : something coined

co·in·cide vb **co·in·cid·ed; co·in·cid·ing 1** : to occupy the same space **2** : to happen at the same time **3** : to agree exactly

co·in·ci·dence n **1** : a coinciding in space or time **2** : two things that happen at the same time by accident but seem to have some connection

coke n : gray lumps of fuel made by heating soft coal in a closed chamber until some of its gases have passed off

col- — see COM-

col·an·der n : a utensil with small holes for draining foods

¹cold adj **1** : having a low temperature or one much below normal **2** : lacking warmth of feeling : UNFRIENDLY **3** : suffering from lack of warmth — **cold·ly** adv — **cold·ness** n

²cold n **1** : a condition of low temperature : cold weather **2** : the bodily feeling produced by lack of warmth : CHILL **3** : COMMON COLD

cold–blood·ed adj **1** : lacking or showing a lack of normal human feelings **2** : having a body temperature that varies with the temperature of the environment **3** : sensitive to cold

co·le·us n : a plant of the mint family grown for its many-colored leaves

col·ic n : sharp pain in the bowels — **col·icky** adj

col·i·se·um n : a large structure (as a stadium) for athletic contests or public entertainment

col·lab·o·rate vb **col·lab·o·rat·ed; col·lab·o·rat·ing 1** : to work with others (as in writing a book) **2** : to cooperate with an enemy force that has taken over one's country

col·lage n : a work of art made by gluing pieces of different materials to a flat surface

¹col·lapse vb **col·lapsed; col·laps·ing 1** : to break down completely : fall in **2** : to shrink together suddenly **3** : to suffer a physical or mental breakdown **4** : to fold together

²collapse n : the act or an instance of collapsing : BREAKDOWN

col·laps·ible adj : capable of collapsing or possible to collapse

¹col·lar n **1** : a band, strap, or chain worn around the neck or the neckline of a garment **2** : a part of the harness of draft animals fitted over the shoulders **3** : something (as a ring to hold a pipe in place) that is like a collar — **col·lar·less** adj

²collar vb **1** : to seize by or as if by the collar : CAPTURE, GRAB **2** : to put a collar on

col·lar·bone n : a bone of the shoulder joined to the breastbone and the shoulder blade

col·league n : an associate in a profession : a fellow worker

col·lect vb **1** : to bring or come together into one body or place **2** : to gather from a number of sources **3** : to gain or regain control of **4** : to receive payment for

col·lect·ed adj : ³CALM 2

col·lec·tion n **1** : the act or process of gathering together **2** : something collected and especially a group of objects gathered for study or exhibition **3** : a gathering of money (as for charitable purposes)

col·lec·tive adj **1** : having to do with a number of persons or things thought of as a whole **2** : done or shared by a number of persons as a group — **col·lec·tive·ly** adj

col·lec·tor n **1** : a person or thing that collects **2** : a person whose business it is to collect money

col·lege n : a school higher than a high school

col·le·giate adj **1** : having to do with a college **2** : of, relating to, or characteristic of college students

col·lide vb **col·lid·ed; col·lid·ing 1** : to strike against each other **2** : ¹CLASH 2

col·lie n : a large usually long-coated dog of a Scottish breed used to herd sheep

col·li·sion n : an act or instance of colliding

col·lo·qui·al adj : used in or suited to familiar and informal conversation

col·lo·qui·al·ism n : a colloquial word or expression

co·logne n : a perfumed liquid made up of alcohol and fragrant oils

¹co·lon n : the main part of the large intestine

²colon n : a punctuation mark : used mostly to call attention to what follows (as a list, explanation, or quotation)

col·o·nel n : a commissioned officer in the Army, Air Force, or Marine Corps ranking above a lieutenant colonel

¹co·lo·ni·al adj **1** : of, relating to, or characteristic of a colony **2** often cap : of or relating to the original thirteen colonies that formed the United States

²**colonial** *n* : a member of or a person living in a colony

col·o·nist *n* **1** : a person living in a colony **2** : a person who helps to found a colony

col·o·nize *vb* **col·o·nized; col·o·niz·ing 1** : to establish a colony in or on **2** : to settle in a colony

col·on·nade *n* : a row of columns usually supporting the base of a roof structure

col·o·ny *n, pl* **col·o·nies 1** : a group of people sent out by a state to a new territory : the territory in which these people settle **2** : a distant territory belonging to or under the control of a nation **3** : a group of living things of one kind living together **4** : a group of people with common qualities or interests located in close association

¹**col·or** *n* **1** : the appearance of a thing apart from size and shape when light strikes it **2** : a hue other than black, white, or gray **3** : outward show : APPEARANCE **4** : the normal rosy tint of skin **5** : ¹BLUSH **6 colors** *pl* : an identifying flag **7 colors** *pl* : military service **8** : ¹INTEREST 6 **9** : the quality of sound in music

²**color** *vb* **1** : to give color to **2** : to change the color of **3** : MISREPRESENT **4** : to take on or change color : BLUSH

col·or·ation *n* : use or arrangement of colors or shades : COLORING

color–blind *adj* : unable to tell some colors apart

col·ored *adj* : having color

col·or·ful *adj* **1** : having bright colors **2** : full of variety or interest

col·or·ing *n* **1** : the act of applying colors **2** : something that produces color **3** : the effect produced by the use of color **4** : natural color : COMPLEXION

col·or·less *adj* **1** : having no color **2** : WAN, PALE **3** : ¹DULL 8

co·los·sal *adj* : very large : HUGE

colt *n* **1** : FOAL **2** : a young male horse

col·um·bine *n* : a plant related to the buttercups that has leaves with three parts and showy flowers usually with five petals ending in spurs

col·umn *n* **1** : one of two or more vertical sections of a printed page **2** : a special regular feature in a newspaper or magazine **3** : a pillar supporting a roof or gallery **4** : something like a column in shape, position, or use **5** : a long straight row (as of soldiers)

col·um·nist *n* : a writer of a column in a newspaper or magazine

com- *or* **col-** *or* **con-** *prefix* : with : together : jointly — usually *com-* before *b, p,* or *m, col-* before *l* and *con-* before other sounds

co·ma *n* : a deep sleeplike state caused by sickness or injury

¹**comb** *n* **1** : a toothed implement used to smooth and arrange the hair or worn in the hair to hold it in place **2** : a toothed instrument used for separating fibers (as of wool or flax) **3** : a fleshy crest often with points suggesting teeth on the head of a fowl and some related birds **4** : ¹HONEYCOMB 1

²**comb** *vb* **1** : to smooth, arrange, or untangle with a comb **2** : to search over or through carefully

¹**com·bat** *n* **1** : a fight or contest between individuals or groups **2** : ¹CONFLICT 2 **3** : active military fighting

²**com·bat** *vb* **com·bat·ed** *or* **com·bat·ted; com·bat·ing** *or* **com·bat·ting** : to fight with : fight against : OPPOSE

¹**com·bat·ant** *n* : a person who takes part in a combat

²**combatant** *adj* : engaging in or ready to engage in combat

com·bi·na·tion *n* **1** : a result or product of combining or being combined **2** : a union of persons or groups for a purpose **3** : a series of letters or numbers which when dialed by a disk on a lock will operate or open the lock **4** : a union of different things

combination lock *n* : a lock with one or more dials or rings marked usually with numbers which are used to open the lock by moving them in a certain order to certain positions

¹**com·bine** *vb* **com·bined; com·bin·ing** : to join together so as to make or to seem one thing : UNITE, MIX

²**com·bine** *n* **1** : a union of persons or groups of persons especially for business or political benefits **2** : a machine that harvests and threshes grain

com·bus·ti·ble *adj* **1** : possible to burn **2** : catching fire or burning easily

com·bus·tion *n* : the process of burning

come *vb* **came; come; com·ing 1** : to move toward : APPROACH **2** : to reach the point of being or becoming **3** : to add up : AMOUNT **4** : to take place **5** : ORIGINATE 2, ARISE **6** : to be available **7** : ¹REACH 2

co·me·di·an *n* **1** : an actor who plays comic roles **2** : an amusing person

com·e·dy *n, pl* **com·e·dies 1** : an amusing play that has a happy ending **2** : an amusing and often ridiculous event

come·ly *adj* **come·li·er; come·li·est** : pleasing to the sight : good-looking

com·et *n* : a bright celestial body that develops a cloudy tail as it moves in an orbit around the sun

come to *vb* : to become conscious again

¹com·fort *vb* 1 : to give hope and strength to : CHEER 2 : to ease the grief or trouble of

²comfort *n* 1 : acts or words that comfort 2 : the feeling of the one that is comforted 3 : something that makes a person comfortable

com·fort·able *adj* 1 : giving comfort and especially physical ease 2 : more than what is needed 3 : physically at ease — com·fort·ably *adj*

com·fort·er *n* 1 : one that gives comfort 2 : ¹QUILT

com·ic *adj* 1 : of, relating to, or characteristic of comedy 2 : FUNNY 1

com·i·cal *adj* : FUNNY 1, RIDICULOUS — com·i·cal·ly *adv*

comic book *n* : a magazine made up of a series of comic strips

comic strip *n* : a series of cartoons that tell a story or part of a story

com·ma *n* : a punctuation mark, used chiefly to show separation of words or word groups within a sentence

¹com·mand *vb* 1 : to order with authority 2 : to have power or control over : be commander of 3 : to have for one's use 4 : to demand as right or due : EXACT 5 : to survey from a good position

²command *n* 1 : the act of commanding 2 : an order given 3 : the ability to control and use : MASTERY 4 : the authority, right, or power to command : CONTROL 5 : the people, area, or unit (as of soldiers and weapons) under a commander 6 : a position from which military operations are directed

com·man·dant *n* : a commanding officer

com·mand·er *n* : a commissioned officer in the Navy or Coast Guard ranking above a lieutenant commander

commander in chief : a person who holds supreme command of the armed forces of a nation

com·mand·ment *n* : something given as a command and especially one of the Ten Commandments in the Bible

com·man·do *n, pl* com·man·dos *or* com·man·does 1 : a band or unit of troops trained for making surprise raids into enemy territory 2 : a member of a commando unit

command sergeant major *n* : a noncommissioned officer in the Army ranking above a first sergeant

com·mem·o·rate *vb* com·mem·o·rat·ed; com·mem·o·rat·ing 1 : to call or recall to mind 2 : to observe with a ceremony 3 : to serve as a memorial of

com·mem·o·ra·tion *n* 1 : the act of commemorating 2 : something (as a ceremony) that commemorates

com·mence *vb* com·menced; com·menc·ing : BEGIN, START

com·mence·ment *n* 1 : the act or the time of commencing : BEGINNING 2 : graduation exercises

com·mend *vb* 1 : to give into another's care : ENTRUST 2 : to speak of with approval : PRAISE

com·men·da·tion *n* : ²PRAISE 1, APPROVAL

¹com·ment *n* 1 : an expression of opinion either in speech or writing 2 : mention of something that deserves notice

²comment *vb* : to make a comment : REMARK

com·men·ta·tor *n* 1 : a person who makes comments 2 : a person who reports and discusses news events (as over radio)

com·merce *n* : the buying and selling of goods especially on a large scale and between different places : TRADE

¹com·mer·cial *adj* 1 : having to do with commerce 2 : having financial profit as the chief goal — com·mer·cial·ly *adv*

²commercial *n* : an advertisement broadcast on radio or television

com·mer·cial·ize *vb* com·mer·cial·ized; com·mer·cial·iz·ing : to manage with the idea of making a profit

¹com·mis·sion *n* 1 : an order or instruction granting the power to perform various acts or duties : the right or duty in question 2 : a certificate that gives military or naval rank and authority : the rank and authority given 3 : authority to act as agent for another : a task or piece of business entrusted to an agent 4 : a group of persons given orders and authority to perform specified duties 5 : an act of doing something wrong 6 : a fee paid to an agent for taking care of a piece of business

²commission *vb* 1 : to give a commission to 2 : to put (a ship) into service

commissioned officer *n* : an officer in the armed forces who ranks above the enlisted persons or warrant officers and who is appointed by a commission from the president

com·mis·sion·er *n* 1 : a member of a commission 2 : an official who is the head of a government department

com·mit *vb* com·mit·ted; com·mit·ting 1 : to make secure or put in safekeeping : ENTRUST 2 : to place in or send to a prison or mental institution 3 : to bring about : PERFORM 4 : to pledge or assign to a certain course or use — com·mit·ment *n*

com·mit·tee *n* : a group of persons appointed or elected to consider some subject of interest or to perform some duty

com·mod·i·ty *n, pl* com·mod·i·ties : something produced by agriculture, mining, or manufacture

com·mo·dore n **1** : a former wartime commissioned officer rank in the Navy and Coast Guard between the ranks of captain and rear admiral **2** : the chief officer of a yacht club **3** : the senior captain of a line of merchant ships

¹com·mon adj **1** : having to do with, belonging to, or used by everybody : PUBLIC **2** : belonging to or shared by two or more individuals or by the members of a family or group **3** : ¹GENERAL 1 **4** : occurring or appearing frequently **5** : not above the average in rank, excellence, or social position **6** : falling below ordinary standards (as in quality or manners) : INFERIOR **7** : COARSE 4, VULGAR

²common n : land (as a park) owned and used by a community — **in common** : shared together

common cold n : a contagious disease which causes the lining of the nose and throat to be sore, swollen, and red and in which there is usually much mucus and coughing and sneezing

common denominator n : a common multiple of the denominators of a number of fractions

com·mon·er n : one of the common people

common multiple n : a multiple of each of two or more numbers

common noun n : a noun that names a class of persons or things or any individual of a class and that may occur with a limiting modifier (as a, the, some, or every)

¹com·mon·place n : something that is often seen or met with

²commonplace adj : often seen or met with : ORDINARY

common sense n : ordinary good sense and judgment

com·mon·wealth n **1** : a political unit (as a nation or state) **2** : a state of the United States and especially Kentucky, Massachusetts, Pennsylvania, or Virginia

com·mo·tion n : noisy excitement and confusion : TURMOIL

¹com·mune vb **com·muned; com·mun·ing** : to be in close accord or communication with someone or something

²com·mune n : a community in which individuals have close personal ties to each other and share property and duties

com·mu·ni·ca·ble adj : possible to communicate

com·mu·ni·cate vb **com·mu·ni·cat·ed; com·mu·ni·cat·ing** **1** : to make known **2** : to pass (as a disease) from one to another

: SPREAD **3** : to get in touch (as by telephone)

com·mu·ni·ca·tion n **1** : the exchange (as by speech or letter) of information between persons **2** : information communicated **3 communications** pl : a system of sending messages (as by telephone) **4 communications** pl : a system of routes for moving troops, supplies, and vehicles

com·mu·nion n **1** : an act or example of sharing **2** : a religious ceremony commemorating with bread and wine the last supper of Jesus **3** : the act of receiving the sacrament **4** : friendly communication **5** : a body of Christians having a common faith and discipline

com·mu·nism n **1** : a social system in which property and goods are held in common **2** : a theory that supports communism

com·mu·nist n **1** : a person who believes in communism **2** cap : a member or follower of a Communist party or plan for change

com·mu·ni·ty n, pl **com·mu·ni·ties 1** : the people living in a certain place (as a village or city) : the area itself **2** : a natural group (as of kinds of plants and animals) living together and depending on one another for various necessities of life **3** : a group of people with common interests living together **4** : people in general : PUBLIC **5** : common ownership or participation

com·mu·ta·tive adj : being a property of a mathematical operation (as addition or multiplication) in which the result of combining elements is independent of the order in which they are taken

com·mute vb **com·mut·ed; com·mut·ing 1** : to change (as a penalty) to something less severe **2** : to travel back and forth regularly — **com·mut·er** n

¹com·pact adj **1** : closely united or packed **2** : arranged so as to save space **3** : not wordy : BRIEF — **com·pact·ly** adv — **com·pact·ness** n

²com·pact n **1** : a small case for cosmetics **2** : a somewhat small automobile

³com·pact n : AGREEMENT 2

compact disc n : a small plastic disc on which information (as music or computer data) is recorded

com·pan·ion n **1** : a person or thing that accompanies another **2** : one of a pair of matching things **3** : a person employed to live with and serve another

com·pan·ion·ship n : FELLOWSHIP 1, COMPANY

com·pan·ion·way n : a ship's stairway from one deck to another

com·pa·ny n, pl **com·pa·nies 1** : FELLOWSHIP 1 **2** : a person's companions or associates **3** : guests or visitors especially at one's home **4** : a group of persons or things **5** : a body of soldiers and especially an infantry unit normally led by a captain **6** : a band of musical or dramatic performers **7** : the officers and crew of a ship **8** : an association of persons carrying on a business

com·pa·ra·ble *adj* : being similar or about the same

¹com·par·a·tive *adj* **1** : of, relating to, or being the form of an adjective or adverb that shows a degree of comparison that is greater or less than its positive degree **2** : measured by comparisons : RELATIVE — **com·par·a·tive·ly** *adv*

²comparative *n* : the comparative degree or a comparative form in a language

com·pare *vb* **com·pared; com·par·ing 1** : to point out as similar : LIKEN **2** : to examine for likenesses or differences **3** : to appear in comparison to others **4** : to state the positive, comparative, and superlative forms of an adjective or adverb

com·par·i·son *n* **1** : the act of comparing : the condition of being compared **2** : an examination of two or more objects to find the likenesses and differences between them **3** : change in the form and meaning of an adjective or an adverb (as by adding *-er* or *-est* to the word or by adding *more* or *most* before the word) to show different levels of quality, quantity, or relation

com·part·ment *n* **1** : one of the parts into which a closed space is divided **2** : a separate division or section

com·pass *n* **1** : BOUNDARY, CIRCUMFERENCE **2** : a closed-in space **3** : ¹RANGE 6, SCOPE **4** : a device having a magnetic needle that indicates direction on the earth's surface by pointing toward the north **5** : a device that indicates direction by means other than a magnetic needle **6** : an instrument for drawing circles or marking measurements consisting of two pointed legs joined at the top by a pivot — usually used in pl.

com·pas·sion *n* : pity for and a desire to help another

com·pas·sion·ate *adj* : having or showing compassion

com·pat·i·ble *adj* : capable of existing together in harmony

com·pa·tri·ot *n* : a person from one's own country

com·pel *vb* **com·pelled; com·pel·ling** : to make (as a person) do something by the use of physical, moral, or mental pressure : FORCE

com·pen·sate *vb* **com·pen·sat·ed; com-**

pen·sat·ing 1 : to make up for **2** : ¹RECOMPENSE, PAY

com·pen·sa·tion *n* **1** : something that makes up for or is given to make up for something else **2** : money paid regularly

com·pete *vb* **com·pet·ed; com·pet·ing** : to strive for something (as a prize or a reward) for which another is also striving

com·pe·tence *n* : the quality or state of being competent

com·pe·tent *adj* : CAPABLE 1, EFFICIENT

com·pe·ti·tion *n* **1** : the act or process of competing **2** : a contest in which all who take part compete for the same thing

com·pet·i·tive *adj* : relating to, characterized by, or based on competition

com·pet·i·tor *n* : someone or something that competes especially in the selling of goods or services : RIVAL

com·pile *vb* **com·piled; com·pil·ing 1** : to collect into a volume or list **2** : to collect information from books or documents and arrange it in a new form

com·pla·cence *n* : calm or satisfied feeling about one's self or one's position

com·pla·cen·cy *n* : COMPLACENCE

com·pla·cent *adj* : feeling or showing complacence

com·plain *vb* **1** : to express grief, pain, or discontent : find fault **2** : to accuse someone of wrongdoing — **com·plain·er** *n*

com·plaint *n* **1** : expression of grief, pain, or discontent **2** : a cause or reason for complaining **3** : a sickness or disease of the body **4** : a charge of wrongdoing against a person

¹com·ple·ment *n* : something that completes or fills : the number required to complete or make perfect

²com·ple·ment *vb* : to form or serve as a complement to

com·ple·men·ta·ry *adj* : serving as a complement

¹com·plete *adj* **1** : having no part lacking : ENTIRE **2** : brought to an end **3** : THOROUGH 1 — **com·plete·ness** *n*

²complete *vb* **com·plet·ed; com·plet·ing 1** : to bring to an end : FINISH **2** : to make whole or perfect

com·plete·ly *adv* : as much as possible : in every way or detail

com·ple·tion *n* : the act or process of completing : the condition of being complete

com·plex *adj* **1** : made up of two or more parts **2** : not simple

complex fraction *n* : a fraction with a fraction or mixed number in the numerator or denominator or both

com·plex·ion *n* **1** : the color or appearance

of the skin and especially of the face **2** : general appearance or impression

com·plex·i·ty *n, pl* **com·plex·i·ties** **1** : the quality or condition of being complex **2** : something complex

com·pli·cate *vb* **com·pli·cat·ed; com·pli·cat·ing** : to make or become complex or difficult

com·pli·ca·tion *n* **1** : a confused situation **2** : something that makes a situation more difficult

¹com·pli·ment *n* **1** : an act or expression of praise, approval, respect, or admiration **2 compliments** *pl* : best wishes

²com·pli·ment *vb* : to pay a compliment to

com·pli·men·ta·ry *adj* **1** : expressing or containing a compliment **2** : given free as a courtesy or favor

com·ply *vb* **com·plied; com·ply·ing** : to act in agreement with another's wishes or in obedience to a rule

com·po·nent *n* : one of the parts or units of a combination, mixture, or system

com·pose *vb* **com·posed; com·pos·ing** **1** : to form by putting together **2** : to be the parts or materials of **3** : to put in order : SETTLE

com·posed *adj* : being calm and in control of oneself

com·pos·er *n* **1** : a person who composes **2** : a writer of music

com·pos·ite *adj* : made up of different parts or elements

composite number *n* : an integer that is a product of two or more whole numbers each greater than 1

com·po·si·tion *n* **1** : the act of composing (as by writing) **2** : the manner in which the parts of a thing are put together **3** : MAKEUP 1, CONSTITUTION **4** : a literary, musical, or artistic production **5** : a short piece of writing done as a school exercise

com·post *n* : decayed organic material used to improve soil for growing crops

com·po·sure *n* : calmness especially of mind, manner, or appearance

¹com·pound *vb* **1** : to mix or unite together into a whole **2** : to form by combining separate things

²com·pound *adj* : made of or by the union of two or more parts

³com·pound *n* **1** : a word made up of parts that are themselves words **2** : something (as a chemical) that is formed by combining two or more parts or elements

⁴com·pound *n* : an enclosed area containing a group of buildings

compound fracture *n* : a breaking of a bone in which bone fragments stick out through the flesh

com·pre·hend *vb* **1** : to understand fully **2** : to take in : INCLUDE

com·pre·hen·sion *n* : ability to understand

com·pre·hen·sive *adj* : including much : INCLUSIVE — **com·pre·hen·sive·ness** *n*

¹com·press *vb* **1** : to press or squeeze together **2** : to reduce the volume of by pressure

²com·press *n* : a pad (as of folded cloth) applied firmly to a part of the body (as to check bleeding)

com·pres·sion *n* : the process of compressing : the state of being compressed

com·pres·sor *n* **1** : one that compresses **2** : a machine for compressing something (as air)

com·prise *vb* **com·prised; com·pris·ing** **1** : to be made up of : consist of **2** : ²FORM 3

¹com·pro·mise *n* **1** : an agreement over a dispute reached by each side changing or giving up some demands **2** : the thing agreed upon as a result of a compromise

²compromise *vb* **com·pro·mised; com·pro·mis·ing** **1** : to settle by compromise **2** : to expose to risk, suspicion, or disgrace

com·pul·sion *n* **1** : an act of compelling : the state of being compelled **2** : a force that compels **3** : a very strong urge to do something

com·pul·so·ry *adj* **1** : required by or as if by law **2** : having the power of forcing someone to do something

com·pu·ta·tion *n* **1** : the act or action of computing **2** : a result obtained by computing

com·pute *vb* **com·put·ed; com·put·ing** : to find out by using mathematics

com·put·er *n* : an automatic electronic machine that can store, recall, and process data

com·put·er·ize *vb* **com·put·er·ized; com·put·er·iz·ing** **1** : to carry out, control, or produce on a computer **2** : to equip with computers **3** : to put in a form that a computer can use

com·rade *n* : COMPANION 1

¹con *adv* : on the negative side

²con *n* : an opposing argument, person, or position

con- — see COM-

con·cave *adj* : hollow or rounded inward like the inside of a bowl

con·ceal *vb* **1** : to hide from sight **2** : to keep secret

con·ceal·ment *n* **1** : the act of hiding : the state of being hidden **2** : a hiding place

con·cede *vb* **con·ced·ed; con·ced·ing** **1** : to grant as a right or privilege **2** : to admit to be true

con·ceit *n* : too much pride in oneself or one's ability

con·ceit·ed *adj* : VAIN 2

con·ceiv·able *adj* : possible to conceive, imagine, or understand

con·ceive *vb* **con·ceived; con·ceiv·ing 1** : to form an idea of : IMAGINE **2** : THINK 2

con·cen·trate *vb* **con·cen·trat·ed; con·cen·trat·ing 1** : to bring or come to or direct toward a common center **2** : to make stronger or thicker by removing something (as water) **3** : to fix one's powers, efforts, or attentions on one thing

con·cen·tra·tion *n* **1** : the act or process of concentrating : the state of being concentrated **2** : close mental attention to a subject

con·cept *n* **1** : ^{2}THOUGHT 4 **2** : a general idea

^{1}con·cern *vb* **1** : to relate to : be about **2** : to be of interest or importance to : AFFECT **3** : to be a care, trouble, or distress to **4** : ENGAGE 3, OCCUPY

^{2}concern *n* **1** : something that relates to or involves a person : AFFAIR **2** : a state of interest and uncertainty **3** : a business organization

con·cerned *adj* : being worried and disturbed

con·cern·ing *prep* : relating to : ABOUT

con·cert *n* **1** : AGREEMENT 1 **2** : a musical performance by several voices or instruments or by both

con·cer·ti·na *n* : a small musical instrument like an accordion

con·cer·to *n, pl* **con·cer·tos** : a musical composition usually in three parts for orchestra with one or more principal instruments

con·ces·sion *n* **1** : the act or an instance of granting something **2** : something granted **3** : a special right or privilege given by an authority

conch *n, pl* **conchs** *or* **conch·es** : a very large sea snail with a tall thick spiral shell

con·cil·i·ate *vb* **con·cil·i·at·ed; con·cil·i·at·ing 1** : to bring into agreement : RECONCILE **2** : to gain or regain the goodwill or favor of

con·cise *adj* : expressing much in few words

con·clude *vb* **con·clud·ed; con·clud·ing 1** : to bring or come to an end : FINISH **2** : to form an opinion **3** : to bring about as a result

con·clu·sion *n* **1** : final decision reached by reasoning **2** : the last part of something **3** : a final settlement

con·clu·sive *adj* : DECISIVE 1 — **con·clu·sive·ly** *adv*

con·coct *vb* **1** : to prepare (as food) by putting several different things together **2** : to make up : DEVISE

con·cord *n* : a state of agreement

con·course *n* **1** : a flocking, moving, or flowing together (as of persons or streams) : GATHERING **2** : a place where roads or paths meet **3** : an open space or hall (as in a mall or railroad terminal) where crowds gather

^{1}con·crete *adj* **1** : ^{1}MATERIAL 1, REAL **2** : made of or relating to concrete

^{2}con·crete *n* : a hardened mixture of cement, sand, and water with gravel or broken stone used in construction (as of pavements and buildings)

con·cur *vb* **con·curred; con·cur·ring 1** : to act or happen together **2** : to be in agreement (as in action or opinion) : ACCORD

con·cus·sion *n* **1** : a sharp hard blow or the effect of this **2** : injury to the brain by jarring (as from a blow)

con·demn *vb* **1** : to declare to be wrong **2** : to declare guilty **3** : ^{2}SENTENCE **4** : to declare to be unfit for use

con·dem·na·tion *n* **1** : ^{1}CENSURE 1, BLAME **2** : the act of judicially condemning **3** : the state of being condemned

con·den·sa·tion *n* **1** : the act or process of condensing **2** : something that has been condensed

con·dense *vb* **con·densed; con·dens·ing** : to make or become more compact, more concise, closer, or denser : CONCENTRATE

con·de·scend *vb* **1** : to stoop to a level considered lower than one's own **2** : to grant favors with a show of being better than others

^{1}con·di·tion *n* **1** : something agreed upon or necessary if some other thing is to take place **2 conditions** *pl* : state of affairs **3** : state of being **4** : situation in life **5** : state of health or fitness

^{2}condition *vb* **1** : to put into the proper or desired condition **2** : to change the habits of usually by training

con·di·tion·al *adj* : depending on a condition

con·dor *n* : a very large American vulture having a bare head and neck and a frill of white feathers on the neck

^{1}con·duct *n* **1** : the act or way of carrying something on **2** : personal behavior

^{2}con·duct *vb* **1** : ^{2}GUIDE 1 **2** : to carry on or out from a position of command : LEAD **3** : BEHAVE 1 **4** : to have the quality of transmitting light, heat, sound, or electricity

con·duc·tion *n* **1** : the act of transporting something **2** : transmission through a conductor

con·duc·tor *n* **1** : a person in charge of a public means of transportation (as a train) **2** : a person or thing that directs or leads **3** : a substance or body capable of transmitting light, electricity, heat, or sound

cone *n* **1** : the scaly fruit of certain trees (as the pine or fir) **2** : a solid body tapering evenly to a point from a circular base **3** : something resembling a cone in shape **4** : an ice-cream holder **5** : a cell of the retina of the eye that is sensitive to colored light

con·fec·tion *n* : a fancy dish or sweet : DEL-ICACY, CANDY

con·fec·tion·er *n* : a maker of or dealer in confections (as candies)

con·fec·tion·ery *n, pl* **con·fec·tion·er·ies 1** : sweet things to eat (as candy) **2** : a confectioner's business or place of business

con·fed·er·a·cy *n, pl* **con·fed·er·a·cies 1** : a league of persons, parties, or states **2** *cap* : the eleven southern states that seceded from the United States in 1860 and 1861

¹con·fed·er·ate *adj* **1** : united in a league **2** *cap* : of or relating to the Confederacy

²confederate *n* **1** : a member of a confederacy **2** : ACCOMPLICE **3** *cap* : a soldier of or a person who sided with the Confederacy

³con·fed·er·ate *vb* **con·fed·er·at·ed; con·fed·er·at·ing** : to unite in an alliance or confederacy

con·fer *vb* **con·ferred; con·fer·ring 1** : BE-STOW, PRESENT **2** : to compare views especially in studying a problem

con·fer·ence *n* : a meeting for discussion or exchange of opinions

con·fess *vb* **1** : to tell of or make known (as something private or damaging to oneself) **2** : to make known one's sins to God or to a priest

con·fes·sion *n* **1** : an act of confessing **2** : an admission of guilt **3** : a formal statement of religious beliefs

con·fide *vb* **con·fid·ed; con·fid·ing 1** : to have or show faith **2** : to show confidence by telling secrets **3** : to tell in confidence **4** : ENTRUST 2

con·fi·dence *n* **1** : a feeling of trust or belief **2** : SELF-CONFIDENCE **3** : reliance on another's secrecy or loyalty **4** : ²SECRET

con·fi·dent *adj* : having or showing confidence — **con·fi·dent·ly** *adv*

con·fi·den·tial *adj* **1** : ¹SECRET 1 **2** : ²INTI-MATE 2 **3** : trusted with secret matters — **con·fi·den·tial·ly** *adv*

con·fine *vb* **con·fined; con·fin·ing 1** : to keep within limits **2** : to shut up : IM-PRISON **3** : to keep indoors — **con·fine·ment** *n*

con·fines *n pl* : the boundary or limits of something

con·firm *vb* **1** : to make firm or firmer (as in a habit, in faith, or in intention) : STRENGTHEN **2** : APPROVE 2, ACCEPT **3** : to administer the rite of confirmation to **4** : to make sure of the truth of

con·fir·ma·tion *n* **1** : an act of confirming **2** : a religious ceremony admitting a person to full privileges in a church or synagogue **3** : something that confirms

con·firmed *adj* **1** : being firmly established **2** : unlikely to change

con·fis·cate *vb* **con·fis·cat·ed; con·fis·cat·ing** : to seize by or as if by public authority

con·fla·gra·tion *n* : a large destructive fire

¹con·flict *n* **1** : an extended struggle : BAT-TLE **2** : a clashing disagreement (as between ideas or interests)

²con·flict *vb* : to be in opposition

con·form *vb* **1** : to make or be like : AGREE, ACCORD **2** : COMPLY

con·for·mi·ty *n, pl* **con·for·mi·ties 1** : agreement in form, manner, or character **2** : action in accordance with some standard or authority

con·found *vb* : to throw into disorder : mix up : CONFUSE

con·front *vb* **1** : to face especially in challenge : OPPOSE **2** : to cause to face or meet

con·fuse *vb* **con·fused; con·fus·ing 1** : to make mentally foggy or uncertain : PER-PLEX **2** : to make embarrassed **3** : to fail to tell apart

con·fu·sion *n* **1** : an act or instance of confusing **2** : the state of being confused

con·geal *vb* **1** : to change from a fluid to a solid state by or as if by cold : FREEZE **2** : to make or become hard, stiff, or thick

con·ge·nial *adj* **1** : alike or sympathetic in nature, disposition, or tastes **2** : existing together in harmony **3** : tending to please or satisfy

con·gest *vb* : to make too crowded or full : CLOG

¹con·glom·er·ate *adj* : made up of parts from various sources or of various kinds

²conglomerate *n* : a mass (as a rock) formed of fragments from various sources

con·grat·u·late *vb* **con·grat·u·lat·ed; con·grat·u·lat·ing** : to express pleasure on account of success or good fortune

con·grat·u·la·tion *n* **1** : the act of congratulating **2** : an expression of joy or pleasure at another's success or good fortune — usually used in pl.

con·gre·gate *vb* **con·gre·gat·ed; con·gre·gat·ing** : to collect or gather into a crowd or group : ASSEMBLE

con·gre·ga·tion *n* **1** : a gathering or collection of persons or things **2** : an assembly of persons gathered especially for religious worship **3** : the membership of a church or synagogue

con·gress *n* **1** : a formal meeting of delegates for discussion and action : CONFER-

ENCE **2** : the chief lawmaking body of a nation and especially of a republic that in the United States is made up of separate houses of senators and representatives

con·gress·man *n, pl* **con·gress·men** : a member of a congress and especially of the United States House of Representatives

con·gress·wom·an *n, pl* **con·gress·wom·en** : a woman member of a congress and especially of the United States House of Representatives

con·gru·ent *adj* : having the same size and shape

con·ic *adj* **1** : CONICAL **2** : of or relating to a cone

con·i·cal *adj* : shaped like a cone

co·ni·fer *n* : any of a group of mostly evergreen trees and shrubs (as pines) that produce cones — **co·nif·er·ous** *adj*

1con·jec·ture *n* : [2]GUESS

2conjecture *vb* **con·jec·tured; con·jec·tur·ing** : [1]GUESS 1, SURMISE

con·junc·tion *n* **1** : a joining together : UNION **2** : a word or expression that joins together sentences, clauses, phrases, or words

con·jure *vb* **con·jured; con·jur·ing** **1** : to beg earnestly or solemnly : BESEECH **2** : to practice magical arts **3** : IMAGINE 1

con·nect *vb* **1** : to join or link together **2** : to attach by close personal relationship **3** : to bring together in thought — **con·nec·tor** *n*

con·nec·tion *n* **1** : the act of connecting **2** : the fact or condition of being connected : RELATIONSHIP **3** : a thing that connects : BOND, LINK **4** : a person connected with others (as by kinship) **5** : a social, professional, or commercial relationship **6** : the act or the means of continuing a journey by transferring (as to another train)

con·nois·seur *n* : a person qualified to act as a judge in matters involving taste and appreciation

con·quer *vb* **1** : to get or gain by force : win by fighting **2** : OVERCOME 1

con·quer·or *n* : one that conquers : VICTOR

con·quest *n* **1** : the act or process of conquering : VICTORY **2** : something that is conquered

con·quis·ta·dor *n, pl* **con·quis·ta·do·res** *or* **con·quis·ta·dors** : a leader in the Spanish conquest especially of Mexico and Peru in the sixteenth century

con·science *n* : knowledge of right and wrong and a feeling that one should do what is right

con·sci·en·tious *adj* **1** : guided by or agreeing with one's conscience **2** : using or done with careful attention

con·scious *adj* **1** : aware of facts or feelings **2** : known or felt by one's inner self **3** : mentally awake or active **4** : INTENTIONAL — **con·scious·ly** *adv*

con·scious·ness *n* **1** : the condition of being conscious **2** : the upper level of mental life involving conscious thought and the will

con·se·crate *vb* **con·se·crat·ed; con·se·crat·ing** **1** : to declare to be sacred or holy : set apart for the service of God **2** : to dedicate to a particular purpose

con·sec·u·tive *adj* : following one another in order without gaps

1con·sent *vb* : to express willingness or approval : AGREE

2consent *n* : approval of or agreement with what is done or suggested by another person

con·se·quence *n* **1** : something produced by a cause or following from a condition **2** : real importance

con·se·quent *adj* : following as a result or effect

con·se·quent·ly *adv* : as a result

con·ser·va·tion *n* **1** : PROTECTION 1, PRESERVATION **2** : planned management of natural resources (as timber) to prevent waste, destruction, or neglect

1con·ser·va·tive *adj* **1** : favoring a policy of keeping things as they are : opposed to change **2** : favoring established styles and standards — **con·ser·va·tive·ly** *adv*

2conservative *n* : a person who holds conservative views : a cautious person

con·ser·va·to·ry *n, pl* **con·ser·va·to·ries** **1** : GREENHOUSE **2** : a place of instruction in some special study (as music)

1con·serve *vb* **con·served; con·serv·ing** : to keep in a safe condition : SAVE

2con·serve *n* **1** : a candied fruit **2** : a rich fruit preserve

con·sid·er *vb* **1** : to think over carefully : PONDER, REFLECT **2** : to treat in a kind or thoughtful way **3** : to think of in a certain way : BELIEVE

con·sid·er·able *adj* : rather large in extent, amount, or size — **con·sid·er·ably** *adv*

con·sid·er·ate *adj* : thoughtful of the rights and feelings of others

con·sid·er·ation *n* **1** : careful thought : DELIBERATION **2** : thoughtfulness for other people **3** : something that needs to be considered before deciding or acting **4** : a payment made in return for something

con·sign *vb* **1** : ENTRUST 2 **2** : to give, transfer, or deliver to another **3** : to send (as goods) to an agent to be sold or cared for — **con·sign·ment** *n*

con·sist *vb* : to be made up or composed

con·sis·ten·cy *n, pl* **con·sis·ten·cies** **1** : degree of compactness, firmness, or stickiness **2** : agreement or harmony between parts or elements **3** : a sticking with one way of thinking or acting

con·sis·tent *adj* : showing consistency — **con·sis·tent·ly** *adv*

con·so·la·tion *n* **1** : the act of consoling : the state of being consoled **2** : something that lessens disappointment, misery, or grief

¹con·sole *n* **1** : the part of an organ at which the organist sits and which contains the keyboard and controls **2** : a panel or cabinet on which are dials and switches for controlling an electronic or mechanical device **3** : a radio, phonograph, or television cabinet that stands on the floor

²con·sole *vb* **con·soled; con·sol·ing** : to comfort in a time of grief or distress

con·sol·i·date *vb* **con·sol·i·dat·ed; con·sol·i·dat·ing** **1** : to join together into one whole : UNITE **2** : STRENGTHEN

con·so·nant *n* **1** : a speech sound (as \p\, \n\, or \s\) produced by narrowing or closing the breath channel at one or more points **2** : a letter in the English alphabet other than *a, e, i, o,* or *u*

¹con·sort *n* : a wife or husband especially of a king or queen

²con·sort *vb* : to go together as companions : ASSOCIATE

con·spic·u·ous *adj* **1** : easily seen **2** : attracting attention : PROMINENT

con·spir·a·cy *n, pl* **con·spir·a·cies** **1** : the act of conspiring or plotting **2** : an agreement among conspirators **3** : a group of conspirators

con·spir·a·tor *n* : a person who conspires

con·spire *vb* **con·spired; con·spir·ing** **1** : to make an agreement especially in secret to do an unlawful act : PLOT **2** : to act together

con·sta·ble *n* : a police officer usually of a village or small town

con·stan·cy *n* : firmness and loyalty in one's beliefs or personal relationships

con·stant *adj* **1** : always faithful and true **2** : remaining steady and unchanged **3** : occurring over and over again — **con·stant·ly** *adv*

con·stel·la·tion *n* : any of eighty-eight groups of stars forming patterns

con·ster·na·tion *n* : amazement, alarm, or disappointment that makes one feel helpless or confused

con·sti·pate *vb* **con·sti·pat·ed; con·sti·pat·ing** : to cause constipation in

con·sti·pa·tion *n* : difficult or infrequent passage of dry hard material from the bowels

¹con·stit·u·ent *n* **1** : one of the parts or materials of which something is made : ELEMENT, INGREDIENT **2** : any of the voters who elect a person to represent them

²constituent *adj* **1** : serving to form or make up a unit or whole **2** : having power to elect or appoint or to make or change a constitution

con·sti·tute *vb* **con·sti·tut·ed; con·sti·tut·ing** **1** : to appoint to an office or duty **2** : SET UP **2** **3** : to make up : FORM

con·sti·tu·tion *n* **1** : the bodily makeup of an individual **2** : the basic structure of something **3** : the basic beliefs and laws of a nation, state, or social group by which the powers and duties of the government are established and certain rights are guaranteed to the people

¹con·sti·tu·tion·al *adj* **1** : having to do with a person's bodily or mental makeup **2** : of, relating to, or in agreement with a constitution (as of a nation)

²constitutional *n* : an exercise (as a walk) taken for one's health

con·strain *vb* : COMPEL, FORCE

con·straint *n* **1** : COMPULSION **1, 2** **2** : a keeping back of one's natural feelings

con·strict *vb* : to make narrower or smaller by drawing together : SQUEEZE

con·stric·tion *n* : an act or instance of constricting

con·stric·tor *n* : a snake (as a boa) that kills prey by crushing in its coils

con·struct *vb* : to make or form by combining parts

con·struc·tion *n* **1** : the arrangement of words and the relationship between words in a sentence **2** : the process, art, or manner of constructing **3** : something built or put together : STRUCTURE **4** : INTERPRETATION

construction paper *n* : a thick paper available in many colors for school art work

con·struc·tive *adj* : helping to develop or improve something

con·strue *vb* **con·strued; con·stru·ing** : to understand or explain the sense or intention of

con·sul *n* : an official appointed by a government to live in a foreign country in order to look after the commercial interests of citizens of the appointing country

con·sult *vb* **1** : to seek the opinion or advice of **2** : to seek information from **3** : to talk something over

con·sul·ta·tion *n* **1** : a discussion between doctors on a case or its treatment **2** : the act of consulting

con·sume *vb* **con·sumed; con·sum·ing** **1** : to destroy by or as if by fire **2** : to use up

: SPEND **3** : to eat or drink up **4** : to take up the interest or attention of

con·sum·er *n* **1** : one that consumes **2** : a person who buys and uses up goods

con·sump·tion *n* **1** : the act or process of consuming and especially of using up something (as food or coal) **2** : a wasting away of the body especially from tuberculosis of the lungs

¹con·tact *n* **1** : a meeting or touching of persons or things **2** : a person one knows who has influence especially in the business or political world

²contact *vb* **1** : to come or bring into contact **2** : to get in touch or communication with

³contact *adj* : involving or activated by contact

contact lens *n* : a thin lens used to correct bad eyesight and worn right over the cornea of the eye

con·ta·gion *n* **1** : the passing of a disease from one individual to another as a result of some contact between them **2** : a contagious disease

con·ta·gious *adj* : spreading by contagion

con·tain *vb* **1** : to keep within limits : RESTRAIN, CHECK **2** : to have within : HOLD **3** : to consist of or include

con·tain·er *n* : something into which other things can be put (as for storage)

con·tam·i·nate *vb* **con·tam·i·nat·ed; con·tam·i·nat·ing** **1** : to soil, stain, or infect by contact or association **2** : to make unfit for use by adding something harmful or unpleasant

con·tem·plate *vb* **con·tem·plat·ed; con·tem·plat·ing** **1** : to view with careful and thoughtful attention **2** : to have in mind : plan on

con·tem·pla·tion *n* **1** : the act of thinking about spiritual things : MEDITATION **2** : the act of looking at or thinking about something for some time **3** : a looking ahead to some future event

¹con·tem·po·rary *adj* **1** : living or occurring at the same period of time **2** : MODERN 1

²contemporary *n, pl* **con·tem·po·rar·ies** : a person who lives at the same time or is of about the same age as another

con·tempt *n* **1** : the act of despising : the state of mind of one who despises **2** : the state of being despised

con·tempt·ible *adj* : deserving contempt

con·temp·tu·ous *adj* : feeling or showing contempt : SCORNFUL

con·tend *vb* **1** : COMPETE **2** : to try hard to deal with **3** : to argue or state earnestly

¹con·tent *adj* : pleased and satisfied with what one has or is

²content *vb* : to make content : SATISFY

³content *n* : freedom from care or discomfort

⁴con·tent *n* **1** : something contained — usually used in pl. **2** : the subject or topic treated (as in a book) — usually used in pl. **3** : the important part or meaning (as of a book) **4** : the amount contained or possible to contain

con·tent·ed *adj* : satisfied or showing satisfaction with one's possessions or one's situation in life

con·ten·tion *n* **1** : an act or instance of contending **2** : an idea or point for which a person argues (as in a debate or argument) **3** : COMPETITION 2

con·tent·ment *n* : freedom from worry or restlessness : peaceful satisfaction

¹con·test *vb* : to make (something) a cause of dispute or fighting

²con·test *n* : a struggle for victory : COMPETITION

con·tes·tant *n* : one who takes part in a contest

con·ti·nent *n* **1** : one of the great divisions of land on the globe (as Africa, Antarctica, Asia, Australia, Europe, North America, or South America) **2** *cap* : the continent of Europe

con·ti·nen·tal *adj* : of or relating to a continent

con·tin·gent *adj* : depending on something else that may or may not exist or occur

con·tin·u·al *adj* **1** : going on without stopping **2** : occurring again and again at short intervals — **con·tin·u·al·ly** *adv*

con·tin·u·ance *n* **1** : the act of continuing **2** : the quality of being continual

con·tin·u·a·tion *n* **1** : the making longer of a state or activity **2** : a going on after stopping **3** : a thing or part by which something is continued

con·tin·ue *vb* **con·tin·ued; con·tinu·ing** **1** : to do or cause to do the same thing without changing or stopping **2** : to begin again after stopping

con·ti·nu·i·ty *n, pl* **con·ti·nu·i·ties** : the quality or state of being continuous

con·tin·u·ous *adj* : continuing without a stop — **con·tin·u·ous·ly** *adv*

con·tort *vb* : to give an unusual appearance or unnatural shape to by twisting

con·tor·tion *n* **1** : a twisting or a being twisted out of shape **2** : a contorted shape or thing

con·tour *n* **1** : the outline of a figure, body, or surface **2** : a line or a drawing showing an outline

contra- *prefix* **1** : against : contrary : contrasting **2** : pitched below normal bass

con·tra·band *n* **1** : goods forbidden by law to be owned or to be brought into or out of a country **2** : smuggled goods

¹con·tract *n* **1** : an agreement that the law can force one to keep **2** : a writing made to show the terms and conditions of a contract

²con·tract *vb* **1** : to agree by contract **2** : to become sick with : CATCH **3** : to draw together and make shorter and broader **4** : to make or become smaller : SHRINK **5** : to make (as a word) shorter by dropping sounds or letters

con·trac·tion *n* **1** : the act or process of contracting : the state of being contracted **2** : a shortening of a word or word group by leaving out a sound or letter **3** : a form (as *don't* or *they've*) produced by contraction

con·tra·dict *vb* **1** : to deny the truth of a statement : say the opposite of what someone else has said **2** : to be opposed to

con·tra·dic·tion *n* : something (as a statement) that contradicts something else

con·tra·dic·to·ry *adj* : involving, causing, or being a contradiction

con·tral·to *n, pl* **con·tral·tos** **1** : the lowest female singing voice : ALTO **2** : a singer with a contralto voice

con·trap·tion *n* : GADGET

¹con·trary *n, pl* **con·trar·ies** : something opposite or contrary — **on the contrary** : just the opposite : NO

²con·trary *adj* **1** : exactly opposite **2** : being against what is usual or expected **3** : not favorable **4** : unwilling to accept control or advice

¹con·trast *vb* **1** : to show noticeable differences **2** : to compare two persons or things so as to show the differences between them

²con·trast *n* **1** : difference or the amount of difference (as in color or brightness) between adjacent parts **2** : difference or amount of difference between related or similar things

con·trib·ute *vb* **con·trib·ut·ed; con·trib·ut·ing** **1** : to give along with others **2** : to have a share in something **3** : to supply (as an article) for publication especially in a magazine — **con·trib·u·tor** *n*

con·tri·bu·tion *n* **1** : the act of contributing **2** : the sum or thing contributed

con·trite *adj* : feeling or showing sorrow for some wrong that one has done : REPENTANT

con·triv·ance *n* : something (as a scheme or a mechanical device) produced with skill and cleverness

con·trive *vb* **con·trived; con·triv·ing** **1** : ²PLAN 1, PLOT **2** : to form or make in some skillful or clever way **3** : to manage to bring about or do

¹con·trol *vb* **con·trolled; con·trol·ling** **1** : to keep within bounds : RESTRAIN **2** : to have power over

²control *n* **1** : the power or authority to control or command **2** : ability to control **3** : SELF-RESTRAINT **4** : REGULATION **5** : a device used to start, stop, or change the operation of a machine or system **6** : something used in an experiment or study to provide a check on results

con·tro·ver·sial *adj* : relating to or causing controversy

con·tro·ver·sy *n, pl* **con·tro·ver·sies** **1** : an often long or heated discussion of something about which there is great difference of opinion **2** : ¹QUARREL 2

co·nun·drum *n* : ¹RIDDLE

con·va·lesce *vb* **con·va·lesced; con·va·lesc·ing** : to regain health and strength gradually after sickness or injury

con·va·les·cence *n* : the period or process of convalescing

¹con·va·les·cent *adj* : passing through convalescence

²convalescent *n* : a person who is convalescent

con·vec·tion *n* : motion in a gas (as air) or a liquid in which the warmer portions rise and the colder portions sink

con·vene *vb* **con·vened; con·ven·ing** **1** : ASSEMBLE 3 **2** : to cause to assemble

con·ve·nience *n* **1** : the quality or state of being convenient **2** : personal comfort **3** : OPPORTUNITY 1 **4** : something that gives comfort or advantage

con·ve·nient *adj* **1** : suited to a person's comfort or ease **2** : suited to a certain use **3** : easy to get to — **con·ve·nient·ly** *adv*

con·vent *n* **1** : a group of nuns living together **2** : a house or a set of buildings occupied by a community of nuns

con·ven·tion *n* **1** : AGREEMENT 2 **2** : a custom or a way of acting and doing things that is widely accepted and followed **3** : a meeting of persons gathered together for a common purpose

con·ven·tion·al *adj* **1** : behaving according to convention **2** : used or accepted through convention

con·ver·sa·tion *n* : talking or a talk between two or more people

con·verse *vb* **con·versed; con·vers·ing** : to have a conversation

con·ver·sion *n* **1** : the act of converting : the state of being converted **2** : a change in the nature or form of a thing **3** : a change of religion

¹con·vert *vb* **1** : to change from one belief,

religion, view, or party to another **2** : to change from one form to another **3** : to exchange for an equivalent

²con·vert n : a person who has been converted

¹con·vert·ible adj : possible to change in form or use

²convertible n **1** : something that is convertible **2** : an automobile with a top that can be raised, lowered, or removed

con·vex adj : rounded like the outside of a ball or circle

con·vey vb **con·veyed; con·vey·ing 1** : to carry from one place to another : TRANSPORT **2** : to serve as a way of carrying **3** : IMPART 2, COMMUNICATE

con·vey·ance n **1** : the act of conveying **2** : something used to carry goods or passengers

¹con·vict vb : to prove or find guilty

²con·vict n : a person serving a prison sentence usually for a long time

con·vic·tion n **1** : the act of convicting : the state of being convicted **2** : the state of mind of a person who is sure that what he or she believes or says is true **3** : a strong belief or opinion

con·vince vb **con·vinced; con·vinc·ing** : to argue so as to make a person agree or believe

con·vinc·ing adj : causing one to believe or agree : PERSUASIVE — **con·vinc·ing·ly** adv

con·vulse vb **con·vulsed; con·vuls·ing** : to shake violently or with jerky motions

con·vul·sion n **1** : an attack of violent involuntary muscular contractions : FIT **2** : a violent disturbance : UPHEAVAL

con·vul·sive adj : being or producing a convulsion — **con·vul·sive·ly** adv

¹coo vb **cooed; coo·ing 1** : to make the soft sound made by doves and pigeons or one like it **2** : to talk fondly or lovingly

²coo n, pl **coos** : the sound made in cooing

¹cook n : a person who prepares food for eating

²cook vb **1** : to prepare food for eating by the use of heat **2** : to go through the process of being cooked

cook·book n : a book of cooking recipes and directions

cook·ie or **cooky** n, pl **cook·ies** : a small sweet cake

cook·out n : an outing at which a meal is cooked and served outdoors

cook up vb : to think up : DEVISE

¹cool adj **1** : somewhat cold : not warm **2** : not letting or keeping in heat **3** : ³CALM 2 **4** : not friendly or interested : INDIFFERENT — **cool·ly** adv

²cool vb : to make or become cool

³cool n : a cool time or place

cool·er n : a container for keeping food or drink cool

coon n : RACCOON

¹coop n : a building for housing poultry

²coop vb : to restrict to a small space

coo·per n : a worker who makes or repairs wooden casks, tubs, or barrels

co·op·er·ate vb **co·op·er·at·ed; co·op·er·at·ing** : to act or work together so as to get something done

co·op·er·a·tion n : the act or process of cooperating

¹co·op·er·a·tive adj **1** : willing to cooperate or work with others **2** : of, relating to, or organized as a cooperative

²cooperative n : an association formed to enable its members to buy or sell to better advantage

¹co·or·di·nate adj : equal in rank or importance

²co·or·di·nate vb **co·or·di·nat·ed; co·or·di·nat·ing** : to work or cause to work together smoothly

co·or·di·na·tion n : smooth working together (as of parts)

cop n : POLICE OFFICER

cope vb **coped; cop·ing** : to struggle or try to manage especially with some success

copi·er n **1** : a person who copies **2** : a machine for making copies (as of letters or drawings)

co·pi·lot n : an assistant airplane pilot

co·pi·ous adj : very plentiful : ABUNDANT — **co·pi·ous·ly** adv

cop·per n **1** : a tough reddish metallic chemical element that is one of the best conductors of heat and electricity **2** : a copper or bronze coin

cop·per·head n : a mottled reddish brown poisonous snake of the eastern United States

cop·pice n : a thicket, grove, or growth of small trees

co·pra n : dried coconut meat

copse n : COPPICE

¹copy n, pl **cop·ies 1** : something that is made to look exactly like something else : DUPLICATE **2** : one of the total number of books, magazines, or papers printed at one time **3** : written or printed material to be set in type

²copy vb **cop·ied; copy·ing 1** : to make a copy of : DUPLICATE **2** : IMITATE 1 3

¹copy·right n : the legal right to be the only one to reproduce, publish, and sell the contents and form of a literary or artistic work

²copyright vb : to get a copyright on

¹cor·al n **1** : a stony or horny material consisting of the skeletons of tiny colonial sea animals related to the jellyfishes and including one kind that is red and used in jewelry **2 :** one or a colony of the animals that form coral **3 :** a dark pink

²coral *adj* **1 :** made of coral **2 :** of the color of coral

coral snake *n* **:** a small poisonous American snake brightly ringed with red, black, and yellow or white

cord *n* **1 :** material like a small thin rope that is used mostly for tying things **2 :** something like a cord **3 :** an amount of firewood equal to a pile of wood eight feet long, four feet high, and four feet wide or 128 cubic feet (about 3.6 cubic meters) **4 :** a rib or ridge woven into cloth **5 :** a ribbed fabric **6 :** a small insulated cable used to connect an electrical appliance with an outlet

cord·ed *adj* **:** having or drawn into ridges or cords

cor·dial *adj* **:** being warm and friendly — **cor·dial·ly** *adv*

cor·dial·i·ty *n* **:** sincere affection and kindness

cor·du·roy *n* **1 :** a heavy ribbed usually cotton cloth **2 corduroys** *pl* **:** trousers made of corduroy **3 :** logs laid crosswise side by side to make a road surface

¹core *n* **1 :** the central part of some fruits (as pineapples or pears) **2 :** the central part of a heavenly body (as the earth or sun) **3 :** the basic or central part of something

²core *vb* **cored; cor·ing :** to remove the core from

¹cork *n* **1 :** the light but tough material that is the outer layer of bark of a tree (**cork oak**) and is used especially for stoppers and insulation **2 :** a usually cork stopper for a bottle or jug

²cork *vb* **:** to stop with a cork

¹cork·screw *n* **:** a pointed spiral piece of metal with a handle that is screwed into corks to draw them from bottles

²corkscrew *adj* **:** like a corkscrew

cor·mo·rant *n* **:** a large black seabird with a long neck and a slender hooked beak

¹corn *n* **1 :** the seeds or grain of a cereal plant (as wheat or oats) **2 :** INDIAN CORN **3 :** a plant whose seeds are corn

²corn *vb* **:** to preserve by packing with salt or by soaking in salty water

³corn *n* **:** a hardening and thickening of the skin (as on a person's toe)

corn·cob *n* **:** the woody core on which grains of Indian corn grow

cor·nea *n* **:** the transparent outer layer of the front of the eye covering the pupil and iris

¹cor·ner *n* **1 :** the point or place where edges or sides meet **2 :** the place where two streets or roads meet **3 :** a piece used to mark, form, or protect a corner (as of a book) **4 :** a place away from ordinary life or business **5 :** a position from which escape or retreat is difficult or impossible — **cor·nered** *adj*

²corner *adj* **1 :** located at a corner **2 :** used or usable in or on a corner

³corner *vb* **1 :** to drive into a corner **2 :** to put in a difficult position

cor·net *n* **:** a brass musical instrument similar to but shorter than a trumpet

corn·flow·er *n* **:** a European plant related to the daisies that is often grown for its bright heads of blue, pink, or white flowers

cor·nice *n* **1 :** an ornamental piece that forms the top edge of the front of a building or pillar **2 :** an ornamental molding placed where the walls meet the ceiling of a room

corn·meal *n* **:** meal ground from corn

corn·stalk *n* **:** a stalk of Indian corn

corn·starch *n* **:** a fine starch made from Indian corn and used as a thickening agent in cooking

corn syrup *n* **:** a syrup made from cornstarch and used chiefly in baked goods and candy

cor·nu·co·pia *n* **:** a container in the shape of a horn overflowing with fruits and flowers used as a symbol of plenty

corny *adj* **corn·i·er; corn·i·est :** so simple, sentimental, or old-fashioned as to be annoying

co·rol·la *n* **:** the part of a flower that is formed by the petals

cor·o·nary *adj* **:** of or relating to the heart or its blood vessels

cor·o·na·tion *n* **:** the act or ceremony of crowning a king or queen

cor·o·net *n* **1 :** a small crown worn by a person of noble but less than royal rank **2 :** an ornamental wreath or band worn around the head

¹cor·po·ral *adj* **:** of or relating to the body **:** BODILY

²corporal *n* **:** a noncommissioned officer ranking above a private in the Army or above a lance corporal in the Marine Corps

cor·po·ra·tion *n* **:** a group authorized by law to carry on an activity (as a business) with the rights and duties of a single person

cor·po·re·al *adj* **:** having, consisting of, or relating to a physical body

corps *n, pl* **corps 1 :** an organized branch of a country's military forces **2 :** a group of persons acting under one authority

corpse *n* **:** a dead body

cor·pu·lent *adj* **:** very stout and heavy **:** extremely fat

cor·pus·cle *n* **:** one of the very small cells that float freely in the blood

¹**cor·ral** *n* : an enclosure for keeping or capturing animals

²**corral** *vb* **cor·ralled; cor·ral·ling 1** : to confine in or as if in a corral **2** : to get hold of or control over

¹**cor·rect** *vb* **1** : to make or set right **2** : to change or adjust so as to bring to some standard or to a required condition **3** : to punish in order to improve **4** : to show how a thing can be improved or made right

²**correct** *adj* **1** : meeting or agreeing with some standard : APPROPRIATE **2** : free from mistakes : ACCURATE — **cor·rect·ly** *adv* — **cor·rect·ness** *n*

cor·rec·tion *n* **1** : the act of correcting **2** : a change that makes something right **3** : PUNISHMENT 1

cor·re·spond *vb* **1** : to be alike : AGREE **2** : to be equivalent **3** : to communicate with a person by exchange of letters

cor·re·spon·dence *n* **1** : agreement between certain things **2** : communication by means of letters : the letters exchanged

cor·re·spon·dent *n* **1** : a person with whom another person communicates by letter **2** : a person who sends news stories or comment to a newspaper, magazine, or broadcasting company especially from a distant place

cor·ri·dor *n* : a passage into which rooms open

cor·rode *vb* **cor·rod·ed; cor·rod·ing** : to wear away little by little (as by rust or acid)

cor·ro·sion *n* : the process or effect of corroding

cor·ro·sive *adj* : tending or able to corrode

cor·ru·gate *vb* **cor·ru·gat·ed; cor·ru·gat·ing** : to make wrinkles in or shape into wavy folds

¹**cor·rupt** *vb* **1** : to change (as in morals, manners, or actions) from good to bad **2** : to influence a public official in an improper way (as by a bribe)

²**corrupt** *adj* **1** : morally bad : EVIL **2** : behaving in a bad or improper way : doing wrong — **cor·rupt·ly** *adv* — **cor·rupt·ness** *n*

cor·rup·tion *n* **1** : physical decay or rotting **2** : lack of honesty **3** : the causing of someone else to do something wrong **4** : a being changed for the worse

cor·sage *n* : a bouquet of flowers usually worn on the shoulder

corse·let *or* **cors·let** *n* : the body armor worn by a knight especially on the upper part of the body

cor·set *n* : a tight undergarment worn to support or give shape to waist and hips

cos·met·ic *n* : material (as a cream, lotion, or powder) used to beautify especially the complexion

cos·mic *adj* : of or relating to the whole universe

cosmic ray *n* : a stream of very penetrating particles that enter the earth's atmosphere from outer space at high speed

cos·mo·naut *n* : a Soviet astronaut

cos·mos *n* **1** : the orderly universe **2** : a tall garden plant related to the daisies that has showy white, pink, or rose-colored flower heads

¹**cost** *n* **1** : the amount paid or charged for something : PRICE **2** : loss or penalty involved in gaining something

²**cost** *vb* **cost; cost·ing 1** : to have a price of **2** : to cause one to pay, spend, or lose

cost·ly *adj* **cost·li·er; cost·li·est 1** : of great cost or value : EXPENSIVE, DEAR **2** : made at great expense or sacrifice

¹**cos·tume** *n* **1** : style of clothing, ornaments, and hair used especially during a certain period, in a certain region, or by a certain class or group **2** : special or fancy dress (as for wear on the stage or at a masquerade) **3** : a person's outer garments

²**costume** *vb* **cos·tumed; cos·tum·ing 1** : to provide with a costume **2** : to design costumes for

¹**cot** *n* : a small house : COTTAGE, HUT

²**cot** *n* : a narrow bed often made to fold up

cot·tage *n* **1** : a small usually frame house for one family **2** : a small house for vacation use

cottage cheese *n* : a very soft cheese made from soured skim milk

¹**cot·ton** *n* **1** : a soft fluffy material made up of twisted hairs that surrounds the seeds of a tall plant (**cotton plant**) related to the mallows and that is spun into yarn **2** : thread, yarn, or cloth made from cotton

²**cotton** *adj* : made of cotton

cotton gin *n* : a machine for removing seeds from cotton

cot·ton·mouth *n* : MOCCASIN 2

cot·ton·seed *n* : the seed of the cotton plant from which comes a meal rich in protein and an oil used especially in cooking

cot·ton·tail *n* : a small rabbit with a white tail

cot·ton·wood *n* : any of several poplar trees that have seeds with bunches of hairs suggesting cotton and that include some which grow rapidly

couch *n* : a piece of furniture (as a bed or sofa) that one can sit or lie on

cou·gar *n* : a large yellowish brown North American wild animal related to the domestic cat

¹**cough** *vb* **1** : to force air from the lungs

with a sharp short noise or series of noises **2 :** to get rid of by coughing

²cough *n* **1 :** a condition in which there is severe or frequent coughing **2 :** an act or sound of coughing

could *past of* CAN **1 —** used as a helping verb in the past **2 —** used as a polite form instead of *can*

couldn't : could not

coun·cil *n* **:** a group of persons appointed or elected to make laws or give advice

coun·cil·or *or* **coun·cil·lor** *n* **:** a member of a council

¹coun·sel *n* **1 :** advice given **2 :** the discussion of reasons for or against a thing : an exchange of opinions **3** *pl* **counsel :** a lawyer engaged in the trial and management of a case in court

²counsel *vb* **coun·seled** *or* **coun·selled; coun·sel·ing** *or* **coun·sel·ling 1 :** to give counsel : ADVISE **2 :** to seek counsel

coun·sel·or *or* **coun·sel·lor** *n* **1 :** a person who gives counsel **2 :** LAWYER **3 :** a supervisor of campers or activities at a summer camp

¹count *vb* **1 :** to add one by one in order to find the total number in a collection **2 :** to name the numerals in order up to a particular point **3 :** to name the numbers one by one or by groups **4 :** to include in counting or thinking about **5 :** to consider or judge to be **6 :** to include or leave out by or as if by counting **7 :** RELY, DEPEND **8 :** ²PLAN 1 **9 :** to have value, force, or importance

²count *n* **1 :** the act or process of counting **2 :** a total arrived at by counting **3 :** any one charge in a legal declaration or indictment

³count *n* **:** a European nobleman whose rank is like that of a British earl

count·down *n* **:** a counting off of the time remaining before an event (as the launching of a rocket)

¹coun·te·nance *n* **:** the human face or its expression

²countenance *vb* **coun·te·nanced; coun·te·nanc·ing :** to give approval or tolerance to

¹count·er *n* **1 :** a piece (as of plastic or ivory) used in counting or in games **2 :** a level surface usually higher than a table that is used for selling, serving food, displaying things, or working on

²count·er *n* **1 :** one that counts **2 :** a device for showing a number or amount

³coun·ter *vb* **1 :** to act in opposition to : OPPOSE **2 :** RETALIATE

⁴coun·ter *adv* **:** in another or opposite direction

⁵coun·ter *n* **:** an answering or opposing force or blow

⁶coun·ter *adj* **:** moving or acting in an opposite way : CONTRARY

coun·ter- *prefix* **1 :** opposite **2 :** opposing **3 :** like : matching **4 :** duplicate : substitute

coun·ter·act *vb* **:** to act against so as to prevent something from acting in its own way

coun·ter·clock·wise *adv or adj* **:** in a direction opposite to that in which the hands of a clock move

¹coun·ter·feit *adj* **1 :** made in exact imitation of something genuine and meant to be taken as genuine **2 :** not sincere

²counterfeit *vb* **1 :** PRETEND 2 **2 :** to imitate or copy especially in order to deceive **— coun·ter·feit·er** *n*

³counterfeit *n* **:** something made to imitate another thing with the desire to deceive

coun·ter·part *n* **:** a person or thing that is very like or corresponds to another person or thing

coun·ter·point *n* **:** one or more independent melodies added above or below and in harmony with a given melody

coun·ter·sign *n* **:** a secret signal that must be given by a person wishing to pass a guard **:** PASSWORD

count·ess *n* **1 :** the wife or widow of a count or an earl **2 :** a woman who holds the rank of a count or an earl in her own right

counting number *n* **:** NATURAL NUMBER

count·less *adj* **:** too many to be counted

coun·try *n, pl* **coun·tries 1 :** REGION 1, DISTRICT **2 :** a land lived in by a people with a common government **3 :** the people of a nation **4 :** open rural land away from big towns and cities

country and western *n* **:** music coming from or imitating the folk music of the southern United States or the Western cowboy

coun·try·man *n, pl* **coun·try·men 1 :** a person born in the same country as another **:** a fellow citizen **2 :** a person living or raised in the country

coun·try·side *n* **:** a rural area or its people

coun·ty *n, pl* **coun·ties :** a division of a state or country for local government

cou·pé *or* **coupe** *n* **1 :** a carriage with four wheels and an enclosed body seating two persons and with an outside seat for the driver in front **2 :** an enclosed two-door automobile for usually two persons

¹cou·ple *n* **1 :** two persons who are paired together or closely associated **2 :** two things of the same kind that are connected or that are thought of together

²couple *vb* **cou·pled; cou·pling 1 :** to join or link together : CONNECT **2 :** to join in pairs

cou·plet *n* : two rhyming lines of verse one after another

cou·pling *n* **1** : the act of bringing or coming together **2** : something that joins or connects two parts or things

cou·pon *n* **1** : a ticket or form that allows the holder to receive some service, payment, or discount **2** : a part of an advertisement meant to be cut out for use as an order blank

cour·age *n* : the strength of mind that makes one able to meet danger and difficulties with firmness

cou·ra·geous *adj* : having or showing courage — **cou·ra·geous·ly** *adv*

¹course *n* **1** : motion from one point to another : progress in space or time **2** : the path over which something moves **3** : direction of motion **4** : a natural channel for water **5** : way of doing something **6** : a series of acts or proceedings arranged in regular order **7** : a series of studies leading to a diploma or a degree **8** : a part of a meal served at one time **9** : a continuous level range of brick or masonry throughout a wall — **of course** : as might be expected

²course *vb* **coursed; cours·ing 1** : to run through or over **2** : to move rapidly : RACE

¹court *n* **1** : the home of a ruler **2** : a ruler's assembly of advisers and officers as a governing power **3** : the family and people who follow a ruler **4** : an open space completely or partly surrounded by buildings **5** : a short street **6** : a space arranged for playing a certain game **7** : an official meeting led by a judge for settling legal questions or the place where it is held **8** : respect meant to win favor

²court *vb* **1** : to try to gain or get the support of : SEEK **2** : to seem to be asking for : TEMPT **3** : to seek the liking of

cour·te·ous *adj* : showing respect and consideration for others : POLITE — **cour·te·ous·ly** *adv* — **cour·te·ous·ness** *n*

cour·te·sy *n, pl* **cour·te·sies 1** : the quality or state of being courteous **2** : a courteous act or expression **3** : something that is a favor and not a right

court·house *n* **1** : a building in which courts of law are held **2** : a building in which county offices are housed

court·i·er *n* : a member of a royal court

court·ly *adj* **court·li·er; court·li·est** : suitable to a royal court : ELEGANT, POLITE

court·ship *n* : the act or process of courting or seeking the liking of someone

court·yard *n* : ¹COURT 4

cous·in *n* : a child of one's uncle or aunt

cove *n* : a small sheltered inlet or bay

cov·e·nant *n* : a formal or solemn agreement

¹cov·er *vb* **1** : to provide protection to or against **2** : to maintain a check on especially by patrolling **3** : to hide from sight or knowledge **4** : to place or spread something over **5** : to dot thickly **6** : to form a cover or covering over **7** : to take into account **8** : to have as one's field of activity or interest **9** : to pass over or through

²cover *n* **1** : something that protects, shelters, or hides **2** : something that is placed over or about another thing : LID, TOP **3** : a binding or a protecting case **4** : a covering (as a blanket) used on a bed **5** : an envelope or wrapper for mail

cov·er·age *n* **1** : insurance against something **2** : the value or amount of insurance

cov·er·all *n* : an outer garment that combines shirt and pants and is worn to protect one's regular clothes — usually used in pl.

covered wagon *n* : a large long wagon with a curving canvas top

cov·er·ing *n* : something (as a roof or an envelope) that covers or conceals

cov·er·let *n* : BEDSPREAD

¹co·vert *adj* : made or done secretly — **co·vert·ly** *adv* — **co·vert·ness** *n*

²covert *n* **1** : a hiding place (as a thicket that gives shelter to game animals) **2** : one of the small feathers around the bottom of the quills on the wings and tail of a bird

cov·et *vb* : to wish for greatly or with envy

cov·et·ous *adj* : having or showing too much desire for wealth or possessions or for something belonging to another person

cov·ey *n, pl* **coveys 1** : a small flock (as of quail) **2** : ¹GROUP

¹cow *n* : the mature female of cattle or of an animal (as the moose) of which the male is called *bull*

²cow *vb* : to lower the spirits or courage of : make afraid

cow·ard *n* : a person who shows dishonorable fear

cow·ard·ice *n* : dishonorable fear

cow·ard·ly *adj* : being or behaving like a coward — **cow·ard·li·ness** *n*

cow·bell *n* : a bell hung around the neck of a cow to tell where it is

cow·bird *n* : a small American blackbird that lays its eggs in the nests of other birds

cow·boy *n* : a man or boy who works on a ranch or performs at a rodeo

cow·catch·er *n* : a strong frame on the front of a railroad engine for moving things blocking the track

cow·er *vb* : to shrink away or crouch down shivering (as from fear)

cow·girl *n* : a girl or woman who works on a ranch or performs at a rodeo

cow·hand *n* : a person who works on a cattle ranch

cow·herd *n* : a person who tends cows

cow·hide *n* **1** : the hide of cattle or leather made from it **2** : a whip of rawhide or braided leather

cowl *n* : a hood or long hooded cloak especially of a monk

cow·lick *n* : a small bunch of hair that sticks out and will not lie flat

cow·pox *n* : a disease of cattle that when given to humans (as by vaccination) protects from smallpox

cow·punch·er *n* : COWBOY

cow·slip *n* **1** : a common Old World primrose with yellow or purple flowers **2** : MARSH MARIGOLD

cox·swain *n* : the person who steers a boat

coy *adj* : falsely shy or modest

coy·ote *n* : a small wolf chiefly of western North America

¹co·zy *adj* **co·zi·er; co·zi·est** : enjoying or providing warmth and comfort — **co·zi·ly** *adv* — **co·zi·ness** *n*

²cozy *n, pl* **co·zies** : a padded covering for a container (as a teapot) to keep the contents hot

¹crab *n* : a sea animal related to the lobsters but having a flat shell and a small abdomen pressed against the underside of the body

²crab *vb* **crabbed; crab·bing** : to find fault : COMPLAIN

³crab *n* : a person who is usually cross

crab apple *n* **1** : a small wild sour apple **2** : a cultivated apple with small usually brightly colored acid fruit

crab·bed *adj* : CRABBY

crab·by *adj* **crab·bi·er; crab·bi·est** : being cross and irritable

crab·grass *n* : a weedy grass with coarse stems that root at the joints

¹crack *vb* **1** : to break or cause to break with a sudden sharp sound **2** : to make or cause to make a sound of cracking as if breaking **3** : to break often without completely separating into parts **4** : to tell (a joke) especially in a clever way **5** : to lose self-control : break down **6** : to change in tone quality **7** : to strike or receive a sharp blow

²crack *n* **1** : a sudden sharp noise **2** : a sharp clever remark **3** : a narrow break or opening **4** : a broken tone of the voice **5** : the beginning moment **6** : a sharp blow **7** : ²ATTEMPT

³crack *adj* : of high quality or ability

crack·er *n* : a dry thin baked food made of flour and water

¹crack·le *vb* **crack·led; crack·ling 1** : to make many small sharp noises **2** : to form little cracks in a surface

²crackle *n* : the noise of repeated small cracks (as of burning wood)

crack–up *n* **1** : BREAKDOWN **2** : ²CRASH 3, WRECK

crack up *vb* : to cause or have a crack-up

¹cra·dle *n* **1** : a baby's bed or cot usually on rockers **2** : place of beginning **3** : a framework or support resembling a baby's cradle in appearance or use **4** : a rocking device used in panning gold **5** : a support for a telephone receiver

²cradle *vb* **cra·dled; cra·dling 1** : to hold or support in or as if in a cradle **2** : to wash (as earth or sand) in a miner's cradle

craft *n* **1** : skill in making things especially with the hands **2** : an occupation or trade requiring skill with the hands or as an artist **3** : skill in deceiving for a bad purpose : CUNNING **4** : the members of a trade or a trade group **5** *pl usually* **craft** : a boat especially when of small size **6** *pl usually* **craft** : AIRCRAFT

crafts·man *n, pl* **crafts·men 1** : a person who works at a trade or handicraft **2** : a highly skilled worker in any field

crafty *adj* **craft·i·er; craft·i·est** : skillful at deceiving others : CUNNING — **craft·i·ly** *adv* — **craft·i·ness** *n*

crag *n* : a steep rock or cliff

crag·gy *adj* **crag·gi·er; crag·gi·est** : having many crags

cram *vb* **crammed; cram·ming 1** : to stuff or pack tightly **2** : to fill full **3** : to study hard just before a test

¹cramp *n* **1** : a sudden painful involuntary tightening of a muscle **2** : sharp pain in the abdomen — usually used in pl.

²cramp *vb* **1** : to cause cramp in **2** : to hold back from free action or expression : HAMPER

cran·ber·ry *n, pl* **cran·ber·ries** : a sour bright red berry that is eaten in sauces and jelly and is the fruit of an evergreen swamp plant related to the blueberries

¹crane *n* **1** : a tall wading bird that looks like a heron but is related to the rails **2** : a machine with a swinging arm for lifting and carrying heavy weights **3** : a mechanical arm that swings freely from a center and is used to support or carry a weight

²crane *vb* **craned; cran·ing** : to stretch one's neck to see better

cra·ni·al *adj* : of or relating to the cranium

cra·ni·um *n, pl* **cra·ni·ums** *or* **cra·nia 1** : SKULL **2** : the part of the skull enclosing the brain

¹crank *n* **1** : a bent armlike part with a handle that is turned to start or run machinery **2** : a person with strange ideas **3** : a cross or irritable person

²**crank** *vb* : to start or run by turning a crank

cranky *adj* **crank·i·er; crank·i·est** : easily angered or irritated — **crank·i·ness** *n*

cran·ny *n, pl* **cran·nies** : a small break or slit (as in a cliff)

crap·pie *n* : either of two sunfishes native to the Great Lakes and Mississippi valley of which the larger and darker one (**black crappie**) is an important sport fish and the other (**white crappie**) is used as a table fish

¹**crash** *vb* **1** : to break or go to pieces with or as if with violence and noise : SMASH **2** : to fall or strike something with noise and damage **3** : to hit or cause to hit something with force and noise **4** : to make or cause to make a loud noise **5** : to move or force a way roughly and noisily

²**crash** *n* **1** : a loud sound (as of things smashing) **2** : a breaking to pieces by or as if by hitting something : SMASH, COLLISION **3** : the crashing of something **4** : a sudden weakening or failure (as of a business or prices)

¹**crate** *n* : a box or frame of wooden slats or boards for holding and protecting something in shipment

²**crate** *vb* **crat·ed; crat·ing** : to pack in a crate

cra·ter *n* **1** : a hollow in the shape of a bowl around the opening of a volcano or geyser **2** : a hole (as in the surface of the earth or moon) formed by an impact (as of a meteorite)

cra·vat *n* : NECKTIE

crave *vb* **craved; crav·ing** **1** : to ask for earnestly **2** : to want greatly : long for

cra·ven *adj* : COWARDLY

crav·ing *n* : a great desire or longing

craw *n* **1** : ¹CROP 2 **2** : the stomach of an animal

craw·fish *n, pl* **crawfish** : CRAYFISH

¹**crawl** *vb* **1** : to move slowly with the body close to the ground : move on hands and knees **2** : to go very slowly or carefully **3** : to be covered with or have the feeling of being covered with creeping things

²**crawl** *n* **1** : the act or motion of crawling **2** : a swimming stroke that looks a little like crawling

cray·fish *n, pl* **crayfish** **1** : a freshwater shellfish that looks like the related lobster but is much smaller **2** : a spiny saltwater shellfish that looks like the related lobster but lacks very large claws

¹**cray·on** *n* : a stick of white or colored chalk or of colored wax used for writing or drawing

²**crayon** *vb* : to draw or color with a crayon

craze *n* : something that is very popular for a short while

cra·zy *adj* **cra·zi·er; cra·zi·est** **1** : having a diseased or abnormal mind : INSANE **2** : not sensible or logical **3** : very excited or pleased — **cra·zi·ly** *adv* — **cra·zi·ness** *n*

¹**creak** *vb* : to make a long scraping or squeaking sound

²**creak** *n* : a long squeaking or scraping noise

creaky *adj* **creak·i·er; creak·i·est** : making or likely to make a creaking sound — **creak·i·ly** *adv*

¹**cream** *n* **1** : the oily yellowish part of milk **2** : a food prepared with cream **3** : something having the smoothness and thickness of cream **4** : the best part **5** : a pale yellow

²**cream** *vb* **1** : to furnish, prepare, or treat with cream **2** : to rub or beat (as butter) until creamy

cream·ery *n, pl* **cream·er·ies** : DAIRY 1, 3

creamy *adj* **cream·i·er; cream·i·est** **1** : full of or containing cream **2** : like cream in appearance, color, or taste — **cream·i·ness** *n*

¹**crease** *n* : a line or mark usually made by folding or wrinkling

²**crease** *vb* **creased; creas·ing** **1** : to make a crease in or on **2** : to become creased

cre·ate *vb* **cre·at·ed; cre·at·ing** : to cause to exist : bring into existence : PRODUCE

cre·a·tion *n* **1** : the act of bringing the world into existence out of nothing **2** : the act of making, inventing, or producing something **3** : something created by human intelligence or imagination **4** : the created world

cre·a·tive *adj* : able to create especially new and original things — **cre·a·tive·ly** *adv* — **cre·a·tive·ness** *n*

cre·a·tor *n* **1** : one that creates or produces **2** *cap* : GOD 1

crea·ture *n* **1** : a living being **2** : a lower animal **3** : PERSON 1

cred·i·ble *adj* : possible to believe : deserving belief — **cred·i·bly** *adv*

¹**cred·it** *n* **1** : the balance in an account in a person's favor **2** : trust given to a customer for future payment for goods purchased **3** : time given for payment **4** : belief or trust in the truth of something **5** : good reputation especially for honesty : high standing **6** : a source of honor or pride **7** : recognition or honor received for some quality or work **8** : a unit of schoolwork

²**credit** *vb* **1** : BELIEVE 2 **2** : to place something in a person's favor on (a business account) **3** : to give credit or honor to for something

cred·it·able *adj* : good enough to deserve praise

cred·i·tor *n* : a person to whom a debt is owed

cred·u·lous *adj* : quick to believe especially without very good reasons

creed *n* **1** : a statement of the basic beliefs of a religious faith **2** : a set of guiding rules or beliefs

creek *n* : a stream of water usually larger than a brook and smaller than a river

creel *n* : a basket for holding a catch of fish

¹creep *vb* **crept; creep·ing 1** : to move along with the body close to the ground or floor : move slowly on hands and knees : CRAWL **2** : to move or advance slowly, timidly, or quietly **3** : to grow or spread along the ground or along a surface

²creep *n* **1** : a creeping movement **2** : a feeling as of insects crawling over one's skin : a feeling of horror — usually used in pl.

creep·er *n* **1** : one that creeps **2** : a small bird that creeps about trees and bushes in search of insects **3** : a plant (as ivy) that grows by spreading over a surface

creepy *adj* **creep·i·er; creep·i·est 1** : having or causing a feeling as of insects creeping on the skin **2** : causing fear : SCARY — **creep·i·ness** *n*

cre·mate *vb* **cre·mat·ed; cre·mat·ing** : to burn (as a dead body) to ashes

cre·ma·tion *n* : the act or practice of cremating

crepe *n* : a thin crinkled fabric (as of silk or wool)

crepe paper *n* : paper with a crinkled or puckered look and feel

crept *past of* CREEP

cre·scen·do *n, pl* **cre·scen·dos** *or* **cre·scen·does** : a gradual increase in the loudness of music

¹cres·cent *n* **1** : the shape of the visible moon during about the first week after new moon or the last week before the next new moon **2** : something shaped like a crescent moon

²crescent *adj* : shaped like the new moon

cress *n* : any of several salad plants of the mustard group

crest *n* **1** : a showy growth (as of flesh or feathers) on the head of an animal **2** : an emblem or design on a helmet (as of a knight) or over a coat of arms **3** : something forming the top of something else — **crest·ed** *adj*

crest·fall·en *adj* : feeling disappointment and loss of pride

crev·ice *n* : a narrow opening (as in the earth) caused by cracking or splitting : FISSURE

crew *n* **1** : a gathering of people **2** : a group of people working together **3** : the group of people who operate a ship, train, or airplane

crib *n* **1** : a manger for feeding animals **2** : a small bed frame with high sides for a child **3** : a building or bin for storing

¹crick·et *n* : a small leaping insect noted for the chirping notes of the males

²cricket *n* : a game played on a large field with bats, ball, and wickets by two teams of eleven players each

cri·er *n* : one who calls out orders or announcements

crime *n* **1** : the doing of an act forbidden by law : the failure to do an act required by law **2** : an act that is sinful, foolish, or disgraceful

¹crim·i·nal *adj* **1** : being or guilty of crime **2** : relating to crime or its punishment — **crim·i·nal·ly** *adv*

²criminal *n* : a person who has committed a crime

crim·son *n* : a deep purplish red

cringe *vb* **cringed; cring·ing 1** : to shrink in fear : COWER **2** : to behave in a very humble way : FAWN

crin·kle *vb* **crin·kled; crin·kling 1** : to form or cause little waves or wrinkles on the surface : WRINKLE **2** : ¹RUSTLE 1

crin·kly *adj* **crin·kli·er; crin·kli·est** : full of small wrinkles

¹crip·ple *n* : a lame or disabled person

²cripple *vb* **crip·pled; crip·pling 1** : to cause to become a cripple **2** : to make useless or imperfect

cri·sis *n, pl* **cri·ses 1** : a turning point for better or worse in a disease **2** : an unstable or critical time or state of affairs

¹crisp *adj* **1** : being thin and hard and easily crumbled **2** : pleasantly firm and fresh **3** : having a sharp distinct outline **4** : being clear and brief **5** : pleasantly cool and invigorating : BRISK

²crisp *vb* : to make or become crisp

criss·cross *vb* **1** : to mark with or make lines that cross one another **2** : to go or pass back and forth

crit·ic *n* **1** : a person who makes or gives a judgment of the value, worth, beauty, or quality of something **2** : a person given to finding fault or complaining

crit·i·cal *adj* **1** : inclined to criticize especially in an unfavorable way **2** : consisting of or involving criticism or the judgment of critics **3** : using or involving careful judgment **4** : of, relating to, or being a turning point or crisis — **crit·i·cal·ly** *adv*

crit·i·cism *n* **1** : the act of criticizing and especially of finding fault **2** : a critical remark or comment **3** : a careful judgment or review especially by a critic

crit·i·cize *vb* **crit·i·cized; crit·i·ciz·ing 1** : to examine and judge as a critic **2** : to find fault with

¹croak *vb* **1** : to make a deep harsh sound **2** : to speak in a hoarse throaty voice

²croak *n* : a hoarse harsh sound or cry

¹cro·chet *n* : work done or a fabric formed by crocheting

²crochet *vb* : to make (something) or create a fabric with a hooked needle by forming and interlacing loops in a thread

crock *n* : a thick pot or jar of baked clay

crock·ery *n* : EARTHENWARE

croc·o·dile *n* : a very large animal related to the alligator that crawls on short legs about tropical marshes and rivers

cro·cus *n* : a plant related to the irises that has grasslike leaves and is often planted for its white, yellow, or purple spring flowers

cro·ny *n, pl* **cro·nies** : a close companion : CHUM

¹crook *vb* : ²BEND 2, CURVE

²crook *n* **1** : a shepherd's staff with one end curved into a hook **2** : a dishonest person (as a thief or swindler) **3** : a curved or hooked part of a thing : BEND

crook·ed *adj* **1** : having bends and curves **2** : not set or placed straight **3** : DISHONEST — **crook·ed·ly** *adv* — **crook·ed·ness** *n*

croon *vb* : to hum or sing in a low soft voice

¹crop *n* **1** : a short riding whip **2** : an enlargement just above the stomach of a bird or insect in which food is stored for a while **3** : the amount gathered or harvested : HARVEST **4** : BATCH 3, LOT

²crop *vb* **cropped; crop·ping 1** : to remove (as by cutting or biting) the upper or outer parts of : TRIM **2** : to grow or yield a crop (as of grain) : cause (land) to bear a crop **3** : to come or appear when not expected

cro·quet *n* : a game in which players drive wooden balls with mallets through a series of wickets set out on a lawn

cro·quette *n* : a roll or ball of hashed meat, fish, or vegetables fried in deep fat

¹cross *n* **1** : a structure consisting of one bar crossing another at right angles **2** *often cap* : the structure on which Jesus was crucified used as a symbol of Christianity and of the Christian religion **3** : sorrow or suffering as test of patience or virtue **4** : an object or mark shaped like a cross **5** : a mixing of breeds, races, or kinds : the product of such a mixing

²cross *vb* **1** : to lie or be situated across **2** : to divide by passing through or across (a line or area) : INTERSECT **3** : to move, pass, or extend across or past **4** : to make the sign of the cross upon or over (as in prayer)

5 : to cancel by marking crosses on or by drawing a line through **6** : to place one over the other **7** : to act against : OPPOSE **8** : to draw a line across **9** : to cause (an animal or plant) to breed with one of another kind : produce hybrids **10** : to pass going in opposite directions

³cross *adj* **1** : lying, falling, or passing across **2** : ²CONTRARY 1 **3** : hard to get along with : IRRITABLE — **cross·ly** *adv* — **cross·ness** *n*

cross·bar *n* : a bar, piece, or stripe placed crosswise or across something

cross·bones *n pl* : two leg or arm bones placed or pictured as lying across each other

cross·bow *n* : a short bow mounted crosswise near the end of a wooden stock that shoots short arrows

cross–ex·am·ine *vb* **cross–ex·am·ined; cross–ex·am·in·ing** : to question (a person) in an effort to show that statements or answers given earlier were false — **cross–ex·am·in·er** *n*

cross–eyed *adj* : having one or both eyes turned toward the nose

cross·ing *n* **1** : a point where two lines, tracks, or streets cross each other **2** : a place provided for going across a street, railroad tracks, or a stream **3** : a voyage across a body of water

cross·piece *n* : something placed so as to cross something else

cross–ref·er·ence *n* : a reference made from one place to another (as in a dictionary)

cross·roads *n sing or pl* : a place where roads cross

cross section *n* **1** : a cutting made across something (as a log or an apple) **2** : a representation of a cross section **3** : a number of persons or things selected from a group to stand for the whole

cross·walk *n* : a specially paved or marked path for people walking across a street or road

cross·wise *adv* : so as to cross something : ACROSS

cross·word puzzle *n* : a puzzle in which words are filled into a pattern of numbered squares in answer to clues so that they read across and down

crotch *n* : an angle formed by the spreading apart of two legs or branches or of a limb from its trunk

¹crouch *vb* : to stoop or bend low with the arms and legs close to the body

²crouch *n* : the position of crouching

croup *n* : a children's disease in which a hoarse cough and hard breathing are present

¹crow *n* : a glossy black bird that has a harsh cry

²crow vb **1** : to make the loud shrill sound that a rooster makes **2** : to make sounds of delight **3** : ²BOAST 1

³crow n **1** : the cry of a rooster **2** : a cry of triumph

crow·bar n : a metal bar used as a lever (as for prying things apart)

¹crowd vb **1** : to press or push forward **2** : to press close **3** : to collect in numbers : THRONG **4** : to fill or pack by pressing together

²crowd n **1** : a large number of persons collected together : THRONG **2** : the population as a whole : ordinary people **3** : a group of people having a common interest

¹crown n **1** : a wreath or band especially as a mark of victory or honor **2** : a royal headdress **3** : the highest part (as of a tree or mountain) **4** : the top of the head **5** : the top part of a hat **6** : the part of a tooth outside of the gum **7** : something suggesting a crown **8** cap : royal power or authority or one having such power **9** : any of various coins (as a British coin worth five shillings) — **crowned** adj

²crown vb **1** : to place a crown on : make sovereign **2** : to declare officially to be **3** : to give something as a mark of honor or reward **4** : ²TOP 2 **5** : to bring to a successful conclusion : COMPLETE, PERFECT **6** : to put an artificial crown on a damaged tooth **7** : to hit on the head

crow's nest n : a partly enclosed place to stand high on the mast of a ship for use as a lookout

cru·cial adj **1** : being a final or very important test or decision : DECISIVE **2** : very important : SIGNIFICANT

cru·ci·ble n : a pot made of a substance not easily damaged by fire that is used for holding something to be treated under great heat

cru·ci·fix n : a cross with a figure of Christ crucified on it

cru·ci·fix·ion n **1** : an act of crucifying **2** cap : the crucifying of Christ on the cross

cru·ci·fy vb **cru·ci·fied; cru·ci·fy·ing 1** : to put to death by nailing or binding the hands and feet to a cross **2** : to treat cruelly : TORTURE, PERSECUTE

crude adj **crud·er; crud·est 1** : in a natural state and not changed by special treatment : RAW **2** : not having or showing good manners : VULGAR **3** : planned or done in a rough or unskilled way — **crude·ly** adv — **crude·ness** n

cru·el adj **cru·el·er** or **cru·el·ler; cru·el·est** or **cru·el·lest 1** : ready to hurt others **2** : causing or helping to cause suffering — **cru·el·ly** adv

cru·el·ty n, pl **cru·el·ties 1** : the quality or state of being cruel **2** : cruel treatment

cru·et n : a bottle for holding vinegar, oil, or sauce for table use

¹cruise vb **cruised; cruis·ing 1** : to travel by ship often stopping at a series of ports **2** : to travel for pleasure **3** : to travel at the best operating speed

²cruise n : an act or instance of cruising

cruis·er n **1** : a warship that is smaller than a battleship **2** : a police car used for patrolling streets and equipped with radio for communicating with headquarters **3** : a motorboat equipped for living aboard

crul·ler n : a small sweet cake made of egg batter usually cut in strips or twists and fried in deep fat

¹crumb n **1** : a small piece especially of bread **2** : a little bit

²crumb vb : to break into crumbs : CRUMBLE

crum·ble vb **crum·bled; crum·bling 1** : to break into small pieces **2** : to fall to pieces : fall into ruin

crum·bly adj **crum·bli·er; crum·bli·est** : easily crumbled

crum·ple vb **crum·pled; crum·pling 1** : to press or crush out of shape : RUMPLE **2** : to become crumpled **3** : ¹COLLAPSE 1

¹crunch vb **1** : to chew or grind with a crushing noise **2** : to make the sound of being crushed or squeezed

²crunch n : an act or sound of crunching

¹cru·sade n **1** cap : one of the military expeditions made by Christian countries in the eleventh, twelfth, and thirteenth centuries to recover the Holy Land from the Muslims **2** : a campaign to get things changed for the better

²crusade vb **cru·sad·ed; cru·sad·ing** : to take part in a crusade

cru·sad·er n : a person who takes part in a crusade

¹crush vb **1** : to squeeze together so as to change or destroy the natural shape or condition **2** : ¹HUG 1 **3** : to break into fine pieces by pressure **4** : OVERWHELM 2 **5** : OPPRESS 1

²crush n **1** : an act of crushing **2** : a tightly packed crowd **3** : a foolish or very strong liking : INFATUATION

crust n **1** : the hardened outside surface of bread **2** : a hard dry piece of bread **3** : the pastry cover of a pie **4** : a hard outer covering or surface layer **5** : the outer part of the earth

crus·ta·cean n : any of a large group of mostly water animals (as crabs, lobsters, and shrimps) with a body made of segments, a firm outer shell, two pairs of antennae, and limbs that are jointed

crusty *adj* **crust·i·er; crust·i·est** **1** : having or being a crust **2** : ³CROSS 3

crutch *n* **1** : a support usually made with a piece at the top to fit under the armpit that is used by a lame person as an aid in walking **2** : something (as a prop or support) like a crutch in shape or use

¹cry *vb* **cried; cry·ing** **1** : to make a loud call or cry : SHOUT, EXCLAIM **2** : to shed tears : WEEP **3** : to utter a special sound or call **4** : to make known to the public : call out

²cry *n, pl* **cries** **1** : a loud call or shout (as of pain, fear, or joy) **2** : ¹APPEAL 2 **3** : a fit of weeping **4** : the special sound made by an animal

cry·ba·by *n, pl* **cry·ba·bies** : a person who cries easily or who complains often

¹crys·tal *n* **1** : quartz that is colorless and transparent or nearly so **2** : something transparent like crystal **3** : a body formed by a substance hardening so that it has flat surfaces in an even arrangement **4** : a clear colorless glass of very good quality **5** : the transparent cover over a clock or watch dial

²crystal *adj* : made of or being like crystal : CLEAR

crys·tal·line *adj* **1** : made of crystal or composed of crystals **2** : like crystal : TRANSPARENT

crys·tal·lize *vb* **crys·tal·lized; crys·tal·liz·ing** **1** : to form or cause to form crystals or grains **2** : to take or cause to take definite form

cub *n* **1** : the young of various animals (as the bear, fox, or lion) **2** : CUB SCOUT

cub·by·hole *n* : a snug place (as for storing things)

¹cube *n* **1** : a solid body having six equal square sides **2** : the product obtained by multiplying the square of a number by the number itself

²cube *vb* **cubed; cub·ing** **1** : to take (a number) as a factor three times **2** : to form into a cube or divide into cubes

cu·bic *adj* : being the volume of a cube whose edge is a specified unit

cu·bi·cal *adj* **1** : having the form of a cube **2** : relating to volume

cu·bit *n* : a unit of length usually equal to about forty-six centimeters

Cub Scout *n* : a member of a program of the Boy Scouts for boys in the first through fifth grades in school

cuck·oo *n, pl* **cuckoos** **1** : any of several related birds (as a grayish brown European bird) that mostly lay their eggs in the nests of other birds for them to hatch **2** : the call of the European cuckoo

cu·cum·ber *n* : a long usually green-skinned vegetable that is used in salads and as pickles and is the fruit of a vine related to the melons and gourds

cud *n* : a portion of food brought up from the first stomach of some animals (as the cow and sheep) to be chewed again

cud·dle *vb* **cud·dled; cud·dling** **1** : to hold close for warmth or comfort or in affection **2** : to lie close : NESTLE, SNUGGLE

¹cud·gel *n* : a short heavy club

²cudgel *vb* **cud·geled** *or* **cud·gelled; cud·gel·ing** *or* **cud·gel·ling** : to beat with or as if with a cudgel

¹cue *n* **1** : a word, phrase, or action in a play serving as a signal for the next actor to speak or to do something **2** : something serving as a signal or suggestion : HINT

²cue *n* : a straight tapering stick used in playing billiards and pool

¹cuff *n* **1** : a band or turned-over piece at the end of a sleeve **2** : the turned-back hem of a trouser leg

²cuff *vb* : to strike especially with or as if with the palm of the hand : SLAP

³cuff *n* : ²SLAP 1

¹cull *vb* **1** : to select from a group **2** : to identify and remove the culls from

²cull *n* : something rejected from a group or lot as not as good as the rest

cul·mi·nate *vb* **cul·mi·nat·ed; cul·mi·nat·ing** : to reach the highest point

cul·pa·ble *adj* : deserving blame

cul·prit *n* **1** : one accused of or charged with a crime or fault **2** : one guilty of a crime or fault

cul·ti·vate *vb* **cul·ti·vat·ed; cul·ti·vat·ing** **1** : to prepare land for the raising of crops **2** : to raise or assist the growth of crops by tilling or by labor and care **3** : to improve or develop by careful attention, training, or study : devote time and thought to **4** : to seek the company and friendship of

cul·ti·vat·ed *adj* **1** : raised or produced under cultivation **2** : having or showing good education and proper manners

cul·ti·va·tion *n* **1** : the act or process of cultivating especially the soil **2** : REFINEMENT 2

cul·ti·va·tor *n* **1** : one (as a farmer) that cultivates something **2** : a tool or machine for loosening the soil between rows of a crop

cul·tur·al *adj* : of or relating to culture — **cul·tur·al·ly** *adv*

cul·ture *n* **1** : CULTIVATION 1 **2** : the raising or development (as of a crop or product) by careful attention **3** : the improvement of the mind, tastes, and manners through careful training **4** : a certain stage, form, or kind of civilization

cul·tured *adj* **1** : having or showing refinement in taste, speech, or manners **2** : produced under artificial conditions

cul·vert *n* : a drain or waterway crossing under a road or railroad

cum·ber·some *adj* : hard to handle or manage because of size or weight

cu·mu·la·tive *adj* : increasing (as in force, strength, or amount) by one addition after another

cu·mu·lus *n, pl* **cu·mu·li** : a massive cloud form having a flat base and rounded outlines often piled up like a mountain

1cu·ne·i·form *adj* **1** : shaped like a wedge **2** : made up of or written with marks or letters shaped like wedges

2cuneiform *n* : cuneiform writing

1cun·ning *adj* **1** : skillful and clever at using special knowledge or at getting something done **2** : showing craftiness and trickery **3** : CUTE, PRETTY

2cunning *n* **1** : SKILL 1, DEXTERITY **2** : cleverness in getting what one wants often by tricks or deceiving

1cup *n* **1** : something to drink out of in the shape of a small bowl usually with a handle **2** : the contents of a cup : CUPFUL **3** : a trophy in the shape of a cup with two handles **4** : something like a cup in shape or use

2cup *vb* **cupped; cup·ping** : to curve into the shape of a cup

cup·board *n* : a closet usually with shelves for dishes or food

cup·cake *n* : a small cake baked in a mold shaped like a cup

cup·ful *n, pl* **cup·fuls** *or* **cups·ful** **1** : the amount held by a cup **2** : a half pint : eight ounces (about 236 milliliters)

cu·pid *n* : a picture or statue of Cupid the Roman god of love often as a winged child with a bow and arrow

cu·pid·i·ty *n* : excessive desire for wealth : GREED

cu·po·la *n* **1** : a rounded roof or ceiling : DOME **2** : a small structure built on top of a roof

cur *n* : a worthless or mongrel dog

cur·able *adj* : possible to cure

cu·rate *n* : a member of the clergy who assists the rector or vicar of a church

1curb *n* **1** : a chain or strap on a horse's bit used to control the horse by pressing against the lower jaw **2** : 1CHECK 2 **3** : an enclosing border (as of stone or concrete) often along the edge of a street

2curb *vb* : to control by or furnish with a curb

curb·ing *n* **1** : material for making a curb **2** : 1CURB 3

curd *n* : the thickened or solid part of sour or partly digested milk

cur·dle *vb* **cur·dled; cur·dling** : to change into curd : COAGULATE

1cure *n* **1** : a method or period of medical treatment **2** : recovery or relief from a disease **3** : 1REMEDY 1

2cure *vb* **cured; cur·ing** **1** : to make or become healthy or sound again **2** : to prepare by a chemical or physical process for use or storage **3** : to undergo a curing process

cur·few *n* **1** : a rule requiring certain or all people to be off the streets or at home at a stated time **2** : a signal (as the ringing of a bell) formerly given to announce the beginning of a curfew **3** : the time when a curfew is sounded

cu·rio *n, pl* **cu·ri·os** : a rare or unusual article : CURIOSITY

cu·ri·os·i·ty *n, pl* **cu·ri·os·i·ties** **1** : an eager desire to learn and often to learn what does not concern one **2** : something strange or unusual **3** : an object or article valued because it is strange or rare

cu·ri·ous *adj* **1** : eager to learn : INQUISITIVE **2** : attracting attention by being strange or unusual : ODD — **cu·ri·ous·ly** *adv*

1curl *vb* **1** : to twist or form into ringlets **2** : to take or move in a curved form

2curl *n* **1** : a lock of hair that coils : RINGLET **2** : something having a spiral or winding form : COIL **3** : the action of curling : the state of being curled

curly *adj* **curl·i·er; curl·i·est** **1** : tending to curl **2** : having curls

cur·rant *n* **1** : a small seedless raisin used in baking and cooking **2** : a sour red or white edible berry produced by a low spreading shrub related to the gooseberry

cur·ren·cy *n, pl* **cur·ren·cies** **1** : common use or acceptance **2** : money in circulation

1cur·rent *adj* **1** : now passing **2** : occurring in or belonging to the present time **3** : generally and widely accepted, used, or practiced

2current *n* **1** : a body of fluid moving in a specified direction **2** : the swiftest part of a stream **3** : the general course : TREND **4** : a flow of charges of electricity

cur·ric·u·lum *n, pl* **cur·ric·u·la** *or* **cur·ric·u·lums** : all the courses of study offered by a school

cur·ry *vb* **cur·ried; cur·ry·ing** : to rub and clean the coat of

1curse *n* **1** : a calling for harm or injury to come to someone **2** : a word or an expression used in cursing or swearing **3** : evil or misfortune that comes as if in answer to a curse **4** : a cause of great harm or evil

2curse *vb* **cursed; curs·ing** **1** : to call upon

divine power to send harm or evil upon **2** : SWEAR 5   **3** : to bring unhappiness or evil upon : AFFLICT

cur·sor *n* : a symbol (as an arrow or blinking line) on a computer screen that shows where the user is working

curt *adj* : rudely brief in language

cur·tail *vb* : to shorten or reduce by cutting off the end or a part of

¹cur·tain *n*   **1** : a piece of material (as cloth) hung up to darken, hide, divide, or decorate   **2** : something that covers, hides, or separates like a curtain

²curtain *vb*   **1** : to furnish with curtains   **2** : to hide or shut off with a curtain

¹curt·sy *or* **curt·sey** *vb* **curt·sied** *or* **curt·seyed**; **curt·sy·ing** *or* **curt·sey·ing** : to lower the body slightly by bending the knees as an act of politeness or respect

²curtsy *or* **curtsey** *n, pl* **curtsies** *or* **curt·seys** : an act of politeness or respect made mainly by women and consisting of a slight lowering of the body by bending the knees

cur·va·ture *n*   **1** : a curving or bending   **2** : the state of being curved

¹curve *vb* **curved**; **curv·ing**   **1** : to turn or change from a straight line or course   **2** : to cause to curve

²curve *n*   **1** : a bending or turning without angles : BEND   **2** : something curved   **3** : a ball thrown so that it moves away from a straight course

¹cush·ion *n*   **1** : a soft pillow or pad to rest on or against   **2** : something like a cushion in use, shape, or softness   **3** : something that serves to soften or lessen the effects of something bad or unpleasant

²cushion *vb*   **1** : to place on or as if on a cushion   **2** : to furnish with a cushion   **3** : to soften or lessen the force or shock of

cusp *n* : a point or pointed end (as on the crown of a tooth)

cus·pid *n* : ¹CANINE 1

cuss *vb* : SWEAR 5

cus·tard *n* : a sweetened mixture of milk and eggs baked, boiled, or frozen

cus·to·di·an *n* : one that guards and protects or takes care of

cus·to·dy *n*   **1** : direct responsibility for care and control   **2** : the state of being arrested or held by police

¹cus·tom *n*   **1** : the usual way of doing things : the usual practice   **2** **customs** *pl* : duties or taxes paid on imports or exports   **3** : support given to a business by its customers

²custom *adj*   **1** : made or done to personal order   **2** : specializing in custom work

cus·tom·ary *adj*   **1** : based on or existing by custom   **2** : commonly done or observed

cus·tom·er *n* : a person who buys from or uses the services of a company especially regularly

¹cut *vb* **cut**; **cut·ting**   **1** : to penetrate or divide with or as if with an edged tool : CLEAVE   **2** : to undergo shaping or penetrating with an edged tool   **3** : to experience the growth of through the gum   **4** : to hurt someone's feelings   **5** : to strike sharply or at an angle   **6** : to make less   **7** : ²CROSS 3, INTERSECT   **8** : to shape by carving or grinding   **9** : ¹SWERVE   **10** : to go by a short or direct path or course   **11** : to divide into two parts   **12** : to stop or cause to stop   **13** : ¹SNUB

²cut *n*   **1** : something cut or cut off   **2** : ¹SHARE 1   **3** : something (as a gash or wound) produced by or as if by cutting   **4** : a passage made by digging or cutting   **5** : a pictorial illustration (as in a book)   **6** : something done or said that hurts the feelings   **7** : a straight path or course   **8** : a cutting stroke or blow   **9** : the way in which a thing is cut, formed, or made   **10** : REDUCTION 1

cute *adj* **cut·er**; **cut·est**   **1** : KEEN 4, SHREWD   **2** : attractive especially in looks or actions

cu·ti·cle *n*   **1** : an outer layer (as of skin or a leaf) often produced by the cells beneath   **2** : a dead or horny layer of skin especially around a fingernail

cut·lass *n* : a short heavy curved sword

cut·lery *n*   **1** : cutting tools (as knives and scissors)   **2** : utensils used in cutting, serving, and eating food

cut·let *n*   **1** : a small slice of meat cut for broiling or frying   **2** : a piece of food shaped like a cutlet

cut·out *n* : something cut out or intended to be cut out from something else

cut out *vb* : to form by cutting

cut·ter *n*   **1** : someone or something that cuts   **2** : a boat used by warships for carrying passengers and stores to and from the shore   **3** : a small sailing boat with one mast   **4** : a small armed boat used by the Coast Guard

cut·ting *n* : a part (as a shoot) of a plant able to grow into a whole new plant

cut·tle·fish *n* : a sea animal with ten arms that is related to the squid and octopus

cut·up *n* : a person who clowns or acts in a noisy manner

cut·worm *n* : a moth caterpillar that has a smooth body and feeds on the stems of plants at night

-cy *n suffix, pl* **-cies**   **1** : action : practice   **2** : rank : office   **3** : body : class   **4** : state : quality

cy·a·nide *n* : any of several compounds containing carbon and nitrogen and including two very poisonous substances

cy·cad *n* : a tropical tree like a palm but related to the conifers

1cy·cle *n* **1** : a period of time taken up by a series of events or actions that repeat themselves again and again in the same order **2** : a complete round or series **3** : a long period of time : AGE **4** : BICYCLE **5** : TRICYCLE **6** : MOTORCYCLE

2cycle *vb* **cy·cled; cy·cling** : to ride a cycle

cy·clist *n* : a person who rides a cycle and especially a bicycle

cy·clone *n* **1** : a storm or system of winds that rotates about a center of low atmospheric pressure in a counterclockwise direction north of the equator and a clockwise direction south of the equator and that moves forward at a speed of thirty to fifty kilometers per hour and often brings heavy rain **2** : TORNADO

cy·clops *n, pl* **cyclops** : WATER FLEA

cyl·in·der *n* : a long round body whether hollow or solid

cy·lin·dri·cal *adj* : having the shape of a cylinder

cym·bal *n* : either of a pair of brass plates that are clashed together to make a sharp ringing sound and that together form a musical percussion instrument

cy·press *n* : any of various evergreen trees that are related to the pines, bear cones, and have strong reddish wood which is not easily damaged by moisture

cyst *n* **1** : an abnormal sac in a living body **2** : a covering like a cyst or a body (as a spore) with such a covering

cy·to·plasm *n* : the protoplasm of a cell except for the nucleus

czar *n* : the ruler of Russia until the 1917 revolution

cza·ri·na *n* **1** : the wife of a czar **2** : a woman who has the rank of czar

D

d *n, pl* **d's** *or* **ds** *often cap* **1** : the fourth letter of the English alphabet **2** : 500 in Roman numerals **3** : a grade that shows a student's work is poor

1dab *n* **1** : a sudden poke **2** : a small amount **3** : a light quick touch

2dab *vb* **dabbed; dab·bing** **1** : to strike or touch lightly **2** : to apply with light or uneven strokes — **dab·ber** *n*

dab·ble *vb* **dab·bled; dab·bling** **1** : to wet by splashing : SPATTER **2** : to paddle in or as if in water **3** : to work without real interest or effort — **dab·bler** *n*

dace *n, pl* **dace** : any of several small fishes related to the carps

dachs·hund *n* : a small hound with a long body, very short legs, and long drooping ears

dad *n* : 1FATHER 1

dad·dy *n, pl* **daddies** : 1FATHER 1

dad·dy long·legs *n, pl* **daddy longlegs** **1** : an insect like a spider but with a small rounded body and long slender legs **2** : a slender two-winged fly with long legs

daf·fo·dil *n* : a plant that grows from a bulb and has long slender leaves and yellow, white, or pinkish flowers suggesting trumpets and having a scalloped edge and leaflike parts at the base

daft *adj* : FOOLISH, CRAZY — **daft·ly** *adv* — **daft·ness** *n*

dag·ger *n* : a short knife used for stabbing

dahl·ia *n* : a tall plant related to the daisies and widely grown for its bright flowers

1dai·ly *adj* **1** : occurring, done, produced, or issued every day or every weekday **2** : given or paid for one day

2daily *adv* : every day

3daily *n, pl* **dai·lies** : a newspaper published every weekday

1dain·ty *n, pl* **dain·ties** : DELICACY 1

2dainty *adj* **dain·ti·er; dain·ti·est** **1** : tasting good **2** : pretty in a delicate way **3** : having or showing delicate taste — **dain·ti·ly** *adv* — **dain·ti·ness** *n*

dairy *n, pl* **dair·ies** **1** : a place where milk is stored or is made into butter and cheese **2** : a farm that produces milk **3** : a company or a store that sells milk products

dairy·ing *n* : the business of producing milk or milk products

dairy·maid *n* : a woman or girl who works in a dairy

dairy·man *n, pl* **dairy·men** : a man who operates a dairy farm or works in a dairy

da·is *n* : a raised platform (as in a hall or large room)

dai·sy *n, pl* **daisies** : any of a large group of plants with flower heads consisting of one or more rows of white or colored flowers like petals around a central disk of tiny often yellow flowers closely packed together

dale *n* : VALLEY

dal·ly *vb* **dal·lied; dal·ly·ing** **1** : to act playfully **2** : to waste time **3** : LINGER, DAWDLE

dal·ma·tian *n, often cap* : a large dog having a short white coat with black or brown spots

1dam *n* : a female parent — used especially of a domestic animal

2dam *n* : a barrier (as across a stream) to hold back a flow of water

3dam *vb* **dammed; dam·ming** : to hold back or block with or as if with a dam

1dam·age *n* **1** : loss or harm due to injury **2 damages** *pl* : money demanded or paid according to law for injury or damage

2damage *vb* **dam·aged; dam·ag·ing** : to cause damage to

dam·ask *n* : a fancy cloth used especially for household linen

dame *n* : a woman of high rank or social position

1damn *vb* **1** : to condemn to everlasting punishment especially in hell **2** : to declare to be bad or a failure **3** : to swear at : CURSE

2damn *n* : the word *damn* used as a curse

dam·na·ble *adj* : very bad : OUTRAGEOUS — **dam·na·bly** *adv*

1damned *adj* **damned·er; damned·est 1** : DAMNABLE **2** : REMARKABLE

2damned *adv* : to a high degree : VERY

1damp *n* **1** : a harmful gas found especially in coal mines **2** : MOISTURE

2damp *vb* : DAMPEN

3damp *adj* : slightly wet : MOIST — **damp·ly** *adv* — **damp·ness** *n*

damp·en *vb* **1** : to make dull or less active **2** : to make or become damp — **damp·en·er** *n*

damp·er *n* **1** : something that checks, discourages, or deadens **2** : a valve or movable plate for controlling a flow of air

dam·sel *n* : GIRL 1, MAIDEN

1dance *vb* **danced; danc·ing 1** : to glide, step, or move through a series of movements usually in time to music **2** : to move about or up and down quickly and lightly **3** : to perform or take part in as a dancer — **danc·er** *n*

2dance *n* **1** : an act of dancing **2** : a social gathering for dancing **3** : a set of movements or steps for dancing usually in time to special music **4** : the art of dancing

dan·de·li·on *n* : a weedy plant related to the daisies that has a ring of long deeply toothed leaves often eaten as cooked greens or in salad and bright yellow flowers with hollow stems

dan·druff *n* : thin dry whitish flakes that form on the scalp and come off freely

1dan·dy *n, pl* **dandies 1** : a man who pays a great deal of attention to his clothes **2** : an excellent or unusual example

2dandy *adj* **dan·di·er; dan·di·est** : very good

Dane *n* : a person born or living in Denmark

dan·ger *n* **1** : the state of not being protected from harm or evil : PERIL **2** : something that may cause injury or harm

dan·ger·ous *adj* **1** : full of danger **2** : able or likely to injure — **dan·ger·ous·ly** *adv*

dan·gle *vb* **dan·gled; dan·gling 1** : to hang loosely especially with a swinging or jerking motion **2** : to depend on something else **3** : to cause to dangle

1Dan·ish *adj* : of or relating to Denmark, the Danes, or Danish

2Danish *n* **1** : the language of the Danes **2** : a piece of Danish pastry

Danish pastry *n* : a pastry made of rich raised dough

dank *adj* : unpleasantly wet or moist — **dank·ly** *adv* — **dank·ness** *n*

dap·per *adj* : neat and trim in dress or appearance

dap·ple *vb* **dap·pled; dap·pling** : to mark or become marked with rounded spots of color

1dare *vb* **dared; dar·ing 1** : to have courage enough for some purpose : be bold enough — sometimes used as a helping verb **2** : to challenge to do something especially as a proof of courage

2dare *n* : a demand that one do something difficult or dangerous as proof of courage

dare·dev·il *n* : a person so bold as to be reckless

1dar·ing *adj* : ready to take risks : BOLD, VENTURESOME — **dar·ing·ly** *adv*

2daring *n* : bold fearlessness : readiness to take chances

1dark *adj* **1** : being without light or without much light **2** : not light in color **3** : not bright and cheerful : GLOOMY **4** : being without knowledge and culture — **dark·ish** *adj* — **dark·ly** *adv* — **dark·ness** *n*

2dark *n* **1** : absence of light **2** : a place or time of little or no light

dark·en *vb* **1** : to make or grow dark or darker **2** : to make or become gloomy — **dark·en·er** *n*

dark·room *n* : a usually small lightproof room used in developing photographic plates and film

1dar·ling *n* **1** : a dearly loved person **2** : 1FAVORITE

2darling *adj* **1** : dearly loved **2** : very pleasing : CHARMING

1darn *vb* : to mend by interlacing threads

2darn *n* : a place that has been darned

3darn *n* : 2DAMN

darning needle *n* : DRAGONFLY

1dart *n* **1** : a small pointed object that is meant to be thrown **2 darts** *pl* : a game in which darts are thrown at a target **3** : a quick sudden movement **4** : a stitched fold in a garment

²dart *vb* : to move or shoot out suddenly and quickly

¹dash *vb* **1** : to knock, hurl, or shove violently **2** : ²SMASH 1 **3** : ¹SPLASH 2 **4** : DESTROY 1 **5** : to complete or do hastily **6** : to move with sudden speed

²dash *n* **1** : a sudden burst or splash **2** : a punctuation mark — that is used most often to show a break in the thought or structure of a sentence **3** : a small amount : TOUCH **4** : liveliness in style and action **5** : a sudden rush or attempt **6** : a short fast race **7** : a long click or buzz forming a letter or part of a letter (as in telegraphy) **8** : DASHBOARD

dash·board *n* : a panel across an automobile or aircraft below the windshield usually containing dials and controls

dash·ing *adj* : having clothes or manners that are very fancy and stylish

das·tard *n* : a mean and sneaky coward

das·tard·ly *adj* : of or like a dastard — **das·tard·li·ness** *n*

da·ta *n sing or pl* **1** : facts about something that can be used in calculating, reasoning, or planning **2** : DATUM

da·ta·base *n* : a collection of data that is organized especially to be used by a computer

¹date *n* : the sweet brownish fruit of an Old World palm (**date palm**)

²date *n* **1** : the day, month, or year of a happening **2** : a statement of time on something (as a coin, letter, book, or building) **3** : APPOINTMENT 3 **4** : a person with whom one has a social engagement

³date *vb* **dat·ed; dat·ing 1** : to find or show the date of **2** : to write the date on **3** : to make or have a date with **4** : to belong to or have survived from a time **5** : to show to be old-fashioned or belonging to a past time

da·tum *n, pl* **da·ta** *or* **datums** : a single piece of information : FACT

¹daub *vb* **1** : to cover with something soft and sticky **2** : to paint or color carelessly or badly — **daub·er** *n*

²daub *n* : something daubed on : SMEAR

daugh·ter *n* **1** : a female child or offspring **2** : a woman or girl associated with or thought of as a child of something (as a country, race, or religion) — **daugh·ter·ly** *adj*

daugh·ter–in–law *n, pl* **daugh·ters–in–law** : the wife of one's son

daunt *vb* : DISCOURAGE 1, INTIMIDATE

daunt·less *adj* : bravely determined — **daunt·less·ly** *adv* — **daunt·less·ness** *n*

dau·phin *n* : the oldest son of a king of France

dav·en·port *n* : a large sofa

da·vit *n* : one of a pair of posts fitted with ropes and pulleys and used for supporting and lowering a ship's boat

daw·dle *vb* **daw·dled; daw·dling 1** : to spend time wastefully : DALLY **2** : to move slowly and without purpose — **daw·dler** *n*

¹dawn *vb* **1** : to begin to grow light as the sun rises **2** : to start becoming plain or clear

²dawn *n* **1** : the time when the sun comes up in the morning **2** : a first appearance : BEGINNING

day *n* **1** : the time between sunrise and sunset : DAYLIGHT **2** : the time the earth takes to make one turn on its axis **3** : a period of twenty-four hours beginning at midnight **4** : a specified day or date **5** : a specified period : AGE **6** : the time set apart by custom or law for work

day·bed *n* : a couch with low head and foot pieces

day·break *n* : ²DAWN 1

¹day·dream *n* : a happy or pleasant imagining about oneself or one's future

²daydream *vb* : to have a daydream — **day·dream·er** *n*

day·light *n* **1** : the light of day **2** : DAYTIME **3** : ²DAWN 1 **4** *pl* : normal soundness of the mind

daylight saving time *n* : time usually one hour ahead of standard time

day·time *n* : the period of daylight

¹daze *vb* **dazed; daz·ing** : to stun especially by a blow

²daze *n* : a dazed state

daz·zle *vb* **daz·zled; daz·zling 1** : to confuse or be confused by too much light or by moving lights **2** : to confuse, surprise, or delight by being or doing something special and unusual — **daz·zler** *n* — **daz·zling·ly** *adv*

DDT *n* : a chemical formerly used as an insecticide but found to damage the environment

de- *prefix* **1** : do the opposite of **2** : reverse of **3** : remove or remove from a specified thing **4** : reduce **5** : get off of

dea·con *n* **1** : an official in some Christian churches ranking just below a priest **2** : a church member who has special duties (as helping a minister)

¹dead *adj* **1** : no longer living : LIFELESS **2** : having the look of death **3** : ¹NUMB 1 **4** : very tired **5** : never having lived : INANIMATE **6** : lacking motion, activity, energy, or power to function **7** : no longer in use : OBSOLETE **8** : lacking warmth, vigor, or liveliness **9** : ACCURATE, PRECISE **10** : being sudden and complete **11** : ¹COMPLETE 1, TOTAL

²dead *n, pl* **dead 1** *dead pl* : those that are dead **2** : the time of greatest quiet

³dead *adv* **1** : in a whole or complete manner **2** : suddenly and completely **3** : ²STRAIGHT

dead·en *vb* : to take away some of the force of : make less

dead end *n* : an end (as of a street) with no way out

dead heat *n* : a contest that ends in a tie

dead letter *n* : a letter that cannot be delivered by the post office or returned to the sender

dead·line *n* : a date or time by which something must be done

¹dead·lock *n* : a stopping of action because both sides in a struggle are equally strong and neither will give in

²deadlock *vb* : to bring or come to a deadlock

¹dead·ly *adj* **dead·li·er; dead·li·est** **1** : causing or capable of causing death **2** : meaning or hoping to kill or destroy **3** : very accurate **4** : causing spiritual death **5** : suggestive of death **6** : ¹EXTREME 1 — **dead·li·ness** *n*

²deadly *adv* **1** : in a way suggestive of death **2** : to an extreme degree

deaf *adj* **1** : wholly or partly unable to hear **2** : unwilling to hear or listen — **deaf·ness** *n*

deaf·en *vb* **1** : to make deaf **2** : to stun with noise

deaf–mute *n* : a person who can neither hear nor speak

¹deal *n* **1** : an indefinite amount **2** : one's turn to deal the cards in a card game

²deal *vb* **dealt; deal·ing** **1** : to give out one or a few at a time **2** : ¹GIVE 5, ADMINISTER **3** : to have to do **4** : to take action **5** : to buy and sell regularly : TRADE — **deal·er** *n*

³deal *n* **1** : an agreement to do business **2** : treatment received **3** : a secret agreement **4** : ¹BARGAIN 2

deal·ing *n* **1** : ³DEAL 1 **2** : a way of acting or doing business

dean *n* **1** : a church official in charge of a cathedral **2** : the head of a section (as a college) of a university **3** : an official in charge of students or studies in a school or college — **dean·ship** *n*

¹dear *adj* **1** : greatly loved or cared about **2** — used as form of address especially in letters **3** : high-priced **4** : deeply felt : EARNEST — **dear·ly** *adv* — **dear·ness** *n*

²dear *adv* : at a high price

³dear *n* : a loved one : DARLING

dearth *n* : SCARCITY, LACK

death *n* **1** : the end or ending of life **2** : the cause of loss of life **3** : the state of being dead **4** : DESTRUCTION 2 — **death·less** *adj* — **death·like** *adj*

death·bed *n* **1** : the bed a person dies in **2** : the last hours of life

death·blow *n* : a fatal or crushing blow or event

¹death·ly *adj* : of, relating to, or suggesting death

²deathly *adv* : in a way suggesting death

de·bar *vb* **de·barred; de·bar·ring** : to keep from having or doing something

de·base *vb* **de·based; de·bas·ing** : to make less good or valuable than before — **de·base·ment** *n*

de·bat·able *adj* : possible to question or argue about

¹de·bate *n* **1** : a discussion or argument carried on between two teams **2** : DISCUSSION

²debate *vb* **de·bat·ed; de·bat·ing** **1** : to discuss a question by giving arguments on both sides : take part in a debate **2** : to consider reasons for and against — **de·bat·er** *n*

de·bil·i·tate *vb* **de·bil·i·tat·ed; de·bil·i·tat·ing** : to make feeble : WEAKEN

de·bil·i·ty *n, pl* **de·bil·i·ties** : a weakened state especially of health

¹deb·it *vb* : to record as a debit

²debit *n* : a business record showing money paid out or owed

deb·o·nair *adj* : gaily and gracefully charming — **deb·o·nair·ly** *adv* — **deb·o·nair·ness** *n*

de·bris *n, pl* **de·bris** : the junk or pieces left from something broken down or destroyed

debt *n* **1** : ¹SIN **2** : something owed to another **3** : the condition of owing money

debt·or *n* : a person who owes a debt

de·but *n* **1** : a first public appearance **2** : the formal entrance of a young woman into society

deb·u·tante *n* : a young woman making her debut

deca- *or* **dec-** *or* **deka-** *or* **dek-** *prefix* : ten

de·cade *n* : a period of ten years

deca·gon *n* : a closed figure having ten angles and ten sides

de·cal *n* : a design made to be transferred (as to glass) from specially prepared paper

deca·logue *n, often cap* : the ten commandments of God given to Moses on Mount Sinai

de·camp *vb* : to go away suddenly and usually secretly : run away

de·cant·er *n* : an ornamental glass bottle used especially for serving wine

de·cap·i·tate *vb* **de·cap·i·tat·ed; de·cap·i·tat·ing** : to cut off the head of : BEHEAD

¹de·cay *vb* : to weaken in health or soundness (as by aging or rotting)

²decay *n* **1** : the state of something that is decayed or decaying : a spoiled or rotting condition **2** : a gradual getting worse or failing **3** : a natural change of a radioactive element into another form of the same element or into a different element

1de·cease n : DEATH 1

2decease vb **de·ceased; de·ceas·ing** : 1DIE 1

de·ce·dent n : a dead person

de·ceit n **1** : the act or practice of deceiving : DECEPTION **2** : a statement or act that misleads a person or causes him or her to believe what is false : TRICK

de·ceit·ful adj : full of deceit : not honest — **de·ceit·ful·ly** adv — **de·ceit·ful·ness** n

de·ceive vb **de·ceived; de·ceiv·ing** **1** : to cause to believe what is not true : MISLEAD **2** : to be dishonest and misleading — **de·ceiv·er** n

de·cel·er·ate vb **de·cel·er·at·ed; de·cel·er·at·ing** : to slow down

De·cem·ber n : the twelfth month of the year

de·cen·cy n, pl **de·cen·cies** **1** : a way or habit of conducting oneself that is decent : modest or proper behavior **2** : something that is right and proper

de·cent adj **1** : meeting an accepted standard of good taste (as in speech, dress, or behavior) **2** : being moral and good : not dirty **3** : fairly good — **de·cent·ly** adv

de·cep·tion n **1** : the act of deceiving **2** : 1TRICK 1

de·cep·tive adj : tending or able to deceive — **de·cep·tive·ly** adv

deci- prefix : tenth part

deci·bel n : a unit for measuring the relative loudness of sounds

de·cide vb **de·cid·ed; de·cid·ing** **1** : to make a judgment on **2** : to bring to an end **3** : to make or cause to make a choice

de·cid·ed adj **1** : UNMISTAKABLE **2** : free from doubt — **de·cid·ed·ly** adv

de·cid·u·ous adj : made up of or having a part that falls off at the end of a period of growth and use

1dec·i·mal adj **1** : based on the number 10 : numbered or counting by tens **2** : expressed in or including a decimal

2decimal n : a proper fraction in which the denominator is 10 or 10 multiplied one or more times by itself and is indicated by a point (**decimal point**) placed at the left of the numerator

deci·me·ter n : a unit of length equal to one tenth meter

de·ci·pher vb **1** : to translate from secret writing : DECODE **2** : to make out the meaning of something not clear

de·ci·sion n **1** : the act or result of deciding **2** : promptness and firmness in deciding

de·ci·sive adj **1** : deciding or able to decide a question or dispute **2** : RESOLUTE **3**

: 1CLEAR 7, UNMISTAKABLE — **de·ci·sive·ly** adv — **de·ci·sive·ness** n

1deck n **1** : a floor that goes from one side of a ship to the other **2** : something like the deck of a ship **3** : a pack of playing cards

2deck vb : to dress or decorate especially in a showy way

dec·la·ra·tion n **1** : an act of declaring **2** : something declared or a document containing such a declaration

de·clar·a·tive adj : making a statement

de·clare vb **de·clared; de·clar·ing** **1** : to make known in a clear or formal way **2** : to state as if certain

1de·cline vb **de·clined; de·clin·ing** **1** : to bend or slope downward **2** : to pass toward a lower, worse, or weaker state **3** : to refuse to accept, do, or agree

2decline n **1** : a gradual weakening in body or mind **2** : a change to a lower state or level **3** : the time when something is nearing its end

de·code vb **de·cod·ed; de·cod·ing** : to change a message in code into ordinary language

de·com·pose vb **de·com·posed; de·com·pos·ing** **1** : to separate a thing into its parts or into simpler compounds **2** : to break down in decaying — **de·com·pos·er** n

de·com·po·si·tion n **1** : the process of decomposing **2** : the state of being decomposed

dec·o·rate vb **dec·o·rat·ed; dec·o·rat·ing** **1** : to make more attractive by adding something nice looking **2** : to award a decoration of honor to

dec·o·ra·tion n **1** : the act of decorating **2** : 1ORNAMENT 1 **3** : a badge of honor

dec·o·ra·tive adj : serving to decorate : ORNAMENTAL

dec·o·ra·tor n : a person who decorates especially the rooms of houses

de·co·rum n : proper behavior

1de·coy n : a person or thing (as an artificial bird) used to lead or lure into a trap or snare

2decoy vb : to lure by or as if by a decoy

1de·crease vb **de·creased; de·creas·ing** : to grow less or cause to grow less

2de·crease n **1** : the process of decreasing **2** : REDUCTION 2

1de·cree n : an order or decision given by a person or group in authority

2decree vb **de·creed; de·cree·ing** : to order by a decree

de·crep·it adj : worn out or weakened by age or use

de·cre·scen·do n : a gradual decrease in the loudness of music

ded·i·cate vb **ded·i·cat·ed; ded·i·cat·ing** **1**

: to set apart for some purpose and especially for a sacred or serious purpose : DEVOTE **2** : to address or write something in (as a book) as a compliment to someone

ded·i·ca·tion *n* **1** : an act of dedicating **2** : something written in dedicating a book **3** : devotion to the point of giving up what one needs or loves

de·duct *vb* : to take away an amount of something : SUBTRACT

de·duc·tion *n* **1** : SUBTRACTION **2** : an amount deducted

1deed *n* **1** : a usually fine or brave act or action : FEAT **2** : a legal document containing the record of an agreement or especially of a transfer of real estate

2deed *vb* : to transfer by a deed

deem *vb* : to hold as an opinion

1deep *adj* **1** : reaching down far below the surface **2** : reaching far back from the front or outer part **3** : hard to understand **4** : located well below the surface or well within the boundaries of **5** : fully developed : PROFOUND **6** : dark and rich in color **7** : low in tone **8** : completely busy — **deep·ly** *adv*

2deep *adv* : to a great depth : DEEPLY

3deep *n* **1** : a very deep place or part **2** : OCEAN 1

deep·en *vb* : to make or become deep or deeper

deep fat *n* : hot fat or oil deep enough in a cooking utensil to cover the food to be fried

deep–fry *vb* : to cook in deep fat

deer *n, pl* **deer** : any of a group of mammals that chew the cud and have cloven hoofs and in the male antlers which are often branched

deer·skin *n* : leather made from the skin of a deer or a garment made of such leather

de·face *vb* **de·faced; de·fac·ing** : to destroy or mar the face or surface of — **de·face·ment** *n* — **de·fac·er** *n*

1de·fault *n* : failure to do something required by law or duty

2default *vb* : to fail to do one's duty — **de·fault·er** *n*

1de·feat *vb* **1** : to bring to nothing **2** : to win victory over

2defeat *n* : loss of a contest or battle

de·fect *n* : a lack of something necessary for completeness or perfection

de·fec·tive *adj* : lacking something necessary : FAULTY

de·fend *vb* **1** : to protect from danger or attack **2** : to act or speak in favor of when others are opposed — **de·fend·er** *n*

de·fense *n* **1** : the act of defending **2** : something that defends or protects **3** : a defensive team — **de·fense·less** *adj*

1de·fen·sive *adj* **1** : serving or meant to defend or protect **2** : of or relating to the attempt to keep an opponent from scoring (as in a game) — **de·fen·sive·ly** *adv*

2defensive *n* : a defensive position or attitude

1de·fer *vb* **de·ferred; de·fer·ring** : to put off to a future time — **de·fer·ment** *n*

2defer *vb* **de·ferred; de·fer·ring** : to yield to the opinion or wishes of another

def·er·ence *n* : respect and consideration for the wishes of another

de·fi·ance *n* **1** : an act of defying **2** : a willingness to resist

de·fi·ant *adj* : showing defiance — **de·fi·ant·ly** *adv*

de·fi·cien·cy *n, pl* **de·fi·cien·cies** : the state of being without something necessary and especially something required for health

de·fi·cient *adj* : lacking something necessary for completeness or health

def·i·cit *n* : a shortage especially in money needed

de·file *vb* **de·filed; de·fil·ing** **1** : to make filthy **2** : 1CORRUPT 1 **3** : 2DISHONOR — **de·file·ment** *n*

de·fine *vb* **de·fined; de·fin·ing** **1** : to set or mark the limits of **2** : to make distinct in outline **3** : to find out and explain the meaning of — **de·fin·er** *n*

def·i·nite *adj* **1** : having certain or distinct limits **2** : clear in meaning **3** : UNQUESTIONABLE — **def·i·nite·ly** *adv* — **def·i·nite·ness** *n*

definite article *n* : the article *the* used to show that the following noun refers to one or more specific persons or things

def·i·ni·tion *n* **1** : an act of defining **2** : a statement of the meaning of a word or a word group **3** : clearness of outline or detail

de·flate *vb* **de·flat·ed; de·flat·ing** **1** : to let the air or gas out of something that has been blown up **2** : to reduce in size or importance

de·flect *vb* : to turn aside

de·for·est *vb* : to clear of forests

de·form *vb* : to spoil the form or the natural appearance of

de·for·mi·ty *n, pl* **de·for·mi·ties** **1** : the condition of being deformed **2** : a flaw or blemish in something and especially in the body of a person or animal

de·fraud *vb* : to take or keep something from by deceit : CHEAT

de·frost *vb* **1** : to thaw out **2** : to remove ice from — **de·frost·er** *n*

deft *adj* : quick and neat in action : SKILLFUL — **deft·ly** *adv* — **deft·ness** *n*

de·fy *vb* **de·fied; de·fy·ing** **1** : to challenge

to do something thought to be impossible
: DARE　**2** : to refuse boldly to obey or yield
to　**3** : to resist the effects of or attempts at

deg·ra·da·tion *n*　**1** : an act of degrading　**2**
: the state of being degraded

de·grade *vb* **de·grad·ed; de·grad·ing**　**1**
: to reduce from a higher to a lower rank or
degree　**2** : to bring to a low state : DEBASE,
CORRUPT

de·gree *n*　**1** : a step in a series　**2** : amount
of something as measured by a series of
steps　**3** : one of the three forms an adjective or adverb may have when it is compared　**4** : a title given (as to students) by a
college or university　**5** : one of the divisions marked on a measuring instrument (as
a thermometer)　**6** : a 360th part of the circumference of a circle　**7** : a line or space of
the staff in music or the difference in pitch
between two notes

de·hu·mid·i·fy *vb* **de·hu·mid·i·fied; de·hu-
mid·i·fy·ing** : to take moisture from (as the
air) — **de·hu·mid·i·fi·er** *n*

de·hy·drate *vb* **de·hy·drat·ed; de·hy·drat-
ing**　**1** : to take water from (as foods)　**2** : to
lose water or body fluids

de·ice *vb* **de·iced; de·ic·ing** : to free or keep
free of ice — **de·ic·er** *n*

de·i·fy *vb* **de·i·fied; de·i·fy·ing** : to make a
god of

deign *vb* : CONDESCEND 1

de·i·ty *n, pl* **de·i·ties**　**1** *cap* : GOD 1　**2**
: GOD 2, GODDESS

de·ject·ed *adj* : low in spirits — **de·ject·ed·
ly** *adv*

de·jec·tion *n* : a dejected state

deka- *or* **dek-** — see DECA-

¹de·lay *n*　**1** : a putting off of something　**2**
: the time during which something is de-
layed

²delay *vb*　**1** : to put off　**2** : to stop or prevent for a time　**3** : to move or act slowly

¹del·e·gate *n* : a person sent with power to
act for another or others

²del·e·gate *vb* **del·e·gat·ed; del·e·gat·ing**
1 : to entrust to another　**2** : to make responsible for getting something done

del·e·ga·tion *n*　**1** : the act of delegating　**2**
: one or more persons chosen to represent
others

de·lete *vb* **de·let·ed; de·let·ing** : to take out
from something written especially by eras-
ing, crossing out, or cutting

de·le·tion *n*　**1** : an act of deleting　**2** : something deleted

¹de·lib·er·ate *vb* **de·lib·er·at·ed; de·lib·er-
at·ing** : to think about carefully

²de·lib·er·ate *adj*　**1** : showing careful
thought　**2** : done or said on purpose　**3**

: slow in action : not hurried — **de·lib·er·
ate·ly** *adv* — **de·lib·er·ate·ness** *n*

de·lib·er·a·tion *n*　**1** : careful thought : CON-
SIDERATION　**2** : the quality of being deliberate

del·i·ca·cy *n, pl* **del·i·ca·cies**　**1** : something
pleasing to eat that is rare or a luxury　**2**
: fineness of structure　**3** : weakness of
body : FRAILTY　**4** : a situation needing
careful handling　**5** : consideration for the
feelings of others

del·i·cate *adj*　**1** : pleasing because of fineness or mildness　**2** : able to sense very
small differences　**3** : calling for skill and
careful treatment　**4** : easily damaged　**5**
: SICKLY 1　**6** : requiring tact — **del·i·cate·
ly** *adv*

del·i·ca·tes·sen *n* : a store where prepared
foods (as salads and cooked meats) are sold

de·li·cious *adj* : giving great pleasure especially to the taste or smell — **de·li·cious·ly**
adv — **de·li·cious·ness** *n*

¹de·light *n*　**1** : great pleasure or satisfaction
: JOY　**2** : something that gives great pleasure

²delight *vb*　**1** : to take great pleasure　**2** : to
give joy or satisfaction to

de·light·ed *adj* : very pleased

de·light·ful *adj* : giving delight : very pleasing — **de·light·ful·ly** *adv*

de·lir·i·ous *adj*　**1** : suffering delirium　**2**
: wildly excited — **de·lir·i·ous·ly** *adv*

de·lir·i·um *n*　**1** : a condition of mind in
which thought and speech are confused and
which often goes along with a high fever　**2**
: wild excitement

de·liv·er *vb*　**1** : to set free : RESCUE　**2**
: ¹TRANSFER 2　**3** : to help in childbirth　**4**
: ²UTTER 2　**5** : to send to an intended target
— **de·liv·er·er** *n*

de·liv·er·ance *n* : an act of delivering or the
state of being delivered : a setting free

de·liv·ery *n, pl* **de·liv·er·ies**　**1** : a setting
free (as from something that hampers or
holds one back)　**2** : the transfer of something from one place or person to another
3 : the act of giving birth　**4** : speaking or
manner of speaking (as of a formal speech)
5 : the act or way of throwing

dell *n* : a small valley usually covered with
trees

del·phin·i·um *n* : a tall plant related to the
buttercups and often grown for its large
stalks of showy flowers

del·ta *n* : a piece of land in the shape of a triangle or fan made by deposits of mud and
sand at the mouth of a river

de·lude *vb* **de·lud·ed; de·lud·ing** : DE-
CEIVE, MISLEAD

¹del·uge *n*　**1** : a flooding of land by water

: FLOOD **2** : a drenching rain **3** : a sudden huge stream of something

²deluge *vb* **del·uged; del·ug·ing 1** : ²FLOOD 1 **2** : to overwhelm as if with a deluge

de·lu·sion *n* **1** : an act of deluding or the state of being deluded **2** : a false belief that continues in spite of the facts

de·luxe *adj* : very fine or luxurious

delve *vb* **delved; delv·ing 1** : DIG **2** : to work hard looking for information in written records — **delv·er** *n*

¹de·mand *n* **1** : an act of demanding **2** : an expressed desire to own or use something **3** : a seeking or being sought after

²demand *vb* **1** : to claim as one's right **2** : to ask earnestly or in the manner of a command **3** : to call for : REQUIRE — **de·mand·er** *n*

de·mean *vb* **de·meaned; de·mean·ing** : to behave or conduct (oneself) usually in a proper way

de·mean·or *n* : outward manner or behavior

de·ment·ed *adj* : INSANE 1, MAD — **de·ment·ed·ly** *adv*

de·mer·it *n* : a mark placed against a person's record for doing something wrong

demi- *prefix* **1** : half **2** : one that partly belongs to a specified type or class

demi·god *n* : one who is partly divine and partly human

de·mo·bi·lize *vb* **de·mo·bi·lized; de·mo·bi·liz·ing** : to let go from military service

de·moc·ra·cy *n, pl* **de·moc·ra·cies 1** : government by the people : majority rule **2** : government in which the highest power is held by the people and is usually used through representatives **3** : a political unit (as a nation) governed by the people **4** : belief in or practice of the idea that all people are socially equal

dem·o·crat *n* : one who believes in or practices democracy

dem·o·crat·ic *adj* **1** : of, relating to, or favoring political democracy **2** : believing in or practicing the idea that people are socially equal — **dem·o·crat·i·cal·ly** *adv*

de·mol·ish *vb* **1** : to destroy by breaking apart **2** : to ruin completely : SHATTER

de·mon *n* **1** : an evil spirit : DEVIL **2** : a person of great energy or skill

dem·on·strate *vb* **dem·on·strat·ed; dem·on·strat·ing 1** : to show clearly **2** : to prove or make clear by reasoning **3** : to explain (as in teaching) by use of examples or experiments **4** : to show to people the good qualities of an article or a product **5** : to make a public display (as of feelings or military force)

dem·on·stra·tion *n* **1** : an outward expression (as a show of feelings) **2** : an act or a means of demonstrating **3** : a showing or using of an article for sale to display its good points **4** : a parade or a gathering to show public feeling

de·mon·stra·tive *adj* **1** : pointing out the one referred to and showing that it differs from others **2** : showing feeling freely

dem·on·stra·tor *n* **1** : a person who makes or takes part in a demonstration **2** : a manufactured article used for demonstration

de·mor·al·ize *vb* **de·mor·al·ized; de·mor·al·iz·ing** : to weaken the discipline or spirit of

de·mote *vb* **de·mot·ed; de·mot·ing** : to reduce to a lower grade or rank

de·mure *adj* **1** : MODEST 3 **2** : pretending to be modest : COY — **de·mure·ly** *adv* — **de·mure·ness** *n*

den *n* **1** : the shelter or resting place of a wild animal **2** : a quiet or private room in a home **3** : a hiding place (as for thieves)

de·na·ture *vb* **de·na·tured; de·na·tur·ing** : to make alcohol unfit for humans to drink

den·drite *n* : any of the usually branched fibers that carry nerve impulses toward a nerve cell body

de·ni·al *n* **1** : a refusal to give or agree to something asked for **2** : a refusal to admit the truth of a statement **3** : a refusal to accept or believe in someone or something **4** : a cutting down or limiting

den·im *n* **1** : a firm often coarse cotton cloth **2 denims** *pl* : overalls or pants of usually blue denim

de·nom·i·na·tion *n* **1** : a name especially for a class of things **2** : a religious body made up of a number of congregations having the same beliefs **3** : a value in a series of values (as of money)

de·nom·i·na·tor *n* : the part of a fraction that is below the line

de·note *vb* **de·not·ed; de·not·ing 1** : to serve as a mark or indication of **2** : to have the meaning of : MEAN

de·nounce *vb* **de·nounced; de·nounc·ing 1** : to point out as wrong or evil : CONDEMN **2** : to inform against : ACCUSE — **de·nounce·ment** *n* — **de·nounc·er** *n*

dense *adj* **dens·er; dens·est 1** : having its parts crowded together : THICK **2** : STUPID 1 — **dense·ly** *adv* — **dense·ness** *n*

den·si·ty *n, pl* **den·si·ties 1** : the state of being dense **2** : the amount of something in a specified volume or area

¹dent *vb* **1** : to make a dent in or on **2** : to become marked by a dent

²dent *n* : a notch or hollow made in a surface by a blow or by pressure

den·tal *adj* : of or relating to the teeth or dentistry — **den·tal·ly** *adv*

dental floss *n* : flat thread used for cleaning between teeth

den·ti·frice *n* : a powder, paste, or liquid used in cleaning the teeth

den·tin *or* **den·tine** *n* : a hard bony material that makes up the main part of a tooth

den·tist *n* : a person whose profession is the care, treatment, and repair of the teeth

den·tist·ry *n* : the profession or practice of a dentist

den·ture *n* : a set of false teeth

de·nude *vb* **de·nud·ed; de·nud·ing** : to strip of covering : make bare

de·ny *vb* **de·nied; de·ny·ing** 1 : to declare not to be true 2 : to refuse to grant 3 : DISOWN, REPUDIATE

de·odor·ant *n* : something used to remove or hide unpleasant odors

de·odor·ize *vb* **de·odor·ized; de·odor·iz·ing** : to remove odor and especially a bad smell from

de·part *vb* 1 : to go away or go away from : LEAVE 2 : ¹DIE 1 3 : to turn aside

de·part·ment *n* : a special part or division of an organization (as a government or college)

department store *n* : a store having individual departments for different kinds of goods

de·par·ture *n* 1 : a going away 2 : a setting out (as on a new course) 3 : a turning away or aside (as from a way of doing things)

de·pend *vb* 1 : to rely for support 2 : to be determined by or based on some action or condition 3 : ²TRUST 1, RELY

de·pend·able *adj* : TRUSTWORTHY, RELIABLE — **de·pend·ably** *adv*

de·pen·dence *n* 1 : a condition of being influenced and caused by something else 2 : a state of being dependent on someone or something 3 : ¹TRUST 1, RELIANCE

¹de·pen·dent *adj* 1 : CONTINGENT 2 : relying on someone else for support 3 : requiring something (as a drug) to feel or act normally

²dependent *n* : a person who depends upon another for support

de·pict *vb* 1 : to represent by a picture 2 : to describe in words

de·plete *vb* **de·plet·ed; de·plet·ing** : to reduce in amount by using up

de·plor·able *adj* 1 : deserving to be deplored : REGRETTABLE 2 : very bad : WRETCHED — **de·plor·ably** *adv*

de·plore *vb* **de·plored; de·plor·ing** 1 : to regret strongly 2 : to consider deserving of disapproval

de·port *vb* 1 : BEHAVE 1, CONDUCT 2 : to force (a person who is not a citizen) to leave a country

de·port·ment *n* : BEHAVIOR 1

de·pose *vb* **de·posed; de·pos·ing** : to remove from a high office

¹de·pos·it *vb* 1 : to place for or as if for safekeeping 2 : to put money in a bank 3 : to give as a pledge that a purchase will be made or a service used 4 : to lay down : PUT 5 : to let fall or sink

²deposit *n* 1 : the state of being deposited 2 : money that is deposited in a bank 3 : something given as a pledge or as part payment 4 : something laid or thrown down 5 : mineral matter built up in nature

de·pos·i·tor *n* : a person who makes a deposit especially of money in a bank

de·pot *n* 1 : a place where military supplies are kept 2 : STOREHOUSE 1 3 : a railroad or bus station

de·pre·ci·ate *vb* **de·pre·ci·at·ed; de·pre·ci·at·ing** 1 : to lower the price or value of 2 : BELITTLE 3 : to lose value

de·press *vb* 1 : to press down 2 : to lessen the activity or strength of 3 : to lower the spirits of : make sad and dull

de·pres·sant *adj or n* : SEDATIVE

de·pres·sion *n* 1 : an act of depressing : a state of being depressed 2 : a hollow place or part 3 : low spirits 4 : a period of low activity in business with much unemployment

de·pri·va·tion *n* 1 : an act or instance of depriving 2 : the state of being deprived

de·prive *vb* **de·prived; de·priv·ing** : to take something away from or keep from having or doing something

depth *n* 1 : a deep place in a body of water (as a sea or a lake) 2 : measurement from top to bottom or from front to back 3 : the innermost part of something : MIDDLE, MIDST 4 : ABUNDANCE, COMPLETENESS 5 : the quality of being deep

depth charge *n* : an explosive for use underwater especially against submarines

dep·u·tize *vb* **dep·u·tized; dep·u·tiz·ing** : to appoint as deputy

dep·u·ty *n, pl* **dep·u·ties** : a person appointed to act for or in place of another

de·rail *vb* : to cause to leave the rails — **de·rail·ment** *n*

de·range *vb* **de·ranged; de·rang·ing** 1 : to put out of order : DISARRANGE 2 : to make insane — **de·range·ment** *n*

der·by *n, pl* **der·bies** 1 : a horse race for three-year-olds usually held every year 2 : a stiff felt hat with a narrow brim and a rounded top

de·ride *vb* **de·rid·ed; de·rid·ing** : to laugh at in scorn : make fun of : RIDICULE

der·i·va·tion *n* **1** : the formation of a word from an earlier word or root **2** : ETYMOLOGY **3** : ORIGIN 3, SOURCE **4** : an act or process of deriving

1de·riv·a·tive *n* **1** : a word formed by derivation **2** : something derived

2derivative *adj* : derived from something else — **de·riv·a·tive·ly** *adv*

de·rive *vb* **de·rived; de·riv·ing** **1** : to receive or obtain from a source **2** : to trace the derivation of **3** : to come from a certain source

der·mal *adj* : of or relating to skin

der·mis *n* : the inner sensitive layer of the skin

de·rog·a·to·ry *adj* : intended to hurt the reputation of a person or thing

der·rick *n* **1** : a machine for moving or lifting heavy weights by means of a long beam fitted with ropes and pulleys **2** : a framework or tower over an oil well for supporting machinery

de·scend *vb* **1** : to come or go down from a higher place or level to a lower one **2** : to come down in sudden attack **3** : to come down from an earlier time **4** : to come down from a source : DERIVE **5** : to be handed down to an heir **6** : to sink in a social or moral scale : STOOP

de·scen·dant *n* : one that is descended from a particular ancestor or family

de·scent *n* **1** : a coming or going down **2** : one's line of ancestors **3** : a downward slope **4** : a sudden attack

de·scribe *vb* **de·scribed; de·scrib·ing** **1** : to write or tell about : give an account of **2** : to draw the outline of — **de·scrib·er** *n*

de·scrip·tion *n* **1** : an account of something especially of a kind that presents a picture to a person who reads or hears it **2** : 1SORT 1, KIND

de·scrip·tive *adj* : serving to describe — **de·scrip·tive·ly** *adv*

des·e·crate *vb* **des·e·crat·ed; des·e·crat·ing** : to treat a sacred place or sacred object shamefully or with great disrespect

de·seg·re·gate *vb* **de·seg·re·gat·ed; de·seg·re·gat·ing** : to end segregation in : free of any law or practice setting apart members of a certain race

de·seg·re·ga·tion *n* : the act or process or an instance of desegregating

1des·ert *n* : a dry barren region where only a few special kinds of plants can grow without an artificial water supply

2desert *adj* : of, relating to, or being a desert

3de·sert *n* **1** : worthiness of reward or punishment **2** : a just reward or punishment

4de·sert *vb* **1** : to leave usually without intending to return **2** : to leave a person or a thing that one should stay with **3** : to fail in time of need — **de·sert·er** *n*

de·serve *vb* **de·served; de·serv·ing** : to be worthy of : MERIT

de·served·ly *adv* : as one deserves

de·serv·ing *adj* : WORTHY

1de·sign *vb* **1** : to think up and plan out in the mind **2** : to set apart for or have as a special purpose : INTEND **3** : to make a pattern or sketch of — **de·sign·er** *n*

2design *n* **1** : 1PLAN 2, SCHEME **2** : a planned intention **3** : a secret purpose : PLOT **4** : a preliminary sketch, model, or plan **5** : an arrangement of parts in a structure or a work of art **6** : a decorative pattern

des·ig·nate *vb* **des·ig·nat·ed; des·ig·nat·ing** **1** : to mark or point out : INDICATE **2** : to appoint or choose for a special purpose : NAME **3** : to call by a name or title

des·ig·na·tion *n* **1** : an act of designating **2** : a name, sign, or title that identifies something

de·sign·ing *adj* : CRAFTY

de·sir·able *adj* **1** : having pleasing qualities : ATTRACTIVE **2** : worth having or seeking — **de·sir·ably** *adv*

1de·sire *vb* **de·sired; de·sir·ing** **1** : to long for : wish for in earnest **2** : to express a wish for : REQUEST

2desire *n* **1** : a strong wish : LONGING **2** : a wish made known : REQUEST **3** : something desired

de·sist *vb* : to stop something one is doing

desk *n* : a piece of furniture with a flat or sloping surface for use in writing or reading

1des·o·late *adj* **1** : ABANDONED **2** : having no comfort or companionship : LONELY **3** : left neglected or in ruins **4** : CHEERLESS, GLOOMY

2des·o·late *vb* **des·o·lat·ed; des·o·lat·ing** : to make or leave desolate

des·o·la·tion *n* **1** : the state of being desolated : RUIN **2** : sadness resulting from grief or loneliness

1de·spair *vb* : to give up or lose all hope or confidence

2despair *n* **1** : loss of hope : a feeling of complete hopelessness **2** : a cause of hopelessness

des·per·ate *adj* **1** : being beyond or almost beyond hope : causing despair **2** : reckless because of despair : RASH — **des·per·ate·ly** *adv* — **des·per·ate·ness** *n*

des·per·a·tion *n* : a state of hopeless despair leading to recklessness

de·spi·ca·ble *adj* : deserving to be despised — **de·spi·ca·bly** *adv*

de·spise *vb* **de·spised; de·spis·ing** : to

consider as beneath one's notice or respect : feel scorn and dislike for

de·spite *prep* : in spite of

de·spoil *vb* : to rob of possessions or belongings — PLUNDER — **de·spoil·er** *n*

de·spon·den·cy *n* : MELANCHOLY, DEJECTION

de·spon·dent *adj* : feeling quite discouraged or depressed : being in very low spirits — **de·spon·dent·ly** *adv*

des·pot *n* : a ruler having absolute power and authority and especially one who rules cruelly

des·sert *n* : a course of sweet food, fruit, or cheese served at the end of a meal

des·ti·na·tion *n* : a place that one starts out for or that something is sent to

des·tine *vb* **des·tined; des·tin·ing** **1** : to decide in advance on the future condition, use, or action of **2** : to set aside for a special purpose

des·ti·ny *n, pl* **des·ti·nies** **1** : the fate or lot to which a person or thing is destined **2** : the course of events held to be arranged by a superhuman power

des·ti·tute *adj* **1** : lacking something needed or desirable **2** : very poor

de·stroy *vb* **1** : to put an end to : do away with **2** : ¹KILL 1

de·stroy·er *n* **1** : one that destroys **2** : a small fast warship armed with guns, depth charges, torpedoes, and sometimes missiles

de·struc·ti·ble *adj* : possible to destroy

de·struc·tion *n* **1** : the act or process of destroying something **2** : the state or fact of being destroyed : RUIN **3** : something that destroys

de·struc·tive *adj* **1** : causing destruction **2** : not positive or helpful — **de·struc·tive·ly** *adv* — **de·struc·tive·ness** *n*

de·tach *vb* : to separate from something else or from others especially for a certain purpose — **de·tach·able** *adj*

de·tached *adj* **1** : not joined or connected : SEPARATE **2** : not taking sides or being influenced by others — **de·tached·ly** *adv*

de·tach·ment *n* **1** : SEPARATION 1 **2** : a body of troops or ships sent on special duty **3** : a keeping apart : lack of interest in worldly concerns **4** : IMPARTIALITY

¹de·tail *n* **1** : a dealing with something item by item **2** : a small part : ITEM **3** : a soldier or group of soldiers picked for special duty

²detail *vb* **1** : to report in detail : give the details of **2** : to select for some special duty

de·tailed *adj* : including many details

de·tain *vb* **1** : to hold or keep in or as if in prison **2** : to stop especially from going on : DELAY — **de·tain·ment** *n*

de·tect *vb* : to learn of the existence, presence, or fact of

de·tec·tion *n* : the act of detecting : the state or fact of being detected : DISCOVERY

¹de·tec·tive *adj* **1** : able to detect or used in detecting something **2** : of or relating to detectives or their work

²detective *n* : a person (as a police officer) whose business is solving crimes and catching criminals or gathering information that is not easy to get

de·ten·tion *n* **1** : the act of detaining : the state of being detained : CONFINEMENT **2** : a forced delay

de·ter *vb* **de·terred; de·ter·ring** : to discourage or prevent from doing something

¹de·ter·gent *adj* : able to clean : used in cleaning

²detergent *n* : a substance that is like soap in its ability to clean

de·te·ri·o·rate *vb* **de·te·ri·o·rat·ed; de·te·ri·o·rat·ing** : to make or become worse or of less value

de·ter·mi·na·tion *n* **1** : a coming to a decision or the decision reached **2** : a settling or making sure of the position, size, or nature of something **3** : firm or fixed intention

de·ter·mine *vb* **de·ter·mined; de·ter·min·ing** **1** : to fix exactly and with certainty **2** : to come to a decision **3** : to learn or find out exactly **4** : to be the cause of or reason for

de·ter·mined *adj* **1** : free from doubt **2** : not weak or uncertain : FIRM — **de·ter·mined·ly** *adv*

de·ter·min·er *n* : a word belonging to a group of noun modifiers that can occur before descriptive adjectives modifying the same noun

de·test *vb* : to dislike very much

de·test·able *adj* : causing or deserving strong dislike — **de·test·ably** *adv*

de·throne *vb* **de·throned; de·thron·ing** : to drive from a throne : DEPOSE — **de·throne·ment** *n*

¹de·tour *n* : a roundabout way that temporarily replaces part of a regular route

²detour *vb* : to use or follow a detour

de·tract *vb* : to take away (as from value or importance)

det·ri·ment *n* : injury or damage or its cause : HARM

dev·as·tate *vb* **dev·as·tat·ed; dev·as·tat·ing** : to reduce to ruin : lay waste

dev·as·ta·tion *n* : the action of devastating : the state of being devastated

de·vel·op *vb* **1** : to make or become plain little by little : UNFOLD **2** : to apply chemicals to exposed photographic material (as a film) in order to bring out the picture **3** : to bring out the possibilities of : IMPROVE **4** : to make more available or usable **5** : to gain gradually **6** : to grow toward maturity — **de·vel·op·er** *n*

de·vel·oped *adj* : having many large industries and a complex economic system

de·vel·op·ment *n* **1** : the act or process of developing : a result of developing **2** : the state of being developed

de·vi·ate *vb* **de·vi·at·ed; de·vi·at·ing** : to turn aside from a course, principle, standard, or topic

de·vice *n* **1** : a scheme to deceive : TRICK **2** : a piece of equipment or mechanism for a special purpose **3** : ²DESIRE 2, WILL

¹dev·il *n* **1** *often cap* : the personal supreme spirit of evil **2** : an evil spirit : DEMON, FIEND **3** : a wicked or cruel person **4** : a reckless or dashing person **5** : a mischievous person **6** : a person to be pitied

²devil *vb* **dev·iled** *or* **dev·illed; dev·il·ing** *or* **dev·il·ling 1** : to chop fine and season highly **2** : ¹TEASE, ANNOY

dev·il·ment *n* : reckless mischief

de·vise *vb* **de·vised; de·vis·ing** : to think up : PLAN, INVENT — **de·vis·er** *n*

de·void *adj* : entirely lacking

de·vote *vb* **de·vot·ed; de·vot·ing 1** : to set apart for a special purpose **2** : to give up to entirely or in part

de·vot·ed *adj* **1** : completely loyal **2** : AFFECTIONATE, LOVING — **de·vot·ed·ly** *adv*

de·vo·tion *n* **1** : a religious exercise or practice (as prayers) especially for use in private worship **2** : an act of devoting : the quality of being devoted **3** : deep love or affection

de·vour *vb* **1** : to eat up greedily **2** : CONSUME 1 **3** : to take in eagerly by the senses or mind

de·vout *adj* **1** : devoted to religion **2** : warmly sincere and earnest — **de·vout·ly** *adv* — **de·vout·ness** *n*

dew *n* : moisture condensed on cool surfaces at night

dew·ber·ry *n, pl* **dew·ber·ries** : a sweet edible berry that grows on a prickly vine and is related to the blackberries

dew·lap *n* : a hanging fold of skin under the neck of some animals

dew point *n* : the temperature at which the moisture in the air begins to turn to dew

dewy *adj* **dew·i·er; dew·i·est** : moist with or as if with dew — **dew·i·ly** *adv* — **dew·i·ness** *n*

dex·ter·i·ty *n, pl* **dex·ter·i·ties 1** : skill and ease in bodily activity **2** : mental skill or quickness

dex·ter·ous *or* **dex·trous** *adj* **1** : skillful with the hands **2** : mentally skillful and clever **3** : done with skill — **dex·ter·ous·ly** *adv* — **dex·ter·ous·ness** *n*

di·a·be·tes *n* : a disease in which too little insulin is produced and the body cannot use sugar and starch in the normal way

di·a·bet·ic *n* : a person with diabetes

di·a·crit·i·cal mark *n* : a mark used with a letter or group of letters to show a pronunciation different from that given a letter or group of letters not marked or marked in a different way

di·a·dem *n* : a band for the head worn especially by monarchs

di·ag·nose *vb* **di·ag·nosed; di·ag·nos·ing** : to recognize (as a disease) by signs and symptoms

di·ag·no·sis *n, pl* **di·ag·no·ses** : the art or act of recognizing a disease from its signs and symptoms

¹di·ag·o·nal *adj* **1** : running from one corner to the opposite corner of a figure with four sides **2** : running in a slanting direction — **di·ag·o·nal·ly** *adv*

²diagonal *n* : a diagonal line, direction, or pattern

¹di·a·gram *n* : a drawing, sketch, plan, or chart that makes something clearer or easier to understand

²diagram *vb* **di·a·gramed** *or* **di·a·grammed; di·a·gram·ing** *or* **di·a·gram·ming** : to put in the form of a diagram

¹di·al *n* **1** : the face of a watch or clock **2** : SUNDIAL **3** : a face or series of marks on which some measurement or other number is shown usually by means of a pointer **4** : a disk usually with a knob or holes that may be turned to operate something (as a telephone)

²dial *vb* **di·aled** *or* **di·alled; di·al·ing** *or* **di·al·ling** : to use a dial to operate or select

di·a·lect *n* **1** : a form of a language belonging to a certain region **2** : a form of a language used by the members of a certain occupation or class

di·a·logue *or* **di·a·log** *n* **1** : a conversation between two or more persons **2** : conversation given in a written story or a play

di·am·e·ter *n* **1** : a straight line that joins two points of a figure or body and passes through the center **2** : the distance through the center of an object from one side to the other : THICKNESS

di·a·mond *n* **1** : a very hard mineral that is a form of carbon, is usually nearly colorless, and is used especially in jewelry **2** : a flat figure ♦ like one of the surfaces of certain cut diamonds **3** : INFIELD 1

di·a·per *n* : a piece of absorbent material drawn up between the legs of a baby and fastened about the waist

di·a·phragm *n* **1** : a muscular wall separating the chest from the abdomen **2** : a thin circular plate (as in a microphone) that vibrates when sound strikes it

di·ar·rhea *n* : abnormally frequent and watery bowel movements

di·a·ry *n, pl* **di·a·ries 1** : a daily record especially of personal experiences and thoughts **2** : a book for keeping a diary

¹dice *n, pl* **dice** : a small cube marked on each face with one to six spots and used usually in pairs in games

²dice *vb* **diced; dic·ing** : to cut into small cubes

dick·er *vb* : ²BARGAIN, HAGGLE

¹dic·tate *vb* **dic·tat·ed; dic·tat·ing 1** : to speak or read for someone else to write down or for a machine to record **2** : to say or state with authority : ORDER

²dictate *n* : a statement made or direction given with authority : COMMAND

dic·ta·tion *n* **1** : the giving of orders often without thought of whether they are reasonable or fair **2** : the dictating of words **3** : something dictated or taken down from dictation

dic·ta·tor *n* **1** : a person who rules with total authority and often in a cruel or brutal manner **2** : a person who dictates — **dic·ta·tor·ship** *n*

dic·ta·to·ri·al *adj* : of, relating to, or like a dictator or a dictatorship

dic·tion *n* **1** : choice of words especially with regard to correctness, clearness, and effectiveness **2** : ENUNCIATION

dic·tio·nary *n, pl* **dic·tio·nar·ies 1** : a book giving the meaning and usually the pronunciation of words listed in alphabetical order **2** : an alphabetical reference book explaining words and phrases of a field of knowledge **3** : a book listing words of one language in alphabetical order with definitions in another language

did *past of* DO

didn't : did not

¹die *vb* **died; dy·ing 1** : to stop living **2** : to pass out of existence **3** : to disappear little by little **4** : to wish eagerly **5** : ¹STOP 4

²die *n* **1** *pl* **dice** : ¹DICE **2** *pl* **dies** : a device for forming or cutting material by pressure

die·sel *n* **1** : DIESEL ENGINE **2** : a vehicle driven by a diesel engine

diesel engine *n* : an engine in which the mixture of air and fuel is compressed until enough heat is created to ignite the mixture

¹di·et *n* **1** : the food and drink that a person or animal usually takes **2** : the kind and amount of food selected or allowed in certain circumstances (as ill health)

²diet *vb* : to eat or cause to eat less or according to certain rules — **di·et·er** *n*

³diet *adj* : reduced in calories

di·e·tary *adj* : of or relating to a diet or to rules of diet

di·e·ti·tian *or* **di·e·ti·cian** *n* : a person trained to apply the principles of nutrition to the planning of food and meals

dif·fer *vb* **1** : to be not the same : be unlike **2** : DISAGREE 2

dif·fer·ence *n* **1** : what makes two or more persons or things different **2** : a disagreement about something **3** : REMAINDER 2

dif·fer·ent *adj* **1** : not of the same kind **2** : not the same — **dif·fer·ent·ly** *adv*

dif·fer·en·ti·ate *vb* **dif·fer·en·ti·at·ed; dif·fer·en·ti·at·ing 1** : to make or become different **2** : to recognize or state the difference between

dif·fer·en·ti·a·tion *n* : the process of change by which immature living structures develop to maturity

dif·fi·cult *adj* **1** : hard to do or make **2** : hard to deal with **3** : hard to understand

dif·fi·cul·ty *n, pl* **dif·fi·cul·ties 1** : the state of being difficult **2** : great effort **3** : OBSTACLE **4** : a difficult situation : TROUBLE

dif·fi·dent *adj* **1** : lacking confidence **2** : RESERVED 1 — **dif·fi·dent·ly** *adv*

dif·fuse *vb* **dif·fused; dif·fus·ing** : to undergo diffusion

dif·fu·sion *n* : the mixing of particles of liquids or gases so that they move from a region of high concentration to one of lower concentration

¹dig *vb* **dug; dig·ging 1** : to turn up, loosen, or remove the soil **2** : to form by removing earth **3** : to uncover or search by or as if by turning up earth **4** : DISCOVER, UNCOVER **5** : ¹PROD 1, POKE **6** : to work hard — **dig·ger** *n*

²dig *n* **1** : ²POKE, THRUST **2** : a nasty remark

¹di·gest *n* : information in shortened form

²di·gest *vb* **1** : to think over and get straight in the mind **2** : to change (food) into simpler forms that can be taken in and used by the body **3** : to become digested

di·gest·ible *adj* : possible to digest

di·ges·tion *n* : the process or power of digesting something (as food)

di·ges·tive *adj* : of, relating to, or functioning in digestion

dig·it *n* **1** : any of the numerals 1 to 9 and the symbol 0 **2** : ¹FINGER 1, ¹TOE 1

dig·i·tal *adj* **1** : of, relating to, or done with a finger or toe **2** : of, relating to, or using calculation directly with digits rather than through measurable physical quantities **3** : of or relating to data in the form of numerical digits **4** : providing displayed or recorded information in numerical digits from an automatic device — **dig·i·tal·ly** *adv*

dig·ni·fied *adj* : having or showing dignity

dig·ni·fy *vb* **dig·ni·fied; dig·ni·fy·ing** : to give dignity or importance to

dig·ni·tary *n, pl* **dig·ni·tar·ies** : a person of high position or honor

dig·ni·ty *n, pl* **dig·ni·ties** **1** : the quality or state of being worthy of honor and respect **2** : high rank or office **3** : a dignified look or way of behaving

dike *or* **dyke** *n* : a bank of earth thrown up from a ditch or heaped up to form a boundary or to control water

di·lap·i·dat·ed *adj* : partly fallen apart or ruined from age or from lack of care

di·late *vb* **di·lat·ed; di·lat·ing** : to make or grow larger or wider

di·lem·ma *n* : a situation in which a person has to choose between things that are all bad or unsatisfactory

dil·i·gence *n* : careful and continued work

dil·i·gent *adj* : showing steady and earnest care and effort — **dil·i·gent·ly** *adv*

dill *n* : an herb related to the carrot with fragrant leaves and seeds used mostly in flavoring pickles

dil·ly·dal·ly *vb* **dil·ly·dal·lied; dil·ly·dal·ly·ing** : to waste time : DAWDLE

di·lute *vb* **di·lut·ed; di·lut·ing** : to make thinner or more liquid

di·lu·tion *n* **1** : the act of diluting : the state of being diluted **2** : something (as a solution) that is diluted

¹dim *adj* **dim·mer; dim·mest** **1** : not bright or distinct : FAINT **2** : not seeing or understanding clearly — **dim·ly** *adv* — **dim·ness** *n*

²dim *vb* **dimmed; dim·ming** **1** : to make or become dim **2** : to reduce the light from

dime *n* : a United States coin worth ten cents

di·men·sion *n* : the length, width, or height of something

di·men·sion·al *adj* : of or relating to dimensions

di·min·ish *vb* **1** : to make less or cause to seem less **2** : BELITTLE **3** : DWINDLE — **di·min·ish·ment** *n*

di·min·u·en·do *n, pl* **di·min·u·en·dos** *or* **di·min·u·en·does** : DECRESCENDO

di·min·u·tive *adj* : very small : TINY

dim·mer *n* : a device for regulating the brightness of an electric lighting unit (as the lights of a room)

¹dim·ple *n* : a slight hollow spot especially in the cheek or chin

²dimple *vb* **dim·pled; dim·pling** : to mark with or form dimples

¹din *n* : loud confused noise

²din *vb* **dinned; din·ning** **1** : to make a din **2** : to repeat again and again in order to impress on someone's mind

dine *vb* **dined; din·ing** **1** : to eat dinner **2** : to give a dinner to

din·er *n* **1** : a person eating dinner **2** : a railroad dining car or a restaurant in the shape of one

di·nette *n* : a separate area or small room used for dining

ding·dong *n* : the sound of a bell ringing

din·ghy *n, pl* **dinghies** **1** : a small light rowboat **2** : a rubber life raft

din·gle *n* : a small narrow wooded valley

din·gy *adj* **din·gi·er; din·gi·est** : rather dark and dirty — **din·gi·ness** *n*

din·ner *n* **1** : the main meal of the day **2** : BANQUET

di·no·saur *n* : any of a group of extinct mostly land-dwelling reptiles that lived millions of years ago

dint *n* **1** : the force or power of something **2** : ²DENT

di·o·cese *n* : the district over which a bishop has authority

¹dip *vb* **dipped; dip·ping** **1** : to sink or push briefly into a liquid **2** : to take out with or as if with a ladle **3** : to lower and quickly raise again : drop or sink and quickly rise again **4** : to sink out of sight **5** : to slope downward

²dip *n* **1** : a plunge into water for fun or exercise : a short swim **2** : a downward slope **3** : something obtained by or used in dipping **4** : a tasty sauce into which solid food may be dipped

diph·the·ria *n* : a contagious disease in which the air passages become coated with a membrane that often makes breathing difficult

diph·thong *n* : two vowel sounds joined in one syllable to form one speech sound

di·plo·ma *n* : a certificate that shows a person has finished a course or graduated from a school

di·plo·ma·cy *n* **1** : the work of keeping up relations between the governments of different countries **2** : skill in dealing with others

dip·lo·mat *n* **1** : a person whose work is diplomacy **2** : a person who is good at not saying or doing things that hurt or make people angry

dip·lo·mat·ic *adj* **1** : of or relating to diplomats and their work **2** : TACTFUL — **dip·lo·mat·i·cal·ly** *adv*

dip·per *n* **1** : one that dips **2** : a ladle or scoop for dipping

dire *adj* **1** : causing horror or terror

: DREADFUL **2** : very great — **dire·ly** *adv* — **dire·ness** *n*

¹di·rect *vb* **1** : to put an address on (as a letter) **2** : ¹AIM 3, TURN **3** : to show or tell the way **4** : to guide the production of **5** : ¹ORDER 2, COMMAND

²direct *adj* **1** : going from one point to another without turning or stopping : STRAIGHT **2** : going straight to the point **3** : being in an unbroken family line — **di·rect·ness** *n*

³direct *adv* : DIRECTLY 1

direct current *n* : an electric current flowing in one direction only

di·rec·tion *n* **1** : SUPERVISION, MANAGEMENT **2** : an order or instruction to be followed **3** : the path along which something moves, lies, or points

di·rect·ly *adv* **1** : in a direct course or way **2** : right away : IMMEDIATELY

direct object *n* : a word that represents the main goal or the result of the action of a verb

di·rec·tor *n* : a person who directs something

di·rec·to·ry *n, pl* **di·rec·to·ries** : a book containing an alphabetical list of names and addresses

dirge *n* : a song or hymn of grief

di·ri·gi·ble *n* : AIRSHIP

dirk *n* : a long dagger with a straight blade

dirt *n* **1** : a filthy or soiling substance (as mud or dust) **2** : ²SOIL

¹dirty *adj* **dirt·i·er; dirt·i·est 1** : soiled or polluted by dirt or impurities **2** : UNFAIR, MEAN **3** : INDECENT, VULGAR **4** : not clear in color **5** : showing dislike or anger — **dirt·i·ness** *n*

²dirty *vb* **dirt·ied; dirty·ing** : to make or become dirty

dis- *prefix* **1** : do the opposite of **2** : deprive of **3** : expel from **4** : opposite or absence of **5** : not

dis·abil·i·ty *n, pl* **dis·abil·i·ties 1** : the state of being disabled : lack of power to do something **2** : something that disables

dis·able *vb* **dis·abled; dis·abling** : to make unable or incapable : CRIPPLE — **dis·able·ment** *n*

dis·ad·van·tage *n* : something that makes it hard for a person to succeed or do something

dis·ad·van·ta·geous *adj* : making it harder for a person to succeed or do something — **dis·ad·van·ta·geous·ly** *adv* — **dis·ad·van·ta·geous·ness** *n*

dis·agree *vb* **dis·agreed; dis·agree·ing 1** : to be unlike each other : be different **2** : to have unlike ideas or opinions **3** : QUARREL **4** : to have an unpleasant effect

dis·agree·able *adj* **1** : UNPLEASANT **2**

: having a bad disposition : PEEVISH — **dis·agree·ably** *adv*

dis·agree·ment *n* **1** : the act or fact of disagreeing **2** : the condition of being different **3** : a difference of opinion

dis·ap·pear *vb* **1** : to stop being visible : pass out of sight **2** : to stop existing

dis·ap·pear·ance *n* : the act or fact of disappearing

dis·ap·point *vb* : to fail to satisfy the hope or expectation of

dis·ap·point·ment *n* **1** : the act of disappointing **2** : the condition or feeling of being disappointed **3** : one that disappoints

dis·ap·prov·al *n* : the feeling of not liking or agreeing with something or someone

dis·ap·prove *vb* **dis·ap·proved; dis·ap·prov·ing** : to dislike or be against something

dis·arm *vb* **1** : to take weapons from **2** : to reduce the size and strength of the armed forces of a country **3** : to make harmless **4** : to remove any feelings of doubt, mistrust, or unfriendliness : win over — **dis·ar·ma·ment** *n*

dis·ar·range *vb* **dis·ar·ranged; dis·ar·rang·ing** : to make all mussed up or mixed up — **dis·ar·range·ment** *n*

di·sas·ter *n* : something (as a flood or a tornado) that happens suddenly and causes much suffering or loss : CALAMITY

di·sas·trous *adj* : being or resulting in a disaster — **di·sas·trous·ly** *adv*

dis·band *vb* : to break up and stop being a group — **dis·band·ment** *n*

dis·bar *vb* **dis·barred; dis·bar·ring** : to deprive (a lawyer) of the rights of membership in the legal profession — **dis·bar·ment** *n*

dis·be·lief *n* : refusal or inability to believe

dis·be·lieve *vb* **dis·be·lieved; dis·be·liev·ing** : to think not to be true or real — **dis·be·liev·er** *n*

dis·burse *vb* **dis·bursed; dis·burs·ing** : to pay out — **dis·burse·ment** *n*

disc *variant of* DISK

¹dis·card *vb* **1** : to throw down an unwanted playing card from one's hand **2** : to get rid of as useless or unwanted

²dis·card *n* **1** : the act of discarding **2** : something discarded

dis·cern *vb* : to see, recognize, or understand something

¹dis·charge *vb* **dis·charged; dis·charg·ing 1** : to relieve of a load or burden : UNLOAD **2** : SHOOT 1, 2, FIRE **3** : to set free **4** : to dismiss from service **5** : to let go or let off **6** : to give forth the contents (as a fluid) **7** : to get rid of by paying or doing

²dis·charge *n* **1** : the act of discharging, unloading, or releasing **2** : a certificate of release or payment **3** : a firing off **4** : a flowing out (as of blood or pus) **5** : a firing of a person from a job **6** : complete separation from military service

dis·ci·ple *n* **1** : a person who accepts and helps to spread the teachings of another **2** : APOSTLE 1

¹**dis·ci·pline** *n* **1** : strict training that corrects or strengthens **2** : PUNISHMENT 1 **3** : habits and ways of acting that are gotten through practice **4** : a system of rules

²**discipline** *vb* **dis·ci·plined; dis·ci·plin·ing** **1** : to punish for the sake of discipline **2** : to train in self-control or obedience **3** : to bring under control

disc jockey *n* : a radio announcer who plays records

dis·claim *vb* : to deny being part of or responsible for

dis·close *vb* **dis·closed; dis·clos·ing** : to make known : REVEAL

dis·clo·sure *n* **1** : an act of disclosing **2** : something disclosed

dis·col·or *vb* : to change in color especially for the worse

dis·col·or·a·tion *n* **1** : change of color **2** : a discolored spot

dis·com·fort *n* : the condition of being uncomfortable

dis·con·cert *vb* : to make confused and a little upset

dis·con·nect *vb* : to undo the connection of

dis·con·nect·ed *adj* : INCOHERENT — **dis·con·nect·ed·ly** *adv*

dis·con·so·late *adj* : too sad to be cheered up — **dis·con·so·late·ly** *adv*

¹**dis·con·tent** *vb* : to make dissatisfied

²**discontent** *n* : the condition of being dissatisfied

dis·con·tent·ed *adj* : not contented — **dis·con·tent·ed·ly** *adv*

dis·con·tin·ue *vb* **dis·con·tin·ued; dis·con·tinu·ing** : to bring to an end : STOP

dis·cord *n* : lack of agreement or harmony

dis·cord·ant *adj* : being in disagreement : not being in harmony

¹**dis·count** *n* : an amount taken off a regular price

²**dis·count** *vb* **1** : to lower the amount of a bill, debt, or charge usually in return for cash or quick payment **2** : to believe only partly

dis·cour·age *vb* **dis·cour·aged; dis·cour·ag·ing** **1** : to make less determined, hopeful, or sure of oneself **2** : DETER **3** : to try to persuade not to do something — **dis·cour·age·ment** *n*

¹**dis·course** *n* **1** : CONVERSATION **2** : a long talk or composition about a subject

²**dis·course** *vb* **dis·coursed; dis·cours·ing** : to talk especially for a long time

dis·cour·te·ous *adj* : not polite : RUDE — **dis·cour·te·ous·ly** *adv*

dis·cour·te·sy *n, pl* **dis·cour·te·sies** **1** : rude behavior **2** : a rude act

dis·cov·er *vb* : to find out, see, or learn of especially for the first time : FIND — **dis·cov·er·er** *n*

dis·cov·ery *n, pl* **dis·cov·er·ies** **1** : an act of discovering **2** : something discovered

¹**dis·cred·it** *vb* **1** : to refuse to accept as true **2** : to cause to seem dishonest or untrue

²**discredit** *n* : loss of good name or respect

dis·creet *adj* : having or showing good judgment especially in conduct or speech — **dis·creet·ly** *adv*

dis·cre·tion *n* **1** : good sense in making decisions **2** : the power of deciding for oneself

dis·crim·i·nate *vb* **dis·crim·i·nat·ed; dis·crim·i·nat·ing** **1** : to be able to tell the difference between things **2** : to treat some people better than others without any fair or proper reason

dis·crim·i·na·tion *n* **1** : the act of discriminating **2** : the ability to see differences **3** : the treating of some people better than others without any fair or proper reason

dis·crim·i·na·to·ry *adj* : showing discrimination : being unfair

dis·cus *n, pl* **dis·cus·es** : an object that is shaped like a disk and hurled for distance in a track-and-field event

dis·cuss *vb* **1** : to argue or consider fully and openly **2** : to talk about

dis·cus·sion *n* : conversation or debate for the purpose of understanding a question or subject

¹**dis·dain** *n* : a feeling of scorn for something considered beneath oneself — **dis·dain·ful** *adj* — **dis·dain·ful·ly** *adv*

²**disdain** *vb* **1** : to think oneself far too good for something or someone **2** : to refuse because of scorn

dis·ease *n* **1** : a change in a living body (as of a person or plant) that interferes with its normal functioning : ILLNESS **2** : an instance or a kind of disease — **dis·eased** *adj*

dis·em·bark *vb* : to go or put ashore from a ship

dis·en·tan·gle *vb* **dis·en·tan·gled; dis·en·tan·gling** : to straighten out : UNTANGLE — **dis·en·tan·gle·ment** *n*

dis·fa·vor *n* **1** : DISAPPROVAL **2** : the state of being disliked

dis·fig·ure *vb* **dis·fig·ured; dis·fig·ur·ing** : to spoil the looks of — **dis·fig·ure·ment** *n*

dis·fran·chise *vb* **dis·fran·chised; dis-**

fran·chis·ing : to take away the right to vote — **dis·fran·chise·ment** *n*

1dis·grace *vb* **dis·graced; dis·grac·ing** : to bring shame to — **dis·grac·er** *n*

2disgrace *n* **1** : the condition of being looked down on : loss of respect **2** : 1DIS-HONOR 1 **3** : a cause of shame

dis·grace·ful *adj* : bringing or deserving disgrace — **dis·grace·ful·ly** *adv* — **dis·grace·ful·ness** *n*

dis·grun·tle *vb* **dis·grun·tled; dis·grun·tling** : to make grouchy or cross

1dis·guise *vb* **dis·guised; dis·guis·ing** **1** : to change the looks of so as to conceal identity **2** : to keep from revealing

2disguise *n* **1** : clothing put on to hide one's true identity or to imitate another's **2** : an outward appearance that hides what something really is

1dis·gust *n* : the strong dislike one feels for something nasty and sickening

2disgust *vb* : to cause to feel disgust — **dis·gust·ed·ly** *adv*

dis·gust·ing *adj* : causing disgust — **dis·gust·ing·ly** *adv*

1dish *n* **1** : a hollowed out vessel for serving food at table **2** : the contents of a dish

2dish *vb* : to put into a dish : SERVE

dis·heart·en *vb* : DISCOURAGE 1 — **dis·heart·en·ing·ly** *adv*

di·shev·eled *or* **di·shev·elled** *adj* : mussed up : UNTIDY

dis·hon·est *adj* : not honest or trustworthy — **dis·hon·est·ly** *adv*

dis·hon·es·ty *n* : lack of honesty : the quality of being dishonest

1dis·hon·or *n* **1** : loss of honor or good name **2** : a cause of disgrace

2dishonor *vb* : to bring shame on : DIS-GRACE

dis·hon·or·able *adj* : not honorable : SHAMEFUL — **dis·hon·or·ably** *adv*

dis·il·lu·sion *vb* : to free from mistaken beliefs or foolish hopes — **dis·il·lu·sion·ment** *n*

dis·in·fect *vb* : to free from germs that might cause disease

1dis·in·fec·tant *n* : something that frees from germs

2disinfectant *adj* : serving to disinfect

dis·in·her·it *vb* : to deprive (an heir) of the right to inherit

dis·in·te·grate *vb* **dis·in·te·grat·ed; dis·in·te·grat·ing** : to separate or break up into small parts or pieces

dis·in·te·gra·tion *n* : the act or process of disintegrating : the state of being disintegrated

dis·in·ter·est·ed *adj* **1** : not interested **2**

: free of selfish interest — **dis·in·ter·est·ed·ly** *adv* — **dis·in·ter·est·ed·ness** *n*

dis·joint·ed *adj* : not clear and orderly — **dis·joint·ed·ly** *adv*

disk *or* **disc** *n* **1** : something that is or appears to be flat and round **2** *usually disc* : a phonograph record **3** : a round flat plate coated with a magnetic substance on which data for a computer is stored — **disk·like** *adj*

disk·ette *n* : FLOPPY DISK

1dis·like *n* : a strong feeling of not liking or approving

2dislike *vb* **dis·liked; dis·lik·ing** : to feel dislike for

dis·lo·cate *vb* **dis·lo·cat·ed; dis·lo·cat·ing** : to displace a bone from its normal connections with another bone

dis·lo·ca·tion *n* : the state of being dislocated

dis·lodge *vb* **dis·lodged; dis·lodg·ing** : to force out of a resting place or a place of hiding or defense

dis·loy·al *adj* : not loyal — **dis·loy·al·ly** *adv*

dis·loy·al·ty *n*, *pl* **dis·loy·al·ties 1** : lack of loyalty **2** : a disloyal act

dis·mal *adj* : very gloomy and depressing

dis·man·tle *vb* **dis·man·tled; dis·man·tling 1** : to strip of furniture or equipment **2** : to take completely apart (as for storing or repair) — **dis·man·tle·ment** *n*

1dis·may *vb* : to cause to be unable to act because of surprise, fear, or confusion

2dismay *n* **1** : sudden loss of courage or determination because of fear **2** : a feeling of fear or disappointment

dis·miss *vb* **1** : to send away **2** : to discharge from an office or job **3** : to decide not to think about

dis·miss·al *n* : the act of dismissing : the state or fact of being dismissed

dis·mount *vb* **1** : to get down from something (as a horse or bicycle) **2** : to cause to fall off or get off **3** : to take (as a cannon) off a support **4** : to take apart (as a machine)

dis·obe·di·ence *n* : an act or the fact of disobeying

dis·obe·di·ent *adj* : not obeying — **dis·obe·di·ent·ly** *adv*

dis·obey *vb* **dis·obeyed; dis·obey·ing** : to refuse, neglect, or fail to obey

1dis·or·der *vb* **1** : to disturb the order of **2** : to disturb the regular or normal functioning of

2disorder *n* **1** : lack of order or of orderly arrangement : CONFUSION **2** : an abnormal state of body or mind : SICKNESS

dis·or·der·ly *adj* **1** : not behaving quietly or

well : UNRULY **2** : not neat or orderly —
dis·or·der·li·ness n
dis·or·ga·nize vb **dis·or·ga·nized; dis·or·ga·niz·ing** : to break up the regular arrangement or system of
dis·own vb : to refuse to accept any longer as one's own
dis·par·age vb **dis·par·aged; dis·par·ag·ing** : to speak of as unimportant or not much good : BELITTLE — **dis·par·age·ment** n
dis·pas·sion·ate adj : not influenced by strong feeling : CALM, IMPARTIAL — **dis·pas·sion·ate·ly** adv
¹**dis·patch** vb **1** : to send away quickly to a certain place or for a certain reason **2** : ¹KILL 1 — **dis·patch·er** n
²**dispatch** n **1** : MESSAGE **2** : a news story sent in to a newspaper **3** : SPEED 1
dis·pel vb **dis·pelled; dis·pel·ling** : to drive away
dis·pense vb **dis·pensed; dis·pens·ing** **1** : to give out in shares : DISTRIBUTE **2** : ADMINISTER 2 **3** : to put up or prepare medicine in a form ready for use — **dispense with** : to do or get along without
dis·pens·er n : a container that gives out something one at a time or a little at a time
dis·perse vb **dis·persed; dis·pers·ing** : to break up and scatter
dispir·it vb : to take away the cheerfulness or enthusiasm of
dis·place vb **dis·placed; dis·plac·ing** **1** : to remove from the usual or proper place **2** : to remove from office : DISCHARGE **3** : to take the place of : REPLACE — **dis·place·ment** n
¹**dis·play** vb **1** : to put (something) in plain sight **2** : to make clear the existence or presence of : show plainly
²**display** n : a showing of something
dis·please vb **dis·pleased; dis·pleas·ing** : to be or do something that makes (a person) cross or not pleased or satisfied
dis·plea·sure n : a feeling of dislike and irritation : DISSATISFACTION
dis·pos·able adj : made to be thrown away after use
dis·pos·al n **1** : ARRANGEMENT 1 **2** : a getting rid of **3** : right or power to use : CONTROL
dis·pose vb **dis·posed; dis·pos·ing** **1** : to put in place : ARRANGE **2** : to make ready and willing — **dis·pos·er** n — **dispose of** **1** : to finish with **2** : to get rid of
dis·po·si·tion n **1** : ARRANGEMENT 1 **2** : one's usual attitude or mood **3** : TENDENCY 2, LIKING
dis·pro·por·tion n : lack of normal or usual proportions

dis·prove vb **dis·proved; dis·prov·ing** : to show to be false
dis·put·able adj : not yet proved : DEBATABLE — **dis·put·ably** adv
¹**dis·pute** vb **dis·put·ed; dis·put·ing** **1** : ARGUE 2 **2** : to question or deny the truth or rightness of **3** : to fight over — **dis·put·er** n
²**dispute** n **1** : ARGUMENT 2, DEBATE **2** : ¹QUARREL 2
dis·qual·i·fy vb **dis·qual·i·fied; dis·qual·i·fy·ing** : to make or declare unfit or not qualified
¹**dis·qui·et** vb : to make uneasy or worried : DISTURB
²**disquiet** n : an uneasy feeling
dis·qui·et·ing adj : causing worry or uneasiness — **dis·qui·et·ing·ly** adv
¹**dis·re·gard** vb : to pay no attention to
²**disregard** n : the act of disregarding : the state of being disregarded
dis·re·pair n : the condition of needing repair
dis·rep·u·ta·ble adj : not respectable — **dis·rep·u·ta·bly** adv
dis·re·spect n : lack of respect : DISCOURTESY — **dis·re·spect·ful** adj — **dis·re·spect·ful·ly** adv
dis·robe vb **dis·robed; dis·rob·ing** : UNDRESS
dis·rupt vb : to throw into disorder : BREAK UP
dis·sat·is·fac·tion n : a being dissatisfied
dis·sat·is·fy vb **dis·sat·is·fied; dis·sat·is·fy·ing** : to fail to satisfy : DISPLEASE
dis·sect vb : to cut or take apart especially for examination
dis·sen·sion n : disagreement in opinion : DISCORD
¹**dis·sent** vb : DISAGREE 2 — **dis·sent·er** n
²**dissent** n : difference of opinion
dis·ser·vice n : a harmful, unfair, or unjust act
dis·sim·i·lar adj : not similar : DIFFERENT
dis·si·pate vb **dis·si·pat·ed; dis·si·pat·ing** **1** : to break up and drive off : DISPERSE **2** : to scatter or waste foolishly : SQUANDER
dis·si·pat·ed adj : enjoying bad, foolish, or harmful activities
dis·si·pa·tion n **1** : the act of dissipating or the state of being dissipated **2** : a dissipated way of life
dis·so·lute adj : having or showing bad morals or behavior — **dis·so·lute·ly** adv — **dis·so·lute·ness** n
dis·solve vb **dis·solved; dis·solv·ing** **1** : to mix or cause to mix with a liquid so that the result is a liquid that is the same throughout **2** : to bring to an end : TERMI-

NATE **3** : to fade away as if by melting or breaking up

dis·so·nance *n* : an unpleasant combination of musical sounds

dis·suade *vb* **dis·suad·ed; dis·suad·ing** : to persuade or advise not to do something

dis·tance *n* **1** : how far from each other two points or places are **2** : the quality or state of not being friendly : RESERVE **3** : a distant point or region

dis·tant *adj* **1** : separated in space or time **2** : REMOTE 1 **3** : not closely related **4** : ¹COLD 2, UNFRIENDLY — **dis·tant·ly** *adv*

dis·taste *n* : ¹DISLIKE

dis·taste·ful *adj* : UNPLEASANT

dis·tend *vb* : EXPAND 2, SWELL

dis·till *also* **dis·til** *vb* **dis·tilled; dis·till·ing** : to obtain or purify by distillation — **dis·till·er** *n*

dis·til·la·tion *n* : the process of heating a liquid or solid until it sends off a gas or vapor and then cooling the gas or vapor until it becomes liquid

dis·tinct *adj* **1** : real and different from each other **2** : easy to see, hear, or understand — **dis·tinct·ly** *adv* — **dis·tinct·ness** *n*

dis·tinc·tion *n* **1** : the seeing or pointing out of a difference **2** : DIFFERENCE 1 **3** : great worth : EXCELLENCE **4** : something that makes a person or thing special or different

dis·tinc·tive *adj* **1** : clearly marking a person or a thing as different from others **2** : having or giving a special look or way — **dis·tinc·tive·ly** *adv* — **dis·tinc·tive·ness** *n*

dis·tin·guish *vb* **1** : to recognize by some mark or quality **2** : to know the difference **3** : to set apart as different or special

dis·tin·guish·able *adj* : possible to recognize or tell apart from others

dis·tin·guished *adj* : widely known and admired

dis·tort *vb* **1** : to tell in a way that is misleading : MISREPRESENT **2** : to twist out of shape — **dis·tort·er** *n*

dis·tor·tion *n* : the act of distorting : the state or fact of being distorted

dis·tract *vb* **1** : to draw the mind or attention to something else **2** : to upset or trouble in mind to the point of confusion

dis·trac·tion *n* **1** : the act of distracting : the state of being distracted **2** : complete confusion of mind **3** : something that makes it hard to pay attention

¹dis·tress *n* **1** : suffering or pain of body or mind **2** : DANGER 1 — **dis·tress·ful** *adj*

²distress *vb* : to cause distress to — **dis·tress·ing·ly** *adv*

dis·trib·ute *vb* **dis·trib·ut·ed; dis·trib·ut·ing** **1** : to divide among several or many **2** : to spread out so as to cover something **3** : to divide or. separate especially into classes : SORT — **dis·trib·u·tor** *n*

dis·tri·bu·tion *n* **1** : the act of distributing **2** : the way things are distributed **3** : something distributed

dis·trib·u·tive *adj* **1** : of or relating to distribution **2** : producing the same answer when operating on the sum of several numbers as when operating on each and collecting the results — **dis·trib·u·tive·ly** *adv*

dis·trict *n* **1** : an area or section (as of a city or nation) set apart for some purpose **2** : an area or region with some special feature

¹dis·trust *n* : a lack of trust or confidence : SUSPICION — **dis·trust·ful** *adj* — **dis·trust·ful·ly** *adv*

²distrust *vb* : to have no trust or confidence in

dis·turb *vb* **1** : to interfere with : INTERRUPT **2** : to change the arrangements of : move from its place **3** : to trouble the mind of : UPSET **4** : to make confused or disordered

dis·tur·bance *n* **1** : the act of disturbing : the state of being disturbed **2** : ²DISORDER 1, COMMOTION

dis·use *n* : lack of use

dis·used *adj* : not used any more

¹ditch *n* : a long narrow channel or trench dug in the earth

²ditch *vb* **1** : to dig a ditch in or around (as for drainage) **2** : to get rid of : DISCARD **3** : to make a forced landing in an airplane on water

dith·er *n* : a very nervous or excited state

dit·ty *n, pl* **ditties** : a short simple song

di·van *n* : a large couch often with no back or arms

¹dive *vb* **dived** *or* **dove; div·ing** **1** : to plunge into water headfirst **2** : SUBMERGE 1 **3** : to fall fast **4** : to descend in an airplane at a steep angle **5** : to shove suddenly into or at something — **div·er** *n*

²dive *n* **1** : an act of diving **2** : a quick drop (as of prices)

di·verse *adj* : different from each other : UNLIKE — **di·verse·ly** *adv* — **di·verse·ness** *n*

di·ver·sion *n* **1** : an act or instance of diverting or turning aside **2** : something that relaxes, amuses, or entertains

di·ver·si·ty *n, pl* **di·ver·si·ties** : the condition or fact of being different

di·vert *vb* **1** : to turn aside : turn from one course or use to another **2** : to turn the attention away : DISTRACT **3** : to give pleasure : AMUSE

¹di·vide *vb* **di·vid·ed; di·vid·ing** **1** : to separate into two or more parts or pieces **2** : to give out in shares **3** : to be or make different in opinion or interest **4** : to subject to

mathematical division **5** : to branch off
: FORK — **di·vid·er** *n*

²divide *n* : WATERSHED 1

div·i·dend *n* **1** : a sum to be divided and
given out **2** : a number to be divided by
another number

¹di·vine *adj* **1** : of or relating to God or a
god **2** : being in praise of God : RELIGIOUS,
HOLY **3** : GODLIKE — **di·vine·ly** *adv*

²divine *n* : a member of the clergy

di·vin·i·ty *n, pl* **di·vin·i·ties** **1** : the quality
or state of being divine **2** : DEITY **3** : the
study of religion

di·vis·i·ble *adj* : possible to divide or separate

di·vi·sion *n* **1** : the act or process of dividing : the state of being divided **2** : a part or
portion of a whole **3** : a large military unit
4 : something that divides, separates, or
marks off **5** : the finding out of how many
times one number is contained in another **6**
: a group of plants that ranks above the class
in scientific classification and is the highest
group of the plant kingdom

di·vi·sor *n* : the number by which a dividend
is divided

¹di·vorce *n* **1** : a complete legal ending of a
marriage **2** : complete separation

²divorce *vb* **di·vorced; di·vorc·ing** **1** : to
make or keep separate **2** : to end one's
marriage legally : get a divorce

di·vulge *vb* **di·vulged; di·vulg·ing** : to
make public : REVEAL, DISCLOSE

dix·ie·land *n* : lively jazz music in a style developed in New Orleans

diz·zy *adj* **diz·zi·er; diz·zi·est** **1** : having
the feeling of whirling **2** : confused or unsteady in mind **3** : causing a dizzy feeling
— **diz·zi·ly** *adv* — **diz·zi·ness** *n*

DNA *n* : a complicated organic acid that carries genetic information in the chromosomes

¹do *vb* **did; done; do·ing; does** **1** : to
cause (as an act or action) to happen
: CARRY OUT, PERFORM **2** : ²ACT 2, BE-
HAVE **3** : to meet one's needs : SUCCEED **4**
: ¹FINISH 1 — used in the past participle **5**
: to put forth : EXERT **6** : to work on, prepare, or put in order **7** : to work at as a paying job **8** : to serve the purpose : SUIT **9**
— used as a helping verb (1) before the subject in a question, (2) in a negative statement, (3) for emphasis, and (4) as a substitute for a preceding predicate — **do away
with** **1** : to get rid of **2** : ¹KILL 1

²do *n* : the first note of the musical scale

doc·ile *adj* : easily taught, led, or managed
— **doc·ile·ly** *adv*

¹dock *vb* **1** : to cut off the end of **2** : to take
away a part of

²dock *n* **1** : an artificial basin for ships that
has gates to keep the water in or out **2** : a
waterway usually between two piers to receive ships **3** : a wharf or platform for
loading or unloading materials

³dock *vb* **1** : to haul or guide into a dock **2**
: to come or go into a dock **3** : to join (as
two spacecraft) mechanically while in
space

⁴dock *n* : the place in a court where a prisoner stands or sits during trial

¹doc·tor *n* : a person (as a physician or veterinarian) skilled and specializing in the art
of healing

²doctor *vb* **1** : to use remedies on or for **2**
: to practice medicine

doc·trine *n* : something (as a rule or principle) that is taught, believed in, or considered
to be true

doc·u·ment *n* **1** : a written or printed paper
that gives information about or proof of
something **2** : a computer file (as a letter,
essay, or chart) typed in by a user

¹dodge *n* : a sudden movement to one side

²dodge *vb* **dodged; dodg·ing** **1** : to move
suddenly aside or to and fro **2** : to avoid by
moving quickly **3** : EVADE — **dodg·er** *n*

dodge ball *n* : a game in which players stand
in a circle and try to hit a player inside the
circle by throwing a large inflated ball

do·do *n, pl* **dodoes** *or* **dodos** : a large heavy
bird unable to fly that once lived on some of
the islands of the Indian ocean

doe *n* : the female of an animal (as a deer)
the male of which is called *buck*

do·er *n* : one that does

does *present third sing of* DO

doesn't : does not

doff *vb* : to take off (as one's hat as an act of
politeness)

¹dog *n* **1** : a domestic animal that eats meat
and is related to the wolves and foxes **2** : a
device (as a metal bar with a hook at the
end) for holding, gripping, or fastening
something — **dog·like** *adj*

²dog *vb* **dogged; dog·ging** : to hunt, track,
or follow like a hound

dog·cart *n* **1** : a cart pulled by dogs **2** : a
light one-horse carriage with two seats back
to back

dog·catch·er *n* : an official paid to catch and
get rid of stray dogs

dog days *n pl* : the hot period between early
July and early September

dog–eared *adj* : having a lot of pages with
corners turned over

dog·fish *n* : any of several small sharks
often seen near shore

dog·ged *adj* : stubbornly determined —
dog·ged·ly *adv* — **dog·ged·ness** *n*

dog·gy or **dog·gie** n, pl **doggies** : a usually small or young dog

dog·house n : a shelter for a dog — **in the doghouse** : in trouble over some wrongdoing

dog·ma n **1** : something firmly believed **2** : a belief or set of beliefs taught by a church

dog·mat·ic adj **1** : of or relating to dogma **2** : seeming or sounding absolutely certain about something — **dog·mat·i·cal·ly** adv

¹**dog·trot** n : a slow trot

²**dogtrot** vb **dog·trot·ted; dog·trot·ting** : to move at a dogtrot

dog·wood n : any of several shrubs and small trees with clusters of small flowers often surrounded by four showy leaves that look like petals

doi·ly n, pl **doilies** : a small often ornamental mat used on a table

do·ings n pl : things that are done or that go on

dol·drums n pl **1** : a spell of low spirits **2** : a part of the ocean near the equator known for its calms

¹**dole** n **1** : a giving out especially of food, clothing, or money to the needy **2** : something given out as charity

²**dole** vb **doled; dol·ing 1** : to give out as charity **2** : to give in small portions

dole·ful adj : full of grief : SAD — **dole·ful·ly** adv — **dole·ful·ness** n

doll n : a small figure of a human being used especially as a child's plaything

dol·lar n : any of various coins or pieces of paper money (as of the United States or Canada) equal to 100 cents

dolly n, pl **dollies 1** : DOLL **2** : a platform on a roller or on wheels for moving heavy things

dol·phin n **1** : a small whale with teeth and a long nose **2** : either of two large food fishes of the sea

dolt n : a stupid person — **dolt·ish** adj — **dolt·ish·ly** adv — **dolt·ish·ness** n

-**dom** n suffix **1** : dignity : office **2** : realm : jurisdiction **3** : state or fact of being **4** : those having a certain office, occupation, interest, or character

do·main n **1** : land under the control of a ruler or a government **2** : a field of knowledge or activity

dome n : a bulge or a rounded top or roof that looks like half of a ball — **domed** adj

¹**do·mes·tic** adj **1** : of or relating to a household or a family **2** : of, relating to, made in, or done in one's own country **3** : living with or under the care of human beings : TAME — **do·mes·ti·cal·ly** adv

²**domestic** n : a household servant

do·mes·ti·cate vb **do·mes·ti·cat·ed; do·**

mes·ti·cat·ing : to bring under the control of and make usable by humans

do·mi·cile n : a dwelling place

dom·i·nance n : the state or fact of being dominant

dom·i·nant adj : controlling or being over all others — **dom·i·nant·ly** adv

dom·i·nate vb **dom·i·nat·ed; dom·i·nat·ing** : to have a commanding position or controlling power over

dom·i·neer vb : to rule or behave in a bossy way

do·min·ion n **1** : ruling or controlling power : SOVEREIGNTY **2** : a territory under the control of a ruler : DOMAIN

dom·i·no n, pl **dom·i·noes** or **dom·i·nos** : one of a set of flat oblong dotted pieces used in playing a game (**dominoes**)

don vb **donned; don·ning** : to put on

do·nate vb **do·nat·ed; do·nat·ing** : to make a gift of : CONTRIBUTE — **do·na·tor** n

do·na·tion n : a giving of something without charge : the thing given (as to charity)

done past participle of DO

don·key n, pl **donkeys 1** : an animal related to but smaller than the horse that has short hair in mane and tail and very large ears **2** : a silly or stupid person

do·nor n : one who gives, donates, or presents — **do·nor·ship** n

don't : do not

¹**doo·dle** vb **doo·dled; doo·dling** : to make a doodle — **doo·dler** n

²**doodle** n : a scribble, design, or sketch done while thinking about something else

doo·dle·bug n : ANT LION

¹**doom** n **1** : a decision made by a court : SENTENCE **2** : a usually unhappy end : FATE

²**doom** vb **1** : to give judgment against : CONDEMN **2** : to make sure that something bad will happen

dooms·day n : the day of final judgment : the end of the world

door n **1** : a usually swinging or sliding frame or barrier by which an entrance (as into a house) is closed and opened **2** : a part of a piece of furniture like a house's door **3** : DOORWAY

door·man n, pl **door·men** : a person who tends a door of a building

door·step n : a step or a series of steps before an outer door

door·way n : the opening or passage that a door closes

door·yard n : a yard outside the door of a house

dope n **1** : a thick sticky material (as one used to make pipe joints tight) **2** : a narcotic substance **3** : a stupid person **4** : IN-FORMATION 2

dop·ey *adj* **dop·i·er; dop·i·est** **1** : lacking alertness and activity : SLUGGISH **2** : STUPID 2

dorm *n* : DORMITORY

dor·mant *adj* : being in an inactive state for the time being

dor·mer *n* **1** : a window placed upright in a sloping roof **2** : the structure containing a dormer window

dor·mi·to·ry *n, pl* **dor·mi·to·ries** **1** : a sleeping room especially for several people **2** : a residence hall having many sleeping rooms

dor·mouse *n, pl* **dor·mice** : a small European animal that is like a squirrel, lives in trees, and feeds on nuts

dor·sal *adj* : of, relating to, or being on or near the surface of the body that in humans is the back but in most animals is the upper surface — **dor·sal·ly** *adv*

do·ry *n, pl* **dories** : a boat with a flat bottom, high sides that curve upward and outward, and a sharp bow

¹**dose** *n* : a measured amount (as of a medicine) to be used at one time

²**dose** *vb* **dosed; dos·ing** : to give medicine to

¹**dot** *n* **1** : a small point, mark, or spot **2** : a certain point in time **3** : a short click forming a letter or part of a letter (as in telegraphy)

²**dot** *vb* **dot·ted; dot·ting** : to mark with or as if with dots

dote *vb* **dot·ed; dot·ing** : to be foolishly fond — **dot·er** *n* — **dot·ing·ly** *adv*

¹**dou·ble** *adj* **1** : having a twofold relation or character : DUAL **2** : made up of two parts or members **3** : being twice as great or as many **4** : folded in two **5** : having more than the usual number of petals

²**double** *vb* **dou·bled; dou·bling** **1** : to make or become twice as great or as many : multiply by two **2** : to make of two thicknesses **3** : CLENCH 2 **4** : to become bent or folded usually in the middle **5** : to take the place of another **6** : to turn sharply and go back over the same course

³**double** *adv* **1** : DOUBLY **2** : two together

⁴**double** *n* **1** : something that is twice another **2** : a hit in baseball that enables the batter to reach second base **3** : one that is very like another

double bass *n* : an instrument of the violin family that is the largest member and has the deepest tone

dou·ble–cross *vb* : BETRAY 2

dou·ble·head·er *n* : two games played one right after the other on the same day

dou·ble–joint·ed *adj* : having a joint that permits unusual freedom of movement of the parts that are joined

double play *n* : a play in baseball by which two base runners are put out

dou·blet *n* : a close-fitting jacket worn by men in Europe especially in the sixteenth century

dou·ble–talk *n* : language that seems to make sense but is actually a mixture of sense and nonsense

dou·bloon *n* : an old gold coin of Spain and Spanish America

dou·bly *adv* : to twice the amount or degree

¹**doubt** *vb* **1** : to be uncertain about **2** : to lack confidence in : DISTRUST **3** : to consider unlikely — **doubt·er** *n* — **doubt·ing·ly** *adv*

²**doubt** *n* **1** : uncertainty of belief or opinion **2** : the condition of being undecided **3** : a lack of confidence : DISTRUST

doubt·ful *adj* **1** : not clear or certain as to fact **2** : of a questionable kind **3** : undecided in opinion **4** : not certain in outcome — **doubt·ful·ly** *adv*

doubt·less *adv* **1** : without doubt **2** : in all probability

dough *n* **1** : a soft mass of moistened flour or meal thick enough to knead or roll **2** : MONEY 1, 2

dough·nut *n* : a small ring of sweet dough fried in fat

dough·ty *adj* **dough·ti·er; dough·ti·est** : very strong and brave — **dough·ti·ly** *adv* — **dough·ti·ness** *n*

dour *adj* : looking or being stern or sullen — **dour·ly** *adv* — **dour·ness** *n*

douse *vb* **doused; dous·ing** **1** : to stick into water **2** : to throw a liquid on **3** : to put out : EXTINGUISH

¹**dove** *n* : any of various mostly small pigeons

²**dove** *past of* DIVE

dowdy *adj* **dowd·i·er; dowd·i·est** **1** : not neatly or well dressed or cared for **2** : not stylish — **dowd·i·ly** *adv* — **dowd·i·ness** *n*

dow·el *n* : a pin or peg used for fastening together two pieces of wood

¹**down** *adv* **1** : toward or in a lower position **2** : to a lying or sitting position **3** : toward or to the ground, floor, or bottom **4** : in cash **5** : in a direction opposite to up **6** : to or in a lower or worse condition **7** : from a past time **8** : to or in a state of less activity

²**down** *prep* : down in : down along : down on : down through

³**down** *vb* : to go or cause to go or come down

⁴**down** *adj* **1** : being in a low position **2** : directed or going downward **3** : being at a lower level **4** : low in spirits : DOWNCAST

5down *n* : a low or falling period

6down *n* : a rolling grassy upland — usually used in pl.

7down *n* **1** : soft fluffy feathers (as of young birds) **2** : something soft and fluffy like down — **down·like** *adj*

down·beat *n* : the first beat of a measure of music

down·cast *adj* **1** : low in spirit : SAD **2** : directed down

down·fall *n* : a sudden fall (as from power, happiness, or a high position) or the cause of such a fall — **down·fall·en** *adj*

1down·grade *n* : a downward slope (as of a road)

2downgrade *vb* **down·grad·ed; down·grad·ing** : to lower in grade, rank, position, or standing

down·heart·ed *adj* : DOWNCAST 1 — **down·heart·ed·ly** *adv* — **down·heart·ed·ness** *n*

1down·hill *adv* : 1DOWNWARD 1

2down·hill *adj* : sloping downhill

down payment *n* : a part of a price paid when something is bought or delivered leaving a balance to be paid later

down·pour *n* : a heavy rain

1down·right *adv* : REALLY, VERY

2downright *adj* : 2OUTRIGHT 1, ABSOLUTE

down·stage *adv or adj* : toward or at the front of a theatrical stage

1down·stairs *adv* : down the stairs : on or to a lower floor

2down·stairs *adj* : situated on a lower floor or on the main or first floor

3down·stairs *n sing or pl* : the lower floor of a building

down·stream *adv* : in the direction a stream is flowing

down·town *adv or adj* : to, toward, or in the main business district

1down·ward *or* **down·wards** *adv* **1** : from a higher place or condition to a lower one **2** : from an earlier time

2downward *adj* : going or moving down

down·wind *adv or adj* : in the direction the wind is blowing

downy *adj* **down·i·er; down·i·est 1** : like down **2** : covered with down

dow·ry *n, pl* **dowries** : the property that a woman brings to her husband in marriage

1doze *vb* **dozed; doz·ing** : to sleep lightly — **doz·er** *n*

2doze *n* : a light sleep

doz·en *n, pl* **dozens** *or* **dozen** : a group of twelve

1drab *n* : a light olive brown

2drab *adj* **drab·ber; drab·best 1** : of the color drab **2** : lacking change and interest : DULL — **drab·ly** *adv* — **drab·ness** *n*

1draft *n* **1** : the act of pulling or hauling : the thing or amount pulled **2** : the act or an instance of drinking or inhaling : the portion drunk or inhaled at one time **3** : a medicine prepared for drinking **4** : something represented in words or lines : DESIGN, PLAN **5** : a quick sketch or outline from which a final work is produced **6** : the act of drawing out liquid (as from a cask) : a portion of liquid drawn out **7** : the depth of water a ship needs in order to float **8** : a picking of persons for required military service **9** : an order made by one party to another to pay money to a third party **10** : a current of air **11** : a device to regulate an air supply (as in a stove)

2draft *adj* **1** : used for pulling loads **2** : TENTATIVE **3** : ready to be drawn from a container

3draft *vb* **1** : to pick especially for required military service **2** : to make a draft of : OUTLINE **3** : COMPOSE 1, PREPARE — **draft·er** *n*

drafts·man *n, pl* **drafts·men** : a person who draws plans (as for machinery) — **draftsman·ship** *n*

drafty *adj* **draft·i·er; draft·i·est** : exposed to a draft or current of air — **draft·i·ness** *n*

1drag *n* **1** : something without wheels (as a sledge for carrying heavy loads) that is dragged, pulled, or drawn along or over a surface **2** : something used for dragging (as a device used underwater to catch something) **3** : something that stops or holds back progress **4** : a dull event, person, or thing

2drag *vb* **dragged; drag·ging 1** : to haul slowly or heavily **2** : to move with distressing slowness or difficulty **3** : to pass or cause to pass slowly **4** : to hang or lag behind **5** : to trail along on the ground **6** : to search or fish with a drag

drag·gle *vb* **drag·gled; drag·gling 1** : to make or become wet and dirty by dragging **2** : to follow slowly : STRAGGLE

drag·net *n* **1** : a net to be drawn along in order to catch something **2** : a network of planned actions for going after and catching a criminal

drag·on *n* : an imaginary animal usually pictured as a huge serpent or lizard with wings and large claws

drag·on·fly *n, pl* **drag·on·flies** : a large insect with a long slender body and four wings

dra·goon *n* : a soldier on horseback

drag race *n* : a race for two vehicles at a time from a standstill to a point a quarter mile away

1drain *vb* **1** : to draw off or flow off gradually or completely **2** : to make or become dry or empty a little at a time **3** : to let out surface or surplus water **4** : ¹EXHAUST 3

²drain *n* **1** : a means of draining (as a pipe, channel, or sewer) **2** : the act of draining **3** : a using up a little at a time

drain·age *n* **1** : an act of draining **2** : something that is drained off **3** : a method of draining : system of drains

drain·pipe *n* : a pipe for drainage

drake *n* : a male duck

dra·ma *n* **1** : a written work that tells a story through action and speech and is meant to be acted out on a stage **2** : dramatic art, literature, or affairs

dra·mat·ic *adj* **1** : of or relating to the drama **2** : like that of the drama : VIVID — **dra·mat·i·cal·ly** *adv*

dra·ma·tist *n* : PLAYWRIGHT

dra·ma·tize *vb* **dram·a·tized; dram·a·tiz·ing** **1** : to make into a drama **2** : to present or represent in a dramatic manner — **dra·ma·ti·za·tion** *n*

drank *past of* DRINK

¹drape *vb* **draped; drap·ing** **1** : to decorate or cover with or as if with folds of cloth **2** : to arrange or hang in flowing lines

²drape *n* **1 drapes** *pl* : DRAPERY 2 **2** : arrangement in or of folds **3** : the cut or hang of clothing

drap·ery *n, pl* **drap·er·ies** **1** : a decorative fabric hung in loose folds **2** : curtains of heavy fabric often used over thinner curtains

dras·tic *adj* **1** : acting rapidly and strongly **2** : severe in effect : HARSH — **dras·ti·cal·ly** *adv*

draught *chiefly Brit variant of* DRAFT

¹draw *vb* **drew; drawn; draw·ing** **1** : to cause to move by pulling : cause to follow **2** : to move or go usually steadily or a little at a time **3** : ATTRACT 1 **4** : to call forth : PROVOKE **5** : INHALE **6** : to bring or pull out **7** : to bring or get from a source **8** : to need (a certain depth) to float in **9** : to take or receive at random **10** : to bend (a bow) by pulling back the string **11** : to cause to shrink or pucker : WRINKLE **12** : to leave (a contest) undecided : TIE **13** : to produce a likeness of by making lines on a surface : SKETCH **14** : to write out in proper form — often used with *up* **15** : FORMULATE **16** : to produce or make use of a current of air

²draw *n* **1** : the act or result of drawing **2** : a tie game or contest **3** : something that draws attention **4** : a gully shallower than a ravine

draw·back *n* : ¹HANDICAP 3

draw·bridge *n* : a bridge made to be drawn up, down, or aside to permit or prevent passage

draw·er *n* **1** : one that draws **2** : a sliding boxlike compartment (as in a desk) **3 drawers** *pl* : an undergarment for the lower part of the body

draw·ing *n* **1** : an act or instance of drawing lots **2** : the act or art of making a figure, plan, or sketch by means of lines **3** : a picture made by drawing

drawing room *n* : a formal room for entertaining company

¹drawl *vb* : to speak slowly with vowel sounds drawn out beyond their usual length

drawl *n* : a drawling way of speaking

draw on *vb* : to come closer : APPROACH

draw out *vb* : to cause or encourage to speak freely

draw·string *n* : a string, cord, or tape used to close a bag, control fullness in clothes, or open or close curtains

draw up *vb* **1** : to arrange (as a body of troops) in order **2** : to straighten (oneself) to an erect posture **3** : to bring or come to a stop

dray *n* : a strong low cart or wagon without sides for hauling heavy loads

¹dread *vb* **1** : to fear greatly **2** : to be very unwilling to meet or face

²dread *n* : great fear especially of harm to come

³dread *adj* : causing great fear or anxiety

dread·ful *adj* **1** : causing a feeling of dread **2** : very disagreeable, unpleasant, or shocking — **dread·ful·ly** *adv* — **dread·ful·ness** *n*

dread·nought *n* : a very large battleship

¹dream *n* **1** : a series of thoughts, pictures, or feelings occurring during sleep **2** : a dreamlike creation of the imagination : DAYDREAM **3** : something notable for its pleasing quality **4** : a goal that is longed for : IDEAL — **dream·like** *adj*

²dream *vb* **dreamed** *or* **dreamt; dream·ing** **1** : to have a dream or dreams **2** : to spend time having daydreams **3** : to think of as happening or possible — **dream·er** *n*

dream·land *n* : an unreal delightful country existing only in imagination or in dreams

dream·less *adj* : having no dreams — **dream·less·ly** *adv* — **dream·less·ness** *n*

dreamy *adj* **dream·i·er; dream·i·est** **1** : tending to spend time dreaming **2** : having the quality of a dream **3** : being quiet and soothing **4** : SUPERB — **dream·i·ly** *adv* — **dream·i·ness** *n*

drea·ry *adj* **drea·ri·er; drea·ri·est** : DISMAL, GLOOMY — **drea·ri·ly** *adv* — **drea·ri·ness** *n*

¹dredge *vb* **dredged; dredg·ing** : to dig or gather with or as if with a dredge — **dredg·er** *n*

²dredge *n* **1** : a heavy iron frame with a net

attached to be dragged (as for gathering oysters) over the sea bottom **2** : a machine for scooping up or removing earth usually by buckets on an endless chain or by a suction tube **3** : a barge used in dredging

dregs *n pl* **1** : solids that settle out of a liquid **2** : the worst or most useless part

drench *vb* : to wet thoroughly

¹dress *vb* **1** : to make or set straight (as soldiers on parade) **2** : to put clothes on : CLOTHE **3** : to wear formal or fancy clothes **4** : to trim or decorate for display **5** : to treat with remedies and bandage **6** : to arrange by combing, brushing, or curling **7** : to prepare (a meat animal) for food **8** : to apply fertilizer to

²dress *n* **1** : CLOTHING 1, APPAREL **2** : an outer garment with a skirt for a woman or child

¹dress·er *n* : a piece of furniture (as a chest or a bureau) with a mirror

²dresser *n* : a person who dresses in a certain way

dress·ing *n* **1** : the act or process of one who dresses **2** : a sauce added to a food (as a salad) **3** : a seasoned mixture used as a stuffing (as for a turkey) **4** : material used to cover an injury **5** : something used as a fertilizer

dress·mak·er *n* : a person who makes dresses

dress·mak·ing *n* : the process or occupation of making dresses

dress up *vb* **1** : to put on one's best or formal clothes **2** : to put on strange or fancy clothes

dressy *adj* **dress·i·er; dress·i·est** **1** : showy in dress **2** : suitable for formal occasions

drew *past of* DRAW

¹drib·ble *vb* **drib·bled; drib·bling** **1** : to fall or let fall in small drops : TRICKLE **2** : ¹SLOBBER, DROOL **3** : to move forward by bouncing, tapping, or kicking

²dribble *n* **1** : a trickling flow **2** : the act of dribbling a ball

drib·let *n* **1** : a small amount **2** : a falling drop

dri·er *or* **dry·er** *n* **1** : something that removes or absorbs moisture **2** : a substance that speeds up the drying of oils, paints, and inks **3** *usually dryer* : a device for drying

¹drift *n* **1** : the motion or course of something drifting **2** : a mass of matter (as snow or sand) piled in a heap by the wind **3** : a course something appears to be taking **4** : the meaning of something said or implied

²drift *vb* **1** : to float or to be driven along by winds, waves, or currents **2** : to move

along without effort or purpose **3** : to pile up in drifts — **drift·er** *n*

drift·wood *n* : wood drifted or floated by water

¹drill *vb* **1** : to bore with a drill **2** : to teach by means of repeated practice — **drill·er** *n*

²drill *n* **1** : a tool for making holes in hard substances **2** : the training of soldiers (as in marching) **3** : regular strict training and instruction in a subject

³drill *n* : a farming implement for making holes or furrows and planting seeds in them

⁴drill *vb* : to sow seeds with or as if with a drill

drily *variant of* DRYLY

¹drink *vb* **drank; drunk; drink·ing** **1** : to swallow liquid **2** : to absorb a liquid **3** : to take in through the senses **4** : to drink alcoholic liquor — **drink·er** *n*

²drink *n* **1** : BEVERAGE **2** : alcoholic liquor

drink·able *adj* : suitable or safe for drinking

¹drip *vb* **dripped; drip·ping** **1** : to fall or let fall in or as if in drops **2** : to let fall drops of liquid

²drip *n* **1** : a falling in drops **2** : dripping liquid **3** : the sound made by falling drops

¹drive *vb* **drove; driv·en; driv·ing** **1** : to push or force onward **2** : to direct the movement or course of **3** : to go or carry in a vehicle under one's own control **4** : to set or keep in motion or operation **5** : to carry through : CONCLUDE **6** : to force to work or to act **7** : to bring into a specified condition — **driv·er** *n*

²drive *n* **1** : a trip in a carriage or automobile **2** : a collecting and driving together of animals **3** : DRIVEWAY **4** : an often scenic public road **5** : an organized usually thorough effort to carry out a purpose **6** : the means for giving motion to a machine or machine part **7** : a device that transfers information to and from a storage material (as tape or disks)

drive-in *adj* : designed and equipped to serve customers while they remain in their automobiles

drive·way *n* : a private road leading from the street to a house or garage

¹driz·zle *n* : a fine misty rain

²drizzle *vb* **driz·zled; driz·zling** : to rain in very small drops

droll *adj* : having an odd or amusing quality — **droll·ness** *n* — **drol·ly** *adv*

drom·e·dary *n, pl* **drom·e·dar·ies** **1** : a speedy camel trained for riding **2** : the camel of western Asia and northern Africa that has only one hump

¹drone *n* **1** : a male bee **2** : a lazy person : one who lives on the labor of others

2**drone** *vb* **droned; dron·ing :** to make or to speak with a low dull monotonous hum

3**drone** *n* **:** a droning sound

drool *vb* **:** to let liquid flow from the mouth **:** SLOBBER

1**droop** *vb* **1 :** to sink, bend, or hang down **2 :** to become sad or weak

2**droop** *n* **:** the condition or appearance of drooping

1**drop** *n* **1 :** the amount of liquid that falls naturally in one rounded mass **2 drops** *pl* **:** a dose of medicine measured by drops **3 :** something (as a small round candy) that is shaped like a liquid drop **4 :** an instance of dropping **5 :** the distance of a fall

2**drop** *vb* **dropped; drop·ping 1 :** to fall or let fall in drops **2 :** to let fall **3 :** to lower in pitch and volume **4 :** SEND 1 **5 :** to let go **:** DISMISS **6 :** to knock down **:** cause to fall **7 :** to go lower **8 :** to make a brief visit **9 :** to pass into a less active state **10 :** to withdraw from membership or from taking part **11 :** LOSE 4

drop·let *n* **:** a tiny drop

drop·out *n* **:** one that drops out especially from school or a training program

drop·per *n* **1 :** one that drops **2 :** a short glass tube with a rubber bulb used to measure out liquids by drops

drought *n* **1 :** lack of rain or water **2 :** a long period of dry weather

1**drove** *n* **1 :** a group of animals being driven or moving in a body **2 :** a crowd of people moving or acting together

2**drove** *past of* DRIVE

drov·er *n* **:** a worker who drives cattle or sheep

drown *vb* **1 :** to suffocate in a liquid and especially in water **2 :** to cover with water **:** FLOOD **3 :** to overpower especially with noise

1**drowse** *vb* **drowsed; drows·ing :** to be half asleep **:** sleep lightly

2**drowse** *n* **:** a light sleep **:** DOZE

drowsy *adj* **drows·i·er; drows·i·est 1 :** ready to fall asleep **2 :** making one sleepy — **drows·i·ly** *adv* — **drows·i·ness** *n*

drub *vb* **drubbed; drub·bing 1 :** to beat severely **2 :** to defeat completely

drudge *n* **:** a person who does hard or dull work

drudg·ery *n, pl* **drudg·er·ies :** hard or dull work

1**drug** *n* **1 :** a substance used as a medicine or in making medicines **2 :** medicine used to deaden pain or bring sleep **3 :** a substance that may harm or make an addict of a person who uses it

2**drug** *vb* **drugged; drug·ging 1 :** to poison

with or as if with a drug **2 :** to dull a person's senses with drugs

drug·gist *n* **:** a seller of drugs and medicines **:** PHARMACIST

drug·store *n* **:** a retail store where medicines and often other things are sold **:** PHARMACY

1**drum** *n* **1 :** a percussion instrument usually consisting of a metal or wooden cylinder with flat ends covered by tightly stretched skin **2 :** a sound of or like a drum **3 :** an object shaped like a drum

2**drum** *vb* **drummed; drum·ming 1 :** to beat a drum **2 :** to beat or sound like a drum **3 :** to gather together by or as if by beating a drum **4 :** to drive or force by steady or repeated effort **5 :** to beat or tap in a rhythmic way

drum major *n* **:** the marching leader of a band or drum corps

drum ma·jor·ette *n* **:** a girl who is a drum major

drum·mer *n* **1 :** a person who plays a drum **2 :** a traveling salesman

drum·stick *n* **1 :** a stick for beating a drum **2 :** the lower section of the leg of a fowl

1**drunk** *past participle of* DRINK

2**drunk** *adj* **1 :** being so much under the influence of alcohol that normal thinking and acting become difficult or impossible **2 :** controlled by some feeling as if under the influence of alcohol

3**drunk** *n* **1 :** a period of drinking too much alcoholic liquor **2 :** a drunken person

drunk·ard *n* **:** a person who is often drunk

drunk·en *adj* **1 :** 2DRUNK 1 **2 :** resulting from being drunk — **drunk·en·ly** *adv* — **drunk·en·ness** *n*

1**dry** *adj* **dri·er; dri·est 1 :** free or freed from water or liquid **:** not wet or moist **2 :** having little or no rain **3 :** lacking freshness **:** STALE **4 :** not being in or under water **5 :** THIRSTY 1, 2 **6 :** no longer liquid or sticky **7 :** containing no liquid **8 :** not giving milk **9 :** not producing phlegm **10 :** amusing in a sharp or acid way **11 :** UNINTERESTING **12 :** not sweet — **dry·ly** *adv* — **dry·ness** *n*

2**dry** *vb* **dried; dry·ing :** to make or become dry

dry cell *n* **:** a small cell producing electricity by means of chemicals in a sealed container

dry–clean *vb* **:** to clean (fabrics) with chemical solvents

dry cleaner *n* **:** one whose business is dry cleaning

dry cleaning *n* **1 :** the cleaning of fabrics with a substance other than water **2 :** something that is dry-cleaned

dryer *variant of* DRIER

dry goods *n pl* : cloth goods (as fabrics, lace, and ribbon)

dry ice *n* : solidified carbon dioxide used chiefly to keep something very cold

du·al *adj* : consisting of two parts : having two like parts : DOUBLE — **du·al·ly** *adv*

¹**dub** *vb* **dubbed; dub·bing** **1** : to make a knight of by a light tapping on the shoulder with a sword **2** : ²NAME 1, NICKNAME

²**dub** *vb* **dubbed; dub·bing** : to add (sound effects) to a film or broadcast

du·bi·ous *adj* **1** : causing doubt : UNCERTAIN **2** : feeling doubt **3** : QUESTIONABLE **1** — **du·bi·ous·ly** *adv*

duch·ess *n* **1** : the wife or widow of a duke **2** : a woman who holds the rank of a duke in her own right

¹**duck** *n* : any of a group of swimming birds that have broad flat bills and are smaller than the related geese and swans

²**duck** *vb* **1** : to push or pull under water for a moment **2** : to lower the head or body suddenly **3** : ²DODGE 1 **4** : ²DODGE 2 **5** : to avoid a duty, question, or responsibility

³**duck** *n* **1** : a coarse usually cotton fabric rather like canvas **2 ducks** *pl* : clothes (as trousers) made of duck

duck·bill *n* : PLATYPUS

duck·ling *n* : a young duck

duck·weed *n* : a very small stemless plant that floats in fresh water

duct *n* : a pipe, tube, or vessel that carries something (as a bodily secretion, water, or hot air) — **duct·less** *adj*

ductless gland *n* : ENDOCRINE GLAND

dud *n* **1 duds** *pl* : CLOTHING **2** : a complete failure **3** : a missile that fails to explode

dude *n* : a man who pays too much attention to his clothes

¹**due** *adj* **1** : owed or owing as a debt or a right **2** : SUITABLE **3** : being a result — used with *to* **4** : required or expected to happen

²**due** *n* **1** : something owed : DEBT **2 dues** *pl* : a regular or legal charge or fee

³**due** *adv* : DIRECTLY 1

¹**du·el** *n* **1** : a combat between two persons fought with deadly weapons by agreement and in the presence of witnesses **2** : a contest between two opponents

²**duel** *vb* **du·eled** or **du·elled; du·el·ing** or **du·el·ling** : to fight in a duel — **du·el·ist** *n*

du·et *n* **1** : a musical composition for two performers **2** : two performers playing or singing together

due to *prep* : because of

dug *past of* DIG

dug·out *n* **1** : a boat made by hollowing out

a log **2** : a shelter dug in a hillside or in the ground **3** : a low shelter facing a baseball diamond and containing the players' bench

duke *n* : a member of the highest rank of the British nobility

¹**dull** *adj* **1** : mentally slow : STUPID **2** : LISTLESS **3** : slow in action : SLUGGISH **4** : not sharp in edge or point : BLUNT **5** : lacking brightness or luster **6** : not clear and ringing **7** : CLOUDY 1, OVERCAST **8** : not interesting : TEDIOUS **9** : slightly grayish — **dull·ness** or **dul·ness** *n* — **dul·ly** *adv*

²**dull** *vb* : to make or become dull

du·ly *adv* : in a due or suitable manner, time, or degree

dumb *adj* **1** : lacking the normal power of speech **2** : normally unable to speak **3** : not willing to speak : SILENT **4** : STUPID 1, FOOLISH — **dumb·ly** *adv* — **dumb·ness** *n*

dumb·bell *n* **1** : a short bar with two weighted balls or disks at the ends usually used in pairs for strengthening the arms **2** : a stupid person

dumb·found or **dum·found** *vb* : to cause to become speechless with astonishment : AMAZE

dumb·wait·er *n* : a small elevator for carrying food and dishes or other small items from one floor to another

dum·my *n, pl* **dummies** **1** : a person who does not have or seems not to have the power of speech **2** : a stupid person **3** : an imitation used as a substitute for something

¹**dump** *vb* : to let fall in a heap : get rid of

²**dump** *n* **1** : a place for dumping something (as trash) **2** : a place for storage of military materials or the materials stored **3** : a messy or shabby place

dump·ling *n* : a small mass of dough cooked by boiling or steaming

dumps *n pl* : low spirits

dumpy *adj* **dump·i·er; dump·i·est** : short and thick in build — **dump·i·ness** *n*

¹**dun** *n* : a slightly brownish dark gray

²**dun** *vb* **dunned; dun·ning** : to make repeated demands upon for payment

dunce *n* : a stupid person

dune *n* : a hill or ridge of sand piled up by the wind

dung *n* : FECES

dun·ga·ree *n* **1** : a heavy cotton cloth **2 dungarees** *pl* : pants or work clothes made of dungaree

dun·geon *n* : a dark usually underground prison

dung·hill *n* : a pile of manure

dunk *vb* : to dip (as a doughnut) into liquid (as coffee)

duo *n, pl* **du·os** **1** : a duet especially for two performers at two pianos **2** : ¹PAIR 1

¹dupe *n* : a person who has been or is easily deceived or cheated

²dupe *vb* **duped; dup·ing** : to make a dupe of : TRICK

du·plex *adj* : ¹DOUBLE 2

¹du·pli·cate *adj* **1** : having two parts exactly the same or alike **2** : being the same as another

²du·pli·cate *vb* **du·pli·cat·ed; du·pli·cat·ing** **1** : to make double **2** : to make an exact copy of

³du·pli·cate *n* : a thing that is exactly like another

du·pli·ca·tion *n* **1** : the act or process of duplicating **2** : the state of being duplicated

du·ra·bil·i·ty *n* : ability to last or to stand hard or continued use

du·ra·ble *adj* : able to last a long time — **du·ra·ble·ness** *n* — **du·ra·bly** *adv*

du·ra·tion *n* : the time during which something exists or lasts

dur·ing *prep* **1** : throughout the course of **2** : at some point in the course of

dusk *n* **1** : the darker part of twilight especially at night **2** : partial darkness

dusky *adj* **dusk·i·er; dusk·i·est** **1** : somewhat dark in color **2** : somewhat dark : DIM — **dusk·i·ness** *n*

¹dust *n* **1** : fine dry powdery particles (as of earth) : a fine powder **2** : the powdery remains of bodies once alive **3** : something worthless **4** : the surface of the ground — **dust·less** *adj*

²dust *vb* **1** : to make free of dust : brush or wipe away dust **2** : to sprinkle with or as if with fine particles — **dust·er** *n*

dust·pan *n* : a pan shaped like a shovel and used for sweepings

dust storm *n* : a violent wind carrying dust across a dry region

dusty *adj* **dust·i·er; dust·i·est** **1** : filled or covered with dust **2** : like dust

¹Dutch *adj* : of or relating to the Netherlands, its people, or the Dutch language

²Dutch *n* **1** **Dutch** *pl* : the people of the Netherlands **2** : the language of the Dutch

Dutch door *n* : a door divided so that the lower part can be shut while the upper part remains open

Dutch treat *n* : a treat for which each person pays his or her own way

du·ti·ful *adj* : having or showing a sense of duty — **du·ti·ful·ly** *adv* — **du·ti·ful·ness** *n*

du·ty *n, pl* **duties** **1** : conduct owed to parents and those in authority **2** : the action required by one's position or occupation **3** : something a person feels he or she ought to do **4** : a tax especially on imports into a country

¹dwarf *n, pl* **dwarfs** *also* **dwarves** **1** : a person, animal, or plant much below normal size **2** : a small legendary being usually pictured as a deformed and ugly person

²dwarf *vb* **1** : to prevent from growing to natural size : STUNT **2** : to cause to appear smaller

³dwarf *adj* : of less than the usual size

dwell *vb* **dwelt** *or* **dwelled; dwell·ing** **1** : to stay for a while **2** : to live in a place : RESIDE **3** : to keep the attention directed — **dwell·er** *n*

dwell·ing *n* : RESIDENCE 2, 3

dwin·dle *vb* **dwin·dled; dwin·dling** : to make or become less

¹dye *n* : a coloring matter

²dye *vb* **dyed; dye·ing** : to give a new color to

dye·stuff *n* : material used for dyeing

dying *present participle of* DIE

dyke *variant of* DIKE

dy·nam·ic *adj* : full of energy : ACTIVE, FORCEFUL

¹dy·na·mite *n* : an explosive used in blasting

²dynamite *vb* **dy·na·mit·ed; dy·na·mit·ing** : to blow up with dynamite — **dy·na·mit·er** *n*

dy·na·mo *n, pl* **dy·na·mos** : a machine for producing electric current

dy·nas·ty *n, pl* **dy·nas·ties** : a series of rulers of the same family

dys·en·tery *n* : a disease in which much watery material mixed with mucus and blood is passed from the bowels

E

e *n, pl* **e's** *or* **es** *often cap* **1** : the fifth letter of the English alphabet **2** : a grade that shows a student's work is failing

¹each *adj* : being one of two or more individuals

²each *pron* : each one

³each *adv* : to or for each : APIECE

each other *pron* : each of two or more in a shared action or relationship

ea·ger *adj* : desiring very much : IMPATIENT — **ea·ger·ly** *adv* — **ea·ger·ness** *n*

ea·gle *n* : any of several large birds of prey noted for keen sight and powerful flight

ea·glet *n* : a young eagle

-ean — see -AN

¹ear *n* **1** : the organ of hearing **2** : the sense of hearing **3** : willing or sympathetic attention **4** : something like an ear in shape or position — **eared** *adj*

²ear *n* : the seed-bearing head of a cereal grass

ear·ache *n* : an ache or pain in the ear

ear·drum *n* : the membrane that separates the outer and middle parts of the ear and vibrates when sound waves strike it

earl *n* : a member of the British nobility ranking below a marquess and above a viscount

¹ear·ly *adv* **ear·li·er; ear·li·est** **1** : at or near the beginning of a period of time or a series **2** : before the usual time

²early *adj* **ear·li·er; ear·li·est** : occurring near the beginning or before the usual time

ear·muff *n* : one of a pair of coverings joined by a flexible band and worn to protect the ears from cold or noise

earn *vb* **1** : to get for services given **2** : to deserve especially as a reward or punishment

ear·nest *adj* : not light or playful — **ear·nest·ly** *adv* — **ear·nest·ness** *n*

earn·ings *n pl* : money received as wages or gained as profit

ear·phone *n* : a device that converts electrical energy into sound and is worn over the opening of the ear or inserted into it

ear·ring *n* : an ornament worn on the ear lobe

ear·shot *n* : the range within which an unaided human voice can be heard

earth *n* **1** : ²SOIL 1 **2** : areas of land as distinguished from the sea and the air **3** *often cap* : the planet that we live on

earth·en *adj* : made of earth

earth·en·ware *n* : things (as dishes) made of baked clay

earth·ly *adj* **1** : having to do with or belonging to the earth : not heavenly **2** : IMAGINABLE, POSSIBLE

earth·quake *n* : a shaking or trembling of a portion of the earth

earth·worm *n* : a worm that has a long body made up of similar segments and lives in damp soil

earthy *adj* **earth·i·er; earth·i·est** **1** : consisting of or like earth **2** : PRACTICAL 4 **3** : not polite : CRUDE

ear·wig *n* : an insect with long slender feelers and a large forcepslike organ at the end of its abdomen

¹ease *n* **1** : freedom from pain or trouble : comfort of body or mind **2** : freedom from any feeling of difficulty or embarrassment

²ease *vb* **eased; eas·ing** **1** : to free from discomfort or worry : RELIEVE **2** : to make less tight : LOOSEN **3** : to move very carefully

ea·sel *n* : a frame for holding a flat surface in an upright position

eas·i·ly *adv* **1** : in an easy manner : without difficulty **2** : without doubt or question

¹east *adv* : to or toward the east

²east *adj* : placed toward, facing, or coming from the east

³east *n* **1** : the direction of sunrise : the compass point opposite to west **2** *cap* : regions or countries east of a certain point

Eas·ter *n* : a Christian church festival observed in memory of the Resurrection

Easter lily *n* : a white garden lily that blooms in spring

east·er·ly *adj or adv* **1** : toward the east **2** : from the east

east·ern *adj* **1** *often cap* : of, relating to, or like that of the East **2** : lying toward or coming from the east

east·ward *adv or adj* : toward the east

easy *adj* **eas·i·er; eas·i·est** **1** : not hard to do or get : not difficult **2** : not hard to please **3** : free from pain, trouble, or worry **4** : COMFORTABLE **5** : showing ease : NATURAL

eat *vb* **ate; eat·en; eat·ing** **1** : to chew and swallow food **2** : to take a meal or meals **3** : to destroy as if by eating : CORRODE — **eat·er** *n*

eat·able *adj* : fit to be eaten

eaves *n sing or pl* : the lower edge of a roof that sticks out past the wall

eaves·drop *vb* **eaves·dropped; eaves·drop·ping** : to listen secretly to private conversation

¹ebb *n* **1** : the flowing out of the tide **2** : a

passing from a high to a low point or the time of this

2ebb *vb* **1** : to flow out or away : RECEDE **2** : 1DECLINE **2**, WEAKEN

1eb·o·ny *n, pl* **eb·o·nies** : a hard heavy wood that wears well and comes from tropical trees related to the persimmon

2ebony *adj* **1** : made of or like ebony **2** : 1BLACK **1**

1ec·cen·tric *adj* **1** : acting or thinking in a strange way **2** : not of the usual or normal kind

2eccentric *n* : an eccentric person

ec·cle·si·as·ti·cal *adj* : of or relating to the church or its affairs

1echo *n, pl* **ech·oes** : the repeating of a sound caused by the reflection of sound waves

2echo *vb* **ech·oed; echo·ing 1** : to send back or repeat a sound **2** : to say what someone else has already said

éclair *n* : an oblong pastry with whipped cream or custard filling

1eclipse *n* **1** : a complete or partial hiding of the sun caused by the moon's passing between the sun and the earth **2** : a darkening of the moon caused by the moon's entering the shadow of the earth **3** : the hiding of any celestial body by another **4** : a falling into disgrace or out of use or public favor

2eclipse *vb* **eclipsed; eclips·ing 1** : to cause an eclipse of **2** : to be or do much better than : OUTSHINE

eco·log·i·cal *adj* : of or relating to the science of ecology or the ecology of a particular environment and the living things in it

ecol·o·gist *n* : a specialist in ecology

ecol·o·gy *n* **1** : a branch of science dealing with the relation of living things to their environment **2** : the pattern of relations between living things and their environment

eco·nom·ic *adj* **1** : of or relating to economics **2** : of, relating to, or based on the making, selling, and using of goods and services

eco·nom·i·cal *adj* **1** : using what one has carefully and without waste : FRUGAL **2** : operating with little waste or at a saving — **eco·nom·i·cal·ly** *adv*

eco·nom·ics *n* : the science that studies and explains facts about the making, selling, and using of goods and services

econ·o·mize *vb* **econ·o·mized; econ·o·miz·ing 1** : to practice economy : be thrifty **2** : to reduce expenses : SAVE

econ·o·my *n, pl* **econ·o·mies 1** : the careful use of money and goods : THRIFT **2** : the way an economic system (as of a country or a period in history) is organized

eco·sys·tem *n* : the whole group of living

and nonliving things that make up an environment and affect each other

ec·sta·sy *n, pl* **ec·sta·sies** : very great happiness : extreme delight

ec·stat·ic *adj* : of, relating to, or showing ecstasy

ec·ze·ma *n* : a disease in which the skin is red, itchy, and marred by scaly or crusted spots

1-ed *vb suffix or adj suffix* **1** — used to form the past participle of verbs **2** : having : showing **3** : having the characteristics of

2-ed *vb suffix* — used to form the past tense of verbs

1ed·dy *n, pl* **eddies** : a current of air or water running against the main current or in a circle

2eddy *vb* **ed·died; ed·dy·ing** : to move in an eddy

1edge *n* **1** : the cutting side of a blade **2** : the line where a surface ends : MARGIN, BORDER — **edged** *adj* — **on edge** : NERVOUS **3**, TENSE

2edge *vb* **edged; edg·ing 1** : to give an edge to **2** : to move slowly and little by little

edge·ways *or* **edge·wise** *adv* : with the edge in front : SIDEWAYS

ed·i·ble *adj* : fit or safe to eat

edict *n* : a command or law given or made by an authority (as a ruler)

ed·i·fice *n* : a large or impressive building (as a church)

ed·it *vb* **1** : to correct, revise, and get ready for publication : collect and arrange material to be printed **2** : to be in charge of the publication of something (as an encyclopedia or a newspaper) that is the work of many writers

edi·tion *n* **1** : the form in which a book is published **2** : the whole number of copies of a book, magazine, or newspaper published at one time **3** : one of several issues of a newspaper for a single day

ed·i·tor *n* **1** : a person who edits **2** : a person who writes editorials

1ed·i·to·ri·al *adj* **1** : of or relating to an editor **2** : being or like an editorial

2editorial *n* : a newspaper or magazine article that gives the opinions of its editors or publishers

ed·u·cate *vb* **ed·u·cat·ed; ed·u·cat·ing 1** : to provide schooling for **2** : to develop the mind and morals of especially by formal instruction : TRAIN — **ed·u·ca·tor** *n*

ed·u·ca·tion *n* **1** : the act or process of educating or of being educated **2** : knowledge, skill, and development gained from study or training **3** : the study or science of the methods and problems of teaching

ed·u·ca·tion·al *adj* **1** : having to do with education **2** : offering information or something of value in learning — **ed·u·ca·tion·al·ly** *adv*

¹-ee *n suffix* **1** : person who receives or benefits from a specified thing or action **2** : person who does a specified thing

²-ee *n suffix* **1** : a certain and especially a small kind of **2** : one like or suggesting

eel *n* : a long snakelike fish with a smooth slimy skin

e'en *adv* : EVEN

-eer *n suffix* : person who is concerned with or conducts or produces as a profession

e'er *adv* : EVER

ee·rie *also* **ee·ry** *adj* **ee·ri·er; ee·ri·est** : causing fear and uneasiness : STRANGE

ef·face *vb* **ef·faced; ef·fac·ing** : to erase or blot out completely

¹ef·fect *n* **1** : an event, condition, or state of affairs that is produced by a cause **2** : EXECUTION 1, OPERATION **3** : REALITY 1, FACT **4** : the act of making a certain impression **5** : ¹INFLUENCE 1 **6 effects** *pl* : personal property or possessions

²effect *vb* : BRING ABOUT

ef·fec·tive *adj* **1** : producing or able to produce a desired effect **2** : IMPRESSIVE **3** : being in actual operation — **ef·fec·tive·ly** *adv* — **ef·fec·tive·ness** *n*

ef·fec·tu·al *adj* : producing or able to produce a desired effect

ef·fi·ca·cy *n, pl* **ef·fi·ca·cies** : power to produce effects : efficient action

ef·fi·cien·cy *n, pl* **ef·fi·cien·cies** : the quality or degree of being efficient

ef·fi·cient *adj* : capable of bringing about a desired result with little waste (as of time or energy) — **ef·fi·cient·ly** *adv*

ef·fort *n* **1** : hard work of mind or body : EXERTION **2** : a serious attempt : TRY

ef·fort·less *adj* : showing or needing little or no effort — **ef·fort·less·ly** *adv*

¹egg *vb* : INCITE, URGE

²egg *n* **1** : a shelled oval or rounded body by which some animals (as birds or snakes) reproduce and from which the young hatches out **2** : an egg cell usually together with its protective coverings

egg cell *n* : a cell produced by an ovary that when fertilized by a sperm cell can develop into an embryo and finally a new mature being

egg·nog *n* : a drink made of eggs beaten with sugar, milk or cream, and often alcoholic liquor

egg·plant *n* : an oval vegetable with a usually glossy purplish skin and white flesh that is the fruit of a plant related to the tomato

egg·shell *n* : the shell of an egg

egret *n* : any of various herons that have long plumes during the breeding season

¹Egyp·tian *adj* : of or relating to Egypt or the Egyptians

²Egyptian *n* **1** : a person who is born or lives in Egypt **2** : the language of the ancient Egyptians

ei·der *n* : a large northern sea duck that is mostly white above and black below and has very soft down

ei·der·down *n* **1** : the down of the eider used for filling quilts and pillows **2** : a quilt filled with down

¹eight *adj* : being one more than seven

²eight *n* : one more than seven : two times four : 8

¹eigh·teen *adj* : being one more than seventeen

²eighteen *n* : one more than seventeen : three times six : 18

¹eigh·teenth *adj* : coming right after seventeenth

²eighteenth *n* : number eighteen in a series

¹eighth *adj* : coming right after seventh

²eighth *n* **1** : number eight in a series **2** : one of eight equal parts

¹eight·i·eth *adj* : coming right after seventy-ninth

²eightieth *n* : number eighty in a series

¹eighty *adj* : being eight times ten

²eighty *n* : eight times ten : 80

¹ei·ther *adj* **1** : ¹EACH **2** : being one or the other

²either *pron* : the one or the other

³either *conj* — used before words or phrases the last of which follows "or" to show that they are choices or possibilities

ejac·u·late *vb* **ejac·u·lat·ed; ejac·u·lat·ing** : EXCLAIM

eject *vb* : to drive out or throw off or out

eke out *vb* **eked out; ek·ing out** **1** : to add to bit by bit **2** : to get with great effort

¹elab·o·rate *adj* : worked out with great care or with much detail — **elab·o·rate·ly** *adv*

²elab·o·rate *vb* **elab·o·rat·ed; elab·o·rat·ing** : to work out in detail

elapse *vb* **elapsed; elaps·ing** : to slip past : go by

¹elas·tic *adj* : capable of returning to original shape or size after being stretched, pressed, or squeezed together

²elastic *n* **1** : an elastic fabric made of yarns containing rubber **2** : a rubber band

elas·tic·i·ty *n* : the quality or state of being elastic

elate *vb* **elat·ed; elat·ing** : to fill with joy or pride

ela·tion *n* : the quality or state of being elated

¹el·bow n 1 : the joint of the arm or of the same part of an animal's forelimb 2 : a part (as of a pipe) bent like an elbow

²elbow vb : to push or force a way through with the elbows

¹el·der n : a shrub or small tree related to the honeysuckles that has flat clusters of white flowers followed by fruits like berries

²elder adj : being older than another person

³elder n 1 : one who is older 2 : a person having authority because of age and experience 3 : an official in some churches

el·der·ber·ry n, pl **el·der·ber·ries** : the juicy black or red fruit of the elder

el·der·ly adj : somewhat old : past middle age

el·dest adj : being oldest of a group of people (as siblings)

¹elect adj : chosen for office but not yet holding office

²elect vb 1 : to select by vote 2 : to make a choice

elec·tion n : an electing or being elected especially by vote

elec·tive adj : chosen or filled by election

elec·tor n : a person qualified or having the right to vote in an election

electr- or **electro-** prefix 1 : electricity 2 : electric 3 : electric and 4 : electrically

elec·tric or **elec·tri·cal** adj 1 : of or relating to electricity or its use 2 : heated, moved, made, or run by electricity 3 : having a thrilling effect 4 : giving off sounds through an electronic amplifier — **elec·tri·cal·ly** adv

electric eel : a large South American eel-shaped fish having organs that are able to give a severe electric shock

elec·tri·cian n : a person who installs, operates, or repairs electrical equipment

elec·tric·i·ty n 1 : an important form of energy that is found in nature but that can be artificially produced by rubbing together two unlike things (as glass and silk), by the action of chemicals, or by means of a generator 2 : electric current

elec·tri·fy vb **elec·tri·fied**; **elec·tri·fy·ing** 1 : to charge with electricity 2 : to equip for use of electric power 3 : to supply with electric power 4 : to excite suddenly and sharply : THRILL

elec·tro·cute vb **elec·tro·cut·ed**; **elec·tro·cut·ing** : to kill by an electric shock

elec·trode n : a conductor (as a metal or carbon) used to make electrical contact with a part of an electrical circuit that is not metallic

elec·trol·y·sis n : the producing of chemical changes by passage of an electric current through a liquid

elec·tro·lyte n : a substance (as an acid or salt) that when dissolved (as in water) conducts an electric current

elec·tro·lyt·ic adj : of or relating to electrolysis or an electrolyte

elec·tro·mag·net n : a piece of iron encircled by a coil of wire through which an electric current is passed to magnetize the iron

elec·tro·mag·net·ic adj : of or relating to a magnetic field produced by an electric current

electromagnetic wave n : a wave (as a radio wave or wave of light) that travels at the speed of light and consists of a combined electric and magnetic effect

elec·tron n : a very small particle that has a negative charge of electricity and travels around the nucleus of an atom

elec·tron·ic adj 1 : of, relating to, or using the principles of electronics 2 : operating by means of or using an electronic device (as a computer) — **elec·tron·i·cal·ly** adv

electronic mail n : E-MAIL

elec·tron·ics n : a science that deals with the giving off, action, and effects of electrons in vacuums, gases, and semiconductors and with devices using such electrons

electron tube n : a device in which conduction of electricity by electrons takes place through a vacuum or a gas within a sealed container and which has various uses (as in radio and television)

elec·tro·scope n : an instrument for discovering the presence of an electric charge on a body and for finding out whether the charge is positive or negative

el·e·gance n 1 : refined gracefulness 2 : decoration that is rich but in good taste

el·e·gant adj : showing good taste (as in dress or manners) : having or showing beauty and refinement — **el·e·gant·ly** adv

el·e·gy n, pl **el·e·gies** : a sad or mournful poem usually expressing sorrow for one who is dead

el·e·ment n 1 : one of the parts of which something is made up 2 : something that must be learned before one can advance 3 : a member of a mathematical set 4 : any of more than 100 substances that cannot by ordinary chemical means be separated into different substances

el·e·men·ta·ry adj : of or relating to the beginnings or first principles of a subject

el·e·phant n : a huge thickset mammal with the nose drawn out into a long trunk and two large curved tusks

el·e·vate vb **el·e·vat·ed**; **el·e·vat·ing** : to lift up : RAISE

el·e·va·tion n 1 : height especially above

sea level : ALTITUDE **2** : a raised place (as a hill) **3** : the act of elevating : the condition of being elevated

el·e·va·tor n **1** : a device (as an endless belt) for raising material **2** : a floor or little room that can be raised or lowered for carrying persons or goods from one level to another **3** : a building for storing grain **4** : a winglike device on an airplane to produce motion up or down

¹elev·en adj : being one more than ten

²eleven n : one more than ten : 11

¹elev·enth adj : coming right after tenth

²eleventh n : number eleven in a series

elf n, pl **elves** : an often mischievous fairy

elf·in adj **1** : of or relating to elves **2** : having a strange beauty or charm

el·i·gi·ble adj : worthy or qualified to be chosen

elim·i·nate vb **elim·i·nat·ed; elim·i·nat·ing** : to get rid of : do away with

elim·i·na·tion n : a getting rid especially of waste from the body

elk n **1** : the moose of Europe and Asia **2** : a large North American deer with curved antlers having many branches

el·lipse n : a closed curve that looks like a circle pulled out on opposite sides

el·lip·ti·cal or **el·lip·tic** adj : of or like an ellipse

elm n : a tall shade tree with a broad rather flat top and spreading branches

el·o·cu·tion n : the art of reading or speaking well in public

elo·dea n : a common floating water plant with small green leaves

elon·gate vb **elon·gat·ed; elon·gat·ing** : to make or grow longer

elope vb **eloped; elop·ing** : to run away to be married — **elope·ment** n

el·o·quence n **1** : speaking or writing that is forceful and able to persuade **2** : the art or power of speaking or writing with force and in a way to persuade

el·o·quent adj **1** : expressing oneself or expressed clearly and with force **2** : clearly showing some feeling or meaning — **el·o·quent·ly** adv

¹else adv **1** : in a different way or place or at a different time **2** : if the facts are or were different : if not

²else adj **1** : being other and different **2** : being in addition

else·where adv : in or to another place

elude vb **elud·ed; elud·ing** : to avoid or escape by being quick, skillful, or tricky

elu·sive adj **1** : clever in eluding **2** : hard to understand or define

elves pl of ELF

em- — see EN-

E–mail n : messages sent and received electronically (as between computer terminals linked by telephone lines)

e–mail vb : to send E-mail — **e–mailer** n

eman·ci·pate vb **eman·ci·pat·ed; eman·ci·pat·ing** : to set free from control or slavery : LIBERATE

eman·ci·pa·tion n : a setting free

em·balm vb : to treat a dead body so as to preserve it from decay — **em·balm·er** n

em·bank·ment n : a raised bank or wall to carry a roadway, prevent floods, or hold back water

em·bar·go n, pl **em·bar·goes** : an order of a government prohibiting commercial shipping from leaving its ports

em·bark vb **1** : to go on or put on board a ship or an airplane **2** : to begin some project or task

em·bar·rass vb **1** : to involve in financial difficulties **2** : to cause to feel confused and distressed : FLUSTER

em·bas·sy n, pl **em·bas·sies** **1** : an ambassador and his assistants **2** : the residence or office of an ambassador

em·bed or **im·bed** vb **em·bed·ded** or **im·bed·ded; em·bed·ding** or **im·bed·ding** : to set solidly in or as if in a bed

em·bel·lish vb : to add ornamental details to — **em·bel·lish·ment** n

em·ber n : a glowing piece of coal or wood in the ashes from a fire

em·bez·zle vb **em·bez·zled; em·bez·zling** : to take (property entrusted to one's care) dishonestly for one's own use

em·bit·ter vb : to make bitter : stir bitter feeling in

em·blem n : an object or a likeness of an object used to suggest a thing that cannot be pictured : SYMBOL

em·body vb **em·bod·ied; em·body·ing** **1** : to bring together so as to form a body or system **2** : to make a part of a body or system **3** : to represent in visible form

em·boss vb : to ornament with a raised pattern or design

¹em·brace vb **em·braced; em·brac·ing** **1** : to clasp in the arms **2** : to enclose on all sides **3** : to take up readily or gladly **4** : TAKE IN 5, INCLUDE

²embrace n : an encircling with the arms : HUG

em·broi·der vb **1** : to make or fill in a design with needlework **2** : to decorate with needlework **3** : to add to the interest of (as a story) with details far beyond the truth

em·broi·dery n, pl **em·broi·der·ies** **1** : needlework done to decorate cloth **2** : the act or art of embroidering

em·bryo n, pl **em·bry·os** **1** : an animal in

the earliest stages of growth when its basic structures are being formed **2** : a tiny young plant inside a seed

1em·er·ald *n* : a precious stone of a rich green color

2emerald *adj* : brightly or richly green

emerge *vb* **emerged; emerg·ing 1** : to come out or into view (as from water or a hole) **2** : to become known especially as a result of study or questioning

emer·gen·cy *n, pl* **emer·gen·cies** : an unexpected situation calling for prompt action

em·ery *n, pl* **em·er·ies** : a mineral used in the form of powder or grains for polishing and grinding

-emia *or* **-ae·mia** *n suffix* : condition of having a specified disorder of the blood

em·i·grant *n* : a person who emigrates

em·i·grate *vb* **em·i·grat·ed; em·i·grat·ing** : to leave a country or region to settle somewhere else

em·i·gra·tion *n* : a going away from one region or country to live in another

em·i·nence *n* **1** : the condition of being eminent **2** : a piece of high ground : HILL

em·i·nent *adj* : standing above others in rank, merit, or worth

em·is·sary *n, pl* **em·is·sar·ies** : a person sent on a mission to represent another

emit *vb* **emit·ted; emit·ting** : to give out : send forth

emo·tion *n* **1** : strong feeling **2** : a mental and bodily reaction (as anger or fear) accompanied by strong feeling

emo·tion·al *adj* **1** : of or relating to the emotions **2** : likely to show or express emotion **3** : expressing emotion — **emo·tion·al·ly** *adv*

em·per·or *n* : the supreme ruler of an empire

em·pha·sis *n, pl* **em·pha·ses 1** : a forcefulness of expression that gives special importance to something **2** : special force given to one or more words or syllables in speaking or reading **3** : special importance given to something

em·pha·size *vb* **em·pha·sized; em·pha·siz·ing** : to give emphasis to

em·phat·ic *adj* : showing or spoken with emphasis

em·phy·se·ma *n* : a disease in which the lungs become stretched and inefficient

em·pire *n* **1** : a group of territories or peoples under one ruler **2** : a country whose ruler is called an emperor **3** : the power or rule of an emperor

1em·ploy *vb* **1** : to make use of **2** : to use the services of : hire for wages or salary

2employ *n* : the state of being employed

em·ploy·ee *or* **em·ploye** *n* : a person who works for pay in the service of an employer

em·ploy·er *n* : one that employs others

em·ploy·ment *n* **1** : OCCUPATION 1, ACTIVITY **2** : the act of employing : the state of being employed

em·pow·er *vb* : to give authority or legal power to

em·press *n* **1** : the wife of an emperor **2** : a woman who is the ruler of an empire in her own right

1emp·ty *adj* **emp·ti·er; emp·ti·est 1** : containing nothing **2** : not occupied or lived in : VACANT — **emp·ti·ness** *n*

2empty *vb* **emp·tied; emp·ty·ing 1** : to make empty : remove the contents of **2** : to transfer by emptying a container **3** : to become empty **4** : 1DISCHARGE 6

emp·ty–hand·ed *adj* **1** : having nothing in the hands **2** : having gotten or gained nothing

emp·ty–head·ed *adj* : having a merry silly nature

emu *n* : an Australian bird that is like but smaller than the related ostrich and runs very fast

em·u·late *vb* **em·u·lat·ed; em·u·lat·ing** : to try hard to equal or do better than

em·u·la·tion *n* : ambition or effort to equal or do better than others

emul·si·fy *vb* **emul·si·fied; emul·si·fy·ing** : to make an emulsion of

emul·sion *n* : a material consisting of a mixture of liquids so that fine drops of one liquid are scattered throughout the other

en- *also* **em-** *prefix* **1** : put into or on to : go into or on to **2** : cause to be **3** : provide with — in all senses usually *em-* before *b, m, or p*

1-en *also* **-n** *adj suffix* : made of : consisting of

2-en *vb suffix* **1** : become or cause to be **2** : cause or come to have

en·able *vb* **en·abled; en·abling** : to give strength, power, or ability to : make able

en·act *vb* **1** : to make into law **2** : to act the part of (as in a play) — **en·act·ment** *n*

1enam·el *vb* **enam·eled** *or* **enam·elled; enam·el·ing** *or* **enam·el·ling** : to cover with or as if with enamel

2enamel *n* **1** : a glassy substance used for coating the surface of metal, glass, and pottery **2** : the hard outer surface of the teeth **3** : a paint that forms a hard glossy coat

en·camp *vb* : to set up and occupy a camp

en·camp·ment *n* **1** : the act of making a camp **2** : CAMP

en·case *vb* **en·cased; en·cas·ing** : to enclose in or as if in a case

-ence *n suffix* : action or process

en·chant *vb* **1** : to put under a spell by or as

if by charms or magic **2** : to please greatly — **en·chant·er** *n* — **en·chant·ment** *n*

en·chant·ing *adj* : very attractive : CHARM-ING

en·chant·ress *n* : a woman who enchants : WITCH, SORCERESS

en·cir·cle *vb* **en·cir·cled; en·cir·cling 1** : to form a circle around : SURROUND **2** : to pass completely around

en·close *or* **in·close** *vb* **en·closed** *or* **in·closed; en·clos·ing** *or* **in·clos·ing 1** : to close in all around : SURROUND **2** : to put in the same parcel or envelope with something else

en·clo·sure *or* **in·clo·sure** *n* **1** : the act of enclosing **2** : an enclosed space **3** : something (as a fence) that encloses **4** : something enclosed (as in a letter)

en·com·pass *vb* **1** : ENCIRCLE 1 **2** : IN-CLUDE

1en·core *n* **1** : a demand for the repeating of something on a program made by applause from an audience **2** : a further appearance or performance given in response to applause

2encore *vb* **en·cored; en·cor·ing** : to call for an encore

1en·coun·ter *vb* **1** : to meet as an enemy : FIGHT **2** : to meet face-to-face or unexpectedly

2encounter *n* **1** : a meeting with an enemy : COMBAT **2** : a meeting face-to-face and often by chance

en·cour·age *vb* **en·cour·aged; en·cour·ag·ing 1** : to give courage, spirit, or hope to : HEARTEN **2** : to give help to : AID

en·cour·age·ment *n* **1** : the act of encouraging : the state of being encouraged **2** : something that encourages

en·croach *vb* **1** : to take over the rights or possessions of another little by little or in secret **2** : to go beyond the usual or proper limits

en·crust *also* **in·crust** *vb* : to cover with or as if with a crust

en·cum·ber *vb* **1** : to weigh down : BURDEN **2** : HINDER, HAMPER

-en·cy *n suffix, pl* **-en·cies** : quality or state

en·cy·clo·pe·dia *n* : a book or a set of books containing information on all branches of learning in articles arranged alphabetically by subject

1end *n* **1** : the part near the boundary of an area **2** : the point (as of time or space) where something ceases to exist **3** : the first or last part of a thing **4** : DEATH 1, DE-STRUCTION **5** : 1PURPOSE, GOAL

2end *vb* : to bring or come to an end : STOP

en·dan·ger *vb* : 2RISK 1

en·dear *vb* : to make dear or beloved

en·dear·ment *n* : a word or an act that shows love or affection

1en·deav·or *vb* : to make an effort : TRY

2endeavor *n* : a serious determined effort

end·ing *n* : the final part : END

en·dive *n* : either of two plants related to the daisies and often used in salads

end·less *adj* **1** : having or seeming to have no end **2** : joined at the ends — **end·less·ly** *adv* — **end·less·ness** *n*

en·do·crine gland *n* : any of several glands (as the thyroid or pituitary) that secrete hormones directly into the blood

en·dorse *or* **in·dorse** *vb* **en·dorsed** *or* **in·dorsed; en·dors·ing** *or* **in·dors·ing 1** : to sign one's name on the back of (a check) to obtain payment **2** : to give one's support to openly — **en·dorse·ment** *n*

en·dow *vb* **1** : to provide with money for support **2** : to provide with something freely or naturally

en·dow·ment *n* : the providing of a permanent fund for support or the fund provided

end·point *n* : either of two points that mark the ends of a line segment or a point that marks the end of a ray

en·dur·ance *n* : the ability to put up with strain, suffering, or hardship

en·dure *vb* **en·dured; en·dur·ing 1** : to continue in existence : LAST **2** : to put up with (as pain) patiently or firmly

end·ways *adv or adj* **1** : on end **2** : with the end forward **3** : 1LENGTHWISE

en·e·ma *n* : the injection of liquid into the bowel or the liquid injected

en·e·my *n, pl* **en·e·mies 1** : one that hates another : one that attacks or tries to harm another **2** : something that harms or threatens **3** : a nation with which one's own country is at war or a person belonging to such a nation

en·er·get·ic *adj* : having or showing energy : ACTIVE, VIGOROUS — **en·er·get·i·cal·ly** *adv*

en·er·gy *n, pl* **en·er·gies 1** : ability to be active : strength of body or mind to do things or to work **2** : usable power or the resources (as oil) for producing such power

en·fold *vb* **1** : to wrap up : cover with or as if with folds **2** : 1EMBRACE 1

en·force *vb* **en·forced; en·forc·ing 1** : to demand and see that one gets **2** : to put into force — **en·force·ment** *n*

en·gage *vb* **en·gaged; en·gag·ing 1** : to pledge (as oneself) to do something : PROM-ISE **2** : to catch and hold fast (as the attention) **3** : to take part in something **4** : to enter into contest or battle with **5** : to arrange for the services or use of : HIRE **6** : to put or become in gear : MESH

en·gaged *adj* **1** : busy with some activity **2** : pledged to be married

en·gage·ment *n* **1** : the act of engaging : the state of being engaged **2** : EMPLOYMENT 2 **3** : an appointment at a certain time and place **4** : a fight between armed forces

en·gag·ing *adj* : ATTRACTIVE

en·gen·der *vb* : to cause to be or develop : PRODUCE

en·gine *n* **1** : a mechanical tool or device **2** : a machine for driving or operating something especially by using the energy of steam, gasoline, or oil **3** : ¹LOCOMOTIVE

¹en·gi·neer *n* **1** : a member of a military group devoted to engineering work **2** : a person who specializes in engineering **3** : a person who runs or has charge of an engine or of machinery or technical equipment

²engineer *vb* **1** : to plan, build, or manage as an engineer **2** : to plan out : CONTRIVE

en·gi·neer·ing *n* : a science by which the properties of matter and the sources of energy in nature are made useful to man in structures (as roads and dams), machines (as automobiles and computers), and products (as plastics and radios)

¹En·glish *adj* : of or relating to England, its people, or the English language

²English *n* **1** : the language of England, the United States, and some other countries now or at one time under British rule **2 English** *pl* : the people of England

English horn *n* : a woodwind instrument that is similar to an oboe but is longer and has a deeper tone

en·grave *vb* **en·graved; en·grav·ing 1** : to cut or carve (as letters or designs) on a hard surface **2** : to cut lines, letters, figures, or designs on or into (a hard surface) often for use in printing **3** : to print from a cut surface — **en·grav·er** *n*

en·grav·ing *n* **1** : the art of cutting something especially into the surface of wood, stone, or metal **2** : a print made from an engraved surface

en·gross *vb* : to take up the whole interest of

en·gulf *vb* : to flow over and swallow up

en·hance *vb* **en·hanced; en·hanc·ing** : to make greater or better

enig·ma *n* : something hard to understand

en·joy *vb* **1** : to take pleasure or satisfaction in **2** : to have for one's use or benefit

en·joy·able *adj* : being a source of pleasure

en·joy·ment *n* **1** : the action or condition of enjoying something **2** : something that gives pleasure

en·large *vb* **en·larged; en·larg·ing** : to make or grow larger : EXPAND

en·large·ment *n* **1** : an act of enlarging **2**

: the state of being enlarged **3** : a photographic print made larger than the negative

en·light·en *vb* : to give knowledge to

en·list *vb* **1** : to join the armed forces as a volunteer **2** : to obtain the help of — **en·list·ment** *n*

en·list·ed man *n* : a man or woman serving in the armed forces who ranks below a commissioned officer or warrant officer

en·liv·en *vb* : to put life or spirit into : make active or cheerful

en·mi·ty *n, pl* **en·mi·ties** : hatred especially when shared : ILL WILL

enor·mous *adj* : unusually large : HUGE — **enor·mous·ly** *adv*

¹enough *adj* : equal to the needs or demands

²enough *adv* : in sufficient amount or degree

³enough *pron* : a sufficient number or amount

en·rage *vb* **en·raged; en·rag·ing** : to fill with rage : ANGER

en·rich *vb* **1** : to make rich or richer **2** : to improve the quality of food by adding vitamins and minerals **3** : to make more fertile

en·roll *or* **en·rol** *vb* **en·rolled; en·roll·ing** : to include (as a name) on a roll or list

en·roll·ment *or* **en·rol·ment** *n* **1** : the act of enrolling or being enrolled **2** : the number of persons enrolled

en route *adv* : on or along the way

en·sem·ble *n* : a group of musicians or dancers performing together

en·shrine *vb* **en·shrined; en·shrin·ing** : to cherish as if sacred

en·sign *n* **1** : a flag flown as the symbol of nationality **2** : a commissioned officer of the lowest rank in the Navy or Coast Guard

en·slave *vb* **en·slaved; en·slav·ing** : to make a slave of

en·sue *vb* **en·sued; en·su·ing** : to come after in time or as a result : FOLLOW

en·sure *vb* **en·sured; en·sur·ing** : to make sure, certain, or safe : GUARANTEE

en·tan·gle *vb* **en·tan·gled; en·tan·gling 1** : to make tangled or confused **2** : to catch in a tangle — **en·tan·gle·ment** *n*

en·ter *vb* **1** : to come or go in or into **2** : to put into a list : write down **3** : to become a member or a member of : JOIN **4** : to become a party to or take an interest in something **5** : PENETRATE 1, PIERCE **6** : to cause to be admitted (as to a school)

en·ter·prise *n* **1** : an undertaking requiring courage and energy **2** : willingness to engage in daring or difficult action **3** : a business organization or activity

en·ter·pris·ing *adj* : bold and energetic in trying or experimenting

en·ter·tain *vb* **1** : to greet in a friendly way and provide for especially in one's home

: have as a guest **2** : to have in mind **3** : to provide amusement for

en·ter·tain·er *n* : a person who performs for public entertainment

en·ter·tain·ment *n* **1** : the act of entertaining or amusing **2** : something (as a show) that is a form of amusement or recreation

en·thrall *or* **en·thral** *vb* **en·thralled; en·thrall·ing** : to hold the attention of completely : CHARM

en·throne *vb* **en·throned; en·thron·ing** **1** : to seat on a throne **2** : to place in a high position

en·thu·si·asm *n* : strong feeling in favor of something

en·thu·si·ast *n* : a person filled with enthusiasm

en·thu·si·as·tic *adj* : full of enthusiasm : EAGER

en·thu·si·as·ti·cal·ly *adv* : with enthusiasm

en·tice *vb* **en·ticed; en·tic·ing** : to attract by raising hope or desire : TEMPT

en·tire *adj* : complete in all parts or respects — **en·tire·ly** *adv*

en·tire·ty *n, pl* **en·tire·ties** **1** : a state of completeness **2** : ²WHOLE 2

en·ti·tle *vb* **en·ti·tled; en·ti·tling** **1** : to give a title to **2** : to give a right or claim to

en·trails *n pl* : the internal parts of an animal

¹en·trance *n* **1** : the act of entering **2** : a door, gate, or way for entering **3** : permission to enter : ADMISSION

²en·trance *vb* **en·tranced; en·tranc·ing** **1** : to put into a trance **2** : to fill with delight and wonder

en·trap *vb* **en·trapped; en·trap·ping** : to catch in or as if in a trap

en·treat *vb* : to ask in an earnest way

en·treaty *n, pl* **en·treat·ies** : an act of entreating : PLEA

en·trust *or* **in·trust** *vb* **1** : to give care of something to as a trust **2** : to give to another with confidence

en·try *n, pl* **en·tries** **1** : the act of entering : ENTRANCE **2** : a place (as a hall or door) through which entrance is made **3** : the act of making (as in a book or a list) a written record of something **4** : something entered in a list or a record **5** : a person or thing entered in a contest

en·twine *vb* **en·twined; en·twin·ing** : to twist or twine together or around

enu·mer·ate *vb* **enu·mer·at·ed; enu·mer·at·ing** **1** : ¹COUNT 1 **2** : to name one after another : LIST

enun·ci·ate *vb* **enun·ci·at·ed; enun·ci·at·ing** **1** : ANNOUNCE 1 **2** : to pronounce words or parts of words

enun·ci·a·tion *n* : clearness of pronunciation

en·vel·op *vb* : to put a covering completely around : wrap up or in

en·ve·lope *n* : an enclosing cover or wrapper (as for a letter)

en·vi·ous *adj* : feeling or showing envy — **en·vi·ous·ly** *adv* — **en·vi·ous·ness** *n*

en·vi·ron·ment *n* **1** : SURROUNDINGS **2** : the surrounding conditions or forces (as soil, climate, and living things) that influence the form and ability to survive of a plant or animal or ecological community **3** : the social and cultural conditions that influence the life of a person or human community

en·voy *n* **1** : a representative sent by one government to another **2** : MESSENGER

¹en·vy *n, pl* **envies** **1** : a feeling of discontent at another's good fortune together with a desire to have the same good fortune oneself **2** : a person or a thing that is envied

²envy *vb* **en·vied; en·vy·ing** : to feel envy toward or because of

en·zyme *n* : one of the substances produced by body cells that help bodily chemical activities (as digestion) to take place but are not destroyed in so doing

eon *variant of* AEON

¹ep·ic *adj* : of, relating to, or characteristic of an epic

²epic *n* : a long poem that tells the story of a hero's deeds

¹ep·i·dem·ic *adj* : spreading widely and affecting large numbers of people at the same time

²epidemic *n* **1** : a rapidly spreading outbreak of disease **2** : something that spreads or develops rapidly like an epidemic disease

epi·der·mis *n* **1** : a thin outer layer of skin covering the dermis **2** : any of various thin outer layers of plants or animals

ep·i·sode *n* : an event or one of a series of events that stands out clearly in one's life, in history, or in a story

epis·tle *n* : ¹LETTER 2

ep·i·taph *n* : a brief statement on a tombstone in memory of a dead person

ep·och *n* : a period marked by unusual or important events

¹equal *adj* **1** : exactly the same in number, amount, degree, rank, or quality **2** : evenly balanced **3** : having enough strength, ability, or means : ADEQUATE — **equal·ly** *adv*

²equal *vb* **equaled** *or* **equalled; equal·ing** *or* **equal·ling** : to be equal to

³equal *n* : one that is equal to another

equal·i·ty *n, pl* **equal·i·ties** : the condition or state of being equal

equal·ize *vb* **equal·ized; equal·iz·ing** : to make equal or even

equa·tion *n* **1** : a statement of the equality

of two mathematical expressions **2** : an expression representing a chemical reaction by means of chemical symbols

equa·tor *n* : an imaginary circle around the earth everywhere equally distant from the north pole and the south pole

equa·to·ri·al *adj* **1** : of, relating to, or lying near the equator **2** : of, coming from, or suggesting the region at or near the equator

eques·tri·an *adj* : of or relating to horses or to the riding or riders of horses

equi·lat·er·al *adj* : having all sides of equal length

equi·lib·ri·um *n* **1** : a state of balance between opposing weights, forces, or influences **2** : the normal bodily adjustment of a person or animal in relation to its environment

equi·nox *n* : either of the two times each year when the sun's center crosses the equator and day and night (as on March 21 and September 23) are everywhere of equal length

equip *vb* **equipped; equip·ping** : to make ready for a purpose by supplying what is necessary

equip·ment *n* **1** : an act of equipping **2** : supplies and tools needed for a special purpose

1equiv·a·lent *adj* : alike or equal in number, value, or meaning

2equivalent *n* : something equivalent

1-er *adj suffix or adv suffix* — used to form the comparative degree of adjectives and adverbs of one syllable and of some adjectives and adverbs of two or more syllables

2-er *also* **-ier** *or* **-yer** *n suffix* **1** : a person whose work or business is connected with **2** : a person or thing belonging to or associated with **3** : a native of : resident of **4** : one that has **5** : one that produces **6** : one that does or performs a specified action **7** : one that is a suitable object of a specified action **8** : one that is

era *n* **1** : a period of time starting from some special date or event **2** : an important period of history

erad·i·cate *vb* **erad·i·cat·ed; erad·i·cat·ing** : to remove by or as if by tearing up by the roots : destroy completely

erase *vb* **erased; eras·ing** : to cause to disappear by rubbing or scraping

eras·er *n* : something (as a piece of rubber or a felt pad) for erasing marks

era·sure *n* **1** : an act of erasing **2** : something erased

1ere *prep* : ²BEFORE 3

1ere *prep* : ²BEFORE 3

2ere *conj* : ³BEFORE 2

1erect *adj* : being straight up and down — **erect·ly** *adv* — **erect·ness** *n*

2erect *vb* **1** : to put up by fitting together materials or parts **2** : to set straight up — **erec·tor** *n*

er·mine *n* : a weasel of northern regions that is valued for its winter coat of white fur with a tail tipped in black

erode *vb* **erod·ed; erod·ing** : to eat into : wear away : destroy by wearing away

ero·sion *n* : the act of eroding : the state of being eroded

err *vb* **1** : to make a mistake **2** : to do wrong : SIN

er·rand *n* **1** : a short trip made to take care of some business **2** : the business done on an errand

er·rant *adj* **1** : wandering in search of adventure **2** : straying from a proper course

er·rat·ic *adj* : not following the usual or expected course

er·ro·ne·ous *adj* : INCORRECT 1

er·ror *n* : a failure to be correct or accurate : MISTAKE

erupt *vb* **1** : to burst forth or cause to burst forth **2** : to break through a surface **3** : to break out (as with a skin rash)

erup·tion *n* **1** : a bursting forth **2** : a breaking out (as of a skin rash) or the resulting rash

-ery *n suffix, pl* **-er·ies** **1** : qualities considered as a group : character : -NESS **2** : art : practice **3** : place of doing, keeping, producing, or selling **4** : collection : aggregate **5** : state or condition

1-es *n pl suffix* **1** — used to form the plural of most nouns that end in *s*, *z*, *sh*, *ch*, or a final *y* that changes to *i* and of some nouns ending in *f* that changes to *v* **2** : ¹-s 2

2-es *vb suffix* — used to form the third person singular present of most verbs that end in *s*, *z*, *sh*, *ch*, or a final *y* that changes to *i*

es·ca·la·tor *n* : a moving stairway arranged like an endless belt

es·ca·pade *n* : a daring or reckless adventure

1es·cape *vb* **es·caped; es·cap·ing** **1** : to get away : get free or clear **2** : to keep free of : AVOID **3** : to fail to be noticed or remembered by **4** : to leak out from some enclosed place

2escape *n* **1** : the act of escaping **2** : a way of escaping

1es·cort *n* **1** : one (as a person or group) that accompanies another to give protection or show courtesy **2** : the man who goes on a date with a woman

2es·cort *vb* : to accompany as an escort

1-ese *adj suffix* : of, relating to, or coming from a certain place or country

2-ese *n suffix, pl* **-ese** **1** : native or resident of a specified place or country **2** : language of a particular place, country, or nationality **3** : speech or literary style of a specified place, person, or group

Es·ki·mo *n, pl* **Es·ki·mos** : a member of a group of peoples of Alaska, northern Canada, Greenland, and northeastern Siberia

Eskimo dog *n* : a sled dog of northern North America

esoph·a·gus *n, pl* **esoph·a·gi** : the tube that leads from the mouth through the throat to the stomach

es·pe·cial *adj* : SPECIAL — **es·pe·cial·ly** *adv*

es·pi·o·nage *n* : the practice of spying : the use of spies

es·py *vb* **es·pied; es·py·ing** : to catch sight of

-ess *n suffix* : female

¹es·say *vb* : ¹TRY 6

²es·say *n* **1** : ²ATTEMPT **2** : a usually short piece of writing dealing with a subject from a personal point of view

es·say·ist *n* : a writer of essays

es·sence *n* **1** : the basic part of something **2** : a substance made from a plant or drug and having its special qualities **3** : ¹PERFUME 2

¹es·sen·tial *adj* **1** : forming or belonging to the basic part of something **2** : important in the highest degree — **es·sen·tial·ly** *adv*

²essential *n* : something that is essential

-est *adj suffix or adv suffix* — used to form the superlative degree of adjectives and adverbs of one syllable and of some adjectives and adverbs of two or more syllables

es·tab·lish *vb* **1** : to bring into being : FOUND **2** : to put beyond doubt : PROVE

es·tab·lish·ment *n* **1** : the act of establishing **2** : a place for residence or for business

es·tate *n* **1** : ¹STATE 1 **2** : the property of all kinds that a person leaves at death **3** : a fine country house on a large piece of land

¹es·teem *n* : high regard

²esteem *vb* : to think well or highly of

esthetic *variant of* AESTHETIC

¹es·ti·mate *vb* **es·ti·mat·ed; es·ti·mat·ing 1** : to give or form a general idea of (as the value, size, or cost of something) **2** : to form an opinion

²es·ti·mate *n* **1** : an opinion or judgment especially of the value or quality of something **2** : an approximation of the size or cost of something

es·ti·ma·tion *n* **1** : the making of an estimate : JUDGMENT **2** : an estimate formed : OPINION

et cet·era : and others of the same kind : and so forth : and so on

etch *vb* : to produce designs or figures on metal or glass by lines eaten into the substance by acid

etch·ing *n* **1** : the art or process of producing drawings or pictures by printing from etched plates **2** : a picture made from an etched plate

eter·nal *adj* **1** : lasting forever : having no beginning and no end **2** : continuing without interruption

eter·ni·ty *n, pl* **eter·ni·ties 1** : time without end **2** : the state after death **3** : a period of time that seems to be endless

-eth — see -TH

ether *n* **1** : the clear upper part of the sky **2** : a light flammable liquid used to dissolve fats and as an anesthetic

ethe·re·al *adj* **1** : HEAVENLY 1 **2** : very delicate : AIRY

eth·i·cal *adj* **1** : of or relating to ethics **2** : following accepted rules of behavior

eth·ics *n sing or pl* **1** : a branch of philosophy dealing with moral duty and with questions of what is good and bad **2** : the rules of moral behavior governing an individual or a group

eth·nic *adj* : of or relating to races or large groups of people classed according to common characteristics and customs — **eth·ni·cal·ly** *adv*

et·i·quette *n* : the rules governing the proper way to behave or to do something

-ette *n suffix* **1** : little one **2** : female **3** : imitation

et·y·mol·o·gy *n, pl* **et·y·mol·o·gies** : the history of a word shown by tracing it or its parts back to the earliest known forms and meanings both in its own language and any other language from which it may have been taken

eu·ca·lyp·tus *n, pl* **eu·ca·lyp·ti** *or* **eu·ca·lyp·tus·es** : a tree of a kind native mainly to western Australia and widely grown for shade, timber, gum, and oil

Eu·cha·rist *n* : COMMUNION 2

eu·gle·na *n* : any of numerous tiny single-celled organisms that contain chlorophyll, swim about by means of a flagellum, and are often classified in science as algae

eu·ro *n, pl* **euros** : a coin or bill used by countries of the European Union

¹Eu·ro·pe·an *adj* : of or relating to Europe or the Europeans

²European *n* : a native or resident of Europe

evac·u·ate *vb* **evac·u·at·ed; evac·u·at·ing 1** : to make empty : empty out **2** : to discharge waste matter from the body **3** : to remove troops or people from a place of danger

evade *vb* **evad·ed; evad·ing** : to get away from or avoid meeting directly

eval·u·ate *vb* **eval·u·at·ed; eval·u·at·ing** : to find or estimate the value of

eval·u·a·tion *n* : the act or result of evaluating

evan·ge·list *n* : a Christian preacher who goes about from place to place trying to change or increase people's religious feelings

evap·o·rate *vb* **evap·o·rat·ed; evap·o·rat·ing** **1** : to change into vapor **2** : to disappear without being seen to go **3** : to remove some of the water from something (as by heating)

evap·o·ra·tion *n* : the process of evaporating

eve *n* **1** : EVENING **2** : the evening or day before a special day **3** : the period just before an important event

¹even *adj* **1** : being without breaks or bumps **2** : staying the same over a period of time **3** : being on the same line or level **4** : equal in size, number, or amount **5** : ¹EQUAL 2, FAIR **6** : possible to divide by two — **even·ly** *adv* — **even·ness** *n*

²even *adv* **1** : at the very time : JUST **2** : INDEED **3** — used to stress an extreme or highly unlikely condition or instance **4** : to a greater extent or degree : STILL **5** : so much as

³even *vb* : to make or become even

eve·ning *n* : the final part of the day and early part of the night

evening star *n* : a bright planet (as Venus) seen in the western sky after sunset

event *n* **1** : something usually of importance that happens **2** : a social occasion (as a party) **3** : the fact of happening **4** : a contest in a program of sports

event·ful *adj* **1** : filled with events **2** : very important

even·tide *n* : EVENING

even·tu·al *adj* : coming at some later time — **even·tu·al·ly** *adv*

ev·er *adv* **1** : at all times : ALWAYS **2** : at any time **3** : in any way

ev·er·glade *n* : a swampy grassland

¹ev·er·green *n* **1** : an evergreen plant (as a pine or a laurel) **2 evergreens** *pl* : branches and leaves of evergreens used for decorations

²evergreen *adj* : having leaves that stay green through more than one growing season

ev·er·last·ing *adj* **1** : lasting forever : ETERNAL **2** : going on for a long time or for too long a time — **ev·er·last·ing·ly** *adv*

ev·er·more *adj* : FOREVER 1

ev·ery *adj* : being each of a group or series without leaving out any

ev·ery·body *pron* : every person

ev·ery·day *adj* : used or suitable for every day : ORDINARY

ev·ery·one *pron* : every person

ev·ery·thing *pron* : every thing : ALL

ev·ery·where *adv* : in or to every place or part

evict *vb* : to put out from property by legal action

ev·i·dence *n* **1** : an outward sign : INDICATION **2** : material presented to a court to help find the truth in a matter

ev·i·dent *adj* : clear to the sight or to the mind : PLAIN — **ev·i·dent·ly** *adv*

¹evil *adj* **1** : morally bad : WICKED **2** : causing harm : tending to injure

²evil *n* **1** : something that brings sorrow, trouble, or destruction **2** : the fact of suffering or wrongdoing

evoke *vb* **evoked; evok·ing** : to call forth or up : SUMMON

evo·lu·tion *n* **1** : the process of development of an animal or a plant **2** : the theory that the various kinds of existing animals and plants have come from kinds that existed in the past

evolve *vb* **evolved; evolv·ing** : to grow or develop out of something

ewe *n* : a female sheep

ex- *prefix* **1** : out of : outside **2** : former

¹ex·act *vb* : to demand and get by force or threat

²exact *adj* : showing close agreement with fact : ACCURATE — **ex·act·ly** *adv* — **ex·act·ness** *n*

ex·act·ing *adj* : making many or difficult demands upon a person : TRYING

ex·ag·ger·ate *vb* **ex·ag·ger·at·ed; ex·ag·ger·at·ing** : to enlarge a fact or statement beyond what is true

ex·ag·ger·a·tion *n* **1** : the act of exaggerating **2** : an exaggerated statement

ex·alt *vb* **1** : to raise in rank or power **2** : to praise highly

ex·am *n* : EXAMINATION

ex·am·i·na·tion *n* **1** : the act of examining or state of being examined **2** : a test given to determine progress, fitness, or knowledge

ex·am·ine *vb* **ex·am·ined; ex·am·in·ing** **1** : to look at or check carefully **2** : to question closely

ex·am·ple *n* **1** : a sample of something taken to show what the whole is like : INSTANCE **2** : something to be imitated : MODEL **3** : something that is a warning to others **4** : a problem to be solved to show how a rule works

ex·as·per·ate *vb* **ex·as·per·at·ed; ex·as·per·at·ing** : to make angry

ex·as·per·a·tion *n* : extreme annoyance : ANGER

ex·ca·vate *vb* **ex·ca·vat·ed; ex·ca·vat·ing** **1** : to hollow out : form a hole in **2** : to make by hollowing out **3** : to dig out and remove **4** : to expose to view by digging away a covering (as of earth)

ex·ca·va·tion *n* **1** : the act of excavating **2** : a hollow place formed by excavating

ex·ceed *vb* **1** : to go or be beyond the limit of **2** : to be greater than

ex·ceed·ing·ly *adv* : to a very great degree

ex·cel *vb* **ex·celled; ex·cel·ling** : to do better than others : SURPASS

ex·cel·lence *n* **1** : high quality **2** : an excellent quality : VIRTUE

ex·cel·lent *adj* : very good of its kind — **ex·cel·lent·ly** *adv*

1ex·cept *prep* **1** : not including **2** : other than : BUT

2except *vb* : to leave out from a number or a whole : EXCLUDE

3except *conj* : if it were not for the fact that : ONLY

ex·cep·tion *n* **1** : the act of leaving out **2** : a case to which a rule does not apply **3** : an objection or a reason for objecting

ex·cep·tion·al *adj* **1** : forming an exception **2** : better than average : SUPERIOR — **ex·cep·tion·al·ly** *adv*

1ex·cess *n* **1** : a state of being more than enough **2** : the amount by which something is more than what is needed or allowed

2excess *adj* : more than is usual or acceptable

ex·ces·sive *adj* : showing excess — **ex·ces·sive·ly** *adv*

1ex·change *n* **1** : a giving or taking of one thing in return for another : TRADE **2** : the act of substituting one thing for another **3** : the act of giving and receiving between two groups **4** : a place where goods or services are exchanged

2exchange *vb* **ex·changed; ex·chang·ing** : to give in exchange : TRADE, SWAP

ex·cit·able *adj* : easily excited

ex·cite *vb* **ex·cit·ed; ex·cit·ing** **1** : to increase the activity of **2** : to stir up feeling in : ROUSE

ex·cite·ment *n* **1** : the state of being excited : AGITATION **2** : something that excites or stirs up

ex·cit·ing *adj* : producing excitement

ex·claim *vb* : to cry out or speak out suddenly or with strong feeling

ex·cla·ma·tion *n* **1** : a sharp or sudden cry of strong feeling **2** : strong expression of anger or complaint

exclamation point *n* : a punctuation mark ! used mostly to show a forceful way of speaking or strong feeling

ex·clam·a·to·ry *adj* : containing or using exclamation

ex·clude *vb* **ex·clud·ed; ex·clud·ing** : to shut out : keep out

ex·clu·sion *n* : the act of excluding : the state of being excluded

ex·clu·sive *adj* **1** : excluding or trying to exclude others **2** : 4SOLE **2 3** : ENTIRE, COMPLETE **4** : not including — **ex·clu·sive·ly** *adv*

ex·crete *vb* **ex·cret·ed; ex·cret·ing** : to separate and give off waste matter from the body usually as urine or sweat

ex·cre·tion *n* **1** : the process of excreting **2** : waste material excreted

ex·cre·to·ry *adj* : of or relating to excretion : used in excreting

ex·cur·sion *n* **1** : a brief pleasure trip **2** : a trip at special reduced rates

ex·cus·able *adj* : possible to excuse

1ex·cuse *vb* **ex·cused; ex·cus·ing** **1** : to make apology for **2** : to overlook or pardon as of little importance **3** : to let off from doing something **4** : to be an acceptable reason for

2ex·cuse *n* **1** : the act of excusing **2** : something offered as a reason for being excused **3** : something that excuses or is a reason for excusing

ex·e·cute *vb* **ex·e·cut·ed; ex·e·cut·ing** **1** : to put into effect : CARRY OUT, PERFORM **2** : to put to death according to a legal order **3** : to make according to a design

ex·e·cu·tion *n* **1** : a carrying through of something to its finish **2** : a putting to death as a legal penalty

1ex·ec·u·tive *adj* **1** : fitted for or relating to the carrying of things to completion **2** : concerned with or relating to the carrying out of the law and the conduct of public affairs

2executive *n* **1** : the executive branch of a government **2** : a person who manages or directs

ex·em·pli·fy *vb* **ex·em·pli·fied; ex·em·pli·fy·ing** : to show by example

1ex·empt *adj* : free or released from some condition or requirement that other persons must meet or deal with

2exempt *vb* : to make exempt

ex·emp·tion *n* **1** : the act of exempting : the state of being exempt **2** : something that is exempted

1ex·er·cise *n* **1** : the act of putting into use, action, or practice **2** : bodily activity for the sake of health **3** : a school lesson or other task performed to develop skill : practice work : DRILL **4 exercises** *pl* : a program of songs, speeches, and announcing of awards and honors

2exercise *vb* **ex·er·cised; ex·er·cis·ing** **1** : to put into use : EXERT **2** : to use again and again to train or develop **3** : to take part in bodily activity for the sake of health or training

ex·ert *vb* **1** : to put forth (as strength) : bring into play **2** : to put (oneself) into action or to tiring effort

ex·er·tion *n* **1** : the act of exerting **2** : use of strength or ability

ex·hale *vb* **ex·haled; ex·hal·ing 1** : to breathe out **2** : to send forth : give off

¹ex·haust *vb* **1** : to draw out or let out completely **2** : to use up completely **3** : to tire out : FATIGUE

²exhaust *n* **1** : the gas that escapes from an engine **2** : a system of pipes through which exhaust escapes

ex·haus·tion *n* **1** : the act of exhausting **2** : the condition of being exhausted

¹ex·hib·it *vb* **1** : to show by outward signs : REVEAL **2** : to put on display

²exhibit *n* **1** : an article or collection shown in an exhibition **2** : an article presented as evidence in a law court

ex·hi·bi·tion *n* **1** : the act of exhibiting **2** : a public showing (as of athletic skill or works of art)

ex·hil·a·rate *vb* **ex·hil·a·rat·ed; ex·hil·a·rat·ing** : to make cheerful or lively

ex·hort *vb* : to try to influence by words or advice : urge strongly

¹ex·ile *n* **1** : the sending or forcing of a person away from his or her own country or the situation of a person who is sent away **2** : a person who is expelled from his or her own country

²exile *vb* **ex·iled; ex·il·ing** : to force to leave one's own country

ex·ist *vb* **1** : to have actual being : be real **2** : to continue to live **3** : to be found : OCCUR

ex·is·tence *n* **1** : the fact or the condition of being or of being real **2** : the state of being alive : LIFE

¹ex·it *n* **1** : the act of going out of or away from a place : DEPARTURE **2** : a way of getting out of a place

²exit *vb* : to go out : LEAVE, DEPART

ex·o·dus *n* : the going out or away of a large number of people

ex·or·bi·tant *adj* : going beyond the limits of what is fair, reasonable, or expected

exo·sphere *n* : the outer fringe region of the atmosphere

ex·ot·ic *adj* : introduced from a foreign country

ex·pand *vb* **1** : to open wide : UNFOLD **2** : to take up or cause to take up more space **3** : to work out in greater detail

ex·panse *n* : a wide area or stretch

ex·pan·sion *n* : the act of expanding or the state of being expanded : ENLARGEMENT

ex·pect *vb* **1** : to look for or look forward to something that ought to or probably will happen **2** : to consider to be obliged

ex·pec·tant *adj* : looking forward to or waiting for something

ex·pec·ta·tion *n* : a looking forward to or waiting for something

ex·pe·di·ent *adj* : suitable for bringing about a desired result often without regard to what is fair or right — **ex·pe·di·ent·ly** *adv*

ex·pe·di·tion *n* **1** : a journey for a particular purpose (as for exploring) **2** : the people making an expedition

ex·pel *vb* **ex·pelled; ex·pel·ling 1** : to force out **2** : to drive away

ex·pend *vb* **1** : to pay out : SPEND **2** : to use up

ex·pen·di·ture *n* **1** : the act of spending (as money, time, or energy) **2** : something that is spent

ex·pense *n* **1** : something spent or required to be spent : COST **2** : a cause for spending

ex·pen·sive *adj* : COSTLY 1 — **ex·pen·sive·ly** *adv*

¹ex·pe·ri·ence *n* **1** : the actual living through an event or events **2** : the skill or knowledge gained by actually doing a thing **3** : something that one has actually done or lived through

²experience *vb* **ex·pe·ri·enced; ex·pe·ri·enc·ing** : to have experience of : UNDERGO

ex·pe·ri·enced *adj* : made skillful or wise through experience

¹ex·per·i·ment *n* : a trial or test made to find out about something

²ex·per·i·ment *vb* : to make experiments

ex·per·i·men·tal *adj* : of, relating to, or based on experiment

¹ex·pert *adj* : showing special skill or knowledge gained from experience or training — **ex·pert·ly** *adv* — **ex·pert·ness** *n*

²ex·pert *n* : a person with special skill or knowledge of a subject

ex·pi·ra·tion *n* : an act or instance of expiring

ex·pire *vb* **ex·pired; ex·pir·ing 1** : ¹DIE 1 **2** : to come to an end **3** : to breathe out : EXHALE

ex·plain *vb* **1** : to make clear : CLARIFY 2 **2** : to give the reasons for or cause of — **ex·plain·able** *adj*

ex·pla·na·tion *n* **1** : the act or process of explaining **2** : a statement that makes something clear

ex·plan·a·to·ry *adj* : giving explanation : helping to explain

ex·plic·it *adj* : so clear in statement that there is no doubt about the meaning

ex·plode *vb* **ex·plod·ed; ex·plod·ing 1** : to burst or cause to burst with violence and noise **2** : to burst forth

¹ex·ploit *n* : a brave or daring act

²ex·ploit *vb* **1** : to get the value or use out of **2** : to make use of unfairly for one's own benefit

ex·plo·ra·tion *n* : the act or an instance of exploring

ex·plore *vb* **ex·plored; ex·plor·ing 1** : to search through or into : examine closely **2** : to go into or through for purposes of discovery

ex·plor·er *n* : a person (as a traveler seeking new geographical or scientific information) who explores something

ex·plo·sion *n* **1** : the act of exploding : a sudden and noisy bursting (as of a bomb) **2** : a sudden outburst of feeling

¹ex·plo·sive *adj* **1** : able to cause explosion **2** : likely to explode — **ex·plo·sive·ly** *adv*

²explosive *n* : an explosive substance

ex·po·nent *n* : a numeral written above and to the right of a number to show how many times the number is to be used as a factor

¹ex·port *vb* : to send or carry abroad especially for sale in foreign countries

²ex·port *n* **1** : something that is exported **2** : the act of exporting

ex·pose *vb* **ex·posed; ex·pos·ing 1** : to leave without protection, shelter, or care **2** : to let light strike the photographic film or plate in taking a picture **3** : to put on exhibition : display for sale **4** : to make known

ex·po·si·tion *n* **1** : an explaining of something **2** : a public exhibition

ex·po·sure *n* **1** : an act of making something public **2** : the condition of being exposed **3** : the act of letting light strike a photographic film or the time during which a film is exposed **4** : a section of a roll of film for one picture **5** : position with respect to direction

ex·pound *vb* **1** : EXPLAIN 1, INTERPRET **2** : to talk especially for a long time

¹ex·press *adj* **1** : clearly stated **2** : of a certain sort **3** : sent or traveling at high speed

²express *n* **1** : a system for the special transportation of goods **2** : a vehicle (as a train or elevator) run at special speed with few or no stops

³express *vb* **1** : to make known especially in words **2** : to represent by a sign or symbol **3** : to send by express

ex·pres·sion *n* **1** : the act or process of expressing especially in words **2** : a meaningful word or saying **3** : a way of speaking, singing, or playing that shows mood or feeling **4** : the look on one's face — **ex·pres·sion·less** *adj*

ex·pres·sive *adj* : expressing something : full of expression — **ex·pres·sive·ly** *adv* — **ex·pres·sive·ness** *n*

ex·press·way *n* : a divided highway for rapid traffic

ex·pul·sion *n* : the act of expelling : the state of being expelled

ex·qui·site *adj* **1** : finely made or done **2** : very pleasing (as through beauty or fitness) **3** : very severe : INTENSE

ex·tend *vb* **1** : ¹STRETCH 2 **2** : to hold out **3** : to make longer **4** : ENLARGE **5** : to stretch out or across something

ex·ten·sion *n* **1** : a stretching out : an increase in length or time **2** : a part forming an addition or enlargement

ex·ten·sive *adj* : having wide extent : BROAD

ex·tent *n* **1** : the distance or range over which something extends **2** : the point, degree, or limit to which something extends

¹ex·te·ri·or *adj* : EXTERNAL

²exterior *n* : an exterior part or surface

ex·ter·mi·nate *vb* **ex·ter·mi·nat·ed; ex·ter·mi·nat·ing** : to get rid of completely : wipe out

¹ex·ter·nal *adj* : situated on or relating to the outside : OUTSIDE

²external *n* : something that is external

ex·tinct *adj* **1** : no longer active **2** : no longer existing

ex·tinc·tion *n* **1** : an act of extinguishing or an instance of being extinguished **2** : the state of being extinct

ex·tin·guish *vb* **1** : to cause to stop burning **2** : to cause to die out : DESTROY — **ex·tin·guish·er** *n*

ex·tol *vb* **ex·tolled; ex·tol·ling** : to praise highly : GLORIFY

¹ex·tra *adj* : being more than what is usual, expected, or due

²extra *n* **1** : something extra **2** : an added charge **3** : a special edition of a newspaper **4** : a person hired for a group scene (as in a movie)

³extra *adv* : beyond the usual size, amount, or degree

extra- *prefix* : outside : beyond

¹ex·tract *vb* **1** : to remove by pulling **2** : to get out by pressing, distilling, or by a chemical process **3** : to choose and take out for separate use

²ex·tract *n* **1** : a selection from a writing **2** : a product obtained by extraction

ex·trac·tion *n* **1** : an act of extracting **2** : ORIGIN 1, DESCENT

ex·tra·cur·ric·u·lar *adj* : of or relating to those activities (as athletics) that are offered by a school but are not part of the course of study

ex·traor·di·nary *adj* : so unusual as to be remarkable — **ex·traor·di·nari·ly** *adv*

ex·trav·a·gance *n* **1** : the wasteful or careless spending of money **2** : something that is extravagant **3** : the quality or fact of being extravagant

ex·trav·a·gant *adj* **1** : going beyond what is reasonable or suitable **2** : wasteful especially of money — **ex·trav·a·gant·ly** *adv*

¹ex·treme *adj* **1** : existing to a very great degree **2** : farthest from a center — **ex·treme·ly** *adv*

²extreme *n* **1** : something as far as possible from a center or from its opposite **2** : the greatest possible degree : MAXIMUM

ex·trem·i·ty *n, pl* **ex·trem·i·ties 1** : the farthest limit, point, or part **2** : an end part of a limb of the body (as a foot) **3** : an extreme degree (as of emotion or distress)

ex·tri·cate *vb* **ex·tri·cat·ed; ex·tri·cat·ing** : to free from entanglement or difficulty

ex·ult *vb* : to be in high spirits : REJOICE

ex·ul·tant *adj* : full of or expressing joy or triumph — **ex·ul·tant·ly** *adv*

-ey — see -Y

¹eye *n* **1** : the organ of seeing **2** : the abil-ity to see **3** : the ability to recognize **4** : GLANCE **5** : close attention : WATCH **6** : JUDGMENT 1 **7** : something like or suggesting an eye **8** : the center of something — **eyed** *adj* — **eye·less** *adj*

²eye *vb* **eyed; eye·ing** *or* **ey·ing** : to look at : watch closely

eye·ball *n* : the whole eye

eye·brow *n* : the arch or ridge over the eye : the hair on the ridge over the eye

eye·drop·per *n* : DROPPER 2

eye·glass *n* **1** : a glass lens used to help one to see clearly **2 eyeglasses** *pl* : a pair of glass lenses set in a frame and used to help one to see clearly

eye·lash *n* : a single hair of the fringe on the eyelid

eye·let *n* **1** : a small hole (as in cloth or leather) for a lace or rope **2** : GROMMET

eye·lid *n* : the thin movable cover of an eye

eye·piece *n* : the lens or combination of lenses at the eye end of an optical instrument (as a microscope or telescope)

eye·sight *n* : ¹SIGHT 4, VISION

eye·sore *n* : something displeasing to the sight

eye·strain *n* : a tired or irritated state of the eyes (as from too much use)

eye·tooth *n, pl* **eye·teeth** : a canine tooth of the upper jaw

ey·rie *n* : AERIE

F

f *n, pl* **f's** *or* **fs** *often cap* **1** : the sixth letter of the English alphabet **2** : a grade that shows a student's work is failing

fa *n* : the fourth note of the musical scale

fa·ble *n* **1** : a story that is not true **2** : a story in which animals speak and act like people and which is usually meant to teach a lesson

fab·ric *n* **1** : the basic structure **2** : CLOTH 1 **3** : a structural plan or material

fab·u·lous *adj* **1** : like a fable especially in being marvelous or beyond belief **2** : told in or based on fable

fa·cade *n* : the face or front of a building

¹face *n* **1** : the front part of the head **2** : an expression of the face **3** : outward appearance **4** : GRIMACE **5** : DIGNITY 1, PRESTIGE **6** : a front, upper, or outer surface **7** : one of the flat surfaces that bound a solid

²face *vb* **faced; fac·ing 1** : to cover the front or surface of **2** : to have the front or face toward **3** : to oppose firmly

fac·et *n* : one of the small flat surfaces on a cut gem

fa·ce·tious *adj* : intended or trying to be funny

face–to–face *adv or adj* : in person

fa·cial *adj* : of or relating to the face — **fa·cial·ly** *adv*

fa·cil·i·tate *vb* **fa·cil·i·tat·ed; fa·cil·i·tat·ing** : to make easier

fa·cil·i·ty *n, pl* **fa·cil·i·ties 1** : freedom from difficulty **2** : ease in doing something : APTITUDE **3** : something that makes an action, operation, or activity easier

fac·sim·i·le *n* **1** : an exact copy **2** : a system of transmitting and reproducing printed matter or pictures by means of signals sent over telephone lines

fact *n* **1** : something (as an event or an act) that really exists or has occurred **2** : physical reality or actual experience

¹fac·tor *n* **1** : something that helps produce a result **2** : any of the numbers that when multiplied together form a product

²factor *vb* : to find the factors of a number

fac·to·ry *n, pl* **fac·to·ries** : a place where goods are manufactured

fac·tu·al *adj* : of, relating to, or based on facts — **fac·tu·al·ly** *adv*

fac·ul·ty *n, pl* **fac·ul·ties** 1 : ability to do something : TALENT 2 : one of the powers of the mind or body 3 : the teachers in a school or college

fad *n* : a way of doing or an interest widely followed for a time

fade *vb* **fad·ed; fad·ing** 1 : to dry up : WITHER 2 : to lose or cause to lose brightness of color 3 : to grow dim or faint

Fahr·en·heit *adj* : relating to or having a temperature scale on which the boiling point of water is at 212 degrees above the zero of the scale and the freezing point is at 32 degrees above zero

¹**fail** *vb* 1 : to lose strength : WEAKEN 2 : to die away 3 : to stop functioning 4 : to fall short 5 : to be or become absent or not enough 6 : to be unsuccessful 7 : to become bankrupt 8 : DISAPPOINT, DESERT 9 : ¹NEGLECT 2

²**fail** *n* : FAILURE 1

fail·ing *n* : a slight moral weakness or flaw

fail·ure *n* 1 : a failing to do or perform 2 : a state of being unable to work in a normal way 3 : a lack of success 4 : BANKRUPTCY 5 : a falling short 6 : a breaking down 7 : a person or thing that has failed

¹**faint** *adj* 1 : lacking courage : COWARDLY 2 : being weak or dizzy and likely to collapse 3 : lacking strength : FEEBLE 4 : not clear or plain : DIM — **faint·ly** *adv* — **faint·ness** *n*

²**faint** *vb* : to lose consciousness

³**faint** *n* : an act or condition of fainting

faint·heart·ed *adj* : TIMID

¹**fair** *adj* 1 : attractive in appearance : BEAUTIFUL 2 : not stormy or cloudy 3 : not favoring one over another 4 : observing the rules 5 : being within the foul lines 6 : not dark : BLOND 7 : neither good nor bad — **fair·ness** *n*

²**fair** *adv* : in a fair manner

³**fair** *n* 1 : a gathering of buyers and sellers at a certain time and place for trade 2 : an exhibition (as of livestock or farm products) usually along with entertainment and amusements 3 : a sale of articles for a charitable purpose

fair·ground *n* : an area set aside for fairs, circuses, or exhibitions

fair·ly *adv* 1 : in a manner of speaking : QUITE 2 : in a fair manner : JUSTLY 3 : for the most part : RATHER

¹**fairy** *n, pl* **fair·ies** : an imaginary being who has the form of a very tiny human being and has magic powers

²**fairy** *adj* : of, relating to, or like a fairy

fairy·land *n* 1 : the land of fairies 2 : a place of delicate beauty or magical charm

fairy tale *n* 1 : a story about fairies 2 : a small lie : FIB

faith *n* 1 : loyalty to duty or to a person 2 : belief in God 3 : firm belief even in the absence of proof 4 : a system of religious beliefs : RELIGION

faith·ful *adj* 1 : RELIABLE 2 : firm in devotion or support 3 : true to the facts : ACCURATE — **faith·ful·ly** *adv* — **faith·ful·ness** *n*

faith·less *adj* : not true to allegiance or duty — **faith·less·ly** *adv* — **faith·less·ness** *n*

¹**fake** *adj* : ¹COUNTERFEIT

²**fake** *n* : a person or thing that is not really what is pretended

³**fake** *vb* **faked; fak·ing** 1 : to change or treat in a way that gives a false effect 2 : ²COUNTERFEIT 2 3 : PRETEND 1

fal·con *n* 1 : a hawk trained for use in hunting small game 2 : any of several small hawks with long wings and swift flight

fal·con·ry *n* : the art or sport of hunting with a falcon

¹**fall** *vb* **fell; fall·en; fall·ing** 1 : to come or go down freely by the force of gravity 2 : to come as if by falling 3 : to become lower (as in degree or value) 4 : to topple from an upright position 5 : to collapse wounded or dead 6 : to become captured 7 : to occur at a certain time 8 : to pass from one condition of body or mind to another — **fall short** : be lacking in something

²**fall** *n* 1 : the act or an instance of falling 2 : AUTUMN 3 : a thing or quantity that falls 4 : a loss of greatness : DOWNFALL 5 : WATERFALL — usually used in pl. 6 : a decrease in size, amount, or value 7 : the distance something falls

fal·la·cy *n, pl* **fal·la·cies** 1 : a false or mistaken idea 2 : false reasoning

fall back *vb* : ²RETREAT

fall·out *n* : the usually radioactive particles falling through the atmosphere as a result of the explosion of an atomic bomb

fall out *vb* : ²QUARREL 2

¹**fal·low** *n* : land for crops that lies idle

²**fallow** *vb* : to till without planting a crop

³**fallow** *adj* : not tilled or planted

fallow deer *n* : a small European deer with broad antlers and a pale yellowish coat spotted with white in summer

¹**false** *adj* **fals·er; fals·est** 1 : not true, genuine, or honest 2 : not faithful or loyal 3 : not based on facts or sound judgment — **false·ly** *adv* — **false·ness** *n*

²**false** *adv* : in a false or misleading manner

false·hood *n* 1 : ³LIE 2 : the habit of lying

fal·si·fy *vb* **fal·si·fied; fal·si·fy·ing** : to make false

fal·si·ty n, pl **fal·si·ties 1** : something false **2** : the quality or state of being false

fal·ter vb **1** : to move unsteadily : WAVER **2** : to hesitate in speech **3** : to hesitate in purpose or action

fame n : the fact or condition of being known to and usually thought well of by the public : RENOWN

famed adj : known widely and well : FAMOUS

fa·mil·ial adj : of, relating to, or typical of a family

fa·mil·iar adj **1** : closely acquainted : INTIMATE **2** : INFORMAL 1 **3** : too friendly or bold **4** : often seen or experienced **5** : having a good knowledge of

fa·mil·iar·i·ty n, pl **fa·mil·iar·i·ties 1** : close friendship : INTIMACY **2** : good knowledge of something **3** : INFORMALITY 1

fa·mil·iar·ize vb **fa·mil·iar·ized; fa·mil·iar·iz·ing** : to make familiar

fam·i·ly n, pl **fam·i·lies 1** : a group of persons who come from the same ancestor **2** : a group of persons living under one roof or one head **3** : a group of things sharing certain characteristics **4** : a social group made up of parents and their children **5** : a group of related plants or animals that ranks above the genus and below the order in scientific classification

fam·ine n **1** : a very great and general lack of food **2** : a great shortage

fam·ish vb : to suffer from hunger : STARVE

fam·ished adj : very hungry

fa·mous adj : very well-known

fa·mous·ly adv : very well

¹fan n **1** : something (as a hand-waved semicircular device or a mechanism with rotating blades) for producing a current of air **2** : something like a fan — **fan·like** adj

²fan vb **fanned; fan·ning 1** : to move air with a fan **2** : to direct a current of air upon with a fan

³fan n : an enthusiastic follower or admirer

¹fa·nat·ic adj : too enthusiastic or devoted

²fanatic n : a fanatic person

fan·ci·ful adj **1** : showing free use of the imagination **2** : coming from fancy rather than reason — **fan·ci·ful·ly** adv — **fan·ci·ful·ness** n

¹fan·cy vb **fan·cied; fan·cy·ing 1** : ¹LIKE 1, ENJOY **2** : IMAGINE 1

²fancy n, pl **fancies 1** : the power of the mind to think of things that are not present or real : IMAGINATION **2** : LIKING **3** : IDEA 2, NOTION

³fancy adj **fan·ci·er; fan·ci·est 1** : not plain or ordinary **2** : being above the average (as in quality or price) **3** : done with

great skill and grace — **fan·ci·ly** adv — **fan·ci·ness** n

fang n **1** : a long sharp tooth by which animals seize and hold their prey **2** : one of the usually two long hollow or grooved teeth by which a poisonous snake injects its poison — **fanged** adj

fan·tas·tic adj **1** : produced by or like something produced by the fancy **2** : barely believable — **fan·tas·ti·cal·ly** adv

fan·ta·sy or **phan·ta·sy** n, pl **fan·ta·sies** or **phan·ta·sies 1** : IMAGINATION 1 **2** : something produced by the imagination

¹far adv **far·ther** or **fur·ther; far·thest** or **fur·thest 1** : at or to a great distance in space or time **2** : to a great extent : MUCH **3** : to or at a definite distance or point **4** : to an advanced point

²far adj **far·ther** or **fur·ther; far·thest** or **fur·thest 1** : very distant in space or time **2** : LONG 3 **3** : the more distant of two

far·away adj **1** : REMOTE 1, DISTANT **2** : PREOCCUPIED

¹fare vb **fared; far·ing** : to get along : SUCCEED

²fare n **1** : the money a person pays to travel (as on a bus) **2** : a person paying a fare **3** : FOOD 1

¹fare·well n : an expression of good wishes at parting — often used as an interjection

²fare·well adj : of or relating to a time or act of leaving : FINAL

far·fetched adj : not likely to be true

¹farm n **1** : a piece of land used for raising crops or animals **2** : an area of water where fish or shellfish are grown

²farm vb : to work on or run a farm — **farm·er** n

farm·hand n : a farm laborer

farm·house n : the dwelling house of a farm

farm·yard n : the yard around or enclosed by farm buildings

far–off adj : distant in time or space

far–reach·ing adj : EXTENSIVE

far·sight·ed adj **1** : able to see distant things more clearly than near ones **2** : able to judge how something will work out in the future — **far·sight·ed·ness** n

¹far·ther adv **1** : at or to a greater distance or more advanced point **2** : ²BESIDES

²farther adj : more distant

¹far·thest adj : most distant

²farthest adv **1** : to or at the greatest distance in space or time **2** : to the most advanced point

fas·ci·nate vb **fas·ci·nat·ed; fas·ci·nat·ing 1** : to seize and hold the attention of **2** : to attract greatly

fas·ci·na·tion n : the state of being fascinated

fas·cism *n* : a political system headed by a dictator in which the government controls business and labor and opposition is not permitted

fas·cist *n, often cap* : one who approves of or practices fascism

¹fash·ion *n* **1** : the make or form of something **2** : MANNER 2, WAY **3** : the popular style of a thing at a certain time

²fashion *vb* : to give shape or form to : MOLD

fash·ion·able *adj* : following the fashion or established style — **fash·ion·ably** *adv*

¹fast *adj* **1** : firmly placed **2** : totally loyal **3** : moving, operating, or acting quickly **4** : taking a short time **5** : indicating ahead of the correct time **6** : not likely to fade

²fast *adv* **1** : in a fast or fixed way **2** : to the full extent : SOUND **3** : with great speed

³fast *vb* **1** : to go without eating **2** : to eat in small amounts or only certain foods

⁴fast *n* **1** : the act of fasting **2** : a period of fasting

fas·ten *vb* **1** : to attach or join by or as if by pinning, tying, or nailing **2** : to fix firmly **3** : to become fixed or joined — **fas·ten·er** *n*

fas·ten·ing *n* : something that holds another thing in or in the right position

fast–food *adj* : of, relating to, or specializing in food that can be prepared and served quickly — **fast–food** *n*

fas·tid·i·ous *adj* : hard to please : very particular

¹fat *adj* **fat·ter; fat·test** **1** : having much body fat **2** : ¹THICK 1 **3** : richly rewarding or profitable **4** : swollen up — **fat·ness** *n*

²fat *n* **1** : animal or plant tissue containing much greasy or oily material **2** : any of numerous compounds of carbon, hydrogen, and oxygen that make up most of animal or plant fat and that are important to nutrition as sources of energy **3** : a solid fat as distinguished from an oil **4** : the best or richest part

fa·tal *adj* **1** : FATEFUL **2** : causing death : MORTAL — **fa·tal·ly** *adv*

fa·tal·i·ty *n, pl* **fa·tal·i·ties** : a death resulting from a disaster or accident

fate *n* **1** : a power beyond human control that is held to determine what happens : DESTINY **2** : something that happens as though determined by fate : FORTUNE **3** : final outcome

fate·ful *adj* : having serious results — **fate·ful·ly** *adv* — **fate·ful·ness** *n*

¹fa·ther *n* **1** : a male parent **2** *cap* : GOD 1 **3** : ANCESTOR **4** : one who cares for another as a father might **5** : one deserving the respect and love given to a father **6** : a

person who invents or begins something **7** : PRIEST — used especially as a title — **fa·ther·hood** *n* — **fa·ther·less** *adj*

²father *vb* **1** : to become the father of **2** : to care for as a father

fa·ther–in–law *n, pl* **fa·thers–in–law** : the father of one's husband or wife

fa·ther·land *n* : one's native land

fa·ther·ly *adj* **1** : of or like a father **2** : showing the affection or concern of a father

¹fath·om *n* : a unit of length equal to six feet (about 1.8 meters) used chiefly in measuring the depth of water

²fathom *vb* **1** : to measure the depth of water by means of a special line **2** : to see into and come to understand

¹fa·tigue *n* : a state of being very tired

²fatigue *vb* **fa·tigued; fa·tigu·ing** : to tire by work or exertion

fat·ten *vb* : to make or become fat

fat·ty *adj* **fat·ti·er; fat·ti·est** : containing or like fat

fau·cet *n* : a fixture for controlling the flow of a liquid (as from a pipe or cask)

fault *n* **1** : a weakness in character : FAILING **2** : FLAW, IMPERFECTION **3** : ERROR **4** : responsibility for something wrong **5** : a crack in the earth's crust along which movement occurs — **at fault** : BLAMEWORTHY

fault·less *adj* : free from fault : PERFECT — **fault·less·ly** *adv* — **fault·less·ness** *n*

faulty *adj* **fault·i·er; fault·i·est** : having a fault or blemish : IMPERFECT — **fault·i·ly** *adv* — **fault·i·ness** *n*

faun *n* : a Roman god of country life represented as part goat and part man

fau·na *n* : the animal life typical of a region, period, or special environment

¹fa·vor *n* **1** : APPROVAL, LIKING **2** : a preferring of one side over another : PARTIALITY **3** : an act of kindness **4** : a small gift or decorative item

²favor *vb* **1** : to regard with favor **2** : OBLIGE 3 **3** : to prefer especially unfairly **4** : to make possible or easier **5** : to look like

fa·vor·able *adj* **1** : showing favor **2** : PROMISING — **fa·vor·able·ness** *n* — **fa·vor·ably** *adv*

¹fa·vor·ite *n* : a person or a thing that is favored above others

²favorite *adj* : being a favorite

¹fawn *vb* **1** : to show affection — used especially of a dog **2** : to try to win favor by behavior that shows lack of self-respect

²fawn *n* **1** : a young deer **2** : a light grayish brown

¹fax *n* **1** : FACSIMILE 2 **2** : a machine used

to send or receive material by facsimile **3**
: something sent or received by facsimile

²**fax** *vb* : to send material by facsimile

faze *vb* **fazed; faz·ing** : DAUNT

¹**fear** *vb* : to be afraid of : feel fear

²**fear** *n* : a strong unpleasant feeling caused
by being aware of danger or expecting
something bad to happen

fear·ful *adj* **1** : causing fear **2** : filled with
fear **3** : showing or caused by fear — **fear-
ful·ly** *adv* — **fear·ful·ness** *n*

fear·less *adj* : free from fear : BRAVE —
fear·less·ly *adv* — **fear·less·ness** *n*

fear·some *adj* : causing fear

fea·si·ble *adj* : possible to do or carry out

¹**feast** *n* **1** : a fancy meal **2** : a religious
festival

²**feast** *vb* **1** : to eat well **2** : ²DELIGHT 1

feat *n* : an act showing courage, strength, or
skill

¹**feath·er** *n* **1** : one of the light horny
growths that make up the outer covering of
a bird **2** : VARIETY 3, SORT — **feath·ered**
adj — **feath·er·less** *adj*

²**feather** *vb* : to grow or form feathers

feather bed *n* **1** : a mattress filled with
feathers **2** : a bed with a feather mattress

feath·ery *adj* **1** : like a feather or tuft of
feathers **2** : covered with feathers

¹**fea·ture** *n* **1** : a single part (as the nose or
the mouth) of the face **2** : something especially noticeable **3** : a main attraction **4**
: a special story in a newspaper or magazine

²**feature** *vb* **fea·tured; fea·tur·ing** : to stand
out or cause to stand out

Feb·ru·ary *n* : the second month of the year

fe·ces *n pl* : body waste that passes out from
the intestine

fed·er·al *adj* : of or relating to a nation
formed by the union of several states or nations

fee *n* **1** : a fixed charge **2** : a charge for
services

fee·ble *adj* **fee·bler; fee·blest** **1** : lacking
in strength or endurance **2** : not loud —
fee·ble·ness *n* — **fee·bly** *adv*

¹**feed** *vb* **fed; feed·ing** **1** : to give food to or
give as food **2** : to take food into the body
: EAT **3** : to supply with something necessary (as to growth or operation) — **feed·er** *n*

²**feed** *n* : food especially for livestock

¹**feel** *vb* **felt; feel·ing** **1** : to be aware of
through physical contact **2** : to examine or
test by touching **3** : to be conscious of **4**
: to seem especially to the touch **5** : to
sense oneself to be

²**feel** *n* **1** : SENSATION 2, FEELING **2** : the
quality of something as learned through or
as if through touch

feel·er *n* **1** : a long flexible structure (as an

insect's antenna) that is an organ of touch
2 : a suggestion or remark made to find out
the views of other people

feel·ing *n* **1** : the sense by which a person
knows whether things are hard or soft, hot
or cold, heavy or light **2** : a sensation of
temperature or pressure **3** : a state of mind
4 feelings *pl* : the state of a person's emotions **5** : the condition of being aware **6**
: IMPRESSION 4

feet *pl of* FOOT

feign *vb* : PRETEND 2

¹**feint** *n* : a pretended blow or attack at one
point or in one direction to take attention
away from the point or direction one really
intends to attack

²**feint** *vb* : to make a feint

¹**fe·line** *adj* **1** : of or relating to cats or the
cat family **2** : like or like that of a cat

²**feline** *n* : a feline animal : CAT

¹**fell** *vb* : to cut or knock down

²**fell** *past of* FALL

¹**fel·low** *n* **1** : COMPANION 1, COMRADE **2**
: an equal in rank, power, or character **3**
: one of a pair : MATE **4** : a male person

²**fellow** *adj* : being a companion, mate, or
equal

fel·low·man *n, pl* **fel·low·men** : a fellow
human being

fel·low·ship *n* **1** : friendly relationship existing among persons **2** : a group with similar interests

fel·on *n* : ²CRIMINAL

fel·o·ny *n, pl* **fel·o·nies** : a very serious
crime

¹**felt** *n* : a heavy material made by rolling and
pressing fibers together

²**felt** *past of* FEEL

¹**fe·male** *adj* **1** : of, relating to, or being the
sex that bears young or lays eggs **2** : having
a pistil but no stamens **3** : of, relating to, or
characteristic of females — **fe·male·ness** *n*

²**female** *n* : a female being

fem·i·nine *adj* **1** : ¹FEMALE 1 **2** : ¹FEMALE 3

fem·i·nism *n* **1** : the theory that women and
men should have equal rights and opportu-
nities **2** : organized activity on behalf of
women's rights and interests — **fem·i·nist** *n*
or adj

fen *n* : low land covered by water

¹**fence** *n* : a barrier (as of wood or wire) to
prevent escape or entry or to mark a boundary

²**fence** *vb* **fenced; fenc·ing** **1** : to enclose
with a fence **2** : to practice fencing —
fenc·er *n*

fenc·ing *n* : the sport of having a pretended
fight with blunted swords

fend *vb* **1** : REPEL 1 **2** : to try to get along
without help

fend·er *n* **1** : a frame on the lower front of a locomotive or streetcar to catch or throw off anything that is hit **2** : a guard over an automobile or cycle wheel

1fer·ment *vb* : to undergo or cause to undergo fermentation

2fer·ment *n* **1** : something (as yeast) that causes fermentation **2** : a state of excitement

fer·men·ta·tion *n* : a chemical breaking down of an organic material that is controlled by an enzyme and usually does not require oxygen

fern *n* : a plant that produces spores instead of seeds and no flowers and whose leaves are usually divided into many parts — **fern·like** *adj*

fe·ro·cious *adj* : FIERCE 1, SAVAGE — **fe·ro·cious·ly** *adv* — **fe·ro·cious·ness** *n*

fe·roc·i·ty *n*, *pl* **fe·roc·i·ties** : the quality or state of being ferocious

1fer·ret *n* : a domesticated animal with usually white or light brown or gray fur that is descended from the European polecat

2ferret *vb* **1** : to hunt with a ferret **2** : to find by eager searching

Fer·ris wheel *n* : an amusement device consisting of a large vertical wheel that is driven by a motor and has seats around its rim

1fer·ry *vb* **fer·ried; fer·ry·ing 1** : to carry by boat over a body of water **2** : to cross by a ferry **3** : to deliver an airplane under its own power **4** : to transport in an airplane

2ferry *n*, *pl* **fer·ries 1** : a place where persons or things are ferried **2** : FERRYBOAT

fer·ry·boat *n* : a boat used to ferry passengers, vehicles, or goods

fer·tile *adj* **1** : producing much vegetation or large crops **2** : capable of developing and growing

fer·til·i·ty *n* : the condition of being fertile

fer·til·iza·tion *n* **1** : an act or process of making fertile **2** : the joining of an egg cell and a sperm cell to form the first stage of an embryo

fer·til·ize *vb* **fer·til·ized; fer·til·iz·ing** : to make fertile or more fertile

fer·til·iz·er *n* : material added to soil to make it more fertile

fer·vent *adj* : very warm in feeling : ARDENT — **fer·vent·ly** *adv*

fer·vor *n* : strong feeling or expression

fes·ter *vb* : to become painfully red and sore and usually full of pus

fes·ti·val *n* **1** : a time of celebration **2** : a program of cultural events or entertainment

fes·tive *adj* **1** : having to do with a feast or festival **2** : very merry and joyful

fes·tiv·i·ty *n*, *pl* **fes·tiv·i·ties 1** : a festive state **2** : festive activity : MERRYMAKING

1fes·toon *n* : an ornament (as a chain) hanging between two points

2festoon *vb* : to hang or form festoons on

fetch *vb* **1** : to go after and bring back **2** : to bring as a price : sell for

fetch·ing *adj* : very attractive — **fetch·ing·ly** *adv*

1fet·ter *n* **1** : a shackle for the feet **2** : something that holds back : RESTRAINT

2fetter *vb* **1** : to put fetters on **2** : to keep from moving or acting freely

fe·tus *n* : an animal not yet born or hatched but more developed than an embryo

1feud *n* : a long bitter quarrel carried on especially between families or clans and usually having acts of violence and revenge

2feud *vb* : to carry on a feud

feu·dal *adj* : of or relating to feudalism

feu·dal·ism *n* : a system of social organization existing in medieval Europe in which a vassal served a lord and received protection and land in return

fe·ver *n* **1** : a rise of body temperature above normal **2** : a disease in which fever is present

fe·ver·ish *adj* **1** : having a fever **2** : of, relating to, or being fever **3** : showing great emotion or activity : HECTIC — **fe·ver·ish·ly** *adv* — **fe·ver·ish·ness** *n*

1few *pron* : not many : a small number

2few *adj* : not many but some

3few *n* : a small number of individuals

fez *n*, *pl* **fez·zes** : a round red felt hat that usually has a tassel but no brim

fi·as·co *n*, *pl* **fi·as·coes** : a complete failure

1fib *n* : an unimportant lie

2fib *vb* **fibbed; fib·bing** : to tell a fib — **fib·ber** *n*

fi·ber *or* **fi·bre** *n* : a long slender threadlike structure

fi·ber·glass *also* **fi·bre·glass** *n* **1** : glass in the form of fibers used in various products (as filters and insulation) **2** : a material of plastic and fiberglass

fiber op·tics *n pl* : thin transparent fibers of glass or plastic that transmit light throughout their length

fi·brous *adj* : containing, consisting of, or like fibers

-fi·ca·tion *n suffix* : the act or process of or the result of

fick·le *adj* : INCONSTANT — **fick·le·ness** *n*

fic·tion *n* **1** : something told or written that is not fact **2** : a made-up story

fic·tion·al *adj* : of, relating to, or suggesting fiction — **fic·tion·al·ly** *adv*

fic·ti·tious *adj* : not real

1fid·dle *n* : VIOLIN

²fiddle *vb* **fid·dled; fid·dling** **1** : to play on a fiddle **2** : to move the hands or fingers restlessly **3** : to spend time in aimless activity **4** : TAMPER — **fid·dler** *n*

fid·dle·sticks *n* : NONSENSE 1 — used as an interjection

fi·del·i·ty *n* **1** : LOYALTY **2** : ACCURACY

fidg·et *vb* : to move in a restless or nervous way

fidg·ets *n pl* : uneasy restlessness shown by nervous movements

fidg·ety *adj* : tending to fidget

fief *n* : an estate given to a vassal by a feudal lord

¹field *n* **1** : a piece of open, cleared, or cultivated land **2** : a piece of land put to a special use or giving a special product **3** : an open space **4** : an area of activity or influence **5** : a background on which something is drawn, painted, or mounted

²field *adj* : of or relating to a field

³field *vb* : to catch or stop and throw a ball

field·er *n* : a baseball player other than the pitcher or catcher on the team that is not at bat

field glasses *n pl* : a hand-held instrument for seeing at a distance that is made up of two telescopes usually without prisms

field goal *n* : a score in football made by kicking the ball through the goal during ordinary play

fiend *n* **1** : DEMON 1, DEVIL **2** : a very wicked or cruel person — **fiend·ish** *adj*

fierce *adj* **fierc·er; fierc·est** **1** : likely to attack **2** : having or showing very great energy or enthusiasm **3** : wild or threatening in appearance — **fierce·ly** *adv* — **fierce·ness** *n*

fi·ery *adj* **fi·er·i·er; fi·er·i·est** **1** : being on fire **2** : hot like a fire **3** : full of spirit

fi·es·ta *n* : FESTIVAL 1, CELEBRATION

fife *n* : a small musical instrument like a flute that produces a shrill sound

¹fif·teen *adj* : being one more than fourteen

²fifteen *n* : one more than fourteen : three times five : 15

¹fif·teenth *adj* : coming right after fourteenth

²fifteenth *n* : number fifteen in a series

¹fifth *adj* : coming right after fourth

²fifth *n* **1** : number five in a series **2** : one of five equal parts

¹fif·ti·eth *adj* : coming right after forty-ninth

²fiftieth *n* : number fifty in a series

¹fif·ty *adj* : being five times ten

²fifty *n* : five times ten : 50

fig *n* : an edible fruit that is oblong or shaped like a pear and that grows on a tree related to the mulberry

¹fight *vb* **fought; fight·ing** **1** : to take part in a fight : COMBAT **2** : to try hard **3** : to struggle against — **fight·er** *n*

²fight *n* **1** : a meeting in battle or in physical combat **2** : ¹QUARREL 2 **3** : strength or desire for fighting

¹fig·ure *n* **1** : a symbol (as 1, 2, 3) that stands for a number : NUMERAL **2 figures** *pl* : ARITHMETIC 2 **3** : value or price expressed in figures **4** : the shape or outline of something **5** : the shape of the body especially of a person **6** : an illustration in a printed text **7** : ¹PATTERN 3 **8** : a series of movements in a dance **9** : an outline traced by a series of movements (as by an ice skater) **10** : a well-known or important person

²figure *vb* **fig·ured; fig·ur·ing** **1** : to decorate with a pattern **2** : CALCULATE 1

fig·ure·head *n* : a figure, statue, or bust on the bow of a ship

figure of speech : an expression (as a simile or a metaphor) that uses words in other than a plain or literal way

figure out *vb* : to work out in the mind

fil·a·ment *n* **1** : a fine thread **2** : a fine wire (as in a light bulb) that is made to glow by the passage of an electric current **3** : the stalk of a plant stamen that bears the anther — **fil·a·men·tous** *adj*

fil·bert *n* : the hazel or its nut

filch *vb* : PILFER

¹file *n* : a steel tool with sharp ridges or teeth for smoothing or rubbing down hard substances

²file *vb* **filed; fil·ing** : to rub, smooth, or cut away with a file

³file *vb* **filed; fil·ing** **1** : to arrange in order **2** : to enter or record officially

⁴file *n* **1** : a device for keeping papers or records **2** : a collection of papers or records kept in a file **3** : a collection of data treated as a unit by a computer

⁵file *n* : a row of persons or things arranged one behind the other

⁶file *vb* **filed; fil·ing** : to move in a file

fil·ial *adj* **1** : of, relating to, or suitable for a son or daughter **2** : being or having the relation of offspring

¹fill *vb* **1** : to make or become full **2** : to occupy fully **3** : to spread through **4** : to stop up : PLUG **5** : to write information on or in : COMPLETE **6** : to do the duties of **7** : to supply according to directions

²fill *n* **1** : an amount that satisfies **2** : material for filling something

fill·er *n* **1** : one that fills **2** : a material used for filling

fil·let *n* : a piece of lean boneless meat or fish

fill·ing *n* : a substance used to fill something else

filling station *n* : SERVICE STATION

fil·ly *n, pl* **fillies** : a female foal : a young female horse

¹film *n* **1** : a thin coating or layer **2** : a roll of material prepared for taking pictures **3** : MOVIE

²film *vb* **1** : to cover or become covered with film **2** : to photograph on a film **3** : to make a movie

film·strip *n* : a strip of film for projecting still pictures on a screen

filmy *adj* **film·i·er; film·i·est** : of, like, or made of film

¹fil·ter *n* **1** : a device or a mass of material (as sand) with tiny openings through which a gas or liquid is passed to separate out something which it contains **2** : a transparent material that absorbs light of some colors and is used for changing light (as in photography)

²filter *vb* **1** : to pass through a filter **2** : to remove by means of a filter

filth *n* : disgusting dirt

filthy *adj* **filth·i·er; filth·i·est** : disgustingly dirty — **filth·i·ness** *n*

fil·tra·tion *n* : the process of filtering

fin *n* **1** : any of the thin parts that stick out from the body of a water animal and especially a fish and are used in moving or guiding the body through the water **2** : something shaped like a fin

¹fi·nal *adj* **1** : not to be changed : CONCLUSIVE **2** : coming or happening at the end — **fi·nal·ly** *adv*

²final *n* **1** : the last match or game of a tournament **2** : a final examination in a course

fi·na·le *n* : the close or end of something (as a musical work)

fi·nal·i·ty *n* : the condition of being final

¹fi·nance *n* **1 finances** *pl* : money available to a government, business, or individual **2** : the system that includes the circulation of money, the providing of banks and credit, and the making of investments

²finance *vb* **fi·nanced; fi·nanc·ing** : to provide money for

fi·nan·cial *adj* : having to do with finance or with finances — **fi·nan·cial·ly** *adv*

fin·an·cier *n* : a specialist in finance and especially in the financing of businesses

finch *n* : a small songbird (as a sparrow, bunting, or canary) that eats seeds

¹find *vb* **found; find·ing** **1** : to come upon by chance **2** : to come upon by searching, study, or effort **3** : to decide on **4** : to know by experience **5** : to gain or regain the use of — **find fault** : to criticize in an unfavorable way

²find *n* : something found

find·er *n* **1** : one that finds **2** : a device on a camera that shows the view being photographed

find out *vb* : to learn by studying or watching : DISCOVER

¹fine *n* : a sum of money to be paid as a punishment

²fine *vb* **fined; fin·ing** : to punish by a fine

³fine *adj* **fin·er; fin·est** **1** : very small or thin **2** : not coarse **3** : very good in quality or appearance — **fine·ly** *adv* — **fine·ness** *n*

⁴fine *adv* : very well

fin·ery *n, pl* **fin·er·ies** : stylish or showy clothes and jewelry

¹fin·ger *n* **1** : one of the five divisions of the end of the hand including the thumb **2** : something that is like or does the work of a finger **3** : the part of a glove into which a finger goes — **fin·ger·like** *adj*

²finger *vb* : to touch with the fingers : HANDLE

fin·ger·board *n* : a strip on the neck of a stringed instrument (as a guitar) against which the fingers press the strings to change the pitch

finger hole *n* : any of a group of holes in a wind instrument that may be covered with a finger to change the pitch

fin·ger·ling *n* : a young fish

fin·ger·nail *n* : the hard covering at the end of a finger

¹fin·ger·print *n* : the pattern of marks made by pressing a finger on a surface especially when the pattern is made in ink in order to identify a person

²fingerprint *vb* : to take the fingerprints of

fin·icky *adj* : very hard to please : FUSSY — **fin·ick·i·ness** *n*

¹fin·ish *vb* **1** : to bring or come to an end : COMPLETE, TERMINATE **2** : to put a final coat or surface on

²finish *n* **1** : ¹END 2, CONCLUSION **2** : the final treatment or coating of a surface or the appearance given by finishing

fi·nite *adj* : having certain limits

Finn *n* : a person born or living in Finland

finned *adj* : having fins

¹Finn·ish *adj* : of or relating to Finland, its people, or the Finnish language

²Finnish *n* : the language of the Finns

fiord *variant of* FJORD

fir *n* : a tall evergreen tree related to the pine that yields useful lumber

¹fire *n* **1** : the light and heat and especially the flame produced by burning **2** : fuel that is burning (as in a fireplace or stove) **3** : the destructive burning of something (as a building or a forest) **4** : a being lively : ENTHUSIASM **5** : the shooting of firearms — **on fire** : actively burning — **under fire** **1**

: exposed to the firing of enemy guns **2** : under attack

²fire *vb* **fired; fir·ing 1** : to set on fire **2** : EXCITE 2, STIR **3** : to dismiss from employment **4** : to set off : EXPLODE **5** : ¹SHOOT 2 **6** : to subject to great heat

fire·arm *n* : a small weapon from which shot or a bullet is driven by the explosion of gunpowder

fire·bug *n* : a person who sets destructive fires on purpose

fire·crack·er *n* : a paper tube containing an explosive to be set off for amusement

fire engine *n* : a truck equipped to fight fires

fire escape *n* : a stairway that provides a way of escape from a building in case of fire

fire extinguisher *n* : something (as a metal container filled with chemicals) that is used to put out a fire

fire·fight·er *n* : a person whose job is to put out fires

fire·fly *n, pl* **fire·flies** : a small beetle producing a soft light

fire·house *n* : FIRE STATION

fire·man *n, pl* **fire·men 1** : FIREFIGHTER **2** : a person who tends a fire (as in a large furnace)

fire·place *n* : a structure with a hearth on which an open fire can be built for heating or especially outdoors for cooking

fire·plug *n* : HYDRANT

fire·proof *adj* : not easily burned : made safe against fire

fire·side *n* **1** : a place near the hearth **2** : ¹HOME 1

fire station *n* : a building housing fire engines and usually firefighters

fire·wood *n* : wood cut for fuel

fire·work *n* **1** : a device that makes a display of light or noise by the burning of explosive or flammable materials **2 fireworks** *pl* : a display of fireworks

¹firm *adj* **1** : STRONG 1, VIGOROUS **2** : having a solid compact texture **3** : not likely to be changed **4** : not easily moved or shaken : FAITHFUL **5** : showing no weakness — **firm·ly** *adv* — **firm·ness** *n*

²firm *n* : BUSINESS 2

fir·ma·ment *n* : the arch of the sky

¹first *adj* **1** : being number one **2** : coming before all others

²first *adv* **1** : before any other **2** : for the first time

³first *n* **1** : number one in a series **2** : something or someone that is first

first aid *n* : care or treatment given to an ill or injured person before regular medical help can be gotten

first·hand *adj or adv* : coming right from the original source

first lieutenant *n* : a commissioned officer in the Army, Air Force, or Marine Corps ranking above a second lieutenant

first–rate *adj* : EXCELLENT

first sergeant *n* **1** : a noncommissioned officer serving as the chief assistant to a military commander **2** : a noncommissioned officer ranking above a sergeant first class in the Army or above a gunnery sergeant in the Marine Corps

firth *n* : a narrow arm of the sea

¹fish *n, pl* **fish** *or* **fish·es 1** : an animal that lives in water — usually used in combination **2** : any of a large group of vertebrate animals that live in water, breathe with gills, and usually have fins and scales — **fish·like** *adj*

²fish *vb* **1** : to attempt to catch fish **2** : to try to find or to find out something by groping

fish·er·man *n, pl* **fish·er·men** : a person who fishes

fish·ery *n, pl* **fish·er·ies 1** : the business of catching fish **2** : a place for catching fish

fish·hook *n* : a hook used for catching fish

fishy *adj* **fish·i·er; fish·i·est 1** : of or like fish **2** : QUESTIONABLE

fis·sion *n* **1** : a splitting or breaking into parts **2** : a method of reproduction in which a living cell or body divides into two or more parts each of which grows into a whole new individual **3** : the splitting of an atomic nucleus with the release of large amounts of energy

fis·sure *n* : a narrow opening or crack

fist *n* : the hand with the fingers doubled tight into the palm

¹fit *adj* **fit·ter; fit·test 1** : good enough **2** : healthy in mind and body — **fit·ness** *n*

²fit *n* : a sudden attack or outburst

³fit *vb* **fit·ted; fit·ting 1** : to be suitable for or to **2** : to be the right shape or size **3** : to bring to the right shape or size **4** : EQUIP

⁴fit *n* **1** : the way something fits **2** : a piece of clothing that fits

fit·ful *adj* : IRREGULAR 4

¹fit·ting *adj* : ²APPROPRIATE, SUITABLE — **fit·ting·ly** *adv*

²fitting *n* : a small accessory part

¹five *adj* : being one more than four

²five *n* **1** : one more than four : 5 **2** : the fifth in a set or series

¹fix *vb* **1** : to make firm or secure **2** : to cause to combine chemically **3** : to set definitely : ESTABLISH **4** : to get ready : PREPARE **5** : ¹REPAIR 1, MEND — **fix·er** *n*

²fix *n* : an unpleasant or difficult position

fixed *adj* **1** : not changing : SET **2** : not moving : INTENT — **fix·ed·ly** *adv*

fixed star *n* : a star so distant that its motion can be measured only by very careful observations over long periods

fix·ture *n* : something attached as a permanent part

¹fizz *vb* : to make a hissing or sputtering sound

²fizz *n* **1** : a hissing or sputtering sound **2** : a bubbling drink

¹fiz·zle *vb* **fiz·zled; fiz·zling** : to fail after a good start

²fizzle *n* : FAILURE 3

fjord *or* **fiord** *n* : a narrow inlet of the sea between cliffs or steep slopes

flab·by *adj* **flab·bi·er; flab·bi·est** : not hard and firm : SOFT — **flab·bi·ness** *n*

¹flag *n* : a piece of cloth with a special design or color that is used as a symbol (as of a nation) or as a signal

²flag *vb* **flagged; flag·ging** : to signal with or as if with a flag

³flag *vb* **flagged; flag·ging** : to become weak

fla·gel·lum *n, pl* **fla·gel·la** : a long whiplike structure by which some tiny plants and animals move

flag·man *n, pl* **flag·men** : a person who signals with a flag

flag·on *n* : a container for liquids usually having a handle, spout, and lid

flag·pole *n* : a pole from which a flag flies

fla·grant *adj* : so bad as to be impossible to overlook — **fla·grant·ly** *adv*

flag·ship *n* : the ship carrying the commander of a group of ships and flying a flag that tells the commander's rank

flag·staff *n, pl* **flag·staffs** : FLAGPOLE

flag·stone *n* : a piece of hard flat rock used for paving

¹flail *n* : a tool for threshing grain by hand

²flail *vb* : to hit with or as if with a flail

flair *n* : natural ability

¹flake *n* : a small thin flat piece

²flake *vb* **flaked; flak·ing** : to form or separate into flakes

flaky *adj* **flak·i·er; flak·i·est** : tending to flake — **flak·i·ness** *n*

flam·boy·ant *adj* : liking or making a dashing show — **flam·boy·ant·ly** *adv*

¹flame *n* **1** : the glowing gas that makes up part of a fire **2** : a condition or appearance suggesting a flame

²flame *vb* **flamed; flam·ing** : to burn with or as if with a flame

flame·throw·er *n* : a device that shoots a burning stream of fuel

fla·min·go *n, pl* **fla·min·gos** *or* **fla·min·goes** : a waterbird with very long neck and legs, scarlet wings, and a broad bill bent downward at the end

flam·ma·ble *adj* : capable of being easily set on fire and of burning quickly

¹flank *n* **1** : the fleshy part of the side between the ribs and the hip **2** : ¹SIDE 3 **3** : the right or left side of a formation (as of soldiers)

²flank *vb* **1** : to pass around the flank of **2** : to be located at the side of : BORDER

flank·er *n* : a football player stationed wide of the formation

flan·nel *n* : a soft cloth made of wool or cotton

¹flap *n* **1** : something broad and flat or limber that hangs loose **2** : the motion made by something broad and limber (as a sail or wing) moving back and forth or the sound produced

²flap *vb* **flapped; flap·ping** **1** : to give a quick light blow **2** : to move with a beating or fluttering motion

flap·jack *n* : PANCAKE

¹flare *vb* **flared; flar·ing** **1** : to burn with an unsteady flame **2** : to shine with great or sudden light **3** : to become angry **4** : to spread outward

²flare *n* **1** : a sudden blaze of light **2** : a blaze of light used to signal, light up something, or attract attention **3** : a device or material used to produce a flare **4** : a sudden outburst (as of sound or anger) **5** : a spreading outward : a part that spreads outward

¹flash *vb* **1** : to shine in or like a sudden flame **2** : to send out in or as if in flashes **3** : to come or pass very suddenly **4** : to make a sudden display (as of feeling)

²flash *n* **1** : a sudden burst of or as if of light **2** : a very short time

³flash *adj* : beginning suddenly and lasting only a short time

flash·light *n* : a small portable electric light that runs on batteries

flashy *adj* **flash·i·er; flash·i·est** : GAUDY

flask *n* : a container like a bottle with a flat or rounded body

¹flat *adj* **flat·ter; flat·test** **1** : having a smooth level surface **2** : spread out on or along a surface **3** : having a broad smooth surface and little thickness **4** : ²OUTRIGHT 1, POSITIVE **5** : FIXED 1 **6** : having nothing lacking or left over : EXACT **7** : INSIPID **8** : having lost air pressure **9** : lower than the true musical pitch **10** : lower by a half step in music **11** : free from gloss — **flat·ly** *adv* — **flat·ness** *n*

²flat *n* **1** : a level place : PLAIN **2** : a flat part or surface **3** : a note or tone that is a half step lower than the note named **4** : a sign ♭ meaning that the pitch of a musical note is to be lower by a half step **5** : a deflated tire

³flat *adv* **1** : on or against a flat surface **2** : below the true musical pitch

⁴flat *n* : an apartment on one floor

flat·boat *n* : a large boat with a flat bottom and square ends

flat·fish *n* : a fish (as the flounder) that swims on its side and has both eyes on the upper side

flat·iron *n* : ¹IRON

flat·ten *vb* : to make or become flat

flat·ter *vb* **1** : to praise but not sincerely **2** : to show too favorably — **flat·ter·er** *n* — **flat·ter·ing·ly** *adv*

flat·tery *n, pl* **flat·ter·ies** : praise that is not deserved or meant

flaunt *vb* **1** : to wave or flutter in a showy way **2** : to make too much show of : PARADE

¹fla·vor *n* **1** : the quality of something that affects the sense of taste **2** : a substance added to food to give it a desired taste — **fla·vored** *adj*

²flavor *vb* : to give or add a flavor to

fla·vor·ing *n* : ¹FLAVOR 2

flaw *n* : a small often hidden fault

flax *n* : a plant with blue flowers that is grown for its fiber from which linen is made and for its seed from which oil and livestock feed are obtained

flax·en *adj* **1** : made of flax **2** : having a light straw color

flax·seed *n* : the seed of flax from which linseed oil comes and which is used in medicine

flay *vb* **1** : ²SKIN **2** : to scold severely

flea *n* : a small bloodsucking insect that has no wings and a hard body

¹fleck *vb* : to mark with small streaks or spots

²fleck *n* **1** : ¹SPOT 2, MARK **2** : ¹FLAKE, PARTICLE

fledg·ling *n* : a young bird that has just grown the feathers needed to fly

flee *vb* **fled; flee·ing** : to run away or away from : FLY

¹fleece *n* : the woolly coat of an animal and especially a sheep

²fleece *vb* **fleeced; fleec·ing** : to take money or property from by trickery

fleecy *adj* **fleec·i·er; fleec·i·est** : covered with, made of, or like fleece

¹fleet *n* **1** : a group of warships under one command **2** : a country's navy **3** : a group of ships or vehicles that move together or are under one management

²fleet *adj* : very swift — **fleet·ly** *adv* — **fleet·ness** *n*

Fleet Admiral *n* : the highest ranking com-

missioned officer in the Navy ranking above an admiral

flesh *n* **1** : the soft and especially the edible muscular parts of an animal's body **2** : a fleshy edible plant part (as the pulp of a fruit) — **fleshed** *adj*

fleshy *adj* **flesh·i·er; flesh·i·est** **1** : like or consisting of flesh **2** : rather stout

flew *past of* FLY

flex *vb* : to bend often again and again

flex·i·bil·i·ty *n* : the quality or state of being flexible

flex·i·ble *adj* **1** : possible to bend or flex **2** : able or suitable to meet new situations — **flex·i·bly** *adv*

¹flick *n* : a light snapping stroke

²flick *vb* : to strike or move with a quick motion

¹flick·er *vb* : to burn unsteadily

²flicker *n* **1** : a quick small movement **2** : a flickering light

³flicker *n* : a large North American woodpecker

fli·er *or* **fly·er** *n* **1** : one that flies **2** : AVIATOR

¹flight *n* **1** : an act or instance of passing through the air by the use of wings **2** : a passing through the air or space **3** : the distance covered in a flight **4** : a scheduled trip by an airplane **5** : a group of similar things flying through the air together **6** : a passing above or beyond ordinary limits **7** : a continuous series of stairs

²flight *n* : the act of running away

flight·less *adj* : unable to fly

flighty *adj* **flight·i·er; flight·i·est** **1** : easily excited : SKITTISH **2** : not wise or sober : FRIVOLOUS

flim·sy *adj* **flim·si·er; flim·si·est** : not strong or solid — **flim·si·ly** *adv* — **flim·si·ness** *n*

flinch *vb* : to draw back from or as if from pain

¹fling *vb* **flung; fling·ing** **1** : to move suddenly **2** : to throw hard or without care

²fling *n* **1** : an act of flinging **2** : a time of freedom for pleasure

flint *n* : a very hard stone that produces a spark when struck by steel

flint·lock *n* : an old-fashioned firearm using a flint for striking a spark to fire the charge

¹flip *vb* **flipped; flip·ping** : to move or turn by or as if by tossing

²flip *n* : an act of flipping : TOSS

flip·pant *adj* : not respectful : SAUCY — **flip·pant·ly** *adv*

flip·per *n* **1** : a broad flat limb (as of a seal) specialized for swimming **2** : a flat rubber shoe with the front expanded into a paddle used in swimming

¹flirt *vb* : to show a liking for someone of the opposite sex just for the fun of it

²flirt *n* : a person who flirts a lot

flit *vb* **flit·ted; flit·ting** : to move by darting about

¹float *n* **1** : something that floats in or on the surface of a liquid **2** : a cork or bob that holds up the baited end of a fishing line **3** : a floating platform anchored near a shore for the use of swimmers or boats **4** : a hollow ball that controls the flow or level of the liquid it floats on (as in a tank) **5** : a vehicle with a platform used to carry an exhibit in a parade

²float *vb* **1** : to rest on the surface of a liquid **2** : to drift on or through or as if on or through a fluid **3** : to cause to float — **float·er** *n*

¹flock *n* **1** : a group of animals (as geese or sheep) living or kept together **2** : a group someone (as a minister) watches over

²flock *vb* : to gather or move in a crowd

floe *n* : a sheet or mass of floating ice

flog *vb* **flogged; flog·ging** : to beat severely with a rod or whip

¹flood *n* **1** : a huge flow of water that rises and spreads over the land **2** : the flowing in of the tide **3** : a very large number or amount

²flood *vb* **1** : to cover or become filled with water **2** : to fill as if with a flood

flood·light *n* : a lamp that gives a bright broad beam of light

flood·plain *n* : low flat land along a stream that is flooded when the steam overflows

flood·wa·ter *n* : the water of a flood

¹floor *n* **1** : the part of a room on which one stands **2** : the lower inside surface of a hollow structure **3** : a ground surface **4** : a story of a building

²floor *vb* **1** : to cover or provide with a floor **2** : to knock down

floor·ing *n* **1** : ¹FLOOR 1 **2** : material for floors

¹flop *vb* **flopped; flop·ping** **1** : to flap about **2** : to drop or fall limply **3** : ¹FAIL 6

²flop *n* **1** : the act or sound of flopping **2** : FAILURE 3

¹flop·py *adj* **flop·pi·er; flop·pi·est** : being soft and flexible

²floppy *n, pl* **floppies** : FLOPPY DISK

floppy disk *n* : a small flexible plastic disk with a magnetic coating on which computer data can be stored

flo·ra *n* : the plant life typical of a region, period, or special environment

flo·ral *adj* : of or relating to flowers

flo·ret *n* : a small flower

flo·rist *n* : a person who sells flowers and ornamental plants

¹floss *n* **1** : soft thread used in embroidery **2** : fluffy material full of fibers

²floss *vb* : to use dental floss on (one's teeth)

flo·til·la *n* : a fleet of usually small ships

¹flounce *vb* **flounced; flounc·ing** : to move with exaggerated jerky motions

²flounce *n* : a strip of fabric attached by its upper edge

¹floun·der *n* : a flatfish used for food

²flounder *vb* **1** : to struggle to move or get footing **2** : to behave or do something in a clumsy way

flour *n* : the finely ground meal of a cereal grain and especially of wheat

¹flour·ish *vb* **1** : to grow well : THRIVE **2** : to do well : PROSPER **3** : to make sweeping movements with

²flourish *n* **1** : a fancy bit of decoration added to something (as handwriting) **2** : a sweeping motion

flout *vb* : to show lack of respect for : DISREGARD

¹flow *vb* **1** : to move in a stream **2** : to glide along smoothly **3** : to hang loose and waving

²flow *n* **1** : an act of flowing **2** : the rise of the tide **3** : a smooth even movement : STREAM

¹flow·er *n* **1** : a plant part that produces seed **2** : a plant grown chiefly for its showy flowers **3** : the state of bearing flowers **4** : the best part or example — **flow·ered** *adj* — **flow·er·less** *adj*

²flower *vb* : to produce flowers

flower head *n* : a tight cluster of small flowers that are arranged so that the whole looks like a single flower

flowering plant *n* : a seed plant whose seeds are produced in the ovary of a flower

flow·er·pot *n* : a pot in which to grow plants

flow·ery *adj* **1** : having many flowers **2** : full of fine words — **flow·er·i·ness** *n*

flown *past participle of* FLY

flu *n* **1** : INFLUENZA **2** : any of several virus diseases something like a cold

fluc·tu·ate *vb* **fluc·tu·at·ed; fluc·tu·at·ing** : to change continually and especially up and down

flue *n* : an enclosed passage (as in a chimney) for smoke or air

flu·en·cy *n* : the ability to speak easily and well

flu·ent *adj* **1** : able to speak easily and well **2** : that is smooth and correct : GOOD — **flu·ent·ly** *adv*

¹fluff *n* : ⁷DOWN, NAP

²fluff *vb* : to make or become fluffy

fluffy *adj* **fluff·i·er; fluff·i·est** : having, covered with, or like down

¹flu·id *adj* **1** : capable of flowing like a

liquid or gas **2** : being smooth and easy —
flu·id·ly *adv*
²**fluid** *n* : something that tends to flow and
take the shape of its container
flung *past of* FLING
flunk *vb* : ¹FAIL 6
fluo·res·cent *adj* **1** : giving out visible light
when exposed to external radiation **2** : producing visible light by means of a fluores-
cent coating **3** : extremely bright or glowing
fluo·ri·date *vb* **fluo·ri·dat·ed; fluo·ri·dat-
ing** : to add a fluoride to (as drinking water)
to reduce tooth decay
fluo·ri·da·tion *n* : the act of fluoridating
fluo·ride *n* : a compound of fluorine
fluo·rine *n* : a yellowish flammable irritating
gaseous chemical element
¹**flur·ry** *n, pl* **flurries** **1** : a gust of wind **2**
: a brief light snowfall **3** : a brief outburst
(as of activity)
²**flurry** *vb* **flur·ried; flur·ry·ing** : ¹FLUSTER,
EXCITE
¹**flush** *vb* : to begin or cause to begin flight
suddenly
²**flush** *n* **1** : an act of flushing **2** : ¹BLUSH 1
³**flush** *vb* **1** : ²BLUSH **2** : to pour water over
or through
⁴**flush** *adj* : having one edge or surface even
with the next
⁵**flush** *adv* : so as to be flush
¹**flus·ter** *vb* : to make nervous and confused
: UPSET
²**fluster** *n* : a state of nervous confusion
¹**flute** *n* : a woodwind instrument in the form
of a hollow slender tube open at only one
end that is played by blowing across a hole
near the closed end
²**flute** *vb* **flut·ed; flut·ing** : to make a sound
like that of a flute
¹**flut·ter** *vb* **1** : to move the wings rapidly
without flying or in making short flights **2**
: to move with a quick flapping motion **3**
: to move about busily without getting much
done
²**flutter** *n* : an act of fluttering
¹**fly** *vb* **flew; flown; fly·ing** **1** : to move in or
pass through the air with wings **2** : to move
through the air or before the wind **3** : to
float or cause to float, wave, or soar in the
wind **4** : to run away : FLEE **5** : to move or
pass swiftly **6** : to operate or travel in an
aircraft
²**fly** *n, pl* **flies** **1** : a flap of material to cover
a fastening in a garment **2** : the outer can-
vas of a tent that has a double top **3** : a
baseball hit high in the air
³**fly** *n, pl* **flies** **1** : a winged insect **2** : any
of a large group of mostly stout-bodied
two-winged insects (as the common house-

fly) **3** : a fishhook made to look like an insect
fly·catch·er *n* : a small bird that eats flying
insects
flyer *variant of* FLIER
fly·ing boat *n* : a seaplane with a hull designed to support it on the water
flying fish *n* : a fish with large fins that let it
jump from the water and move for a dis-
tance through the air
fly·pa·per *n* : sticky paper to catch and kill
flies
fly·speck *n* : a spot of feces left by a fly on a
surface
fly·way *n* : a route regularly followed by migratory birds
¹**foal** *n* : a young animal of the horse family
especially while less than one year old
²**foal** *vb* : to give birth to a foal
¹**foam** *n* : a mass of tiny bubbles that forms
in or on the surface of liquids or in the
mouths or on the skins of animals
²**foam** *vb* : to produce or form foam
foamy *adj* **foam·i·er; foam·i·est** : covered
with or looking like foam — **foam·i·ness**
n
fo·cal *adj* : of, relating to, or having a focus
¹**fo·cus** *n, pl* **fo·cus·es** *or* **fo·ci** **1** : a point
at which rays (as of light, heat, or sound)
meet after being reflected or bent : the point
at which an image is formed **2** : the distance from a lens or mirror to a focus **3** : an
adjustment (as of a person's eyes or glasses)
that gives clear vision **4** : a center of activity or interest
²**focus** *vb* **fo·cused** *or* **fo·cussed; fo·cus-
ing** *or* **fo·cus·sing** **1** : to bring or come to
a focus **2** : to adjust the focus of
fod·der *n* : coarse dry food (as stalks of
corn) for livestock
foe *n* : an enemy especially in war
¹**fog** *n* **1** : fine particles of water floating in
the air at or near the ground **2** : a confused
state of mind
²**fog** *vb* **fogged; fog·ging** : to cover or become covered with fog
fog·gy *adj* **fog·gi·er; fog·gi·est** **1** : filled
with fog **2** : confused as if by fog — **fog-
gi·ness** *n*
fog·horn *n* : a loud horn sounded in a fog to
give warning
fo·gy *n, pl* **fogies** : a person with old-fashioned ideas
foi·ble *n* : an unimportant weakness or failing
¹**foil** *vb* : to keep from succeeding or from
reaching a goal
²**foil** *n* **1** : a very thin sheet of metal **2**
: something that makes another thing more
noticeable by being very different from it

³foil *n* : a fencing weapon having a light flexible blade with a blunt point

¹fold *n* : an enclosure or shelter for sheep

²fold *vb* : to pen up (sheep) in a fold

³fold *vb* **1** : to double something over itself **2** : to clasp together **3** : ¹EMBRACE 1

⁴fold *n* **1** : a part doubled or laid over another part : PLEAT **2** : a bend produced in a rock layer by pressure **3** : a crease made by folding something (as a newspaper)

-fold *suffix* **1** : multiplied by a specified number : times — in adjectives and adverbs **2** : having so many parts

fold·er *n* **1** : one that folds **2** : a folded printed sheet **3** : a folded cover or large envelope for loose papers

fo·li·age *n* : the leaves of a plant (as a tree) — **fo·li·aged** *adj*

¹folk *or* **folks** *n pl* **1** : persons of a certain class, kind, or group **2 folks** *pl* : people in general **3 folks** *pl* : the members of one's family : one's relatives

²folk *adj* : created by the common people

folk·lore *n* : customs, beliefs, stories, and sayings of a people handed down from generation to generation

folk·sing·er *n* : a person who sings songs (**folk songs**) created by and long sung among the common people

folk·tale *n* : a story made up and handed down by the common people

fol·low *vb* **1** : to go or come after or behind **2** : to be led or guided by : OBEY **3** : to proceed along **4** : to work in or at something as a way of life **5** : to come after in time or place **6** : to result from **7** : to keep one's eyes or attention on — **fol·low·er** *n* — **follow suit 1** : to play a card that belongs to the same group (as hearts or spades) as the one led **2** : to do the same thing someone else has just done

¹fol·low·ing *adj* : coming just after

²following *n* : a group of followers

follow through *vb* : to complete an action

follow up *vb* : to show continued interest in or take further action regarding

fol·ly *n, pl* **follies 1** : lack of good sense **2** : a foolish act or idea

fond *adj* **1** : having a liking or love **2** : AFFECTIONATE, LOVING — **fond·ly** *adv* — **fond·ness** *n*

fon·dle *vb* **fon·dled; fon·dling** : to touch or handle in a tender or loving manner

font *n* : a basin to hold water for baptism

food *n* **1** : material containing carbohydrates, fats, proteins, and supplements (as minerals and vitamins) that is taken in by and used in the living body for growth and repair and as a source of energy for activities **2** : inorganic substances taken in by green plants and used to build organic nutrients **3** : organic materials formed by plants and used in their growth and activities **4** : solid food as distinguished from drink

food chain *n* : a sequence of organisms in which each depends on the next and usually lower member as a source of food

food·stuff *n* : a substance with food value

¹fool *n* **1** : a person without good sense or judgment **2** : JESTER 1

²fool *vb* **1** : to spend time idly **2** : to meddle or tamper with something **3** : to speak or act in a playful way or in fun : JOKE **4** : ²TRICK

fool·har·dy *adj* **fool·har·di·er; fool·har·di·est** : foolishly adventurous or bold

fool·ish *adj* : showing or resulting from lack of good sense : SENSELESS — **fool·ish·ly** *adv* — **fool·ish·ness** *n*

fool·proof *adj* : done, made, or planned so well that nothing can go wrong

¹foot *n, pl* **feet 1** : the end part of the leg of an animal or person : the part of an animal on which it stands or moves **2** : a unit of length equal to twelve inches (about .3 meter) **3** : something like a foot in position or use — **on foot** : by walking

²foot *vb* **1** : to go on foot **2** : ¹PAY 2

foot·ball *n* **1** : a game played with a blown up oval ball on a large field by two teams of eleven players that move the ball by kicking, passing, or running with it **2** : the ball used in football

foot·ed *adj* **1** : having a foot or feet **2** : having such or so many feet

foot·fall *n* : the sound of a footstep

foot·hill *n* : a hill at the foot of higher hills

foot·hold *n* : a place where the foot may be put (as for climbing)

foot·ing *n* **1** : a firm position or placing of the feet **2** : FOOTHOLD **3** : position in relation to others **4** : social relationship

foot·lights *n pl* : a row of lights set across the front of a stage floor

foot·man *n, pl* **foot·men** : a male servant who lets visitors in and waits on table

foot·note *n* : a note at the bottom of a page

foot·path *n* : a path for walkers

foot·print *n* : a track left by a foot

foot·sore *adj* : having sore feet from walking a lot

foot·step *n* **1** : a step of the foot **2** : the distance covered by a step **3** : FOOTPRINT

foot·stool *n* : a low stool to support the feet

foot·work *n* : the skill with which the feet are moved (as in boxing)

¹for *prep* **1** : by way of getting ready **2** : toward the goal of **3** : in order to reach **4**

: as being **5** : because of **6** — used to show who or what is to receive something **7** : in order to help or defend **8** : directed at : AGAINST **9** : in exchange as equal to **10** : with regard to : CONCERNING **11** : taking into account **12** : through the period of

²for *conj* : BECAUSE

¹for·age *n* : food (as pasture) for browsing or grazing animals

²forage *vb* **for·aged; for·ag·ing** : ¹SEARCH 1

for·ay *n* : ¹RAID

for·bear *vb* **for·bore; for·borne; for·bear·ing 1** : to hold back **2** : to control oneself when provoked

for·bid *vb* **for·bade** *or* **for·bad; for·bid·den; for·bid·ding** : to order not to do something

for·bid·ding *adj* : tending to frighten or discourage

¹force *n* **1** : POWER 4 **2** : the state of existing and being enforced : EFFECT **3** : a group of persons gathered together and trained for action **4** : power or violence used on a person or thing **5** : an influence (as a push or pull) that tends to produce a change in the speed or direction of motion of something

²force *vb* **forced; forc·ing 1** : to make (as a person) do something **2** : to get or make by using force **3** : to break open by force **4** : to speed up the development of

force·ful *adj* : having much force : VIGOROUS — **force·ful·ly** *adv* — **force·ful·ness** *n*

for·ceps *n, pl* **forceps** : an instrument for grasping, holding, or pulling on things especially in delicate operations (as by a jeweler or surgeon)

forc·ible *adj* **1** : got, made, or done by force or violence **2** : showing a lot of force or energy — **forc·ibly** *adv*

¹ford *n* : a shallow place in a body of water where one can wade across

²ford *vb* : to cross by wading

¹fore *adv* : in or toward the front

²fore *adj* : being or coming before in time, place, or order

³fore *n* : ¹FRONT 2 .

⁴fore *interj* — used by a golfer to warn someone within range of a hit ball

fore- *prefix* **1** : earlier : beforehand **2** : at the front : in front **3** : front part of something specified

fore–and–aft *adj* : being in line with the length of a ship

fore·arm *n* : the part of the arm between the elbow and the wrist

fore·bear *n* : ANCESTOR

fore·bod·ing *n* : a feeling that something bad is going to happen

¹fore·cast *vb* **forecast** *or* **fore·cast·ed; fore·cast·ing** : to predict often after

thought and study of available evidence — **fore·cast·er** *n*

²forecast *n* : a prediction of something in the future

fore·cas·tle *n* **1** : the forward part of the upper deck of a ship **2** : quarters for the crew in the forward part of a ship

fore·fa·ther *n* : ANCESTOR

fore·fin·ger *n* : INDEX FINGER

fore·foot *n, pl* **fore·feet** : one of the front feet of an animal with four feet

fore·front *n* : the very front : VANGUARD

forego *variant of* FORGO

fore·go·ing *adj* : being before in time or place

fore·gone conclusion *n* : something felt to be sure to happen

fore·ground *n* : the part of a picture or scene that seems to be nearest to and in front of the person looking at it

fore·hand *n* : a stroke (as in tennis) made with the palm of the hand turned in the direction in which the hand is moving

fore·head *n* : the part of the face above the eyes

for·eign *adj* **1** : located outside of a place or country and especially outside of one's country **2** : belonging to a place or country other than the one under consideration **3** : relating to or having to do with other nations **4** : not normal or wanted

for·eign·er *n* : a person who is from a foreign country

fore·leg *n* : a front leg

fore·limb *n* : an arm, fin, wing, or leg that is or occupies the position of a foreleg

fore·man *n, pl* **fore·men** : the leader of a group of workers

fore·mast *n* : the mast nearest the bow of the ship

¹fore·most *adj* : first in time, place, or order : most important

²foremost *adv* : in the first place

fore·noon *n* : MORNING

fore·quar·ter *n* : the front half of a side of the body or carcass of an animal with four feet

fore·run·ner *n* : one that comes before especially as a sign of the coming of another

fore·see *vb* **fore·saw; fore·seen; fore·see·ing** : to see or know about beforehand

fore·sight *n* **1** : the act or power of foreseeing **2** : care for the future : PRUDENCE

for·est *n* : a growth of trees and underbrush covering a large area — **for·est·ed** *adj*

fore·stall *vb* : to keep out, interfere with, or prevent by steps taken in advance

forest ranger *n* : a person in charge of the management and protection of a part of a public forest

for·est·ry *n* : the science and practice of caring for forests — **for·est·er** *n*

fore·tell *vb* **fore·told; fore·tell·ing** : to tell of a thing before it happens

fore·thought *n* : a thinking or planning for the future

for·ev·er *adv* **1** : for a limitless time **2** : at all times

for·ev·er·more *adv* : FOREVER 1

fore·word *n* : PREFACE

¹for·feit *n* : something forfeited

²forfeit *vb* : to lose or lose the right to something through a fault, error, or crime

¹forge *n* : a furnace or a place with a furnace where metal is shaped and worked by heating and hammering

²forge *vb* **forged; forg·ing 1** : to shape and work metal by heating and hammering **2** : to produce something that is not genuine : COUNTERFEIT — **forg·er** *n*

³forge *vb* **forged; forg·ing** : to move forward slowly but steadily

forg·ery *n, pl* **forg·er·ies 1** : the crime of falsely making or changing a written paper or signing someone else's name **2** : something that has been forged

for·get *vb* **for·got; for·got·ten** *or* **for·got; for·get·ting 1** : to be unable to think of or recall **2** : to fail by accident to do (something) : OVERLOOK

for·get·ful *adj* : forgetting easily — **for·get·ful·ly** *adv* — **for·get·ful·ness** *n*

for·get–me–not *n* : a small low plant with bright blue flowers

for·give *vb* **for·gave; for·giv·en; for·giv·ing** : to stop feeling angry at or hurt by

for·give·ness *n* : the act of forgiving or the state of being forgiven

for·go *or* **fore·go** *vb* **for·went** *or* **fore·went; for·gone** *or* **fore·gone; for·go·ing** *or* **fore·go·ing** : to hold oneself back from : GIVE UP

¹fork *n* **1** : an implement having a handle and two or more prongs for taking up (as in eating), pitching, or digging **2** : something like a fork in shape **3** : the place where something divides or branches **4** : one of the parts into which something divides or branches — **forked** *adj*

²fork *vb* **1** : to divide into branches **2** : to pitch or lift with a fork

for·lorn *adj* : sad from being left alone — **for·lorn·ly** *adv*

¹form *n* **1** : the shape and structure of something **2** : an established way of doing something **3** : a printed sheet with blank spaces for information **4** : a mold in which concrete is placed to set **5** : ¹SORT 1, KIND **6** : a plan of arrangement or design (as for a work of art) **7** : one of the different pro-

nunciations, spellings, or inflections a word may have

²form *vb* **1** : to give form or shape to **2** : DEVELOP 5 **3** : to come or bring together in making **4** : to take form : come into being

¹for·mal *adj* : following established form, custom, or rule — **for·mal·ly** *adv*

²formal *n* : something (as a dress) formal in character

for·mal·i·ty *n, pl* **for·mal·i·ties 1** : the quality or state of being formal **2** : an established way of doing something

for·ma·tion *n* **1** : a forming of something **2** : something that is formed **3** : an arrangement of something (as persons or ships)

for·mer *adj* : coming before in time

for·mer·ly *adv* : at an earlier time

for·mi·da·ble *adj* **1** : exciting fear or awe **2** : offering serious difficulties

form·less *adj* : having no regular form or shape — **form·less·ly** *adv* — **form·less·ness** *n*

for·mu·la *n* **1** : a direction giving amounts of the substances for the preparation of something (as a medicine) **2** : a milk mixture or substitute for feeding a baby **3** : a general fact or rule expressed in symbols **4** : an expression in symbols giving the makeup of a substance **5** : an established form or method

for·mu·late *vb* **for·mu·lat·ed; for·mu·lat·ing** : to state definitely and clearly

for·sake *vb* **for·sook; for·sak·en; for·sak·ing** : to give up or leave entirely

for·syth·ia *n* : a bush often grown for its bright yellow flowers that appear in early spring

fort *n* : a strong or fortified place

forth *adv* **1** : onward in time, place, or order **2** : out into view

forth·com·ing *adj* **1** : being about to appear **2** : ready or available when needed

forth·right *adj* : going straight to the point clearly and firmly — **forth·right·ly** *adv*

forth·with *adv* : without delay : IMMEDIATELY

¹for·ti·eth *adj* : coming right after thirty-ninth

²fortieth *n* : number forty in a series

for·ti·fi·ca·tion *n* **1** : the act of fortifying **2** : something that strengthens or protects

for·ti·fy *vb* **for·ti·fied; for·ti·fy·ing 1** : to make strong (as by building defenses) **2** : ENRICH 2, 3

for·ti·tude *n* : strength of mind that lets a person meet and put up with trouble

fort·night *n* : two weeks

for·tress *n* : a fortified place

for·tu·nate *adj* **1** : bringing some unexpected good **2** : receiving some unexpected good : LUCKY — **for·tu·nate·ly** adv

for·tune n **1** : favorable results that come partly by chance **2** : what happens to a person : good or bad luck **3** : what is to happen to one in the future **4** : WEALTH

for·tune–tell·er n : a person who claims to foretell future events

1for·ty adj : being four times ten

2forty n : four times ten : 40

for·ty–nin·er n : a person in the California gold rush of 1849

fo·rum n **1** : the marketplace or public place of an ancient Roman city serving as the center for public business **2** : a program of open discussion

1for·ward adj **1** : near, at, or belonging to the front part **2** : lacking proper modesty or reserve **3** : moving, tending, or leading to a position in front

2forward adv : to or toward what is in front

3forward vb **1** : to help onward : ADVANCE **2** : to send on or ahead

4forward n : a player at or near the front of his or her team or near the opponent's goal

for·wards adv : 2FORWARD

fos·sil n : a trace or print or the remains of a plant or animal of a past age preserved in earth or rock

1fos·ter adj : giving, receiving, or sharing parental care even though not related by blood or legal ties

2foster vb **1** : to give parental care to **2** : to help the growth and development of

fought past of FIGHT

1foul adj **1** : disgusting in looks, taste, or smell **2** : full of or covered with dirt **3** : being vulgar or insulting **4** : being wet and stormy **5** : very unfair **6** : breaking a rule in a game or sport **7** : being outside the foul lines — **foul·ly** adv — **foul·ness** n

2foul n **1** : a breaking of the rules in a game or sport **2** : a foul ball in baseball

3foul vb **1** : to make or become foul or filthy **2** : to make a foul **3** : to become or cause to become entangled

foul line n : either of two straight lines running from the rear corner of home plate through first and third base to the boundary of a baseball field

foul play n : VIOLENCE 1

1found past of FIND

2found vb : ESTABLISH 1

foun·da·tion n **1** : the act of founding **2** : the support upon which something rests

1found·er n : a person who founds something

2foun·der vb : 1SINK 1

found·ling n : an infant found after being abandoned by unknown parents

found·ry n, pl **foundries** : a building or factory where metals are cast

foun·tain n **1** : a spring of water **2** : SOURCE 1 **3** : an artificial stream or spray of water (as for drinking or ornament) or the device from which it comes

fountain pen n : a pen with ink inside that is fed as needed to the writing point

1four adj : being one more than three

2four n **1** : one more than three : two times two : 4 **2** : the fourth in a set or series

four·fold adj : being four times as great or as many

four·score adj : 1EIGHTY

four·some adj : a group of four persons or things

1four·teen adj : being one more than thirteen

2fourteen n : one more than thirteen : two times seven : 14

1four·teenth adj : coming right after thirteenth

2fourteenth n : number fourteen in a series

1fourth adj : coming right after third

2fourth n **1** : number four in a series **2** : one of four equal parts

Fourth of July n : INDEPENDENCE DAY

fowl n, pl **fowl** or **fowls** **1** : BIRD **2** : a common domestic rooster or hen **3** : the flesh of a mature domestic fowl for use as food

fox n : a wild animal closely related to the dog that has a sharp snout, pointed ears, and a long bushy tail

foxy adj **fox·i·er**; **fox·i·est** : cunning and careful in planning and action — **fox·i·ly** adv — **fox·i·ness** n

foy·er n **1** : a lobby especially in a theater **2** : an entrance hall

fra·cas n : a noisy quarrel : BRAWL

frac·tion n **1** : a part of a whole : FRAGMENT **2** : a number (as $1/2$, $2/3$, $17/100$) that indicates one or more equal parts of a whole or group and that may be considered as indicating also division of the number above the line by the number below the line

frac·tion·al adj **1** : of, relating to, or being a fraction **2** : fairly small

1frac·ture n **1** : a breaking or being broken (as of a bone) **2** : damage or an injury caused by breaking

2fracture vb **frac·tured**; **frac·tur·ing** : to cause a fracture in : BREAK

frag·ile adj : easily broken : DELICATE

frag·ment n : a part broken off or incomplete

frag·men·tary adj : made up of fragments : INCOMPLETE

fra·grance n : a sweet or pleasant smell

fra·grant adj : sweet or pleasant in smell — **fra·grant·ly** adv

frail adj : very delicate or weak in structure or being

frail·ty *n, pl* **frailties** 1 : the quality or state of being weak 2 : a weakness of character

¹frame *vb* **framed; fram·ing** 1 : ²FORM 1, CONSTRUCT 2 : to enclose in a frame

²frame *n* 1 : the structure of an animal and especially a human body : PHYSIQUE 2 : an arrangement of parts that give form or support to something 3 : an open case or structure for holding or enclosing something 4 : a particular state or mood

³frame *adj* : having a wooden frame

frame·work *n* : a basic supporting part or structure

franc *n* 1 : a French coin or bill 2 : any of various coins or bills used in countries where French is widely spoken

Fran·co- *prefix* 1 : French and 2 : French

frank *adj* : free in speaking one's feelings and opinions — **frank·ly** *adv* — **frank·ness** *n*

frank·furt·er *n* : a cooked sausage (as of beef or beef and pork)

frank·in·cense *n* : a fragrant gum that is burned for its sweet smell

fran·tic *adj* : wildly excited

fran·ti·cal·ly *adv* : in a frantic way

fra·ter·nal *adj* 1 : having to do with brothers 2 : made up of members banded together like brothers

fra·ter·ni·ty *n, pl* **fra·ter·ni·ties** : a society of boys or men (as in a college)

fraud *n* 1 : TRICKERY, DECEIT 2 : an act of deceiving : TRICK 3 : a person who pretends to be what he or she is not

fraud·u·lent *adj* : based on or done by fraud — **fraud·u·lent·ly** *adv*

fraught *adj* : full of some quality

¹fray *n* : ²FIGHT 1, BRAWL

²fray *vb* : to wear into shreds

fraz·zle *n* : a tired or nervous condition

¹freak *n* : a strange, abnormal, or unusual person, thing, or event

²freak *adj* : being or suggesting a freak : IMPROBABLE

¹freck·le *n* : a small brownish spot on the skin

²freckle *vb* **freck·led; freck·ling** : to mark or become marked with freckles

¹free *adj* **fre·er; fre·est** 1 : having liberty : not being a slave 2 : not controlled by others 3 : released or not suffering from something unpleasant or painful 4 : given without charge 5 : not held back by fear or distrust : OPEN 6 : not blocked : CLEAR 7 : not combined — **free·ly** *adv*

²free *vb* **freed; free·ing** : to make or set free

³free *adv* 1 : in a free manner : FREELY 2 : without charge

freed·man *n, pl* **freed·men** : a person freed from slavery

free·dom *n* 1 : the condition of being free : LIBERTY, INDEPENDENCE 2 : ability to move or act freely 3 : the quality of being very frank : CANDOR 4 : free and unlimited use

free·hand *adj or adv* : done without mechanical aids

free·man *n, pl* **free·men** : a free person : one who is not a slave

free·stand·ing *adj* : standing alone or on its own foundation free of attachment or support

free·way *n* : an expressway that can be used without paying tolls

¹freeze *vb* **froze; fro·zen; freez·ing** 1 : to harden into or be hardened into a solid (as ice) by loss of heat 2 : to be or become uncomfortably cold 3 : to damage by cold 4 : to clog or become clogged by ice 5 : to become fixed or motionless

²freeze *n* 1 : a period of freezing weather : cold weather 2 : an act or instance of freezing 3 : the state of being frozen

freez·er *n* : a compartment or room used to freeze food or keep it frozen

freezing point *n* : the temperature at which a liquid becomes solid

¹freight *n* 1 : the amount paid (as to a shipping company) for carrying goods 2 : goods or cargo carried by a ship, train, truck, or airplane 3 : the carrying (as by truck) of goods from one place to another 4 : a train that carries freight

²freight *vb* : to send by freight

freight·er *n* : a ship or airplane used to carry freight

¹French *adj* : of or relating to France, its people, or the French language

²French *n* 1 **French** *pl* : the people of France 2 : the language of the French

french fry *n, often cap 1st F* : a strip of potato fried in deep fat

French horn *n* : a circular brass musical instrument with a large opening at one end and a mouthpiece shaped like a small funnel

fren·zied *adj* : very excited and upset

fren·zy *n, pl* **frenzies** : great and often wild or disorderly activity

fre·quen·cy *n, pl* **fre·quen·cies** 1 : frequent repetition 2 : rate of repetition

¹fre·quent *vb* : to visit often

²fre·quent *adj* : happening often — **fre·quent·ly** *adv*

fresh *adj* 1 : not salt 2 : PURE 1, BRISK 3 : not frozen, canned, or pickled 4 : not stale, sour, or spoiled 5 : not dirty or rumpled 6 : NEW 6 7 : newly made or received 8 : IMPUDENT — **fresh·ly** *adv* — **fresh·ness** *n*

fresh·en *vb* : to make or become fresh

fresh·et *n* : a sudden overflowing of a stream

fresh·man *n, pl* **fresh·men** : a first year student (as in college)

fresh·wa·ter *adj* : of, relating to, or living in fresh water

¹fret *vb* **fret·ted; fret·ting** : to make or become worried

²fret *n* : an irritated or worried state

³fret *n* : a design of short lines or bars

⁴fret *n* : one of a series of ridges fixed across the fingerboard of a stringed musical instrument — **fret·ted** *adj*

fret·ful *adj* : likely to fret : IRRITABLE — **fret·ful·ly** *adv* — **fret·ful·ness** *n*

fri·ar *n* : a member of a Roman Catholic religious order for men

fric·tion *n*   **1** : the rubbing of one thing against another   **2** : resistance to motion between bodies in contact   **3** : disagreement among persons or groups

Fri·day *n* : the sixth day of the week

friend *n*   **1** : a person who has a strong liking for and trust in another person   **2** : a person who is not an enemy   **3** : a person who aids or favors something — **friend·less** *adj*

friend·ly *adj* **friend·li·er; friend·li·est**   **1** : showing friendship   **2** : being other than an enemy — **friend·li·ness** *n*

friend·ship *n* : the state of being friends

frieze *n* : a band or stripe (as around a building) used as a decoration

frig·ate *n*   **1** : a square-rigged warship   **2** : a modern warship that is smaller than a destroyer

fright *n*   **1** : sudden terror : great fear   **2** : something that frightens or is ugly or shocking

fright·en *vb* : to make afraid : TERRIFY — **fright·en·ing·ly** *adv*

fright·ful *adj*   **1** : causing fear or alarm   **2** : SHOCKING, OUTRAGEOUS — **fright·ful·ly** *adv* — **fright·ful·ness** *n*

frig·id *adj*   **1** : freezing cold   **2** : not friendly — **frig·id·ly** *adv* — **frig·id·ness** *n*

frill *n*   **1** : ²RUFFLE   **2** : something added mostly for show

frilly *adj* **frill·i·er; frill·i·est** : having frills

¹fringe *n*   **1** : a border or trimming made by or made to look like the loose ends of the cloth   **2** : something suggesting a fringe

²fringe *vb* **fringed; fring·ing**   **1** : to decorate with a fringe   **2** : to serve as a fringe for

frisk *vb* : to move around in a lively or playful way

frisky *adj* **frisk·i·er; frisk·i·est** : tending to frisk : PLAYFUL, LIVELY

¹frit·ter *n* : a small amount of fried batter often containing fruit or meat

²fritter *vb* : to waste on unimportant things

friv·o·lous *adj*   **1** : of little importance : TRIVIAL   **2** : lacking in seriousness : PLAYFUL

frizzy *adj* **frizz·i·er; frizz·i·est** : very curly

fro *adv* : in a direction away

frock *n* : a woman's or girl's dress

frog *n*   **1** : a tailless animal with smooth skin and webbed feet that spends more of its time in water than the related toad   **2** : an ornamental fastening for a garment — **frog in one's throat** : HOARSENESS

frog·man *n, pl* **frog·men** : a swimmer equipped to work underwater for long periods of time

¹frol·ic *vb* **frol·icked; frol·ick·ing** : to play about happily : ROMP

²frolic *n* : FUN 1, GAIETY

frol·ic·some *adj* : given to frolic : PLAYFUL

from *prep*   **1** — used to show a starting point   **2** — used to show a point of separation   **3** — used to show a material, source, or cause

frond *n* : a large leaf (as of a palm or fern) with many divisions or something like such a leaf

¹front *n*   **1** : a region in which active warfare is taking place   **2** : the forward part or surface   **3** : the boundary between bodies of air at different temperatures

²front *vb* : ²FACE 2

³front *adj* : of, relating to, or situated at the front

fron·tal *adj* : of, relating to, or directed at the front

fron·tier *n*   **1** : a border between two countries   **2** : the edge of the settled part of a country

fron·tiers·man *n, pl* **fron·tiers·men** : a person living on the frontier

¹frost *n*   **1** : temperature cold enough to cause freezing   **2** : a covering of tiny ice crystals on a cold surface formed from the water vapor in the air

²frost *vb* : to cover with frost or with something suggesting frost

frost·bite *n* : slight freezing of a part of the body or the effect of this

frost·ing *n*   **1** : ICING   **2** : a dull finish on glass

frosty *adj* **frost·i·er; frost·i·est**   **1** : cold enough to produce frost   **2** : covered with or appearing to be covered with frost — **frost·i·ly** *adv* — **frost·i·ness** *n*

¹froth *n* : bubbles formed in or on liquids

²froth *vb* : to produce or form froth

frothy *adj* **froth·i·er; froth·i·est** : full of or made up of froth — **froth·i·ness** *n*

¹frown *vb*   **1** : to wrinkle the forehead (as in anger or thought)   **2** : to look with disapproval

²frown *n* : a wrinkling of the brow

froze *past of* FREEZE

frozen *past participle of* FREEZE

fru·gal *adj* : careful in spending or using resources — **fru·gal·ly** *adv*

¹fruit *n* **1** : a pulpy or juicy plant part (as rhubarb or a strawberry) that is often eaten as a dessert and is distinguished from a vegetable **2** : a reproductive body of a seed plant that consists of the ripened ovary of a flower with its included seeds **3** : ²RESULT 1, PRODUCT — **fruit·ed** *adj*

²fruit *vb* : to bear or cause to bear fruit

fruit·cake *n* : a rich cake containing nuts, dried or candied fruits, and spices

fruit·ful *adj* **1** : very productive **2** : bringing results — **fruit·ful·ly** *adv* — **fruit·ful·ness** *n*

fruit·less *adj* **1** : not bearing fruit **2** : UNSUCCESSFUL — **fruit·less·ly** *adv* — **fruit·less·ness** *n*

fruity *adj* **fruit·i·er; fruit·i·est** : relating to or suggesting fruit

frus·trate *vb* **frus·trat·ed; frus·trat·ing 1** : to prevent from carrying out a purpose **2** : ¹DEFEAT 1 **3** : DISCOURAGE 1

frus·tra·tion *n* : DISAPPOINTMENT 2, DEFEAT

¹fry *vb* **fried; fry·ing** : to cook in fat

²fry *n, pl* **fry 1** : recently hatched or very young fishes **2** : persons of a particular group

fudge *n* : a soft creamy candy often containing nuts

¹fu·el *n* : a substance (as oil) that can be burned to produce heat or power

²fuel *vb* **fu·eled** *or* **fu·elled; fu·el·ing** *or* **fu·el·ling** : to supply with or take on fuel

¹fu·gi·tive *adj* : running away or trying to escape

²fugitive *n* : a person who is running away

¹-ful *adj suffix* **1** : full of **2** : characterized by **3** : having the qualities of **4** : -ABLE

²-ful *n suffix* : number or quantity that fills or would fill

ful·crum *n, pl* **fulcrums** *or* **ful·cra** : the support on which a lever turns in lifting something

ful·fill *or* **ful·fil** *vb* **ful·filled; ful·fill·ing 1** : ACCOMPLISH **2** : SATISFY 1 — **ful·fill·ment** *n*

¹full *adj* **1** : containing as much as possible or normal **2** : ¹COMPLETE 1 **3** : plump and rounded in outline **4** : having much material — **full·ness** *n*

²full *adv* **1** : ²VERY 1 **2** : COMPLETELY

³full *n* **1** : the highest state, extent, or degree **2** : the complete amount

full moon *n* : the moon with its whole disk lighted

ful·ly *adv* **1** : COMPLETELY **2** : at least

¹fum·ble *vb* **fum·bled; fum·bling** : to feel about for or handle something clumsily

²fumble *n* : an act of fumbling

¹fume *n* : a disagreeable smoke, vapor, or gas — usually used in pl.

²fume *vb* **fumed; fum·ing 1** : to give off fumes **2** : to show bad temper : be angry

fu·mi·gate *vb* **fu·mi·gat·ed; fu·mi·gat·ing** : to disinfect by exposing to smoke, vapor, or gas

fun *n* **1** : someone or something that provides amusement or enjoyment **2** : a good time : AMUSEMENT **3** : words or actions to make someone or something an object of unkind laughter

¹func·tion *n* **1** : the action for which a person or thing is specially fitted or used : PURPOSE **2** : a large important ceremony or social affair

²function *vb* : to serve a certain purpose : WORK

function key *n* : any of a set of keys on a computer keyboard that have or can be programmed to have special functions

fund *n* **1** : ¹STOCK 4, SUPPLY **2** : a sum of money for a special purpose **3 funds** *pl* : available money

¹fun·da·men·tal *adj* : being or forming a foundation : BASIC, ESSENTIAL — **fun·da·men·tal·ly** *adv*

²fundamental *n* : a basic part

fu·ner·al *n* : the ceremonies held for a dead person (as before burial)

fun·gi·cide *n* : a substance used to kill fungi — **fun·gi·cid·al** *adj*

fun·gous *or* **fun·gal** *adj* : of, relating to, or caused by fungi

fun·gus *n, pl* **fun·gi** *also* **fun·gus·es** : any of a group of plantlike organisms (as mushrooms, molds, and rusts) that have no chlorophyll and must live on other plants or animals or on decaying material

fun·nel *n* **1** : a utensil usually shaped like a hollow cone with a tube extending from the point and used to catch and direct a downward flow (as of liquid) **2** : a large pipe for the escape of smoke or for ventilation (as on a ship)

fun·nies *n pl* : comic strips or a section containing comic strips (as in a newspaper)

fun·ny *adj* **fun·ni·er; fun·ni·est 1** : causing laughter **2** : STRANGE 3

fur *n* **1** : a piece of the pelt of an animal **2** : an article of clothing made with fur **3** : the hairy coat of a mammal especially when fine, soft, and thick — **furred** *adj*

fu·ri·ous *adj* **1** : very angry **2** : very active : VIOLENT — **fu·ri·ous·ly** *adv*

furl *vb* : to wrap or roll close to or around something

fur·long *n* : a unit of length equal to 220 yards (about 201 meters)

fur·lough *n* : a leave of absence from duty

fur·nace *n* : an enclosed structure in which heat is produced (as for heating a house or for melting metals)

fur·nish *vb* 1 : to provide with what is needed 2 : to supply to someone or something

fur·nish·ings *n pl* : articles of furniture for a room or building

fur·ni·ture *n* : movable articles used to furnish a room

fur·ri·er *n* : a dealer in furs

¹fur·row *n* 1 : a trench made by or as if by a plow 2 : a narrow groove : WRINKLE

²furrow *vb* : to make furrows in

fur·ry *adj* **fur·ri·er; fur·ri·est** 1 : like fur 2 : covered with fur

¹fur·ther *adv* 1 : ¹FARTHER 1 2 : ²BESIDES, ALSO 3 : to a greater degree or extent

²further *vb* : to help forward : PROMOTE

³further *adj* 1 : ²FARTHER 2 : going or extending beyond : ADDITIONAL

fur·ther·more *adv* : MOREOVER

fur·ther·most *adj* : most distant : FARTHEST

fur·thest *adv or adj* : FARTHEST

fur·tive *adj* : done in a sneaky or sly manner — **fur·tive·ly** *adv* — **fur·tive·ness** *n*

fu·ry *n, pl* **furies** 1 : violent anger : RAGE 2 : wild and dangerous force

¹fuse *vb* **fused; fus·ing** 1 : to change into a liquid or to a plastic state by heat 2 : to unite by or as if by melting together

²fuse *n* : a device having a metal wire or strip that melts and interrupts an electrical circuit when the current becomes too strong

³fuse *n* 1 : a cord that is set afire to ignite an explosive by carrying fire to it 2 *usually* **fuze** : a device for setting off a bomb or torpedo

fu·se·lage *n* : the central body part of an airplane that holds the crew, passengers, and cargo

fu·sion *n* 1 : a fusing or melting together 2 : union by or as if by melting 3 : union of atomic nuclei to form heavier nuclei resulting in the release of enormous quantities of energy

¹fuss *n* 1 : unnecessary activity or excitement often over something unimportant 2 : ¹PROTEST 2 3 : a great show of interest

²fuss *vb* : to make a fuss

fussy *adj* **fuss·i·er; fuss·i·est** 1 : inclined to complain or whine 2 : needing much attention to details 3 : hard to please

fu·tile *adj* : having no result or effect : USELESS — **fu·tile·ly** *adv* — **fu·tile·ness** *n*

fu·til·i·ty *n* : the quality or state of being futile

¹fu·ture *adj* : coming after the present

²future *n* 1 : future time 2 : the chance of future success

fuze *variant of* FUSE

fuzz *n* : fine light particles or fibers

fuzzy *adj* **fuzz·i·er; fuzz·i·est** 1 : covered with or looking like fuzz 2 : not clear — **fuzz·i·ly** *adv* — **fuzz·i·ness** *n*

-fy *vb suffix* **-fied; -fy·ing** 1 : make : form into 2 : make similar to

G

g *n, pl* **g's** *or* **gs** *often cap* 1 : the seventh letter of the English alphabet 2 : a unit of force equal to the weight of a body on which the force acts

¹gab *vb* **gabbed; gab·bing** : to talk in an idle way

²gab *n* : idle talk : CHATTER

gab·ar·dine *n* : a firm cloth with diagonal ribs and a hard smooth finish

¹gab·ble *vb* **gab·bled; gab·bling** : ¹CHATTER 2

²gabble *n* : loud or fast talk that has no meaning

gab·by *adj* **gab·bi·er; gab·bi·est** : given to talking a lot : TALKATIVE

ga·ble *n* : the triangular part of an outside wall of a building formed by the sides of the roof sloping down from the ridgepole to the eaves

gad *vb* **gad·ded; gad·ding** : to roam about : WANDER

gad·about *n* : a person who goes from place to place without much reason

gad·fly *n, pl* **gad·flies** 1 : a large biting fly 2 : a person who is an annoying pest

gad·get *n* : an interesting, unfamiliar, or unusual device

gaff *n* 1 : an iron hook with a handle 2 : something hard to take

¹gag *vb* **gagged; gag·ging** 1 : to keep from speaking or crying out by or as if by stopping up the mouth 2 : to cause to feel like vomiting : RETCH

²gag *n* 1 : something that gags 2 : ¹JOKE 1, 2

gage *variant of* GAUGE

gai·ety *n, pl* **gai·eties** 1 : MERRYMAKING 1 2 : bright spirits or manner

gai·ly *adv* 1 : in a merry or lively way 2 : in a bright or showy way

¹gain *n* 1 : advantage gained or increased : PROFIT 2 : an increase in amount, size, or degree

²gain *vb* **1** : to get hold of often by effort or with difficulty : WIN **2** : to get to : REACH **3** : to get advantage : PROFIT — **gain·er** *n*
gain·ful *adj* : producing gain
gait *n* : way of walking or running
¹ga·la *n* : a large showy entertainment celebrating a special occasion
²gala *adj* : of or being a gala
ga·lac·tic *adj* : of or relating to a galaxy
gal·axy *n, pl* **gal·ax·ies** **1** : MILKY WAY GALAXY **2** : one of billions of collections of stars, gas, and dust that make up the universe
gale *n* **1** : a strong wind **2** : a wind of from about fourteen to twenty-four meters per second **3** : OUTBURST 1
ga·le·na *n* : a bluish gray mineral that is the main ore of lead
¹gall *n* **1** : bile especially when obtained from an animal and used in the arts or medicine **2** : insolent boldness
²gall *n* : a sore spot (as on a horse's back) caused by rubbing
³gall *vb* **1** : to make sore by rubbing **2** : IR-RITATE 1
⁴gall *n* : a swelling or growth on a twig or leaf
gal·lant *adj* **1** : showing no fear : BRAVE **2** : CHIVALROUS 2, NOBLE **3** : very polite to women
gal·lant·ry *n* **1** : polite attention shown to women **2** : COURAGE, BRAVERY
gall·blad·der *n* : a small sac in which bile from the liver is stored
gal·le·on *n* : a large sailing ship of the time of Columbus and later
gal·lery *n, pl* **gal·ler·ies** **1** : a long narrow room or hall usually with windows along one side **2** : an indoor structure (as in a theater or church) built out from one or more walls **3** : a room or hall used for a special purpose (as showing pictures)
gal·ley *n, pl* **galleys** **1** : a large low ship of olden times moved by oars and sails **2** : the kitchen of a ship
galley slave *n* : a person forced to row on a galley
gal·li·vant *vb* : GAD
gal·lon *n* : a unit of liquid capacity equal to four quarts (about 3.8 liters)
¹gal·lop *vb* : to go or cause to go at a gallop
²gallop *n* **1** : a fast springing way of running of an animal with four feet and especially a horse **2** : a ride or run at a gallop
gal·lows *n, pl* **gallows** *or* **gal·lows·es** : a structure from which criminals are hanged
ga·losh *n* : an overshoe worn in snow or wet weather
gal·va·nize *vb* **gal·va·nized; gal·va·niz·ing** **1** : to excite or stir by or as if by an electric shock **2** : to coat with zinc for protection

¹gam·ble *vb* **gam·bled; gam·bling** **1** : to play a game in which something (as money) is risked : BET **2** : to take risks on the chance of gain : take a chance
²gamble *n* : something that is risky to do
gam·bler *n* : a person who gambles
gam·bol *vb* **gam·boled** *or* **gam·bolled; gam·bol·ing** *or* **gam·bol·ling** : to run or skip about playfully : FROLIC
¹game *n* **1** : AMUSEMENT, PLAY **2** : a contest carried on according to rules with the players in direct opposition to each other **3** : animals hunted for sport or for food **4** : the meat from game animals
²game *adj* **gam·er; gam·est** **1** : full of spirit or eagerness **2** : of or relating to animals that are hunted
game·cock *n* : a rooster trained for fighting
game·keep·er *n* : a person in charge of the breeding and protection of game animals or birds on private land
game·ly *adv* : with spirit and courage
game·ness *n* : the quality or state of being spirited and courageous
game show *n* : a television program on which contestants compete for prizes in a game (as a quiz)
game warden *n* : a person who sees that fishing and hunting laws are obeyed
gam·ing *n* : the practice of gambling
gam·ma rays *n pl* : very penetrating rays like X rays but of shorter wavelength
gamy *adj* **gam·i·er; gam·i·est** : having the flavor of wild game especially when slightly spoiled
gan·der *n* : a male goose
gang *n* **1** : a group of persons working or going about together **2** : a group of persons acting together to do something illegal
gan·gli·on *n, pl* **gan·glia** : a mass of nerve cells especially outside the brain or spinal cord
gang·plank *n* : a movable bridge from a ship to the shore
gan·grene *n* : death of body tissue when the blood supply is cut off
gang·ster *n* : a member of a gang of criminals
gang·way *n* **1** : a way into, through, or out of an enclosed space **2** : GANGPLANK
gan·net *n* : a large bird that eats fish and spends much time far from land
gan·try *n, pl* **gantries** **1** : a structure over railroad tracks for holding signals **2** : a movable structure for preparing a rocket for launching
gap *n* **1** : an opening made by a break or a coming apart **2** : an opening between mountains **3** : a hole or space where something is missing

¹gape vb **gaped; gap·ing 1** : to open the mouth wide **2** : to stare with open mouth **3** : to open or part widely

²gape n : an act or instance of gaping

¹ga·rage n : a building where automobiles or trucks are repaired or kept when not in use

²garage vb **ga·raged; ga·rag·ing** : to keep or put in a garage

¹garb n : style or kind of clothing

²garb vb : CLOTHE 1

gar·bage n : waste food especially from a kitchen

gar·ble vb **gar·bled; gar·bling** : to change or twist the meaning or sound of

¹gar·den n **1** : a piece of ground in which fruits, flowers, or vegetables are grown **2** : an enclosure for the public showing of plants or animals

²garden vb : to make or work in a garden

gar·den·er n : a person who gardens especially for pay

gar·de·nia n : a large white or yellowish flower with a fragrant smell

¹gar·gle vb **gar·gled; gar·gling** : to rinse the throat with a liquid kept in motion by air forced through it from the lungs

²gargle n **1** : a liquid used in gargling **2** : a gargling sound

gar·goyle n : a waterspout in the form of a strange or frightening human or animal figure sticking out at the roof or eaves of a building

gar·ish adj : too bright or showy : GAUDY

¹gar·land n : a wreath or rope of leaves or flowers

²garland vb : to form into or decorate with a garland

gar·lic n : a plant related to the onion and grown for its bulbs that have a strong smell and taste and are used to flavor foods

gar·ment n : an article of clothing

gar·ner vb : to gather in and store

gar·net n : a deep red mineral used as a gem

¹gar·nish vb : to add decorations or seasoning (as to food)

²garnish n : something used in garnishing

gar·ret n : a room or unfinished part of a house just under the roof

¹gar·ri·son n : a place in which troops are regularly stationed

²garrison vb **1** : to station troops in **2** : to send (troops) to a garrison

gar·ter n : a band worn to hold up a stocking or sock

garter snake n : any of numerous harmless American snakes with stripes along the back

¹gas n, pl **gas·es 1** : a substance (as oxygen or hydrogen) having no fixed shape and tending to expand without limit **2** : a gas or a mixture of gases used as a fuel or to make one unconscious (as for an operation) **3** : a fluid that poisons the air or makes breathing difficult **4** : GASOLINE

²gas vb **gassed; gas·sing; gas·ses 1** : to treat with gas **2** : to poison with gas **3** : to supply with gas

gas·eous adj : of or relating to gas

¹gash n : a long deep cut

²gash vb : to make a long deep cut in

gas mask n : a mask connected to a chemical air filter and used to protect the face and lungs from poisonous gases

gas·o·line n : a flammable liquid made especially from gas found in the earth and from petroleum and used mostly as an automobile fuel

¹gasp vb **1** : to breathe with difficulty : PANT **2** : to utter with quick difficult breaths

²gasp n **1** : the act of gasping **2** : something gasped

gas station n : SERVICE STATION

gas·tric juice n : an acid liquid made by the stomach that helps to digest food

gate n **1** : an opening in a wall or fence often with a movable frame or door for closing it **2** : a part of a barrier (as a fence) that opens and closes like a door

¹gath·er vb **1** : to bring or come together **2** : to pick out and collect **3** : to gain little by little **4** : to get an idea : CONCLUDE **5** : to draw together in folds

²gather n : the result of gathering cloth : PUCKER

gath·er·ing n : a coming together of people : MEETING

gau·cho n, pl **gauchos** : a South American cowboy

gaudy adj **gaud·i·er; gaud·i·est** : too showy

¹gauge or **gage** n **1** : measurement according to a standard **2** : SIZE 2 **3** : an instrument for measuring, testing, or registering

²gauge or **gage** vb **gauged** or **gaged; gaug·ing** or **gag·ing 1** : to measure exactly **2** : to find out the capacity or contents of **3** : ¹ESTIMATE 1, JUDGE

gaunt adj : very thin and bony (as from illness or starvation)

¹gaunt·let n **1** : a glove made of small metal plates and worn with a suit of armor **2** : a glove with a wide cuff that covers and protects the wrist and part of the arm

²gauntlet n : a double file of persons who beat someone forced to run between them

gauze n : a thin transparent fabric

gauzy adj **gauz·i·er; gauz·i·est** : thin and transparent like gauze

gave past of GIVE

gav·el n : a mallet with which the person in

charge raps to call a meeting or court to order

gawk *vb* : to stare stupidly

gawky *adj* **gawk·i·er; gawk·i·est** : AWKWARD 1, CLUMSY — **gawk·i·ly** *adv* — **gawk·i·ness** *n*

gay *adj* **gay·er; gay·est** 1 : MERRY 2 : brightly colored

¹**gaze** *vb* **gazed; gaz·ing** : to fix the eyes in a long steady look

²**gaze** *n* : a long steady look

ga·zelle *n* : a swift graceful antelope with large bright eyes

ga·zette *n* 1 : NEWSPAPER 2 : a journal giving official information

gaz·et·teer *n* : a geographical dictionary

ga·zil·lion *n* : a large number — **gazillion** *adj*

¹**gear** *n* 1 : EQUIPMENT 2 2 : a group of parts that has a specific function in a machine 3 : a toothed wheel : COGWHEEL 4 : the position the gears of a machine are in when they are ready to work 5 : one of the adjustments in a motor vehicle that determine the direction of travel and the relative speed between the engine and the motion of the vehicle

²**gear** *vb* 1 : to make ready for operation 2 : to make suitable

gear·shift *n* : a mechanism by which gears are connected and disconnected

gee *interj* — used to show surprise or enthusiasm

geese *pl of* GOOSE

Gei·ger counter *n* : an instrument for detecting the presence of cosmic rays or radioactive substances

gel·a·tin *n* 1 : a protein obtained by boiling animal tissues and used especially as food 2 : an edible jelly formed with gelatin

gem *n* : a usually valuable stone cut and polished for jewelry

Gem·i·ni *n* 1 : a constellation between Taurus and Cancer imagined as twins 2 : the third sign of the zodiac or a person born under this sign

gen·der *n* : SEX 1

gene *n* : a unit of DNA that controls the development of a single characteristic in an individual

genera *pl of* GENUS

¹**gen·er·al** *adj* 1 : having to do with the whole 2 : not specific or detailed 3 : not specialized

²**general** *n* : a commissioned officer in the Army, Air Force, or Marine Corps ranking above a lieutenant general

gen·er·al·iza·tion *n* 1 : the act of generalizing 2 : a general statement

gen·er·al·ize *vb* **gen·er·al·ized; gen·er·al·iz·ing** : to put in the form of a general rule : draw or state a general conclusion from a number of different items or instances

gen·er·al·ly *adv* : as a rule : USUALLY

General of the Air Force : the highest ranking commissioned officer in the Air Force ranking above a general

General of the Army : the highest ranking commissioned officer in the Army ranking above a general

gen·er·ate *vb* **gen·er·at·ed; gen·er·at·ing** : to cause to come into being

gen·er·a·tion *n* 1 : those having the same parents and being a step in a line from one ancestor 2 : a group of individuals born about the same time 3 : the act of generating something

gen·er·a·tor *n* : DYNAMO

gen·er·os·i·ty *n, pl* **gen·er·os·i·ties** 1 : willingness to give or to share 2 : a generous act

gen·er·ous *adj* 1 : free in giving or sharing 2 : ABUNDANT — **gen·er·ous·ly** *adv*

gen·e·sis *n, pl* **gen·e·ses** : a coming into being

ge·net·ic *adj* : of or relating to genetics

genetic code *n* : the arrangement of chemical groups within the genes by which genetic information is passed on

ge·net·i·cist *n* : a specialist in genetics

ge·net·ics *n* : a branch of biology that deals with the heredity and variation of living things

ge·nial *adj* : pleasantly cheerful — **ge·nial·ly** *adv*

ge·nie *n* : a magic spirit believed to take human form and serve the person who calls it

gen·i·tal *adj* : of or relating to reproduction or sex

ge·nius *n* 1 : great natural ability 2 : a very gifted person

gen·tian *n* : an herb with smooth opposite leaves and usually blue flowers

¹**gen·tile** *n, often cap* : a person who is not Jewish

²**gentile** *adj, often cap* : of or relating to people not Jewish

gen·til·i·ty *n* 1 : good birth and family 2 : the qualities of a well-bred person 3 : good manners

gen·tle *adj* **gen·tler; gen·tlest** 1 : easily handled : not wild 2 : not harsh or stern : MILD 3 : ¹MODERATE 1 — **gen·tle·ness** *n*

gen·tle·folk *n pl* : GENTRY 1

gen·tle·man *n, pl* **gen·tle·men** 1 : a man of good birth and position 2 : a man of good education and social position 3 : a man with very good manners 4 : MAN — used in the plural when speaking to a group of men — **gen·tle·man·ly** *adj*

gen·tle·wom·an *n, pl* **gen·tle·wom·en** 1 : a woman of good birth and position 2 : a woman with very good manners : LADY 2

gen·tly *adv* : in a gentle manner

gen·try *n* 1 : people of good birth, breeding, and education 2 : people of a certain class

gen·u·flect *vb* : to kneel on one knee and rise again as an act of deep respect

gen·u·ine *adj* 1 : being just what it seems to be : REAL 2 : HONEST 1, SINCERE — **gen·u·ine·ly** *adv* — **gen·u·ine·ness** *n*

ge·nus *n, pl* **gen·era** : a group of related plants or animals that ranks below the family in scientific classification and is made up of one or more species

geo- *prefix* 1 : earth 2 : geographical

geo·chem·is·try *n* : chemistry that deals with the earth's crust

geo·graph·ic *or* **geo·graph·i·cal** *adj* : of or relating to geography

ge·og·ra·phy *n* 1 : a science that deals with the location of living and nonliving things on earth and the way they affect one another 2 : the natural features of an area

geo·log·ic *or* **geo·log·i·cal** *adj* : of or relating to geology

ge·ol·o·gist *n* : a specialist in geology

ge·ol·o·gy *n* 1 : a science that deals with the history of the earth and its life especially as recorded in rocks 2 : the geologic features (as mountains or plains) of an area

geo·mag·net·ic *adj* : of or relating to the magnetism of the earth

geo·met·ric *adj* : of or relating to geometry

ge·om·e·try *n* : a branch of mathematics that deals with points, lines, angles, surfaces, and solids

ge·ra·ni·um *n* : an herb often grown for its bright flowers

ger·bil *n* : a small Old World leaping desert rodent

germ *n* 1 : a bit of living matter capable of forming a new individual 2 : a source from which something develops 3 : a microbe that causes disease

¹Ger·man *n* 1 : a person born or living in Germany 2 : the language spoken mainly in Germany, Austria, and parts of Switzerland

²German *adj* : of or relating to Germany, the Germans, or the German language

ger·ma·ni·um *n* : a white hard brittle element used as a semiconductor

germ cell *n* : a reproductive cell (as an egg or sperm cell)

ger·mi·cide *n* : a substance that destroys germs

ger·mi·nate *vb* **ger·mi·nat·ed; ger·mi·nat·ing** : ¹SPROUT

ger·mi·na·tion *n* : a beginning of development (as of a seed)

ges·tic·u·late *vb* **ges·tic·u·lat·ed; ges·tic·u·lat·ing** : to make gestures especially when speaking

¹ges·ture *n* 1 : a motion of the limbs or body that expresses an idea or a feeling 2 : something said or done that shows one's feelings

²gesture *vb* **ges·tured; ges·tur·ing** : to make or direct with a gesture

get *vb* **got; got** *or* **got·ten; get·ting** 1 : to gain possession of (as by receiving, earning, buying, or winning) 2 : ARRIVE 1 3 : GO 1, MOVE 4 : BECOME 1 5 : ¹CATCH 7 6 : to cause to be 7 : UNDERSTAND 1 8 : PERSUADE — **get ahead** : to achieve success (as in business) — **get around** 1 : to get the better of 2 : EVADE — **get at** 1 : to reach with or as if with the hand 2 : to turn one's attention to 3 : to try to prove or make clear — **get away with** : to do (as something wrong) without being caught — **get back at** : to get even with — **get even** : to get revenge — **get even with** : to pay back for a real or imagined injury — **get one's goat** : to make one angry or annoyed — **get over** : to recover from — **get together** 1 : to bring or come together 2 : to reach agreement — **get wind of** : to become aware of : hear about

get along *vb* 1 : to approach old age 2 : to meet one's needs 3 : to stay friendly

get by *vb* 1 : GET ALONG 2 2 : to succeed with the least possible effort or accomplishment

get off *vb* 1 : START 2 : to escape punishment or harm

get out *vb* 1 : ESCAPE 2 : to become known

get–to·geth·er *n* : an informal social gathering

get up *vb* 1 : to arise from bed 2 : to rise to one's feet 3 : PREPARE, ORGANIZE 4 : DRESS

gey·ser *n* : a spring that now and then shoots up hot water and steam

ghast·ly *adj* **ghast·li·er; ghast·li·est** 1 : HORRIBLE, SHOCKING 2 : like a ghost : PALE

ghet·to *n, pl* **ghettos** *or* **ghettoes** : a part of a city in which members of a minority group live because of social, legal, or economic pressure

ghost *n* : the spirit of a dead person thought of as living in an unseen world or as appearing to living people

ghost·ly *adj* **ghost·li·er; ghost·li·est** : of, relating to, or like a ghost

ghost town *n* : a town deserted because some nearby natural resource has been used up

ghoul *n* **1** : an evil being of legend that robs graves and feeds on corpses **2** : someone whose activities suggest those of a ghoul

¹gi·ant *n* **1** : an imaginary person of great size and strength **2** : a person or thing that is very large or powerful

²giant *adj* : much larger than ordinary : HUGE

giant panda *n* : a large black-and-white mammal of the bear family found mainly in central China

gib·ber·ish *n* : confused meaningless talk

gib·bon *n* : a small ape of southeastern Asia that has long arms and legs and lives mostly in trees

¹gibe *or* **jibe** *vb* **gibed; gib·ing** : ¹JEER

²gibe *or* **jibe** *n* : ²JEER

gib·let *n* : an edible inner organ (as the heart or liver) of a fowl

gid·dy *adj* **gid·di·er; gid·di·est** **1** : having a feeling of whirling or spinning about : DIZZY **2** : causing dizziness **3** : SILLY **3** — **gid·di·ness** *n*

gift *n* **1** : a special ability : TALENT **2** : something given : PRESENT

gift·ed *adj* : having great ability

gig *n* **1** : a long light boat for a ship's captain **2** : a light carriage having two wheels and pulled by a horse

giga·byte *n* : a unit of computer information storage capacity equal to 1,073,741,824 bytes

gi·gan·tic *adj* : like a giant (as in size, weight, or strength)

gig·gle *vb* **gig·gled; gig·gling** : to laugh with repeated short high sounds

Gi·la monster *n* : a large black and orange poisonous lizard of the southwestern United States

gild *vb* **gild·ed** *or* **gilt; gild·ing** : to cover with a thin coating of gold

¹gill *n* : a unit of liquid capacity equal to a quarter of a pint (about 120 milliliters)

²gill *n* : an organ (as of a fish) for taking oxygen from water

¹gilt *n* : gold or something like gold applied to a surface

²gilt *n* : a young female hog

gim·let *n* : a small tool for boring

¹gin *n* : a machine to separate seeds from cotton

²gin *vb* **ginned; gin·ning** : to separate seeds from cotton in a gin

³gin *n* : a strong alcoholic liquor flavored with juniper berries

gin·ger *n* : a hot spice obtained from the root

of a tropical plant and used to season foods (as cookies) or in medicine

ginger ale *n* : a soft drink flavored with ginger

gin·ger·bread *n* : a dark cake flavored with ginger and molasses

gin·ger·ly *adv* : with great caution or care

gin·ger·snap *n* : a thin brittle cookie flavored with ginger

ging·ham *n* : a cotton cloth in plain weave

gipsy *variant of* GYPSY

gi·raffe *n* : a spotted mammal of Africa that has a long neck and chews the cud

gird *vb* **gird·ed** *or* **girt; gird·ing** : to encircle or fasten with or as if with a belt or cord

gird·er *n* : a horizontal main supporting beam

¹gir·dle *n* **1** : something (as a belt or sash) that encircles or binds **2** : a light corset worn below the waist

²girdle *vb* **gir·dled; gir·dling** **1** : to bind with or as if with a girdle, belt, or sash : ENCIRCLE **2** : to strip a ring of bark from a tree trunk

girl *n* **1** : a female child or young woman **2** : a female servant **3** : GIRLFRIEND

girl·friend *n* **1** : a female friend **2** : a regular female companion of a boy or man

girl·hood *n* : the state or time of being a girl

girl·ish *adj* : of, relating to, or having qualities often felt to be typical of a girl — **girl·ish·ly** *adv* — **girl·ish·ness** *n*

Girl Scout *n* : a member of the Girl Scouts of the United States of America

girth *n* **1** : a band put around the body of an animal to hold something (as a saddle) on its back **2** : the measure or distance around something

gist *n* : the main point of a matter

¹give *vb* **gave; giv·en; giv·ing** **1** : to hand over to be kept : PRESENT **2** : ¹PAY 1 **3** : ²UTTER **4** : FURNISH, PROVIDE **5** : to cause to have **6** : to let someone or something have **7** : to yield slightly **8** : to yield as a product : PRODUCE — **give way** **1** : to yield oneself without control **2** : to break down : COLLAPSE

²give *n* : the quality of being able to bend under pressure

give in *vb* **1** : ¹OFFER 2 **2** : ¹SURRENDER 1, YIELD

giv·en *adj* **1** : being likely to have or do something **2** : decided on beforehand

given name *n* : a first name (as *John* or *Susan*)

give up *vb* **1** : to let go : ABANDON **2** : to stop trying : QUIT

giz·zard *n* : a large muscular part of the

digestive tube (as of a bird) in which food is churned and ground small

gla·cial *adj* **1** : very cold **2** : of or relating to glaciers

gla·cier *n* : a large body of ice moving slowly down a slope or over a wide area of land

glad *adj* **glad·der; glad·dest 1** : being happy and joyful **2** : bringing or causing joy **3** : very willing — **glad·ly** *adv* — **glad·ness** *n*

glad·den *vb* : to make glad

glade *n* : a grassy open space in a forest

glad·i·a·tor *n* : a person taking part in a fight to the death as public entertainment for the ancient Romans

glad·i·o·lus *n, pl* **glad·i·o·li** *or* **gladiolus** *or* **glad·i·o·lus·es** : a plant with long stiff pointed leaves and stalks of brightly colored flowers

glad·some *adj* : giving or showing joy

glam·or·ous *adj* : full of glamour

glam·our *or* **glam·or** *n* **1** : appeal or attractiveness especially when it is misleading **2** : tempting or fascinating personal attraction

¹**glance** *vb* **glanced; glanc·ing 1** : to strike at an angle and fly off to one side **2** : to give a quick look

²**glance** *n* : a quick look

gland *n* : an organ in the body that prepares a substance to be used by the body or given off from it

glan·du·lar *adj* : of or relating to glands

¹**glare** *vb* **glared; glar·ing 1** : to shine with a harsh bright light **2** : to look fiercely or angrily

²**glare** *n* **1** : a harsh bright light **2** : a fierce or angry look

glar·ing *adj* **1** : so bright as to be harsh **2** : ANGRY, FIERCE **3** : very noticeable : OBVIOUS

¹**glass** *n* **1** : a hard brittle usually transparent substance commonly made from sand heated with chemicals **2** : something made of glass **3 glasses** *pl* : EYEGLASS 2 **4** : the contents of a glass

²**glass** *vb* : to fit or protect with glass

glass·blow·ing *n* : the art of shaping a mass of melted glass by blowing air into it through a tube

glass·ful *n* : the amount a glass will hold

glass·ware *n* : articles of glass

glassy *adj* **glass·i·er; glass·i·est 1** : like glass (as in smoothness) **2** : not shiny or bright : DULL

¹**glaze** *vb* **glazed; glaz·ing 1** : to set glass in **2** : to cover with a glassy surface **3** : to become shiny or glassy in appearance

²**glaze** *n* : a glassy surface or coating

gla·zier *n* : a person who sets glass in window frames

¹**gleam** *n* **1** : a faint, soft, or reflected light **2** : a small bright light **3** : a short or slight appearance

²**gleam** *vb* **1** : to shine with a soft light **2** : to give out gleams of light

glean *vb* **1** : to gather from a field what is left by the harvesters **2** : to gather (as information) little by little with patient effort

glee *n* : great joy : DELIGHT

glee club *n* : a singing group organized especially as a social activity in a school or college

glee·ful *adj* : full of glee

glen *n* : a narrow hidden valley

glib *adj* **glib·ber; glib·best** : speaking or spoken with careless ease and often with little regard for the truth — **glib·ly** *adv* — **glib·ness** *n*

¹**glide** *vb* **glid·ed; glid·ing** : to move with a smooth silent motion

²**glide** *n* : the act or action of gliding

glid·er *n* **1** : an aircraft without an engine that glides on air currents **2** : a porch seat hung from a frame (as by chains)

¹**glim·mer** *vb* : to shine faintly and unsteadily

²**glimmer** *n* : a faint unsteady light

¹**glimpse** *vb* **glimpsed; glimps·ing** : to catch a quick view of

²**glimpse** *n* : a short hurried look

¹**glint** *vb* : to shine with tiny bright flashes

²**glint** *n* : a brief flash

glis·ten *vb* : to shine with a soft reflected light

glitch *n* : a usually minor problem

¹**glit·ter** *vb* **1** : to sparkle brightly **2** : to sparkle with light that is harsh and cold **3** : to be very bright and showy

²**glitter** *n* : sparkling brightness

gloat *vb* : to gaze at or think about something with great satisfaction and often with mean or selfish satisfaction

glob·al *adj* **1** : shaped like a globe **2** : having to do with the whole earth

globe *n* **1** : a round object : BALL, SPHERE **2** : EARTH 3 **3** : a round model of the earth or heavens

globe–trot·ter *n* : a person who travels widely

glob·u·lar *adj* : shaped like a globe : SPHERICAL

glob·ule *n* : a small round mass

glock·en·spiel *n* : a portable musical instrument consisting of a series of metal bars played with hammers

gloom *n* **1** : partial or complete darkness **2** : a sad mood

gloomy *adj* **gloom·i·er; gloom·i·est 1** : partly or completely dark **2** : SAD 1, BLUE

3 : causing lowness of spirits **4** : not hopeful : PESSIMISTIC

glo·ri·fi·ca·tion n : the act of glorifying : the state of being glorified

glo·ri·fy vb **glo·ri·fied; glo·ri·fy·ing 1** : to honor or praise as divine : WORSHIP **2** : to give honor and praise to **3** : to show in a way that looks good

glo·ri·ous adj **1** : having or deserving glory **2** : having great beauty or splendor **3** : DELIGHTFUL

¹glo·ry n, pl **glories 1** : praise, honor, and admiration given to a person by others **2** : something that brings honor, praise, or fame **3** : BRILLIANCE, SPLENDOR **4** : HEAVEN 2

²glory vb **glo·ried; glo·ry·ing** : to rejoice proudly : be proud or boastful

¹gloss n **1** : brightness from a smooth surface : LUSTER, SHEEN **2** : a falsely attractive surface appearance

²gloss vb **1** : to give a gloss to **2** : to smooth over : explain away

glos·sa·ry n, pl **glos·sa·ries** : a list of the hard or unusual words used in a book given with their meanings

glossy adj **gloss·i·er; gloss·i·est** : smooth and shining on the surface

glove n : a covering for the hand having a separate section for each finger

¹glow vb **1** : to shine with or as if with great heat **2** : to show strong bright color **3** : to be or to look warm and flushed (as with exercise)

²glow n **1** : light such as comes from something that is very hot but not flaming **2** : brightness or warmth of color **3** : a feeling of physical warmth (as from exercise) **4** : warmth of feeling

glow·er vb : to stare angrily : SCOWL

glow·worm n : an insect or insect larva that gives off light

glu·cose n : a sugar in plant saps and fruits that is the usual form in which carbohydrate is taken in by the animal body

¹glue n : a substance used to stick things tightly together

²glue vb **glued; glu·ing** : to stick with or as if with glue

glu·ey adj **glu·i·er; glu·i·est 1** : sticky like glue **2** : covered with glue

glum adj **glum·mer; glum·mest 1** : ¹SULKY **2** : seeming gloomy and sad — **glum·ly** adv — **glum·ness** n

¹glut vb **glut·ted; glut·ting 1** : to make quite full : fill completely **2** : to flood with goods so that supply is greater than demand

²glut n : too much of something

glu·ti·nous adj : like glue : STICKY — **glu·ti·nous·ly** adv

glut·ton n : a person or animal that overeats — **glut·ton·ous** adj — **glut·ton·ous·ly** adv

glut·tony n, pl **glut·ton·ies** : the act or habit of eating or drinking too much

glyc·er·in or **glyc·er·ine** n : a sweet thick liquid that is found in various oils and fats and is used to moisten or dissolve things

gly·co·gen n : a white tasteless starchy substance that is the chief stored carbohydrate of animals

G–man n, pl **G–men** : a special agent of the Federal Bureau of Investigation

gnarled adj : being full of knots, twisted, and rugged

gnash vb : to strike or grind (the teeth) together (as in anger)

gnat n : a very small two-winged fly

gnaw vb **gnawed; gnaw·ing** : to bite so as to wear away little by little : bite or chew upon

gnome n : one of an imaginary race of dwarfs believed to live inside the earth and guard treasure

gnu n, pl **gnu** or **gnus** : a large African antelope with a head like that of an ox, curving horns, a short mane, and a tail somewhat like that of a horse

go vb **went; gone; go·ing; goes 1** : to pass from one place to or toward another **2** : to move away : LEAVE **3** : to become lost, used, or spent **4** : to continue its course or action : RUN **5** : to make its own special sound **6** : to be suitable : MATCH **7** : to reach some state

¹goad n **1** : a pointed rod used to keep an animal moving **2** : something that stirs one to action

²goad vb : to drive or stir with a goad

goal n **1** : the point at which a race or journey is to end **2** : an area to be reached safely in certain games **3** : ¹PURPOSE **4** : an object into which a ball or puck must be driven in various games in order to score **5** : a scoring of one or more points by driving a ball or puck into a goal

goal·ie n : GOALKEEPER

goal·keep·er n : a player who defends a goal

goal·post n : one of two usually upright posts often with a crossbar that serve as the goal in various games

goal·tend·er n : GOALKEEPER

goat n : a horned animal that chews the cud and is related to but more lively than the sheep — **goat·like** adj

goa·tee n : a small beard trimmed to a point

goat·herd n : a person who tends goats

goat·skin n : the skin of a goat or leather made from it

gob n : ¹LUMP

¹gob·ble *vb* **gob·bled; gob·bling** : to eat fast or greedily

²gobble *vb* **gob·bled; gob·bling** : to make the call of a turkey or a similar sound

³gobble *n* : the loud harsh call of a turkey

go—be·tween *n* : a person who acts as a messenger or peacemaker

gob·let *n* : a drinking glass with a foot and stem

gob·lin *n* : an ugly imaginary creature with evil or sly ways

god *n* **1** *cap* : the Being considered the holy and ruling power who made and sustains all things of the universe **2** : a being believed to have more than human powers **3** : a natural or artificial object worshiped as divine **4** : something believed to be the most important thing in existence

god·child *n*, *pl* **god·chil·dren** : a person for whom another person is sponsor at baptism

god·dess *n* : a female god

god·fa·ther *n* : a boy or man who is sponsor for a child at its baptism

god·less *adj* **1** : not believing in God or a god **2** : WICKED 1, EVIL — **god·less·ness** *n*

god·like *adj* : like or suitable for God or a god

god·ly *adj* **god·li·er; god·li·est** : DEVOUT 1, PIOUS — **god·li·ness** *n*

god·moth·er *n* : a girl or woman who is sponsor for a child at its baptism

god·par·ent *n* : a sponsor at baptism

god·send *n* : some badly needed thing that comes unexpectedly

goes *present 3d sing of* GO

go—get·ter *n* : a very active and aggressive person

gog·gle *vb* **gog·gled; gog·gling** **1** : to roll the eyes **2** : to stare with bulging or rolling eyes

gog·gle—eyed *adj* : having bulging or rolling eyes

gog·gles *n pl* : eyeglasses worn to protect the eyes (as from dust, sun, or wind)

go·ings—on *n pl* : things that happen

goi·ter *n* : a swelling on the front of the neck caused by enlargement of the thyroid gland

gold *n* **1** : a soft yellow metallic chemical element used especially in coins and jewelry **2** : gold coins **3** : MONEY 3 **4** : a deep yellow

gold·en *adj* **1** : like, made of, or containing gold **2** : of the color of gold **3** : very good or desirable **4** : being prosperous and happy

gold·en·rod *n* : a plant with tall stiff stems topped with rows of tiny yellow flower heads on slender branches

golden rule *n* : a rule that one should treat others as one would want others to treat oneself

gold·finch *n* **1** : a European finch with a yellow patch on each wing **2** : an American finch that looks like the canary

gold·fish *n* : a small usually golden yellow or orange carp often kept in aquariums

gold·smith *n* : a person who makes or deals in articles of gold

golf *n* : a game played by driving a small ball (**golf ball**) with one of a set of clubs (**golf clubs**) around an outdoor course (**golf course**) and into various holes in as few strokes as possible

golf·er *n* : a person who plays golf

gol·ly *interj* — used to express surprise or annoyance

gon·do·la *n* **1** : a long narrow boat used in the canals of Venice, Italy **2** : a freight car with no top **3** : an enclosure that hangs from a balloon and carries passengers or instruments

gone *adj* **1** : ADVANCED 1 **2** : INFATUATED **3** : ¹DEAD 1 **4** : WEAK 1, LIMP

gon·er *n* : one whose case is hopeless

gong *n* : a metallic disk that produces a harsh ringing tone when struck

¹good *adj* **bet·ter; best** **1** : suitable for a use : SATISFACTORY **2** : being at least the amount mentioned **3** : CONSIDERABLE **4** : DESIRABLE, ATTRACTIVE **5** : HELPFUL, KIND **6** : behaving well **7** : being honest and upright **8** : showing good sense or judgment **9** : better than average

²good *n* **1** : something good **2** : WELFARE 1, BENEFIT **3 goods** *pl* : WARE 2 **4 goods** *pl* : personal property **5 goods** *pl* : a length of cloth

¹good—bye *or* **good—by** *interj* — used as a farewell remark

²good—bye *or* **good—by** *n* : a farewell remark

good—heart·ed *adj* : having a kindly generous disposition — **good—heart·ed·ly** *adv* — **good—heart·ed·ness** *n*

good—hu·mored *adj* : GOOD-NATURED — **good—hu·mored·ly** *adv* — **good—hu·mored·ness** *n*

good·ly *adj* **good·li·er; good·li·est** **1** : of pleasing appearance **2** : LARGE, CONSIDERABLE

good—na·tured *adj* : having or showing a pleasant disposition — **good—na·tured·ly** *adv*

good·ness *n* **1** : the quality or state of being good **2** : excellence of morals and behavior

good—tem·pered *adj* : not easily angered or upset

good·will *n* **1** : kindly feelings **2** : the value of the trade a business has built up

goody n, pl **good·ies** : something especially good to eat

¹goof n 1 : a stupid or silly person 2 : ²BLUNDER

²goof vb : to make a blunder

goofy adj **goof·i·er; goof·i·est** : SILLY 1

goose n, pl **geese** 1 : a waterbird with webbed feet that is related to the smaller duck and the larger swan 2 : a female goose 3 : the flesh of a goose used as food 4 : a silly person

goose·ber·ry n, pl **goose·ber·ries** : the sour berry of a thorny bush related to the currant

goose bumps n pl : a roughness of the skin caused by cold, fear, or a sudden feeling of excitement

goose·flesh n : GOOSE BUMPS

goose pimples n pl : GOOSE BUMPS

go·pher n 1 : a burrowing animal that is about the size of a rat and has strong claws on the forefeet and very large outside cheek pouches 2 : a striped ground squirrel of the prairies 3 : a burrowing American land tortoise

¹gore n : shed or clotted blood

²gore vb **gored; gor·ing** : to pierce or wound with a horn or tusk

¹gorge n : a narrow steep-walled canyon or part of a canyon

²gorge vb **gorged; gorg·ing** : to eat greedily

gor·geous adj : very beautiful — **gor·geous·ly** adv — **gor·geous·ness** n

go·ril·la n : a very large ape of the forests of central Africa that lives mostly on the ground

gory adj **gor·i·er; gor·i·est** : covered with gore

gos·ling n : a young goose

gos·pel n 1 often cap : the teachings of Christ and the apostles 2 : something told or accepted as being absolutely true

gos·sa·mer adj : very light and flimsy

¹gos·sip n 1 : a person who repeats stories about other people 2 : talk or rumors having no worth

²gossip vb : to spread gossip

got past of GET

gotten past participle of GET

¹gouge n 1 : a chisel with a curved blade for scooping or cutting holes 2 : a hole or groove made with or as if with a gouge

²gouge vb **gouged; goug·ing** : to dig out with or as if with a gouge

gou·lash n : a beef stew made with vegetables and paprika

gourd n : the fruit of a vine (**gourd vine**) related to the pumpkin and melon

gour·met n : a person who appreciates fine food and drink

gov·ern vb 1 : ²RULE 2 2 : to influence the actions and conduct of : CONTROL

gov·ern·able adj : possible to govern

gov·ern·ess n : a woman who teaches and trains a child especially in a private home

gov·ern·ment n 1 : control and direction of public business (as of a city or a nation) 2 : a system of control : an established form of political rule 3 : the persons making up a governing body

gov·ern·men·tal adj : of or relating to government or the government

gov·er·nor n 1 : a person who governs and especially the elected head of a state of the United States 2 : a device attached to an engine for controlling its speed

gov·er·nor·ship n 1 : the office or position of governor 2 : the term of office of a governor

gown n 1 : a woman's dress 2 : a loose robe

¹grab vb **grabbed; grab·bing** : ¹SNATCH

²grab n : the act or an instance of grabbing

¹grace n 1 : GOODWILL 1, FAVOR 2 : a short prayer at a meal 3 : pleasing and attractive behavior or quality 4 : the condition of being in favor 5 : a sense of what is proper 6 : an extra note or notes in music (as a trill) added for ornamentation 7 : beauty and ease of movement

²grace vb **graced; grac·ing** 1 : to do credit to : HONOR 2 : to make more attractive : ADORN

grace·ful adj : showing grace or beauty in form or action — **grace·ful·ly** adv — **grace·ful·ness** n

grace·less adj : lacking grace — **grace·less·ly** adv — **grace·less·ness** n

gra·cious adj 1 : being kind and courteous 2 : GRACEFUL — **gra·cious·ly** adv — **gra·cious·ness** n

grack·le n : a large blackbird with shiny feathers that show changeable green, purple, and bronze colors

¹grade n 1 : a position in a scale of rank, quality, or order 2 : a class of things that are of the same rank, quality, or order 3 : a division of a school course representing a year's work 4 : the group of pupils in a school grade 5 **grades** pl : the elementary school system 6 : a mark or rating especially in school 7 : the degree of slope (as of a road or railroad track) : SLOPE

²grade vb **grad·ed; grad·ing** 1 : to arrange in grades : SORT 2 : to make level or evenly sloping 3 : to give a grade to 4 : to assign to a grade

grade school n : a school including the first six or the first eight grades

grad·u·al adj : moving or happening by steps or degrees — **grad·u·al·ly** adv

¹grad·u·ate *n* : a person who has completed the required course of study in a college or school

²grad·u·ate *vb* **grad·u·at·ed; grad·u·at·ing** : to become a graduate : finish a course of study

grad·u·a·tion *n* **1** : the act or process of graduating **2** : COMMENCEMENT 2

Graeco- — see GRECO-

¹graft *n* **1** : a grafted plant **2** : the act of grafting **3** : something (as skin or a bud) used in grafting **4** : something (as money or advantage) gotten in a dishonest way and especially by betraying a public trust

²graft *vb* **1** : to insert a twig or bud from one plant into another plant so they are joined and grow together **2** : to join one thing to another as if by grafting **3** : to gain money or advantage in a dishonest way — **graft·er** *n*

grain *n* **1** : the edible seed or seedlike fruit of some grasses (as wheat or oats) or a few other plants (as buckwheat) **2** : plants that produce grain **3** : a small hard particle **4** : a tiny amount : BIT **5** : a unit of weight equal to 0.0648 gram **6** : the arrangement of fibers in wood — **grained** *adj*

gram *or* **gramme** *n* : a unit of mass in the metric system equal to $1/1000$ kilogram

-gram *n suffix* : drawing : writing : record

gram·mar *n* **1** : the study of the classes of words and their uses and relations in sentences **2** : the study of what is good and bad to use in speaking and writing **3** : speech or writing judged according to the rules of grammar

gram·mat·i·cal *adj* : of, relating to, or following the rules of grammar — **gram·mat·i·cal·ly** *adv*

gra·na·ry *n, pl* **gra·na·ries** : a storehouse for grain

grand *adj* **1** : higher in rank than others : FOREMOST **2** : great in size **3** : COMPREHENSIVE, INCLUSIVE **4** : showing wealth or high social standing **5** : IMPRESSIVE **6** : very good — **grand·ly** *adv* — **grand·ness** *n*

grand·aunt *n* : GREAT-AUNT

grand·child *n, pl* **grand·chil·dren** : a child of one's son or daughter

grand·daugh·ter *n* : a daughter of one's son or daughter

gran·dee *n* : a man of high rank especially in Spain or Portugal

gran·deur *n* : impressive greatness (as of power or nature)

grand·fa·ther *n* **1** : the father of one's father or mother **2** : ANCESTOR — **grand·fa·ther·ly** *adj*

grandfather clock *n* : a tall clock standing directly on the floor

grand·ma *n* : GRANDMOTHER 1

grand·moth·er *n* **1** : the mother of one's father or mother **2** : a female ancestor — **grand·moth·er·ly** *adj*

grand·neph·ew *n* : a grandson of one's brother or sister

grand·niece *n* : a granddaughter of one's brother or sister

grand·pa *n* : GRANDFATHER 1

grand·par·ent *n* : a parent of one's father or mother

grand·son *n* : a son of one's son or daughter

grand·stand *n* : the main stand (as on an athletic field) for spectators

grand·un·cle *n* : GREAT-UNCLE

gran·ite *n* : a very hard rock that is used for building and for monuments

gran·ny *n, pl* **gran·nies** : GRANDMOTHER 1

granny knot *n* : a knot that is not very firm and is often made accidentally instead of a square knot

¹grant *vb* **1** : to agree to **2** : to give as a favor or right **3** : to admit (something not yet proved) to be true

²grant *n* **1** : the act of granting **2** : GIFT 2

grape *n* : a juicy berry that has a smooth green or whitish to deep red, purple, or black skin and grows in clusters on a woody vine (**grapevine**)

grape·fruit *n* : a large fruit with a yellow skin that is related to the orange and lemon

graph *n* : a diagram that by means of dots and lines shows a system of relationships between things

-graph *n suffix* **1** : something written **2** : instrument for making or sending records

¹graph·ic *adj* **1** : being written, drawn, printed, or engraved **2** : told or described in a clear vivid way **3** : of or relating to the pictorial arts or to printing — **graph·i·cal·ly** *adv*

²graphic *n* **1** : a picture, map, or graph used for illustration **2** **graphics** *pl* : a display (as of pictures or graphs) generated by a computer on a screen or printer

graph·ite *n* : a soft black carbon used in making lead pencils and as a lubricant

-g·ra·phy *n suffix, pl* **-g·ra·phies** : writing or picturing in a special way, by a special means, or of a special thing

grap·nel *n* : a small anchor with several claws that can be used to anchor a boat or to take and keep a hold on an object (as another boat or something under water)

¹grap·ple *n* **1** : the act of grappling or seizing **2** : a device for grappling

²grapple *vb* **grap·pled; grap·pling** **1** : to

seize or hold with an instrument (as a hook) **2** : to seize and struggle with another

¹grasp *vb* **1** : to seize and hold with or as if with the hand : GRIP **2** : to make the motion of seizing : CLUTCH **3** : UNDERSTAND 1, COMPREHEND

²grasp *n* **1** : the act of grasping : a grip of the hand **2** : ²CONTROL 1, HOLD **3** : the power of seizing and holding : REACH **4** : ¹UNDERSTANDING 1, COMPREHENSION

grasp·ing *adj* : GREEDY 2

grass *n* **1** : plants suitable for or eaten by grazing animals **2** : any of a large natural group of green plants with jointed stems, long slender leaves, and stalks of clustered flowers **3** : GRASSLAND — **grass·like** *adj*

grass·hop·per *n* : a common leaping insect that feeds on plants

grass·land *n* : land covered with herbs (as grass and clover) rather than shrubs and trees

grassy *adj* **grass·i·er; grass·i·est** : of, like, or covered with grass

¹grate *vb* **grat·ed; grat·ing** **1** : to break into small pieces by rubbing against something rough **2** : to grind or rub against something with a scratching noise **3** : to have a harsh effect

²grate *n* **1** : a frame containing parallel or crossed bars (as in a window) **2** : a frame of iron bars for holding burning fuel

grate·ful *adj* **1** : feeling or showing thanks **2** : providing pleasure or comfort — **grate·ful·ly** *adv* — **grate·ful·ness** *n*

grat·er *n* : a device with a rough surface for grating

grat·i·fi·ca·tion *n* **1** : the act of gratifying : the state of being gratified **2** : something that gratifies

grat·i·fy *vb* **grat·i·fied; grat·i·fy·ing** : to give pleasure or satisfaction to

grat·ing *n* : ²GRATE 1

grat·i·tude *n* : the state of being grateful

¹grave *n* : a hole in the ground for burying a dead body

²grave *adj* **grav·er; grav·est** **1** : deserving serious thought : IMPORTANT **2** : having a serious look or way of acting — **grave·ly** *adv* — **grave·ness** *n*

grav·el *n* : small pieces of rock and pebbles larger than grains of sand

grav·el·ly *adj* **1** : containing or made up of gravel **2** : sounding harsh or scratchy

grave·stone *n* : a monument on a grave

grave·yard *n* : CEMETERY

grav·i·tate *vb* **grav·i·tat·ed; grav·i·tat·ing** : to move or be drawn toward something

grav·i·ta·tion *n* **1** : a force of attraction that tends to draw particles or bodies together **2** : the act or process of gravitating

grav·i·ty *n, pl* **grav·i·ties** **1** : the condition of being grave **2** : the attraction of bodies by gravitation toward the center of the earth **3** : GRAVITATION 1

gra·vy *n, pl* **gravies** : a sauce made from the juice of cooked meat

¹gray *or* **grey** *adj* **1** : of the color gray **2** : having gray hair **3** : lacking cheer or brightness — **gray·ness** *n*

²gray *or* **grey** *n* **1** : something gray in color **2** : a color that is a blend of black and white

³gray *or* **grey** *vb* : to make or become gray

gray·ish *adj* : somewhat gray

¹graze *vb* **grazed; graz·ing** **1** : to eat grass **2** : to supply with grass or pasture

²graze *vb* **grazed; graz·ing** **1** : to rub lightly in passing : barely touch **2** : to scrape by rubbing against something

³graze *n* : a scrape or mark caused by grazing

¹grease *n* **1** : a more or less solid substance obtained from animal fat by melting **2** : oily material **3** : a thick lubricant

²grease *vb* **greased; greas·ing** **1** : to smear with grease **2** : to lubricate with grease

grease·paint *n* : actors' makeup

greasy *adj* **greas·i·er; greas·i·est** **1** : smeared with grease **2** : like or full of grease

great *adj* **1** : very large in size : HUGE **2** : large in number : NUMEROUS **3** : long continued **4** : much beyond the average or ordinary **5** : IMPORTANT 1, DISTINGUISHED **6** : remarkable in knowledge or skill **7** : GRAND 6 — **great·ly** *adv*

great–aunt *n* : an aunt of one's father or mother

great–grand·child *n, pl* **great–grand·children** : a grandson (**great–grandson**) or granddaughter (**great–granddaughter**) of one's son or daughter

great–grand·par·ent *n* : a grandfather (**great–grandfather**) or grandmother (**great–grandmother**) of one's father or mother

great–un·cle *n* : an uncle of one's father or mother

grebe *n* : any of a group of swimming and diving birds related to the loons

Gre·cian *adj* : ²GREEK

Gre·co– *or* **Grae·co–** *prefix* **1** : Greece : Greeks **2** : Greek and

greed *n* : greedy desire (as for money or food)

greedy *adj* **greed·i·er; greed·i·est** **1** : having a strong appetite for food or drink : very hungry **2** : trying to grab more than one needs or more than one's share — **greed·i·ly** *adv* — **greed·i·ness** *n*

¹Greek *n* **1** : a person born or living in Greece **2** : the language of the Greeks

²Greek *adj* : of or relating to Greece, its people, or the Greek language

¹green *adj* **1** : of the color green **2** : covered with green vegetation **3** : made of green plants or of the leafy parts of plants **4** : not ripe **5** : not fully processed, treated, or seasoned **6** : lacking training or experience **7** : supporting the preservation or improvement of the natural environment (as by controlling pollution) **8** : helping to preserve the environment (as by being recyclable or not polluting) — **green·ly** *adv* — **green·ness** *n*

²green *n* **1** : a color that ranges between blue and yellow **2** **greens** *pl* : leafy parts of plants used for decoration or food **3** : a grassy plain or plot

green·ery *n, pl* **green·er·ies** : green plants or foliage

green·horn *n* : a person who is new at something

green·house *n* : a building with glass walls and roof for growing plants

greenhouse effect *n* : warming of the lower atmosphere of the earth that occurs when radiation from the sun is absorbed by the earth and then given off again and absorbed by carbon dioxide and water vapor in the atmosphere

green·ish *adj* : somewhat green

green·ling *n* : any of a group of food and sport fishes of the Pacific coast

green manure *n* : a leafy crop (as of clover) plowed under to improve the soil

green thumb *n* : an unusual ability to make plants grow

green·wood *n* : a forest green with leaves

greet *vb* **1** : to speak to in a friendly polite way upon arrival or meeting **2** : to receive or react to in a certain way **3** : to present itself to — **greet·er** *n*

greet·ing *n* **1** : an expression of pleasure on meeting someone **2** : SALUTATION **2** **3** : an expression of good wishes

gre·gar·i·ous *adj* : tending to live together with or associate with others of one's own kind — **gre·gar·i·ous·ly** *adv* — **gre·gar·i·ous·ness** *n*

gre·nade *n* : a small bomb designed to be thrown by hand or fired (as by a rifle)

gren·a·dier *n* : a member of a European regiment formerly armed with grenades

grew *past of* GROW

grey *variant of* GRAY

grey·hound *n* : a tall swift dog with a smooth coat and good eyesight

grid *n* **1** : a group of electrical conductors that form a network **2** : a network of horizontal and perpendicular lines (as for locating places on a map)

grid·dle *n* : a flat surface or pan on which food is cooked

griddle cake *n* : PANCAKE

grid·iron *n* **1** : a grate with parallel bars for broiling food **2** : a football field

grief *n* **1** : very deep sorrow **2** : a cause of sorrow **3** : MISHAP

griev·ance *n* **1** : a cause of uneasiness or annoyance **2** : a formal complaint

grieve *vb* **grieved; griev·ing** **1** : to cause grief to **2** : to feel or show grief

griev·ous *adj* **1** : causing suffering **2** : SERIOUS **5**, GRAVE

¹grill *vb* **1** : to broil on a grill **2** : to distress with continued questioning

²grill *n* **1** : a grate on which food is broiled **2** : a dish of broiled food **3** : a simple restaurant

grille *or* **grill** *n* : an often ornamental arrangement of bars (as of metal) forming a barrier or screen

grim *adj* **grim·mer; grim·mest** **1** : ¹SAVAGE **2**, CRUEL **2** : harsh in appearance : STERN **3** : UNYIELDING **2** **4** : FRIGHTFUL **1** — **grim·ly** *adv* — **grim·ness** *n*

¹gri·mace *n* : a twisting of the face (as in disgust)

²grim·ace *vb* **grim·aced; grim·ac·ing** : to make a grimace

grime *n* : dirt rubbed into a surface

grimy *adj* **grim·i·er; grim·i·est** : full of grime : DIRTY

¹grin *vb* **grinned; grin·ning** : to draw back the lips and show the teeth

²grin *n* : an act of grinning

¹grind *vb* **ground; grind·ing** **1** : to make or be made into meal or powder by rubbing **2** : to wear down, polish, or sharpen by friction **3** : to rub together with a scraping noise **4** : to operate or produce by or as if by turning a crank

²grind *n* **1** : an act of grinding **2** : steady hard work

grind·stone *n* : a flat round stone that turns on an axle and is used for sharpening tools and for shaping and smoothing

¹grip *vb* **gripped; grip·ping** **1** : to grasp firmly **2** : to hold the interest of

²grip *n* **1** : a strong grasp **2** : strength in holding : POWER **3** : ¹HANDLE **4** : a small suitcase

grippe *n* : a disease like or the same as influenza

gris·ly *adj* **gris·li·er; gris·li·est** : HORRIBLE, GHASTLY

grist *n* : grain to be ground or that is already ground

gris·tle *n* : CARTILAGE — **gris·tli·ness** *n* — **gris·tly** *adj*

grist·mill *n* : a mill for grinding grain

¹**grit** *n* **1** : rough hard bits especially of sand **2** : strength of mind or spirit

²**grit** *vb* **grit·ted; grit·ting** : ¹GRIND 3, GRATE

grits *n pl* : coarsely ground hulled grain

grit·ty *adj* **grit·ti·er; grit·ti·est 1** : containing or like grit **2** : bravely refusing to yield : PLUCKY — **grit·ti·ness** *n*

griz·zled *adj* : streaked or mixed with gray

griz·zly *adj* **griz·zli·er; griz·zli·est** : GRIZZLED, GRAYISH

grizzly bear *n* : a large powerful usually brownish yellow bear of western North America

¹**groan** *vb* **1** : to make or express with a deep moaning sound **2** : to creak under a strain

²**groan** *n* : a low moaning sound

gro·cer *n* : a dealer in food

gro·cery *n, pl* **gro·cer·ies 1** *groceries pl* : the goods sold by a grocer **2** : a grocer's store

grog·gy *adj* **grog·gi·er; grog·gi·est** : weak and confused and unsteady on one's feet — **grog·gi·ly** *adv* — **grog·gi·ness** *n*

groin *n* : the fold or area where the abdomen joins the thigh

grom·met *n* : an eyelet of firm material to strengthen or protect an opening

¹**groom** *n* **1** : a servant especially in charge of horses **2** : BRIDEGROOM

²**groom** *vb* **1** : to make neat and attractive (as by cleaning and brushing) **2** : to make fit or ready

¹**groove** *n* **1** : a narrow channel made in a surface (as by cutting) **2** : ¹ROUTINE

²**groove** *vb* **grooved; groov·ing** : to form a groove in

groovy *adj* **groov·i·er; groov·i·est** : very good : EXCELLENT

grope *vb* **groped; grop·ing 1** : to feel one's way **2** : to seek by or as if by feeling around

gros·beak *n* : a finch with a strong conical bill

¹**gross** *adj* **1** : GLARING 3 **2** : BIG 1 3 : ¹THICK 3 **4** : consisting of a whole before anything is deducted **5** : COARSE 4, VULGAR

²**gross** *n* : the whole before anything is deducted

³**gross** *n, pl* **gross** : twelve dozen

gro·tesque *adj* : very strange and unexpected : FANTASTIC

grot·to *n, pl* **grottoes 1** : ¹CAVE, CAVERN **2** : an artificial structure like a cave

¹**grouch** *n* **1** : a fit of bad temper **2** : a person with a bad disposition

²**grouch** *vb* : ¹GRUMBLE 1, COMPLAIN

grouchy *adj* **grouch·i·er; grouch·i·est** : having a bad disposition : CANTANKEROUS — **grouch·i·ly** *adv* — **grouch·i·ness** *n*

¹**ground** *n* **1** : the bottom of a body of water **2** **grounds** *pl* : SEDIMENT 1 **3** : a reason for a belief, action, or argument **4** : the surface or material upon which something is made or displayed or against which it appears **5** : the surface of the earth : SOIL **6** : an area used for some purpose **7 grounds** *pl* : the land around and belonging to a building **8** : an area to be won or defended as if in a battle

²**ground** *vb* **1** : to instruct in basic knowledge or understanding **2** : to run or cause to run aground **3** : to connect electrically with the ground **4** : to prevent (a plane or pilot) from flying

³**ground** *past of* GRIND

ground crew *n* : the mechanics and technicians who take care of an airplane

ground·hog *n* : WOODCHUCK

ground·less *adj* : being without foundation or reason

ground swell *n* : a broad deep ocean swell caused by a distant storm or earthquake

ground·work *n* : FOUNDATION 2

¹**group** *n* : a number of persons or things that form one whole

²**group** *vb* : to arrange in or put into a group

¹**grouse** *n, pl* **grouse** : a game bird that is much like the domestic fowl

²**grouse** *vb* **groused; grous·ing** : ¹GRUMBLE 1, GROUCH

grove *n* : a small wood or a planting of trees

grov·el *vb* **grov·eled** *or* **grov·elled; grov·el·ing** *or* **grov·el·ling 1** : to creep or lie face down on the ground (as in fear) **2** : CRINGE — **grov·el·er** *or* **grov·el·ler** *n*

grow *vb* **grew; grown; grow·ing 1** : to spring up and develop to maturity **2** : to be able to live and develop **3** : to be related in some way by reason of growing **4** : ¹INCREASE, EXPAND **5** : BECOME 1 **6** : to cause to grow : RAISE — **grow·er** *n*

¹**growl** *vb* **1** : to make a rumbling noise **2** : to make a growl **3** : ¹GRUMBLE 1

²**growl** *n* **1** : a deep threatening sound (as of a dog) **2** : a grumbling or muttered complaint

grown *adj* : having reached full growth : MATURE

¹**grown–up** *adj* : ¹ADULT

²**grown–up** *n* : an adult person

growth *n* **1** : a stage or condition in growing **2** : a process of growing **3** : a gradual increase **4** : something (as a covering of plants) produced by growing

grow up *vb* : to become adult

¹grub *vb* **grubbed; grub·bing 1 :** to root out by digging : DIG **2 :** to work hard

²grub *n* **1 :** a soft thick wormlike larva (as of a beetle) **2 :** FOOD 1

grub·by *adj* **grub·bi·er; grub·bi·est :** ¹DIRTY 1 — **grub·bi·ly** *adv* — **grub·bi·ness** *n*

¹grub·stake *n* **:** supplies or funds given to a prospector in return for a promise of a share in the finds

²grubstake *vb* **grub·staked; grub·stak·ing :** to provide with a grubstake

¹grudge *vb* **grudged; grudg·ing :** BEGRUDGE

²grudge *n* **:** a feeling of sullen dislike that lasts a long time

gru·el *n* **:** a thin porridge

gru·el·ing *or* **gru·el·ling** *adj* **:** calling for much effort

grue·some *adj* **:** HORRIBLE, GHASTLY — **grue·some·ly** *adv* — **grue·some·ness** *n*

gruff *adj* **:** rough in speech or manner : HARSH — **gruff·ly** *adv* — **gruff·ness** *n*

¹grum·ble *vb* **grum·bled; grum·bling 1 :** to complain or mutter in discontent **2 :** ¹RUMBLE

²grumble *n* **1 :** the act of grumbling **2 :** ²RUMBLE

grumpy *adj* **grump·i·er; grump·i·est :** GROUCHY, CROSS — **grump·i·ly** *adv* — **grump·i·ness** *n*

¹grunt *vb* **:** to make a grunt — **grunt·er** *n*

²grunt *n* **:** a deep short sound (as of a hog)

¹guar·an·tee *n* **1 :** GUARANTOR **2 :** the act of guaranteeing **3 :** a promise that something will work the way it should **4 :** SECURITY 2

²guarantee *vb* **guar·an·teed; guar·an·tee·ing 1 :** to promise to answer for the debt or duty of another person **2 :** to give a guarantee on or about

guar·an·tor *n* **:** a person who gives a guarantee

¹guard *n* **1 :** the act or duty of keeping watch **2 :** a person or a body of persons that guards against injury or danger **3 :** a device giving protection

²guard *vb* **1 :** to protect from danger : DEFEND **2 :** to watch over so as to prevent escape **3 :** to keep careful watch

guard·ed *adj* **:** CAUTIOUS

guard·house *n* **1 :** a building used as a headquarters by soldiers on guard duty **2 :** a military jail

guard·ian *n* **1 :** a person who guards or looks after something : CUSTODIAN **2 :** a person who legally has the care of another person or of that person's property — **guard·ian·ship** *n*

guard·room *n* **:** a room used by a military guard while on duty

guards·man *n, pl* **guards·men :** a member of a military guard

gu·ber·na·to·ri·al *adj* **:** of or relating to a governor

gud·geon *n* **:** any of several small fishes

guer·ril·la *or* **gue·ril·la** *n* **:** a member of a band of persons carrying on warfare but not part of a regular army

¹guess *vb* **1 :** to judge without sure knowledge **2 :** to solve correctly **3 :** THINK 2, BELIEVE — **guess·er** *n*

²guess *n* **:** an opinion formed by guessing

guess·work *n* **:** work done or results gotten by guessing

guest *n* **1 :** a person entertained in one's house or at one's table **2 :** a person using a hotel, motel, inn, or restaurant

¹guf·faw *n* **:** a burst of loud laughter

²guffaw *vb* **:** to laugh noisily

guid·ance *n* **:** the act or process of guiding or being guided : DIRECTION

¹guide *n* **:** someone or something (as a book) that leads, directs, or shows the right way

²guide *vb* **guid·ed; guid·ing 1 :** to show the way to **2 :** DIRECT, INSTRUCT

guide·book *n* **:** a book of information for travelers

guide·post *n* **:** a post with signs giving directions for travelers

guide word *n* **:** either of the terms at the head of a page of an alphabetical reference work (as a dictionary) usually showing the first and last entries on the page

guild *n* **:** an association of persons with similar aims or common interests

guile *n* **:** sly trickery — **guile·ful** *adj* — **guile·ful·ly** *adv*

¹guil·lo·tine *n* **:** a machine for cutting off a person's head with a heavy blade that slides down two grooved posts

²guillotine *vb* **guil·lo·tined; guil·lo·tin·ing :** to cut off a person's head with a guillotine

guilt *n* **1 :** the fact of having done something wrong and especially something punishable by law **2 :** conduct that causes one to feel shame or regret or the feeling experienced — **guilt·less** *adj*

guilty *adj* **guilt·i·er; guilt·i·est 1 :** having done wrong **2 :** aware of, suffering from, or showing guilt — **guilt·i·ly** *adv* — **guilt·i·ness** *n*

guin·ea *n* **:** an old British gold coin

guinea fowl *n* **:** an African bird related to the pheasants that has a bare head and neck and usually dark gray feathers with white speckles and is sometimes raised for food

guinea pig *n* **:** a stocky rodent with short ears and a very short tail

guise *n* **1 :** a style of dress **2 :** outward appearance

gui·tar *n* : a musical instrument with six strings played by plucking or strumming

gulch *n* : RAVINE

gulf *n* **1** : a part of an ocean or sea extending into the land **2** : CHASM, ABYSS **3** : a wide separation (as in age)

gull *n* : a waterbird with webbed feet that is usually blue-gray or whitish in color and has a thick strong bill

gul·let *n* : THROAT 2, ESOPHAGUS

gull·ible *adj* : easily tricked or misled

gul·ly *n, pl* **gullies** : a trench worn in the earth by running water

¹gulp *vb* **1** : to swallow eagerly or in large amounts at a time **2** : to keep back as if by swallowing **3** : to catch the breath as if after a long drink

²gulp *n* **1** : the act of gulping **2** : a large swallow

¹gum *n* : the flesh along the jaws at the roots of the teeth

²gum *n* **1** : a sticky substance obtained from plants that hardens on drying **2** : a substance like a plant gum (as in stickiness) **3** : CHEWING GUM

³gum *vb* **gummed; gum·ming** : to smear, stick together, or clog with or as if with gum

gum·bo *n, pl* **gumbos** : a rich soup thickened with okra pods

gum·drop *n* : a candy usually made from corn syrup and gelatin

gum·my *adj* **gum·mi·er; gum·mi·est** **1** : consisting of, containing, or covered with gum **2** : GLUEY, STICKY

gump·tion *n* : ¹SPIRIT 5, COURAGE

¹gun *n* **1** : CANNON 1 **2** : a portable firearm (as a rifle, shotgun, or pistol) **3** : something like a gun in shape or function **4** : a discharge of a gun (as in a salute)

²gun *vb* **gunned; gun·ning** **1** : to hunt with a gun **2** : to open the throttle of quickly so as to increase speed

gun·boat *n* : a small armed ship for use in coastal waters

gun·fire *n* : the firing of guns

gun·man *n, pl* **gun·men** : a criminal armed with a gun

gun·ner *n* : a person who operates a gun

gun·nery *n* : the use of guns

gunnery sergeant *n* : a noncommissioned officer in the Marine Corps ranking above a staff sergeant

gun·ny *n, pl* **gun·nies** **1** : coarse jute sacking **2** : BURLAP

gun·pow·der *n* : an explosive powder used in guns and blasting

gun·shot *n* **1** : a shot from a gun **2** : the effective range of a gun

gun·wale *n* : the upper edge of a ship's side

gup·py *n, pl* **guppies** : a small tropical minnow often kept as an aquarium fish

¹gur·gle *vb* **gur·gled; gur·gling** **1** : to flow in a broken uneven noisy current **2** : to sound like a liquid flowing with a gurgle

²gurgle *n* : a sound of or like gurgling liquid

¹gush *vb* **1** : ¹SPOUT 1 3 **2** : to be too affectionate or enthusiastic

²gush *n* : a sudden free pouring out

gush·er *n* : an oil well with a large natural flow

gust *n* **1** : a sudden brief rush of wind **2** : a sudden outburst (as of emotion)

gusty *adj* **gust·i·er; gust·i·est** : WINDY

¹gut *n* **1** : ENTRAILS — usually used in pl. **2** : the digestive tube or a part of this **3** : CATGUT **4 guts** *pl* : COURAGE

²gut *vb* **gut·ted; gut·ting** **1** : to remove the entrails from **2** : to destroy the inside of

¹gut·ter *n* **1** : a trough along the eaves of a house to catch and carry off water **2** : a low area (as at the side of a road) to carry off surface water

²gutter *vb* **1** : to flow in small streams **2** : to have wax flowing down the sides after melting through the rim

¹guy *n* : a rope, chain, rod, or wire (**guy wire**) attached to something to steady it

²guy *n* : PERSON 1, FELLOW

gym *n* : GYMNASIUM

gym·na·si·um *n* : a room or building for sports events or gymnastics

gym·nast *n* : a person who is skilled in gymnastics

gym·nas·tic *adj* : of or relating to gymnastics

gym·nas·tics *n sing or pl* : physical exercises for developing skill, strength, and control in the use of the body or a sport in which such exercises are performed

Gyp·sy *or* **Gip·sy** *n, pl* **Gyp·sies** *or* **Gip·sies** : a member of a group of people coming from India to Europe long ago and living a wandering way of life

gypsy moth *n* : a moth whose caterpillar has a spotty grayish look and does great damage to trees by eating the leaves

gy·rate *vb* **gy·rat·ed; gy·rat·ing** : to move in a circle around a center : SPIN

gy·ro·scope *n* : a wheel mounted to spin rapidly so that its axis is free to turn in various directions

gy·ro·scop·ic *adj* : of or relating to a gyroscope

H

h *n, pl* **h's** *or* **hs** *often cap* : the eighth letter of the English alphabet

ha *interj* — used to show surprise or joy

hab·it *n* **1** : clothing worn for a special purpose **2** : usual way of behaving **3** : a way of acting or doing that has become fixed by being repeated often **4** : characteristic way of growing

hab·it·able *adj* : suitable or fit to live in

hab·i·tat *n* : the place where a plant or animal grows or lives in nature

hab·i·ta·tion *n* **1** : the act of living in a place **2** : a place to live

ha·bit·u·al *adj* **1** : being or done by habit **2** : doing or acting by force of habit **3** : ¹REGULAR — **ha·bit·u·al·ly** *adv* — **ha·bit·u·al·ness** *n*

ha·ci·en·da *n* **1** : a large estate especially in a Spanish-speaking country **2** : the main house of a hacienda

¹hack *vb* **1** : to cut with repeated chopping blows **2** : to cough in a short broken way **3** : to write computer programs for enjoyment **4** : to gain access to a computer illegally

²hack *n* : a short broken cough

³hack *n* **1** : a horse let out for hire or used for varied work **2** : a person who works for pay at a routine writing job **3** : a writer who is not very good

hack·er *n* **1** : one that hacks **2** : a person who is unskilled at a particular activity **3** : an expert at programming and solving problems with a computer **4** : a person who illegally gains access to a computer system

hack·les *n pl* : hairs (as on the neck of a dog) that can be made to stand up

hack·ney *n, pl* **hack·neys** : a horse for ordinary riding or driving

hack·saw *n* : a saw used for cutting hard materials (as metal) that consists of a frame and a blade with small teeth

had *past of* HAVE

had·dock *n, pl* **haddock** *or* **haddocks** : a food fish related to but smaller than the cod

hadn't : had not

haf·ni·um *n* : a gray metallic chemical element

hag *n* **1** : WITCH 1 **2** : an ugly old woman

hag·gard *adj* : having a hungry, tired, or worried look

hag·gle *vb* **hag·gled; hag·gling** : to argue especially over a price — **hag·gler** *n*

ha–ha *interj* — used to show amusement or scorn

hai·ku *n, pl* **haiku** **1** : a Japanese verse form without rhyme having three lines with the first and last lines having five syllables and the middle having seven **2** : a poem written in this form

¹hail *n* **1** : small lumps of ice and snow that fall from the clouds sometimes during thunderstorms **2** : ¹VOLLEY 1

²hail *vb* **1** : to fall as hail **2** : to pour down like hail

³hail *interj* — used to show enthusiastic approval

⁴hail *vb* **1** : GREET 1, WELCOME **2** : to call out to — **hail from** : to come from

⁵hail *n* : an exclamation of greeting, approval, or praise

hail·stone *n* : a lump of hail

hail·storm *n* : a storm that brings hail

hair *n* **1** : a threadlike growth from the skin of a person or lower animal **2** : a covering or growth of hairs (as on one's head) **3** : something (as a growth on a leaf) like an animal hair — **haired** *adj* — **hair·less** *adj* — **hair·like** *adj*

hair·brush *n* : a brush for the hair

hair·cut *n* : the act, process, or result of cutting the hair

hair·do *n, pl* **hairdos** : a way of arranging a person's hair

hair·dress·er *n* : one who dresses or cuts hair — **hair·dress·ing** *n*

hair·pin *n* : a pin in the shape of a U for holding the hair in place

hair–rais·ing *adj* : causing terror, excitement, or great surprise

hair·style *n* : HAIRDO

hairy *adj* **hair·i·er; hair·i·est** : covered with hair — **hair·i·ness** *n*

¹hale *adj* : being strong and healthy

²hale *vb* **haled; hal·ing** : to force to go

¹half *n, pl* **halves** **1** : one of two equal parts into which something can be divided **2** : a part of something that is about equal to the remainder **3** : one of a pair

²half *adj* **1** : being one of two equal parts **2** : amounting to about a half : PARTIAL

³half *adv* **1** : to the extent of half **2** : not completely

half brother *n* : a brother by one parent only

half·heart·ed *adj* : lacking spirit or interest — **half·heart·ed·ly** *adv* — **half·heart·ed·ness** *n*

half–knot *n* : a knot in which two rope ends are wrapped once around each other and which is used to start other knots

half–life *n, pl* **half–lives** : the time required for half of the atoms of a radioactive substance to change composition

half sister *n* : a sister by one parent only

¹half·way *adv* : at or to half the distance

²halfway *adj* **1** : midway between two points **2** : PARTIAL **3**

half–wit *n* : a very stupid person — **half–witted** *adj*

hal·i·but *n, pl* **halibut** *or* **halibuts** : a very large flatfish much used for food

hall *n* **1** : a large building used for public purposes **2** : a building (as of a college) set apart for a special purpose **3** : an entrance room **4** : CORRIDOR **5** : AUDITORIUM

hal·le·lu·jah *interj* — used to express praise, joy, or thanks

hal·low *vb* : to set apart for holy purposes : treat as sacred

Hal·low·een *n* : October 31 observed with parties and with the playing of tricks by children during the evening

hal·lu·ci·na·tion *n* : the seeing of objects or the experiencing of feelings that are not real but are usually the result of mental disorder or the effect of a drug

hal·lu·ci·no·gen *n* : a drug that causes hallucinations — **hal·lu·ci·no·gen·ic** *adj*

hall·way *n* : CORRIDOR

ha·lo *n, pl* **halos** *or* **haloes** **1** : a circle of light around the sun or moon caused by tiny ice crystals in the air **2** : a circle drawn or painted around the head of a person in a picture as a symbol of holiness

¹halt *vb* : HESITATE **1**

²halt *n* : ¹END **2**

³halt *vb* **1** : to stop or cause to stop marching or traveling **2** : ²END

hal·ter *n* **1** : a rope or strap for leading or tying an animal **2** : a headstall to which a halter may be attached **3** : a brief blouse usually without a back and fastened by straps around the neck

halve *vb* **halved; halv·ing** **1** : to divide into halves **2** : to reduce to one half

halves *pl of* HALF

hal·yard *n* : a rope for raising or lowering a sail

ham *n* **1** : a buttock with the connected thigh **2** : a cut of meat consisting of a thigh usually of pork **3** : an operator of an amateur radio station

ham·burg·er *or* **ham·burg** *n* **1** : ground beef **2** : a sandwich made of a patty of ground beef in a split bun

ham·let *n* : a small village

¹ham·mer *n* **1** : a tool consisting of a head fastened to a handle and used for pounding (as in driving nails) **2** : something like a hammer in shape or action **3** : a heavy metal ball with a flexible handle thrown for distance in a track-and-field contest (**hammer throw**)

²hammer *vb* **1** : to strike with a hammer **2** : to fasten (as by nailing) with a hammer **3** : to produce by or as if by means of repeated blows

ham·mock *n* : a swinging cot usually made of canvas or netting

¹ham·per *vb* : to keep from moving or acting freely

²hamper *n* : a large basket usually with a cover

ham·ster *n* : a stocky rodent with a short tail and large cheek pouches

¹hand *n* **1** : the part of the arm fitted (as in humans) for handling, grasping, and holding **2** : a bodily structure (as the hind foot of an ape) like the human hand in function or form **3** : something like a hand **4** : ²CONTROL **1** **5** : one side of a problem **6** : a pledge especially of marriage **7** : HANDWRITING **8** : ABILITY **1** **9** : a unit of measure equal to about ten centimeters **10** : ²HELP **1**, ASSISTANCE **11** : a part or share in doing something **12** : an outburst of applause **13** : the cards held by a player in a card game **14** : a hired worker : LABORER — **at hand** : near in time or place — **by hand** : with the hands — **in hand** **1** : in one's possession or control **2** : in preparation — **off one's hands** : out of one's care — **on hand** **1** : in present possession **2** : ³PRESENT **1** — **out of hand** : out of control

²hand *vb* : to give or pass with the hand

hand·bag *n* : a bag used for carrying money and small personal articles

hand·ball *n* : a game played by hitting a small rubber ball against a wall or board with the hand

hand·bill *n* : a printed sheet (as of advertising) distributed by hand

hand·book *n* : a book of facts usually about one subject

hand·car *n* : a small railroad car that is made to move by hand or by a small motor

hand·cart *n* : a cart drawn or pushed by hand

¹hand·cuff *n* : a metal fastening that can be locked around a person's wrist

²handcuff *vb* : to put handcuffs on

hand·ed *adj* : using a particular hand or number of hands

hand·ful *n, pl* **handfuls** *or* **hands·ful** **1** : as much or as many as the hand will grasp **2** : a small amount or number

¹hand·i·cap *n* **1** : a contest in which one more skilled is given a disadvantage and one less skilled is given an advantage **2** : the disadvantage or advantage given in a contest **3** : a disadvantage that makes progress or success difficult

²handicap *vb* **hand·i·capped; hand·i·capping** **1** : to give a handicap to **2** : to put at a disadvantage

hand·i·craft n 1 : an occupation (as weaving or pottery making) that requires skill with the hands 2 : articles made by one working at handicraft

hand·i·ly adv : in a handy manner : EASILY

hand·i·work n : work done by the hands

hand·ker·chief n, pl **hand·ker·chiefs** : a small usually square piece of cloth used for wiping the face, nose, or eyes

¹**han·dle** n : the part by which something (as a dish or tool) is picked up or held — **han·dled** adj

²**handle** vb **han·dled; han·dling** 1 : to touch, feel, hold, or move with the hand 2 : to manage with the hands 3 : to deal with (as in writing or speaking) 4 : MANAGE 1, DIRECT 5 : to deal with or act on 6 : to deal or trade in — **han·dler** n

han·dle·bars n pl : a bar (as on a bicycle) that has a handle at each end and is used for steering

hand·made adj : made by hand rather than by machine

hand–me–downs n pl : used clothes

hand organ n : a small musical instrument cranked by hand

hand·out n : something (as food) given to a beggar

hand·rail n : a rail to be grasped by the hand for support

hands down adv : without question : EASILY

hand·shake n : a clasping of hands by two people (as in greeting)

hand·some adj **hand·som·er; hand·som·est** 1 : CONSIDERABLE 2 : more than enough 3 : having a pleasing and impressive appearance

hand·spring n : a feat of tumbling in which the body turns forward or backward in a full circle from a standing position and lands first on the hands and then on the feet

hand·stand n : a stunt in which a person balances the body in the air upside down supported on the hands

hand–to–hand adj : involving bodily contact

hand·work n : work done by hand and not by machine

hand·writ·ing n : writing done by hand

handy adj **hand·i·er; hand·i·est** 1 : within easy reach 2 : easy to use or manage 3 : VERSATILE 2 4 : DEXTEROUS 1

¹**hang** vb **hung** also **hanged; hang·ing** 1 : to fasten or be fastened to something without support from below : SUSPEND 2 : to kill or be killed by suspending (as from a gallows) by a rope tied around the neck 3 : to fasten so as to allow free motion forward and backward 4 : to cause to droop — **hang on to** : to hold or keep with determination

²**hang** n 1 : the way in which a thing hangs 2 : MEANING 1 3 : KNACK 1

han·gar n : a shelter for housing and repairing aircraft

hang·er n : a device on which something hangs

hang·man n, pl **hang·men** : one who hangs criminals

hang·nail n : a bit of skin hanging loose about a fingernail

hang·out n : a place where a person spends much idle time or goes often

hang·over n 1 : something (as a surviving custom) that remains from what is past 2 : a sick uncomfortable state that comes from drinking too much liquor

han·ker vb : to have a great desire

han·som n : a light covered carriage that has two wheels and a driver's seat elevated at the rear

Ha·nuk·kah n : a Jewish holiday lasting eight days and celebrating the cleansing and second dedication of the Temple after the Syrians were driven out of Jerusalem in 165 B.C.

hap·haz·ard adj : marked by lack of plan, order, or direction — **hap·haz·ard·ly** adv — **hap·haz·ard·ness** n

hap·less adj : ¹UNFORTUNATE 1

hap·pen vb 1 : to occur or come about by chance 2 : to take place 3 : to have opportunity : CHANCE 4 : to come especially by way of injury or harm

hap·pen·ing n : something that happens

hap·py adj **hap·pi·er; hap·pi·est** 1 : FORTUNATE 1, LUCKY 2 : being suitable for something 3 : enjoying one's condition : CONTENT 4 : JOYFUL 5 : feeling or showing pleasure : GLAD — **hap·pi·ly** adv — **hap·pi·ness** n

hap·py–go–lucky adj : free from care

ha·rangue n : a scolding speech or writing

ha·rass vb 1 : to worry and hinder by repeated attacks 2 : to annoy again and again — **ha·rass·ment** n

¹**har·bor** n 1 : a place of safety and comfort : REFUGE 2 : a part of a body of water (as a sea or lake) so protected as to be a place of safety for ships : PORT

²**harbor** vb 1 : to give shelter to 2 : to have or hold in the mind

¹**hard** adj 1 : not easily cut, pierced, or divided : not soft 2 : high in alcoholic content 3 : containing substances that prevent lathering with soap 4 : difficult to put up with : SEVERE 5 : UNFEELING 2 6 : carried on with steady and earnest effort 7 : DILIGENT, ENERGETIC 8 : sounding as in cold and geese — used of c and g 9 : difficult to do or to understand

2hard *adv* **1** : with great effort or energy **2** : in a violent way **3** : with pain, bitterness, or resentment

hard copy *n* : a copy of information (as from computer storage) produced on paper in normal size

hard disk *n* **1** : a rigid metal disk used to store computer data **2** : HARD DRIVE

hard drive *n* : a computer-data storage device containing one or more hard disks

hard·en *vb* **1** : to make or become hard or harder **2** : to make or become hardy or strong **3** : to make or become stubborn or unfeeling — **hard·en·er** *n*

hard·head·ed *adj* **1** : STUBBORN 1 **2** : using or showing good judgment — **hard·head·ed·ly** *adv* — **hard·head·ed·ness** *n*

hard·heart·ed *adj* : showing or feeling no pity : UNFEELING — **hard·heart·ed·ly** *adv* — **hard·heart·ed·ness** *n*

hard·ly *adv* : only just : BARELY

hard·ness *n* : the quality or state of being hard

hard palate *n* : the bony front part of the roof of the mouth

hard·ship *n* : something (as a loss or injury) that is hard to put up with

hard·tack *n* : a hard biscuit made of flour and water without salt

hard·ware *n* **1** : things (as tools, cutlery, or parts of machines) made of metal **2** : items of equipment or their parts used for a particular purpose

1hard·wood *n* : the usually hard wood of a tree belonging to the group bearing broad leaves as distinguished from the wood of a tree (as a pine) with leaves that are needles

2hardwood *adj* : having or made of hardwood

har·dy *adj* **har·di·er; har·di·est 1** : BOLD 1, BRAVE **2** : able to stand weariness, hardship, or severe weather — **har·di·ness** *n*

hare *n* : a timid animal like the related rabbit but having young that are born with the eyes open and a furry coat

hare·brained *adj* : FOOLISH

hark *vb* : LISTEN

1harm *n* **1** : physical or mental damage : INJURY **2** : MISCHIEF 1

2harm *vb* : to cause harm to : HURT

harm·ful *adj* : causing harm : INJURIOUS — **harm·ful·ly** *adv* — **harm·ful·ness** *n*

harm·less *adj* : not harmful — **harm·less·ly** *adv* — **harm·less·ness** *n*

har·mon·ic *adj* : of or relating to musical harmony rather than melody or rhythm — **har·mon·i·cal·ly** *adv*

har·mon·i·ca *n* : a small musical instrument held in the hand and played by the mouth : MOUTH ORGAN

har·mo·ni·ous *adj* **1** : having a pleasant sound : MELODIOUS **2** : combining so as to produce a pleasing result **3** : showing harmony in action or feeling — **har·mo·ni·ous·ly** *adv* — **har·mo·ni·ous·ness** *n*

har·mo·nize *vb* **har·mo·nized; har·mo·niz·ing 1** : to play or sing in harmony **2** : to be in harmony — **har·mo·niz·er** *n*

har·mo·ny *n, pl* **har·mo·nies 1** : the playing of musical tones together in chords **2** : a pleasing arrangement of parts **3** : AGREEMENT 1, ACCORD

1har·ness *n* : an arrangement of straps and fastenings placed on an animal so as to control it or prepare it to pull a load

2harness *vb* **1** : to put a harness on **2** : to put to work : UTILIZE

1harp *n* : a musical instrument consisting of a triangular frame set with strings that are plucked by the fingers

2harp *vb* : to call attention to something over and over again

1har·poon *n* : a barbed spear used especially for hunting whales and large fish

2harpoon *vb* : to strike with a harpoon

harp·si·chord *n* : a keyboard instrument similar to a piano with strings that are plucked

1har·row *n* : a heavy frame set with metal teeth or disks used in farming for breaking up and smoothing soil

2harrow *vb* **1** : to drag a harrow over (plowed ground) **2** : 2DISTRESS

har·ry *vb* **har·ried; har·ry·ing** : HARASS

harsh *adj* **1** : having a coarse surface : rough to the touch **2** : disagreeable to any of the senses **3** : causing physical discomfort **4** : SEVERE 1 — **harsh·ly** *adv* — **harsh·ness** *n*

1har·vest *n* **1** : the season when crops are gathered **2** : the gathering of a crop **3** : a ripe crop (as of grain)

2harvest *vb* : to gather in a crop

har·vest·er *n* **1** : one that gathers by or as if by harvesting **2** : a machine for harvesting field crops

has *present 3d sing of* HAVE

1hash *vb* : to chop into small pieces

2hash *n* **1** : cooked meat and vegetables chopped together and browned **2** : 2JUMBLE

hash·ish *n* : a drug from the hemp plant that is used for its intoxicating effects

hash over *vb* : to talk about : DISCUSS

hasn't : has not

hasp *n* : a fastener (as for a door) consisting of a hinged metal strap that fits over a staple and is held by a pin or padlock

has·sle *n* **1** : a loud angry argument **2** : a

brief fight **3** : something that annoys or bothers

has·sock *n* : a firm stuffed cushion used as a seat or leg rest

haste *n* **1** : quickness of motion or action : SPEED **2** : hasty action

has·ten *vb* : to move or act fast : HURRY

hasty *adj* **hast·i·er; hast·i·est 1** : done or made in a hurry **2** : made, done, or decided without proper care and thought — **hast·i·ly** *adv*

hat *n* : a covering for the head having a crown and usually a brim

1hatch *n* **1** : an opening in the deck of a ship or in the floor or roof of a building **2** : a small door or opening (as in an airplane) **3** : the cover for a hatch

2hatch *vb* **1** : to produce from eggs **2** : to come forth from an egg **3** : to develop usually in secret

hatch·ery *n, pl* **hatch·er·ies** : a place for hatching eggs

hatch·et *n* : a small ax with a short handle

hatch·way *n* : a hatch usually having a ladder or stairs

1hate *n* : deep and bitter dislike

2hate *vb* **hat·ed; hat·ing** : to feel great dislike toward

hate·ful *adj* **1** : full of hate **2** : causing or deserving hate — **hate·ful·ly** *adv* — **hate·ful·ness** *n*

ha·tred *n* : 1HATE

hat·ter *n* : a person who makes, sells, or cleans and repairs hats

haugh·ty *adj* **haugh·ti·er; haugh·ti·est** : acting as if other people are not as good as oneself — **haugh·ti·ly** *adv* — **haugh·ti·ness** *n*

1haul *vb* **1** : to pull or drag with effort **2** : to transport in a vehicle

2haul *n* **1** : the act of hauling **2** : an amount collected **3** : the distance or route over which a load is moved

haunch *n* **1** : HIP **2** : HINDQUARTER

1haunt *vb* **1** : to visit often **2** : to come to mind frequently **3** : to visit or live in as a ghost

2haunt *n* : a place often visited

have *vb, past & past participle* **had;** *present participle* **hav·ing;** *present 3d sing* **has 1** : to hold for one's use or as property **2** : to consist of **3** : to be forced or feel obliged **4** : to stand in some relationship to **5** : OBTAIN, GAIN, GET **6** : to possess as a characteristic **7** : 2EXERCISE 1 **8** : to be affected by **9** : to be in : CARRY ON **10** : to hold in the mind **11** : to cause to be **12** : to cause to **13** : 1PERMIT 1 **14** : 2TRICK **15** : to give birth to **16** : to partake of **17** — used as a helping verb with the past participle of another verb

ha·ven *n* : a safe place

haven't : have not

hav·er·sack *n* : a bag worn over one shoulder for carrying supplies

hav·oc *n* **1** : wide destruction **2** : great confusion and lack of order

Ha·wai·ian *n* **1** : a person born or living in Hawaii **2** : the language of the Hawaiians

1hawk *n* : a bird of prey that has a strong hooked bill and sharp curved claws and is smaller than most eagles

2hawk *vb* : to make a harsh coughing sound in clearing the throat

3hawk *vb* : to offer for sale by calling out in the street — **hawk·er** *n*

haw·ser *n* : a large rope for towing or tying up a ship

haw·thorn *n* : any of several thorny shrubs or small trees with shiny leaves, white, pink, or red flowers, and small red fruits

1hay *n* : any of various herbs (as grasses) cut and dried for use as fodder

2hay *vb* : to cut plants for hay

hay fever *n* : a sickness like a cold usually affecting people sensitive to plant pollen

hay·loft *n* : a loft in a barn or stable for storing hay

hay·mow *n* : HAYLOFT

hay·stack *n* : a large pile of hay stored outdoors

hay·wire *adj* **1** : working badly or in an odd way **2** : CRAZY 1, WILD

1haz·ard *n* : a source of danger

2hazard *vb* : to risk something : take a chance

haz·ard·ous *adj* : DANGEROUS — **haz·ard·ous·ly** *adv* — **haz·ard·ous·ness** *n*

1haze *n* : fine dust, smoke, or fine particles of water in the air

2haze *vb* **hazed; haz·ing** : to make or become hazy or cloudy

ha·zel *n* **1** : a shrub or small tree that bears an edible nut **2** : a light brown

ha·zel·nut *n* : the nut of a hazel

hazy *adj* **haz·i·er; haz·i·est 1** : partly hidden by haze **2** : not clear in thought or meaning : VAGUE — **haz·i·ly** *adv* — **haz·i·ness** *n*

H–bomb *n* : HYDROGEN BOMB

he *pron* **1** : that male one **2** : a or the person : 3ONE 2

1head *n* **1** : the part of the body containing the brain, eyes, ears, nose, and mouth **2** : 1MIND 2 **3** : control of the mind or feelings **4** : the side of a coin or medal usually thought of as the front **5** : each person among a number **6** *pl* **head** : a unit of number **7** : something like a head in position or use 8 : the place a stream begins 9 : a skin stretched across one or both ends of a drum 10 : DIRECTOR, LEADER 11 : a compact mass of plant parts (as leaves or flowers) 12 : a part of a machine, tool, or weapon that performs the main work 13 : a place of leadership or honor 14 : CLIMAX, CRISIS — **out of one's head** : DELIRIOUS 1 — **over one's head** : beyond one's understanding

2head adj 1 : 2CHIEF 1 2 : located at the head 3 : coming from in front

3head vb 1 : to provide with or form a head 2 : to be or put oneself at the head of 3 : to be or get in front of 4 : to go or cause to go in a certain direction

head·ache n 1 : pain in the head 2 : something that annoys or confuses

head·band n : a band worn on or around the head

head·board n : a board forming the head (as of a bed)

head·dress n : a covering or ornament for the head

head·ed adj : having such a head or so many heads

head·first adv : with the head in front

head·gear n : something worn on the head

head·ing n : something (as a title or an address) at the top or beginning (as of a letter)

head·land n : a point of high land sticking out into the sea

head·light n : a light at the front of a vehicle

1head·line n : a title of an article in a newspaper

2headline vb **head·lined; head·lin·ing** : to provide with a headline

1head·long adv 1 : HEADFIRST 2 : without waiting to think through

2headlong adj 1 : 1RASH, IMPULSIVE 2 : plunging headfirst

head·mas·ter n : a man who heads the staff of a private school

head·mis·tress n : a woman who heads the staff of a private school

head–on adv or adj : with the front hitting or facing an object

head·phone n : an earphone held over the ear by a band worn on the head

head·quar·ters n sing or pl : a place where a leader gives out orders

head·stall n : an arrangement of straps or rope that fits around the head of an animal and forms part of a bridle or halter

head start n : an advantage given at the beginning (as to a school child or a runner)

head·stone n : a stone at the head of a grave

head·strong adj : always wanting one's own way

head·wait·er n : the head of the staff of a restaurant or of the dining room of a hotel

head·wa·ters n pl : the beginning and upper part of a stream

head·way n 1 : movement in a forward direction (as of a ship) 2 : 1PROGRESS 2

heal vb 1 : 2CURE 1 2 : to return to a sound or healthy condition — **heal·er** n

health n 1 : the condition of being free from illness or disease 2 : the overall condition of the body

health·ful adj : good for the health — **health·ful·ly** adv — **health·ful·ness** n

healthy adj **health·i·er; health·i·est** 1 : being sound and well : not sick 2 : showing good health 3 : aiding or building up health — **health·i·ly** adv — **health·i·ness** n

1heap n 1 : things or material piled together 2 : a large number or amount

2heap vb 1 : to throw or lay in a heap : make into a pile 2 : to provide in large amounts 3 : to fill to capacity

hear vb **heard; hear·ing** 1 : to take in through the ear : have the power of hearing 2 : to gain knowledge of by hearing 3 : to listen to with care and attention — **hear·er** n

hear·ing n 1 : the act or power of taking in sound through the ear : the sense by which a person hears 2 : EARSHOT 3 : a chance to be heard or known

hearing aid n : an electronic device used by a partly deaf person to make sounds louder

hear·ken vb : LISTEN

hear·say n : something heard from another : RUMOR

hearse n : a vehicle for carrying the dead to the grave

heart n 1 : a hollow organ of the body that expands and contracts to move blood through the arteries and veins 2 : something shaped like a heart 3 : the part nearest the center 4 : the most essential part 5 : human feelings 6 : COURAGE — **by heart** : so as to be able to repeat from memory

heart·ache n : 1SORROW 1, 2

heart·beat n : a single contracting and expanding of the heart

heart·break n : very great or deep grief

heart·break·ing adj : causing great sorrow

heart·bro·ken adj : overcome by sorrow

heart·en vb : to give new hope or courage to

heart·felt adj : deeply felt : SINCERE

hearth n 1 : an area (as of brick) in front of a fireplace 2 : the floor of a fireplace 3 : 1HOME 1

hearth·stone n : a stone forming a hearth

heart·i·ly adv 1 : with sincerity or enthusiasm 2 : COMPLETELY

heart·less adj : UNFEELING 2, CRUEL — **heart·less·ly** adv — **heart·less·ness** n

heart·sick *adj* : DESPONDENT

heart·wood *n* : the usually dark wood in the center of a tree

hearty *adj* **heart·i·er; heart·i·est** **1** : friendly and enthusiastic **2** : strong, healthy, and active **3** : having a good appetite **4** : AMPLE — **heart·i·ness** *n*

¹**heat** *vb* : to make or become warm or hot

²**heat** *n* **1** : a condition of being hot : WARMTH **2** : high temperature **3** : a form of energy that causes a body to rise in temperature **4** : strength of feeling or force of action **5** : a single race in a contest that includes two or more races

heat·ed *adj* **1** : HOT 1 **2** : ANGRY — **heat·ed·ly** *adv*

heat·er *n* : a device for heating

heath *n* **1** : any of a group of low, woody, and often evergreen plants that grow on poor, sour, wet soil **2** : a usually open level area of land on which heaths can grow

¹**hea·then** *adj* **1** : of or relating to the heathen **2** : UNCIVILIZED 1

²**heathen** *n, pl* **heathens** *or* **heathen 1** : a person who does not know about and worship the God of the Bible : PAGAN **2** : an uncivilized person

heath·er *n* : an evergreen heath of northern and mountainous areas with pink flowers and needlelike leaves

¹**heave** *vb* **heaved** *or* **hove; heav·ing 1** : to raise with an effort **2** : HURL, THROW **3** : to utter with an effort **4** : to rise and fall again and again **5** : to be thrown or raised up

²**heave** *n* **1** : an effort to lift or raise **2** : a forceful throw **3** : an upward motion (as of the chest in breathing)

heav·en *n* **1** : SKY 1 — usually used in pl. **2** *often cap* : the dwelling place of God and of the blessed dead **3** *cap* : GOD 1 **4** : a place or condition of complete happiness

heav·en·ly *adj* **1** : of or relating to heaven or the heavens **2** : of or relating to the Heaven of God and the blessed dead **3** : entirely delightful

heav·i·ly *adv* **1** : with or as if with weight **2** : in a slow and difficult way **3** : very much

heavy *adj* **heavi·er; heavi·est 1** : having great weight **2** : hard to put up with **3** : burdened by something important or troubling **4** : having little strength or energy **5** : unusually great in amount, force, or effect — **heav·i·ness** *n*

¹**He·brew** *adj* : of or relating to the Hebrew peoples or Hebrew

²**Hebrew** *n* **1** : a member of any of a group of peoples including the ancient Jews **2** : JEW **3** : the language of the Hebrews

hec·tic *adj* : filled with excitement, activity, or confusion

hecto- *prefix* : hundred

hec·to·me·ter *n* : a unit of length in the metric system equal to 100 meters

he'd : he had : he would

¹**hedge** *n* : a fence or boundary made up of a thick growth of shrubs or low trees

²**hedge** *vb* **hedged; hedg·ing 1** : to surround or protect with a hedge **2** : to avoid giving a direct or exact answer or promise

hedge·hog *n* **1** : a European mammal that eats insects, has sharp spines mixed with the hair on its back, and is able to roll itself up into a ball **2** : PORCUPINE

hedge·row *n* : a hedge of shrubs or trees around a field

¹**heed** *vb* : to pay attention to : MIND

²**heed** *n* : ATTENTION 1 — **heed·ful** *adj* — **heed·ful·ly** *adv*

heed·less *adj* : not taking heed : CARELESS — **heed·less·ly** *adv* — **heed·less·ness** *n*

¹**heel** *n* **1** : the back part of the human foot behind the arch and below the ankle **2** : the part of an animal's limb corresponding to a person's heel **3** : one of the crusty ends of a loaf of bread **4** : a part (as of a stocking) that covers the human heel **5** : the solid part of a shoe that supports the heel **6** : a rear, low, or bottom part **7** : a mean selfish person — **heel·less** *adj*

²**heel** *vb* : to lean to one side

heft *vb* : to test the weight of by lifting

hefty *adj* **heft·i·er; heft·i·est** : HEAVY 1

heif·er *n* : a young cow

height *n* **1** : the highest point or greatest degree **2** : the distance from the bottom to the top of something standing upright **3** : distance upward

height·en *vb* **1** : to make greater : INCREASE **2** : to make or become high or higher

heir *n* **1** : a person who inherits or has the right to inherit property after the death of its owner **2** : a person who has legal claim to a title or a throne when the person holding it dies

heir·ess *n* : a female heir

heir·loom *n* : a piece of personal property handed down in a family from one generation to another

held *past of* HOLD

he·li·cop·ter *n* : an aircraft supported in the air by horizontal propellers

he·li·port *n* : a place for a helicopter to land and take off

he·li·um *n* : a very light gaseous chemical element that is found in various natural gases, will not burn, and is used in balloons

hell *n* **1** : a place where souls are believed to survive after death **2** : a place or state of punishment for the wicked after death : the home of evil spirits **3** : a place or state of misery or wickedness — **hell·ish** *adj*

he'll : he shall : he will

hell·ben·der *n* : a large American salamander that lives in water

hel·lo *interj* — used as a greeting or to express surprise

helm *n* **1** : a lever or wheel for steering a ship **2** : a position of control

hel·met *n* : a protective covering for the head

¹help *vb* **1** : to provide with what is useful in achieving an end : AID, ASSIST **2** : to give relief from pain or disease **3** : PREVENT 1 **4** : ¹SERVE 9

²help *n* **1** : an act or instance of helping : AID **2** : the state of being helped **3** : a person or a thing that helps **4** : a body of hired helpers

help·er *n* **1** : one that helps **2** : a less skilled person who helps a skilled worker

help·ful *adj* : providing help — **help·ful·ly** *adv* — **help·ful·ness** *n*

help·ing *n* : a serving of food

helping verb *n* : a verb (as *am, may,* or *will*) that is used with another verb to express person, number, mood, or tense

help·less *adj* : not able to help or protect oneself — **help·less·ly** *adv* — **help·less·ness** *n*

hel·ter–skel·ter *adv* : in great disorder

¹hem *n* : a border of a cloth article made by folding back an edge and sewing it down

²hem *vb* **hemmed; hem·ming 1** : to finish with or make a hem **2** : SURROUND

hemi- *prefix* : half

hemi·sphere *n* **1** : one of the halves of the earth as divided by the equator into northern and southern parts (**northern hemisphere, southern hemisphere**) or by a meridian into two parts so that one half (**eastern hemisphere**) to the east of the Atlantic ocean includes Europe, Asia, and Africa and the half (**western hemisphere**) to the west includes North and South America and surrounding waters **2** : a half of a sphere **3** : either the left or the right half of the cerebrum

hemi·spher·ic *or* **hemi·spher·i·cal** *adj* : of or relating to a hemisphere

hem·lock *n* **1** : a poisonous plant of the carrot family **2** : an evergreen tree of the pine family

he·mo·glo·bin *n* : the coloring material of the red blood cells that carry oxygen from the lungs to the tissues

hem·or·rhage *n* : great loss of blood by bleeding

hemp *n* : a tall plant grown for its tough woody fiber that is used in making rope and for its flowers and leaves that yield drugs (as marijuana)

hen *n* **1** : a female domestic fowl **2** : a female bird

hence *adv* **1** : from this place **2** : from this time **3** : as a result : THEREFORE

hence·forth *adv* : from this time on

hench·man *n, pl* **hench·men** : a trusted follower or supporter

hep·a·ti·tis *n* : a disease which is caused by a virus and in which the liver is damaged and there is yellowing of the skin and fever

hepta- *or* **hept-** *prefix* : seven

hep·ta·gon *n* : a closed figure having seven angles and seven sides

¹her *adj* : of or relating to her or herself

²her *pron objective case of* SHE

¹her·ald *n* **1** : an official messenger **2** : a person who brings news or announces something

²herald *vb* : to give notice of : ANNOUNCE

he·ral·dic *adj* : of or relating to heralds or heraldry

her·ald·ry *n* : the art or science of tracing a person's ancestors and determining what coat of arms his or her family has the right to

herb *n* **1** : a plant with soft stems that die down at the end of the growing season **2** : a plant or plant part used in medicine or in seasoning foods

her·biv·o·rous *adj* : eating or living on plants

¹herd *n* : a number of animals of one kind kept or living together

²herd *vb* **1** : to gather or join in a herd **2** : to form into or move as a herd — **herd·er** *n*

herds·man *n, pl* **herds·men** : one who owns or tends a flock or herd

¹here *adv* **1** : in or at this place **2** : ¹NOW 1 **3** : to or into this place : HITHER

²here *n* : this place

here·abouts *or* **here·about** *adv* : near or around this place

¹here·af·ter *adv* **1** : after this **2** : in some future time or state

²hereafter *n* **1** : ²FUTURE 1 **2** : life after death

here·by *adv* : by means of this

he·red·i·tary *adj* **1** : capable of being passed from parent to offspring **2** : received or passing from an ancestor to an heir

he·red·i·ty *n, pl* **he·red·i·ties** : the passing on of characteristics (as looks or ability) from parents to offspring

here·in *adv* : in this

here·of *adv* : of this

here·on *adv* : on this

her·e·sy *n, pl* **her·e·sies** **1** : the holding of religious beliefs opposed to church doctrine : such a belief **2** : an opinion opposed to a generally accepted belief

her·e·tic *n* : a person who believes or teaches something opposed to accepted beliefs (as of a church)

he·ret·i·cal *adj* : of, relating to, or being heresy

here·to·fore *adv* : HITHERTO

here·up·on *adv* : right after this

here·with *adv* : with this

her·i·tage *n* : something that comes to one from one's ancestors

her·mit *n* : one who lives apart from others especially for religious reasons

he·ro *n, pl* **heroes** **1** : a person admired for great deeds or fine qualities **2** : one who shows great courage **3** : the chief male character in a story, play, or poem

he·ro·ic *adj* **1** : of, relating to, or like heroes **2** : COURAGEOUS, DARING — **he·ro·ical·ly** *adv*

her·o·in *n* : a very harmful drug that comes from morphine

her·o·ine *n* **1** : a woman admired for great deeds or fine qualities **2** : the chief female character in a story, poem, or play

her·o·ism *n* **1** : great courage especially for a noble purpose **2** : the qualities of a hero

her·on *n* : a wading bird that has long legs and a long neck and feeds on frogs, lizards, and small fish

her·ring *n* : a widely used food fish of the north Atlantic ocean

hers *pron* : that which belongs to her

her·self *pron* : her own self

he's : he is : he has

hes·i·tan·cy *n* : the quality or state of being hesitant

hes·i·tant *adj* : feeling or showing hesitation — **hes·i·tant·ly** *adv*

hes·i·tate *vb* **hes·i·tat·ed; hes·i·tat·ing** **1** : to pause because of forgetfulness or uncertainty **2** : to speak or say in a weak or broken way

hes·i·ta·tion *n* : an act or instance of hesitating

hew *vb* **hewed** *or* **hewn; hew·ing** **1** : to chop down **2** : to shape by cutting with an ax

hex *n* : a harmful spell : JINX

hexa- *or* **hex-** *prefix* : six

hexa·gon *n* : a closed figure having six angles and six sides

hex·ag·o·nal *adj* : having six sides — **hex·ag·o·nal·ly** *adv*

hey *interj* — used to call attention or to express surprise or joy

hey·day *n* : the time of greatest strength, energy, or success

hi *interj* — used especially as a greeting

hi·ber·nate *vb* **hi·ber·nat·ed; hi·ber·nat·ing** : to pass the winter in a resting state — **hi·ber·na·tor** *n*

hi·ber·na·tion *n* : the state of one that hibernates

1hic·cup *n* : a gulping sound caused by sudden movements of muscles active in breathing

2hiccup *vb* **hic·cuped** *also* **hic·cupped; hic·cup·ing** *also* **hic·cup·ping** : to make a hiccup

hick·o·ry *n, pl* **hick·o·ries** : a tall tree related to the walnuts that has strong tough elastic wood and bears an edible nut (**hickory nut**) in a hard shell

1hide *vb* **hid; hid·den** *or* **hid; hid·ing** **1** : to put or stay out of sight **2** : to keep secret **3** : to screen from view

2hide *n* : the skin of an animal whether fresh or prepared for use

hide–and–go–seek *n* : HIDE-AND-SEEK

hide–and–seek *n* : a game in which one player covers his or her eyes and after giving the others time to hide goes looking for them

hide·away *n* : [1]RETREAT 3, HIDEOUT

hid·eous *adj* : very ugly or disgusting : FRIGHTFUL — **hid·eous·ly** *adv* — **hid·eous·ness** *n*

hide·out *n* : a secret place for hiding (as from the police)

hi·ero·glyph·ic *n* : any of the symbols in the picture writing of ancient Egypt

hi–fi *n* **1** : HIGH FIDELITY **2** : equipment for reproduction of sound with high fidelity

hig·gle·dy–pig·gle·dy *adv or adj* : in confusion : TOPSY-TURVY

1high *adj* **1** : extending to a great distance above the ground **2** : having a specified elevation : TALL **3** : of greater degree, size, amount, or cost than average **4** : of more than usual importance **5** : having great force **6** : pitched or sounding above some other sound

2high *adv* : at or to a high place or degree

3high *n* **1** : the space overhead : SKY **2** : a region of high barometric pressure **3** : a high point or level **4** : the arrangement of gears in an automobile giving the highest speed of travel

high·brow *n* : a person of great learning or culture

high fidelity *n* : the reproduction of sound with a high degree of accuracy

high·land *n* : high or hilly country

1high·light *n* : a very interesting event or detail

2highlight *vb* **high·light·ed; high·light·ing** **1** : EMPHASIZE **2** : to be a highlight of

high·ly *adv* **1** : to a high degree : very much **2** : with much approval

high·ness *n* **1** : the quality or state or being high **2** — used as a title for a person of very high rank

high school *n* : a school usually including the ninth to twelfth or tenth to twelfth grades

high seas *n pl* : the open part of a sea or ocean

high–spir·it·ed *adj* : LIVELY 1

high–strung *adj* : very sensitive or nervous

high tide *n* : the tide when the water is at its greatest height

high·way *n* : a main road

high·way·man *n, pl* **high·way·men** : a person who robs travelers on a road

¹hike *vb* **hiked; hik·ing** : to take a long walk — **hik·er** *n*

²hike *n* : a long walk especially for pleasure or exercise

hi·lar·i·ous *adj* : enjoying or causing hilarity : MERRY — **hi·lar·i·ous·ly** *adv* — **hi·lar·i·ous·ness** *n*

hi·lar·i·ty *n* : noisy fun

¹hill *n* **1** : a usually rounded elevation of land lower than a mountain **2** : a little heap or mound of earth **3** : several seeds or plants planted in a group rather than a row

²hill *vb* **1** : to form into a heap **2** : to draw earth around the roots or base of

hill·bil·ly *n, pl* **hill·bil·lies** : a person from a backwoods area

hill·ock *n* : a small hill

hill·side *n* : the part of a hill between the top and the foot

hill·top *n* : the highest part of a hill

hilly *adj* **hill·i·er; hill·i·est** : having many hills

hilt *n* : a handle especially of a sword or dagger

him *pron objective case of* HE

him·self *pron* : his own self

hind *adj* : being at the end or back : REAR

hin·der *vb* : to make slow or difficult

hind·quar·ter *n* : the back half of a complete side of a four-footed animal or carcass

hin·drance *n* : something that hinders : OBSTACLE

hind·sight *n* : understanding of something only after it has happened

¹hinge *n* : a jointed piece on which a door, gate, or lid turns or swings

²hinge *vb* **hinged; hing·ing** **1** : to attach by or provide with hinges **2** : DEPEND 2

¹hint *n* **1** : information that helps one guess an answer or do something more easily **2** : a small amount : TRACE

²hint *vb* : to suggest something without plainly asking or saying it

hin·ter·land *n* : a region far from cities

hip *n* : the part of the body that curves out below the waist on each side

hip·pie *or* **hip·py** *n, pl* **hippies** : a usually young person who typically has long hair, is against the values and practices of society, and often lives together with others

hip·po *n, pl* **hip·pos** : HIPPOPOTAMUS

hip·po·pot·a·mus *n, pl* **hip·po·pot·a·mus·es** *or* **hip·po·pot·a·mi** : a large hoglike animal with thick hairless skin that eats plants and lives in African rivers

hire *vb* **hired; hir·ing** **1** : ¹EMPLOY 2 **2** : to get the temporary use of in return for pay **3** : to take a job

¹his *adj* : of or relating to him or himself

²his *pron* : that which belongs to him

¹His·pan·ic *adj* : of or relating to people of Latin American origin

²Hispanic *n* : a person of Latin American origin

¹hiss *vb* **1** : to make a hiss **2** : to show dislike by hissing

²hiss *n* : a sound like a long \s\ sometimes used as a sign of dislike

his·to·ri·an *n* : a person who studies or writes about history

his·tor·ic *adj* : famous in history

his·tor·i·cal *adj* **1** : of, relating to, or based on history **2** : known to be true — **his·tor·i·cal·ly** *adv*

his·to·ry *n, pl* **his·to·ries** **1** : a telling of events : STORY **2** : a written report of past events **3** : a branch of knowledge that records and explains past events

¹hit *vb* **hit; hit·ting** **1** : to touch or cause to touch with force **2** : to strike or cause to strike something aimed at **3** : to affect as if by a blow **4** : OCCUR 2 **5** : to happen to get : come upon **6** : to arrive at — **hit·ter** *n*

²hit *n* **1** : a blow striking an object aimed at **2** : COLLISION **3** : something very successful **4** : a batted baseball that enables the batter to reach base safely

hit–and–run *adj* : being or involving a driver who does not stop after being in an automobile accident

¹hitch *vb* **1** : to move by jerks **2** : to fasten by or as if by a hook or knot **3** : HITCHHIKE

²hitch *n* **1** : a jerky movement or pull **2** : an unexpected stop or obstacle **3** : a knot used for a temporary fastening

hitch·hike *vb* **hitch·hiked; hitch·hik·ing** : to travel by getting free rides in passing vehicles — **hitch·hik·er** *n*

hith·er *adv* : to this place

hith·er·to *adv* : up to this time

HIV *n* : a virus that causes AIDS by destroying large numbers of cells that help the human body fight infection

hive *n* **1** : a container for housing honeybees **2** : a colony of bees **3** : a place swarming with busy people

hives *n pl* : an allergic condition in which the skin breaks out in large red itching patches

ho *interj* — used especially to attract attention

¹hoard *n* : a supply usually of something of value stored away or hidden

²hoard *vb* : to gather and store away — **hoard·er** *n*

hoar·frost *n* : ¹FROST 2

hoarse *adj* **hoars·er; hoars·est** **1** : harsh in sound **2** : having a rough voice — **hoarse·ly** *adv* — **hoarse·ness** *n*

hoary *adj* **hoar·i·er; hoar·i·est** : gray or white with age

¹hoax *vb* : to trick into thinking something is true or real when it isn't

²hoax *n* **1** : an act meant to fool or deceive **2** : something false passed off as real

¹hob·ble *vb* **hob·bled; hob·bling** **1** : to walk with difficulty : LIMP **2** : to tie the legs of to make movement difficult

²hobble *n* **1** : a limping walk **2** : something used to hobble an animal

hob·by *n, pl* **hobbies** : an interest or activity engaged in for pleasure

hob·by·horse *n* **1** : a stick with a horse's head on which children pretend to ride **2** : ROCKING HORSE

hob·gob·lin *n* **1** : a mischievous elf **2** : BOGEY 2

hob·nail *n* : a short nail with a large head driven into soles of heavy shoes to protect against wear — **hob·nailed** *adj*

ho·bo *n, pl* **hoboes** : ¹VAGRANT

hock·ey *n* : a game played on ice or in a field by two teams who try to drive a puck or ball through a goal by hitting it with a stick

hod *n* **1** : a wooden tray or trough that has a long handle and is used to carry mortar or bricks **2** : a bucket for holding or carrying coal

hodge·podge *n* : a disorderly mixture

¹hoe *n* : a tool with a long handle and a thin flat blade used for weeding and cultivating

²hoe *vb* **hoed; hoe·ing** : to weed or loosen the soil around plants with a hoe

¹hog *n* **1** : an adult domestic swine **2** : a greedy or dirty person

²hog *vb* **hogged; hog·ging** : to take more than one's share

ho·gan *n* : a dwelling of some American Indians made of logs or sticks covered with earth

hog·gish *adj* : very selfish or greedy — **hog·gish·ly** *adv* — **hog·gish·ness** *n*

hogs·head *n* **1** : a very large cask **2** : a

unit of liquid measure equal to sixty-three gallons (about 238 liters)

¹hoist *vb* : to lift up especially with a pulley

²hoist *n* **1** : an act of hoisting **2** : a device used for lifting heavy loads

¹hold *vb* **held; hold·ing** **1** : to have or keep in one's possession or under one's control **2** : to limit the movement or activity of : RESTRAIN **3** : to make accept a legal or moral duty **4** : to have or keep in one's grasp **5** : ¹SUPPORT 4 **6** : to take in and have within : CONTAIN **7** : to have in mind **8** : CONSIDER 3, REGARD **9** : to carry on by group action **10** : to continue in the same way or state : LAST **11** : to remain fast or fastened **12** : to bear or carry oneself

²hold *n* **1** : the act or way of holding : GRIP **2** : ¹INFLUENCE 1 **3** : a note or rest in music kept up longer than usual

³hold *n* **1** : the part of a ship below the decks in which cargo is stored **2** : the cargo compartment of an airplane

hold·er *n* : one that holds

hold out *vb* : to refuse to yield or agree

hold·up *n* **1** : robbery by an armed robber **2** : ¹DELAY

hold up *vb* **1** : ²DELAY 2 **2** : to rob while threatening with a weapon

hole *n* **1** : an opening into or through something **2** : CAVITY **3** : DEN 1, BURROW

hol·i·day *n* **1** : a day of freedom from work especially when celebrating some event **2** : VACATION

ho·li·ness *n* **1** : the quality or state of being holy **2** — used as a title for persons of high religious position

¹hol·ler *vb* : to cry out : SHOUT

²holler *n* : ²SHOUT, CRY

¹hol·low *n* **1** : a low spot in a surface **2** : VALLEY **3** : CAVITY

²hollow *adj* **1** : curved inward : SUNKEN **2** : having a space inside : not solid **3** : suggesting a sound made in an empty place **4** : not sincere — **hol·low·ly** *adv* — **hol·low·ness** *n*

³hollow *vb* : to make or become hollow

hol·ly *n, pl* **hollies** : an evergreen tree or shrub that has shiny leaves with prickly edges and red berries much used for Christmas decorations

hol·ly·hock *n* : a plant with large rounded leaves and tall stalks of bright showy flowers

ho·lo·caust *n* : a complete destruction especially by fire

ho·lo·gram *n* : a three-dimensional picture made by laser light reflected onto a photographic substance without the use of a camera

hol·ster *n* : a usually leather case in which a pistol is carried or worn

ho·ly *adj* **ho·li·er; ho·li·est** **1** : set apart for the service of God or of a divine being : SACRED **2** : having a right to expect complete devotion **3** : pure in spirit

hom- *or* **homo-** *prefix* : one and the same : similar : alike

hom·age *n* **1** : a feudal ceremony in which a person pledges loyalty to a lord and becomes a vassal **2** : ¹RESPECT 2

¹home *n* **1** : the house in which one or one's family lives **2** : the place where one was born or grew up **3** : HABITAT **4** : a place for the care of persons unable to care for themselves **5** : the social unit formed by a family living together **6** : ¹HOUSE 1 **7** : the goal or point to be reached in some games — **home·less** *adj*

²home *adv* **1** : to or at home **2** : to the final place or limit

home·land *n* : native land

home·like *adj* : like a home (as in comfort and kindly warmth)

home·ly *adj* **home·li·er; home·li·est** **1** : suggesting home life **2** : not handsome

home·made *adj* : made in the home

home·mak·er *n* : a person who manages a household especially as a wife and mother — **home·mak·ing** *n or adj*

home page *n* : the page of a World Wide Web site that is usually seen first and that usually contains links to the other pages of the site or to other sites

home plate *n* : the base that a baseball runner must touch to score

hom·er *n* : HOME RUN

home·room *n* : a schoolroom where pupils of the same class report at the start of each day

home run *n* : a hit in baseball that enables the batter to go around all the bases and score

home·school *vb* : to teach school subjects to one's children at home

home·school·er *n* **1** : one that homeschools **2** : a child who is homeschooled

home·sick *adj* : longing for home and family — **home·sick·ness** *n*

¹home·spun *adj* **1** : spun or made at home **2** : made of homespun **3** : not fancy : SIMPLE

²homespun *n* : a loosely woven usually woolen or linen fabric originally made from homespun yarn

¹home·stead *n* **1** : a home and the land around it **2** : a piece of land gained from United States public lands by living on and farming it

²homestead *vb* : to acquire or settle on public land for use as a homestead — **home·stead·er** *n*

home·ward *or* **home·wards** *adv or adj* : toward home

home·work *n* : work (as school lessons) to be done at home

hom·ey *adj* **hom·i·er; hom·i·est** : HOMELIKE — **hom·ey·ness** *or* **hom·i·ness** *n*

ho·mi·cide *n* : a killing of one human being by another

hom·ing pigeon *n* : a racing pigeon trained to return home

hom·i·ny *n* : hulled corn with the germ removed

homo- — see HOM-

ho·mog·e·nize *vb* **ho·mog·e·nized; ho·mog·e·niz·ing** : to reduce the particles in (as milk or paint) to the same size and spread them evenly in the liquid

ho·mo·graph *n* : one of two or more words spelled alike but different in meaning or origin or pronunciation

hom·onym *n* **1** : HOMOPHONE **2** : HOMOGRAPH **3** : one of two or more words spelled and pronounced alike but different in meaning

ho·mo·phone *n* : one of two or more words pronounced alike but different in meaning or origin or spelling

hone *vb* **honed; hon·ing** : to sharpen with or as if with a fine abrasive stone

hon·est *adj* **1** : free from fraud or trickery : STRAIGHTFORWARD **2** : not given to cheating, stealing, or lying : UPRIGHT, TRUSTWORTHY **3** : being just what is indicated : REAL, GENUINE

hon·es·ty *n* : the quality or state of being honest

hon·ey *n* **1** : a sweet sticky fluid made by bees from the liquid drawn from flowers **2** : an outstanding example

hon·ey·bee *n* : a bee whose honey is used by people as food

¹hon·ey·comb *n* **1** : a mass of wax cells built by honeybees in their nest to contain young bees and stores of honey **2** : something like a honeycomb in structure or appearance

²honeycomb *vb* : to make or become full of holes like a honeycomb

hon·ey·dew melon *n* : a pale muskmelon with greenish sweet flesh and smooth skin

¹hon·ey·moon *n* **1** : a holiday taken by a recently married couple **2** : a period of harmony especially just after marriage

²honeymoon *vb* : to have a honeymoon — **hon·ey·moon·er** *n*

hon·ey·suck·le *n* : a climbing vine or a bush with fragrant white, yellow, or red flowers

¹honk *vb* : to make a honk

honk

²**honk** n 1 : the cry of a goose 2 : a sound like the cry of a goose

¹**hon·or** n 1 : public admiration : REPUTATION 2 : outward respect : RECOGNITION 3 : PRIVILEGE 4 — used especially as a title for an official of high rank (as a judge) 5 : a person whose worth brings respect or fame 6 : evidence or a symbol of great respect 7 : high moral standards of behavior

²**honor** vb 1 : ²RESPECT 2 : to give an honor to

hon·or·able adj 1 : bringing about or deserving honor 2 : observing ideas of honor or reputation 3 : having high moral standards of behavior : ETHICAL, UPRIGHT

hon·or·ary adj : given or done as an honor

¹**hood** n 1 : a covering for the head and neck and sometimes the face 2 : something like a hood 3 : the movable covering for an automobile engine — **hood·ed** adj

²**hood** vb : to cover with or as if with a hood

-hood n suffix 1 : state : condition : quality : nature 2 : instance of a specified state or quality 3 : individuals sharing a specified state or character

hood·lum n : a brutal ruffian : THUG

hood·wink vb : to mislead by trickery

hoof n, pl **hooves** or **hoofs** 1 : a covering of horn that protects the ends of the toes of some animals (as horses, oxen, or swine) 2 : a hoofed foot (as of a horse) — **hoofed** adj

¹**hook** n 1 : a curved device (as a piece of bent metal) for catching, holding, or pulling something 2 : something curved or bent like a hook — **by hook or by crook** : in any way : fairly or unfairly

²**hook** vb 1 : to bend in the shape of a hook 2 : to catch or fasten with a hook

hook·worm n : a small worm that lives in the intestines and makes people sick by sucking their blood

hoop n 1 : a circular band used for holding together the strips that make up the sides of a barrel or tub 2 : a circular figure or object 3 : a circle or series of circles of flexible material (as wire) used for holding a woman's skirt out from the body

hooray variant of HURRAH

¹**hoot** vb 1 : to utter a loud shout usually to show disapproval 2 : to make the noise of an owl or a similar cry 3 : to express by hoots

²**hoot** n 1 : a sound of hooting 2 : the least bit

¹**hop** vb **hopped**; **hop·ping** 1 : to move by short quick jumps 2 : to jump on one foot 3 : to jump over 4 : to get aboard by or as if by hopping 5 : to make a quick trip especially by air

²**hop** n 1 : a short quick jump especially on one leg 2 : ²DANCE 2 3 : a short trip especially by air

³**hop** n 1 : a twining vine whose greenish flowers look like cones 2 **hops** pl : the dried flowers of the hop plant used chiefly in making beer and ale and in medicine

¹**hope** vb **hoped**; **hop·ing** : to desire especially with expectation that the wish will be granted

²**hope** n 1 : ¹TRUST 1 2 : desire together with the expectation of getting what is wanted 3 : a cause for hope 4 : something hoped for

hope·ful adj 1 : full of hope 2 : giving hope : PROMISING — **hope·ful·ly** adv — **hope·ful·ness** n

hope·less adj 1 : having no hope 2 : offering no hope — **hope·less·ly** adv — **hope·less·ness** n

hop·per n 1 : one that hops 2 : an insect that moves by leaping 3 : a container usually shaped like a funnel for delivering material (as grain or coal) into a machine or a bin 4 : a tank holding liquid and having a device for releasing its contents through a pipe

hop·scotch n : a game in which a player tosses a stone into sections of a figure drawn on the ground and hops through the figure and back to pick up the stone

horde n : MULTITUDE, SWARM

ho·ri·zon n 1 : the line where the earth or sea seems to meet the sky 2 : the limit of a person's outlook or experience

¹**hor·i·zon·tal** adj : level with the horizon — **hor·i·zon·tal·ly** adv

²**horizontal** n : something (as a line or plane) that is horizontal

hor·mone n : any of various chemical substances secreted by body cells especially into the blood and acting on cells or organs of the body usually at a distance from the place of origin

horn n 1 : one of the hard bony growths on the head of many hoofed animals (as cattle, goats, or sheep) 2 : the material of which horns are composed or a similar material 3 : something made from a horn 4 : something shaped like a horn 5 : a musical or signaling instrument made from an animal's horn 6 : a brass musical instrument (as a trumpet or French horn) 7 : a usually electrical device that makes a noise like that of a horn — **horned** adj — **horn·less** adj — **horn·like** adj

horned toad n : a small harmless lizard with scales and hard pointed growths on the skin

hor·net n : a large wasp that can give a severe sting

horn of plenty : CORNUCOPIA

horny *adj* **horn·i·er; horn·i·est** : like or made of horn

hor·ri·ble *adj* : causing horror : TERRIBLE — **hor·ri·bly** *adv*

hor·rid *adj* **1** : HORRIBLE **2** : very unpleasant : DISGUSTING — **hor·rid·ly** *adv*

hor·ri·fy *vb* **hor·ri·fied; hor·ri·fy·ing** : to cause to feel horror

hor·ror *n* **1** : great and painful fear, dread, or shock **2** : great dislike **3** : a quality or thing that causes horror

horse *n* **1** : a large hoofed animal that feeds on grasses and is used as a work animal and for riding **2** : a frame that supports something (as wood while being cut) **3** : a piece of gymnasium equipment used for vaulting exercises — **horse·less** *adj* — **from the horse's mouth** : from the original source

¹horse·back *n* : the back of a horse

²horseback *adv* : on horseback

horse·car *n* **1** : a streetcar drawn by horses **2** : a car for transporting horses

horse chestnut *n* : a shiny brown nut that is unfit to eat and is the fruit of a tall tree with leaves divided into fingerlike parts and large flower clusters shaped like cones

horse·fly *n, pl* **horse·flies** : a large swift two-winged fly the females of which suck blood from animals

horse·hair *n* **1** : the hair of a horse especially from the mane or tail **2** : cloth made from horsehair

horse latitudes *n pl* : either of two regions in the neighborhoods of 30° north and 30° south of the equator marked by calms and light changeable winds

horse·man *n, pl* **horse·men** **1** : a horseback rider **2** : a person skilled in handling horses — **horse·man·ship** *n*

horse opera *n* : a movie or a radio or television play about cowboys

horse·play *n* : rough play

horse·pow·er *n* : a unit of power that equals the work done in raising 550 pounds one foot in one second

horse·rad·ish *n* : a hot relish made from the root of an herb of the mustard family

horse·shoe *n* **1** : a protective iron plate that is nailed to the rim of a horse's hoof **2** : something shaped like a horseshoe **3** **horseshoes** *pl* : a game in which horseshoes are tossed at a stake in the ground

horse·tail *n* : any of a group of primitive plants that produce spores and have hollow stems with joints and leaves reduced to sheaths about the joints

horse·whip *vb* **horse·whipped; horse·whip·ping** : to beat severely with a whip made to be used on a horse

horse·wom·an *n, pl* **horse·wom·en** : a woman skilled in riding on horseback or in handling horses

hors·ey *or* **horsy** *adj* **hors·i·er; hors·i·est** : of or relating to horses or horsemen and horsewomen

ho·san·na *interj* — used as a cry of approval, praise, or love

¹hose *n, pl* **hose** *or* **hos·es** **1** *pl* **hose** : STOCKING, SOCK **2** : a flexible tube for carrying fluid

²hose *vb* **hosed; hos·ing** : to spray, water, or wash with a hose

ho·siery *n* : stockings or socks in general

hos·pi·ta·ble *adj* **1** : friendly and generous in entertaining guests **2** : willing to deal with something new — **hos·pi·ta·bly** *adv*

hos·pi·tal *n* : a place where the sick and injured are cared for

hos·pi·tal·i·ty *n* : friendly and generous treatment of guests

hos·pi·tal·ize *vb* **hos·pi·tal·ized; hos·pi·tal·iz·ing** : to place in a hospital for care and treatment — **hos·pi·tal·iza·tion** *n*

¹host *n* **1** : ARMY 1 **2** : MULTITUDE

²host *n* : one who receives or entertains guests

³host *n, often cap* : the bread used in Christian Communion

hos·tage *n* : a person given or held to make certain that promises will be kept

hos·tel *n* : a place providing inexpensive lodging for use by young travelers

host·ess *n* : a woman who receives or entertains guests

hos·tile *adj* **1** : of or relating to an enemy **2** : UNFRIENDLY

hos·til·i·ty *n, pl* **hos·til·i·ties** **1** : a hostile state, attitude, or action **2** **hostilities** *pl* : acts of warfare

hot *adj* **hot·ter; hot·test** **1** : having a high temperature **2** : easily excited **3** : having or causing the sensation of an uncomfortable degree of body heat **4** : recently made or received **5** : close to something sought **6** : PUNGENT **7** : RADIOACTIVE **8** : recently stolen — **hot·ly** *adv* — **hot·ness** *n*

hot·bed *n* : a bed of heated earth covered by glass for growing tender plants early in the season

hot dog *n* : a frankfurter and especially a cooked one served in a long split roll

ho·tel *n* : a place that provides lodging and meals for the public : INN

hot·head *n* : a person who is easily excited or angered — **hot·head·ed** *adj*

hot·house *n* : a heated building enclosed by glass for growing plants

hot plate *n* : a small portable appliance for heating or cooking

hot rod *n* : an automobile rebuilt for high speed and fast acceleration

hot water *n* : a difficult or distressing situation : TROUBLE

1hound *n* : a dog with drooping ears and deep bark that is used in hunting and follows game by the sense of smell

2hound *vb* : to hunt, chase, or annoy without ceasing

hour *n* **1** : one of the twenty-four divisions of a day : sixty minutes **2** : the time of day **3** : a fixed or particular time **4** : a measure of distance figured by the amount of time it takes to cover it

hour·glass *n* : a device for measuring time in which sand runs from the upper into the lower part of a glass in an hour

1hour·ly *adv* : at or during every hour

2hourly *adj* **1** : occurring every hour **2** : figured by the hour

1house *n, pl* **hous·es 1** : a place built for people to live in **2** : something (as a nest or den) used by an animal for shelter **3** : a building in which something is kept **4** : ¹HOUSEHOLD **5** : FAMILY 1 **6** : a body of persons assembled to make the laws for a country **7** : a business firm **8** : the audience in a theater or concert hall — **on the house** : free of charge

2house *vb* **1** : to provide with living quarters or shelter **2** : CONTAIN 3

house·boat *n* : a roomy pleasure boat fitted for use as a place to live

house·boy *n* : a boy or man hired to do housework

house·fly *n, pl* **house·flies** : a two-winged fly that is common about houses and often carries disease germs

1house·hold *n* : all the persons who live as a family in one house

2household *adj* **1** : of or relating to a household **2** : FAMILIAR

house·hold·er *n* : one who lives in a dwelling alone or as the head of a household

house·keep·er *n* : a person employed to take care of a house

house·keep·ing *n* : the care and management of a house

house·maid *n* : a woman or girl hired to do housework

house·moth·er *n* : a woman who acts as hostess, supervisor, and often housekeeper in a residence for young people

house·plant *n* : a plant grown or kept indoors

house·top *n* : ¹ROOF 1

house·warm·ing *n* : a party to celebrate moving into a new home

house·wife *n, pl* **house·wives** : a married woman in charge of a household

house·work *n* : the actual labor involved in housekeeping

hous·ing *n* **1** : dwellings provided for a number of people **2** : something that covers or protects

hove *past of* HEAVE

hov·el *n* : a small poorly built usually dirty house

hov·er *vb* **1** : to hang fluttering in the air or on the wing **2** : to move to and fro near a place

1how *adv* **1** : in what way : by what means **2** : for what reason **3** : to what degree, number, or amount **4** : in what state or condition — **how about** : what do you say to or think of — **how come** : ¹WHY — **how do you do** : HELLO

2how *conj* : in what manner or condition

how·ev·er *adv* **1** : to whatever degree or extent **2** : in whatever way **3** : in spite of that

1howl *vb* **1** : to make a loud long mournful sound like that of a dog **2** : to cry out loudly (as with pain)

2howl *n* **1** : a loud long mournful sound made by dogs **2** : a long loud cry (as of distress, disappointment, or rage) **3** : COMPLAINT 1 **4** : something that causes laughter

HTML *n* : a computer language that is used to create pages on the World Wide Web that can include text, pictures, sound, video, and links to other Web pages

hub *n* **1** : the center of a wheel, propeller, or fan **2** : a center of activity

hub·bub *n* : UPROAR

huck·le·ber·ry *n, pl* **huck·le·ber·ries** : a dark edible berry with many hard seeds that grows on a bush related to the blueberry

huck·ster *n* **1** : PEDDLER, HAWKER **2** : a writer of advertising

1hud·dle *vb* **hud·dled; hud·dling 1** : to crowd, push, or pile together **2** : to get together to talk something over **3** : to curl up

2huddle *n* **1** : a closely packed group **2** : a private meeting or conference

hue *n* **1** : ¹COLOR 1 **2** : a shade of a color

1huff *vb* : to give off puffs (as of air or steam)

2huff *n* : a fit of anger or temper

huffy *adj* **huff·i·er; huff·i·est 1** : easily offended : PETULANT **2** : ¹SULKY — **huff·i·ly** *adv* — **huff·i·ness** *n*

1hug *vb* **hugged; hug·ging 1** : to clasp in the arms : EMBRACE **2** : to keep close to

2hug *n* : ²EMBRACE

huge *adj* **hug·er; hug·est** : very large : VAST

hulk *n* **1** : a person or thing that is bulky or clumsy **2** : the remains of an old or wrecked ship

hulk·ing *adj* : very large and strong : MASSIVE

¹hull *n* **1** : the outside covering of a fruit or seed **2** : the frame or body of a ship, flying boat, or airship

²hull *vb* : to remove the hulls of — **hull·er** *n*

hul·la·ba·loo *n, pl* **hul·la·ba·loos** : a confused noise : HUBBUB, COMMOTION

¹hum *vb* **hummed; hum·ming 1** : to utter a sound like a long \m\ **2** : to make the buzzing noise of a flying insect **3** : to sing with closed lips **4** : to give forth a low murmur of sounds **5** : to be very busy or active

²hum *n* : the act or an instance of humming : the sound produced by humming

¹hu·man *adj* **1** : of, relating to, being, or characteristic of people as distinct from lower animals **2** : having human form or characteristics

²human *n* : a human being — **hu·man·like** *adj*

hu·mane *adj* : having sympathy and consideration for others — **hu·mane·ly** *adv* — **hu·mane·ness** *n*

¹hu·man·i·tar·i·an *n* : a person devoted to and working for the health and happiness of other people

²humanitarian *adj* : of, relating to, or characteristic of humanitarians

hu·man·i·ty *n, pl* **hu·man·i·ties 1** : KINDNESS 2, SYMPATHY **2** : the quality or state of being human **3** *humanities pl* : studies (as literature, history, and art) concerned primarily with human culture **4** : the human race

hu·man·ly *adv* : within the range of human ability

¹hum·ble *adj* **hum·bler; hum·blest 1** : not bold or proud : MODEST **2** : expressing a spirit of respect for the wishes of another **3** : low in rank or condition — **hum·bly** *adv*

²humble *vb* **hum·bled; hum·bling 1** : to make humble **2** : to destroy the power of

¹hum·bug *n* **1** : FRAUD 3 **2** : NONSENSE 1

²humbug *vb* **hum·bugged; hum·bug·ging** : DECEIVE 1

hum·ding·er *n* : something striking or extraordinary

hum·drum *adj* : MONOTONOUS

hu·mid *adj* : MOIST

hu·mid·i·fy *vb* **hu·mid·i·fied; hu·mid·i·fy·ing** : to make (as the air of a room) more moist — **hu·mid·i·fi·er** *n*

hu·mid·i·ty *n, pl* **hu·mid·i·ties** : the degree of wetness especially of the atmosphere : MOISTURE

hu·mil·i·ate *vb* **hu·mil·i·at·ed; hu·mil·i·at·ing** : to lower the pride or self-respect of

hu·mil·i·a·tion *n* **1** : the state of being humiliated **2** : an instance of being humiliated

hu·mil·i·ty *n* : the quality of being humble

hum·ming·bird *n* : a tiny brightly colored American bird whose wings make a humming sound in flight

hum·mock *n* **1** : a rounded mound of earth : KNOLL **2** : a ridge or pile of ice

¹hu·mor *n* **1** : state of mind : MOOD **2** : the amusing quality of something **3** : the ability to see or report the amusing quality of things

²humor *vb* : to give in to the wishes of

hu·mor·ist *n* : a person who writes or talks in a humorous way

hu·mor·ous *adj* : full of humor : FUNNY — **hu·mor·ous·ly** *adv*

hump *n* **1** : a rounded bulge or lump (as on the back of a camel) **2** : a difficult part (as of a task) — **humped** *adj*

hump·back *n* **1** : a humped back **2** : HUNCHBACK 2 — **hump·backed** *adj*

hu·mus *n* : the dark rich part of earth formed from decaying material

¹hunch *vb* **1** : to bend one's body into an arch or hump **2** : to draw up close together or into an arch

²hunch *n* **1** : HUMP 1 **2** : a strong feeling about what will happen

hunch·back *n* **1** : HUMPBACK 1 **2** : a person with a humped or crooked back

¹hun·dred *n* **1** : ten times ten : 100 **2** : a very large number

²hundred *adj* : being 100

¹hun·dredth *adj* : coming right after ninety-ninth

²hundredth *n* : number 100 in a series

hung *past of* HANG

¹hun·ger *n* **1** : a desire or a need for food **2** : a strong desire

²hunger *vb* **1** : to feel hunger **2** : to have a strong desire

hun·gry *adj* **hun·gri·er; hun·gri·est 1** : feeling or showing hunger **2** : having a strong desire — **hun·gri·ly** *adv*

hunk *n* : a large lump or piece

¹hunt *vb* **1** : to follow after in order to capture or kill **2** : to try to find

²hunt *n* : an instance or the practice of hunting

hunt·er *n* **1** : a person who hunts game **2** : a dog or horse used or trained for hunting **3** : a person who searches for something

hunts·man *n, pl* **hunts·men** : HUNTER 1

¹hur·dle *n* **1** : a barrier to be jumped in a race (*hurdles*) **2** : OBSTACLE

²hurdle *vb* **hur·dled; hur·dling 1** : to leap over while running **2** : OVERCOME

hur·dy–gur·dy *n, pl* **hur·dy–gur·dies** : HAND ORGAN

hurl *vb* : to throw with force

hur·rah *or* **hoo·ray** *also* **hur·ray** *interj* — used to express joy, approval, or encouragement

hur·ri·cane *n* : a tropical cyclone with winds of thirty-three meters per second or greater usually accompanied by rain, thunder, and lightning

hur·ried *adj* **1** : going or working with speed : FAST **2** : done in a hurry — **hur·ried·ly** *adv*

1hur·ry *vb* **hur·ried; hur·ry·ing** **1** : to carry or cause to go with haste **2** : to move or act with haste **3** : to speed up

2hurry *n* : a state of eagerness or urgent need : extreme haste

1hurt *vb* **hurt; hurt·ing** **1** : to feel or cause pain **2** : to do harm to : DAMAGE **3** : 2DISTRESS, OFFEND **4** : to make poorer or more difficult

2hurt *n* **1** : an injury or wound to the body **2** : SUFFERING 1, ANGUISH **3** : 1WRONG

hurt·ful *adj* : causing injury or suffering

hur·tle *vb* **hur·tled; hur·tling** **1** : to rush suddenly or violently **2** : to drive or throw violently

1hus·band *n* : a married man

2husband *vb* : to manage with thrift : use carefully

hus·band·ry *n* **1** : the management or wise use of resources : THRIFT **2** : the business and activities of a farmer

1hush *vb* : to make or become quiet, calm, or still : SOOTHE

2hush *n* : 1QUIET

hush–hush *adj* : 1SECRET 1, CONFIDENTIAL

1husk *n* : the outer covering of a fruit or seed

2husk *vb* : to strip the husk from — **husk·er** *n*

1hus·ky *adj* **hus·ki·er; hus·ki·est** : HOARSE — **hus·ki·ly** *adv* — **hus·ki·ness** *n*

2husky *n, pl* **huskies** : a strong dog with a thick coat used to pull sleds in the Arctic

3husky *n, pl* **huskies** : a husky person or thing

4husky *adj* **hus·ki·er; hus·ki·est** : STRONG 1, BURLY — **hus·ki·ness** *n*

1hus·tle *vb* **hus·tled; hus·tling** **1** : to push, crowd, or force forward roughly **2** : HURRY

2hustle *n* : energetic activity

hus·tler *n* : an energetic person who works fast

hut *n* : a small roughly made and often temporary dwelling

hutch *n* **1** : a low cupboard usually having open shelves on top **2** : a pen or coop for an animal

hy·a·cinth *n* : a plant of the lily family with stalks of fragrant flowers shaped like bells

1hy·brid *n* **1** : an animal or plant whose parents differ in some hereditary characteristic or belong to different groups (as breeds, races, or species) **2** : something that is of mixed origin or composition

2hybrid *adj* : of or relating to a hybrid : of mixed origin

hydr- *or* **hydro-** *prefix* **1** : water **2** : hydrogen

hy·drant *n* : a pipe with a spout through which water may be drawn from the main pipes

hy·drau·lic *adj* **1** : operated, moved, or brought about by means of water **2** : operated by liquid forced through a small hole or through a tube — **hy·drau·li·cal·ly** *adv*

hy·dro·car·bon *n* : a substance containing only carbon and hydrogen

hy·dro·chlo·ric acid *n* : a strong acid formed by dissolving in water a gas made up of hydrogen and chlorine

hy·dro·elec·tric *adj* : relating to or used in the making of electricity by waterpower

hy·dro·gen *n* : a colorless, odorless, and tasteless flammable gas that is the lightest of the chemical elements

hydrogen bomb *n* : a bomb whose great power is due to the sudden release of energy when the central portions of hydrogen atoms unite

hydrogen peroxide *n* : a liquid chemical containing hydrogen and oxygen and used for bleaching and as an antiseptic

hy·dro·pho·bia *n* : RABIES

hy·dro·plane *n* **1** : a speedboat whose hull is completely or partly raised as it glides over the water **2** : SEAPLANE

hy·e·na *n* : a large mammal of Asia and Africa that lives on flesh

hy·giene *n* **1** : a science that deals with the bringing about and keeping up of good health in the individual and the group **2** : conditions or practices necessary for health

hy·gien·ic *adj* : of, relating to, or leading toward health or hygiene — **hy·gien·i·cal·ly** *adv*

hy·gien·ist *n* : a person skilled in hygiene and especially in a specified branch of hygiene

hy·grom·e·ter *n* : an instrument for measuring the humidity of the air

hymn *n* : a song of praise especially to God

hym·nal *n* : a book of hymns

hyper- *prefix* : excessively

hy·per·link *n* : an electronic link that allows a computer user to move directly from a marked place in a hypertext document to another in the same or a different document — **hyperlink** *vb*

hy·per·sen·si·tive *adj* : very sensitive

hy·per·text *n* : an arrangement of the information in a computer database that allows the user to get other information by clicking on text displayed on the screen

hy·pha *n, pl* **hy·phae** : one of the fine threads that make up the body of a fungus

¹hy·phen *n* : a mark - used to divide or to compound words or word elements

²hyphen *vb* : HYPHENATE

hy·phen·ate *vb* **hy·phen·at·ed; hy·phen·at·ing** : to connect or mark with a hyphen

hyp·no·sis *n* : a state which resembles sleep but is produced by a person who can then make suggestions to which the hypnotized person will respond

hyp·no·tism *n* : the study or act of producing a state like sleep in which the person in this state will respond to suggestions made by the hypnotist

hyp·no·tist *n* : a person who practices hypnotism

hyp·no·tize *vb* **hyp·no·tized; hyp·no·tiz·ing** : to affect by or as if by hypnotism

hy·poc·ri·sy *n, pl* **hy·poc·ri·sies** : a pretending to be what one is not or to believe or feel what one does not

hyp·o·crite *n* : a person who practices hypocrisy

hy·pot·e·nuse *n* : the side of a right triangle that is opposite the right angle

hy·poth·e·sis *n, pl* **hy·poth·e·ses** : something not proved but assumed to be true for purposes of argument or further study or investigation

hy·po·thet·i·cal *adj* **1** : involving or based on a hypothesis **2** : being merely supposed — **hy·po·thet·i·cal·ly** *adv*

hys·te·ria *n* **1** : a nervous disorder in which one loses control over the emotions **2** : a wild uncontrolled outburst of emotion — **hys·ter·i·cal** *adj* — **hys·ter·i·cal·ly** *adv*

hys·ter·ics *n sing or pl* : a fit of uncontrollable laughing or crying : HYSTERIA

I

i *n, pl* **i's** *or* **is** *often cap* **1** : the ninth letter of the English alphabet **2** : one in Roman numerals

I *pron* : the person speaking or writing

-ial *adj suffix* : ¹-AL

-ian — see -AN

ibex *n, pl* **ibex** *or* **ibex·es** : a wild goat of the Old World with horns that curve backward

-ibility — see -ABILITY

ibis *n, pl* **ibis** *or* **ibis·es** : a bird related to the herons but having a slender bill that curves down

-ible — see -ABLE

-ic *adj suffix* **1** : of, relating to, or having the form of : being **2** : coming from, consisting of, or containing **3** : in the manner of **4** : associated or dealing with : using **5** : characterized by : exhibiting : affected with

-ical *adj suffix* : -IC

¹ice *n* **1** : frozen water **2** : a substance like ice **3** : a frozen dessert usually made with sweetened fruit juice

²ice *vb* **iced; ic·ing** **1** : to coat or become coated with ice **2** : to chill with ice : supply with ice **3** : to cover with icing

ice·berg *n* : a large floating mass of ice that has broken away from a glacier

ice·boat *n* : a boatlike frame driven by sails and gliding over ice on runners

ice·bound *adj* : surrounded or blocked by ice

ice·box *n* : REFRIGERATOR

ice·break·er *n* : a ship equipped to make and keep open a channel through ice

ice cap *n* : a large more or less level glacier flowing outward in all directions from its center

ice–cold *adj* : very cold

ice cream *n* : a frozen food containing sweetened and flavored cream or butterfat

ice–skate *vb* : to skate on ice — **ice skat·er** *n*

ici·cle *n* : a hanging mass of ice formed from dripping water

ic·ing *n* : a sweet coating for baked goods

icon *n* **1** : a picture that represents something **2** : a religious image usually painted on a small wooden panel **3** : a small picture or symbol on a computer screen that suggests a function that the computer can perform

-ics *n sing or pl suffix* **1** : study : knowledge : skill : practice **2** : characteristic actions or qualities

icy *adj* **ic·i·er; ic·i·est** **1** : covered with, full of, or being ice **2** : very cold **3** : UN-FRIENDLY — **ic·i·ly** *adv* — **ic·i·ness** *n*

I'd : I had : I should : I would

idea *n* **1** : a plan of action : INTENTION **2** : something imagined or pictured in the mind : NOTION **3** : a central meaning or purpose

¹ide·al *adj* **1** : existing only in the mind **2** : having no flaw : PERFECT — **ide·al·ly** *adv*

²ideal *n* **1** : a standard of perfection, beauty, or excellence **2** : a perfect type

iden·ti·cal *adj* **1** : being one and the same **2** : being exactly alike or equal

identification

iden·ti·fi·ca·tion *n* **1** : an act of identifying : the state of being identified **2** : something that shows or proves identity

iden·ti·fy *vb* **iden·ti·fied; iden·ti·fy·ing 1** : to think of as identical **2** : ¹ASSOCIATE 2 **3** : to find out or show the identity of

iden·ti·ty *n, pl* **iden·ti·ties 1** : the fact or condition of being exactly alike : SAMENESS **2** : INDIVIDUALITY 1 **3** : the fact of being the same person or thing as claimed

id·i·o·cy *n, pl* **id·i·o·cies 1** : great lack of intelligence **2** : something very stupid or foolish

id·i·om *n* : an expression that cannot be understood from the meanings of its separate words but must be learned as a whole

id·i·ot *n* **1** : a person of very low intelligence **2** : a silly or foolish person

id·i·ot·ic *adj* : showing idiocy : FOOLISH, STUPID — **id·i·ot·i·cal·ly** *adv*

¹idle *adj* **idler; idlest 1** : not based on facts **2** : not working or in use **3** : LAZY 1 — **idle·ness** *n* — **idly** *adv*

²idle *vb* **idled; idling 1** : to spend time doing nothing **2** : to run without being connected for doing useful work — **idler** *n*

idol *n* **1** : an image worshiped as a god **2** : a much loved person or thing

idol·ize *vb* **idol·ized; idol·iz·ing** : to make an idol of : love or admire too much

-ie *also* **-y** *n suffix, pl* **-ies** : little one

-ier — see ²-ER

if *conj* **1** : in the event that **2** : WHETHER 1

-ify *vb suffix* **-ified; -ify·ing** : -FY

ig·loo *n, pl* **igloos** : an Eskimo house often made of blocks of snow and shaped like a dome

ig·ne·ous *adj* : formed by hardening of melted mineral material

ig·nite *vb* **ig·nit·ed; ig·nit·ing 1** : to set on fire : LIGHT **2** : to catch fire

ig·ni·tion *n* **1** : the act or action of igniting **2** : the process or means (as an electric spark) of igniting a fuel mixture

ig·no·ble *adj* : DISHONORABLE — **ig·no·bly** *adv*

ig·no·rance *n* : the state of being ignorant

ig·no·rant *adj* **1** : having little or no knowledge : not educated **2** : not knowing : UNAWARE **3** : resulting from or showing lack of knowledge — **ig·no·rant·ly** *adv*

ig·nore *vb* **ig·nored; ig·nor·ing** : to pay no attention to

igua·na *n* : a very large tropical American lizard with a ridge of tall scales along its back

il- — see IN-

¹ill *adj* **worse; worst 1** : ¹EVIL 2 **2** : causing suffering or distress **3** : not normal or sound **4** : not in good health **5** : ¹UNFOR-TUNATE 1, UNLUCKY **6** : UNKIND, UNFRIENDLY **7** : not right or proper

²ill *adv* **worse; worst 1** : with displeasure **2** : in a harsh way **3** : SCARCELY 1, HARDLY **4** : in a faulty way

³ill *n* **1** : the opposite of good **2** : SICKNESS 2 **3** : ²TROUBLE 2

I'll : I shall : I will

il·le·gal *adj* : contrary to law : UNLAWFUL — **il·le·gal·ly** *adv*

il·leg·i·ble *adj* : impossible to read — **il·leg·i·bly** *adv*

il·le·git·i·mate *adj* : not legitimate — **il·le·git·i·mate·ly** *adv*

il·lic·it *adj* : not permitted : UNLAWFUL — **il·lic·it·ly** *adv*

il·lit·er·a·cy *n* : the quality or state of being illiterate

¹il·lit·er·ate *adj* **1** : unable to read or write **2** : showing lack of education — **il·lit·er·ate·ly** *adv*

²illiterate *n* : an illiterate person

ill—man·nered *adj* : not polite

ill—na·tured *adj* : having a bad disposition — **ill—na·tured·ly** *adv*

ill·ness *n* : SICKNESS 1 2

il·log·i·cal *adj* : not using or following good reasoning — **il·log·i·cal·ly** *adv*

ill—tem·pered *adj* : ILL-NATURED

ill—treat *vb* : to treat in a cruel or improper way — **ill—treat·ment** *n*

il·lu·mi·nate *vb* **il·lu·mi·nat·ed; il·lu·mi·nat·ing 1** : to supply with light : light up **2** : to make clear : EXPLAIN

il·lu·mi·na·tion *n* **1** : the action of illuminating : the state of being illuminated **2** : the amount of light

ill—use *vb* : ILL-TREAT

il·lu·sion *n* **1** : a misleading image presented to the eye **2** : the state or fact of being led to accept as true something unreal or imagined **3** : a mistaken idea

il·lu·sive *adj* : ILLUSORY

il·lu·so·ry *adj* : based on or producing illusion : DECEPTIVE

il·lus·trate *vb* **il·lus·trat·ed; il·lus·trat·ing 1** : to make clear by using examples **2** : to supply with pictures or diagrams meant to explain or decorate **3** : to serve as an example

il·lus·tra·tion *n* **1** : the action of illustrating : the condition of being illustrated **2** : an example or instance used to make something clear **3** : a picture or diagram that explains or decorates

il·lus·tra·tive *adj* : serving or meant to illustrate

il·lus·tra·tor *n* : an artist who makes illustrations (as for books)

il·lus·tri·ous *adj* : EMINENT

ill will *n* : unfriendly feeling

im- — see IN-

I'm : I am

¹im·age *n* **1** : something (as a statue) made to look like a person or thing **2** : a picture of a person or thing formed by a device (as a mirror or lens) **3** : a person very much like another **4** : a mental picture of something not present : IMPRESSION **5** : a graphic representation

²image *vb* **im·aged; im·ag·ing 1** : to describe in words or pictures **2** : REFLECT 2

imag·in·able *adj* : possible to imagine

imag·i·nary *adj* : existing only in the imagination : not real

imag·i·na·tion *n* **1** : the act, process, or power of forming a mental picture of something not present and especially of something one has not known or experienced **2** : creative ability **3** : a creation of the mind

imag·i·na·tive *adj* **1** : of, relating to, or showing imagination **2** : having a lively imagination — **imag·i·na·tive·ly** *adv*

imag·ine *vb* **imag·ined; imag·in·ing 1** : to form a mental picture of **2** : THINK 2

¹im·be·cile *n* : a person of such low intelligence as to need help in simple personal care

²imbecile *or* **im·be·cil·ic** *adj* : of very low intelligence : very stupid

im·be·cil·i·ty *n, pl* **im·be·cil·i·ties 1** : the quality or state of being imbecile **2** : something very foolish

imbed *variant of* EMBED

im·i·tate *vb* **im·i·tat·ed; im·i·tat·ing 1** : to follow as a pattern, model, or example **2** : to be or appear like : RESEMBLE **3** : to copy exactly : MIMIC

¹im·i·ta·tion *n* **1** : an act of imitating **2** : ¹COPY 1

²imitation *adj* : like something else and especially something better

im·i·ta·tive *adj* **1** : involving imitation **2** : given to imitating

im·mac·u·late *adj* **1** : having no stain or blemish : PURE **2** : perfectly clean — **im·mac·u·late·ly** *adv*

im·ma·te·ri·al *adj* : not important : INSIGNIFICANT

im·ma·ture *adj* : not yet fully grown or ripe — **im·ma·ture·ly** *adv*

im·mea·sur·able *adj* : impossible to measure — **im·mea·sur·ably** *adv*

im·me·di·ate *adj* **1** : acting or being without anything else between **2** : being next in line or nearest in relationship **3** : closest in importance **4** : acting or being without any delay **5** : not far away in time or space

im·me·di·ate·ly *adv* **1** : with nothing between **2** : right away

im·mense *adj* : very great in size or amount : HUGE — **im·mense·ly** *adv*

im·men·si·ty *n, pl* **im·men·si·ties** : the quality or state of being immense

im·merse *vb* **im·mersed; im·mers·ing 1** : to plunge into something (as a fluid) that surrounds or covers **2** : to become completely involved with

im·mi·grant *n* : a person who comes to a country to live there

im·mi·grate *vb* **im·mi·grat·ed; im·mi·grat·ing** : to come into a foreign country to live

im·mi·gra·tion *n* : an act or instance of immigrating

im·mi·nent *adj* : being about to happen — **im·mi·nent·ly** *adv*

im·mo·bile *adj* : unable to move or be moved

im·mo·bi·lize *vb* **im·mo·bi·lized; im·mo·bi·liz·ing** : to fix in place : make immovable

im·mod·est *adj* : not modest — **im·mod·est·ly** *adv*

im·mod·es·ty *n* : lack of modesty

im·mor·al *adj* : not moral : BAD 4 — **im·mor·al·ly** *adv*

im·mo·ral·i·ty *n, pl* **im·mo·ral·i·ties 1** : the quality or state of being immoral **2** : an immoral act or custom

¹im·mor·tal *adj* : living or lasting forever — **im·mor·tal·ly** *adv*

²immortal *n* **1** : an immortal being **2** : a person of lasting fame

im·mor·tal·i·ty *n* **1** : the quality or state of being immortal : endless life **2** : lasting fame or glory

im·mov·able *adj* : impossible to move : firmly fixed — **im·mov·ably** *adv*

im·mune *adj* **1** : ¹EXEMPT **2** : having a strong or special power to resist

immune system *n* : the system of the body that fights infection and disease and that includes especially the white blood cells and antibodies and the organs that produce them

im·mu·ni·ty *n, pl* **im·mu·ni·ties 1** : EXEMPTION 1 **2** : power to resist infection whether natural or acquired (as by vaccination)

im·mu·ni·za·tion *n* : treatment (as with a vaccine) to produce immunity to a disease

im·mu·nize *vb* **im·mu·nized; im·mu·niz·ing** : to make immune

imp *n* **1** : a small demon **2** : a mischievous child

im·pact *n* **1** : a striking together of two bodies **2** : a strong effect

im·pair *vb* : to make less (as in quantity, value, or strength) or worse : DAMAGE

im·pale *vb* **im·paled; im·pal·ing** : to pierce with something pointed

im·part vb **1** : to give or grant from a supply **2** : to make known

im·par·tial adj : not partial or biased : FAIR, JUST — **im·par·tial·ly** adv

im·par·tial·i·ty n : the quality or state of being impartial

im·pass·able adj : impossible to pass, cross, or travel

im·pas·sioned adj : showing very strong feeling

im·pas·sive adj : not feeling or showing emotion — **im·pas·sive·ly** adv

im·pa·tience n **1** : lack of patience **2** : restless or eager desire

im·pa·tient adj **1** : not patient **2** : showing or coming from impatience **3** : restless and eager — **im·pa·tient·ly** adv

im·peach vb : to charge a public official formally with misconduct in office

im·pede vb **im·ped·ed; im·ped·ing** : to disturb the movement or progress of

im·ped·i·ment n **1** : something that impedes **2** : a defect in speech

im·pel vb **im·pelled; im·pel·ling** : to urge or drive forward or into action : FORCE

im·pend vb : to threaten to occur very soon

im·pen·e·tra·ble adj **1** : impossible to penetrate **2** : impossible to understand — **im·pen·e·tra·bly** adv

im·pen·i·tent adj : not penitent

im·per·a·tive adj **1** : expressing a command, request, or strong encouragement **2** : impossible to avoid or ignore : URGENT

im·per·cep·ti·ble adj **1** : not perceptible by the senses or by the mind **2** : very small or gradual — **im·per·cep·ti·bly** adv

im·per·fect adj : not perfect : FAULTY — **im·per·fect·ly** adv

im·per·fec·tion n **1** : the quality or state of being imperfect **2** : FLAW, FAULT

im·pe·ri·al adj : of or relating to an empire or its ruler — **im·pe·ri·al·ly** adv

im·per·il vb **im·per·iled** or **im·per·illed; im·per·il·ing** or **im·per·il·ling** : to place in great danger : ENDANGER

im·per·ish·able adj : INDESTRUCTIBLE — **im·per·ish·ably** adv

im·per·son·al adj : not referring or belonging to a specific person — **im·per·son·al·ly** adv

im·per·son·ate vb **im·per·son·at·ed; im·per·son·at·ing** : to pretend to be another person

im·per·son·a·tion n : the act of impersonating

im·per·ti·nence n **1** : the quality or state of being impertinent **2** : a rude act or remark

im·per·ti·nent adj : INSOLENT, RUDE — **im·per·ti·nent·ly** adv

im·per·turb·able adj : hard to disturb or upset — **im·per·turb·ably** adv

im·per·vi·ous adj : not letting something enter or pass through

im·pet·u·ous adj : IMPULSIVE, RASH — **im·pet·u·ous·ly** adv

im·pi·ous adj : not pious : IRREVERENT — **im·pi·ous·ly** adv

imp·ish adj : MISCHIEVOUS **3** — **imp·ish·ly** adv

im·pla·ca·ble adj : impossible to please, satisfy, or change — **im·pla·ca·bly** adv

im·plant vb : to fix or set securely or deeply

im·ple·ment n : an article (as a tool) intended for a certain use

im·pli·cate vb **im·pli·cat·ed; im·pli·cat·ing** : to show to be connected or involved

im·pli·ca·tion n **1** : the act of implicating : the state of being implicated **2** : the act of implying **3** : something implied

im·plic·it adj **1** : understood though not put clearly into words **2** : ABSOLUTE **2** — **im·plic·it·ly** adv

im·plore vb **im·plored; im·plor·ing** : to call upon with a humble request : BESEECH

im·ply vb **im·plied; im·ply·ing** : to express indirectly : suggest rather than say plainly

im·po·lite adj : not polite — **im·po·lite·ly** adv — **im·po·lite·ness** n

¹im·port vb **1** : ²MEAN **3** **2** : to bring (as goods) into a country usually for selling

²im·port n **1** : MEANING **1** **2** : IMPORTANCE **3** : something brought into a country

im·por·tance n : the quality or state of being important : SIGNIFICANCE

im·por·tant adj **1** : SIGNIFICANT **2** : having power or authority — **im·por·tant·ly** adv

im·por·ta·tion n **1** : the act or practice of importing **2** : something imported

im·por·tu·nate adj : making a nuisance of oneself with requests and demands — **im·por·tu·nate·ly** adv

im·por·tune vb **im·por·tuned; im·por·tun·ing** : to beg or urge so much as to be a nuisance

im·pose vb **im·posed; im·pos·ing** **1** : to establish or apply as a charge or penalty **2** : to force someone to accept or put up with **3** : to take unfair advantage

im·pos·ing adj : impressive because of size, dignity, or magnificence

im·pos·si·bil·i·ty n, pl **im·pos·si·bil·i·ties** **1** : the quality or state of being impossible **2** : something impossible

im·pos·si·ble adj **1** : incapable of being or of occurring **2** : HOPELESS **2** **3** : very bad or unpleasant — **im·pos·si·bly** adv

im·pos·tor n : a person who pretends to be someone else in order to deceive

im·pos·ture *n* : the act or conduct of an impostor

im·po·tence *n* : the quality or state of being impotent

im·po·tent *adj* : lacking in power or strength — **im·po·tent·ly** *adv*

im·pound *vb* : to shut up in or as if in an enclosed place

im·pov·er·ish *vb* **1** : to make poor **2** : to use up the strength or richness of

im·prac·ti·cal *adj* : not practical — **im·prac·ti·cal·ly** *adv*

im·pre·cise *adj* : not clear or exact — **im·pre·cise·ly** *adv*

im·preg·nate *vb* **im·preg·nat·ed; im·preg·nat·ing** **1** : to make fertile or fruitful **2** : to cause (a material) to be filled with something

im·press *vb* **1** : to fix in or on one's mind **2** : to move or affect strongly

im·pres·sion *n* **1** : the act or process of impressing **2** : something (as a design) made by pressing or stamping **3** : something that impresses or is impressed on one's mind **4** : a memory or belief that is vague or uncertain

im·pres·sion·able *adj* : easy to impress or influence

im·pres·sive *adj* : having the power to impress the mind or feelings — **im·pres·sive·ly** *adv*

¹im·print *vb* **1** : to mark by pressure : STAMP **2** : to fix firmly

²im·print *n* : something imprinted or printed : IMPRESSION

im·pris·on *vb* : to put in prison

im·pris·on·ment *n* : the act of imprisoning : the state of being imprisoned

im·prob·a·bil·i·ty *n* : the quality or state of being improbable

im·prob·a·ble *adj* : not probable — **im·prob·a·bly** *adv*

im·prop·er *adj* : not proper, right, or suitable — **im·prop·er·ly** *adv*

improper fraction *n* : a fraction whose numerator is equal to or larger than the denominator

im·prove *vb* **im·proved; im·prov·ing** : to make or become better — **im·prov·er** *n*

im·prove·ment *n* **1** : the act or process of improving **2** : increased value or excellence **3** : something that adds to the value or appearance (as of a house)

im·prov·i·sa·tion *n* **1** : the act or art of improvising **2** : something that is improvised

im·pro·vise *vb* **im·pro·vised; im·pro·vis·ing** **1** : to compose, recite, or sing without studying or practicing ahead of time **2** : to make, invent, or arrange with whatever is at hand

im·pu·dence *n* : impudent behavior or speech : INSOLENCE, DISRESPECT

im·pu·dent *adj* : being bold and disrespectful : INSOLENT — **im·pu·dent·ly** *adv*

im·pulse *n* **1** : a force that starts a body into motion **2** : the motion produced by a starting force **3** : a sudden stirring up of the mind and spirit to do something **4** : the wave of change that passes along a stimulated nerve and carries information to the brain

im·pul·sive *adj* **1** : acting or tending to act on impulse **2** : resulting from a sudden impulse — **im·pul·sive·ly** *adv*

im·pure *adj* **1** : not pure : UNCLEAN, DIRTY **2** : mixed with something else that is usually not as good — **im·pure·ly** *adv*

im·pu·ri·ty *n, pl* **im·pu·ri·ties** **1** : the quality or state of being impure **2** : something that is or makes impure

¹in *prep* **1** : enclosed or surrounded by : WITHIN **2** : INTO 1 **3** : DURING **4** : WITH 7 **5** — used to show a state or condition **6** — used to show manner or purpose **7** : INTO 2

²in *adv* **1** : to or toward the inside **2** : to or toward some particular place **3** : ¹NEAR 1 **4** : into the midst of something **5** : to or at its proper place **6** : on the inner side : WITHIN **7** : at hand or on hand

³in *adj* **1** : being inside or within **2** : headed or bound inward

¹in- *or* **il-** *or* **im-** *or* **ir-** *prefix* : not : NON-, UN- — usually *il-* before *l* and *im-* before *b, m,* or *p* and *ir-* before *r* and *in-* before other sounds

²in- *or* **il-** *or* **im-** *or* **ir-** *prefix* **1** : in : within : into : toward : on — usually *il-* before *l, im-* before *b, m,* or *p, ir-* before *r,* and *in-* before other sounds **2** : EN-

in·abil·i·ty *n* : the condition of being unable to do something : lack of ability

in·ac·ces·si·bil·i·ty *n* : the quality or state of being inaccessible

in·ac·ces·si·ble *adj* : hard or impossible to get to or at

in·ac·cu·ra·cy *n, pl* **in·ac·cu·ra·cies** **1** : lack of accuracy **2** : ERROR, MISTAKE

in·ac·cu·rate *adj* : not right or correct : not exact — **in·ac·cu·rate·ly** *adv*

in·ac·tive *adj* : not active : IDLE

in·ac·tiv·i·ty *n* : the state of being inactive

in·ad·e·qua·cy *n, pl* **in·ad·e·qua·cies** : the condition of being not enough or not good enough

in·ad·e·quate *adj* : not enough or not good enough

in·ad·vis·able *adj* : not wise to do : UNWISE

in·alien·able *adj* : impossible to take away or give up

inane *adj* : silly and pointless — **inane·ly** *adv*

in·an·i·mate *adj* : not living : LIFELESS

in·ap·pro·pri·ate *adj* : not appropriate — **in·ap·pro·pri·ate·ly** *adv*

in·as·much as *conj* : considering that : ²SINCE 2

in·at·ten·tion *n* : failure to pay attention

in·at·ten·tive *adj* : not paying attention — **in·at·ten·tive·ly** *adv*

in·au·di·ble *adj* : impossible to hear — **in·au·di·bly** *adv*

in·au·gu·ral *adj* : of or relating to an inauguration

in·au·gu·rate *vb* **in·au·gu·rat·ed; in·au·gu·rat·ing** 1 : to introduce into office with suitable ceremonies : INSTALL 2 : to celebrate the opening of 3 : to bring into being or action

in·au·gu·ra·tion *n* : an act or ceremony of inaugurating

in·born *adj* : INSTINCTIVE

in·breed *vb* **in·bred; in·breed·ing** : to breed with closely related individuals

in·can·des·cent *adj* : white or glowing with great heat

incandescent lamp *n* : a lamp whose light is produced by the glow of a wire heated by an electric current

in·ca·pa·ble *adj* : not able to do something

¹**in·cense** *n* 1 : material used to produce a perfume when burned 2 : the perfume given off by burning incense

²**in·cense** *vb* **in·censed; in·cens·ing** : to make very angry

in·cen·tive *n* : something that makes a person try or work hard or harder

in·ces·sant *adj* : going on and on : not stopping or letting up — **in·ces·sant·ly** *adv*

¹**inch** *n* : a unit of length equal to ¹/₃₆ yard or 2.54 centimeters

²**inch** *vb* : to move a little bit at a time

in·ci·dent *n* : an often unimportant happening that may form a part of a larger event

¹**in·ci·den·tal** *adj* 1 : happening by chance 2 : of minor importance

²**incidental** *n* : something incidental

in·ci·den·tal·ly *adv* : as a matter of less interest or importance

in·cin·er·ate *vb* **in·cin·er·at·ed; in·cin·er·at·ing** : to burn to ashes

in·cin·er·a·tor *n* : a furnace or a container for burning waste materials

in·cise *vb* **in·cised; in·cis·ing** : to cut into : CARVE, ENGRAVE

in·ci·sion *n* : a cutting into something or the cut or wound that results

in·ci·sor *n* : a tooth (as any of the four front teeth of the human upper or lower jaw) for cutting

in·cite *vb* **in·cit·ed; in·cit·ing** : to move to action : stir up : ROUSE

in·clem·ent *adj* : STORMY 1

in·cli·na·tion *n* 1 : an act or the action of bending or leaning 2 : a usually favorable feeling toward something 3 : ¹SLANT, TILT

¹**in·cline** *vb* **in·clined; in·clin·ing** 1 : to cause to bend or lean 2 : to be drawn to an opinion or course of action 3 : ¹SLOPE, LEAN

²**in·cline** *n* : ²SLOPE 2

in·clined *adj* 1 : having an inclination 2 : having a slope

inclose, inclosure *variant of* ENCLOSE, ENCLOSURE

in·clude *vb* **in·clud·ed; in·clud·ing** : to take in or have as part of a whole

in·clu·sion *n* 1 : an act of including : the state of being included 2 : something included

in·clu·sive *adj* 1 : covering everything or all important points 2 : including the stated limits and all in between

in·cog·ni·to *adv or adj* : with one's identity kept secret

in·co·her·ence *n* : the quality or state of being incoherent

in·co·her·ent *adj* : not connected in a clear or logical way — **in·co·her·ent·ly** *adv*

in·come *n* : a gain usually measured in money that comes in from labor, business, or property

income tax *n* : a tax on the income of a person or business

in·com·pa·ra·ble *adj* : MATCHLESS — **in·com·pa·ra·bly** *adv*

in·com·pat·i·ble *adj* : not able to live or work together in harmony — **in·com·pat·i·bly** *adv*

in·com·pe·tence *n* : the state or fact of being incompetent

in·com·pe·tent *adj* : not able to do a good job — **in·com·pe·tent·ly** *adv*

in·com·plete *adj* : not complete : not finished — **in·com·plete·ly** *adv*

in·com·pre·hen·si·ble *adj* : impossible to understand — **in·com·pre·hen·si·bly** *adv*

in·con·ceiv·able *adj* 1 : impossible to imagine or put up with 2 : hard to believe — **in·con·ceiv·ably** *adv*

in·con·gru·ous *adj* : not harmonious, suitable, or proper — **in·con·gru·ous·ly** *adv*

in·con·sid·er·ate *adj* : careless of the rights or feelings of others

in·con·sis·tent *adj* 1 : not being in agreement 2 : not keeping to the same thoughts or practices : CHANGEABLE

in·con·spic·u·ous *adj* : not easily seen or noticed — **in·con·spic·u·ous·ly** *adv*

¹**in·con·ve·nience** *n* 1 : the quality or state of being inconvenient 2 : something inconvenient

²in·con·ve·nience *vb* in·con·ve·nienced; in·con·ve·nienc·ing : to cause inconvenience to

in·con·ve·nient *adj* : not convenient — in·con·ve·nient·ly *adv*

in·cor·po·rate *vb* in·cor·po·rat·ed; in·cor·po·rat·ing 1 : to join or unite closely into a single mass or body 2 : to make a corporation of

in·cor·po·ra·tion *n* : an act of incorporating : the state of being incorporated

in·cor·rect *adj* 1 : not correct : not accurate or true : WRONG 2 : showing no care for duty or for moral or social standards — in·cor·rect·ly *adv* — in·cor·rect·ness *n*

¹in·crease *vb* in·creased; in·creas·ing : to make or become greater (as in size)

²in·crease *n* 1 : the act of increasing 2 : something added (as by growth)

in·creas·ing·ly *adv* : more and more

in·cred·i·ble *adj* : too strange or unlikely to be believed — in·cred·i·bly *adv*

in·cre·du·li·ty *n* : the quality or state of being incredulous

in·cred·u·lous *adj* : feeling or showing disbelief : SKEPTICAL — in·cred·u·lous·ly *adv*

in·crim·i·nate *vb* in·crim·i·nat·ed; in·crim·i·nat·ing : to charge with or involve in a crime or fault : ACCUSE

incrust *variant of* ENCRUST

in·cu·bate *vb* in·cu·bat·ed; in·cu·bat·ing 1 : to sit upon eggs to hatch them by warmth 2 : to keep under conditions good for hatching or development

in·cu·ba·tion *n* 1 : an act of incubating : the state of being incubated 2 : the time between infection with germs and the appearance of disease symptoms

in·cu·ba·tor *n* 1 : an apparatus that provides enough heat to hatch eggs artificially 2 : an apparatus to help the growth of tiny newborn babies

in·cum·bent *n* : the holder of an office or position

in·cur *vb* in·curred; in·cur·ring : to bring upon oneself

in·cur·able *adj* : impossible to cure — in·cur·ably *adv*

in·debt·ed *adj* : being in debt : owing something — in·debt·ed·ness *n*

in·de·cen·cy *n, pl* in·de·cen·cies 1 : lack of decency 2 : an indecent act or word

in·de·cent *adj* : not decent : COARSE, VULGAR

in·de·ci·sion *n* : a swaying between two or more courses of action

in·de·ci·sive *adj* 1 : not decisive or final 2 : finding it hard to make decisions — in·de·ci·sive·ly *adv* — in·de·ci·sive·ness *n*

in·deed *adv* : in fact : TRULY

in·de·fen·si·ble *adj* : impossible to defend

in·def·i·nite *adj* 1 : not clear or fixed in meaning or details 2 : not limited (as in amount or length) — in·def·i·nite·ly *adv*

indefinite article *n* : either of the articles *a* or *an* used to show that the following noun refers to any person or thing of the kind named

in·del·i·ble *adj* 1 : impossible to erase, remove, or blot out 2 : making marks not easily removed — in·del·i·bly *adv*

in·del·i·cate *adj* : not polite or proper : COARSE — in·del·i·cate·ly *adv*

in·dent *vb* : to set (as the first line of a paragraph) in from the margin

in·den·ta·tion *n* 1 : a cut or dent in something 2 : the action of indenting or the state of being indented

in·de·pen·dence *n* : the quality or state of being independent

Independence Day *n* : July 4 observed as a legal holiday in honor of the adoption of the Declaration of Independence in 1776

¹in·de·pen·dent *adj* 1 : not under the control or rule of another 2 : not connected with something else : SEPARATE 3 : not depending on anyone else for money to live on 4 : able to make up one's own mind — in·de·pen·dent·ly *adv*

²independent *n* : an independent person (as a voter who belongs to no political party)

in·de·scrib·able *adj* : impossible to describe — in·de·scrib·ably *adv*

in·de·struc·ti·ble *adj* : impossible to destroy — in·de·struc·ti·bly *adv*

¹in·dex *n, pl* in·dex·es *or* in·di·ces 1 : a list of names or topics (as in a book) given in alphabetical order and showing where each is to be found 2 : POINTER 1 3 : ¹SIGN 5, INDICATION

²index *vb* 1 : to provide with an index 2 : to list in an index

index finger *n* : the finger next to the thumb

¹In·di·an *n* 1 : a person born or living in India 2 : AMERICAN INDIAN

²Indian *adj* 1 : of or relating to India or its peoples 2 : of or relating to the American Indians or their languages

Indian club *n* : a wooden club swung for exercise

Indian corn *n* : a tall American cereal grass widely grown for its large ears of grain which are used as food or for feeding livestock

Indian pipe *n* : a waxy white leafless woodland herb with nodding flowers

Indian summer *n* : a period of mild weather in late autumn or early winter

in·di·cate *vb* in·di·cat·ed; in·di·cat·ing 1 : to point out or point to 2 : to state or express briefly

in·di·ca·tion *n* **1** : the act of indicating **2** : something that indicates

in·dic·a·tive *adj* **1** : representing an act or state as a fact that can be known or proved **2** : pointing out

in·di·ca·tor *n* **1** : one that indicates **2** : a pointer on a dial or scale **3** : ¹DIAL 3, GAUGE 3

indices *pl of* INDEX

in·dict *vb* : to charge with an offense or crime : ACCUSE — **in·dict·ment** *n*

in·dif·fer·ence *n* **1** : the condition or fact of being indifferent **2** : lack of interest

in·dif·fer·ent *adj* **1** : having no choice : showing neither interest nor dislike **2** : neither good nor bad — **in·dif·fer·ent·ly** *adv*

in·di·gest·ible *adj* : not digestible : not easy to digest

in·di·ges·tion *n* : discomfort caused by slow or painful digestion

in·dig·nant *adj* : filled with or expressing indignation — **in·dig·nant·ly** *adv*

in·dig·na·tion *n* : anger caused by something unjust or unworthy

in·dig·ni·ty *n, pl* **in·dig·ni·ties** **1** : an act that injures one's dignity or self-respect **2** : treatment that shows a lack of respect

in·di·go *n, pl* **in·di·gos** *or* **in·di·goes** **1** : a blue dye made artificially and formerly obtained from plants (**indigo plants**) **2** : a dark grayish blue

in·di·rect *adj* **1** : not straight or direct **2** : not straightforward **3** : not having a plainly seen connection — **in·di·rect·ly** *adv* — **in·di·rect·ness** *n*

indirect object *n* : an object that represents the secondary goal of the action of its verb

in·dis·creet *adj* : not discreet — **in·dis·creet·ly** *adv*

in·dis·cre·tion *n* **1** : lack of discretion **2** : an indiscreet act or remark

in·dis·crim·i·nate *adj* : showing lack of discrimination

in·dis·pens·able *adj* : ¹ESSENTIAL 2 — **in·dis·pens·ably** *adv*

in·dis·posed *adj* **1** : somewhat unwell **2** : not willing

in·dis·po·si·tion *n* : the condition of being indisposed : a slight illness

in·dis·put·able *adj* : not disputable : UNQUESTIONABLE — **in·dis·put·ably** *adv*

in·dis·tinct *adj* : not distinct — **in·dis·tinct·ly** *adv* — **in·dis·tinct·ness** *n*

in·dis·tin·guish·able *adj* : impossible to distinguish clearly — **in·dis·tin·guish·ably** *adv*

¹**in·di·vid·u·al** *adj* **1** : of or relating to an individual **2** : intended for one person **3** : ¹PARTICULAR 1, SEPARATE **4** : having a special quality : DISTINCTIVE 1 — **in·di·vid·u·al·ly** *adv*

²**individual** *n* **1** : a single member of a class **2** : a single human being

in·di·vid·u·al·i·ty *n, pl* **in·di·vid·u·al·i·ties** **1** : the qualities that set one person or thing off from all others **2** : the quality or state of being an individual

in·di·vis·i·ble *adj* : impossible to divide or separate — **in·di·vis·i·bly** *adv*

in·doc·tri·nate *vb* **in·doc·tri·nat·ed; in·doc·tri·nat·ing** **1** : INSTRUCT 1, TEACH **2** : to teach the ideas, opinions, or beliefs of a certain group

in·doc·tri·na·tion *n* : the act or process of indoctrinating

in·do·lence *n* : LAZINESS

in·do·lent *adj* : LAZY, IDLE

in·dom·i·ta·ble *adj* : UNCONQUERABLE — **in·dom·i·ta·bly** *adv*

in·door *adj* **1** : of or relating to the inside of a building **2** : done, used, or belonging within a building

in·doors *adv* : in or into a building

indorse *variant of* ENDORSE

in·du·bi·ta·ble *adj* : being beyond question or doubt — **in·du·bi·ta·bly** *adv*

in·duce *vb* **in·duced; in·duc·ing** **1** : to lead on to do something **2** : to bring about : CAUSE **3** : to produce (as an electric current) by induction

in·duce·ment *n* **1** : the act of inducing **2** : something that induces

in·duct *vb* **1** : to place in office : INSTALL **2** : to take in as a member of a military service

in·duc·tion *n* **1** : the act or process of inducting **2** : the production of an electrical or magnetic effect through the influence of a nearby magnet, electrical current, or electrically charged body

in·dulge *vb* **in·dulged; in·dulg·ing** **1** : to give in to one's own or another's desires : HUMOR **2** : to allow oneself the pleasure of having or doing something

in·dul·gence *n* **1** : the act of indulging : the state of being indulgent **2** : an indulgent act **3** : something indulged in

in·dul·gent *adj* : characterized by indulgence : LENIENT — **in·dul·gent·ly** *adv*

in·dus·tri·al *adj* **1** : of, relating to, or engaged in industry **2** : having highly developed industries — **in·dus·tri·al·ly** *adv*

in·dus·tri·al·ist *n* : a person owning or engaged in the management of an industry

in·dus·tri·al·i·za·tion *n* : the process of industrializing : the state of being industrialized

in·dus·tri·al·ize *vb* **in·dus·tri·al·ized; in·dus·tri·al·iz·ing** : to make or become industrial

in·dus·tri·ous *adj* : working hard and

steadily : DILIGENT — **in·dus·tri·ous·ly** adv

in·dus·try n, pl **in·dus·tries** 1 : the habit of working hard and steadily 2 : businesses that provide a certain product or service 3 : manufacturing activity

-ine adj suffix : of, relating to, or like

in·ed·i·ble adj : not fit for food

in·ef·fec·tive adj : not producing the desired effect — **in·ef·fec·tive·ly** adv

in·ef·fec·tu·al adj : not producing the proper or usual effect — **in·ef·fec·tu·al·ly** adv

in·ef·fi·cien·cy n, pl **in·ef·fi·cien·cies** : the state or an instance of being inefficient

in·ef·fi·cient adj 1 : not effective : INEFFECTUAL 2 : not able or willing to do something well — **in·ef·fi·cient·ly** adv

in·elas·tic adj : not elastic

in·el·i·gi·bil·i·ty n : the condition or fact of being ineligible

in·el·i·gi·ble adj : not eligible

in·ept adj 1 : not suited to the occasion 2 : lacking in skill or ability — **in·ept·ly** adv — **in·ept·ness** n

in·equal·i·ty n, pl **in·equal·i·ties** 1 : the quality of being unequal or uneven 2 : an instance of being uneven

in·ert adj : unable or slow to move or react — **in·ert·ly** adv — **in·ert·ness** n

in·er·tia n 1 : a property of matter by which it remains at rest or in motion in the same straight line unless acted upon by some external force 2 : a tendency not to move or change

in·er·tial adj : of or relating to inertia

in·es·cap·able adj : INEVITABLE — **in·es·cap·ably** adv

in·ev·i·ta·bil·i·ty n : the quality or state of being inevitable

in·ev·i·ta·ble adj : sure to happen : CERTAIN — **in·ev·i·ta·bly** adv

in·ex·act adj : INACCURATE — **in·ex·act·ly** adv — **in·ex·act·ness** n

in·ex·cus·able adj : not to be excused — **in·ex·cus·ably** adv

in·ex·haust·ible adj : plentiful enough not to give out or be used up — **in·ex·haust·ibly** adv

in·ex·o·ra·ble adj : RELENTLESS — **in·ex·o·ra·bly** adv

in·ex·pe·di·ent adj : not suitable or advisable

in·ex·pen·sive adj : [1]CHEAP 1 — **in·ex·pen·sive·ly** adv — **in·ex·pen·sive·ness** n

in·ex·pe·ri·ence n : lack of experience

in·ex·pe·ri·enced adj : having little or no experience

in·ex·pli·ca·ble adj : impossible to explain or account for — **in·ex·pli·ca·bly** adv

in·ex·press·ible adj : being beyond one's power to express : INDESCRIBABLE — **in·ex·press·ibly** adv

in·fal·li·ble adj 1 : not capable of being wrong 2 : not likely to fail : SURE — **in·fal·li·bly** adv

in·fa·mous adj 1 : having an evil reputation 2 : DETESTABLE — **in·fa·mous·ly** adv

in·fa·my n, pl **in·fa·mies** 1 : an evil reputation 2 : an infamous act

in·fan·cy n, pl **in·fan·cies** 1 : early childhood 2 : a beginning or early period of existence

[1]**in·fant** n 1 : a child in the first period of life 2 : [2]MINOR

[2]**infant** adj 1 : of or relating to infancy 2 : intended for young children

in·fan·tile adj : CHILDISH

infantile paralysis n : POLIO

in·fan·try n, pl **in·fan·tries** : a branch of an army composed of soldiers trained to fight on foot

in·fat·u·at·ed adj : having a foolish or very strong love or admiration

in·fat·u·a·tion n : the state of being infatuated

in·fect vb 1 : to cause disease germs to be present in or on 2 : to pass on a germ or disease to 3 : to enter and cause disease in 4 : to cause to share one's feelings

in·fec·tion n 1 : the act or process of infecting : the state of being infected 2 : any disease caused by germs

in·fec·tious adj 1 : passing from one to another in the form of a germ 2 : capable of being easily spread

in·fer vb **in·ferred**; **in·fer·ring** 1 : to arrive at as a conclusion 2 : [2]SURMISE 3 : to point out 4 : HINT, SUGGEST

in·fer·ence n 1 : the act or process of inferring 2 : something inferred

[1]**in·fe·ri·or** adj 1 : situated lower down (as in place or importance) 2 : of little or less importance, value, or merit

[2]**inferior** n : an inferior person or thing

in·fe·ri·or·i·ty n 1 : the state of being inferior 2 : a sense of being inferior

in·fer·nal adj 1 : of or relating to hell 2 : very bad or unpleasant : DAMNABLE — **in·fer·nal·ly** adv

in·fer·tile adj : not fertile

in·fest vb : to spread or swarm in or over in a troublesome manner

in·fi·del n : a person who does not believe in a certain religion

in·fi·del·i·ty n, pl **in·fi·del·i·ties** 1 : lack of belief in a certain religion 2 : DISLOYALTY

in·field n 1 : the diamond-shaped part of a baseball field inside the bases and home plate 2 : the players in the infield

in·field·er *n* : a baseball player who plays in the infield

in·fi·nite *adj* **1** : having no limits of any kind **2** : seeming to be without limits — **in·fi·nite·ly** *adv*

in·fin·i·tive *n* : a verb form serving as a noun or as a modifier and at the same time taking objects and adverbial modifiers

in·fin·i·ty *n, pl* **in·fin·i·ties** **1** : the quality of being infinite **2** : a space, quantity, or period of time that is without limit

in·firm *adj* : weak or frail in body (as from age or disease)

in·fir·ma·ry *n, pl* **in·fir·ma·ries** : a place for the care and housing of infirm or sick people

in·fir·mi·ty *n, pl* **in·fir·mi·ties** : the condition of being infirm

in·flame *vb* **in·flamed; in·flam·ing** **1** : to excite to too much action or feeling **2** : to cause to redden or grow hot (as from anger) **3** : to make or become sore, red, and swollen

in·flam·ma·ble *adj* **1** : FLAMMABLE **2** : easily inflamed : EXCITABLE

in·flam·ma·tion *n* **1** : the act of inflaming : the state of being inflamed **2** : a bodily response to injury in which heat, redness, and swelling are present

in·flam·ma·to·ry *adj* **1** : tending to excite anger or disorder **2** : causing or having inflammation

in·flat·able *adj* : possible to inflate

in·flate *vb* **in·flat·ed; in·flat·ing** **1** : to swell or fill with air or gas **2** : to cause to increase beyond proper limits

in·fla·tion *n* **1** : an act of inflating : the state of being inflated **2** : a continual rise in the price of goods and services

in·flect *vb* **1** : to change a word by inflection **2** : to change the pitch of a person's voice

in·flec·tion *n* **1** : a change in the pitch of a person's voice **2** : a change in a word that shows a grammatical difference (as of number, person, or tense)

in·flec·tion·al *adj* : of or relating to inflection

in·flex·i·ble *adj* **1** : not easily bent or twisted : RIGID **2** : not easily influenced or persuaded : FIRM

in·flict *vb* **1** : to give by or as if by striking **2** : to cause to be put up with

in·flo·res·cence *n* : the arrangement of flowers on a stalk

1in·flu·ence *n* **1** : the act or power of producing an effect without apparent force or direct authority **2** : a person or thing that influences

2influence *vb* **in·flu·enced; in·flu·enc·ing** : to have an influence on

in·flu·en·tial *adj* : having influence

in·flu·en·za *n* : a very contagious virus disease like a severe cold with fever

in·fo·mer·cial *n* : a television program that is a long commercial often including a discussion or demonstration

in·form *vb* **1** : to let a person know something **2** : to give information so as to accuse or cause suspicion — **in·form·er** *n*

in·for·mal *adj* **1** : not formal **2** : suitable for ordinary or everyday use — **in·for·mal·ly** *adv*

in·for·mal·i·ty *n, pl* **in·for·mal·i·ties** **1** : the quality or state of being informal **2** : an informal act

in·form·ant *n* : a person who informs

in·for·ma·tion *n* **1** : the giving or getting of knowledge **2** : knowledge obtained from investigation, study, or instruction **3** : NEWS 3

information superhighway *n* : INTERNET

in·for·ma·tive *adj* : giving information : INSTRUCTIVE

in·frac·tion *n* : VIOLATION

in·fra·red *adj* : being, relating to, or producing rays like light but lying outside the visible spectrum at its red end

in·fre·quent *adj* **1** : seldom happening : RARE **2** : not placed, made, or done at frequent intervals — **in·fre·quent·ly** *adv*

in·fringe *vb* **in·fringed; in·fring·ing** **1** : to fail to obey or act in agreement with : VIOLATE **2** : to go further than is right or fair to another : ENCROACH — **in·fringe·ment** *n*

in·fu·ri·ate *vb* **in·fu·ri·at·ed; in·fu·ri·at·ing** : to make furious : ENRAGE

in·fuse *vb* **in·fused; in·fus·ing** **1** : to put in as if by pouring **2** : to steep without boiling — **in·fu·sion** *n*

1-ing *n suffix* **1** : action or process **2** : product or result of an action or process **3** : something used in or connected with making or doing

2-ing *vb suffix or adj suffix* — used to form the present participle and sometimes to form adjectives that do not come from a verb

in·ge·nious *adj* : showing ingenuity : CLEVER — **in·ge·nious·ly** *adv*

in·ge·nu·ity *n, pl* **in·ge·nu·ities** : skill or cleverness in discovering, inventing, or planning

in·gen·u·ous *adj* **1** : FRANK, STRAIGHTFORWARD **2** : NAIVE 1 — **in·gen·u·ous·ly** *adv* — **in·gen·u·ous·ness** *n*

in·got *n* : a mass of metal cast into a shape that is easy to handle or store

in·gra·ti·ate *vb* **in·gra·ti·at·ed; in·gra·ti·at·ing** : to gain favor for by effort

in·gra·ti·at·ing *adj* **1** : PLEASING **2** : intended to gain someone's favor — **in·gra·ti·at·ing·ly** *adv*

in·grat·i·tude *n* : lack of gratitude

in·gre·di·ent *n* : one of the substances that make up a mixture

in·hab·it *vb* : to live or dwell in

in·hab·i·tant *n* : one who lives in a place permanently

in·ha·la·tion *n* : the act or an instance of inhaling

in·hale *vb* **in·haled; in·hal·ing** **1** : to draw in by breathing **2** : to breathe in

in·hal·er *n* : a device used for inhaling medicine

in·her·ent *adj* : belonging to or being a part of the nature of a person or thing — **in·her·ent·ly** *adv*

in·her·it *vb* **1** : to get by legal right from a person at his or her death **2** : to get by heredity

in·her·i·tance *n* **1** : the act of inheriting **2** : something inherited

in·hib·it *vb* : to prevent or hold back from doing something

in·hos·pi·ta·ble *adj* : not friendly or generous : not showing hospitality — **in·hos·pi·ta·bly** *adv*

in·hu·man *adj* **1** : lacking pity or kindness **2** : unlike what might be expected by a human — **in·hu·man·ly** *adv*

in·hu·mane *adj* : not humane

in·hu·man·i·ty *n, pl* **in·hu·man·i·ties** : a cruel act or attitude

in·iq·ui·tous *adj* : WICKED 1

in·iq·ui·ty *n, pl* **in·iq·ui·ties** : ¹SIN 1

¹ini·tial *adj* **1** : of, relating to, or being a beginning **2** : placed or standing at the beginning : FIRST

²initial *n* **1** : the first letter of a name **2** : a large letter beginning a text or a paragraph

³initial *vb* **ini·tialed** *or* **ini·tialled; ini·tial·ing** *or* **ini·tial·ling** : to mark with an initial or with one's initials

ini·ti·ate *vb* **ini·ti·at·ed; ini·ti·at·ing** **1** : to set going **2** : to admit into a club by special ceremonies

ini·ti·a·tion *n* **1** : the act or an instance of initiating : the process of being initiated **2** : the ceremonies with which a person is made a member of a club

ini·tia·tive *n* **1** : a first step or movement **2** : energy shown in initiating action : ENTERPRISE

in·ject *vb* **1** : to throw or drive into something **2** : to force a fluid into (as a part of the body) for medical reasons

in·jec·tion *n* **1** : an act or instance of injecting **2** : something injected

in·junc·tion *n* : a court order commanding or forbidding the doing of some act

in·jure *vb* **in·jured; in·jur·ing** **1** : to do an injustice to : WRONG **2** : to cause pain or harm to

in·ju·ri·ous *adj* : causing injury

in·ju·ry *n, pl* **in·ju·ries** **1** : an act that damages or hurts **2** : hurt, damage, or loss suffered

in·jus·tice *n* **1** : violation of a person's rights **2** : an unjust act

¹ink *n* : a usually liquid material for writing or printing

²ink *vb* : to put ink on

in·kling *n* : a vague notion : HINT

ink·stand *n* : a small stand for holding ink and pens

ink·well *n* : a container for ink

inky *adj* **ink·i·er; ink·i·est** **1** : consisting of or like ink **2** : soiled with or as if with ink

in·laid *adj* **1** : set into a surface in a decorative design **2** : decorated with a design or material set into a surface

¹in·land *adj* : of or relating to the part of a country away from the coast

²inland *n* : the part of a country away from the coast or boundaries

³inland *adv* : into or toward the area away from a coast

in–law *n* : a relative by marriage

¹in·lay *vb* **in·laid; in·lay·ing** : to set into a surface for decoration or strengthening

²in·lay *n* : inlaid work : material used in inlaying

in·let *n* **1** : a small or narrow bay **2** : an opening for intake

in·mate *n* **1** : one of a group living in a single residence **2** : a person confined in an institution (as an asylum or prison)

in·most *adj* : INNERMOST

inn *n* : a place that provides a place to sleep and food for travelers

in·ner *adj* **1** : located farther in **2** : of or relating to the mind or spirit

inner ear *n* : the inner hollow part of the ear that contains sense organs which perceive sound and help keep the body properly balanced

in·ner·most *adj* : farthest inward

in·ning *n* : a division of a baseball game that consists of a turn at bat for each team

inn·keep·er *n* : the person who runs an inn

in·no·cence *n* : the quality or state of being innocent

in·no·cent *adj* **1** : free from sin : PURE **2** : free from guilt or blame **3** : free from evil influence or effect : HARMLESS — **in·no·cent·ly** *adv*

in·noc·u·ous *adj* : not harmful

in·no·va·tion *n* **1** : the introduction of something new **2** : a new idea, method, or device : NOVELTY

in·nu·mer·a·ble *adj* : too many to be counted

in·oc·u·late *vb* **in·oc·u·lat·ed; in·oc·u·lat·ing** : to inject a serum, vaccine, or weakened germ into to protect against or treat a disease

in·oc·u·la·tion *n* **1** : the act or an instance of inoculating **2** : material used in inoculating

in·of·fen·sive *adj* **1** : not harmful **2** : PEACEFUL 1 **3** : not offensive

in·op·por·tune *adj* : INCONVENIENT

¹in·put *n* **1** : something (as power, a signal, or data) that is put into a machine or system **2** : the point at which an input is made **3** : the act of or process of putting in

²input *vb* **in·put·ted** *or* **input; in·put·ting** : to enter (as data) into a computer

in·quest *n* : an official investigation especially into the cause of a death

in·quire *vb* **in·quired; in·quir·ing 1** : to ask about **2** : to make an investigation **3** : to ask a question — **in·quir·er** *n* — **in·quir·ing·ly** *adv*

in·qui·ry *n, pl* **in·qui·ries 1** : the act of inquiring **2** : a request for information **3** : a thorough examination

in·quis·i·tive *adj* **1** : given to seeking information **2** : tending to ask questions — **in·quis·i·tive·ly** *adv* — **in·quis·i·tive·ness** *n*

in·sane *adj* **1** : not normal or healthy in mind **2** : used by or for people who are insane — **in·sane·ly** *adv*

in·san·i·ty *n* : the condition of being insane : mental illness

in·sa·tia·ble *adj* : impossible to satisfy

in·scribe *vb* **in·scribed; in·scrib·ing 1** : to write, engrave, or print as a lasting record **2** : to write, engrave, or print something on or in

in·scrip·tion *n* : something that is inscribed

in·sect *n* **1** : a small and often winged animal that has six jointed legs and a body formed of three parts **2** : an animal (as a spider or a centipede) similar to the true insects

in·sec·ti·cide *n* : a chemical used to kill insects

in·se·cure *adj* : not safe or secure — **in·se·cure·ly** *adv*

in·se·cu·ri·ty *n* : the quality or state of being insecure

in·sen·si·ble *adj* **1** : UNCONSCIOUS 2 **2** : not able to feel **3** : not aware of or caring about something

in·sen·si·tive *adj* : not sensitive : lacking feeling — **in·sen·si·tive·ly** *adv*

in·sen·si·tiv·i·ty *n* : lack of sensitivity

in·sep·a·ra·bil·i·ty *n* : the quality or state of being inseparable

in·sep·a·ra·ble *adj* : impossible to separate — **in·sep·a·ra·bly** *adv*

¹in·sert *vb* **1** : to put in **2** : to set in and make fast

²in·sert *n* : something that is or is meant to be inserted

in·ser·tion *n* **1** : the act or process of inserting **2** : ²INSERT

¹in·set *n* : ²INSERT

²inset *vb* **in·set** *or* **in·set·ted; in·set·ting** : ¹INSERT 2

¹in·side *n* **1** : an inner side, surface, or space : INTERIOR **2** : ENTRAILS — usually used in pl.

²inside *adv* **1** : on the inner side **2** : in or into the interior

³inside *adj* **1** : of, relating to, or being on or near the inside **2** : relating or known to a certain few people

⁴inside *prep* **1** : to or on the inside of **2** : before the end of : WITHIN

in·sid·er *n* : a person having information not generally available

in·sight *n* : the power or act of seeing what's really important about a situation

in·sig·nia *or* **in·sig·ne** *n, pl* **insignia** *or* **in·sig·ni·as** : an emblem of a certain office, authority, or honor

in·sig·nif·i·cance *n* : the quality or state of being insignificant

in·sig·nif·i·cant *adj* : not significant : UNIMPORTANT — **in·sig·nif·i·cant·ly** *adv*

in·sin·cere *adj* : not sincere — **in·sin·cere·ly** *adv*

in·sin·cer·i·ty *n* : lack of sincerity

in·sin·u·ate *vb* **in·sin·u·at·ed; in·sin·u·at·ing** : to bring or get in little by little or in a secret way **2** : ²HINT, IMPLY

in·sip·id *adj* **1** : having little taste or flavor : TASTELESS **2** : not interesting or challenging : DULL

in·sist *vb* **1** : to place special stress or great importance **2** : to make a demand

in·sis·tence *n* : the quality or state of being insistent

in·sis·tent *adj* : demanding attention : PERSISTENT — **in·sis·tent·ly** *adv*

in·so·lence *n* : lack of respect for rank or authority

in·so·lent *adj* : showing insolence — **in·so·lent·ly** *adv*

in·sol·u·bil·i·ty *n* : the quality or state of being insoluble

in·sol·u·ble *adj* **1** : having no solution or explanation **2** : difficult or impossible to dissolve — **in·sol·u·bly** *adv*

in·spect *vb* **1** : to examine closely **2** : to view and examine in an official way

in·spec·tion *n* : the act of inspecting

in·spec·tor *n* : a person who makes inspections

in·spi·ra·tion *n* **1** : the act of breathing in

2 : the act or power of arousing the mind or the emotions 3 : the state of being inspired 4 : something that is or seems inspired 5 : an inspiring agent or influence

in·spire vb **in·spired; in·spir·ing** 1 : to move or guide by divine influence 2 : to give inspiration to : ENCOURAGE 3 : AROUSE 2 4 : to bring about : CAUSE 5 : INHALE

in·sta·bil·i·ty n : the quality or state of being unstable

in·stall vb 1 : to put in office with ceremony 2 : to set up for use or service

in·stal·la·tion n 1 : the act of installing : the state of being installed 2 : something installed for use

¹in·stall·ment or **in·stal·ment** n : INSTALLATION 1

²installment n : one of the parts of a series

in·stance n 1 : EXAMPLE 1 2 : a certain point in an action or process

¹in·stant n : MOMENT 1

²instant adj 1 : happening or done at once 2 : partially prepared by the manufacturer so that only final mixing is needed 3 : made to dissolve quickly in a liquid

in·stan·ta·neous adj 1 : happening in an instant 2 : done without delay — **in·stan·ta·neous·ly** adv

in·stant·ly adv : IMMEDIATELY 2

in·stead adv : as a substitute

in·stead of prep : as a substitute for : rather than

in·step n : the arched middle part of the human foot in front of the ankle joint

in·sti·gate vb **in·sti·gat·ed; in·sti·gat·ing** : PROVOKE 2, INCITE

in·still vb : to put into the mind little by little

in·stinct n 1 : a natural ability 2 : an act or course of action in response to a stimulus that is automatic rather than learned 3 : behavior based on automatic reactions

in·stinc·tive adj : of or relating to instinct : resulting from instinct — **in·stinc·tive·ly** adv

¹in·sti·tute vb **in·sti·tut·ed; in·sti·tut·ing** 1 : ESTABLISH 1 2 : to set going : INAUGURATE

²institute n 1 : an organization for the promotion of a cause 2 : a place for study usually in a special field

in·sti·tu·tion n 1 : the act of instituting : ESTABLISHMENT 2 : an established custom, practice, or law 3 : an established organization

in·sti·tu·tion·al adj : of or relating to an institution

in·struct vb 1 : to help to get knowledge to : TEACH 2 : to give information to 3 : to give commands to : DIRECT

in·struc·tion n 1 : LESSON 3 2 **instructions** pl : DIRECTION 2, ORDER 3 **instructions** pl : an outline of how something is to be done 4 : the practice or method used by a teacher

in·struc·tive adj : helping to give knowledge — **in·struc·tive·ly** adv

in·struc·tor n : TEACHER

in·stru·ment n 1 : a way of getting something done 2 : a device for doing a particular kind of work 3 : a device used to produce music 4 : a legal document (as a deed) 5 : a measuring device

in·stru·men·tal adj 1 : acting to get something done 2 : of or relating to an instrument 3 : being music played on an instrument rather than sung — **in·stru·men·tal·ly** adv

in·sub·or·di·nate adj : unwilling to obey authority : DISOBEDIENT

in·sub·or·di·na·tion n : failure to obey authority

in·sub·stan·tial adj 1 : not real : IMAGINARY 2 : not firm or solid — **in·sub·stan·tial·ly** adv

in·suf·fer·able adj : impossible to endure : INTOLERABLE — **in·suf·fer·ably** adv

in·suf·fi·cien·cy n, pl **in·suf·fi·cien·cies** 1 : the quality or state of being insufficient 2 : a shortage of something

in·suf·fi·cient adj : not sufficient : INADEQUATE — **in·suf·fi·cient·ly** adv

in·su·late vb **in·su·lat·ed; in·su·lat·ing** 1 : to separate from others : ISOLATE 2 : to separate a conductor of electricity, heat, or sound from other conducting bodies by means of something that will not conduct electricity, heat, or sound

in·su·la·tion n 1 : the act of insulating : the state of being insulated 2 : material used in insulating

in·su·la·tor n 1 : a material (as rubber or glass) that is a poor conductor of electricity or heat 2 : a device made of an electrical insulating material and used for separating or supporting electrical conductors

in·su·lin n : a hormone from the pancreas that prevents or controls diabetes

¹in·sult vb : to treat with disrespect or scorn

²in·sult n : an act or expression showing disrespect or scorn

in·sur·ance n 1 : the act of insuring : the state of being insured 2 : the business of insuring persons or property 3 : a contract by which someone guarantees for a fee to pay someone else for the value of property lost or damaged (as through theft or fire) or usually a specified amount for injury or death 4 : the amount for which something is insured

in·sure *vb* **in·sured; in·sur·ing 1** : to give or get insurance on or for **2** : ENSURE — **in·sur·er** *n*

in·sured *n* : a person whose life or property is insured

¹in·sur·gent *n* : ²REBEL

²insurgent *adj* : REBELLIOUS 1

in·sur·rec·tion *n* : an act or instance of rebelling against a government

in·tact *adj* : not touched especially by anything that harms

in·take *n* **1** : a place where liquid or air is taken into something (as a pump) **2** : the act of taking in **3** : something taken in

¹in·tan·gi·ble *adj* **1** : not possible to touch **2** : not possible to think of as matter or substance

²intangible *n* : something intangible

in·te·ger *n* : a number that is a natural number (as 1, 2, or 3), the negative of a natural number (as –1, –2, –3), or 0

in·te·gral *adj* : needed to make something complete

in·te·grate *vb* **in·te·grat·ed; in·te·grat·ing 1** : to form into a whole : UNITE **2** : to make a part of a larger unit **3** : to make open to all races

integrated circuit *n* : a tiny group of electronic devices and their connections that is produced in or on a small slice of material (as silicon)

in·te·gra·tion *n* : an act, process, or instance of integrating

in·teg·ri·ty *n* **1** : the condition of being free from damage or defect **2** : total honesty and sincerity

in·tel·lect *n* **1** : the power of knowing **2** : the capacity for thought especially when highly developed **3** : a person with great powers of thinking and reasoning

¹in·tel·lec·tu·al *adj* **1** : of or relating to the intellect or understanding **2** : having or showing greater than usual intellect **3** : requiring study and thought — **in·tel·lec·tu·al·ly** *adv*

²intellectual *n* : an intellectual person

in·tel·li·gence *n* **1** : the ability to learn and understand **2** : NEWS 3, INFORMATION **3** : an agency that obtains information about an enemy or a possible enemy

in·tel·li·gent *adj* : having or showing intelligence or intellect — **in·tel·li·gent·ly** *adv*

in·tel·li·gi·ble *adj* : possible to understand — **in·tel·li·gi·bly** *adv*

in·tem·per·ance *n* : lack of self-control (as in satisfying an appetite)

in·tem·per·ate *adj* **1** : not moderate or mild **2** : lacking or showing a lack of self-control (as in the use of alcoholic drinks) — **in·tem·per·ate·ly** *adv*

in·tend *vb* : to have in mind as a purpose or aim : PLAN

in·tense *adj* **1** : ¹EXTREME 1 **2** : done with great energy, enthusiasm, or effort **3** : having very strong feelings — **in·tense·ly** *adv*

in·ten·si·fi·ca·tion *n* : the act or process of intensifying

in·ten·si·fy *vb* **in·ten·si·fied; in·ten·si·fy·ing** : to make or become intense or more intensive : HEIGHTEN

in·ten·si·ty *n, pl* **in·ten·si·ties 1** : extreme strength or force **2** : the degree or amount of a quality or condition

¹in·ten·sive *adj* **1** : involving special effort or concentration : THOROUGH **2** — used to stress something

²intensive *n* : an intensive word

¹in·tent *n* **1** : ¹PURPOSE, INTENTION **2** : MEANING 1

²intent *adj* **1** : showing concentration or great attention **2** : showing great determination — **in·tent·ly** *adv* — **in·tent·ness** *n*

in·ten·tion *n* **1** : a determination to act in a particular way **2** : ¹PURPOSE, AIM **3** : MEANING 1, INTENT

in·ten·tion·al *adj* : done by intention : not accidental — **in·ten·tion·al·ly** *adv*

in·ter *vb* **in·terred; in·ter·ring** : BURY 1

inter- *prefix* **1** : between : among : together **2** : mutual : mutually : reciprocal : reciprocally **3** : located, occurring, or carried on between

in·ter·act *vb* : to act upon one another

in·ter·ac·tion *n* : the action or influence of people, groups, or things on one another

in·ter·ac·tive *adj* **1** : active between people, groups, or things **2** : of, relating to, or allowing two-way electronic communications (as between a person and a computer) — **in·ter·ac·tive·ly** *adv*

in·ter·cede *vb* **in·ter·ced·ed; in·ter·ced·ing 1** : to try to help settle differences between unfriendly individuals or groups **2** : to plead for the needs of someone else

in·ter·cept *vb* : to take, seize, or stop before reaching an intended destination — **in·ter·cep·tor** *n*

in·ter·ces·sion *n* : the act of interceding

in·ter·ces·sor *n* : a person who intercedes

¹in·ter·change *vb* **in·ter·changed; in·ter·chang·ing** : to put each in the place of the other : EXCHANGE

²in·ter·change *n* **1** : an act or instance of interchanging **2** : a joining of highways that permits moving from one to the other without crossing traffic lanes

in·ter·change·able *adj* : possible to interchange — **in·ter·change·ably** *adv*

in·ter·com *n* : a communication system with a microphone and loudspeaker at each end in·ter·course *n* : dealings between persons or groups

in·ter·de·pen·dence *n* : the quality or state of being interdependent

in·ter·de·pen·dent *adj* : depending on one another — in·ter·de·pen·dent·ly *adv*

¹in·ter·est *n* 1 : a right, title, or legal share in something 2 : WELFARE 1, BENEFIT 3 : the money paid by a borrower for the use of borrowed money 4 **interests** *pl* : a group financially interested in an industry or business 5 : a feeling of concern, curiosity, or desire to be involved with something 6 : the quality of attracting special attention or arousing curiosity 7 : something in which one is interested

²**interest** *vb* 1 : to persuade to become involved in 2 : to arouse and hold the interest of

in·ter·est·ed *adj* : having or showing interest

in·ter·est·ing *adj* : holding the attention : arousing interest — in·ter·est·ing·ly *adv*

in·ter·fere *vb* in·ter·fered; in·ter·fer·ing 1 : to be in opposition : CLASH 2 : to take a part in the concerns of others

in·ter·fer·ence *n* 1 : the act or process of interfering 2 : something that interferes

in·ter·im *n* : INTERVAL 1

¹in·te·ri·or *adj* 1 : being or occurring within the limits : INNER 2 : far from the border or shore : INLAND

²**interior** *n* : the inner part of something

in·ter·ject *vb* : to put between or among other things

in·ter·jec·tion *n* 1 : an interjecting of something 2 : something interjected 3 : a word or cry (as "ouch") expressing sudden or strong feeling

in·ter·lace *vb* in·ter·laced; in·ter·lac·ing : to unite by or as if by lacing together

in·ter·lock *vb* : to lock together

in·ter·lop·er *n* : INTRUDER

in·ter·lude *n* 1 : an entertainment between the acts of a play 2 : a period or event that comes between others 3 : a musical composition between parts of a longer composition or of a drama

in·ter·mar·riage *n* : marriage between members of different groups

in·ter·mar·ry *vb* in·ter·mar·ried; in·ter·mar·ry·ing : to become connected by intermarriage

in·ter·me·di·ary *n, pl* in·ter·me·di·ar·ies : GO-BETWEEN

¹in·ter·me·di·ate *adj* : being or occurring in the middle or between — in·ter·me·di·ate·ly *adv*

²**intermediate** *n* : someone or something that is intermediate

in·ter·ment *n* : BURIAL

in·ter·mi·na·ble *adj* : ENDLESS 1 — in·ter·mi·na·bly *adv*

in·ter·min·gle *vb* in·ter·min·gled; in·ter·min·gling : to mix together

in·ter·mis·sion *n* 1 : ¹PAUSE 1, INTERRUPTION 2 : a temporary halt (as between acts of a play)

in·ter·mit·tent *adj* : starting, stopping, and starting again — in·ter·mit·tent·ly *adv*

¹in·tern *vb* : to force to stay within certain limits especially during a war — in·tern·ment *n*

²in·tern *or* in·terne *n* : a medical school graduate getting practical experience in a hospital — in·tern·ship *n*

³in·tern *vb* : to work as an intern

in·ter·nal *adj* 1 : being within something : INTERIOR, INNER 2 : having to do with the inside of the body 3 : of or relating to the domestic affairs of a country — in·ter·nal·ly *adv*

in·ter·na·tion·al *adj* : of, relating to, or affecting two or more nations — in·ter·na·tion·al·ly *adv*

In·ter·net *n* : a communications system that connects groups of computers and databases all over the world

in·ter·plan·e·tary *adj* : existing, carried on, or operating between planets

in·ter·play *n* : INTERACTION

in·ter·pose *vb* in·ter·posed; in·ter·pos·ing 1 : to put between 2 : to introduce between parts of a conversation 3 : to be or come between

in·ter·po·si·tion *n* 1 : the act of interposing : the state of being interposed 2 : something that interposes or is interposed

in·ter·pret *vb* 1 : to tell the meaning of : EXPLAIN, TRANSLATE 2 : to understand according to one's own belief, judgment, or interest 3 : to bring out the meaning of — in·ter·pret·er *n*

in·ter·pre·ta·tion *n* : the act or the result of interpreting

in·ter·pre·ta·tive *adj* : designed or serving to interpret

in·ter·pre·tive *adj* : INTERPRETATIVE

in·ter·ra·cial *adj* : of or involving members of different races

in·ter·re·late *vb* in·ter·re·lat·ed; in·ter·re·lat·ing : to bring into or have a relationship with each other

in·ter·re·la·tion *n* : relation with each other — in·ter·re·la·tion·ship *n*

in·ter·ro·gate *vb* in·ter·ro·gat·ed; in·ter·ro·gat·ing : to question thoroughly

in·ter·ro·ga·tion *n* : the act of interrogating

interrogation point *n* : QUESTION MARK

in·ter·rog·a·tive *adj* : asking a question

in·ter·rog·a·to·ry *adj* : containing or expressing a question

in·ter·rupt *vb* **1** : to stop or hinder by breaking in **2** : to put or bring a difference into

in·ter·rup·tion *n* : an act of interrupting : a state of being interrupted

in·ter·scho·las·tic *adj* : existing or carried on between schools

in·ter·sect *vb* : to cut or divide by passing through or across : CROSS

in·ter·sec·tion *n* **1** : the act or process of intersecting **2** : the place or point where two or more things (as streets) intersect : CROSSING **3** : the set of mathematical elements common to two or more sets

in·ter·sperse *vb* **in·ter·spersed; in·ter·spers·ing 1** : to insert here and there **2** : to insert something at various places in or among

in·ter·state *adj* : existing between or including two or more states

in·ter·stel·lar *adj* : existing or taking place among the stars

in·ter·twine *vb* **in·ter·twined; in·ter·twin·ing** : to twine or cause to twine about one another

in·ter·val *n* **1** : a space of time between events or states **2** : a space between things **3** : the difference in pitch between two tones

in·ter·vene *vb* **in·ter·vened; in·ter·ven·ing 1** : to come between events, places, or points of time **2** : to interfere with something so as to stop, settle, or change

in·ter·ven·tion *n* : the act or fact of intervening

¹in·ter·view *n* **1** : a meeting face to face to give or get information or advice **2** : a written report of an interview for publication

²interview *vb* : to meet and question in an interview — **in·ter·view·er** *n*

in·ter·weave *vb* **in·ter·wove; in·ter·wo·ven; in·ter·weav·ing 1** : to weave together **2** : INTERMINGLE

in·tes·ti·nal *adj* : of or relating to the intestine

in·tes·tine *n* : the lower narrower part of the digestive canal in which most of the digestion and absorption of food occurs and through which waste material passes to be discharged

in·ti·ma·cy *n, pl* **in·ti·ma·cies** : the state or an instance of being intimate

¹in·ti·mate *vb* **in·ti·mat·ed; in·ti·mat·ing** : to express (as an idea) indirectly : HINT

²in·ti·mate *adj* **1** : most private : PERSONAL **2** : marked by very close association **3** : suggesting comfortable warmth or privacy : COZY — **in·ti·mate·ly** *adv*

³in·ti·mate *n* : a very close friend

in·ti·ma·tion *n* **1** : the act of intimating **2** : ¹HINT 1

in·tim·i·date *vb* **in·tim·i·dat·ed; in·tim·i·dat·ing** : to frighten especially by threats

in·tim·i·da·tion *n* : the act of intimidating : the state of being intimidated

in·to *prep* **1** : to the inside of **2** : to the state, condition, or form of **3** : so as to hit : AGAINST

in·tol·er·a·ble *adj* : UNBEARABLE — **in·tol·er·a·bly** *adv*

in·tol·er·ance *n* : the quality or state of being intolerant

in·tol·er·ant *adj* : not tolerant — **in·tol·er·ant·ly** *adv*

in·to·na·tion *n* : the rise and fall in pitch of the voice in speech

in·tox·i·cate *vb* **in·tox·i·cat·ed; in·tox·i·cat·ing 1** : to make drunk **2** : to make wildly excited or enthusiastic

in·tox·i·ca·tion *n* **1** : an unhealthy state that is or is like a poisoning **2** : the state of one who has drunk too much liquor : DRUNKENNESS

in·tra·mu·ral *adj* : being or occurring within the limits usually of a school

in·tran·si·tive *adj* : not having or containing a direct object

in·trep·id *adj* : feeling no fear : BOLD — **in·trep·id·ly** *adv*

in·tri·ca·cy *n, pl* **in·tri·ca·cies 1** : the quality or state of being intricate **2** : something intricate

in·tri·cate *adj* **1** : having many closely combined parts or elements **2** : very difficult to follow or understand — **in·tri·cate·ly** *adv*

¹in·trigue *vb* **in·trigued; in·tri·gu·ing 1** : ²PLOT 2, SCHEME **2** : to arouse the interest or curiosity of

²in·trigue *n* : a secret or sly scheme often for selfish purposes

in·tro·duce *vb* **in·tro·duced; in·tro·duc·ing 1** : to bring into practice or use **2** : to lead or bring in especially for the first time **3** : to cause to be acquainted : make known **4** : to bring forward for discussion **5** : to put in : INSERT — **in·tro·duc·er** *n*

in·tro·duc·tion *n* **1** : the action of introducing **2** : something introduced **3** : the part of a book that leads up to and explains what will be found in the main part **4** : the act of making persons known to each other

in·tro·duc·to·ry *adj* : serving to introduce : PRELIMINARY

in·trude *vb* **in·trud·ed; in·trud·ing 1** : to force in, into, or on especially where not right or proper **2** : to come or go in without an invitation or right — **in·trud·er** *n*

in·tru·sion *n* : the act of intruding

intrust *variant of* ENTRUST

in·tu·i·tion n : a knowing or something known without mental effort

in·un·date vb **in·un·dat·ed; in·un·dat·ing** : to cover with a flood : OVERFLOW

in·un·da·tion n : [1]FLOOD 1

in·vade vb **in·vad·ed; in·vad·ing** 1 : to enter by force to conquer or plunder 2 : to show lack of respect for — **in·vad·er** n

[1]in·val·id adj : not valid

[2]in·va·lid adj 1 : SICKLY 1 2 : of or relating to a sick person

[3]in·va·lid n : a sick or disabled person — **in·va·lid·ism** n

in·val·i·date vb **in·val·i·dat·ed; in·val·i·dat·ing** : to weaken or destroy the effect of

in·valu·able adj : having value too great to be estimated : PRICELESS

in·var·i·a·bil·i·ty n : the quality or state of being invariable

in·vari·able adj : not changing or capable of change — **in·vari·ably** adv

in·va·sion n : an act of invading

in·vei·gle vb **in·vei·gled; in·vei·gling** : to win over or obtain by flattery

in·vent vb 1 : to think up : make up 2 : to create or produce for the first time — **in·ven·tor** n

in·ven·tion n 1 : an original device or process 2 : [3]LIE 3 : the act or process of inventing

in·ven·tive adj : CREATIVE

[1]in·ven·to·ry n, pl **in·ven·to·ries** 1 : a list of items (as goods on hand) 2 : the act or process of making an inventory

[2]inventory vb **in·ven·to·ried; in·ven·to·ry·ing** : to make an inventory of

[1]in·verse adj 1 : opposite in order, nature, or effect 2 : being a mathematical operation that is opposite in effect to another operation — **in·verse·ly** adv

[2]inverse n : something inverse

in·vert vb 1 : to turn inside out or upside down 2 : to reverse the order or position of

[1]in·ver·te·brate adj : having no backbone

[2]invertebrate n : an invertebrate animal

[1]in·vest vb 1 : to give power or authority to 2 : BESIEGE 1

[2]invest vb 1 : to put out money in order to gain a financial return 2 : to put out (as effort) in support of a usually worthy cause — **in·ves·tor** n

in·ves·ti·gate vb **in·ves·ti·gat·ed; in·ves·ti·gat·ing** : to study by close and careful observation — **in·ves·ti·ga·tor** n

in·ves·ti·ga·tion n : the act or process of investigating

in·ves·ti·ture n : the act of placing in office

in·vest·ment n 1 : the investing of money 2 : a sum of money invested 3 : a property in which money is invested

in·vig·o·rate vb **in·vig·o·rat·ed; in·vig·o·rat·ing** : to give life and energy to

in·vin·ci·bil·i·ty n : the quality or state of being invincible

in·vin·ci·ble adj : impossible to defeat — **in·vin·ci·bly** adv

in·vi·o·la·ble adj 1 : too sacred to be treated with disrespect 2 : impossible to harm or destroy by violence

in·vi·o·late adj : not violated

in·vis·i·bil·i·ty n : the quality or state of being invisible

in·vis·i·ble adj 1 : impossible to see 2 : being out of sight 3 : IMPERCEPTIBLE 1 — **in·vis·i·ble·ness** n — **in·vis·i·bly** adv

in·vi·ta·tion n 1 : the act of inviting 2 : the written or spoken expression by which a person is invited

in·vite vb **in·vit·ed; in·vit·ing** 1 : to tend to bring on 2 : to request the presence or company of 3 : [1]WELCOME 2

in·vit·ing adj : ATTRACTIVE — **in·vit·ing·ly** adv

in·vo·ca·tion n : a prayer for blessing or guidance at the beginning of a meeting or a service

[1]in·voice n : a list of goods shipped usually showing the price and the terms of sale

[2]invoice vb **in·voiced; in·voic·ing** : to make an invoice of

in·voke vb **in·voked; in·vok·ing** 1 : to call on for aid or protection (as in prayer) 2 : to call forth by magic 3 : to appeal to as an authority or for support

in·vol·un·tary adj 1 : not made or done willingly or from choice 2 : not under the control of the will — **in·vol·un·tari·ly** adv

in·volve vb **in·volved; in·volv·ing** 1 : to draw into a situation : ENGAGE 2 : INCLUDE 3 : to be sure to or need to be accompanied by — **in·volve·ment** n

in·volved adj : COMPLEX 2

in·vul·ner·a·bil·i·ty n : the quality or state of being invulnerable

in·vul·ner·a·ble adj 1 : impossible to injure or damage 2 : safe from attack — **in·vul·ner·a·bly** adv

[1]in·ward adj 1 : situated on the inside : INNER 2 : of or relating to the mind or spirit 3 : directed toward the interior

[2]inward or **in·wards** adv 1 : toward the inside or center 2 : toward the mind or spirit

in·ward·ly adv 1 : in the mind or spirit 2 : beneath the surface 3 : to oneself : PRIVATELY 4 : toward the inside

io·dine n 1 : a chemical element found in seawater and seaweeds and used especially in medicine and photography 2 : a solution of iodine in alcohol used to kill germs

io·dize *vb* **io·dized; io·diz·ing** : to add iodine to

ion *n* : an atom or group of atoms that carries an electric charge

-ion *suffix* **1** : act or process **2** : result of an act or process **3** : state or condition

ion·ize *vb* **ion·ized; ion·iz·ing** : to change into ions

ion·o·sphere *n* : the part of the earth's atmosphere beginning at an altitude of about 40 kilometers, extending outward 400 kilometers or more, and containing electrically charged particles

io·ta *n* : a tiny amount : JOT

IOU *n* : a written promise to pay a debt

-ious *adj suffix* : -OUS

ir- — see IN-

iras·ci·ble *adj* : easily angered

irate *adj* : ANGRY — **irate·ly** *adv* — **irate·ness** *n*

ire *n* : ²ANGER, WRATH

ir·i·des·cence *n* : a shifting and constant change of colors producing rainbow effects

ir·i·des·cent *adj* : having iridescence — **ir·i·des·cent·ly** *adv*

irid·i·um *n* : a hard brittle heavy metallic chemical element

iris *n* **1** : the colored part around the pupil of an eye **2** : a plant with long pointed leaves and large usually brightly colored flowers

¹Irish *adj* : of or relating to Ireland, its people, or the Irish language

²Irish *n* **1 Irish** *pl* : the people of Ireland **2** : a language of Ireland

irk *vb* : to make weary, irritated, or bored

irk·some *adj* : causing boredom : TIRESOME — **irk·some·ness** *n*

¹iron *n* **1** : a heavy silvery white metallic chemical element that rusts easily, is strongly attracted by magnets, occurs in meteorites and combined in minerals, and is necessary in biological processes **2** : something made of iron **3 irons** *pl* : handcuffs or chains used to bind or to hinder movement **4** : a device that is heated and used for pressing cloth

²iron *adj* **1** : made of or relating to iron **2** : like iron

³iron *vb* : to press with a heated iron — **iron·er** *n*

iron·ic *or* **iron·i·cal** *adj* : relating to, containing, or showing irony — **iron·i·cal·ly** *adv*

iron lung *n* : an apparatus in which a person whose breathing is damaged (as by polio) can be placed to help the breathing

iron·work *n* **1** : work in iron **2 ironworks** *pl* : a mill where iron or steel is smelted or heavy iron or steel products are made

iro·ny *n, pl* **iro·nies 1** : the use of words that mean the opposite of what one really intends **2** : a result opposite to what was expected

ir·ra·di·ate *vb* **ir·ra·di·at·ed; ir·ra·di·at·ing 1** : to cast rays of light on **2** : to affect or treat with radiations (as X rays)

ir·ra·di·a·tion *n* **1** : the giving off of radiant energy (as heat) **2** : exposure to irradiation (as of X rays)

ir·ra·tio·nal *adj* **1** : not able to reason **2** : not based on reason — **ir·ra·tio·nal·ly** *adv*

ir·rec·on·cil·able *adj* : impossible to bring into harmony

ir·re·cov·er·able *adj* : impossible to recover or set right

ir·re·deem·able *adj* : impossible to redeem

ir·re·duc·ible *adj* : not possible to reduce

ir·re·fut·able *adj* : impossible to refute : INDISPUTABLE

ir·reg·u·lar *adj* **1** : not following custom or rule **2** : not following the usual manner of inflection **3** : not even or having the same shape on both sides **4** : not continuous or coming at set times — **ir·reg·u·lar·ly** *adv*

ir·reg·u·lar·i·ty *n, pl* **ir·reg·u·lar·i·ties 1** : the quality or state of being irregular **2** : something irregular

ir·rel·e·vance *n* **1** : the quality or state of being irrelevant **2** : something irrelevant

ir·rel·e·vant *adj* : not relevant — **ir·rel·e·vant·ly** *adv*

ir·re·li·gious *adj* : not having or acting as if one has religious emotions or beliefs

ir·rep·a·ra·ble *adj* : impossible to get back or to make right — **ir·rep·a·ra·bly** *adv*

ir·re·place·able *adj* : impossible to replace

ir·re·press·ible *adj* : impossible to repress or control

ir·re·proach·able *adj* : being beyond reproach

ir·re·sist·ible *adj* : impossible to resist — **ir·re·sist·ibly** *adv*

ir·res·o·lute *adj* : uncertain how to act or proceed — **ir·res·o·lute·ly** *adv*

ir·re·spec·tive of *prep* : without regard to

ir·re·spon·si·bil·i·ty *n* : the quality or state of being irresponsible

ir·re·spon·si·ble *adj* : having or showing little or no sense of responsibility — **ir·re·spon·si·bly** *adv*

ir·re·triev·able *adj* : impossible to get back — **ir·re·triev·ably** *adv*

ir·rev·er·ence *n* **1** : lack of reverence **2** : something said or done that is irreverent

ir·rev·er·ent *adj* : not reverent : DISRESPECTFUL — **ir·rev·er·ent·ly** *adv*

ir·re·vers·i·ble *adj* : impossible to reverse

ir·rev·o·ca·ble *adj* : impossible to take away or undo — **ir·rev·o·ca·bly** *adv*

ir·ri·gate *vb* **ir·ri·gat·ed; ir·ri·gat·ing 1** : to

supply (as land) with water by artificial means **2** : to flush with a liquid

ir·ri·ga·tion *n* : an act or process of irrigating

ir·ri·ta·bil·i·ty *n* : the quality or state of being irritable

ir·ri·ta·ble *adj* : easily irritated — **ir·ri·ta·bly** *adv*

¹**ir·ri·tant** *adj* : tending to cause irritation

²**irritant** *n* : something that irritates

ir·ri·tate *vb* **ir·ri·tat·ed; ir·ri·tat·ing 1** : to cause anger or impatience in : ANNOY **2** : to make sensitive or sore

ir·ri·ta·tion *n* **1** : the act of irritating : the state of being irritated **2** : ²IRRITANT

is *present 3d sing of* BE

-ish *adj suffix* **1** : of, relating to, or being **2** : characteristic of **3** : somewhat **4** : about

isin·glass *n* : mica in thin sheets

Is·lam *n* : a religion based on belief in Allah as the only God, in Muhammad as his prophet, and in the Koran — **Is·lam·ic** *adj*

is·land *n* **1** : an area of land surrounded by water and smaller than a continent **2** : something suggesting an island in its isolation

is·land·er *n* : a person who lives on an island

isle *n* : a usually small island

is·let *n* : a small island

-ism *n suffix* **1** : act : practice : process **2** : manner of action or behavior like that of a specified person or thing **3** : state : condition **4** : teachings : theory : cult : system

isn't : is not

iso·bar *n* : a line on a map to indicate areas having the same atmospheric pressure

iso·late *vb* **iso·lat·ed; iso·lat·ing** : to place or keep apart from others

iso·la·tion *n* : the act of isolating : the condition of being isolated

isos·ce·les triangle *n* : a triangle having two sides of equal length

ISP *n* : a company that provides access to the Internet for a fee : Internet service provider

¹**Is·rae·li** *adj* : of or relating to the Republic of Israel or the Israelis

²**Israeli** *n* : a person born or living in the Republic of Israel

Is·ra·el·ite *n* : a member of the Hebrew people having Jacob as an ancestor

is·su·ance *n* : the act of issuing

¹**is·sue** *n* **1** : the action of going, coming, or flowing out **2** : OFFSPRING, PROGENY **3** : what finally happens : RESULT **4** : something that is disputed **5** : a giving off (as of blood) from the body **6** : the act of bringing out, offering, or making available **7** : the thing or the whole quantity of things given out at one time

²**issue** *vb* **is·sued; is·su·ing 1** : to go, come, or flow out **2** : ¹RESULT 1 **3** : to dis-

tribute officially **4** : to send out for sale or circulation

-ist *n suffix* **1** : performer of a specified action : maker : producer **2** : one who plays a specified musical instrument or operates a specified mechanical device **3** : one who specializes in a specified art or science or skill **4** : one who follows or favors a specified teaching, practice, system, or code of behavior

isth·mus *n* : a neck of land separating two bodies of water and connecting two larger areas of land

¹**it** *pron* **1** : the thing, act, or matter about which these words are spoken or written **2** : the whole situation **3** — used with little meaning of its own in certain kinds of sentences

²**it** *n* : the player who has to do something special in a children's game

¹**Ital·ian** *n* **1** : a person born or living in Italy **2** : the language of the Italians

²**Italian** *adj* : of or relating to Italy, its people, or the Italian language

¹**ital·ic** *adj* : of or relating to a type style with letters that slant to the right (as in *"these characters are italic"*)

²**italic** *n* : an italic letter or italic type

ital·i·cize *vb* **ital·i·cized; ital·i·ciz·ing 1** : to print in italics **2** : UNDERLINE 1

¹**itch** *vb* : to have or cause an itch

²**itch** *n* **1** : an uneasy irritating sensation in the skin **2** : a skin disorder in which an itch is present **3** : a restless usually constant desire

itchy *adj* **itch·i·er; itch·i·est** : that itches

it'd : it had : it would

-ite *n suffix* **1** : native : resident **2** : descendant **3** : adherent : follower

item *n* **1** : a single thing in a list, account, or series **2** : a brief piece of news

item·ize *vb* **item·ized; item·iz·ing** : to set down one by one : LIST

¹**itin·er·ant** *adj* : traveling from place to place

²**itinerant** *n* : a person who travels about

-itis *n suffix* : inflammation of

it'll : it shall : it will

its *adj* : of or relating to it or itself

it's 1 : it is **2** : it has

it·self *pron* : its own self

-ity *n suffix, pl* **-ities** : quality : state : degree

I've : I have

-ive *adj suffix* : that does or tends to do a specified action

ivo·ry *n, pl* **ivo·ries 1** : the hard creamy-white material of which the tusks of a tusked mammal (as an elephant) are made **2** : a very pale yellow

ivy *n, pl* **ivies 1** : a woody vine with evergreen leaves, small yellowish flowers, and black berries often found growing on buildings **2** : a plant like ivy

-i·za·tion *n suffix* : action : process : state

-ize *vb suffix* **-ized; -iz·ing 1** : cause to be or be like : form or cause to be formed into **2** : cause to experience a specified action **3** : saturate, treat, or combine with **4** : treat like **5** : engage in a specified activity

J

j *n, pl* **j's** *or* **js** *often cap* : the tenth letter of the English alphabet

¹jab *vb* **jabbed; jab·bing** : to poke quickly or suddenly with or as if with something sharp

²jab *n* : a quick or sudden poke

¹jab·ber *vb* : to talk too fast or not clearly enough to be understood

²jabber *n* : confused talk : GIBBERISH

¹jack *n* **1** : a playing card marked with the figure of a man **2** : a device for lifting something heavy a short distance **3** : JACK-ASS 1 **4** : a small six-pointed usually metal object used in a children's game (**jacks**) **5** : a small national flag flown by a ship **6** : a socket used with a plug to connect one electric circuit with another

²jack *vb* : to move or lift by or as if by a jack

jack·al *n* : any of several Old World wild dogs like but smaller than wolves

jack·ass *n* **1** : a male donkey **2** : DONKEY 1 **3** : a stupid person

jack·daw *n* : a European bird somewhat like a crow

jack·et *n* **1** : a short coat or coatlike garment **2** : an outer cover or casing

Jack Frost *n* : frost or frosty weather thought of as a person

jack–in–the–box *n, pl* **jack–in–the–box·es** *or* **jacks–in–the–box** : a small box out of which a comical toy figure springs when the lid is raised

jack–in–the–pul·pit *n, pl* **jack–in–the–pul·pits** *or* **jacks–in–the–pul·pit** : a plant that grows in moist shady woods and has a stalk of tiny yellowish flowers protected by a leaf bent over like a hood

¹jack·knife *n, pl* **jack·knives** : a knife with folding blade or blades that can be carried in one's pocket

²jackknife *vb* **jack·knifed; jack·knif·ing** : to double up like a jackknife

jack–of–all–trades *n, pl* **jacks–of–all–trades** : a person who can do several kinds of work fairly well

jack–o'–lan·tern *n* : a lantern made of a pumpkin cut to look like a human face

jack·pot *n* : a large and often unexpected success or reward

jack·rab·bit *n* : a large North American hare with very long ears and long hind legs

jade *n* : a usually green mineral used for jewelry and carvings

jag·ged *adj* : having a sharply uneven edge or surface — **jag·ged·ly** *adv*

jag·uar *n* : a large yellowish brown black-spotted animal of the cat family found from Texas to Paraguay

¹jail *n* : PRISON

²jail *vb* : to shut up in or as if in a prison

jail·bird *n* : a person who is or has been locked up in prison

jail·break *n* : escape from prison by the use of force

jail·er *or* **jail·or** *n* : a keeper of a prison

ja·lopy *n, pl* **ja·lop·ies** : a worn shabby old automobile or airplane

¹jam *vb* **jammed; jam·ming 1** : to crowd, squeeze, or wedge into a tight position **2** : to put into action hard or suddenly **3** : to hurt by pressure **4** : to be or cause to be stuck or unable to work because a part is wedged tight **5** : to cause interference in (radio or television signals)

²jam *n* **1** : a crowded mass of people or things that blocks something **2** : a difficult state of affairs

³jam *n* : a food made by boiling fruit with sugar until it is thick

jamb *n* : a vertical piece forming the side of an opening (as for a doorway)

jam·bo·ree *n* **1** : a large jolly get-together **2** : a national or international camping assembly of boy scouts

¹jan·gle *vb* **jan·gled; jan·gling** : to make or cause to make a harsh sound

²jangle *n* : a harsh often ringing sound

jan·i·tor *n* : a person who takes care of a building (as a school)

Jan·u·ary *n* : the first month of the year

¹Jap·a·nese *adj* : of or relating to Japan, its people, or the Japanese language

²Japanese *n, pl* **Japanese 1** : a person born or living in Japan **2** : the language of the Japanese

Japanese beetle *n* : a small glossy green or brown Asian beetle that has gotten into the United States where it is a harmful pest whose larvae feed on roots and whose adults eat leaves and fruits

¹jar *vb* **jarred; jar·ring 1** : to make a harsh unpleasant sound **2** : to have a disagreeable effect **3** : to shake or cause to shake hard

²jar *n* **1** : a harsh sound **2** : ²JOLT 1 **3** : ²SHOCK 3

³**jar** *n* : a usually glass or pottery container with a wide mouth

jar·gon *n* **1** : the special vocabulary of an activity or group **2** : language that is not clear and is full of long words

jas·mine *n* : any of various mostly climbing plants of warm regions with fragrant flowers

jas·per *n* : an opaque usually red, green, brown, or yellow stone used for making ornamental objects (as vases)

¹**jaunt** *vb* : to make a short trip for pleasure

²**jaunt** *n* : a short pleasure trip

jaun·ty *adj* **jaun·ti·er; jaun·ti·est** : lively in manner or appearance — **jaun·ti·ly** *adv* — **jaun·ti·ness** *n*

Ja·va man *n* : a small-brained prehistoric human known from skulls found in Java

jav·e·lin *n* **1** : a light spear **2** : a slender rod thrown for distance in a track-and-field contest (**javelin throw**)

jaw *n* **1** : either of the bony structures that support the soft parts of the mouth and usually bear teeth on their edge **2** : a part of an invertebrate animal (as an insect) that resembles or does the work of a jaw **3** : one of a pair of moving parts that open and close for holding or crushing something

jaw·bone *n* : JAW 1

jay *n* : a noisy bird related to the crow but with brighter colors

jay·walk *vb* : to cross a street in a place or in a way that is against traffic regulations — **jay·walk·er** *n*

jazz *n* : lively American music that developed from ragtime

jeal·ous *adj* **1** : demanding complete faithfulness **2** : feeling a mean resentment toward someone more successful than oneself **3** : CAREFUL 1, WATCHFUL — **jeal·ous·ly** *adv*

jeal·ou·sy *n, pl* **jeal·ou·sies** : a jealous attitude or feeling

jeans *n pl* : pants made of a heavy cotton cloth

¹**jeer** *vb* **1** : to speak or cry out in scorn **2** : to scorn or mock with jeers

²**jeer** *n* : a scornful remark or sound : TAUNT

Je·ho·vah *n* : GOD 1

jell *vb* **1** : to become as firm as jelly : SET **2** : to take shape

¹**jel·ly** *n, pl* **jellies** : a soft springy food made from fruit juice boiled with sugar, from meat juices, or from gelatin — **jel·ly·like** *adj*

²**jelly** *vb* **jel·lied; jel·ly·ing** **1** : JELL 1 **2** : to make jelly

jelly bean *n* : a chewy bean-shaped candy

jel·ly·fish *n* : a free-swimming sea animal related to the corals that has a jellylike body shaped like a saucer

jen·net *n* : a female donkey

jeop·ar·dize *vb* **jeop·ar·dized; jeop·ar·diz·ing** : to expose to danger

jeop·ar·dy *n* : DANGER 1

¹**jerk** *n* **1** : a short quick pull or jolt **2** : a foolish person

²**jerk** *vb* **1** : to give a quick sharp pull or twist to **2** : to move with jerks

jer·kin *n* : a close-fitting sleeveless jacket that extends to or just over the hips

jerky *adj* **jerk·i·er; jerk·i·est** : moving with sudden starts and stops — **jerk·i·ly** *adv* — **jerk·i·ness** *n*

jer·sey *n, pl* **jerseys** **1** : a knitted cloth (as of wool or cotton) used mostly for clothing **2** : a close-fitting knitted garment (as a shirt)

¹**jest** *n* **1** : a comic act or remark : JOKE **2** : a playful mood or manner

²**jest** *vb* : to make jests : JOKE

jest·er *n* **1** : a person formerly kept in royal courts to amuse people **2** : a person who often jests

Je·sus *n* : the founder of the Christian religion

¹**jet** *n* **1** : a black mineral that is often used for jewelry **2** : a very dark black

²**jet** *vb* **jet·ted; jet·ting** : ¹SPURT 1

³**jet** *n* **1** : a rush of liquid, gas, or vapor through a narrow opening or a nozzle **2** : a nozzle for a jet of gas or liquid **3** : JET ENGINE **4** : JET AIRPLANE

jet airplane *n* : an airplane powered by a jet engine

jet engine *n* : an engine in which fuel burns to produce a jet of heated air and gases that shoot out from the rear and drive the engine forward

jet plane *n* : JET AIRPLANE

jet–pro·pelled *adj* : driven forward or onward by a jet engine

jet·sam *n* : goods thrown overboard to lighten a ship in danger of sinking

jet stream *n* : high-speed winds blowing from a westerly direction several kilometers above the earth's surface

jet·ti·son *vb* : to throw out especially from a ship or an airplane

jet·ty *n, pl* **jetties** **1** : a pier built to change the path of the current or tide or to protect a harbor **2** : a landing wharf

Jew *n* : a person who is a descendant of the ancient Hebrews or whose religion is Judaism

jew·el *n* **1** : an ornament of precious metal often set with precious stones and worn on the person **2** : a person who is greatly admired **3** : GEM **4** : a bearing in a watch made of crystal or a precious stone

jew·el·er *or* **jew·el·ler** *n* : a person who

makes or deals in jewelry and related articles (as silverware)

jew·el·ry *n* : ornamental pieces (as rings or necklaces) worn on the person

Jew·ish *adj* : of or relating to Jews or Judaism

Jew's harp *or* **Jews' harp** *n* : a small musical instrument that is held in the mouth and struck with the finger to give off a tone

jib *n* : a three-cornered sail extending forward from the foremast

¹jibe *variant of* GIBE

²jibe *vb* **jibed; jib·ing 1** : to shift suddenly from side to side **2** : to change the course of a boat so that the sail jibes

³jibe *vb* **jibed; jib·ing** : to be in agreement

jif·fy *n, pl* **jiffies** : MOMENT 1

¹jig *n* : a lively dance

²jig *vb* **jigged; jig·ging** : to dance a jig

¹jig·gle *vb* **jig·gled; jig·gling** : to move or cause to move with quick little jerks

²jiggle *n* : a quick little jerk

jig·saw *n* : a machine saw used to cut curved and irregular lines or openwork patterns

jigsaw puzzle *n* : a puzzle made by cutting a picture into small pieces that must be fitted together again

jim·son·weed *n* : a coarse poisonous weedy plant related to the potato that is sometimes grown for its showy white or purple flowers

¹jin·gle *vb* **jin·gled; jin·gling** : to make or cause to make a light clinking sound

²jingle *n* **1** : a light clinking sound **2** : a short verse or song that repeats bits in a catchy way — **jin·gly** *adj*

jinx *n* : a bringer of bad luck

jit·ters *n pl* : extreme nervousness

jit·tery *adj* : very nervous

job *n* **1** : a piece of work usually done on order at an agreed rate **2** : something produced by or as if by work **3** : a regular paying employment **4** : a special duty or function — **job·less** *adj*

jock·ey *n, pl* **jockeys 1** : a professional rider in a horse race **2** : OPERATOR 1

¹jog *vb* **jogged; jog·ging 1** : to give a slight shake or push to : NUDGE **2** : to rouse to alertness **3** : to move or cause to move at a jog **4** : to run slowly (as for exercise) — **jog·ger** *n*

²jog *n* **1** : a slight shake or push **2** : a slow jolting gait (as of a horse) **3** : a slow run

³jog *n* : a short change in direction

jog·gle *vb* **jog·gled; jog·gling** : to shake or cause to shake slightly

john·ny·cake *n* : a bread made of cornmeal, water or milk, and leavening with or without flour, shortening, and eggs

join *vb* **1** : to come, bring, or fasten together **2** : ADJOIN **3** : to come or bring into close

association **4** : to come into the company of **5** : to become a member of **6** : to take part in a group activity **7** : to combine the elements of

¹joint *n* **1** : a part of the skeleton where two pieces come together usually in a way that allows motion **2** : a part of a plant stem where a leaf or branch develops : NODE **3** : a place where two things or parts are joined — **joint·ed** *adj*

²joint *adj* **1** : joined together **2** : done by or shared by two or more — **joint·ly** *adv*

joist *n* : any of the small timbers or metal beams laid crosswise in a building to support a floor or ceiling

¹joke *n* **1** : something said or done to cause laughter or amusement **2** : a very short story with a funny ending that is a surprise **3** : something not worthy of being taken seriously

²joke *vb* **joked; jok·ing 1** : to say or do something as a joke **2** : to make jokes

jok·er *n* **1** : a person who jokes **2** : an extra card used in some card games

jok·ing·ly *adv* : in a joking manner

jol·li·ty *n* : the state of being jolly

¹jol·ly *adj* **jol·li·er; jol·li·est** : full of fun or high spirits

²jolly *adv* : ²VERY 1

¹jolt *vb* **1** : to move or cause to move with a sudden jerky motion **2** : to cause to be upset

²jolt *n* **1** : an abrupt jerky blow or movement **2** : a sudden shock or disappointment

jon·quil *n* : a plant related to the daffodil but with fragrant yellow or white flowers with a short central tube

josh *vb* **1** : ²KID 1 **2** : ²JOKE

jos·tle *vb* **jos·tled; jos·tling** : to knock against so as to jar : push roughly

¹jot *n* : the least bit

²jot *vb* **jot·ted; jot·ting** : to write briefly or in a hurry : make a note of

jounce *vb* **jounced; jounc·ing** : to move, fall, or bounce so as to shake

jour·nal *n* **1** : a brief record (as in a diary) of daily happenings **2** : a daily record (as of business dealings) **3** : a daily newspaper **4** : a magazine that reports on things of special interest to a particular group

jour·nal·ism *n* **1** : the business of collecting and editing news (as for newspapers, radio, or television) **2** : writing of general or popular interest

jour·nal·ist *n* : an editor or reporter of the news

¹jour·ney *n, pl* **jour·neys** : a traveling from one place to another

²journey *vb* **jour·neyed; jour·ney·ing** : to go on a journey : TRAVEL — **jour·ney·er** *n*

jour·ney·man *n, pl* **jour·ney·men** : a worker who has learned a trade and usually works for another person by the day

¹joust *vb* : to take part in a joust : TILT

²joust *n* : a combat on horseback between two knights with lances

jo·vial *adj* : ¹JOLLY — **jo·vial·ly** *adv*

¹jowl *n* : loose flesh (as a double chin) hanging from the lower jaw and throat

²jowl *n* **1** : an animal's jaw and especially the lower jaw **2** : CHEEK 1

joy *n* **1** : a feeling of pleasure or happiness that comes from success, good fortune, or a sense of well-being **2** : something that gives pleasure or happiness

joy·ful *adj* : feeling, causing, or showing joy — **joy·ful·ly** *adv* — **joy·ful·ness** *n*

joy·ous *adj* : JOYFUL — **joy·ous·ly** *adv* — **joy·ous·ness** *n*

joy·stick *n* : a control lever (as for a computer display or an airplane) capable of motion in two or more directions

ju·bi·lant *adj* : expressing great joy especially with shouting : noisily happy

ju·bi·lee *n* **1** : a fiftieth anniversary **2** : time of celebration

Ju·da·ism *n* : a religion developed among the ancient Hebrews that stresses belief in one God and faithfulness to the moral laws of the Old Testament

¹judge *vb* **judged; judg·ing** **1** : to form an opinion after careful consideration **2** : to act as a judge (as in a trial) **3** : THINK 2

²judge *n* **1** : a public official whose duty is to decide questions brought before a court **2** : a person appointed to decide in a contest or competition **3** : a person with the experience to give a meaningful opinion : CRITIC

judg·ment *or* **judge·ment** *n* **1** : a decision or opinion (as of a court) given after judging **2** : an opinion or estimate formed by examining and comparing **3** : the ability for judging

ju·di·cial *adj* : of or relating to the providing of justice — **ju·di·cial·ly** *adv*

ju·di·cious *adj* : having, using, or showing good judgment : WISE — **ju·di·cious·ly** *adv* — **ju·di·cious·ness** *n*

ju·do *n* : a Japanese form of wrestling in which each person tries to throw or pin the opponent

jug *n* : a large deep usually earthenware or glass container with a narrow mouth and a handle

jug·gle *vb* **jug·gled; jug·gling** **1** : to keep several things moving in the air at the same time **2** : to mix things up in order to deceive **3** : to hold or balance insecurely — **jug·gler** *n*

juice *n* **1** : the liquid part that can be squeezed out of vegetables and fruit **2** : the fluid part of meat

juicy *adj* **juic·i·er; juic·i·est** : having much juice — **juic·i·ness** *n*

Ju·ly *n* : the seventh month of the year

¹jum·ble *vb* **jum·bled; jum·bling** : to mix in a confused mass

²jumble *n* : a disorderly mass or pile

jum·bo *n, pl* **jumbos** : something very large of its kind

¹jump *vb* **1** : to spring into the air : LEAP **2** : to make a sudden movement : START **3** : to have or cause a sudden sharp increase **4** : to make a hasty judgement **5** : to make a sudden attack **6** : to pass over or cause to pass over with or as if with a leap — **jump the gun 1** : to start in a race before the starting signal **2** : to do something before the proper time

²jump *n* **1** : an act or instance of jumping : LEAP **2** : a sudden involuntary movement : START **3** : a sharp sudden increase **4** : an initial advantage

jum·per *n* **1** : a loose blouse or jacket often worn by workmen **2** : a sleeveless dress worn usually with a blouse

jumpy *adj* **jump·i·er; jump·i·est** : NERVOUS 3

jun·co *n, pl* **juncos** *or* **juncoes** : a small mostly gray American finch usually having a pink bill

junc·tion *n* **1** : an act of joining **2** : a place or point of meeting

June *n* : the sixth month of the year

jun·gle *n* **1** : a thick or tangled growth of plants **2** : a large area of land usually in a tropical region covered with a thick tangled growth of plants

¹ju·nior *adj* **1** : being younger — used to distinguish a son from a father with the same name **2** : lower in rank **3** : of or relating to juniors

²junior *n* **1** : a person who is younger or lower in rank than another **2** : a student in the next-to-last year (as at high school)

ju·ni·per *n* : any of various evergreen trees and shrubs related to the pines but having tiny berrylike cones

¹junk *n* **1** : old iron, glass, paper, or waste : RUBBISH **2** : a poorly made product

²junk *vb* : to get rid of as worthless : SCRAP

³junk *n* : a sailing ship of Chinese waters

junk food *n* : food that is high in calories but low in nutritional content

Ju·pi·ter *n* : the planet that is fifth in order of distance from the sun and is the largest of the planets with a diameter of about 140,000 kilometers

ju·ror *n* : a member of a jury

ju·ry *n, pl* **juries** **1** : a body of persons

sworn to seek for and try to learn the truth about a matter put before them for decision **2** : a committee that judges and awards prizes (as at an exhibition)

1just *adj* **1** : having a foundation in fact or reason : REASONABLE **2** : agreeing with a standard of correctness **3** : morally right or good **4** : legally right — **just·ly** *adv*

2just *adv* **1** : exactly as wanted **2** : very recently **3** : by a very small amount **4** : by a very short distance **5** : nothing more than **6** : ²VERY 2

jus·tice *n* **1** : just or right action or treatment **2** : ²JUDGE 1 **3** : the carrying out of law **4** : the quality of being fair or just

jus·ti·fi·able *adj* : possible to justify — **jus·ti·fi·ably** *adv*

jus·ti·fi·ca·tion *n* **1** : the act or an instance of justifying **2** : something that justifies

jus·ti·fy *vb* **jus·ti·fied; jus·ti·fy·ing** : to prove or show to be just, right, or reasonable

jut *vb* **jut·ted; jut·ting** : to extend or cause to extend above or beyond a surrounding area

jute *n* : a strong glossy fiber from a tropical plant used chiefly for making sacks and twine

1ju·ve·nile *adj* **1** : incompletely developed : IMMATURE **2** : of, relating to, or characteristic of children or young people

2juvenile *n* : a young person : YOUTH

K

k *n, pl* **k's** *or* **ks** *often cap* **1** : the eleventh letter of the English alphabet **2** : THOUSAND **3** : KILOBYTE

kale *n* : a hardy cabbage with wrinkled leaves that do not form a head

ka·lei·do·scope *n* **1** : a tube containing bits of colored glass or plastic and two mirrors at one end that shows many different patterns as it is turned **2** : a changing pattern or scene

kan·ga·roo *n, pl* **kan·ga·roos** : any of numerous leaping mammals of Australia and nearby islands that feed on plants and have long powerful hind legs, a thick tail used as a support in standing or walking, and in the female a pouch on the abdomen in which the young are carried

ka·o·lin *n* : a very pure white clay used in making porcelain

kar·a·o·ke *n* : a device that plays music to which the user sings along and that records the user's singing with the music

kar·at *n* : a unit of fineness for gold

ka·ra·te *n* : an Oriental art of self-defense in which an attacker is defeated by kicks and punches

ka·ty·did *n* : any of several large green American grasshoppers with males that make shrill noises

kay·ak *n* **1** : an Eskimo canoe made of a frame covered with skins except for a small opening in the center **2** : a boat styled like an Eskimo kayak

ka·zoo *n, pl* **ka·zoos** : a toy musical instrument containing a membrane which produces a buzzing tone when one hums into the mouth hole

KB *n* : KILOBYTE

1keel *n* : a timber or plate running lengthwise along the center of the bottom of a ship and usually sticking out from the bottom

2keel *vb* : to turn over

keel over *vb* : to fall suddenly (as in a faint)

keen *adj* **1** : having a fine edge or point : SHARP **2** : seeming to cut or sting **3** : full of enthusiasm : EAGER **4** : having or showing mental sharpness **5** : very sensitive (as in seeing or hearing) — **keen·ly** *adv* — **keen·ness** *n*

1keep *vb* **kept; keep·ing** **1** : to be faithful to : FULFILL **2** : to act properly in relation to **3** : PROTECT **4** : to take care of : TEND **5** : to continue doing something **6** : to have in one's service or at one's disposal **7** : to preserve a record in **8** : to have on hand regularly for sale **9** : to continue to have in one's possession or power **10** : to prevent from leaving : DETAIN **11** : to hold back **12** : to remain or cause to remain in a given place, situation, or condition **13** : to continue in an unspoiled condition **14** : ¹REFRAIN

2keep *n* **1** : the strongest part of a castle in the Middle Ages **2** : the necessities of life — **for keeps** **1** : with the understanding that one may keep what is won **2** : for a long time : PERMANENTLY

keep·er *n* : a person who watches, guards, or takes care of something

keep·ing *n* **1** : watchful attention : CARE **2** : a proper or fitting relationship : HARMONY

keep·sake *n* : something kept or given to be kept in memory of a person, place, or happening

keep up *vb* **1** : MAINTAIN 1 **2** : to stay well informed about something **3** : to continue without interruption **4** : to stay even with others (as in a race)

keg *n* **1** : a small barrel holding about 114 liters **2** : the contents of a keg

kelp *n* : a large coarse brown seaweed

ken *n* **1** : range of vision : SIGHT **2** : range of understanding

ken·nel *n* **1** : a shelter for a dog **2** : a place where dogs are bred or housed

kept *past of* KEEP

ker·chief *n, pl* **kerchiefs** **1** : a square of cloth worn as a head covering or as a scarf **2** : HANDKERCHIEF

ker·nel *n* **1** : the inner softer part of a seed, fruit stone, or nut **2** : the whole grain or seed of a cereal

ker·o·sene *or* **ker·o·sine** *n* : a thin oil obtained from petroleum and used as a fuel and solvent

ketch *n* : a fore-and-aft rigged ship with two masts

ketch·up *n* : a thick seasoned sauce usually made from tomatoes

ket·tle *n* **1** : a pot for boiling liquids **2** : TEAKETTLE

ket·tle·drum *n* : a large brass or copper drum that has a rounded bottom and can be varied in pitch

1key *n* **1** : an instrument by which the bolt of a lock (as on a door) is turned **2** : a device having the form or function of a key **3** : a means of gaining or preventing entrance, possession, or control **4** : something (as a map legend) that gives an explanation : SOLUTION **5** : one of the levers with a flat surface that is pressed with a finger to activate a mechanism of a machine or instrument **6** : a system of seven musical tones arranged in relation to a keynote from which the system is named **7** : a characteristic way (as of thought) **8** : a small switch for opening or closing an electric circuit

2key *vb* **keyed; key·ing** **1** : to regulate the musical pitch of **2** : to bring into harmony

3key *adj* : of great importance : most important

4key *n* : a low island or reef

key·board *n* **1** : a row of keys by which a musical instrument (as a piano) is played **2** : a portable electronic musical instrument with a keyboard like that of a piano **3** : the whole arrangement of keys (as on a typewriter)

key·hole *n* : a hole for receiving a key

key·note *n* **1** : the first and harmonically fundamental tone of a scale **2** : the fundamental fact, idea, or mood

key·stone *n* **1** : the wedge-shaped piece at the top of an arch that locks the other pieces in place **2** : something on which other things depend for support

key up *vb* : to make nervous or tense

kha·ki *n* **1** : a light yellowish brown **2** : a light yellowish brown cloth used especially for military uniforms

khan *n* **1** : a Mongolian leader **2** : a local chieftain or man of rank in some countries of central Asia

ki·bitz·er *n* : a person who looks on and often offers unwanted advice especially at a card game

1kick *vb* **1** : to strike out or hit with the foot **2** : to object strongly : PROTEST **3** : to spring back when fired

2kick *n* **1** : a blow with the foot **2** : a sudden moving (as of a ball) with the foot **3** : the sudden move backward of a gun when fired **4** : a feeling of or cause for objection **5** : a feeling or source of pleasure

kick·ball *n* : a form of baseball played with a large rubber ball that is kicked instead of hit with a bat

kick·off *n* : a kick that puts the ball into play (as in football or soccer)

kick off *vb* **1** : to make a kickoff **2** : BEGIN 1

1kid *n* **1** : the young of a goat or a related animal **2** : the flesh, fur, or skin of a kid or something (as leather) made from one of these **3** : CHILD — **kid·dish** *adj*

2kid *vb* **kid·ded; kid·ding** **1** : to deceive or trick as a joke **2** : 1TEASE — **kid·der** *n*

kid·nap *vb* **kid·napped** *or* **kid·naped; kid·nap·ping** *or* **kid·nap·ing** : to carry away a person by force or by fraud and against his or her will — **kid·nap·per** *or* **kid·nap·er** *n*

kid·ney *n, pl* **kid·neys** : either of a pair of organs near the backbone that give off waste from the body in the form of urine

kidney bean *n* : a common garden bean and especially one having large dark red seeds

1kill *vb* **1** : to end the life of : SLAY **2** : to put an end to **3** : to use up **4** : 1DEFEAT 1

2kill *n* **1** : an act of killing **2** : an animal killed

kill·deer *n* : a grayish brown North American plover that has a shrill mournful call

1kill·er *n* : one that kills

2killer *adj* **1** : very impressive or effective **2** : very difficult **3** : causing death or ruin

kill·joy *n* : a person who spoils the pleasure of others

kiln *n* : a furnace or oven in which something (as pottery) is hardened, burned, or dried

ki·lo *n, pl* **kilos** : KILOGRAM

kilo- *prefix* : thousand

ki·lo·byte *n* : a unit of computer information storage equal to 1024 bytes

ki·lo·gram *n* : a metric unit of weight equal to 1000 grams

ki·lo·me·ter *n* : a metric unit of length equal to 1000 meters

kilo·watt *n* : a unit of electrical power equal to 1000 watts

kilt *n* : a knee-length pleated skirt usually of tartan worn by men in Scotland

kil·ter *n* : proper condition

ki·mo·no *n, pl* **ki·mo·nos** 1 : a loose robe with wide sleeves that is traditionally worn with a broad sash as an outer garment by the Japanese 2 : a loose dressing gown worn chiefly by women

kin *n* 1 : a person's relatives 2 : KINSMAN

-kin *also* **-kins** *n suffix* : little

¹**kind** *n* : a group of persons or things that can be recognized as belonging together or having something in common

²**kind** *adj* 1 : wanting or liking to do good and to bring happiness to others : CONSID-ERATE 2 : showing or growing out of gentleness or goodness of heart

kin·der·gar·ten *n* : a school or a class for very young children

kind·heart·ed *adj* : having or showing a kind and sympathetic nature — **kind·heart-ed·ly** *adv* — **kind·heart·ed·ness** *n*

kin·dle *vb* **kin·dled; kin·dling** 1 : to set on fire : LIGHT 2 : to stir up : EXCITE

kin·dling *n* : material that burns easily and is used for starting a fire

¹**kind·ly** *adj* **kind·li·er; kind·li·est** 1 : pleasant or wholesome in nature 2 : sympathetic or generous in nature — **kind·li-ness** *n*

²**kindly** *adv* 1 : in a willing manner 2 : in a kind manner 3 : in an appreciative manner 4 : in an obliging manner

kind·ness *n* 1 : a kind deed : FAVOR 2 : the quality or state of being kind

kind of *adv* : to a moderate degree : SOME-WHAT

¹**kin·dred** *n* 1 : a group of related individuals 2 : a person's relatives

²**kindred** *adj* : alike in nature or character

kin·folk *n* : ¹KINDRED 2

king *n* 1 : a male ruler of a country who usually inherits his position and rules for life 2 : a chief among competitors 3 : the chief piece in the game of chess 4 : a playing card bearing the figure of a king 5 : a piece in checkers that has reached the opponent's back row — **king·ly** *adj*

king·dom *n* 1 : a country whose ruler is a king or queen 2 : one of the three basic divisions (**animal kingdom, plant kingdom, mineral kingdom**) into which natural objects are commonly grouped 3 : a major category in scientific biological classification that ranks above the phylum and division and is the highest and broadest group

king·fish·er *n* : any of a group of usually crested birds with a short tail, long sharp bill, and bright feathers

king·let *n* : a small bird resembling a warbler

king–size *or* **king–sized** *adj* : unusually large

¹**kink** *n* 1 : a short tight twist or curl (as in a thread or rope) 2 : ¹CRAMP 1 3 : an imperfection that makes something hard to use or work — **kinky** *adj*

²**kink** *vb* : to form or cause to form a kink in

-kins — see -KIN

kin·ship *n* : the quality or state of being kin

kins·man *n, pl* **kins·men** : a relative usually by birth

kins·wom·an *n, pl* **kins·wom·en** : a woman who is a relative usually by birth

¹**kiss** *vb* 1 : to touch with the lips as a mark of love or greeting 2 : to touch gently or lightly

²**kiss** *n* 1 : a loving touch with the lips 2 : a gentle touch or contact 3 : a bite-size candy often wrapped in paper or foil

kit *n* 1 : a set of articles for personal use 2 : a set of tools or supplies 3 : a set of parts to be put together 4 : a container (as a bag or case) for a kit

kitch·en *n* : a room in which cooking is done

kitch·en·ette *n* : a small kitchen

kitchen garden *n* : a piece of land where vegetables are grown for household use

kite *n* 1 : a hawk with long narrow wings and deeply forked tail that feeds mostly on insects and small reptiles 2 : a light covered frame for flying in the air at the end of a long string

kith *n* : familiar friends and neighbors or relatives

kit·ten *n* : a young cat — **kit·ten·ish** *adj*

kit·ty *n, pl* **kitties** : CAT, KITTEN

ki·wi *n* : a New Zealand bird that is unable to fly

knack *n* 1 : a clever or skillful way of doing something : TRICK 2 : a natural ability : TALENT

knap·sack *n* : a carrying case or pouch slung from the shoulders over the back

knave *n* 1 : RASCAL 1 2 : ¹JACK 1

knead *vb* 1 : to work and press into a mass with or as if with the hands 2 : ²MASSAGE — **knead·er** *n*

knee *n* 1 : the joint or region in which the thigh and lower leg come together 2 : something resembling a knee 3 : the part of a garment covering the knee

knee·cap *n* : a thick flat movable bone forming the front part of the knee

kneel *vb* **knelt** *or* **kneeled; kneel·ing** : to bend the knee : support oneself on one's knees

¹**knell** *vb* 1 : to ring slowly and solemnly : TOLL 2 : to summon, announce, or warn by a knell

²**knell** *n* 1 : a stroke or sound of a bell espe-

cially when rung slowly for a death, funeral, or disaster **2** : an indication (as a sound) of the end or failure of something

knew *past of* KNOW

knick·ers *n pl* : loose-fitting short pants gathered just below the knee

knick·knack *n* : a small ornamental object

1knife *n, pl* **knives** **1** : a cutting instrument consisting of a sharp blade fastened to a handle **2** : a cutting blade in a machine

2knife *vb* **knifed; knif·ing** : to stab, slash, or wound with a knife

1knight *n* **1** : a warrior of olden times who fought on horseback, served a king, held a special military rank, and swore to behave in a noble way **2** : a man honored by a sovereign for merit and in Great Britain ranking below a baronet **3** : one of the pieces in the game of chess — **knight·ly** *adj*

2knight *vb* : to make a knight of

knight·hood *n* **1** : the rank, dignity, or profession of a knight **2** : the qualities that a knight should have **3** : knights as a class or body

knit *vb* **knit** *or* **knit·ted; knit·ting** **1** : to form a fabric or garment by interlacing yarn or thread in connected loops with needles (**knitting needles**) **2** : to draw or come together closely as if knitted : unite firmly **3** : 2WRINKLE — **knit·ter** *n*

knob *n* **1** : a rounded lump **2** : a small rounded handle **3** : a rounded hill

1knock *vb* **1** : to strike with a sharp blow **2** : to bump against something **3** : to make a pounding noise **4** : to find fault with

2knock *n* **1** : a sharp blow **2** : a severe misfortune or hardship **3** : a pounding noise

knock·er *n* : a device made like a hinge and fastened to a door for use in knocking

knock–kneed *adj* : having the legs bowed inward

knoll *n* : a small round hill

1knot *n* **1** : an interlacing (as of string or ribbon) that forms a lump or knob **2** : PROBLEM **2** **3** : a bond of union **4** : the inner end of a branch enclosed in a plant stem or a section of this in sawed lumber **5** : a cluster of persons or things **6** : an ornamental bow of ribbon **7** : one nautical mile per hour (about two kilometers per hour)

2knot *vb* **knot·ted; knot·ting** **1** : to tie in or with a knot **2** : to unite closely

knot·hole *n* : a hole in wood where a knot has come out

knot·ty *adj* **knot·ti·er; knot·ti·est** **1** : full of knots **2** : DIFFICULT **3**

know *vb* **knew; known; know·ing** **1** : to have understanding of **2** : to recognize the nature of **3** : to recognize the identity of **4** : to be acquainted or familiar with **5** : to be aware of the truth of **6** : to have a practical understanding of **7** : to have information or knowledge **8** : to be or become aware

know·ing *adj* **1** : having or showing special knowledge, information, or intelligence **2** : shrewdly and keenly alert **3** : INTENTIONAL — **know·ing·ly** *adv*

know–it–all *n* : a person who always claims to know everything

knowl·edge *n* **1** : understanding and skill gained by experience **2** : the state of being aware of something or of having information **3** : range of information or awareness **4** : something learned and kept in the mind : LEARNING

knuck·le *n* : the rounded lump formed by the ends of two bones (as of a finger) where they come together in a joint

ko·ala *n* : a tailless Australian animal with thick fur and big hairy ears, sharp claws for climbing, and a pouch like the kangaroo's for carrying its young

kohl·ra·bi *n* : a cabbage that forms no head but has a fleshy edible stem

kook·a·bur·ra *n* : an Australian kingfisher that has a call resembling loud laughter

Ko·ran *n* : a book of sacred writings accepted by Muslims as revealed to Muhammad by Allah

1Ko·re·an *n* **1** : a person born or living in North Korea or South Korea **2** : the language of the Koreans

2Korean *adj* : of or relating to North Korea or South Korea, the Korean people, or their language

krill *n* : tiny floating sea creatures that are a chief food of whales

kud·zu *n* : an Asian vine of the pea family that is widely grown for hay and for use in erosion control and is often a serious weed in the southeastern United States

kum·quat *n* : a small citrus fruit with sweet rind and sour pulp that is used mostly in preserves

L

l *n, pl* **l's** *or* **ls** *often cap* **1** : the twelfth letter of the English alphabet **2** : fifty in Roman numerals

la *n* : the sixth note of the musical scale

lab *n* : LABORATORY

¹la·bel *n* **1** : a slip (as of paper or cloth) attached to something to identify or describe it **2** : a word or phrase that describes or names something

²label *vb* **la·beled** *or* **la·belled; la·bel·ing** *or* **la·bel·ling** **1** : to attach a label to **2** : to name or describe with or as if with a label

la·bi·al *adj* : of or relating to the lips

¹la·bor *n* **1** : effort that is hard and usually physical **2** : the effort involved in giving birth **3** : something that has to be done : TASK **4** : workers as a body or class

²labor *vb* **1** : to work hard : TOIL **2** : to move slowly or heavily

lab·o·ra·to·ry *n, pl* **lab·o·ra·to·ries** : a room or building in which experiments and tests are done

Labor Day *n* : the first Monday in September observed as a legal holiday to honor the worker

la·bored *adj* : produced or done with effort or difficulty

la·bor·er *n* : a person who works on jobs that require strength rather than skill

la·bo·ri·ous *adj* : requiring much effort — **la·bo·ri·ous·ly** *adv*

labor union *n* : an organization of workers designed to help them get better pay and working conditions

¹lace *vb* **laced; lac·ing** : to fasten with a lace

²lace *n* **1** : a cord or string for pulling and holding together opposite edges (as of a shoe) **2** : an ornamental net of thread or cord usually with a design

lac·er·ate *vb* **lac·er·at·ed; lac·er·at·ing** : to injure by tearing

lac·er·a·tion *n* : a lacerated place or wound

¹lack *vb* **1** : to be missing **2** : to need or be without something

²lack *n* **1** : the fact or state of being absent or needed **2** : something that is absent or needed

¹lac·quer *n* : a material like varnish that dries quickly into a shiny layer (as on wood or metal)

²lacquer *vb* : to coat with lacquer

la·crosse *n* : a ball game played outdoors using a long-handled stick with a shallow net for catching, throwing, and carrying the ball

lacy *adj* **lac·i·er; lac·i·est** : like or made of lace

lad *n* : BOY 1, YOUTH

lad·der *n* : a device used for climbing usually consisting of two long pieces of wood, rope, or metal joined at short distances by horizontal pieces

lad·die *n* : BOY 1, LAD

lad·en *adj* : heavily loaded

¹la·dle *n* : a spoon with a long handle and a deep bowl that is used for dipping

²ladle *vb* **la·dled; la·dling** : to take up and carry in a ladle

la·dy *n, pl* **la·dies** **1** : a woman of high social position **2** : a pleasant well-bred woman or girl **3** : a woman of any kind or class — often used in speaking to a stranger **4** : WIFE **5** : a British noblewoman — used as a title

la·dy·bird *n* : LADYBUG

la·dy·bug *n* : a small rounded beetle that feeds mostly on plant lice

la·dy·like *adj* : WELL-BRED

la·dy·ship *n* : the rank of a lady — used as a title

lady's slipper *or* **lady slipper** *n* : any of several North American wild orchids whose flowers suggest a slipper in shape

¹lag *n* : the act or the amount of lagging

²lag *vb* **lagged; lag·ging** : to move or advance slowly

¹lag·gard *adj* : lagging behind : SLOW

²laggard *n* : a person who lags

la·goon *n* : a shallow channel or pond near or connected to a larger body of water

laid *past of* LAY

lain *past participle of* LIE

lair *n* : the den or resting place of a wild animal

lake *n* : a large inland body of still water

¹lamb *n* : a young sheep usually less than one year old

²lamb *vb* : to give birth to a lamb

lamb·kin *n* : a young lamb

¹lame *adj* **lam·er; lam·est** **1** : not able to get around without pain or difficulty **2** : being stiff and sore **3** : not very convincing : WEAK — **lame·ly** *adv* — **lame·ness** *n*

²lame *vb* **lamed; lam·ing** : to make or become lame

¹la·ment *vb* **1** : to mourn aloud : WAIL **2** : to show sorrow for

²lament *n* **1** : a crying out in sorrow **2** : a sad song or poem

la·men·ta·ble *adj* : REGRETTABLE

lam·en·ta·tion *n* : the act of lamenting

lam·i·nat·ed *adj* : made of layers of material firmly joined together

lamp *n* : a device for producing light

lamp·black *n* : a fine black soot made by

burning material incompletely and used especially to color things black

lam·prey n, pl **lampreys** : a water animal that looks like an eel but has a sucking mouth with no jaws

¹lance n : a weapon with a long handle and a sharp steel head used in olden times by knights on horseback

²lance vb : to cut open with a small sharp instrument

lance corporal n : an enlisted person in the Marine Corps ranking above a private first class

¹land n 1 : the solid part of the surface of the earth 2 : a part of the earth's surface (as a country or a farm) marked off by boundaries 3 : the people of a country — **land·less** adj

²land vb 1 : to go ashore or cause to go ashore from a ship 2 : to cause to reach or come to rest where planned 3 : to catch and bring in 4 : to get for oneself by trying 5 : to come down or bring down and settle on a surface

land breeze n : a breeze blowing toward the sea

land·hold·er n : an owner of land

land·ing n 1 : the act of one that lands 2 : a place for unloading or taking on passengers and cargo 3 : the level part of a staircase (as between flights of stairs)

landing field n : a field where aircraft land and take off

landing strip n : AIRSTRIP

land·la·dy n, pl **land·la·dies** 1 : a woman who owns land or houses that she rents 2 : a woman who runs an inn or rooming house

land·locked adj 1 : shut in or nearly shut in by land 2 : kept from leaving fresh water by some barrier

land·lord n 1 : a man who owns land or houses that he rents 2 : a man who runs an inn or rooming house

land·lub·ber n : a person who lives on land and knows little or nothing about the sea

land·mark n 1 : something (as a building, a large tree, or a statue) that is easy to see and can help a person find the way to a place near it 2 : a very important event 3 : a building of historical importance

land mine n : a mine placed just below the surface of the ground and designed to be exploded by the weight of vehicles or troops passing over it

land·own·er n : a person who owns land

¹land·scape n 1 : a picture of natural scenery 2 : the land that can be seen in one glance

²landscape vb **land·scaped; land·scap-**ing : to improve the natural beauty of a piece of land

land·slide n 1 : the slipping down of a mass of rocks or earth on a steep slope 2 : the material that moves in a landslide 3 : the winning of an election by a very large number of votes

lane n 1 : a narrow path or road (as between fences or hedges) that is not used as a highway 2 : a special route (as for ships) 3 : a strip of road used for a single line of traffic

lan·guage n 1 : the words and expressions used and understood by a large group of people 2 : the speech of human beings 3 : a means of expressing ideas or feelings 4 : a formal system of signs and symbols that is used to carry information 5 : the way in which words are used 6 : the special words used by a certain group or in a certain field 7 : the study of languages

lan·guid adj : having very little strength or energy — **lan·guid·ly** adv — **lan·guid·ness** n

lan·guish vb : to become weak especially from a lack of something needed or wanted — **lan·guish·er** n — **lan·guish·ing** adj — **lan·guish·ing·ly** adv

lan·guor n 1 : weakness or weariness of body or mind 2 : a state of dreamy idleness — **lan·guor·ous** adj — **lan·guor·ous·ly** adv

lank adj 1 : not well filled out : THIN 2 : hanging straight and limp without spring or curl — **lank·ly** adv — **lank·ness** n

lanky adj **lank·i·er; lank·i·est** : being very tall and thin — **lank·i·ly** adv — **lank·i·ness** n

lan·tern n : a usually portable lamp with a protective covering

lan·yard n 1 : a short rope or cord used as a fastening on ships 2 : a cord worn around the neck to hold a knife or whistle 3 : a strong cord with a hook at one end used in firing cannon

¹lap n : the front part of a person between the waist and the knees when seated

²lap vb **lapped; lap·ping** : OVERLAP

³lap n 1 : a part of something that overlaps another part 2 : one time around a race-track 3 : a stage in a trip

⁴lap vb **lapped; lap·ping** 1 : to scoop up food or drink with the tip of the tongue 2 : to splash gently

⁵lap n : the act or sound of lapping

lap·dog n : a dog small enough to be held in the lap

la·pel n : the part of the front of a collar that is turned back

lap·ful *n, pl* **lap·fuls** *or* **laps·ful** : as much as the lap can hold

¹lapse *n* **1** : a slight error or slip **2** : a gradual falling away from a higher to a lower condition **3** : a gradual passing of time

²lapse *vb* **lapsed; laps·ing** **1** : to slip, pass, or fall gradually **2** : to become little used **3** : to come to an end — **laps·er** *n*

lap·top *adj* : small enough to be used on one's lap — **laptop** *n*

lar·board *n* : ³PORT

lar·ce·ny *n, pl* **lar·ce·nies** : the unlawful taking of personal property without the owner's consent : THEFT

larch *n* : a tree related to the pine that sheds its needles each fall

¹lard *vb* : to smear or soil with grease

²lard *n* : a white soft fat from fatty tissue of the hog

lar·der *n* : a place where food is kept

large *adj* **larg·er; larg·est** : more than most others of a similar kind in amount or size : BIG — **large·ness** *n* — **at large** **1** : not locked up : FREE **2** : as a whole **3** : representing a whole state or district

large-heart·ed *adj* : GENEROUS 1

large intestine *n* : the wide lower part of the intestine from which water is absorbed and in which feces are made ready for passage

large·ly *adv* : MOSTLY, CHIEFLY

lar·i·at *n* : a long light rope used to catch livestock or tie up grazing animals

¹lark *n* : any of a group of mostly brownish songbirds of Europe and Asia

²lark *n* : something done for fun : PRANK

lark·spur *n* : a tall branching plant related to the buttercups that is often grown for its stalks of showy blue, purple, pink, or white flowers

lar·va *n, pl* **lar·vae** **1** : a wingless form (as a grub or caterpillar) in which many insects hatch from the egg **2** : an early form of any animal that at birth or hatching is very different from its parents

lar·yn·gi·tis *n* : inflammation of the larynx : a sore throat

lar·ynx *n, pl* **la·ryn·ges** *or* **lar·ynx·es** : the upper part of the windpipe that contains the vocal cords

la·ser *n* : a device that produces a very powerful beam of light

laser printer *n* : a printer for computer output that produces high-quality images formed by a laser

¹lash *vb* **1** : to move violently or suddenly **2** : to hit with a whip — **lash·er** *n*

²lash *n* **1** : a blow with a whip or switch **2** : the flexible part of a whip **3** : a sudden swinging blow **4** : EYELASH

³lash *vb* : to tie down with a rope or chain

lash·ing *n* : something used for tying, wrapping, or fastening

lass *n* : GIRL 1

lass·ie *n* : GIRL 1, LASS

¹las·so *vb* : to catch with a lasso

²lasso *n, pl* **lassos** *or* **lassoes** : a rope or long leather thong with a slipknot for catching animals

¹last *vb* **1** : to go on **2** : to stay in good condition — **last·er** *n*

²last *n* : a block shaped like a foot on which shoes are made

³last *adv* **1** : at the end **2** : most recently

⁴last *adj* **1** : following all the rest : FINAL **2** : most recent **3** : lowest in rank or position **4** : most unlikely

⁵last *n* : a person or thing that is last

last·ing *adj* : continuing for a long while — **last·ing·ly** *adv* — **last·ing·ness** *n*

last·ly *adv* : at or as the end

¹latch *n* : a movable piece that holds a door or gate closed

²latch *vb* : to fasten with a latch

¹late *adj* **lat·er; lat·est** **1** : coming or remaining after the usual or proper time **2** : coming toward the end (as of the day or night) **3** : having died or recently left a certain position **4** : RECENT 2 — **late·ness** *n*

²late *adv* **lat·er; lat·est** **1** : after the usual or proper time **2** : LATELY

late-com·er *n* : a person who arrives late

late·ly *adv* : not long ago : RECENTLY

la·tent *adj* : present but not visible or active — **la·tent·ly** *adv*

lat·er·al *adj* : being on or directed toward the side — **lat·er·al·ly** *adv*

la·tex *n* **1** : a milky plant juice that is the source of rubber **2** : a mixture of water and tiny particles of rubber or plastic used especially in paints

lath *n, pl* **laths** : a thin strip of wood used (as in a wall or ceiling) as a base for plaster

lathe *n* : a machine in which a piece of material is held and turned while being shaped by a tool

¹lath·er *n* **1** : the foam made by stirring soap and water together **2** : foam from sweating

²lather *vb* **1** : to spread lather over **2** : to form a lather

¹Lat·in *adj* **1** : of or relating to the language of the ancient Romans **2** : of or relating to Latin America or the Latin Americans

²Latin *n* **1** : the language of the ancient Romans **2** : a member of a people whose language and customs have descended from the ancient Romans **3** : a person born or living in Latin America

Lat·in–Amer·i·can *adj* : of or relating to Latin America or its people

Latin American *n* : a person born or living in Latin America

lat·i·tude *n* **1** : the distance north or south of the equator measured in degrees **2** : RE-GION 3 **3** : freedom to act or speak as one wishes

lat·ter *adj* **1** : relating to or coming near the end **2** : of, relating to, or being the second of two things referred to

lat·tice *n* **1** : a structure made of thin strips of wood or metal that cross each other to form a network **2** : a window or gate having a lattice

1laud *n* : 2PRAISE 1, ACCLAIM

2laud *vb* : 1PRAISE 1, ACCLAIM

1laugh *vb* : to show amusement, joy, or scorn by smiling and making sounds (as chuckling) in the throat

2laugh *n* : the act or sound of laughing

laugh·able *adj* : causing or likely to cause laughter — **laugh·able·ness** *n* — **laugh·ably** *adv*

laugh·ing·stock *n* : a person or thing that is made fun of

laugh·ter *n* : the action or sound of laughing

1launch *vb* **1** : 1THROW 1 2, HURL **2** : to set afloat **3** : to send off especially with force **4** : to give a start to

2launch *n* : an act of launching

3launch *n* : MOTORBOAT

launch·pad *n* : a nonflammable platform from which a rocket can be launched

laun·der *vb* : to wash or wash and iron clothes — **laun·der·er** *n*

laun·dress *n* : a woman whose work is washing clothes

laun·dry *n, pl* **laundries** **1** : clothes or linens that have been laundered or are to be laundered **2** : a place where laundering is done

laun·dry·man *n, pl* **laun·dry·men** : a man who works in or for a laundry

lau·rel *n* **1** : a small evergreen European tree with shiny pointed leaves used in ancient times to crown victors (as in sports) **2** : any of various plants (as the American **mountain laurel**) that resemble the European laurel **3** : a crown of laurel used as a mark of honor

la·va *n* **1** : melted rock coming from a volcano **2** : lava that has cooled and hardened

lav·a·to·ry *n, pl* **lav·a·to·ries** **1** : a small sink (as in a bathroom) **2** : a room for washing that usually has a toilet **3** : TOILET 3

lav·en·der *n* **1** : a European mint with narrow somewhat woolly leaves and stalks of small sweet-smelling pale violet flowers **2** : a pale purple

1lav·ish *adj* **1** : spending or giving more

than is necessary : EXTRAVAGANT **2** : spent, produced, or given freely — **lav·ish·ly** *adv* — **lav·ish·ness** *n*

2lavish *vb* : to spend, use, or give freely

law *n* **1** : a rule of conduct or action that a nation or a group of people agrees to follow **2** : a whole collection of established rules **3** : a rule or principle that always works the same way under the same conditions **4** : a bill passed by a legislative group **5** : 2PO-LICE **6** *cap* : the first part of the Jewish scriptures **7** : trial in court **8** : the profession of a lawyer

law–abid·ing *adj* : obeying the law

law·break·er *n* : a person who breaks the law

law·ful *adj* **1** : permitted by law **2** : approved by law — **law·ful·ly** *adv* — **law·ful·ness** *n*

law·less *adj* **1** : having no laws : not based on or controlled by law **2** : uncontrolled by law : UNRULY — **law·less·ly** *adv* — **law·less·ness** *n*

law·mak·er *n* : one who takes part in writing and passing laws : LEGISLATOR — **law·mak·ing** *adj or n*

lawn *n* : ground (as around a house) covered with grass that is kept mowed

lawn mower *n* : a machine used to mow the grass on lawns

lawn tennis *n* : TENNIS

law·suit *n* : a complaint brought before a court of law for decision

law·yer *n* : a person whose profession is to handle lawsuits for people or to give advice about legal rights and duties

lax *adj* **1** : not firm or tight : LOOSE **2** : not stern or strict — **lax·ly** *adv* — **lax·ness** *n*

1lax·a·tive *adj* : helpful against constipation

2laxative *n* : a laxative medicine that is nearly always mild

1lay *vb* **laid**; **lay·ing** **1** : to bring down (as with force) **2** : to put down **3** : to produce an egg **4** : to cause to disappear **5** : to spread over a surface **6** : 1PREPARE 1, ARRANGE **7** : to put to : APPLY

2lay *n* : the way a thing lies in relation to something else

3lay *past of* lie

lay·away *n* : something held for a customer until the price is paid

lay away *vb* : to put aside for later use or delivery

lay·er *n* **1** : one that lays something **2** : one thickness of something laid over another

lay in *vb* : to store for later use

lay·man *n, pl* **lay·men** **1** : a person who is not a member of the clergy **2** : a person who is not a member of a certain profession

lay off *vb* **1** : to stop employing (a person) usually temporarily **2** : to let alone

lay·out *n* : ¹PLAN 1, ARRANGEMENT

lay out *vb* 1 : to plan in detail 2 : ARRANGE 1, DESIGN

lay up *vb* 1 : to store up 2 : to be confined by illness or injury

la·zy *adj* **la·zi·er; la·zi·est** 1 : not willing to act or work 2 : ¹SLOW 3, SLUGGISH — **la·zi·ly** *adv* — **la·zi·ness** *n*

leach *vb* 1 : to treat (as earth) with a liquid (as water) to remove something soluble 2 : to remove (as a soluble salt) by leaching

¹**lead** *vb* **led; lead·ing** 1 : to guide on a way often by going ahead 2 : to be at the head of 3 : to go through : LIVE 4 : to reach or go in a certain direction

²**lead** *n* 1 : position at the front 2 : the distance that a person or thing is ahead 3 : the first part of a news story

³**lead** *n* 1 : a heavy soft gray metallic element that is easily bent and shaped 2 : AMMUNITION 1 3 : a long thin piece of graphite used in pencils

lead·en *adj* 1 : made of lead 2 : heavy as lead 3 : dull gray — **lead·en·ly** *adv* — **lead·en·ness** *n*

lead·er *n* : one that leads or is able to lead — **lead·er·ship** *n*

¹**leaf** *n, pl* **leaves** 1 : one of the usually flat green parts that grow from a plant stem and that together make up the foliage 2 : FOLIAGE 3 : a single sheet of a book making two pages 4 : a movable part of a table top — **leaf·less** *adj* — **leaf·like** *adj*

²**leaf** *vb* 1 : to grow leaves 2 : to turn the leaves of a book

leaf·let *n* 1 : a young or small leaf 2 : a division of a compound leaf 3 : PAMPHLET

leaf·stalk *n* : PETIOLE

leafy *adj* **leaf·i·er; leaf·i·est** : having, covered with, or like leaves

¹**league** *n* 1 : a group of nations working together for a common purpose 2 : an association of persons or groups with common interests or goals 3 : ¹CLASS 7

²**league** *vb* **leagued; leagu·ing** : to form a league

¹**leak** *vb* 1 : to enter or escape or let enter or escape usually by accident 2 : to make or become known

²**leak** *n* 1 : a crack or hole that accidentally lets fluid in or out 2 : something that accidentally or secretly causes or permits loss 3 : the act of leaking : LEAKAGE

leak·age *n* 1 : the act or process of leaking 2 : the thing or amount that leaks

leaky *adj* **leak·i·er; leak·i·est** : letting fluid leak in or out — **leak·i·ness** *n*

¹**lean** *vb* 1 : to bend or tilt from a straight position 2 : to bend and rest one's weight on 3 : DEPEND 1, RELY 4 : to tend or move toward in opinion, taste, or desire

²**lean** *adj* 1 : having too little flesh : SKINNY 2 : containing very little fat 3 : not large or plentiful — **lean·ness** *n*

lean–to *n, pl* **lean–tos** 1 : a building that has a roof with only one slope and is usually joined to another building 2 : a rough shelter held up by posts, rocks, or trees

¹**leap** *vb* **leaped** *or* **leapt; leap·ing** 1 : to jump or cause to jump from a surface 2 : to move, act, or pass quickly — **leap·er** *n*

²**leap** *n* 1 : an act of leaping : JUMP 2 : a place leaped over 3 : a distance leaped

leap·frog *n* : a game in which one player bends down and another leaps over the first player

leap year *n* : a year of 366 days with February 29 as the extra day

learn *vb* **learned** *also* **learnt; learn·ing** 1 : to get knowledge of or skill in (by studying or practicing) 2 : MEMORIZE 3 : to become able through practice 4 : to find out 5 : to gain knowledge

learned *adj* : having or showing knowledge or learning

learn·ing *n* 1 : the act of a person who learns 2 : knowledge or skill gained from teaching or study

¹**lease** *n* 1 : an agreement by which a person exchanges property (as real estate) for a period of time for rent or services 2 : the period of time for which property is leased 3 : a piece of property that is leased

²**lease** *vb* **leased; leas·ing** : to give or get the use of (property) in return for services or rent

¹**leash** *n* : a line for leading or holding an animal

²**leash** *vb* : to put on a leash

¹**least** *adj* : smallest in size or degree

²**least** *n* : the smallest or lowest amount or degree

³**least** *adv* : in or to the smallest degree

leath·er *n* 1 : the tanned skin of an animal 2 : something made of leather

leath·ery *adj* : like leather

¹**leave** *vb* **left; leav·ing** 1 : to fail to include or take along 2 : to have remaining 3 : to give by will 4 : to let stay without interference 5 : to go away from 6 : to give up 7 : DELIVER 2

²**leave** *n* 1 : PERMISSION 2 : permitted absence from one's duty or work 3 : the act of leaving and saying good-bye 4 : a period of time during which a person is allowed to be absent from duties

leaved *adj* : having leaves

leaves *pl of* LEAF

leav·ings *n pl* : something left over

¹lec·ture *n* **1** : a talk that teaches something **2** : a severe scolding

²lecture *vb* **lec·tured; lec·tur·ing 1** : to give a lecture **2** : ²SCOLD — **lec·tur·er** *n*

led *past of* LEAD

ledge *n* **1** : a piece projecting from a top or an edge like a shelf **2** : SHELF 2

¹lee *n* **1** : a protecting shelter **2** : the side (as of a ship) sheltered from the wind

²lee *adj* : of or relating to the lee

leech *n* **1** : a bloodsucking worm related to the earthworm **2** : a person who clings like a leech to another person for what can be gained

leek *n* : a garden plant grown for its thick stems which taste like a mild onion

¹leer *vb* : to look with a leer

²leer *n* : a mean or nasty glance

leery *adj* : SUSPICIOUS 2, WARY

¹lee·ward *n* : the lee side

²leeward *adj* : located away from the wind

¹left *adj* **1** : on the same side of the body as the heart **2** : located nearer to the left side of the body than to the right

²left *n* : the left side or the part on the left side

³left *past of* LEAVE

left–hand *adj* **1** : located on the left **2** : LEFT-HANDED

left–hand·ed *adj* **1** : using the left hand better or more easily than the right **2** : done or made with or for the left hand

left·over *n* : something left over

lefty *n, pl* **left·ies** : a left-handed person

leg *n* **1** : one of the limbs of an animal or person that support the body and are used in walking and running **2** : the part of the leg between the knee and the foot **3** : something like a leg in shape or use **4** : the part of a garment that covers the leg **5** : a stage or part of a journey

leg·a·cy *n, pl* **leg·a·cies** : something left to a person by or as if by a will

le·gal *adj* **1** : of or relating to law or lawyers **2** : based on law **3** : allowed by law or rules — **le·gal·ly** *adv*

le·gal·i·ty *n, pl* **le·gal·i·ties** : the quality or state of being legal

le·gal·ize *vb* **le·gal·ized; le·gal·iz·ing** : to make legal — **le·gal·iza·tion** *n*

leg·end *n* **1** : an old story that is widely believed but cannot be proved to be true **2** : writing or a title on an object **3** : a list of symbols used (as on a map)

leg·end·ary *adj* : of, relating to, or like a legend

leg·ged *adj* : having legs

leg·ging *n* : an outer covering for the leg usually of cloth or leather

leg·i·ble *adj* : clear enough to be read — **leg·i·bly** *adv*

le·gion *n* **1** : a group of from 3000 to 6000 soldiers that made up the chief army unit in ancient Rome **2** : ARMY 1 **3** : a very great number

leg·is·late *vb* **leg·is·lat·ed; leg·is·lat·ing** : to make laws — **leg·is·la·tor** *n*

leg·is·la·tion *n* **1** : the action of making laws **2** : the laws that are made

leg·is·la·tive *adj* **1** : having the power or authority to make laws **2** : of or relating to legislation — **leg·is·la·tive·ly** *adv*

leg·is·la·ture *n* : a body of persons having the power to make, change, or cancel laws

le·git·i·ma·cy *n* : the quality or state of being legitimate

le·git·i·mate *adj* **1** : accepted by the law as rightful : LAWFUL **2** : being right or acceptable — **le·git·i·mate·ly** *adv*

leg·less *adj* : having no legs

le·gume *n* : any of a large group of plants (as peas, beans, and clover) with fruits that are pods and root nodules containing bacteria that fix nitrogen

lei·sure *n* **1** : freedom from work **2** : time that is free for use as one wishes

lei·sure·ly *adj* : UNHURRIED

lem·on *n* **1** : an oval yellow fruit with a sour juice that is related to the orange and grows on a small spiny tree **2** : something unsatisfactory : DUD

lem·on·ade *n* : a drink made of lemon juice, sugar, and water

lend *vb* **lent; lend·ing 1** : ²LOAN 1 **2** : to give usually for a time **3** : to make a loan or loans — **lend·er** *n*

length *n* **1** : the measured distance from one end to the other of the longer or longest side of an object **2** : a measured distance **3** : amount of time something takes **4** : the sound of a vowel or syllable as it is affected by the time needed to pronounce it **5** : a piece of something that is long — **at length 1** : very fully **2** : at the end

length·en *vb* : to make or become longer

length·ways *adv* : LENGTHWISE

length·wise *adv or adj* : in the direction of the length

lengthy *adj* **length·i·er; length·i·est** : very long — **length·i·ly** *adv* — **length·i·ness** *n*

le·nient *adj* : being kind and patient — **le·nient·ly** *adv*

lens *n* **1** : a clear curved piece of material (as glass) used to bend the rays of light to form an image **2** : a part of the eye that focuses rays of light so as to form clear images

lent *past of* LEND

len·til *n* : the flattened round edible seed of a plant related to the pea

Leo *n* **1** : a constellation between Cancer

and Virgo imagined as a lion **2** : the fifth sign of the zodiac or a person born under this sign

leop·ard *n* : a large cat of Asia and Africa that has a brownish buff coat with black spots

leop·ard·ess *n* : a female leopard

le·o·tard *n* : a tight one-piece garment worn by dancers or acrobats

le·sion *n* : an abnormal spot or area of the body caused by sickness or injury

¹less *adj* **1** : being fewer **2** : of lower rank, degree, or importance **3** : not so much : a smaller amount of

²less *adv* : not so much or so well

³less *n* **1** : a smaller number or amount **2** : a thing that is poorer than another

⁴less *prep* : ¹MINUS 1

-less *adj suffix* **1** : not having **2** : not able to be acted on or to act in a specified way

less·en *vb* : to make or become less

¹less·er *adj* : of smaller size or importance

²lesser *adv* : ²LESS

les·son *n* **1** : a part of the Scripture read in a church service **2** : a reading or exercise assigned for study **3** : something learned or taught

lest *conj* : for fear that

let *vb* **let; let·ting 1** : to cause to : MAKE **2** : to give use of in return for payment **3** : to allow or permit to **4** : to allow to go or pass

-let *n suffix* **1** : small one **2** : something worn on

let·down *n* : DISAPPOINTMENT 2

let down *vb* **1** : DISAPPOINT **2** : RELAX 3

let on *vb* **1** : ADMIT 3 **2** : PRETEND 1

let's : let us

¹let·ter *n* **1** : one of the marks that are symbols for speech sounds in writing or print and that make up the alphabet **2** : a written or printed communication (as one sent through the mail) **3 letters** *pl* : LITERATURE 2 **4** : the strict or outward meaning **5** : the initial of a school awarded to a student usually for athletic achievement

²letter *vb* : to mark with letters

letter carrier *n* : a person who delivers mail

let·ter·head *n* **1** : stationery having a printed or engraved heading **2** : the heading of a letterhead

let·ter·ing *n* : letters used in an inscription

let·tuce *n* : a garden plant related to the daisies that has large crisp leaves eaten in salad

let up *vb* **1** : to slow down **2** : ¹STOP 4, CEASE

leu·ke·mia *n* : a dangerous disease in which too many white blood cells are formed

le·vee *n* **1** : a bank built along a river to prevent flooding **2** : a landing place along a river

¹lev·el *n* **1** : a device used (as by a carpenter) to find a horizontal line or surface **2** : a horizontal line or surface usually at a named height **3** : a step or stage in height, position, or rank

²level *vb* **lev·eled** *or* **lev·elled; lev·el·ing** *or* **lev·el·ling** : to make or become level, flat, or even — **lev·el·er** *or* **lev·el·ler** *n*

³level *adj* **1** : having a flat even surface **2** : HORIZONTAL **3** : of the same height or rank : EVEN **4** : steady and cool in judgment — **lev·el·ly** *adv* — **lev·el·ness** *n*

¹le·ver *n* **1** : a bar used to pry or move something **2** : a stiff bar for lifting a weight at one point of its length by pressing or pulling at a second point while the bar turns on a support **3** : a bar or rod used to run or adjust something

²lever *vb* : to raise or move with a lever

¹levy *n, pl* **lev·ies 1** : a collection (as of taxes) by authority of the law **2** : the calling of troops into service **3** : something (as taxes) collected by authority of the law

²levy *vb* **lev·ied; levy·ing 1** : to collect legally **2** : to raise or collect troops for service

li·a·ble *adj* **1** : forced by law or by what is right to make good **2** : not sheltered or protected (as from danger or accident) **3** : LIKELY 1

li·ar *n* : a person who tells lies

¹li·bel *n* : something spoken or written that hurts a person's good name

²libel *vb* **li·beled** *or* **li·belled; li·bel·ing** *or* **li·bel·ling** : to hurt by a libel — **li·bel·er** *or* **li·bel·ler** *n*

lib·er·al *adj* **1** : not stingy : GENEROUS **2** : being more than enough **3** : not strict **4** : BROAD 4 — **lib·er·al·ly** *adv*

lib·er·ate *vb* **lib·er·at·ed; lib·er·at·ing** : to set free

lib·er·ty *n, pl* **lib·er·ties 1** : the state of those who are free and independent : FREEDOM **2** : freedom to do what one pleases **3** : the state of not being busy : LEISURE **4** : behavior or an act that is too free

Li·bra *n* **1** : a constellation between Virgo and Scorpio imagined as a pair of scales **2** : the seventh sign of the zodiac or a person born under this sign

li·brar·i·an *n* : a person in charge of a library

li·brary *n, pl* **li·brar·ies 1** : a place where especially literary or reference materials (as books, manuscripts, recordings, or films) are kept for use but not for sale **2** : a collection of such materials

lice *pl of* LOUSE

¹li·cense *or* **li·cence** *n* **1** : permission

granted by qualified authority to do something **2** : a paper showing legal permission **3** : liberty of action that is carried too far

²**license** or **licence** vb **li·censed** or **licenced; li·cens·ing** or **li·cenc·ing** : to permit or authorize by license

li·chen n : a plant made up of an alga and a fungus growing together

¹**lick** vb **1** : to pass the tongue over **2** : to touch or pass over like a tongue **3** : to hit again and again : BEAT **4** : to get the better of — **lick·ing** n

²**lick** n **1** : the act of licking **2** : a small amount **3** : a place (**salt lick**) where salt is found on the top of the ground and animals come to lick it up

lick·e·ty–split adv : at top speed

lic·o·rice n **1** : the dried root of a European plant related to the peas or a juice from it used in medicine and in candy **2** : candy flavored with licorice

lid n **1** : a movable cover **2** : EYELID — **lid·ded** adj — **lid·less** adj

¹**lie** vb **lay; lain; ly·ing** **1** : to stretch out or be stretched out (as on a bed or on the ground) **2** : to be spread flat so as to cover **3** : to be located or placed **4** : to be or stay

²**lie** vb **lied; ly·ing** : to make a statement that one knows to be untrue

³**lie** n : something said or done in the hope of deceiving : an untrue statement

¹**liege** adj **1** : having the right to receive service and loyalty **2** : owing or giving service to a lord

²**liege** n **1** : VASSAL 1 **2** : a feudal lord

lieu·ten·ant n **1** : an official who acts for a higher official **2** : a first lieutenant or second lieutenant (as in the Army) **3** : a commissioned officer in the Navy or Coast Guard ranking above a lieutenant junior grade

lieutenant colonel n : a commissioned officer in the Army, Air Force, or Marine Corps ranking above a major

lieutenant commander n : a commissioned officer in the Navy or Coast Guard ranking above a lieutenant

lieutenant general n : a commissioned officer in the Army, Air Force, or Marine Corps ranking above a major general

lieutenant junior grade n : a commissioned officer in the Navy or Coast Guard ranking above an ensign

life n, pl **lives** **1** : the quality that separates plants and animals from such things as water or rock : the quality that plants and animals lose when they die **2** : all the experiences that make up the existence of a person : the course of existence **3** : BIOGRAPHY **4** : the period during which a person or thing is alive or exists **5** : a way of living **6** : a living being **7** : ¹SPIRIT 5

life belt n : a life preserver worn like a belt

life·boat n : a sturdy boat (as one carried by a ship) for use in an emergency and especially in saving lives at sea

life buoy n : a life preserver in the shape of a ring

life·guard n : a guard employed at a beach or swimming pool to protect swimmers from drowning

life jacket n : a life preserver in the form of a vest

life·less adj : having no life

life·like adj : very like something that is alive

life·long adj : continuing through life

life preserver n : a device (as a life jacket or life buoy) designed to save a person from drowning by keeping the person afloat

life raft n : a raft usually made of wood or an inflatable material for use by people forced into the water

life·sav·er n : a person trained in lifesaving

life·sav·ing n : the methods that can be used to save lives especially of drowning persons

life–size or **life–sized** adj : of natural size : having the same size as the original

life·style n : the usual way of life of a person, group, or society : the way we live

life·time n : LIFE 4

life vest n : LIFE JACKET

¹**lift** vb **1** : to raise from a lower to a higher position, rate, or amount **2** : to rise from the ground **3** : to move upward and disappear or become scattered — **lift·er** n

²**lift** n **1** : the amount that may be lifted at one time : LOAD **2** : the action or an instance of lifting **3** : help especially in the form of a ride **4** chiefly British : ELEVATOR 2 **5** : an upward force (as on an airplane wing) that opposes the pull of gravity

lift·off n : a vertical takeoff (as by a rocket)

lig·a·ment n : a tough band of tissue or fibers that holds bones together or keeps an organ in place in the body

¹**light** n **1** : the bright form of energy given off by something (as the sun) that lets one see objects **2** : a source (as a lamp) of light **3** : DAYLIGHT 1 **4** : public knowledge **5** : something that helps one to know or understand

²**light** adj **1** : having light : BRIGHT **2** : not dark or deep in color

³**light** vb **light·ed** or **lit; light·ing** **1** : to make or become bright **2** : to burn or cause to burn **3** : to lead with a light

⁴**light** adj **1** : having little weight : not heavy **2** : not strong or violent **3** : not hard to bear, do, pay, or digest **4** : active in motion **5** : not severe **6** : free from care

: HAPPY **7** : intended mainly to entertain —
light·ly adv — **light·ness** n

⁵**light** adv : with little baggage

⁶**light** vb **light·ed** or **lit; light·ing 1**
: ²PERCH, SETTLE **2** : to come by chance

light bulb n : INCANDESCENT LAMP

¹**light·en** vb **1** : to make or become light or
lighter : BRIGHTEN **2** : to grow bright with
lightning — **light·en·er** n

²**lighten** vb : to make or become less heavy
— **light·en·er** n

light·face n : a type having light thin lines —
light·faced adj

light·heart·ed adj : free from worry —
light·heart·ed·ly adv — **light·heart·ed·**
ness n

light·house n : a tower with a powerful light
at the top that is built on the shore to guide
sailors at night

light·ing n : supply of light or of lights

light·ning n : the flashing of light caused by
the passing of electricity from one cloud to
another or between a cloud and the earth

lightning bug n : FIREFLY

light·proof adj : not letting in light

light·weight adj : having less than the usual
or expected weight

light–year n : a unit of length in astronomy
equal to the distance that light travels in one
year or 9,458,000,000,000 kilometers

lik·able or **like·able** adj : easily liked — **lik·**
able·ness n

¹**like** vb **liked; lik·ing 1** : to have a liking for
: ENJOY **2** : to feel toward : REGARD **3**
: CHOOSE 3, PREFER

²**like** n : LIKING, PREFERENCE

³**like** adj **1** : SIMILAR, ALIKE **2** : similar
to or to that of — used after the word modified

⁴**like** prep **1** : similar or similarly to **2**
: typical of **3** : likely to **4** : such as

⁵**like** n : ³EQUAL, COUNTERPART

⁶**like** conj **1** : AS IF **2** : in the same way that
: ²AS 2

like·li·hood n : PROBABILITY 1

¹**like·ly** adj **1** : very possibly going to hap-
pen **2** : seeming to be the truth : BELIEV-
ABLE **3** : giving hope of turning out well
: PROMISING — **like·li·ness** n

²**likely** adv : without great doubt

lik·en vb : COMPARE 1

like·ness n **1** : the state of being like : RE-
SEMBLANCE **2** : a picture of a person : POR-
TRAIT

like·wise adv **1** : in like manner **2** : ALSO

lik·ing n : a being pleased with someone or
something

li·lac n **1** : a bush having clusters of fragrant
grayish pink, purple, or white flowers **2** : a
medium purple

lilt vb : to sing or play in a lively cheerful
manner — **lilt·ing·ly** adv

lily n, pl **lil·ies** : a plant (as the **Easter lily** or
the **tiger lily**) that grows from a bulb and
has a leafy stem and showy funnel-shaped
flowers

lily of the valley : a low plant related to the
lilies that has usually two leaves and a stalk
of fragrant flowers shaped like bells

li·ma bean n : a bean with flat pale green or
white seeds

limb n **1** : any of the paired parts (as an arm,
wing, or leg) of an animal that stick out
from the body and are used mostly in moving or grasping **2** : a large branch of a tree
— **limbed** adj — **limb·less** adj

¹**lim·ber** adj : bending easily — **lim·ber·ly**
adv — **lim·ber·ness** n

²**limber** vb : to make or become limber

¹**lime** n : a white substance made by heating
limestone or shells that is used in making
plaster and cement and in farming

²**lime** vb **limed; lim·ing** : to treat or cover
with lime

³**lime** n : a small greenish yellow fruit that is
related to the lemon and orange

lim·er·ick n : a humorous poem five lines
long

lime·stone n : a rock formed chiefly from
animal remains (as shells or coral) that is
used in building and gives lime when
burned

lime·wa·ter n : a colorless water solution
that contains calcium and turns white when
carbon dioxide is blown through it

¹**lim·it** n **1** : a boundary line **2** : a point beyond which a person or thing cannot go

²**limit** vb : to set limits to

lim·i·ta·tion n **1** : an act or instance of limiting **2** : the quality or state of being limited

lim·it·less adj : having no limits

¹**limp** vb : to walk lamely

²**limp** n : a limping movement or gait

³**limp** adj : not firm or stiff — **limp·ly** adv —
limp·ness n

limy adj **lim·i·er; lim·i·est** : containing lime
or limestone

lin·den n : a shade tree with heart-shaped
toothed leaves, drooping clusters of yellowish white flowers, and hard fruits like peas

¹**line** n **1** : a long thin cord **2** : a pipe carrying a fluid (as steam, water, or oil) **3** : an
outdoor wire carrying electricity for a telephone or power company **4** : a row of letters or words across a page or column **5**
lines pl : the words of a part in a play **6**
: the direction followed by something in
motion **7** : the boundary or limit of a place
or lot **8** : the track of a railway **9** : AGREE-

MENT 1, HARMONY **10** : a course of behavior or thought **11** : FAMILY 1 **12** : a system of transportation **13** : a long narrow mark (as one drawn by a pencil) **14** : the football players whose positions are along the line of scrimmage **15** : a geometric element produced by moving a point : a set of points **16** : ¹OUTLINE 1, CONTOUR **17** : a plan for making or doing something

²**line** *vb* **lined; lin·ing 1** : to mark with a line or lines **2** : to place or be placed in a line along **3** : to form a line : form into lines

³**line** *vb* **lined; lin·ing** : to cover the inner surface of

lin·eage *n* **1** : the ancestors from whom a person is descended **2** : people descended from the same ancestor

lin·ear *adj* **1** : of, relating to, or like a line . : STRAIGHT **2** : involving a single dimension

lin·en *n* **1** : smooth strong cloth or yarn made from flax **2** : household articles (as tablecloths or sheets) or clothing (as shirts or underwear) once often made of linen

line of scrimmage : an imaginary line in football parallel to the goal lines and running through the place where the ball is laid before each play begins

¹**lin·er** *n* : a ship or airplane of a regular transportation line

²**liner** *n* : one that lines or is used to line something

line segment *n* : SEGMENT 3

line-up *n* **1** : a line of persons arranged especially for police identification **2** : a list of players taking part in a game (as baseball)

-ling *n suffix* **1** : one associated with **2** : young, small, or minor one

lin·ger *vb* : to be slow in leaving : DELAY

lin·guist *n* **1** : a person skilled in languages **2** : a person who specializes in linguistics

lin·guis·tics *n* : the study of human speech including the units, nature, structure, and development of language, languages, or a language

lin·i·ment *n* : a liquid medicine rubbed on the skin (as to ease pain)

lin·ing *n* : material that lines an inner surface

¹**link** *n* **1** : a single ring of a chain **2** : something that connects **3** : HYPERLINK

²**link** *vb* : to join with or as if with links

linking verb *n* : an intransitive verb that links a subject with a word or words in the predicate

lin·net *n* : a common small European finch often kept as a cage bird

li·no·leum *n* : a floor covering with a canvas back and a surface of hardened linseed oil and usually cork dust

lin·seed *n* : FLAXSEED

linseed oil *n* : a yellowish oil obtained from flaxseed

lint *n* **1** : loose bits of thread **2** : ¹COTTON 1

lin·tel *n* : a horizontal piece or part across the top of an opening (as of a door) to carry the weight of the structure above it

li·on *n* : a large flesh-eating animal of the cat family that has a brownish buff coat, a tufted tail, and in the male a shaggy mane and that lives in Africa and southern Asia

li·on·ess *n* : a female lion

lip *n* **1** : either of the two folds of flesh that surround the mouth **2** : an edge (as of a flower or a wound) like or of flesh **3** : the edge of a hollow container especially where it is slightly spread out — **lip·less** *adj* — **lip·like** *adj* — **lipped** *adj*

lip·stick *n* : a waxy solid colored cosmetic for the lips usually in stick form

liq·ue·fy *vb* **liq·ue·fied; liq·ue·fy·ing** : to make or become liquid

¹**liq·uid** *adj* **1** : flowing freely like water **2** : neither solid nor gaseous **3** : like liquid in clearness or smoothness **4** : made up of or easily changed into cash — **liq·uid·ly** *adv* — **liq·uid·ness** *n*

²**liquid** *n* : a liquid substance

liq·uor *n* **1** : a liquid substance or solution **2** : a strong alcoholic beverage (as whiskey)

¹**lisp** *vb* : to pronounce the sounds \s\ and \z\ as \th\ and \th\

²**lisp** *n* : the act or habit of lisping

¹**list** *n* : a leaning over to one side

²**list** *vb* : to lean to one side

³**list** *n* : a record or catalog of names or items

⁴**list** *vb* : to put into a list

lis·ten *vb* **1** : to pay attention in order to hear **2** : to give heed : follow advice — **lis·ten·er** *n*

list·less *adj* : too tired or too little interested to want to do things — **list·less·ly** *adv* — **list·less·ness** *n*

lit *past of* LIGHT

li·ter *n* : a metric unit of liquid capacity equal to 1.057 quarts

lit·er·al *adj* **1** : following the ordinary or usual meaning of the words **2** : true to fact — **lit·er·al·ly** *adv* — **lit·er·al·ness** *n*

lit·er·ary *adj* : of or relating to literature

lit·er·ate *adj* **1** : well educated : WELL-BRED **2** : able to read and write

lit·er·a·ture *n* **1** : written works having excellence of form or expression and ideas of lasting and widespread interest **2** : written material (as of a period or on a subject)

lithe *adj* : ¹LIMBER, SUPPLE — **lithe·ly** *adv* — **lithe·ness** *n*

lith·o·sphere *n* : the outer part of the solid earth

lit·mus paper *n* : paper treated with coloring matter that turns red in acid solutions and blue in alkaline solutions

¹lit·ter *n* **1** : a covered and curtained couch having poles and used for carrying a single passenger **2** : a stretcher for carrying a sick or wounded person **3** : material spread out like a bed in places where farm animals (as cows or chickens) are kept to soak up their urine and feces **4** : the young born to an animal at a single time **5** : a messy collection of things scattered about : RUBBISH

²litter *vb* **1** : to cover with litter **2** : to scatter about in disorder

lit·ter·bug *n* : one that litters a public area

¹lit·tle *adj* **lit·tler** *or* **less; lit·tlest** *or* **least** **1** : small in size **2** : small in quantity **3** : small in importance **4** : NARROW-MINDED, MEAN **5** : short in duration or extent — **lit·tle·ness** *n*

²little *adv* **less; least** : in a very small quantity or degree

³little *n* : a small amount or quantity

Little Dipper *n* : a group of seven stars in the northern sky arranged in a form like a dipper with the North Star forming the tip of the handle

li·tur·gi·cal *adj* : of, relating to, or like liturgy

lit·ur·gy *n, pl* **lit·ur·gies** : a religious rite or body of rites

¹live *vb* **lived; liv·ing** **1** : to be alive **2** : to continue in life **3** : DWELL **2** **4** : to pass one's life — **live it up** : to live with great enthusiasm and excitement

²live *adj* **1** : not dead : ALIVE **2** : burning usually without flame **3** : not exploded **4** : of present and continuing interest **5** : charged with an electric current **6** : broadcast at the time of production

live·li·hood *n* : ²LIVING 3

live·long *adj* : during all of

live·ly *adj* **live·li·er; live·li·est** **1** : full of life : ACTIVE **2** : KEEN **4** **3** : full of spirit or feeling : ANIMATED — **live·li·ness** *n*

liv·en *vb* : to make or become lively

live oak *n* : any of several American oaks that have evergreen leaves

liv·er *n* : a large gland of vertebrates (as fishes and humans) that has a rich blood supply, secretes bile, and helps in storing some nutrients and in forming some body wastes

liv·er·ied *adj* : wearing a livery

liv·er·wort *n* : any of a group of flowerless plants that are somewhat like mosses

liv·ery *n, pl* **liv·er·ies** **1** : a special uniform worn by the servants of a wealthy household **2** : the clothing worn to distinguish an association of persons **3** : the care and sta-

bling of horses for pay **4** : the keeping of horses and vehicles for hire or a place (**livery stable**) engaged in this

lives *pl of* LIFE

live·stock *n* : animals kept or raised especially on a farm and for profit

live wire *n* : an alert active forceful person

liv·id *adj* **1** : discolored by bruising **2** : pale as ashes — **liv·id·ly** *adv* — **liv·id·ness** *n*

¹liv·ing *adj* **1** : not dead : ALIVE **2** : ACTIVE **4** **3** : true to life

²living *n* **1** : the condition of being alive **2** : conduct or manner of life **3** : what one has to have to meet one's needs

living room *n* : a room in a house for general family use

liz·ard *n* : any of a group of reptiles having movable eyelids, ears that are outside the body, and usually four legs

lla·ma *n* : a South American hoofed animal that chews the cud

lo *interj* — used to call attention or to show wonder or surprise

¹load *n* **1** : something taken up and carried : BURDEN **2** : a mass or weight supported by something **3** : something that depresses the mind or spirits **4** : a charge for a firearm **5** : the quantity of material loaded into a device at one time

²load *vb* **1** : to put a load in or on **2** : to supply abundantly **3** : to put a load into — **load·er** *n*

¹loaf *n, pl* **loaves** **1** : a usually oblong mass of bread **2** : a dish (as of meat) baked in the form of a loaf

²loaf *vb* : to spend time idly or lazily — **loaf·er** *n*

loam *n* : a soil having the right amount of silt, clay, and sand for good plant growth

loamy *adj* : made up of or like loam

¹loan *n* **1** : money loaned at interest **2** : something loaned for a time to a borrower **3** : permission to use something for a time

²loan *vb* **1** : to give to another for temporary use with the understanding that the same or a like thing will be returned **2** : LEND 3

loath *or* **loth** *adj* : not willing

loathe *vb* **loathed; loath·ing** : to dislike greatly

loathing *n* : very great dislike

loath·some *adj* : very unpleasant : OFFENSIVE — **loath·some·ly** *adv* — **loath·some·ness** *n*

loaves *pl of* LOAF

¹lob *vb* **lobbed; lob·bing** : to send (as a ball) in a high arc by hitting or throwing easily

²lob *n* : a lobbed throw or shot (as in tennis)

lob·by *n, pl* **lobbies** : a hall or entry especially when large enough to serve as a waiting room

lobe *n* : a rounded part — **lobed** *adj*
lob·ster *n* : a large edible sea crustacean with five pairs of legs of which the first pair usually has large claws
¹lo·cal *adj* 1 : of or relating to position in space 2 : relating to a particular place — **lo·cal·ly** *adv*
²local *n* 1 : a public vehicle (as a bus or train) that makes all or most stops on its run 2 : a local branch (as of a lodge or labor union) .
lo·cal·i·ty *n, pl* **lo·cal·i·ties** : a place and its surroundings
lo·cal·ize *vb* **lo·cal·ized; lo·cal·iz·ing** : to make or become local
lo·cate *vb* **lo·cat·ed; lo·cat·ing** 1 : to state and fix exactly the place or limits of 2 : to settle or establish in a locality 3 : to look and find the position of
lo·ca·tion *n* 1 : the act or process of locating 2 : a place fit for some use (as a building)
¹lock *n* : a small bunch of hair or of fiber (as cotton or wool)
²lock *n* 1 : a fastening (as for a door) in which a bolt is operated (as by a key) 2 : the device for exploding the charge or cartridge of a firearm 3 : an enclosure (as in a canal) with gates at each end used in raising or lowering boats as they pass from level to level
³lock *vb* 1 : to fasten with or as if with a lock 2 : to shut in or out by or as if by means of a lock 3 : to make fast by the linking of parts together
lock·er *n* : a cabinet, compartment, or chest for personal use or for storing frozen food at a low temperature
lock·et *n* : a small ornamental case usually worn on a chain
lock·jaw *n* : TETANUS
lock·smith *n* : a worker who makes or repairs locks
lock·up *n* : PRISON
lo·co *adj* : not sane : CRAZY
lo·co·mo·tion *n* : the act or power of moving from place to place
lo·co·mo·tive *n* : a vehicle that moves under its own power and is used to haul cars on a railroad
lo·cust *n* 1 : a grasshopper that moves in huge swarms and eats up the plants in its course 2 : CICADA 3 : a hardwood tree with feathery leaves and drooping flower clusters
lode·stone *n* 1 : a rocky substance having magnetic properties 2 : something that attracts strongly
¹lodge *vb* **lodged; lodg·ing** 1 : to provide temporary quarters for 2 : to use a place

for living or sleeping 3 : to come to rest 4 : ³FILE 2
²lodge *n* 1 : a house set apart for residence in a special season or by an employee on an estate 2 : the meeting place of a branch of a secret society
lodg·er *n* : a person who lives in a rented room in another's house
lodging *n* 1 : a temporary living or sleeping place 2 **lodgings** *pl* : a room or rooms in the house of another person rented as a place to live
loft *n* 1 : an upper room or upper story of a building 2 : a balcony in a church 3 : an upper part of a barn
lofty *adj* **loft·i·er; loft·i·est** 1 : PROUD 1 2 : of high rank or fine quality 3 : rising to a great height — **loft·i·ly** *adv* — **loft·i·ness** *n*
¹log *n* 1 : a large piece of rough timber : a long piece of a tree trunk trimmed and ready for sawing 2 : a device for measuring the speed of a ship 3 : the daily record of a ship's speed and progress 4 : the record of a ship's voyage or of an aircraft's flight 5 : a record of how something (as a piece of equipment) works in actual use
²log *vb* **logged; log·ging** 1 : to engage in cutting and hauling logs for timber 2 : to put details of or about in a log
log·ger·head *n* : a very large sea turtle found in the warmer parts of the Atlantic ocean
log·ic *n* 1 : a science that deals with the rules and tests of sound thinking and reasoning 2 : sound reasoning
log·i·cal *adj* 1 : having to do with logic 2 : according to the rules of logic 3 : according to what is reasonably expected — **log·i·cal·ly** *adv* — **log·i·cal·ness** *n*
log on *vb* : to establish a connection to and begin using a computer or network
-logy *n suffix* : area of knowledge : science
loin *n* 1 : the part of the body between the hip and the lower ribs 2 : a piece of meat (as beef) from the loin of an animal
loi·ter *vb* 1 : to linger on one's way 2 : to hang around idly — **loi·ter·er** *n*
loll *vb* 1 : to hang loosely : DANGLE 2 : to lie around lazily
lol·li·pop *or* **lol·ly·pop** *n* : a lump of hard candy on the end of a stick
lone *adj* 1 : having no companion 2 : being by itself
lone·ly *adj* **lone·li·er; lone·li·est** 1 : LONE 1 2 : not often visited 3 : longing for companions — **lone·li·ness** *n*
lone·some *adj* 1 : saddened by a lack of companions 2 : not often visited or traveled over — **lone·some·ly** *adv* — **lone·some·ness** *n*

¹**long** *adj* **lon·ger; lon·gest** **1** : of great length from end to end : not short **2** : having a greater length than breadth **3** : lasting for some time : not brief **4** : having a stated length (as in distance or time) **5** : of, relating to, or being one of the vowel sounds \ā, à, ē, ī, ō, ü\ and sometimes \ä\ and \ȯ\

²**long** *adv* **1** : for or during a long time **2** : for the whole length of **3** : at a distant point of time

³**long** *n* : a long time

⁴**long** *vb* : to wish for something very much — **long·ing·ly** *adv*

long·hand *n* : HANDWRITING

long·horn *n* : any of the half-wild cattle with very long horns that were once common in the southwestern United States

long–horned *adj* : having long horns or antennae

long·ing *n* : an eager desire

long·ish *adj* : somewhat long

lon·gi·tude *n* : distance measured in degrees east or west of a line drawn (as through Greenwich, England) between the north and south poles

lon·gi·tu·di·nal *adj* : placed or running lengthwise — **lon·gi·tu·di·nal·ly** *adv*

long–lived *adj* : living or lasting for a long time

long–range *adj* **1** : capable of traveling or shooting great distances **2** : lasting over or providing for a long period

long·sight·ed *adj* : FARSIGHTED — **long·sight·ed·ness** *n*

long–suf·fer·ing *adj* : very patient and forgiving

long–wind·ed *adj* **1** : too long **2** : given to talking too long

¹**look** *vb* **1** : to use the power of vision : SEE **2** : to appear suitable to **3** : SEEM **1 4** : to turn one's attention or eyes **5** : ²FACE 2 — **look after** : to take care of — **look down on** : to regard with contempt — **look up to** : RESPECT 1

²**look** *n* **1** : an act of looking **2** : the way one appears to others **3** : appearance that suggests what something is or means

looking glass *n* : ¹MIRROR 1

look·out *n* **1** : a careful watch for something expected or feared **2** : a high place from which a wide view is possible **3** : a person who keeps watch

¹**loom** *n* : a device for weaving cloth

²**loom** *vb* : to come into sight suddenly and often with a dim or strange appearance

loon *n* : a large diving bird that lives on fish and has webbed feet, a black head, and a black back spotted with white

¹**loop** *n* **1** : an almost oval form produced when something flexible and thin (as a wire or a rope) crosses itself **2** : something (as a figure or bend) suggesting a flexible loop

²**loop** *vb* : to make a loop or loops in

loop·hole *n* : a way of escaping something

¹**loose** *adj* **loos·er; loos·est** **1** : not tightly fixed or fastened **2** : not pulled tight **3** : not tied up or shut in **4** : not brought together in a package or binding **5** : not respectable **6** : having parts that are not squeezed tightly together **7** : not exact or careful — **loose·ly** *adv* — **loose·ness** *n*

²**loose** *vb* **loosed; loos·ing** **1** : to make loose : UNTIE **2** : to set free

loose–leaf *adj* : arranged so that pages can be put in or taken out

loos·en *vb* : to make or become loose

¹**loot** *n* : something stolen or taken by force

²**loot** *vb* : ¹PLUNDER — **loot·er** *n*

¹**lope** *n* : a gait with long smooth steps

²**lope** *vb* **loped; lop·ing** : to go or ride at a lope

lop–eared *adj* : having ears that droop

lop·sid·ed *adj* : UNBALANCED 1 — **lop·sid·ed·ly** *adv* — **lop·sid·ed·ness** *n*

¹**lord** *n* **1** : a person having power and authority over others **2** *cap* : GOD 1 **3** *cap* : JESUS **3** : a British nobleman or a bishop of the Church of England entitled to sit in the House of Lords — used as a title

²**lord** *vb* : to act in a proud or bossy way toward others

lord·ship *n* : the rank or dignity of a lord — used as a title

lore *n* : common knowledge or belief

lose *vb* **lost; los·ing** **1** : to be unable to find or have at hand : MISLAY **2** : to be deprived of **3** : ²WASTE 2 **4** : to be defeated in **5** : to fail to keep — **los·er** *n* — **lose one's way** : to stray from the right path

loss *n* **1** : the act or fact of losing something **2** : harm or distress that comes from losing something **3** : something that is lost **4** : failure to win

¹**lost** *past of* LOSE

²**lost** *adj* **1** : not used, won, or claimed **2** : unable to find the way **3** : come or brought to a bad end **4** : no longer possessed or known **5** : fully occupied

lot *n* **1** : an object used in deciding something by chance or the use of such an object to decide something **2** : FATE 2 **3** : a piece or plot of land **4** : a large number or amount

loth *variant of* LOATH

lo·tion *n* : a liquid preparation used on the skin for healing or as a cosmetic

lot·tery *n, pl* **lot·ter·ies** : a way of raising money in which many tickets are sold and a few of these are drawn to win prizes

lo·tus *n* : any of various water lilies

¹loud *adj* **1** : not low, soft, or quiet in sound : NOISY **2** : not quiet or calm in expression **3** : too bright or showy to be pleasing — **loud·ly** *adv* — **loud·ness** *n*

²loud *adv* : in a loud manner

loud·speak·er *n* : an electronic device that makes sound louder

¹lounge *vb* **lounged; loung·ing** **1** : to move or act in a slow, tired, or lazy way **2** : to stand, sit, or lie in a relaxed manner

²lounge *n* **1** : a comfortable room where one can relax or lounge **2** : SOFA

louse *n, pl* **lice** **1** : a small, wingless, and usually flat insect that lives on the bodies of warm-blooded animals **2** : PLANT LOUSE

lov·able *adj* : deserving to be loved or admired — **lov·able·ness** *n* — **lov·ably** *adv*

¹love *n* **1** : great and warm affection (as of a child for a parent) **2** : a great liking **3** : a beloved person

²love *vb* **loved; lov·ing** **1** : to feel warm affection for **2** : to like very much — **lov·er** *n*

love·ly *adj* **love·li·er; love·li·est** **1** : very beautiful **2** : very pleasing — **love·li·ness** *n*

lov·ing *adj* : feeling or showing love : AFFECTIONATE — **lov·ing·ly** *adv*

¹low *vb* : to make the calling sound of a cow : MOO

²low *n* : the mooing of a cow : MOO

³low *adj* **1** : not high : not tall **2** : lying or going below the usual level **3** : not loud : SOFT **4** : deep in pitch **5** : ¹PROSTRATE 3 **6** : SAD 1 **7** : less than usual (as in quantity or value) **8** : COARSE 4, VULGAR **9** : not favorable : POOR — **low·ness** *n*

⁴low *n* **1** : something that is low **2** : a region of low barometric pressure **3** : the arrangement of gears in an automobile that gives the lowest speed of travel

⁵low *adv* : so as to be low

¹low·er *adj* **1** : being below the other of two similar persons or things **2** : less advanced

²lower *vb* **1** : to move to a lower level : SINK **2** : to let or pull down **3** : to make or become less (as in value or amount) **4** : to make or become lower

low·land *n* : low flat country

¹low·ly *adv* : in a humble way

²lowly *adj* **low·li·er; low·li·est** : of low rank or condition : HUMBLE — **low·li·ness** *n*

loy·al *adj* **1** : faithful to one's country **2** : faithful to a person or thing one likes or believes in — **loy·al·ly** *adv*

loy·al·ty *n, pl* **loy·al·ties** : the quality or state of being loyal

loz·enge *n* : a small candy often containing medicine

LSD *n* : a dangerous drug that causes hallucinations

lu·bri·cant *n* : something (as oil or grease) that makes a surface smooth or slippery

lu·bri·cate *vb* **lu·bri·cat·ed; lu·bri·cat·ing** **1** : to make smooth or slippery **2** : to apply oil or grease to

lu·bri·ca·tion *n* : the act or process of lubricating or the state of being lubricated

lu·cid *adj* **1** : showing a normal state of mind **2** : easily understood — **lu·cid·ly** *adv* — **lu·cid·ness** *n*

luck *n* **1** : something that happens to a person by or as if by chance **2** : the accidental way events occur **3** : good fortune

lucky *adj* **luck·i·er; luck·i·est** **1** : helped by luck : FORTUNATE **2** : happening because of good luck **3** : thought of as bringing good luck — **luck·i·ly** *adv*

lu·di·crous *adj* : funny because of being ridiculous : ABSURD — **lu·di·crous·ly** *adv* — **lu·di·crous·ness** *n*

lug *vb* **lugged; lug·ging** : to find hard to carry or haul

lug·gage *n* : BAGGAGE

luke·warm *adj* **1** : neither hot nor cold **2** : not very interested or eager

¹lull *vb* : to make or become quiet or less watchful

²lull *n* : a period of calm (as in a storm)

lul·la·by *n, pl* **lul·la·bies** : a song for helping babies to sleep

¹lum·ber *vb* : to move in an awkward way

²lumber *n* : timber especially when sawed into boards

³lumber *vb* : to cut logs : saw logs into lumber

lum·ber·jack *n* : a person who works at lumbering

lum·ber·man *n, pl* **lum·ber·men** : a boss lumberjack

lum·ber·yard *n* : a place where a stock of lumber is kept for sale

lu·mi·nous *adj* : shining brightly — **lu·mi·nous·ly** *adv*

¹lump *n* : a small uneven mass (as a chunk or a swelling)

²lump *vb* **1** : to form into a lump **2** : to group together

lu·nar *adj* **1** : of or relating to the moon **2** : measured by the revolutions of the moon

¹lu·na·tic *adj* **1** : INSANE 1, CRAZY **2** : INSANE 2

²lunatic *n* : an insane person

¹lunch *n* **1** : a light meal especially when eaten in the middle of the day **2** : food prepared for lunch

²lunch *vb* : to eat lunch

lun·cheon *n* **1** : ¹LUNCH 1 **2** : a formal lunch

lung *n* : either of two organs in the chest that are like bags and are the main breathing structure in animals that breathe air

¹lunge *n* : a sudden movement forward

²lunge *vb* **lunged; lung·ing** : to push or drive with force

lung·fish *n* : any of several fishes that breathe with structures like lungs as well as with gills

lu·pine *n* : a plant related to the clovers that has tall spikes of showy flowers like those of sweet peas

¹lurch *n* **1** : a sudden roll of a ship to one side **2** : a swaying staggering movement or gait

²lurch *vb* : to move with a lurch

¹lure *n* **1** : something that attracts or draws one on : TEMPTATION **2** : an artificial bait for catching fish

²lure *vb* **lured; lur·ing** : to tempt or lead away by offering some pleasure or advantage : ENTICE

lu·rid *adj* **1** : looking like glowing fire seen through smoke **2** : SENSATIONAL **2** — **lu·rid·ly** *adv* — **lu·rid·ness** *n*

lurk *vb* : to hide in or about a place

lus·cious *adj* **1** : very sweet and pleasing to taste and smell **2** : delightful to hear, see, or feel — **lus·cious·ly** *adv* — **lus·cious·ness** *n*

lush *adj* **1** : very juicy and fresh **2** : covered with a thick growth — **lush·ly** *adv* — **lush·ness** *n*

lus·ter *or* **lus·tre** *n* : a glow of reflected light : SHEEN

lus·trous *adj* : having luster

lute *n* : an old stringed instrument with a body shaped like a pear and usually paired strings played with the fingers

lux·u·ri·ant *adj* : growing freely and well — **lux·u·ri·ant·ly** *adv*

lux·u·ri·ous *adj* **1** : loving pleasure and luxury **2** : very fine and comfortable — **lux·u·ri·ous·ly** *adv* — **lux·u·ri·ous·ness** *n*

lux·u·ry *n, pl* **lux·u·ries 1** : very rich, pleasant, and comfortable surroundings **2** : something desirable but expensive or hard to get **3** : something pleasant but not really needed for one's pleasure or comfort

¹-ly *adj suffix* **1** : like : similar to **2** : happening in each specified period of time : every

²-ly *adv suffix* **1** : in a specified manner **2** : from a specified point of view

lye *n* : a dangerous compound containing sodium that dissolves in water and is used in cleaning

lying *present participle of* LIE

lymph *n* : a clear liquid like blood without the red cells that nourishes the tissues and carries off wastes

lym·phat·ic *adj* : of or relating to lymph

lynx *n, pl* **lynx** *or* **lynx·es** : any of several wildcats with rather long legs, a short tail, and often ears with small bunches of long hairs at the tip

lyre *n* : a stringed instrument like a harp used by the ancient Greeks

¹lyr·ic *n* **1** : a lyric poem **2 lyrics** *pl* : the words of a popular song

²lyric *adj* **1** : suitable for singing : MUSICAL **2** : expressing personal emotion

lyr·i·cal *adj* : ²LYRIC

M

m *n, pl* **m's** *or* **ms** *often cap* **1** : the thirteenth letter of the English alphabet **2** : 1000 in Roman numerals

ma *n, often cap* : ¹MOTHER 1

ma'am *n* : MADAM

mac·ad·am *n* : a road surface made of small closely packed broken stone

ma·caque *n* : any of several mostly Asian monkeys with short tails

mac·a·ro·ni *n, pl* **macaronis** *or* **macaronies** : a food that is made of a mixture of flour and water formed into tubes and dried

mac·a·roon *n* : a cookie made of the white of eggs, sugar, and ground almonds or coconut

ma·caw *n* : a large parrot of Central and South America with a long tail, a harsh voice, and bright feathers

¹mace *n* : a spice made from the dried outer covering of the nutmeg

²mace *n* : a fancy club carried before certain officials as a sign of authority

ma·chete *n* : a large heavy knife used for cutting sugarcane and underbrush and as a weapon

¹ma·chine *n* **1** : VEHICLE 2 **2** : a device that combines forces, motion, and energy in a way that does some desired work

²machine *vb* **ma·chined; ma·chin·ing** : to shape or finish by tools run by machines

machine gun *n* : an automatic gun for continuous firing

ma·chin·ery *n* **1** : a group of machines **2** : the working parts of a machine **3** : the people and equipment by which something is done

machine shop *n* : a workshop in which metal articles are machined and put together

ma·chin·ist *n* : a person who makes or works on machines

mack·er·el *n, pl* **mackerel** *or* **mackerels** : a food fish of the North Atlantic that is green with blue bars above and silvery below

mack·i·naw *n* : a short heavy woolen coat

ma·cron *n* : a mark {macr} placed over a vowel to show that the vowel is long

mad *adj* **mad·der; mad·dest** **1** : INSANE 1 **2** : done or made without thinking **3** : ANGRY **4** : INFATUATED **5** : having rabies **6** : marked by intense and often disorganized activity — **mad·ly** *adv* — **mad·ness** *n*

mad·am *n, pl* **mes·dames** — used without a name as a form of polite address to a woman

¹**mad·cap** *adj* : likely to do something mad or reckless : done for fun without thinking

²**madcap** *n* : a madcap person

mad·den *vb* : to make mad

made *past of* MAKE

made–up *adj* : showing more imagination than concern with fact

mad·house *n* : a place or scene of complete confusion

mag·a·zine *n* **1** : a storehouse or warehouse for military supplies **2** : a place for keeping explosives in a fort or ship **3** : a container in a gun for holding cartridges **4** : a publication issued at regular intervals (as weekly or monthly)

mag·got *n* : a legless grub that is the larva of a two-winged fly

¹**mag·ic** *n* **1** : the power to control natural forces possessed by certain persons (as wizards and witches) in folk tales and fiction **2** : a power that seems mysterious **3** : something that charms **4** : the art or skill of performing tricks or illusions as if by magic for entertainment

²**magic** *adj* **1** : of or relating to magic **2** : having effects that seem to be caused by magic **3** : giving a feeling of enchantment

mag·i·cal *adj* : ²MAGIC

ma·gi·cian *n* : a person skilled in magic

magic lantern *n* : an early kind of slide projector

mag·is·trate *n* **1** : a chief officer of government **2** : a local official with some judicial power

mag·ma *n* : molten rock within the earth

mag·na·nim·i·ty *n* : the quality of being magnanimous

mag·nan·i·mous *adj* **1** : having a noble and courageous spirit **2** : being generous and forgiving — **mag·nan·i·mous·ly** *adv*

mag·ne·sium *n* : a silvery white metallic chemical element that is lighter than aluminum and is used in lightweight alloys

mag·net *n* : a piece of material (as of iron, steel, or alloy) that is able to attract iron

mag·net·ic *adj* **1** : acting like a magnet **2** : of or relating to the earth's magnetism **3** : having a great power to attract people

magnetic field *n* : the portion of space near a magnetic body within which magnetic forces can be detected

magnetic needle *n* : a narrow strip of magnetized steel that is free to swing around to show the direction of the earth's magnetism

magnetic pole *n* **1** : either of the poles of a magnet **2** : either of two small regions of the earth which are located near the North and South Poles and toward which a compass needle points

magnetic tape *n* : a thin ribbon of plastic coated with a magnetic material on which information (as sound) may be stored

mag·ne·tism *n* **1** : the power to attract that a magnet has **2** : the power to attract others : personal charm

mag·ne·tize *vb* **mag·ne·tized; mag·ne·tiz·ing** : to cause to be magnetic

mag·ne·to *n, pl* **mag·ne·tos** : a small generator used especially to produce the spark in some gasoline engines

mag·nif·i·cent *adj* : having impressive beauty : very grand — **mag·nif·i·cent·ly** *adv*

mag·ni·fy *vb* **mag·ni·fied; mag·ni·fy·ing** **1** : to enlarge in fact or appearance **2** : to cause to seem greater or more important : EXAGGERATE

magnifying glass *n* : a lens that magnifies something seen through it

mag·ni·tude *n* : greatness of size

mag·no·lia *n* : a tree or tall shrub having showy white, pink, yellow, or purple flowers that appear before or sometimes with the leaves

mag·pie *n* : a noisy black-and-white bird related to the jays

ma·hog·a·ny *n, pl* **ma·hog·a·nies** : a strong reddish brown wood that is used especially for furniture and is obtained from several tropical trees

maid *n* **1** : an unmarried girl or woman **2** : a female servant

¹**maid·en** *n* : an unmarried girl or woman

²**maiden** *adj* **1** : UNMARRIED **2** : ¹FIRST 2

maid·en·hair fern *n* : a fern with slender stems and delicate feathery leaves

maid·en·hood *n* : the state or time of being a maiden

maiden name *n* : a woman's family name before she is married

maid of honor : an unmarried woman who stands with the bride at a wedding

¹**mail** *n* **1** : letters, parcels, and papers sent from one person to another through the post office **2** : the whole system used in the public sending and delivering of mail **3** : something that comes in the mail

²**mail** *vb* : to send by mail

³**mail** *n* : a fabric made of metal rings linked together and used as armor

mail·box *n* **1** : a public box in which to place outgoing mail **2** : a private box (as on a house) for the delivery of incoming mail

mail carrier *n* : LETTER CARRIER

mail·man *n*, *pl* **mail·men** : LETTER CARRIER

maim *vb* : to injure badly or cripple by violence

¹**main** *n* **1** : physical strength : FORCE **2** : HIGH SEAS **3** : the chief part : essential point **4** : a principal line, tube, or pipe of a utility system

²**main** *adj* **1** : first in size, rank, or importance : CHIEF **2** : PURE 3, SHEER — **main·ly** *adv*

main·land *n* : a continent or the main part of a continent as distinguished from an offshore island or sometimes from a cape or peninsula

main·mast *n* : the principal mast of a sailing ship

main·sail *n* : the principal sail on the mainmast

main·spring *n* : the principal spring in a mechanical device (as a watch or clock)

main·stay *n* **1** : the large strong rope from the maintop of a ship usually to the foot of the foremast **2** : a chief support

main·tain *vb* **1** : to keep in a particular or desired state **2** : to defend by argument **3** : CARRY ON 3, CONTINUE **4** : to provide for : SUPPORT **5** : to insist to be true

main·te·nance *n* **1** : the act of maintaining : the state of being maintained **2** : UPKEEP

main·top *n* : a platform around the head of a mainmast

maize *n* : INDIAN CORN

ma·jes·tic *adj* : very impressive and dignified : NOBLE — **ma·jes·ti·cal·ly** *adv*

maj·es·ty *n*, *pl* **maj·es·ties** **1** : royal dignity or authority **2** : the quality or state of being majestic **3** — used as a title for a king, queen, emperor, or empress

¹**ma·jor** *adj* **1** : greater in number, quantity, rank, or importance **2** : of or relating to a musical scale of eight notes with half steps between the third and fourth and between the seventh and eighth notes and with whole steps between all the others

²**major** *n* : a commissioned officer in the Army, Air Force, or Marine Corps ranking above a captain

major general *n* : a commissioned officer in the Army, Air Force, or Marine Corps ranking above a brigadier general

ma·jor·i·ty *n*, *pl* **ma·jor·i·ties** **1** : the age at which one is allowed to vote **2** : a number greater than half of a total **3** : the amount by which a majority is more than a minority **4** : a group or party that makes up the greater part of a whole body of persons

¹**make** *vb* **made; mak·ing** **1** : to cause to occur **2** : to form or put together out of material or parts **3** : to combine to produce **4** : to set in order : PREPARE **5** : to cause to be or become **6** : ¹DO 1, PERFORM **7** : to produce by action **8** : COMPEL **9** : GET 1, GAIN **10** : to act so as to be — **make believe** : to act as if something known to be imaginary is real or true — **make good** **1** : FULFILL, COMPLETE **2** : SUCCEED 3

²**make** *n* **1** : the way in which a thing is made : STRUCTURE **2** : ¹BRAND 4

¹**make–be·lieve** *n* : a pretending to believe (as in children's play)

²**make–believe** *adj* : not real : IMAGINARY

make out *vb* **1** : to write out **2** : UNDERSTAND 1 **3** : IDENTIFY 3 **4** : ¹FARE

¹**make·shift** *n* : a thing used as a temporary substitute for another

²**makeshift** *adj* : serving as a temporary substitute

make·up *n* **1** : the way the parts or elements of something are put together or joined **2** : materials used in changing one's appearance (as for a play or other entertainment) **3** : any of various cosmetics (as lipstick or powder)

make up *vb* **1** : to create from the imagination **2** : ²FORM 3, COMPOSE **3** : ¹RECOMPENSE, ATONE **4** : to become friendly again **5** : to put on makeup — **make up one's mind** : to reach a decision

mal- *prefix* **1** : bad : badly **2** : abnormal : abnormally

mal·ad·just·ed *adj* : not properly adjusted

mal·a·dy *n*, *pl* **mal·a·dies** : a disease or ailment of body or mind

ma·lar·ia *n* : a serious disease with chills and fever that is spread by the bite of one kind of mosquito

¹**male** *n* : an individual that produces germ cells (as sperm) that fertilize the eggs of a female

²**male** *adj* **1** : of, relating to, or being the sex that fathers young **2** : bearing stamens but no pistil **3** : of, relating to, or like that of males — **male·ness** *n*

mal·for·ma·tion *n* : something that is badly or wrongly formed

mal·ice *n* : ILL WILL

ma·li·cious *adj* **1** : doing mean things for pleasure **2** : done just to be mean — **ma·li·cious·ly** *adv*

¹**ma·lign** *adj* : MALIGNANT 1

²**malign** *vb* : to say evil things about : SLANDER

ma·lig·nant *adj* **1** : evil in influence or result : INJURIOUS **2** : MALICIOUS 1 **3** : likely to cause death : DEADLY — **ma·lig·nant·ly** *adv*

mall *n* **1** : a shaded walk : PROMENADE **2** : a usually paved or grassy strip between two roadways **3** : a shopping area in a community with a variety of shops around an often covered space for pedestrians

mal·lard *n* : a common wild duck of the northern hemisphere that is the ancestor of the domestic ducks

mal·lea·ble *adj* : capable of being beaten out, extended, or shaped by hammer blows

mal·let *n* **1** : a hammer with a short handle and a barrel-shaped head of wood or soft material used for driving a tool (as a chisel) or for striking a surface without denting it **2** : a club with a short thick rod for a head and a long thin rod for a handle

mal·low *n* : a tall plant related to the hollyhock that has usually lobed leaves and white, rose, or purplish flowers with five petals

mal·nu·tri·tion *n* : faulty nourishment

malt *n* **1** : grain and especially barley soaked in water until it has sprouted **2** : MALTED MILK

malt·ed milk *n* : a beverage made by dissolving a powder made from dried milk and cereals in a liquid (as milk)

mal·treat *vb* : to treat in a rough or unkind way : ABUSE

ma·ma *or* **mam·ma** *n* : ¹MOTHER 1

mam·mal *n* : a warm-blooded animal that feeds its young with milk and has a backbone, two pairs of limbs, and a more or less complete covering of hair

¹mam·moth *n* : a very large hairy extinct elephant with tusks that curve upward

²mammoth *adj* : very large : HUGE

mam·my *n, pl* **mammies** : ¹MOTHER 1

¹man *n, pl* **men** **1** : a human being : PERSON **2** : an adult male human being **3** : the human race : MANKIND **4** : a member of the natural family to which human beings belong including both modern humans and extinct related forms **5** : HUSBAND **6** : an adult male servant or employee **7** : one of the pieces with which various games (as chess or checkers) are played

²man *vb* **manned; man·ning** **1** : to station crew members at **2** : to do the work of operating

man·age *vb* **man·aged; man·ag·ing** **1** : to look after and make decisions about : be the boss of **2** : to achieve what one wants to do

man·age·ment *n* **1** : the managing of something **2** : the people who manage

man·ag·er *n* : a person who manages — **man·ag·er·ship** *n*

man·a·tee *n* : a mainly tropical water-dwelling mammal that eats plants and has a broad rounded tail

man·da·rin *n* : a high public official of the Chinese Empire

man·date *n* **1** : an order from a higher court to a lower court **2** : the instruction given by voters to their elected representatives

man·di·ble *n* **1** : a lower jaw often with its soft parts **2** : either the upper or lower part of the bill of a bird **3** : either of the first pair of mouth parts of some invertebrates (as an insect or crustacean) that often form biting organs

man·do·lin *n* : a small stringed instrument with four pairs of strings played by plucking

mane *n* : long heavy hair growing from the neck or shoulders of an animal (as a horse or lion) — **maned** *adj*

¹ma·neu·ver *n* **1** : a planned movement of troops or ships **2** : a training exercise by armed forces **3** : skillful action or management

²maneuver *vb* **1** : to move in a maneuver **2** : to perform a maneuver **3** : to guide skillfully — **ma·neu·ver·able** *adj*

ma·neu·ver·abil·i·ty *n* : the quality or state of being maneuverable

man·ga·nese *n* : a grayish white brittle metallic chemical element that resembles iron

mange *n* : a contagious skin disease usually of domestic animals in which there is itching and loss of hair

man·ger *n* : an open box in which food for farm animals is placed

man·gle *vb* **man·gled; man·gling** **1** : to cut or bruise with repeated blows **2** : to spoil while making or performing

man·go *n, pl* **man·goes** *or* **man·gos** : a juicy somewhat acid tropical fruit that is yellow or reddish and is borne by an evergreen tree related to the sumac

mangy *adj* **mang·i·er; mang·i·est** **1** : having mange or resulting from mange **2** : SHABBY 2 **3** : SEEDY 2

man·hole *n* : a covered hole (as in a street or tank) large enough to let a person pass through

man·hood *n* **1** : COURAGE **2** : the state of being an adult human male **3** : adult human males

ma·nia *n* **1** : often violent or excited insanity **2** : unreasonable enthusiasm

ma·ni·ac *n* : a violently insane person

¹man·i·cure *n* **1** : MANICURIST **2** : a treatment for the care of the hands and nails

²**manicure** *vb* **man·i·cured; man·i·cur·ing**
: to give a manicure to

man·i·cur·ist *n* : a person who gives mani-
cures

¹**man·i·fest** *adj* : clear to the senses or to the
mind : easy to recognize : OBVIOUS

²**manifest** *vb* : to show plainly

man·i·fes·ta·tion *n* 1 : the act of manifest-
ing 2 : something that makes clear : EVI-
DENCE

man·i·fold *adj* : of many and various kinds

ma·nip·u·late *vb* **ma·nip·u·lat·ed; ma·nip·
u·lat·ing** 1 : to work with the hands or by
mechanical means and especially with skill
2 : to manage skillfully and especially with
intent to deceive

man·kind *n* 1 : human beings 2 : men as
distinguished from women

man·ly *adj* **man·li·er; man·li·est** : having
qualities (as courage) often felt to be proper
for a man — **man·li·ness** *n*

man–made *adj* : made by people rather than
nature

man·na *n* : food supplied by a miracle to the
Israelites in the wilderness

man·ne·quin *n* : a form representing the
human figure used especially for displaying
clothes

man·ner *n* 1 : ¹SORT 1 2 : a way of acting
3 **manners** *pl* : behavior toward or in the
presence of other people

man·ner·ism *n* : a habit (as of looking or
moving in a certain way) that one notices in
a person's behavior

man·ner·ly *adj* : showing good manners
: POLITE

man–of–war *n, pl* **men–of–war** : WARSHIP

man·or *n* : a large estate

man·sion *n* : a large fine house

man·slaugh·ter *n* : the unintentional but unlawful killing of a person

man·tel *n* : a shelf above a fireplace

man·tel·piece *n* 1 : a shelf above a fireplace along with side pieces 2 : MANTEL

man·tis *n, pl* **man·tis·es** *or* **man·tes** : an insect related to the grasshoppers and roaches
that feeds on other insects which are
clasped in the raised front legs

man·tle *n* 1 : a loose sleeveless outer garment 2 : something that covers or wraps 3
: a fold of the body wall of a mollusk that
produces the shell material 4 : the part of
the earth's interior beneath the crust and
above the central core

¹**man·u·al** *adj* 1 : of or relating to the hands
2 : done or operated by the hands — **man·
u·al·ly** *adv*

²**manual** *n* : HANDBOOK

manual training *n* : training in work done
with the hands and in useful arts

¹**man·u·fac·ture** *n* 1 : the making of products by hand or machinery 2 : PRODUC-
TION 2

²**manufacture** *vb* **man·u·fac·tured; man·u·
fac·tur·ing** : to make from raw materials by
hand or machinery — **man·u·fac·tur·er** *n*

ma·nure *n* : material (as animal wastes) used
to fertilize land

man·u·script *n* 1 : a composition or document written by hand especially before the
development of printing 2 : a document
submitted for publication 3 : HANDWRIT-
ING

¹**many** *adj* **more; most** 1 : amounting to a
large number 2 : being one of a large but
not fixed number

²**many** *pron* : a large number

³**many** *n* : a large number

¹**map** *n* 1 : a picture or chart showing features of an area (as the surface of the earth
or the moon) 2 : a picture or chart of the
sky showing the position of stars and planets

²**map** *vb* **mapped; map·ping** 1 : to make a
map of 2 : to plan in detail

ma·ple *n* : any of a group of trees having
deeply notched leaves, fruits with two
wings, and hard pale wood and including
some whose sap is evaporated to a sweet
syrup (**maple syrup**) and a brownish sugar
(**maple sugar**)

mar *vb* **marred; mar·ring** : to make a blemish on : SPOIL

ma·ra·ca *n* : a musical rhythm instrument
made of a dried gourd with seeds or pebbles
inside that is usually played in pairs by
shaking

mar·a·thon *n* 1 : a long-distance running
race 2 : a long hard contest

¹**mar·ble** *n* 1 : limestone that is capable of
taking a high polish and is used in architecture and sculpture 2 : a little ball (as of
glass) used in a children's game (**marbles**)

²**marble** *adj* : made of or like marble

¹**march** *vb* 1 : to move or cause to move
along steadily usually with long even steps
and in step with others 2 : to make steady
progress — **march·er** *n*

²**march** *n* 1 : the action of marching 2 : the
distance covered in marching 3 : a regular
step used in marching 4 : a musical piece
in a lively rhythm with a strong beat that is
suitable to march to

March *n* : the third month of the year

mar·chio·ness *n* 1 : the wife or widow of a
marquess 2 : a woman who holds the rank
of a marquess in her own right

mare *n* : an adult female of the horse or a related animal (as a zebra or donkey)

mar·ga·rine *n* : a food product made usually

from vegetable oils and skim milk and used as a spread or for cooking

mar·gin *n* 1 : the part of a page outside the main body of print or writing 2 : ¹BORDER 1 3 : an extra amount (as of time or money) allowed for use if needed

mari·gold *n* : any of several plants related to the daisies that are grown for their yellow or brownish red and yellow flower heads

mar·i·jua·na *n* : dried leaves and flowers of the hemp plant smoked as a drug

ma·ri·na *n* : a dock or basin providing a place to anchor motorboats and yachts

¹**ma·rine** *adj* 1 : of or relating to the sea 2 : of or relating to the navigation of the sea : NAUTICAL 3 : of or relating to marines

²**marine** *n* 1 : the ships of a country 2 : one of a class of soldiers serving on board a ship or in close cooperation with a naval force

mar·i·ner *n* : SEAMAN 1, SAILOR

mar·i·o·nette *n* : a doll that can be made to move by means of strings : PUPPET

mar·i·tal *adj* : of or relating to marriage

mar·i·time *adj* 1 : of or relating to ocean navigation or trade 2 : bordering on or living near the sea

¹**mark** *n* 1 : something designed or serving to record position 2 : something aimed at : TARGET 3 : the starting line of a race 4 : INDICATION 2 5 : a blemish (as a scratch or stain) made on a surface 6 : a written or printed symbol 7 : a grade or score showing the quality of work or conduct

²**mark** *vb* 1 : to set apart by a line or boundary 2 : to make a mark on 3 : to decide and show the value or quality of by marks : GRADE 4 : to be an important characteristic of 5 : to take notice of — **mark·er** *n*

³**mark** *n* : a German coin or bill

marked *adj* 1 : having a mark or marks 2 : NOTICEABLE

¹**mar·ket** *n* 1 : a meeting of people at a fixed time and place to buy and sell things 2 : a public place where a market is held 3 : a store where foods are sold to the public 4 : the region in which something can be sold

²**market** *vb* : to buy or sell in a market

mar·ket·place *n* : an open square or place in a town where markets or public sales are held

mark·ing *n* : a mark made

marks·man *n*, *pl* **marks·men** : a person who shoots well — **marks·man·ship** *n*

mar·ma·lade *n* : a jam containing pieces of fruit and fruit rind

mar·mo·set *n* : a small monkey of South and Central America with soft fur and a bushy tail

mar·mot *n* : a stocky animal with short legs, coarse fur, and bushy tail that is related to the squirrels

¹**ma·roon** *vb* : to put ashore and abandon on a lonely island or coast

²**maroon** *n* : a dark red

mar·quess *n* : a British nobleman ranking below a duke and above an earl

mar·quis *n* : MARQUESS

mar·quise *n* : MARCHIONESS

mar·riage *n* 1 : the legal relationship into which a man and a woman enter with the purpose of making a home and raising a family 2 : the act of getting married

mar·row *n* : a soft tissue rich in fat and blood vessels that fills the cavities of most bones

mar·ry *vb* **mar·ried**; **mar·ry·ing** 1 : to join in marriage as husband and wife 2 : to give (as one's child) in marriage 3 : to take for husband or wife 4 : to enter into a marriage relationship

Mars *n* : the planet that is fourth in order of distance from the sun, is known for its redness, and has a diameter of about 6800 kilometers

marsh *n* : an area of soft wet land usually overgrown with grasses and related plants

¹**mar·shal** *n* 1 : a person who arranges and directs ceremonies 2 : an officer of the highest rank in some military forces 3 : a federal official having duties similar to those of a sheriff 4 : the head of a division of a city government

²**marshal** *vb* **mar·shaled** *or* **mar·shalled**; **mar·shaling** *or* **mar·shal·ling** : to arrange in order

marsh·mal·low *n* : a soft spongy sweet made from corn syrup, sugar, and gelatin

marsh marigold *n* : a swamp plant with shiny leaves and bright yellow flowers like buttercups

marshy *adj* **marsh·i·er**; **marsh·i·est** : like or being a marsh

mar·su·pi·al *n* : any of a group of mammals (as kangaroos and opossums) that do not develop a true placenta and that usually have a pouch on the female's abdomen in which the young are carried

mart *n* : a trading place : MARKET

mar·ten *n* : a slender animal larger than the related weasels that eats flesh and is sought for its soft gray or brown fur

mar·tial *adj* : having to do with or suitable for war

mar·tin *n* 1 : a European swallow with a forked tail 2 : any of several birds (as the American **purple martin**) resembling or related to the true martin

Mar·tin Lu·ther King Day *n* : the third Monday in January observed as a legal holiday in some states of the United States

¹mar·tyr *n* : a person who suffers greatly or dies rather than give up his or her religion or principles

²martyr *vb* : to put to death for refusing to give up a belief

¹mar·vel *n* : something that causes wonder or astonishment

²marvel *vb* **mar·veled** *or* **mar·velled; mar·vel·ing** *or* **mar·vel·ling** : to be struck with astonishment or wonder

mar·vel·ous *or* **mar·vel·lous** *adj* **1** : causing wonder or astonishment **2** : of the finest kind or quality — **mar·vel·ous·ly** *adv*

mas·cot *n* : a person, animal, or object adopted by a group and believed to bring good luck

mas·cu·line *adj* **1** : of the male sex **2** : ²MALE 3

¹mash *vb* : to make into a soft pulpy mass

²mash *n* **1** : a mixture of ground feeds used for feeding livestock **2** : a mass of something made soft and pulpy by beating or crushing

¹mask *n* **1** : a cover for the face or part of the face used for disguise or protection **2** : something that disguises or conceals **3** : a copy of a face molded in wax or plaster

²mask *vb* : CONCEAL, DISGUISE

ma·son *n* : a person who builds or works with stone, brick, or cement

ma·son·ry *n, pl* **ma·son·ries** **1** : the art, trade, or occupation of a mason **2** : the work done by a mason **3** : something built of stone, brick, or concrete

masque *n* **1** : ¹MASQUERADE 1 **2** : an old form of dramatic entertainment in which the actors wore masks

¹mas·quer·ade *n* **1** : a party (as a dance) at which people wear masks and costumes **2** : a pretending to be something one is not

²masquerade *vb* **mas·quer·ad·ed; mas·quer·ad·ing** **1** : to disguise oneself **2** : to pass oneself off as something one is not — POSE — **mas·quer·ad·er** *n*

¹mass *n* **1** : an amount of something that holds or clings together **2** : BULK 1, SIZE **3** : the principal part : main body **4** : a large quantity or number **5 masses** *pl* : the body of ordinary or common people

²mass *vb* : to collect into a mass

Mass *n* : a religious service in celebration of the Eucharist

¹mas·sa·cre *n* : the violent and cruel killing of a large number of persons

²massacre *vb* **mas·sa·cred; mas·sa·cring** : to kill in a massacre : SLAUGHTER

¹mas·sage *n* : treatment of the body by rubbing, kneading, and tapping

²massage *vb* **mas·saged; mas·sag·ing** : to give massage to

mas·sive *adj* : very large, heavy, and solid

mast *n* **1** : a long pole that rises from the bottom of a ship and supports the sails and rigging **2** : a vertical or nearly vertical tall pole — **mast·ed** *adj*

¹mas·ter *n* **1** : a male teacher **2** : an artist or performer of great skill **3** : one having authority over another person or thing **4** : EMPLOYER **5** — used as a title for a young boy too young to be called *mister*

²master *vb* **1** : to get control of **2** : to become skillful at

master chief petty officer *n* : a petty officer in the Navy or Coast Guard ranking above a senior chief petty officer

mas·ter·ful *adj* **1** : tending to take control : BOSSY **2** : having or showing great skill

mas·ter·ly *adj* : showing the knowledge or skill of a master

mas·ter·piece *n* : a work done or made with supreme skill

master sergeant *n* : a noncommissioned officer in the Army ranking above a sergeant first class or in the Air Force ranking above a technical sergeant or in the Marine Corps ranking above a gunnery sergeant

mas·tery *n, pl* **mas·ter·ies** **1** : the position or authority of a master **2** : VICTORY 1 **3** : skill that makes one master of something

mast·head *n* : the top of a mast

mas·ti·cate *vb* **mas·ti·cat·ed; mas·ti·cat·ing** : ¹CHEW

mas·tiff *n* : a very large powerful dog with a smooth coat

¹mat *n* **1** : a piece of coarse woven or braided fabric used as a floor or seat covering **2** : a piece of material in front of a door to wipe the shoes on **3** : a piece of material (as cloth or woven straw) used under dishes or vases or as an ornament **4** : a pad or cushion for gymnastics or wrestling **5** : something made up of many tangled strands

²mat *vb* **mat·ted; mat·ting** : to form into a tangled mass

mat·a·dor *n* : a bullfighter who plays the chief human part in a bullfight

¹match *n* **1** : a person or thing that is equal to or as good as another **2** : a thing that is exactly like another thing **3** : two people or things that go well together **4** : MARRIAGE 1 **5** : a contest between two individuals or teams

²match *vb* **1** : to place in competition **2** : to choose something that is the same as another or goes with it **3** : to be the same or suitable to one another

³match *n* **1** : a wick or cord that is made to burn evenly and is used for lighting a charge of powder **2** : a short slender piece of material tipped with a mixture that produces fire when scratched

match·book *n* : a small folder containing rows of paper matches

match·less *adj* : having no equal : better than any other of the same kind — **match·less·ly** *adv*

match·lock *n* : a musket with a hole at the rear of the barrel into which a slowly burning cord is lowered to ignite the charge

¹mate *n* **1** : COMPANION 1, COMRADE **2** : an officer on a ship used to carry passengers or freight who ranks below the captain **3** : either member of a married couple **4** : either member of a breeding pair of animals **5** : either of two matched objects

²mate *vb* **mat·ed; mat·ing** : to join as mates : MARRY

¹ma·te·ri·al *adj* **1** : of, relating to, or made of matter : PHYSICAL **2** : of or relating to a person's bodily needs or wants **3** : having real importance — **ma·teri·al·ly** *adv*

²material *n* **1** : the elements, substance, or parts of which something is made or can be made **2 materials** *pl* : equipment needed for doing something

ma·te·ri·al·ize *vb* **ma·te·ri·al·ized; ma·te·ri·al·iz·ing** **1** : to cause to take on a physical form **2** : to become actual fact

ma·ter·nal *adj* **1** : of or relating to a mother **2** : related through one's mother — **ma·ter·nal·ly** *adv*

ma·ter·ni·ty *n* : the state of being a mother

math *n* : MATHEMATICS

math·e·mat·i·cal *adj* **1** : of or relating to mathematics **2** : ²EXACT — **math·e·mat·i·cal·ly** *adv*

math·e·ma·ti·cian *n* : a specialist in mathematics

math·e·mat·ics *n* : the science that studies and explains numbers, quantities, measurements, and the relations between them

mat·i·nee *or* **mat·i·née** *n* : a musical or dramatic performance in the afternoon

mat·ri·mo·ni·al *adj* : of or relating to marriage

mat·ri·mo·ny *n* : MARRIAGE 1

ma·tron *n* **1** : a married woman **2** : a woman who is in charge of the household affairs of an institution **3** : a woman who looks after women prisoners in a police station or prison

¹mat·ter *n* **1** : something to be dealt with or considered **2** : PROBLEM 2, DIFFICULTY **3** : the substance things are made of : something that takes up space and has weight **4** : material substance of a certain kind or function **5** : PUS **6** : a more or less definite quantity or amount **7** : ¹MAIL 1 — **no matter** : it makes no difference

²matter *vb* : to be of importance

mat·ter–of–fact *adj* : sticking to or concerned with fact

mat·ting *n* : material for mats

mat·tress *n* **1** : a springy pad for use as a resting place usually over springs on a bedstead **2** : a sack that can be filled with air or water and used as a mattress

¹ma·ture *adj* **1** : fully grown or developed : ADULT, RIPE **2** : like that of a mature person

²mature *vb* **ma·tured; ma·tur·ing** : to reach maturity

ma·tu·ri·ty *n* : the condition of being mature : full development

¹maul *n* : a heavy hammer used especially for driving wedges or posts

²maul *vb* **1** : to beat and bruise severely **2** : to handle roughly

mauve *n* : a medium purple, violet, or lilac

maxi- *prefix* : very long or large

max·il·la *n, pl* **max·il·lae 1** : an upper jaw especially of a mammal **2** : either of the pair of mouth parts next behind the mandibles of an arthropod (as an insect or a crustacean)

max·im *n* : a short saying expressing a general truth or rule of conduct

¹max·i·mum *n, pl* **maximums** *or* **max·i·ma** : the highest value : greatest amount

²maximum *adj* : as great as possible in amount or degree

may *helping verb, past* **might**; *present sing & pl* **may 1** : have permission to **2** : be in some degree likely to **3** — used to express a wish **4** — used to express purpose

May *n* : the fifth month of the year

may·be *adv* : possibly but not certainly

mayn't : may not

may·on·naise *n* : a creamy dressing usually made of egg yolk, oil, and vinegar or lemon juice

may·or *n* : an official elected to serve as head of a city or borough

maze *n* : a confusing arrangement of paths or passages

MB *n* : MEGABYTE

me *pron objective case of* I

mead·ow *n* : usually moist and low grassland

mead·ow·lark *n* : a bird that has brownish upper parts and a yellow breast and is about as large as a robin

mea·ger *or* **mea·gre** *adj* **1** : having little flesh : THIN **2** : INSUFFICIENT

¹meal *n* **1** : the food eaten or prepared for eating at one time **2** : the act or time of eating

²meal *n* **1** : usually coarsely ground seeds of a cereal grass and especially of Indian corn **2** : something like meal in texture

mealy *adj* **meal·i·er; meal·i·est** : like meal
— **meal·i·ness** *n*

¹mean *vb* **meant; mean·ing** **1** : to have in
mind as a purpose : INTEND   **2** : to intend
for a particular use   **3** : to have as a meaning : SIGNIFY

²mean *adj* **1** : low in quality, worth, or dignity   **2** : lacking in honor or dignity   **3**
: STINGY 1   **4** : deliberately unkind   **5**
: ASHAMED 1 — **mean·ly** *adv* — **mean-
ness** *n*

³mean *adj* : occurring or being in a middle
position : AVERAGE

⁴mean *n* **1** : a middle point or something
(as a place, time, number, or rate) that falls
at or near a middle point : MODERATION   **2**
: ARITHMETIC MEAN   **3 means** *pl* : something that helps a person to get what he or
she wants   **4 means** *pl* : WEALTH 1 — **by
all means** : CERTAINLY 1 — **by any means**
: in any way — **by means of** : through the
use of — **by no means** : certainly not

me·an·der *vb* **1** : to follow a winding
course   **2** : to wander without a goal or purpose

mean·ing *n* **1** : the idea a person intends to
express by something said or done   **2** : the
quality of communicating something or of
being important

mean·ing·ful *adj* : having a meaning or purpose — **mean·ing·ful·ly** *adv*

mean·ing·less *adj* : having no meaning or
importance

¹mean·time *n* : the time between two events

²meantime *adv* : in the meantime

¹mean·while *n* : ¹MEANTIME

²meanwhile *adv* **1** : ²MEANTIME   **2** : at the
same time

mea·sles *n sing or pl* **1** : a contagious disease in which there are fever and red spots
on the skin   **2** : any of several diseases
(as **German measles**) resembling true
measles

mea·sly *adj* **mea·sli·er; mea·sli·est** : so
small or unimportant as to be rejected with
scorn

mea·sur·able *adj* : capable of being measured

¹mea·sure *n* **1** : EXTENT 2, DEGREE,
AMOUNT   **2** : the size, capacity, or quantity
of something as fixed by measuring   **3**
: something (as a yardstick or cup) used in
measuring   **4** : a unit used in measuring   **5**
: a system of measuring   **6** : the notes and
rests between bar lines on a musical staff   **7**
: a way of accomplishing something   **8** : a
legislative bill or act

²measure *vb* **mea·sured; mea·sur·ing** **1**
: to find out the size, extent, or amount of   **2**
: ¹ESTIMATE 1   **3** : to bring into comparison

4 : to give a measure of : INDICATE   **5** : to
have as its measurement

mea·sure·ment *n* **1** : the act of measuring
2 : the extent, size, capacity, or amount of
something as fixed by measuring   **3** : a system of measures

measure up *vb* : to satisfy needs or requirements

meat *n* **1** : solid food   **2** : the part of something that can be eaten   **3** : animal and especially mammal tissue for use as food   **4**
: the most important part : SUBSTANCE —
meat·less *adj*

me·chan·ic *n* : a person who makes or repairs machines

me·chan·i·cal *adj* **1** : of or relating to machinery   **2** : made or operated by a machine
3 : done or produced as if by a machine
: lacking freshness and individuality — **me-
chan·i·cal·ly** *adv*

me·chan·ics *n sing or pl* **1** : a science dealing with the action of forces on bodies   **2**
: the way something works or things are
done

mech·a·nism *n* **1** : a mechanical device   **2**
: the parts by which a machine operates   **3**
: the parts or steps that make up a process or
activity

mech·a·nize *vb* **mech·a·nized; mech·a·niz-
ing** **1** : to make mechanical or automatic   **2**
: to equip with machinery

med·al *n* : a piece of metal often in the form
of a coin with design and words in honor
of a special event, a person, or an achievement

me·dal·lion *n* **1** : a large medal   **2** : something like a large medal (as in shape)

med·dle *vb* **med·dled; med·dling** : to interest oneself in what is not one's concern

med·dle·some *adj* : given to meddling

media *pl of* MEDIUM

med·i·cal *adj* : of or relating to the science
or practice of medicine or to the treatment
of disease — **med·i·cal·ly** *adv*

med·i·cate *vb* **med·i·cat·ed; med·i·cat·ing**
1 : to use medicine on or for   **2** : to add medicinal material to

med·i·ca·tion *n* **1** : the act or process of
medicating   **2** : medicinal material

me·dic·i·nal *adj* : used or likely to relieve or
cure disease — **me·dic·i·nal·ly** *adv*

med·i·cine *n* **1** : something used to cure or
relieve a disease   **2** : a science or art dealing
with the prevention, cure, or relief of disease

medicine dropper *n* : DROPPER 2

medicine man *n* : a member of a primitive
tribe believed to have magic powers and
called on to cure illnesses and keep away
evil spirits

me·di·eval *or* **me·di·ae·val** *adj* : of or relating to the Middle Ages

me·di·o·cre *adj* : neither good nor bad : ORDINARY

med·i·tate *vb* **med·i·tat·ed; med·i·tat·ing 1** : to consider carefully : PLAN **2** : to spend time in quiet thinking : REFLECT

med·i·ta·tion *n* : the act or an instance of meditating

Med·i·ter·ra·nean *adj* : of or relating to the Mediterranean sea or to the lands or peoples surrounding it

¹**me·di·um** *n, pl* **me·di·ums** *or* **me·dia 1** : something that is between or in the middle **2** : the thing by which or through which something is done **3** : the substance in which something lives or acts **4** : a person through whom other persons try to communicate with the spirits of the dead

²**medium** *adj* : intermediate in amount, quality, position, or degree

med·ley *n, pl* **medleys 1** : MIXTURE 2, JUMBLE **2** : a musical selection made up of a series of different songs or parts of different compositions

me·dul·la ob·lon·ga·ta *n* : the last part of the brain that joins the spinal cord and is concerned especially with control of involuntary activities (as breathing and beating of the heart)

meed *n* : something deserved or earned : REWARD

meek *adj* **1** : putting up with injury or abuse with patience **2** : lacking spirit or self-confidence — **meek·ly** *adv* — **meek·ness** *n*

¹**meet** *vb* **met; meet·ing 1** : to come upon or across **2** : to be at a place to greet or keep an appointment **3** : to approach from the opposite direction **4** : to come together : JOIN, MERGE **5** : to be sensed by **6** : to deal with **7** : to fulfill the requirements of : SATISFY **8** : to become acquainted **9** : to hold a meeting

²**meet** *n* : a meeting for sports competition

meet·ing *n* **1** : the act of persons or things that meet **2** : ASSEMBLY 1

meet·ing·house *n* : a building used for public assembly and especially for Protestant worship

mega·byte *n* : a unit of computer information storage capacity equal to 1,048,576 bytes

mega·phone *n* : a device shaped like a cone that is used to direct the voice and increase its loudness

¹**mel·an·choly** *n* : a sad or gloomy mood

²**melancholy** *adj* : SAD 1

¹**mel·low** *adj* **1** : tender and sweet because of ripeness **2** : made mild by age **3** : being clear, full, and pure : not coarse — **mel·low·ness** *n*

²**mellow** *vb* : to make or become mellow

me·lo·di·ous *adj* : agreeable to the ear because of its melody — **me·lo·di·ous·ly** *adv* — **me·lo·di·ous·ness** *n*

mel·o·dy *n, pl* **mel·o·dies 1** : pleasing arrangement of sounds **2** : a series of musical notes or tones arranged in a definite pattern of pitch and rhythm **3** : the leading part in a musical composition

mel·on *n* : a fruit (as a watermelon) having juicy and usually sweet flesh and growing on a vine related to the gourds

melt *vb* **1** : to change from a solid to a liquid usually through the action of heat **2** : to grow less : DISAPPEAR **3** : to make or become gentle : SOFTEN **4** : to lose clear outline

melting point *n* : the temperature at which a solid melts

mem·ber *n* **1** : a part (as an arm, leg, leaf, or branch) of a person, animal, or plant **2** : one of the individuals (as persons) or units (as species) making up a group **3** : a part of a structure

mem·ber·ship *n* **1** : the state or fact of being a member **2** : the whole number of members

mem·brane *n* : a thin soft flexible layer especially of animal or plant tissue

mem·bra·nous *adj* : made of or like membrane

me·men·to *n, pl* **me·men·tos** *or* **me·men·toes** : something that serves as a reminder

mem·o·ra·ble *adj* : worth remembering : not easily forgotten — **mem·o·ra·bly** *adv*

mem·o·ran·dum *n, pl* **mem·o·ran·dums** *or* **mem·o·ran·da 1** : an informal record or message **2** : a written reminder

¹**me·mo·ri·al** *adj* : serving to preserve the memory of a person or event

²**memorial** *n* : something by which the memory of a person or an event is kept alive : MONUMENT

Memorial Day *n* **1** : May 30 once observed as a legal holiday in remembrance of war dead **2** : the last Monday in May observed as a legal holiday in most states of the United States

mem·o·rize *vb* **mem·o·rized; mem·o·riz·ing** : to learn by heart

mem·o·ry *n, pl* **mem·o·ries 1** : the power or process of remembering **2** : the store of things learned and kept in the mind **3** : the act of remembering and honoring **4** : something remembered **5** : the time within which past events are remembered **6** : a device or part in a computer which can receive and store information for use when wanted **7** : capacity for storing information

men *pl of* MAN

¹men·ace *n* **1** : DANGER **2** **2** : an annoying person

²menace *vb* **men·aced; men·ac·ing** : THREATEN 1

me·nag·er·ie *n* : a collection of confined wild animals

¹mend *vb* **1** : IMPROVE, CORRECT **2** : to restore to a whole condition **3** : to improve in health — **mend·er** *n*

²mend *n* **1** : the process of improving **2** : a mended place

men·folk *or* **men·folks** *n pl* : the men of a family or community

men·ha·den *n, pl* **menhaden** : a fish of the Atlantic coast of the United States that is related to the herrings and is a source of oil and fertilizer

¹me·ni·al *n* : a household servant

²menial *adj* : of, relating to, or suitable for servants : not needing skill

men–of–war *pl of* MAN-OF-WAR

men·stru·a·tion *n* : a periodic discharge of bloody fluid from the uterus

-ment *n suffix* **1** : result, goal, or method of a specified action **2** : action : process **3** : place of a specified action **4** : state : condition

men·tal *adj* **1** : of or relating to the mind **2** : done in the mind — **men·tal·ly** *adv*

men·tal·i·ty *n* : mental power : ability to learn

men·thol *n* : a white crystalline soothing substance from oils of mint

¹men·tion *n* : a brief reference to something

²mention *vb* : to refer to : speak about briefly

menu *n* **1** : a list of dishes served at or available for a meal **2** : the dishes or kinds of food served at a meal **3** : a list shown on a computer screen from which a user can select an operation for the computer to perform

¹me·ow *n* : the cry of a cat

²meow *vb* : to utter a meow

mer·can·tile *adj* : of or relating to merchants or trade

¹mer·ce·nary *n, pl* **mer·ce·nar·ies** : a soldier from a foreign country hired to fight in an army

²mercenary *adj* **1** : doing something only for the pay or reward **2** : greedy for money

mer·chan·dise *n* : goods that are bought and sold in trade

mer·chant *n* **1** : a person who carries on trade especially on a large scale or with foreign countries **2** : STOREKEEPER 2

mer·chant·man *n, pl* **mer·chant·men** : a ship used in trading

merchant marine *n* **1** : the trading ships of a nation **2** : the persons who work in a merchant marine

mer·ci·ful *adj* : having or showing mercy or compassion — **mer·ci·ful·ly** *adv*

mer·ci·less *adj* : having no mercy : PITILESS — **mer·ci·less·ly** *adv*

mer·cu·ric *adj* : of, relating to, or containing mercury

mer·cu·ry *n* **1** : a heavy silvery white metallic chemical element that is liquid at ordinary temperatures **2** : the column of mercury in a thermometer or barometer **3** *cap* : the planet that is nearest the sun and has a diameter of about 4700 kilometers

mer·cy *n, pl* **mer·cies** **1** : kind and gentle treatment of a wrongdoer, an opponent, or some unfortunate person **2** : a kind sympathetic disposition : willingness to forgive, spare, or help **3** : a blessing as an act of divine love **4** : a fortunate happening

mere *adj, superlative* **mer·est** : nothing more than : SIMPLE

mere·ly *adv* : nothing else than : JUST

merge *vb* **merged; merg·ing** : to be or cause to be combined or blended into a single unit

merg·er *n* : a combination of two or more businesses into one

me·rid·i·an *n* **1** : the highest point reached **2** : any imaginary semicircle on the earth reaching from the north to the south pole **3** : a representation of a meridian on a map or globe numbered according to degrees of longitude

me·ringue *n* **1** : a mixture of beaten white of egg and sugar put on pies or cakes and browned **2** : a shell made of baked meringue and filled with fruit or ice cream

me·ri·no *n, pl* **me·ri·nos** **1** : a sheep of a breed that produces a heavy fleece of white fine wool **2** : a fine soft fabric like cashmere

¹mer·it *n* **1** : the condition or fact of deserving well or ill **2** : ²WORTH 1, VALUE **3** : a quality worthy of praise : VIRTUE

²merit *vb* : to be worthy of or have a right to

mer·i·to·ri·ous *adj* : deserving reward or honor : PRAISEWORTHY — **mer·i·to·ri·ous·ly** *adv*

mer·maid *n* : an imaginary sea creature usually shown with a woman's body and a fish's tail

mer·man *n, pl* **mer·men** : an imaginary sea creature usually shown with a man's body and a fish's tail

mer·ri·ment *n* : GAIETY, MIRTH

mer·ry *adj* **mer·ri·er; mer·ri·est** **1** : full of good humor and good spirits : JOYOUS **2**

: full of gaiety or festivity — **mer·ri·ly** *adv*

mer·ry–go–round *n* : a circular revolving platform fitted with seats and figures of animals on which people sit for a ride

mer·ry·mak·er *n* : one taking part in merry-making

mer·ry·mak·ing *n* **1** : merry activity **2** : a festive occasion : PARTY

me·sa *n* : a hill with a flat top and steep sides

mesdames *pl of* MADAM *or of* MRS.

¹mesh *n* **1** : one of the spaces enclosed by the threads of a net or the wires of a sieve or screen **2** : NETWORK 1 **2** **3** : the coming or fitting together of the teeth of two sets of gears

²mesh *vb* : to fit together : INTERLOCK

Mes·o·zo·ic *n* : an era of geological history which extends from the Paleozoic to the Cenozoic and in which dinosaurs are present and the first birds and mammals and flowering plants appear

mes·quite *n* : a spiny shrub or small tree of the southwestern United States and Mexico that is related to the clovers

¹mess *n* **1** : a group of people (as military personnel) who regularly eat together **2** : the meal eaten by a mess **3** : a state of confusion or disorder

²mess *vb* **1** : to take meals with a mess **2** : to make dirty or untidy **3** : to mix up : BUNGLE **4** : to work without serious goal : PUTTER **5** : ²FOOL 2, INTERFERE

mes·sage *n* : a communication in writing, in speech, or by signals

mes·sen·ger *n* : a person who carries a message or does an errand

Messrs. *pl of* MR.

messy *adj* **mess·i·er; mess·i·est** : UNTIDY — **mess·i·ly** *adv* — **mess·i·ness** *n*

met *past of* MEET

met·a·bol·ic *adj* : of or relating to metabolism — **met·a·bol·i·cal·ly** *adv*

me·tab·o·lism *n* : the processes by which a living being uses food to obtain energy and build tissue and disposes of waste material

¹met·al *n* **1** : a substance (as gold, tin, copper, or bronze) that has a more or less shiny appearance, is a good conductor of electricity and heat, and usually can be made into a wire or hammered into a thin sheet **2** : METTLE

²metal *adj* : made of metal

me·tal·lic *adj* **1** : of, relating to, or being a metal **2** : containing or made of metal

met·al·lur·gi·cal *adj* : of or relating to metallurgy

met·al·lur·gy *n* : the science of obtaining metals from their ores and preparing them for use

meta·mor·phic *adj* : formed by the action of pressure, heat, and water that results in a more compact form

meta·mor·pho·sis *n, pl* **meta·mor·pho·ses** : a sudden and very great change especially in appearance or structure

met·a·phor *n* : a figure of speech comparing two unlike things without using *like* or *as*

mete *vb* **met·ed; met·ing** : ALLOT

me·te·or *n* : one of the small pieces of matter in the solar system that enter the earth's atmosphere where friction may cause them to glow and form a streak of light

me·te·or·ic *adj* **1** : of or relating to a meteor or group of meteors **2** : like a meteor in speed or in sudden and temporary brilliance

me·te·or·ite *n* : a meteor that reaches the surface of the earth

me·te·o·rol·o·gist *n* : a specialist in meteorology

me·te·o·rol·o·gy *n* : a science that deals with the atmosphere, weather, and weather forecasting

¹me·ter *n* **1** : a planned rhythm in poetry that is usually repeated **2** : the repeated pattern of musical beats in a measure

²meter *n* : a measure of length on which the metric system is based and which is equal to about 39.37 inches

³meter *n* : an instrument for measuring and sometimes recording the amount of something

-meter *n suffix* : instrument for measuring

meth·od *n* **1** : a certain way of doing something **2** : careful arrangement : PLAN

me·thod·i·cal *adj* **1** : showing or done or arranged by method **2** : following a method out of habit : SYSTEMATIC — **me·thod·i·cal·ly** *adv*

met·ric *adj* **1** : of or relating to measurement **2** : of or relating to the metric system

met·ri·cal *adj* : of or relating to meter (as in poetry or music)

metric system *n* : a system of weights and measures in which the meter is the unit of length and the kilogram is the unit of weight

metric ton *n* : a unit of weight equal to 1000 kilograms

met·ro·nome *n* : a device for marking exact musical tempo by regularly repeated ticks

me·trop·o·lis *n* **1** : the chief or capital city of a country, state, or region **2** : a large or important city

met·ro·pol·i·tan *adj* : of, relating to, or like that of a metropolis

met·tle *n* : strength of spirit : COURAGE — **on one's mettle** : aroused to do one's best

¹mew *vb* : to make a meow or a similar sound

²**mew** *n* : MEOW

¹**Mex·i·can** *adj* : of or relating to Mexico or the Mexicans

²**Mexican** *n* : a person born or living in Mexico

mi *n* : the third note of the musical scale

mi·ca *n* : a mineral that easily breaks into very thin transparent sheets

mice *pl of* MOUSE

micr- *or* **micro-** *prefix* **1** : small : tiny **2** : millionth

mi·crobe *n* : a very tiny and often harmful plant or animal : MICROORGANISM

mi·cro·com·put·er *n* : PERSONAL COMPUTER

mi·cro·film *n* : a film on which something (as printing or a drawing) is recorded in very much smaller size

mi·crom·e·ter *n* **1** : an instrument used with a telescope or microscope for measuring very small distances **2** : MICROMETER CALIPER

micrometer caliper *n* : an instrument having a rod moved by fine screw threads and used for making exact measurements

mi·cro·or·gan·ism *n* : an organism (as a bacterium) of microscopic or less than microscopic size

mi·cro·phone *n* : an instrument in which sound is changed into an electrical effect for transmitting or recording (as in radio or television)

mi·cro·pro·ces·sor *n* : a computer processor contained on an integrated-circuit chip

mi·cro·scope *n* : an instrument with one or more lenses used to help a person to see something very small by making it appear larger

mi·cro·scop·ic *adj* **1** : of, relating to, or conducted with the microscope **2** : so small as to be visible only through a microscope : very tiny — **mi·cro·scop·i·cal·ly** *adv*

¹**mi·cro·wave** *n* **1** : a radio wave between one millimeter and one meter in wavelength **2** : MICROWAVE OVEN

²**microwave** *vb* : to cook or heat in a microwave oven

microwave oven *n* : an oven in which food is cooked by the heat produced as a result of penetration of the food by microwaves

¹**mid** *adj* : being the part in the middle

²**mid** *prep* : AMID

mid·air *n* : a region in the air some distance above the ground

mid·day *n* : NOON

¹**mid·dle** *adj* **1** : equally distant from the ends : CENTRAL **2** : being at neither extreme

²**middle** *n* : the middle part, point, or position : CENTER

middle age *n* : the period of life from about forty to about sixty years of age — **mid·dle–aged** *adj*

Middle Ages *n pl* : the period of European history from about A.D. 500 to about 1500

middle class *n* : a social class between that of the wealthy and the poor

middle school *n* : a school usually including grades 5 to 8 or 6 to 8

mid·dy *n, pl* **middies** **1** : MIDSHIPMAN **2** : a loose blouse with a collar cut wide and square in the back

midge *n* : a very small fly or gnat

midg·et *n* : one (as a person) that is much smaller than usual or normal

mid·night *n* : twelve o'clock at night

mid·rib *n* : the central vein of a leaf

mid·riff *n* **1** : the middle part of the surface of the human body **2** : a part of a garment that covers the midriff

mid·ship·man *n, pl* **mid·ship·men** : a student naval officer

¹**midst** *n* **1** : the inside or central part **2** : a position among the members of a group **3** : the condition of being surrounded

²**midst** *prep* : in the midst of

mid·stream *n* : the part of a stream away from both sides

mid·sum·mer *n* **1** : the middle of summer **2** : the summer solstice

mid·way *adv or adj* : in the middle of the way or distance : HALFWAY

mid·win·ter *n* **1** : the middle of winter **2** : the winter solstice

mid·year *n* : the middle of a year

mien *n* : a person's appearance or way of acting that shows mood or personality

¹**might** *past of* MAY — used as a helping verb to show that something is possible but not likely

²**might** *n* : power that can be used (as by a person or group)

mightn't : might not

¹**mighty** *adj* **might·i·er; might·i·est** **1** : having great power or strength **2** : done by might : showing great power **3** : great in influence, size, or effect — **might·i·ly** *adv*

²**mighty** *adv* : ²VERY 1

mi·grant *n* : one that migrates

mi·grate *vb* **mi·grat·ed; mi·grat·ing** **1** : to move from one country or region to another **2** : to pass from one region to another on a regular schedule

mi·gra·tion *n* **1** : the act or an instance of migrating **2** : a group of individuals that are migrating

mi·gra·to·ry *adj* **1** : having a way of life that includes making migrations **2** : of or relating to migration

mike *n* : MICROPHONE

milch *adj* : giving milk : kept for milking

mild *adj* **1** : gentle in personality or behavior **2** : not strong or harsh in action or effect — **mild·ly** *adv* — **mild·ness** *n*

1mil·dew *n* **1** : a thin whitish growth of fungus on decaying material or on living plants **2** : a fungus that grows as a mildew

2mildew *vb* : to become affected with mildew

mile *n* **1** : a measure of distance (**statute mile**) equal to 5280 feet (1609 meters) **2** : a measure of distance (**geographical mile** or **nautical mile**) equal to about 6076 feet (1852 meters)

mile·age *n* **1** : an amount of money given for traveling expenses at a certain rate per mile **2** : distance or distance covered in miles **3** : the number of miles that something (as a car or tire) will travel before wearing out **4** : the average number of miles a car or truck will travel on a gallon of fuel

mile·stone *n* **1** : a stone showing the distance in miles to a stated place **2** : an important point in progress or development

1mil·i·tary *adj* **1** : of or relating to soldiers, the army, or war **2** : carried on by soldiers : supported by armed force

2military *n, pl* **military** : members of the armed forces

mi·li·tia *n* : a body of citizens having some military training but called into service only in emergencies

1milk *n* **1** : a whitish liquid secreted by the breasts or udder of a female mammal as food for her young **2** : a liquid (as a plant juice) like milk

2milk *vb* : to draw off the milk of (as by pressing or sucking)

milk·maid *n* : DAIRYMAID

milk·man *n, pl* **milk·men** : a person who sells or delivers milk

milk of mag·ne·sia : a white liquid containing an oxide of magnesium in water and used as a laxative

milk shake *n* : a drink made of milk, a flavoring syrup, and ice cream shaken or mixed thoroughly

milk tooth *n* : one of the first and temporary teeth that in humans number twenty

milk·weed *n* : any of a group of plants with milky juice and flowers in dense clusters

milky *adj* **milk·i·er; milk·i·est 1** : like milk in color or thickness **2** : full of or containing milk — **milk·i·ness** *n*

Milky Way *n* **1** : a broad band of light that stretches across the sky and is caused by the light of a very great number of faint stars **2** : MILKY WAY GALAXY

Milky Way galaxy *n* : the galaxy of which the sun and the solar system are a part and which contains the stars that make up the Milky Way

1mill *n* **1** : a building in which grain is ground into flour **2** : a machine used in processing (as by grinding, crushing, stamping, cutting, or finishing) raw material **3** : a factory using machines

2mill *vb* **1** : to grind into flour or powder **2** : to shape or finish by means of a rotating cutter **3** : to give a raised rim to (a coin) **4** : to move about in a circle or in disorder

3mill *n* : one tenth of a cent

mil·len·ni·um *n, pl* **mil·len·nia** *or* **millenniums 1** : a period of 1000 years **2** : a 1000th anniversary or its celebration — **mil·len·ni·al** *adj*

mill·er *n* **1** : a person who works in or runs a flour mill **2** : a moth whose wings seem to be covered with flour or dust

mil·let *n* : an annual grass with clusters of small usually white seeds that is grown as a cereal and for animals to graze

milli- *prefix* : thousandth

mil·li·gram *n* : a unit of weight equal to $1/1000$ gram

mil·li·li·ter *n* : a unit of capacity equal to $1/1000$ liter

mil·li·me·ter *n* : a unit of length equal to $1/1000$ meter

mil·li·ner *n* : a person who makes, trims, or sells women's hats

1mil·lion *n* **1** : one thousand thousands : 1,000,000 **2** : a very large number

2million *adj* : being 1,000,000

mil·lion·aire *n* : a person having a million dollars or more

1mil·lionth *adj* : being last in a series of a million

2millionth *n* : number 1,000,000 in a series

mil·li·pede *n* : an animal that is an arthropod with a long body somewhat like that of a centipede but with two pairs of legs on most of its many body sections

mill·stone *n* : either of two circular stones used for grinding grain

mill wheel *n* : a waterwheel that drives a mill

mim·eo·graph *n* : a machine for making copies of typewritten, written, or drawn matter by means of stencils

1mim·ic *n* : one that mimics another

2mimic *vb* **mim·icked; mim·ick·ing 1** : to imitate very closely **2** : to make fun of by imitating

min·a·ret *n* : a tall slender tower of a mosque with a balcony from which the people are called to prayer

mince *vb* **minced; minc·ing 1** : to cut or chop very fine **2** : to act or speak in an unnaturally dainty way **3** : to keep (what one says) within the bounds of politeness

mince·meat *n* : a mixture of finely chopped and cooked raisins, apples, suet, spices, and sometimes meat that is used chiefly as a filling for pie (**mince pie**)

1mind *n* **1** : MEMORY 1 **2** : the part of a person that feels, understands, thinks, wills, and especially reasons **3** : INTENTION 1 **4** : OPINION 1

2mind *vb* **1** : to pay attention to : HEED **2** : to pay careful attention to and obey **3** : to be bothered about **4** : to object to : DISLIKE **5** : to take charge of

mind·ed *adj* **1** : having a specified kind of mind **2** : greatly interested in one thing

mind·ful *adj* : keeping in mind

1mine *pron* : that which belongs to me

2mine *n* **1** : a pit or tunnel from which minerals (as coal, gold, or diamonds) are taken **2** : an explosive buried in the ground and set to explode when disturbed (as by an enemy soldier or vehicle) **3** : an explosive placed in a case and sunk in the water to sink enemy ships **4** : a rich source of supply

3mine *vb* **mined; min·ing 1** : to dig a mine **2** : to obtain from a mine **3** : to work in a mine **4** : to dig or form mines under a place **5** : to lay military mines in or under — **min·er** *n*

1min·er·al *n* **1** : a naturally occurring substance (as diamond or quartz) that results from processes other than those of plants and animals **2** : a naturally occurring substance (as ore, coal, petroleum, natural gas, or water) obtained for humans to use usually from the ground

2mineral *adj* **1** : of or relating to minerals **2** : containing gases or mineral salts

mineral kingdom *n* : a basic group of natural objects that includes objects consisting of matter that does not come from plants and animals

min·gle *vb* **min·gled; min·gling 1** : to mix or be mixed so that the original parts can still be recognized **2** : to move among others within a group

mini- *prefix* : very short or small

1min·i·a·ture *n* **1** : a copy on a much reduced scale **2** : a very small portrait especially on ivory or metal

2miniature *adj* : very small : represented on a small scale

min·i·mize *vb* **min·i·mized; min·i·miz·ing** : to make as small as possible

1min·i·mum *n, pl* **min·i·ma** *or* **min·i·mums** : the lowest amount

2minimum *adj* : being the least possible

min·ing *n* : the process or business of working mines

1min·is·ter *n* **1** : a Protestant clergyman **2** : a government official at the head of a section of government activities **3** : a person who represents his or her government in a foreign country

2minister *vb* : to give aid or service

min·is·try *n, pl* **min·is·tries 1** : the act of ministering **2** : the office or duties of a minister **3** : a body of ministers **4** : a section of a government headed by a minister

mink *n* **1** : an animal related to the weasel that has partly webbed feet and lives around water **2** : the soft thick usually brown fur of a mink

min·now *n* **1** : any of various small freshwater fishes (as a shiner) related to the carps **2** : a fish that looks like a true minnow

1mi·nor *adj* **1** : less in size, importance, or value **2** : of or relating to a musical scale having the third tone lowered a half step

2minor *n* : a person too young to have full civil rights

mi·nor·i·ty *n, pl* **mi·nor·i·ties 1** : the state of being a minor **2** : a number less than half of a total **3** : a part of a population that is in some ways different from others and that is sometimes disliked or given unfair treatment

min·strel *n* **1** : an entertainer in the Middle Ages who sang verses and played a harp **2** : one of a group of entertainers with blackened faces who sing, dance, and tell jokes

1mint *n* **1** : any of a group of fragrant herbs and shrubs (as catnip or peppermint) with square stems **2** : a piece of candy flavored with mint

2mint *n* **1** : a place where metals are made into coins **2** : a great amount especially of money

3mint *vb* **1** : 2COIN 1 **2** : to make into coin

min·u·end *n* : a number from which another number is to be subtracted

min·u·et *n* : a slow stately dance

1mi·nus *prep* **1** : with the subtraction of : LESS **2** : 1WITHOUT 2

2minus *adj* : located in the lower part of a range

minus sign *n* : a sign – used especially in mathematics to indicate subtraction (as in 8–6=2) or a quantity less than zero (as in –10°)

1min·ute *n* **1** : the sixtieth part of an hour or of a degree : sixty seconds **2** : MOMENT 1 **3 minutes** *pl* : a brief record of what happened during a meeting

2mi·nute *adj* **mi·nut·er; mi·nut·est 1** : very small : TINY **2** : paying attention to small details — **mi·nute·ly** *adv*

min·ute·man *n, pl* **min·ute·men** : a member of a group of armed men ready to fight at a minute's notice immediately before and during the American Revolution

mir·a·cle *n* **1** : an extraordinary event taken as a sign of the power of God **2** : something very rare, unusual, or wonderful

mi·rac·u·lous *adj* : being or being like a miracle — **mi·rac·u·lous·ly** *adv*

mi·rage *n* : an illusion sometimes seen at sea, in the desert, or over hot pavement that looks like a pool of water or a mirror in which distant objects are glimpsed

¹mire *n* : heavy deep mud

²mire *vb* **mired; mir·ing** : to stick or cause to stick fast in mire

¹mir·ror *n* **1** : a glass coated on the back with a reflecting substance **2** : something that gives a true likeness or description

²mirror *vb* : to reflect in or as if in a mirror

mirth *n* : the state of being happy or merry as shown by laughter

mirth·ful *adj* : full of or showing mirth — **mirth·ful·ly** *adv*

mis- *prefix* **1** : in a way that is bad or wrong **2** : bad : wrong **3** : opposite or lack of

mis·ad·ven·ture *n* : an unfortunate or unpleasant event

mis·be·have *vb* **mis·be·haved; mis·be·hav·ing** : to behave badly

mis·car·ry *vb* **mis·car·ried; mis·car·ry·ing** : to go wrong : FAIL

mis·cel·la·neous *adj* : consisting of many things of different sorts

mis·chance *n* **1** : bad luck **2** : a piece of bad luck : MISHAP

mis·chief *n* **1** : injury or damage caused by a person **2** : conduct that annoys or bothers

mis·chie·vous *adj* **1** : harming or intended to do harm **2** : causing or likely to cause minor injury or harm **3** : showing a spirit of irresponsible fun or playfulness — **mis·chie·vous·ly** *adv* — **mis·chie·vous·ness** *n*

¹mis·con·duct *n* : wrong conduct : bad behavior

²mis·con·duct *vb* : to manage badly

mis·count *vb* : to count incorrectly

mis·cre·ant *n* : VILLAIN, RASCAL

mis·cue *n* : ²MISTAKE 2

mis·deal *vb* **mis·dealt; mis·deal·ing** : to deal in an incorrect way

mis·deed *n* : a bad action

mis·di·rect *vb* : to direct incorrectly

mi·ser *n* : a stingy person who lives poorly in order to store up and save money

mis·er·a·ble *adj* **1** : very unsatisfactory **2** : causing great discomfort **3** : very unhappy or distressed : WRETCHED — **mis·er·a·bly** *adv*

mi·ser·ly *adj* : of, relating to, or like a miser

mis·ery *n, pl* **mis·er·ies** : suffering or distress due to being poor, in pain, or unhappy

mis·fit *n* **1** : something that fits badly **2** : a person who cannot adjust to an environment

mis·for·tune *n* **1** : bad luck **2** : an unfortunate situation or event

mis·giv·ing *n* : a feeling of distrust or doubt especially about what is going to happen

mis·guid·ed *adj* : having mistaken ideas or rules of conduct

mis·hap *n* : an unfortunate accident

mis·judge *vb* **mis·judged; mis·judg·ing** : to judge incorrectly or unjustly

mis·lay *vb* **mis·laid; mis·lay·ing** : to put in a place later forgotten : LOSE

mis·lead *vb* **mis·led; mis·lead·ing** : to lead in a wrong direction or into error

mis·place *vb* **mis·placed; mis·plac·ing** **1** : to put in a wrong place **2** : MISLAY

mis·print *n* : a mistake in printing

mis·pro·nounce *vb* **mis·pro·nounced; mis·pro·nounc·ing** : to pronounce in a way considered incorrect

mis·pro·nun·ci·a·tion *n* : incorrect pronunciation

mis·read *vb* **mis·read; mis·read·ing** **1** : to read incorrectly **2** : MISUNDERSTAND 2

mis·rep·re·sent *vb* : to give a false or misleading idea of

¹miss *vb* **1** : to fail to hit, catch, reach, or get **2** : ¹ESCAPE 2 **3** : to fail to have or go to **4** : to be aware of the absence of : want to be with

²miss *n* : failure to hit or catch

³miss *n* **1** — used as a title before the name of an unmarried woman **2** : young lady — used without a name as a form of polite address to a girl or young woman

mis·shap·en *adj* : badly shaped

mis·sile *n* : an object (as a stone, arrow, bullet, or rocket) that is dropped, thrown, shot, or launched usually so as to strike something at a distance

miss·ing *adj* **1** : ¹ABSENT 1 **2** : ²LOST 4

mis·sion *n* **1** : a group of missionaries **2** : a place where the work of missionaries is carried on **3** : a group of persons sent by a government to represent it in a foreign country **4** : a task that is assigned or begun

¹mis·sion·ary *adj* : of or relating to religious missions

²missionary *n, pl* **mis·sion·ar·ies** : a person sent (as to a foreign country) to spread a religious faith

mis·sive *n* : ¹LETTER 2

mis·spell *vb* : to spell in an incorrect way

mis·spend *vb* **mis·spent; mis·spend·ing** : ²WASTE 2

mis·step *n* **1** : a wrong step **2** : ²MISTAKE 2, SLIP

¹mist *n* **1** : particles of water floating in the air or falling as fine rain **2** : something that keeps one from seeing or understanding clearly

²**mist** *vb* **1** : to be or become misty **2** : to become or cause to become dim or blurred **3** : to cover with mist

¹**mis·take** *vb* **mis·took; mis·tak·en; mis·tak·ing 1** : MISUNDERSTAND 2 **2** : to fail to recognize correctly

²**mistake** *n* **1** : a wrong judgment **2** : a wrong action or statement

mis·tak·en *adj* **1** : being in error : judging wrongly **2** : ²WRONG 2, INCORRECT — **mis·tak·en·ly** *adv*

mis·ter *n* **1** *cap* — used sometimes in writing instead of the usual *Mr.* **2** : SIR 2

mis·tle·toe *n* : a green plant with waxy white berries that grows on the branches and trunks of trees

mis·treat *vb* : to treat badly : ABUSE

mis·tress *n* : a woman who has control or authority

¹**mis·trust** *n* : ¹DISTRUST

²**mistrust** *vb* **1** : ²DISTRUST, SUSPECT **2** : to lack confidence in

misty *adj* **mist·i·er; mist·i·est 1** : full of mist **2** : clouded by or as if by mist **3** : VAGUE 3, INDISTINCT — **mist·i·ly** *adv* — **mist·i·ness** *n*

mis·un·der·stand *vb* **mis·un·der·stood; mis·un·der·stand·ing 1** : to fail to understand **2** : to take in a wrong meaning or way

mis·un·der·stand·ing *n* **1** : a failure to understand **2** : DISAGREEMENT 3, QUARREL

¹**mis·use** *vb* **mis·used; mis·us·ing 1** : to use in a wrong way **2** : ²ABUSE 3, MIS·TREAT

²**mis·use** *n* : incorrect or improper use

mite *n* **1** : any of various tiny spiderlike animals often living on plants, animals, and stored foods **2** : a very small coin or amount of money **3** : a very small object or creature

mi·to·sis *n, pl* **mi·to·ses** : a process of cell division in which two new nuclei are formed each containing the original number of chromosomes

mitt *n* **1** : MITTEN **2** : a baseball catcher's or first baseman's glove

mit·ten *n* : a covering for the hand and wrist having a separate division for the thumb only

¹**mix** *vb* **1** : to make into one mass by stirring together : BLEND **2** : to make by combining different things **3** : to become one mass through blending **4** : CONFUSE 1 — **mixer** *n*

²**mix** *n* : MIXTURE 2

mixed *adj* **1** : made up of two or more kinds **2** : made up of persons of both sexes

mixed number *or* **mixed numeral** *n* : a

number (as 1²/₃) made up of a whole number and a fraction

mix·ture *n* **1** : the act of mixing **2** : something mixed or being mixed **3** : two or more substances mixed together in such a way that each remains unchanged

mix-up *n* : an instance of confusion

miz·zen *n* **1** : a fore-and-aft sail set on the mizzenmast **2** : MIZZENMAST

miz·zen·mast *n* : the mast behind or next behind the mainmast

¹**moan** *n* **1** : a long low sound showing pain or grief **2** : a mournful sound

²**moan** *vb* **1** : COMPLAIN 1 **2** : to utter a moan

moat *n* : a deep wide ditch around the walls of a castle or fort that is usually filled with water

¹**mob** *n* **1** : the common masses of people **2** : a rowdy excited crowd

²**mob** *vb* **mobbed; mob·bing** : to crowd about and attack or annoy

¹**mo·bile** *adj* **1** : easily moved : MOVABLE **2** : changing quickly in expression

²**mo·bile** *n* : an artistic structure whose parts can be moved especially by air currents

mo·bi·lize *vb* **mo·bi·lized; mo·bi·liz·ing** : to assemble (as military forces) and make ready for action

moc·ca·sin *n* **1** : a soft shoe with no heel and the sole and sides made of one piece **2** : a poisonous snake of the southern United States

moccasin flower *n* : LADY'S SLIPPER

¹**mock** *vb* **1** : to treat with scorn : RIDICULE **2** : ³MIMIC 2

²**mock** *adj* : not real : MAKE-BELIEVE

mock·ery *n, pl* **mock·er·ies 1** : the act of mocking **2** : a bad imitation : FAKE

mock·ing·bird *n* : a songbird of the southern United States noted for its sweet song and imitations of other birds

mock orange *n* : SYRINGA

¹**mode** *n* **1** : a particular form or variety of something **2** : a form or manner of expressing or acting : WAY

²**mode** *n* : a popular fashion or style

¹**mod·el** *n* **1** : a small but exact copy of a thing **2** : a pattern or figure of something to be made **3** : a person who sets a good example **4** : a person who poses for an artist or photographer **5** : a person who wears and displays garments that are for sale **6** : a special type of a product

²**model** *vb* **mod·eled** *or* **mod·elled; mod·el·ing** *or* **mod·el·ling 1** : to plan or shape after a pattern **2** : to make a model of **3** : to act or serve as a model

³**model** *adj* **1** : worthy of being imitated **2** : being a miniature copy

mo·dem *n* : a device that changes electrical signals from one form to another and is used especially to send or receive computer data over a telephone line

¹mod·er·ate *adj* **1** : neither too much nor too little **2** : neither very good nor very bad **3** : not expensive : REASONABLE — **mod·er·ate·ly** *adv*

²mod·er·ate *vb* **mod·er·at·ed; mod·er·at·ing** : to make or become less violent or severe

mod·er·a·tion *n* **1** : the act of moderating **2** : the condition of being moderate

mod·ern *adj* **1** : of, relating to, or characteristic of the present time or times not long past **2** : of the period from about 1500

mod·ern·ize *vb* **mod·ern·ized; mod·ern·iz·ing** : to make or become modern

mod·est *adj* **1** : having a limited and not too high opinion of oneself and one's abilities : not boastful **2** : limited in size or amount **3** : clean and proper in thought, conduct, and dress — **mod·est·ly** *adv*

mod·es·ty *n* : the quality of being modest

mod·i·fi·ca·tion *n* **1** : the act of modifying **2** : the result of modifying : a slightly changed form

mod·i·fi·er *n* : a word (as an adjective or adverb) used with another word to limit its meaning

mod·i·fy *vb* **mod·i·fied; mod·i·fy·ing** **1** : to make changes in **2** : to lower or reduce in amount or scale **3** : to limit in meaning : QUALIFY

mod·u·late *vb* **mod·u·lat·ed; mod·u·lat·ing** **1** : to bring into proper proportion **2** : to tone down : SOFTEN

mod·ule *n* : an independent unit of a spacecraft

mo·hair *n* : a fabric or yarn made from the long silky hair of an Asian goat

Mohammedan, Mohammedanism *variant of* MUHAMMADAN, MUHAMMADANISM

moist *adj* : slightly wet : DAMP — **moist·ness** *n*

moist·en *vb* : to make moist

mois·ture *n* : a small amount of liquid that causes moistness

mo·lar *n* : a tooth with a broad surface used for grinding : a back tooth

mo·las·ses *n* : a thick brown syrup that drains from sugar as it is being made

¹mold *or* **mould** *n* : light rich crumbly earth that contains decaying material

²mold *or* **mould** *n* **1** : a hollow form in which something is shaped **2** : something shaped in a mold

³mold *or* **mould** *vb* **1** : to work and press into shape **2** : to form in or as if in a mold

⁴mold *n* **1** : an often woolly surface growth of fungus on damp or decaying material **2** : a fungus that forms mold

⁵mold *vb* : to become moldy

mold·er *vb* : to crumble to bits by slow decay

mold·ing *n* **1** : the act or work of a person who molds **2** : a strip of material having a shaped surface and used as a decoration (as on a wall or the edge of a table)

moldy *adj* **mold·i·er; mold·i·est** : covered with or containing mold

¹mole *n* : a small usually brown spot on the skin

²mole *n* : a small burrowing animal with very soft fur and very tiny eyes

mo·lec·u·lar *adj* : of or relating to a molecule

mol·e·cule *n* **1** : the smallest portion of a substance having the properties of the substance **2** : a very small particle

mole·hill *n* : a little ridge of earth pushed up by moles as they burrow underground

mo·lest *vb* : to disturb or injure by interfering

mol·li·fy *vb* **mol·li·fied; mol·li·fy·ing** : to soothe in temper or disposition

mol·lusk *n* : any of a large group of animals (as clams, snails, and octopuses) most of which live in water and have the body protected by a limy shell

molt *or* **moult** *vb* : to shed outer material (as hair, shell, or horns) that will be replaced by a new growth

mol·ten *adj* : melted especially by very great heat

mo·lyb·de·num *n* : a white metallic chemical element used in some steel to give greater strength and hardness

mom *n* : ¹MOTHER 1

mo·ment *n* **1** : a very brief time **2** : IMPORTANCE

mo·men·tary *adj* : lasting only a moment — **mo·men·tar·i·ly** *adv*

mo·men·tous *adj* : very important — **mo·men·tous·ness** *n*

mo·men·tum *n* : the force that a moving body has because of its weight and motion

mom·my *n, pl* **mom·mies** : ¹MOTHER 1

mon- *or* **mono-** *prefix* : one : single : alone

mon·arch *n* **1** : a person who reigns over a kingdom or empire **2** : a large orange and black American butterfly

mon·ar·chy *n, pl* **mon·ar·chies** **1** : a state or country having a monarch **2** : the system of government by a monarch

mon·as·tery *n, pl* **mon·as·ter·ies** : a place where a community of monks live and work

mo·nas·tic *adj* : of or relating to monks or monasteries

Mon·day *n* : the second day of the week

mon·e·tary *adj* : of or relating to money

mon·ey *n, pl* **moneys** *or* **mon·ies** 1 : metal (as gold, silver, or copper) coined or stamped and issued for use in buying and selling 2 : a printed or engraved certificate (**paper money**) legal for use in place of metal money 3 : wealth figured in terms of money

money order *n* : a piece of paper like a check that can be bought (as at a post office) and that tells another office to pay the sum of money printed on it to the one named

¹Mon·go·lian *adj* : of or relating to Mongolia or the Mongolians

²Mongolian *n* : a person born or living in Mongolia

mon·goose *n, pl* **mon·goos·es** : a long thin furry animal that eats snakes, eggs, and rodents

¹mon·grel *n* : one (as a plant, person, or thing) of mixed or uncertain kind or origin

²mongrel *adj* : of mixed or uncertain kind or origin

¹mon·i·tor *n* 1 : a pupil in a school picked for a special duty (as keeping order) 2 : a person or thing that watches or checks something 3 : a video screen used for display (as of television pictures or computer information)

²monitor *vb* : to watch or check for a special reason

monk *n* : a member of a religious group of men who form a community and promise to stay poor, obey all the laws of their community, and not get married

¹mon·key *n, pl* **monkeys** 1 : any of a group of mostly tropical furry animals that have a long tail and that along with the apes are most closely related to humans in the animal kingdom 2 : a mischievous child

²monkey *vb* **mon·keyed; mon·key·ing** 1 : to act in a mischievous way 2 : ²TRIFLE 3, FOOL

mon·key·shine *n* : PRANK

monkey wrench *n* : a wrench with one fixed and one adjustable jaw

monks·hood *n* : a tall poisonous Old World plant related to the buttercups that is grown for its white or purplish flowers that are shaped like hoods or as a source of drugs

mono- — see MON-

mono·gram *n* : a design usually made by combining two or more of a person's initials

mono·plane *n* : an airplane with only one set of wings

mo·nop·o·lize *vb* **mo·nop·o·lized; mo·nop·o·liz·ing** : to get or have complete control over

mo·nop·o·ly *n, pl* **mo·nop·o·lies** 1 : complete control of the entire supply of goods or a service in a certain market 2 : complete possession 3 : a person or group having a monopoly

mono·syl·la·ble *n* : a word of one syllable

mo·not·o·nous *adj* : boring from being always the same — **mo·not·o·nous·ly** *adv*

mo·not·o·ny *n, pl* **mo·not·o·nies** : a boring lack of change

mon·soon *n* 1 : a wind in the Indian ocean and southern Asia that blows from the southwest from April to October and from the northeast from October to April 2 : the rainy season that comes with the southwest monsoon

mon·ster *n* 1 : an animal or plant that is very unlike the usual type 2 : a strange or horrible creature 3 : something unusually large 4 : an extremely wicked or cruel person

mon·strous *adj* 1 : unusually large : ENORMOUS 2 : very bad or wrong 3 : very different from the usual form : ABNORMAL — **mon·strous·ly** *adv*

month *n* : one of the twelve parts into which the year is divided

¹month·ly *adj* 1 : happening, done, or published every month 2 : figured in terms of one month 3 : lasting a month

²monthly *n, pl* **monthlies** : a magazine published every month

mon·u·ment *n* 1 : a structure (as a building, stone, or statue) made to keep alive the memory of a person or event 2 : a work, saying, or deed that lasts or is worth keeping or remembering

¹moo *vb* **mooed; moo·ing** : to make a moo : LOW

²moo *n, pl* **moos** : the low sound made by a cow

¹mood *n* : a state or frame of mind : DISPOSITION

²mood *n* : a set of forms of a verb that show whether the action or state expressed is to be thought of as a fact, a command, or a wish or possibility

moody *adj* **mood·i·er; mood·i·est** : often feeling gloomy or in a bad mood — **mood·i·ly** *adv* — **mood·i·ness** *n*

¹moon *n* 1 : the natural celestial body that shines by reflecting light from the sun and revolves about the earth in about $29^1/_2$ days 2 : SATELLITE 1 3 : MONTH

²moon *vb* : to waste time by daydreaming

moon·beam *n* : a ray of light from the moon

moon·light *n* : the light of the moon

moon·stone *n* : a partly transparent shining stone used as a gem

¹moor *n* : an area of open land that is too wet or too poor for farming

²**moor** *vb* : to fasten in place with cables, lines, or anchors

moor·ing *n* 1 : a place where or an object to which a boat can be fastened 2 : a chain or line by which an object is moored

moor·land *n* : land consisting of moors

moose *n* : a large deerlike animal with broad flattened antlers and humped shoulders that lives in forests of Canada and the northern United States

¹**mop** *n* 1 : a tool for cleaning made of a bundle of cloth or yarn or a sponge fastened to a handle 2 : something that looks like a cloth or yarn mop

²**mop** *vb* **mopped; mop·ping** : to wipe or clean with or as if with a mop

¹**mope** *vb* **moped; mop·ing** : to be in a dull and sad state of mind

²**mope** *n* : a person without any energy or enthusiasm

mo·raine *n* : a pile of earth and stones left by a glacier

¹**mor·al** *adj* 1 : concerned with or relating to what is right and wrong in human behavior 2 : able or fit to teach a lesson 3 : ¹GOOD 7, VIRTUOUS 4 : able to tell right from wrong — **mor·al·ly** *adv*

²**moral** *n* 1 : the lesson to be learned from a story or experience 2 **morals** *pl* : moral conduct 3 **morals** *pl* : moral teachings or rules of behavior

mo·rale *n* : the condition of the mind or feelings (as in relation to enthusiasm, spirit, or hope) of an individual or group

mo·ral·i·ty *n, pl* **mo·ral·i·ties** 1 : moral quality : VIRTUE 2 : moral conduct

mo·rass *n* : MARSH, SWAMP

mor·bid *adj* : not healthy or normal

¹**more** *adj* 1 : greater in amount, number, or size 2 : ¹EXTRA, ADDITIONAL

²**more** *adv* 1 : in addition 2 : to a greater extent — often used with an adjective or adverb to form the comparative

³**more** *n* 1 : a greater amount or number 2 : an additional amount

more·over *adv* : in addition to what has been said : BESIDES

morn *n* : MORNING

morn·ing *n* : the early part of the day : the time from sunrise to noon

morning glory *n* : a vine that climbs by twisting around something and has large bright flowers that close in the sunshine

morning star *n* : any of the planets Venus, Jupiter, Mars, Mercury, or Saturn when rising before the sun

mo·ron *n* : a person with less than ordinary mental ability but able to do simple routine work

mor·phine *n* : a habit-forming drug made from opium and used often to relieve pain

mor·row *n* : the next following day

mor·sel *n* 1 : a small piece of food : BITE 2 : a small amount : a little piece

¹**mor·tal** *adj* 1 : capable of causing death : FATAL 2 : certain to die 3 : very unfriendly 4 : very great or overpowering 5 : ¹HUMAN 1 — **mor·tal·ly** *adv*

²**mortal** *n* : a human being

¹**mor·tar** *n* 1 : a strong deep bowl in which substances are pounded or crushed with a pestle 2 : a short light cannon used to shoot shells high into the air

²**mortar** *n* : a building material made of lime and cement mixed with sand and water that is spread between bricks or stones so as to hold them together when it hardens

mor·ti·fy *vb* **mor·ti·fied; mor·ti·fy·ing** : to embarrass greatly : SHAME

mo·sa·ic *n* : a decoration on a surface made by setting small pieces of glass or stone of different colors into another material so as to make patterns or pictures

Moslem *variant of* MUSLIM

mosque *n* : a Muslim place of worship

mos·qui·to *n, pl* **mos·qui·toes** : a small two-winged fly the female of which punctures the skin of people and animals to suck their blood

moss *n* 1 : any of a class of plants that have no flowers and grow as small leafy stems in cushion-like patches clinging to rocks, bark, or damp ground 2 : any of various plants (as lichens) resembling moss

mossy *adj* **moss·i·er; moss·i·est** : like or covered with moss

¹**most** *adj* 1 : the majority of 2 : greatest in amount or extent

²**most** *adv* 1 : to the greatest or highest level or extent — often used with an adjective or adverb to form the superlative 2 : to a very great extent

³**most** *n* : the greatest amount, number, or part

most·ly *adv* : for the greatest part

mote *n* : a small particle : SPECK

mo·tel *n* : a building or group of buildings which provide lodgings and in which the rooms are usually reached directly from an outdoor parking area

moth *n, pl* **moths** 1 : CLOTHES MOTH 2 : an insect that usually flies at night and has mostly feathery antennae and stouter body, duller coloring, and smaller wings than the related butterflies

¹**moth·er** *n* 1 : a female parent 2 : a nun in charge of a convent 3 : ¹CAUSE 1, ORIGIN — **moth·er·hood** *n* — **moth·er·less** *adj*

²**mother** *adj* 1 : of or having to do with a

mother **2 :** being in the relation of a mother to others **3 :** gotten from or as if from one's mother

³mother *vb* **:** to be or act as a mother to

moth·er·board *n* **:** the main circuit board especially of a small computer

moth·er–in–law *n, pl* **mothers–in–law :** the mother of one's husband or wife

moth·er·ly *adj* **1 :** of, relating to, or characteristic of a mother **2 :** like a mother **:** MATERNAL

moth·er–of–pearl *n* **:** a hard pearly material that lines the shell of some mollusks (as mussels) and is often used for ornamental objects and buttons

¹mo·tion *n* **1 :** a formal plan or suggestion for action offered according to the rules of a meeting **2 :** the act or process of changing place or position **:** MOVEMENT — **mo·tion·less** *adj* — **mo·tion·less·ness** *n*

²motion *vb* **:** to direct or signal by a movement or sign

motion picture *n* **1 :** a series of pictures projected on a screen rapidly one after another so as to give the appearance of a continuous picture in which the objects move **2 :** MOVIE 1

mo·ti·vate *vb* **mo·ti·vat·ed; mo·ti·vat·ing :** to provide with a reason for doing something

¹mo·tive *n* **:** a reason for doing something

²motive *adj* **:** causing motion

mot·ley *adj* **1 :** having various colors **2 :** composed of various often unlike kinds or parts

¹mo·tor *n* **1 :** a machine that produces motion or power for doing work **2 :** ²AUTOMOBILE — **mo·tored** *adj*

²motor *adj* **1 :** causing or controlling activity (as motion) **2 :** equipped with or driven by a motor **3 :** of or relating to an automobile **4 :** designed for motor vehicles or motorists

³motor *vb* **:** ¹DRIVE 3

mo·tor·bike *n* **:** a light motorcycle

mo·tor·boat *n* **:** an often small boat driven by a motor

mo·tor·car *n* **:** ²AUTOMOBILE

mo·tor·cy·cle *n* **:** a vehicle for one or two passengers that has two wheels and is driven by a motor

mo·tor·ist *n* **:** a person who travels by automobile

mo·tor·ize *vb* **mo·tor·ized; mo·tor·iz·ing :** to equip with a motor or with motor-driven vehicles

motor scooter *n* **:** a motorized vehicle having two or three wheels like a child's scooter but having a seat

motor vehicle *n* **:** a motorized vehicle (as an automobile or motorcycle) not operated on rails

mot·tled *adj* **:** having spots or blotches of different colors

mot·to *n, pl* **mottoes 1 :** a phrase or word inscribed on something (as a coin or public building) to suggest its use or nature **2 :** a short expression of a guiding rule of conduct

mould *variant of* MOLD

moult *variant of* MOLT

mound *n* **:** a small hill or heap of dirt (as one made to mark a grave)

¹mount *n* **:** a high hill **:** MOUNTAIN — used especially before a proper name

²mount *vb* **1 :** ASCEND, CLIMB **2 :** to get up onto something **3 :** to increase rapidly in amount **4 :** to prepare for use or display by fastening in position on a support

³mount *n* **:** that on which a person or thing is or can be mounted

moun·tain *n* **1 :** an elevation higher than a hill **2 :** a great mass or huge number

moun·tain·eer *n* **1 :** a person who lives in the mountains **2 :** a mountain climber

mountain goat *n* **:** a goatlike animal of the mountains of western North America with thick white coat and slightly curved black horns

mountain lion *n* **:** COUGAR

moun·tain·ous *adj* **1 :** having many mountains **2 :** like a mountain in size **:** HUGE

moun·tain·side *n* **:** the side of a mountain

moun·tain·top *n* **:** the highest part of a mountain

mount·ing *n* **:** something that serves as a mount **:** SUPPORT

mourn *vb* **:** to feel or show grief or sorrow especially over someone's death — **mourn·er** *n*

mourn·ful *adj* **1 :** full of sorrow or sadness **2 :** causing sorrow — **mourn·ful·ly** *adv* — **mourn·ful·ness** *n*

mourn·ing *n* **1 :** the act of sorrowing **2 :** an outward sign (as black clothes or an arm band) of grief for a person's death

mourning dove *n* **:** a wild dove of the United States named from its mournful cry

mouse *n, pl* **mice 1 :** a furry gnawing animal like the larger related rats **2 :** a person without spirit or courage **3 :** a small movable device that is connected to a computer and used to move the cursor and select functions on the screen — **mouse·like** *adj*

mous·er *n* **:** a cat good at catching mice

moustache *variant of* MUSTACHE

¹mouth *n, pl* **mouths 1 :** the opening through which food passes into the body **:** the space containing the tongue and teeth **2 :** an opening that is like a mouth **3 :** the place where a stream enters a larger body of water

²**mouth** *vb* : to repeat without being sincere or without understanding

mouth·ful *n* **1** : as much as the mouth will hold **2** : the amount put into the mouth at one time

mouth organ *n* : HARMONICA

mouth·piece *n* : the part put to, between, or near the lips

mov·able *or* **move·able** *adj* **1** : possible to move **2** : changing from one date to another

¹**move** *vb* **moved; mov·ing** **1** : to go from one place to another **2** : to change the place or position of : SHIFT **3** : to set in motion : STIR **4** : to cause to act : INFLUENCE **5** : to stir the feelings of **6** : to change position **7** : to suggest according to the rules in a meeting **8** : to change residence

²**move** *n* **1** : the act of moving a piece in a game **2** : the turn of a player to move **3** : an action taken to accomplish something : MANEUVER **4** : the action of moving : MOVEMENT

move·ment *n* **1** : the act or process of moving : an instance of moving **2** : a program or series of acts working toward a desired end **3** : a mechanical arrangement (as of wheels) for causing a particular motion (as in a clock or watch) **4** : RHYTHM 2, METER **5** : a section of a longer piece of music **6** : an emptying of the bowels : the material emptied from the bowels

mov·er *n* : a person or company that moves the belongings of others (as from one home to another)

mov·ie *n* **1** : a story represented in motion pictures **2** : a showing of a movie

mov·ing *adj* **1** : changing place or position **2** : having the power to stir the feelings or sympathics — **mov·ing·ly** *adv*

moving picture *n* : MOTION PICTURE 1

¹**mow** *n* : the part of a barn where hay or straw is stored

²**mow** *vb* **mowed; mowed** *or* **mown; mow·ing** **1** : to cut down with a scythe or machine **2** : to cut the standing plant cover from **3** : to cause to fall in great numbers — **mow·er** *n*

Mr. *n, pl* **Messrs.** — used as a title before a man's name

Mrs. *n, pl* **mes·dames** — used as a title before a married woman's name

Ms. *n* — often used instead of *Miss* or *Mrs.*

¹**much** *adj* **more; most** : great in amount or extent

²**much** *adv* **more; most** **1** : to a great or high level or extent **2** : just about : NEARLY

³**much** *n* : a great amount or part

mu·ci·lage *n* : a water solution of a gum or similar substance used especially to stick things together

muck *n* **1** : soft wet soil or barnyard manure **2** : DIRT 1, FILTH

mu·cous *adj* **1** : of, relating to, or like mucus **2** : containing or producing mucus

mu·cus *n* : a slippery sticky substance produced especially by mucous membranes (as of the nose and throat) which it moistens and protects

mud *n* : soft wet earth or dirt

¹**mud·dle** *vb* **mud·dled; mud·dling** **1** : to be or cause to be confused or bewildered **2** : to mix up in a confused manner **3** : to make a mess of : BUNGLE

²**muddle** *n* : a state of confusion

¹**mud·dy** *adj* **mud·di·er; mud·di·est** **1** : filled or covered with mud **2** : looking like mud **3** : not clear or bright : DULL **4** : being mixed up — **mud·di·ly** *adv* — **mud·di·ness** *n*

²**muddy** *vb* **mud·died; mud·dy·ing** **1** : to soil or stain with or as if with mud **2** : to make cloudy or dull

¹**muff** *n* : a soft thick cover into which both hands can be shoved to protect them from cold

²**muff** *vb* : to handle awkwardly : BUNGLE

muf·fin *n* : a bread made of batter containing eggs and baked in a small container

muf·fle *vb* **muf·fled; muf·fling** **1** : to wrap up so as to hide or protect **2** : to deaden the sound of

muf·fler *n* **1** : a scarf for the neck **2** : a device to deaden the noise of an engine (as of an automobile)

mug *n* : a large drinking cup

mug·gy *adj* **mug·gi·er; mug·gi·est** : being very warm and humid — **mug·gi·ness** *n*

Mu·ham·mad·an *or* **Mo·ham·med·an** *n* : MUSLIM

Mu·ham·mad·an·ism *or* **Mo·ham·med·an·ism** *n* : ISLAM

mul·ber·ry *n, pl* **mul·ber·ries** : a tree that bears edible usually purple fruit like berries and has leaves on which silkworms can be fed

¹**mulch** *n* : a material (as straw or sawdust) spread over the ground to protect the roots of plants from heat, cold, or drying of the soil or to keep fruit clean

²**mulch** *vb* : to cover with mulch

mule *n* **1** : an animal that is an offspring of a donkey and a horse **2** : a stubborn person

mule skinner *n* : a driver of mules

mu·le·teer *n* : a driver of mules

mul·ish *adj* : stubborn like a mule — **mul·ish·ly** *adv* — **mul·ish·ness** *n*

mul·let *n* : any of various freshwater or salt-water food fishes some mostly gray (**gray mullets**) and others red or golden (**red mullets**)

multi- *prefix* **1** : many : much **2** : more than two **3** : many times over

mul·ti·cul·tur·al *adj* : of, relating to, or made up of several different cultures together

1mul·ti·ple *adj* : being more than one

2multiple *n* : the number found by multiplying one number by another

mul·ti·pli·cand *n* : a number that is to be multiplied by another number

mul·ti·pli·ca·tion *n* : a short way of finding out what would be the result of adding a figure the number of times indicated by another figure

mul·ti·pli·er *n* : a number by which another number is multiplied

mul·ti·ply *vb* **mul·ti·plied; mul·ti·ply·ing** **1** : to increase in number : make or become more numerous **2** : to find the product of by means of multiplication

mul·ti·tude *n* : a great number of persons or things

mum *adj* : SILENT 1 4

1mum·ble *vb* **mum·bled; mum·bling** : to speak so that words are not clear

2mumble *n* : speech that is not clear enough to be understood

mum·my *n, pl* **mummies** : a dead body preserved in the manner of the ancient Egyptians

mumps *n sing or pl* : an infectious disease in which there is fever and soreness and swelling of glands and especially of those around the jaw

munch *vb* : to chew with a crunching sound

mu·nic·i·pal *adj* : having to do with the government of a town or city

mu·nic·i·pal·i·ty *n, pl* **mu·nic·i·pal·i·ties** : a town or city having its own local government

mu·ni·tions *n* : military equipment and supplies for fighting : AMMUNITION

1mu·ral *adj* : having to do with a wall

2mural *n* : a painting on a wall

1mur·der *n* : the intentional and unlawful killing of a human being

2murder *vb* **1** : to commit murder **2** : to spoil by performing or using badly — **mur·der·er** *n*

mur·der·ous *adj* **1** : intending or capable of murder : DEADLY **2** : very hard to bear or withstand — **mur·der·ous·ly** *adv*

murk *n* : GLOOM 1, DARKNESS

murky *adj* **murk·i·er; murk·i·est** **1** : very dark or gloomy **2** : FOGGY 1, MISTY — **murk·i·ness** *n*

1mur·mur *n* : a low faint sound

2murmur *vb* **1** : to make a murmur **2** : to say in a voice too low to be heard clearly

mus·ca·dine *n* : a grape of the southern United States

mus·cle *n* **1** : an animal body tissue consisting of long cells that can contract and produce motion **2** : a bodily organ that is a mass of muscle tissue attached at either end (as to bones) so that it can make a body part (as an arm) move **3** : strength or development of the muscles

mus·cle–bound *adj* : having large muscles that do not move and stretch easily

mus·cu·lar *adj* **1** : of, relating to, or being muscle **2** : done by the muscles **3** : STRONG 1

muse *vb* **mused; mus·ing** : PONDER

mu·se·um *n* : a building in which are displayed objects of interest in one or more of the arts or sciences

1mush *n* : cornmeal boiled in water

2mush *vb* : to travel across snow with a sled drawn by dogs

1mush·room *n* **1** : a part of a fungus that bears spores, grows above ground, and suggests an umbrella in shape **2** : a fungus that produces mushrooms **3** : something shaped like a mushroom

2mushroom *vb* : to come into being suddenly or grow and develop rapidly

mushy *adj* **mush·i·er; mush·i·est** : soft like mush

mu·sic *n* **1** : the art of producing pleasing or expressive combinations of tones especially with melody, rhythm, and usually harmony **2** : compositions made according to the rules of music **3** : pleasing sounds **4** : a musical composition set down on paper

1mu·si·cal *adj* **1** : having to do with music or the writing or performing of music **2** : pleasing like music **3** : fond of or talented in music **4** : set to music — **mu·si·cal·ly** *adv*

2musical *n* : a movie or play that tells a story with both speaking and singing

music box *n* : a box that contains a mechanical device which uses gears like those of a clock to play a tune

mu·si·cian *n* : a person who writes, sings, or plays music with skill and especially as a profession

musk *n* **1** : a strong-smelling material from a gland of an Asian deer (**musk deer**) used in perfumes **2** : any of several plants with musky odors

mus·ket *n* : a firearm that is loaded through the muzzle and that was once used by infantry soldiers

mus·ke·teer *n* : a soldier armed with a musket

musk·mel·on *n* : a small round to oval melon with sweet usually green or orange flesh

musk–ox *n* : a shaggy animal like an ox found in Greenland and northern North America

musk·rat *n* : a North American water animal related to the rats that has webbed hind feet and a long scaly tail and is valued for its glossy usually dark brown fur

musky *adj* **musk·i·er; musk·i·est** : suggesting musk in odor — **musk·i·ness** *n*

Mus·lim *or* **Mos·lem** *n* : a person whose religion is Islam

mus·lin *n* : a cotton fabric of plain weave

¹muss *n* : ²DISORDER 1, CONFUSION

²muss *vb* : to make untidy

mus·sel *n* **1** : a sea mollusk that has a long dark shell in two parts and is sometimes used as food **2** : any of various American freshwater clams with shells from which mother-of-pearl is obtained

must *helping verb, present and past all persons* **must** **1** : to be required to **2** : to be very likely to

mus·tache *or* **mous·tache** *n* : the hair growing on the human upper lip

mus·tang *n* : a small hardy horse of western North America that is half wild

mus·tard *n* : a yellow powder that is prepared from the seeds of a plant related to the turnips, has a sharp taste, and is used in medicine and as a seasoning for foods

¹mus·ter *n* **1** : a formal military inspection **2** : an assembled group : COLLECTION

²muster *vb* **1** : to call together (as troops) for roll call or inspection **2** : to bring into being or action

mustn't : must not

musty *adj* **must·i·er; must·i·est** : bad in odor or taste from the effects of dampness or mildew — **must·i·ness** *n*

¹mu·tant *adj* : of, relating to, or resulting from mutation

²mutant *n* : a mutant individual

mu·tate *vb* **mu·tat·ed; mu·tat·ing** **1** : to undergo great changes **2** : to undergo mutation

mu·ta·tion *n* : a change in a gene or a resulting new trait inherited by an individual

¹mute *adj* **mut·er; mut·est** **1** : unable to speak **2** : not speaking : SILENT

²mute *n* **1** : a person who cannot or does not speak **2** : a device on a musical instrument that deadens, softens, or muffles its tone

³mute *vb* **mut·ed; mut·ing** : to muffle or reduce the sound of

mu·ti·late *vb* **mu·ti·lat·ed; mu·ti·lat·ing** : to cut off or destroy a necessary part (as a limb) : MAIM **2** : to make imperfect by cutting or changing

mu·ti·neer *n* : a person who is guilty of mutiny

mu·ti·nous *adj* : being inclined to or in a state of mutiny — **mu·ti·nous·ly** *adv*

¹mu·ti·ny *n, pl* **mu·ti·nies** **1** : refusal to obey authority **2** : a turning of a group (as of sailors) against an officer in authority

²mutiny *vb* **mu·ti·nied; mu·ti·ny·ing** : to refuse to obey authority

mutt *n* : a mongrel dog

mut·ter *vb* **1** : to speak in a low voice with lips partly closed **2** : ¹GRUMBLE 1

mut·ton *n* : the flesh of a mature sheep

mu·tu·al *adj* **1** : given and received in equal amount **2** : having the same relation to one another **3** : shared by two or more at the same time — **mu·tu·al·ly** *adv*

¹muz·zle *n* **1** : the nose and jaws of an animal **2** : a fastening or covering for the mouth of an animal to prevent it from biting or eating **3** : the open end of a gun from which the bullet comes out when the gun is fired

²muzzle *vb* **muz·zled; muz·zling** **1** : to put a muzzle on **2** : to keep from free expression of ideas or opinions

my *adj* : of or relating to me or myself

my·nah *or* **my·na** *n* : an Asian starling that can be trained to pronounce words and is sometimes kept as a cage bird

¹myr·i·ad *n* : a large but not specified or counted number

²myriad *adj* : extremely numerous

myrrh *n* : a brown slightly bitter fragrant material obtained from African and Arabian trees and used especially in perfumes or formerly in incense

myr·tle *n* **1** : an evergreen shrub of southern Europe **2** : ¹PERIWINKLE

my·self *pron* : my own self

mys·te·ri·ous *adj* : containing a mystery : hard to understand : SECRET — **mys·te·ri·ous·ly** *adv* — **mys·te·ri·ous·ness** *n*

mys·tery *n, pl* **mys·ter·ies** **1** : something that is beyond human power to understand **2** : something that has not been explained **3** : a piece of fiction about a mysterious crime

mys·ti·fy *vb* **mys·ti·fied; mys·ti·fy·ing** : CONFUSE 1

myth *n* **1** : a legend that tells about a being with more than human powers or an event which cannot be explained or that explains a religious belief or practice **2** : a person or thing existing only in the imagination

myth·i·cal *adj* **1** : based on or told of in a myth **2** : IMAGINARY

my·thol·o·gy *n, pl* **my·thol·o·gies** : a collection of myths

N

n *n, pl* **n's** *or* **ns** *often cap* : the fourteenth letter of the English alphabet

-n — see -EN

nab *vb* **nabbed; nab·bing** : ¹ARREST 2

¹nag *n* : a usually old or worn-out horse

²nag *vb* **nagged; nag·ging** 1 : to find fault continually : COMPLAIN 2 : to annoy continually or again and again

na·iad *n, pl* **na·iads** *or* **na·ia·des** 1 : a nymph believed in ancient times to be living in lakes, rivers, and springs 2 : the larva of an insect (as a dragonfly) that lives in water

¹nail *n* 1 : the horny scale at the end of each finger and toe 2 : a slender pointed piece of metal driven into or through something for fastening

²nail *vb* : to fasten with or as if with a nail

nail·brush *n* : a brush for cleaning the hands and fingernails

na·ive *or* **na·ïve** *adj* 1 : being simple and sincere 2 : showing lack of experience or knowledge — **na·ive·ly** *adv*

na·ked *adj* 1 : having no clothes on : NUDE 2 : lacking a usual or natural covering 3 : not in its case or covering 4 : stripped of anything misleading : PLAIN 5 : not aided by an artificial device — **na·ked·ly** *adv* — **na·ked·ness** *n*

¹name *n* 1 : a word or combination of words by which a person or thing is known 2 : REPUTATION 2

²name *vb* **named; nam·ing** 1 : to give a name to : CALL 2 : to refer to by name 3 : to nominate for a job of authority : APPOINT 4 : to decide on : CHOOSE 5 : ²MENTION

³name *adj* 1 : of, relating to, or having a name 2 : well known because of wide distribution

name·less *adj* 1 : having no name 2 : not marked with a name 3 : ¹UNKNOWN, ANONYMOUS 4 : not to be described — **name·less·ness** *n*

name·ly *adv* : that is to say

name·sake *n* : a person who has the same name as another and especially one named for another

nan·ny *n, pl* **nannies** : a child's nurse

nanny goat *n* : a female domestic goat

¹nap *vb* **napped; nap·ping** 1 : to sleep briefly especially during the day 2 : to be unprepared

²nap *n* : a short sleep especially during the day

³nap *n* : a hairy or fluffy surface (as on cloth)

nape *n* : the back of the neck

naph·tha *n* : any of various usually flamma-

ble liquids prepared from coal or petroleum and used to dissolve substances or to thin paint

nap·kin *n* : a small square of cloth or paper used at table to wipe the lips or fingers and protect the clothes

nar·cis·sus *n, pl* **narcissus** *or* **nar·cis·sus·es** *or* **nar·cis·si** : a daffodil with flowers that have short tubes, grow separately on the stalk, and come in white, yellow, or a combination of both

¹nar·cot·ic *n* : a drug (as opium) that in small doses dulls the senses, relieves pain, and brings on sleep but in larger doses is a dangerous poison

²narcotic *adj* 1 : acting as or being the source of a narcotic 2 : of or relating to narcotics or their use or control

nar·rate *vb* **nar·rat·ed; nar·rat·ing** : to tell in full detail — **nar·ra·tor** *n*

nar·ra·tion *n* 1 : the act or process or an instance of narrating 2 : ¹NARRATIVE 1

¹nar·ra·tive *n* 1 : something (as a story) that is narrated 2 : the art or practice of narrating

²narrative *adj* : of or relating to narration : having the form of a story

¹nar·row *adj* 1 : of slender or less than usual width 2 : limited in size or extent 3 : not broad or open in mind or views 4 : barely successful : CLOSE — **nar·row·ly** *adv* — **nar·row·ness** *n*

²narrow *vb* : to make or become narrow

³narrow *n* : a narrow passage connecting two bodies of water — usually used in pl.

nar·row—mind·ed *adj* : ¹NARROW 3, INTOLERANT — **nar·row—mind·ed·ly** *adv* — **nar·row—mind·ed·ness** *n*

nar·whal *n* : an arctic marine animal about twenty feet long that is related to the dolphin and in the male has a long twisted ivory tusk

¹na·sal *n* : a nasal sound

²nasal *adj* 1 : of or relating to the nose 2 : uttered with the nose passage open — **na·sal·ly** *adv*

nas·tur·tium *n* : an herb with a juicy stem, roundish leaves, red, yellow, or white flowers, and seeds with a sharp taste

nas·ty *adj* **nas·ti·er; nas·ti·est** 1 : very dirty : FILTHY 2 : INDECENT 3 : ¹MEAN 4 4 : HARMFUL, DANGEROUS 5 : very unpleasant — **nas·ti·ly** *adv* — **nas·ti·ness** *n*

na·tal *adj* : of, relating to, or associated with birth

na·tion *n* 1 : NATIONALITY 3 2 : a community of people made up of one or more nationalities usually with its own territory and government 3 : a usually large independent division of territory : COUNTRY

¹na·tion·al *adj* : of or relating to a nation — na·tion·al·ly *adv*

²national *n* : a citizen of a nation

na·tion·al·ism *n* : devotion to the interests of a certain country

na·tion·al·ist *n* : a person who believes in nationalism

na·tion·al·is·tic *adj* 1 : of, relating to, or favoring nationalism 2 : ¹NATIONAL — na·tion·al·is·ti·cal·ly *adv*

na·tion·al·i·ty *n, pl* na·tion·al·i·ties 1 : the fact or state of belonging to a nation 2 : the state of being a separate nation 3 : a group of people having a common history, tradition, culture, or language

na·tion·al·ize *vb* na·tion·al·ized; na·tion·al·iz·ing : to place under government control

na·tion·wide *adj* : extending throughout a nation

¹na·tive *adj* 1 : NATURAL 1 2 : born in a certain place or country 3 : belonging to one because of one's place of birth 4 : grown, produced, or coming from a certain place

²native *n* : one that is native

Native American *n* : AMERICAN INDIAN

na·tiv·i·ty *n, pl* na·tiv·i·ties 1 : BIRTH 1 2 *cap* : the birth of Christ : CHRISTMAS

nat·ty *adj* nat·ti·er; nat·ti·est : very neat, trim, and stylish — nat·ti·ly *adv* — nat·ti·ness *n*

nat·u·ral *adj* 1 : born in or with one 2 : being such by nature : BORN 3 : found in or produced by nature 4 : of or relating to nature 5 : not made by humans 6 : being simple and sincere 7 : LIFELIKE 8 : being neither sharp nor flat : having neither sharps nor flats — nat·u·ral·ly *adv* — nat·u·ral·ness *n*

nat·u·ral·ist *n* : a student of nature and especially of plants and animals as they live in nature

nat·u·ral·i·za·tion *n* : the act or process of naturalizing : the state of being naturalized

nat·u·ral·ize *vb* nat·u·ral·ized; nat·u·ral·iz·ing 1 : to become or cause to become established as if native 2 : to admit to citizenship

natural number *n* : the number 1 or any number (as 3, 12, 432) obtained by adding 1 to it one or more times

natural resource *n* : something (as a mineral, forest, or kind of animal) that is found in nature and is valuable to humans

na·ture *n* 1 : the basic character of a person or thing 2 : ¹SORT 1, VARIETY 3 : natural

feelings : DISPOSITION, TEMPERAMENT 4 : the material universe 5 : the working of a living body 6 : natural scenery

¹naught *or* nought *pron* : ¹NOTHING 1

²naught *or* nought *n* : ZERO 1, CIPHER

naugh·ty *adj* naugh·ti·er; naugh·ti·est : behaving in a bad or improper way — naugh·ti·ly *adv* — naugh·ti·ness *n*

nau·sea *n* 1 : a disturbed condition of the stomach in which one feels like vomiting 2 : deep disgust : LOATHING

nau·se·ate *vb* nau·se·at·ed; nau·se·at·ing : to affect or become affected with nausea — nau·se·at·ing *adj* — nau·se·at·ing·ly *adv*

nau·seous *adj* 1 : suffering from nausea 2 : causing nausea

nau·ti·cal *adj* : of or relating to sailors, navigation, or ships — nau·ti·cal·ly *adv*

na·val *adj* : of or relating to a navy or warships

nave *n* : the long central main part of a church

na·vel *n* : a hollow in the middle of the abdomen that marks the place where the umbilical cord was attached

nav·i·ga·bil·i·ty *n* : the quality or state of being navigable

nav·i·ga·ble *adj* 1 : deep enough and wide enough to permit passage of ships 2 : possible to steer

nav·i·gate *vb* nav·i·gat·ed; nav·i·gat·ing 1 : to travel by water 2 : to sail over, on, or through 3 : to steer a course in a ship or aircraft 4 : to steer or direct the course of (as a boat)

nav·i·ga·tion *n* 1 : the act or practice of navigating 2 : the science of figuring out the position and course of a ship or aircraft

nav·i·ga·tor *n* : an officer on a ship or aircraft responsible for its navigation

na·vy *n, pl* navies 1 : a nation's ships of war 2 : the complete naval equipment and organization of a nation 3 : a dark blue

¹nay *adv* : ¹NO 2

²nay *n* : ³NO 2

Na·zi *n* : a member of a political party controlling Germany from 1933 to 1945

Ne·an·der·thal man *n* : a long gone ancient human who made tools of stone and lived by hunting

¹near *adv* 1 : at, within, or to a short distance or time 2 : ALMOST, NEARLY

²near *prep* : close to

³near *adj* 1 : closely related or associated 2 : not far away 3 : coming close : NARROW 4 : being the closer of two — near·ly *adv* — near·ness *n*

⁴near *vb* : to come near : APPROACH

near·by *adv or adj* : close at hand

near·sight·ed *adj* : able to see near things more clearly than distant ones — **near·sight·ed·ly** *adv* — **near·sight·ed·ness** *n*

neat *adj* 1 : being simple and in good taste 2 : SKILLFUL 2 3 : showing care and a concern for order — **neat·ly** *adv* — **neat·ness** *n*

neb·u·la *n, pl* **neb·u·las** *or* **neb·u·lae** : any of many clouds of gas or dust seen in the sky among the stars

neb·u·lous *adj* : not clear : VAGUE — **neb·u·lous·ly** *adv* — **neb·u·lous·ness** *n*

¹nec·es·sary *adj* : needing to be had or done : ESSENTIAL — **nec·es·sar·i·ly** *adv*

²necessary *n, pl* **nec·es·sar·ies** : something that is needed

ne·ces·si·tate *vb* **ne·ces·si·tat·ed; ne·ces·si·tat·ing** : to make necessary : REQUIRE

ne·ces·si·ty *n, pl* **ne·ces·si·ties** 1 : the state of things that forces certain actions 2 : very great need 3 : the state of being without or unable to get necessary things : POVERTY 4 : something that is badly needed

neck *n* 1 : the part connecting the head and the main part of the body 2 : the part of a garment covering or nearest to the neck 3 : something like a neck in shape or position — **necked** *adj* — **neck and neck** : so nearly equal (as in a race) that one cannot be said to be ahead of the other

neck·er·chief *n, pl* **neck·er·chiefs** : a square of cloth worn folded around the neck like a scarf

neck·lace *n* : an ornament (as a string of beads) worn around the neck

neck·line *n* : the outline of the neck opening of a garment

neck·tie *n* : a narrow length of material worn around the neck and tied in front

nec·tar *n* 1 : the drink of the Greek and Roman gods 2 : a sweet liquid given off by plants and used by bees in making honey

nec·tar·ine *n* : a peach with a smooth skin

née *or* **nee** *adj* : BORN 1 — used to identify a woman by her maiden name

¹need *n* 1 : something that must be done : OBLIGATION 2 : a lack of something necessary, useful, or desired 3 : something necessary or desired

²need *vb* 1 : to suffer from the lack of something important to life or health 2 : to be necessary 3 : to be without : REQUIRE

need·ful *adj* : ¹NECESSARY — **need·ful·ly** *adv* — **need·ful·ness** *n*

¹nee·dle *n* 1 : a slender pointed usually steel device used to make a hole and pull thread through in sewing 2 : a slender pointed piece of metal or plastic (used for knitting) 3 : a leaf (as of a pine) shaped like a needle 4 : a pointer on a dial 5 : a slender hollow instrument by which material is put into or taken from the body through the skin — **nee·dle·like** *adj*

²needle *vb* **nee·dled; nee·dling** : ¹TEASE, TAUNT

nee·dle·point *n* : embroidery done on canvas usually in simple even stitches across counted threads

need·less *adj* : UNNECESSARY — **need·less·ly** *adv* — **need·less·ness** *n*

nee·dle·work *n* : work (as sewing or embroidery) done with a needle

needn't : need not

needs *adv* : because of necessity

needy *adj* **need·i·er; need·i·est** : very poor — **need·i·ness** *n*

ne'er *adv* : NEVER

ne'er–do–well *n* : a worthless person who will not work

ne·gate *vb* **ne·gat·ed; ne·gat·ing** 1 : to deny the existence or truth of 2 : to cause to be ineffective

ne·ga·tion *n* : the action of negating : DENIAL

¹neg·a·tive *adj* 1 : making a denial 2 : not positive 3 : not helpful 4 : less than zero and shown by a minus sign 5 : of, being, or relating to electricity of which the electron is the unit and which is produced in a hard rubber rod that has been rubbed with wool 6 : having more electrons than protons 7 : being the part toward which the electric current flows from the outside circuit — **neg·a·tive·ly** *adv* — **neg·a·tiv·i·ty** *n*

²negative *n* 1 : something that is the opposite of something else 2 : a negative number 3 : an expression (as the word *no*) that denies or says the opposite 4 : the side that argues or votes against something 5 : a photographic image on film from which a final picture is made

¹ne·glect *vb* 1 : to fail to give the right amount of attention to 2 : to fail to do or look after especially because of carelessness

²neglect *n* 1 : an act or instance of neglecting something 2 : the state of being neglected

ne·glect·ful *adj* : tending to neglect : NEGLIGENT — **ne·glect·ful·ly** *adv* — **ne·glect·ful·ness** *n*

neg·li·gee *n* : a woman's loose robe worn especially while dressing or resting

neg·li·gence *n* 1 : the state of being negligent 2 : an act or instance of being negligent

neg·li·gent *adj* : likely to neglect things : CARELESS — **neg·li·gent·ly** *adv*

neg·li·gi·ble *adj* : so small or unimportant as to deserve little or no attention — **neg·li·gi·bly** *adv*

ne·go·tia·ble *adj* : possible to negotiate — **ne·go·tia·bil·i·ty** *n*

ne·go·ti·ate *vb* **ne·go·ti·at·ed; ne·go·ti·at·ing** 1 : to have a discussion with another in order to settle something 2 : to arrange for by discussing 3 : to give to someone in exchange for cash or something of equal value 4 : to be successful in getting around, through, or over — **ne·go·ti·a·tor** *n*

ne·go·ti·a·tion *n* : the act or process of negotiating or being negotiated

Ne·gro *n, pl* **Ne·groes** 1 : a member of any of the original peoples of Africa south of the Sahara 2 : a person with Negro ancestors — **Negro** *adj*

¹neigh *vb* : to make a neigh

²neigh *n* : the long loud cry of a horse

¹neigh·bor *n* 1 : a person living or a thing located near another 2 : a fellow human being

²neighbor *vb* : to be near or next to — **neigh·bor·ing** *adj*

neigh·bor·hood *n* 1 : a place or region near : VICINITY 2 : an amount, size, or range that is close to 3 : the people living near one another 4 : a section lived in by neighbors

neigh·bor·ly *adj* : of, relating to, or like neighbors : FRIENDLY — **neigh·bor·li·ness** *n*

¹nei·ther *conj* 1 : not either 2 : also not

²neither *pron* : not the one and not the other

³neither *adj* : not either

ne·on *n* 1 : a colorless gaseous chemical element found in very small amounts in the air and used in electric lamps 2 : a lamp in which the gas contains a large proportion of neon 3 : a sign made up of such lamps

neo·phyte *n* 1 : a new convert 2 : BEGINNER, NOVICE

neph·ew *n* : a son of one's brother or sister

Nep·tune *n* : the planet that is eighth in order of distance from the sun and has a diameter of about 45,000 kilometers

nep·tu·ni·um *n* : a radioactive chemical element similar to uranium

nerd *n* 1 : a person who is socially awkward, unattractive, or not fashionable 2 : a person who is extremely devoted to study and learning — **nerdy** *adj*

¹nerve *n* 1 : one of the bands of nerve fibers that join centers (as the brain) of the nervous system with other parts of the body and carry nerve impulses 2 : FORTITUDE, DARING 3 : IMPUDENCE 4 **nerves** *pl* : JITTERS 5 : the sensitive soft inner part of a tooth — **nerve·less** *adj*

²nerve *vb* **nerved; nerv·ing** : to give strength or courage to

nerve cell *n* : a cell of the nervous system with fibers that conduct nerve impulses

nerve fiber *n* : any of the slender extensions of a nerve cell that carry nerve impulses

nerve impulse *n* : a progressive change of a nerve fiber by which information is brought to or orders sent from the central nervous system

ner·vous *adj* 1 : of or relating to nerve cells 2 : of, relating to, or made up of nerves or nervous tissue 3 : easily excited or upset 4 : TIMID — **ner·vous·ly** *adv* — **ner·vous·ness** *n*

nervy *adj* **nerv·i·er; nerv·i·est** 1 : showing calm courage : BOLD 2 : ¹FORWARD 2 3 : NERVOUS 3 — **nerv·i·ness** *n*

-ness *n suffix* : state : condition

¹nest *n* 1 : a shelter made by a bird for its eggs and young 2 : a place where the eggs of some animals other than birds are laid and hatched 3 : a cozy home : a snug shelter 4 : those living in a nest

²nest *vb* : to build or live in a nest

nes·tle *vb* **nes·tled; nes·tling** 1 : to lie close and snug : CUDDLE 2 : to settle as if in a nest

nest·ling *n* : a young bird not yet able to leave the nest

¹net *n* 1 : a fabric made of threads, cords, ropes, or wires that weave in and out with much open space 2 : something made of net 3 : something that traps one as if in a net 4 : NETWORK 2 5 *often cap* : INTERNET

²net *vb* **net·ted; net·ting** 1 : to cover with or as if with a net 2 : to catch in or as if in a net

³net *adj* : remaining after all charges or expenses have been subtracted

⁴net *vb* **net·ted; net·ting** : to gain or produce as profit : CLEAR

net·ting *n* : NETWORK 1 2

net·tle *n* : a tall plant with stinging hairs on the leaves

net·work *n* 1 : a net fabric or structure 2 : an arrangement of lines or channels crossing as in a net 3 : a system of computers connected by communications lines 4 : a group of connected radio or television stations

neu·ron *n* : NERVE CELL

neu·ter *adj* : lacking sex organs : having sex organs that are not fully developed

¹neu·tral *n* 1 : one that does not favor either side in a quarrel, contest, or war 2 : a grayish color 3 : a position of gears (as in the transmission of a motor vehicle) in which they are not in contact

2neutral *adj* **1** : not favoring either side in a quarrel, contest, or war **2** : of or relating to a neutral country **3** : being neither one thing nor the other **4** : having no color that stands out : GRAYISH **5** : neither acid nor basic **6** : not electrically charged

neu·tral·i·ty *n* : the quality or state of being neutral

neu·tral·ize *vb* **neu·tral·ized; neu·tral·iz·ing** **1** : to make chemically neutral **2** : to make ineffective — **neu·tral·i·za·tion** *n* — **neu·tral·iz·er** *n*

neu·tron *n* : a particle that has a mass nearly equal to that of the proton but no electrical charge and that is present in all atomic nuclei except those of hydrogen

nev·er *adv* **1** : not ever : at no time **2** : not to any extent or in any way

nev·er·more *adv* : never again

nev·er·the·less *adv* : even so : HOWEVER

1new *adj* **1** : not old : RECENT **2** : taking the place of one that came before **3** : recently discovered or learned about **4** : not known or experienced before **5** : not accustomed **6** : beginning as a repeating of a previous act or thing **7** : being in a position, place, or state the first time — **new·ness** *n*

2new *adv* : NEWLY, RECENTLY

new·born *adj* **1** : recently born **2** : made new or strong again

new·com·er *n* **1** : one recently arrived : BEGINNER

new·el *n* : a post at the bottom or at a turn of a stairway

new·fan·gled *adj* : of the newest style : NOVEL

new·ly *adv* : not long ago : RECENTLY

new moon *n* **1** : the moon's phase when its dark side is toward the earth **2** : the thin curved outline of the moon seen shortly after sunset for a few days after the new moon

news *n* **1** : a report of recent events **2** : material reported in a newspaper or news magazine or on a newscast **3** : an event that is interesting enough to be reported

news·boy *n* : a person who delivers or sells newspapers

news·cast *n* : a radio or television broadcast of news

news·girl *n* : a girl who delivers or sells newspapers

news·man *n, pl* **news·men** : a person who gathers or reports news

news·pa·per *n* : a paper that is printed and sold usually every day or weekly and that contains news, articles of opinion, features, and advertising

news·pa·per·man *n, pl* **news·pa·per·men** : a man who owns or works on a newspaper

news·pa·per·wom·an *n, pl* **news·pa·per·wom·en** : a woman who owns or works on a newspaper

news·reel *n* : a short motion picture about current events

news·stand *n* : a place where newspapers and magazines are sold

news·wom·an *n, pl* **news·wom·en** : a woman who gathers or reports news

newsy *adj* **news·i·er; news·i·est** : filled with news

newt *n* : a small salamander that lives mostly in water

New Year's Day *n* : January 1 observed as a legal holiday in many countries

1next *adj* : coming just before or after

2next *prep* : NEXT TO

3next *adv* **1** : in the nearest place, time, or order following **2** : at the first time after this

next–door *adj* : located in the next building, apartment, or room

1next to *prep* **1** : BESIDE 1 **2** : following right after

2next to *adv* : very nearly : ALMOST

nib *n* **1** : a pointed object (as the bill of a bird) **2** : the point of a pen

1nib·ble *vb* **nib·bled; nib·bling** : to bite or chew gently or bit by bit — **nib·bler** *n*

2nibble *n* **1** : an act of nibbling **2** : a very small amount

nice *adj* **nic·er; nic·est** **1** : very fussy (as about appearance, manners, or food) **2** : able to recognize small differences between things **3** : PLEASING, PLEASANT **4** : well behaved — **nice·ly** *adv* — **nice·ness** *n*

ni·ce·ty *n, pl* **ni·ce·ties** **1** : something dainty, delicate, or especially nice **2** : a fine detail

niche *n* **1** : an open hollow in a wall (as for a statue) **2** : a place, job, or use for which a person or a thing is best fitted

1nick *n* **1** : a small cut or chip in a surface **2** : the last moment

2nick *vb* : to make a nick in

1nick·el *n* **1** : a hard silvery white metallic chemical element that can be highly polished, resists weathering, and is used in alloys **2** : a United States coin worth five cents

2nickel *vb* **nick·eled** *or* **nick·elled; nick·el·ing** *or* **nick·el·ling** : to plate with nickel

1nick·er *vb* : 1NEIGH, WHINNY

2nicker *n* : 2NEIGH

1nick·name *n* **1** : a usually descriptive name given in addition to the one belonging to an individual **2** : a familiar form of a proper name

2nickname *vb* **nick·named; nick·nam·ing** : to give a nickname to

nic·o·tine *n* : a poisonous substance found in small amounts in tobacco and used especially to kill insects

niece *n* : a daughter of one's brother or sister

nig·gling *adj* : PETTY 1

1nigh *adv* 1 : near in time or place 2 : ALMOST, NEARLY

2nigh *adj* : 3CLOSE 5, NEAR

night *n* 1 : the time between dusk and dawn when there is no sunlight 2 : NIGHTFALL 3 : the darkness of night

night·club *n* : a place of entertainment open at night usually serving food and liquor and having music for dancing

night crawl·er *n* : EARTHWORM

night·fall *n* : the coming of night

night·gown *n* : a loose garment worn in bed

night·hawk *n* 1 : a bird that is related to the whippoorwill, flies mostly at twilight, and eats insects 2 : a person who stays up late at night

night·in·gale *n* : a reddish brown Old World thrush noted for the sweet song of the male

1night·ly *adj* 1 : of or relating to the night or every night 2 : happening or done at night or every night

2nightly *adv* 1 : every night 2 : at or by night

night·mare *n* 1 : a frightening dream 2 : a horrible experience — **night·mar·ish** *adj*

night·shirt *n* : a nightgown like a very long shirt

night·stick *n* : a police officer's club

night·time *n* : NIGHT 1

nil *n* : ZERO 4, NOTHING

nim·ble *adj* **nim·bler; nim·blest** 1 : quick and light in motion : AGILE 2 : quick in understanding and learning : CLEVER — **nim·ble·ness** *n* — **nim·bly** *adv*

nim·bus *n, pl* **nim·bi** *or* **nim·bus·es** : a rain cloud that is evenly gray and that covers the whole sky

nin·com·poop *n* : 1FOOL 1

1nine *adj* : being one more than eight

2nine *n* 1 : one more than eight : three times three : 9 2 : the ninth in a set or series

1nine·teen *adj* : being one more than eighteen

2nineteen *n* : one more than eighteen : 19

1nine·teenth *adj* : coming right after eighteenth

2nineteenth *n* : number nineteen in a series

1nine·ti·eth *adj* : coming right after eighty-ninth

2ninetieth *n* : number ninety in a series

1nine·ty *adj* : being nine times ten

2ninety *n* : nine times ten : 90

nin·ja *n* : a person trained in ancient Japanese arts of fighting and defending oneself

and employed especially for espionage and assassinations

nin·ny *n, pl* **ninnies** : 1FOOL 1

1ninth *adj* : coming right after eighth

2ninth *n* 1 : number nine in a series 2 : one of nine equal parts

1nip *vb* **nipped; nip·ping** 1 : to catch hold of (as with teeth) and squeeze sharply though not very hard 2 : to cut off by or as if by pinching sharply 3 : to stop the growth or progress of 4 : to injure or make numb with cold

2nip *n* 1 : something that nips 2 : the act of nipping 3 : a small portion : BIT

3nip *n* : a small amount of liquor

nip and tuck *adj or adv* : so close that the lead shifts rapidly from one contestant to another

nip·ple *n* 1 : the part of the breast from which a baby or young animal sucks milk 2 : something (as the mouthpiece of a baby's bottle) like a nipple

nip·py *adj* **nip·pi·er; nip·pi·est** : CHILLY

nit *n* : the egg of a louse

ni·trate *n* : a substance that is made from or has a composition as if made from nitric acid

ni·tric acid *n* : a strong liquid acid that contains hydrogen, nitrogen, and oxygen and is used in making fertilizers, explosives, and dyes

ni·tro·gen *n* : a colorless odorless gaseous chemical element that makes up 78 percent of the atmosphere and forms a part of all living tissues

nitrogen cycle *n* : a continuous series of natural processes by which nitrogen passes from air to soil to organisms and back into the air

nitrogen fix·a·tion *n* : the changing of free nitrogen into combined forms especially by bacteria (**nitrogen-fixing bacteria**)

ni·tro·glyc·er·in *or* **ni·tro·glyc·er·ine** *n* : a heavy oily liquid explosive from which dynamite is made

nit·wit *n* : a very silly or stupid person

1no *adv* 1 : not at all : not any 2 : not so — used to express disagreement or refusal 3 — used to express surprise, doubt, or disbelief

2no *adj* 1 : not any 2 : hardly any : very little 3 : not a

3no *n, pl* **noes** *or* **nos** 1 : an act or instance of refusing or denying by the use of the word *no* : DENIAL 2 : a negative vote or decision 3 *noes or nos pl* : persons voting in the negative

no·bil·i·ty *n, pl* **no·bil·i·ties** 1 : the quality or state of being noble 2 : noble rank 3 : the class or a group of nobles

¹no·ble *adj* **no·bler; no·blest** **1** : EMINENT, ILLUSTRIOUS **2** : of very high birth or rank **3** : having very fine qualities **4** : grand in appearance — **no·ble·ness** *n* — **no·bly** *adv*

²noble *n* : a person of noble birth or rank

no·ble·man *n, pl* **no·ble·men** : a man of noble rank

no·ble·wom·an *n, pl* **no·ble·wom·en** : a woman of noble rank

¹no·body *pron* : no person : not anybody

²nobody *n, pl* **no·bod·ies** : a person of no importance

noc·tur·nal *adj* **1** : of, relating to, or happening at night : NIGHTLY **2** : active at night — **noc·tur·nal·ly** *adv*

¹nod *vb* **nod·ded; nod·ding** **1** : to bend the head downward or forward (as in bowing, going to sleep, or indicating "yes") **2** : to move up and down **3** : to show by a nod of the head

²nod *n* : the action of bending the head downward and forward

node *n* : a thickened spot or part (as of a plant stem where a leaf develops)

nod·ule *n* : a small node (as of a clover root)

no·el *n* **1** : a Christmas carol **2** *cap* : the Christmas season

noes *pl of* NO

¹noise *n* **1** : a loud unpleasant sound **2** : ³SOUND 1 — **noise·less** *adj* — **noise·less·ly** *adv* — **noise·less·ness** *n*

²noise *vb* **noised; nois·ing** : to spread by rumor or report

noise·mak·er *n* : a device used to make noise especially at parties

noisy *adj* **nois·i·er; nois·i·est** **1** : making noise **2** : full of noise — **nois·i·ly** *adv* — **nois·i·ness** *n*

¹no·mad *n* **1** : a member of a people having no fixed home but wandering from place to place **2** : WANDERER

²nomad *adj* : NOMADIC 2

no·mad·ic *adj* **1** : of or relating to nomads **2** : roaming about with no special end in mind

nom·i·nal *adj* **1** : being such in name only **2** : very small : TRIFLING — **nom·i·nal·ly** *adv*

nom·i·nate *vb* **nom·i·nat·ed; nom·i·nat·ing** : to choose as a candidate for election, appointment, or honor — **nom·i·na·tor** *n*

nom·i·na·tion *n* **1** : the act or an instance of nominating **2** : the state of being nominated

nom·i·na·tive *adj* : being or belonging to the case of a noun or pronoun that is usually the subject of a verb

nom·i·nee *n* : a person nominated for an office, duty, or position

non- *prefix* : not

non·al·co·hol·ic *adj* : containing no alcohol

non·cha·lance *n* : the state of being nonchalant

non·cha·lant *adj* : having a confident and easy manner — **non·cha·lant·ly** *adv*

non·com·bat·ant *n* **1** : a member (as a chaplain) of the armed forces whose duties do not include fighting **2** : ¹CIVILIAN

non·com·mis·sioned officer *n* : an officer in the Army, Air Force, or Marine Corps appointed from among the enlisted persons

non·com·mit·tal *adj* : not telling or showing what one thinks or has decided — **non·com·mit·tal·ly** *adv*

non·com·mu·ni·ca·ble *adj* : not spread from one individual to another

non·con·duc·tor *n* : a substance that conducts heat, electricity, or sound at a very low rate

non·con·form·ist *n* : a person who does not conform to generally accepted standards or customs

non·de·script *adj* : of no certain class or kind : not easily described

¹none *pron* : not any : not one

²none *adv* **1** : not at all **2** : in no way

non·en·ti·ty *n, pl* **non·en·ti·ties** : someone or something of no importance

¹non·es·sen·tial *adj* : not essential

²nonessential *n* : something that is not essential

none·the·less *adv* : NEVERTHELESS

non·fic·tion *n* : writings that are not fiction

non·flam·ma·ble *adj* : not flammable

non·green *adj* : having no chlorophyll

non·liv·ing *adj* : not living

non·par·ti·san *adj* : not partisan : not committed to one party or side

non·plus *vb* **non·plussed; non·plus·sing** : to cause to be at a loss as to what to say, think, or do : PERPLEX

non·poi·son·ous *adj* : not poisonous

non·prof·it *adj* : not existing or carried on to make a profit

¹non·res·i·dent *adj* : not living in a certain place

²nonresident *n* : a nonresident person

non·sched·uled *adj* : licensed to carry pasengers or freight by air whenever demand requires

non·sec·tar·i·an *adj* : not limited to a particular religious group

non·sense *n* **1** : foolish or meaningless words or actions **2** : things of no importance or value

non·sen·si·cal *adj* : making no sense : ABSURD — **non·sen·si·cal·ly** *adv*

non·smok·er *n* : a person who does not smoke tobacco

non·smok·ing *adj* **1** : not in the habit of

smoking tobacco **2** : reserved for the use of nonsmokers

non·stan·dard *adj* : not standard

non·stop *adv or adj* : without a stop

noo·dle *n* : a food like macaroni made with egg and shaped into flat strips — usually used in pl.

nook *n* **1** : an inner corner **2** : a sheltered or hidden place

noon *n* : the middle of the day : twelve o'clock in the daytime

noon·day *n* : NOON, MIDDAY

no one *pron* : [1]NOBODY

noon·tide *n* : NOON

noon·time *n* : NOON

noose *n* : a loop that passes through a knot at the end of a line so that it gets smaller when the other end of the line is pulled

nor *conj* : and not

norm *n* : [1]AVERAGE 2

[1]**nor·mal** *adj* **1** : of the regular or usual kind : REGULAR **2** : of average intelligence **3** : sound in body or mind — **nor·mal·ly** *adv*

[2]**normal** *n* **1** : one that is normal **2** : [1]AVERAGE 2

nor·mal·cy *n* : NORMALITY

nor·mal·i·ty *n* : the quality or state of being normal

Nor·man *n* **1** : one of the Scandinavians who conquered Normandy in the tenth century **2** : one of the people of mixed Norman and French blood who conquered England in 1066

Norse *n pl* **1** : people of Scandinavia **2** : people of Norway

[1]**north** *adv* : to or toward the north

[2]**north** *adj* : placed toward, facing, or coming from the north

[3]**north** *n* **1** : the direction to the left of one facing east : the compass point opposite to south **2** *cap* : regions or countries north of a point that is mentioned or understood

[1]**North American** *n* : a person born or living in North America

[2]**North American** *adj* : of or relating to North America or the North Americans

north·bound *adj* : going north

[1]**north·east** *adv* : to or toward the direction between north and east

[2]**northeast** *adj* : placed toward, facing, or coming from the northeast

[3]**northeast** *n* **1** : the direction between north and east **2** *cap* : regions or countries northeast of a point that is mentioned or understood

north·east·er·ly *adv or adj* **1** : from the northeast **2** : toward the northeast

north·east·ern *adj* **1** *often cap* : of, relating to, or like that of the Northeast **2** : lying toward or coming from the northeast

north·er·ly *adj or adv* **1** : toward the north **2** : from the north

north·ern *adj* **1** *often cap* : of, relating to, or like that of the North **2** : lying toward or coming from the north

northern lights *n pl* : AURORA BOREALIS

north·land *n, often cap* : land in the north : the north of a country or region

north pole *n* **1** *often cap N&P* : the most northern point of the earth : the northern end of the earth's axis **2** : the end of a magnet that points toward the north when the magnet is free to swing

North Star *n* : the star toward which the northern end of the earth's axis very nearly points

north·ward *adv or adj* : toward the north

[1]**north·west** *adv* : to or toward the direction between north and west

[2]**northwest** *adj* : placed toward, facing, or coming from the northwest

[3]**northwest** *n* **1** : the direction between north and west **2** *cap* : regions or countries northwest of a point that is mentioned or understood

north·west·er·ly *adv or adj* **1** : from the northwest **2** : toward the northwest

north·west·ern *adj* **1** *often cap* : of, relating to, or like that of the Northwest **2** : lying toward or coming from the northwest

[1]**Nor·we·gian** *adj* : of or relating to Norway, its people, or the Norwegian language

[2]**Norwegian** *n* **1** : a person who is born or lives in Norway **2** : the language of the Norwegians

nos *pl of* NO

[1]**nose** *n* **1** : the part of a person's face or an animal's head that contains the nostrils **2** : the sense or organ of smell **3** : something (as a point, edge, or the front of an object) that suggests a nose **4** : an ability to discover — **nosed** *adj*

[2]**nose** *vb* **nosed; nos·ing 1** : to detect by or as if by smell : SCENT **2** : to touch or rub with the nose : NUZZLE **3** : to search in a nosy way : PRY **4** : to move ahead slowly or carefully

nose·bleed *n* : a bleeding at the nose

nose cone *n* : a protective cone forming the forward end of a rocket or missile

nose–dive *vb* **nose–dived; nose–div·ing** : to plunge suddenly or sharply

nose dive *n* **1** : a downward plunge (as of an airplane) **2** : a sudden sharp drop (as in prices)

nos·tal·gia *n* : a wishing for something past

nos·tril *n* : either of the outer openings of the nose through which one breathes

nos·trum *n* : a medicine of secret formula and doubtful worth : a questionable remedy

nosy

nosy or **nos·ey** adj **nos·i·er; nos·i·est** : tending to pry into someone else's business

not adv **1** — used to make a word or group of words negative **2** — used to stand for the negative of a group of words that comes before

¹no·ta·ble adj **1** : deserving special notice : REMARKABLE **2** : DISTINGUISHED, PROMINENT — **no·ta·bly** adv

²notable n : a famous person

no·ta·rize vb **no·ta·rized; no·ta·riz·ing** : to sign as a notary public to show that a document is authentic

no·ta·ry public n, pl **notaries public** or **notary publics** : a public officer who witnesses the making of a document (as a deed) and signs it to show that it is authentic

no·ta·tion n **1** : the act of noting **2** : ²NOTE 5 **3** : a system of signs, marks, or figures used to give specified information

¹notch n **1** : a cut in the shape of a V in an edge or surface **2** : a narrow pass between mountains **3** : DEGREE 1, STEP

²notch vb : to cut or make notches in

¹note vb **not·ed; not·ing 1** : to notice or observe with care **2** : to record in writing **3** : to call attention to in speech or writing

²note n **1** : a musical sound : TONE **2** : a symbol in music that by its shape and position on the staff shows the pitch of a tone and the length of time it is to be held **3** : the musical call or song of a bird **4** : a quality that shows a feeling **5** : something written down often to aid the memory **6** : a printed comment in a book that helps explain part of the text **7** : DISTINCTION 3 **8** : a short written message or letter **9** : careful notice **10** : a promise to pay a debt **11** : a piano key **12** : frame of mind : MOOD

note·book n : a book of blank pages for writing in

not·ed adj : well-known and highly regarded

note·wor·thy adj : worthy of note : REMARKABLE — **note·wor·thi·ness** n

¹noth·ing pron **1** : not anything : no thing **2** : one of no interest, value, or importance

²nothing adv : not at all : in no way

³nothing n **1** : something that does not exist **2** : ZERO 1 4 **3** : something of little or no worth or importance — **noth·ing·ness** n

¹no·tice n **1** : WARNING **2** : an indication that an agreement will end at a specified time **3** : ATTENTION 1, HEED **4** : a written or printed announcement **5** : a brief published criticism (as of a book or play)

²notice vb **no·ticed; no·tic·ing** : to take notice of : pay attention to

no·tice·able adj : deserving notice : likely to be noticed — **no·tice·ably** adv

no·ti·fi·ca·tion n **1** : the act or an instance of notifying **2** : something written or printed that gives notice

no·ti·fy vb **no·ti·fied; no·ti·fy·ing** : to give notice to : INFORM

no·tion n **1** : IDEA 2 **2** : WHIM **3 notions** pl : small useful articles (as buttons, needles, and thread)

no·to·ri·e·ty n : the state of being notorious

no·to·ri·ous adj : widely known for some bad characteristic — **no·to·ri·ous·ly** adv

¹not·with·stand·ing prep : in spite of

²notwithstanding adv : NEVERTHELESS

nou·gat n : a candy consisting of a sugar paste with nuts or fruit pieces

nought variant of NAUGHT

noun n : a word or phrase that is the name of something (as a person, place, or thing) and that is used in a sentence especially as subject or object of a verb or as object of a preposition

nour·ish vb : to cause to grow or live in a healthy state especially by providing with enough good food — **nour·ish·ing** adj

nour·ish·ment n **1** : something (as food) that nourishes **2** : the act of nourishing : the state of being nourished

¹nov·el adj **1** : new and different from what is already known **2** : original or striking in design or appearance

²novel n : a long made-up story that usually fills a book

nov·el·ist n : a writer of novels

nov·el·ty n, pl **nov·el·ties 1** : something new or unusual **2** : the quality or state of being novel **3** : a small article of unusual design intended mainly for decoration or adornment

No·vem·ber n : the eleventh month of the year

nov·ice n **1** : a new member of a religious community who is preparing to take the vows of religion **2** : a person who has no previous experience with something : BEGINNER

¹now adv **1** : at this time **2** : immediately before the present time **3** : in the time immediately to follow **4** — used to express command or introduce an important point **5** : SOMETIMES **6** : in the present state **7** : at the time referred to

²now conj : in view of the fact that : ²SINCE 2

³now n : the present time

now·a·days adv : at the present time

¹no·where adv **1** : not in or at any place **2** : to no place

²nowhere n : a place that does not exist

nox·ious adj : causing harm

noz·zle n : a short tube with a taper or constriction often used on a hose or pipe to direct or speed up a flow of fluid

-n't adv suffix : not

nu·cle·ar adj **1** : of, relating to, or being a nucleus (as of a cell) **2** : of or relating to the nucleus of the atom **3** : produced by a nuclear reaction **4** : of, relating to, or being a weapon whose destructive power comes from an uncontrolled nuclear reaction **5** : relating to or powered by nuclear energy

nu·cle·us n, pl **nu·clei 1** : a central point, group, or mass **2** : a part of cell protoplasm enclosed in a nuclear membrane, containing chromosomes and genes, and concerned especially with the control of vital functions and heredity **3** : the central part of an atom that comprises nearly all of the atomic mass and that consists of protons and neutrons except in hydrogen in which it consists of one proton only

nude adj **nud·er; nud·est** : not wearing clothes : NAKED — **nude·ness** n

¹nudge vb **nudged; nudg·ing** : to touch or push gently (as with the elbow) especially in order to attract attention

²nudge n : a slight push

nu·di·ty n : the quality or state of being nude

nug·get n : a solid lump especially of precious metal

nui·sance n : an annoying person or thing

null adj : having no legal force : not binding : VOID

null and void adj : NULL

¹numb adj **1** : lacking in sensation especially from cold **2** : lacking feelings : INDIFFERENT — **numb·ly** adv — **numb·ness** n

²numb vb : to make or become numb

¹num·ber n **1** : the total of persons, things, or units taken together : AMOUNT **2** : a total that is not specified **3** : a quality of a word form that shows whether the word is singular or plural **4** : NUMERAL **5** : a certain numeral for telling one person or thing from another or from others **6** : one of a series

²number vb **1** : ¹COUNT 1 **2** : INCLUDE **3** : to limit to a certain number **4** : to give a number to **5** : to add up to or have a total of

num·ber·less adj : too many to count

number line n : a line in which points are matched to numbers

nu·mer·al n : a symbol or group of symbols representing a number

nu·mer·a·tion n : a system of counting

nu·mer·a·tor n : the part of a fraction that is above the line

nu·mer·i·cal adj : of or relating to number : stated in numbers — **nu·mer·i·cal·ly** adv

nu·mer·ous adj : consisting of a large number — **nu·mer·ous·ly** adv

num·skull n : a stupid person

nun n : a woman belonging to a religious community and living by vows

nun·cio n, pl **nun·ci·os** : a person who is the pope's representative to a civil government

nup·tial adj : of or relating to marriage or a wedding

nup·tials n pl : WEDDING

¹nurse n **1** : a woman employed for the care of a young child **2** : a person skilled or trained in the care of the sick

²nurse vb **nursed; nurs·ing 1** : to feed at the breast **2** : to take care of (as a young child or a sick person) **3** : to treat with special care

nurse·maid n : ¹NURSE 1

nurs·ery n, pl **nurs·er·ies 1** : a place set aside for small children or for the care of small children **2** : a place where young trees, vines, and plants are grown and usually sold

nurs·ery·man n, pl **nurs·ery·men** : a person whose occupation is the growing of trees, shrubs, and plants

¹nur·ture n **1** : UPBRINGING **2** : something (as food) that nourishes

²nurture vb **nur·tured; nur·tur·ing 1** : to supply with food **2** : EDUCATE 2 **3** : to provide for growth of

¹nut n **1** : a dry fruit or seed with a firm inner kernel and a hard shell **2** : the often edible kernel of a nut **3** : a piece of metal with a hole in it that is fastened to a bolt by means of a screw thread **4** : a foolish or crazy person — **nut·like** adj

²nut vb **nut·ted; nut·ting** : to gather or seek nuts

nut·crack·er n **1** : a device used for cracking the shells of nuts **2** : a bird related to the crows that lives mostly on the seeds of pine trees

nut·hatch n : a small bird that creeps on tree trunks and branches and eats insects

nut·let n **1** : a small nut **2** : a small fruit like a nut

nut·meg n : a spice that is the ground seeds of a small evergreen tropical tree

nu·tri·ent n : a substance used in nutrition

nu·tri·ment n : something that nourishes

nu·tri·tion n : the act or process of nourishing or being nourished : the processes by which a living being takes in and uses nutrients

nu·tri·tion·al adj : of or relating to nutrition

nu·tri·tious adj : providing nutrients : NOURISHING

nu·tri·tive adj **1** : NUTRITIONAL **2** : NUTRITIOUS

nut·ty *adj* **nut·ti·er; nut·ti·est** **1** : not showing good sense **2** : having a flavor like that
of nuts

nuz·zle *vb* **nuz·zled; nuz·zling** **1** : to push
or rub with the nose **2** : to lie close : NESTLE

ny·lon *n* : a synthetic material used in the
making of textiles and plastics

nymph *n* **1** : one of many goddesses in old
legends represented as beautiful young girls
living in the mountains, forests, and waters
2 : an immature insect that differs from the
adult chiefly in the size and proportions of
the body

O

o *n, pl* **o's** *or* **os** *often cap* **1** : the fifteenth
letter of the English alphabet **2** : ZERO 1

O *variant of* OH

oaf *n* : a stupid or awkward person — **oaf-
ish** *adj*

oak *n* : any of various trees and shrubs related to the beech and chestnut whose fruits
are acorns and whose tough wood is much
used for furniture and flooring

oak·en *adj* : made of or like oak

oar *n* : a long pole with a broad blade at one
end used for rowing or steering a boat

oar·lock *n* : a usually U-shaped device for
holding an oar in place

oars·man *n, pl* **oars·men** : a person who
rows a boat

oa·sis *n, pl* **oa·ses** : a fertile or green spot in
a desert

oat *n* **1** : a cereal grass grown for its loose
clusters of seeds that are used for human
food and animal feed **2 oats** *pl* : a crop or
the grain of the oat

oath *n, pl* **oaths** **1** : a solemn appeal to God
or to some deeply respected person or thing
to witness to the truth of one's word or the
sacredness of a promise **2** : a careless or
improper use of a sacred name

oat·meal *n* **1** : oats husked and ground into
meal or flattened into flakes **2** : a hot cereal made from meal or flakes of oats

obe·di·ence *n* : the act of obeying : willingness to obey

obe·di·ent *adj* : willing to obey : likely to
mind — **obe·di·ent·ly** *adv*

obe·lisk *n* : a four-sided pillar that becomes
narrower toward the top and ends in a pyramid

obese *adj* : very fat

obey *vb* **obeyed; obey·ing** **1** : to follow
the commands or guidance of **2** : to comply with : carry out

obit·u·ary *n, pl* **obit·u·ar·ies** : a notice of a
person's death (as in a newspaper)

¹ob·ject *n* **1** : something that may be seen
or felt **2** : something that arouses feelings
in an observer **3** : ¹PURPOSE, AIM **4** : a
noun or a term behaving like a noun that receives the action of a verb or completes the
meaning of a preposition

²ob·ject *vb* **1** : to offer or mention as an objection **2** : to oppose something firmly and
usually with words

ob·jec·tion *n* **1** : an act of objecting **2** : a
reason for or a feeling of disapproval

ob·jec·tion·able *adj* : arousing objection
: OFFENSIVE

¹ob·jec·tive *adj* **1** : being outside of the
mind and independent of it **2** : being or belonging to the case of a noun or pronoun
that is an object of a transitive verb or a
preposition **3** : dealing with facts without
allowing one's feelings to confuse them —
ob·jec·tive·ly *adv*

²objective *n* : ¹PURPOSE, GOAL

ob·jec·tiv·i·ty *n* : the quality or state of being
objective

ob·li·gate *vb* **ob·li·gat·ed; ob·li·gat·ing** **1**
: to make (someone) do something by law
or because it is right **2** : OBLIGE 2

ob·li·ga·tion *n* **1** : an act of making oneself
responsible for doing something **2** : something (as the demands of a promise or
contract) that requires one to do something
3 : something one must do : DUTY **4** : a
feeling of being indebted for an act of kindness

oblige *vb* **obliged; oblig·ing** **1** : ²FORCE 1,
COMPEL **2** : to earn the gratitude of **3** : to
do a favor for or do something as a favor

oblig·ing *adj* : willing to do favors — **oblig-
ing·ly** *adv*

oblique *adj* : neither perpendicular nor parallel — **oblique·ly** *adv*

oblit·er·ate *vb* **oblit·er·at·ed; oblit·er·at·ing**
: to remove or destroy completely

obliv·i·on *n* **1** : the state of forgetting or
having forgotten or of being unaware or
unconscious **2** : the state of being forgotten

obliv·i·ous *adj* : not being conscious or
aware — **obliv·i·ous·ly** *adv* — **obliv·i·ous-
ness** *n*

¹ob·long *adj* : different from a square, circle, or sphere by being longer in one direction than the other

²oblong *n* : an oblong figure or object

ob·nox·ious *adj* : very disagreeable : HATE-
FUL — **ob·nox·ious·ly** *adv* — **ob·nox-
ious·ness** *n*

oboe *n* : a woodwind instrument with two reeds that has a penetrating tone and a range of nearly three octaves

ob·scene *adj* : very shocking to one's sense of what is moral or decent

ob·scen·i·ty *n, pl* **ob·scen·i·ties** **1** : the quality or state of being obscene **2** : something that is obscene

¹ob·scure *adj* **1** : ¹DARK 1, GLOOMY **2** : SECLUDED **3** : not easily understood or clearly expressed **4** : not outstanding or famous

²obscure *vb* **ob·scured; ob·scur·ing** : to make obscure

ob·scu·ri·ty *n, pl* **ob·scu·ri·ties** **1** : the quality or state of being obscure **2** : something that is obscure

ob·serv·able *adj* : NOTICEABLE — **ob·serv·ably** *adv*

ob·ser·vance *n* **1** : an established practice or ceremony **2** : an act of following a custom, rule, or law

ob·ser·vant *adj* : quick to take notice : WATCHFUL, ALERT — **ob·ser·vant·ly** *adv*

ob·ser·va·tion *n* **1** : an act or the power of seeing or of fixing the mind upon something **2** : the gathering of information by noting facts or occurrences **3** : an opinion formed or expressed after observing **4** : the fact of being observed

ob·ser·va·to·ry *n, pl* **ob·ser·va·to·ries** : a place that has instruments for making observations (as of the stars)

ob·serve *vb* **ob·served; ob·serv·ing** **1** : to act in agreement with : OBEY **2** : CELEBRATE **2** **3** : ¹WATCH 5 **4** : ²REMARK 2, SAY — **ob·serv·er** *n*

ob·sess *vb* : to occupy the mind of completely or abnormally

ob·ses·sion *n* : a disturbing and often unreasonable idea or feeling that cannot be put out of the mind

ob·sid·i·an *n* : a smooth dark rock formed by the cooling of lava

ob·so·lete *adj* : no longer in use : OUT-OF-DATE

ob·sta·cle *n* : something that stands in the way or opposes : HINDRANCE

ob·sti·na·cy *n* : the quality or state of being obstinate

ob·sti·nate *adj* **1** : sticking stubbornly to an opinion or purpose **2** : not easily overcome or removed — **ob·sti·nate·ly** *adv*

ob·struct *vb* **1** : to stop up by an obstacle : BLOCK **2** : to be or come in the way of : HINDER

ob·struc·tion *n* **1** : an act of obstructing : the state of being obstructed **2** : something that gets in the way : OBSTACLE

ob·tain *vb* : to gain or get hold of with effort

ob·tain·able *adj* : possible to obtain

ob·tuse *adj* **1** : not pointed or sharp : BLUNT **2** : measuring more than a right angle **3** : not quick or keen of understanding or feeling

ob·vi·ous *adj* : easily found, seen, or understood — **ob·vi·ous·ly** *adv* — **ob·vi·ous·ness** *n*

oc·ca·sion *n* **1** : a suitable opportunity : a good chance **2** : the time of an event **3** : a special event

oc·ca·sion·al *adj* : happening or met with now and then — **oc·ca·sion·al·ly** *adv*

oc·cu·pan·cy *n, pl* **oc·cu·pan·cies** : the act of occupying or taking possession

oc·cu·pant *n* : a person who occupies or takes possession

oc·cu·pa·tion *n* **1** : one's business or profession **2** : the taking possession and control of an area

oc·cu·pa·tion·al *adj* : of or relating to one's occupation — **oc·cu·pa·tion·al·ly** *adv*

oc·cu·py *vb* **oc·cu·pied; oc·cu·py·ing** **1** : to take up the attention or energies of **2** : to fill up (an extent of time or space) **3** : to take or hold possession of **4** : to live in as an owner or tenant

oc·cur *vb* **oc·curred; oc·cur·ring** **1** : to be found or met with : APPEAR **2** : to present itself : come by or as if by chance **3** : to come into the mind

oc·cur·rence *n* **1** : something that occurs **2** : the action or process of occurring

ocean *n* **1** : the whole body of salt water that covers nearly three fourths of the earth **2** : one of the large bodies of water into which the great ocean is divided

oce·an·ic *adj* : of or relating to the ocean

ocean·og·ra·phy *n* : a science that deals with the ocean

oce·lot *n* : a medium-sized American wildcat that is tawny or grayish and blotched with black

o'·clock *adv* : according to the clock

octa- *or* **octo-** *also* **oct-** *prefix* : eight

oc·ta·gon *n* : a flat figure with eight angles and eight sides

oc·tag·o·nal *adj* : having eight sides

oc·tave *n* **1** : a space of eight steps between musical notes **2** : a tone or note that is eight steps above or below another note or tone

oc·tet *n* : a group or set of eight

Oc·to·ber *n* : the tenth month of the year

oc·to·pus *n, pl* **oc·to·pus·es** *or* **oc·to·pi** : a marine animal with no shell that has a rounded body with eight long flexible arms about its base which have sucking disks able to seize and hold things (as prey)

oc·u·lar *adj* : of or relating to the eye or eyesight

odd *adj* **1** : not one of a pair or a set **2** : not capable of being divided by two without leaving a remainder **3** : numbered with an odd number **4** : some more than the number mentioned **5** : not usual, expected, or planned **6** : not usual or traditional — **odd·ly** *adv* — **odd·ness** *n*

odd·ball *n* : a person who behaves strangely

odd·i·ty *n, pl* **odd·i·ties** **1** : something odd **2** : the quality or state of being odd

odds *n pl* **1** : a difference in favor of one thing over another **2** : DISAGREEMENT 1

odds and ends *n pl* : things left over : miscellaneous things

ode *n* : a lyric poem that expresses a noble feeling with dignity

odi·ous *adj* : causing hatred or strong dislike : worthy of hatred

odom·e·ter *n* : an instrument for measuring the distance traveled (as by a vehicle)

odor *n* **1** : a quality of something that one becomes aware of through the sense of smell **2** : a smell whether pleasant or unpleasant — **odored** *adj* — **odor·less** *adj*

odor·ous *adj* : having or giving off an odor

o'er *adv or prep* : OVER

of *prep* **1** : proceeding from : belonging to **2** : CONCERNING **3** — used to show what has been taken away or what one has been freed from **4** : on account of **5** : made from **6** — used to join an amount or a part with the whole which includes it **7** : that is **8** : that has : WITH 8

1off *adv* **1** : from a place or position **2** : from a course : ASIDE **3** : into sleep **4** : so as not to be supported, covering or enclosing, or attached **5** : so as to be discontinued or finished **6** : away from work

2off *prep* **1** : away from the surface or top of **2** : at the expense of **3** : released or freed from **4** : below the usual level of **5** : away from

3off *adj* **1** : more removed or distant **2** : started on the way **3** : not taking place **4** : not operating **5** : not correct : WRONG **6** : not entirely sane **7** : small in degree : SLIGHT **8** : provided for

of·fend *vb* **1** : to do wrong : SIN **2** : to hurt the feelings of : DISTRESS

of·fend·er *n* : a person who offends

of·fense *or* **of·fence** *n* **1** : an act of attacking : ASSAULT **2** : an offensive team **3** : the act of offending : the state of being offended **4** : WRONGDOING, SIN

1of·fen·sive *adj* **1** : relating to or made for or suited to attack **2** : of or relating to the attempt to score in a game or contest **3** : causing displeasure or resentment — **of·fen·sive·ly** *adv* — **of·fen·sive·ness** *n*

2offensive *n* **1** : the state or attitude of one who is making an attack **2** : 2ATTACK 1

1of·fer *vb* **1** : to present as an act of worship : SACRIFICE **2** : to present (something) to be accepted or rejected **3** : to present for consideration : SUGGEST **4** : to declare one's willingness **5** : PUT UP 5

2offer *n* **1** : an act of offering **2** : a price suggested by one prepared to buy : BID

of·fer·ing *n* **1** : the act of one who offers **2** : something offered **3** : a sacrifice offered as part of worship **4** : a contribution to the support of a church

off·hand *adv or adj* : without previous thought or preparation

of·fice *n* **1** : a special duty or post and especially one of authority in government **2** : a place where business is done or a service is supplied

of·fice·hold·er *n* : a person who holds public office

of·fi·cer *n* **1** : a person given the responsibility of enforcing the law **2** : a person who holds an office **3** : a person who holds a commission in the armed forces

1of·fi·cial *n* : OFFICER 2

2official *adj* **1** : of or relating to an office **2** : having authority to perform a duty **3** : coming from or meeting the requirements of an authority **4** : proper for a person in office — **of·fi·cial·ly** *adv*

of·fi·ci·ate *vb* **of·fi·ci·at·ed; of·fi·ci·at·ing** **1** : to perform a ceremony or duty **2** : to act as an officer : PRESIDE

off·ing *n* : the near future or distance

off–line *adj or adv* : not connected to or directly controlled by a computer system

1off·set *n* : something that serves to make up for something else

2offset *vb* **offset; off·set·ting** : to make up for

off·shoot *n* : a branch of a main stem of a plant

1off·shore *adv* : from the shore : at a distance from the shore

2off·shore *adj* **1** : coming or moving away from the shore **2** : located off the shore

off·spring *n, pl* **offspring** *also* **off·springs** : the young of a person, animal, or plant

off·stage *adv or adj* : off or away from the stage

off–the–rec·ord *adj* : given or made in confidence and not for publication

oft *adv* : OFTEN

of·ten *adv* : many times

of·ten·times *adv* : OFTEN

ogle *vb* **ogled; ogling** : to look at (as a person) in a flirting way or with unusual attention or desire

ogre *n* **1** : an ugly giant of fairy tales and

folklore who eats people **2** : a dreaded person or object

oh *or* **O** *interj* **1** — used to express an emotion (as surprise or pain) **2** — used in direct address

1-oid *n suffix* : something resembling a specified object or having a specified quality

2-oid *adj suffix* : resembling : having the form or appearance of

1oil *n* **1** : any of numerous greasy usually liquid substances from plant, animal, or mineral sources that do not dissolve in water and are used especially as lubricants, fuels, and food **2** : PETROLEUM **3** : artists' paints made of pigments and oil **4** : a painting in oils

2oil *vb* : to put oil on or in

oil·cloth *n* : cloth treated with oil or paint so as to be waterproof and used for shelf and table coverings

oily *adj* **oil·i·er; oil·i·est** **1** : of, relating to, or containing oil **2** : covered or soaked with oil — **oil·i·ness** *n*

oint·ment *n* : a semisolid usually greasy medicine for use on the skin

1OK *or* **okay** *adv or adj* : all right

2OK *or* **okay** *n* : APPROVAL

3OK *or* **okay** *vb* **OK'd** *or* **okayed; OK'·ing** *or* **okay·ing** : APPROVE 2, AUTHORIZE

oka·pi *n* : an animal of the African forests related to the giraffe

okra *n* : a plant related to the hollyhocks and grown for its edible green pods which are used in soups and stews

1old *adj* **1** : dating from the distant past : ANCIENT **2** : having lasted or been such for a long time **3** : having existed for a specified length of time **4** : having lived a long time **5** : FORMER **6** : showing the effects of time or use

2old *n* : old or earlier time

old·en *adj* : of or relating to earlier days

Old English *n* : the language of the English people from the earliest documents in the seventh century to about 1100

old–fash·ioned *adj* **1** : of, relating to, or like that of an earlier time **2** : holding fast to old ways : CONSERVATIVE

Old French *n* : the French language from the ninth to the thirteenth century

Old Glory *n* : the flag of the United States

old maid *n* **1** : an elderly unmarried woman **2** : a very neat fussy person **3** : a card game in which cards are matched in pairs and the player holding the extra queen at the end loses

old·ster *n* : an old person

old–time *adj* : 1OLD 1

old–tim·er *n* **1** : 1VETERAN 1 **2** : OLDSTER

old–world *adj* : having old-fashioned charm

oleo·mar·ga·rine *n* : MARGARINE

ol·fac·to·ry *adj* : of or relating to smelling or the sense of smell

ol·ive *n* **1** : an oily fruit that is eaten both ripe and unripe, is the source of an edible oil (**olive oil**), and grows on an evergreen tree with hard smooth shining wood (**olive wood**) **2** : a yellowish green

Olym·pic *adj* : of or relating to the Olympic Games

Olympic Games *n pl* : a series of international athletic contests held in a different country once every four years

om·e·lette *or* **om·e·let** *n* : eggs beaten with milk or water, cooked without stirring until firm, and folded in half often over a filling

omen *n* : a happening believed to be a sign or warning of a future event

om·i·nous *adj* : being a sign of evil or trouble to come — **om·i·nous·ly** *adv* — **om·i·nous·ness** *n*

omis·sion *n* **1** : something omitted **2** : the act of omitting : the state of being omitted

omit *vb* **omit·ted; omit·ting** **1** : to leave out : fail to include **2** : to leave undone : NEGLECT

om·ni·bus *n* : BUS

om·nip·o·tent *adj* : having power or authority without limit : ALMIGHTY

1on *prep* **1** : over and in contact with **2** : AGAINST 3 **3** : near or connected with **4** : 1TO 1 **5** : sometime during **6** : in the state or process of **7** : 2ABOUT 3 **8** : by means of

2on *adv* **1** : in or into contact with a surface **2** : forward in time, space, or action **3** : from one to another **4** : into operation or a position allowing operation

3on *adj* **1** : being in operation **2** : placed so as to allow operation **3** : taking place **4** : having been planned

1once *adv* **1** : one time only **2** : at any one time : EVER **3** : at some time in the past : FORMERLY

2once *n* : one single time — **at once** **1** : at the same time **2** : IMMEDIATELY 2

3once *conj* : as soon as : WHEN

once–over *n* : a quick glance or examination

on·com·ing *adj* : coming nearer

1one *adj* **1** : being a single unit or thing **2** : being a certain unit or thing **3** : being the same in kind or quality **4** : not specified

2one *n* **1** : the number denoting a single unit : 1 **2** : the first in a set or series **3** : a single person or thing

3one *pron* **1** : a single member or individual **2** : any person

one another *pron* : EACH OTHER

one·self *pron* : one's own self

one–sid·ed *adj* **1** : having or happening on

one side only **2** : having one side more developed **3** : favoring one side

one·time *adj* : FORMER

one–way *adj* : moving or allowing movement in one direction only

on·go·ing *adj* : being in progress or movement

on·ion *n* : the edible bulb of a plant related to the lilies that has a sharp odor and taste and is used as a vegetable and to season foods

on–line *adj or adv* : connected to, directly controlled by, or available through a computer system

on·look·er *n* : SPECTATOR

¹on·ly *adj* **1** : best without doubt **2** : alone in or of a class or kind : SOLE

²only *adv* **1** : as a single fact or instance and nothing more or different **2** : no one or nothing other than **3** : in the end **4** : as recently as

³only *conj* : except that

on·o·mato·poe·ia *n* : the forming of a word (as "buzz" or "hiss") in imitation of a natural sound

on·rush *n* : a rushing forward

on·set *n* **1** : ²ATTACK 1 **2** : BEGINNING

on·slaught *n* : a violent attack

on·to *prep* : to a position on or against

¹on·ward *adv* : toward or at a point lying ahead in space or time : FORWARD

²onward *adj* : directed or moving onward

oo·dles *n pl* : a great quantity

¹ooze *n* : soft mud : SLIME

²ooze *vb* **oozed; ooz·ing** : to flow or leak out slowly

opal *n* : a mineral with soft changeable colors that is used as a gem

opaque *adj* **1** : not letting light through : not transparent **2** : not reflecting light : DULL

¹open *adj* **1** : not shut or blocked : not closed **2** : not enclosed or covered **3** : not secret : PUBLIC **4** : to be used, entered, or taken part in by all **5** : easy to enter, get through, or see **6** : not drawn together : spread out **7** : not decided or settled **8** : ready to consider appeals or ideas — **open·ly** *adv* — **open·ness** *n*

²open *vb* **1** : to change or move from a shut condition **2** : to clear by or as if by removing something in the way **3** : to make or become ready for use **4** : to have an opening **5** : BEGIN 1, START — **open·er** *n*

³open *n* : open space : OUTDOORS

open–air *adj* : OUTDOOR

open–and–shut *adj* : ¹PLAIN 3, OBVIOUS

open·heart·ed *adj* **1** : FRANK **2** : GENEROUS 1

open·ing *n* **1** : an act of opening **2** : an

open place : CLEARING **3** : BEGINNING **4** : OCCASION 1 **5** : a job opportunity

open letter *n* : a letter (as one addressed to an official) for the public to see and printed in a newspaper or magazine

open·work *n* : something made or work done so as to show openings through the fabric or material

op·era *n* : a play in which the entire text is sung with orchestral accompaniment

opera glasses *n* : small binoculars of low power for use in a theater

op·er·ate *vb* **op·er·at·ed; op·er·at·ing** **1** : to work or cause to work in a proper way **2** : to take effect **3** : MANAGE 1 **4** : to perform surgery : do an operation on (as a person)

operating system *n* : a program or series of programs that controls the operation of a computer and directs the processing of the user's programs (as by assigning storage space and controlling input and output functions)

op·er·a·tion *n* **1** : the act, process, method, or result of operating **2** : the quality or state of being able to work **3** : a certain piece or kind of surgery **4** : a process (as addition or multiplication) of getting one mathematical expression from others according to a rule **5** : the process of putting military or naval forces into action **6** : a single step performed by a computer in carrying out a program

op·er·a·tion·al *adj* **1** : of or relating to operation or an operation **2** : ready for operation

op·er·a·tor *n* **1** : a person who operates something (as a business) **2** : a person in charge of a telephone switchboard

op·er·et·ta *n* : a light play set to music with speaking, singing, and dancing scenes

opin·ion *n* **1** : a belief based on experience and on seeing certain facts but not amounting to sure knowledge **2** : a judgment about a person or thing **3** : a statement by an expert after careful study

opin·ion·at·ed *adj* : holding to one's opinions too strongly

opi·um *n* : a bitter brownish narcotic drug that is the dried juice of one kind of poppy

opos·sum *n* : a common American animal related to the kangaroos that lives mostly in trees and is active at night

op·po·nent *n* : a person or thing that opposes another

op·por·tu·ni·ty *n, pl* **op·por·tu·ni·ties** **1** : a favorable combination of circumstances, time, and place **2** : a chance to better oneself

op·pose *vb* **op·posed; op·pos·ing** **1** : to

be or place opposite to something **2** : to offer resistance to : stand against : RESIST

¹op·po·site *adj* **1** : being at the other end, side, or corner **2** : being in a position to oppose or cancel out **3** : being as different as possible : CONTRARY

²opposite *n* : either of two persons or things that are as different as possible

³opposite *adv* : on the opposite side

⁴opposite *prep* : across from and usually facing or on the same level with

op·po·si·tion *n* **1** : the state of being opposite **2** : the action of resisting **3** : a group of persons that oppose someone or something **4** *often cap* : a political party opposed to the party in power

op·press *vb* **1** : to cause to feel burdened in spirit **2** : to control or rule in a harsh or cruel way

op·pres·sion *n* **1** : cruel or unjust use of power or authority **2** : a feeling of low spirits

op·pres·sive *adj* **1** : cruel or harsh without just cause **2** : causing a feeling of oppression — **op·pres·sive·ly** *adv*

op·tic *adj* : of or relating to seeing or the eye

op·ti·cal *adj* **1** : of or relating to the science of optics **2** : of or relating to seeing : VISUAL **3** : involving the use of devices that are sensitive to light to get information for a computer

optical fiber *n* : a single fiber used in fiber optics

optical illusion *n* : ILLUSION 1

op·ti·cian *n* : a person who prepares eyeglass lenses and sells glasses

op·tics *n* : a science that deals with the nature and properties of light and the changes that it undergoes and produces

op·ti·mism *n* : a habit of expecting things to turn out for the best

op·ti·mist *n* : an optimistic person

op·ti·mis·tic *adj* : showing optimism : expecting everything to come out all right : HOPEFUL

op·ti·mum *adj* : most desirable or satisfactory

op·tion *n* **1** : the power or right to choose **2** : a right to buy or sell something at a specified price during a specified period

op·tion·al *adj* : left to one's choice : not required

op·tom·e·trist *n* : a person who prescribes glasses or exercise to improve the eyesight

op·u·lent *adj* : having or showing much wealth

or *conj* — used between words or phrases that are choices

¹-or *n suffix* : one that does a specified thing

²-or *n suffix* : condition : activity

or·a·cle *n* **1** : a person (as a priestess in ancient Greece) through whom a god is believed to speak **2** : the place where a god speaks through an oracle **3** : an answer given by an oracle

orac·u·lar *adj* : of, relating to, or serving as an oracle

oral *adj* **1** : ²SPOKEN 1 **2** : of, relating to, given by, or near the mouth — **oral·ly** *adv*

or·ange *n* **1** : a sweet juicy fruit with a reddish yellow rind that grows on an evergreen citrus tree with shining leaves and fragrant white flowers **2** : a color between red and yellow

or·ange·ade *n* : a drink made of orange juice, sugar, and water

orang·utan *or* **orang·ou·tan** *n* : a large ape of Borneo and Sumatra that eats plants, lives in trees, and has very long arms and hairless face, feet, and hands

ora·tion *n* : an important speech given on a special occasion

or·a·tor *n* : a public speaker noted for skill and power in speaking

or·a·tor·i·cal *adj* : of, relating to, or like an orator or oratory — **or·a·tor·i·cal·ly** *adv*

or·a·to·ry *n* **1** : the art of an orator **2** : the style of language used in an oration

orb *n* : something in the shape of a ball (as a planet or the eye)

¹or·bit *n* : the path taken by one body circling around another body

²orbit *vb* **1** : to move in an orbit around : CIRCLE **2** : to send up so as to move in an orbit

or·chard *n* **1** : a place where fruit trees are grown **2** : the trees in an orchard

or·ches·tra *n* **1** : a group of musicians who perform instrumental music using mostly stringed instruments **2** : the front part of the main floor in a theater

or·ches·tral *adj* : of, relating to, or written for an orchestra

or·chid *n* : any of a large group of plants with usually showy flowers with three petals of which the middle petal is enlarged into a lip and differs from the others in shape and color

or·dain *vb* **1** : to make a person a Christian minister or priest by a special ceremony **2** : ²DECREE **3** : DESTINE 1, FATE

or·deal *n* : a severe test or experience

¹or·der *vb* **1** : to put into a particular grouping or sequence : ARRANGE **2** : to give an order to or for

²order *n* **1** : a group of people united (as by living under the same religious rules or by loyalty to common needs or duties) **2 orders** *pl* : the office of a person in the Christian ministry **3** : a group of related plants or animals that ranks above the family and below the class in scientific classification **4** : the arrangement of objects or events in space or time **5** : the way something should be **6** : the state of things when law or authority is obeyed **7** : a certain rule or regulation : COMMAND **8** : good working condition **9** : a written direction to pay a sum of money **10** : a statement of what one wants to buy **11** : goods or items bought or sold — **in order to** : for the purpose of

1or·der·ly *adj* **1** : being in good order : NEAT, TIDY **2** : obeying orders or rules : well-behaved — **or·der·li·ness** *n*

2orderly *n, pl* **or·der·lies** **1** : a soldier who works for an officer especially to carry messages **2** : a person who does cleaning and general work in a hospital

or·di·nal *n* : ORDINAL NUMBER

ordinal number *n* : a number that is used to show the place (as first, fifth, twenty-second) taken by an element in a series

or·di·nance *n* : a law or regulation especially of a city or town

or·di·nar·i·ly *adv* : in the usual course of events : USUALLY

1or·di·nary *n* : the conditions or events that are usual or normal

2ordinary *adj* **1** : to be expected : NORMAL, USUAL **2** : neither good nor bad : AVERAGE **3** : not very good : MEDIOCRE — **or·di·nar·i·ness** *n*

ord·nance *n* **1** : military supplies (as guns, ammunition, trucks, and tanks) **2** : ARTILLERY 1

ore *n* : a mineral mined to obtain a substance (as gold) that it contains

or·gan *n* **1** : a musical instrument played by means of one or more keyboards and having pipes sounded by compressed air **2** : a part of a person, plant, or animal that is specialized to do a particular task **3** : a way of getting something done

or·gan·ic *adj* **1** : relating to an organ of the body **2** : having parts that fit or work together **3** : relating to or obtained from living things **4** : relating to carbon compounds : containing carbon

or·gan·ism *n* **1** : something having many related parts and functioning as a whole **2** : a living being made up of organs and able to carry on the activities of life : a living person, animal, or plant

or·gan·ist *n* : a person who plays an organ

or·ga·ni·za·tion *n* **1** : the act or process of organizing **2** : the state or way of being organized **3** : a group of persons united for a common purpose

or·ga·nize *vb* **or·ga·nized; or·ga·niz·ing** **1** : to make separate parts into one united whole **2** : to arrange in a certain order — **or·ga·niz·er** *n*

ori·ent *vb* **1** : to set or arrange in a position especially so as to be lined up with certain points of the compass **2** : to acquaint with an existing situation or environment — **ori·en·ta·tion** *n*

Ori·en·tal *adj* **1** : [1]ASIAN **2** : of or relating to the region that includes the countries of eastern Asia (as China, Japan, Vietnam, and Korea)

Oriental *n* : a member of any of the native peoples of the Orient

ori·ga·mi *n* : the art of folding paper into three-dimensional figures or designs without cutting the paper or using glue

or·i·gin *n* **1** : a person's ancestry **2** : the rise, beginning, or coming from a source **3** : basic source or cause

1orig·i·nal *n* : something from which a copy or translation can be made

2original *adj* **1** : of or relating to the origin or beginning : FIRST **2** : not copied from anything else : not translated : NEW **3** : able to think up new things : INVENTIVE — **orig·i·nal·ly** *adv*

orig·i·nal·i·ty *n* **1** : the quality or state of being original **2** : the power or ability to think, act, or do something in ways that are new

orig·i·nate *vb* **orig·i·nat·ed; orig·i·nat·ing** **1** : to bring into being : cause to be : INVENT, INITIATE **2** : to come into being — **orig·i·na·tor** *n*

ori·ole *n* **1** : an Old World yellow and black bird related to the crow **2** : an American songbird related to the blackbird and bobolink that has a bright orange and black male

1or·na·ment *n* **1** : something that adds beauty : DECORATION **2** : the act of beautifying

2or·na·ment *vb* : DECORATE 1

1or·na·men·tal *adj* : serving to ornament : DECORATIVE

2ornamental *n* : a plant grown for its beauty

or·na·men·ta·tion *n* **1** : the act or process of ornamenting : the state of being ornamented **2** : something that ornaments

or·nate *adj* : decorated in a fancy way — **or·nate·ly** *adv* — **or·nate·ness** *n*

or·nery *adj* **or·neri·er; or·neri·est** : having a bad disposition

1or·phan *n* : a child whose parents are dead

2orphan *vb* : to cause to become an orphan

or·phan·age *n* : an institution for the care of orphans

or·tho·don·tist *n* : a dentist who adjusts badly placed or irregular teeth

or·tho·dox *adj* **1** : holding established beliefs especially in religion **2** : approved as measuring up to some standard : CONVENTIONAL

1-ory *n suffix, pl* **-ories** : place of or for

2-ory *adj suffix* : of, relating to, or associated with

os·cil·late *vb* **os·cil·lat·ed; os·cil·lat·ing** : to swing back and forth like a pendulum

os·mo·sis *n* : a passing of material and especially water through a membrane (as of a living cell) that will not allow all kinds of molecules to pass

os·prey *n, pl* **ospreys** : a large hawk that feeds chiefly on fish

os·ten·si·ble *adj* : shown in an outward way : APPARENT — **os·ten·si·bly** *adv*

os·ten·ta·tious *adj* : having or fond of unnecessary show

os·tra·cize *vb* **os·tra·cized; os·tra·ciz·ing** : to shut out of a group by the agreement of all

os·trich *n* : a very large bird of Africa and the Arabian Peninsula that often weighs 300 pounds and runs very swiftly but cannot fly

1oth·er *adj* **1** : being the one (as of two or more) left **2** : 1SECOND 1 **3** : 1EXTRA, ADDITIONAL

2other *n* : a remaining or different one

3other *pron* : another thing

oth·er·wise *adv* **1** : in another way **2** : in different circumstances **3** : in other ways

ot·ter *n* : a web-footed animal related to the minks that feeds on fish

ouch *interj* — used especially to express sudden pain

ought *helping verb* **1** — used to show duty **2** — used to show what it would be wise to do **3** — used to show what is naturally expected **4** — used to show what is correct

oughtn't : ought not

ounce *n* **1** : a unit of weight equal to $1/16$ pound (about 28 grams) **2** : a unit of liquid capacity equal to $1/16$ pint (about 30 milliliters)

our *adj* : of or relating to us : done, given, or felt by us

ours *pron* : that which belongs to us

our·selves *pron* : our own selves

-ous *adj suffix* : full of : having : resembling

oust *vb* : to force or drive out (as from office or from possession of something)

oust·er *n* : the act or an instance of ousting or being ousted

1out *adv* **1** : in a direction away from the inside, center, or surface **2** : away from home, business, or the usual or proper place **3** : beyond control or possession **4** : so as to be used up, completed, or discontinued **5** : in or into the open **6** : ALOUD **7** : so as to put out or be put out in baseball

2out *prep* **1** : outward through **2** : outward on or along

3out *adj* **1** : located outside or at a distance **2** : no longer in power or use **3** : not confined : not concealed or covered **4** : 1ABSENT 1 **5** : being no longer at bat and not successful in reaching base **6** : no longer in fashion

4out *n* : PUTOUT

out- *prefix* : in a manner that goes beyond

out–and–out *adj* : THOROUGH 1

out·board motor *n* : a small gasoline engine with an attached propeller that can be fastened to the back end of a small boat

out·break *n* : something (as an epidemic of measles) that breaks out

out·build·ing *n* : a building (as a shed or stable) separate from a main building

out·burst *n* **1** : a sudden violent expression of strong feeling **2** : a sudden increase of activity or growth

1out·cast *adj* : rejected or cast out

2outcast *n* : a person who is cast out by society

out·class *vb* : EXCEL, SURPASS

out·come *n* : 2RESULT 1

out·cry *n, pl* **out·cries** **1** : a loud and excited cry **2** : a strong protest

out·dat·ed *adj* : OBSOLETE, OUTMODED

out·dis·tance *vb* **out·dis·tanced; out·dis·tanc·ing** : to go far ahead of (as in a race)

out·do *vb* **out·did; out·done; out·do·ing; out·does** : to do better than : SURPASS

out·door *adj* **1** : of or relating to the outdoors **2** : used, being, or done outdoors

1out·doors *adv* : outside a building : in or into the open air

2outdoors *n* **1** : the open air **2** : the world away from human dwellings

out·er *adj* **1** : located on the outside or farther out **2** : being beyond the earth's atmosphere or beyond the solar system

out·er·most *adj* : farthest out

out·field *n* : the part of a baseball field beyond the infield and between the foul lines

out·field·er *n* : a baseball player who plays in the outfield

1out·fit *n* **1** : the equipment or clothing for a special use **2** : a group of persons working together or associated in the same activity

2outfit *vb* **out·fit·ted; out·fit·ting** : to supply with an outfit : EQUIP — **out·fit·ter** *n*

out·go *n, pl* **outgoes** : EXPENDITURE 2

out·go·ing *adj* **1** : going out **2** : retiring from a place or position **3** : FRIENDLY 1

out·grow *vb* **out·grew; out·grown; out·grow·ing** **1** : to grow faster than **2** : to grow too large for

out·growth *n* : something that grows out of or develops from something else

out·ing *n* : a brief usually outdoor trip for pleasure

out·land·ish *adj* : very strange or unusual : BIZARRE

out·last *vb* : to last longer than

¹out·law *n* : a lawless person or one who is running away from the law

²outlaw *vb* : to make illegal

out·lay *n* : EXPENDITURE

out·let *n* **1** : a place or opening for letting something out **2** : a way of releasing or satisfying a feeling or impulse **3** : a device (as in a wall) into which the prongs of an electrical plug are inserted for making connection with an electrical circuit

¹out·line *n* **1** : a line that traces or forms the outer limits of an object or figure and shows its shape **2** : a drawing or picture giving only the outlines of a thing : this method of drawing **3** : a short treatment of a subject : SUMMARY

²outline *vb* **out·lined; out·lin·ing** : to make or prepare an outline of

out·live *vb* **out·lived; out·liv·ing** : to live longer than : OUTLAST

out·look *n* **1** : a view from a certain place **2** : a way of thinking about or looking at things **3** : conditions that seem to lie ahead

out·ly·ing *adj* : being far from a central point : REMOTE

out·mod·ed *adj* : no longer in style or in use

out·num·ber *vb* : to be more than in number

out of *prep* **1** : from the inside to the outside of : not in **2** : beyond the limits of **3** : BECAUSE OF **4** : in a group of **5** : ¹WITHOUT **2** **6** : FROM **3**

out–of–bounds *adv or adj* : outside the limits of the playing field

out–of–date *adj* : OUTMODED

out–of–door *or* **out–of–doors** *adj* : OUTDOOR **2**

out–of–doors *n* : ²OUTDOORS

out·pa·tient *n* : a person who visits a hospital for examination or treatment but who does not stay overnight at the hospital

out·post *n* **1** : a guard placed at a distance from a military force or camp **2** : the position taken by an outpost **3** : a settlement on a frontier or in a faraway place

¹out·put *n* **1** : something produced **2** : the information produced by a computer

²output *vb* **out·put·ted** *or* **out·put; out·put·ting** : to produce as output

¹out·rage *n* **1** : an act of violence or cruelty **2** : an act that hurts someone or shows disrespect for a person's feelings **3** : angry feelings caused by injury or insult

²outrage *vb* **out·raged; out·rag·ing** **1** : to cause to suffer violent injury or great insult **2** : to cause to feel anger or strong resentment

out·ra·geous *adj* : going far beyond what is right, decent, or just

¹out·right *adv* **1** : COMPLETELY **2** : without holding back **3** : on the spot : INSTANTLY

²out·right *adj* **1** : being exactly what is said **2** : given without restriction

out·run *vb* **out·ran; out·run; out·run·ning** : to run faster than

out·sell *vb* **out·sold; out·sell·ing** : to sell or be sold more than

out·set *n* : BEGINNING **1**, START

out·shine *vb* **out·shone; out·shin·ing** **1** : to shine brighter than **2** : OUTDO, SURPASS

¹out·side *n* **1** : a place or region beyond an enclosure or boundary **2** : an outer side or surface **3** : the greatest amount or limit : ³MOST

²outside *adj* **1** : of, relating to, or being on the outside **2** : coming from outside : not belonging to a place or group

³outside *adv* : on or to the outside : OUTDOORS

⁴outside *prep* : on or to the outside of : beyond the limits of

out·sid·er *n* : a person who does not belong to a certain party or group

out·size *adj* : unusually large or heavy

out·skirts *n pl* : the area that lies away from the center of a place

out·smart *vb* : OUTWIT

out·spo·ken *adj* : direct or open in expression : BLUNT — **out·spo·ken·ly** *adv* — **out·spo·ken·ness** *n*

out·spread *adj* : spread out

out·stand·ing *adj* **1** : UNPAID **2** : standing out especially because of excellence — **out·stand·ing·ly** *adv*

out·stay *vb* : to stay beyond or longer than

out·stretched *adj* : stretched out

out·strip *vb* **out·stripped; out·strip·ping** **1** : to go faster or farther than **2** : to do better than : EXCEL

¹out·ward *adj* **1** : moving or turned toward the outside or away from a center **2** : showing on the outside

²outward *or* **out·wards** *adv* : toward the outside : away from a center

out·ward·ly *adv* : on the outside : in outward appearance

out·weigh *vb* : to be greater than in weight or importance

out·wit *vb* **out·wit·ted; out·wit·ting** : to get ahead of by cleverness : BEST

out·worn *adj* : no longer useful or accepted

¹oval *n* : a figure or object having the shape of an egg or ellipse

²oval *adj* : having the shape of an oval : EL-LIPTICAL

ova·ry *n, pl* **ova·ries** **1** : an organ of the body in female animals in which eggs are produced **2** : the larger lower part of the pistil of a flower in which the seeds are formed

ova·tion *n* : a making of a loud noise by many people (as by cheering or clapping) to show great liking or respect

ov·en *n* : a heated chamber (as in a stove) for baking, heating, or drying

¹over *adv* **1** : across a barrier or space **2** : in a direction down or forward and down **3** : across the brim **4** : so as to bring the underside up **5** : beyond a limit **6** : more than needed **7** : once more : AGAIN

²over *prep* **1** : above in place : higher than **2** : above in power or value **3** : on or along the surface of **4** : on or to the other side of : ACROSS **5** : down from the top or edge of

³over *adj* **1** : being more than needed : SURPLUS **2** : brought or come to an end

¹over·all *adv* : as a whole : in most ways

²overall *adj* : including everything

over·alls *n pl* : loose pants usually with shoulder straps and a piece in front to cover the chest

over·anx·ious *adj* : much too anxious

over·bear·ing *adj* : acting in a proud or bossy way toward other people

over·board *adv* **1** : over the side of a ship into the water **2** : to extremes of enthusiasm

over·bur·den *vb* : to burden too heavily

over·cast *adj* : clouded over

over·charge *vb* **over·charged; over·charg·ing** : to charge too much

over·coat *n* : a heavy coat worn over indoor clothing

over·come *vb* **over·came; overcome; over·com·ing** **1** : to win a victory over : CONQUER **2** : to make helpless

over·con·fi·dent *adj* : too sure of oneself

over·cooked *adj* : cooked too long

over·crowd *vb* : to cause to be too crowded

over·do *vb* **over·did; over·done; over·do·ing** **1** : to do too much **2** : EXAGGERATE **3** : to cook too long

over·dose *n* : too large a dose (as of a drug)

over·dress *vb* : to dress too well for the occasion

over·due *adj* **1** : not paid when due **2** : delayed beyond an expected time

over·eat *vb* **over·ate; over·eat·en; over·eat·ing** : to eat too much

over·es·ti·mate *vb* **over·es·ti·mat·ed; over·es·ti·mat·ing** : to estimate too highly

over·flight *n* : a passage over an area in an airplane

¹over·flow *vb* **1** : to cover with or as if with water **2** : to flow over the top of **3** : to flow over bounds

²over·flow *n* **1** : a flowing over : FLOOD **2** : something that flows over : SURPLUS

over·grown *adj* : grown too big

¹over·hand *adj* : made with a downward movement of the hand or arm

²overhand *adv* : with an overhand movement

overhand knot *n* : a simple knot often used to prevent the end of a cord from pulling apart

¹over·hang *vb* **over·hung; over·hang·ing** : to stick out or hang over

²overhang *n* : a part that overhangs

¹over·haul *vb* **1** : to make a thorough examination of and make necessary repairs and adjustments on **2** : to catch up with : OVERTAKE

²over·haul *n* : an instance of overhauling

¹over·head *adv* **1** : above one's head **2** : in the sky

²over·head *adj* : placed or passing overhead

³over·head *n* : the general expenses (as for rent or heat) of a business

over·hear *vb* **over·heard; over·hear·ing** : to hear something said to someone else and not meant for one's own ears

over·heat *vb* : to heat too much : become too hot

over·joy *vb* : to make very joyful

¹over·land *adv* : by land rather than by water

²over·land *adj* : going overland

over·lap *vb* **over·lapped; over·lap·ping** : to place or be placed so that a part of one covers a part of another

¹over·lay *vb* **over·laid; over·lay·ing** : to lay or spread over or across

²over·lay *n* : something (as a veneer on wood) that is overlaid

over·load *vb* : to put too great a load on

over·look *vb* **1** : to look over : INSPECT **2** : to look down upon from a higher position **3** : to fail to see : MISS **4** : to pass over without notice or blame : EXCUSE

over·lord *n* : a lord over other lords

over·ly *adv* : by too much

¹over·night *adv* **1** : during or through the night **2** : ²FAST 3, QUICKLY

²overnight *adj* **1** : done or lasting through the night **2** : staying for the night **3** : for use on short trips

over·pass *n* : a crossing (as of two highways or a highway and a railroad) at different levels usually by means of a bridge

over·pow·er *vb* **1** : to overcome by greater force : DEFEAT **2** : to affect by being too strong

over·rate *vb* **over·rat·ed; over·rat·ing** : to value or praise too highly

over·ride *vb* **over·rode; over·rid·den; over·rid·ing** : to push aside as less important

over·ripe *adj* : passed beyond ripeness toward decay

over·rule *vb* **over·ruled; over·rul·ing 1** : to decide against **2** : to set aside a decision or ruling made by someone having less authority

over·run *vb* **over·ran; overrun; over·run·ning 1** : to take over and occupy by force **2** : to run past **3** : to spread over so as to cover

¹over·seas *adv* : beyond or across the sea

²overseas *adj* : of, relating to, or intended for lands across the sea

over·see *vb* **over·saw; over·seen; over·see·ing 1** : INSPECT 1, EXAMINE **2** : SUPERINTEND

over·seer *n* : a person whose business it is to oversee something

over·shad·ow *vb* **1** : to cast a shadow over : DARKEN **2** : to be more important than

over·shoe *n* : a shoe (as of rubber) worn over another for protection

over·shoot *vb* **over·shot; over·shoot·ing** : to miss by going beyond

over·sight *n* **1** : the act or duty of overseeing : watchful care **2** : an error or a leaving something out through carelessness or haste

over·sim·pli·fy *vb* **over·sim·pli·fied; over·sim·pli·fy·ing** : to make incorrect or misleading by simplifying too much

over·size *or* **over·sized** *adj* : larger than the usual or normal size

over·sleep *vb* **over·slept; over·sleep·ing** : to sleep beyond the usual time or beyond the time set for getting up

over·spread *vb* **overspread; over·spread·ing** : to spread over or above

over·state *vb* **over·stat·ed; over·stat·ing** : to put in too strong terms : EXAGGERATE

over·step *vb* **over·stepped; over·step·ping** : to step over or beyond : EXCEED

over·stuffed *adj* : covered completely and deeply with upholstery

over·sup·ply *n, pl* **over·sup·plies** : a supply that is too large

over·take *vb* **over·took; over·tak·en; over·tak·ing 1** : to catch up with and often pass **2** : to come upon suddenly or without warning

¹over·throw *vb* **over·threw; over·thrown; over·throw·ing 1** : OVERTURN 1 **2** : to cause the fall or end of : DEFEAT, DESTROY

²over·throw *n* : an act of overthrowing : the state of being overthrown : DEFEAT, RUIN

over·time *n* : time spent working that is more than one usually works in a day or a week

over·ture *n* **1** : something first offered or suggested with the hope of reaching an agreement **2** : a musical composition played by the orchestra at the beginning of an opera or musical play

over·turn *vb* **1** : to turn over : UPSET **2** : ¹OVERTHROW 2

¹over·weight *n* **1** : weight that is more than is required or allowed **2** : bodily weight that is greater than what is considered normal or healthy

²over·weight *adj* : weighing more than is right, necessary, or allowed

over·whelm *vb* **1** : to cover over completely : SUBMERGE **2** : to overcome completely

¹over·work *vb* **1** : to work or cause to work too much or too hard **2** : to make too much use of

²overwork *n* : too much work

ovip·a·rous *adj* : reproducing by eggs that hatch outside the parent's body

ovule *n* : any of the tiny egglike structures in a plant ovary that can develop into seeds

ovum *n, pl* **ova** : EGG CELL

owe *vb* **owed; ow·ing 1** : to be obligated to pay, give, or return **2** : to be in debt to **3** : to have as a result

owing *adj* : due to be paid

owing to *prep* : BECAUSE OF

owl *n* : a bird with large head and eyes, hooked bill, and strong claws that is active at night and lives on rats and mice, insects, and small birds — **owl·ish** *adj*

owl·et *n* : a young or small owl

¹own *adj* : belonging to oneself or itself

²own *vb* **1** : to have or hold as property : POSSESS **2** : ADMIT 3, CONFESS 1

own·er *n* : a person who owns something

own·er·ship *n* : the state or fact of being an owner

ox *n, pl* **ox·en** *also* **ox 1** : one of our common domestic cattle or a closely related animal **2** : an adult castrated male of domestic cattle used especially for meat or for hauling loads : STEER

ox·bow *n* : a bend in a river in the shape of a U

ox·cart *n* : a cart pulled by oxen

ox·ford *n* : a low shoe laced and tied over the instep

ox·i·da·tion *n* : the process of oxidizing

ox·ide *n* : a compound of oxygen with another element or with a group of elements

ox·i·dize *vb* **ox·i·dized; ox·i·diz·ing** : to combine with oxygen : add oxygen to

ox·y·gen *n* : a chemical element found in the air as a colorless odorless tasteless gas that is necessary for life

oys·ter *n* : a soft gray shellfish that lives on stony bottoms (**oyster beds**) in shallow seawater, has a shell made up of two hinged parts, and is used as food

ozone *n* **1** : a faintly blue form of oxygen that is present in the air in small quantities **2** : pure and refreshing air

ozone layer *n* : a layer of the upper atmosphere that is characterized by high ozone content which blocks most of the sun's radiation from entering the lower atmosphere

P

p *n, pl* **p's** *or* **ps** *often cap* : the sixteenth letter of the English alphabet

pa *n* : ¹FATHER 1

¹pace *n* **1** : rate of moving forward or ahead **2** : a manner of walking **3** : a horse's gait in which the legs on the same side move at the same time **4** : a single step or its length

²pace *vb* **paced; pac·ing 1** : to walk with slow steps **2** : to move at a pace **3** : to measure by steps **4** : to walk back and forth across **5** : to set or regulate the pace of

pa·cif·ic *adj* **1** : making peace : PEACEABLE **2** : ³CALM, PEACEFUL **3** *cap* : relating to the Pacific ocean

pac·i·fy *vb* **pac·i·fied; pac·i·fy·ing** : to make peaceful or quiet : CALM, SOOTHE

¹pack *n* **1** : a bundle arranged for carrying especially on the back of a person or animal **2** : a group of like persons or things : BAND, SET

²pack *vb* **1** : to put into a container or bundle **2** : to put things into **3** : to crowd into so as to fill full : CRAM **4** : to send away — **pack·er** *n*

pack·age *n* **1** : a bundle made up for shipping **2** : a box or case in which goods are shipped or delivered

pack·et *n* : a small package

pack·ing·house *n* : a building for preparing and packing food and especially meat

pact *n* : AGREEMENT 2, TREATY

¹pad *vb* **pad·ded; pad·ding** : to walk or run with quiet steps

²pad *n* **1** : something soft used for protection or comfort : CUSHION **2** : a piece of material that holds ink used in inking rubber stamps **3** : one of the cushioned parts of the underside of the foot of some animals (as a dog) **4** : a floating leaf of a water plant **5** : a tablet of writing or drawing paper

³pad *vb* **pad·ded; pad·ding 1** : to stuff or cover with soft material **2** : to make longer by adding words

pad·ding *n* : material used to pad something

¹pad·dle *vb* **pad·dled; pad·dling** : to move or splash about in the water with the hands or feet : WADE

²paddle *n* **1** : an instrument like an oar used in moving and steering a small boat (as a canoe) **2** : one of the broad boards at the outer edge of a waterwheel or a paddle wheel **3** : an instrument for beating, mixing, or hitting

³paddle *vb* **pad·dled; pad·dling 1** : to move or drive forward with or as if with a paddle **2** : to stir or mix with a paddle : to beat with or as if with a paddle

paddle wheel *n* : a wheel with paddles near its outer edge used to drive a boat

pad·dock *n* **1** : an enclosed area where animals are put to eat grass or to exercise **2** : an enclosed area where racehorses are saddled and paraded

pad·dy *n, pl* **paddies** : wet land in which rice is grown

¹pad·lock *n* : a removable lock that has a curved piece that snaps into a catch

²padlock *vb* : to fasten with a padlock

¹pa·gan *n* : ²HEATHEN 1

²pagan *adj* : of or relating to pagans or their worship : HEATHEN

¹page *n* **1** : a boy being trained to be a knight in the Middle Ages **2** : a person employed (as by a hotel or the United States congress) to carry messages or run errands

²page *vb* **paged; pag·ing** : to call out the name of (a person) in a public place

³page *n* **1** : one side of a printed or written sheet of paper **2** : a large section of computer memory **3** : the block of information found at a single World Wide Web address

pag·eant *n* **1** : a grand and fancy public ceremony and display **2** : an entertainment made up of scenes based on history or legend

pa·go·da *n* : a tower of several stories built as a temple or memorial in the Far East

paid *past of* PAY

pail *n* **1** : a usually round container with a handle : BUCKET **2** : PAILFUL

pail·ful *n, pl* **pail·fuls** *or* **pails·ful** : the amount a pail holds

¹pain *n* **1** : suffering that accompanies a

bodily disorder (as a disease or an injury)
2 : a feeling (as a prick or an ache) that is
caused by something harmful and usually
makes one try to escape its source **3** : suffering of the mind or emotions : GRIEF **4**
pains *pl* : great care or effort — **pain·ful**
adj — **pain·ful·ly** *adv* — **pain·less** *adj*
²**pain** *vb* **1** : to cause pain in or to **2** : to
give or feel pain
pains·tak·ing *adj* : taking pains : showing
care — **pains·tak·ing·ly** *adv*
¹**paint** *vb* **1** : to cover a surface with or as if
with paint **2** : to make a picture or design
by using paints **3** : to describe clearly —
paint·er *n*
²**paint** *n* : a mixture of coloring matter with a
liquid that forms a dry coating when spread
on a surface
paint·brush *n* : a brush for applying paint
paint·ing *n* **1** : a painted work of art **2** : the
art or occupation of painting
¹**pair** *n, pl* **pairs** *also* **pair** **1** : two things
that match or are meant to be used together
2 : a thing having two similar parts that are
connected **3** : a mated couple
²**pair** *vb* **1** : to arrange or join in pairs **2** : to
form a pair : MATCH
pa·ja·mas *n pl* : loose clothes usually consisting of pants and top that match and that
are worn for relaxing or sleeping
¹**Pak·i·stani** *n* : a person born or living in
Pakistan
²**Pakistani** *adj* : of or relating to Pakistan or
the Pakistanis
pal *n* : a close friend
pal·ace *n* **1** : the home of a ruler **2** : a large
or splendid house
pal·at·able *adj* : pleasant to the taste
pal·ate *n* **1** : the roof of the mouth made up
of a bony front part (**hard palate**) and a soft
flexible back part (**soft palate**) **2** : the
sense of taste
¹**pale** *adj* **pal·er; pal·est** **1** : not having the
warm color of a healthy person **2** : not
bright or brilliant **3** : light in color or shade
— **pale·ness** *n*
²**pale** *vb* **paled; pal·ing** : to make or become
pale
Pa·leo·zo·ic *n* : an era of geological history
ending about 230,000,000 years ago which
came before the Mesozoic and in which
vertebrates and land plants first appeared
pal·ette *n* **1** : a thin board or tablet on which
a painter puts and mixes colors **2** : the set of
colors that a painter puts on a palette
pal·i·sade *n* **1** : a fence made of poles to
protect against attack **2** : a line of steep
cliffs
¹**pall** *vb* : to become dull or uninteresting
: lose the ability to give pleasure

²**pall** *n* **1** : a heavy cloth covering for a coffin, hearse, or tomb **2** : something that
makes things dark and gloomy
pall·bear·er *n* : a person who helps to carry
or follows a coffin at a funeral
pal·let *n* **1** : a mattress of straw **2** : a temporary bed on the floor
pal·lid *adj* : ¹PALE 1
pal·lor *n* : paleness of face
¹**palm** *n* : any of a group of mostly tropical
trees, shrubs, and vines with a simple but
often tall stem topped with leaves that are
shaped like feathers or fans
²**palm** *n* **1** : the under part of the hand between the fingers and the wrist **2** : a measure of length of about seven to ten centimeters
³**palm** *vb* : to hide in the hand
pal·met·to *n, pl* **pal·met·tos** *or* **pal·met-
toes** : a low palm with leaves shaped like
fans
palm off *vb* : to get rid of or pass on in a dishonest way
pal·o·mi·no *n, pl* **pal·o·mi·nos** : a small
strong horse that is light tan or cream in
color with a lighter mane and tail
pal·pi·tate *vb* **pal·pi·tat·ed; pal·pi·tat·ing**
: ¹THROB 1
pal·sy *n* **1** : PARALYSIS **2** : an uncontrollable trembling of the body or a part of the
body
pal·try *adj* **pal·tri·er; pal·tri·est** : of little
importance : PETTY
pam·pas *n pl* : wide treeless plains of South
America
pam·per *vb* : to give someone or someone's
desires too much care and attention : IN-
DULGE
pam·phlet *n* : a short publication without a
binding : BOOKLET
¹**pan** *n* **1** : a shallow open container used
for cooking **2** : a container somewhat like
a cooking pan
²**pan** *vb* **panned; pan·ning** : to wash earthy
material so as to collect bits of metal (as
gold)
pan·cake *n* : a flat cake made of thin batter
and cooked on both sides on a griddle
pan·cre·as *n* : a large gland in the abdomen
that produces insulin and a fluid (**pancre-
atic juice**) that aids digestion
pan·cre·at·ic *adj* : of or relating to the pancreas
pan·da *n* **1** : a long-tailed mainly plant-eating mammal that is related to and resembles
the American raccoon, has long reddish fur,
and is found from the Himalayas to China
2 : GIANT PANDA
pan·de·mo·ni·um *n* : wild uproar
pane *n* : a sheet of glass (as in a window)

1pan·el *n* **1** : a group of persons appointed for some service **2** : a group of persons taking part in a discussion or quiz program **3** : a part of something (as a door or a wall) often sunk below the level of the frame **4** : a piece of material (as plywood) made to form part of a surface (as of a wall) **5** : a board into which instruments or controls are set

2panel *vb* **pan·eled** *or* **pan·elled; pan·el·ing** *or* **pan·el·ling** : to supply or decorate with panels

pan·el·ing *n* : panels joined in a continuous surface

pang *n* : a sudden sharp attack or feeling (as of hunger or regret)

1pan·ic *n* : a sudden overpowering fear especially without reasonable cause

2panic *vb* **pan·icked; pan·ick·ing** : to affect or be affected by panic

pan·icky *adj* **1** : like or caused by panic **2** : feeling or likely to feel panic

pan·o·rama *n* : a clear complete view in every direction

pan out *vb* : to give a good result : SUCCEED

pan·sy *n*, *pl* **pansies** : a garden plant related to the violets that has large velvety flowers with five petals usually in shades of yellow, purple, or brownish red

1pant *vb* : to breathe hard or quickly

2pant *n* : a panting breath

pan·ta·loons *n pl* : PANTS

pan·ther *n* **1** : LEOPARD **2** : COUGAR **3** : JAGUAR

pant·ie *or* **panty** *n*, *pl* **pant·ies** : a woman's or child's undergarment with short legs or no legs

1pan·to·mime *n* **1** : a show in which a story is told by using expressions on the face and movements of the body instead of words **2** : a showing or explaining of something through movements of the body and face alone

2pantomime *vb* **pan·to·mimed; pan·to·mim·ing** : to tell through pantomime

pan·try *n*, *pl* **pan·tries** : a small room where food and dishes are kept

pants *n pl* : an outer garment reaching from the waist to the ankle or only to the knee and covering each leg separately

pa·pa *n* : 1FATHER 1

pa·pal *adj* : of or relating to the pope

pa·paw *n* **1** : PAPAYA **2** : the greenish or yellow edible fruit of a North American tree with shiny leaves and purple flowers

pa·pa·ya *n* : a yellow edible fruit that looks like a melon and grows on a tropical American tree

1pa·per *n* **1** : a material made in thin sheets from fibers (as of wood or cloth) **2** : a

sheet or piece of paper **3** : a piece of paper having something written or printed on it : DOCUMENT **4** : NEWSPAPER **5** : WALLPA-PER **6** : a piece of written schoolwork

2paper *vb* : to cover or line with paper (as wallpaper)

3paper *adj* **1** : made of paper **2** : like paper in thinness or weakness

pa·per·back *n* : a book with a flexible paper binding

paper clip *n* : a clip of bent wire used to hold sheets of paper together

pa·pery *adj* : like paper

pa·poose *n* : a baby of North American Indian parents

pa·pri·ka *n* : a mild red spice made from the fruit of some sweet peppers

pa·py·rus *n*, *pl* **pa·py·rus·es** *or* **pa·py·ri** **1** : a tall African plant related to the grasses that grows especially in Egypt **2** : a material like paper made from papyrus by ancient people and used by them to write on

par *n* **1** : a fixed or stated value (as of money or a security) **2** : an equal level **3** : the score set for each hole of a golf course

par·a·ble *n* : a simple story that teaches a moral truth

1para·chute *n* : a folding device of light material shaped like an umbrella and used for making a safe jump from an airplane

2parachute *vb* **para·chut·ed; para·chut·ing** : to transport or come down by parachute

1pa·rade *n* **1** : great show or display **2** : the formation of troops before an officer for inspection **3** : a public procession **4** : a crowd of people walking at an easy pace

2parade *vb* **pa·rad·ed; pa·rad·ing** **1** : to march in an orderly group **2** : SHOW OFF

par·a·dise *n* **1** : the garden of Eden **2** : HEAVEN 2 **3** : a place or state of great happiness

par·a·dox *n* : a statement that seems to be the opposite of the truth or of common sense and yet is perhaps true

par·af·fin *n* : a white odorless tasteless substance obtained from wood, coal, or petroleum and used in coating and sealing and in candles

1para·graph *n* : a part of a piece of writing that is made up of one or more sentences and has to do with one topic or gives the words of one speaker

2paragraph *vb* : to divide into paragraphs

par·a·keet *or* **par·ra·keet** *n* : a small parrot with a long tail

1par·al·lel *adj* : lying or moving in the same direction but always the same distance apart

2parallel *n* **1** : a parallel line or surface **2** : one of the imaginary circles on the earth's surface parallel to the equator that mark latitude **3** : agreement in many or most details **4** : COUNTERPART, EQUAL

³parallel *vb* **1** : to be like or equal to **2** : to move, run, or extend in a direction parallel with

par·al·lel·o·gram *n* : a plane figure with four sides whose opposite sides are parallel and equal

pa·ral·y·sis *n, pl* **pa·ral·y·ses** : partial or complete loss of one's ability to move or feel

par·a·lyze *vb* **par·a·lyzed; par·a·lyz·ing 1** : to affect with paralysis **2** : to destroy or decrease something's energy or ability to act

par·a·me·cium *n, pl* **par·a·me·cia** *also* **par·a·me·ciums** : a tiny water animal that is a single cell shaped like a slipper

par·a·mount *adj* : highest in importance or greatness

par·a·pet *n* **1** : a wall of earth or stone to protect soldiers **2** : a low wall or fence at the edge of a platform, roof, or bridge

¹para·phrase *n* : a way of stating something again by giving the meaning in different words

²paraphrase *vb* **para·phrased; para·phras·ing** : to give the meaning of in different words

par·a·site *n* **1** : a person who lives at the expense of another **2** : a plant or animal that lives in or on some other living thing and gets food and sometimes shelter from it

par·a·sit·ic *adj* : of or relating to parasites or their way of life : being a parasite — **par·a·sit·i·cal·ly** *adv*

par·a·sol *n* : a light umbrella used as a protection against the sun

par·a·troop·er *n* : a soldier trained and equipped to parachute from an airplane

¹par·cel *n* **1** : a plot of land **2** : PACKAGE 1

²parcel *vb* **par·celed** *or* **par·celled; par·cel·ing** *or* **par·cel·ling 1** : to divide and give out by parts **2** : to wrap up into a package

parcel post *n* : a mail service that handles packages

parch *vb* : to dry up from heat and lack of moisture

parch·ment *n* **1** : the skin of a sheep or goat prepared so that it can be written on **2** : a paper similar to parchment

¹par·don *n* **1** : forgiveness for wrong or rude behavior **2** : a setting free from legal punishment

²pardon *vb* **1** : to free from penalty for a fault or crime **2** : to allow (a wrong act) to pass without punishment : FORGIVE

pare *vb* **pared; par·ing 1** : to cut or shave off the outside or the ends of **2** : to reduce as if by cutting

par·ent *n* **1** : a father or mother of a child **2** : an animal or plant that produces offspring or seed

par·ent·age *n* : a line of ancestors : ANCESTRY

pa·ren·tal *adj* : of or relating to parents

pa·ren·the·sis *n, pl* **pa·ren·the·ses 1** : a word, phrase, or sentence inserted in a passage to explain or comment on it **2** : one of a pair of marks ( ) used to enclose a word or group of words or to group mathematical terms to be dealt with as a unit — **par·en·thet·ic** *or* **par·en·thet·i·cal** *adj*

par·fait *n* : a dessert made usually of layers of fruit, syrup, ice cream, and whipped cream

par·ish *n* **1** : a section of a church district under the care of a priest or minister **2** : the persons who live in a parish and attend the parish church **3** : the members of a church **4** : a division in the state of Louisiana that is similar to a county in other states

parish house *n* : a building for the educational and social activities of a church

pa·rish·io·ner *n* : a member or resident of a parish

¹park *n* **1** : an area of land set aside for recreation or for its beauty **2** : an enclosed field for ball games

²park *vb* : to stop (as an auto or truck) and leave it for a while

par·ka *n* : a warm windproof jacket with a hood

park·way *n* : a broad landscaped highway

¹par·ley *n, pl* **parleys** : a discussion with an enemy

²parley *vb* **par·leyed; par·ley·ing** : to hold a discussion of terms with an enemy

par·lia·ment *n* : an assembly that is the highest legislative body of a country (as the United Kingdom)

par·lor *n* **1** : a room for receiving guests and for conversation **2** : a usually small place of business

pa·ro·chi·al *adj* : of, relating to, or supported by a religious body (as a church)

pa·role *n* : an early release of a prisoner

parrakeet *variant of* PARAKEET

par·rot *n* : a brightly colored tropical bird that has a strong hooked bill and is sometimes trained to imitate human speech

¹par·ry *vb* **par·ried; par·ry·ing 1** : to turn aside an opponent's weapon or blow **2** : to avoid by a skillful answer

²parry *n, pl* **par·ries** : an act or instance of parrying

pars·ley *n, pl* **pars·leys** : a garden plant related to the carrot that has finely divided leaves and is used to season or decorate various foods

pars·nip *n* : a vegetable that is the long white root of a plant related to the carrot

par·son *n* : ¹MINISTER 1

par·son·age *n* : a house provided by a church for its pastor to live in

¹part *n* **1** : one of the sections into which something is divided : something less than a whole **2** : a voice or instrument **3** : the music for a voice or instrument **4** : a piece of a plant or animal body **5** : a piece of a machine **6** : a person's share or duty **7** : one of the sides in a disagreement **8** : the role of a character in a play **9** : a line along which the hair is divided

²part *vb* **1** : to leave someone : go away **2** : to divide into parts **3** : to hold apart **4** : to come apart

par·take *vb* **par·took; par·tak·en; par·tak·ing** : to take a share or part

part·ed *adj* : divided into parts

par·tial *adj* **1** : favoring one side of a question over another **2** : fond or too fond of someone or something **3** : of one part only **4** : not complete — **par·tial·ly** *adv*

par·ti·al·i·ty *n, pl* **par·ti·al·i·ties** : the quality or state of being partial

par·tic·i·pant *n* : a person who takes part in something

par·tic·i·pate *vb* **par·tic·i·pat·ed; par·tic·i·pat·ing** : to join with others in doing something

par·tic·i·pa·tion *n* : the act of participating

par·ti·ci·ple *n* : a word formed from a verb but often used like an adjective while keeping some verb characteristics (as tense and the ability to take an object)

par·ti·cle *n* : a very small bit of something

¹par·tic·u·lar *adj* **1** : relating to one person or thing **2** : not usual : SPECIAL **3** : being one of several **4** : concerned about details — **par·tic·u·lar·ly** *adv*

²particular *n* : a single fact or detail

part·ing *n* : a place or point where a division or separation occurs

par·ti·san *n* **1** : a person who aids or approves something (as a party or a point of view) or someone **2** : a soldier who lives and fights behind enemy lines — **par·ti·san·ship** *n*

¹par·ti·tion *n* **1** : an act of dividing into parts **2** : something that divides

²partition *vb* **1** : to divide into shares **2** : to divide into separate parts or areas

part·ly *adv* : somewhat but not completely

part·ner *n* **1** : a person who does or shares something with another **2** : either one of a married pair **3** : one who plays with another person on the same side in a game **4** : one of two or more persons who run a business together

part·ner·ship *n* **1** : the state of being a partner **2** : a group of people in business together

part of speech : a class of words (as adjectives, adverbs, conjunctions, interjections, nouns, prepositions, pronouns, or verbs) identified according to the kinds of ideas they express and the work they do in a sentence

partook *past of* PARTAKE

par·tridge *n, pl* **partridge** *or* **par·tridg·es** : any of several plump game birds related to the chicken

part-time *adj* : involving fewer than the usual hours

par·ty *n, pl* **par·ties** **1** : a group of persons who take one side of a question or share a set of beliefs **2** : a social gathering or the entertainment provided for it **3** : a person or group concerned in some action

¹pass *vb* **1** : ¹MOVE 1, PROCEED **2** : to go away **3** : ¹DIE 1 **4** : to go by or move past **5** : to go or allow to go across, over, or through **6** : to move from one place or condition to another **7** : HAPPEN 2 **8** : to be or cause to be approved **9** : to go successfully through an examination or inspection **10** : to be or cause to be identified or recognized **11** : to transfer or throw to another person — **pass·er** *n*

²pass *n* **1** : an opening or way for passing along or through **2** : a gap in a mountain range

³pass *n* **1** : SITUATION 4 **2** : a written permit to go or come **3** : the act or an instance of passing (as a ball) in a game

pass·able *adj* **1** : fit to be traveled on **2** : barely good enough — **pass·ably** *adv*

pas·sage *n* **1** : the act or process of passing from one place or condition to another **2** : a means (as a hall) of passing or reaching **3** : the passing of a law **4** : a right or permission to go as a passenger **5** : a brief part of a speech or written work

pas·sage·way *n* : a road or way by which a person or thing may pass

pas·sen·ger *n* : someone riding on or in a vehicle

passenger pigeon *n* : a North American wild pigeon once common but now extinct

pass·er·by *n, pl* **pass·ers·by** : someone who passes by

¹pass·ing *n* **1** : the act of passing **2** : DEATH 1

²passing *adj* **1** : going by or past **2** : lasting only for a short time **3** : showing haste or lack of attention **4** : used for passing **5** : showing satisfactory work in a test or course of study

pas·sion *n* **1** *cap* : the suffering of Christ

between the night of the Last Supper and his death **2** : a strong feeling or emotion **3** : strong liking or desire : LOVE **4** : an object of one's love, liking, or desire

pas·sion·ate *adj* **1** : easily angered **2** : showing or affected by strong feeling — **pas·sion·ate·ly** *adv*

pas·sive *adj* **1** : not acting but acted upon **2** : showing that the person or thing represented by the subject is acted on by the verb **3** : offering no resistance — **pas·sive·ly** *adv*

pass out *vb* : to become unconscious : FAINT

Pass·over *n* : a Jewish holiday celebrated in March or April in honor of the freeing of the Hebrews from slavery in Egypt

pass·port *n* : a government document that allows a citizen to leave his or her country

pass up *vb* : to let go by : REFUSE

pass·word *n* : a secret word or phrase that must be spoken by a person before being allowed to pass a guard

¹past *adj* **1** : of or relating to a time that has gone by **2** : expressing a time gone by **3** : no longer serving

²past *prep* **1** : ²BEYOND **2** : going close to and then beyond

³past *n* **1** : a former time **2** : past life or history

⁴past *adv* : so as to pass by or beyond

¹paste *n* **1** : dough for pies or tarts **2** : a soft smooth mixture **3** : a mixture of flour or starch and water used for sticking things together

²paste *vb* **past·ed; past·ing** : to stick on or together with paste

paste·board *n* : a stiff material made of sheets of paper pasted together or of pulp pressed and dried

¹pas·tel *n* **1** : a crayon made by mixing ground coloring matter with a watery solution of a gum **2** : a drawing made with pastel crayons **3** : a soft pale color

²pastel *adj* **1** : made with pastels **2** : light and pale in color

pas·teur·i·za·tion *n* : the process or an instance of pasteurizing

pas·teur·ize *vb* **pas·teur·ized; pas·teur·iz·ing** : to keep a liquid (as milk) for a time at a temperature high enough to kill many harmful germs and then cool it rapidly — **pas·teur·iz·er** *n*

pas·time *n* : something (as a hobby) that helps to make time pass pleasantly

pas·tor *n* : a minister or priest in charge of a church

pas·to·ral *adj* **1** : of or relating to shepherds or peaceful rural scenes **2** : of or relating to the pastor of a church

past·ry *n, pl* **past·ries** **1** : sweet baked

goods (as pies) made mainly of flour and fat **2** : a piece of pastry

¹pas·ture *n* **1** : plants (as grass) for feeding grazing animals **2** : land on which animals graze

²pasture *vb* **pas·tured; pas·tur·ing** **1** : ¹GRAZE 1 **2** : to supply (as cattle) with pasture

¹pat *n* **1** : a light tap with the open hand or a flat instrument **2** : the sound of a pat or tap **3** : a small flat piece (as of butter)

²pat *adj* **pat·ter; pat·test** **1** : exactly suitable **2** : learned perfectly **3** : not changing

³pat *vb* **pat·ted; pat·ting** : to tap or stroke gently with the open hand

¹patch *n* **1** : a piece of cloth used to mend or cover a torn or worn place **2** : a small piece or area different from what is around it

²patch *vb* : to mend or cover with a patch

patch up *vb* : ADJUST 1

patch·work *n* : pieces of cloth of different colors and shapes sewed together

¹pat·ent *adj* **1** : protected by a patent **2** : OBVIOUS, EVIDENT

²pat·ent *n* : a document that gives the inventor of something the only right to make, use, and sell the invention for a certain number of years

³pat·ent *vb* : to get a patent for

pa·ter·nal *adj* **1** : of or relating to a father : FATHERLY **2** : received or inherited from a father **3** : related through the father

path *n, pl* **paths** **1** : a track made by traveling on foot **2** : the way or track in which something moves **3** : a way of life or thought — **path·less** *adj*

pa·thet·ic *adj* : making one feel pity, tenderness, or sorrow

path·way *n* : PATH 1

pa·tience *n* : the ability to be patient or the fact of being patient

¹pa·tient *adj* **1** : putting up with pain or troubles without complaint **2** : showing or involving calm self-control — **pa·tient·ly** *adv*

²patient *n* : a person under medical care and treatment

pa·tio *n, pl* **pa·ti·os** **1** : an inner part of a house that is open to the sky **2** : an open area next to a house that is usually paved

pa·tri·arch *n* **1** : the father and ruler of a family or tribe **2** : a respected old man

pa·tri·ot *n* : a person who loves his or her country and enthusiastically supports it

pa·tri·ot·ic *adj* : having or showing patriotism

pa·tri·ot·ism *n* : love of one's country

¹pa·trol *n* **1** : the action of going around an area for observation or guard **2** : a person or group doing the act of patrolling **3** : a part of a troop of Boy Scouts that consists of two or more boys **4** : a part of a troop of Girl Scouts that usually consists of six or eight girls

²patrol *vb* **pa·trolled; pa·trol·ling** : to go around an area for the purpose of watching or protecting

pa·trol·man *n, pl* **pa·trol·men** : a police officer who has a regular beat

pa·tron *n* **1** : a person who gives generous support or approval **2** : CUSTOMER **3** : a saint to whom a church or society is dedicated

pa·tron·age *n* **1** : the help or encouragement given by a patron **2** : a group of patrons (as of a shop or theater) **3** : the control by officials of giving out jobs, contracts, and favors

pa·tron·ize *vb* **pa·tron·ized; pa·tron·iz·ing** **1** : to act as a patron to or of : SUPPORT **2** : to be a customer of **3** : to treat (a person) as if one were better or more important

¹pat·ter *vb* **1** : to strike again and again with light blows **2** : to run with quick light steps

²patter *n* : a series of quick light sounds

¹pat·tern *n* **1** : something worth copying **2** : a model or guide for making something **3** : a form or figure used in decoration : DESIGN — **pat·terned** *adj*

²pattern *vb* : to make or design by following a pattern

pat·ty *n, pl* **pat·ties** : a small flat cake of chopped food

pau·per *n* : a very poor person

¹pause *n* **1** : a temporary stop **2** : a sign ⌒ above a musical note or rest to show that the note or rest is to be held longer

²pause *vb* **paused; paus·ing** : to stop for a time : make a pause

pave *vb* **paved; pav·ing** : to make a hard surface on (as with concrete or asphalt)

pave·ment *n* **1** : a paved surface (as of a street) **2** : material used in paving

pa·vil·ion *n* **1** : a very large tent **2** : a building usually with open sides that is used as a place for entertainment or shelter in a park or garden

pav·ing *n* : PAVEMENT

¹paw *n* : the foot of a four-footed animal (as the lion, dog, or cat) that has claws

²paw *vb* **1** : to touch in a clumsy or rude way **2** : to touch or scrape with a paw **3** : to beat or scrape with a hoof

¹pawn *n* : the piece of least value in the game of chess

²pawn *n* **1** : something of value given as a guarantee (as of payment of a debt) **2** : the condition of being given as a guarantee

³pawn *vb* : to leave as a guarantee for a loan : PLEDGE

pawn·bro·ker *n* : a person who makes a business of lending money and keeping personal property as a guarantee

pawn·shop *n* : a pawnbroker's shop

¹pay *vb* **paid; pay·ing** **1** : to give (as money) in return for services received or for something bought **2** : to give what is owed **3** : to get revenge on **4** : to give or offer freely **5** : to get a suitable return for cost or trouble : be worth the effort or pains required — **pay·er** *n*

²pay *n* **1** : the act of paying : PAYMENT **2** : the state of being paid or employed for money **3** : SALARY

pay·able *adj* : that may, can, or must be paid

pay·check *n* : a check or money received as wages or salary

pay·ment *n* **1** : the act of paying **2** : money given to pay a debt

pay off *vb* **1** : to pay in full **2** : to have a good result

pay·roll *n* **1** : a list of persons who receive pay **2** : the amount of money necessary to pay the employees of a business

pay up *vb* : to pay in full especially debts that are overdue

PC *n, pl* **PCs** *or* **PC's** : PERSONAL COMPUTER

pea *n, pl* **peas** *also* **pease** **1** : a vegetable that is the round seed found in the pods of a garden plant (**pea vine**) related to the clovers **2** : a plant (as the sweet pea) resembling or related to the garden pea

peace *n* **1** : freedom from public disturbance or war **2** : freedom from upsetting thoughts or feelings **3** : agreement and harmony among persons **4** : an agreement to end a war

peace·able *adj* : PEACEFUL 1 3

peace·ful *adj* **1** : liking peace : not easily moved to argue or fight **2** : full of or enjoying peace, quiet, or calm **3** : not involving fighting — **peace·ful·ly** *adv* — **peace·ful·ness** *n*

peace·mak·er *n* : a person who settles an argument or stops a fight

peace pipe *n* : a decorated pipe of the American Indians used for certain ceremonies

peach *n* **1** : a fruit that is related to the plum and has a sweet juicy pulp, hairy skin, and a large rough stone **2** : a pale yellowish pink color

pea·cock *n* : the male of a very large Asian pheasant with a very long brightly colored tail that can be spread or raised at will, a small crest, and in most forms brilliant blue or green feathers on the neck and shoulders

peak *n* **1** : the part of a cap that sticks out in

front **2** : the pointed top of a hill or mountain **3** : a mountain all by itself **4** : the highest point of development

¹peal *n* **1** : the sound of bells **2** : a loud sound : a series of loud sounds

²peal *vb* : to give out peals

pea·nut *n* : a plant related to the peas that has yellow flowers and is grown for its underground pods of oily nutlike edible seeds which yield a valuable oil (**peanut oil**) or are crushed to form a spread (**peanut butter**)

pear *n* : the fleshy fruit that grows on a tree related to the apple and is commonly larger at the end opposite the stem

pearl *n* **1** : a smooth body with a rich luster that is formed within the shell of some mollusks (as the **pearl oyster** of tropical seas) usually around something irritating (as a grain of sand) which has gotten into the shell **2** : MOTHER-OF-PEARL **3** : something like a pearl in shape, color, or value **4** : a pale bluish gray color

pearly *adj* **pearl·i·er; pearl·i·est** : like a pearl especially in having a shining surface

peas·ant *n* : a farmer owning a small amount of land or a farm worker in European countries

pease *pl of* PEA

peat *n* : a blackish or dark brown material that is the remains of plants partly decayed in water and is dug and dried for use as fuel

peat moss *n* : a spongy brownish moss of wet areas that is often the chief plant making up peat

peb·ble *n* : a small rounded stone

pe·can *n* : an oval edible nut that usually has a thin shell and is the fruit of a tall tree of the central and southern United States related to the walnuts

pec·ca·ry *n, pl* **pec·ca·ries** : either of two mostly tropical American animals that gather in herds, are active at night, and look like but are much smaller than the related pigs

¹peck *n* **1** : a unit of capacity equal to one quarter of a bushel **2** : a great deal : a large quantity

²peck *vb* **1** : to strike or pick up with the bill **2** : to strike with a sharp instrument (as a pick)

³peck *n* **1** : the act of pecking **2** : a mark made by pecking

pe·cu·liar *adj* **1** : one's own : of or limited to some one person, thing, or place **2** : different from the usual : ODD

pe·cu·li·ar·i·ty *n, pl* **pe·cu·li·ar·i·ties** **1** : the quality or state of being peculiar **2** : something peculiar or individual

¹ped·al *n* : a lever worked by the foot or feet

²pedal *vb* **ped·aled** *or* **ped·alled; ped·al·ing** *or* **ped·al·ling** : to use or work the pedals of something

ped·dle *vb* **ped·dled; ped·dling** : to go about especially from house to house with goods for sale

ped·dler *or* **ped·lar** *n* : someone who peddles

ped·es·tal *n* **1** : a support or foot of an upright structure (as a column, statue, or lamp) **2** : a position of high regard

pe·des·tri·an *n* : a person who is walking

pe·di·a·tri·cian *n* : a doctor who specializes in the care of babies and children

ped·i·gree *n* **1** : a table or list showing the line of ancestors of a person or animal **2** : a line of ancestors

pe·dom·e·ter *n* : an instrument that measures the distance one covers in walking

¹peek *vb* **1** : to look slyly or cautiously **2** : to take a quick glance — **peek·er** *n*

²peek *n* : a short or sly look

¹peel *vb* **1** : to strip off the skin or bark of **2** : to strip or tear off **3** : to come off smoothly or in bits

²peel *n* : an outer covering and especially the skin of a fruit

¹peep *vb* : to make a weak shrill sound such as a young bird makes — **peep·er** *n*

²peep *n* : a weak shrill sound

³peep *vb* **1** : to look through or as if through a small hole or a crack : PEEK **2** : to show slightly

⁴peep *n* **1** : a brief or sly look **2** : the first appearance

¹peer *n* **1** : a person of the same rank or kind : EQUAL **2** : a member of one of the five ranks (duke, marquis, earl, viscount, and baron) of the British nobility

²peer *vb* **1** : to look curiously or carefully **2** : to come slightly into view : peep out

peer·less *adj* : having no equal

pee·vish *adj* : complaining a lot : IRRITABLE — **pee·vish·ly** *adv* — **pee·vish·ness** *n*

pee·wee *n* : one that is small

¹peg *n* **1** : a slender piece (as of wood or metal) used especially to fasten things together or to hang things on **2** : a piece driven into the ground to mark a boundary or to hold something **3** : a step or grade in approval or esteem

²peg *vb* **pegged; peg·ging** **1** : to mark or fasten with pegs **2** : to work hard

pel·i·can *n* : a bird with a large bill, webbed feet, and a great pouch on the lower jaw that is used to scoop in fish for food

pel·la·gra *n* : a disease caused by a diet containing too little protein and too little of a necessary vitamin

pel·let *n* **1** : a little ball (as of food or medicine) **2** : a piece of small shot

pell-mell *adv* **1** : in crowded confusion **2** : in a big hurry

¹pelt *n* : a skin of an animal especially with its fur or wool

²pelt *vb* **1** : to strike with repeated blows **2** : HURL, THROW **3** : to beat or pound against something again and again

pel-vis *n* : the bowl-shaped part of the skeleton that supports the lower part of the abdomen and includes the hip bones and the lower bones of the backbone

¹pen *vb* **penned; pen-ning** : to shut in a small enclosure

²pen *n* : a small enclosure especially for animals

³pen *n* : an instrument for writing with ink

⁴pen *vb* **penned; pen-ning** : to write with a pen

pe-nal *adj* : of or relating to punishment

pe-nal-ize *vb* **pe-nal-ized; pe-nal-iz-ing** : to give a penalty to

pen-al-ty *n, pl* **pen-al-ties 1** : punishment for doing something wrong **2** : a loss or handicap given for breaking a rule in a sport or game

pence *pl of* PENNY

¹pen-cil *n* : a device for writing or drawing consisting of a stick of black or colored material enclosed in wood, plastic, or metal

²pencil *vb* **pen-ciled** *or* **pen-cilled; pen-cil-ing** *or* **pen-cil-ling** : to write, mark, or draw with a pencil

pen-dant *n* : an ornament (as on a necklace) allowed to hang free

¹pend-ing *prep* **1** : DURING 1 **2** : while waiting for

²pending *adj* : not yet decided

pen-du-lum *n* : an object hung from a fixed point so as to swing freely back and forth under the action of gravity

pen-e-trate *vb* **pen-e-trat-ed; pen-e-trat-ing 1** : to pass into or through : PIERCE **2** : to see into or understand

pen-e-tra-tion *n* **1** : the act or process of penetrating **2** : keen understanding

pen-guin *n* : a seabird that cannot fly, has very short legs, and is found in the cold regions of the southern hemisphere

pen-i-cil-lin *n* : an antibiotic that is produced by a mold and is used especially against disease-causing round bacteria

pen-in-su-la *n* : a piece of land extending out into a body of water

pe-nis *n, pl* **pe-nes** *or* **pe-nis-es** : a male organ in mammals used for sexual intercourse and for urinating

pen-i-tence *n* : sorrow for one's sins or faults

¹pen-i-tent *adj* : feeling or showing penitence

²penitent *n* : a penitent person

pen-i-ten-tia-ry *n, pl* **pen-i-ten-tia-ries** : a prison for criminals

pen-knife *n, pl* **pen-knives** : a small jackknife

pen-man *n, pl* **pen-men** : a person who uses a pen : WRITER

pen-man-ship *n* : writing with a pen : style or quality of handwriting

pen name *n* : a false name that an author uses on his or her work

pen-nant *n* **1** : a narrow pointed flag used for identification, signaling, or decoration **2** : a flag that serves as the emblem of a championship

pen-ni-less *adj* : very poor : having no money

pen-ny *n, pl* **pennies 1** *or pl* **pence** : a coin of the United Kingdom equal to $1/100$ pound **2** : CENT

¹pen-sion *n* : a sum paid regularly to a person who has retired from work

²pension *vb* : to grant or give a pension to

pen-sive *adj* : lost in sober or sad thought — **pen-sive-ly** *adv* — **pen-sive-ness** *n*

pent *adj* : penned up : shut up

penta- *or* **pent-** *prefix* : five

pen-ta-gon *n* : a flat figure having five angles and five sides

pen-tag-o-nal *adj* : having five sides

pen-tath-lon *n* : an athletic contest made up of five different events in which each person participates

pent-house *n* : an apartment built on the roof of a building

pe-on *n* : a member of the landless laboring class in Spanish America

pe-o-ny *n, pl* **pe-o-nies** : a plant related to the buttercup that lives for years and is widely grown for its very large usually double white, pink, or red flowers

¹peo-ple *n, pl* **people** *or* **peoples 1** : a body of persons making up a race, tribe, or nation **2** : human beings — often used in compounds instead of *persons* **3** : the persons of a certain group or place

²people *vb* **peo-pled; peo-pling 1** : to supply or fill with people **2** : to dwell on or in

¹pep *n* : brisk energy or liveliness

²pep *vb* **pepped; pep-ping** : to put pep into

¹pep-per *n* **1** : a product from the fruit of an East Indian climbing shrub that is sharp in flavor, is used as a seasoning or in medicine, and consists of the whole ground dried berry (**black pepper**) or of the ground seeds alone (**white pepper**) **2** : a plant related to the tomato that is grown for its fruits which may be very sharp in flavor (**hot peppers**) or mild and sweet (**sweet peppers** or **bell peppers**)

²**pepper** *vb* **1** : to season with or as if with pepper **2** : to hit with a shower of blows or objects

pep·per·mint *n* : a mint with stalks of small usually purple flowers that yields an oil (**peppermint oil**) which is sharp in flavor and is used especially to flavor candies

pep·py *adj* **pep·pi·er; pep·pi·est** : full of pep

pep·sin *n* : an enzyme that starts the digestion of proteins in the stomach

per *prep* **1** : to or for each **2** : ACCORDING TO 1

per an·num *adv* : by the year : in or for each year : ANNUALLY

per cap·i·ta *adv or adj* : by or for each person

per·ceive *vb* **per·ceived; per·ceiv·ing 1** : to become aware of through the senses and especially through sight **2** : UNDERSTAND 1

¹**per·cent** *adv or adj* : out of every hundred : measured by the number of units as compared with one hundred

²**percent** *n, pl* **percent** : a part or fraction of a whole expressed in hundredths

per·cent·age *n* **1** : a part of a whole expressed in hundredths **2** : a share of profits

per·cep·ti·ble *adj* : possible to detect

per·cep·tion *n* **1** : an act or the result of grasping with one's mind **2** : the ability to grasp (as meanings and ideas) with one's mind **3** : a judgment formed from information grasped

¹**perch** *n* **1** : a place where birds roost **2** : a raised seat or position

²**perch** *vb* : to sit or rest on or as if on a perch

³**perch** *n, pl* **perch** *or* **perch·es 1** : a European freshwater food fish that is mostly olive green and yellow **2** : any of numerous fishes related to or resembling the European perch

per·chance *adv* : PERHAPS

per·co·late *vb* **per·co·lat·ed; per·co·lat·ing 1** : to trickle or cause to trickle through something porous : OOZE **2** : to prepare (coffee) by passing hot water through ground coffee beans again and again — **per·co·la·tor** *n*

per·co·la·tion *n* : the act or process of percolating

per·cus·sion *n* **1** : a sharp tapping **2** : the striking of an explosive cap to set off the charge in a gun **3** : the musical instruments of a band or orchestra that are played by striking or shaking

percussion instrument *n* : a musical instrument (as a drum, cymbal, or maraca) sounded by striking or shaking

¹**pe·ren·ni·al** *adj* **1** : present all through the year **2** : never ending : CONTINUOUS **3** : living from year to year

²**perennial** *n* : a perennial plant

¹**per·fect** *adj* **1** : lacking nothing : COMPLETE **2** : thoroughly skilled or trained : meeting the highest standards **3** : having no mistake, error, or flaw — **per·fect·ly** *adv*

²**per·fect** *vb* : to make perfect

per·fec·tion *n* **1** : completeness in all parts or details **2** : the highest excellence or skill **3** : a quality or thing that cannot be improved

per·fo·rate *vb* **per·fo·rat·ed; per·fo·rat·ing 1** : to make a hole through : PIERCE **2** : to make many small holes in

per·form *vb* **1** : to carry out : ACCOMPLISH, DO **2** : to do something needing special skill — **per·form·er** *n*

per·for·mance *n* **1** : the carrying out of an action **2** : a public entertainment

¹**per·fume** *n* **1** : a pleasant smell : FRAGRANCE **2** : a liquid used to make things smell nice

²**per·fume** *vb* **per·fumed; per·fum·ing** : to make smell nice : add a pleasant scent to

per·haps *adv* : possibly but not certainly : MAYBE

per·il *n* **1** : the state of being in great danger **2** : a cause or source of danger

per·il·ous *adj* : DANGEROUS 1 — **per·il·ous·ly** *adv*

pe·rim·e·ter *n* **1** : the whole outer boundary of a figure or area **2** : the length of the boundary of a figure

pe·ri·od *n* **1** : a punctuation mark . used chiefly to mark the end of a declarative sentence or an abbreviation **2** : a portion of time set apart by some quality **3** : a portion of time that forms a stage in the history of something **4** : one of the divisions of a school day

pe·ri·od·ic *adj* : occurring at regular intervals

¹**pe·ri·od·i·cal** *adj* **1** : PERIODIC **2** : published at regular intervals — **pe·ri·od·i·cal·ly** *adv*

²**periodical** *n* : a periodical publication (as a magazine)

peri·scope *n* : an instrument containing lenses and mirrors by which a person (as on a submarine) can get a view that would otherwise be blocked

per·ish *vb* : to become destroyed : DIE

per·ish·able *adj* : likely to spoil or decay

¹**per·i·win·kle** *n* : an evergreen plant that spreads along the ground and has shining leaves and blue or white flowers

²**periwinkle** *n* : a small snail that lives along rocky seashores

perk *vb* **1** : to lift in a quick, alert, or bold way **2** : to make fresher in appearance **3** : to become more lively or cheerful

perky *adj* **perk·i·er; perk·i·est** : being lively and cheerful

per·ma·nence *n* : the quality or state of being permanent

per·ma·nent *adj* : lasting or meant to last for a long time : not temporary — **per·ma·nent·ly** *adv*

per·me·able *adj* : having pores or openings that let liquids or gases pass through

per·me·ate *vb* **per·me·at·ed; per·me·at·ing** 1 : to pass through something that has pores or small openings or is in a loose form 2 : to spread throughout

per·mis·sion *n* : the consent of a person in authority

¹per·mit *vb* **per·mit·ted; per·mit·ting** 1 : to give permission : ALLOW 2 : to make possible : give an opportunity

²per·mit *n* : a statement of permission (as a license or pass)

per·ni·cious *adj* : causing great damage or harm

per·ox·ide *n* : an oxide containing much oxygen (as one of hydrogen used as an antiseptic)

¹per·pen·dic·u·lar *adj* 1 : exactly vertical 2 : being at right angles to a line or surface — **per·pen·dic·u·lar·ly** *adv*

²perpendicular *n* : a perpendicular line, surface, or position

per·pe·trate *vb* **per·pe·trat·ed; per·pe·trat·ing** : to bring about or carry out : COMMIT — **per·pe·tra·tor** *n*

per·pet·u·al *adj* 1 : lasting forever : ETERNAL 2 : occurring continually : CONSTANT — **per·pet·u·al·ly** *adv*

per·pet·u·ate *vb* **per·pet·u·at·ed; per·pet·u·at·ing** : to cause to last a long time

per·plex *vb* : to confuse the mind of : BEWILDER

per·plex·i·ty *n, pl* **per·plex·i·ties** 1 : a puzzled or anxious state of mind 2 : something that perplexes

per·se·cute *vb* **per·se·cut·ed; per·se·cut·ing** : to treat continually in a way meant to be cruel and harmful

per·se·cu·tion *n* 1 : the act of persecuting 2 : the state of being persecuted

per·se·ver·ance *n* : the act or power of persevering

per·se·vere *vb* **per·se·vered; per·se·ver·ing** : to keep trying to do something in spite of difficulties

per·sim·mon *n* : a fruit of orange color that looks like a plum and grows on a tree related to the ebonies

per·sist *vb* 1 : to keep on doing or saying something : continue stubbornly 2 : to last on and on : continue to exist or occur

per·sist·ence *n* 1 : the act or fact of persisting 2 : the quality of being persistent : PERSEVERANCE

per·sist·ent *adj* : continuing to act or exist longer than usual — **per·sist·ent·ly** *adv*

per·son *n* 1 : a human being — used in compounds especially by those who prefer to avoid *man* in words that apply to both sexes 2 : the body of a human being 3 : bodily presence 4 : reference to the speaker, to the one spoken to, or to one spoken of as shown especially by means of certain pronouns

per·son·age *n* : an important or famous person

per·son·al *adj* 1 : of, relating to, or belonging to a person : not public : not general 2 : made or done in person 3 : of the person or body 4 : relating to a particular person or his or her qualities 5 : intended for one particular person 6 : relating to oneself — **per·son·al·ly** *adv*

personal computer *n* : a computer designed for an individual user

per·son·al·i·ty *n, pl* **per·son·al·i·ties** 1 : the qualities (as moods or habits) that make one person different from others 2 : a person's pleasing qualities 3 : a person of importance or fame

personal pronoun *n* : a pronoun (as *I, you, it,* or *they*) used as a substitute for a noun that names a definite person or thing

per·son·i·fy *vb* **per·son·i·fied; per·son·i·fy·ing** : to think of or represent as a person

per·son·nel *n* : a group of people employed in a business or an organization

per·spec·tive *n* 1 : the art of painting or drawing a scene so that objects in it seem to have their right shape and to be the right distance apart 2 : the power to understand things in their true relationship to each other 3 : the true relationship of objects or events to one another

per·spi·ra·tion *n* 1 : the act or process of perspiring 2 : salty liquid given off from skin glands

per·spire *vb* **per·spired; per·spir·ing** : to give off salty liquid through the skin

per·suade *vb* **per·suad·ed; per·suad·ing** : to win over to a belief or way of acting by argument or earnest request : CONVINCE

per·sua·sion *n* 1 : the act of persuading 2 : the power to persuade 3 : a way of believing : BELIEF

per·sua·sive *adj* : able or likely to persuade — **per·sua·sive·ly** *adv* — **per·sua·sive·ness** *n*

pert *adj* 1 : SAUCY 1 2 : PERKY

per·tain *vb* 1 : to belong to as a part, quality, or function 2 : to relate to a person or thing

per·ti·nent *adj* : relating to the subject that is being thought about or discussed : RELE-VANT

per·turb *vb* : to disturb in mind : trouble greatly

pe·ruse *vb* **pe·rused; pe·rus·ing** 1 : READ 1 2 : to read through carefully

per·vade *vb* **per·vad·ed; per·vad·ing** : to spread through all parts of : PERMEATE

per·verse *adj* : stubborn in being against what is right or sensible

pe·se·ta *n* : a Spanish coin or bill

pe·so *n, pl* **pesos** 1 : an old silver coin of Spain and Spanish America 2 : a coin of the Philippines or of any of various Latin American countries

pes·si·mist *n* : a pessimistic person

pes·si·mis·tic *adj* 1 : having no hope that one's troubles will end or that success or happiness will come : GLOOMY 2 : having the belief that evil is more common or powerful than good

pest *n* 1 : PESTILENCE 2 : a plant or animal that damages humans or their goods 3 : NUISANCE

pes·ter *vb* : to bother again and again

pes·ti·cide *n* : a substance used to destroy pests

pes·ti·lence *n* : a contagious often fatal disease that spreads quickly

pes·tle *n* : a tool shaped like a small club for crushing substances in a mortar

¹pet *n* 1 : a tame animal kept for pleasure rather than for use 2 : a person who is treated with special kindness or consideration

²pet *adj* 1 : kept or treated as a pet 2 : showing fondness 3 : ²FAVORITE

³pet *vb* **pet·ted; pet·ting** 1 : to stroke or pat gently or lovingly 2 : to kiss and caress

pet·al *n* : one of the often brightly colored modified leaves that make up the corolla of a flower — **pet·aled** *or* **pet·alled** *adj* — **pet·al·less** *adj*

pet·i·ole *n* : the stalk of a leaf

pe·tite *adj* : having a small trim figure

¹pe·ti·tion *n* 1 : an earnest appeal 2 : a document asking for something

²petition *vb* : to make a petition to or for — **pe·ti·tion·er** *n*

pe·trel *n* : a small seabird with long wings that flies far from land

pet·ri·fy *vb* **pet·ri·fied; pet·ri·fy·ing** 1 : to change plant or animal matter into stone or something like stone 2 : to frighten very much

pe·tro·leum *n* : a raw oil that is obtained from wells drilled in the ground and that is the source of gasoline, kerosene, and fuel oils

pet·ti·coat *n* : a skirt worn under a dress or outer skirt

petting zoo *n* : a collection of farm animals or gentle exotic animals for children to pet and feed

pet·ty *adj* **pet·ti·er; pet·ti·est** 1 : small and of no importance 2 : showing or having a mean narrow-minded attitude — **pet·ti·ly** *adv* — **pet·ti·ness** *n*

petty officer *n* : an officer in the Navy or Coast Guard appointed from among the enlisted people

petty officer first class *n* : a petty officer in the Navy or Coast Guard ranking above a petty officer second class

petty officer second class *n* : a petty officer in the Navy or Coast Guard ranking above a petty officer third class

petty officer third class *n* : a petty officer in the Navy or Coast Guard ranking above a seaman

pet·u·lant *adj* : easily put in a bad humor : CROSS

pe·tu·nia *n* : a plant related to the potato grown for its velvety brightly colored flowers that are shaped like funnels

pew *n* : one of the benches with backs and sometimes doors set in rows in a church

pe·wee *n* : a small grayish or greenish brown bird (as a phoebe) that eats flying insects

pew·ter *n* 1 : a metallic substance made mostly of tin sometimes mixed with copper or antimony that is used in making utensils (as pitchers and bowls) 2 : utensils made of pewter

phantasy *variant of* FANTASY

phan·tom *n* : an image or figure that can be sensed (as with the eyes or ears) but that is not real

pha·raoh *n* : a ruler of ancient Egypt

phar·ma·cist *n* : a person skilled or engaged in pharmacy

phar·ma·cy *n, pl* **phar·ma·cies** 1 : the art, practice, or profession of mixing and preparing medicines usually according to a doctor's prescription 2 : the place of business of a pharmacist : DRUGSTORE

phar·ynx *n, pl* **pha·ryn·ges** *also* **phar·ynx·es** : the space behind the mouth into which the nostrils, gullet, and windpipe open — **pha·ryn·geal** *adj*

phase *n* 1 : the way that the moon or a planet looks to the eye at any time in its series of changes with respect to how it shines 2 : a step or part in a series of events or actions : STAGE 3 : a particular part or feature : ASPECT

pheas·ant *n* : a large brightly colored game bird with a long tail that is related to the chicken

phe·nom·e·nal *adj* : very remarkable : EXTRAORDINARY

phe·nom·e·non *n, pl* **phe·nom·e·na** *or* **phe·nom·e·nons** **1** *pl* **phenomena** : an observable fact or event **2** : a rare or important fact or event **3** *pl* **phenomenons** : an extraordinary or exceptional person or thing

1-phil *or* **-phile** *n suffix* : lover : one having a strong attraction to

2-phil *or* **-phile** *adj suffix* : having a fondness for or strong attraction to

phil·an·throp·ic *adj* : of, relating to, or devoted to philanthropy : CHARITABLE — **phil·an·throp·i·cal·ly** *adv*

phi·lan·thro·pist *n* : a person who gives generously to help other people

phi·lan·thro·py *n, pl* **phi·lan·thro·pies** **1** : active effort to help other people **2** : a philanthropic gift **3** : an organization giving or supported by charitable gifts

phil·o·den·dron *n* : any of several plants that can stand shade and are often grown for their showy leaves

phi·los·o·pher *n* **1** : a student of philosophy **2** : a person who takes misfortunes with calmness and courage

phil·o·soph·i·cal *or* **phil·o·soph·ic** *adj* **1** : of or relating to philosophy **2** : showing the wisdom and calm of a philosopher — **phil·o·soph·i·cal·ly** *adv*

phi·los·o·phy *n, pl* **phi·los·o·phies** **1** : the study of the basic ideas about knowledge, right and wrong, reasoning, and the value of things **2** : the philosophical teachings or principles of a person or a group **3** : calmness of temper and judgment

phlox *n, pl* **phlox** *or* **phlox·es** : any of a group of plants grown for their showy clusters of usually white, pink, or purplish flowers

pho·bia *n* : an unreasonable, abnormal, and lasting fear of something

phoe·be *n* : a common American bird that is grayish brown above and yellowish white below and that eats flying insects

phon- *or* **phono-** *prefix* : sound : voice : speech

1phone *n* : 1TELEPHONE

2phone *vb* **phoned; phon·ing** : 2TELEPHONE

pho·neme *n* : one of the smallest units of speech that distinguish one utterance from another

pho·net·ic *adj* : of or relating to spoken language or speech sounds

pho·nics *n* : a method of teaching beginners to read and pronounce words by learning the sound value of letters, letter groups, and syllables

pho·no·graph *n* : an instrument that reproduces sounds recorded on a grooved disk **(phonograph record)**

phos·pho·rus *n* : a white or yellowish waxlike chemical element that gives a faint glow in moist air and is necessary in some form to plant and animal life

1pho·to *n, pl* **photos** : 1PHOTOGRAPH

2photo *vb* : 2PHOTOGRAPH

1pho·to·copy *n* : a copy of usually printed material made using a process in which an image is formed by the action of light on an electrically charged surface

2photocopy *vb* : to make a photocopy of — **pho·to·copi·er** *n*

1pho·to·graph *n* : a picture made by photography

2photograph *vb* : to take a picture of with a camera — **pho·tog·ra·pher** *n*

pho·to·graph·ic *adj* : obtained by or used in photography

pho·tog·ra·phy *n* : the making of pictures by means of a camera that directs the image of an object onto a film made sensitive to light

pho·to·syn·the·sis *n* : the process by which green plants form carbohydrates from carbon dioxide and water in the presence of light — **pho·to·syn·thet·ic** *adj*

1phrase *n* **1** : a brief expression **2** : a group of two or more words that express a single idea but do not form a complete sentence

2phrase *vb* **phrased; phras·ing** : to express in words

phy·lum *n, pl* **phy·la** : a group of animals that ranks above the class in scientific classification and is the highest group of the plant kingdom

phys·i·cal *adj* **1** : of or relating to nature or the world as we see it : material and not mental, spiritual, or imaginary **2** : of the body : BODILY **3** : of or relating to physics — **phys·i·cal·ly** *adv*

phy·si·cian *n* : a specialist in healing human disease : a doctor of medicine

phys·i·cist *n* : a specialist in physics

phys·ics *n* : a science that deals with the facts about matter and motion and includes the subjects of mechanics, heat, light, electricity, sound, and the atomic nucleus

phys·i·o·log·i·cal *or* **phys·i·o·log·ic** *adj* : of or relating to physiology

phys·i·ol·o·gist *n* : a specialist in physiology

phys·i·ol·o·gy *n* **1** : a branch of biology that deals with the working of the living body and its parts (as organs and cells) **2** : the processes and activities by which a living being or any of its parts functions

phy·sique *n* : the build of a person's body

pi *n, pl* **pis** : the symbol π representing the ratio of the circumference of a circle to its diameter or about 3.1416

pi·a·nist *n* : a person who plays the piano

pi·a·no *n, pl* **pianos** : a keyboard instrument having steel wire strings that sound when struck by hammers covered with felt

pi·az·za *n* 1 : a large open square in an Italian town 2 : PORCH, VERANDA

pic·co·lo *n, pl* **pic·co·los** : a small flute whose tones are an octave higher than those of the ordinary flute

¹pick *vb* 1 : to strike or work on with a pointed tool 2 : to remove bit by bit 3 : to gather one by one 4 : CHOOSE 1, SELECT 5 : to eat sparingly or daintily 6 : to steal from 7 : to start (a fight) with someone else deliberately 8 : to unlock without a key 9 : to pluck with the fingers or with a pick — **pick·er** *n* — **pick on** : ¹TEASE

²pick *n* 1 : PICKAX 2 : a slender pointed instrument 3 : a thin piece of metal or plastic used to pluck the strings of a musical instrument 4 : the act or opportunity of choosing 5 : the best ones

pick·ax *n* : a heavy tool with a wooden handle and a blade pointed at one or both ends for loosening or breaking up soil or rock

pick·er·el *n* : any of several fairly small fishes that look like the pike

¹pick·et *n* 1 : a pointed stake or slender post (as for making a fence) 2 : a soldier or a group of soldiers assigned to stand guard 3 : a person stationed before a place of work where there is a strike

²picket *vb* 1 : ²TETHER 2 : to walk or stand in front of as a picket

¹pick·le *n* 1 : a mixture of salt and water or vinegar for keeping foods : BRINE 2 : a difficult or very unpleasant condition 3 : something (as a cucumber) that has been kept in a pickle of salty water or vinegar

²pickle *vb* **pick·led; pick·ling** : to soak or keep in a pickle

pick·pock·et *n* : a thief who steals from pockets and purses

pick·up *n* : a light truck with an open body and low sides

pick up *vb* 1 : to take hold of and lift 2 : to stop for and take along 3 : to gain by study or experience : LEARN 4 : to get by buying : BUY 5 : to come to and follow 6 : to bring within range of hearing 7 : to get back speed or strength

¹pic·nic *n* 1 : an outdoor party with food taken along and eaten in the open 2 : a nice experience

²picnic *vb* **pic·nicked; pic·nick·ing** : to go on a picnic

pic·to·graph *n* : a diagram showing information by means of pictures

pic·to·ri·al *adj* 1 : of or relating to pictures 2 : using pictures

¹pic·ture *n* 1 : an image of something formed on a surface (as by drawing, painting, printing, or photography) 2 : a very clear description 3 : an exact likeness 4 : MOVIE 5 : an image on the screen of a television set

²picture *vb* **pic·tured; pic·tur·ing** 1 : to draw or paint a picture of 2 : to describe very clearly in words 3 : to form a mental image of : IMAGINE

picture graph *n* : PICTOGRAPH

pic·tur·esque *adj* : like a picture : suggesting a painted scene

pie *n* : a food consisting of a crust and a filling (as of fruit or meat)

pie·bald *adj* : spotted or blotched with two colors and especially black and white

¹piece *n* 1 : a part cut, torn, or broken from a thing 2 : one of a group, set, or mass of things 3 : a portion marked off 4 : a single item or example 5 : a definite amount or size in which articles are made for sale or use 6 : something made or written 7 : ¹COIN 1

²piece *vb* **pieced; piec·ing** 1 : to repair or complete by adding a piece or pieces 2 : to make out of pieces

piece·meal *adv* : one piece at a time : little by little

pied *adj* : having blotches of two or more colors

pier *n* 1 : a support for a bridge 2 : a structure built out into the water for use as a place to land or walk or to protect or form a harbor

pierce *vb* **pierced; pierc·ing** 1 : to run into or through : STAB 2 : to make a hole in or through 3 : to force into or through 4 : to penetrate with the eye or mind : see through — **pierc·ing·ly** *adv*

pi·e·ty *n, pl* **pieties** : the state or fact of being pious : devotion to one's God

pig *n* 1 : a swine especially when not yet mature 2 : a person who lives or acts like a pig 3 : a metal cast (as of iron) poured directly from the smelting furnace into a mold

pi·geon *n* : a bird with a stout body, short legs, and smooth feathers

pi·geon-toed *adj* : having the toes turned in

pig·gish *adj* : like a pig especially in greed or dirtiness

pig·gy·back *adv or adj* : on the back or shoulders

piggy bank *n* : a bank for coins often in the shape of a pig

pig·head·ed *adj* : STUBBORN 1 2

pig·ment *n* **1** : a substance that gives color to other substances **2** : coloring matter in persons, animals, and plants

pigmy *variant of* PYGMY

pig·pen *n* **1** : a place where pigs are kept **2** : a dirty place

pig·sty *n* : PIGPEN

pig·tail *n* : a tight braid of hair

¹pike *n, pl* **pike** *or* **pikes** : a long slender freshwater fish with a large mouth

²pike *n* : a long wooden pole with a steel point used long ago as a weapon by soldiers

³pike *n* : TURNPIKE, ROAD

¹pile *n* : a large stake or pointed post driven into the ground to support a foundation

²pile *n* : a mass of things heaped together : HEAP **2** : REACTOR 2

³pile *vb* **piled; pil·ing** **1** : to lay or place in a pile : STACK **2** : to heap in large amounts **3** : to move or push forward in a crowd or group

⁴pile *n* : a velvety surface of fine short raised fibers

pil·fer *vb* : to steal small amounts or articles of small value

pil·grim *n* **1** : a person who travels to a holy place as an act of religious devotion **2** *cap* : one of the English colonists who founded the first permanent settlement in New England at Plymouth in 1620

pil·grim·age *n* : a journey made by a pilgrim

pil·ing *n* : a structure made of piles

pill *n* : medicine or a food supplement in the form of a small rounded mass to be swallowed whole

¹pil·lage *n* : the act of robbing by force especially in war

²pillage *vb* **pil·laged; pil·lag·ing** : to take goods and possessions by force

pil·lar *n* **1** : a large post that supports something (as a roof) **2** : a column standing alone (as for a monument) **3** : something like a pillar : a main support

pil·lo·ry *n, pl* **pil·lo·ries** : a device once used for punishing someone in public consisting of a wooden frame with holes in which the head and hands can be locked

¹pil·low *n* : a bag filled with soft or springy material used as a cushion usually for the head of a person lying down

²pillow *vb* **1** : to lay on or as if on a pillow **2** : to serve as a pillow for

pil·low·case *n* : a removable covering for a pillow

¹pi·lot *n* **1** : a person who steers a ship **2** : a person especially qualified to guide ships into and out of a port or in dangerous waters **3** : a person who flies or is qualified to fly an aircraft

²pilot *vb* : to act as pilot of

pi·mien·to *also* **pi·men·to** *n, pl* **pi·mien·tos** *also* **pi·men·tos** : a sweet pepper with a mild thick flesh

pim·ple *n* : a small swelling of the skin often containing pus — **pim·pled** *adj* — **pim·ply** *adj*

¹pin *n* **1** : a slender pointed piece (as of wood or metal) usually having the shape of a cylinder used to fasten articles together or in place **2** : a small pointed piece of wire with a head used for fastening cloth or paper **3** : something (as an ornament or badge) fastened to the clothing by a pin **4** : one of ten pieces set up as the target in bowling

²pin *vb* **pinned; pin·ning** **1** : to fasten or join with a pin **2** : to hold as if with a pin

pin·a·fore *n* : a sleeveless garment with a low neck worn as an apron or a dress

pin·cer *n* **1** **pincers** *pl* : an instrument with two handles and two jaws for gripping something **2** : a claw (as of a lobster) like pincers

¹pinch *vb* **1** : to squeeze between the finger and thumb or between the jaws of an instrument **2** : to squeeze painfully **3** : to cause to look thin or shrunken **4** : to be thrifty or stingy

²pinch *n* **1** : a time of emergency **2** : a painful pressure or stress **3** : an act of pinching : SQUEEZE **4** : as much as may be picked up between the finger and the thumb

pinch hitter *n* **1** : a baseball player who is sent in to bat for another **2** : a person who does another's work in an emergency

pin·cush·ion *n* : a small cushion in which pins may be stuck when not in use

¹pine *n* : an evergreen tree that has narrow needles for leaves, cones, and a wood that ranges from very soft to hard

²pine *vb* **pined; pin·ing** **1** : to lose energy, health, or weight through sorrow or worry **2** : to long for very much

pine·ap·ple *n* : a large juicy yellow fruit of a tropical plant that has long stiff leaves with spiny margins

pin·ey *also* **piny** *adj* : of, relating to, or like that of pine

pin·feath·er *n* : a new feather just breaking through the skin of a bird

pin·ion *n* **1** : the wing or the end part of the wing of a bird **2** : ¹FEATHER 1

¹pink *n* **1** : any of a group of plants with thick stem joints and narrow leaves that are grown for their showy often fragrant flowers **2** : the highest degree

²pink *n* : a pale red

³pink *adj* : of the color pink

⁴pink vb : to cut cloth, leather, or paper in an ornamental pattern or with an edge with notches

pink·eye n : a very contagious disease of the eyes in which the inner part of the eyelids becomes sore and red

pink·ish adj : somewhat pink

pin·na·cle n **1** : a slender tower generally coming to a narrow point at the top **2** : a high pointed peak **3** : the highest point of development or achievement

pin·point vb : to locate or find out exactly

pint n : a unit of capacity equal to one half quart or sixteen ounces (about .47 liter)

pin·to n, pl **pintos** : a spotted horse or pony

pin·wheel n : a toy with fanlike blades at the end of a stick that spin in the wind

piny variant of PINEY

¹pi·o·neer n **1** : a person who goes before and prepares the way for others to follow **2** : an early settler

²pioneer vb **1** : to explore or open up ways or regions for others to follow **2** : to start up something new or take part in the early development of something

pi·ous adj **1** : showing respect and honor toward God **2** : making a show of being very good

pip n : a small fruit seed

¹pipe n **1** : a musical instrument or part of a musical instrument consisting of a tube (as of wood) played by blowing **2** : one of the tubes in a pipe organ that makes sound when air passes through it **3** : BAGPIPE — usually used in pl. **4** : a long tube or hollow body for transporting a substance (as water, steam, or gas) **5** : a tube with a small bowl at one end for smoking tobacco or for blowing bubbles

²pipe vb **piped; pip·ing 1** : to play on a pipe **2** : to have or utter in a shrill tone **3** : to equip with pipes **4** : to move by means of pipes — **pip·er** n

pipe·line n : a line of pipe with pumps and control devices (as for carrying liquids or gases)

¹pip·ing n **1** : the music or sound of a person or thing that pipes **2** : a quantity or system of pipes **3** : a narrow fold of material used to decorate edges or seams

²piping adj : having a high shrill sound

pip·it n : a small bird like a lark

pi·ra·cy n, pl **pi·ra·cies 1** : robbery on the high seas **2** : the using of another's work or invention without permission

pi·rate n : a robber on the high seas : a person who commits piracy

pis pl of PI

Pi·sces n **1** : a constellation between Aquarius and Aries imagined as two fish **2** : the twelfth sign of the zodiac or a person born under this sign

pis·ta·chio n, pl **pis·ta·chios** : the green edible seed of a small tree related to the sumacs

pis·til n : the central organ in a flower that contains the ovary and produces the seed

pis·tol n : a short gun made to be aimed and fired with one hand

pis·ton n : a disk or short cylinder that slides back and forth inside a larger cylinder and is moved by steam in steam engines and by the explosion of fuel in automobiles

¹pit n **1** : a cavity or hole in the ground **2** : an area set off from and often sunken below neighboring areas **3** : a hollow area usually of the surface of the body **4** : an indented scar (as from a boil) — **pit·ted** adj

²pit vb **pit·ted; pit·ting 1** : to make pits in or scar with pits **2** : to set against another in a fight or contest

³pit n : a hard seed or stone (as of a cherry)

⁴pit vb **pit·ted; pit·ting** : to remove the pits from

¹pitch n **1** : a dark sticky substance left over from distilling tar and used in making roofing paper, in waterproofing seams, and in paving **2** : resin from pine trees

²pitch vb **1** : to set up and fix firmly in place **2** : to throw (as hay) usually upward or away from oneself **3** : to throw a baseball to a batter **4** : to plunge or fall forward **5** : ¹SLOPE **6** : to fix or set at a certain pitch or level **7** : to move in such a way that one end falls while the other end rises

³pitch n **1** : the action or manner of pitching **2** : highness or lowness of sound **3** : amount of slope **4** : the amount or level of something (as a feeling) — **pitched** adj

pitch·blende n : a dark mineral that is a source of radium and uranium

¹pitch·er n : a container usually with a handle and a lip used for holding and pouring out liquids

²pitcher n : a baseball player who pitches

pitch·fork n : a fork with a long handle used in pitching hay or straw

pit·e·ous adj : seeking or deserving pity — **pit·e·ous·ly** adv

pit·fall n **1** : a covered or camouflaged pit used to capture animals or people : TRAP **2** : a danger or difficulty that is hidden or is not easily recognized

pith n **1** : the loose spongy tissue forming the center of the stem in some plants **2** : the important part

piti·able adj : PITIFUL

piti·ful adj **1** : causing a feeling of pity or sympathy **2** : deserving pitying scorn

piti·less adj : having no pity : MERCILESS

pi·tu·i·tary gland *n* : an endocrine organ at the base of the brain producing several hormones of which one affects growth

¹pity *n* **1** : a sympathetic feeling for the distress of others **2** : a reason or cause of pity or regret

²pity *vb* **pit·ied; pity·ing** : to feel pity for

¹piv·ot *n* **1** : a point or a fixed pin on the end of which something turns **2** : something on which something else turns or depends : a central member, part, or point

²pivot *vb* **1** : to turn on or as if on a pivot **2** : to provide with, mount on, or attach by a pivot

pix·ie *or* **pixy** *n, pl* **pix·ies** : a mischievous elf or fairy

piz·za *n* : an open pie made usually of thinly rolled bread dough spread with a spiced mixture (as of tomatoes, cheese, and ground meat) and baked

plac·ard *n* : a large card for announcing or advertising something : POSTER

pla·cate *vb* **pla·cat·ed; pla·cat·ing** : to calm the anger of : SOOTHE

¹place *n* **1** : a short street **2** : an available space : ROOM **3** : a building or spot set apart for a special purpose **4** : a certain region or center of population **5** : a piece of land with a house on it **6** : position in a scale or series in comparison with another or others **7** : a space (as a seat in a theater) set aside for one's use **8** : usual space or use **9** : the position of a figure in a numeral **10** : a public square

²place *vb* **placed; plac·ing** **1** : to put or arrange in a certain place or position **2** : to appoint to a job or find a job for **3** : to identify by connecting with a certain time, place, or happening

place·hold·er *n* : a symbol (as *x*, Δ, *) used in mathematics in the place of a numeral

place·kick *n* : a kick in football made with the ball held in place on the ground

pla·cen·ta *n* : an organ that has a large blood supply and joins the fetus of a mammal to its mother's uterus

pla·gia·rism *n* : an act of stealing and passing off as one's own the ideas or words of another

¹plague *n* **1** : something that causes much distress **2** : a cause of irritation : NUISANCE **3** : a destructive epidemic disease

²plague *vb* **plagued; plagu·ing** **1** : to strike or afflict with disease or distress **2** : ¹TEASE, TORMENT

plaid *n* **1** : TARTAN **2** : a pattern consisting of rectangles formed by crossed lines of various widths

¹plain *adj* **1** : having no pattern or decoration **2** : open and clear to the sight **3**

: clear to the mind **4** : FRANK **5** : of common or average accomplishments or position : ORDINARY **6** : not hard to do : not complicated **7** : not handsome or beautiful

²plain *n* : a large area of level or rolling treeless land

³plain *adv* : in a plain manner

plain·tive *adj* : showing or suggesting sorrow : MOURNFUL, SAD

¹plait *n* **1** : a flat fold : PLEAT **2** : a flat braid (as of hair)

²plait *vb* **1** : ¹PLEAT **2** : ¹BRAID **3** : to make by braiding

¹plan *n* **1** : a drawing or diagram showing the parts or outline of something **2** : a method or scheme of acting, doing, or arranging

²plan *vb* **planned; plan·ning** **1** : to form a plan of or for : arrange the parts of ahead of time **2** : to have in mind : INTEND

¹plane *vb* **planed; plan·ing** **1** : to smooth or level off with a plane **2** : to remove with or as if with a plane

²plane *n* : a tool for smoothing wood

³plane *adj* : HORIZONTAL, FLAT

⁴plane *n* **1** : a surface any two points of which can be joined by a straight line lying wholly within it **2** : a level or flat surface **3** : a level of development **4** : AIRPLANE

plan·et *n* : a celestial body other than a comet or meteor that travels in orbit about the sun

plan·e·tar·i·um *n* : a building in which there is a device for projecting the images of celestial bodies on a ceiling shaped like a dome

plan·e·tary *adj* **1** : of or relating to a planet **2** : having a motion like that of a planet

plank *n* : a heavy thick board

plank·ton *n* : the tiny floating plants and animals of a body of water

¹plant *vb* **1** : to place in the ground to grow **2** : to set firmly in or as if in the ground : FIX **3** : to introduce as a habit **4** : to cause to become established : SETTLE **5** : to stock with something

²plant *n* **1** : any member of the kingdom of living things (as mosses, ferns, grasses, and trees) that usually lack obvious nervous or sense organs and the ability to move about and that have cellulose cell walls **2** : the buildings and equipment of an industrial business or an institution — **plant·like** *adj*

¹plan·tain *n* : any of several common weeds having little or no stem, leaves with parallel veins, and a long stalk of tiny greenish flowers

²plantain *n* : a banana plant having greenish

fruit that is larger, less sweet, and more starchy than the ordinary banana

plan·ta·tion *n* 1 : a group of plants and especially trees planted and cared for 2 : a planted area (as an estate) cultivated by laborers 3 : COLONY 1

plant·er *n* 1 : one (as a farmer or a machine) that plants crops 2 : a person who owns or runs a plantation 3 : a container in which ornamental plants are grown

plant kingdom *n* : a basic group of natural objects that includes all living and extinct plants

plant louse *n* : APHID

plaque *n* 1 : a flat thin piece (as of metal) used for decoration or having writing cut in it 2 : a thin film containing bacteria and bits of food that forms on the teeth

plas·ma *n* : the watery part of blood, lymph, or milk

¹plas·ter *n* : a paste (as of lime, sand, and water) that hardens when it dries and is used for coating walls and ceilings

²plaster *vb* 1 : to cover or smear with or as if with plaster 2 : to paste or fasten on especially so as to cover — **plas·ter·er** *n*

plaster of par·is *often cap 2d P* : a white powder that mixes with water to form a paste that hardens quickly and is used for casts and molds

¹plas·tic *adj* 1 : capable of being molded or modeled 2 : made of plastic

²plastic *n* : any of various manufactured materials that can be molded into objects or formed into films or fibers

¹plate *n* 1 : a thin flat piece of material 2 : metal in sheets 3 : a piece of metal on which something is engraved or molded 4 : HOME PLATE 5 : household utensils made of or plated with gold or silver 6 : a shallow usually round dish 7 : a main course of a meal 8 : a sheet of glass coated with a chemical sensitive to light for use in a camera 9 : an illustration often covering a full page of a book

²plate *vb* **plat·ed; plat·ing** : to cover with a thin layer of metal (as gold or silver)

pla·teau *n, pl* **plateaus** *or* **pla·teaux** : a broad flat area of high land

plat·form *n* 1 : a statement of the beliefs and rules of conduct for which a group stands 2 : a level usually raised surface (as in a railroad station) 3 : a raised floor or stage for performers or speakers 4 : an arrangement of computer components that uses a particular operating system

plat·i·num *n* : a heavy grayish white metallic chemical element

pla·toon *n* : a part of a military company usually made up of two or more squads

platoon sergeant *n* : a noncommissioned officer in the Army ranking above a staff sergeant

plat·ter *n* : a large plate especially for serving meat

platy·pus *n* : a small water-dwelling mammal of Australia that lays eggs and has webbed feet, dense fur, and a bill that resembles that of a duck

plau·si·ble *adj* : seeming to be reasonable — **plau·si·bly** *adv*

¹play *n* 1 : exercise or activity for amusement 2 : the action of or a particular action in a game 3 : one's turn to take part in a game 4 : absence of any bad intention 5 : quick or light movement 6 : freedom of motion 7 : a story presented on stage

²play *vb* 1 : to produce music or sound 2 : to take part in a game of 3 : to take part in sport or recreation : amuse oneself 4 : to handle something idly : TOY 5 : to act on or as if on the stage 6 : PRETEND 1 7 : to perform (as a trick) for fun 8 : to play in a game against 9 : ²ACT 2, BEHAVE 10 : to move swiftly or lightly 11 : to put or keep in action — **play hooky** : to stay out of school without permission

play·act·ing *n* : an acting out of make-believe roles

play·er *n* 1 : a person who plays a game 2 : a person who plays a musical instrument 3 : a device that reproduces sounds or video images that have been recorded (as on magnetic tape)

player piano *n* : a piano containing a mechanical device by which it may be played automatically

play·ful *adj* 1 : full of play : MERRY 2 : HUMOROUS — **play·ful·ly** *adv* — **play·ful·ness** *n*

play·ground *n* : an area used for games and playing

play·house *n* 1 : THEATER 1 2 : a small house for children to play in

playing card *n* : any of a set of cards marked to show rank and suit (**spades, hearts, diamonds,** or **clubs**) and used in playing various games

play·mate *n* : a companion in play

play·pen *n* : a small enclosure in which a baby is placed to play

play·thing *n* : ¹TOY 2

play·wright *n* : a writer of plays

pla·za *n* : a public square in a city or town

plea *n* 1 : an argument in defense : EXCUSE 2 : an earnest appeal

plead *vb* **plead·ed** *or* **pled; plead·ing** 1 : to argue for or against : argue in court 2 : to answer to a charge 3 : to offer as a defense, an excuse, or an apology **4** : to make an earnest appeal : BEG

pleas·ant *adj* **1** : giving pleasure : AGREEABLE **2** : having pleasing manners, behavior, or appearance — **pleas·ant·ly** *adv* — **pleas·ant·ness** *n*

¹please *vb* **pleased; pleas·ing** **1** : to give pleasure or enjoyment to **2** : to be willing : LIKE, CHOOSE

²please *adv* — used to show politeness in asking or accepting

pleas·ing *adj* : giving pleasure : AGREEABLE — **pleas·ing·ly** *adv*

plea·sur·able *adj* : PLEASANT 1

plea·sure *n* **1** : a particular desire **2** : a feeling of enjoyment or satisfaction **3** : something that pleases or delights

¹pleat *vb* : to arrange in folds made by doubling material over on itself

²pleat *n* : a fold (as in cloth) made by doubling material over on itself

pled *past of* PLEAD

¹pledge *n* **1** : something handed over to another to ensure that the giver will keep his or her promise or agreement **2** : something that is a symbol of something else **3** : a promise or agreement that must be kept

²pledge *vb* **pledged; pledg·ing** **1** : to give as a pledge **2** : to hold by a pledge : PROMISE

plen·te·ous *adj* : PLENTIFUL 2

plen·ti·ful *adj* **1** : giving or containing plenty : FRUITFUL **2** : present in large numbers or amount : ABUNDANT — **plen·ti·ful·ly** *adv*

plen·ty *n* : a full supply : more than enough

pleu·ri·sy *n* : a sore swollen state of the membrane that lines the chest often with fever, painful breathing, and coughing

plex·us *n, pl* **plex·us·es** *or* **plex·us** : a network usually of nerves or blood vessels

pli·able *adj* **1** : possible to bend without breaking **2** : easily influenced

pli·ant *adj* : PLIABLE

pli·ers *n pl* : small pincers with long jaws used for bending or cutting wire or handling small things

plight *n* : a usually bad condition or state : PREDICAMENT

plod *vb* **plod·ded; plod·ding** : to move or travel slowly but steadily

¹plot *n* **1** : a small area of ground **2** : the plan or main story of a play or novel **3** : a secret usually evil scheme

²plot *vb* **plot·ted; plot·ting** **1** : to make a map or plan of **2** : to plan or scheme secretly — **plot·ter** *n*

plo·ver *n* : any one of several shorebirds having shorter and stouter bills than the related sandpipers

¹plow *or* **plough** *n* **1** : a farm machine used to cut, lift, and turn over soil **2** : a device (as a snowplow) used to spread or clear away matter on the ground

²plow *or* **plough** *vb* **1** : to open, break up, or work with a plow **2** : to move through or cut as a plow does

plow·share *n* : the part of a plow that cuts the earth

¹pluck *vb* **1** : to pull off : PICK **2** : to remove something (as hairs) by or as if by plucking **3** : to seize and remove quickly : SNATCH **4** : to pull at (a string) and let go

²pluck *n* **1** : a sharp pull : TUG, TWITCH **2** : COURAGE, SPIRIT

plucky *adj* **pluck·i·er; pluck·i·est** : showing courage : BRAVE

¹plug *n* **1** : a piece (as of wood or metal) used to stop up or fill a hole **2** : a device usually on a cord used to make an electrical connection by putting it into another part (as a socket)

²plug *vb* **plugged; plug·ging** **1** : to stop or make tight with a plug **2** : to keep steadily at work or in action **3** : to connect to an electric circuit

plum *n* **1** : a roundish smooth-skinned edible fruit that has an oblong stone and grows on a tree related to the peaches and cherries **2** : a dark reddish purple **3** : a choice or desirable thing : PRIZE

plum·age *n* : the feathers of a bird

¹plumb *n* : a small weight (as of lead) attached to a line and used to show depth or an exactly straight up-and-down line

²plumb *vb* : to measure or test with a plumb

plumb·er *n* : a person who puts in or repairs plumbing

plumb·ing *n* **1** : a plumber's work **2** : a system of pipes for supplying and carrying off water in a building

plume *n* **1** : a large or showy feather of a bird **2** : an ornamental feather or tuft of feathers (as on a hat) — **plumed** *adj*

plum·met *vb* : to fall straight down

¹plump *vb* **1** : to drop or fall heavily or suddenly **2** : to come out in favor of something

²plump *adv* **1** : with a sudden or heavy drop **2** : DIRECTLY 1

³plump *vb* : to make or become rounded or filled out

⁴plump *adj* : having a pleasingly rounded form : well filled out — **plump·ness** *n*

¹plun·der *vb* : to rob or steal especially openly and by force (as during war)

²plunder *n* : something taken by plundering : LOOT

¹plunge *vb* **plunged; plung·ing** **1** : to thrust or force quickly **2** : to leap or dive suddenly   **3** : to rush, move, or force with reckless haste   **4** : to dip or move suddenly downward or forward and downward

²plunge *n* : a sudden dive, rush, or leap

¹plu·ral *adj* : of, relating to, or being a word form used to show more than one

²plural *n* : a form of a word used to show that more than one person or thing is meant

plu·ral·ize *vb* **plu·ral·ized; plu·ral·iz·ing** : to make plural or express in the plural form

¹plus *adj* : falling high in a certain range

²plus *prep* : increased by : with the addition of

¹plush *n* : a cloth like a very thick soft velvet

²plush *adj* : very rich and fine

plus sign *n* : a sign + used in mathematics to show addition (as in 8+6=14) or a quantity greater than zero (as in +10°)

Plu·to *n* : the planet that is farthest away from the sun and has a diameter of about 5800 kilometers

plu·to·ni·um *n* : a radioactive metallic chemical element formed from neptunium and used for releasing atomic energy

¹ply *vb* **plied; ply·ing**   **1** : to use something steadily or forcefully   **2** : to keep supplying   **3** : to work hard and steadily at

²ply *n, pl* **plies** : one of the folds, layers, or threads of which something (as yarn or plywood) is made up

ply·wood *n* : a strong board made by gluing together thin sheets of wood under heat and pressure

pneu·mat·ic *adj*   **1** : of, relating to, or using air, gas, or wind   **2** : moved or worked by the pressure of air   **3** : made to hold or be inflated with compressed air

pneu·mo·nia *n* : a serious disease in which the lungs are inflamed

¹poach *vb* : to cook slowly in liquid

²poach *vb* : to hunt or fish unlawfully on private property

pock *n* : a small swelling like a pimple on the skin (as in smallpox) or the mark it leaves

¹pock·et *n*   **1** : a small bag fastened into a garment for carrying small articles   **2** : a place or thing like a pocket   **3** : a condition of the air (as a down current) that causes an airplane to drop suddenly

²pocket *vb*   **1** : to put something in a pocket   **2** : to take for oneself especially dishonestly

³pocket *adj* : POCKET-SIZE

pock·et·book *n*   **1** : a case for carrying money or papers in the pocket   **2** : HAND-BAG   **3** : amount of income

pock·et·knife *n, pl* **pock·et·knives** : a knife that has one or more blades that fold into the handle and that can be carried in the pocket

pock·et·size *adj* : small enough to fit in a pocket

pock·mark *n* : the mark left by a pock — **pock·marked** *adj*

pod *n* : a fruit (as of the pea or bean) that is dry when ripe and then splits open to free its seeds

po·em *n* : a piece of writing often having rhyme or rhythm which tells a story or describes a feeling

po·et *n* : a writer of poems

po·et·ic *or* **po·et·i·cal** *adj*   **1** : of, relating to, or like that of poets or poetry   **2** : written in verse

po·et·ry *n*   **1** : writing usually with a rhythm that repeats : VERSE   **2** : the writings of a poet

po·go stick *n* : a pole with a strong spring at the bottom and two rests for the feet on which a person stands and bounces along

poin·set·tia *n* : a tropical plant much used at Christmas with showy usually red leaves that grow like petals around its small greenish flowers

¹point *n*   **1** : a separate or particular detail : ITEM   **2** : an individual quality   **3** : the chief idea or meaning (as of a story or a speech)   **4** : ¹PURPOSE, AIM   **5** : a geometric element that has position but no dimensions and is pictured as a small dot   **6** : a particular place or position   **7** : a particular stage or moment   **8** : the sharp end (as of a sword, pin, or pencil)   **9** : a piece of land that sticks out   **10** : a dot in writing or printing   **11** : one of the thirty-two marks indicating direction on a compass   **12** : a unit of scoring in a game — **point·ed** *adj* — **point·less** *adj*

²point *vb*   **1** : to put a point on   **2** : to show the position or direction of something by the finger or by standing in a fixed position   **3** : to direct someone's attention to   **4** : ¹AIM 1, DIRECT

¹point–blank *adj*   **1** : aimed at a target from a short distance away   **2** : ¹BLUNT 2

²point–blank *adv* : in a point-blank manner

point·er *n*   **1** : something that points or is used for pointing   **2** : a large hunting dog with long ears and short hair that is usually white with colored spots, hunts by scent, and points game   **3** : a helpful hint

point of view : a way of looking at or thinking about something

¹poise *vb* **poised; pois·ing** : to hold or make steady by balancing

²poise *n*   **1** : the state of being balanced   **2** : a natural self-confident manner   **3** : BEARING 1

¹poi·son *n* : a substance that by its chemical action can injure or kill a living thing

²poison *vb*   **1** : to injure or kill with poison   **2** : to put poison on or in

poison ivy *n* : a common woody plant related to the sumacs and having leaves with three leaflets that can cause an itchy rash when touched

poison oak *n* : a poison ivy that grows as a bush

poi·son·ous *adj* : containing poison : having or causing an effect of poison

poison sumac *n* : a poisonous American swamp shrub or small tree related to poison ivy

¹poke *vb* **poked; pok·ing 1 :** JAB **2 :** to make by stabbing or piercing **3 :** to stick out, or cause to stick out **4 :** to search over or through usually without purpose : RUMMAGE **5 :** to move slowly or lazily

²poke *n* : a quick thrust : JAB

¹pok·er *n* : a metal rod used for stirring a fire

²po·ker *n* : a card game in which each player bets on the value of his or her hand

poky *or* **pok·ey** *adj* **pok·i·er; pok·i·est 1 :** being small and cramped **2 :** so slow as to be annoying

po·lar *adj* **1 :** of or relating to a pole of the earth or the region around it **2 :** coming from or being like a polar region **3 :** of or relating to a pole of a magnet

polar bear *n* : a large creamy-white bear of arctic regions

Po·lar·is *n* : NORTH STAR

¹pole *n* : a long slender piece (as of wood or metal)

²pole *vb* **poled; pol·ing :** to push or move with a pole

³pole *n* **1 :** either end of an axis and especially of the earth's axis **2 :** either of the two ends of a magnet **3 :** either of the terminals of an electric battery

Pole *n* : a person born or living in Poland

pole·cat *n* **1 :** a brown or black European animal related to the weasel **2 :** SKUNK

pole·star *n* : NORTH STAR

pole vault *n* : a track-and-field contest in which each athlete uses a pole to jump over a high bar

¹po·lice *vb* **po·liced; po·lic·ing :** to keep order in or among

²police *n, pl* **police 1 :** the department of government that keeps order and enforces law, investigates crimes, and makes arrests **2** *police pl* : members of a police force

police dog *n* : a dog trained to help police

po·lice·man *n, pl* **po·lice·men :** a man who is a police officer

police officer *n* : a member of a police force

po·lice·wom·an *n, pl* **po·lice·wom·en :** a woman who is a police officer

¹pol·i·cy *n, pl* **pol·i·cies :** a course of action chosen to guide people in making decisions

²policy *n, pl* **pol·i·cies :** a document that contains the agreement made by an insurance company with a person whose life or property is insured

po·lio *n* : a once common virus disease often affecting children and sometimes causing paralysis

po·lio·my·eli·tis *n* : POLIO

¹pol·ish *vb* **1 :** to make smooth and glossy usually by rubbing **2 :** to smooth or improve in manners, condition, or style — **pol·ish·er** *n*

²polish *n* **1 :** a smooth glossy surface **2** : good manners : REFINEMENT **3 :** a substance prepared for use in polishing

¹Pol·ish *adj* : of or relating to Poland, the Poles, or Polish

²Polish *n* : the language of the Poles

po·lite *adj* **po·lit·er; po·lit·est :** showing courtesy or good manners — **po·lite·ly** *adv* — **po·lite·ness** *n*

po·lit·i·cal *adj* : of or relating to politics, government, or the way government is carried on — **po·lit·i·cal·ly** *adv*

pol·i·ti·cian *n* : a person who is actively taking part in party politics or in conducting government business

pol·i·tics *n sing or pl* **1 :** the science and art of government : the management of public affairs **2 :** activity in or management of the business of political parties

pol·ka *n* : a lively dance for couples or the music for it

¹poll *n* **1 :** the casting or recording of the votes or opinions of a number of persons **2** : the place where votes are cast — usually used in pl.

²poll *vb* **1 :** to receive and record the votes of **2 :** to receive (votes) in an election **3** : to cast a vote or ballot at a poll

pol·lack *or* **pol·lock** *n, pl* **pollack** *or* **pollock :** either of two food fishes of the northern Atlantic and the northern Pacific that are related to the cod

pol·len *n* : the fine usually yellow dust in the anthers of a flower that fertilizes the seeds

pol·li·nate *vb* **pol·li·nat·ed; pol·li·nat·ing** : to place pollen on the stigma of

pol·li·na·tion *n* : the act or process of pollinating

pol·li·wog *or* **pol·ly·wog** *n* : TADPOLE

pol·lut·ant *n* : something that causes pollution

pol·lute *vb* **pol·lut·ed; pol·lut·ing :** to make impure — **pol·lut·er** *n*

pol·lu·tion *n* : the action of polluting or the state of being polluted

po·lo *n* : a game played by teams of players on horseback who drive a wooden ball with long-handled mallets

poly- *prefix* : many : much : MULTI-

poly·es·ter *n* : a synthetic fiber used especially in clothing

poly·gon *n* : a plane figure having three or more straight sides

poly·mer *n* : a chemical compound or mixture of compounds that is formed by combination of smaller molecules and consists basically of repeating structural units

pol·yp *n* : a small sea animal (as a coral) having a tubelike body closed and attached to something (as a rock) at one end and opening at the other with a mouth surrounded by tentacles

pome·gran·ate *n* : a reddish fruit about the size of an orange that has a thick skin and many seeds in a pulp of acid flavor and grows on a tropical Old World tree

1pom·mel *n* : a rounded knob on the handle of a sword or at the front and top of a saddle

2pommel *vb* **pom·meled** *or* **pom·melled; pom·mel·ing** *or* **pom·mel·ling** : PUMMEL

pomp *n* : a show of wealth and splendor

pom·pom *or* **pom·pon** *n* : a fluffy ball used as trimming on clothing

pomp·ous *adj* 1 : making an appearance of importance or dignity 2 : SELF-IMPORTANT — **pomp·ous·ly** *adv* — **pomp·ous·ness** *n*

pon·cho *n, pl* **ponchos** 1 : a Spanish-American cloak like a blanket with a slit in the middle for the head 2 : a waterproof garment like a poncho worn as a raincoat

pond *n* : a body of water usually smaller than a lake

pon·der *vb* : to think over carefully

pon·der·ous *adj* 1 : very heavy 2 : unpleasantly dull

pond scum *n* : a mass of algae in still water or an alga that grows in such masses

pon·iard *n* : a slender dagger

pon·toon *n* 1 : a small boat with a flat bottom 2 : a light watertight float used as one of the supports for a floating bridge 3 : a float attached to the bottom of an airplane for landing on water

po·ny *n, pl* **ponies** : a small horse

pony express *n* : a rapid postal system that operated across the western United States in 1860–61 by changing horses and riders along the way

poo·dle *n* : one of an old breed of active intelligent dogs with heavy coats of solid color

pooh *interj* — used to express contempt or disapproval

1pool *n* 1 : a small deep body of usually fresh water 2 : something like a pool 3 : a small body of standing liquid : PUDDLE 4 : SWIMMING POOL

2pool *n* 1 : a game of billiards played on a table with six pockets 2 : people, money,

or things come together or put together for some purpose

3pool *vb* : to contribute to a common fund or effort

poor *adj* 1 : not having riches or possessions 2 : less than enough 3 : worthy of pity 4 : low in quality or value — **poor·ly** *adv* — **poor·ness** *n*

1pop *vb* **popped; pop·ping** 1 : to burst or cause to burst with a sharp sound 2 : to move suddenly 3 : to fire a gun : SHOOT 4 : to stick out

2pop *n* 1 : a short explosive sound 2 : SODA POP

pop·corn *n* 1 : corn whose kernels burst open when exposed to high heat to form a white or yellowish mass 2 : the kernels after popping

pope *n, often cap* : the head of the Roman Catholic Church

pop·lar *n* : a tree that has rough bark, catkins for flowers, and a white cottonlike substance around its seeds

pop·py *n, pl* **poppies** : a plant with a hairy stem and showy usually red, yellow, or white flowers

pop·u·lace *n* 1 : the common people 2 : POPULATION 1

pop·u·lar *adj* 1 : of, relating to, or coming from the whole body of people 2 : enjoyed or approved by many people — **pop·u·lar·ly** *adv*

pop·u·lar·i·ty *n* : the quality or state of being popular

pop·u·late *vb* **pop·u·lat·ed; pop·u·lat·ing** : to provide with inhabitants

pop·u·la·tion *n* 1 : the whole number of people in a country, city, or area 2 : the people or things living in a certain place

pop·u·lous *adj* : having a large population

por·ce·lain *n* : a hard white ceramic ware used especially for dishes and chemical utensils

porch *n* : a covered entrance to a building usually with a separate roof

por·cu·pine *n* : a gnawing animal having stiff sharp quills among its hairs

1pore *vb* **pored; por·ing** : to read with great attention : STUDY

2pore *n* : a tiny opening (as in the skin or in the soil)

por·gy *n, pl* **porgies** : any of several food fishes of the Mediterranean sea and the Atlantic ocean

pork *n* : the fresh or salted flesh of a pig

po·rous *adj* 1 : full of pores 2 : capable of absorbing liquids

por·poise *n* 1 : a sea animal somewhat like a small whale with a blunt rounded snout 2 : DOLPHIN 1

por·ridge *n* : a food made by boiling meal of a grain or a vegetable (as peas) in water or milk until it thickens

¹port *n* **1** : a place where ships may ride safe from storms **2** : a harbor where ships load or unload cargo **3** : AIRPORT

²port *n* **1** : an opening (as in machinery) for gas, steam, or water to go in or out **2** : PORTHOLE

³port *n* : the left side of a ship or airplane looking forward

por·ta·ble *adj* : possible to carry or move about

por·tage *n* : the carrying of boats or goods overland from one body of water to another

por·tal *n* : a grand or fancy door or gate

port·cul·lis *n* : a heavy iron gate which can be let down to prevent entrance (as to a castle)

por·tend *vb* : to give a sign or warning of beforehand

por·tent *n* : a sign or warning that something is going to happen

por·ter *n* **1** : a person who carries baggage (as at a terminal) **2** : an attendant on a train

port·fo·lio *n, pl* **port·fo·li·os** : a flat case for carrying papers or drawings

port·hole *n* : a small window in the side of a ship or airplane

por·ti·co *n, pl* **por·ti·coes** *or* **por·ti·cos** : a row of columns supporting a roof around or at the entrance of a building

¹por·tion *n* : a part or share of a whole

²portion *vb* : to divide into portions : DISTRIBUTE

por·trait *n* : a picture of a person usually showing the face

por·tray *vb* **1** : to make a portrait of **2** : to picture in words : DESCRIBE **3** : to play the role of

por·tray·al *n* : the act or result of portraying

¹Por·tu·guese *adj* : of or relating to Portugal, its people, or the Portuguese language

²Portuguese *n, pl* **Portuguese** **1** : a person born or living in Portugal **2** : the language of Portugal and Brazil

¹pose *vb* **posed; pos·ing** **1** : to hold or cause to hold a special position of the body **2** : to set forth **3** : to pretend to be what one is not

²pose *n* **1** : a position of the body held for a special purpose **2** : a pretended attitude

po·si·tion *n* **1** : the way in which something is placed or arranged **2** : a way of looking at or considering things **3** : the place where a person or thing is **4** : the rank a person has in an organization or in society **5** : JOB 3

¹pos·i·tive *adj* **1** : definitely and clearly stated **2** : fully confident : CERTAIN **3** : of, relating to, or having the form of an adjec-

tive or adverb that shows no degree of comparison **4** : having a real position or effect **5** : having the light and shade the same as in the original subject **6** : being greater than zero and often shown by a plus sign **7** : of, being, or relating to electricity of a kind that is produced in a glass rod rubbed with silk **8** : having a deficiency of electrons **9** : being the part from which the electric current flows to the external circuit **10** : showing acceptance or approval **11** : showing the presence of what is looked for or suspected to be present — **pos·i·tive·ly** *adv*

²positive *n* : the positive degree or a positive form of an adjective or adverb

pos·sess *vb* **1** : to have and hold as property : OWN **2** : to enter into and control firmly — **pos·ses·sor** *n*

pos·ses·sion *n* **1** : the act of possessing or holding as one's own : OWNERSHIP **2** : something that is held as one's own property

¹pos·ses·sive *adj* **1** : being or belonging to the case of a noun or pronoun that shows possession **2** : showing the desire to possess or control

²possessive *n* : a noun or pronoun in the possessive case

pos·si·bil·i·ty *n, pl* **pos·si·bil·i·ties** **1** : the state or fact of being possible **2** : something that may happen

pos·si·ble *adj* **1** : being within the limits of one's ability **2** : being something that may or may not happen **3** : able or fitted to be or to become

pos·si·bly *adv* **1** : by any possibility **2** : PERHAPS

pos·sum *n* : OPOSSUM

¹post *n* : a piece of solid substance (as metal or timber) placed firmly in an upright position and used especially as a support

²post *vb* **1** : to fasten on a post, wall, or bulletin board **2** : to make known publicly as if by posting a notice **3** : to forbid persons from entering or using by putting up warning notices

³post *vb* **1** : to ride or travel with haste **2** : to send by mail : MAIL **3** : to make familiar with a subject

⁴post *n* **1** : the place at which a soldier or guard is stationed **2** : a place where a body of troops is stationed **3** : a place or office to which a person is appointed **4** : a trading settlement

⁵post *vb* : to station at a post

post- *prefix* : after : later : following : behind

post·age *n* : a fee for postal service

post·al *adj* : of or relating to the post office or the handling of mail

postal card *n* **1** : a blank card with a postage stamp printed on it **2** : POSTCARD 1

post·card *n* **1** : a card on which a message may be sent by mail without an envelope **2** : POSTAL CARD 1

post·er *n* : a usually large sheet with writing or pictures on it that is displayed as a notice, advertisement, or for decoration

pos·ter·i·ty *n* **1** : the line of individuals descended from one ancestor **2** : all future generations

post·man *n, pl* **post·men** : LETTER CARRIER

post·mark *n* : a mark put on a piece of mail especially for canceling the postage stamp

post·mas·ter *n* : a person in charge of a post office

post·mis·tress *n* : a woman in charge of a post office

post office *n* **1** : a government agency in charge of the mail **2** : a place where mail is received, handled, and sent out

post·paid *adv* : with postage paid by the sender

post·pone *vb* **post·poned; post·pon·ing** : to put off till some later time — **post·pone·ment** *n*

post·script *n* : a note added at the end of a finished letter or book

¹**pos·ture** *n* : the position of one part of the body with relation to other parts : the general way of holding the body

²**posture** *vb* **pos·tured; pos·tur·ing** : to take on a particular posture : POSE

po·sy *n, pl* **posies** **1** : ¹FLOWER 1, 2 **2** : BOUQUET

¹**pot** *n* **1** : a deep rounded container for household purposes **2** : the amount a pot will hold

²**pot** *vb* **pot·ted; pot·ting** **1** : to put or pack in a pot **2** : to plant (as a flower) in a pot to grow — often used with *up*

pot·ash *n* : potassium or a compound of potassium

po·tas·si·um *n* : a silvery soft light metallic chemical element found especially in minerals

po·ta·to *n, pl* **po·ta·toes** : the thick edible underground tuber of a widely grown American plant related to the tomato

potato chip *n* : a very thin slice of white potato fried crisp and salted

po·tent *adj* **1** : having power or authority **2** : very effective : STRONG

po·ten·tial *adj* : existing as a possibility — **po·ten·tial·ly** *adv*

pot·hole *n* : a deep round hole (as in a stream bed or a road)

po·tion *n* : a drink especially of a medicine or of a poison

pot·shot *n* : a shot taken in a casual manner or at an easy target

¹**pot·ter** *n* : a person who makes pottery

²**potter** *vb* : PUTTER

pot·tery *n, pl* **pot·ter·ies** **1** : a place where clay articles (as pots, dishes, and vases) are made **2** : the art of making clay articles **3** : articles made from clay that is shaped while moist and hardened by heat

pouch *n* **1** : a small bag with a drawstring **2** : a bag often with a lock for carrying goods or valuables **3** : a bag of folded skin and flesh especially for carrying the young (as on the abdomen of a kangaroo) or for carrying food (as in the cheek of many animals of the rat family)

poul·tice *n* : a soft and heated mass usually containing medicine and spread on the body surface to relieve pain, inflammation, or congestion

poul·try *n* : birds (as chickens, turkeys, ducks, and geese) grown to furnish meat or eggs for human food

¹**pounce** *vb* **pounced; pounc·ing** **1** : to swoop on and seize something with or as if with claws **2** : to leap or attack very quickly

²**pounce** *n* : an act of pouncing : a sudden swooping or springing on something

¹**pound** *n* **1** : a measure of weight equal to sixteen ounces (about .45 kilogram) **2** : a coin or bill used in the United Kingdom and several other countries

²**pound** *n* : a public enclosure where stray animals are kept

³**pound** *vb* **1** : to crush to a powder or pulp by beating **2** : to strike heavily again and again **3** : to move along heavily

pour *vb* **1** : to flow or cause to flow in a stream **2** : to let loose something without holding back **3** : to rain hard

¹**pout** *vb* : to show displeasure by pushing out one's lips

²**pout** *n* : an act of pouting

pov·er·ty *n* **1** : the condition of being poor : lack of money or possessions **2** : a lack of something desirable

¹**pow·der** *vb* **1** : to sprinkle with or as if with fine particles of something **2** : to reduce to powder **3** : to use face powder

²**powder** *n* **1** : the fine particles made (as by pounding or crushing) from a dry substance **2** : something (as a food, medicine, or cosmetic) made in or changed to the form of a powder **3** : an explosive used in shooting and in blasting

powder horn *n* : a cow or ox horn made into a flask for carrying gunpowder

pow·dery *adj* **1** : made of or like powder **2** : easily crumbled **3** : sprinkled with powder

¹**pow·er** *n* **1** : possession of control, authority, or influence over others **2** : a nation that has influence among other nations **3** : the ability to act or to do **4** : physical might : STRENGTH **5** : the number of times as shown by an exponent a number is used as a factor to obtain a product **6** : force or energy used to do work **7** : the rate of speed at which work is done **8** : the number of times an optical instrument magnifies the apparent size of the object viewed — **pow·er·less** *adj*

²**power** *vb* : to supply with power

³**power** *adj* : relating to, supplying, or using mechanical or electrical power

pow·er·ful *adj* : full of or having power, strength, or influence — **pow·er·ful·ly** *adv*

pow·er·house *n* **1** : POWER PLANT **2** : a person or thing having unusual strength or energy

power plant *n* : a building in which electric power is generated

pow·wow *n* **1** : a North American Indian ceremony or conference **2** : a meeting for discussion

prac·ti·ca·ble *adj* : possible to do or put into practice

prac·ti·cal *adj* **1** : engaged in some work **2** : of or relating to action and practice rather than ideas or thought **3** : capable of being made use of **4** : ready to do things rather than just plan or think about them

practical joke *n* : a joke made up of something done rather than said : a trick played on someone

prac·ti·cal·ly *adv* **1** : ACTUALLY **2** : ALMOST

¹**prac·tice** *or* **prac·tise** *vb* **prac·ticed** *or* **prac·tised; prac·tic·ing** *or* **prac·tis·ing** **1** : to work at often so as to learn well **2** : to engage in often or usually **3** : to follow or work at as a profession

²**practice** *also* **practise** *n* **1** : actual performance : USE **2** : a usual way of doing **3** : repeated action for gaining skill

prai·rie *n* : a large area of level or rolling grassland

prairie chicken *n* : a grouse of the Mississippi valley

prairie dog *n* : a burrowing animal related to the woodchuck but about the size of a large squirrel that lives in large colonies

prairie schooner *n* : a long covered wagon used by pioneers to cross the prairies

¹**praise** *vb* **praised; prais·ing** **1** : to express approval of **2** : to glorify God or a saint especially in song

²**praise** *n* **1** : an expression of approval **2** : ¹WORSHIP 1

praise·wor·thy *adj* : worthy of praise

prance *vb* **pranced; pranc·ing** **1** : to rise onto or move on the hind legs **2** : to ride on a prancing horse **3** : ¹STRUT

prank *n* : a mischievous act : PRACTICAL JOKE

prat·tle *vb* **prat·tled; prat·tling** : to talk a great deal without much meaning

prawn *n* : an edible shellfish that looks like a shrimp

pray *vb* **1** : to ask earnestly : BEG **2** : to address God with adoration, pleading, or thanksgiving

prayer *n* **1** : a request addressed to God **2** : the act of praying to God **3** : a set form of words used in praying **4** : a religious service that is mostly prayers

praying mantis *n* : MANTIS

pre- *prefix* **1** : earlier than : before **2** : beforehand **3** : in front of : front

preach *vb* **1** : to give a sermon **2** : to urge publicly : ADVOCATE

preach·er *n* **1** : a person who preaches **2** : ¹MINISTER 1

pre·am·ble *n* : an introduction (as to a law) that often gives the reasons for the parts that follow

pre·car·i·ous *adj* **1** : depending on chance or unknown conditions : UNCERTAIN **2** : lacking steadiness or security — **pre·car·i·ous·ly** *adv* — **pre·car·i·ous·ness** *n*

pre·cau·tion *n* **1** : care taken beforehand **2** : something done beforehand to prevent evil or bring about good results

pre·cede *vb* **pre·ced·ed; pre·ced·ing** : to be or go before in importance, position, or time

pre·ce·dent *n* : something that can be used as a rule or as a model to be followed in the future

pre·ced·ing *adj* : going before : PREVIOUS

pre·cious *adj* **1** : very valuable **2** : greatly loved : DEAR

prec·i·pice *n* : a very steep and high face of rock or mountain : CLIFF

pre·cip·i·tate *vb* **pre·cip·i·tat·ed; pre·cip·i·tat·ing** **1** : to cause to happen suddenly or unexpectedly **2** : to change from a vapor to a liquid or solid and fall as rain or snow **3** : to separate from a solution

pre·cip·i·ta·tion *n* **1** : unwise haste **2** : water or the amount of water that falls to the earth as hail, mist, rain, sleet, or snow

pre·cise *adj* **1** : exactly stated or explained **2** : very clear **3** : very exact : ACCURATE — **pre·cise·ly** *adv* — **pre·cise·ness** *n*

pre·ci·sion *n* : the quality or state of being precise

pre·co·cious *adj* : showing qualities or abilities of an adult at an unusually early age — **pre·co·cious·ly** *adv* — **pre·co·cious·ness** *n*

pre—Co·lum·bi·an *adj* : preceding or belonging to the time before the arrival of Columbus in America

pred·a·tor *n* : an animal that lives mostly by killing and eating other animals

pred·a·to·ry *adj* : living by preying upon other animals

pre·de·ces·sor *n* : a person who has held a position or office before another

pre·dic·a·ment *n* : a bad or difficult situation : FIX

pred·i·cate *n* : the part of a sentence or clause that tells what is said about the subject

predicate adjective *n* : an adjective that occurs in the predicate after a linking verb and describes the subject

predicate noun *n* : a noun that occurs in the predicate after a linking verb and refers to the same person or thing as the subject

pre·dict *vb* : to figure out and tell beforehand

pre·dic·tion *n* **1** : an act of predicting **2** : something that is predicted

pre·dom·i·nance *n* : the quality or state of being predominant

pre·dom·i·nant *adj* : greater than others in number, strength, influence, or authority

pre·dom·i·nate *vb* **pre·dom·i·nat·ed; pre·dom·i·nat·ing** : to be predominant

preen *vb* **1** : to smooth with or as if with the bill **2** : to make one's appearance neat and tidy

pre·fab·ri·cate *vb* **pre·fab·ri·cat·ed; pre·fab·ri·cat·ing** : to manufacture the parts of something beforehand so that it can be built by putting the parts together

pref·ace *n* : a section at the beginning that introduces a book or a speech

pre·fer *vb* **pre·ferred; pre·fer·ring** : to like better

pref·er·a·ble *adj* : deserving to be preferred : more desirable — **pref·er·a·bly** *adv*

pref·er·ence *n* **1** : a choosing of or special liking for one person or thing rather than another **2** : the power or chance to choose : CHOICE **3** : a person or thing that is preferred

¹pre·fix *vb* **1** : to put or attach at the beginning of a word : add as a prefix

²prefix *n* : a letter or group of letters that comes at the beginning of a word and has a meaning of its own

preg·nan·cy *n, pl* **preg·nan·cies** : the state of being pregnant

preg·nant *adj* **1** : carrying unborn offspring **2** : full of meaning

pre·hen·sile *adj* : adapted for grasping by wrapping around

pre·his·tor·ic *adj* : of, relating to, or being in existence in the period before written history began

¹prej·u·dice *n* **1** : injury or damage to a case at law or to one's rights **2** : a liking or dislike for one rather than another without good reason

²prejudice *vb* **prej·u·diced; prej·u·dic·ing** **1** : to cause damage to (as a case at law) **2** : to cause prejudice in

prel·ate *n* : a clergyman (as a bishop) of high rank

¹pre·lim·i·nary *n, pl* **pre·lim·i·nar·ies** : something that is preliminary

²preliminary *adj* : coming before the main part : INTRODUCTORY

prel·ude *n* **1** : something that comes before and prepares for the main or more important parts **2** : a short musical introduction (as for an opera) **3** : a piece (as an organ solo) played at the beginning of a church service

pre·ma·ture *adj* : happening, coming, or done before the usual or proper time : too early — **pre·ma·ture·ly** *adv*

pre·med·i·tate *vb* **pre·med·i·tat·ed; pre·med·i·tat·ing** : to think about and plan beforehand

¹pre·mier *adj* : first in position or importance : CHIEF

²premier *n* : PRIME MINISTER

¹pre·miere *adj* : ²CHIEF 2

²premiere *n* : a first showing or performance

prem·ise *n* **1** : a statement taken to be true and on which an argument or reasoning may be based **2** **premises** *pl* : a piece of land with the buildings on it

pre·mi·um *n* **1** : a prize to be gained by some special act **2** : a sum over and above the stated value **3** : the amount paid for a contract of insurance

pre·mo·lar *n* : any of the teeth that come between the canines and the molars and in humans are normally two in each side of each jaw

pre·mo·ni·tion *n* : a feeling that something is going to happen

pre·oc·cu·pied *adj* : lost in thought

prepaid *past of* PREPAY

prep·a·ra·tion *n* **1** : the act of making ready beforehand for some special reason **2** : something that prepares **3** : something prepared for a particular purpose

pre·par·a·to·ry *adj* : preparing or serving to prepare for something

pre·pare *vb* **pre·pared; pre·par·ing** **1** : to make ready beforehand for some particular reason **2** : to put together the elements of

pre·pay *vb* **pre·paid; pre·pay·ing** : to pay or pay for beforehand

prep·o·si·tion *n* : a word or group of words that combines with a noun or pronoun to form a phrase that usually acts as an adverb, adjective, or noun

prep·o·si·tion·al *adj* : of, relating to, or containing a preposition

pre·pos·ter·ous *adj* : making little or no sense : FOOLISH

pre·req·ui·site *n* : something that is needed beforehand or is necessary to prepare for something else

pre·scribe *vb* **pre·scribed; pre·scrib·ing** **1** : to lay down as a rule of action : ORDER **2** : to order or direct the use of as a remedy

pre·scrip·tion *n* **1** : a written direction or order for the preparing and use of a medicine **2** : a medicine that is prescribed

pres·ence *n* **1** : the fact or condition of being present **2** : position close to a person **3** : a person's appearance

presence of mind : ability to think clearly and act quickly in an emergency

¹pres·ent *n* : something presented or given : GIFT

²pre·sent *vb* **1** : to introduce one person to another **2** : to take (oneself) into another's presence **3** : to bring before the public **4** : to make a gift to **5** : to give as a gift **6** : to offer to view : SHOW, DISPLAY,

³pres·ent *adj* **1** : not past or future : now going on **2** : being before or near a person or in sight : being at a certain place and not elsewhere **3** : pointing out or relating to time that is not past or future

⁴pres·ent *n* : the present time : right now

pre·sent·able *adj* : having a satisfactory or pleasing appearance

pre·sen·ta·tion *n* **1** : an introduction of one person to another **2** : an act of presenting **3** : something offered or given

pres·ent·ly *adv* **1** : before long : SOON **2** : at the present time : NOW

pres·er·va·tion *n* : a keeping from injury, loss, or decay

¹pre·serve *vb* **pre·served; pre·serv·ing** **1** : to keep or save from injury or ruin : PROTECT **2** : to prepare (as by canning or pickling) fruits or vegetables for keeping **3** : MAINTAIN 1, CONTINUE — **pre·serv·er** *n*

²preserve *n* **1** : fruit cooked in sugar or made into jam or jelly — often used in pl. **2** : an area where game or fish are protected

pre·side *vb* **pre·sid·ed; pre·sid·ing** **1** : to act as chairperson of a meeting **2** : to be in charge

pres·i·den·cy *n, pl* **pres·i·den·cies** **1** : the office of president **2** : the term during which a president holds office

pres·i·dent *n* **1** : a person who presides over a meeting **2** : the chief officer of a company or society **3** : the head of the government and chief executive officer of a modern republic

pres·i·den·tial *adj* : of or relating to a president or the presidency

¹press *n* **1** : ²CROWD 1, THRONG **2** : a machine that uses pressure to shape, flatten, squeeze, or stamp **3** : a closet for clothing **4** : the act of pressing : PRESSURE **5** : a printing or publishing business **6** : the newspapers and magazines of a country

²press *vb* **1** : to bear down upon : push steadily against **2** : to squeeze so as to force out the juice or contents **3** : to flatten out or smooth by bearing down upon especially by ironing **4** : to ask or urge strongly **5** : to force or push one's way

press·ing *adj* : needing one's immediate attention

pres·sure *n* **1** : the action of pressing or bearing down upon **2** : a force or influence that cannot be avoided **3** : the force with which one body presses against another **4** : the need to get things done

pres·tige *n* : importance in the eyes of people : REPUTE

pres·to *adv or adj* : suddenly as if by magic

pre·sume *vb* **pre·sumed; pre·sum·ing** **1** : to undertake without permission or good reason : DARE **2** : to suppose to be true without proof

pre·sump·tion *n* **1** : presumptuous behavior or attitude **2** : a strong reason for believing something to be so **3** : something believed to be so but not proved

pre·sump·tu·ous *adj* : going beyond what is proper — **pre·sump·tu·ous·ly** *adv* — **pre·sump·tu·ous·ness** *n*

pre·tend *vb* **1** : to make believe : SHAM **2** : to put forward as true something that is not true — **pre·tend·er** *n*

pre·tense *or* **pre·tence** *n* **1** : a claim usually not supported by facts **2** : an effort to reach a certain condition or quality

pre·ten·tious *adj* : having or showing pretenses : SHOWY — **pre·ten·tious·ly** *adv* — **pre·ten·tious·ness** *n*

¹pret·ty *adj* **pret·ti·er; pret·ti·est** : pleasing to the eye or ear especially because of being graceful or delicate — **pret·ti·ly** *adv* — **pret·ti·ness** *n*

²pret·ty *adv* : in some degree : FAIRLY

pret·zel *n* : a brown cracker that is salted and is usually hard and shaped like a loose knot

pre·vail *vb* **1** : to win a victory **2** : to succeed in convincing **3** : to be or become usual, common, or widespread

prev·a·lence *n* : the state of being prevalent

prev·a·lent *adj* : accepted, practiced, or happening often or over a wide area

pre·vent *vb* **1** : to keep from happening **2** : to hold or keep back — **pre·vent·able** *adj*

pre·ven·tion *n* : the act or practice of preventing something

pre·ven·tive *adj* : used for prevention

pre·view *n* : a showing of something (as a movie) before regular showings

pre·vi·ous *adj* : going before in time or order : PRECEDING — **pre·vi·ous·ly** *adv*

¹**prey** *n* **1** : an animal hunted or killed by another animal for food **2** : a person that is helpless and unable to escape attack : VICTIM **3** : the act or habit of seizing or pouncing upon

²**prey** *vb* **1** : to seize and eat something as prey **2** : to have a harmful effect

¹**price** *n* **1** : the quantity of one thing given or asked for something else : the amount of money paid or to be paid **2** : ²REWARD **3** : the cost at which something is gotten or done

²**price** *vb* **priced; pric·ing** **1** : to set a price on **2** : to ask the price of

price·less *adj* : too valuable to have a price : not to be bought at any price

¹**prick** *n* **1** : a mark or small wound made by a pointed instrument **2** : something sharp or pointed **3** : a sensation of being pricked

²**prick** *vb* **1** : to pierce slightly with a sharp point **2** : to have or to cause a feeling of or as if of being pricked **3** : to point upward

prick·er *n* : ¹PRICKLE 1

¹**prick·le** *n* **1** : a small sharp point (as a thorn) **2** : a slight stinging pain

²**prickle** *vb* **prick·led; prick·ling** : ²PRICK 2

prick·ly *adj* **prick·li·er; prick·li·est** **1** : having prickles **2** : being or having a pricking

prickly pear *n* : a usually spiny cactus with flat branching joints and a sweet pulpy fruit shaped like a pear

¹**pride** *n* **1** : too high an opinion of one's own ability or worth : a feeling of being better than others **2** : a reasonable and justifiable sense of one's own worth : SELF-RESPECT **3** : a sense of pleasure that comes from some act or possession **4** : something of which one is proud

²**pride** *vb* **prid·ed; prid·ing** : to think highly of (oneself)

priest *n* : a person who has the authority to lead or perform religious ceremonies

priest·ess *n* : a woman who is a priest

prim *adj* **prim·mer; prim·mest** : very fussy about one's appearance or behavior — **prim·ly** *adv*

pri·mar·i·ly *adv* : in the first place

¹**pri·ma·ry** *adj* **1** : first in time or development **2** : most important : PRINCIPAL **3** : not made or coming from something else : BASIC **4** : of, relating to, or being the

heaviest of three levels of stress in pronunciation

²**primary** *n, pl* **pri·ma·ries** : an election in which members of a political party nominate candidates for office

primary color *n* : any of a set of colors from which all other colors may be made with the colors for light being red, green, and blue and for pigments or paint being red, yellow, and blue

pri·mate *n* : any of a group of mammals that includes humans together with the apes and monkeys and a few related forms

¹**prime** *n* **1** : the first part : the earliest stage **2** : the period in life when a person is best in health, looks, or strength **3** : the best individual or part

²**prime** *adj* **1** : first in time : ORIGINAL **2** : having no factor except itself and one **3** : first in importance, rank, or quality

³**prime** *vb* **primed; prim·ing** **1** : to put a first color or coating on (an unpainted surface) **2** : to put into working order by filling **3** : to tell what to say beforehand : COACH

prime minister *n* : the chief officer of the government in some countries

¹**prim·er** *n* **1** : a small book for teaching children to read **2** : a book of first instructions on a subject

²**prim·er** *n* **1** : a device (as a cap) for setting off an explosive **2** : material used to prime a surface

pri·me·val *adj* : belonging to the earliest time : PRIMITIVE

prim·i·tive *adj* **1** : of or belonging to very early times **2** : of or belonging to an early stage of development

primp *vb* : to dress or arrange in a careful or fussy manner

prim·rose *n* : a low perennial plant with large leaves growing from the base of the stem and showy often yellow or pink flowers

prince *n* **1** : MONARCH 1 **2** : the son of a monarch **3** : a nobleman of very high or the highest rank

prin·cess *n* : a daughter or granddaughter of a monarch : a female member of a royal family

¹**prin·ci·pal** *adj* : highest in rank or importance : CHIEF — **prin·ci·pal·ly** *adv*

²**principal** *n* **1** : a leading or most important person or thing **2** : the head of a school **3** : a sum of money that is placed to earn interest, is owed as a debt, or is used as a fund

prin·ci·pal·i·ty *n, pl* **prin·ci·pal·i·ties** : a small territory that is ruled by a prince

principal parts *n pl* : the infinitive, the past tense, and the past and present participles of an English verb

prin·ci·ple *n* **1** : a general or basic truth on

which other truths or theories can be based
2 : a rule of conduct   **3** : a law or fact of nature which makes possible the working of a
machine or device

¹print *n*   **1** : a mark made by pressure   **2**
: something which has been stamped with
an impression or formed in a mold   **3**
: printed matter   **4** : printed letters   **5** : a
picture, copy, or design taken from an engraving or photographic negative   **6** : cloth
upon which a design is stamped

²print *vb*   **1** : to put or stamp in or on   **2** : to
make a copy of by pressing paper against an
inked surface (as type or an engraving)   **3**
: to stamp with a design by pressure   **4**
: PUBLISH 2   **5** : PRINT OUT   **6** : to write in
separate letters like those made by a typewriter   **7** : to make a picture from a photographic negative

print·er *n*   **1** : a person whose business is
printing   **2** : a machine that produces print-
outs

print·ing *n*   **1** : the process of putting something in printed form   **2** : the art, practice,
or business of a printer

printing press *n* : a machine that makes
printed copies

print·out *n* : a printed record produced by a
computer

print out *vb* : to make a printout of

¹pri·or *n* : a monk who is head of a priory

²prior *adj*   **1** : being or happening before
something else   **2** : being more important
than something else

pri·or·ess *n* : a nun who is head of a priory

pri·or·i·ty *n, pl* **pri·or·i·ties** : the quality or
state of coming before another in time or
importance

prior to *prep* : in advance of : BEFORE

pri·o·ry *n, pl* **pri·o·ries** : a religious house
under a prior or prioress

prism *n* : a transparent object that usually
has three sides and bends light so that it
breaks up into rainbow colors

pris·on *n* : a place where criminals are
locked up

pris·on·er *n* : a person who has been captured or locked up

pri·va·cy *n*   **1** : the state of being out of the
sight and hearing of other people   **2** : SE-
CRECY 2

¹pri·vate *adj*   **1** : having to do with or for the
use of a single person or group : not public
2 : not holding any public office   **3** : ¹SE-
CRET 1 — **pri·vate·ly** *adv* — **pri·vate·ness**
n

²private *n* : an enlisted person of the lowest
rank in the Marine Corps or of either of the
two lowest ranks in the Army

pri·va·teer *n*   **1** : an armed private ship per-

mitted by its government to make war on
ships of an enemy country   **2** : a sailor on a
privateer

private first class *n* : an enlisted person in
the Army or Marine Corps ranking above a
private

priv·et *n* : a shrub with white flowers that is
related to the lilac and is often used for
hedges

priv·i·lege *n* : a right or liberty granted as a
favor or benefit especially to some and not
others

priv·i·leged *adj* : having more things and a
better chance in life than most people

¹prize *n*   **1** : something won or to be won in
a contest   **2** : something unusually valuable
or eagerly sought

²prize *adj*   **1** : awarded a prize   **2** : awarded
as a prize   **3** : outstanding of its kind

³prize *vb* **prized; priz·ing**   **1** : to estimate
the value of   **2** : to value highly : TREASURE

⁴prize *n* : something taken (as in war) by
force especially at sea

prize·fight·er *n* : a professional boxer

¹pro *n, pl* **pros** : an argument or evidence in
favor of something

²pro *adv* : in favor of something

³pro *n or adj* : PROFESSIONAL

pro- *prefix* : approving : in favor of

prob·a·bil·i·ty *n, pl* **prob·a·bil·i·ties**   **1** : the
quality or state of being probable   **2** : something probable

prob·a·ble *adj* : reasonably sure but not certain of happening or being true : LIKELY

prob·a·bly *adv* : very likely

pro·ba·tion *n* : a period of trial for finding
out or testing a person's fitness (as for a job)

¹probe *n*   **1** : a slender instrument for examining a cavity (as a deep wound)   **2** : a careful investigation

²probe *vb* **probed; prob·ing**   **1** : to examine
with or as if with a probe   **2** : to investigate
thoroughly

prob·lem *n*   **1** : something to be worked out
or solved   **2** : a person or thing that is hard
to understand or deal with

pro·bos·cis *n* : a long flexible hollow bodily
structure (as the trunk of an elephant or the
beak of a mosquito)

pro·ce·dure *n*   **1** : the manner or method in
which a business or action is carried on   **2**
: an action or series of actions

pro·ceed *vb*   **1** : to come from a source   **2**
: to go or act by an orderly method   **3** : to
go forward or onward : ADVANCE

pro·ceed·ing *n*   **1** : PROCEDURE 2   **2** **proceedings** *pl* : things that happen

pro·ceeds *n pl* : the money or profit that
comes from a business deal

¹pro·cess *n*   **1** : ²ADVANCE 1   **2** : a series of actions, motions, or operations leading to some result **3** : the carrying on of a legal action

²process *vb* **1** : to change by a special treatment **2** : to take care of according to a routine **3** : to take in and organize for use in a variety of ways

pro·ces·sion *n* **1** : continuous forward movement : PROGRESSION **2** : a group of individuals moving along in an orderly often ceremonial way

pro·ces·sor *n* **1** : a person or machine that processes **2** : COMPUTER **3** : the part of a computer that operates on data

pro·claim *vb* : to announce publicly : DE-CLARE

proc·la·ma·tion *n* **1** : the act of proclaiming **2** : something proclaimed

pro·cure *vb* **pro·cured; pro·cur·ing 1** : OB-TAIN **2** : to bring about or cause to be done

¹prod *vb* **prod·ded; prod·ding 1** : to poke with something **2** : to stir a person or animal to action

²prod *n* **1** : something used for prodding **2** : an act of prodding **3** : a sharp urging or reminder

¹prod·i·gal *adj* : carelessly wasteful

²prodigal *n* : somebody who wastes money carelessly

prod·i·gy *n, pl* **prod·i·gies 1** : an amazing event or action : WONDER **2** : an unusually talented child

¹pro·duce *vb* **pro·duced; pro·duc·ing 1** : to bring to view : EXHIBIT **2** : to bring forth : YIELD **3** : to prepare (as a play) for public presentation **4** : MANUFACTURE — **pro·duc·er** *n*

²pro·duce *n* **1** : something produced **2** : fresh fruits and vegetables

prod·uct *n* **1** : the number resulting from the multiplication of two or more numbers **2** : something produced by manufacture, labor, thought, or growth

pro·duc·tion *n* **1** : something produced **2** : the act of producing **3** : the amount produced

pro·duc·tive *adj* **1** : having the power to produce plentifully **2** : producing something

¹pro·fane *vb* **pro·faned; pro·fan·ing** : to treat with great disrespect — **pro·fan·er** *n*

²profane *adj* : showing no respect for God or holy things — **pro·fane·ly** *adv* — **pro·fane·ness** *n*

pro·fan·i·ty *n, pl* **pro·fan·i·ties** : profane language

pro·fess *vb* **1** : to declare openly **2** : PRE-TEND **2**

pro·fes·sion *n* **1** : a public declaring or claiming **2** : an occupation (as medicine,

law, or teaching) that is not mechanical or agricultural and that requires special education **3** : the people working in a profession

¹pro·fes·sion·al *adj* **1** : of, relating to, or like that of a profession **2** : taking part in an activity (as a sport) that others do for pleasure in order to make money — **pro·fes·sion·al·ly** *adv*

²professional *n* : a person whose work is professional

pro·fes·sor *n* : a teacher especially of the highest rank at a college or university

prof·fer *vb* : ¹OFFER **2**

pro·fi·cient *adj* : very good at doing something : EXPERT — **pro·fi·cient·ly** *adv*

pro·file *n* : something (as a head) seen or drawn from the side

¹prof·it *n* **1** : the gain or benefit from something **2** : the gain after all the expenses are subtracted from the total amount received — **prof·it·less** *adj*

²profit *vb* **1** : to get some good out of something : GAIN **2** : to be of use to (someone)

prof·it·able *adj* : producing profit — **prof·it·ably** *adv*

pro·found *adj* **1** : having or showing great knowledge and understanding **2** : very deeply felt — **pro·found·ly** *adv* — **pro·found·ness** *n*

pro·fuse *adj* : very plentiful — **pro·fuse·ly** *adv* — **pro·fuse·ness** *n*

pro·fu·sion *n* : a plentiful supply : PLENTY

prog·e·ny *n, pl* **prog·e·nies** : human descendants or animal offspring

¹pro·gram *n* **1** : a brief statement or written outline (as of a concert or play) **2** : PER-FORMANCE **2 3** : a plan of action **4** : a set of step-by-step instructions that tell a computer to do something with data

²program *vb* **pro·grammed; pro·gram·ming** : to provide with a program

pro·gram·mer *n* : a person who creates and tests programs for computers

¹prog·ress *n* **1** : a moving toward a goal **2** : gradual improvement

²pro·gress *vb* **1** : to move forward : AD-VANCE **2** : to move toward a higher, better, or more advanced stage

pro·gres·sion *n* **1** : the act of progressing or moving forward **2** : a continuous and connected series (as of acts, events, or steps)

pro·gres·sive *adj* **1** : of, relating to, or showing progress **2** : taking place gradually or step by step **3** : favoring or working for gradual political change and social improvement by action of the government — **pro·gres·sive·ly** *adv* — **pro·gres·sive·ness** *n*

pro·hib·it *vb* **1** : to forbid by authority **2** : to make impossible

pro·hi·bi·tion *n* **1** : the act of prohibiting something **2** : the forbidding by law of the sale or manufacture of alcoholic liquids for use as beverages

¹proj·ect *n* **1** : a plan or scheme to do something **2** : a task or problem in school **3** : a group of houses or apartment buildings built according to a single plan

²pro·ject *vb* **1** : to stick out **2** : to cause to fall on a surface

pro·jec·tile *n* : something (as a bullet or rocket) that is thrown or driven forward especially from a weapon

pro·jec·tion *n* **1** : something that sticks out **2** : the act or process of projecting on a surface (as by means of motion pictures or slides)

pro·jec·tor *n* : a machine for projecting images on a screen

pro·lif·ic *adj* : producing young or fruit in large numbers

pro·long *vb* : to make longer than usual or expected

prom *n* : a usually formal dance given by a high school or college class

prom·e·nade *n* **1** : a walk or ride for pleasure or to be seen **2** : a place for walking

prom·i·nence *n* **1** : the quality, condition, or fact of being prominent : DISTINCTION **2** : something (as a mountain) that is prominent

prom·i·nent *adj* **1** : sticking out beyond the surface **2** : attracting attention (as by size or position) : CONSPICUOUS **3** : DISTINGUISHED, EMINENT — **prom·i·nent·ly** *adv*

¹prom·ise *n* **1** : a statement by a person that he or she will do or not do something **2** : a cause or ground for hope

²promise *vb* **prom·ised; prom·is·ing** **1** : to give a promise about one's own actions **2** : to give reason to expect

prom·is·ing *adj* : likely to turn out well

prom·on·to·ry *n, pl* **prom·on·to·ries** : a high point of land sticking out into the sea

pro·mote *vb* **pro·mot·ed; pro·mot·ing** **1** : to move up in position or rank **2** : to help (something) to grow or develop

pro·mo·tion *n* **1** : a moving up in position or rank **2** : the promoting of something (as growth of health)

¹prompt *vb* **1** : to lead to do something **2** : to remind of something forgotten or poorly learned **3** : to be the cause of : INSPIRE — **prompt·er** *n*

²prompt *adj* **1** : quick and ready to act **2** : being on time : PUNCTUAL **3** : done at once : given without delay — **prompt·ly** *adv* — **prompt·ness** *n*

prone *adj* **1** : likely to be or act a certain way **2** : having the front surface downward — **prone·ness** *n*

prong *n* **1** : one of the sharp points of a fork **2** : a slender part that sticks out (as a point of an antler)

prong·horn *n* : an animal like an antelope that lives in the treeless parts of the western United States and Mexico

pro·noun *n* : a word used as a substitute for a noun

pro·nounce *vb* **pro·nounced; pro·nounc·ing** **1** : to state in an official or solemn way **2** : to use the voice to make the sounds of **3** : to say correctly

pro·nounced *adj* : very noticeable

pro·nun·ci·a·tion *n* : the act or way of pronouncing a word or words

¹proof *n* **1** : evidence of truth or correctness **2** : ¹TEST 1 **3** : a printing (as from type) prepared for study and correction **4** : a test print made from a photographic negative

²proof *adj* : able to keep out something that could be harmful — usually used in compounds

proof·read *vb* **proof·read; proof·read·ing** : to read over and fix mistakes in (written or printed matter) — **proof·read·er** *n*

¹prop *n* : something that props or supports

²prop *vb* **propped; prop·ping** **1** : to keep from falling or slipping by providing a support under or against **2** : to give help, encouragement, or support to

³prop *n* : PROPERTY 3

pro·pa·gan·da *n* : an organized spreading of certain ideas or the ideas spread in such a way

prop·a·gate *vb* **prop·a·gat·ed; prop·a·gat·ing** **1** : to have or cause to have offspring **2** : to cause (as an idea or belief) to spread out and affect a greater number or wider area

prop·a·ga·tion *n* : an act or process of propagating

pro·pel *vb* **pro·pelled; pro·pel·ling** : to push or drive usually forward or onward

pro·pel·ler *n* : a device having a hub fitted with blades that is made to turn rapidly by an engine and that drives a ship, power boat, or airplane

prop·er *adj* **1** : referring to one individual only **2** : belonging naturally to a particular group or individual : CHARACTERISTIC **3** : considered in its true or basic meaning **4** : having or showing good manners **5** : APPROPRIATE, SUITABLE

proper fraction *n* : a fraction in which the numerator is smaller than the denominator

prop·er·ly *adv* **1** : in a fit or suitable way **2** : according to fact

proper noun *n* : a noun that names a particular person, place, or thing

prop·er·ty *n, pl* **prop·er·ties** **1** : a special quality of a thing **2** : something (as land or money) that is owned **3** : something other than scenery or costumes that is used in a play or movie

proph·e·cy *n, pl* **proph·e·cies** **1** : the sayings of a prophet **2** : something foretold : PREDICTION

proph·e·sy *vb* **proph·e·sied; proph·e·sy·ing** **1** : to speak or write as a prophet **2** : FORETELL, PREDICT

proph·et *n* **1** : one who declares publicly a message that one believes has come from God or a god **2** : a person who predicts the future

pro·phet·ic *adj* : of or relating to a prophet or prophecy

¹pro·por·tion *n* **1** : the size, number, or amount of one thing or group of things as compared to that of another thing or group of things **2** : a balanced or pleasing arrangement **3** : a statement of the equality of two ratios (as $4/_2 = {}^{10}/_5$) **4** : a fair or just share **5** : DIMENSION

²proportion *vb* **1** : to adjust something to fit with something else **2** : to make the parts of fit well with each other

pro·por·tion·al *adj* : being in proportion to something else — **pro·por·tion·al·ly** *adv*

pro·pos·al *n* **1** : a stating or putting forward of something for consideration **2** : something proposed : PLAN **3** : an offer of marriage

pro·pose *vb* **pro·posed; pro·pos·ing** **1** : to make a suggestion to be thought over and talked about : SUGGEST **2** : to make plans : INTEND **3** : to suggest for filling a place or office **4** : to make an offer of marriage

prop·o·si·tion *n* **1** : something proposed **2** : a statement to be proved, explained, or discussed

pro·pri·e·tor *n* : a person who owns something : OWNER

pro·pri·ety *n, pl* **pro·pri·eties** **1** : the quality or state of being proper **2** : correctness in manners or behavior **3** *proprieties pl* : the rules and customs of behavior followed by nice people

pro·pul·sion *n* **1** : the act or process of propelling **2** : something that propels

pros *pl of* PRO

prose *n* **1** : the ordinary language that people use in speaking or writing **2** : writing without the repeating rhythm that is used in verse

pros·e·cute *vb* **pros·e·cut·ed; pros·e·cut·ing** **1** : to follow up to the end : keep at **2**

: to carry on a legal action against an accused person to prove his or her guilt

pros·e·cu·tion *n* **1** : the act of prosecuting especially a criminal case in court **2** : the one bringing charges of crime against a person being tried **3** : the state's lawyers in a criminal case

pros·e·cu·tor *n* : a person who prosecutes especially a criminal case as lawyer for the state

¹pros·pect *n* **1** : a wide view **2** : an imagining of something to come **3** : something that is waited for or expected : POSSIBILITY **4** : a possible buyer or customer **5** : a likely candidate

²prospect *vb* : to explore especially for mineral deposits

pro·spec·tive *adj* **1** : likely to come about **2** : likely to become — **pro·spec·tive·ly** *adv*

pros·pec·tor *n* : a person who explores a region in search of valuable minerals (as metals or oil)

pros·per *vb* **1** : to succeed or make money in something one is doing **2** : ¹FLOURISH 1, THRIVE

pros·per·i·ty *n* : the state of being prosperous or successful

pros·per·ous *adj* **1** : having or showing success or financial good fortune **2** : strong and healthy in growth — **pros·per·ous·ly** *adv*

¹pros·trate *adj* **1** : stretched out with face on the ground **2** : spread out parallel to the ground **3** : lacking strength or energy

²prostrate *vb* **pros·trat·ed; pros·trat·ing** **1** : to throw or put into a prostrate position **2** : to bring to a weak and powerless condition

pro·tect *vb* : to cover or shield from something that would destroy or injure : GUARD

pro·tec·tion *n* **1** : the act of protecting : the state of being protected **2** : a protecting person or thing

pro·tec·tive *adj* : giving or meant to give protection — **pro·tec·tive·ly** *adv* — **pro·tec·tive·ness** *n*

pro·tec·tor *n* : a person or thing that protects or is intended to protect

pro·tein *n* : a nutrient containing nitrogen that is found in all living plant or animal cells, is a necessary part of the diet, and is supplied especially by such foods as meat, milk, and eggs

¹pro·test *n* **1** : the act of protesting **2** : a complaint or objection against an idea, an act, or a way of doing things

²pro·test *vb* **1** : to declare positively : ASSERT **2** : to complain strongly about

¹Prot·es·tant *n* : a member of a Christian

church other than the Eastern Orthodox Church and the Roman Catholic Church

²Protestant *adj* : of or relating to Protestants

pro·ton *n* : a very small particle that occurs in the nucleus of every atom and has a positive charge of electricity

pro·to·plasm *n* : the usually colorless and jellylike living part of cells

pro·to·zo·an *n* : any of a large group of mostly microscopic animals whose body is a single cell

pro·tract *vb* : to make longer : draw out in time or space

pro·trac·tor *n* : an instrument used for drawing and measuring angles

pro·trude *vb* **pro·trud·ed; pro·trud·ing** : to stick out or cause to stick out

proud *adj* **1** : having or showing a feeling that one is better than others : HAUGHTY **2** : having a feeling of pleasure or satisfaction : very pleased **3** : having proper self-respect — **proud·ly** *adv*

prove *vb* **proved; proved** *or* **prov·en; prov·ing** **1** : to test by experiment or by a standard **2** : to convince others of the truth of something by showing the facts **3** : to test the answer to and check the way of solving an arithmetic problem

prov·erb *n* : a short well-known saying containing a wise thought : MAXIM, ADAGE

pro·ver·bi·al *adj* : of, relating to, or being a proverb — **pro·ver·bi·al·ly** *adv*

pro·vide *vb* **pro·vid·ed; pro·vid·ing** **1** : to look out for or take care of beforehand **2** : to make as a condition **3** : to give something that is needed

pro·vid·ed *conj* : IF 1

pro·vid·er *n* : one that provides something

prov·i·dence *n* **1** *often cap* : help or care from God or heaven **2** *cap* : God as the guide and protector of all human beings **3** : PRUDENCE, THRIFT

prov·ince *n* **1** : a part of a country having a government of its own (as one of the divisions of the Dominion of Canada) **2** **provinces** *pl* : the part or parts of a country far from the capital or chief city **3** : an area of activity or authority

pro·vin·cial *adj* **1** : of, relating to, or coming from a province **2** : lacking the social graces and sophistication of the city

¹pro·vi·sion *n* **1** : the act of providing **2** : something done beforehand **3** : a stock or store of food — usually used in pl. **4** : ¹CONDITION 1

²provision *vb* : to supply with provisions

prov·o·ca·tion *n* **1** : the act of provoking **2** : something that provokes

pro·voc·a·tive *adj* : serving or likely to

cause a reaction (as interest, curiosity, or anger) — **pro·voc·a·tive·ly** *adv*

pro·voke *vb* **pro·voked; pro·vok·ing** **1** : to cause to become angry **2** : to bring about

pro·vok·ing *adj* : causing mild anger — **pro·vok·ing·ly** *adv*

prow *n* : the bow of a ship

prow·ess *n* **1** : great bravery especially in battle **2** : very great ability

prowl *vb* : to move about quietly and secretly like a wild animal hunting prey — **prowl·er** *n*

proxy *n, pl* **prox·ies** **1** : authority to act for another or a paper giving such authority **2** : a person with authority to act for another

prude *n* : a person who cares too much about proper speech and conduct — **prud·ish** *adj*

pru·dence *n* : skill and good sense in taking care of oneself or of one's doings

pru·dent *adj* **1** : clever and careful in action or judgment **2** : careful in trying to avoid mistakes — **pru·dent·ly** *adv*

¹prune *n* : a dried plum

²prune *vb* **pruned; prun·ing** **1** : to cut off dead or unwanted parts of a bush or tree **2** : to cut out useless or unwanted parts (as unnecessary words or phrases in a composition)

¹pry *vb* **pried; pry·ing** : to be nosy about something

²pry *vb* **pried; pry·ing** **1** : to raise or open or try to do so with a lever **2** : to get at with great difficulty

pry·ing *adj* : rudely nosy

psalm *n* **1** : a sacred song or poem **2** *cap* : one of the hymns that make up the Old Testament Book of Psalms

psy·chi·a·trist *n* : a specialist in psychiatry

psy·chi·a·try *n* : a branch of medicine dealing with problems of the mind, emotions, or behavior

psy·cho·log·i·cal *adj* **1** : of or relating to psychology **2** : directed toward or meant to influence the mind

psy·chol·o·gist *n* : a specialist in psychology

psy·chol·o·gy *n* : the science that studies facts about the mind and its activities especially in human beings

pu·ber·ty *n* : the age at or period during which a person becomes able to reproduce sexually

¹pub·lic *adj* **1** : of or relating to the people as a whole **2** : of, relating to, or working for a government or community **3** : open to all **4** : known to many people : not kept secret **5** : WELL-KNOWN, PROMINENT — **pub·lic·ly** *adv*

²public *n* **1** : the people as a whole **2** : a group of people having common interests

pub·li·ca·tion n **1** : the act or process of publishing **2** : a printed work (as a book or magazine) made for sale or distribution

pub·lic·i·ty n **1** : public interest and approval **2** : something (as favorable news) used to attract public interest and approval

pub·li·cize vb **pub·li·cized; pub·li·ciz·ing** : to give publicity to

public school n : a free school paid for by taxes and run by a local government

pub·lish vb **1** : to make widely known **2** : to bring printed works (as books) before the public usually for sale — **pub·lish·er** n

puck n : a rubber disk used in hockey

¹puck·er vb : to draw or cause to draw up into folds or wrinkles

²pucker n : a fold or wrinkle in a normally even surface

pud·ding n : a soft spongy or creamy dessert

pud·dle n : a very small pool (as of dirty or muddy water)

pudgy adj **pudg·i·er; pudg·i·est** : being short and plump : CHUBBY

pueb·lo n, pl **pueb·los** : an Indian village of Arizona or New Mexico made up of groups of stone or adobe houses with flat roofs

¹Puer·to Ri·can adj : of or relating to Puerto Rico or the Puerto Ricans

²Puerto Rican n : a person born or living in Puerto Rico

¹puff vb **1** : to blow in short gusts **2** : to breathe hard : PANT **3** : to send out small whiffs or clouds (as of smoke) **4** : to swell up or become swollen with or as if with air

²puff n **1** : a quick short sending or letting out of air, smoke, or steam **2** : a slight swelling **3** : a soft pad for putting powder on the skin

puf·fin n : a seabird related to the auks that has a short thick neck and a deep grooved bill marked with several colors

puffy adj **puff·i·er; puff·i·est 1** : blowing in puffs **2** : BREATHLESS 1 **3** : somewhat swollen **4** : like a puff : FLUFFY

pug n **1** : a small dog having a thick body, a large round head, a square snout, a curled tail, and usually short hair **2** : a nose turning up at the tip and usually short and thick

¹pull vb **1** : to separate from a firm or a natural attachment **2** : to use force on so as to cause or tend to cause movement toward the force **3** : to stretch repeatedly **4** : ¹MOVE 1 **5** : to draw apart : TEAR, REND

²pull n **1** : the act or an instance of pulling **2** : the effort put forth in moving **3** : a device for pulling something **4** : a force that pulls

pul·let n : a young hen

pul·ley n, pl **pulleys** : a wheel that has a grooved rim in which a belt, rope, or chain

runs and that is used to change the direction of a pulling force and in combination to increase the force applied for lifting

pull·over n : a garment (as a sweater) that is put on by being pulled over the head

pull through vb : to survive a very difficult or dangerous period

pul·mo·nary adj : of or relating to the lungs

¹pulp n **1** : the soft juicy part of a fruit or vegetable **2** : a mass of vegetable matter from which the moisture has been squeezed **3** : the soft sensitive tissue inside a tooth **4** : a material prepared usually from wood or rags and used in making paper

²pulp vb : to make into a pulp

pul·pit n **1** : a raised place in which a clergyman stands while preaching or conducting a religious service **2** : preachers in general

pulp·wood n : wood (as of aspen or spruce) from which wood pulp is made

pulpy adj **pulp·i·er; pulp·i·est** : like or made of pulp

pul·sate vb **pul·sat·ed; pul·sat·ing** : to have or show a pulse or beats

pul·sa·tion n : pulsating movement or action

pulse n **1** : a regular beating or throbbing (as of the arteries) **2** : one complete beat of a pulse or the number of these in a given period (as a minute)

pul·ver·ize vb **pul·ver·ized; pul·ver·iz·ing** : to beat or grind into a powder or dust

pu·ma n : COUGAR

pum·ice n : a very light porous volcanic glass that is used in powder form for smoothing and polishing

pum·mel vb **pum·meled** or **pum·melled; pum·mel·ing** or **pum·mel·ling** : to strike again and again

¹pump n : a device for raising, moving, or compressing fluids

²pump vb **1** : to raise, move, or compress by using a pump **2** : to free (as from water or air) by the use of a pump **3** : to fill by using a pump **4** : to draw, force, or drive onward in the manner of a pump **5** : to question again and again to find out something — **pump·er** n

pum·per·nick·el n : a dark rye bread

pump·kin n : a large round orange or yellow fruit of a vine related to the squash vine that is used as a vegetable or as feed for farm animals

¹pun n : a form of joking in which a person uses a word in two senses

²pun vb **punned; pun·ning** : to make a pun

¹punch vb **1** : to care for (range cattle) **2** : to strike with the fist **3** : to press or strike by or as if by punching **4** : to pierce or stamp with a punch

²**punch** *n* : a blow with or as if with the fist

³**punch** *n* : a tool for piercing, stamping, or cutting

⁴**punch** *n* : a drink containing several things and often including wine or liquor

punc·tu·al *adj* : acting at the right time : not late

punc·tu·ate *vb* **punc·tu·at·ed; punc·tu·at·ing** : to mark or divide with punctuation marks

punc·tu·a·tion *n* **1** : the act of punctuating **2** : a system of using marks (**punctuation marks**) such as commas and periods to make clear the meaning of written matter

¹**punc·ture** *n* **1** : an act of puncturing **2** : a hole or wound made by puncturing

²**puncture** *vb* **punc·tured; punc·tur·ing 1** : to pierce with something pointed **2** : to make useless or destroy as if by a puncture

pun·gent *adj* : giving a sharp or biting sensation — **pun·gent·ly** *adv*

pun·ish *vb* **1** : to make suffer for a fault or crime **2** : to make someone suffer for (as a crime)

pun·ish·able *adj* : deserving to be punished

pun·ish·ment *n* **1** : the act of punishing : the state or fact of being punished **2** : the penalty for a fault or crime

¹**punk** *n* : a petty gangster or hoodlum

²**punk** *adj* **1** : poor in quality **2** : UNWELL, SICK

¹**punt** *vb* : to kick a ball dropped from the hands before it hits the ground — **punt·er** *n*

²**punt** *n* : an act or instance of punting a ball

pu·ny *adj* **pu·ni·er; pu·ni·est** : small and weak in size or power

pup *n* **1** : PUPPY **2** : one of the young of any of several animals (as a seal)

pu·pa *n, pl* **pu·pae** *or* **pupas** : an insect (as a bee, moth, or beetle) in an intermediate inactive stage of its growth in which it is enclosed in a cocoon or case

pu·pal *adj* : of, relating to, or being a pupa

¹**pu·pil** *n* : a child in school or under the care of a teacher

²**pupil** *n* : the opening in the iris through which light enters the eye

pup·pet *n* **1** : a doll moved by hand or by strings or wires **2** : one (as a person or government) whose acts are controlled by another

pup·py *n, pl* **puppies** : a young dog

¹**pur·chase** *vb* **pur·chased; pur·chas·ing** : to get by paying money

²**purchase** *n* **1** : an act of purchasing **2** : something purchased **3** : a firm hold or grasp or a safe place to stand

pure *adj* **pur·er; pur·est 1** : not mixed with anything else : free from everything that might injure or lower the quality **2** : free

from sin : INNOCENT, CHASTE **3** : nothing other than : ABSOLUTE — **pure·ly** *adv* — **pure·ness** *n*

pure·bred *adj* : bred from ancestors of a single breed for many generations

¹**purge** *vb* **purged; purg·ing 1** : to make clean **2** : to have or cause frequent bowel movements **3** : to get rid of

²**purge** *n* **1** : an act or instance of purging **2** : the removal of members thought to be treacherous or disloyal

pu·ri·fi·ca·tion *n* : an act or instance of purifying or of being purified

pu·ri·fy *vb* **pu·ri·fied; pu·ri·fy·ing** : to make pure : free from impurities

pu·ri·tan *n* **1** *cap* : a member of a sixteenth and seventeenth century Protestant group in England and New England opposing formal customs of the Church of England **2** : a person who practices or preaches or follows a stricter moral code than most people

pu·ri·ty *n* **1** : freedom from dirt or impurities **2** : freedom from sin or guilt

pur·ple *n* : a color between red and blue

pur·plish *adj* : somewhat purple

¹**pur·pose** *n* : something set up as a goal to be achieved : INTENTION, AIM — **on purpose** : PURPOSELY

²**purpose** *vb* **pur·posed; pur·pos·ing** : to have as one's intention : INTEND

pur·pose·ful *adj* : having a clear purpose or aim — **pur·pose·ful·ly** *adv* — **pur·pose·ful·ness** *n*

pur·pose·ly *adv* : with a clear or known purpose

purr *vb* : to make the low murmuring sound of a contented cat or a similar sound

¹**purse** *n* **1** : a bag or pouch for money **2** : HANDBAG **3** : the contents of a purse : MONEY **1 4** : a sum of money offered as a prize or collected as a present

²**purse** *vb* **pursed; purs·ing** : to draw into folds

pur·sue *vb* **pur·sued; pur·su·ing 1** : to follow after in order to catch or destroy : CHASE **2** : to follow with an end in view **3** : to go on with : FOLLOW — **pur·su·er** *n*

pur·suit *n* **1** : the act of pursuing **2** : ACTIVITY 2, OCCUPATION

pus *n* : thick yellowish matter (as in an abscess or a boil)

¹**push** *vb* **1** : to press against with force so as to drive or move away **2** : to force forward, downward, or outward **3** : to go or make go ahead

²**push** *n* **1** : a sudden thrust : SHOVE **2** : a steady applying of force in a direction away from the body from which it comes

push button *n* : a small button or knob that

when pushed operates something usually by closing an electric circuit

push·cart *n* : a cart pushed by hand

push·over *n* **1** : an opponent that is easy to defeat **2** : something easily done

pushy *adj* **push·i·er; push·i·est** : too aggressive : FORWARD

puss *n* : CAT 1

pussy *n, pl* **puss·ies** : CAT 1

pussy willow *n* : a willow with large silky catkins

put *vb* **put; put·ting 1** : to place in or move into a particular position **2** : to bring into a specified state or condition **3** : to cause to stand for or suffer something **4** : to give expression to **5** : to give up to or urge to an activity **6** : to think something to have : ATTRIBUTE **7** : to begin a voyage — **put forward** : PROPOSE 1

put away *vb* **1** : to give up : DISCARD **2** : to take in food and drink

put by *vb* : to lay aside : SAVE

put down *vb* **1** : to bring to an end by force **2** : to consider to belong to a particular class or to be due to a particular cause

put in *vb* **1** : to ask for **2** : to spend time in a place or activity

put off *vb* : DEFER

put on *vb* **1** : to dress oneself in **2** : PRETEND 2, SHAM **3** : ¹PRODUCE 4

put down *vb* **1** : to bring to an end by force **2** : to consider to belong to a particular class or to be due to a particular cause

put in *vb* **1** : to ask for **2** : to spend time in a place or activity

put off *vb* : DEFER

put on *vb* **1** : to dress oneself in **2** : PRETEND 2, SHAM **3** : ¹PRODUCE 4

put·out *n* : the causing of a batter or runner to be out in baseball

put out *vb* **1** : to make use of **2** : EXTINGUISH 1 **3** : ¹MAKE 2 **4** : IRRITATE 1,

ANNOY **5** : to cause to be out (as in baseball)

pu·trid *adj* **1** : ROTTEN 1 **2** : coming from or suggesting something rotten

put·ter *vb* : to act or work without much purpose

put through *vb* : to conclude with success

¹put·ty *n, pl* **putties** : a soft cement (as for holding glass in a window frame)

²putty *vb* **put·tied; put·ty·ing** : to cement or seal up with putty

put up *vb* **1** : to make (as food) ready or safe for later use **2** : NOMINATE **3** : to give or get shelter and often food **4** : ¹BUILD 1 **5** : to make by action or effort — **put up to** : to urge or cause to do something wrong or unexpected — **put up with** : to stand for : TOLERATE

¹puz·zle *vb* **puz·zled; puz·zling 1** : CONFUSE 1, PERPLEX **2** : to solve by thought or by clever guessing

²puzzle *n* **1** : something that puzzles : MYSTERY **2** : a question, problem, or device intended to test one's skill or cleverness

¹pyg·my *also* **pig·my** *n, pl* **pygmies** *also* **pigmies** : a person or thing very small for its kind : DWARF

²pygmy *adj* : very small

¹pyr·a·mid *n* **1** : a large structure built especially in ancient Egypt that usually has a square base and four triangular sides meeting at a point and that contains tombs **2** : something that has the shape of a pyramid **3** : a solid with a polygon for its base and three or more triangles for its sides which meet to form the top

²pyramid *vb* : to build up in the form of a pyramid

pyre *n* : a heap of wood for burning a dead body

py·thon *n* : any of various large snakes of the Old World tropics that are related to the boas

Q

q *n, pl* **q's** *or* **qs** *often cap* : the seventeenth letter of the English alphabet

¹quack *vb* : to make the cry of a duck

²quack *n* : a cry made by or as if by quacking

³quack *n* : an ignorant person who pretends to have medical knowledge and skill

⁴quack *adj* **1** : of, relating to, or like that of a quack **2** : pretending to cure disease

quadri- *or* **quadr-** *or* **quadru-** *prefix* **1** : four **2** : fourth

quad·ri·lat·er·al *n* : a figure of four sides and four angles

quad·ru·ped *n* : an animal having four feet

qua·dru·plet *n* **1** : one of four offspring

born at one birth **2** : a combination of four of a kind

¹quail *n, pl* **quail** *or* **quails** : any of various mostly small plump game birds (as the bobwhite) that are related to the chicken

²quail *vb* : to lose courage : shrink in fear

quaint *adj* **1** : being or looking unusual or different **2** : pleasingly old-fashioned or unfamiliar — **quaint·ly** *adv* — **quaint·ness** *n*

¹quake *vb* **quaked; quak·ing 1** : to shake usually from shock or lack of stability **2** : to tremble or shudder usually from cold or fear

²**quake** n : an instance (as an earthquake) of shaking or trembling

qual·i·fi·ca·tion n   **1** : the act or an instance of qualifying   **2** : the state of being qualified   **3** : a special skill, knowledge, or ability that fits a person or thing for a particular work or position   **4** : LIMITATION 1

qual·i·fy vb **qual·i·fied; qual·i·fy·ing   1** : to narrow down or make less general in meaning : LIMIT   **2** : to make less harsh or strict : SOFTEN   **3** : to fit by training, skill, or ability for a special purpose   **4** : to show the skill or ability needed to be on a team or take part in a contest

qual·i·ty n, pl **qual·i·ties   1** : basic and individual nature   **2** : how good or bad something is   **3** : high social rank   **4** : what sets a person or thing apart : CHARACTERISTIC

qualm n   **1** : a sudden attack of illness, faintness, or nausea   **2** : a sudden fear   **3** : a feeling of doubt or uncertainty that one's behavior is honest or right — **qualm·ish** adj

quan·da·ry n, pl **quan·da·ries** : a state of doubt or puzzled confusion

quan·ti·ty n, pl **quan·ti·ties   1** : ²AMOUNT, NUMBER   **2** : a large number or amount

¹**quar·an·tine** n   **1** : a halting or forbidding of the moving of people or things out of a certain area to prevent the spread of disease or pests   **2** : a period during which a person with a contagious disease is under quarantine   **3** : a place (as a hospital) where persons are kept in quarantine

²**quarantine** vb **quar·an·tined; quar·an·tin·ing** : to put or hold in quarantine

¹**quar·rel** n   **1** : a cause of disagreement or complaint   **2** : an angry difference of opinion

²**quarrel** vb **quar·reled** or **quar·relled; quar·rel·ing** or **quar·rel·ling   1** : to find fault   **2** : to argue actively : SQUABBLE

quar·rel·some adj : usually ready to quarrel

¹**quar·ry** n, pl **quar·ries** : an animal or bird hunted as game or prey

²**quarry** n, pl **quar·ries** : an open pit usually for obtaining building stone, slate, or limestone

³**quarry** vb **quar·ried; quar·ry·ing   1** : to dig or take from or as if from a quarry   **2** : to make a quarry in — **quar·ri·er** n

quart n : a measure of capacity that equals two pints (about .95 liter)

¹**quar·ter** n   **1** : one of four equal parts into which something can be divided   **2** : a United States coin worth twenty-five cents   **3** : someone or something (as a place, direction, or group) not clearly identified   **4** : a particular division or district of a city   **5 quarters** pl : a dwelling place   **6** : MERCY 1

²**quarter** vb   **1** : to divide into four usually equal parts   **2** : to provide with lodgings or shelter

³**quarter** adj : consisting of or equal to a quarter

quar·ter·deck n : the part of the upper deck that is located toward the rear of a ship

quarter horse n : a stocky muscular saddle horse capable of high speed over short distances

¹**quar·ter·ly** adv : four times a year

²**quarterly** adj : coming or happening every three months

³**quarterly** n, pl **quar·ter·lies** : a magazine published four times a year

quar·ter·mas·ter n : an army officer who provides clothing and supplies for troops

quar·tet also **quar·tette** n : a group or set of four

quartz n : a common mineral often found in the form of colorless transparent crystals but sometimes (as in amethysts, agates, and jaspers) brightly colored

qua·ver vb   **1** : ¹TREMBLE 1, SHAKE   **2** : to sound in shaky tones

quay n : a paved bank or a solid artificial landing for loading and unloading ships

quea·sy adj **quea·si·er; quea·si·est   1** : somewhat nauseated   **2** : full of doubt

queen n   **1** : the wife or widow of a king   **2** : a woman who rules a kingdom in her own right   **3** : a woman of high rank, power, or attractiveness   **4** : the most powerful piece in the game of chess   **5** : a playing card bearing the figure of a queen   **6** : a fully developed adult female of social bees, ants, or termites — **queen·ly** adj

queer adj : oddly unlike the usual or normal — **queer·ly** adv

quell vb   **1** : to put down by force   **2** : ⁴QUIET 1, CALM

quench vb   **1** : to put out (as a fire)   **2** : to end by satisfying

¹**que·ry** n, pl **queries   1** : ¹QUESTION 1   **2** : a question in the mind : DOUBT

²**query** vb **que·ried; que·ry·ing   1** : to put as a question   **2** : to ask questions about especially in order to clear up a doubt   **3** : to ask questions of especially to obtain official or expert information

¹**quest** n : an act or instance of seeking : SEARCH

²**quest** vb : to search for

¹**ques·tion** n   **1** : something asked   **2** : a topic discussed or argued about   **3** : a suggestion to be voted on   **4** : an act or instance of asking   **5** : OBJECTION 1, DISPUTE

²**question** vb   **1** : to ask questions of or about   **2** : to doubt the correctness of

ques·tion·able adj   **1** : not certain or exact

: DOUBTFUL **2** : not believed to be true, sound, or proper

question mark *n* : a punctuation mark ? used chiefly at the end of a sentence to indicate a direct question

ques·tion·naire *n* : a set of questions to be asked of a number of persons to collect facts about knowledge or opinions

1queue *n* **1** : PIGTAIL **2** : a waiting line

2queue *vb* **queued; queu·ing** *or* **queue·ing** : to form or line up in a queue

quib·ble *vb* **quib·bled; quib·bling 1** : to talk about unimportant things rather than the main point **2** : to find fault especially over unimportant points — **quib·bler** *n*

1quick *adj* **1** : very swift : SPEEDY **2** : mentally alert **3** : easily stirred up — **quick·ly** *adv* — **quick·ness** *n*

2quick *n* **1** : a very tender area of flesh (as under a fingernail) **2** : one's innermost feelings

3quick *adv* : in a quick manner : FAST

quick·en *vb* **1** : REVIVE 1 **2** : AROUSE 2 **3** : to make or become quicker : HASTEN **4** : to begin or show active growth

quick·sand *n* : a deep mass of loose sand mixed with water into which heavy objects sink

quick·sil·ver *n* : MERCURY 1

quick–tem·pered *adj* : easily made angry

quick–wit·ted *adj* : mentally alert

1qui·et *n* : the quality or state of being quiet

2quiet *adj* **1** : marked by little or no motion or activity : CALM **2** : GENTLE 2, MILD **3** : not disturbed : PEACEFUL **4** : free from noise or uproar : STILL **5** : not showy (as in color or style) **6** : SECLUDED — **qui·et·ly** *adv* — **qui·et·ness** *n*

3quiet *adv* : in a quiet manner : QUIETLY

4quiet *vb* **1** : to cause to be quiet : CALM **2** : to become quiet

qui·etude *n* : the state of being quiet : REST

quill *n* **1** : a large stiff feather **2** : the hollow tubelike part of a feather **3** : a spine of a hedgehog or porcupine **4** : a pen made from a feather

1quilt *n* : a bed cover made of two pieces of cloth with a filling of wool, cotton, or down held together by patterned stitching

2quilt *vb* : to stitch or sew together as in making a quilt

quince *n* : a hard yellow fruit that grows on a shrubby tree related to the apple and is used especially in preserves

qui·nine *n* : a bitter drug obtained from cinchona bark and used to treat malaria

quin·tet *n* : a group or set of five

quin·tu·plet *n* **1** : a combination of five of a kind **2** : one of five offspring born at one birth

quirk *n* : a sudden turn, twist, or curve

quit *vb* **quit; quit·ting** : to finish doing, using, dealing with, working on, or handling : LEAVE

quite *adv* **1** : beyond question or doubt : COMPLETELY **2** : more or less : RATHER

quit·ter *n* : a person who gives up too easily

1quiv·er *n* : a case for carrying arrows

2quiver *vb* : to move with a slight trembling motion

3quiver *n* : the act or action of quivering

1quiz *n, pl* **quiz·zes** : a short oral or written test

2quiz *vb* **quizzed; quiz·zing** : to ask a lot of questions of

quoit *n* : a ring (as of rope) tossed at a peg in a game (**quoits**)

quo·rum *n* : the number of members of a group needed at a meeting in order for business to be legally carried on

quo·ta *n* : a share assigned to each member of a group

quo·ta·tion *n* **1** : material (as a passage from a book) that is quoted **2** : the act or process of quoting

quotation mark *n* : one of a pair of punctuation marks " " or ' ' used chiefly to indicate the beginning and end of a direct quotation

quote *vb* **quot·ed; quot·ing** : to repeat (someone else's words) exactly

quo·tient *n* : the number obtained by dividing one number by another

R

r *n, pl* **r's** *or* **rs** *often cap* : the eighteenth letter of the English alphabet

rab·bi *n, pl* **rab·bis 1** : ¹MASTER 1, TEACHER — used as a term of address for Jewish religious leaders **2** : a professionally trained leader of a Jewish congregation

rab·bit *n* : a gnawing mammal that burrows and is smaller and has shorter ears than the related hare

rab·ble *n* **1** : a crowd that is noisy and hard to control : MOB **2** : a group of people looked down upon as ignorant and hard to handle

ra·bid *adj* **1** : very angry : FURIOUS **2** : going to extreme lengths (as in interest or opinion) **3** : affected with rabies — **ra·bid·ly** *adv* — **ra·bid·ness** *n*

ra·bies *n* : a deadly disease of the nervous

system caused by a virus that is usually passed on through the bite of an infected animal

rac·coon *n* : a small North American animal that lives in trees, eats flesh, is active mostly at night, and is sometimes hunted for sport, for its edible flesh, or for its coat of long fluffy fur

¹**race** *n* **1** : a strong or rapid current of water **2** : a contest of speed **3** : a contest involving progress toward a goal

²**race** *vb* **raced; rac·ing 1** : to take part in a race **2** : to go, move, or drive at top speed **3** : to cause an engine of a motor vehicle in neutral to run fast

³**race** *n* **1** : a group of individuals with the same ancestors **2** : one of the three, four, or five great divisions based on easily seen things (as skin color) into which human beings are usually divided

race·course *n* : a place for racing

race·horse *n* : a horse bred or kept for racing

rac·er *n* **1** : one that races or is used for racing **2** : any of several long slender active snakes (as a common American blacksnake)

race·track *n* : a usually oval course on which races are run

ra·cial *adj* : of, relating to, or based on race — **ra·cial·ly** *adv*

¹**rack** *n* **1** : an instrument of torture for stretching the body **2** : a frame or stand for storing or displaying things

²**rack** *vb* **1** : to cause to suffer torture, pain, or sorrow **2** : to stretch or strain violently

¹**rack·et** *n* : a light bat consisting of a handle and a frame with a netting stretched tight across it

²**racket** *n* **1** : a loud confused noise **2** : a dishonest scheme for obtaining money (as by cheating or threats)

·**rack·e·teer** *n* : a person who gets money or advantages by using force or threats

racy *adj* **rac·i·er; rac·i·est** : full of energy or keen enjoyment

ra·dar *n* : a radio device for detecting the position of things in the distance and the direction of moving objects (as distant airplanes or ships)

ra·di·ance *n* : the quality or state of being radiant : SPLENDOR

ra·di·ant *adj* **1** : giving out or reflecting rays of light **2** : glowing with love, confidence, or joy **3** : transmitted by radiation

radiant energy *n* : energy sent out in the form of electromagnetic waves

ra·di·ate *vb* **ra·di·at·ed; ra·di·at·ing 1** : to send out rays : SHINE **2** : to come forth in the form of rays **3** : to spread around from or as if from a center

ra·di·a·tion *n* **1** : the process of radiating and especially of giving off radiant energy in the form of waves or particles **2** : something that is radiated

ra·di·a·tor *n* : a device to heat air (as in a room) or to cool an object (as an automobile engine)

¹**rad·i·cal** *adj* **1** : departing sharply from the usual or ordinary : EXTREME **2** : of or relating to radicals in politics — **rad·i·cal·ly** *adv*

²**radical** *n* : a person who favors rapid and sweeping changes especially in laws and methods of government

radii *pl of* RADIUS

¹**ra·dio** *adj* **1** : of or relating to radiant energy **2** : of, relating to, or used in radio

²**radio** *n, pl* **ra·di·os 1** : the sending or receiving of signals by means of electromagnetic waves without a connecting wire **2** : a radio receiving set **3** : a radio message **4** : the radio broadcasting industry

³**radio** *vb* : to communicate or send a message to by radio

ra·dio·ac·tive *adj* : of, caused by, or exhibiting radioactivity

ra·dio·ac·tiv·i·ty *n* : the giving off of rays of energy or particles by the breaking apart of atoms of certain elements (as uranium)

radio wave *n* : an electromagnetic wave used in radio, television, or radar communication

rad·ish *n* : the fleshy edible root of a plant related to the mustards

ra·di·um *n* : a strongly radioactive element found in very small quantities in various minerals (as pitchblende) and used in the treatment of cancer

ra·di·us *n, pl* **ra·dii 1** : the bone on the thumb side of the human forearm or a corresponding bone in lower forms **2** : a straight line extending from the center of a circle to the circumference or from the center of a sphere to the surface **3** : a nearly circular area defined by a radius

raf·fle *n* : the sale of chances for a prize whose winner is the one whose ticket is picked at a drawing

¹**raft** *n* : a flat structure (as a group of logs fastened together) for support or transportation on water

²**raft** *n* : a large amount or number

raf·ter *n* : one of the usually sloping timbers that support a roof

rag *n* **1** : a waste or worn piece of cloth **2 rags** *pl* : shabby or very worn clothing

rag·a·muf·fin *n* : a poorly clothed and often dirty child

¹**rage** *n* **1** : very strong and uncontrolled anger : FURY **2** : violent action (as of wind or sea) **3** : FAD

²**rage** *vb* **raged; rag·ing** **1** : to be in a rage **2** : to continue out of control

rag·ged *adj* **1** : having a rough or uneven edge or outline **2** : very worn : TATTERED **3** : wearing tattered clothes **4** : done in an uneven way — **rag·ged·ly** *adv* — **rag·ged·ness** *n*

rag·gedy *adj* : RAGGED 2, 3

rag·man *n, pl* **rag·men** : a collector of or dealer in rags

rag·time *n* : jazz music that has a lively melody and a steady rhythm like a march

rag·weed *n* : a common coarse weed with pollen that irritates the eyes and noses of some persons

¹**raid** *n* : a sudden attack or invasion

²**raid** *vb* : to make a raid on — **raid·er** *n*

¹**rail** *n* **1** : a bar extending from one support to another and serving as a guard or barrier **2** : a bar of steel forming a track for wheeled vehicles **3** : RAILROAD

²**rail** *vb* : to provide with a railing

³**rail** *n* : any of a family of wading birds related to the cranes and hunted as game birds

⁴**rail** *vb* : to scold or complain in harsh or bitter language

rail·ing *n* **1** : a barrier (as a fence) made up of rails and their supports **2** : material for making rails

rail·lery *n, pl* **rail·ler·ies** : an act or instance of making fun of someone in a good-natured way

¹**rail·road** *n* **1** : a permanent road that has parallel steel rails that make a track for cars **2** : a railroad together with the lands, buildings, locomotives, cars, and other equipment that belong to it

²**railroad** *vb* : to work on a railroad

rail·way *n* : ¹RAILROAD 1

rai·ment *n* : CLOTHING 1

¹**rain** *n* **1** : water falling in drops from the clouds **2** : a fall of rain **3** : rainy weather **4** : a heavy fall of objects

²**rain** *vb* **1** : to fall as water in drops from the clouds **2** : to send down rain **3** : to fall like rain **4** : to give in large amounts — **rain cats and dogs** : to rain very hard

rain·bow *n* : an arc of colors that appears in the sky opposite the sun and is caused by the sun shining through rain, mist, or spray

rain·coat *n* : a coat of waterproof or water-resistant material

rain·drop *n* : a drop of rain

rain·fall *n* **1** : ¹RAIN 2 **2** : amount of precipitation

rain forest *n* : a woodland with a high annual rainfall and very tall trees and that is often found in tropical regions

rain·proof *adj* : not letting in rain

rain·storm *n* : a storm of or with rain

rain·wa·ter *n* : water falling or fallen as rain

rainy *adj* **rain·i·er; rain·i·est** : having much rain

¹**raise** *vb* **raised; rais·ing** **1** : to cause to rise : LIFT **2** : to give life to : AROUSE **3** : to set upright by lifting or building **4** : PROMOTE 1, ELEVATE **5** : ²END **6** : COLLECT 2 **7** : to look after the growth and development of : GROW **8** : to bring up a child : REAR **9** : to give rise to : PROVOKE **10** : to bring to notice **11** : ¹INCREASE **12** : to make light and airy **13** : to cause to form on the skin — **rais·er** *n*

²**raise** *n* : an increase in amount (as of pay)

rai·sin *n* : a sweet grape dried for food

ra·ja *or* **ra·jah** *n* : an Indian prince

¹**rake** *n* : a garden tool with a long handle and a bar with teeth or prongs at the end

²**rake** *vb* **raked; rak·ing** **1** : to gather, loosen, or smooth with a rake **2** : to search through : RANSACK **3** : to sweep the length of with gunfire

³**rake** *n* : a person with bad morals and conduct

¹**ral·ly** *vb* **ral·lied; ral·ly·ing** **1** : to bring or come together for a common purpose **2** : to bring back to order **3** : to rouse from low spirits or weakness **4** : ¹REBOUND 2

²**rally** *n, pl* **rallies** **1** : the act of rallying **2** : a big meeting held to arouse enthusiasm

¹**ram** *n* **1** : a male sheep **2** : BATTERING RAM

²**ram** *vb* **rammed; ram·ming** **1** : to strike or strike against with violence **2** : to force in, down, or together by driving or pressing **3** : ²FORCE 2

RAM *n* : RANDOM-ACCESS MEMORY

Ram·a·dan *n* : the ninth month of the Islamic calendar observed as sacred with fasting practiced daily from dawn to sunset

¹**ram·ble** *vb* **ram·bled; ram·bling** **1** : to go aimlessly from place to place : WANDER **2** : to talk or write without a clear purpose or point **3** : to grow or extend irregularly

²**ramble** *n* : a long stroll with no particular destination

ram·bler *n* : a hardy climbing rose with large clusters of small flowers

ram·bunc·tious *adj* : UNRULY — **ram·bunc·tious·ly** *adv* — **ram·bunc·tious·ness** *n*

ram·i·fi·ca·tion *n* **1** : a branching out **2** : one thing that comes from another like a branch

ram·i·fy *vb* **ram·i·fied; ram·i·fy·ing** : to spread out or split up into branches or divisions

ramp *n* : a sloping passage or roadway connecting different levels

ram·page *n* : a course of violent or reckless action or behavior

ram·pant *adj* : not checked in growth or spread — **ram·pant·ly** *adv*

ram·part *n* : a broad bank or wall raised as a protective barrier

ram·rod *n* : a rod for ramming the charge down the barrel in a firearm that is loaded through the muzzle

ram·shack·le *adj* : ready to fall down

ran *past of* RUN

¹**ranch** *n* 1 : a place for the raising of livestock (as cattle) on range 2 : a farm devoted to a special crop

²**ranch** *vb* : to live or work on a ranch — **ranch·er** *n*

ran·cid *adj* : having the strong disagreeable smell or taste of stale oil or fat — **ran·cid·ness** *n*

ran·cor *n* : deep hatred

ran·cor·ous *adj* : showing rancor — **ran·cor·ous·ly** *adv*

ran·dom *adj* : lacking a clear plan, purpose, or pattern — **ran·dom·ly** *adv* — **ran·dom·ness** *n*

ran·dom–ac·cess *adj* : permitting access to stored data in any order the user desires

random–access memory *n* : a computer memory that provides the main storage available to the user for programs and data

rang *past of* RING

¹**range** *n* 1 : a series of things in a line 2 : a cooking stove 3 : open land over which livestock may roam and feed 4 : the distance a gun will shoot 5 : a place where shooting is practiced 6 : the distance or amount included or gone over : SCOPE 7 : a variety of choices within a scale

²**range** *vb* **ranged; rang·ing** 1 : to set in a row or in proper order 2 : to set in place among others of the same kind 3 : to roam over or through 4 : to come within an upper and a lower limit

rang·er *n* 1 : FOREST RANGER 2 : a member of a body of troops who range over a region 3 : a soldier specially trained in close-range fighting and in raiding tactics

rangy *adj* **rang·i·er; rang·i·est** : tall and slender in body build — **rang·i·ness** *n*

¹**rank** *adj* 1 : strong and active in growth 2 : ¹EXTREME 1 3 : having an unpleasant smell — **rank·ly** *adv* — **rank·ness** *n*

²**rank** *n* 1 : ³ROW 1, SERIES 2 : a line of soldiers standing side by side 3 **ranks** *pl* : the body of enlisted persons in an army 4 : position within a group 5 : high social position 6 : official grade or position

³**rank** *vb* 1 : to arrange in lines or in a formation 2 : to arrange in a classification 3 : to take or have a certain position in a group

ran·kle *vb* **ran·kled; ran·kling** : to cause anger, irritation, or bitterness

ran·sack *vb* 1 : to search thoroughly 2 : to search through in order to rob

¹**ran·som** *n* 1 : something paid or demanded for the freedom of a captured person 2 : the act of ransoming

²**ransom** *vb* : to free from captivity or punishment by paying a price — **ran·som·er** *n*

rant *vb* : to talk loudly and wildly — **rant·er** *n*

¹**rap** *n* : a sharp blow or knock

²**rap** *vb* **rapped; rap·ping** : to give a quick sharp blow : ¹KNOCK 1

³**rap** *vb* **rapped; rap·ping** 1 : to talk freely and informally 2 : to perform rap music

⁴**rap** *n* 1 : an informal talk : CHAT 2 : a rhythmic chanting often in unison of rhymed verses to a musical accompaniment

ra·pa·cious *adj* 1 : very greedy 2 : PREDATORY — **ra·pa·cious·ly** *adv* — **ra·pa·cious·ness** *n*

¹**rape** *n* : a plant related to the mustards that is grown for animals to graze on and for its seeds used as birdseed and as a source of oil

²**rape** *vb* **raped; rap·ing** : to have sexual intercourse with by force

³**rape** *n* : an act of raping

rap·id *adj* : very fast — **rap·id·ly** *adv*

ra·pid·i·ty *n* : the quality or state of being rapid

rap·ids *n pl* : a part of a river where the current flows very fast usually over rocks

ra·pi·er *n* : a straight sword with a narrow blade having two sharp edges

rap·port *n* : friendly relationship : ACCORD

rapt *adj* : showing complete delight or interest

rap·ture *n* : a strong feeling of joy, delight, or love

¹**rare** *adj* **rar·er; rar·est** 1 : not thick or compact : THIN 2 : very fine : EXCELLENT 3 : very uncommon

²**rare** *adj* **rar·er; rar·est** : cooked so that the inside is still red

rar·e·fy *vb* **rar·e·fied; rar·e·fy·ing** : to make or become less dense or solid

rare·ly *adv* : not often : SELDOM

rar·i·ty *n, pl* **rar·i·ties** 1 : the quality, state, or fact of being rare 2 : something that is uncommon

ras·cal *n* 1 : a mean or dishonest person 2 : a mischievous person

¹**rash** *adj* : too hasty in decision, action, or speech — **rash·ly** *adv* — **rash·ness** *n*

²**rash** *n* : a breaking out of the skin with red spots (as in measles)

¹**rasp** *vb* 1 : to rub with or as if with a rough file 2 : IRRITATE 1 3 : to make a harsh sound

²**rasp** *n* 1 : a coarse file with cutting points

instead of lines **2 :** a rasping sound or sensation

rasp·ber·ry *n, pl* **rasp·ber·ries :** a sweet edible red, black, or purple berry

¹rat *n* **1 :** a gnawing animal with brown, black, white, or grayish fur that looks like but is larger than the mouse **2 :** a person who betrays friends

²rat *vb* **rat·ted; rat·ting 1 :** to betray one's friends **2 :** to hunt or catch rats

¹rate *n* **1 :** a price or charge set according to a scale or standard **2 :** amount of something measured in units of something else — **at any rate :** in any case

²rate *vb* **rat·ed; rat·ing 1 :** CONSIDER 3, REGARD **2 :** to have a rating **:** RANK **3 :** to have a right to **:** DESERVE

rath·er *adv* **1 :** more willingly **2 :** more correctly or truly **3 :** INSTEAD **4 :** ²SOMEWHAT

rat·i·fi·ca·tion *n* **:** the act or process of ratifying

rat·i·fy *vb* **rat·i·fied; rat·i·fy·ing :** to give legal approval to (as by a vote)

rat·ing *n* **:** a position within a grading system

ra·tio *n, pl* **ra·tios :** the relationship in number or quantity between two or more things

¹ra·tion *n* **1 :** a food allowance for one day **2 rations** *pl* **:** ¹PROVISION 3 **3 :** the amount one is allowed by authority

²ration *vb* **1 :** to control the amount one can use **2 :** to use sparingly

ra·tio·nal *adj* **1 :** having the ability to reason **2 :** relating to, based on, or showing reason — **ra·tio·nal·ly** *adv*

ra·tio·nale *n* **:** a basic explanation or reason for something

ra·tio·nal·ize *vb* **ra·tio·nal·ized; ra·tio·nal·iz·ing :** to find believable but untrue reasons for (one's conduct)

rat·ter *n* **:** a dog or cat that catches rats

¹rat·tle *vb* **rat·tled; rat·tling 1 :** to make or cause to make a rapid series of short sharp sounds **2 :** to move with a clatter **3 :** to say or do in a brisk lively way **4 :** to disturb the calmness of **:** UPSET

²rattle *n* **1 :** a series of short sharp sounds **2 :** a device (as a toy) for making a rattling sound **3 :** a rattling organ at the end of a rattlesnake's tail

rat·tler *n* **:** RATTLESNAKE

rat·tle·snake *n* **:** a poisonous American snake with a rattle at the end of its tail

rat·tle·trap *n* **:** something (as an old car) rickety and full of rattles

rau·cous *adj* **1 :** being harsh and unpleasant **2 :** behaving in a rough and noisy way — **rau·cous·ly** *adv* — **rau·cous·ness** *n*

¹rav·age *n* **:** violently destructive action or effect

²ravage *vb* **rav·aged; rav·ag·ing :** to attack or act upon with great violence — **rav·ag·er** *n*

rave *vb* **raved; rav·ing 1 :** to talk wildly or as if crazy **2 :** to talk with great enthusiasm

rav·el *vb* **rav·eled** *or* **rav·elled; rav·el·ing** *or* **rav·el·ling :** UNRAVEL 1

¹ra·ven *n* **:** a large shiny black bird like a crow that is found in northern regions

²raven *adj* **:** shiny and black like a raven's feathers

rav·en·ous *adj* **:** very hungry — **rav·en·ous·ly** *adv*

ra·vine *n* **:** a small narrow valley with steep sides that is larger than a gully and smaller than a canyon

rav·ish *vb* **1 :** to seize and take away by force **2 :** to overcome with a feeling and especially one of joy or delight

raw *adj* **1 :** not cooked **2 :** being in or nearly in the natural state **3 :** lacking a normal or usual finish **4 :** having the skin rubbed off **5 :** not trained or experienced **6 :** unpleasantly damp or cold — **raw·ly** *adv* — **raw·ness** *n*

raw·hide *n* **1 :** a whip of untanned hide **2 :** untanned cattle skin

¹ray *n* **:** a flat broad fish related to the sharks that has its eyes on the top of its head

²ray *n* **1 :** one of the lines of light that appear to be given off by a bright object **2 :** a thin beam of radiant energy (as light) **3 :** light cast in rays **4 :** any of a group of lines that spread out from the same center **5 :** a straight line extending from a point in one direction only **6 :** a plant or animal structure like a ray **7 :** a tiny bit **:** PARTICLE

ray·on *n* **:** a cloth made from fibers produced chemically from cellulose

raze *vb* **razed; raz·ing :** to destroy completely by knocking down or breaking to pieces **:** DEMOLISH

ra·zor *n* **:** a sharp cutting instrument used to shave off hair

razz *vb* **:** to make fun of **:** TEASE

re *n* **:** the second note of the musical scale

re- *prefix* **1 :** again **2 :** back **:** backward

¹reach *vb* **1 :** to stretch out **:** EXTEND **2 :** to touch or move to touch or take by sticking out a part of the body (as the hand) or something held in the hand **3 :** to extend or stretch to **4 :** to arrive at **:** COME **5 :** to communicate with

²reach *n* **1 :** an unbroken stretch (as of a river) **2 :** the act of reaching especially to take hold of something **3 :** ability to stretch (as an arm) so as to touch something

re·act *vb* **1 :** to act or behave in response (as to stimulation or an influence) **2 :** to oppose a force or influence — usually used with against **3** : to go through a chemical reaction

re·ac·tion n **1** : an instance of reacting **2** : a response (as of body or mind) to a stimulus (as a treatment, situation, or stress) **3** : a chemical change that is brought about by the action of one substance on another and results in a new substance being formed

re·ac·tion·ary adj : of, relating to, or favoring old-fashioned political or social ideas

re·ac·tor n **1** : one that reacts **2** : a device using atomic energy to produce heat

read vb **read; read·ing** **1** : to understand language through written symbols for speech sounds **2** : to speak aloud written or printed words **3** : to learn from what one has seen in writing or printing **4** : to discover or figure out the meaning of **5** : to give meaning to **6** : to show by letters or numbers — **read between the lines** : to understand more than is directly stated

read·able adj : able to be read easily

read·er n **1** : one that reads **2** : a book for learning or practicing reading

read·ing n **1** : something read or for reading **2** : the form in which something is written : VERSION **3** : the number or fact shown on an instrument

read–only memory n : a usually small computer memory that contains special-purpose information (as a program) which cannot be changed

read·out n **1** : information from an automatic device (as a computer) that is recorded (as on a disk) or presented in a form that can be seen **2** : an electronic device that presents information in a form that can be seen

¹ready adj **read·i·er; read·i·est** **1** : prepared for use or action **2** : likely to do something **3** : WILLING 1 **4** : showing ease and promptness **5** : available right away : HANDY — **read·i·ly** adv — **read·i·ness** n

²ready vb **read·ied; ready·ing** : to make ready : PREPARE

ready–made adj : made beforehand in large numbers

re·al adj **1** : of, relating to, or made up of land and buildings **2** : not artificial : GENUINE **3** : not imaginary : ACTUAL — **re·al·ness** n

real estate n : property consisting of buildings and land

re·al·ism n : willingness to face facts or to give in to what is necessary

re·al·is·tic adj **1** : true to life or nature **2** : ready to see things as they really are and to deal with them sensibly — **re·al·is·ti·cal·ly** adv

re·al·i·ty n, pl **re·al·i·ties** **1** : actual existence **2** : someone or something real or actual

re·al·iza·tion n : the action of realizing : the state of being realized

re·al·ize vb **re·al·ized; re·al·iz·ing** **1** : to bring into being : ACCOMPLISH **2** : to get as a result of effort : GAIN **3** : to be aware of : UNDERSTAND

re·al·ly adv **1** : in fact **2** : without question

realm n **1** : KINGDOM 1 **2** : field of activity or influence

real time n : the actual time during which something takes place — **real–time** adj

re·al·ty n : REAL ESTATE

¹ream n **1** : a quantity of paper that may equal 480, 500, or 516 sheets **2 reams** pl : a great amount

²ream vb **1** : to shape or make larger with a reamer **2** : to clean or clear with a reamer

ream·er n : a tool with cutting edges for shaping or enlarging a hole

reap vb **1** : to cut (as grain) or clear (as a field) with a sickle, scythe, or machine **2** : HARVEST

reap·er n **1** : a worker who harvests crops **2** : a machine for reaping grain

re·ap·pear vb : to appear again

¹rear vb **1** : to put up by building : CONSTRUCT **2** : to raise or set on end **3** : to take care of the breeding and raising of **4** : BRING UP **5** : to rise high **6** : to rise up on the hind legs

²rear n **1** : the part (as of an army) or area farthest from the enemy **2** : the space or position at the back

³rear adj : being at the back

rear admiral n : a commissioned officer in the Navy or Coast Guard ranking above a captain

re·ar·range vb **re·ar·ranged; re·ar·rang·ing** : to arrange again usually in a different way

¹rea·son n **1** : a statement given to explain a belief or an act **2** : a good basis **3** : ¹CAUSE 1 **4** : the power to think **5** : a sound mind

²reason vb **1** : to talk with another so as to influence his or her actions or opinions **2** : to use the power of reason

rea·son·able adj **1** : not beyond what is usual or expected : MODERATE **2** : ¹CHEAP 1, INEXPENSIVE **3** : able to reason — **rea·son·able·ness** n — **rea·son·ably** adv

re·as·sure vb **re·as·sured; re·as·sur·ing** **1** : to assure again **2** : to give fresh confidence to : free from fear

¹re·bate vb **re·bat·ed; re·bat·ing** : to make a rebate or to give as a rebate

²rebate n : a returning of part of a payment or of an amount owed

¹**reb·el** *adj* **1** : being or fighting against one's government or ruler **2** : not obeying

²**rebel** *n* : a person who refuses to give in to authority

³**re·bel** *vb* **re·belled; re·bel·ling 1** : to be or fight against authority and especially the authority of one's government **2** : to feel or show anger or strong dislike

re·bel·lion *n* **1** : open opposition to authority **2** : an open fight against one's government

re·bel·lious *adj* **1** : taking part in rebellion **2** : tending to fight against or disobey authority — **re·bel·lious·ly** *adv* — **re·bel·lious·ness** *n*

re·birth *n* **1** : a new or second birth **2** : a return to importance

re·born *adj* : born again

¹**re·bound** *vb* **1** : to spring back on hitting something **2** : to get over a disappointment

²**re·bound** *n* **1** : the action of rebounding : RECOIL **2** : an immediate reaction to a disappointment

¹**re·buff** *vb* : to refuse or criticize sharply

²**rebuff** *n* : a refusal to meet an advance or offer

re·build *vb* **re·built; re·build·ing 1** : to make many or important repairs to or changes in **2** : to build again

¹**re·buke** *vb* **re·buked; re·buk·ing** : to criticize severely

²**rebuke** *n* : an expression of strong disapproval

re·bus *n* : a riddle or puzzle made up of letters, pictures, and symbols whose names sound like the syllables and words of a phrase or sentence

re·but *vb* **re·but·ted; re·but·ting** : to prove to be wrong especially by argument or by proof that the opposite is right

¹**re·call** *vb* **1** : to ask or order to come back **2** : to bring back to mind **3** : CANCEL 2, REVOKE

²**re·call** *n* **1** : a command to return **2** : remembrance of what has been learned or experienced

re·cap·ture *vb* **re·cap·tured; re·cap·tur·ing 1** : to capture again **2** : to experience again

re·cede *vb* **re·ced·ed; re·ced·ing 1** : to move back or away **2** : to slant backward

¹**re·ceipt** *n* **1** : RECIPE **2** : the act of receiving **3 receipts** *pl* : something received **4** : a written statement saying that money or goods have been received

²**receipt** *vb* **1** : to give a receipt for **2** : to mark as paid

re·ceive *vb* **re·ceived; re·ceiv·ing 1** : to take or get something that is given, paid, or sent **2** : to let enter one's household or company : WELCOME **3** : to be at home to visitors **4** : ²EXPERIENCE **5** : to change incoming radio waves into sounds or pictures

re·ceiv·er *n* **1** : one that receives **2** : a device for changing electricity or radio waves into light or sound

re·cent *adj* **1** : of or relating to a time not long past **2** : having lately appeared to come into being : NEW, FRESH — **re·cent·ly** *adv* — **re·cent·ness** *n*

re·cep·ta·cle *n* : something used to receive and contain smaller objects

re·cep·tion *n* **1** : the act or manner of receiving **2** : a social gathering at which someone is often formally introduced or welcomed **3** : the receiving of a radio or television broadcast

re·cep·tion·ist *n* : an office employee who greets callers

re·cep·tive *adj* : able or willing to receive ideas — **re·cep·tive·ly** *adv* — **re·cep·tive·ness** *n*

re·cep·tor *n* : a cell or group of cells that receives stimuli : SENSE ORGAN

¹**re·cess** *n* **1** : a secret or hidden place **2** : a hollow cut or built into a surface (as a wall) **3** : a brief period for relaxation between work periods

²**recess** *vb* **1** : to put into a recess **2** : to interrupt for or take a recess

re·ces·sion *n* : a period of reduced business activity

re·ces·sive *adj* : not dominant

rec·i·pe *n* : a set of instructions for making something (as a food dish) by combining various things

re·cip·i·ent *n* : one that receives

re·cip·ro·cal *n* : one of a pair of numbers (as 9 and $1/9$ or $2/3$ and $3/2$) whose product is one

re·cit·al *n* **1** : a reciting of something **2** : a public performance given by one musician **3** : a public performance by music or dance pupils

rec·i·ta·tion *n* **1** : a complete telling or listing of something **2** : the reciting before an audience of something memorized **3** : a student's oral reply to questions

re·cite *vb* **re·cit·ed; re·cit·ing 1** : to repeat from memory **2** : to tell about in detail **3** : to answer questions about a lesson

reck·less *adj* : being or given to wild careless behavior — **reck·less·ly** *adv* — **reck·less·ness** *n*

reck·on *vb* **1** : ¹COUNT 1, COMPUTE **2** : to regard or think of as : CONSIDER

re·claim *vb* **1** : to make better in behavior or character : REFORM **2** : to change to a desirable condition or state **3** : to obtain from a waste product or by-product

rec·la·ma·tion *n* : the act or process of reclaiming : the state of being reclaimed

re·cline *vb* **re·clined; re·clin·ing** **1** : to lean backward **2** : to lie down

rec·og·ni·tion *n* **1** : the act of recognizing **2** : special attention or notice

rec·og·nize *vb* **rec·og·nized; rec·og·niz·ing** **1** : to know and remember upon seeing **2** : to be willing to acknowledge **3** : to take approving notice of **4** : to show one is acquainted with

¹re·coil *vb* **1** : to draw back **2** : to spring back to a former position

²recoil *n* **1** : the act or action of recoiling **2** : a springing back (as of a gun just fired) **3** : the distance through which something (as a spring) recoils

rec·ol·lect *vb* : to call to mind : REMEMBER

rec·ol·lec·tion *n* **1** : the act or power of recalling to mind : MEMORY **2** : something remembered

rec·om·mend *vb* **1** : to present or support as worthy or fit **2** : to make acceptable **3** : to make a suggestion : ADVISE

rec·om·men·da·tion *n* **1** : the act of recommending **2** : a thing or course of action recommended **3** : something that recommends

¹rec·om·pense *vb* **rec·om·pensed; rec·om·pens·ing** : to pay for or pay back

²recompense *n* : a return for something done, suffered, or given : PAYMENT

rec·on·cile *vb* **rec·on·ciled; rec·on·cil·ing** **1** : to make friendly again **2** : ¹SETTLE 7, ADJUST **3** : to make agree **4** : to cause to give in or accept

re·con·di·tion *vb* : to restore to good condition (as by repairing or replacing parts)

re·con·nais·sance *n* : a survey (as of enemy territory) to get information

re·con·noi·ter *vb* : to make a reconnaissance (as in preparation for military action)

re·con·sid·er *vb* : to consider again especially with a view to change

re·con·sid·er·a·tion *n* : the act of reconsidering : the state of being reconsidered

re·con·struct *vb* : to construct again : REBUILD, REMODEL

¹re·cord *vb* **1** : to set down in writing **2** : to register permanently **3** : to change sound or visual images into a form (as on magnetic tape) that can be listened to or watched at a later time

²rec·ord *n* **1** : the state or fact of being recorded **2** : something written to preserve an account **3** : the known or recorded facts about a person or thing **4** : a recorded top performance **5** : something on which sound or visual images have been recorded

³rec·ord *adj* : outstanding among other like things

re·cord·er *n* **1** : a person or device that

records **2** : a musical instrument like a long hollow whistle with eight finger holes

re·cord·ing *n* : ²RECORD 5

¹re·count *vb* : to tell all about : NARRATE

²re·count *vb* : to count again

³re·count *n* : a counting again (as of election votes)

re·course *n* **1** : a turning for help or protection **2** : a source of help or strength

re·cov·er *vb* **1** : to get back : REGAIN **2** : to regain normal health, self-confidence, or position **3** : to make up for **4** : RECLAIM 2

re—cov·er *vb* : to cover again

re·cov·ery *n, pl* **re·cov·er·ies** : the act, process, or an instance of recovering

rec·re·a·tion *n* **1** : a refreshing of mind or body after work or worry **2** : a means of refreshing mind or body

¹re·cruit *vb* **1** : to form or strengthen with new members **2** : to get the services of **3** : to restore or increase the health or vigor of

²recruit *n* : a newcomer to a field of activity

rect·an·gle *n* : a four-sided figure with right angles and with opposite sides parallel

rect·an·gu·lar *adj* : shaped like a rectangle

rec·ti·fy *vb* **rec·ti·fied; rec·ti·fy·ing** : to set or make right

rec·tor *n* : PASTOR

rec·tum *n, pl* **rec·tums** *or* **rec·ta** : the last part of the large intestine

re·cu·per·ate *vb* **re·cu·per·at·ed; re·cu·per·at·ing** : to regain health or strength

re·cu·per·a·tion *n* : a getting back to health or strength

re·cur *vb* **re·curred; re·cur·ring** : to occur or appear again

re·cur·rence *n* : the state of occurring again and again

re·cy·cla·ble *adj* : that can be recycled

re·cy·cle *vb* **re·cy·cled; re·cy·cling** : to process (as paper, glass, or cans) in order to regain materials for human use

¹red *adj* **red·der; red·dest** **1** : of the color red **2** : of or relating to Communism or Communists — **red·ness** *n*

²red *n* **1** : the color of fresh blood or of the ruby **2** : something red in color **3** : a person who seeks or favors revolution **4** : COMMUNIST 2

red·bird *n* : any of several birds (as a cardinal) with mostly red feathers

red blood cell *n* : one of the tiny reddish cells of the blood that have no nuclei and carry oxygen from the lungs to the tissues

red·breast *n* : a bird (as a robin) with a reddish breast

red·cap *n* : PORTER 1

red cell *n* : RED BLOOD CELL

red·coat *n* : a British soldier especially during the Revolutionary War

red corpuscle

red corpuscle *n* : RED BLOOD CELL
red·den *vb* : to make or become red
red·dish *adj* : somewhat red
re·deem *vb* **1** : to buy back **2** : to ransom, free, or rescue through payment or effort **3** : to free from sin **4** : to make good : FULFILL **5** : to make up for — **re·deem·er** *n*
re·demp·tion *n* : the act or process or an instance of redeeming
red–hand·ed *adv or adj* : in the act of doing something wrong
red·head *n* : a person having reddish hair
red–hot *adj* **1** : glowing red with heat **2** : very active and emotional
re·di·rect *vb* : to change the course or direction of
re·dis·cov·er *vb* : to discover again
red–let·ter *adj* : of special importance : MEMORABLE
re·do *vb* **re·did; re·done; re·do·ing** : to do over or again
re·dress *vb* : to set right : REMEDY
red tape *n* : usually official rules and regulations that waste people's time
re·duce *vb* **re·duced; re·duc·ing** **1** : to make smaller or less **2** : to force to surrender **3** : to lower in grade or rank **4** : to change from one form into another **5** : to lose weight by dieting
re·duc·tion *n* **1** : the act of reducing : the state of being reduced **2** : something made by reducing **3** : the amount by which something is reduced
red·wood *n* : a tall timber tree of California that bears cones and has a light long-lasting brownish red wood
reed *n* **1** : a tall slender grass of wet areas that has stems with large joints **2** : a stem or a growth or mass of reeds **3** : a thin flexible piece of cane, plastic, or metal fastened to the mouthpiece or over an air opening in a musical instrument (as a clarinet or accordion) and set in vibration by an air current (as the breath)
reef *n* : a chain of rocks or ridge of sand at or near the surface of water
¹reek *n* : a strong or unpleasant smell
²reek *vb* : to have a strong or unpleasant smell
¹reel *n* **1** : a device that can be turned round and round and on which something flexible may be wound **2** : a quantity of something wound on a reel
²reel *vb* **1** : to wind on a reel **2** : to pull by the use of a reel
³reel *vb* **1** : to whirl around **2** : to be in a confused state **3** : to fall back (as from a blow) **4** : to walk or move unsteadily : STAGGER
⁴reel *n* : a reeling motion

⁵reel *n* : a lively folk dance
re·elect *vb* : to elect for another term
reel off *vb* : to tell or recite rapidly or easily
re·en·ter *vb* : to enter again
re·es·tab·lish *vb* : to establish again
re·fer *vb* **re·ferred; re·fer·ring** **1** : to send or direct to some person or place for treatment, aid, information, or decision **2** : to call attention
¹ref·er·ee *n* **1** : a person to whom something that is to be investigated or decided is referred **2** : a sports official with final authority for conducting a game or match
²referee *vb* **ref·er·eed; ref·er·ee·ing** : to act or be in charge of as referee
ref·er·ence *n* **1** : the act of referring **2** : a relation to or concern with something **3** : something that refers a reader to another source of information **4** : a person of whom questions can be asked about the honesty or ability of another person **5** : a written statement about someone's honesty or ability **6** : a work (as a dictionary) that contains useful information
ref·er·en·dum *n, pl* **ref·er·en·da** *or* **ref·er·en·dums** : the idea or practice of letting the voters approve or disapprove laws
¹re·fill *vb* : to fill or become filled again
²re·fill *n* : a new or fresh supply of something
re·fine *vb* **re·fined; re·fin·ing** **1** : to bring to a pure state **2** : to make better : IMPROVE
re·fined *adj* **1** : having or showing good taste or training **2** : freed from impurities : PURE
re·fine·ment *n* **1** : the act or process of refining **2** : excellence of manners, feelings, or tastes **3** : something meant to improve something else
re·fin·ery *n, pl* **re·fin·er·ies** : a building and equipment for refining metals, oil, or sugar
re·fin·ish *vb* : to give (as furniture) a new surface
re·fit *vb* **re·fit·ted; re·fit·ting** : to get ready for use again
re·flect *vb* **1** : to bend or throw back (waves of light, sound, or heat) **2** : to give back an image or likeness of in the manner of a mirror **3** : to bring as a result **4** : to bring disapproval or blame **5** : to think seriously
re·flec·tion *n* **1** : the return of light or sound waves from a surface **2** : an image produced by or as if by a mirror **3** : something that brings blame or disgrace **4** : an opinion formed or a remark made after careful thought **5** : careful thought
re·flec·tor *n* : a shiny surface for reflecting light or heat
re·flex *n* : an action that occurs automatically when a sense organ is stimulated
reflex act *n* : REFLEX

re·for·est *vb* : to renew forest growth by planting seeds or young trees

re·for·es·ta·tion *n* : the act of reforesting

1re·form *vb* **1** : to make better or improve by removal of faults **2** : to correct or improve one's own behavior or habits

2reform *n* **1** : improvement of what is bad **2** : a removal or correction of a wrong or an error

ref·or·ma·tion *n* : the act of reforming : the state of being reformed

re·for·ma·to·ry *n, pl* **re·for·ma·to·ries** : an institution for reforming usually young or first offenders

re·form·er *n* : a person who works for reform

re·fract *vb* : to cause to go through refraction

re·frac·tion *n* : the bending of a ray when it passes at an angle from one medium into another in which its speed is different (as when light passes from air into water)

re·frac·to·ry *adj* **1** : STUBBORN 3 **2** : capable of enduring very high temperatures

1re·frain *vb* : to hold oneself back

2refrain *n* : a phrase or verse repeated regularly in a poem or song

re·fresh *vb* : to make fresh or fresher : RE-VIVE — **re·fresh·er** *n*

re·fresh·ment *n* **1** : the act of refreshing : the state of being refreshed **2** : something (as food or drink) that refreshes — often used in pl.

re·frig·er·ate *vb* **re·frig·er·at·ed; re·frig·er·at·ing** : to make or keep cold or cool

re·frig·er·a·tor *n* : a device or room for keeping articles (as food) cool

re·fu·el *vb* : to provide with or take on more fuel

ref·uge *n* **1** : shelter or protection from danger or distress **2** : a place that provides shelter or protection

ref·u·gee *n* : a person who flees for safety usually to a foreign country

1re·fund *vb* : to give back : REPAY

2re·fund *n* : a sum of money refunded

re·fus·al *n* : the act of refusing

1re·fuse *vb* **re·fused; re·fus·ing** **1** : to say one will not accept **2** : to say one will not do, give, or allow something

2ref·use *n* : TRASH 1, RUBBISH

re·fute *vb* **re·fut·ed; re·fut·ing** : to prove wrong by argument or evidence — **re·fut·er** *n*

re·gain *vb* **1** : to gain or get again : get back **2** : to get back to : reach again

re·gal *adj* : of, relating to, or suitable for a monarch : ROYAL — **re·gal·ly** *adv*

re·gale *vb* **re·galed; re·gal·ing** **1** : to entertain richly **2** : to give pleasure or amusement to

1re·gard *n* **1** : 2LOOK 1 **2** : CONSIDERA-TION 2 **3** : a feeling of respect **4 regards** *pl* : friendly greetings **5** : a point to be considered

2regard *vb* **1** : to pay attention to **2** : to show respect or consideration for **3** : to have a high opinion of **4** : to look at **5** : to think of : CONSIDER

re·gard·ing *prep* : relating to : ABOUT

re·gard·less *adv* : come what may

regardless of *prep* : in spite of

re·gat·ta *n* : a rowing, speedboat, or sailing race or a series of such races

re·gen·er·ate *vb* **re·gen·er·at·ed; re·gen·er·at·ing** : to form (as a lost part) once more

re·gent *n* **1** : a person who governs a kingdom (as during the childhood of the monarch) **2** : a member of a governing board (as of a state university)

re·gime *n* : a form or system of government or management

reg·i·men *n* : a systematic course of treatment

reg·i·ment *n* : a military unit made up usually of a number of battalions

re·gion *n* **1** : an area having no definite boundaries **2** : VICINITY 2 **3** : a broad geographical area

re·gion·al *adj* : of, relating to, or characteristic of a certain region

1reg·is·ter *n* **1** : a written record or list containing regular entries of items or details **2** : a book or system of public records **3** : a device for regulating ventilation or the flow of heated air from a furnace **4** : a mechanical device (as a **cash register**) that records items

2register *vb* **1** : to enter or enroll in a register (as a list of voters, students, or guests) **2** : to record automatically **3** : to get special protection for by paying extra postage **4** : to show by expression and bodily movements

reg·is·tra·tion *n* **1** : the act of registering **2** : an entry in a register **3** : the number of persons registered **4** : a document showing that something is registered

reg·is·try *n, pl* **reg·is·tries** : a place where registration takes place

1re·gret *vb* **re·gret·ted; re·gret·ting** **1** : to mourn the loss or death of **2** : to be sorry for

2regret *n* **1** : sorrow aroused by events beyond one's control **2** : an expression of sorrow **3 regrets** *pl* : a note politely refusing to accept an invitation

re·gret·ful *adj* : full of regret — **re·gret·ful·ly** *adv*

re·gret·ta·ble *adj* : deserving regret — **re·gret·ta·bly** *adv*

re·group *vb* : to form into a new grouping

reg·u·lar *adj* **1** : formed, built, or arranged according to an established rule, law, principle, or type **2** : even or balanced in form or structure **3** : steady in practice or occurrence **4** : following established usages or rules **5** : [1]NORMAL 1 **6** : of, relating to, or being a permanent army — **reg·u·lar·ly** *adv*

reg·u·lar·i·ty *n* : the quality or state of being regular

reg·u·late *vb* **reg·u·lat·ed; reg·u·lat·ing 1** : to govern or direct by rule **2** : to bring under the control of authority **3** : to bring order or method to **4** : to fix or adjust the time, amount, degree, or rate of — **reg·u·la·tor** *n*

reg·u·la·tion *n* **1** : the act of regulating : the state of being regulated **2** : a rule or order telling how something is to be done or having the force of law

re·hears·al *n* : a private performance or practice session in preparation for a public appearance

re·hearse *vb* **re·hearsed; re·hears·ing** : to practice in private in preparation for a public performance

[1]reign *n* **1** : the authority or rule of a monarch **2** : the time during which a monarch rules

[2]reign *vb* **1** : to rule as a monarch **2** : to be usual or widespread

re·im·burse *vb* **re·im·bursed; re·im·burs·ing** : to pay back : REPAY — **re·im·burse·ment** *n*

[1]rein *n* **1** : a line or strap attached at either end of the bit of a bridle to control an animal — usually used in pl. **2** : an influence that slows, limits, or holds back **3** : controlling or guiding power

[2]rein *vb* : to check, control, or stop by or as if by reins

re·in·car·na·tion *n* : rebirth of the soul in a new body

rein·deer *n, pl* **reindeer** : a large deer that has antlers in both the male and the female and is found in northern regions

re·in·force *vb* **re·in·forced; re·in·forc·ing 1** : to strengthen with extra troops or ships **2** : to strengthen with new force, assistance, material, or support

re·in·force·ment *n* **1** : the act of reinforcing : the state of being reinforced **2** : something that reinforces

re·in·state *vb* **re·in·stat·ed; re·in·stat·ing** : to place again in a former position or condition — **re·in·state·ment** *n*

re·it·er·ate *vb* **re·it·er·at·ed; re·it·er·at·ing** : to say or do over again or repeatedly

[1]re·ject *vb* **1** : to refuse to admit, believe, or receive **2** : to throw away as useless or unsatisfactory **3** : to refuse to consider

[2]re·ject *n* : a rejected person or thing

re·jec·tion *n* **1** : the act of rejecting : the state of being rejected **2** : something rejected

re·joice *vb* **re·joiced; re·joic·ing 1** : to give joy to : GLADDEN **2** : to feel joy

re·join *vb* **1** : to join again : return to **2** : to reply sharply

re·join·der *n* : [2]REPLY

[1]re·lapse *n* : a fresh period of an illness after an improvement

[2]re·lapse *vb* **re·lapsed; re·laps·ing** : to slip or fall back into a former condition after a change for the better

re·late *vb* **re·lat·ed; re·lat·ing 1** : to give an account of : NARRATE **2** : to show or have a relationship to or between : CONNECT

re·lat·ed *adj* : connected by common ancestry or by marriage

re·la·tion *n* **1** : the act of telling or describing **2** : CONNECTION 2 **3** : a related person : RELATIVE **4** : RELATIONSHIP 2 **5** : REFERENCE 2, RESPECT **6 relations** *pl* : business or public affairs

re·la·tion·ship *n* **1** : the state of being related or connected **2** : connection by blood or marriage

[1]rel·a·tive *n* : a person connected with another by blood or marriage

[2]relative *adj* **1** : RELEVANT **2** : existing in comparison to something else — **rel·a·tive·ly** *adv*

re·lax *vb* **1** : to make or become loose or less tense **2** : to make or become less severe or strict **3** : to rest or enjoy oneself away from one's usual duties

re·lax·a·tion *n* **1** : the act or fact of relaxing or of being relaxed **2** : a relaxing activity or pastime

[1]re·lay *n* **1** : a fresh supply (as of horses or people) arranged to relieve others **2** : a race between teams in which each team member covers a certain part of the course

[2]re·lay *vb* **re·layed; re·lay·ing** : to pass along by stages

[1]re·lease *vb* **re·leased; re·leas·ing 1** : to set free (as from prison) **2** : to relieve from something that holds or burdens **3** : to give up in favor of another **4** : to permit to be published, sold, or shown — **re·leas·er** *n*

[2]release *n* **1** : relief or rescue from sorrow, suffering, or trouble **2** : a discharge from an obligation **3** : a giving up of a right or claim **4** : a setting free : the state of being freed **5** : a device for holding or releasing a mechanism **6** : the act of permitting publication or performance **7** : matter released for publication or performance

re·lent *vb* : to become less severe, harsh, or strict

re·lent·less *adj* : very stern or harsh — **re·lent·less·ly** *adv* — **re·lent·less·ness** *n*

rel·e·vance *n* : relation to the matter at hand

rel·e·vant *adj* : having something to do with the matter at hand — **rel·e·vant·ly** *adv*

re·li·abil·i·ty *n* : the quality or state of being reliable

re·li·able *adj* : fit to be trusted : DEPENDABLE — **re·li·ably** *adv*

re·li·ance *n* 1 : the act of relying 2 : the condition or attitude of one who relies

rel·ic *n* 1 : an object treated with great respect because of its connection with a saint or martyr 2 : something left behind after decay or disappearance

re·lief *n* 1 : removal or lightening of something painful or troubling 2 : WELFARE 2 3 : military assistance in or rescue from a position of difficulty 4 : release from a post or from performance of a duty 5 : elevation of figures or designs from the background (as in sculpture) 6 : elevations of a land surface

re·lieve *vb* **re·lieved; re·liev·ing** 1 : to free partly or wholly from a burden or from distress 2 : to release from a post or duty 3 : to break the sameness of — **re·liev·er** *n*

re·li·gion *n* 1 : the service and worship of God or the supernatural 2 : a system of religious beliefs and practices

re·li·gious *adj* 1 : relating to or showing devotion to God or to the powers or forces believed to govern life 2 : of or relating to religion 3 : very devoted and faithful — **re·li·gious·ly** *adv* — **re·li·gious·ness** *n*

re·lin·quish *vb* : GIVE UP 1 : let go of

¹**rel·ish** *n* 1 : a pleasing taste 2 : great enjoyment 3 : a highly seasoned food eaten with other food to add flavor

²**relish** *vb* 1 : to be pleased by : ENJOY 2 : to like the taste of

re·live *vb* **re·lived; re·liv·ing** : to experience again (as in the imagination)

re·luc·tance *n* : the quality or state of being reluctant

re·luc·tant *adj* : showing doubt or unwillingness — **re·luc·tant·ly** *adv*

re·ly *vb* **re·lied; re·ly·ing** : to place faith or confidence : DEPEND

re·main *vb* 1 : to be left after others have been removed, subtracted, or destroyed 2 : to be something yet to be done or considered 3 : to stay after others have gone 4 : to continue unchanged

re·main·der *n* 1 : a remaining group or part 2 : the number left after a subtraction 3 : the number left over from the dividend after division that is less than the divisor

re·mains *n pl* 1 : whatever is left over or behind 2 : a dead body

re·make *vb* **re·made; re·mak·ing** : to make again or in a different form

¹**re·mark** *n* 1 : a telling of something in speech or writing 2 : a brief comment

²**remark** *vb* 1 : to take note of : OBSERVE 2 : to make a comment

re·mark·able *adj* : worth noticing : UNUSUAL — **re·mark·able·ness** *n* — **re·mark·ably** *adv*

re·match *n* : a second meeting between the same contestants

re·me·di·al *adj* : intended to make something better — **re·me·di·al·ly** *adv*

¹**rem·e·dy** *n, pl* **rem·e·dies** 1 : a medicine or treatment that cures or relieves 2 : something that corrects an evil

²**remedy** *vb* **rem·e·died; rem·e·dy·ing** : to provide or serve as a remedy for

re·mem·ber *vb* 1 : to bring to mind or think of again 2 : to keep in mind 3 : to pass along greetings from

re·mem·brance *n* 1 : the act of remembering 2 : something remembered 3 : something (as a souvenir) that brings to mind a past experience

re·mind *vb* : to cause to remember — **re·mind·er** *n*

rem·i·nisce *vb* **rem·i·nisced; rem·i·nisc·ing** : to talk or think about things in the past

rem·i·nis·cence *n* 1 : a recalling or telling of a past experience 2 **reminiscences** *pl* : a story of one's memorable experiences

rem·i·nis·cent *adj* 1 : of, relating to, or engaging in reminiscence 2 : reminding one of something else

re·miss *adj* : careless in the performance of work or duty — **re·miss·ly** *adv* — **re·miss·ness** *n*

re·mit *vb* **re·mit·ted; re·mit·ting** 1 : ²PARDON 2 2 : to send money (as in payment) — **re·mit·ter** *n*

re·mit·tance *n* : money sent in payment

rem·nant *n* : something that remains or is left over

re·mod·el *vb* **re·mod·eled** *or* **re·mod·elled; re·mod·el·ing** *or* **re·mod·el·ling** : to change the structure of

re·mon·strate *vb* **re·mon·strat·ed; re·mon·strat·ing** : ²PROTEST 2

re·morse *n* : deep regret for one's sins or for acts that wrong others — **re·morse·ful** *adj* — **re·morse·less** *adj*

¹**re·mote** *adj* **re·mot·er; re·mot·est** 1 : far off in place or time 2 : SECLUDED 3 : not closely connected or related 4 : small in

degree **5** : distant in manner : ALOOF — **re-mote-ly** *adv* — **re-mote-ness** *n*

²remote *n* : REMOTE CONTROL

remote control *n* **1** : control (as by a radio signal) of operation from a point some distance away **2** : a device for controlling something from a distance

re-mov-able *adj* : possible to remove

re-mov-al *n* : the act of removing : the fact of being removed

re-move *vb* **re-moved; re-mov-ing 1** : to move by lifting or taking off or away **2** : to dismiss from office **3** : to get rid of

re-mov-er *n* : something (as a chemical) used in removing a substance

Re-nais-sance *n* **1** : the period of European history between the fourteenth and seventeenth centuries marked by a fresh interest in ancient art and literature and by the beginnings of modern science **2** *often not cap* : a movement or period of great activity in literature, science, and the arts

re-name *vb* **re-named; re-nam-ing** : to give a new name to

rend *vb* **rent; rend-ing** : to tear apart by force

ren-der *vb* **1** : to obtain by heating **2** : to furnish or give to another **3** : to cause to be or become **4** : PERFORM 2

ren-dez-vous *n, pl* **ren-dez-vous 1** : a place agreed on for a meeting **2** : a planned meeting

ren-di-tion *n* : an act or a result of rendering

ren-e-gade *n* : a person who deserts a faith, cause, or party

re-nege *vb* **re-neged; re-neg-ing** : to go back on a promise or agreement

re-new *vb* **1** : to make or become new, fresh, or strong again **2** : to make, do, or begin again **3** : to put in a fresh supply of **4** : to continue in force for a new period

re-new-al *n* **1** : the act of renewing : the state of being renewed **2** : something renewed

re-nounce *vb* **re-nounced; re-nounc-ing 1** : to give up, abandon, or resign usually by a public declaration **2** : REPUDIATE 1, DISCLAIM

ren-o-vate *vb* **ren-o-vat-ed; ren-o-vat-ing** : to put in good condition again — **ren-o-va-tor** *n*

re-nown *n* : the state of being widely and favorably known

re-nowned *adj* : having renown

¹rent *n* : money paid for the use of another's property — **for rent** : available for use at a price

²rent *vb* **1** : to take and hold property under an agreement to pay rent **2** : to give the possession and use of in return for rent **3** : to be for rent

³rent *past of* REND

⁴rent *n* : an opening (as in cloth) made by tearing

¹rent-al *n* : an amount paid or collected as rent

²rental *adj* : of, relating to, or available for rent

rent-er *n* : a person who pays rent for something (as a place to live)

re-open *vb* : to open again

re-or-ga-nize *vb* **re-or-ga-nized; re-or-ga-niz-ing** : to organize again

¹re-pair *vb* **1** : to put back in good condition **2** : to make up for

²repair *n* **1** : the act or process of repairing **2** : ¹CONDITION 3

rep-a-ra-tion *n* **1** : the act of making up for a wrong **2** : something paid by a country losing a war to the winner to make up for damages done in the war

re-past *n* : ¹MEAL

re-pay *vb* **re-paid; re-pay-ing 1** : to pay back **2** : to make a return payment to

re-pay-ment *n* : the act or an instance of paying back

re-peal *vb* : to do away with especially by legislative action

¹re-peat *vb* **1** : to state or tell again **2** : to say from memory : RECITE **3** : to make or do again — **re-peat-er** *n*

²repeat *n* **1** : the act of repeating **2** : something repeated

re-peat-ed *adj* : done or happening again and again — **re-peat-ed-ly** *adv*

re-pel *vb* **re-pelled; re-pel-ling 1** : to drive back **2** : to turn away : REJECT **3** : to keep out : RESIST **4** : ²DISGUST

re-pel-lent *n* : a substance used to keep off pests (as insects)

re-pent *vb* **1** : to feel sorrow for one's sin and make up one's mind to do what is right **2** : to feel sorry for something done : REGRET

re-pen-tance *n* : the action or process of repenting

re-pen-tant *adj* : feeling or showing regret for something one has done — **re-pen-tant-ly** *adv*

re-per-cus-sion *n* **1** : a return action or effect **2** : a widespread, indirect, or unexpected effect of something said or done

rep-er-toire *n* : a list or supply of plays, operas, or pieces that a company or person is prepared to perform

rep-er-to-ry *n, pl* **rep-er-to-ries** : REPERTOIRE

rep-e-ti-tion *n* **1** : the act or an instance of repeating **2** : something repeated

re-place *vb* **re-placed; re-plac-ing 1** : to put back in a former or proper place **2** : to take the place of **3** : to put something new in the place of

re·place·ment *n* **1** : the act of replacing : the state of being replaced **2** : ¹SUBSTITUTE

re·plen·ish *vb* : to make full or complete once more — **re·plen·ish·er** *n* — **re·plen·ish·ment** *n*

re·plete *adj* : well supplied — **re·plete·ness** *n*

rep·li·ca *n* : a very exact copy

¹**re·ply** *vb* **re·plied; re·ply·ing** : to say or do in answer : RESPOND

²**reply** *n, pl* **re·plies** : something said, written, or done in answer

¹**re·port** *n* **1** : ¹RUMOR **2** : REPUTATION 1 **3** : a usually complete description or statement **4** : an explosive noise

²**report** *vb* **1** : to describe or tell something **2** : to prepare or present an account of something (as for television or a newspaper) **3** : to present oneself **4** : to make known to the proper authorities **5** : to make a charge of misconduct against — **re·port·er** *n*

report card *n* : a report on a student's grades that is regularly sent by a school to the student's parents or guardian

¹**re·pose** *vb* **re·posed; re·pos·ing** **1** : to lay at rest **2** : to lie at rest

²**repose** *n* **1** : a state of resting and especially sleep after effort or strain **2** : freedom from disturbance or excitement : CALM

rep·re·sent *vb* **1** : to present a picture, image, or likeness of : PORTRAY **2** : to be a sign or symbol of **3** : to act for or in place of

rep·re·sen·ta·tion *n* **1** : one (as a picture or symbol) that represents something else **2** : the act of representing : the state of being represented (as in a legislative body)

¹**rep·re·sen·ta·tive** *adj* **1** : serving to represent **2** : standing or acting for another **3** : carried on by elected representatives **4** : being a typical example of the thing mentioned

²**representative** *n* **1** : a typical example (as of a group or class) **2** : a person who represents another (as in a legislature)

re·press *vb* : to hold in check by or as if by pressure

¹**re·prieve** *vb* **re·prieved; re·priev·ing** : to delay the punishment of (as a prisoner sentenced to die)

²**reprieve** *n* **1** : a postponing of a prison or death sentence **2** : a temporary relief

¹**rep·ri·mand** *n* : a severe or formal criticism : CENSURE

²**reprimand** *vb* : to criticize (a person) severely or formally

re·pri·sal *n* : an act in return for harm done by another

¹**re·proach** *n* **1** : something that calls for blame or disgrace **2** : an expression of disapproval

²**reproach** *vb* : to find fault with : BLAME

re·pro·duce *vb* **re·pro·duced; re·pro·duc·ing** **1** : to produce again **2** : to produce another living thing of the same kind — **re·pro·duc·er** *n*

re·pro·duc·tion *n* **1** : the act or process of reproducing **2** : ¹COPY 1

re·pro·duc·tive *adj* : of, relating to, capable of, or concerned with reproduction

re·proof *n* : blame or criticism for a fault

re·prove *vb* **re·proved; re·prov·ing** : to express blame or disapproval of : SCOLD

rep·tile *n* : any of a group of vertebrates (as snakes, lizards, turtles, and alligators) that are cold-blooded, breathe air, and usually have the skin covered with scales or bony plates

re·pub·lic *n* **1** : a government having a chief of state who is not a monarch and who is usually a president **2** : a government in which supreme power lies in the citizens through their right to vote **3** : a state or country having a republican government

¹**re·pub·li·can** *n* : a person who favors a republican form of government

²**republican** *adj* : of, relating to, or like a republic

re·pu·di·ate *vb* **re·pu·di·at·ed; re·pu·di·at·ing** **1** : to refuse to have anything to do with **2** : to refuse to accept, admit, or pay

¹**re·pulse** *vb* **re·pulsed; re·puls·ing** **1** : to drive or beat back : REPEL **2** : to treat with discourtesy : SNUB

²**repulse** *n* **1** : ²REBUFF, SNUB **2** : the action of driving back an attacker

re·pul·sive *adj* : causing disgust — **re·pul·sive·ly** *adv* — **re·pul·sive·ness** *n*

rep·u·ta·ble *adj* : having a good reputation — **rep·u·ta·bly** *adv*

rep·u·ta·tion *n* **1** : overall quality or character as seen or judged by people in general **2** : notice by other people of some quality or ability

¹**re·pute** *vb* **re·put·ed; re·put·ing** : CONSIDER 3

²**repute** *n* **1** : REPUTATION 1 **2** : good reputation : HONOR

¹**re·quest** *n* **1** : an asking for something **2** : something asked for **3** : the condition of being requested

²**request** *vb* **1** : to make a request to or of **2** : to ask for

re·qui·em *n* **1** : a mass for a dead person **2** : a musical service or hymn in honor of the dead

re·quire *vb* **re·quired; re·quir·ing 1 :** to have a need for **2 :** ¹ORDER 2, COMMAND

re·quire·ment *n* **:** something that is required or necessary

¹**req·ui·site** *adj* **:** needed for reaching a goal or achieving a purpose

²**requisite** *n* **:** REQUIREMENT

re·read *vb* **re·read; re·read·ing :** to read again

¹**res·cue** *vb* **res·cued; res·cu·ing :** to free from danger or evil **:** SAVE — **res·cu·er** *n*

²**rescue** *n* **:** an act of rescuing

re·search *n* **:** careful study and investigation for the purpose of discovering and explaining new knowledge — **re·search·er** *n*

re·sem·blance *n* **:** the quality or state of resembling something else

re·sem·ble *vb* **re·sem·bled; re·sem·bling :** to be like or similar to

re·sent *vb* **:** to feel annoyance or anger at

re·sent·ment *n* **:** a feeling of angry displeasure at a real or imagined wrong, insult, or injury

res·er·va·tion *n* **1 :** an act of reserving **2 :** an arrangement to have something (as a hotel room) held for one's use **3 :** something (as land) reserved for a special use **4 :** something that limits

¹**re·serve** *vb* **re·served; re·serv·ing 1 :** to keep in store for future or special use **2 :** to hold over to a future time or place **3 :** to arrange to have set aside and held for one's use

²**reserve** *n* **1 :** something stored or available for future use **2 reserves** *pl* **:** military forces held back or available for later use **3 :** an area of land set apart **4 :** an act of reserving **5 :** caution in one's words and behavior

re·served *adj* **1 :** cautious in words and actions **2 :** kept or set apart for future or special use

res·er·voir *n* **:** a place where something (as water) is kept in store for future use

re·set *vb* **re·set; re·set·ting :** to set again

re·ship·ment *n* **:** an act of shipping again

re·side *vb* **re·sid·ed; re·sid·ing 1 :** to live permanently and continuously **:** DWELL **2 :** to have its place **:** EXIST

res·i·dence *n* **1 :** the act or fact of residing **2 :** the place where one actually lives **3 :** a building used for a home **4 :** the time during which a person lives in a place

¹**res·i·dent** *adj* **1 :** living in a place for some length of time **2 :** serving in a full-time position at a certain place

²**resident** *n* **:** a person who lives in a place

res·i·den·tial *adj* **1 :** used as a residence or by residents **2 :** suitable for or containing residences

res·i·due *n* **:** whatever remains after a part is taken, set apart, or lost

re·sign *vb* **1 :** to give up by a formal or official act **2 :** to prepare to accept something usually unpleasant

res·ig·na·tion *n* **1 :** an act of resigning **2 :** a letter or written statement that gives notice of resignation **3 :** the feeling of a person who is resigned

re·signed *adj* **:** giving in patiently (as to loss or sorrow) — **re·sign·ed·ly** *adv*

res·in *n* **1 :** a yellowish or brownish substance obtained from the gum or sap of some trees (as the pine) and used in varnishes and medicine **2 :** any of various manufactured products that are similar to natural resins in properties and are used especially as plastics

re·sist *vb* **1 :** to withstand the force or effect of **2 :** to fight against **:** OPPOSE

re·sis·tance *n* **1 :** an act or instance of resisting **2 :** the ability to resist **3 :** an opposing or slowing force **4 :** the opposition offered by a substance to the passage through it of an electric current

re·sis·tant *adj* **:** giving or capable of resistance

res·o·lute *adj* **:** firmly determined — **res·o·lute·ly** *adv* — **res·o·lute·ness** *n*

res·o·lu·tion *n* **1 :** the act of resolving **2 :** the act of solving **:** SOLUTION **3 :** something decided on **4 :** firmness of purpose **5 :** a statement expressing the feelings, wishes, or decisions of a group

¹**re·solve** *vb* **re·solved; re·solv·ing 1 :** to find an answer to **:** SOLVE **2 :** to reach a firm decision about something **3 :** to declare or decide by a formal resolution and vote

²**resolve** *n* **1 :** something resolved **2 :** firmness of purpose

res·o·nance *n* **:** the quality or state of being resonant

res·o·nant *adj* **:** being or making sound with a rich vibrating quality — **res·o·nant·ly** *adv*

¹**re·sort** *n* **1 :** one that is looked to for help **2 :** HANGOUT **3 :** a place where people go for pleasure, sport, or a change

²**resort** *vb* **1 :** to go often or again and again **2 :** to seek aid, relief, or advantage

re·sound *vb* **1 :** to become filled with sound **:** REVERBERATE **2 :** to sound loudly

re·source *n* **1 :** a new or a reserve source of supply or support **2 resources** *pl* **:** a usable stock or supply (as of money or products) **3 :** the ability to meet and deal with situations

re·source·ful *adj* **:** clever in dealing with problems — **re·source·ful·ly** *adv* — **re·source·ful·ness** *n*

¹**re·spect** *n* **1 :** relation to or concern with

something specified **2** : high or special regard : ESTEEM **3 respects** *pl* : an expression of regard or courtesy **4** : ¹DETAIL 2
²respect *vb* **1** : to consider worthy of high
regard : ESTEEM **2** : to pay attention to —
re·spect·er *n*

re·spect·able *adj* **1** : deserving respect **2**
: decent or correct in conduct : PROPER **3**
: fair in size or quantity **4** : fit to be seen
: PRESENTABLE — **re·spect·ably** *adv*

re·spect·ful *adj* : showing respect — **re-
spect·ful·ly** *adv* — **re·spect·ful·ness** *n*

re·spect·ing *prep* : CONCERNING

re·spec·tive *adj* : not the same or shared
: SEPARATE — **re·spec·tive·ly** *adv*

re·spell *vb* : to spell again or in another way

res·pi·ra·tion *n* **1** : the act or process of
breathing **2** : the physical and chemical
processes (as breathing and oxidation) by
which a living being gets the oxygen it
needs to live

res·pi·ra·tor *n* **1** : a device covering the
mouth or nose especially to prevent the
breathing in of something harmful **2** : a
device used for aiding one to breathe

res·pi·ra·to·ry *adj* : of, relating to, or concerned with respiration

re·spire *vb* **re·spired; re·spir·ing** : BREATHE
1

res·pite *n* **1** : a short delay **2** : a period of
rest or relief

re·splen·dent *adj* : shining brightly : SPLEN-
DID — **re·splen·dent·ly** *adv*

re·spond *vb* **1** : to say something in return
: REPLY **2** : to act in response : REACT

re·sponse *n* **1** : an act or instance of reply-
ing : ANSWER **2** : words said or sung by the
people or choir in a religious service **3** : a
reaction of a living being (as to a drug)

re·spon·si·bil·i·ty *n, pl* **re·spon·si·bil·i·ties**
1 : the quality or state of being responsible
2 : the quality of being dependable **3**
: something for which one is responsible

re·spon·si·ble *adj* **1** : getting the credit or
blame for one's acts or decisions **2** : RELI-
ABLE **3** : needing a person to take charge
of or be trusted with things of importance
— **re·spon·si·bly** *adv*

re·spon·sive *adj* **1** : giving response **2**
: quick to respond or react in a sympathetic
way — **re·spon·sive·ly** *adv* — **re·spon-
sive·ness** *n*

¹rest *n* **1** : ¹SLEEP 1 **2** : freedom from activity or work **3** : a state of not moving or
not doing anything **4** : a place for resting
or stopping **5** : a silence in music **6** : a
symbol in music that stands for a certain period of silence in a measure **7** : something
used for support

²rest *vb* **1** : to get rest by lying down

: SLEEP **2** : to give rest to **3** : to lie dead **4**
: to not take part in work or activity **5** : to
sit or lie fixed or supported **6** : DEPEND 2
7 : to fix or be fixed in trust or confidence

³rest *n* : something that is left over : RE-
MAINDER

re·state·ment *n* : a saying again or in another way

res·tau·rant *n* : a public eating place

rest·ful *adj* **1** : giving rest **2** : giving a feeling of rest : QUIET — **rest·ful·ly** *adv* —
rest·ful·ness *n*

rest·ing *adj* : DORMANT

res·tive *adj* **1** : resisting control **2** : not
being at ease — **res·tive·ly** *adv* — **res·tive-
ness** *n*

rest·less *adj* **1** : having or giving no rest **2**
: not quiet or calm — **rest·less·ly** *adv* —
rest·less·ness *n*

res·to·ra·tion *n* **1** : an act of restoring : the
condition of being restored **2** : something
(as a building) that has been restored

re·store *vb* **re·stored; re·stor·ing** **1** : to
give back : RETURN **2** : to put back into use
or service **3** : to put or bring back to an earlier or original state

re·strain *vb* **1** : to keep from doing something **2** : to keep back : CURB — **re·strain-
er** *n*

re·straint *n* **1** : the act of restraining : the
state of being restrained **2** : a restraining
force or influence **3** : control over one's
thoughts or feelings

re·strict *vb* : to keep within bounds : set limits to

re·stric·tion *n* **1** : something (as a law or
rule) that restricts **2** : an act of restricting
: the condition of being restricted

re·stric·tive *adj* : serving or likely to restrict
— **re·stric·tive·ly** *adv* — **re·stric·tive-
ness** *n*

¹re·sult *vb* **1** : to come about as an effect **2**
: to end as an effect

²result *n* **1** : something that comes about as
an effect or end **2** : a good effect

re·sume *vb* **re·sumed; re·sum·ing** **1** : to
take or occupy again **2** : to begin again

re·sump·tion *n* : the act of resuming

res·ur·rect *vb* **1** : to raise from the dead
: bring back to life **2** : to bring to view or
into use again

res·ur·rec·tion *n* **1** *cap* : the rising of Christ
from the dead **2** *often cap* : the rising again
to life of all human dead before the final
judgment **3** : a coming back into use or importance

re·sus·ci·tate *vb* **re·sus·ci·tat·ed; re·sus-
ci·tat·ing** : to bring back from apparent
death or unconsciousness — **re·sus·ci·ta-
tor** *n*

¹re·tail *vb* : to sell in small amounts to people for their own use — **re·tail·er** *n*

²retail *n* : the sale of products or goods in small amounts to people for their own use

³retail *adj* : of, relating to, or engaged in selling by retail

re·tain *vb* **1** : to keep in one's possession or control **2** : to hold safe or unchanged

re·tal·i·ate *vb* **re·tal·i·at·ed; re·tal·i·at·ing** : to get revenge by returning like for like

re·tal·i·a·tion *n* : the act or an instance of retaliating

re·tard *vb* : to slow up : keep back : DELAY — **re·tard·er** *n*

re·tard·ed *adj* : very slow especially in mind

retch *vb* : to vomit or try to vomit

re·ten·tion *n* **1** : the act of retaining : the state of being retained **2** : the power of retaining

ret·i·na *n, pl* **retinas** *or* **ret·i·nae** : the membrane that lines the back part of the eyeball and is the sensitive part for seeing

re·tire *vb* **re·tired; re·tir·ing** **1** : to get away from action or danger : RETREAT **2** : to go away especially to be alone **3** : to give up one's job permanently : quit working **4** : to go to bed **5** : to take out of circulation — **re·tire·ment** *n*

re·tired *adj* : not working at active duties or business

re·tir·ing *adj* : ¹SHY 2, RESERVED

¹re·tort *vb* **1** : to answer back : reply angrily or sharply **2** : to reply with an argument against

²retort *n* : a quick, clever, or angry reply

re·trace *vb* **re·traced; re·trac·ing** : to go over once more

re·tract *vb* **1** : to pull back or in **2** : to take back (as an offer or statement) : WITHDRAW

¹re·tread *vb* **re·tread·ed; re·tread·ing** : to put a new tread on the cord fabric of (a tire)

²re·tread *n* : a retreaded tire

¹re·treat *n* **1** : an act of going away from something dangerous, difficult, or disagreeable **2** : a military signal for turning away from the enemy **3** : a place of privacy or safety : REFUGE **4** : a period in which a person goes away to pray, think quietly, and study

²retreat *vb* : to make a retreat

re·trieve *vb* **re·trieved; re·triev·ing** **1** : to find and bring in killed or wounded game **2** : to make good a loss or damage : RECOVER — **re·triev·er** *n*

ret·ro—rock·et *n* : a rocket (as on a space vehicle) used to slow forward motion

ret·ro·spect *n* : a looking back on things past

¹re·turn *vb* **1** : to come or go back **2** : ²AN-

SWER 1, REPLY **3** : to make an official report of **4** : to bring, carry, send, or put back : RESTORE **5** : ¹YIELD 4, PRODUCE **6** : REPAY 1

²return *n* **1** : the act of coming back to or from a place or condition **2** : RECURRENCE **3** : a report of the results of voting **4** : a statement of income to be taxed **5** : the profit from labor, investment, or business **6** : the act of returning something (as to an earlier place or condition) **7** : something given (as in payment)

³return *adj* **1** : played or given in return **2** : used for returning

re·union *n* **1** : the act of reuniting : the state of being reunited **2** : a reuniting of persons after being apart

re·unite *vb* **re·unit·ed; re·unit·ing** : to come or bring together again after being apart

rev *vb* **revved; rev·ving** : to increase the number of revolutions per minute of (a motor)

re·veal *vb* **1** : to make known **2** : to show clearly ·

re·veil·le *n* : a signal sounded at about sunrise on a bugle or drum to call soldiers or sailors to duty

¹rev·el *vb* **rev·eled** *or* **rev·elled; rev·el·ing** *or* **rev·el·ling** **1** : to be social in a wild noisy way **2** : to take great pleasure

²revel *n* : a noisy or merry celebration

rev·e·la·tion *n* **1** : an act of revealing **2** : something revealed

rev·el·ry *n, pl* **rev·el·ries** : rough and noisy merrymaking

¹re·venge *vb* **re·venged; re·veng·ing** : to cause harm or injury in return for

²revenge *n* **1** : an act or instance of revenging **2** : a desire to repay injury for injury **3** : a chance for getting satisfaction

re·venge·ful *adj* : given to or seeking revenge

rev·e·nue *n* **1** : the income from an investment **2** : money collected by a government (as through taxes)

re·ver·ber·ate *vb* **re·ver·ber·at·ed; re·ver·ber·at·ing** : to continue in or as if in a series of echoes

re·vere *vb* **re·vered; re·ver·ing** : to think of with reverence

¹rev·er·ence *n* : honor and respect mixed with love and awe

²reverence *vb* **rev·er·enced; rev·er·enc·ing** : to show reverence to or toward

rev·er·end *adj* **1** : worthy of honor and respect **2** — used as a title for a member of the clergy

rev·er·ent *adj* : very respectful — **rev·er·ent·ly** *adv*

rev·er·ie *or* **rev·ery** *n, pl* **rev·er·ies** **1**

: ¹DAYDREAM 2 : the condition of being lost in thought

re·ver·sal n : an act or the process of reversing

¹re·verse adj 1 : opposite to a previous or normal condition 2 : acting or working in a manner opposite to the usual — re·verse·ly adv

²reverse vb re·versed; re·vers·ing 1 : to turn completely around or upside down or inside out 2 : ANNUL 3 : to go or cause to go in the opposite direction

³reverse n 1 : something opposite to something else : CONTRARY 2 : an act or instance of reversing 3 : the back part of something 4 : a gear that reverses something

re·vert vb : to come or go back

¹re·view n 1 : a military parade put on for high officers 2 : a general survey 3 : a piece of writing about the quality of a book, performance, or show 4 : a fresh study of material studied before

²review vb 1 : to look at a thing again : study or examine again 2 : to make an inspection of (as troops) 3 : to write a review about (as a book) 4 : to look back on — re·view·er n

re·vile vb re·viled; re·vil·ing : to speak to or yell at in an insulting way — re·vil·er n

re·vise vb re·vised; re·vis·ing 1 : to look over again to correct or improve 2 : to make a new version of

re·viv·al n 1 : a reviving of interest (as in art) 2 : a new presentation of a play or movie 3 : a gaining back of strength or importance 4 : a meeting or series of meetings led by a preacher to stir up religious feelings or to make converts

re·vive vb re·vived; re·viv·ing 1 : to bring back or come back to life, consciousness, freshness, or activity 2 : to bring back into use

re·voke vb re·voked; re·vok·ing : to take away or cancel

¹re·volt vb 1 : to rebel against the authority of a ruler or government 2 : to be or cause to be disgusted or shocked

²revolt n : REBELLION, INSURRECTION

rev·o·lu·tion n 1 : the action by a celestial body of going round in a fixed course 2 : completion of a course (as of years) : CYCLE 3 : a turning round a center or axis : ROTATION 4 : a single complete turn (as of a wheel) 5 : a sudden, extreme, or complete change (as in manner of living or working) 6 : the overthrow of one government and the substitution of another by the governed

rev·o·lu·tion·ary adj 1 : of, relating to, or involving revolution 2 : ¹RADICAL 2

rev·o·lu·tion·ist n : a person taking part in or supporting a revolution

rev·o·lu·tion·ize vb rev·o·lu·tion·ized; rev·o·lu·tion·iz·ing : to change greatly or completely

re·volve vb re·volved; re·volv·ing 1 : to think over carefully 2 : to move in an orbit 3 : ROTATE 1

re·volv·er n : a pistol having a revolving cylinder holding several bullets all of which may be shot without loading again

re·vue n : a theatrical entertainment consisting usually of short and often funny sketches and songs

¹re·ward vb : to give a reward to or for

²reward n : something (as money) given or offered in return for a service (as the return of something lost)

re·word vb : to state in different words

re·write vb re·wrote; re·writ·ten; re·writ·ing : to write over again especially in a different form

rhap·so·dy n, pl rhap·so·dies : a written or spoken expression of extreme praise or delight

rhea n : a tall flightless South American bird that has three toes on each foot and is like but smaller than the ostrich

rheu·mat·ic adj : of, relating to, or suffering from rheumatism — rheu·mat·i·cal·ly adv

rheu·ma·tism n : any of several disorders in which muscles or joints are red, hot, and painful

rhi·no n, pl rhino or rhi·nos : RHINOCEROS

rhi·noc·er·os n, pl rhi·noc·er·os·es or rhinoceros : a large mammal of Africa and Asia with a thick skin, three toes on each foot, and one or two heavy upright horns on the snout

rho·do·den·dron n : a shrub or tree with long usually shiny and evergreen leaves and showy clusters of white, pink, red, or purple flowers

rhom·bus n : a parallelogram whose sides are equal

rhu·barb n : a plant with broad green leaves and thick juicy pink or red stems that are used for food

¹rhyme or rime n 1 : close similarity in the final sounds of two or more words or lines of verse 2 : a verse composition that rhymes

²rhyme or rime vb rhymed or rimed; rhym·ing or rim·ing 1 : to make rhymes 2 : to end with the same sound 3 : to cause lines or words to end with a similar sound

rhythm n 1 : a flow of rising and falling sounds produced in poetry by a regular repeating of stressed and unstressed syllables 2 : a flow of sound in music having regular accented beats **3** : a movement or activity in which some action repeats regularly

rhyth·mic *or* **rhyth·mi·cal** *adj* : having rhythm — **rhyth·mi·cal·ly** *adv*

¹rib *n* **1** : one of the series of curved bones that are joined in pairs to the backbone of humans and other vertebrates and help to stiffen the body wall **2** : something (as a piece of wire supporting the fabric of an umbrella) that is like a rib in shape or use **3** : one of the parallel ridges in a knitted or woven fabric — **ribbed** *adj*

²rib *vb* **ribbed; rib·bing 1** : to provide or enclose with ribs **2** : to form ribs in (a fabric) in knitting or weaving

rib·bon *n* **1** : a narrow strip of fabric (as silk) used for trimming or for tying or decorating packages **2** : a long narrow strip like a ribbon **3** : TATTER 1, SHRED

rice *n* : an annual cereal grass widely grown in warm wet regions for its grain that is a chief food in many parts of the world

rich *adj* **1** : having great wealth **2** : ¹VALUABLE 1, EXPENSIVE **3** : containing much sugar, fat, or seasoning **4** : high in fuel content **5** : deep and pleasing in color or tone **6** : ABUNDANT **7** : FERTILE 1 — **rich·ly** *adv* — **rich·ness** *n*

rich·es *n pl* : things that make one rich : WEALTH

rick·ets *n* : a disease in which the bones are soft and deformed and which usually attacks the young and is caused by lack of the vitamin that controls the use of calcium and phosphorus

rick·ety *adj* : SHAKY, UNSOUND

rick·sha *or* **rick·shaw** *n* : a small hooded carriage with two wheels that is pulled by one person and was used originally in Japan

¹ric·o·chet *n* : a bouncing off at an angle (as of a bullet off a wall)

²ricochet *vb* **ric·o·cheted; ric·o·chet·ing** : to bounce off at an angle

rid *vb* **rid** *also* **rid·ded; rid·ding** : to free from something : RELIEVE

rid·dance *n* : the act of ridding : the state of being rid of something

¹rid·dle *n* : a puzzling question to be solved or answered by guessing

²riddle *vb* **rid·dled; rid·dling** : to pierce with many holes

¹ride *vb* **rode; rid·den; rid·ing 1** : to go on an animal's back or in a vehicle (as a car) **2** : to sit on and control so as to be carried along **3** : to float or move on water **4** : to travel over a surface **5** : CARRY 1 — **rid·er** *n*

²ride *n* **1** : a trip on horseback or by vehicle **2** : a mechanical device (as a merry-go-round) that one rides for fun **3** : a means of transportation

ridge *n* **1** : a range of hills or mountains **2** : a raised strip **3** : the line made where two sloping surfaces come together — **ridged** *adj*

ridge·pole *n* : the highest horizontal timber in a sloping roof to which the upper ends of the rafters are fastened

¹rid·i·cule *n* : the act of making fun of someone

²ridicule *vb* **rid·i·culed; rid·i·cul·ing** : to make fun of : DERIDE

ri·dic·u·lous *adj* : causing or deserving ridicule : ABSURD — **ri·dic·u·lous·ly** *adv* — **ri·dic·u·lous·ness** *n*

riff·raff *n* : RABBLE 2

¹ri·fle *vb* **ri·fled; ri·fling 1** : to search through fast and roughly especially in order to steal **2** : ¹STEAL 2

²rifle *n* : a gun having a long barrel with spiral grooves on its inside

rift *n* **1** : an opening made by splitting or separation : CLEFT **2** : a break in friendly relations

¹rig *vb* **rigged; rig·ging 1** : to fit out (as a ship) with rigging **2** : CLOTHE 1 2, DRESS **3** : EQUIP **4** : to set up usually for temporary use

²rig *n* **1** : the shape, number, and arrangement of sails on a ship of one class or type that sets it apart from ships of other classes or types **2** : apparatus for a certain purpose

rig·ging *n* : lines and chains used on a ship especially for moving the sails and supporting the masts and spars

¹right *adj* **1** : being just or good : UPRIGHT **2** : ACCURATE, CORRECT **3** : SUITABLE, APPROPRIATE **4** : STRAIGHT 1 **5** : of, relating to, located on, or being the side of the body away from the heart **6** : located nearer to the right hand **7** : being or meant to be the side on top, in front, or on the outside **8** : healthy in mind or body — **right·ly** *adv* — **right·ness** *n*

²right *n* **1** : the ideal of what is right and good **2** : something to which one has a just claim **3** : the cause of truth or justice **4** : the right side or a part that is on or toward the right side

³right *adv* **1** : according to what is right **2** : in the exact location or position : PRECISELY **3** : in a direct line or course : STRAIGHT **4** : according to truth or fact **5** : in the right way : CORRECTLY **6** : all the way **7** : without delay : IMMEDIATELY **8** : on or to the right

⁴right *vb* **1** : to make right (something wrong or unjust) **2** : to adjust or restore to a proper state or condition **3** : to bring or bring back to a vertical position **4** : to become vertical

right angle *n* : an angle formed by two lines that are perpendicular to each other — **right–an·gled** *adj*

righ·teous *adj* : doing or being what is right — **righ·teous·ly** *adv* — **righ·teous·ness** *n*

right·ful *adj* : LAWFUL 2, PROPER — **right·ful·ly** *adv* — **right·ful·ness** *n*

right–hand *adj* 1 : located on the right 2 : RIGHT-HANDED 3 : relied on most of all

right–hand·ed *adj* 1 : using the right hand more easily than the left 2 : done or made with or for the right hand 3 : CLOCKWISE

right–of–way *n, pl* **rights–of–way** 1 : the right to pass over someone else's land 2 : the right of some traffic to go before other traffic

right triangle *n* : a triangle having a right angle

rig·id *adj* 1 : not flexible : STIFF 2 : STRICT 1, SEVERE — **rig·id·ly** *adv* — **rig·id·ness** *n*

rig·ma·role *n* : NONSENSE 1

rig·or *n* : a harsh severe condition (as of discipline or weather)

rig·or·ous *adj* 1 : very strict 2 : hard to put up with : HARSH — **rig·or·ous·ly** *adv* — **rig·or·ous·ness** *n*

rill *n* : a very small brook

rim *n* 1 : an outer edge especially of something curved 2 : the outer part of a wheel — **rimmed** *adj*

¹rime *n* : ¹FROST 2

²rime *variant of* RHYME

rind *n* : a usually hard or tough outer layer

¹ring *n* 1 : a circular band worn as an ornament or used for holding or fastening 2 : something circular in shape 3 : a place for exhibitions (as at a circus) or contests (as in boxing) 4 : a group of persons who work together for selfish or dishonest purposes — **ringed** *adj* — **ring·like** *adj*

²ring *vb* **ringed; ring·ing** 1 : to place or form a ring around : to throw a ring over (a peg or hook) in a game (as quoits)

³ring *vb* **rang; rung; ring·ing** 1 : to make or cause to make a rich vibrating sound when struck 2 : to sound a bell 3 : to announce by or as if by striking a bell 4 : to sound loudly 5 : to be filled with talk or report 6 : to repeat loudly 7 : to seem to be a certain way 8 : to call on the telephone

⁴ring *n* 1 : a clear ringing sound made by vibrating metal 2 : a tone suggesting that of a bell 3 : a loud or continuing noise 4 : something that suggests a certain quality 5 : a telephone call

ring·lead·er *n* : a leader especially of a group of persons who cause trouble

ring·let *n* : a long curl

ring·worm *n* : a contagious skin disease with discolored rings on the skin

rink *n* : a place for skating

¹rinse *vb* **rinsed; rins·ing** 1 : to wash lightly with water 2 : to cleanse (as of soap) with clear water 3 : to treat (hair) with a rinse

²rinse *n* 1 : an act of rinsing 2 : a liquid used for rinsing 3 : a solution that temporarily tints hair

¹ri·ot *n* 1 : public violence, disturbance, or disorder 2 : a colorful display

²riot *vb* : to create or take part in a riot

¹rip *vb* **ripped; rip·ping** : to cut or tear open — **rip·per** *n*

²rip *n* : ³TEAR 2

ripe *adj* **rip·er; rip·est** 1 : fully grown and developed 2 : having mature knowledge, understanding, or judgment 3 : ¹READY 1 — **ripe·ness** *n*

rip·en *vb* : to make or become ripe

¹rip·ple *vb* **rip·pled; rip·pling** 1 : to become or cause to become covered with small waves 2 : to make a sound like that of water flowing in small waves

²ripple *n* 1 : the disturbing of the surface of water 2 : a sound like that of rippling water

¹rise *vb* **rose; ris·en; ris·ing** 1 : to get up from lying, kneeling, or sitting 2 : to get up from sleep or from one's bed 3 : to return from death 4 : to take up arms 5 : to appear above the horizon 6 : to go up : ASCEND 7 : to swell in size or volume 8 : to become encouraged 9 : to gain a higher rank or position 10 : to increase in amount or number 11 : ARISE 3 12 : to come into being : ORIGINATE 13 : to show oneself equal to a demand or test — **ris·er** *n*

²rise *n* 1 : an act of rising : a state of being risen 2 : BEGINNING 1, ORIGIN 3 : an increase in amount, number, or volume 4 : an upward slope 5 : a spot higher than surrounding ground 6 : an angry reaction

¹risk *n* : possibility of loss or injury

²risk *vb* 1 : to expose to danger 2 : to take the risk or danger of

risky *adj* **risk·i·er; risk·i·est** : DANGEROUS 1

rite *n* 1 : a set form of conducting a ceremony 2 : a ceremonial act or action

rit·u·al *n* 1 : an established form for a ceremony 2 : a system of rites

¹ri·val *n* : one of two or more trying to get what only one can have

²rival *adj* : having the same worth

³rival *vb* **ri·valed** *or* **ri·valled; ri·val·ing** *or* **ri·val·ling** 1 : to be in competition with 2 : ²EQUAL

ri·val·ry *n, pl* **ri·val·ries** : the act of rivaling : the state of being a rival : COMPETITION

riv·er *n* 1 : a natural stream of water larger than a brook or creek 2 : a large stream

riv·et *n* : a bolt with a head at one end used for uniting two or more pieces by passing the shank through a hole in each piece and then beating or pressing down the plain end so as to make a second head

riv·u·let *n* : a small stream

roach *n* : COCKROACH

road *n*   **1** : an open way for vehicles, persons, and animals   **2** : PATH 3, ROUTE

road·bed *n*   **1** : the foundation of a road or railroad   **2** : the traveled surface of a road

road·side *n* : the strip of land along a road : the side of a road

road·way *n*   **1** : the strip of land over which a road passes   **2** : the part of the surface of a road traveled by vehicles

roam *vb* : to go from place to place with no fixed purpose or direction — **roam·er** *n*

¹roan *adj* : of a dark color (as black or brown) sprinkled with white

²roan *n* : an animal (as a horse) with a roan coat

¹roar *vb*   **1** : to utter a long full loud sound   **2** : to laugh loudly — **roar·er** *n*

²roar *n* : a long shout, bellow, or loud confused noise

¹roast *vb*   **1** : to cook with dry heat (as in an oven)   **2** : to be or make very hot — **roast·er** *n*

²roast *n*   **1** : a piece of meat roasted or suitable for roasting   **2** : an outing at which food is roasted

³roast *adj* : cooked by roasting

rob *vb* **robbed; rob·bing**   **1** : to take something away from a person or place in secrecy or by force, threat, or trickery   **2** : to keep from getting something due, expected, or desired — **rob·ber** *n*

rob·bery *n, pl* **rob·ber·ies** : the act or practice of robbing

¹robe *n*   **1** : a long loose or flowing garment   **2** : a covering for the lower part of the body

²robe *vb* **robed; rob·ing**   **1** : to put on a robe   **2** : ¹DRESS 2

rob·in *n*   **1** : a small European thrush with a yellowish red throat and breast   **2** : a large North American thrush with a grayish back and dull reddish breast

ro·bot *n*   **1** : a machine that looks and acts like a human being   **2** : a capable but unfeeling person

ro·bust *adj* : strong and vigorously healthy — **ro·bust·ly** *adv* — **ro·bust·ness** *n*

¹rock *vb*   **1** : to move back and forth as in a cradle   **2** : to sway or cause to sway back and forth

²rock *n*   **1** : a rocking movement   **2** : popular music played on instruments that are amplified electronically

³rock *n*   **1** : a large mass of stone   **2** : solid mineral deposits   **3** : something like a rock in firmness : SUPPORT

rock·er *n*   **1** : a curving piece of wood or metal on which an object (as a cradle) rocks   **2** : a structure or device that rocks on rockers   **3** : a mechanism that works with a rocking motion

¹rock·et *n*   **1** : a firework that is driven through the air by the gases produced by a burning substance   **2** : a jet engine that operates like a firework rocket but carries the oxygen needed for burning its fuel   **3** : a bomb, missile, or vehicle that is moved by a rocket

²rocket *vb*   **1** : to rise swiftly   **2** : to travel rapidly in or as if in a rocket

rock·ing chair *n* : a chair mounted on rockers

rocking horse *n* : a toy horse mounted on rockers

rock 'n' roll *or* **rock and roll** *n* : ²ROCK 2

rock salt *n* : common salt in large crystals

rocky *adj* **rock·i·er; rock·i·est** : full of or consisting of rocks — **rock·i·ness** *n*

rod *n*   **1** : a straight slender stick or bar   **2** : a stick or bundle of twigs used in whipping a person   **3** : a measure of length equal to $16\frac{1}{2}$ feet (about 5 meters)   **4** : any of the sensory bodies shaped like rods in the retina that respond to faint light   **5** : a light flexible pole often with line and a reel attached used in fishing — **rod·like** *adj*

rode *past of* RIDE

ro·dent *n* : any of a group of mammals (as squirrels, rats, mice, and beavers) with sharp front teeth used in gnawing

ro·deo *n, pl* **ro·de·os**   **1** : a roundup of cattle   **2** : an exhibition that features cowboy skills (as riding and roping)

¹roe *n, pl* **roe** *or* **roes**   **1** : ROE DEER   **2** : DOE

²roe *n* : the eggs of a fish especially while still held together in a membrane

roe·buck *n* : a male roe deer

roe deer *n* : a small deer of Europe and Asia with erect antlers forked at the tip

rogue *n*   **1** : a dishonest or wicked person   **2** : a pleasantly mischievous person

rogu·ish *adj* : being or like a rogue — **rogu·ish·ly** *adv* — **rogu·ish·ness** *n*

role *n*   **1** : a character assigned or taken on   **2** : a part played by an actor or singer   **3** : ¹FUNCTION 1

¹roll *n*   **1** : a writing that may be rolled up : SCROLL   **2** : an official list of names   **3** : something or a quantity of something that is rolled up or rounded as if rolled   **4** : a small piece of baked bread dough

²roll *vb*   **1** : to move by turning over and over on a surface without sliding   **2** : to shape or become shaped in rounded form   **3**

: to make smooth, even, or firm with a roller **4** : to move on rollers or wheels **5** : to sound with a full echoing tone or with a continuous beating sound **6** : to go by : PASS **7** : to flow in a continuous stream **8** : to move with a side-to-side sway

³roll *n* **1** : a sound produced by rapid strokes on a drum **2** : a heavy echoing sound **3** : a rolling movement or action

roll·er *n* **1** : a turning cylinder over or on which something is moved or which is used to press, shape, or smooth something **2** : a rod on which something (as a map) is rolled up **3** : a small wheel **4** : a long heavy wave on the sea

roller coaster *n* : an elevated railway (as in an amusement park) with sharp curves and steep slopes on which cars roll

roller skate *n* : a skate that has wheels instead of a runner

rolling pin *n* : a cylinder (as of wood) used to roll out dough

ROM *n* : READ-ONLY MEMORY

¹Ro·man *n* **1** : a person born or living in Rome **2** : a citizen of an ancient empire centered on Rome **3** *not cap* : roman letters or type

²Roman *adj* **1** : of or relating to Rome or the Romans **2** *not cap* : of or relating to a type style with upright characters (as in "these definitions")

¹ro·mance *n* **1** : an old tale of knights and noble ladies **2** : an adventure story **3** : a love story **4** : a love affair **5** : an attraction or appeal to one's feelings

²romance *vb* **ro·manced; ro·manc·ing** : to have romantic thoughts or ideas

Roman numeral *n* : a numeral in a system of figures based on the ancient Roman system

ro·man·tic *adj* **1** : not founded on fact : IMAGINARY **2** : IMPRACTICAL **3** : stressing or appealing to the emotions or imagination **4** : of, relating to, or associated with love — **ro·man·ti·cal·ly** *adv*

¹romp *n* : rough and noisy play : FROLIC

²romp *vb* : to play in a rough and noisy way

romp·er *n* : a young child's one-piece garment having legs that can be unfastened around the inside — usually used in pl.

¹roof *n, pl* **roofs** **1** : the upper covering part of a building **2** : something like a roof in form, position, or purpose — **roofed** *adj*

²roof *vb* : to cover with a roof

roof·ing *n* : material for a roof

roof·tree *n* : RIDGEPOLE

¹rook *n* : an Old World bird similar to the related crows

²rook *vb* : ¹CHEAT 1, SWINDLE

³rook *n* : one of the pieces in the game of chess

rook·ie *n* : BEGINNER, RECRUIT

¹room *n* **1** : available space **2** : a divided part of the inside of a building **3** : the people in a room **4 rooms** *pl* : LODGING 2 **5** : a suitable opportunity

²room *vb* : to provide with or live in lodgings

room·er *n* : LODGER

rooming house *n* : a house for renting furnished rooms to lodgers

room·mate *n* : one of two or more persons sharing a room or dwelling

roomy *adj* **room·i·er; room·i·est** : SPACIOUS — **room·i·ness** *n*

¹roost *n* : a support on which birds perch

²roost *vb* : to settle on a roost

roost·er *n* : an adult male chicken

¹root *n* **1** : a leafless underground part of a plant that stores food and holds the plant in place **2** : the part of something by which it is attached **3** : something like a root especially in being a source of support or growth **4** : SOURCE 1 **5** : ¹CORE 3 **6** : a word or part of a word from which other words are obtained by adding a prefix or suffix — **root·ed** *adj*

²root *vb* **1** : to form or cause to form roots **2** : to attach by or as if by roots **3** : UPROOT 1

³root *vb* : to turn up or dig with the snout

⁴root *vb* : ²CHEER 2 — **root·er** *n*

root beer *n* : a sweet drink flavored with extracts of roots and herbs

¹rope *n* **1** : a large stout cord of strands (as of fiber or wire) twisted or braided together **2** : a noose used for hanging **3** : a row or string (as of beads) made by braiding, twining, or threading

²rope *vb* **roped; rop·ing** **1** : to bind, fasten, or tie with a rope **2** : to set off or divide by a rope **3** : ¹LASSO — **rop·er** *n*

ro·sa·ry *n, pl* **ro·sa·ries** : a string of beads used in counting prayers

¹rose *past of* RISE

²rose *n* **1** : a showy and often fragrant white, yellow, pink, or red flower that grows on a prickly shrub (**rose·bush**) with compound leaves **2** : a moderate purplish red

rose·mary *n* : a fragrant mint that has branching woody stems and is used in cooking and in perfumes

ro·sette *n* : a badge or ornament of ribbon gathered in the shape of a rose

rose·wood *n* : a reddish or purplish wood streaked with black and that is valued for making furniture

Rosh Ha·sha·nah *n* : the Jewish New Year observed as a religious holiday in September or October

ros·in *n* : a hard brittle yellow to dark red substance obtained especially from pine trees and used in varnishes and on violin bows

ros·ter *n* : an orderly list usually of people belonging to some group

ros·trum *n, pl* **rostrums** *or* **ros·tra** : a stage or platform for public speaking

rosy *adj* **ros·i·er; ros·i·est** **1** : of the color rose **2** : PROMISING, HOPEFUL

¹rot *vb* **rot·ted; rot·ting** **1** : to undergo decay : SPOIL **2** : to go to ruin

²rot *n* **1** : the process of rotting : the state of being rotten **2** : a disease of plants or of animals in which tissue decays

ro·ta·ry *adj* **1** : turning on an axis like a wheel **2** : having a rotating part

ro·tate *vb* **ro·tat·ed; ro·tat·ing** **1** : to turn about an axis or a center **2** : to do or cause to do something in turn **3** : to pass in a series

ro·ta·tion *n* **1** : the act of rotating especially on an axis **2** : the growing of different crops in the same field usually in a regular order

rote *n* : repeating from memory of forms or phrases with little or no attention to meaning

ro·tor *n* **1** : the part of an electrical machine that turns **2** : a system of spinning horizontal blades that support a helicopter in the air

rot·ten *adj* **1** : having rotted **2** : morally bad **3** : very unpleasant or worthless — **rot·ten·ly** *adv* — **rot·ten·ness** *n*

ro·tund *adj* **1** : somewhat round **2** : ⁴PLUMP — **ro·tund·ly** *adv* — **ro·tund·ness** *n*

rouge *n* : a cosmetic used to give a red color to cheeks or lips

¹rough *adj* **1** : uneven in surface **2** : not calm **3** : being harsh or violent **4** : coarse or rugged in nature or look **5** : not complete or exact — **rough·ly** *adv* — **rough·ness** *n*

²rough *n* **1** : uneven ground covered with high grass, brush, and stones **2** : something in a crude or unfinished state

³rough *vb* **1** : ROUGHEN **2** : to handle roughly : BEAT **3** : to make or shape roughly — **rough it** : to live without ordinary comforts

rough·age *n* : coarse food (as bran) whose bulk increases the activity of the bowel

rough·en *vb* : to make or become rough

rough·neck *n* : a rough person : ROWDY

¹round *adj* **1** : having every part of the surface or circumference the same distance from the center **2** : shaped like a cylinder **3** : ⁴PLUMP **4** : ¹COMPLETE 1, FULL **5** : nearly correct or exact **6** : LARGE **7** : moving in or forming a circle **8** : having curves rather than angles — **round·ish** *adj* — **round·ly** *adv* — **round·ness** *n*

²round *adv* : ¹AROUND

³round *n* **1** : something (as a circle or globe) that is round **2** : a song in which three or four singers sing the same melody and words one after another at intervals **3** : a round or curved part (as a rung of a ladder) **4** : an indirect path **5** : a regularly covered route **6** : a series or cycle of repeated actions or events **7** : one shot fired by a soldier or a gun **8** : ammunition for one shot **9** : a unit of play in a contest or game **10** : a cut of beef especially between the rump and the lower leg

⁴round *vb* **1** : to make or become round **2** : to go or pass around **3** : to bring to completion **4** : to express as a round number **5** : to follow a winding course

⁵round *prep* : ²AROUND 123

round·about *adj* : not direct

round·house *n, pl* **round·hous·es** : a circular building where locomotives are kept or repaired

round trip *n* : a trip to a place and back usually over the same route

round·up *n* **1** : the gathering together of animals on the range by circling them in vehicles or on horseback and driving them in **2** : a gathering together of scattered persons or things **3** : ²SUMMARY

round up *vb* **1** : to collect (as cattle) by circling in vehicles or on horseback and driving **2** : to gather in or bring together

round·worm *n* : any of a group of worms with long round bodies that are not segmented and that include serious parasites of people and animals

rouse *vb* **roused; rous·ing** **1** : ¹AWAKE 1 **2** : to stir up : EXCITE

¹rout *n* **1** : a state of wild confusion or disorderly retreat **2** : a disastrous defeat

²rout *vb* **1** : to put to flight **2** : to defeat completely

¹route *n* : a regular, chosen, or assigned course of travel

²route *vb* **rout·ed; rout·ing** **1** : to send or transport by a selected route **2** : to arrange and direct the order of (as a series of factory operations)

¹rou·tine *n* : a standard or usual way of doing

²routine *adj* **1** : ²COMMONPLACE, ORDINARY **2** : done or happening in a standard or usual way — **rou·tine·ly** *adv*

rove *vb* **roved; rov·ing** : to wander without definite plan or direction — **rov·er** *n*

¹row *vb* **1** : to move a boat by means of oars **2** : to travel or carry in a rowboat

²row *n* : an act or instance of rowing

³row *n* **1** : a series of persons or things in an orderly sequence **2** : ¹WAY 1, STREET

⁴row *n* : a noisy disturbance or quarrel

row·boat *n* : a boat made to be rowed

¹row·dy *adj* **row·di·er; row·di·est** : coarse or rough in behavior — **row·di·ness** *n*

²rowdy *n, pl* **rowdies** : a rowdy person

roy·al *adj* **1** : of or relating to a sovereign : REGAL **2** : fit for a king or queen — **roy·al·ly** *adv*

roy·al·ty *n, pl* **roy·al·ties** **1** : royal status or power **2** : royal character or conduct **3** : members of a royal family **4** : a share of a product or profit (as of a mine) claimed by the owner for allowing another to use the property **5** : payment made to the owner of a patent or copyright for the use of it

¹rub *vb* **rubbed; rub·bing** **1** : to move along the surface of a body with pressure **2** : to wear away or chafe with friction **3** : to cause discontent, irritation, or anger **4** : to scour, polish, erase, or smear by pressure and friction — **rub the wrong way** : to cause to be angry : IRRITATE

²rub *n* **1** : something that gets in the way : DIFFICULTY **2** : something that is annoying **3** : the act of rubbing

rub·ber *n* **1** : something used in rubbing **2** : an elastic substance obtained from the milky juice of some tropical plants **3** : a synthetic substance like rubber **4** : something (as an overshoe) made of rubber

rubber band *n* : a continuous band made of rubber for holding things together : ELASTIC

rubber stamp *n* : a stamp with a printing face of rubber

rub·bish *n* : TRASH

rub·ble *n* : a confused mass of broken or worthless things

ru·ble *n* : a Russian coin or bill

ru·by *n, pl* **rubies** **1** : a precious stone of a deep red color **2** : a deep purplish red

ruck·us *n* : ⁴ROW

rud·der *n* : a movable flat piece attached at the rear of a ship or aircraft for steering

rud·dy *adj* **rud·di·er; rud·di·est** : having a healthy reddish color — **rud·di·ness** *n*

rude *adj* **rud·er; rud·est** **1** : roughly made **2** : not refined or cultured : UNCOUTH **3** : IMPOLITE — **rude·ly** *adv* — **rude·ness** *n*

ru·di·ment *n* : a basic principle

ru·di·men·ta·ry *adj* **1** : ELEMENTARY, SIMPLE **2** : not fully developed

rue *vb* **rued; ru·ing** : to feel sorrow or regret for

rue·ful *adj* **1** : exciting pity or sympathy **2** : MOURNFUL 1, REGRETFUL

ruff *n* **1** : a large round collar of pleated muslin or linen worn by men and women in the sixteenth and seventeenth centuries **2**

: a fringe of long hair or feathers on the neck of an animal or bird

ruf·fi·an *n* : a brutal cruel person

¹ruf·fle *vb* **ruf·fled; ruf·fling** **1** : to disturb the smoothness of **2** : ¹TROUBLE 1, VEX **3** : to erect (as feathers) in or like a ruff **4** : to make into or provide with a ruffle

²ruffle *n* : a strip of fabric gathered or pleated on one edge

rug *n* : a piece of thick heavy fabric usually with a nap or pile used especially as a floor covering

rug·ged *adj* **1** : having a rough uneven surface **2** : involving hardship **3** : STRONG 9, TOUGH — **rug·ged·ly** *adv* — **rug·ged·ness** *n*

¹ru·in *n* **1** : complete collapse or destruction **2** **ruins** *pl* : the remains of something destroyed **3** : a cause of destruction

²ruin *vb* **1** : to reduce to ruins **2** : to damage beyond repair **3** : ³BANKRUPT

ru·in·ous *adj* : causing or likely to cause ruin : DESTRUCTIVE — **ru·in·ous·ly** *adv*

¹rule *n* **1** : a guide or principle for conduct or action **2** : an accepted method, custom, or habit **3** : the exercise of authority or control : GOVERNMENT **4** : the time of a particular sovereign's reign **5** : RULER 2

²rule *vb* **ruled; rul·ing** **1** : ¹CONTROL 2, DIRECT **2** : to exercise authority over : GOVERN **3** : to be supreme or outstanding in **4** : to give or state as a considered decision **5** : to mark with lines drawn along the straight edge of a ruler

rul·er *n* **1** : ¹SOVEREIGN 1 **2** : a straight strip (as of wood or metal) with a smooth edge that is marked off in units and used for measuring or as a guide in drawing straight lines

rum *n* : an alcoholic liquor made from sugarcane or molasses

¹rum·ble *vb* **rum·bled; rum·bling** : to make or move with a low heavy rolling sound

²rumble *n* : a low heavy rolling sound

¹ru·mi·nant *n* : an animal (as a cow) that chews the cud

²ruminant *adj* **1** : chewing the cud **2** : of or relating to the group of hoofed mammals that chew the cud

ru·mi·nate *vb* **ru·mi·nat·ed; ru·mi·nat·ing** **1** : to engage in thought : MEDITATE **2** : to bring up and chew again what has been previously swallowed

¹rum·mage *vb* **rum·maged; rum·mag·ing** : to make an active search especially by moving about, turning over, or looking through the contents of a place or container

²rummage *n* : a confused collection of different articles

rum·my *n* : a card game in which each player

tries to lay down cards in groups of three or more

¹ru·mor *n* **1** : widely held opinion having no known source : HEARSAY **2** : a statement or story that is in circulation but has not been proven to be true

²rumor *vb* : to tell by rumor : spread a rumor

rump *n* **1** : the back part of an animal's body where the hips and thighs join **2** : a cut of beef between the loin and the round

rum·ple *vb* **rum·pled; rum·pling** : ²WRINKLE, MUSS

rum·pus *n* : ⁴ROW, FRACAS

¹run *vb* **ran; run; run·ning** **1** : to go at a pace faster than a walk **2** : to take to flight **3** : to move freely about as one wishes **4** : to go rapidly or hurriedly **5** : to do something by or as if by running **6** : to take part in a race **7** : to move on or as if on wheels **8** : to go back and forth often according to a fixed schedule **9** : to migrate or move in schools **10** : ²FUNCTION, OPERATE **11** : to continue in force **12** : to pass into a specified condition **13** : ¹FLOW 1 **14** : DISSOLVE 1 **15** : to give off liquid **16** : to tend to develop a specified feature or quality **17** : ¹STRETCH 2 **18** : to be in circulation **19** : ²TRACE 4 **20** : to pass over, across, or through **21** : to slip through or past **22** : to cause to penetrate **23** : to cause to go **24** : INCUR — **run into** : to meet by chance

²run *n* **1** : an act or the action of running **2** : a continuous series especially of similar things **3** : sudden heavy demands from depositors, creditors, or customers **4** : the quantity of work turned out in a continuous operation **5** : the usual or normal kind **6** : the distance covered in a period of continuous traveling **7** : a regular course or trip **8** : freedom of movement **9** : a way, track, or path frequented by animals **10** : an enclosure for animals where they may feed and exercise **11** : a score made in baseball by a base runner reaching home plate **12** : ²SLOPE 1 **13** : a ravel in a knitted fabric

¹run·away *n* **1** : ²FUGITIVE **2** : a horse that is running out of control

²runaway *adj* : running away : escaping from control

run–down *adj* **1** : being in poor condition **2** : being in poor health

¹rung *past participle of* RING

²rung *n* **1** : a rounded part placed as a crosspiece between the legs of a chair **2** : one of the crosspieces of a ladder

run–in *n* : an angry dispute : QUARREL

run·ner *n* **1** : one that runs **2** : MESSENGER **3** : a thin piece or part on or in which something slides **4** : a slender creeping branch of a plant that roots at the end or at the joints to form new plants **5** : a plant that forms or spreads by runners **6** : a long narrow carpet (as for a hall)

run·ner–up *n, pl* **run·ners–up** : the competitor in a contest who finishes next to the winner

run·ny *adj* : running or likely to run

run out *vb* **1** : to come to an end : EXPIRE **2** : to become exhausted or used up — **run out of** : to use up the available supply of

run over *vb* : ¹OVERFLOW 2

runt *n* : an unusually small person or animal

run·way *n* **1** : a path beaten by animals in going to and from feeding grounds **2** : a paved strip of ground on a landing field for the landing and takeoff of aircraft

ru·pee *n* : any of various coins (as of India or Pakistan)

¹rup·ture *n* **1** : a break in peaceful or friendly relations **2** : a breaking or tearing apart (as of body tissue) **3** : a condition in which a body part (as a loop of intestine) bulges through the weakened wall of the cavity that contains it

²rupture *vb* **rup·tured; rup·tur·ing** **1** : to part by violence : BREAK **2** : to produce a rupture in **3** : to have a rupture

ru·ral *adj* : of or relating to the country, country people or life, or agriculture

rural free delivery *n* : the free delivery of mail on routes in country districts

ruse *n* : ¹TRICK 4, ARTIFICE

¹rush *n* : a grasslike marsh plant with hollow stems used in chair seats and mats

²rush *vb* **1** : to move forward or act with great haste or eagerness **2** : to perform in a short time or at high speed **3** : ¹ATTACK 1, CHARGE — **rush·er** *n*

³rush *n* **1** : a violent forward motion **2** : a burst of activity or speed **3** : an eager migration of people usually to a new place in search of wealth

⁴rush *adj* : demanding special speed

¹Rus·sian *adj* : of or relating to Russia, its people, or the Russian language

²Russian *n* **1** : a person born or living in Russia **2** : a language of the Russians

¹rust *n* **1** : a reddish coating formed on metal (as iron) when it is exposed especially to moist air **2** : a plant disease caused by fungi that makes spots on plants **3** : a fungus that causes a rust — **rust·like** *adj*

²rust *vb* : to make or become rusty

¹rus·tic *adj* **1** : of, relating to, or suitable for the country **2** : ¹PLAIN 5, SIMPLE

²rustic *n* : a person living or raised in the country

¹rus·tle *vb* **rus·tled; rus·tling** **1** : to make or cause to make a rustle **2** : to steal (as cattle) from the range — **rus·tler** *n*

²**rustle** *n* : a quick series of small sounds

rusty *adj* **rust·i·er; rust·i·est** **1** : affected by rust **2** : less skilled and slow through lack of practice or old age — **rust·i·ness** *n*

¹**rut** *n* **1** : a track worn by a wheel or by habitual passage **2** : ¹ROUTINE

²**rut** *vb* **rut·ted; rut·ting** : to make a rut in

ru·ta·ba·ga *n* : a turnip with a large yellow root

ruth·less *adj* : having no pity : CRUEL — **ruth·less·ly** *adv* — **ruth·less·ness** *n*

-ry *n suffix, pl* **-ries** : -ERY

rye *n* : a hardy cereal grass grown especially for its edible seeds that are used in flour and animal feeds and in making whiskey

S

s *n, pl* **s's** *or* **ss** *often cap* **1** : the nineteenth letter of the English alphabet **2** : a grade rating a student's work as satisfactory

¹**-s** *n pl suffix* — used to form the plural of most nouns that do not end in *s, z, sh, ch,* or *y* following a consonant and with or without an apostrophe to form the plural of abbreviations, numbers, letters, and symbols used as nouns

²**-s** *adv suffix* — used to form adverbs showing usual or repeated action or state

³**-s** *vb suffix* — used to form the third person singular present of most verbs that do not end in *s, z, sh, ch,* or *y* following a consonant

-'s *n suffix or pron suffix* — used to form the possessive of singular nouns, of plural nouns not ending in *s,* and of some pronouns

Sab·bath *n* **1** : the seventh day of the week in the Jewish calendar beginning at sundown on Friday and lasting until sundown on Saturday **2** : the first day of the week (as Sunday) kept for rest and worship

sa·ber *or* **sa·bre** *n* : a cavalry sword with a curved blade

saber–toothed tiger *n* : a very large prehistoric cat with long sharp curved eyeteeth

Sa·bin vaccine *n* : a material that is taken by mouth to prevent polio

sa·ble *n* **1** : the color black **2** : a meat-eating animal of northern Europe and Asia that is related to the marten and prized for its soft rich brown fur

¹**sab·o·tage** *n* : deliberate destruction of or damage to property or machinery (as by enemy agents) to block production or a nation's war effort

²**sabotage** *vb* **sab·o·taged; sab·o·tag·ing** : to damage or block by sabotage

sac *n* : a baglike part of a plant or animal often containing a liquid — **sac·like** *adj*

sa·chem *n* : a North American Indian chief

¹**sack** *n* **1** : ¹BAG 1 **2** : a sack and its contents

²**sack** *vb* : to put into a sack

³**sack** *vb* : to loot after capture

⁴**sack** *n* : the looting of a city by its conquerors

sack·ing *n* : a strong rough cloth (as burlap) from which sacks are made

sac·ra·ment *n* : a religious act or ceremony that is considered especially sacred

sa·cred *adj* **1** : HOLY 1 **2** : RELIGIOUS 2 **3** : deserving to be respected and honored — **sa·cred·ness** *n*

¹**sac·ri·fice** *n* **1** : the act or ceremony of making an offering to God or a god especially on an altar **2** : something offered as a religious act **3** : an unselfish giving **4** : a loss of profit

²**sacrifice** *vb* **sac·ri·ficed; sac·ri·fic·ing** **1** : to offer or kill as a sacrifice **2** : to give for the sake of something else **3** : to sell at a loss

sad *adj* **sad·der; sad·dest** **1** : filled with sorrow or unhappiness **2** : causing or showing sorrow or gloom — **sad·ly** *adv* — **sad·ness** *n*

sad·den *vb* : to make or become sad

¹**sad·dle** *n* **1** : a seat (as for a rider on horseback) that is padded and usually covered with leather **2** : something like a saddle in shape, position, or use

²**saddle** *vb* **sad·dled; sad·dling** **1** : to put a saddle on **2** : to put a load on : BURDEN

saddle horse *n* : a horse suited for or trained for riding

sa·fa·ri *n* : a hunting trip especially in Africa

¹**safe** *adj* **saf·er; saf·est** **1** : free or secure from harm or danger **2** : successful in reaching base in baseball **3** : giving protection or security against danger **4** : HARMLESS **5** : unlikely to be wrong : SOUND **6** : not likely to take risks : CAREFUL — **safe·ly** *adv* — **safe·ness** *n*

²**safe** *n* : a metal chest for keeping something (as money) safe

¹**safe·guard** *n* : something that protects and gives safety

²**safeguard** *vb* : to keep safe

safe·keep·ing *n* : the act of keeping safe : protection from danger or loss

safe·ty *n* : freedom from danger : SECURITY

safety belt *n* : a belt for holding a person to something (as a car seat)

safety pin *n* : a pin that is bent back on itself

to form a spring and has a guard that covers the point

saf·fron *n* **1** : an orange powder used especially to color or flavor foods that consists of the dried stigmas of a crocus with purple flowers **2** : an orange to orange yellow

¹**sag** *vb* **sagged; sag·ging 1** : to sink, settle, or hang below the natural or right level **2** : to become less firm or strong

²**sag** *n* : a sagging part or area

sa·ga *n* : a story of heroic deeds

sa·ga·cious *adj* : quick and wise in understanding and judging — **sa·ga·cious·ly** *adv* — **sa·ga·cious·ness** *n*

¹**sage** *adj* : ²WISE 1 — **sage·ly** *adv*

²**sage** *n* : a very wise person

³**sage** *n* **1** : a mint that grows as a low shrub and has grayish green leaves used to flavor foods **2** : a mint grown for its showy usually scarlet flowers **3** : SAGEBRUSH

sage·brush *n* : a western American plant related to the daisies that grows as a low shrub and has a bitter juice and sharp smell

Sag·it·tar·i·us *n* **1** : a constellation between Scorpio and Capricorn imagined as a centaur **2** : the ninth sign of the zodiac or a person born under this sign

sa·gua·ro *n, pl* **sa·gua·ros** : a giant cactus of the southwestern United States

said *past of* SAY

¹**sail** *n* **1** : a sheet of fabric (as canvas) used to catch enough wind to move boats through the water or over ice **2** : the sails of a ship considered as a group **3** : a trip in a sailing vessel

²**sail** *vb* **1** : to travel on a boat moved by the wind **2** : to travel by water **3** : to move or pass over by ship **4** : to manage or direct the motion of (a boat or ship moved by the wind) **5** : to move or glide along

sail·boat *n* : a boat equipped with sails

sail·fish *n* : a fish related to the swordfish but with a large sail-like fin on its back

sail·or *n* : a person who sails

saint *n* **1** : a good and holy person and especially one who is declared to be worthy of special honor **2** : a person who is very good especially about helping others

Saint Ber·nard *n* : a very large powerful dog bred originally in the Swiss Alps

saint·ly *adj* : like a saint or like that of a saint — **saint·li·ness** *n*

sake *n* **1** : ¹PURPOSE **2** : WELFARE 1, BENEFIT

sal·able *or* **sale·able** *adj* : good enough to sell : likely to be bought

sal·ad *n* **1** : a dish of raw usually mixed vegetables served with a dressing **2** : a cold dish of meat, shellfish, fruit, or vegetables served with a dressing

sal·a·man·der *n* : any of a group of animals that are related to the frogs but look like lizards

sa·la·mi *n* : a highly seasoned sausage of pork and beef

sal·a·ry *n, pl* **sal·a·ries** : a fixed amount of money paid at regular times for work done

sale *n* **1** : an exchange of goods or property for money **2** : the state of being available for purchase **3** : ¹AUCTION **4** : a selling of goods at lowered prices

sales·clerk *n* : a person who sells in a store

sales·man *n, pl* **sales·men** : a person who sells either in a territory or in a store

sales·per·son *n* : one who sells especially in a store

sales tax *n* : a tax paid by the buyer on goods bought

sales·wom·an *n, pl* **sales·wom·en** : a woman who sells either in a territory or in a store

sa·li·va *n* : a watery fluid that contains enzymes which break down starch and is secreted into the mouth from glands in the neck

sal·i·vary *adj* : of, relating to, or producing saliva

Salk vaccine *n* : a material given by injection to prevent polio

sal·low *adj* : of a grayish greenish yellow color

¹**sal·ly** *n, pl* **sallies 1** : a rushing out to attack especially by besieged soldiers **2** : a funny remark

²**sally** *vb* **sal·lied; sal·ly·ing** : to rush out

salm·on *n* **1** : a large fish (**Atlantic salmon**) of the northern Atlantic Ocean valued for food and sport **2** : any of several fishes (**Pacific salmon**) of the northern Pacific Ocean valued for food and sport

sa·loon *n* **1** : a large public hall (as on a passenger ship) **2** : a place where liquors are sold and drunk : BAR

sal·sa *n* **1** : a spicy sauce of tomatoes, onions, and hot peppers **2** : popular music of Latin American origin with characteristics of jazz and rock

¹**salt** *n* **1** : a colorless or white substance that consists of sodium and chlorine and is used in seasoning foods, preserving meats and fish, and in making soap and glass **2** : a compound formed by replacement of hydrogen in an acid by a metal or group of elements that act like a metal

²**salt** *vb* : to add salt to

³**salt** *adj* : containing salt : SALTY

salt·wa·ter *adj* : of, relating to, or living in salt water

salty *adj* **salt·i·er; salt·i·est** : of, tasting of, or containing salt

sal·u·ta·tion n 1 : an act or action of greeting 2 : a word or phrase used as a greeting at the beginning of a letter

¹**sa·lute** vb **sa·lut·ed; sa·lut·ing** 1 : to address with expressions of kind wishes, courtesy, or honor 2 : to honor by a standard military ceremony 3 : to give a sign of respect to (as a military officer) especially by a smart movement of the right hand to the forehead

²**salute** n 1 : GREETING 1, SALUTATION 2 : a military show of respect or honor 3 : the position taken or the movement made to salute a military officer

¹**sal·vage** n 1 : money paid for saving a wrecked or endangered ship or its cargo or passengers 2 : the act of saving a ship 3 : the saving of possessions in danger of being lost 4 : something that is saved (as from a wreck)

²**salvage** vb **sal·vaged; sal·vag·ing** : to recover (something usable) especially from wreckage

sal·va·tion n 1 : the saving of a person from the power and the results of sin 2 : something that saves

¹**salve** n : a healing or soothing ointment

²**salve** vb **salved; salv·ing** : to quiet or soothe with or as if with a salve

¹**same** adj 1 : not another : IDENTICAL 2 : UNCHANGED 3 : very much alike

²**same** pron : something identical with or like another

same·ness n 1 : the quality or state of being the same 2 : MONOTONY

sam·pan n : a Chinese boat with a flat bottom that is usually moved with oars

¹**sam·ple** n : a part or piece that shows the quality of the whole

²**sample** vb **sam·pled; sam·pling** : to judge the quality of by samples : TEST

sam·pler n : a piece of cloth with letters or verses embroidered on it

san·a·to·ri·um n : a place for the care and treatment usually of people recovering from illness or having a disease likely to last a long time

sanc·tion n 1 : approval by someone in charge 2 : an action short of war taken by several nations to make another nation behave

sanc·tu·ary n, pl **sanc·tu·ar·ies** 1 : a holy or sacred place 2 : the most sacred part (as near the altar) of a place of worship 3 : a building for worship 4 : a place of safety 5 : the state of being protected

¹**sand** n 1 : loose material in grains produced by the natural breaking up of rocks 2 : a soil made up mostly of sand

²**sand** vb 1 : to sprinkle with sand 2 : to smooth or clean with sand or sandpaper — **sand·er** n

san·dal n : a shoe that is a sole held in place by straps

san·dal·wood n : the fragrant yellowish heartwood of an Asian tree

sand·bag n : a bag filled with sand and used as a weight (as on a balloon) or as part of a wall or dam

sand·bar n : a ridge of sand formed in water by tides or currents

sand dollar n : a flat round sea urchin

sand·man n, pl **sand·men** : a genie said to make children sleepy by sprinkling sand in their eyes

¹**sand·pa·per** n : paper that has rough material (as sand) glued on one side and is used for smoothing and polishing

²**sandpaper** vb : to rub with sandpaper

sand·pip·er n : a small shorebird related to the plovers

sand·stone n : rock made of sand held together by a natural cement

sand·storm n : a storm of wind (as in a desert) that drives clouds of sand

¹**sand·wich** n : two or more slices of bread or a split roll with a filling (as meat or cheese) between them

²**sandwich** vb : to fit in between things

sandy adj **sand·i·er; sand·i·est** 1 : full of or covered with sand 2 : of a yellowish gray color

sane adj **san·er; san·est** 1 : having a healthy and sound mind 2 : very sensible — **sane·ness** n

sang past of SING

san·i·tar·i·um n : SANATORIUM

san·i·tary adj 1 : of or relating to health or hygiene 2 : free from filth, infection, or other dangers to health

san·i·ta·tion n 1 : the act or process of making sanitary 2 : the act of keeping things sanitary

san·i·ty n : the state of being sane

sank past of SINK

San·ta Claus n : the spirit of Christmas as represented by a jolly old man in a red suit

¹**sap** n : a watery juice that circulates through a higher plant and carries food and nutrients

²**sap** vb **sapped; sap·ping** : to weaken or exhaust little by little

sap·ling n : a young tree

sap·phire n : a clear bright blue precious stone

sap·wood n : young wood found just beneath the bark of a tree and usually lighter in color than the heartwood

sar·casm n : the use of words that normally mean one thing to mean just the opposite usually to hurt someone's feelings or show scorn

sar·cas·tic *adj* **1** : showing or related to sarcasm **2** : having the habit of sarcasm — **sar·cas·ti·cal·ly** *adv*

sar·dine *n* : a young or very small fish often preserved in oil and used for food

sa·ri *n* : a piece of clothing worn mainly by women of India that is a long light cloth wrapped around the body

sar·sa·pa·ril·la *n* : the dried root of a tropical American plant used especially as a flavoring

¹sash *n* : a broad band of cloth worn around the waist or over the shoulder

²sash *n* **1** : a frame for a pane of glass in a door or window **2** : the movable part of a window

¹sass *n* : a rude fresh reply

²sass *vb* : to reply to in a rude fresh way

sas·sa·fras *n* : a tall tree of eastern North America whose dried root bark was formerly used in medicine or as a flavoring

sassy *adj* **sass·i·er; sass·i·est** : given to or made up of sass

sat *past of* SIT

Sa·tan *n* : ¹DEVIL 1

satch·el *n* : a small bag for carrying clothes or books

sat·el·lite *n* **1** : a smaller body that revolves around a planet **2** : a vehicle sent out from the earth to revolve around the earth, moon, sun, or a planet **3** : a country controlled by another more powerful country

sat·in *n* : a cloth (as of silk) with a shiny surface

sat·ire *n* : writing or cartoons meant to make fun of and often show the weaknesses of someone or something

sa·tir·i·cal *adj* : of, relating to, or showing satire

sat·is·fac·tion *n* **1** : the act of satisfying : the condition of being satisfied **2** : something that satisfies

sat·is·fac·to·ry *adj* : causing satisfaction — **sat·is·fac·to·ri·ly** *adv* — **sat·is·fac·to·ri·ness** *n*

sat·is·fy *vb* **sat·is·fied; sat·is·fy·ing** **1** : to carry out the terms of (as a contract) **2** : to make contented **3** : to meet the needs of **4** : CONVINCE

sat·u·rate *vb* **sat·u·rat·ed; sat·u·rat·ing** : to soak full or fill to the limit

Sat·ur·day *n* : the seventh day of the week

Sat·urn *n* : the planet that is sixth in distance from the sun and has a diameter of about 115,000 kilometers

sa·tyr *n* : a forest god of the ancient Greeks believed to have the ears and the tail of a horse or goat

sauce *n* **1** : a tasty liquid poured over food **2** : stewed fruit

sauce·pan *n* : a small deep cooking pan with a handle

sau·cer *n* : a small shallow dish often with a slightly lower center for holding a cup

saucy *adj* **sauc·i·er; sauc·i·est** **1** : being rude usually in a lively and playful way **2** : ²TRIM — **sauc·i·ly** *adv* — **sauc·i·ness** *n*

sau·er·kraut *n* : finely cut cabbage soaked in a salty mixture

saun·ter *vb* : to walk in a slow relaxed way : STROLL

sau·ro·pod *n* : any of a group of plant-eating dinosaurs (as a brontosaurus)

sau·sage *n* **1** : spicy ground meat (as pork) usually stuffed in casings **2** : a roll of sausage in a casing

¹sav·age *adj* **1** : not tamed : WILD **2** : being cruel and brutal : FIERCE — **sav·age·ly** *adv* — **sav·age·ness** *n*

²savage *n* **1** : a person belonging to a group with a low level of civilization **2** : a cruel person

sav·age·ry *n, pl* **sav·age·ries** **1** : an uncivilized condition **2** : savage behavior

¹save *vb* **saved; sav·ing** **1** : to free from danger **2** : to keep from being ruined : PRESERVE **3** : to put aside for later use **4** : to keep from being spent, wasted, or lost **5** : to make unnecessary

²save *prep* : ¹EXCEPT

sav·ing *n* **1** : the act of rescuing **2** : something saved **3** **savings** *pl* : money put aside (as in a bank)

sav·ior *or* **sav·iour** *n* **1** : a person who saves from ruin or danger **2** *cap* : JESUS

sa·vo·ry *adj* : pleasing to the taste or smell

¹saw *past of* SEE

²saw *n* **1** : a tool with a tooth-edged blade for cutting hard material **2** : a machine that operates a toothed blade

³saw *vb* **sawed; sawed** *or* **sawn; saw·ing** : to cut or shape with a saw

⁴saw *n* : a common saying : PROVERB

saw·dust *n* : tiny bits (as of wood) which fall from something being sawed

saw·horse *n* : a frame or rack on which wood is rested while being sawed

saw·mill *n* : a mill or factory having machinery for sawing logs

saw–toothed *adj* : having an edge or outline like the teeth of a saw

sax·o·phone *n* : a musical wind instrument with a reed mouthpiece and a bent tubelike metal body with keys

¹say *vb* **said; say·ing** **1** : to express in words **2** : to give as one's opinion or decision : DECLARE **3** : ¹REPEAT 2, RECITE

²**say** *n* **1** : an expression of opinion **2** : the power to decide or help decide

say·ing *n* : PROVERB

scab *n* **1** : a crust that forms over and protects a sore or wound **2** : a plant disease in which crusted spots form on stems or leaves

scab·bard *n* : a protective case or sheath for the blade of a sword or dagger

scab·by *adj* **scab·bi·er; scab·bi·est 1** : having scabs **2** : diseased with scab

sca·bies *n, pl* **scabies** : an itch or mange caused by mites living as parasites in the skin

scaf·fold *n* **1** : a raised platform built as a support for workers and their tools and materials **2** : a platform on which a criminal is executed

¹**scald** *vb* **1** : to burn with or as if with hot liquid or steam **2** : to pour very hot water over **3** : to bring to a heat just below the boiling point

²**scald** *n* : an injury caused by scalding

¹**scale** *n* **1** : either pan of a balance or the balance itself **2** : an instrument or machine for weighing

²**scale** *vb* **scaled; scal·ing 1** : to weigh on scales **2** : to have a weight of

³**scale** *n* **1** : one of the small stiff plates that cover much of the body of some animals (as fish and snakes) **2** : a thin layer or part (as a special leaf that protects a plant bud) suggesting a fish scale — **scaled** *adj* — **scale·less** *adj* — **scale·like** *adj*

⁴**scale** *vb* **scaled; scal·ing 1** : to remove the scales of **2** : ²FLAKE

⁵**scale** *vb* **scaled; scal·ing 1** : to climb by or as if by a ladder **2** : to regulate or set according to a standard — often used with *down* or *up*

⁶**scale** *n* **1** : a series of tones going up or down in pitch in fixed steps **2** : a series of spaces marked off by lines and used for measuring distances or amounts **3** : a number of like things arranged in order from the highest to the lowest **4** : the size of a picture, plan, or model of a thing compared to the size of the thing itself **5** : a standard for measuring or judging

scale insect *n* : any of a group of insects that are related to the plant lice, suck the juices of plants, and have winged males and wingless females which look like scales attached to the plant

¹**scal·lop** *n* **1** : an edible shellfish that is a mollusk with a ribbed shell in two parts **2** : any of a series of rounded half-circles that form a border on an edge (as of lace)

²**scallop** *vb* **1** : to bake with crumbs, butter, and milk **2** : to embroider, cut, or edge with scallops

¹**scalp** *n* : the part of the skin and flesh of the head usually covered with hair

²**scalp** *vb* : to remove the scalp from

scaly *adj* **scal·i·er; scal·i·est** : covered with or like scales

scamp *n* : RASCAL

¹**scam·per** *vb* : to run or move lightly

²**scamper** *n* : a playful scampering or scurrying

scan *vb* **scanned; scan·ning 1** : to read or mark verses so as to show stress and rhythm **2** : to examine or look over **3** : to examine with a sensing device (as a scanner) especially to obtain information

scan·dal *n* **1** : something that causes a general feeling of shame : DISGRACE **2** : talk that injures a person's good name

scan·dal·ous *adj* **1** : being or containing scandal **2** : very bad or objectionable

Scan·di·na·vian *n* : a person born or living in Scandinavia

scan·ner *n* : a device that converts a printed image (as text or a photograph) into a form a computer can use (as for displaying on the screen)

¹**scant** *adj* **1** : barely enough **2** : not quite full **3** : having only a small supply

²**scant** *vb* : to give or use less than needed : be stingy with

scanty *adj* **scant·i·er; scant·i·est** : barely enough

¹**scar** *n* **1** : a mark left after injured tissue has healed **2** : an ugly mark (as on furniture) **3** : the lasting effect of some unhappy experience

²**scar** *vb* **scarred; scar·ring** : to mark or become marked with a scar

scar·ab *n* : a large dark beetle used in ancient Egypt as a symbol of eternal life

scarce *adj* **scarc·er; scarc·est 1** : not plentiful **2** : hard to find : RARE — **scarce·ness** *n*

scarce·ly *adv* **1** : only just **2** : certainly not

scar·ci·ty *n, pl* **scar·ci·ties** : the condition of being scarce

¹**scare** *vb* **scared; scar·ing** : to be or become frightened suddenly

²**scare** *n* **1** : a sudden fright **2** : a widespread state of alarm

scare·crow *n* : a crude human figure set up to scare away birds and animals from crops

scarf *n, pl* **scarves** *or* **scarfs 1** : a piece of cloth worn loosely around the neck or on the head **2** : a long narrow strip of cloth used as a cover (as on a bureau)

scar·la·ti·na *n* : a mild scarlet fever

¹**scar·let** *n* : a bright red

²**scarlet** *adj* : of the color scarlet

scarlet fever *n* : a contagious disease in

which there is a sore throat, a high fever, and a rash

scary *adj* **scar·i·er; scar·i·est** : causing fright

scat *vb* **scat·ted; scat·ting** : to go away quickly

scat·ter *vb* **1** : to toss, sow, or place here and there **2** : to separate and go in different ways

scat·ter·brain *n* : a flighty thoughtless person — **scat·ter·brained** *adj*

scav·en·ger *n* **1** : a person who picks over junk or garbage for useful items **2** : an animal that lives on decayed material

scene *n* **1** : a division of an act in a play **2** : a single interesting or important happening in a play or story **3** : the place and time of the action in a play or story **4** : the painted screens and slides used as backgrounds on the stage : SCENERY **5** : something that attracts or holds one's gaze : VIEW **6** : a display of anger or misconduct

scen·ery *n* **1** : the painted scenes used on a stage and the furnishings that go with them **2** : outdoor scenes or views

sce·nic *adj* **1** : of or relating to stage scenery **2** : giving views of natural scenery

¹scent *n* **1** : an odor left by some animal or person no longer in a place or given off (as by flowers) at a distance **2** : a usual or particular and often agreeable odor **3** : power or sense of smell **4** : a course followed by someone in search or pursuit of something **5** : ¹PERFUME 2

²scent *vb* **1** : to become aware of or follow through the sense of smell **2** : to get a hint of **3** : to fill with an odor : PERFUME

scep·ter *or* **scep·tre** *n* : a rod carried by a ruler as a sign of authority

¹sched·ule *n* **1** : a written or printed list **2** : a list of the times set for certain events : TIMETABLE **3** : AGENDA, PROGRAM

²schedule *vb* **sched·uled; sched·ul·ing** : to form into or add to a schedule

¹scheme *n* **1** : a plan or program of something to be done : PROJECT **2** : a secret plan : PLOT **3** : an organized design

²scheme *vb* **schemed; schem·ing** : to form a scheme — **schem·er** *n*

Schick test *n* : a test to find out whether a person might easily catch diphtheria

schol·ar *n* **1** : a student in a school : PUPIL **2** : a person who knows a great deal about one or more subjects

schol·ar·ly *adj* : like that of or suitable to learned persons

schol·ar·ship *n* **1** : the qualities of a scholar : LEARNING **2** : money given a student to help pay for further education

scho·las·tic *adj* : of or relating to schools, pupils, or education

¹school *n* **1** : a place for teaching and learning **2** : a session of school **3** : SCHOOLHOUSE **4** : the teachers and pupils of a school **5** : a group of persons who share the same opinions and beliefs

²school *vb* : TEACH 2, TRAIN

³school *n* : a large number of one kind of fish or water animals swimming together

school·bag *n* : a bag for carrying schoolbooks

school·book *n* : a book used in schools

school·boy *n* : a boy who goes to school

school·girl *n* : a girl who goes to school

school·house *n, pl* **school·hous·es** : a building used as a place for teaching and learning

school·ing *n* : EDUCATION 1

school·mas·ter *n* : a man who has charge of a school or teaches in a school

school·mate *n* : a fellow pupil

school·mis·tress *n* : a woman who has charge of a school or teaches in a school

school·room *n* : CLASSROOM

school·teach·er *n* : a person who teaches in a school

school·work *n* : lessons done at school or assigned to be done at home

school·yard *n* : the playground of a school

schoo·ner *n* : a ship usually having two masts with the mainmast located toward the center and the shorter mast toward the front

schwa *n* **1** : an unstressed vowel that is the usual sound of the first and last vowels of the English word *America* **2** : the symbol ə commonly used for a schwa and sometimes also for a similarly pronounced stressed vowel (as in *cut*)

sci·ence *n* **1** : a branch of knowledge in which what is known is presented in an orderly way **2** : a branch of study that is concerned with collecting facts and forming laws to explain them

sci·en·tif·ic *adj* **1** : of or relating to science or scientists **2** : using or applying the methods of science — **sci·en·tif·i·cal·ly** *adv*

sci·en·tist *n* : a person who knows much about science or does scientific work

scis·sors *n sing or pl* : a cutting instrument with two blades fastened together so that the sharp edges slide against each other

scoff *vb* : to show great disrespect with mocking laughter or behavior

¹scold *n* : a person given to criticizing and blaming others

²scold *vb* : to find fault with or criticize in an angry way — **scold·ing** *n*

¹scoop n **1** : a large deep shovel for digging, dipping, or shoveling **2** : a shovellike tool or utensil for digging into a soft substance and lifting out some of it **3** : a motion made with or as if with a scoop **4** : the amount held by a scoop

²scoop vb **1** : to take out or up with or as if with a scoop **2** : to make by scooping

scoot vb : to go suddenly and fast

scoot·er n **1** : a vehicle consisting of a narrow base mounted between a front and a back wheel and guided by a handle attached to the front wheel **2** : MOTOR SCOOTER

scope n **1** : space or opportunity for action or thought **2** : the area or amount covered, reached, or viewed

scorch vb **1** : to burn on the surface **2** : to burn so as to brown or dry out

¹score n **1** : a group of twenty things : TWENTY **2** : a line (as a scratch) made with or as if with something sharp **3** : a record of points made or lost (as in a game) **4** : DEBT 2 **5** : a duty or an injury kept in mind for later action **6** : ¹GROUND 3, REASON **7** : the written or printed form of a musical composition — **score·less** adj

²score vb **scored; scor·ing** **1** : to set down in an account : RECORD **2** : to keep the score in a game **3** : to cut or mark with a line, scratch, or notch **4** : to make or cause to make a point in a game **5** : ACHIEVE 2, WIN **6** : ²GRADE 3, MARK

¹scorn n **1** : an emotion involving both anger and disgust **2** : a person or thing very much disliked

²scorn vb : to show scorn for

scorn·ful adj : feeling or showing scorn — **scorn·ful·ly** adv

Scor·pio n **1** : a constellation between Libra and Sagittarius imagined as a scorpion **2** : the eighth sign of the zodiac or a person born under this sign

scor·pi·on n : an animal related to the spiders that has a long jointed body ending in a slender tail with a poisonous stinger at the end

Scot n : a person born or living in Scotland

¹Scotch adj : ¹SCOTTISH

²Scotch n pl : ²SCOTTISH

scot–free adj : completely free from duty, harm, or punishment

¹Scot·tish adj : of or relating to Scotland or the Scottish

²Scottish n pl : the people of Scotland

scoun·drel n : a mean or wicked person : VILLAIN

¹scour vb **1** : to rub hard with a rough substance in order to clean **2** : to free or clear from impurities by or as if by rubbing

²scour n : an action or result of scouring

³scour vb : to go or move swiftly about, over, or through in search of something

¹scourge n **1** : ²WHIP 1 **2** : a cause of widespread or great suffering

²scourge vb **scourged; scourg·ing** **1** : to whip severely : FLOG **2** : to cause severe suffering to : AFFLICT

¹scout vb **1** : to go about in search of information **2** : to make a search

²scout n **1** : a person, group, boat, or plane that scouts **2** : the act of scouting **3** often cap : BOY SCOUT **4** often cap : GIRL SCOUT

scout·ing n : the act of one that scouts often cap : the general activities of Boy Scout and Girl Scout groups

scout·mas·ter n : the leader of a troop of Boy Scouts

scow n : a large boat with a flat bottom and square ends that is used chiefly for loading and unloading ships and for carrying rubbish

¹scowl vb : ¹FROWN 1

²scowl n : an angry look

scram vb **scrammed; scram·ming** : to go away at once

¹scram·ble vb **scram·bled; scram·bling** **1** : to move or climb quickly on hands and knees **2** : to work hard to win or escape something **3** : to mix together in disorder **4** : to cook the mixed whites and yolks of eggs by stirring them while frying

²scramble n : the act or result of scrambling

¹scrap n **1 scraps** pl : pieces of leftover food **2** : a small bit **3** : waste material (as metal) that can be made fit to use again

²scrap vb **scrapped; scrap·ping** **1** : to break up (as a ship) into scrap **2** : to throw away as worthless

³scrap n : ¹QUARREL 2, FIGHT

scrap·book n : a blank book in which clippings or pictures are kept

¹scrape vb **scraped; scrap·ing** **1** : to remove by repeated strokes of a sharp or rough tool **2** : to clean or smooth by rubbing **3** : to rub or cause to rub so as to make a harsh noise : SCUFF **4** : to hurt or roughen by dragging against a rough surface **5** : to get with difficulty and a little at a time — **scrap·er** n

²scrape n **1** : the act of scraping **2** : a sound, mark, or injury made by scraping **3** : a disagreeable or trying situation

¹scratch vb **1** : to scrape or injure with claws, nails, or an instrument **2** : to make a scraping noise **3** : to erase by scraping

²scratch n : a mark or injury made by scratching

scratchy adj **scratch·i·er; scratch·i·est** : likely to scratch or make sore or raw

¹scrawl *vb* : to write quickly and carelessly
: SCRIBBLE

²scrawl *n* : something written carelessly or
without skill

scraw·ny *adj* **scraw·ni·er; scraw·ni·est**
: poorly nourished : SKINNY

¹scream *vb* : to cry out (as in fright) with a
loud and shrill sound

²scream *n* : a long cry that is loud and shrill

¹screech *n* : a shrill harsh cry usually expressing terror or pain

²screech *vb* : to cry out usually in terror or
pain

¹screen *n* **1** : a curtain or wall used to hide
or to protect **2** : a network of wire set in a
frame for separating finer parts from
coarser parts (as of sand) **3** : a frame that
holds a usually wire netting and is used to
keep out pests (as insects) **4** : the flat surface on which movies are projected **5** : the
surface on which the image appears in an
electronic display (as on a television set or
computer terminal)

²screen *vb* **1** : to hide or protect with or as
if with a screen **2** : to separate or sift with
a screen

screen saver *n* : a computer program that
usually displays images on the screen of a
computer that is on but not in use so as to
prevent damage to the screen

¹screw *n* **1** : a nail-shaped or rod-shaped
piece of metal with a winding ridge around
its length used for fastening and holding
pieces together **2** : the act of screwing tight
: TWIST **3** : PROPELLER

²screw *vb* **1** : to attach or fasten with a
screw **2** : to operate, tighten, or adjust with
a screw **3** : to turn or twist on a thread on
or like that on a screw

screw·driv·er *n* : a tool for turning screws

¹scrib·ble *vb* **scrib·bled; scrib·bling** : to
write quickly or carelessly — **scrib·bler** *n*

²scribble *n* : something scribbled

scribe *n* **1** : a teacher of Jewish law **2** : a
person who copies writing (as in a book)

scrim·mage *n* **1** : a confused struggle **2**
: the action between two football teams
when one attempts to move the ball down
the field

script *n* **1** : the written form of a play or
movie or the lines to be said by a radio or
television performer **2** : a type used in
printing that resembles handwriting **3**
: HANDWRITING

scrip·ture *n* **1** *cap* : BIBLE 1 **2** : writings
sacred to a religious group

¹scroll *n* **1** : a roll of paper or parchment on
which something is written or engraved **2**
: an ornament resembling a length of paper
usually rolled at both ends

²scroll *vb* : to move words or images up or
down a display screen as if by unrolling a
scroll

¹scrub *n* **1** : a thick growth of small or
stunted shrubs or trees **2** : one of poor size
or quality

²scrub *vb* **scrubbed; scrub·bing** : to rub
hard in washing

³scrub *n* : the act or an instance or a period
of scrubbing

scrub·by *adj* **scrub·bi·er; scrub·bi·est 1**
: of poor size or quality **2** : covered with
scrub

scruff *n* : the loose skin on the back of the
neck

scruffy *adj* **scruff·i·er; scruff·i·est** : dirty or
shabby in appearance

scru·ple *n* **1** : a sense of right and wrong
that keeps one from doing as one pleases **2**
: a feeling of guilt when one does wrong
: QUALM

scru·pu·lous *adj* : having or showing very
careful and strict regard for what is right
and proper : CONSCIENTIOUS — **scru·pu-
lous·ly** *adv*

scuff *vb* **1** : to scrape the feet while walking
2 : to become rough or scratched through
wear

¹scuf·fle *vb* **scuf·fled; scuf·fling 1** : to
struggle in a confused way at close quarters
2 : to shuffle one's feet

²scuffle *n* : a rough confused struggle

scull *n* **1** : an oar used at the rear of a boat
to drive it forward **2** : one of a pair of short
oars **3** : a boat driven by one or more pairs
of sculls

sculp·tor *n* : one that sculptures

¹sculp·ture *n* **1** : the action or art of making
statues by carving or chiseling (as in wood
or stone), by modeling (as in clay), or by
casting (as in melted metal) **2** : work produced by sculpture

²sculpture *vb* **sculp·tured; sculp·tur·ing**
: to make sculptures

scum *n* **1** : a film of matter that rises to the
top of a boiling or fermenting liquid **2** : a
coating on the surface of still water

scurf *n* : thin dry scales or a coating of these
(as on a leaf or the skin)

¹scur·ry *vb* **scur·ried; scur·ry·ing** : to move
in a brisk way

²scurry *n, pl* **scur·ries** : the act or an instance of scurrying

¹scur·vy *n* : a disease caused by lack of
vitamin C in which the teeth loosen, the
gums soften, and there is bleeding under the
skin

²scurvy *adj* **scur·vi·er; scur·vi·est** : ¹MEAN
4, CONTEMPTIBLE

¹scut·tle *n* : a pail or bucket for carrying coal

²scuttle n : a small opening with a lid or cover (as in the deck of a ship)

³scuttle vb **scut·tled; scut·tling** : to sink by cutting holes through the bottom or sides

⁴scuttle vb **scut·tled; scut·tling** : to run rapidly from view

scythe n : a tool with a curved blade on a long curved handle that is used to mow grass or grain by hand

sea n **1** : a body of salt water not as large as an ocean and often nearly surrounded by land **2** : OCEAN 1 **3** : rough water **4** : something suggesting a sea's great size or depth

sea anemone n : a hollow sea animal with a flowerlike cluster of tentacles about its mouth

sea·bird n : a bird (as a gull) that lives about the open ocean

sea·coast n : the shore of the sea

sea cucumber n : a sea animal related to the starfishes and sea urchins that has a long flexible muscular body shaped like a cucumber

sea dog n : an experienced sailor

sea·far·er n : a person who travels over the ocean : MARINER

¹sea·far·ing adj : of, given to, or employed in seafaring

²seafaring n : a traveling over the sea as work or as recreation

sea·food n : edible saltwater fish and shellfish

sea·go·ing adj : suitable or used for sea travel

sea gull n : a gull that lives near the sea

sea horse n : a small fish with a head which looks like that of a horse

¹seal n **1** : a sea mammal that swims with flippers, lives mostly in cold regions, mates and bears young on land, eats flesh, and is hunted for fur, hides, or oil **2** : the soft dense fur of a northern seal

²seal n **1** : something (as a pledge) that makes safe or secure **2** : a device with a cut or raised design or figure that can be stamped or pressed into wax or paper **3** : a piece of wax stamped with a design and used to seal a letter or package **4** : a stamp that may be used to close a letter or package **5** : something that closes tightly **6** : a closing that is tight and perfect

³seal vb **1** : to mark with a seal **2** : to close or make fast with or as if with a seal — **seal·er** n

sea level n : the surface of the sea midway between the average high and low tides

sea lion n : a very large seal of the Pacific Ocean

seal·skin n : ¹SEAL 2

¹seam n **1** : the fold, line, or groove made by sewing together or joining two edges or two pieces of material **2** : a layer of a mineral or metal

²seam vb **1** : to join with a seam **2** : to mark with a line, scar, or wrinkle

sea·man n, pl **sea·men** **1** : a person who helps in the handling of a ship at sea : SAILOR **2** : an enlisted person in the Navy or Coast Guard ranking above a seaman apprentice

seaman apprentice n : an enlisted person in the Navy or Coast Guard ranking above a seaman recruit

seaman recruit n : an enlisted person of the lowest rank in the Navy or Coast Guard

seam·stress n : a woman who earns her living by sewing

sea·plane n : an airplane that can rise from and land on water

sea·port n : a port, harbor, or town within reach of seagoing ships

sear vb **1** : to dry by or as if by heat : PARCH **2** : to scorch or make brown on the surface by heat

¹search vb **1** : to go through carefully and thoroughly in an effort to find something **2** : to look in the pockets or the clothing of for something hidden — **search·ing·ly** adv

²search n : an act or instance of searching

search engine n : computer software used to search data (as text or a database) for requested information

search·light n : a lamp for sending a beam of bright light

sea·shell n : the shell of a sea creature

sea·shore n : the shore of a sea

sea·sick adj : sick at the stomach from the pitching or rolling of a ship — **sea·sick·ness** n

sea·side n : SEACOAST

¹sea·son n **1** : one of the four quarters into which a year is commonly divided **2** : a period of time associated with something special

²season vb **1** : to make pleasant to the taste by use of seasoning **2** : to make suitable for use (as by aging or drying)

sea·son·al adj : of, relating to, or coming only at a certain season

sea·son·ing n : something added to food to give it more flavor

¹seat n **1** : something (as a chair) used to sit in or on **2** : the part of something on which one rests in sitting **3** : the place on or at which a person sits **4** : a place that serves as a capital or center — **seat·ed** adj

²seat vb **1** : to place in or on a seat **2** : to provide seats for

seat belt *n* : a strap (as in an automobile or airplane) designed to hold a person in a seat

sea urchin *n* : a rounded shellfish related to the starfishes that lives on or burrows in the sea bottom and is covered with spines

sea·wall *n* : a bank or a wall to prevent sea waves from cutting away the shore

sea·wa·ter *n* : water in or from the sea

sea·weed *n* : an alga (as a kelp) that grows in the sea

se·clud·ed *adj* : hidden from sight

se·clu·sion *n* : the condition of being secluded

¹sec·ond *adj* **1** : being next after the first **2** : next lower in rank, value, or importance than the first

²second *adv* : in the second place or rank

³second *n* : one that is second

⁴second *n* **1** : a sixtieth part of a minute of time or of a degree **2** : MOMENT 1, INSTANT

⁵second *vb* : to support a motion or nomination so that it may be debated or voted on

sec·ond·ary *adj* **1** : second in rank, value, or importance **2** : of, relating to, or being the second of three levels of stress in pronunciation **3** : derived from or coming after something original or primary

sec·ond·hand *adj* **1** : not new : having had a previous owner **2** : selling used goods

second lieutenant *n* : a commissioned officer of the lowest rank in the Army, Air Force, or Marine Corps

sec·ond·ly *adv* : in the second place

sec·ond–rate *adj* : of ordinary quality or value

se·cre·cy *n, pl* **se·cre·cies** **1** : the habit of keeping things secret **2** : the quality or state of being secret or hidden

¹se·cret *adj* **1** : hidden from the knowledge of others **2** : done or working in secrecy — **se·cret·ly** *adv*

²secret *n* : something kept or planned to be kept from others' knowledge

sec·re·tary *n, pl* **sec·re·tar·ies** **1** : a person who is employed to take care of records and letters for another person **2** : an officer of a business corporation or society who has charge of the letters and records and who keeps minutes of meetings **3** : a government official in charge of the affairs of a department **4** : a writing desk with a top section for books

¹se·crete *vb* **se·cret·ed; se·cret·ing** : to produce and give off as a secretion

²secrete *vb* **se·cret·ed; se·cret·ing** : to put in a hiding place

se·cre·tion *n* **1** : the act or process of secreting some substance **2** : a substance formed in and given off by a gland that usu-

ally performs a useful function in the body **3** : a concealing or hiding of something

se·cre·tive *adj* : not open or frank

sect *n* : a group within a religion which has a special set of teachings or a special way of doing things

¹sec·tion *n* **1** : a part cut off or separated **2** : a part of a written work **3** : the appearance that a thing has or would have if cut straight through **4** : a part of a country, group of people, or community

²section *vb* : to cut into sections

sec·tor *n* : a part of an area or of a sphere of activity

sec·u·lar *adj* **1** : not concerned with religion or the church **2** : not bound by a monk's vows : not belonging to a religious order

¹se·cure *adj* **se·cur·er; se·cur·est** **1** : free from danger or risk **2** : strong or firm enough to ensure safety **3** : ¹SURE 5, ASSURED

²secure *vb* **se·cured; se·cur·ing** **1** : to make safe **2** : to fasten tightly **3** : to get hold of : ACQUIRE

se·cu·ri·ty *n, pl* **se·cu·ri·ties** **1** : the state of being secure : SAFETY **2** : something given as a pledge of payment **3** : something (as a stock certificate) that is evidence of debt or ownership

se·dan *n* **1** : SEDAN CHAIR **2** : a closed automobile seating four or more persons that has two or four doors and a permanent top

sedan chair *n* : a portable and often covered chair made to hold one person and to be carried on two poles by two men

se·date *adj* : quiet and steady in manner or conduct — **se·date·ly** *adv* — **se·date·ness** *n*

¹sed·a·tive *adj* : tending to calm or to relieve tension

²sedative *n* : a sedative medicine

sedge *n* : a plant that is like grass but has solid stems and grows in tufts in marshes

sed·i·ment *n* **1** : the material from a liquid that settles to the bottom **2** : material (as stones and sand) carried onto land or into water by water, wind, or a glacier

sed·i·men·ta·ry *adj* : of, relating to, or formed from sediment

se·duce *vb* **se·duced; se·duc·ing** : to persuade to do wrong

¹see *vb* **saw; seen; see·ing** **1** : to have the power of sight : view with the eyes **2** : to have experience of : UNDERGO **3** : to understand the meaning or importance of **4** : to make sure **5** : to attend to **6** : to meet with **7** : ACCOMPANY 1, ESCORT

²see *n* **1** : the city in which a bishop's church is located **2** : DIOCESE

¹seed *n* **1** : a tiny resting plant closed in a protective coat and able to develop under suitable conditions into a plant like the one that produced it **2** : a small structure (as a spore or a tiny dry fruit) other than a true seed by which a plant reproduces itself **3** : the descendants of one individual **4** : a source of development or growth : GERM 2 — **seed·ed** *adj* — **seed·less** *adj*

²seed *vb* **1** : ²SOW 2, PLANT **2** : to produce or shed seeds **3** : to take the seeds out of

seed·case *n* : a dry hollow fruit (as a pod) that contains seeds

seed·ling *n* **1** : a young plant grown from seed **2** : a young tree before it becomes a sapling

seed plant *n* : a plant that reproduces by true seeds

seed·pod *n* : POD

seedy *adj* **seed·i·er; seed·i·est 1** : having or full of seeds **2** : poor in condition or quality

seek *vb* **sought; seek·ing 1** : to try to find **2** : to try to win or get **3** : to make an attempt

seem *vb* **1** : to give the impression of being : APPEAR **2** : to suggest to one's own mind

seem·ing *adj* : APPARENT 3 — **seem·ing·ly** *adv*

seen *past participle of* SEE

seep *vb* : to flow slowly through small openings

seer *n* : a person who predicts events

¹see·saw *n* **1** : an up-and-down or backward-and-forward motion or movement **2** : a children's game of riding on the ends of a plank balanced in the middle with one end going up while the other goes down **3** : the plank used in seesaw

²seesaw *vb* **1** : to ride on a seesaw **2** : to move like a seesaw

seethe *vb* **seethed; seeth·ing 1** : to move without order as if boiling **2** : to be in a state of great excitement

seg·ment *n* **1** : any of the parts into which a thing is divided or naturally separates **2** : a part cut off from a figure (as a circle) by means of a line or plane **3** : a part of a straight line included between two points — **seg·ment·ed** *adj*

seg·re·gate *vb* **seg·re·gat·ed; seg·re·gat·ing** : to set apart from others

seg·re·ga·tion *n* **1** : an act, process, or instance of segregating **2** : enforced separation of a race, class, or group from the rest of society

seize *vb* **seized; seiz·ing 1** : to take possession of by force **2** : to take hold of suddenly or with force

sei·zure *n* : an act of seizing : the state of being seized

sel·dom *adv* : not often : RARELY

¹se·lect *adj* **1** : chosen to include the best or most suitable individuals **2** : of special value or excellence

²select *vb* : to pick out from a number or group : CHOOSE

se·lec·tion *n* **1** : the act or process of selecting **2** : something that is chosen

se·lec·tive *adj* : involving or based on selection

se·le·ni·um *n* : a gray powdery chemical element used chiefly in electronic devices

self *n, pl* **selves 1** : a person regarded as an individual apart from everyone else **2** : a special side of a person's character

self- *prefix* **1** : oneself or itself **2** : of or by oneself or itself **3** : to, with, for, or toward oneself or itself

self–ad·dressed *adj* : addressed for return to the sender

self–cen·tered *adj* : SELFISH

self–con·fi·dence *n* : confidence in oneself and one's abilities

self–con·scious *adj* : too much aware of one's feelings or appearance when in the presence of other people — **self–con·scious·ly** *adv* — **self–con·scious·ness** *n*

self–con·trol *n* : control over one's own impulses, emotions, or actions

self–de·fense *n* : the act of defending oneself or one's property

self–ev·i·dent *adj* : having no need of proof

self–gov·ern·ing *adj* : having self-government

self–gov·ern·ment *n* : government by action of the people making up a community : democratic government

self–im·por·tant *adj* : believing or acting as if one's importance is greater than it really is

self·ish *adj* : taking care of oneself without thought for others — **self·ish·ness** *n*

self·less *adj* : not selfish — **self·less·ly** *adv* — **self·less·ness** *n*

self–pro·pelled *adj* : containing within itself the means for its own movement

self–re·li·ance *n* : trust in one's own efforts and abilities

self–re·spect *n* **1** : a proper regard for oneself as a human being **2** : regard for one's standing or position

self–re·straint *n* : proper control over one's actions or emotions

self–right·eous *adj* : strongly convinced of the rightness of one's actions or beliefs

self·same *adj* : exactly the same

self–serv·ice *n* : the serving of oneself with things to be paid for to a cashier usually upon leaving

sell *vb* **sold; sell·ing** **1** : to betray a person or duty **2** : to exchange in return for money or something else of value **3** : to be sold or priced — **sell·er** *n*

selves *pl of* SELF

sem·a·phore *n* **1** : a device for sending signals that can be seen by the receiver **2** : a system of sending signals with two flags held one in each hand

sem·blance *n* : outward appearance

se·mes·ter *n* : either of two terms that make up a school year

semi- *prefix* **1** : half **2** : partly : not completely **3** : partial

semi·cir·cle *n* : half of a circle

semi·cir·cu·lar *adj* : having the form of a semicircle

semi·co·lon *n* : a punctuation mark ; that can be used to separate parts of a sentence which need clearer separation than would be shown by a comma, to separate main clauses which have no conjunction between, and to separate phrases and clauses containing commas

semi·con·duc·tor *n* : a solid substance whose ability to conduct electricity is between that of a conductor and that of an insulator

¹semi·fi·nal *adj* : coming before the final round in a tournament

²semi·fi·nal *n* : a semifinal match or game

sem·i·nary *n, pl* **sem·i·nar·ies** **1** : a private school at or above the high school level **2** : a school for the training of priests, ministers, or rabbis

semi·sol·id *adj* : having the qualities of both a solid and a liquid

sen·ate *n* **1** : the upper and smaller branch of a legislature in a country or state **2** : a governing body

sen·a·tor *n* : a member of a senate

send *vb* **sent; send·ing** **1** : to cause to go **2** : to set in motion by physical force **3** : to cause to happen **4** : to cause someone to pass a message on or do an errand **5** : to give an order or request to come or go **6** : to bring into a certain condition — **send·er** *n*

¹se·nior *n* **1** : a person older or higher in rank than someone else **2** : a student in the final year of high school or college

²senior *adj* **1** : being older — used to distinguish a father from a son with the same name **2** : higher in rank or office **3** : of or relating to seniors in a high school or college

senior airman *n* : an enlisted person in the Air Force who ranks above airman first class but who has not been made sergeant

senior chief petty officer *n* : a petty officer in the Navy or Coast Guard ranking above a chief petty officer

senior master sergeant *n* : a noncommissioned officer in the Air Force ranking above a master sergeant

sen·sa·tion *n* **1** : awareness (as of noise or heat) or a mental process (as seeing or smelling) resulting from stimulation of a sense organ **2** : an indefinite bodily feeling **3** : a state of excited interest or feeling **4** : a cause or object of excited interest

sen·sa·tion·al *adj* : causing or meant to cause great interest

¹sense *n* **1** : a meaning or one of a set of meanings a word, phrase, or story may have **2** : a specialized function or mechanism (as sight, taste, or touch) of the body that involves the action and effect of a stimulus on a sense organ **3** : a particular sensation or kind of sensation **4** : awareness arrived at through or as if through the senses **5** : an awareness or understanding of something **6** : the ability to make wise decisions **7** : good reason or excuse

²sense *vb* **sensed; sens·ing** : to be or become conscious of

sense·less *adj* **1** : UNCONSCIOUS 2 **2** : STUPID 2 — **sense·less·ly** *adv* — **sense·less·ness** *n*

sense organ *n* : a bodily structure (as the retina of the eye) that reacts to a stimulus (as light) and activates associated nerves so that they carry impulses to the brain

sen·si·bil·i·ty *n, pl* **sen·si·bil·i·ties** **1** : the ability to receive or feel sensations **2** : the emotion or feeling of which a person is capable

sen·si·ble *adj* **1** : possible to take in by the senses or mind **2** : capable of feeling or perceiving **3** : showing or containing good sense or reason — **sen·si·ble·ness** *n* — **sen·si·bly** *adv*

sen·si·tive *adj* **1** : capable of responding to stimulation **2** : easily or strongly affected, impressed, or hurt **3** : readily changed or affected by the action of a certain thing — **sen·si·tive·ly** *adv* — **sen·si·tive·ness** *n*

sen·si·tiv·i·ty *n* : the quality or state of being sensitive

sen·so·ry *adj* : of or relating to sensation or the senses

sen·su·al *adj* : relating to the pleasing of the senses

sent *past of* SEND

¹sen·tence *n* **1** : JUDGMENT 1 **2** : punishment set by a court **3** : a group of words that makes a statement, asks a question, or expresses a command, wish, or exclamation **4** : a mathematical statement (as an equation) in words or symbols

²**sen·tence** *vb* **sen·tenced; sen·tenc·ing** : to give a sentence to

sen·ti·ment *n* **1** : a thought or attitude influenced by feeling **2** : OPINION 1 **3** : tender feelings of affection or yearning

sen·ti·men·tal *adj* **1** : influenced strongly by sentiment **2** : primarily affecting the emotions

sen·ti·nel *n* : SENTRY

sen·try *n, pl* **sentries** : a person (as a soldier) on duty as a guard

se·pal *n* : one of the specialized leaves that form the calyx of a flower

¹**sep·a·rate** *vb* **sep·a·rat·ed; sep·a·rat·ing** **1** : to set or keep apart **2** : to make a distinction between **3** : to cease to be together : PART

²**sep·a·rate** *adj* **1** : set or kept apart **2** : divided from each other **3** : not shared : INDIVIDUAL **4** : having independent existence

sep·a·rate·ly *adv* : apart from others

sep·a·ra·tion *n* **1** : the act of separating : the state of being separated **2** : a point or line at which something is divided

sep·a·ra·tor *n* : a machine for separating cream from milk

Sep·tem·ber *n* : the ninth month of the year

sep·tet *n* : a group or set of seven

sep·ul·cher *or* **sep·ul·chre** *n* : ¹GRAVE, TOMB

se·quel *n* **1** : an event that follows or comes afterward : RESULT **2** : a book that continues a story begun in another

se·quence *n* **1** : the condition or fact of following or coming after something else **2** : ²RESULT 1, SEQUEL **3** : the order in which things are or should be connected, related, or dated

se·quin *n* : a bit of shiny metal or plastic used as an ornament usually on clothing

se·quoia *n* **1** : a California tree that grows almost 100 meters tall and has needles as leaves and small egg-shaped cones **2** : REDWOOD

se·ra·pe *n* : a colorful woolen shawl or blanket

ser·e·nade *n* : music sung or played at night under the window of a lady

se·rene *adj* **1** : ¹CLEAR 2 **2** : being calm and quiet — **se·rene·ly** *adv* — **se·rene·ness** *n*

se·ren·i·ty *n* : the quality or state of being serene

serf *n* : a servant or laborer of olden times who was treated as part of the land worked on and went along with the land if it was sold

serge *n* : a woolen cloth that wears well

ser·geant *n* **1** : a noncommissioned officer in the Army or Marine Corps ranking above a corporal or in the Air Force ranking above an airman first class **2** : an officer in a police force

sergeant first class *n* : a noncommissioned officer in the Army ranking above a staff sergeant

sergeant major *n* **1** : the chief noncommissioned officer at a military headquarters **2** : a noncommissioned officer in the Marine Corps ranking above a first sergeant **3** : a staff sergeant major or command sergeant major in the Army

¹**se·ri·al** *adj* : arranged in or appearing in parts or numbers that follow a regular order — **se·ri·al·ly** *adv*

²**serial** *n* : a story appearing (as in a magazine or on television) in parts at regular intervals

se·ries *n, pl* **series** : a number of things or events arranged in order and connected by being alike in some way

se·ri·ous *adj* **1** : thoughtful or quiet in appearance or manner **2** : requiring much thought or work **3** : being in earnest : not light or casual **4** : IMPORTANT 1 **5** : being such as to cause distress or harm — **se·ri·ous·ly** *adv* — **se·ri·ous·ness** *n*

ser·mon *n* **1** : a speech usually by a priest, minister, or rabbi for the purpose of giving religious instruction **2** : a serious talk to a person about his or her conduct

ser·pent *n* : a usually large snake

se·rum *n* : the liquid part that can be separated from coagulated blood, contains antibodies, and is sometimes used to prevent or cure disease

ser·vant *n* : a person hired to perform household or personal services

¹**serve** *vb* **served; serv·ing** **1** : to be a servant **2** : to give the service and respect due **3** : ²WORSHIP 1 **4** : to put in : SPEND **5** : to be of use : answer some purpose **6** : to provide helpful services **7** : to be enough for **8** : to hold an office : perform a duty **9** : to help persons to food or set out helpings of food or drink **10** : to furnish with something needed or desired **11** : to make a serve (as in tennis)

²**serve** *n* : an act of putting the ball or shuttlecock in play (as in tennis or badminton)

¹**ser·vice** *n* **1** : the occupation or function of serving or working as a servant **2** : the work or action of one that serves **3** : ²HELP 1, USE **4** : a religious ceremony **5** : a helpful or useful act : good turn **6** : ²SERVE **7** : a set of dishes or silverware **8** : a branch of public employment or the people working in it **9** : a nation's armed forces **10** : an organization for supplying some public

demand or keeping up and repairing something

²**service** vb **ser·viced; ser·vic·ing** : to work at taking care of or repairing

ser·vice·able adj 1 : fit for or suited to some use 2 : lasting or wearing well in use — **ser·vice·able·ness** n

ser·vice·man n, pl **ser·vice·men** : a male member of the armed forces

service station n : a place for servicing motor vehicles especially with gasoline and oil

ser·vile adj 1 : of or suitable to a slave 2 : lacking spirit or independence

serv·ing n : a helping of food

ser·vi·tude n : the condition of a slave

ses·sion n 1 : a single meeting (as of a court, lawmaking body, or school) 2 : a whole series of meetings 3 : the time during which a court, congress, or school meets

¹**set** vb **set; set·ting** 1 : to cause to sit 2 : to cover and warm eggs to hatch them 3 : to put or fix in a place or condition 4 : to arrange in a desired and especially a normal position 5 : ¹START 5 6 : to cause to be, become, or do 7 : to fix at a certain amount : SETTLE 8 : to furnish as a model 9 : to put in order for immediate use 10 : to provide (as words or verses) with music 11 : to fix firmly 12 : to become or cause to become firm or solid 13 : to form and bring to maturity 14 : to pass below the horizon : go down — **set about** : to begin to do — **set forth** : to start out

²**set** n 1 : the act or action of setting : the condition of being set 2 : a number of persons or things of the same kind that belong or are used together 3 : the form or movement of the body or its parts 4 : an artificial setting for a scene of a play or motion picture 5 : a group of tennis games that make up a match 6 : a collection of mathematical elements 7 : an electronic apparatus

³**set** adj 1 : fixed by authority 2 : not very willing to change 3 : ¹READY 1

set·back n : a slowing of progress : a temporary defeat

set down vb 1 : to place at rest on a surface 2 : to land an aircraft

set in vb : to make its appearance : BEGIN

set off vb 1 : to cause to stand out 2 : to set apart 3 : to cause to start 4 : EXPLODE 1 5 : to start a journey

set on vb : to urge to attack or chase

set out vb 1 : UNDERTAKE 1 2 : to begin on a course or journey

set·tee n : a long seat with a back

set·ter n 1 : one that sets 2 : a large dog that has long hair and is used in hunting birds

set·ting n 1 : the act of one that sets 2 : that in which something is set or mounted 3 : the background (as time and place) of the action of a story or play 4 : a batch of eggs for hatching

¹**set·tle** vb **set·tled; set·tling** 1 : to place so as to stay 2 : to come to rest 3 : to sink gradually to a lower level 4 : to sink in a liquid 5 : to make one's home 6 : to apply oneself 7 : to fix by agreement 8 : to put in order 9 : to make quiet : CALM 10 : DECIDE 1 11 : to complete payment on 12 : ADJUST 1

²**settle** n : a long wooden bench with arms and a high solid back

set·tle·ment n 1 : the act of settling : the condition of being settled 2 : final payment (as of a bill) 3 : the act or fact of establishing colonies 4 : a place or region newly settled 5 : a small village 6 : an institution that gives help to people in a crowded part of a city

set·tler n : a person who settles in a new region : COLONIST

set up vb 1 : to place or secure in position 2 : to put in operation : FOUND, ESTABLISH

¹**sev·en** adj : being one more than six

²**seven** n : one more than six : 7

¹**sev·en·teen** adj : being one more than sixteen

²**seventeen** n : one more than sixteen : 17

¹**sev·en·teenth** adj : coming right after sixteenth

²**seventeenth** n : number seventeen in a series

¹**sev·enth** adj : coming right after sixth

²**seventh** n 1 : number seven in a series 2 : one of seven equal parts

¹**sev·en·ti·eth** adj : coming right after sixtyninth

²**seventieth** n : number seventy in a series

¹**sev·en·ty** adj : being seven times ten

²**seventy** n : seven times ten : 70

sev·er vb 1 : to put or keep apart : DIVIDE 2 : to come or break apart

¹**sev·er·al** adj 1 : separate or distinct from others : DIFFERENT 2 : consisting of more than two but not very many

²**several** pron : a small number : more than two but not many

se·vere adj **se·ver·er; se·ver·est** 1 : very strict : HARSH 2 : serious in feeling or manner : GRAVE 3 : not using unnecessary ornament : PLAIN 4 : hard to bear or deal with — **se·vere·ly** adv — **se·vere·ness** n

se·ver·i·ty n : the quality or state of being severe

sew vb **sewed; sewn** or **sewed; sew·ing** 1 : to join or fasten by stitches 2 : to work with needle and thread

sew·age *n* : waste materials carried off by sewers

¹sew·er *n* : one that sews

²sew·er *n* : a usually covered drain to carry off water and waste

sew·er·age *n* **1** : SEWAGE **2** : the removal and disposal of sewage by sewers **3** : a system of sewers

sew·ing *n* **1** : the act, method, or occupation of one that sews **2** : material being sewed or to be sewed

sex *n* **1** : either of two divisions of living things and especially humans, one made up of males, the other of females **2** : the things that make males and females different from each other **3** : sexual activity

sex·ism *n* : distinction and especially unjust distinction based on sex and made against one person or group (as women) in favor of another

sex·ist *adj* : based on or showing sexism — **sexist** *n*

sex·tet *n* : a group or set of six

sex·ton *n* : an official of a church who takes care of church buildings and property

sex·u·al *adj* **1** : of or relating to sex or the sexes **2** : of, relating to, or being the form of reproduction in which germ cells from two parents combine in fertilization to form a new individual — **sex·u·al·ly** *adv*

shab·by *adj* **shab·bi·er; shab·bi·est 1** : dressed in worn clothes **2** : faded and worn from use or wear **3** : not fair or generous — **shab·bi·ly** *adv* — **shab·bi·ness** *n*

shack *n* : HUT, SHANTY

¹shack·le *n* **1** : a ring or band that prevents free use of the legs or arms **2** : something that prevents free action **3** : a U-shaped metal device for joining or fastening something

²shackle *vb* **shack·led; shack·ling 1** : to bind or fasten with a shackle **2** : HINDER

shad *n, pl* **shad** : any of several sea fishes related to the herrings that have deep bodies, swim up rivers to spawn, and are important food fish

¹shade *n* **1** : partial darkness **2** : space sheltered from light or heat and especially from the sun **3 shades** *pl* : the shadows that gather as darkness falls **4** : GHOST, SPIRIT **5** : something that blocks off or cuts down light **6** : the darkening of some objects in a painting or drawing to suggest that they are in shade **7** : the darkness or lightness of a color **8** : a very small difference or amount

²shade *vb* **shad·ed; shad·ing 1** : to shelter from light or heat **2** : to mark with shades of light or color **3** : to show or begin to

have slight differences of color, value, or meaning

¹shad·ow *n* **1** : ¹SHADE 1 **2** : a reflected image **3** : shelter from danger or view **4** : the dark figure cast on a surface by a body that is between the surface and the light **5** : PHANTOM **6 shadows** *pl* : darkness caused by the setting of the sun **7** : a very little bit : TRACE

²shadow *vb* **1** : to cast a shadow upon **2** : to cast gloom over **3** : to follow and watch closely especially in a secret way

shad·owy *adj* **1** : not realistic **2** : full of shadow

shady *adj* **shad·i·er; shad·i·est 1** : sheltered from the sun's rays **2** : not right or honest — **shad·i·ness** *n*

shaft *n* **1** : the long handle of a weapon (as a spear) **2** : one of two poles between which a horse is hitched to pull a wagon or carriage **3** : an arrow or its narrow stem **4** : a narrow beam of light **5** : a long narrow part especially when round **6** : the handle of a tool or instrument **7** : a bar to support rotating pieces of machinery or to give them motion **8** : a tall monument (as a column) **9** : a mine opening made for finding or mining ore **10** : an opening or passage straight down through the floors of a building

shag·gy *adj* **shag·gi·er; shag·gi·est 1** : covered with or made up of a long, coarse, and tangled growth (as of hair or vegetation) **2** : having a rough or hairy surface — **shag·gi·ly** *adv* — **shag·gi·ness** *n*

¹shake *vb* **shook; shak·en; shak·ing 1** : to tremble or make tremble : QUIVER **2** : to make less firm : WEAKEN **3** : to move back and forth or to and fro **4** : to cause to be, become, go, or move by or as if by a shake

²shake *n* : the act or motion of shaking

shak·er *n* : one that shakes or is used in shaking

shaky *adj* **shak·i·er; shak·i·est** : easily shaken : UNSOUND — **shak·i·ly** *adv* — **shak·i·ness** *n*

shale *n* : a rock with a fine grain formed from clay, mud, or silt

shall *helping verb, past* **should**; *present sing & pl* **shall 1** : am or are going to or expecting to : WILL **2** : is or are forced to : MUST

¹shal·low *adj* **1** : not deep **2** : showing little knowledge, thought, or feeling — **shal·low·ness** *n*

²shallow *n* : a shallow place in a body of water — usually used in pl.

¹sham *n* : ³COUNTERFEIT, IMITATION

²sham *adj* : not real : FALSE

³sham *vb* **shammed; sham·ming** : to act in a deceiving way

sham·ble *vb* **sham·bled; sham·bling** : to walk in an awkward unsteady way

sham·bles *n sing or pl* : a place or scene of disorder or destruction

1shame *n* **1** : a painful emotion caused by having done something wrong or improper **2** : ability to feel shame **3** : 1DISHONOR 1, DISGRACE **4** : something that brings disgrace or causes shame or strong regret

2shame *vb* **shamed; sham·ing 1** : to make ashamed **2** : 2DISHONOR **3** : to force by causing to feel shame

shame·faced *adj* : seeming ashamed — **shame·faced·ly** *adv* — **shame·faced·ness** *n*

shame·ful *adj* : bringing shame : DISGRACE-FUL — **shame·ful·ly** *adv* — **shame·ful·ness** *n*

shame·less *adj* : having no shame — **shame·less·ly** *adv* — **shame·less·ness** *n*

1sham·poo *vb* : to wash the hair and scalp

2shampoo *n, pl* **sham·poos 1** : a washing of the hair **2** : a cleaner made for washing the hair

sham·rock *n* : a plant (as some clovers) that has leaves with three leaflets and is used as an emblem by the Irish

shank *n* **1** : the lower part of the human leg : the equivalent part of a lower animal **2** : the part of a tool that connects the working part with a part by which it is held or moved

shan't : shall not

shan·ty *n, pl* **shanties** : a small roughly built shelter or dwelling

1shape *vb* **shaped; shap·ing 1** : to give a certain form or shape to **2** : DEVISE **3** : to make fit especially for some purpose : ADAPT **4** : to take on a definite form or quality : DEVELOP — **shap·er** *n*

2shape *n* **1** : outward appearance : FORM **2** : the outline of a body : FIGURE **3** : definite arrangement and form **4** : 1CONDITION 3 — **shaped** *adj*

shape·less *adj* **1** : having no fixed or regular shape **2** : not shapely — **shape·less·ly** *adv* — **shape·less·ness** *n*

shape·ly *adj* **shape·li·er; shape·li·est** : having a pleasing shape — **shape·li·ness** *n*

1share *n* **1** : a portion belonging to one person **2** : the part given or belonging to one of a number of persons owning something together **3** : any of the equal portions into which a property or corporation is divided

2share *vb* **shared; shar·ing 1** : to divide and distribute in portions **2** : to use, experience, or enjoy with others **3** : to take a part

share·crop *vb* **share·cropped; share·crop·ping** : to farm another's land for a share of the crop or profit — **share·crop·per** *n*

1shark *n* : any of a group of mostly fierce sea fishes that are typically gray, have a skeleton of cartilage, and include some forms that may attack humans

2shark *n* : a sly greedy person who takes advantage of others

1sharp *adj* **1** : having a thin edge or fine point **2** : brisk and cold **3** : QUICK-WITTED, SMART **4** : ATTENTIVE 1 **5** : having very good ability to see or hear **6** : ENERGETIC, BRISK **7** : SEVERE 1, ANGRY **8** : very trying to the feelings : causing distress **9** : strongly affecting the senses **10** : ending in a point or edge **11** : involving an abrupt change **12** : DISTINCT 2 **13** : raised in pitch by a half step **14** : higher than true pitch — **sharp·ly** *adv* — **sharp·ness** *n*

2sharp *adv* **1** : in a sharp manner **2** : at an exact time

3sharp *n* **1** : a note or tone that is a half step higher than the note named **2** : a sign # that tells that a note is to be made higher by a half step

sharp·en *vb* : to make or become sharp or sharper — **sharp·en·er** *n*

shat·ter *vb* **1** : to break or fall to pieces **2** : to damage badly : RUIN, WRECK

1shave *vb* **shaved; shaved** *or* **shav·en; shav·ing 1** : to cut or trim off with a sharp blade **2** : to make bare or smooth by cutting the hair from **3** : to trim closely

2shave *n* **1** : an operation of shaving **2** : a narrow escape

shav·ing *n* : a thin slice or strip sliced off with a cutting tool

shawl *n* : a square or oblong piece of cloth used especially by women as a loose covering for the head and shoulders

she *pron* : that female one

sheaf *n, pl* **sheaves 1** : a bundle of stalks and ears of grain **2** : a group of things fastened together — **sheaf·like** *adj*

shear *vb* **sheared; sheared** *or* **shorn; shear·ing 1** : to cut the hair or wool from : CLIP **2** : to strip of as if by cutting **3** : to cut or break sharply — **shear·er** *n*

shears *n pl* : a cutting tool like a pair of large scissors

sheath *n, pl* **sheaths 1** : a case for a blade (as of a knife) **2** : a covering (as the outer wings of a beetle) suggesting a sheath in form or use

sheathe *vb* **sheathed; sheath·ing 1** : to put into a sheath **2** : to cover with something that protects

sheath·ing *n* : the first covering of boards or of waterproof material on the outside wall of a frame house or on a timber roof

sheaves *pl of* SHEAF

¹shed *vb* **shed; shed·ding** **1** : to give off in drops **2** : to cause (blood) to flow from a cut or wound **3** : to spread abroad **4** : REPEL 3 **5** : to cast (as a natural covering) aside

²shed *n* : a structure built for shelter or storage

she'd : she had : she would

sheen *n* : a bright or shining condition : LUSTER

sheep *n, pl* **sheep** **1** : an animal related to the goat that is raised for meat or for its wool and skin **2** : a weak helpless person who is easily led

sheep·fold *n* : a pen or shelter for sheep

sheep·herd·er *n* : a worker in charge of a flock of sheep

sheep·ish *adj* **1** : like a sheep **2** : embarrassed especially over being found out in a fault — **sheep·ish·ly** *adv* — **sheep·ish·ness** *n*

sheep·skin *n* : the skin of a sheep or leather prepared from it

¹sheer *adj* **1** : very thin or transparent **2** : THOROUGH 1, ABSOLUTE **3** : very steep — **sheer·ly** *adv* — **sheer·ness** *n*

²sheer *adv* **1** : COMPLETELY **2** : straight up or down

¹sheet *n* **1** : a broad piece of cloth (as an article of bedding used next to the body) **2** : a broad piece of paper (as for writing or printing) **3** : a broad surface **4** : something that is very thin as compared with its length and width — **sheet·like** *adj*

²sheet *n* : a rope or chain used to adjust the angle at which the sail of a boat is set to catch the wind

sheikh *or* **sheik** *n* : an Arab chief

shek·el *n* **1** : any of various ancient units of weight (as of the Hebrews) **2** : a coin weighing one shekel

shelf *n, pl* **shelves** **1** : a flat piece (as of board or metal) set above a floor (as on a wall or in a bookcase) to hold things **2** : something (as a sandbar or ledge of rock) that suggests a shelf

¹shell *n* **1** : a stiff hard covering of an animal (as a turtle, oyster, or beetle) **2** : the tough outer covering of an egg **3** : the outer covering of a nut, fruit, or seed especially when hard or tough and fibrous **4** : something like a shell (as in shape, function, or material) **5** : a narrow light racing boat rowed by one or more persons **6** : a metal or paper case holding the explosive charge and the shot or object to be fired from a gun or cannon — **shelled** *adj*

²shell *vb* **1** : to take out of the shell or husk **2** : to remove the kernels of grain from (as a cob of Indian corn) **3** : to shoot shells at or upon

she'll : she shall : she will

¹shel·lac *n* : a varnish made from a material given off by an Asian insect dissolved usually in alcohol

²shellac *vb* **shel·lacked; shel·lack·ing** : to coat with shellac

shell·fish *n, pl* **shellfish** : an invertebrate animal that lives in water and has a shell — used mostly of edible forms (as oysters or crabs)

¹shel·ter *n* **1** : something that covers or protects **2** : the condition of being protected

²shelter *vb* **1** : to be a shelter for : provide with shelter **2** : to find and use a shelter

shelve *vb* **shelved; shelv·ing** **1** : to place or store on shelves **2** : ¹DEFER

shelves *pl of* SHELF

¹shep·herd *n* : a person who takes care of sheep

²shepherd *vb* : to care for as or as if a shepherd

shep·herd·ess *n* : a woman who takes care of sheep

sher·bet *n* : a frozen dessert of fruit juice to which milk, the white of egg, or gelatin is added before freezing

sher·iff *n* : the officer of a county who is in charge of enforcing the law

she's : she is : she has

Shet·land pony *n* : any of a breed of small stocky horses with shaggy coats

¹shield *n* **1** : a broad piece of armor carried on the arm to protect oneself in battle **2** : something that serves as a defense or protection

²shield *vb* : to cover or screen with or as if with a shield

¹shift *vb* **1** : to exchange for another of the same kind **2** : to change or remove from one person or place to another **3** : to change the arrangement of gears transmitting power (as in an automobile) **4** : to get along without help : FEND

²shift *n* **1** : the act of shifting : TRANSFER **2** : a group of workers who work together during a scheduled period of time **3** : the period during which one group of workers is working **4** : GEARSHIFT

shift·less *adj* : lacking in ambition and energy : LAZY — **shift·less·ly** *adv* — **shift·less·ness** *n*

shifty *adj* **shift·i·er; shift·i·est** : not worthy of trust : TRICKY — **shift·i·ly** *adv* — **shift·i·ness** *n*

shil·ling *n* : an old British coin equal to $1/20$ pound

shim·mer *vb* : to shine with a wavering light : GLIMMER

¹**shin** *n* : the front part of the leg below the knee

²**shin** *vb* **shinned; shin·ning** : to climb (as a pole) by grasping with arms and legs and moving oneself upward by repeated jerks

¹**shine** *vb* **shone** *or* **shined; shin·ing 1** : to give light **2** : to be glossy : GLEAM **3** : to be outstanding **4** : to make bright by polishing

²**shine** *n* **1** : brightness from light given off or reflected **2** : fair weather : SUNSHINE **3** : ²POLISH 1

shin·er *n* **1** : a small silvery American freshwater fish related to the carp **2** : an eye discolored by injury : a black eye

¹**shin·gle** *n* **1** : a small thin piece of building material (as wood or an asbestos composition) for laying in overlapping rows as a covering for the roof or sides of a building **2** : a small sign

²**shingle** *vb* **shin·gled; shin·gling** : to cover with shingles

shin·ny *vb* **shin·nied; shin·ny·ing** : ²SHIN

shiny *adj* **shin·i·er; shin·i·est** : bright in appearance

¹**ship** *n* **1** : a large seagoing boat **2** : a ship's crew **3** : AIRSHIP, AIRPLANE **4** : a vehicle for traveling beyond the earth's atmosphere

²**ship** *vb* **shipped; ship·ping 1** : to put or receive on board for transportation by water **2** : to cause to be transported **3** : to take into a ship or boat **4** : to sign on as a crew member on a ship

-ship *n suffix* **1** : state : condition : quality **2** : office : rank : profession **3** : skill **4** : something showing a quality or state of being **5** : one having a specified rank

ship·board *n* **1** : a ship's side **2** : ¹SHIP 1

ship·ment *n* **1** : the act of shipping **2** : the goods shipped

ship·ping *n* **1** : the body of ships in one place or belonging to one port or country **2** : the act or business of a person who ships goods

ship·shape *adj* : being neat and orderly : TIDY

¹**ship·wreck** *n* **1** : a wrecked ship **2** : the loss or destruction of a ship

²**shipwreck** *vb* **1** : to cause to experience shipwreck **2** : to destroy (a ship) by driving ashore or sinking

ship·yard *n* : a place where ships are built or repaired

shirk *vb* **1** : to get out of doing what one ought to do **2** : AVOID

shirt *n* **1** : a garment for the upper part of the body usually with a collar, sleeves, a front opening, and a tail long enough to be tucked inside pants or a skirt **2** : UNDERSHIRT

¹**shiv·er** *vb* : to be made to shake (as by cold or fear) : QUIVER

²**shiver** *n* : an instance of shivering

¹**shoal** *adj* : ¹SHALLOW 1

²**shoal** *n* **1** : a place where a sea, lake, or river is shallow **2** : a bank or bar of sand just below the surface of the water

³**shoal** *n* : ³SCHOOL

¹**shock** *n* **1** : a bunch of sheaves of grain or stalks of corn set on end in the field

²**shock** *n* **1** : the sudden violent collision of bodies in a fight **2** : a violent shake or jerk **3** : a sudden and violent disturbance of mind or feelings **4** : a state of bodily collapse that usually follows severe crushing injuries, burns, or hemorrhage **5** : the effect of a charge of electricity passing through the body of a person or animal

³**shock** *vb* **1** : to strike with surprise, horror, or disgust **2** : to affect by electrical shock **3** : to drive into or out of by or as if by a shock

⁴**shock** *n* : a thick bushy mass (as of hair)

shock·ing *adj* : causing horror or disgust — **shock·ing·ly** *adv*

shod·dy *adj* **shod·di·er; shod·di·est** : poorly done or made — **shod·di·ly** *adv* — **shod·di·ness** *n*

¹**shoe** *n* **1** : an outer covering for the human foot usually having a thick and somewhat stiff sole and heel and a lighter upper part **2** : something (as a horseshoe) like a shoe in appearance or use

²**shoe** *vb* **shod** *also* **shoed; shoe·ing** : to put a shoe on : furnish with shoes

shoe·horn *n* : a curved piece (as of metal) to help in putting on a shoe

shoe·lace *n* : a lace or string for fastening a shoe

shoe·mak·er *n* : a person who makes or repairs shoes

shoe·string *n* : SHOELACE

shone *past of* SHINE

shoo *vb* : to wave, scare, or send away by or as if by crying *shoo*

shook *past of* SHAKE

¹**shoot** *vb* **shot; shoot·ing 1** : to let fly or cause to be driven forward with force **2** : to cause a missile to be driven out of **3** : to cause a weapon to discharge a missile **4** : to force (a marble) forward by snapping the thumb **5** : to hit or throw (as a ball or puck) toward a goal **6** : to score by shooting **7** : ²PLAY 2 **8** : to strike with a missile from a bow or gun **9** : to push or slide into or out of a fastening **10** : to thrust forward swiftly **11** : to grow rapidly **12** : to go,

move, or pass rapidly **13** : to pass swiftly along or through **14** : to stream out suddenly : SPURT — **shoot·er** *n*

²shoot *n* **1** : the part of a plant that grows above ground or as much of this as comes from a single bud **2** : a hunting party or trip

shooting star *n* : a meteor appearing as a temporary streak of light in the night sky

¹shop *n* **1** : a worker's place of business **2** : a building or room where goods are sold at retail : STORE **3** : a place in which workers are doing a particular kind of work

²shop *vb* **shopped; shop·ping** : to visit shops for the purpose of looking over and buying goods — **shop·per** *n*

shop·keep·er *n* : STOREKEEPER 2

shop·lift·er *n* : a person who steals merchandise on display in stores

¹shore *n* : the land along the edge of a body of water (as the sea)

²shore *vb* **shored; shor·ing** : to support with one or more bracing timbers

shore·bird *n* : any of various birds (as the plovers) that frequent the seashore

shore·line *n* : the line where a body of water touches the shore

shorn *past participle of* SHEAR

¹short *adj* **1** : not long or tall **2** : not great in distance **3** : brief in time **4** : cut down to a brief length **5** : not coming up to the regular standard **6** : less in amount than expected or called for **7** : less than : not equal to **8** : not having enough **9** : FLAKY, CRUMBLY **10** : of, relating to, or being one of the vowel sounds \ə, a, e, i, ù\ and sometimes \ä\ and \ò\ — **short·ness** *n*

²short *adv* **1** : with suddenness **2** : so as not to reach as far as expected

³short *n* **1** : something shorter than the usual or regular length **2 shorts** *pl* : pants that reach to or almost to the knees **3 shorts** *pl* : short underpants **4** : SHORT CIRCUIT

short·age *n* : a lack in the amount needed : DEFICIT

short·cake *n* : a dessert made usually of rich biscuit dough baked and served with sweetened fruit

short circuit *n* : an electric connection made between points in an electric circuit between which current does not normally flow

short·com·ing *n* : FAULT 1

short·cut *n* : a shorter, quicker, or easier way

short·en *vb* : to make or become short or shorter

short·en·ing *n* : a fatty substance (as lard) used to make pastry flaky

short·hand *n* : a method of rapid writing by using symbols for sounds or words

short·horn *n* : any of a breed of beef cattle developed in England and including good producers of milk from which a separate dairy breed (**milking shorthorn**) has come

short–lived *adj* : living or lasting only a short time

short·ly *adv* **1** : in a few words : BRIEFLY **2** : in or within a short time : SOON

short–sight·ed *adj* : NEARSIGHTED

short–stop *n* : a baseball infielder whose position is between second and third base

¹shot *n* **1** : the act of shooting **2** *pl* **shot** : a bullet, ball, or pellet for a gun or cannon **3** : something thrown, cast forth, or let fly with force **4** : ²ATTEMPT, TRY **5** : the flight of a missile or the distance it travels : RANGE **6** : a person who shoots **7** : a heavy metal ball thrown for distance in a track-and-field contest (**shot put**) **8** : a stroke or throw at a goal **9** : an injection of something (as medicine) into the body

²shot *past of* SHOOT

shot·gun *n* : a gun with a long barrel used to fire shot at short range

should *past of* SHALL **1** : ought to **2** : happen to **3** — used as a politer or less assured form of *shall*

¹shoul·der *n* **1** : the part of the body of a person or animal where the arm or foreleg joins the body **2** : the part of a garment at the wearer's shoulder **3** : a part that resembles a person's shoulder **4** : the edge of a road

²shoulder *vb* **1** : to push with one's shoulder **2** : to accept as one's burden or duty

shoulder blade *n* : the flat triangular bone in a person's or animal's shoulder

shouldn't : should not

¹shout *vb* : to make a sudden loud cry (as of joy, pain, or sorrow)

²shout *n* : a sudden loud cry

¹shove *vb* **shoved; shov·ing** **1** : to push with steady force **2** : to push along or away carelessly or rudely

²shove *n* : the act or an instance of shoving

¹shov·el *n* **1** : a broad scoop used to lift and throw loose material (as snow) **2** : as much as a shovel will hold

²shovel *vb* **shov·eled** *or* **shov·elled; shov·el·ing** *or* **shov·el·ling** **1** : to lift or throw with a shovel **2** : to dig or clean out with a shovel **3** : to throw or carry roughly or in a mass as if with a shovel

¹show *vb* **showed; shown** *or* **showed; show·ing** **1** : to place in sight : DISPLAY **2** : REVEAL **2** **3** : to give from or as if from a position of authority **4** : TEACH 1, INSTRUCT **5** : PROVE 2 **6** : ¹DIRECT 3, USHER **7** : to be noticeable

²show *n* **1** : a display made for effect **2**

: an appearance meant to deceive : PRE-
TENSE **3** : an appearance or display that is
basically true or real **4** : an entertainment
or exhibition especially by performers (as
on TV or the stage)

show·boat *n* : a river steamboat used as a
traveling theater

show·case *n* : a protective glass case in
which things are displayed

¹show·er *n* **1** : a short fall of rain over a
small area **2** : something like a shower **3**
: a party where gifts are given especially to
a bride or a pregnant woman **4** : a bath in
which water is showered on a person or a
device for providing such a bath

²shower *vb* **1** : to wet with fine spray or
drops **2** : to fall in or as if in a shower **3**
: to provide in great quantity **4** : to bathe in
a shower

show·man *n, pl* **show·men** **1** : the producer of a theatrical show **2** : a person having a special skill for presenting something
in a dramatic way

shown *past participle of* SHOW

show off *vb* : to make an obvious display of
one's abilities or possessions

show up *vb* **1** : to reveal the true nature of
: EXPOSE **2** : APPEAR 2

showy *adj* **show·i·er; show·i·est** **1** : attracting attention : STRIKING **2** : given to or
being too much outward display : GAUDY —
show·i·ly *adv* — **show·i·ness** *n*

shrank *past of* SHRINK

shrap·nel *n* **1** : a shell designed to burst and
scatter the metal balls with which it is filled
along with jagged fragments of the case **2**
: metal pieces from an exploded bomb,
shell, or mine

¹shred *n* **1** : a long narrow piece torn or cut
off : STRIP **2** : ²BIT 1, PARTICLE

²shred *vb* **shred·ded; shred·ding** : to cut or
tear into shreds

shrew *n* **1** : a small mouselike animal with
a long pointed snout and tiny eyes that lives
on insects and worms **2** : an unpleasant
quarrelsome woman

shrewd *adj* : showing quick practical cleverness : ASTUTE — **shrewd·ly** *adv* —
shrewd·ness *n*

¹shriek *vb* : to utter a sharp shrill cry

²shriek *n* : a sharp shrill cry

shrike *n* : a grayish or brownish bird with a
hooked bill that feeds mostly on insects and
often sticks them on thorns before eating
them

¹shrill *vb* : to make a high sharp piercing
sound : SCREAM

²shrill *adj* : having a sharp high sound —
shrill·ness *n* — **shril·ly** *adv*

shrimp *n* **1** : a small shellfish related to the

crabs and lobsters **2** : a small or unimportant person or thing — **shrimp·like** *adj*

shrine *n* **1** : a case or box for sacred relics
(as the bones of saints) **2** : the tomb of a
holy person (as a saint) **3** : a place that is
considered sacred

shrink *vb* **shrank** *also* **shrunk; shrunk;
shrink·ing** **1** : to curl up or withdraw in or
as if in fear or pain **2** : to make or become
smaller

shrink·age *n* : the amount by which something shrinks or becomes less

shriv·el *vb* **shriv·eled** *or* **shriv·elled; shriv-
el·ing** *or* **shriv·el·ling** : to shrink and become dry and wrinkled

¹shroud *n* **1** : the cloth placed over or
around a dead body **2** : something that
covers or shelters like a shroud **3** : one of
the ropes that go from the masthead of a
boat to the sides to support the mast

²shroud *vb* : to cover with or as if with a
shroud

shrub *n* : a woody plant having several
stems and smaller than most trees

shrub·bery *n, pl* **shrub·ber·ies** : a group or
planting of shrubs

shrug *vb* **shrugged; shrug·ging** : to draw
or hunch up the shoulders usually to express
doubt, uncertainty, or lack of interest

shrunk *past & past participle of* SHRINK

shrunk·en *adj* : made or grown smaller (as
in size or value)

¹shuck *n* : a covering shell or husk

²shuck *vb* : to free (as an ear of corn) from
the shuck

¹shud·der *vb* : to tremble with fear or horror
or from cold

²shudder *n* : an act of shuddering : SHIVER

¹shuf·fle *vb* **shuf·fled; shuf·fling** **1** : to
push out of sight or mix in a disorderly mass
2 : to mix cards to change their order in the
pack **3** : to move from place to place **4**
: to move in a clumsy dragging way

²shuffle *n* **1** : an act of shuffling **2** : ²JUM-
BLE **3** : a clumsy dragging walk

shun *vb* **shunned; shun·ning** : to avoid
purposely or by habit

shunt *vb* **1** : to turn off to one side or out of
the way : SHIFT **2** : to switch (as a train)
from one track to another

shut *vb* **shut; shut·ting** **1** : to close or become closed **2** : to close so as to prevent
entrance or leaving : BAR **3** : to keep in a
place by enclosing or by blocking the way
out : IMPRISON **4** : to close by bringing
parts together

shut–in *n* : a sick person kept indoors

shut·out *n* : a game in which one side fails to
score

shut·ter *n* **1** : a movable cover for a window **2** : a device in a camera that opens to let in light when a picture is taken

¹shut·tle *n* **1** : an instrument used in weaving to carry the thread back and forth from side to side through the threads that run lengthwise **2** : a vehicle (as a bus or train) that goes back and forth over a short route **3** : SPACE SHUTTLE

²shuttle *vb* **shut·tled; shut·tling** : to move back and forth rapidly or often

shut·tle·cock *n* : a light object (as a piece of cork with feathers stuck in it) used in badminton

¹shy *adj* **shi·er** *or* **shy·er; shi·est** *or* **shy·est** **1** : easily frightened : TIMID **2** : not feeling comfortable around people : not wanting or able to call attention to oneself : BASHFUL **3** : having less than a full or an expected amount or number — **shy·ly** *adv* — **shy·ness** *n*

²shy *vb* **shied; shy·ing** **1** : to draw back in dislike or distaste **2** : to move quickly to one side in fright

sick *adj* **1** : affected with disease or ill health : not well **2** : of, relating to, or intended for use in or during illness **3** : affected with or accompanied by nausea **4** : badly upset by strong emotion (as shame or fear) **5** : tired of something from having too much of it **6** : filled with disgust

sick·bed *n* : a bed on which a sick person lies

sick·en *vb* : to make or become sick

sick·en·ing *adj* : causing sickness or disgust — **sick·en·ing·ly** *adv*

sick·le *n* : a tool with a sharp curved metal blade and a short handle used to cut grass

sick·ly *adj* **sick·li·er; sick·li·est** **1** : somewhat sick : often ailing **2** : caused by or associated with ill health **3** : not growing well : SPINDLY

sick·ness *n* **1** : ill health : ILLNESS **2** : a specific disease : MALADY **3** : NAUSEA 1

¹side *n* **1** : the right or left part of the trunk of the body **2** : a place, space, or direction away from or beyond a central point or line **3** : a surface or line forming a border or face of an object **4** : an outer part of a thing considered as facing in a certain direction **5** : a position viewed as opposite to another **6** : a body of contestants **7** : a line of ancestors traced back from either parent

²side *adj* **1** : of, relating to, or being on the side **2** : aimed toward or from the side **3** : related to something in a minor or unimportant way **4** : being in addition to a main portion

³side *vb* **sid·ed; sid·ing** : to take the same side

side·arm *adv* : with the arm moving out to the side

side·board *n* : a piece of furniture for holding dishes, silverware, and table linen

sid·ed *adj* : having sides often of a stated number or kind

side·line *n* **1** : a line marking the side of a playing field or court **2** : a business or a job done in addition to one's regular occupation

¹side·long *adv* : out of the corner of one's eye

²sidelong *adj* **1** : made to one side or out of the corner of one's eye **2** : INDIRECT 2

side·show *n* : a small show off to the side of a main show or exhibition (as of a circus)

side·step *vb* **side·stepped; side·step·ping** **1** : to take a step to the side **2** : to avoid by a step to the side **3** : to avoid answering or dealing with

side·track *vb* **1** : to transfer from a main railroad line to a side line **2** : to turn aside from a main purpose or direction

side·walk *n* : a usually paved walk at the side of a street or road

side·ways *adv or adj* **1** : from one side **2** : with one side forward **3** : to one side

side·wise *adv or adj* : SIDEWAYS

sid·ing *n* **1** : a short railroad track connected with the main track **2** : material (as boards or metal pieces) used to cover the outside walls of frame buildings

si·dle *vb* **si·dled; si·dling** : to go or move with one side forward

siege *n* **1** : the moving of an army around a fortified place to capture it **2** : a lasting attack (as of illness)

si·er·ra *n* : a range of mountains especially with jagged peaks

si·es·ta *n* : a nap or rest especially at midday

sieve *n* : a utensil with meshes or holes to separate finer particles from coarser ones or solids from liquids

sift *vb* **1** : to pass or cause to pass through a sieve **2** : to separate or separate out by or as if by passing through a sieve **3** : to test or examine carefully — **sift·er** *n*

¹sigh *vb* **1** : to take or let out a long loud breath often as an expression of sadness or weariness **2** : to make a sound like sighing **3** : YEARN

²sigh *n* : the act or a sound of sighing

¹sight *n* **1** : something that is seen : SPECTACLE **2** : something that is worth seeing **3** : something that is peculiar, funny, or messy **4** : the function, process, or power of seeing : the sense by which one becomes aware of the position, form, and color of objects **5** : the act of seeing **6** : the presence of an object within the field of vision **7** : the distance a person can see **8** : a device (as a small metal bead on a gun barrel) that aids the eye in aiming or in finding the direction of an object

²sight *vb* **1 :** to get sight of : SEE **2 :** to look at through or as if through a sight

sight·less *adj* **:** lacking sight : BLIND

sight·seer *n* **:** a person who goes about to see places and things of interest

¹sign *n* **1 :** a motion, action, or movement of the hand that means something **2 :** one of the twelve parts of the zodiac **3 :** a symbol (as + or ÷) indicating a mathematical operation **4 :** a public notice that advertises something or gives information **5 :** something that indicates what is to come **6 :** ¹TRACE 2

²sign *vb* **1 :** to make or place a sign on **2 :** to represent or show by a sign or signs **3 :** to write one's name on to show that one accepts, agrees with, or will be responsible for **4 :** to communicate by using sign language

¹sig·nal *n* **1 :** a sign, event, or word that serves to start some action **2 :** a sound, a movement of part of the body, or an object that gives warning or a command **3 :** a radio wave that transmits a message or effect (as in radio or television)

²signal *vb* **sig·naled** *or* **sig·nalled; sig·nal·ing** *or* **sig·nal·ling 1 :** to notify by a signal **2 :** to communicate by signals

³signal *adj* **1 :** unusually great **2 :** used for signaling

sig·na·ture *n* **1 :** the name of a person written by that person **2 :** a sign or group of signs placed at the beginning of a staff in music to show the key (**key signature**) or the meter (**time signature**)

sign·board *n* **:** a board with a sign or notice on it

sig·nif·i·cance *n* **1 :** MEANING 1 **2 :** IMPORTANCE

sig·nif·i·cant *adj* **1 :** having meaning and especially a special or hidden meaning **2 :** IMPORTANT 1

sig·ni·fy *vb* **sig·ni·fied; sig·ni·fy·ing 1 :** ²MEAN 3, DENOTE **2 :** to show especially by a sign : make known **3 :** to have importance

sign language *n* **:** a system of hand movements used for communication (as by people who are deaf)

sign·post *n* **:** a post with a sign (as for directing travelers)

si·lage *n* **:** fodder fermented (as in a silo) to produce a good juicy feed for livestock

¹si·lence *n* **1 :** the state of keeping or being silent **2 :** the state of there being no sound or noise : STILLNESS

²silence *vb* **si·lenced; si·lenc·ing 1 :** to stop the noise or speech of : cause to be silent **2 :** SUPPRESS 1

si·lent *adj* **1 :** not speaking : not talkative **2 :** free from noise or sound : STILL **3 :** done or felt without being spoken **4 :** making no mention **5 :** not active in running a business **6 :** not pronounced

¹sil·hou·ette *n* **1 :** a drawing or picture of the outline of an object filled in with a solid usually black color **2 :** a profile portrait done in silhouette **3 :** ¹OUTLINE 1

²silhouette *vb* **sil·hou·ett·ed; sil·hou·ett·ing :** to represent by a silhouette : show against a light background

sil·i·con *n* **:** a chemical element that is found combined as the most common element next to oxygen in the earth's crust and is used especially in electronic devices

silk *n* **1 :** a fine fiber that is spun by many insect larvae usually to form their cocoon or by spiders to make their webs and that includes some kinds used for weaving cloth **2 :** thread, yarn, or fabric made from silk **3 :** something suggesting silk

silk·en *adj* **1 :** made of or with silk **2 :** like silk especially in its soft and smooth feel

silk·worm *n* **:** a yellowish hairless caterpillar that is the larva of an Asian moth (**silk moth** or **silkworm moth**), is raised in captivity on mulberry leaves, and produces a strong silk that is the silk most used for thread or cloth

silky *adj* **silk·i·er; silk·i·est :** soft and smooth as silk

sill *n* **1 :** a horizontal supporting piece at the base of a structure **2 :** a heavy horizontal piece (as of wood) that forms the bottom part of a window frame or a doorway

sil·ly *adj* **sil·li·er; sil·li·est 1 :** not very intelligent **2 :** showing a lack of common sense **3 :** not serious or important — **sil·li·ness** *n*

si·lo *n, pl* **silos :** a covered trench, pit, or especially a tall round building in which silage is made and stored

¹silt *n* **1 :** particles of small size left as sediment from water **2 :** a soil made up mostly of silt and containing little clay

²silt *vb* **:** to choke, fill, cover, or block with silt

¹sil·ver *n* **1 :** a soft white metallic chemical element that takes a high polish and is used for money, jewelry and ornaments, and table utensils **2 :** coin made of silver **3 :** SILVERWARE **4 :** a medium gray

²silver *adj* **1 :** made of, coated with, or yielding silver **2 :** having the color of silver

³silver *vb* **:** to coat with or as if with silver

sil·ver·smith *n* **:** a person who makes objects of silver

sil·ver·ware *n* : things (as knives, forks, and spoons) made of silver, silver-plated metal, or stainless steel

sil·very *adj* : having a shine like silver

sim·i·lar *adj* : having qualities in common — **sim·i·lar·ly** *adv*

sim·i·lar·i·ty *n, pl* **sim·i·lar·i·ties** : the quality or state of being similar : RESEMBLANCE

sim·i·le *n* : a figure of speech comparing two unlike things using *like* or *as*

sim·mer *vb* 1 : to cook gently at or just below the boiling point 2 : to be on the point of bursting out with violence or anger

sim·ple *adj* **sim·pler; sim·plest** 1 : INNOCENT 1, MODEST 2 : not rich or important 3 : lacking in education, experience, or intelligence 4 : not fancy 5 : having few parts : not complicated 6 : ABSOLUTE 2 7 : not hard to understand or solve 8 : EASY 1, STRAIGHTFORWARD

sim·ple·ton *n* : a foolish or stupid person

sim·plic·i·ty *n, pl* **sim·plic·i·ties** 1 : the quality or state of being simple or plain and not complicated or difficult 2 : SINCERITY 3 : directness or clearness in speaking or writing

sim·pli·fy *vb* **sim·pli·fied; sim·pli·fy·ing** : to make simple or simpler : make easier

sim·ply *adv* 1 : in a clear way 2 : in a plain way 3 : DIRECTLY 1, CANDIDLY 4 : 2ONLY 1, MERELY 5 : in actual fact : REALLY, TRULY

si·mul·ta·neous *adj* : existing or taking place at the same time — **si·mul·ta·neous·ly** *adv*

¹sin *n* 1 : an action that breaks a religious law 2 : an action that is or is felt to be bad

²sin *vb* **sinned; sin·ning** : to be guilty of a sin

¹since *adv* 1 : from a definite past time until now 2 : before the present time : AGO 3 : after a time in the past

²since *conj* 1 : in the period after 2 : BECAUSE

³since *prep* 1 : in the period after 2 : continuously from

sin·cere *adj* 1 : HONEST 2, STRAIGHTFORWARD 2 : being what it seems to be : GENUINE — **sin·cere·ly** *adv*

sin·cer·i·ty *n* : freedom from fraud or deception : HONESTY

sin·ew *n* : TENDON

sin·ewy *adj* 1 : full of tendons : TOUGH, STRINGY 2 : STRONG 1, POWERFUL

sin·ful *adj* : being or full of sin : WICKED

sing *vb* **sang** *or* **sung; sung; sing·ing** 1 : to produce musical sounds with the voice 2 : to express in musical tones 3 : ¹CHANT 2 4 : to make musical sounds 5 : to make

a small shrill sound 6 : to speak with enthusiasm 7 : to do something with song — **sing·er** *n*

¹singe *vb* **singed; singe·ing** 1 : to burn lightly or on the surface : SCORCH 2 : to remove the hair, down, or fuzz from by passing briefly over a flame

²singe *n* : a slight burn

¹sin·gle *adj* 1 : not married 2 : being alone : being the only one 3 : made up of or having only one 4 : having but one row of petals or rays 5 : being a separate whole : INDIVIDUAL 6 : of, relating to, or involving only one person

²single *vb* **sin·gled; sin·gling** : to select or distinguish (as one person or thing) from a number or group

³single *n* 1 : a separate individual person or thing 2 : a hit in baseball that enables the batter to reach first base

sin·gle–hand·ed *adj* 1 : done or managed by one person or with one hand 2 : working alone : lacking help

sin·gly *adv* : one by one : INDIVIDUALLY

¹sin·gu·lar *adj* 1 : of, relating to, or being a word form used to show not more than one 2 : ¹SUPERIOR 2, EXCEPTIONAL 3 : of unusual quality : UNIQUE 4 : STRANGE 3, ODD

²singular *n* : a form of a word used to show that only one person or thing is meant

sin·is·ter *adj* 1 : ¹EVIL 1, CORRUPT 2 : threatening evil, harm, or danger

¹sink *vb* **sank** *or* **sunk; sunk; sink·ing** 1 : to move or cause to move downward so as to be swallowed up 2 : to fall or drop to a lower level 3 : to lessen in amount 4 : to cause to penetrate 5 : to go into or become absorbed 6 : to form by digging or boring 7 : to spend (money) unwisely

²sink *n* : a basin usually with water faucets and a drain fixed to a wall or floor

sin·ner *n* : a sinful person

si·nus *n* : any of several spaces in the skull mostly connected with the nostrils

¹sip *vb* **sipped; sip·ping** : to take small drinks of

²sip *n* 1 : the act of sipping 2 : a small amount taken by sipping

¹si·phon *n* 1 : a bent pipe or tube through which a liquid can be drawn by air pressure up and over the edge of a container 2 : a tubelike organ in an animal and especially a mollusk or arthropod used to draw in or squirt out a fluid

²siphon *vb* : to draw off by a siphon

sir *n* 1 *cap* — used as a title before the given name of a knight or a baronet 2 — used without a name as a form of polite address to a man

¹**sire** *n* **1** *often cap* : ¹FATHER 1 **2** : ANCES-
TOR **3** : the male parent of an animal

²**sire** *vb* **sired; sir·ing** : to become the father
of

si·ren *n* : a device that makes a loud shrill
warning sound and is often operated by
electricity

sir·loin *n* : a cut of beef taken from the part
just in front of the rump

sirup *variant of* SYRUP

si·sal *n* **1** : a long strong white fiber used to
make rope and twine **2** : a Mexican agave
whose leaves yield sisal

sis·ter *n* **1** : a female person or animal related to another person or animal by having
one or both parents in common **2** : a member of a religious society of women : NUN
3 : a woman related to another by a common tie or interest — **sis·ter·ly** *adj*

sis·ter·hood *n* **1** : the state of being a sister
2 : women joined in a group

sis·ter–in–law *n, pl* **sis·ters–in–law 1** : the
sister of one's husband or wife **2** : the wife
of one's brother

sit *vb* **sat; sit·ting 1** : to rest upon the part
of the body where the hips and legs join **2**
: to cause (as oneself) to be seated **3**
: ²PERCH **4** : to hold a place as a member of
an official group **5** : to hold a session **6**
: to pose for a portrait or photograph **7** : to
be located **8** : to remain quiet or still

site *n* **1** : the space of ground a building
rests upon **2** : the place where something
(as a town or event) is found or took place
3 : a place on the Internet at which an individual or organization provides information
to others

sit·ting *n* **1** : an act of one that sits : the time
taken in such a sitting **2** : SESSION 1

sitting room *n* : LIVING ROOM

sit·u·at·ed *adj* **1** : having its place **2**
: being in such financial circumstances

sit·u·a·tion *n* **1** : LOCATION **2**, PLACE **2**
: position or place of employment : JOB **3**
: position in life : STATUS **4** : the combination of surrounding conditions

¹**six** *adj* : being one more than five

²**six** *n* : one more than five : two times three
: 6

six–gun *n* : a revolver having six chambers

six·pence *n* **1** : the sum of six pence **2** : an
old British coin worth six pence

six–shoot·er *n* : SIX-GUN

¹**six·teen** *adj* : being one more than fifteen

²**sixteen** *n* : one more than fifteen : four
times four : 16

¹**six·teenth** *adj* : coming right after fifteenth

²**sixteenth** *n* : number sixteen in a series

¹**sixth** *adj* : coming right after fifth

²**sixth** *n* **1** : number six in a series **2** : one
of six equal parts

¹**six·ti·eth** *adj* : coming right after fifty-ninth

²**sixtieth** *n* : number sixty in a series

¹**six·ty** *adj* : being six times ten

²**sixty** *n* : six times ten : 60

siz·able *or* **size·able** *adj* : fairly large

size *n* **1** : amount of space occupied : BULK
2 : the measurements of a thing **3** : one of
a series of measures especially of manufactured articles (as clothing) — **sized** *adj*

siz·zle *vb* **siz·zled; siz·zling** : to make a
hissing or sputtering noise in or as if in frying or burning

¹**skate** *n* : a very flat fish related to the
sharks that has large and nearly triangular
fins

²**skate** *n* **1** : a metal runner fitting the sole
of the shoe or a shoe with a permanently attached metal runner used for gliding on ice
2 : ROLLER SKATE

³**skate** *vb* **skat·ed; skat·ing 1** : to glide
along on skates **2** : to slide or move as if on
skates — **skat·er** *n*

skate·board *n* : a short board mounted on
small wheels that is used for coasting and
often for performing athletic stunts —
skate·board·er *n* — **skate·board·ing** *n*

skein *n* : a quantity of yarn or thread
arranged in a loose coil

skel·e·tal *adj* : of, relating or attached to,
forming, or like a skeleton

skel·e·ton *n* **1** : a firm supporting or protecting structure or framework of a living
being : the usually bony framework of a
vertebrate (as a fish, bird, or human) **2**
: FRAMEWORK

skep·ti·cal *adj* : having or showing doubt

¹**sketch** *n* **1** : a rough outline or drawing
showing the main features of something to
be written, painted, or built **2** : a short written composition (as a story or essay)

²**sketch** *vb* **1** : to make a sketch, rough
draft, or outline of **2** : to draw or paint
sketches

sketchy *adj* **sketch·i·er; sketch·i·est 1**
: like a sketch : roughly outlined **2** : lacking completeness or clearness

¹**ski** *n, pl* **skis** : one of a pair of narrow
wooden, metal, or plastic strips bound one
on each foot and used in gliding over snow
or water

²**ski** *vb* **skied; ski·ing** : to glide on skis —
ski·er *n*

¹**skid** *n* **1** : a support (as a plank) used to
raise and hold an object **2** : one of the logs,
planks, or rails along or on which something heavy is rolled or slid **3** : the act of
skidding : SLIDE

²**skid** *vb* **skid·ded; skid·ding 1** : to roll or

slide on skids **2** : to slide sideways **3** : ¹SLIDE 1, SLIP

skiff *n* **1** : a small light rowboat **2** : a sailboat light enough to be rowed

ski·ing *n* : the art or sport of gliding and jumping on skis

skill *n* **1** : ability that comes from training or practice **2** : a developed or acquired ability

skilled *adj* **1** : having skill **2** : requiring skill and training

skil·let *n* : a frying pan

skill·ful *or* **skil·ful** *adj* **1** : having or showing skill : EXPERT **2** : done or made with skill — **skill·ful·ly** *adv*

skim *vb* **skimmed; skim·ming 1** : to clean a liquid of scum or floating substance : remove (as cream or film) from the top part of a liquid **2** : to read or examine quickly and not thoroughly **3** : to throw so as to skip along the surface of water **4** : to pass swiftly or lightly over

skim milk *n* : milk from which the cream has been taken

skimp *vb* : to give too little or just enough attention or effort to or funds for

skimpy *adj* **skimp·i·er; skimp·i·est** : not enough especially because of skimping : SCANTY

¹**skin** *n* **1** : the hide especially of a small animal or one that has fur **2** : the outer limiting layer of an animal body that in vertebrate animals (as humans) is made up of two layers of cells forming an inner dermis and an outer epidermis **3** : an outer or surface layer (as of a fruit) — **skin·less** *adj* — **skinned** *adj*

²**skin** *vb* **skinned; skin·ning 1** : to strip, scrape, or rub off the skin of **2** : to remove an outer layer from (as by peeling)

skin dive *vb* : to swim below the surface of water with a face mask and sometimes a portable breathing device — **skin diver** *n*

skin·ny *adj* **skin·ni·er; skin·ni·est** : very thin

¹**skip** *vb* **skipped; skip·ping 1** : to move lightly with leaps and bounds **2** : to bound or cause to bound off one point after another : SKIM **3** : to leap over lightly and nimbly **4** : to pass over or omit an item, space, or step **5** : to fail to attend

²**skip** *n* **1** : a light bounding step **2** : a way of moving by hops and steps

skip·per *n* : the master of a ship and especially of a fishing, trading, or pleasure boat

¹**skir·mish** *n* **1** : a minor fight in war **2** : a minor dispute or contest

²**skirmish** *vb* : to take part in a skirmish

¹**skirt** *n* **1** : a woman's or girl's garment or part of a garment that hangs from the waist

down **2** : either of two flaps on a saddle covering the bars on which the stirrups are hung **3** : a part or attachment serving as a rim, border, or edging

²**skirt** *vb* **1** : ²BORDER **2** : to go or pass around or about the outer edge of

skit *n* : a brief sketch in play form

skit·tish *adj* : easily frightened

skulk *vb* : to hide or move in a sly or sneaking way

skull *n* : the case of bone or cartilage that forms most of the skeleton of the head and face, encloses the brain, and supports the jaws

skunk *n* **1** : a North American animal related to the weasels and minks that has coarse black and white fur and can squirt out a fluid with a very unpleasant smell **2** : a mean person who deserves to be scorned

sky *n, pl* **skies 1** : the upper air : the vast arch or dome that seems to spread over the earth **2** : WEATHER, CLIMATE

sky·lark *n* : a European lark noted for its song

sky·light *n* : a window or group of windows in a roof or ceiling

sky·line *n* **1** : the line where earth and sky seem to meet : HORIZON **2** : an outline against the sky

sky·rock·et *n* : ¹ROCKET 1

sky·scrap·er *n* : a very tall building

sky·writ·ing *n* : writing formed in the sky by means of smoke or vapor released from an airplane

slab *n* : a flat thick piece or slice (as of stone, wood, or bread)

¹**slack** *adj* **1** : CARELESS 2, NEGLIGENT **2** : not energetic : SLOW **3** : not tight or firm **4** : not busy or active

²**slack** *vb* : to make or become looser, slower, or less energetic : LOOSEN, SLACKEN

³**slack** *n* **1** : a stopping of movement or flow **2** : a part (as of a rope or sail) that hangs loose without strain **3** **slacks** *pl* : pants especially for informal wear

slack·en *vb* **1** : to make slower or less energetic : slow up **2** : to make less tight or firm : LOOSEN

slag *n* : the waste left after the melting of ores and the separation of the metal from them

slain *past participle of* SLAY

slake *vb* **slaked; slak·ing 1** : QUENCH 2 **2** : to cause solid lime to heat and crumble by treating it with water

¹**slam** *n* **1** : a severe blow **2** : a noisy violent closing : BANG

²**slam** *vb* **slammed; slam·ming 1** : to strike or beat hard **2** : to shut with noisy

force : BANG **3** : to put or place with force **4** : to criticize harshly

¹slan·der *vb* : to make a false and spiteful statement against : DEFAME

²slander *n* : a false and spiteful statement that damages another person's reputation

slang *n* : an informal nonstandard vocabulary composed mostly of invented words, changed words, and exaggerated or humorous figures of speech

¹slant *n* : a direction, line, or surface that is neither level nor straight up and down : SLOPE

²slant *vb* : to turn or incline from a straight line or level : SLOPE

³slant *adj* : not level or straight up and down

slant·wise *adv or adj* : so as to slant : at a slant : in a slanting position

¹slap *vb* **slapped; slap·ping 1** : to strike with or as if with the open hand **2** : to make a sound like that of slapping **3** : to put, place, or throw with careless haste or force

²slap *n* **1** : a quick sharp blow especially with the open hand **2** : a noise like that of a slap

¹slash *vb* **1** : to cut by sweeping blows : GASH **2** : to whip or strike with or as if with a cane **3** : to reduce sharply

²slash *n* **1** : an act of slashing **2** : a long cut or slit made by slashing

slat *n* : a thin narrow strip of wood, plastic, or metal

slate *n* **1** : a fine-grained usually bluish gray rock that splits into thin layers or plates and is used mostly for roofing and blackboards **2** : a framed piece of slate used to write on

¹slaugh·ter *n* **1** : the act of killing **2** : the killing and dressing of animals for food **3** : destruction of many lives especially in battle

²slaughter *vb* **1** : ²BUTCHER 1 **2** : ¹MASSACRE

slaugh·ter·house *n, pl* **slaugh·ter·hous·es** : an establishment where animals are killed and dressed for food

Slav *n* : a person speaking a Slavic language as a native tongue

¹slave *n* **1** : a person who is owned by another person and can be sold at the owner's will **2** : one who is like a slave in not being his or her own master **3** : DRUDGE

²slave *vb* **slaved; slav·ing** : to work like a slave

slave·hold·er *n* : an owner of slaves

slav·ery *n* **1** : hard tiring labor : DRUDGERY **2** : the state of being a slave : BONDAGE **3** : the custom or practice of owning slaves

Slav·ic *adj* : of, relating to, or characteristic of the Slavs or their languages

slav·ish *adj* **1** : of or characteristic of slaves **2** : following or copying something or someone without questioning

slay *vb* **slew; slain; slay·ing** : ¹KILL 1 — **slay·er** *n*

¹sled *n* **1** : a vehicle on runners for carrying loads especially over snow **2** : a small vehicle with runners used mostly by children for sliding on snow and ice

²sled *vb* **sled·ded; sled·ding** : to ride or carry on a sled

¹sledge *n* : SLEDGEHAMMER

²sledge *n* : a strong heavy sled

sledge·ham·mer *n* : a large heavy hammer usually used with both hands

¹sleek *vb* : ¹SLICK

²sleek *adj* **1** : smooth and glossy as if polished **2** : having a plump healthy look

¹sleep *n* **1** : a natural periodic loss of consciousness during which the body rests and refreshes itself **2** : an inactive state (as hibernation or trance) like true sleep **3** : DEATH — **sleep·less** *adj* — **sleep·less·ness** *n*

²sleep *vb* **slept; sleep·ing** : to take rest in sleep : be or lie asleep

sleep·er *n* **1** : one that sleeps **2** : a horizontal beam to support something on or near ground level **3** : a railroad car with berths for sleeping

sleep·walk·er *n* : a person who walks about while asleep — **sleep·walk·ing** *n*

sleepy *adj* **sleep·i·er; sleep·i·est 1** : ready to fall asleep : DROWSY **2** : not active, noisy, or busy — **sleep·i·ness** *n*

¹sleet *n* : frozen or partly frozen rain

²sleet *vb* : to shower sleet

sleeve *n* **1** : the part of a garment covering the arm **2** : a part that fits over or around something like a sleeve — **sleeved** *adj* — **sleeve·less** *adj*

¹sleigh *n* : an open usually horse-drawn vehicle with runners for use on snow or ice

²sleigh *vb* : to drive or ride in a sleigh

sleight of hand : skill and quickness in the use of the hands especially in doing magic tricks

slen·der *adj* **1** : gracefully thin **2** : narrow for its height **3** : very little

slept *past of* SLEEP

slew *past of* SLAY

¹slice *vb* **sliced; slic·ing 1** : to cut with or as if with a knife **2** : to cut into thin flat pieces

²slice *n* : a thin flat piece cut from something

¹slick *vb* : to make sleek or smooth

²slick *adj* **1** : having a smooth surface : SLIPPERY **2** : CRAFTY, CLEVER

slick·er *n* : a long loose raincoat

¹slide *vb* **slid; slid·ing 1** : to move or cause

to move smoothly over a surface : GLIDE **2**
: to move or pass smoothly and without
much effort

²slide *n* **1** : the act or motion of sliding **2**
: a loosened mass that slides : AVALANCHE
3 : a surface down which a person or thing
slides **4** : something that operates or adjusts by sliding **5** : a transparent picture
that can be projected on a screen **6** : a glass
plate for holding an object to be examined
under a microscope

¹slight *adj* **1** : not large or stout **2**
: FLIMSY, FRAIL **3** : not important : TRIV-
IAL **4** : small of its kind or in amount —
slight·ly *adv*

²slight *vb* : to treat without proper care, respect, or courtesy

³slight *n* **1** : an act or an instance of slight-
ing **2** : the state or an instance of being
slighted

slight·ing *adj* : showing a lack of respect or
caring

¹slim *adj* **slim·mer; slim·mest 1** : SLEN-
DER 1 **2** : very small

²slim *vb* **slimmed; slim·ming** : to make or
become slender

slime *n* **1** : soft slippery mud **2** : a soft
slippery material (as on the skin of a slug or
catfish)

slimy *adj* **slim·i·er; slim·i·est 1** : having
the feel or look of slime **2** : covered with
slime

¹sling *vb* **slung; sling·ing 1** : to throw with
a sudden sweeping motion : FLING **2** : to
hurl with a sling

²sling *n* **1** : a device (as a short strap with a
string attached at each end) for hurling
stones **2** : SLINGSHOT **3** : a device (as a
rope or chain) by which something is lifted
or carried **4** : a hanging bandage put
around the neck to hold up the arm or hand

³sling *vb* **slung; sling·ing 1** : to put in or
move or support with a sling **2** : to hang
from two points

sling·shot *n* : a forked stick with an elastic
band attached for shooting small stones

slink *vb* **slunk; slink·ing** : to move or go by
or as if by creeping especially so as not to
be noticed (as in fear or shame)

¹slip *vb* **slipped; slip·ping 1** : to move easily and smoothly **2** : to move quietly
: STEAL **3** : to pass or let pass or escape
without being noted, used, or done **4** : to
get away from **5** : to escape the attention of
6 : to slide into or out of place or away from
a support **7** : to slide on a slippery surface
so as to lose one's balance **8** : to put on or
take off a garment quickly and carelessly

²slip *n* **1** : a ramp where ships can be landed
or repaired **2** : a place for a ship between

two piers **3** : a secret or quick departure or
escape **4** : a small mistake : BLUNDER **5**
: the act or an instance of slipping down or
out of place **6** : a sudden mishap **7** : a fall
from some level or standard : DECLINE **8**
: an undergarment made in dress length
with straps over the shoulders **9** : PILLOW-
CASE

³slip *n* **1** : a piece of a plant cut for planting
or grafting **2** : a long narrow piece of material **3** : a piece of paper used for some
record **4** : a young and slender person

⁴slip *vb* **slipped; slip·ping** : to take slips
from (a plant)

slip·cov·er *n* : a cover (as for a sofa or chair)
that may be slipped off and on

slip·knot *n* : a knot made by tying the end of
a line around the line itself to form a loop so
that the size of the loop may be changed by
slipping the knot

slip·per *n* : a light low shoe that is easily
slipped on the foot

slip·pery *adj* **slip·per·i·er; slip·per·i·est 1**
: having a surface smooth or wet enough to
make something slide or make one lose
one's footing or hold **2** : not to be trusted
: TRICKY

slip·shod *adj* : very careless : SLOVENLY

slip up *vb* : to make a mistake

¹slit *n* : a long narrow cut or opening

²slit *vb* **slit; slit·ting** : to make a long narrow
cut in : SLASH

slith·er *vb* : ¹GLIDE

¹sliv·er *n* : a long slender piece cut or torn
off : SPLINTER

²sliver *vb* : to cut or form into slivers

¹slob·ber *vb* : to let saliva or liquid dribble
from the mouth

²slobber *n* : dripping saliva

slo·gan *n* : a word or phrase used by a party,
a group, or a business to attract attention (as
to its goal, worth, or beliefs)

sloop *n* : a sailing boat with one mast and a
fore-and-aft mainsail and jib

¹slop *n* **1** : thin tasteless drink or liquid
food **2** : liquid spilled or splashed **3**
: food waste or gruel fed to animals **4**
: body waste

²slop *vb* **slopped; slop·ping 1** : to spill or
spill something on or over **2** : to feed slop
to

¹slope *vb* **sloped; slop·ing** : to take a slanting direction

²slope *n* **1** : a piece of slanting ground (as a
hillside) **2** : upward or downward slant

slop·py *adj* **slop·pi·er; slop·pi·est 1** : wet
enough to spatter easily **2** : careless in
work or in appearance

slosh *vb* **1** : to walk with trouble through
water, mud, or slush **2** : ¹SPLASH 1, 2, 3

¹slot *n* : a narrow opening, groove, or passage

²slot *vb* **slot·ted; slot·ting** : to cut a slot in

sloth *n* **1** : the state of being lazy **2** : an animal of Central and South America that hangs back downward and moves slowly along the branches of trees on whose leaves, twigs, and fruits it feeds

¹slouch *n* **1** : a lazy worthless person **2** : a lazy drooping way of standing, sitting, or walking

²slouch *vb* : to walk, stand, or sit with a slouch

slough *n* : a wet marshy or muddy place

slov·en·ly *adj* : personally untidy

¹slow *adj* **1** : not as smart or as quick to understand as most people **2** : not easily aroused or excited **3** : moving, flowing, or going at less than the usual speed **4** : indicating less than is correct **5** : not lively or active — **slow·ly** *adv* — **slow·ness** *n*

²slow *adv* : in a slow way

³slow *vb* : to make or go slow or slower

slow·poke *n* : a very slow person

sludge *n* : a soft muddy mass resulting from sewage treatment

¹slug *n* : a long wormlike land mollusk that is related to the snails but has an undeveloped shell or none at all

²slug *n* **1** : a small piece of shaped metal **2** : BULLET **3** : a metal disk often used in place of a coin

³slug *n* : a hard blow especially with the fist

⁴slug *vb* **slugged; slug·ging** : to hit hard with the fist or with a bat

slug·gard *n* : a lazy person

slug·ger *n* : a boxer or baseball batter who hits hard

slug·gish *adj* : slow in movement or reaction — **slug·gish·ly** *adv* — **slug·gish·ness** *n*

¹sluice *n* **1** : an artificial passage for water with a gate for controlling its flow or changing its direction **2** : a device for controlling the flow of water **3** : a sloping trough for washing ore or for floating logs

²sluice *vb* **sluiced; sluic·ing 1** : to wash in a stream of water running through a sluice **2** : ³FLUSH 2, DRENCH

slum *n* : a very poor crowded dirty section especially of a city

¹slum·ber *vb* : to be asleep

²slumber *n* : ¹SLEEP

¹slump *vb* **1** : to drop or slide down suddenly : COLLAPSE **2** : ²SLOUCH **3** : to drop sharply

²slump *n* : a big or continued drop especially in prices, business, or performance

slung *past of* SLING

slunk *past of* SLINK

¹slur *n* **1** : an insulting remark **2** : STIGMA 1, STAIN

²slur *vb* **slurred; slur·ring 1** : to pass over without proper mention or stress **2** : to run one's speech together so that it is hard to understand

³slur *n* : a slurred way of talking

slush *n* : partly melted snow

sly *adj* **sli·er** *or* **sly·er; sli·est** *or* **sly·est 1** : both clever and tricky **2** : being sneaky and dishonest **3** : MISCHIEVOUS 3 — **sly·ly** *adv* — **sly·ness** *n* — **on the sly** : so as not to be seen or caught : SECRETLY

¹smack *n* : a slight taste, trace, or touch of something

²smack *vb* : to have a flavor, trace, or suggestion

³smack *vb* **1** : to close and open the lips noisily especially in eating **2** : to kiss usually loudly or hard **3** : to make or give a smack : SLAP

⁴smack *n* **1** : a quick sharp noise made by the lips (as in enjoyment of some taste) **2** : a loud kiss **3** : a noisy slap or blow

¹small *adj* **1** : little in size **2** : few in numbers or members **3** : little in amount **4** : not very much **5** : UNIMPORTANT **6** : operating on a limited scale **7** : lacking in strength **8** : not generous : MEAN **9** : made up of units of little worth **10** : ¹HUMBLE 3, MODEST **11** : lowered in pride **12** : being letters that are not capitals — **small·ness** *n*

²small *n* : a part smaller and usually narrower than the rest

small intestine *n* : the long narrow upper part of the intestine in which food is mostly digested and from which digested food is absorbed into the body

small·pox *n* : an acute disease in which fever and skin eruptions occur and which is believed to be extinct due to vaccination against the virus causing it

¹smart *adj* **1** : BRISK, SPIRITED **2** : quick to learn or do : BRIGHT **3** : SAUCY 1 **4** : stylish in appearance — **smart·ly** *adv* — **smart·ness** *n*

²smart *vb* **1** : to cause or feel a sharp stinging pain **2** : to feel distress

³smart *n* : a stinging pain usually in one spot

smart al·eck *n* : a person who likes to show off

¹smash *n* **1** : a violent blow or attack **2** : the action or sound of smashing **3** : a striking success

²smash *vb* **1** : to break in pieces : SHATTER **2** : to drive or move violently **3** : to destroy completely : WRECK **4** : to go to pieces : COLLAPSE

¹smear *n* : a spot or streak made by or as if by an oily or sticky substance : SMUDGE

²smear *vb* **1** : to spread or soil with something oily or sticky : DAUB **2** : to spread over a surface **3** : to blacken the good name of

¹smell *vb* **smelled** *or* **smelt; smell·ing 1** : to become aware of the odor of by means of sense organs located in the nose **2** : to detect by means or use of the sense of smell **3** : to have or give off an odor

²smell *n* **1** : the sense by which a person or animal becomes aware of an odor **2** : the sensation one gets through the sense of smell : ODOR, SCENT

¹smelt *n, pl* **smelts** *or* **smelt** : a small food fish that looks like the related trouts, lives in coastal sea waters, and swims up rivers to spawn

²smelt *vb* : to melt (as ore) in order to separate the metal : REFINE

smelt·er *n* **1** : a person whose work or business is smelting **2** : a place where ores or metals are smelted

¹smile *vb* **smiled; smil·ing 1** : to have, produce, or show a smile **2** : to look with amusement or scorn **3** : to express by a smile

²smile *n* : an expression on the face in which the lips curve upward especially to show amusement or pleasure

smite *vb* **smote; smit·ten; smit·ing** : to strike hard especially with the hand or a weapon

smith *n* **1** : a worker in metals **2** : BLACK-SMITH

smithy *n, pl* **smith·ies** : the workshop of a smith and especially of a blacksmith

smock *n* : a loose outer garment worn especially for protection of clothing

smog *n* : a fog made heavier and thicker by the action of sunlight on air polluted by smoke and automobile fumes

¹smoke *n* **1** : the gas of burning materials (as coal, wood, or tobacco) made visible by particles of carbon floating in it **2** : a mass or column of smoke : SMUDGE **3** : the act of smoking tobacco

²smoke *vb* **smoked; smok·ing 1** : to give out smoke **2** : to draw in and breathe out the fumes of burning tobacco **3** : to drive (as mosquitoes) away by smoke **4** : to expose (as meat) to smoke to give flavor and keep from spoiling — **smok·er** *n*

smoke de·tec·tor *n* : a device that sounds an alarm automatically when it detects smoke

smoke·house *n, pl* **smoke·hous·es** : a building where meat or fish is cured with smoke

smoke·stack *n* : a large chimney or a pipe for carrying away smoke (as on a factory or ship)

smoky *adj* **smok·i·er; smok·i·est 1** : giving off smoke especially in large amounts **2** : like that of smoke **3** : filled with or darkened by smoke

¹smol·der *or* **smoul·der** *n* : a slow often smoky fire

²smolder *or* **smoulder** *vb* **1** : to burn slowly usually with smoke and without flame **2** : to burn inwardly

¹smooth *adj* **1** : not rough or uneven in surface **2** : not hairy **3** : free from difficulties or things in the way **4** : moving or progressing without breaks, sudden changes, or shifts **5** : able to make things seem right or easy or good : GLIB — **smooth·ly** *adv* — **smooth·ness** *n*

²smooth *vb* **1** : to make smooth **2** : ¹POL-ISH 2, REFINE **3** : to free from trouble or difficulty

smote *past of* SMITE

smoth·er *vb* **1** : to overcome by depriving of air or exposing to smoke or fumes : SUF-FOCATE **2** : to become suffocated **3** : to cover up : SUPPRESS **4** : to cover thickly

¹smudge *vb* **smudged; smudg·ing** : to soil or blur by rubbing or smearing

²smudge *n* **1** : a blurred spot or streak : SMEAR **2** : a smoky fire (as to drive away mosquitoes or protect fruit from frost)

smug *adj* **smug·ger; smug·gest** : very satisfied with oneself — **smug·ly** *adv*

smug·gle *vb* **smug·gled; smug·gling 1** : to export or import secretly and unlawfully especially to avoid paying taxes **2** : to take or bring secretly — **smug·gler** *n*

smut *n* **1** : something (as a particle of soot) that soils or blackens **2** : a destructive disease of plants (as cereal grasses) in which plant parts (as seeds) are replaced by masses of dark spores of the fungus that causes the disease **3** : a fungus that causes smut

snack *n* : a light meal : LUNCH

¹snag *n* **1** : a stump or stub of a tree branch especially when hidden under water **2** : a rough or broken part sticking out from something **3** : an unexpected difficulty

²snag *vb* **snagged; snag·ging** : to catch or damage on or as if on a snag

snail *n* **1** : a small slow-moving mollusk with a spiral shell into which it can draw itself for safety **2** : a person who moves slowly

¹snake *n* **1** : a limbless crawling reptile that has a long body and lives usually on large insects or small animals and birds **2** : a horrid or treacherous person

²snake *vb* **snaked; snak·ing** : to crawl, wind, or move like a snake

snaky *adj* **snak·i·er; snak·i·est 1 :** of or like a snake **2 :** full of snakes

¹snap *vb* **snapped; snap·ping 1 :** to grasp or grasp at something suddenly with the mouth or teeth **2 :** to grasp at something eagerly **3 :** to get, take, or buy at once **4 :** to speak or utter sharply or irritably **5 :** to break or break apart suddenly and often with a cracking noise **6 :** to make or cause to make a sharp or crackling sound **7 :** to close or fit in place with a quick movement **8 :** to put into or remove from a position suddenly or with a snapping sound **9 :** to close by means of snaps or fasteners **10 :** to act or be acted on with snap **11 :** to take a snapshot of

²snap *n* **1 :** the act or sound of snapping **2 :** something that is easy and presents no problems **3 :** a small amount : BIT **4 :** a sudden spell of harsh weather **5 :** a catch or fastening that closes or locks with a click **6 :** a thin brittle cookie **7 :** SNAPSHOT **8 :** smartness of movement or speech : ENERGY

³snap *adj* **1 :** made suddenly or without careful thought **2 :** closing with a click or by means of a device that snaps **3 :** very easy

snap·drag·on *n* : a garden plant with stalks of mostly white, pink, crimson, or yellow flowers with two lips

snap·per *n* **1 :** one that snaps **2 :** SNAPPING TURTLE **3 :** an active sea fish important for sport and food

snap·ping tur·tle *n* : a large American turtle that catches its prey with a snap of the powerful jaws

snap·py *adj* **snap·pi·er; snap·pi·est 1 :** full of life : LIVELY **2 :** briskly cold : CHILLY **3 :** STYLISH, SMART

snap·shot *n* : a photograph taken usually with an inexpensive hand-held camera

¹snare *n* **1 :** a trap (as a noose) for catching small animals and birds **2 :** something by which one is entangled, trapped, or deceived

²snare *vb* **snared; snar·ing :** to catch or entangle by or as if by use of a snare

snare drum *n* : a small drum with two heads that has strings stretched across its lower head to produce a rattling sound

¹snarl *vb* : to get into a tangle

²snarl *n* **1 :** a tangle usually of hairs or thread : KNOT **2 :** a tangled situation

³snarl *vb* **1 :** to growl with a showing of teeth **2 :** to speak in an angry way **3 :** to utter with a growl

⁴snarl *n* : an angry growl

¹snatch *vb* : to take hold of or try to take hold of something quickly or suddenly

²snatch *n* **1 :** an act of snatching **2 :** a brief period **3 :** something brief, hurried, or in small bits

¹sneak *vb* **sneaked** *or* **snuck; sneak·ing :** to move, act, bring, or put in a sly or secret way

²sneak *n* **1 :** a person who acts in a sly or secret way **2 :** the act or an instance of sneaking

sneak·er *n* : a canvas shoe with a rubber sole

sneaky *adj* **sneak·i·er; sneak·i·est :** behaving in a sly or secret way or showing that kind of behavior

¹sneer *vb* **1 :** to smile or laugh while making a face that shows scorn **2 :** to speak or write in a scorning way

²sneer *n* : a sneering expression or remark

¹sneeze *vb* **sneezed; sneez·ing :** to force out the breath in a sudden loud violent action

²sneeze *n* : an act or instance of sneezing

¹snick·er *vb* : to give a small and often mean or sly laugh

²snicker *n* : an act or sound of snickering

¹sniff *vb* **1 :** to draw air into the nose in short breaths loud enough to be heard **2 :** to show scorn **3 :** to smell by taking short breaths

²sniff *n* **1 :** the act or sound of sniffing **2 :** an odor or amount sniffed

snif·fle *vb* **snif·fled; snif·fling 1 :** to sniff repeatedly **2 :** to speak with sniffs

snif·fles *n pl* : a common cold in which the main symptom is a runny nose

¹snig·ger *vb* : ¹SNICKER

²snigger *n* : ²SNICKER

¹snip *n* **1 :** a small piece that is snipped off **2 :** an act or sound of snipping

²snip *vb* **snipped; snip·ping :** to cut or cut off with or as if with shears or scissors

¹snipe *n, pl* **snipes** *or* **snipe :** a game bird that lives in marshes and has a long straight bill

²snipe *vb* **sniped; snip·ing :** to shoot from a hiding place (as at individual enemy soldiers) — **snip·er** *n*

snob *n* : a person who imitates, admires, or wants to be friends with people of higher position and looks down on or avoids those felt to be less important

snob·bish *adj* : of, relating to, or being a snob

¹snoop *vb* : to look or search especially in a sneaking or nosy way

²snoop *n* : SNOOPER

snoop·er *n* : a person who snoops

snoot *n* : ¹NOSE 1

¹snooze *vb* **snoozed; snooz·ing :** to take a nap

²snooze *n* : a short sleep : NAP

¹**snore** *vb* **snored; snor·ing** : to breathe with a rough hoarse noise while sleeping

²**snore** *n* : an act or sound of snoring

¹**snort** *vb* : to force air through the nose with a rough harsh sound

²**snort** *n* : an act or sound of snorting

snout *n* **1** : a long projecting nose (as of a pig) **2** : the front part of a head (as of a weevil) that sticks out like the snout of a pig **3** : a usually large and ugly human nose

¹**snow** *n* **1** : small white crystals of ice formed directly from the water vapor of the air **2** : a fall of snowflakes : a mass of snowflakes fallen to earth

²**snow** *vb* **1** : to fall or cause to fall in or as snow **2** : to cover or shut in with snow

snow·ball *n* : a round mass of snow pressed or rolled together

snow·bird *n* : a small bird (as a junco) seen mostly in winter

snow—blind *or* **snow—blind·ed** *adj* : having the eyes red and swollen and unable to see from the effect of glare reflected from snow — **snow blindness** *n*

snow·bound *adj* : shut in by snow

snow·drift *n* : a bank of drifted snow

snow·fall *n* **1** : a fall of snow **2** : the amount of snow that falls in a single storm or in a certain period

snow·flake *n* : a snow crystal : a small mass of snow crystals

snow·man *n, pl* **snow·men** : snow shaped to look like a person

snow·mo·bile *n* : a motor vehicle designed for travel on snow

snow·plow *n* : any of various devices used for clearing away snow

¹**snow·shoe** *n* : a light frame of wood strung with a net (as of rawhide) and worn under one's shoe to prevent sinking into soft snow

²**snowshoe** *vb* **snow·shoed; snow·shoe·ing** : to go on snowshoes

snow·storm *n* : a storm of falling snow

snowy *adj* **snow·i·er; snow·i·est** **1** : having or covered with snow **2** : white like snow

¹**snub** *vb* **snubbed; snub·bing** : to ignore or treat rudely on purpose

²**snub** *n* : an act or an instance of snubbing

snub—nosed *adj* : having a stubby and usually slightly turned-up nose

snuck *past of* SNEAK

¹**snuff** *vb* **1** : to cut or pinch off the burned end of the wick of a candle **2** : EXTINGUISH 1

²**snuff** *vb* : to draw through or into the nose with force

³**snuff** *n* : powdered tobacco that is chewed, placed against the gums, or drawn in through the nostrils

¹**snuf·fle** *vb* **snuf·fled; snuf·fling** : to breathe noisily through a nose that is partly blocked

²**snuffle** *n* : the sound made in snuffling

snug *adj* **snug·ger; snug·gest** **1** : fitting closely and comfortably **2** : COMFORTABLE 1, COZY **3** : offering protection or a hiding place — **snug·ly** *adv*

snug·gle *vb* **snug·gled; snug·gling** **1** : to curl up comfortably or cozily : CUDDLE **2** : to pull in close to one

¹**so** *adv* **1** : in the way indicated **2** : in the same way : ALSO **3** : ¹THEN 2 **4** : to an indicated extent or way **5** : to a great degree : VERY, EXTREMELY **6** : to a definite but not specified amount **7** : most certainly : INDEED **8** : THEREFORE

²**so** *conj* **1** : in order that **2** : and therefore

³**so** *pron* **1** : the same : THAT **2** : approximately that

¹**soak** *vb* **1** : to lie covered with liquid **2** : to place in a liquid to wet or as if to wet thoroughly **3** : to enter or pass through something by or as if by tiny holes : PERMEATE **4** : to draw out by or as if by soaking in a liquid **5** : to draw in by or as if by absorption

²**soak** *n* : the act or process of soaking : the state of being soaked

¹**soap** *n* : a substance that is usually made by the action of alkali on fat, dissolves in water, and is used for washing

²**soap** *vb* : to rub soap over or into something

soap·stone *n* : a soft stone having a soapy or greasy feeling

soap·suds *n pl* : SUDS

soapy *adj* **soap·i·er; soap·i·est** **1** : smeared with or full of soap **2** : containing or combined with soap **3** : like soap

soar *vb* : to fly or sail through the air often at a great height

¹**sob** *vb* **sobbed; sob·bing** **1** : to cry or express with gasps and catching in the throat **2** : to make a sobbing sound

²**sob** *n* **1** : an act of sobbing **2** : a sound of or like that of sobbing

¹**so·ber** *adj* **1** : not drinking too much : TEMPERATE **2** : not drunk **3** : having a serious attitude : SOLEMN **4** : having a quiet color **5** : not fanciful or imagined

²**sober** *vb* : to make or become sober

so—called *adj* : usually but often wrongly so named

soc·cer *n* : a game played between two teams of eleven players in which a round inflated ball is moved toward a goal usually by kicking

so·cia·ble *adj* **1** : liking to be around other people : FRIENDLY **2** : involving pleasant social relations

¹so·cial *adj* 1 : FRIENDLY 1, SOCIABLE 2 : of or relating to human beings as a group 3 : living or growing naturally in groups or communities 4 : of, relating to, or based on rank in a particular society 5 : of or relating to fashionable society — **so·cial·ly** *adv*

²social *n* : a friendly gathering usually for a special reason

so·cial·ism *n* : a theory or system of government based on public ownership and control of the means of production and distribution of goods

so·cial·ist *n* : a person who believes in socialism

social studies *n pl* : the studies (as civics, history, and geography) that deal with human relationships and the way society works

so·ci·ety *n, pl* so·ci·et·ies 1 : friendly association with others 2 : human beings viewed as a system within which the individual lives : all of the people 3 : a group of persons with a common interest or purpose 4 : a part of a community thought of as different in some way 5 : the group or set of fashionable persons

¹sock *n, pl* socks *or* sox : a knitted or woven covering for the foot usually reaching past the ankle and sometimes to the knee

²sock *vb* : ¹HIT 1, PUNCH

³sock *n* : ²PUNCH

sock·et *n* : a hollow thing or place that receives or holds something

sock·eye *n* : a small Pacific salmon that is the source of most of the salmon with red flesh that we eat

¹sod *n* : the layer of the soil filled with roots (as of grass)

²sod *vb* sod·ded; sod·ding : to cover with sod

so·da *n* 1 : a powdery substance like salt used in washing and in making glass or soap 2 : SODIUM BICARBONATE 3 : SODA WATER 4 : SODA POP 5 : a sweet drink made of soda water, flavoring, and ice cream

soda fountain *n* : a counter where soft drinks and ice cream are served

soda pop *n* : a flavored beverage containing carbon dioxide

soda water *n* : water with carbon dioxide added

sod·den *adj* : SOGGY

so·di·um *n* : a soft waxy silver-white chemical element occurring in nature in combined form (as in salt)

sodium bicarbonate *n* : a white powder used in cooking and medicine

sodium chlo·ride *n* : ¹SALT 1

so·fa *n* : a long upholstered seat usually with a back and arms

¹soft *adj* 1 : having a pleasing or comfortable effect 2 : not bright or glaring 3 : quiet in pitch or volume 4 : smooth or delicate in appearance or feel 5 : not violent 6 : EASY 1 7 : sounding as in *ace* and *gem* — used of *c* and *g* 8 : easily affected by emotions 9 : lacking in strength 10 : not hard, solid, or firm 11 : free from substances that prevent lathering of soap 12 : not containing alcohol — **soft·ness** *n*

²soft *adv* : SOFTLY

soft·ball *n* 1 : a game like baseball played with a larger ball 2 : the ball used in softball

soft·en *vb* : to make or become soft or softer — **soft·en·er** *n*

soft·ly *adv* : in a soft way : QUIETLY, GENTLY

soft·ware *n* : the programs and related information used by a computer

soft·wood *n* : the wood of a cone-bearing tree (as a pine or spruce)

sog·gy *adj* sog·gi·er; sog·gi·est : heavy with water or moisture

¹soil *vb* : to make or become dirty

²soil *n* 1 : the loose finely divided surface material of the earth in which plants have their roots 2 : COUNTRY 2, LAND — **soil·less** *adj*

¹so·journ *n* : a temporary stay

²sojourn *vb* : to stay as a temporary resident

sol *n* : the fifth note of the musical scale

so·lar *adj* 1 : of or relating to the sun 2 : measured by the earth's course around the sun 3 : produced or made to work by the action of the sun's light or heat

solar system *n* : the sun and the planets, asteroids, comets, and meteors that revolve around it

sold *past of* SELL

¹sol·der *n* : a metal or a mixture of metals used when melted to join or mend surfaces of metal

²solder *vb* : to join together or repair with solder

sol·dier *n* : a person in military service : an enlisted person who is not a commissioned officer

¹sole *n* : a flatfish that has a small mouth and small eyes set close together and is a popular food fish

²sole *n* 1 : the bottom of the foot 2 : the bottom of a shoe, slipper, or boot

³sole *vb* soled; sol·ing : to furnish with a sole

⁴sole *adj* 1 : ¹SINGLE 2, ONLY 2 : limited or belonging only to the one mentioned

sole·ly *adv* 1 : without another : ALONE 2 : ²ONLY 2

sol·emn *adj* 1 : celebrated with religious ceremony : SACRED 2 : ¹FORMAL 3 : done or made seriously and thoughtfully **4** : very serious **5** : being dark and gloomy : SOMBER — **sol·emn·ly** *adv*

so·lem·ni·ty *n, pl* **so·lem·ni·ties 1** : a solemn ceremony, event, day, or speech **2** : formal dignity

so·lic·it *vb* **1** : to come to with a request or plea **2** : to try to get

¹sol·id *adj* **1** : not hollow **2** : not loose or spongy : COMPACT **3** : neither liquid nor gaseous **4** : made firmly and well **5** : being without a break, interruption, or change **6** : UNANIMOUS **7** : RELIABLE, DEPENDABLE **8** : of one material, kind, or color — **sol·id·ly** *adv* — **sol·id·ness** *n*

²solid *n* **1** : something that has length, width, and thickness **2** : a solid substance : a substance that keeps its size and shape

so·lid·i·fy *vb* **so·lid·i·fied; so·lid·i·fy·ing** : to make or become solid

so·lid·i·ty *n, pl* **so·lid·i·ties** : the quality or state of being solid

sol·i·taire *n* : a card game played by one person alone

sol·i·tary *adj* **1** : all alone **2** : seldom visited : LONELY **3** : growing or living alone : not one of a group or cluster

sol·i·tude *n* **1** : the quality or state of being alone or away from others : SECLUSION **2** : a lonely place

¹so·lo *n, pl* **solos 1** : music played or sung by one person either alone or with accompaniment **2** : an action (as in a dance) in which there is only one performer

²solo *adv or adj* : ²ALONE 2

³solo *vb* : to fly solo in an airplane

so·lo·ist *n* : a person who performs a solo

sol·stice *n* : the time of the year when the sun is farthest north (**summer solstice**, about June 22) or south (**winter solstice**, about December 22) of the equator

sol·u·ble *adj* **1** : capable of being dissolved in liquid **2** : capable of being solved or explained

so·lu·tion *n* **1** : the act or process of solving **2** : the result of solving a problem **3** : the act or process by which a solid, liquid, or gas is dissolved in a liquid **4** : a liquid in which something has been dissolved

solve *vb* **solved; solv·ing** : to find the answer to or a solution for

sol·vent *n* : a usually liquid substance in which other substances can be dissolved or dispersed

som·ber *or* **som·bre** *adj* **1** : being dark and gloomy : DULL **2** : showing or causing low spirits

som·bre·ro *n, pl* **som·bre·ros** : a tall hat of felt or straw with a very wide brim worn especially in the Southwest and Mexico

¹some *adj* **1** : being one unknown or not specified **2** : being one, a part, or an unspecified number of something **3** : being of an amount or number that is not mentioned **4** : being at least one and sometimes all of

²some *pron* : a certain number or amount

¹-some *adj suffix* : distinguished by a specified thing, quality, state, or action

²-some *n suffix* : group of so many members

¹some·body *pron* : some person

²somebody *n, pl* **some·bod·ies** : a person of importance

some·day *adv* : at some future time

some·how *adv* : in one way or another

some·one *pron* : some person

¹som·er·sault *n* : a moving of the body through one complete turn in which the feet move up and over the head

²somersault *vb* : to turn a somersault

some·thing *pron* **1** : a thing that is not surely known or understood **2** : a thing or amount that is clearly known but not named **3** : SOMEWHAT

some·time *adv* **1** : at a future time **2** : at a time not known or not specified

some·times *adv* : now and then : OCCASIONALLY

some·way *adv* : SOMEHOW

¹some·what *pron* : some amount or extent

²somewhat *adv* : to some extent

some·where *adv* **1** : in, at, or to a place not known or named **2** : at some time not specified

son *n* **1** : a male child or offspring **2** : a man or boy closely associated with or thought of as a child of something (as a country, race, or religion)

so·na·ta *n* : a musical composition usually for a single instrument consisting of three or four separate sections in different forms and keys

song *n* **1** : vocal music **2** : poetic composition : POETRY **3** : a short musical composition of words and music **4** : a small amount

song·bird *n* : a bird that sings

song·ster *n* : a person or a bird that sings

son·ic *adj* : using, produced by, or relating to sound waves

sonic boom *n* : a sound like an explosion made by an aircraft traveling at supersonic speed

son–in–law *n, pl* **sons–in–law** : the husband of one's daughter

son·ny *n, pl* **son·nies** : a young boy — used mostly to address a stranger

so·no·rous *adj* **1** : producing sound (as when struck) **2** : loud, deep, or rich sound : RESONANT

soon *adv* **1** : without delay : before long **2** : in a prompt way : QUICKLY **3** : ¹EARLY 2 **4** : by choice : WILLINGLY

soot *n* : a black powder formed when something is burned : the very fine powder that colors smoke

soothe *vb* **soothed; sooth·ing** **1** : to please by praise or attention **2** : RELIEVE 1 **3** : to calm down : COMFORT

sooth·say·er *n* : a person who claims to foretell events

sooty *adj* **soot·i·er; soot·i·est** **1** : soiled with soot **2** : like soot especially in color

sop *vb* **sopped; sop·ping** **1** : to soak or dip in or as if in liquid **2** : to mop up (as water)

soph·o·more *n* : a student in his or her second year at a high school or college

so·pra·no *n, pl* **so·pra·nos** **1** : the highest part in harmony having four parts **2** : the highest singing voice of women or boys **3** : a person having a soprano voice **4** : an instrument having a soprano range or part

sor·cer·er *n* : a person who practices sorcery or witchcraft : WIZARD

sor·cer·ess *n* : a woman who practices sorcery or witchcraft : WITCH

sor·cery *n, pl* **sor·cer·ies** : the use of magic : WITCHCRAFT

sor·did *adj* **1** : very dirty : FOUL **2** : of low moral quality : VILE

¹**sore** *adj* **sor·er; sor·est** **1** : causing distress **2** : very painful or sensitive : TENDER **3** : hurt or red and swollen so as to be or seem painful **4** : ANGRY — **sore·ly** *adv* — **sore·ness** *n*

²**sore** *n* : a sore spot (as an ulcer) on the body usually with the skin broken or bruised and often with infection

sor·ghum *n* **1** : a tall grass that looks like Indian corn and is used for forage and grain **2** : syrup from the juice of a sorghum

so·ror·i·ty *n, pl* **so·ror·i·ties** : a club of girls or women especially at a college

¹**sor·rel** *n* **1** : an animal (as a horse) of a sorrel color **2** : a brownish orange to light brown

²**sorrel** *n* : any of several plants with sour juice

¹**sor·row** *n* **1** : sadness or grief caused by loss (as of something loved) **2** : a cause of grief or sadness **3** : a feeling of regret

²**sorrow** *vb* : to feel or express sorrow : GRIEVE

sor·row·ful *adj* **1** : full of or showing sorrow **2** : causing sorrow

sor·ry *adj* **sor·ri·er; sor·ri·est** **1** : feeling sorrow or regret **2** : causing sorrow, pity, or scorn : WRETCHED

¹**sort** *n* **1** : a group of persons or things that have something in common : KIND **2** : PER-SON 1, INDIVIDUAL **3** : general disposition : NATURE — **out of sorts** **1** : not feeling well **2** : easily angered : IRRITABLE

²**sort** *vb* : to separate and arrange according to kind or class : CLASSIFY

SOS *n* **1** : an international radio code distress signal used especially by ships and airplanes calling for help **2** : a call for help

¹**so–so** *adv* : fairly well

²**so–so** *adj* : neither very good nor very bad

sought *past of* SEEK

soul *n* **1** : the spiritual part of a person believed to give life to the body **2** : the essential part of something **3** : a person who leads or stirs others to action : LEADER **4** : a person's moral and emotional nature **5** : human being : PERSON

¹**sound** *adj* **1** : free from disease or weakness **2** : free from flaw or decay **3** : ¹SOLID 4, FIRM **4** : free from error **5** : based on the truth **6** : THOROUGH 1 **7** : ¹DEEP 5, UNDISTURBED **8** : showing good sense : WISE — **sound·ly** *adv* — **sound·ness** *n*

²**sound** *adv* : to the full extent

³**sound** *n* **1** : the sensation experienced through the sense of hearing : an instance or occurrence of this **2** : one of the noises that together make up human speech **3** : the suggestion carried or given by something heard or read **4** : hearing distance : EARSHOT — **sound·less** *adj* — **sound·less·ly** *adv*

⁴**sound** *vb* **1** : to make or cause to make a sound or noise **2** : PRONOUNCE 2 **3** : to make known : PROCLAIM **4** : to order, signal, or indicate by a sound **5** : to make or give an impression : SEEM

⁵**sound** *n* : a long stretch of water that is wider than a strait and often connects two larger bodies of water or forms a channel between the mainland and an island

⁶**sound** *vb* **1** : to measure the depth of (as by a weighted line dropped down from the surface) **2** : to find or try to find the thoughts or feelings of a person

sound·proof *adj* : capable of keeping sound from entering or escaping

sound wave *n* : a wave that is produced when a sound is made and is responsible for carrying the sound to the ear

soup *n* : a liquid food made from the liquid in which vegetables, meat, or fish have been cooked and often containing pieces of solid food

¹**sour** *adj* **1** : having an acid taste **2** : having become acid through spoiling **3** : suggesting decay **4** : not pleasant or friendly **5** : acid in reaction — **sour·ish** *adj* — **sour·ly** *adv* — **sour·ness** *n*

²**sour** *vb* : to make or become sour

source n **1** : the cause or starting point of something **2** : the beginning of a stream of water **3** : one that supplies information

sou·sa·phone n : a large circular tuba designed to rest on the player's shoulder and used chiefly in marching bands

¹south adv : to or toward the south

²south adj : placed toward, facing, or coming from the south

³south n **1** : the direction to the right of one facing east : the compass point opposite to north **2** cap : regions or countries south of a point that is mentioned or understood

¹South American adj : of or relating to South America or the South Americans

²South American n : a person born or living in South America

south·bound adj : going south

¹south·east adv : to or toward the southeast

²southeast n **1** : the direction between south and east **2** cap : regions or countries southeast of a point that is mentioned or understood

³southeast adj : placed toward, facing, or coming from the southeast

south·east·er·ly adv or adj **1** : from the southeast **2** : toward the southeast

south·east·ern adj **1** often cap : of, relating to, or like that of the Southeast **2** : lying toward or coming from the southeast

south·er·ly adj or adv **1** : toward the south **2** : from the south

south·ern adj **1** often cap : of, relating to, or like that of the South **2** : lying toward or coming from the south

South·ern·er n : a person who is born or lives in the South

south·paw n : a person (as a baseball pitcher) who is left-handed

south pole n, often cap S&P **1** : the most southern point of the earth : the southern end of the earth's axis **2** : the end of a magnet that points toward the south when the magnet is free to swing

south·ward adv or adj : toward the south

¹south·west adv : to or toward the southwest

²southwest n **1** : the direction between south and west **2** cap : regions or countries southwest of a point that is mentioned or understood

³southwest adj : placed toward, facing, or coming from the southwest

south·west·er·ly adv or adj **1** : from the southwest **2** : toward the southwest

south·west·ern adj **1** : lying toward or coming from the southwest **2** often cap : of, relating to, or like that of the Southwest

sou·ve·nir n : something that serves as a reminder

sou'·west·er n : a waterproof hat with wide slanting brim that is longer in back than in front

¹sov·er·eign n **1** : a person (as a king or queen) or body of persons having the highest power and authority in a state **2** : an old British gold coin

²sovereign adj **1** : highest in power or authority **2** : having independent authority

sov·er·eign·ty n, pl **sov·er·eign·ties** **1** : supreme power especially over a political unit **2** : freedom from outside control **3** : one (as a country) that is sovereign

¹sow n : an adult female hog

²sow vb **sowed; sown** or **sowed; sow·ing** **1** : to plant or scatter (as seed) for growing **2** : to cover with or as if with scattered seed for growing **3** : to set in motion : cause to exist — **sow·er** n

sow bug n : WOOD LOUSE

sox pl of SOCK

soy·bean n : an annual Asian plant related to the clovers that is widely grown for its edible seeds which yield an oil rich in protein

soybean oil n : a pale yellow oil that is obtained from soybeans and is used chiefly as a food and in paints and soaps

¹space n **1** : a period of time **2** : a part of a distance, area, or volume that can be measured **3** : a certain place set apart or available **4** : the area without limits in which all things exist and move **5** : the region beyond the earth's atmosphere **6** : an empty place

²space vb **spaced; spac·ing** : to place with space between

space·craft n, pl **spacecraft** : a vehicle for travel beyond the earth's atmosphere

space·man n, pl **space·men** : a person who travels outside the earth's atmosphere

space·ship n : SPACECRAFT

space shuttle n : a spacecraft designed to transport people and cargo between earth and space that can be used repeatedly

space station n : an artificial satellite designed to stay in orbit permanently and to be occupied by humans for long periods

space suit n : a suit equipped to keep its wearer alive in space

spa·cious adj : having ample space

¹spade n : a digging tool made to be pushed into the ground with the foot

²spade vb **spad·ed; spad·ing** : to dig with a spade

spa·ghet·ti n : a food made of a mixture of flour and water and dried in the form of strings that are prepared for eating by boiling

¹span n **1** : the distance from the end of the

thumb to the end of the little finger when the hand is stretched wide open **2** : a limited portion of time **3** : the spread (as of an arch) from one support to another

²span *vb* **spanned; span·ning 1** : to measure by or as if by the hand stretched wide open **2** : to reach or extend across **3** : to place or construct a span over

³span *n* : two animals (as mules) worked or driven as a pair

span·gle *n* : SEQUIN

Span·iard *n* : a person born or living in Spain

span·iel *n* : a small or medium-sized dog with a thick wavy coat, long drooping ears, and usually short legs

¹Span·ish *adj* : of or relating to Spain, its people, or the Spanish language

²Spanish *n* **1** : the language of Spain and the countries colonized by Spaniards **2 Spanish** *pl* : the people of Spain

spank *vb* : to strike on the buttocks with the open hand

spank·ing *adj* : BRISK 1, LIVELY

¹spar *n* : a long rounded piece of wood or metal (as a mast, yard, or boom) to which a sail is fastened

²spar *vb* **sparred; spar·ring 1** : to box or make boxing movements with the fists for practice or in fun **2** : ²SKIRMISH

¹spare *vb* **spared; spar·ing 1** : to keep from being punished or harmed : show mercy to **2** : to free of the need to do something **3** : to keep from using or spending **4** : to give up especially as not really needed **5** : to have left over

²spare *adj* **spar·er; spar·est 1** : held in reserve **2** : being over what is needed **3** : somewhat thin **4** : SCANTY

³spare *n* **1** : a spare or duplicate piece or part **2** : the knocking down of all ten bowling pins with the first two balls

spare·ribs *n pl* : a cut of pork ribs separated from the bacon strips

spar·ing *adj* : careful in the use of money or supplies — **spar·ing·ly** *adv*

¹spark *n* **1** : a small bit of burning material **2** : a hot glowing bit struck from a mass (as by steel on flint) **3** : a short bright flash of electricity between two points **4** : ²SPARKLE 1 **5** : ¹TRACE 2

²spark *vb* **1** : to give off or cause to give off sparks **2** : to set off

¹spar·kle *vb* **spar·kled; spar·kling 1** : to throw off sparks **2** : to give off small flashes of light **3** : to be lively or active

²sparkle *n* **1** : a little flash of light **2** : the quality of sparkling

spar·kler *n* : a firework that throws off very bright sparks as it burns

spark plug *n* : a device used in an engine to produce a spark that ignites a fuel mixture

spar·row *n* : a small brownish bird related to the finches

sparrow hawk *n* : a small hawk or falcon

sparse *adj* **spars·er; spars·est** : not thickly grown or settled — **sparse·ly** *adv*

spasm *n* **1** : a sudden involuntary and usually violent contracting of muscles **2** : a sudden, violent, and temporary effort, emotion, or outburst

spas·mod·ic *adj* : relating to or affected by spasm : involving spasms — **spas·mod·i·cal·ly** *adv*

¹spat *past of* SPIT

²spat *n* : a cloth or leather covering for the instep and ankle

³spat *n* : a brief unimportant quarrel

spa·tial *adj* : of or relating to space

¹spat·ter *vb* **1** : to splash with drops or small bits of something wet **2** : to scatter by splashing

²spatter *n* **1** : the act or sound of spattering **2** : a drop or splash spattered on something : a spot or stain due to spattering

spat·u·la *n* : a knifelike instrument with a broad flexible blade that is used mostly for spreading or mixing soft substances or for lifting

¹spawn *vb* : to produce or deposit eggs or spawn

²spawn *n* : the eggs of a water animal (as an oyster or fish) that produces many small eggs

spay *vb* : to remove the ovaries of (a female animal)

speak *vb* **spoke; spo·ken; speak·ing 1** : to utter words : TALK **2** : to utter in words **3** : to mention in speech or writing **4** : to use or be able to use in talking

speak·er *n* **1** : a person who speaks **2** : a person who conducts a meeting **3** : LOUDSPEAKER

¹spear *n* **1** : a weapon with a long straight handle and sharp head or blade used for throwing or jabbing **2** : an instrument with a sharp point and curved hooks used in spearing fish

²spear *vb* : to strike or pierce with or as if with a spear

³spear *n* : a usually young blade or sprout (as of grass)

¹spear·head *n* **1** : the head or point of a spear **2** : the person, thing, or group that is the leading force (as in a development or an attack)

²spearhead *vb* : to serve as leader of

spear·mint *n* : a common mint used for flavoring

spe·cial adj **1** : UNUSUAL, EXTRAORDINARY **2** : liked very well **3** : UNIQUE 2 **4** : ¹EXTRA **5** : meant for a particular purpose or occasion — **spe·cial·ly** adv

spe·cial·ist n **1** : a person who studies or works at a special occupation or branch of learning **2** : a person working in a special skill in the Army in any of the four ranks equal to the ranks of corporal through sergeant first class

spe·cial·ize vb **spe·cial·ized; spe·cial·iz·ing 1** : to limit one's attention or energy to one business, subject, or study **2** : to change and develop so as to be suited for some particular use or living conditions

spe·cial·ty n, pl **spe·cial·ties 1** : a product of a special kind or of special excellence **2** : something a person specializes in

spe·cies n, pl **species 1** : a class of things of the same kind and with the same name : KIND, SORT **2** : a category of plants or animals that ranks below a genus in scientific classification and that is made up of individuals able to produce young with one another

spe·cif·ic adj **1** : being an actual example of a certain kind of thing **2** : clearly and exactly presented or stated **3** : of, relating to, or being a species

spec·i·fi·ca·tion n **1** : the act or process of specifying **2** : a single specified item **3** : a description of work to be done or materials to be used — often used in pl.

spec·i·fy vb **spec·i·fied; spec·i·fy·ing 1** : to mention or name exactly and clearly **2** : to include in a specification

spec·i·men n : a part or a single thing that shows what the whole thing or group is like : SAMPLE

speck n **1** : a small spot or blemish **2** : a very small amount : BIT

¹speck·le n : a small mark (as of color)

²speckle vb **speck·led; speck·ling** : to mark with speckles

spec·ta·cle n **1** : an unusual or impressive public display (as a big parade) **2** **spectacles** pl : a pair of glasses held in place by parts passing over the ears

spec·tac·u·lar adj : STRIKING, SHOWY

spec·ta·tor n : a person who looks on (as at a sports event)

spec·ter or **spec·tre** n : GHOST

spec·trum n, pl **spec·tra** or **spec·trums** : the group of different colors including red, orange, yellow, green, blue, indigo, and violet seen when light passes through a prism and falls on a surface or when sunlight is affected by drops of water (as in a rainbow)

spec·u·late vb **spec·u·lat·ed; spec·u·lat·ing 1** : MEDITATE 2 **2** : to engage in a business deal in which much profit may be made although at a big risk

spec·u·la·tion n **1** : ²GUESS **2** : the taking of a big risk in business in hopes of making a big profit

speech n **1** : the communication or expression of thoughts in spoken words **2** : something that is spoken **3** : a public talk **4** : a form of communication (as a language or dialect) used by a particular group **5** : the power of expressing or communicating thoughts by speaking

speech·less adj **1** : unable to speak **2** : not speaking for a time : SILENT

¹speed n **1** : quickness in movement or action **2** : rate of moving or doing

²speed vb **sped** or **speed·ed; speed·ing 1** : to move or cause to move fast : HURRY **2** : to go or drive at too high a speed **3** : to increase the speed of : ACCELERATE

speed·boat n : a fast motorboat

speed bump n : a low raised ridge across a roadway (as in a parking lot) to limit vehicle speed

speed·om·e·ter n **1** : an instrument that measures speed **2** : an instrument that measures speed and records distance traveled

speedy adj **speed·i·er; speed·i·est** : moving or taking place fast — **speed·i·ly** adv

¹spell vb **1** : to name, write, or print in order the letters of a word **2** : to make up the letters of **3** : to amount to : MEAN

²spell n **1** : a spoken word or group of words believed to have magic power : CHARM **2** : a very strong influence

³spell n **1** : one's turn at work or duty **2** : a period spent in a job or occupation **3** : a short period of time **4** : a stretch of a specified kind of weather **5** : a period of bodily or mental distress or disorder

⁴spell vb : to take the place of for a time : RELIEVE

spell·bound adj : held by or as if by a spell

spell·er n **1** : a person who spells words **2** : a book with exercises for teaching spelling

spell·ing n **1** : the forming of words from letters **2** : the letters composing a word

spelling checker also **spell check** or **spell checker** n : a computer program that shows the user any words that might be incorrectly spelled

spend vb **spent; spend·ing 1** : to use up : pay out **2** : to wear out : EXHAUST **3** : to use wastefully : SQUANDER **4** : to cause or allow (as time) to pass

spend·thrift n : one who spends wastefully

spent adj **1** : used up **2** : drained of energy

sperm n : SPERM CELL

sperm cell n : a male germ cell

sperm whale *n* : a large whale of warm seas hunted mostly for its oil (**sperm oil**)

spew *vb* : to pour out

sphere *n* **1** : a body (as the moon) shaped like a ball **2** : a figure so shaped that every point on its surface is an equal distance from the center of the figure **3** : a field of influence or activity

spher·i·cal *adj* : relating to or having the form of a sphere

sphinx *n* : an Egyptian figure having the body of a lion and the head of a man, a ram, or a hawk

¹spice *n* **1** : a plant product (as pepper or nutmeg) that has a strong pleasant smell and is used to flavor food **2** : something that adds interest

²spice *vb* **spiced; spic·ing** : to season with or as if with spices

spick–and–span *or* **spic–and–span** *adj* **1** : quite new and unused **2** : very clean and neat

spicy *adj* **spic·i·er; spic·i·est** **1** : flavored with or containing spice **2** : somewhat shocking or indecent

spi·der *n* **1** : a wingless animal somewhat like an insect but having eight legs instead of six and a body divided into two parts instead of three **2** : a cast-iron frying pan

spi·der·web *n* : the silken web spun by most spiders and used as a resting place and a trap for prey

spig·ot *n* **1** : a plug used to stop the vent in a barrel **2** : FAUCET

¹spike *n* **1** : a very large nail **2** : one of the metal objects attached to the heel and sole of a shoe (as a baseball shoe) to prevent slipping **3** : something pointed like a spike

²spike *vb* **spiked; spik·ing** **1** : to fasten with spikes **2** : to pierce or cut with or on a spike

³spike *n* **1** : an ear of grain **2** : a long usually rather narrow flower cluster in which the blossoms grow very close to a central stem

¹spill *vb* **spilled** *also* **spilt; spill·ing** **1** : to cause (blood) to flow by wounding : ¹SHED **2** : to cause or allow to fall, flow, or run out so as to be wasted or scattered **3** : to flow or run out, over, or off and become wasted or scattered **4** : to make known

²spill *n* **1** : an act of spilling **2** : a fall especially from a horse or vehicle **3** : something spilled

¹spin *vb* **spun; spin·ning** **1** : to make yarn or thread from (fibers) **2** : to make (yarn or thread) from fibers **3** : to form threads or a web or cocoon by giving off a sticky fluid that quickly hardens into silk **4** : to turn or cause to turn round and round rapidly : TWIRL **5** : to feel as if in a whirl **6** : to make up and tell using the imagination **7** : to move swiftly on wheels or in a vehicle **8** : to make, shape, or produce by or as if by whirling

²spin *n* **1** : a rapid whirling motion **2** : a short trip in or on a wheeled vehicle

spin·ach *n* : a leafy plant that is grown for use as food

spi·nal *adj* : of, relating to, or located near the backbone or the spinal cord — **spi·nal·ly** *adv*

spinal column *n* : BACKBONE 1

spinal cord *n* : the thick cord of nervous tissue that extends from the brain down the back, fills the cavity of the backbone, and is concerned especially with reflex action

spin·dle *n* **1** : a slender round rod or stick with narrowed ends by which thread is twisted in spinning and on which it is wound **2** : something (as an axle or shaft) which is shaped or turned like a spindle or on which something turns

spin·dly *adj* **spin·dli·er; spin·dli·est** : being thin and long or tall and usually feeble or weak

spine *n* **1** : BACKBONE 1 **2** : a stiff pointed part growing from the surface of a plant or animal

spine·less *adj* **1** : lacking spines **2** : having no backbone **3** : lacking spirit, courage, or determination

spin·et *n* **1** : an early harpsichord with one keyboard and only one string for each note **2** : a small upright piano

spin·ning jen·ny *n, pl* **spin·ning jen·nies** : an early machine for spinning wool or cotton by means of many spindles

spinning wheel *n* : a small machine driven by the hand or foot that is used to spin yarn or thread

spin·ster *n* : an unmarried woman past the usual age for marrying

spiny *adj* **spin·i·er; spin·i·est** : covered with spines

spi·ra·cle *n* : an opening (as in the head of a whale or the abdomen of an insect) for breathing

¹spi·ral *adj* **1** : winding or circling around a center and gradually getting closer to or farther away from it **2** : circling around a center like the thread of a screw — **spi·ral·ly** *adv*

²spiral *n* **1** : a single turn or coil in a spiral object **2** : something that has a spiral form

³spiral *vb* **spi·raled** *or* **spi·ralled; spi·ral·ing** *or* **spi·ral·ling** : to move in a spiral path

spire *n* **1** : a pointed roof especially of a tower **2** : STEEPLE

spi·rea *or* **spi·raea** *n* : a shrub related to the roses that bears clusters of small white or pink flowers

¹spir·lt *n* **1** : a force within a human being thought to give the body life, energy, and power : SOUL **2** *cap* : the active presence of God in human life : the third person of the Trinity **3** : a being (as a ghost) whose existence cannot be explained by the known laws of nature **4** : ¹MOOD **5** : a lively or brisk quality **6** : an attitude governing one's actions **7** : PERSON 1 **8** : an alcoholic liquor — usually used in pl. **9 spirits** *pl* : a solution in alcohol **10** : real meaning or intention — **spir·it·less** *adj*

²spirit *vb* : to carry off secretly or mysteriously

spir·it·ed *adj* : full of courage or energy

¹spir·i·tu·al *adj* **1** : of, relating to, or consisting of spirit : not bodily or material **2** : of or relating to sacred or religious matters — **spir·i·tu·al·ly** *adv*

²spiritual *n* : a religious folk song developed especially among Negroes of the southern United States

¹spit *n* **1** : a thin pointed rod for holding meat over a fire **2** : a small point of land that runs out into a body of water

²spit *vb* **spit** *or* **spat**; **spit·ting 1** : to cause (as saliva) to spurt from the mouth **2** : to express by or as if by spitting **3** : to give off usually briskly : EMIT **4** : to rain lightly or snow in flurries

³spit *n* **1** : SALIVA **2** : the act of spitting **3** : a foamy material given out by some insects **4** : perfect likeness

¹spite *n* : dislike or hatred for another person with a wish to torment, anger, or defeat — **in spite of** : without being prevented by

²spite *vb* **spit·ed**; **spit·ing** : ANNOY, ANGER

spite·ful *adj* : filled with or showing spite : MALICIOUS — **spite·ful·ly** *adv*

spit·tle *n* **1** : SALIVA **2** : ³SPIT 3

¹splash *vb* **1** : to hit (something liquid or sloppy) and cause to move and scatter roughly **2** : to wet or soil by spattering with water or mud **3** : to move or strike with a splashing sound **4** : to spread or scatter like a splashed liquid

²splash *n* **1** : splashed material **2** : a spot or smear from or as if from splashed liquid **3** : the sound or action of splashing

¹splat·ter *vb* : ¹SPLASH, SPATTER

²splatter *n* : ²SPLASH

spleen *n* : an organ near the stomach that destroys worn-out red blood cells and produces some of the white blood cells

splen·did *adj* **1** : having or showing splendor : BRILLIANT **2** : impressive in beauty,

excellence, or magnificence **3** : GRAND **4** — **splen·did·ly** *adv*

splen·dor *n* **1** : great brightness **2** : POMP, GLORY

¹splice *vb* **spliced**; **splic·ing 1** : to unite (as two ropes) by weaving together **2** : to unite (as rails or pieces of film) by connecting the ends together

²splice *n* : a joining or joint made by splicing

splint *n* **1** : a thin flexible strip of wood woven together with others in making a chair seat or basket **2** : a device for keeping a broken or displaced bone in place

¹splin·ter *n* : a thin piece split or torn off lengthwise : SLIVER

²splinter *vb* : to break into splinters

¹split *vb* **split**; **split·ting 1** : to divide lengthwise or by layers **2** : to separate the parts of by putting something between **3** : to burst or break apart or in pieces **4** : to divide into shares or sections

²split *n* **1** : a product or result of splitting : CRACK **2** : the act or process of splitting : DIVISION **3** : the feat of lowering oneself to the floor or leaping into the air with the legs extended in a straight line and in opposite directions

³split *adj* : divided by or as if by splitting

¹spoil *n* : stolen goods : PLUNDER

²spoil *vb* **spoiled** *or* **spoilt**; **spoil·ing 1** : ¹PLUNDER, ROB **2** : to damage badly : RUIN **3** : to damage the quality or effect of **4** : to decay or lose freshness, value, or usefulness by being kept too long **5** : to damage the disposition of by letting get away with too much

spoil·age *n* : the action of spoiling or condition of being spoiled

¹spoke *past of* SPEAK

²spoke *n* : one of the bars or rods extending from the hub of a wheel to the rim

¹spoken *past participle of* SPEAK

²spo·ken *adj* **1** : expressed in speech : ORAL **2** : used in speaking **3** : speaking in a specified manner

spokes·man *n, pl* **spokes·men** : SPOKESPERSON

spokes·per·son *n* : a person who speaks for another or for a group

spokes·wom·an *n, pl* **spokes·wom·en** : a woman who is a spokesperson

¹sponge *n* **1** : a springy mass of horny fibers that forms the skeleton of a group of sea animals, is able to absorb water freely, and is used for cleaning **2** : any of a group of water animals that have the form of hollow cell colonies made up of two layers and that include those whose skeletons are sponges **3** : a manufactured product (as of rubber or plastic) having the springy absorbent quality of natural sponge 4 : a pad of folded gauze used in surgery and medicine — **sponge·like** adj

²**sponge** vb **sponged; spong·ing** 1 : to clean or wipe with a sponge 2 : to absorb with or like a sponge 3 : to get something or live at the expense of another

spongy adj **spong·i·er; spong·i·est** : like a sponge in appearance or in ability to absorb : soft and full of holes or moisture

¹**spon·sor** n 1 : a person who takes the responsibility for some other person or thing 2 : GODPARENT 3 : a person or an organization that pays for or plans and carries out a project or activity 4 : a person or an organization that pays the cost of a radio or television program — **spon·sor·ship** n

²**sponsor** vb : to act as sponsor for

spon·ta·ne·ous adj 1 : done, said, or produced freely and naturally 2 : acting or taking place without outside force or cause — **spon·ta·ne·ous·ly** adv

spontaneous combustion n : a bursting of material into flame from the heat produced within itself through chemical action

spook n : GHOST, SPECTER

spooky adj **spook·i·er; spook·i·est** 1 : like a ghost 2 : suggesting the presence of ghosts

¹**spool** n : a small cylinder which has a rim or ridge at each end and a hole from end to end for a pin or spindle and on which material (as thread, wire, or tape) is wound

²**spool** vb : to wind on a spool

¹**spoon** n : a utensil with a shallow bowl and a handle used especially in cooking and eating

²**spoon** vb : to take up in or as if in a spoon

spoon·bill n : a wading bird related to the ibises and having a bill which widens and flattens at the tip

spoon·ful n, pl **spoon·fuls** or **spoons·ful** : as much as a spoon can hold

spore n : a reproductive body of various plants and some lower animals that consists of a single cell and is able to produce a new individual — **spored** adj

¹**sport** vb 1 : to amuse oneself : FROLIC 2 : to speak or act in fun 3 : SHOW OFF

²**sport** n 1 : PASTIME, RECREATION 2 : physical activity (as running or an athletic game) engaged in for pleasure 3 : FUN 4 : a person thought of with respect to the ideals of sportsmanship

sports·man n, pl **sports·men** : a person who engages in or is interested in sports and especially outdoor sports (as hunting and fishing)

sports·man·ship n : fair play, respect for opponents, and gracious behavior in winning or losing

sports·wom·an n, pl **sports·wom·en** : a woman who engages in or is interested in sports and especially outdoor sports

¹**spot** n 1 : something bad that others know about one : FAULT 2 : a small part that is different (as in color) from the main part 3 : an area soiled or marked (as by dirt) 4 : a particular place — **spot·ted** adj — **on the spot** 1 : right away : IMMEDIATELY 2 : at the place of action 3 : in difficulty or danger

²**spot** vb **spot·ted; spot·ting** 1 : to mark or be marked with spots 2 : to single out : IDENTIFY

spot·less adj : free from spot or blemish : perfectly clean or pure — **spot·less·ly** adv — **spot·less·ness** n

¹**spot·light** n 1 : a spot of light used to show up a particular area, person, or thing (as on a stage) 2 : public notice 3 : a light to direct a narrow strong beam of light on a small area

²**spotlight** vb **spot·light·ed** or **spot·lit; spot·light·ing** 1 : to light up with a spotlight 2 : to bring to public attention

spotted owl n : a rare brown owl with white spots and dark stripes that is found from British Columbia to southern California and central Mexico

spot·ty adj **spot·ti·er; spot·ti·est** 1 : having spots 2 : not always the same especially in quality

spouse n : a married person : HUSBAND, WIFE

¹**spout** vb 1 : to shoot out (liquid) with force 2 : to speak with a long and quick flow of words so as to sound important 3 : to flow out with force : SPURT

²**spout** n 1 : a tube, pipe, or hole through which something (as rainwater) spouts 2 : a sudden strong stream of fluid

¹**sprain** n 1 : a sudden or severe twisting of a joint with stretching or tearing of ligaments 2 : a sprained condition

²**sprain** vb : to injure by a sudden or severe twist

sprang past of SPRING

¹**sprawl** vb 1 : to lie or sit with arms and legs spread out 2 : to spread out in an uneven or awkward way

²**sprawl** n : the act or posture of sprawling

¹**spray** n : a green or flowering branch or a usually flat arrangement of these

²**spray** n 1 : liquid flying in fine drops like water blown from a wave 2 : a burst of fine mist (as from an atomizer) 3 : a device (as an atomizer) for scattering a spray of liquid or mist

³**spray** vb 1 : to scatter or let fall in a spray

2 : to scatter spray on or into — **spray·er** *n*

spray gun *n* : a device for spraying paints, varnishes, or insect poisons

¹spread *vb* spread; **spread·ing** **1** : to open over a larger area **2** : to stretch out : EXTEND **3** : SCATTER 1, STREW **4** : to give out over a period of time or among a group **5** : to put a layer of on a surface **6** : to cover something with **7** : to prepare for a meal : SET **8** : to pass from person to person **9** : to stretch or move apart

²spread *n* **1** : the act or process of spreading **2** : extent of spreading **3** : a noticeable display in a magazine or newspaper **4** : a food to be spread on bread or crackers **5** : a very fine meal : FEAST **6** : a cloth cover for a table or bed **7** : distance between two points

spree *n* : an outburst of activity

sprig *n* : a small shoot or twig

spright·ly *adj* spright·li·er; spright·li·est : full of spirit : LIVELY

¹spring *vb* sprang *or* sprung; sprung; **spring·ing** **1** : to appear or grow quickly **2** : to come from by birth or descent **3** : to come into being : ARISE **4** : to move suddenly upward or forward : LEAP **5** : to have (a leak) appear **6** : to move quickly by elastic force **7** : ²WARP 1 **8** : to cause to operate suddenly

²spring *n* **1** : a source of supply (as of water coming up from the ground) **2** : the season between winter and summer including in the northern hemisphere usually the months of March, April, and May **3** : a time or season of growth or development **4** : an elastic body or device that recovers its original shape when it is released after being squeezed or stretched **5** : the act or an instance of leaping up or forward **6** : elastic power or force

spring·board *n* : a flexible board usually fastened at one end and used for jumping high in the air in gymnastics or diving

spring peep·er *n* : a small frog that lives in trees and makes a high peeping sound heard mostly in spring

spring·time *n* : the season of spring

springy *adj* spring·i·er; spring·i·est **1** : ¹ELASTIC **2** : having or showing a lively and energetic movement

¹sprin·kle *vb* sprin·kled; sprin·kling **1** : to scatter in drops **2** : to scatter over or in or among **3** : to rain lightly — **sprin·kler** *n*

²sprinkle *n* **1** : a light rain **2** : SPRINKLING

sprin·kling *n* : a very small number or amount

¹sprint *vb* : to run at top speed especially for a short distance — **sprint·er** *n*

²sprint *n* **1** : a short run at top speed **2** : a race over a short distance

sprite *n* : ELF, FAIRY

sprock·et *n* : one of many points that stick up on the rim of a wheel (**sprocket wheel**) shaped so as to fit into the links of a chain

¹sprout *vb* : to produce or cause to produce fresh young growth

²sprout *n* : a young stem of a plant especially when coming directly from a seed or root

¹spruce *vb* spruced; spruc·ing : to make something or oneself neat or stylish in appearance

²spruce *adj* spruc·er; spruc·est : neat or stylish in appearance

³spruce *n* : an evergreen tree shaped like a cone with a thick growth of short needles, drooping cones, and light soft wood

sprung *past of* SPRING

spry *adj* spri·er *or* spry·er; spri·est *or* spry·est : LIVELY 1, ACTIVE

spun *past of* SPIN

spunk *n* : COURAGE, SPIRIT

¹spur *n* **1** : a pointed device fastened to the back of a rider's boot and used to urge a horse on **2** : something that makes one want to do something : INCENTIVE **3** : a stiff sharp point (as a horny spine on the leg of a rooster) **4** : a mass of jagged rock coming out from the side of a mountain **5** : a short section of railway track coming away from the main line — **spurred** *adj*

²spur *vb* spurred; spur·ring **1** : to urge a horse on with spurs **2** : INCITE

spurn *vb* : to reject with scorn

¹spurt *vb* **1** : to pour out suddenly : SPOUT **2** : ¹SQUIRT

²spurt *n* : a sudden pouring out : JET

³spurt *n* : a brief burst of increased effort

⁴spurt *vb* : to make a spurt

¹sput·ter *vb* **1** : to spit or squirt bits of food or saliva noisily from the mouth **2** : to speak in a hasty or explosive way in confusion or excitement **3** : to make explosive popping sounds

²sputter *n* : the act or sound of sputtering

¹spy *vb* spied; spy·ing **1** : to watch secretly **2** : to catch sight of : SEE

²spy *n, pl* spies **1** : a person who watches the movement or actions of others especially in secret **2** : a person who tries secretly to get information especially about an unfriendly country or its plans and actions

spy·glass *n* : a small telescope

squab *n* : a young pigeon especially when about four weeks old and ready for use as food

¹squab·ble *n* : a noisy quarrel usually over unimportant things

²squabble *vb* **squab·bled; squab·bling** : to quarrel noisily for little or no reason

squad *n* **1** : a small group of soldiers **2** : a small group working or playing together

squad car *n* : CRUISER 2

squad·ron *n* : a group especially of cavalry riders, military airplanes, or naval ships moving and working together

squal·id *adj* : filthy or degraded from a lack of care or money

¹squall *vb* : to let out a harsh cry or scream

²squall *n* : a sudden strong gust of wind often with rain or snow

squa·lor *n* : the quality or state of being squalid

squan·der *vb* : to spend foolishly : WASTE

¹square *n* **1** : an instrument having at least one right angle and two or more straight edges used to mark or test right angles **2** : a flat figure that has four equal sides and four right angles **3** : something formed like a square **4** : the product of a number or amount multiplied by itself **5** : an open place or area where two or more streets meet **6** : ¹BLOCK 6, 7

²square *adj* **squar·er; squar·est 1** : having four equal sides and four right angles **2** : forming a right angle **3** : multiplied by itself **4** : having outlines that suggest sharp corners rather than curves **5** : being a unit of area consisting of a square whose sides have a given length **6** : having a specified length in each of two equal dimensions **7** : exactly adjusted **8** : ¹JUST 3, FAIR **9** : leaving no balance : EVEN **10** : large enough to satisfy — **square·ly** *adv*

³square *vb* **squared; squar·ing 1** : to make square : form with right angles, straight edges, and flat surfaces **2** : to make straight **3** : to multiply a number by itself **4** : AGREE 4 **5** : ²BALANCE 1, SETTLE

square knot *n* : a knot made of two half-knots tied in opposite directions and typically used to join the ends of two cords

square–rigged *adj* : having the principal sails extended on yards fastened in a horizontal position to the masts at their center

square root *n* : a factor of a number that when multiplied by itself gives the number

¹squash *vb* : to beat or press into a soft or flat mass : CRUSH

²squash *n* : the fruit of any of several plants related to the gourds that is cooked as a vegetable or used for animal feed

¹squat *vb* **squat·ted; squat·ting 1** : to crouch by bending the knees fully so as to sit on or close to the heels **2** : to settle without any right on land that one does not own **3** : to settle on government land in order to become the owner of the land

²squat *adj* **squat·ter; squat·test 1** : bent in a deep crouch **2** : low to the ground **3** : having a short thick body

³squat *n* **1** : the act of squatting **2** : a squatting posture

¹squawk *vb* **1** : to make a harsh short scream **2** : to complain or protest loudly or with strong feeling

²squawk *n* **1** : a harsh short scream **2** : a noisy complaint

¹squeak *vb* **1** : to make a short shrill cry **2** : to get, win, or pass with trouble : barely succeed

²squeak *n* : a sharp shrill cry or sound

squeaky *adj* **squeak·i·er; squeak·i·est** : likely to squeak

¹squeal *vb* **1** : to make a sharp long shrill cry or noise **2** : INFORM 2

²squeal *n* : a shrill sharp cry or noise

¹squeeze *vb* **squeezed; squeez·ing 1** : to press together from the opposite sides or parts of : COMPRESS **2** : to get by squeezing **3** : to force or crowd in by compressing

²squeeze *n* : an act or instance of squeezing

squid *n* : a sea mollusk that is related to the octopus but has a long body and ten arms

¹squint *adj* : not able to look in the same direction — used of the two eyes

²squint *vb* **1** : to have squint eyes **2** : to look or peer with the eyes partly closed

³squint *n* **1** : the condition of being cross-eyed **2** : the action or an instance of squinting

¹squire *n* **1** : a person who carries the shield or armor of a knight **2** : ¹ESCORT 1 **3** : an owner of a country estate

²squire *vb* **squired; squir·ing** : to act as a squire or escort for

squirm *vb* **1** : to twist about like an eel or a worm **2** : to feel very embarrassed

squir·rel *n* : a small gnawing animal (as the common American **red squirrel** and **gray squirrel**) usually with a bushy tail and soft fur and strong hind legs for leaping

¹squirt *vb* : to shoot out liquid in a thin stream : SPURT

²squirt *n* **1** : an instrument for squirting liquid **2** : a small powerful stream of liquid : JET **3** : the action of squirting

¹stab *n* **1** : a wound produced by or as if by a pointed weapon **2** : ²THRUST 1 **3** : ³TRY, EFFORT

²stab *vb* **stabbed; stab·bing 1** : to wound or pierce with a stab **2** : ¹DRIVE 2, THRUST

sta·bil·i·ty *n, pl* **sta·bil·i·ties** : the condition of being stable

sta·bi·lize *vb* **sta·bi·lized; sta·bi·liz·ing** : to make or become stable — **sta·bi·liz·er** *n*

¹sta·ble *n* : a building in which domestic animals are housed and cared for

²stable *vb* **sta·bled; sta·bling** : to put or keep in a stable

³stable *adj* **sta·bler; sta·blest** 1 : not easily changed or affected 2 : not likely to change suddenly or greatly 3 : LASTING 4 : RELIABLE

stac·ca·to *adj* 1 : cut short so as not to sound connected 2 : played or sung with breaks between notes

¹stack *n* 1 : a large pile (as of hay) usually shaped like a cone 2 : a neat pile of objects usually one on top of the other 3 : a large number or amount 4 : CHIMNEY 1, SMOKESTACK 5 : a structure with shelves for storing books

²stack *vb* : to arrange in or form a stack : PILE

sta·di·um *n, pl* **sta·di·ums** *or* **sta·dia** : a large outdoor structure with rows of seats for spectators at sports events

staff *n, pl* **staffs** *or* **staves** 1 : a pole, stick, rod, or bar used as a support or as a sign of authority 2 : something that is a source of strength 3 : the five parallel lines with their four spaces on which music is written 4 *pl* **staffs** : a group of persons serving as assistants to or employees under a chief 5 *pl* **staffs** : a group of military officers who plan and manage for a commanding officer

staff sergeant *n* : a noncommissioned officer in the Army, Air Force, or Marine Corps ranking above a sergeant

staff sergeant major *n* : a noncommissioned officer in the Army ranking above a master sergeant

¹stag *n* 1 : an adult male deer especially of the larger kind 2 : a man who goes to a social gathering without escorting a woman

²stag *adj* : intended or thought suitable for men only

¹stage *n* 1 : a raised floor (as for speaking or giving plays) 2 : a place where something important happens 3 : the theatrical profession or art 4 : a step forward in a journey, a task, a process, or a development : PHASE 5 : STAGECOACH

²stage *vb* **staged; stag·ing** : to produce or show to the public on or as if on the stage

stage·coach *n* : a coach pulled by horses that runs on a schedule from place to place carrying passengers and mail

¹stag·ger *vb* 1 : to move unsteadily from side to side as if about to fall : REEL 2 : to cause to move unsteadily 3 : to cause great surprise or shock in 4 : to place or arrange in a zigzag but balanced way

²stagger *n* : a reeling or unsteady walk

stag·nant *adj* 1 : not flowing 2 : not active or brisk : DULL

stag·nate *vb* **stag·nat·ed; stag·nat·ing** : to be or become stagnant

¹stain *vb* 1 : to soil or discolor especially in spots 2 : ²COLOR 2, TINGE 3 : ¹CORRUPT 1 4 : ¹DISGRACE

²stain *n* 1 : ¹SPOT 3, DISCOLORATION 2 : a mark of guilt or disgrace : STIGMA 3 : something (as a dye) used in staining — **stain·less** *adj*

stainless steel *n* : an alloy of steel and chromium that is resistant to stain, rust, and corrosion

stair *n* 1 : a series of steps or flights of steps for going from one level to another — often used in pl. 2 : one step of a stairway

stair·case *n* : a flight of stairs with their supporting structure and railings

stair·way *n* : one or more flights of stairs usually with connecting landings

¹stake *n* 1 : a pointed piece (as of wood) driven or to be driven into the ground as a marker or to support something 2 : a post to which a person is tied to be put to death by burning 3 : something that is put up to be won or lost in gambling 4 : the prize in a contest 5 : ¹SHARE 1, INTEREST — **at stake** : in a position to be lost if something goes wrong

²stake *vb* **staked; stak·ing** 1 : to mark the limits of by stakes 2 : to fasten or support (as plants) with stakes 3 : ²BET 1 4 : to give money to or help (as with a project)

sta·lac·tite *n* : a deposit hanging from the roof or side of a cave in the shape of an icicle formed by the partial evaporating of dripping water containing lime

sta·lag·mite *n* : a deposit like an upside down stalactite formed by the dripping of water containing lime onto the floor of a cave

¹stale *adj* **stal·er; stal·est** 1 : having lost a good taste or quality through age 2 : used or heard so often as to be dull 3 : not so strong, energetic, or effective as before — **stale·ly** *adv* — **stale·ness** *n*

²stale *vb* **staled; stal·ing** : to make or become stale

¹stalk *n* 1 : a plant stem especially when not woody 2 : a slender supporting structure — **stalked** *adj* — **stalk·less** *adj*

²stalk *vb* 1 : to hunt slowly and quietly 2 : to walk in a stiff or proud manner 3 : to move through or follow as if stalking prey — **stalk·er** *n*

³stalk *n* 1 : the act of stalking 2 : a stalking way of walking

¹stall *n* 1 : a compartment for one animal in a stable 2 : a space set off (as for parking an automobile) 3 : a seat in a church choir : a church pew 4 : a booth, stand, or counter where business may be carried on or articles may be displayed for sale

²stall *vb* **1** : to put or keep in a stall **2** : to stop or cause to stop usually by accident

³stall *n* : a trick to deceive or delay

⁴stall *vb* : to distract attention or make excuses to gain time

stal·lion *n* : a male horse

stal·wart *adj* : STURDY, RESOLUTE

sta·men *n* : the male organ of a flower that produces pollen and that consists of an anther and a filament

stam·i·na *n* : VIGOR 1, ENDURANCE

¹stam·mer *vb* : to speak with involuntary stops and much repeating — **stam·mer·er** *n*

²stammer *n* : an act or instance of stammering

¹stamp *vb* **1** : to bring the foot down hard and with noise **2** : to put an end to by or as if by hitting with the bottom of the foot **3** : to mark or cut out with a tool or device having a design **4** : to attach a postage stamp to **5** : CHARACTERIZE 1

²stamp *n* **1** : a device or instrument for stamping **2** : the mark made by stamping **3** : a sign of a special quality **4** : the act of stamping **5** : a small piece of paper or a mark attached to something to show that a tax or fee has been paid

¹stam·pede *n* **1** : a wild dash or flight of frightened animals **2** : a sudden foolish action or movement of a crowd of people

²stampede *vb* **stam·ped·ed; stam·ped·ing** **1** : to run or cause (as cattle) to run away in panic **2** : to act or cause to act together suddenly and without thought

stance *n* : way of standing : POSTURE

stanch *vb* : to stop or check the flow of (as blood)

¹stand *vb* **stood; stand·ing** **1** : to be in or take a vertical position on one's feet **2** : to take up or stay in a specified position or condition **3** : to have an opinion **4** : to rest, remain, or set in a usually vertical position **5** : to be in a specified place **6** : to stay in effect **7** : to put up with : ENDURE **8** : UNDERGO **9** : to perform the duty of — **stand by** : to be or remain loyal or true to — **stand for** **1** : to be a symbol for : REPRESENT **2** : to put up with : PERMIT

²stand *n* **1** : an act of standing **2** : a halt for defense or resistance **3** : a place or post especially where one stands : STATION **4** : a structure containing rows of seats for spectators of a sport or spectacle **5** : a raised area (as for speakers or performers) **6** : a stall or booth often outdoors for a small business **7** : a small structure (as a rack or table) on or in which something may be placed **8** : POSITION 2

¹stan·dard *n* **1** : a figure used as a symbol by an organized body of people **2** : the personal flag of the ruler of a state **3** : something set up as a rule for measuring or as a model **4** : an upright support

²standard *adj* **1** : used as or matching a standard **2** : regularly and widely used **3** : widely known and accepted to be of good and permanent value

stan·dard·ize *vb* **stan·dard·ized; stan·dard·iz·ing** : to make standard or alike

standard time *n* : the time established by law or by common usage over a region or country

stand by *vb* **1** : to be present **2** : to be or get ready to act

¹stand·ing *adj* **1** : ¹ERECT **2** : not flowing : STAGNANT **3** : remaining at the same level or amount until canceled **4** : PERMANENT

²standing *n* **1** : the action or position of one that stands **2** : length of existence or service **3** : POSITION 4, STATUS

stand out *vb* : to be easily seen or recognized

stand·point *n* : a way in which things are thought about : POINT OF VIEW

stand·still *n* : the condition of not being active or busy : STOP

stand up *vb* **1** : to stay in good condition **2** : to fail to keep an appointment with — **stand up for** : DEFEND **2** — **stand up to** : to face boldly

stank *past of* STINK

stan·za *n* : a group of lines forming a division of a poem

¹sta·ple *n* **1** : a piece of metal shaped like a U with sharp points to be driven into a surface to hold something (as a hook, rope, or wire) **2** : a short thin wire with bent ends that is driven through papers and clinched to hold them together or driven through thin material to fasten it to a surface

²staple *vb* **sta·pled; sta·pling** : to fasten with staples

³staple *n* **1** : a chief product of business or farming of a place **2** : something that is used widely and often **3** : the chief part of something **4** : fiber (as cotton or wool) suitable for spinning into yarn

⁴staple *adj* **1** : much used, needed, or enjoyed usually by many people **2** : ¹PRINCIPAL, CHIEF

sta·pler *n* : a device that staples

¹star *n* **1** : any of those celestial bodies except planets which are visible at night and look like fixed points of light **2** : a star or especially a planet that is believed in astrology to influence one's life **3** : a figure or thing (as a medal) with five or more points that represents or suggests a star **4** : the principal member of a theater or opera company **5** : a very talented or popular performer

²star *vb* **starred; star·ring 1** : to sprinkle or decorate with or as if with stars **2** : to mark with a star as being special or very good **3** : to mark with an asterisk **4** : to present in the role of a star **5** : to play the most important role **6** : to perform in an outstanding manner

star·board *n* : the right side of a ship or airplane looking forward

¹starch *vb* : to stiffen with starch

²starch *n* : a white odorless tasteless substance that is the chief storage form of carbohydrates in plants, is an important food, and has also various household and business uses (as for stiffening clothes)

starchy *adj* **starch·i·er; starch·i·est** : like or containing starch

¹stare *vb* **stared; star·ing** : to look at hard and long often with wide-open eyes

²stare *n* : the act or an instance of staring

star·fish *n* : any of a group of sea animals mostly having five arms that spread out from a central disk and feeding mostly on mollusks

¹stark *adj* **1** : ¹BARREN 2, DESOLATE **2** : ¹UTTER, ABSOLUTE

²stark *adv* : COMPLETELY

star·light *n* : the light given by the stars

star·ling *n* : a dark brown or in summer greenish black European bird about the size of a robin that is now common and often a pest in the United States

star·lit *adj* : lighted by the stars

star·ry *adj* **star·ri·er; star·ri·est** : full of stars **2** : of, relating to, or consisting of stars **3** : shining like stars

Stars and Stripes *n sing or pl* : the flag of the United States

¹start *vb* **1** : to move suddenly and quickly : give a sudden twitch or jerk (as in surprise) **2** : to come or bring into being or action **3** : to stick out or seem to stick out **4** : SET OUT 2 **5** : to set going

²start *n* **1** : a sudden movement **2** : a brief act, movement, or effort **3** : a beginning of movement, action, or development **4** : a place of beginning (as of a race)

start·er *n* : someone or something that starts something or causes something else to start

star·tle *vb* **star·tled; star·tling 1** : to cause to move or jump (as in surprise or fear) **2** : to frighten suddenly but slightly

star·tling *adj* : causing a moment of fright or surprise

star·va·tion *n* : the act or an instance of starving : the condition of being starved

starve *vb* **starved; starv·ing 1** : to suffer or die or cause to suffer or die from lack of food **2** : to suffer or cause to suffer from a lack of something other than food

¹state *n* **1** : manner or condition of being **2** : a body of people living in a certain territory under one government : the government of such a body of people **3** : one of the divisions of a nation having a federal government

²state *vb* **stat·ed; stat·ing 1** : to set by rule, law, or authority : FIX **2** : to express especially in words

state·house *n* : the building where the legislature of a state meets

state·ly *adj* **state·li·er; state·li·est 1** : having great dignity **2** : impressive especially in size : IMPOSING — **state·li·ness** *n*

state·ment *n* **1** : something that is stated : REPORT, ACCOUNT **2** : a brief record of a business account

state·room *n* : a private room on a ship or a train

states·man *n, pl* **states·men** : a person who is active in government and who gives wise leadership in making policies

¹stat·ic *adj* **1** : showing little change or action **2** : of or relating to charges of electricity (as one produced by friction) that do not flow

²static *n* : noise produced in a radio or television receiver by atmospheric or electrical disturbances

¹sta·tion *n* **1** : the place or position where a person or thing stands or is assigned to stand or remain **2** : a regular stopping place (as on a bus line) : DEPOT **3** : a post or area of duty **4** : POSITION 4, RANK **5** : a place for specialized observation or for a public service **6** : a collection of radio or television equipment for transmitting or receiving **7** : the place where a radio or television station is

²station *vb* : to assign to or set in a station or position : POST

sta·tion·ary *adj* **1** : having been set in a certain place or post : IMMOBILE **2** : not changing : STABLE

sta·tion·ery *n* : writing paper and envelopes

station wagon *n* : an automobile that is longer on the inside than a sedan and has one or more folding or removable seats but no separate luggage compartment

stat·ue *n* : an image or likeness (as of a person or animal) sculptured, modeled, or cast in a solid substance (as marble or bronze)

stat·ure *n* **1** : natural height (as of a person) **2** : quality or fame one has gained (as by growth or development)

sta·tus *n* **1** : position or rank of a person or thing **2** : state of affairs : SITUATION

stat·ute *n* : LAW 4

staunch *adj* **1** : strongly built : SUBSTAN-TIAL **2** : LOYAL 2, STEADFAST — **staunch·ly** *adv*

¹stave *n* **1** : a wooden stick : STAFF **2** : one of a number of narrow strips of wood or iron plates placed edge to edge to form the sides, covering, or lining of something (as a barrel or keg)

²stave *vb* **staved** *or* **stove; stav·ing 1** : to break in the staves of **2** : to smash a hole in : crush or break inward

stave off *vb* : to keep away : ward off

staves *pl of* STAFF

¹stay *n* : a strong rope or wire used to steady or brace something (as a mast)

²stay *vb* : to fasten (as a smokestack) with stays

³stay *vb* **1** : to stop going forward : PAUSE **2** : ¹REMAIN 3, 4 **3** : to stand firm **4** : to live for a while **5** : ²CHECK 1, HALT

⁴stay *n* **1** : the action of bringing to a stop : the state of being stopped **2** : a period of living in a place

⁵stay *n* **1** : ¹PROP, SUPPORT **2** : a thin firm strip (as of steel or plastic) used to stiffen a garment (as a corset) or part of a garment (as a shirt collar)

⁶stay *vb* : to hold up

stead *n* **1** : ²AVAIL — used mostly in the phrase *stand one in good stead* **2** : the place usually taken or duty carried out by the one mentioned

stead·fast *adj* **1** : not changing : RESOLUTE **2** : LOYAL 2 — **stead·fast·ly** *adv* — **stead·fast·ness** *n*

¹steady *adj* **steadi·er; steadi·est 1** : firmly fixed in position **2** : direct or sure in action **3** : showing little change **4** : not easily upset **5** : RELIABLE — **stead·i·ly** *adv* — **stead·i·ness** *n*

²steady *vb* **stead·ied; steady·ing** : to make, keep, or become steady

steak *n* **1** : a slice of meat and especially beef **2** : a slice of a large fish (as salmon)

¹steal *vb* **stole; sto·len; steal·ing 1** : to come or go quietly or secretly **2** : to take and carry away (something that belongs to another person) without right and with the intention of keeping **3** : to get more than one's share of attention during **4** : to take or get for oneself secretly or without permission

²steal *n* **1** : the act or an instance of stealing **2** : ¹BARGAIN 2

stealth *n* : sly or secret action

stealthy *adj* **stealth·i·er; stealth·i·est** : done in a sly or secret manner — **stealth·i·ly** *adv*

¹steam *n* **1** : the vapor into which water is changed when heated to the boiling point **2** : steam when kept under pressure so that it supplies heat and power **3** : the mist formed when water vapor cools **4** : driving force : POWER

²steam *vb* **1** : to rise or pass off as steam **2** : to give off steam or vapor **3** : to move or travel by or as if by the power of steam **4** : to expose to steam (as for cooking)

steam·boat *n* : a boat driven by steam

steam engine *n* : an engine driven by steam

steam·er *n* **1** : a container in which something is steamed **2** : a ship driven by steam **3** : an engine, machine, or vehicle run by steam

steam·roll·er *n* : a machine formerly driven by steam that has wide heavy rollers for pressing down and smoothing roads

steam·ship *n* : STEAMER 2

steam shovel *n* : a power machine for digging that was formerly operated by steam

steed *n* : a usually lively horse

¹steel *n* **1** : a hard and tough metal made by treating iron with great heat and mixing carbon with it **2** : an article (as a sword) made of steel

²steel *vb* : to fill with courage or determination

³steel *adj* : made of or like steel

steely *adj* **steel·i·er; steel·i·est 1** : made of steel **2** : like steel (as in hardness or color)

¹steep *adj* **1** : having a very sharp slope : almost straight up and down **2** : too great or high — **steep·ly** *adv* — **steep·ness** *n*

²steep *vb* **1** : to soak in a liquid **2** : to fill with or involve deeply

stee·ple *n* **1** : a tall pointed structure usually built on top of a church tower **2** : a church tower

stee·ple·chase *n* **1** : a horse race across country **2** : a race on a course that has hedges, walls, and ditches to be crossed

¹steer *n* : a castrated bull usually raised for beef

²steer *vb* **1** : to control a course or the course of : GUIDE **2** : to follow a course of action **3** : to be guided

steering wheel *n* : a wheel for steering something by hand

stego·sau·rus *n* : a large plant-eating dinosaur having bony plates along its back and tail with spikes at the end of the tail

¹stem *n* **1** : the main stalk of a plant that develops buds and sprouts and usually grows above ground **2** : a plant part (as a leafstalk or flower stalk) that supports some other part **3** : the bow of a ship **4** : a line of ancestors : STOCK **5** : the basic part of a word to which prefixes or suffixes may be added

6 : something like a stalk or shaft — **stem-less** adj

²stem vb **stemmed; stem-ming 1** : to make progress against **2** : to check or hold back the progress of

³stem vb **stemmed; stem-ming 1** : to come from a certain source **2** : to remove the stem from

⁴stem vb **stemmed; stem-ming** : to stop or check by or as if by damming

stemmed adj : having a stem

¹sten-cil n **1** : a material (as a sheet of paper, thin wax, or woven fabric) with cut out lettering or a design through which ink, paint, or metallic powder is forced onto a surface to be printed **2** : a pattern, design, or print produced with a stencil

²stencil vb **sten-ciled** or **sten-cilled; sten-cil-ing** or **sten-cil-ling 1** : to mark or paint with a stencil **2** : to produce with a stencil

ste-nog-ra-pher n : one employed chiefly to take and make a copy of dictation

¹step n **1** : a rest or place for the foot in going up or down : STAIR 2 **2** : a movement made by raising one foot and putting it down in another spot **3** : a combination of foot and body movements in a repeated pattern **4** : manner of walking **5** : FOOTPRINT **6** : the sound of a footstep **7** : the space passed over in one step **8** : a short distance **9** : the height of one stair **10 steps** pl : ¹COURSE 3 **11** : a level, grade, or rank in a scale or series : a stage in a process **12** : ¹MEASURE 7 **13** : a space in music between two notes of a scale or staff that may be a single degree of the scale (**half step**) or two degrees (**whole step**) — **in step** : with one's foot or feet moving in time with other feet or in time to music

²step vb **stepped; step-ping 1** : to move by taking a step or steps **2** : ¹DANCE 1 **3** : to go on foot : WALK **4** : to move at a good speed **5** : to press down with the foot **6** : to come as if at a single step **7** : to measure by steps

step–by–step adj or adv : moving or happening by steps one after the other

step-fa-ther n : the husband of one's mother after the death or divorce of one's real father

step-lad-der n : a light portable set of steps with a hinged frame for steadying

step-moth-er n : the wife of one's father after the death or divorce of one's real mother

steppe n : land that is dry, usually rather level, and covered with grass in regions (as much of southeastern Europe and parts of Asia) of wide temperature range

step-ping–stone n **1** : a stone on which to step (as in crossing a stream) **2** : a means of progress or advancement

step up vb : to increase especially by a series of steps

-ster n suffix **1** : one that does or handles or operates **2** : one that makes or uses **3** : one that is associated with or takes part in **4** : one that is

ste-reo n, pl **ste-re-os 1** : stereophonic reproduction **2** : a stereophonic sound system

ste-reo-phon-ic adj : of or relating to sound reproduction designed to create the effect of listening to the original

ste-reo-scope n : an optical instrument that blends two pictures of one subject taken from slightly different points of view into one image that seems to be three-dimensional

¹ste-reo-type vb **1** : to make a printing plate by casting melted metal in a mold **2** : to form a fixed mental picture of

²stereotype n **1** : a printing plate of a complete page made by casting melted metal in a mold **2** : a fixed idea that many people have about a thing or a group and that may often be untrue or only partly true

ste-reo-typed adj : following a pattern or stereotype : lacking individuality

ste-reo-typ-i-cal also **ste-reo-typ-ic** adj : based on or characteristic of a stereotype — **ste-reo-typ-i-cal-ly** adv

ster-ile adj **1** : not able to produce fruit, crops, or offspring : not fertile **2** : free from living germs

ster-il-ize vb **ster-il-ized; ster-il-iz-ing** : to make sterile and especially free from harmful germs

¹ster-ling n **1** : British money **2** : sterling silver : articles made from sterling silver

²sterling adj **1** : of or relating to British sterling **2** : being or made of an alloy of 925 parts of silver with 75 parts of copper **3** : EXCELLENT

¹stern adj **1** : hard and severe in nature or manner **2** : firm and not changeable — **stern-ly** adv — **stern-ness** n

²stern n : the rear end of a boat

ster-num n, pl **ster-nums** or **ster-na** : BREASTBONE

stetho-scope n : an instrument used by doctors for listening to sounds produced in the body and especially in the chest

¹stew n **1** : food (as meat with vegetables) prepared by slow boiling **2** : a state of excitement, worry, or confusion

²stew vb **1** : to boil slowly : SIMMER **2** : to become excited or worried

stew-ard n **1** : a manager of a very large

home, an estate, or an organization **2** : a person employed to manage the supply and distribution of food (as on a ship) **3** : a worker who serves and looks after the needs of passengers (as on an airplane or ship)

stew·ard·ess *n* : a woman who looks after passengers (as on an airplane or ship)

¹stick *n* **1** : a cut or broken branch or twig **2** : a long thin piece of wood **3** : WALKING STICK 1 **4** : something like a stick in shape or use

²stick *vb* **stuck; stick·ing 1** : to stab with something pointed **2** : to cause to penetrate **3** : to put in place by or as if by pushing **4** : to push out, up, into, or under **5** : to put in a specified place or position **6** : to remain in a place, situation, or environment **7** : to halt the movement or action of **8** : BAFFLE **9** : to burden with something unpleasant **10** : to cling or cause to cling **11** : to become blocked or jammed

stick·er *n* : something (as a slip of paper with gum or glue on its back) that can be stuck to a surface

stick·le·back *n* : a small scaleless fish with sharp spines on its back

sticky *adj* **stick·i·er; stick·i·est 1** : ADHESIVE 1 **2** : coated with a sticky substance **3** : MUGGY, HUMID **4** : tending to stick — **stick·i·ness** *n*

stiff *adj* **1** : not easily bent **2** : not easily moved **3** : FIRM 5 **4** : hard fought : STUBBORN **5** : not easy or graceful in manner : FORMAL **6** : POWERFUL, STRONG **7** : not flowing easily : being thick and heavy **8** : SEVERE 1 **9** : DIFFICULT 1 — **stiff·ly** *adv* — **stiff·ness** *n*

stiff·en *vb* : to make or become stiff or stiffer — **stiff·en·er** *n*

sti·fle *vb* **sti·fled; sti·fling 1** : to kill by depriving of or die from lack of oxygen or air : SMOTHER **2** : to keep in check by deliberate effort

stig·ma *n, pl* **stig·ma·ta** *or* **stig·mas 1** : a mark of disgrace or discredit **2** : the upper part of the pistil of a flower which receives the pollen grains and on which they complete their development

stile *n* **1** : a step or set of steps for crossing a fence or wall **2** : TURNSTILE

sti·let·to *n, pl* **sti·let·tos** *or* **sti·let·toes** : a slender pointed dagger

¹still *adj* **1** : having no motion **2** : making no sound **3** : free from noise and confusion : QUIET — **still·ness** *n*

²still *vb* : to make or become still : QUIET

³still *adv* **1** : without motion **2** : up to this or that time **3** : NEVERTHELESS **4** : ²EVEN 4

⁴still *n* : ¹QUIET, SILENCE

⁵still *n* **1** : a place where alcoholic liquors are made **2** : a device used in distillation

still·born *adj* : born dead

stilt *n* **1** : one of a pair of tall poles each with a high step or loop for the support of a foot used to lift the person wearing them above the ground in walking **2** : a stake or post used to support a structure above ground or water level

stilt·ed *adj* : not easy and natural

¹stim·u·lant *n* **1** : something (as a drug) that makes the body or one of its parts more active for a while **2** : STIMULUS 1

²stimulant *adj* : stimulating or tending to stimulate

stim·u·late *vb* **stim·u·lat·ed; stim·u·lat·ing 1** : to make active or more active : ANIMATE, AROUSE **2** : to act toward as a bodily stimulus or stimulant

stim·u·la·tion *n* : an act or result of stimulating

stim·u·lus *n, pl* **stim·u·li 1** : something that stirs or urges to action **2** : an influence that acts usually from outside the body to partly change bodily activity (as by exciting a sense organ)

¹sting *vb* **stung; sting·ing 1** : to prick painfully usually with a sharp or poisonous stinger **2** : to suffer or affect with sharp quick burning pain **3** : to cause to suffer severely

²sting *n* **1** : an act of stinging **2** : a wound or pain caused by or as if by stinging **3** : STINGER

sting·er *n* : a sharp organ by which an animal (as a wasp or scorpion) wounds and often poisons an enemy

sting·ray *n* : a very flat fish with a stinging spine on its whiplike tail

stin·gy *adj* **stin·gi·er; stin·gi·est 1** : not generous : giving or spending as little as possible **2** : very small in amount — **stin·gi·ly** *adv* — **stin·gi·ness** *n*

¹stink *vb* **stank** *or* **stunk; stunk; stink·ing 1** : to give off or cause to have a strong unpleasant smell **2** : to be of very bad quality

²stink *n* : a strong unpleasant smell

stink·bug *n* : a bug that gives off a bad smell

stinky *adj* : having a strong unpleasant smell

¹stint *vb* : to be stingy or saving

²stint *n* : an amount of work given to be done

¹stir *vb* **stirred; stir·ring 1** : to make or cause to make a usually slight movement or change of position **2** : to make active (as by pushing, beating, or prodding) **3** : to mix, dissolve, or make by a continued circular movement **4** : AROUSE 2

²stir *n* **1** : a state of upset or activity **2** : a slight movement **3** : the act of stirring

stir·ring *adj* : LIVELY 3, MOVING

stir·rup *n* : either of a pair of small light frames often of metal hung by straps from a saddle and used as a support for the foot of a horseback rider

¹stitch *n* 1 : a sudden sharp pain especially in the side 2 : one in-and-out movement of a threaded needle in sewing : a portion of thread left in the material after one such movement 3 : a single loop of thread or yarn around a tool (as a knitting needle or crochet hook) 4 : a method of stitching

²stitch *vb* 1 : to fasten or join with stitches 2 : to make, mend, or decorate with or as if with stitches 3 : SEW 2

¹stock *n* 1 **stocks** *pl* : a wooden frame with holes for the feet or the feet and hands once used to punish a wrongdoer publicly 2 : the wooden part by which a rifle or shotgun is held during firing 3 : an original (as a person, race, or language) from which others descend 4 : the whole supply or amount on hand 5 : farm animals : LIVESTOCK, CATTLE 6 : the ownership element in a business which is divided into shares that can be traded independently 7 : liquid in which meat, fish, or vegetables have been simmered — **in stock** : on hand : in the store and available for purchase

²stock *vb* 1 : to provide with or get stock or a stock 2 : to get or keep a stock of

³stock *adj* 1 : kept regularly in stock 2 : commonly used : STANDARD

stock·ade *n* 1 : a line of strong posts set in the ground to form a defense 2 : an enclosure formed by stakes driven into the ground

stock·bro·ker *n* : a person who handles orders to buy and sell stocks

stock·hold·er *n* : an owner of stock

stock·ing *n* : a close-fitting usually knit covering for the foot and leg

stock market *n* : a place where shares of stock are bought and sold

stocky *adj* **stock·i·er**; **stock·i·est** : compact, sturdy, and relatively thick in build : THICKSET

stock·yard *n* : a yard for stock and especially for keeping livestock about to be slaughtered or shipped

¹stole *past of* STEAL

²stole *n* : a long wide scarf worn about the shoulders

stolen *past participle of* STEAL

¹stom·ach *n* 1 : the pouch into which food goes after it leaves the mouth and has passed down the throat 2 : ABDOMEN 1 3 : ²DESIRE 1, LIKING

²stomach *vb* : to bear patiently : put up with

stomp *vb* : to walk heavily or noisily : STAMP

¹stone *n* 1 : earth or mineral matter hardened in a mass : ROCK 2 : a piece of rock coarser than gravel 3 : GEM 4 : a stony mass sometimes present in a diseased organ 5 : the kernel of a fruit in its hard case 6 *pl usually* **stone** : an English measure of weight equaling fourteen pounds (about 6.5 kilograms)

²stone *vb* **stoned**; **ston·ing** 1 : to throw stones at 2 : to remove the stones of

³stone *adj* : of, relating to, or made of stone

Stone Age *n* : the oldest period in which human beings are known to have existed : the age during which stone tools were used

stone–blind *adj* : completely blind

stone–deaf *adj* : completely deaf

stony *adj* **ston·i·er**; **ston·i·est** 1 : full of stones 2 : insensitive as stone : UNFEELING 3 : hard as stone

stood *past of* STAND

stool *n* 1 : a seat without back or arms supported by three or four legs or by a central post 2 : FOOTSTOOL 3 : a mass of material discharged from the intestine

¹stoop *vb* 1 : to bend down or over 2 : to carry the head and shoulders or the upper part of the body bent forward 3 : to do something that is beneath one

²stoop *n* : a forward bend of the head and shoulders

³stoop *n* : a porch, platform, or stairway at the entrance of a house or building

¹stop *vb* **stopped**; **stop·ping** 1 : to close an opening by filling or blocking it : PLUG 2 : to hold back : RESTRAIN 3 : to halt the movement or progress of 4 : to come to an end : CEASE 5 : to make a visit : STAY

²stop *n* 1 : ¹END 2, FINISH 2 : a set of organ pipes of one tone quality : a control knob for such a set 3 : something that delays, blocks, or brings to a halt 4 : STOPPER, PLUG 5 : the act of stopping : the state of being stopped 6 : a halt in a journey : STAY 7 : a stopping place

stop·light *n* 1 : a light on the rear of a motor vehicle that goes on when the driver presses the brake pedal 2 : a signal light used in controlling traffic

stop·over *n* : a stop made during a journey

stop·page *n* : the act of stopping : the state of being stopped

stop·per *n* : something (as a cork or plug) used to stop openings

stop·watch *n* : a watch having a hand that can be started and stopped for exact timing (as of a race)

stor·age *n* 1 : space or a place for storing 2 : an amount stored 3 : the act of storing

: the state of being stored **4** : the price charged for storing something

storage battery *n* : a battery that can be renewed by passing an electric current through it

¹store *vb* **stored; stor·ing** **1** : to provide with what is needed : SUPPLY **2** : to place or leave something in a location (as a warehouse, library, or computer memory) to keep for later use or disposal **3** : to put somewhere for safekeeping

²store *n* **1 stores** *pl* : something collected and kept for future use **2** : a large quantity, supply, or number **3** : a place where goods are sold : SHOP — **in store** : ¹READY 1

store·house *n, pl* **store·hous·es** **1** : a building for storing goods **2** : a large supply or source

store·keep·er *n* **1** : a person in charge of supplies (as in a factory) **2** : an owner or manager of a store or shop

store·room *n* : a room for storing things not in use

stork *n* : a large Old World wading bird that looks like the related herons and includes one European form (the **white stork**) that often nests on roofs and chimneys

¹storm *n* **1** : a heavy fall of rain, snow, or sleet often with strong wind **2** : a violent outburst **3** : a violent attack on a defended position

²storm *vb* **1** : to blow hard and rain or snow heavily **2** : to make a mass attack against **3** : to be very angry : RAGE **4** : to rush about violently

stormy *adj* **storm·i·er; storm·i·est** **1** : relating to or affected by a storm **2** : displaying anger and excitement — **storm·i·ness** *n*

¹sto·ry *n, pl* **sto·ries** **1** : a report about incidents or events : ACCOUNT **2** : a short often amusing tale **3** : a tale shorter than a novel **4** : a widely told rumor **5** : ³LIE, FALSEHOOD

²sto·ry *or* **sto·rey** *n, pl* **sto·ries** *or* **sto·reys** : a set of rooms or an area making up one floor level of a building

stout *adj* **1** : of strong character : BRAVE, FIRM **2** : of a strong or lasting sort : STURDY, TOUGH **3** : bulky in body : FLESHY — **stout·ly** *adv* — **stout·ness** *n*

¹stove *n* : a structure usually of iron or steel that burns fuel or uses electricity to provide heat (as for cooking or heating)

²stove *past of* STAVE

stove·pipe *n* : a metal pipe to carry away smoke from a stove

stow *vb* **1** : to put away : STORE **2** : to arrange in an orderly way : PACK **3** : ²LOAD 1

stow·away *n* : a person who hides (as in a ship or airplane) to travel free

strad·dle *vb* **strad·dled; strad·dling** **1** : to stand, sit, or walk with the legs spread wide apart **2** : to stand, sit, or ride with a leg on either side of **3** : to favor or seem to favor two opposite sides of

strag·gle *vb* **strag·gled; strag·gling** **1** : to wander from a straight course or way : STRAY **2** : to trail off from others of its kind — **strag·gler** *n*

¹straight *adj* **1** : following the same direction throughout its length : not having curves, bends, or angles **2** : not straying from the main point or proper course **3** : not straying from what is right or honest **4** : correctly ordered or arranged — **straight·ness** *n*

²straight *adv* : in a straight manner, course, or line

straight·en *vb* **1** : to make or become straight **2** : to put in order

straight·for·ward *adj* : being plain and honest : FRANK — **straight·for·ward·ly** *adv* — **straight·for·ward·ness** *n*

straight·way *adv* : IMMEDIATELY 2

¹strain *n* **1** : a line of ancestors to whom a person is related **2** : a group of individuals that cannot be told from related kinds by appearance alone **3** : a quality or disposition that runs through a family or race **4** : a small amount : TRACE **5** : MELODY 2, AIR

²strain *vb* **1** : to stretch or be stretched, pulled, or used to the limit **2** : to stretch beyond a proper limit **3** : to try one's hardest **4** : to injure or be injured by too much or too hard use or. effort **5** : to press or pass through a strainer : FILTER

³strain *n* **1** : the act of straining **2** : the state of being strained **3** : ²OVERWORK, WORRY **4** : bodily injury resulting from strain or from a wrench or twist that stretches muscles and ligaments

strained *adj* **1** : not easy or natural **2** : brought close to war

strain·er *n* : a device (as a screen, sieve, or filter) to hold back solid pieces while a liquid passes through

strait *n* **1** : a narrow channel connecting two bodies of water **2** : ¹DISTRESS 1, NEED — often used in pl.

¹strand *n* : the land bordering a body of water : SHORE, BEACH

²strand *vb* **1** : to run, drive, or cause to drift onto a strand : run aground **2** : to leave in a strange or unfavorable place especially without any chance to get away

³strand *n* **1** : one of the fibers, threads, strings, or wires twisted or braided to make a cord, rope, or cable **2** : something long or twisted like a rope

strange *adj* **strang·er; strang·est 1** : of or relating to some other person, place, or thing **2** : UNFAMILIAR 1 **3** : exciting curiosity, surprise, or wonder because of not being usual or ordinary **4** : ill at ease : SHY — **strange·ly** *adv* — **strange·ness** *n*

strang·er *n* **1** : one who is not in the place where one's home is : FOREIGNER **2** : GUEST 1, VISITOR **3** : a person whom one does not know or has not met

stran·gle *vb* **stran·gled; stran·gling 1** : to choke to death by squeezing the throat **2** : to choke in any way — **stran·gler** *n*

¹strap *n* : a narrow strip of flexible material (as leather) used especially for fastening, binding, or wrapping

²strap *vb* **strapped; strap·ping 1** : to fasten with or attach by means of a strap **2** : BIND 1, 2, CONSTRICT **3** : to whip with a strap

strap·ping *adj* : LARGE, STRONG

strat·a·gem *n* : a trick in war to deceive or outwit the enemy

stra·te·gic *adj* **1** : of, relating to, or showing the use of strategy **2** : useful or important in strategy

strat·e·gy *n, pl* **strat·e·gies 1** : the skill of using military, naval, and air forces to win a war **2** : a clever plan or method

strato·sphere *n* : an upper portion of the atmosphere more than eleven kilometers above the earth where temperature changes little and clouds rarely form

stra·tum *n, pl* **stra·ta** : LAYER 2

stra·tus *n, pl* **stra·ti** : a cloud extending over a large area at an altitude of from 600 to 2000 meters

straw *n* **1** : stalks especially of grain after threshing **2** : a single dry coarse plant stalk : a piece of straw **3** : a slender tube for sucking up a beverage

straw·ber·ry *n, pl* **straw·ber·ries** : the juicy edible usually red fruit of a low plant with white flowers and long slender runners

¹stray *n* : a domestic animal that is wandering at large because it is lost or has been abandoned

²stray *vb* **1** : to wander from a group or from the proper place : ROAM **2** : to go off from a straight or the right course

³stray *adj* **1** : having strayed or been lost **2** : occurring here and there : RANDOM

¹streak *n* **1** : a line or mark of a different color or composition from its background **2** : a narrow band of light **3** : a small amount : TRACE, STRAIN **4** : a short series of something — **streaked** *adj*

²streak *vb* **1** : to make streaks in or on **2** : to move swiftly : RUSH

¹stream *n* **1** : a body of water (as a brook or river) flowing on the earth **2** : a flow of liquid **3** : a steady series (as of words or events) following one another

²stream *vb* **1** : to flow in or as if in a stream **2** : to give out a bodily fluid in large amounts **3** : to become wet with flowing liquid **4** : to trail out at full length **5** : to pour in large numbers

stream·er *n* **1** : a flag that streams in the wind : PENNANT **2** : a long narrow wavy strip (as of ribbon on a hat) suggesting a banner floating in the wind **3 streamers** *pl* : AURORA BOREALIS

stream·lined *adj* **1** : designed or constructed to make motion through water or air easier or as if for this purpose **2** : made shorter, simpler, or more efficient

street *n* **1** : a public way especially in a city, town, or village **2** : the people living along a street

street·car *n* : a passenger vehicle that runs on rails and operates mostly on city streets

strength *n* **1** : the quality of being strong **2** : power to resist force **3** : power to resist attack **4** : intensity of light, color, sound, or odor **5** : force as measured in numbers

strength·en *vb* : to make, grow, or become stronger

stren·u·ous *adj* **1** : very active : ENERGETIC **2** : showing or requiring much energy — **stren·u·ous·ly** *adv*

strep·to·my·cin *n* : a substance produced by a soil bacterium and used especially in treating tuberculosis

¹stress *n* **1** : a force that tends to change the shape of a body **2** : something that causes bodily or mental tension : a state of tension resulting from a stress **3** : special importance given to something **4** : relative prominence of sound : a syllable carrying this stress : ACCENT

²stress *vb* **1** : to expose to stress : STRAIN **2** : ¹ACCENT 1 **3** : to give special importance to

stress mark *n* : a mark used with a written syllable in the respelling of a word to show that this syllable is to be stressed when spoken

¹stretch *vb* **1** : to reach out : EXTEND, SPREAD **2** : to draw out in length or width or both : EXPAND, ENLARGE **3** : to draw up from a cramped, stooping, or relaxed position **4** : to pull tight **5** : to cause to reach or continue **6** : EXAGGERATE **7** : to become extended without breaking

²stretch *n* **1** : the act of extending or drawing out beyond ordinary or normal limits **2** : the extent to which something may be stretched **3** : the act or an instance of stretching the body or one of its parts **4** : a continuous extent in length, area, or time

stretch·er *n* **1** : one that stretches **2** : a light bedlike device for carrying sick or injured persons

strew *vb* **strewed; strewed** *or* **strewn; strew·ing 1** : to spread by scattering **2** : to cover by or as if by scattering something

strick·en *adj* **1** : hit or wounded by or as if by a missile **2** : troubled with disease, misfortune, or sorrow

strict *adj* **1** : permitting no avoidance or escape **2** : kept with great care : ABSOLUTE **3** : carefully observing something (as a rule or principle) : EXACT, PRECISE — **strict·ly** *adv* — **strict·ness** *n*

¹stride *vb* **strode; strid·den; strid·ing 1** : to walk or run with long even steps **2** : to step over : STRADDLE

²stride *n* **1** : a long step : the distance covered by such a step **2** : a step forward : ADVANCE **3** : a way of striding

strife *n* **1** : bitter and sometimes violent disagreement **2** : ²STRUGGLE 1, CONTENTION

¹strike *vb* **struck; struck** *or* **strick·en; strik·ing 1** : GO 1, PROCEED **2** : to touch or hit with force **3** : to lower (as a flag or sail) usually in salute or surrender **4** : to come into contact or collision with **5** : to make a military attack : FIGHT **6** : to remove or cancel with or as if with the stroke of a pen **7** : to make known by sounding or cause to sound **8** : to affect usually suddenly **9** : to produce by stamping with a die or punch **10** : to produce by or as if by a blow **11** : to cause to ignite by scratching **12** : to agree on the arrangements of **13** : to make an impression on **14** : to come upon : DISCOVER **15** : to stop work in order to obtain a change in conditions of work

²strike *n* **1** : an act or instance of striking **2** : a stopping of work by workers to force an employer to agree to demands **3** : a discovery of a valuable mineral deposit **4** : a baseball pitch that is swung at or that passes through a certain area over home plate (**strike zone**) and that counts against the batter **5** : DISADVANTAGE, HANDICAP **6** : the knocking down of all ten bowling pins with the first ball **7** : a military attack

strike·out *n* : an out in baseball that results from a batter's striking out

strike out *vb* : to be out in baseball by getting three strikes as a batter

strik·ing *adj* : attracting attention : REMARKABLE — **strik·ing·ly** *adv*

¹string *n* **1** : a small cord used to bind, fasten, or tie **2** : a thin tough plant structure (as the fiber connecting the halves of a bean pod) **3** : the gut, wire, or plastic cord of a musical instrument that vibrates to produce a tone **4 strings** *pl* : the stringed instruments of an orchestra **5** : a group, series, or line of objects threaded on a string or arranged as if strung together

²string *vb* **strung; string·ing 1** : to provide with strings **2** : to make tense **3** : ²THREAD 4 **4** : to tie, hang, or fasten with string **5** : to remove the strings of **6** : to set or stretch out in a line

string bass *n* : DOUBLE BASS

string bean *n* : a bean grown primarily for its pods which are eaten before the seeds are full grown

stringed instrument *n* : a musical instrument (as a violin, guitar, or banjo) sounded by plucking or striking or by drawing a bow across tight strings

string·er *n* : a long strong piece of wood or metal used for support or strengthening in building (as under a floor)

stringy *adj* **string·i·er; string·i·est** : containing, consisting of, or like string

¹strip *vb* **stripped; strip·ping 1** : to remove clothes : UNDRESS **2** : to remove a covering or surface layer from **3** : to take away all duties, honors, or special rights **4** : to remove furniture, equipment, or accessories from **5** : to tear or damage the thread of a screw or bolt

²strip *n* : a long narrow piece or area

strip–crop·ping *n* : the growing of a food crop (as potatoes) in alternate strips with a crop (as grass) that forms sod and helps keep the soil from being worn away

¹stripe *vb* **striped; strip·ing** : to make stripes on

²stripe *n* **1** : a line or long narrow division or section of something different in color or appearance from the background **2** : a piece of material often with a special design worn (as on a sleeve) to show military rank or length of service

striped *adj* : having stripes

strive *vb* **strove; striv·en** *or* **strived; striv·ing 1** : to carry on a conflict or effort : CONTEND **2** : to try hard

strode *past of* STRIDE

¹stroke *vb* **stroked; strok·ing** : to rub gently in one direction

²stroke *n* **1** : the act of striking : BLOW **2** : a single unbroken movement especially in one direction : one of a series of repeated movements (as in swimming or rowing a boat) **3** : the hitting of a ball in a game (as golf or tennis) **4** : a sudden action or process that results in something being struck **5** : a sudden or unexpected example **6** : a sudden weakening or loss of consciousness and powers of voluntary movement that results from the breaking or blocking of an artery in the brain **7** : effort by which something is done or the results of such effort **8** : the sound of striking (as of a clock or bell) **9** : a mark made by a single movement of a brush, pen, or tool

¹stroll *vb* : to walk in a leisurely manner : RAMBLE

²stroll *n* : a leisurely walk : RAMBLE

stroll·er *n* : a small carriage in which a baby can sit and be pushed around

strong *adj* **stron·ger; stron·gest 1** : having great power in the muscles **2** : HEALTHY 1 2, ROBUST **3** : having great resources **4** : of a specified number **5** : PERSUASIVE **6** : having much of some quality **7** : moving with speed and force **8** : ENTHUSIASTIC, ZEALOUS **9** : not easily injured or overcome **10** : well established : FIRM — **strong·ly** *adv*

strong·hold *n* : FORTRESS

strove *past of* STRIVE

struck *past of* STRIKE

struc·tur·al *adj* **1** : of, relating to, or affecting structure **2** : used or formed for use in construction

struc·ture *n* **1** : something built (as a house or dam) **2** : the manner in which something is built : CONSTRUCTION **3** : the arrangement or relationship of parts or organs

¹strug·gle *vb* **strug·gled; strug·gling 1** : to make a great effort to overcome someone or something : STRIVE **2** : to move with difficulty or with great effort

²struggle *n* **1** : a violent effort **2** : ²FIGHT 1, CONTEST

strum *vb* **strummed; strum·ming** : to play on a stringed instrument by brushing the strings with the fingers

strung *past of* STRING

¹strut *vb* **strut·ted; strut·ting** : to walk in a stiff proud way

²strut *n* **1** : a bar or brace used to resist lengthwise pressure **2** : a strutting step or walk

¹stub *n* **1** : a short part remaining after the rest has been removed or used up **2** : a small part of a check kept as a record of what was on the detached check

²stub *vb* **stubbed; stub·bing** : to strike (as the toe) against an object

stub·ble *n* **1** : the stem ends of herbs and especially cereal grasses left in the ground after harvest **2** : a rough growth or surface like stubble in a field : a short growth of beard

stub·born *adj* **1** : refusing to change an opinion or course of action in spite of difficulty or urging **2** : PERSISTENT **3** : difficult to handle, manage, or treat — **stub·born·ly** *adv* — **stub·born·ness** *n*

stub·by *adj* **stub·bi·er; stub·bi·est** : short and thick like a stub

stuc·co *n, pl* **stuc·cos** *or* **stuc·coes** : a plaster for coating walls

stuck *past of* STICK

stuck–up *adj* : VAIN 2, CONCEITED

¹stud *n* **1** : one of the smaller vertical braces of the walls of a building to which the wall materials are fastened **2** : a removable device like a button used to fasten something or as an ornament **3** : one of the metal cleats used on a snow tire to provide a better grip

²stud *vb* **stud·ded; stud·ding 1** : to supply or cover with or as if with studs **2** : to set thickly together

stu·dent *n* : a person who studies especially in school : PUPIL

stu·dio *n, pl* **stu·di·os 1** : the place where an artist, sculptor, or photographer works **2** : a place for the study of an art **3** : a place where movies are made **4** : a place from which radio or television programs are broadcast

stu·di·ous *adj* : devoted to and fond of study

¹study *n, pl* **stud·ies 1** : use of the mind to get knowledge **2** : a careful investigation or examination of something **3** : a room especially for study, reading, or writing

²study *vb* **stud·ied; study·ing 1** : to use the mind to learn about something by reading, investigating, or memorizing **2** : to give close attention to

¹stuff *n* **1** : materials, supplies, or equipment that people need or use **2** : writing, speech, or ideas of little value **3** : something mentioned or understood but not named **4** : basic part of something : SUBSTANCE

²stuff *vb* **1** : to fill by packing or crowding things in : CRAM **2** : OVEREAT, GORGE **3** : to fill with a stuffing **4** : to stop up : CONGEST **5** : to force into something : THRUST

stuff·ing *n* **1** : material used in filling up or stuffing something **2** : a mixture (as of bread crumbs and seasonings) used to stuff meat, vegetables, eggs, or poultry

stuffy *adj* **stuff·i·er; stuff·i·est 1** : needing fresh air **2** : stuffed or choked up **3** : ¹DULL 8

¹stum·ble *vb* **stum·bled; stum·bling 1** : to trip in walking or running **2** : to walk unsteadily **3** : to speak or act in a clumsy manner **4** : to come unexpectedly or accidentally

stumble

2stumble *n* : an act or instance of stumbling

1stump *n* **1** : the part of something (as an arm, a tooth, or a pencil) that remains after the rest has been removed, lost, or worn away : STUB **2** : the part of a tree that remains in the ground after the tree is cut down

2stump *vb* **1** : PERPLEX, BAFFLE **2** : to walk or walk over heavily, stiffly, or clumsily as if with a wooden leg **3** : 2STUB

stun *vb* **stunned; stun·ning 1** : to make dizzy or senseless by or as if by a blow **2** : to affect with shock or confusion : fill with disbelief

stung *past of* STING

stunk *past of* STINK

stun·ning *adj* **1** : able or likely to make a person senseless or confused **2** : unusually lovely or attractive : STRIKING

1stunt *vb* : to hold back the normal growth of

2stunt *n* : an unusual or difficult performance or act

stu·pe·fy *vb* **stu·pe·fied; stu·pe·fy·ing 1** : to make stupid, groggy, or numb **2** : ASTONISH, ASTOUND

stu·pen·dous *adj* : amazing especially because of great size or height

stu·pid *adj* **1** : slow or dull of mind **2** : showing or resulting from a dull mind or a lack of proper attention **3** : not interesting or worthwhile — **stu·pid·ly** *adv*

stu·pid·i·ty *n, pl* **stu·pid·i·ties 1** : the quality or state of being stupid **2** : a stupid thought, action, or remark

stu·por *n* : a condition in which the senses or feelings become dull

stur·dy *adj* **stur·di·er; stur·di·est 1** : firmly built or made **2** : strong and healthy in body : ROBUST **3** : RESOLUTE — **stur·di·ly** *adv* — **sturd·i·ness** *n*

stur·geon *n* : a large food fish with tough skin and rows of bony plates

1stut·ter *vb* : to speak or say in a jerky way with involuntary repeating or interruption of sounds

2stutter *n* : the act or an instance of stuttering

1sty *n, pl* **sties** : PIGPEN

2sty *or* **stye** *n, pl* **sties** *or* **styes** : a painful red swelling on the edge of an eyelid

1style *n* **1** : the narrow middle part of the pistil of a flower **2** : a way of speaking or writing **3** : an individual way of doing something **4** : a method or manner that is felt to be very respectable, fashionable, or proper : FASHION

2style *vb* **styled; styl·ing 1** : to identify by some descriptive term : CALL **2** : to design and make in agreement with an accepted or a new style

styl·ish *adj* : having style : FASHIONABLE — **styl·ish·ly** *adv* — **styl·ish·ness** *n*

sty·lus *n, pl* **sty·li** *or* **sty·lus·es** : a pointed instrument used in ancient times for writing on wax tablets

1sub *n* : 1SUBSTITUTE

2sub *vb* **subbed; sub·bing** : to act as a substitute

3sub *n* : SUBMARINE

sub- *prefix* **1** : under : beneath : below **2** : lower in importance or rank : lesser **3** : division or part of **4** : so as to form, stress, or deal with lesser parts or relations

sub·di·vide *vb* **sub·di·vid·ed; sub·di·vid·ing 1** : to divide the parts of into more parts **2** : to divide into several parts

sub·di·vi·sion *n* **1** : the act of subdividing **2** : one of the parts into which something is subdivided

sub·due *vb* **sub·dued; sub·du·ing 1** : to overcome in battle **2** : to bring under control **3** : to reduce the brightness or strength of : SOFTEN

sub·head *or* **sub·head·ing** *n* : a heading under which one of the divisions of a subject is listed

1sub·ject *n* **1** : a person under the authority or control of another **2** : a person who owes loyalty to a monarch or state **3** : a course of study **4** : an individual that is studied or experimented on **5** : the person or thing discussed : TOPIC **6** : the word or group of words about which the predicate makes a statement

2subject *adj* **1** : owing obedience or loyalty to another **2** : likely to be affected by **3** : depending on

3sub·ject *vb* **1** : to bring under control or rule **2** : to cause to put up with

sub·lime *adj* **1** : grand or noble in thought, expression, or manner **2** : having beauty enough or being impressive enough to arouse a mixed feeling of admiration and wonder

submarine *n* : a naval ship designed to operate underwater

sub·merge *vb* **sub·merged; sub·merg·ing 1** : to put under or plunge into water **2** : to cover or become covered with or as if with water

sub·mis·sion *n* **1** : the act of submitting something (as for consideration or comment) **2** : the condition of being humble or obedient **3** : the act of submitting to power or authority

sub·mis·sive *adj* : willing to submit to others

sub·mit *vb* **sub·mit·ted; sub·mit·ting 1** : to leave to the judgment or approval of someone else **2** : to put forward as an opinion, reason, or idea **3** : to yield to the authority, control, or choice of another

¹sub·or·di·nate *adj* **1** : being in a lower class or rank : INFERIOR **2** : yielding to or controlled by authority

²subordinate *n* : one that is subordinate

³sub·or·di·nate *vb* **sub·or·di·nat·ed; sub·or·di·nat·ing** : to make subordinate

sub·scribe *vb* **sub·scribed; sub·scrib·ing** **1** : to make known one's approval by or as if by signing **2** : to agree to give or contribute by signing one's name with the amount promised **3** : to place an order (as for a newspaper) with payment or a promise to pay — **sub·scrib·er** *n*

sub·scrip·tion *n* **1** : an act or instance of subscribing **2** : a thing or amount subscribed

sub·se·quent *adj* : following in time, order, or place — **sub·se·quent·ly** *adv*

sub·set *n* : a mathematical set each of whose members is also a member of a larger set

sub·side *vb* **sub·sid·ed; sub·sid·ing** **1** : to become lower : SINK **2** : to become quiet or less

sub·sist *vb* : to continue living or being

sub·sis·tence *n* : the smallest amount (as of food and clothing) necessary to support life

sub·soil *n* : a layer of soil lying just under the topsoil

sub·stance *n* **1** : ESSENCE 1 **2** : the most important part **3** : material of a certain kind **4** : material belongings : WEALTH

sub·stan·dard *adj* : being below what is standard

sub·stan·tial *adj* **1** : made up of or relating to substance **2** : ABUNDANT **3** : PROSPEROUS 1 **4** : firmly constructed **5** : large in amount

¹sub·sti·tute *n* : a person or thing that takes the place of another

²substitute *vb* **sub·sti·tut·ed; sub·sti·tut·ing** **1** : to put in the place of another **2** : to serve as a substitute

sub·sti·tu·tion *n* : the act or process of substituting

sub·tle *adj* **sub·tler; sub·tlest** **1** : DELICATE 1 **2** : SHREWD, KEEN **3** : CLEVER 2, SLY — **sub·tly** *adv*

sub·top·ic *n* : a topic (as in a composition) that is a division of a main topic

sub·tract *vb* : to take away (as one part or number from another) : DEDUCT

sub·trac·tion *n* : the subtracting of one number from another

sub·tra·hend *n* : a number that is to be subtracted from another number

sub·urb *n* **1** : a part of a city or town near its outer edge **2** : a smaller community

close to a city **3** **suburbs** *pl* : the area of homes close to or surrounding a city — **sub·ur·ban** *adj or n*

sub·way *n* **1** : an underground tunnel **2** : a usually electric underground railway

suc·ceed *vb* **1** : to come after : FOLLOW **2** : to take the place of a ruler or leader who has died, resigned, or been removed **3** : to be successful

suc·cess *n* **1** : satisfactory completion of something **2** : the gaining of wealth, respect, or fame **3** : a person or thing that succeeds

suc·cess·ful *adj* **1** : resulting or ending well or in success **2** : gaining or having gained success — **suc·cess·ful·ly** *adv*

suc·ces·sion *n* **1** : the order, act, or right of succeeding to a throne, title, or property **2** : a series of persons or things that follow one after another

suc·ces·sive *adj* : following in order and without interruption — **suc·ces·sive·ly** *adv*

suc·ces·sor *n* : a person who succeeds to a throne, title, property, or office

suc·cor *n* : ²HELP 1, RELIEF

suc·cu·lent *adj* : JUICY

suc·cumb *vb* **1** : to yield to force or pressure **2** : ¹DIE 1

¹such *adj* **1** : of a kind just specified or to be specified **2** : of the same class, type, or sort : SIMILAR **3** : so great : so remarkable

²such *pron* : that sort of person, thing, or group

suck *vb* **1** : to draw in liquid and especially mother's milk with the mouth **2** : to draw liquid from by action of the mouth **3** : to allow to dissolve gradually in the mouth **4** : to put (as a thumb) into the mouth and draw on as if sucking **5** : ABSORB 1

suck·er *n* **1** : one that sucks : SUCKLING **2** : a freshwater fish related to the carps that has thick soft lips for sucking in food **3** : a new stem from the roots or lower part of a plant **4** : LOLLIPOP **5** : a person easily fooled or cheated

suck·le *vb* **suck·led; suck·ling** : to feed from the breast or udder

suck·ling *n* : a young mammal still sucking milk from its mother

suc·tion *n* **1** : the act or process of sucking **2** : the process of drawing something into a space (as in a pump) by removing air from the space **3** : the force caused by suction

sud·den *adj* **1** : happening or coming quickly and unexpectedly **2** : met with unexpectedly **3** : ¹STEEP 1 **4** : HASTY 2 — **sud·den·ly** *adv* — **sud·den·ness** *n*

suds *n pl* **1** : soapy water especially when foamy **2** : the foam on soapy water

sue *vb* **sued; su·ing :** to seek justice or right by bringing legal action

suede *n* **:** leather tanned and rubbed so that it is soft and has a nap

su·et *n* **:** the hard fat about the kidneys in beef and mutton from which tallow is made

suf·fer *vb* **1 :** to feel pain **2 :** to experience something unpleasant **3 :** to bear loss or damage **4 :** ¹PERMIT — **suf·fer·er** *n*

suf·fer·ing *n* **1 :** the state or experience of one that suffers **2 :** a cause of distress **:** HARDSHIP

suf·fice *vb* **suf·ficed; suf·fic·ing 1 :** to satisfy a need **2 :** to be enough for

suf·fi·cient *adj* **:** enough to achieve a goal or fill a need — **suf·fi·cient·ly** *adv*

suf·fix *n* **:** a letter or group of letters that comes at the end of a word and has a meaning of its own

suf·fo·cate *vb* **suf·fo·cat·ed; suf·fo·cat·ing 1 :** to kill by stopping the breath or depriving of oxygen to breathe **2 :** to be or become choked or smothered **3 :** to have or cause to have a feeling of smothering

suf·fo·ca·tion *n* **:** the act of suffocating or state of being suffocated

suf·frage *n* **:** the right to vote

¹sug·ar *n* **1 :** a sweet substance obtained from sugarcane, sugar beets, or maple syrup **2 :** any of numerous soluble and usually sweet carbohydrates

²sugar *vb* **1 :** to mix, cover, or sprinkle with sugar **2 :** to make something less hard to take or put up with **3 :** to change to crystals of sugar

sugar beet *n* **:** a large beet with white roots that is grown as a source of sugar

sug·ar·cane *n* **:** a tall strong grass with jointed stems widely raised in tropical regions for the sugar it yields

sugar maple *n* **:** an American maple tree with hard strong wood and a sweet sap that yields maple syrup and maple sugar

sug·gest *vb* **1 :** to put (as a thought or desire) into a person's mind **2 :** to offer as an idea **3 :** to bring into one's mind through close connection or association

sug·ges·tion *n* **1 :** the act or process of suggesting **2 :** a thought or plan that is suggested **3 :** ¹HINT 2

sug·ges·tive *adj* **1 :** giving a suggestion **2 :** full of suggestions **:** PROVOCATIVE **3 :** suggesting something improper or indecent

sui·cide *n* **1 :** the act of killing oneself purposely **2 :** a person who commits suicide

¹suit *n* **1 :** an action in court for enforcing a right or claim **2 :** an earnest request **3 :** COURTSHIP **4 :** a number of things used

together **:** SET **5 :** all the playing cards of one kind (as spades) in a pack

²suit *vb* **1 :** to be suitable or satisfactory **2 :** to make suitable **:** ADAPT **3 :** to be proper for or pleasing with **4 :** to meet the needs or desires of

suit·abil·i·ty *n* **:** the quality or state of being suitable

suit·able *adj* **:** being fit or right for a use or group — **suit·ably** *adv*

suit·case *n* **:** a flat rectangular traveling bag

suite *n* **1 :** a number of connected rooms (as in a hotel) **2 :** a set of matched furniture for a room

suit·or *n* **:** a man who courts a woman

sul·fur *or* **sul·phur** *n* **:** a yellow chemical element that is found widely in nature and is used in making chemicals and paper

sul·fu·rous *or* **sul·phu·rous** *adj* **:** containing or suggesting sulfur

¹sulk *vb* **:** to be sullenly silent or irritable

²sulk *n* **1 :** the state of one sulking **2 :** a sulky mood or spell

¹sulky *adj* **sulk·i·er; sulk·i·est :** sulking or given to sulking

²sulky *n, pl* **sulk·ies :** a light vehicle with two wheels, a seat for the driver only, and usually no body

sul·len *adj* **1 :** not sociable **:** SULKY **2 :** GLOOMY 1, DREARY — **sul·len·ly** *adv*

sul·tan *n* **:** a ruler especially of a Muslim state

sul·ta·na *n* **:** the wife, mother, sister, or daughter of a sultan

sul·try *adj* **sul·tri·er; sul·tri·est :** very hot and humid

¹sum *n* **1 :** a quantity of money **2 :** the whole amount **3 :** the result obtained by adding numbers **4 :** a problem in arithmetic

²sum *vb* **summed; sum·ming :** to find the sum of by adding or counting

su·mac *or* **su·mach** *n* **:** any of a group of trees, shrubs, or woody vines having leaves with many leaflets and loose clusters of red or white berries

sum·ma·rize *vb* **sum·ma·rized; sum·ma·riz·ing :** to tell in or reduce to a summary

¹sum·ma·ry *adj* **1 :** expressing or covering the main points briefly **:** CONCISE **2 :** done without delay

²summary *n, pl* **sum·ma·ries :** a short statement of the main points (as in a book or report)

¹sum·mer *n* **1 :** the season between spring and autumn which is in the northern hemisphere usually the months of June, July, and August **2 :** YEAR 2

²summer *vb* **:** to pass the summer

sum·mer·time *n* **:** the summer season

sum·mery *adj* : of, relating to, or typical of summer

sum·mit *n* : the highest point (as of a mountain) : TOP

sum·mon *vb* **1** : to call or send for : CONVENE **2** : to order to appear before a court of law **3** : to call into being : AROUSE — **sum·mon·er** *n*

sum·mons *n, pl* **sum·mons·es** **1** : the act of summoning **2** : a call by authority to appear at a place named or to attend to some duty **3** : a written order to appear in court

sump·tu·ous *adj* : very expensive or luxurious

sum up *vb* : SUMMARIZE

¹sun *n* **1** : the celestial body whose light makes our day : the member of the solar system round which the planets revolve **2** : a celestial body like our sun **3** : SUNSHINE 1

²sun *vb* **sunned; sun·ning** **1** : to expose to or as if to the rays of the sun **2** : to sun oneself

sun·bathe *vb* **sun·bathed; sun·bath·ing** : ²SUN 2

sun·beam *n* : a ray of sunlight

sun·block *n* : a strong sunscreen

sun·bon·net *n* : a bonnet with a wide curving brim that shades the face and usually a ruffle at the back that protects the neck from the sun

¹sun·burn *vb* **sun·burned** *or* **sun·burnt; sun·burn·ing** : to burn or discolor by the sun

²sunburn *n* : a sore red state of the skin caused by too much sunlight

sun·dae *n* : a serving of ice cream topped with fruit, syrup, or nuts

Sun·day *n* : the first day of the week : the Christian Sabbath

Sunday school *n* : a school held on Sunday in a church for religious education

sun·di·al *n* : a device to show the time of day by the position of the shadow cast onto a marked plate by an object with a straight edge

sun·down *n* : SUNSET

sun·dries *n pl* : various small articles or items

sun·dry *adj* : more than one or two : VARIOUS

sun·fish *n, pl* **sunfish** *or* **sun·fish·es** : any of numerous mostly small and brightly colored American freshwater fishes related to the perches

sun·flow·er *n* : a tall plant often grown for its large flower heads with brown center and yellow petals or for its edible oily seeds

sung *past of* SING

sun·glass·es *n pl* : glasses to protect the eyes from the sun

sunk *past of* SINK

sunk·en *adj* **1** : lying at the bottom of a body of water **2** : fallen in : HOLLOW **3** : built or settled below the surrounding or normal level

sun·less *adj* : being without sunlight : DARK

sun·light *n* : SUNSHINE

sun·lit *adj* : lighted by the sun

sun·ny *adj* **sun·ni·er; sun·ni·est** **1** : bright with sunshine **2** : MERRY 1, CHEERFUL

sun·rise *n* **1** : the apparent rise of the sun above the horizon : the light and color that go with this **2** : the time at which the sun rises

sun·screen *n* : a substance used on the skin to help protect it from the sun's ultraviolet radiation

sun·set *n* **1** : the apparent passing of the sun below the horizon : the light and color that go with this **2** : the time at which the sun sets

sun·shade *n* : something (as a parasol) used to protect from the sun's rays

sun·shine *n* **1** : the sun's light or direct rays : the warmth and light given by the sun's rays **2** : something that spreads warmth or happiness

sun·stroke *n* : a disorder marked by high fever and collapse and caused by too much sun

sun·tan *n* : a browning of skin exposed to the sun

sun·up *n* : SUNRISE

sun·ward *adv or adj* : toward or facing the sun

su·per *adj* **1** : very great **2** : very good

super- *prefix* **1** : more than **2** : extremely : very

su·perb *adj* : outstandingly excellent, impressive, or beautiful

su·per·com·put·er *n* : a large very fast computer used especially for scientific computations

su·per·fi·cial *adj* **1** : of or relating to the surface or appearance only **2** : not thorough : SHALLOW — **su·per·fi·cial·ly** *adv*

su·per·flu·ous *adj* : going beyond what is enough or necessary : EXTRA

su·per·he·ro *n* : a fictional hero having extraordinary or superhuman powers

su·per·high·way *n* : an expressway for high-speed traffic

su·per·hu·man *adj* : going beyond normal human power, size, or ability

su·per·in·tend *vb* : to have or exercise the charge of

su·per·in·ten·dent *n* : a person who looks

after or manages something (as schools or a building)

¹su·pe·ri·or *adj* **1** : situated higher up : higher in rank, importance, numbers, or quality **2** : excellent of its kind : BETTER **3** : feeling that one is better or more important than others : ARROGANT

²superior *n* **1** : one that is higher than another in rank, importance, or quality **2** : the head of a religious house or order

su·pe·ri·or·i·ty *n* : the state or fact of being superior

¹su·per·la·tive *adj* **1** : of, relating to, or being the form of an adjective or adverb that shows the highest or lowest degree of comparison **2** : better than all others : SUPREME

²superlative *n* : the superlative degree or a superlative form in a language

su·per·mar·ket *n* : a self-service market selling foods and household items

su·per·nat·u·ral *adj* : of or relating to something beyond or outside of nature or the visible universe

su·per·sede *vb* **su·per·sed·ed; su·per·sed·ing** : to take the place or position of

su·per·son·ic *adj* **1** : relating to or being vibrations too rapid to be heard **2** : having a speed from one to five times that of sound

su·per·sti·tion *n* : beliefs or practices resulting from ignorance, fear of the unknown, or trust in magic or chance

su·per·sti·tious *adj* : of, relating to, showing, or influenced by superstition

su·per·vise *vb* **su·per·vised; su·per·vis·ing** : SUPERINTEND, OVERSEE

su·per·vi·sion *n* : the act of supervising : MANAGEMENT

su·per·vi·sor *n* **1** : a person who supervises **2** : an officer in charge of a unit or an operation of a business, government, or school

sup·per *n* **1** : the evening meal especially when dinner is eaten at midday **2** : refreshments served late in the evening especially at a social gathering

sup·plant *vb* : to take the place of another usually unfairly

sup·ple *adj* **sup·pler; sup·plest** **1** : ADAPTABLE **2** : capable of bending or of being bent easily without stiffness, creases, or damage

¹sup·ple·ment *n* : something that supplies what is needed or adds to something else

²sup·ple·ment *vb* : to add to : COMPLETE

sup·ple·men·ta·ry *adj* : added as a supplement : ADDITIONAL

sup·pli·cate *vb* **sup·pli·cat·ed; sup·pli·cat·ing** : to ask or beg in a humble way : BESEECH

sup·pli·ca·tion *n* : the act of supplicating

¹sup·ply *vb* **sup·plied; sup·ply·ing** **1** : to

provide for : SATISFY **2** : to make available : FURNISH

²supply *n, pl* **sup·plies** **1** : the amount of something that is needed or can be gotten **2** : ²STORE 1 **3** : the act or process of supplying something

¹sup·port *vb* **1** : to take sides with : FAVOR **2** : to provide evidence for : VERIFY **3** : to pay the costs of : MAINTAIN **4** : to hold up or in position : serve as a foundation or prop for **5** : to keep going : SUSTAIN — **sup·port·er** *n*

²support *n* **1** : the act of supporting : the condition of being supported **2** : one that supports

sup·pose *vb* **sup·posed; sup·pos·ing** **1** : to think of as true or as a fact for the sake of argument **2** : BELIEVE 2, THINK **3** : ¹GUESS 1

sup·posed *adj* **1** : believed to be true or real **2** : forced or required to do something — **sup·pos·ed·ly** *adv*

sup·press *vb* **1** : to put down (as by authority or force) : SUBDUE **2** : to hold back : REPRESS

sup·pres·sion *n* : an act or instance of suppressing : the state of being suppressed

su·prem·a·cy *n, pl* **su·prem·a·cies** : the highest rank, power, or authority

su·preme *adj* **1** : highest in rank, power, or authority **2** : highest in degree or quality : UTMOST **3** : ¹EXTREME 1, FINAL — **su·preme·ly** *adv*

Supreme Being *n* : GOD 1

Supreme Court *n* : the highest court of the United States consisting of a chief justice and eight associate justices

¹sure *adj* **sur·er; sur·est** **1** : firmly established : STEADFAST **2** : RELIABLE, TRUSTWORTHY **3** : having no doubt : CONFIDENT **4** : not to be doubted : CERTAIN **5** : bound to happen **6** : bound as if by fate

²sure *adv* : SURELY 2, 3

sure·ly *adv* **1** : with confidence : CONFIDENTLY **2** : without doubt **3** : beyond question : REALLY

¹surf *n* **1** : the waves of the sea that splash on the shore **2** : the sound, splash, and foam of breaking waves

²surf *vb* **1** : to ride the surf (as on a surfboard) **2** : to scan a wide range of offerings (as on television or the Internet) for something that is interesting or fills a need

¹sur·face *n* **1** : the outside or any one side of an object **2** : the outside appearance

²surface *adj* **1** : of or relating to a surface : acting on a surface **2** : not deep or real

³surface *vb* **sur·faced; sur·fac·ing** **1** : to give a surface to : make smooth (as by sanding or paving) **2** : to come to the surface

surf·board *n* : a long narrow board that floats and is ridden in surfing

surf·ing *n* : the sport of riding waves in to shore usually while standing on a surfboard

¹surge *vb* **surged; surg·ing** 1 : to rise and fall with much action 2 : to move in or as if in waves

²surge *n* 1 : an onward rush like that of a wave 2 : a large wave

sur·geon *n* : a doctor who specializes in surgery

sur·gery *n, pl* **sur·ger·ies** 1 : a branch of medicine concerned with the correction of defects, the repair and healing of injuries, and the treatment of diseased conditions by operation 2 : the work done by a surgeon

sur·gi·cal *adj* : of, relating to, or associated with surgery or surgeons

sur·ly *adj* **sur·li·er; sur·li·est** : having a mean rude disposition : UNFRIENDLY

¹sur·mise *n* : a thought or idea based on very little evidence : ²GUESS

²surmise *vb* **sur·mised; sur·mis·ing** : to form an idea on very little evidence : ¹GUESS 1

sur·mount *vb* 1 : OVERCOME 1 2 : to get to the top of 3 : to be at the top of

sur·name *n* : a family name : a last name

sur·pass *vb* 1 : to be greater, better, or stronger than : EXCEED 2 : to go beyond the reach or powers of

¹sur·plus *n* : an amount left over : EXCESS

²surplus *adj* : left over : EXTRA

¹sur·prise *n* 1 : an act or instance of coming upon without warning 2 : something that surprises 3 : ASTONISHMENT, AMAZEMENT

²surprise *vb* **sur·prised; sur·pris·ing** 1 : to attack without warning : capture by an unexpected attack 2 : to come upon without warning 3 : to cause to feel wonder or amazement because of being unexpected

sur·pris·ing *adj* : causing surprise : UNEXPECTED — **sur·pris·ing·ly** *adv*

¹sur·ren·der *vb* 1 : to give oneself or something over to the power, control, or possession of another especially under force : YIELD 2 : RELINQUISH

²surrender *n* : the act of giving up or yielding oneself or something into the possession or control of someone else

sur·rey *n, pl* **surreys** : a pleasure carriage that has two wide seats and four wheels and is drawn by horses

sur·round *vb* : to enclose on all sides : ENCIRCLE

sur·round·ings *n pl* : the circumstances, conditions, or things around an individual : ENVIRONMENT

¹sur·vey *vb* **sur·veyed; sur·vey·ing** 1 : to look over : EXAMINE 2 : to find out the size, shape, or position of (as an area of land) 3 : to gather information from : make a survey of

²sur·vey *n, pl* **surveys** 1 : the action or an instance of surveying 2 : something that is surveyed 3 : a careful examination to learn facts 4 : a history or description that covers a large subject briefly

sur·vey·ing *n* 1 : the act or occupation of a person who makes surveys 2 : a branch of mathematics that teaches how to measure the earth's surface and record these measurements accurately

sur·vey·or *n* : a person who surveys or whose occupation is surveying

sur·viv·al *n* 1 : a living or continuing longer than another person or thing 2 : one that survives

sur·vive *vb* **sur·vived; sur·viv·ing** 1 : to remain alive : continue to exist 2 : to live longer than or past the end of — **sur·vi·vor** *n*

sus·cep·ti·ble *adj* 1 : of such a nature as to permit 2 : having little resistance 3 : easily affected or impressed by

¹sus·pect *adj* : thought of with suspicion

²sus·pect *n* : a person who is suspected

³sus·pect *vb* 1 : to have doubts of : DISTRUST 2 : to imagine to be guilty without proof 3 : to suppose to be true or likely

sus·pend *vb* 1 : to force to give up some right or office for a time 2 : to stop or do away with for a time 3 : to stop operation or action for a time 4 : to hang especially so as to be free except at one point

sus·pend·er *n* : one of a pair of supporting straps that fasten to trousers or a skirt and pass over the shoulders

sus·pense *n* : uncertainty or worry about the result of something

sus·pen·sion *n* 1 : the act or an instance of suspending 2 : the state of being suspended 3 : the period during which someone or something is suspended

sus·pi·cion *n* 1 : an act or instance of suspecting or the state of being suspected 2 : a feeling that something is wrong : DOUBT

sus·pi·cious *adj* 1 : likely to arouse suspicion 2 : likely to suspect or distrust 3 : showing distrust

sus·tain *vb* 1 : to give support or relief to : HELP 2 : to provide with what is needed 3 : to keep up : PROLONG 4 : to hold up the weight of : PROP 5 : to keep up the spirits of 6 : to put up with without giving in 7 : ²EXPERIENCE 8 : to allow or uphold as true, legal, or fair 9 : CONFIRM 1, PROVE

sus·te·nance *n* 1 : ²LIVING 3, SUBSISTENCE

2 : the act of sustaining : the state of being sustained **3 :** ²SUPPORT 2

¹swab *n* **1 :** a yarn mop especially as used on a ship **2 :** a wad of absorbent material usually wound around the end of a small stick and used for applying or removing material (as medicine or makeup)

²swab *vb* **swabbed; swab·bing 1 :** to clean with or as if with a swab **2 :** to apply medication to with a swab

¹swag·ger *vb* **:** to walk with a proud strut

²swagger *n* **:** an act or instance of swaggering

¹swal·low *n* **:** any of a group of small migratory birds with long wings, forked tails, and a graceful flight

²swallow *vb* **1 :** to take into the stomach through the mouth and throat **2 :** to perform the actions used in swallowing something **3 :** to take in as if by swallowing : ENGULF **4 :** to accept or believe without question, protest, or anger **5 :** to keep from expressing or showing : REPRESS

³swallow *n* **1 :** an act of swallowing **2 :** an amount that can be swallowed at one time

swam *past of* SWIM

¹swamp *n* **:** wet spongy land often partly covered with water

²swamp *vb* **1 :** to fill or cause to fill with water : sink after filling with water **2 :** OVERWHELM 2

swampy *adj* **swamp·i·er; swamp·i·est :** of, relating to, or like a swamp

swan *n* **:** a usually white waterbird with a long neck and a heavy body that is related to but larger than the geese

¹swap *vb* **swapped; swap·ping :** to give in exchange : make an exchange : TRADE

²swap *n* **:** ¹EXCHANGE 1, TRADE

¹swarm *n* **1 :** a large number of bees that leave a hive together to form a new colony elsewhere **2 :** a large moving crowd (as of people or insects)

²swarm *vb* **1 :** to form a swarm and leave the hive **2 :** to move or gather in a swarm or large crowd **3 :** to be filled with a great number : TEEM

swar·thy *adj* **swar·thi·er; swar·thi·est :** having a dark complexion

¹swat *vb* **swat·ted; swat·ting :** to hit with a quick hard blow

²swat *n* **:** a hard blow

swath *or* **swathe** *n* **1 :** a sweep of a scythe or machine in mowing or the path cut in one course **2 :** a row of cut grass (as grain)

¹sway *n* **1 :** a slow swinging back and forth or from side to side **2 :** a controlling influence or force : RULE

²sway *vb* **1 :** to swing slowly back and forth or from side to side **2 :** to change often between one point, position, or opinion and another **3 :** ²INFLUENCE

swear *vb* **swore; sworn; swear·ing 1 :** to make a statement or promise under oath : VOW **2 :** to give an oath to **3 :** to bind by an oath **4 :** to take an oath **5 :** to use bad or vulgar language : CURSE

¹sweat *vb* **sweat** *or* **sweat·ed; sweat·ing 1 :** to give off salty moisture through the pores of the skin : PERSPIRE **2 :** to collect moisture on the surface **3 :** to work hard enough to perspire

²sweat *n* **1 :** PERSPIRATION 2 **2 :** moisture coming from or collecting in drops on a surface **3 :** the condition of one sweating

sweat·er *n* **:** a knitted or crocheted jacket or pullover

sweat gland *n* **:** any of numerous small skin glands that give off perspiration

Swede *n* **:** a person born or living in Sweden

¹Swed·ish *adj* **:** of or relating to Sweden, the Swedes, or Swedish

²Swedish *n* **:** the language of the Swedes

¹sweep *vb* **swept; sweep·ing 1 :** to remove with a broom or brush **2 :** to clean by removing loose dirt or small trash with a broom or brush **3 :** to move over or across swiftly with force or destruction **4 :** to move or gather as if with a broom or brush **5 :** to touch a surface as if with a brush **6 :** to drive along with steady force **7 :** to move the eyes or an instrument through a wide curve — **sweep·er** *n*

²sweep *n* **1 :** something that sweeps or works with a sweeping motion **2 :** an act or instance of sweeping **3 :** a complete or easy victory **4 :** a curving movement, course, or line **5 :** ¹RANGE 6, SCOPE **6 :** CHIMNEY SWEEP

¹sweep·ing *n* **1 :** the act or action of one that sweeps **2 sweepings** *pl* **:** things collected by sweeping

²sweeping *adj* **1 :** moving or extending in a wide curve or over a wide area **2 :** EXTENSIVE

sweep·stakes *n, sing or pl* **:** a contest in which money or prizes are given to winners picked by chance (as by drawing names from a box)

¹sweet *adj* **1 :** pleasing to the taste **2 :** containing or tasting of sugar **3 :** pleasing to the mind or feelings : AGREEABLE **4 :** ¹KINDLY 2, MILD **5 :** FRAGRANT **6 :** pleasing to the ear or eye **7 :** much loved : DEAR **8 :** not sour, stale, or spoiled **9 :** FRESH 1 — **sweet·ish** *adj* — **sweet·ly** *adv* — **sweet·ness** *n*

²sweet *n* **1 :** something (as candy) that is sweet to the taste **2 :** ¹DARLING 1, DEAR

sweet corn *n* **:** an Indian corn with kernels

rich in sugar that is cooked as a vegetable while young

sweet·en *vb* : to make or become sweet or sweeter

sweet·en·ing *n* **1** : the act or process of making sweet **2** : something that sweetens

sweet·heart *n* : a person whom one loves

sweet·meat *n* : a food (as a piece of candy or candied fruit) rich in sugar

sweet pea *n* : a climbing plant related to the peas that is grown for its fragrant flowers of many colors

sweet potato *n* : the large sweet edible root of a tropical vine somewhat like a morning glory

sweet wil·liam *n, often cap W* : a European pink grown for its thick flat clusters of many-colored flowers

¹swell *vb* **swelled; swelled** *or* **swol·len; swell·ing** **1** : to enlarge in an abnormal way usually by pressure from within or by growth **2** : to grow or make bigger (as in size or value) **3** : to stretch upward or outward : BULGE **4** : to fill or become filled with emotion

²swell *n* **1** : a becoming larger (as in size or value) **2** : a long rolling wave or series of waves in the open sea **3** : a very fashionably dressed person

³swell *adj* **1** : STYLISH, FASHIONABLE **2** : EXCELLENT, FIRST-RATE

swell·ing *n* : a swollen lump or part

swel·ter *vb* : to suffer, sweat, or be faint from heat

swept *past of* SWEEP

¹swerve *vb* **swerved; swerv·ing** : to turn aside suddenly from a straight line or course

²swerve *n* : an act or instance of swerving

¹swift *adj* **1** : moving or capable of moving with great speed **2** : occurring suddenly **3** : ¹READY 3, ALERT **— swift·ly** *adv* **— swift·ness** *n*

²swift *adv* : SWIFTLY

³swift *n* : a small usually sooty black bird that is related to the hummingbirds but looks like a swallow

swig *n* : the amount drunk at one time : GULP

¹swill *vb* : to eat or drink greedily

²swill *n* **1** : ¹SLOP 3 **2** : GARBAGE, REFUSE

¹swim *vb* **swam; swum; swim·ming** **1** : to move through or in water by moving arms, legs, fins, or tail **2** : to glide smoothly and quietly **3** : to float on or in or be covered with or as if with a liquid **4** : to be dizzy : move or seem to move dizzily **5** : to cross by swimming **— swim·mer** *n*

²swim *n* **1** : an act or period of swimming **2** : the main current of activity

swimming *adj* **1** : capable of swimming **2** : used in or for swimming

swimming pool *n* : a tank (as of concrete or plastic) made for swimming

swim·suit *n* : a garment for swimming or bathing

¹swin·dle *vb* **swin·dled; swin·dling** : to get money or property from by dishonest means : CHEAT

²swindle *n* : an act or instance of swindling

swin·dler *n* : a person who swindles

swine *n, pl* **swine** : a hoofed domestic animal that comes from the wild boar, has a long snout and bristly skin, and is widely raised for meat

swine·herd *n* : a person who tends swine

¹swing *vb* **swung; swing·ing** **1** : to move rapidly in a sweeping curve **2** : to throw or toss in a circle or back and forth **3** : to sway to and fro **4** : to hang or be hung so as to move freely back and forth or in a curve **5** : to turn on a hinge or pivot **6** : to manage or handle successfully **7** : to march or walk with free swaying movements

²swing *n* **1** : an act of swinging **2** : a swinging movement, blow, or rhythm **3** : the distance through which something swings **4** : a swinging seat usually hung by overhead ropes **5** : a style of jazz marked by lively rhythm and played mostly for dancing

¹swipe *n* : a strong sweeping blow

²swipe *vb* **swiped; swip·ing** : ¹STEAL 2

¹swirl *vb* : to move with a whirling or twisting motion

²swirl *n* **1** : a whirling mass or motion : EDDY **2** : whirling confusion **3** : a twisting shape or mark

¹swish *vb* : to make, move, or strike with a soft rubbing or hissing sound

²swish *n* **1** : a hissing sound (as of a whip cutting the air) or a light sweeping or rubbing sound (as of a silk skirt) **2** : a swishing movement

¹Swiss *n, pl* **Swiss** : a person born or living in Switzerland

²Swiss *adj* : of or relating to Switzerland or the Swiss

¹switch *n* **1** : a narrow flexible whip, rod, or twig **2** : an act of switching **3** : a blow with a switch or whip **4** : a change from one thing to another **5** : a device for adjusting the rails of a track so that a train or streetcar may be turned from one track to another **6** : SIDING 1 **7** : a device for making, breaking, or changing the connections in an electrical circuit

²switch *vb* **1** : to strike or whip with or as if with a switch **2** : to lash from side to side **3** : to turn, shift, or change by operating a switch **4** : to make a shift or change

switchboard

switch·board *n* : a panel for controlling the operation of a number of electric circuits used especially to make and break telephone connections

1swiv·el *n* : a device joining two parts so that one or both can turn freely (as on a bolt or pin)

2swivel *vb* **swiv·eled** *or* **swiv·elled; swiv·el·ing** *or* **swiv·el·ling** : to turn on or as if on a swivel

swollen *past participle of* SWELL

1swoon *vb* : 2FAINT

2swoon *n* : 3FAINT

1swoop *vb* : to rush down or pounce suddenly like a hawk attacking its prey

2swoop *n* : an act or instance of swooping

sword *n* : a weapon having a long blade usually with a sharp point and edge

sword·fish *n, pl* **swordfish** *or* **sword·fish·es** : a very large ocean food fish having a long swordlike beak formed by the bones of the upper jaw

swords·man *n, pl* **swords·men** : a person who fights with a sword

swore *past of* SWEAR

sworn *past participle of* SWEAR

swum *past participle of* SWIM

swung *past of* SWING

syc·a·more *n* **1** : the common fig tree of Egypt and Asia Minor **2** : an American tree with round fruits and bark that forms flakes

syl·lab·ic *adj* **1** : of, relating to, or being syllables **2** : not accompanied by a vowel sound in the same syllable

syl·lab·i·cate *vb* **syl·lab·i·cat·ed; syl·lab·i·cat·ing** : SYLLABIFY

syl·lab·i·ca·tion *n* : the forming of syllables : the dividing of words into syllables

syl·lab·i·fi·ca·tion *n* : SYLLABICATION

syl·lab·i·fy *vb* **syl·lab·i·fied; syl·lab·i·fy·ing** : to form or divide into syllables

syl·la·ble *n* **1** : a unit of spoken language that consists of one or more vowel sounds alone or of a syllabic consonant alone or of either of these preceded or followed by one or more consonant sounds **2** : one or more letters (as *syl, la,* and *ble*) in a written word (as *syl·la·ble*) usually separated from the rest of the word by a centered dot or a hyphen and used as guides to the division of the word at the end of a line

sym·bol *n* **1** : something that stands for something else : EMBLEM **2** : a letter, character, or sign used instead of a word to represent a quantity, position, relationship, direction, or something to be done

sym·bol·ic *or* **sym·bol·i·cal** *adj* : of, relating to, or using symbols or symbolism

sym·bol·ize *vb* **sym·bol·ized; sym·bol·iz·ing** : to serve as a symbol of

sym·met·ri·cal *or* **sym·met·ric** *adj* : having or showing symmetry

sym·me·try *n, pl* **sym·me·tries** : close agreement in size, shape, and position of parts that are on opposite sides of a dividing line or center : an arrangement involving regular and balanced proportions

sym·pa·thet·ic *adj* **1** : fitting one's mood or disposition **2** : feeling sympathy **3** : feeling favorable — **sym·pa·thet·i·cal·ly** *adv*

sym·pa·thize *vb* **sym·pa·thized; sym·pa·thiz·ing** **1** : to feel or show sympathy **2** : to be in favor of something

sym·pa·thy *n, pl* **sym·pa·thies** **1** : a relationship between persons or things in which whatever affects one similarly affects the other **2** : readiness to think or feel alike : similarity of likes, interest, or aims that makes a bond of goodwill **3** : readiness to favor or support **4** : the act of or capacity for entering into the feelings or interests of another **5** : sorrow or pity for another **6** : a showing of sorrow for another's loss, grief, or misfortune

sym·phon·ic *adj* : of or relating to a symphony or symphony orchestra

sym·pho·ny *n, pl* **sym·pho·nies** **1** : harmonious arrangement (as of sound or color) **2** : a usually long musical composition for a full orchestra **3** : a large orchestra of wind, string, and percussion instruments

symp·tom *n* **1** : a noticeable change in the body or its functions typical of a disease **2** : INDICATION 2, SIGN

syn·a·gogue *or* **syn·a·gog** *n* : a Jewish house of worship

syn·apse *n* : the point at which a nerve impulse passes from one nerve cell to another

syn·co·pa·tion *n* : a temporary accenting of a normally weak beat in music to vary the rhythm

syn·o·nym *n* : a word having the same or almost the same meaning as another word in the same language

syn·on·y·mous *adj* : alike in meaning

syn·tax *n* : the way in which words are put together to form phrases, clauses, or sentences

syn·the·size *vb* **syn·the·sized; syn·the·siz·ing** : to build up from simpler materials

syn·thet·ic *adj* : produced artificially especially by chemical means : produced by human beings

sy·rin·ga *n* : a garden shrub with often fragrant flowers of a white or cream color

sy·ringe *n* : a device used to force fluid into or withdraw it from the body or its cavities

syr·up *or* **sir·up** *n* **1** : a thick sticky solu-

-tion of sugar and water often containing flavoring or a medicine **2** : the juice of a fruit or plant with some of the water removed

sys·tem *n* **1** : a group of parts combined to form a whole that works or moves as a unit **2** : a body that functions as a whole **3** : a group of bodily organs that together carry on some vital function **4** : an orderly plan or method of governing or arranging **5** : regular method or order : ORDERLINESS

sys·tem·at·ic *adj* **1** : having, using, or acting on a system **2** : carrying out a plan with thoroughness or regularity — **sys·tem·at·i·cal·ly** *adv*

sys·tem·ic *adj* : of or relating to the body as a whole

T

t *n, pl* **t's** *or* **ts** *often cap* : the twentieth letter of the English alphabet — **to a T** : just fine : EXACTLY

tab *n* **1** : a short flap or tag attached to something for filing, pulling, or hanging **2** : a careful watch

tab·by *n, pl* **tabbies** **1** : a domestic cat with a gray or tawny coat striped and spotted with black **2** : a female domestic cat

tab·er·na·cle *n* **1** *often cap* : a structure of wood hung with curtains used in worship by the Israelites during their wanderings in the wilderness with Moses **2** : a house of worship

¹ta·ble *n* **1** : a piece of furniture having a smooth flat top on legs **2** : food to eat **3** : the people around a table **4** : short list **5** : an arrangement in rows or columns for reference

²table *vb* **ta·bled; ta·bling** **1** : TABULATE **2** : to put on a table

tab·leau *n, pl* **tableaus** *or* **tab·leaux** : a scene or event shown by a group of persons who remain still and silent

ta·ble·cloth *n* : a covering spread over a dining table before the places are set

ta·ble·land *n* : PLATEAU

ta·ble·spoon *n* **1** : a large spoon used mostly for dishing up food **2** : TABLESPOONFUL

ta·ble·spoon·ful *n, pl* **tablespoonfuls** *or* **ta·ble·spoons·ful** **1** : as much as a tablespoon will hold **2** : a unit of measure used in cooking equal to three teaspoonfuls (about fifteen milliliters)

tab·let *n* **1** : a thin flat slab used for writing, painting, or drawing **2** : a number of sheets of writing paper glued together at one edge **3** : a flat and usually round mass of material containing medicine

table tennis *n* : a game played on a table by two or four players who use paddles to hit a small hollow plastic ball back and forth over a net

ta·ble·ware *n* : utensils (as of china, glass, or silver) for use at the table

tab·u·late *vb* **tab·u·lat·ed; tab·u·lat·ing** : to put in the form of a table

tac·it *adj* : understood or made known without being put into words — **tac·it·ly** *adv*

¹tack *n* **1** : a small nail with a sharp point and usually a broad flat head for fastening a light object or material to a solid surface **2** : the direction a ship is sailing as shown by the position the sails are set in or the movement of a ship with the sails set in a certain position **3** : a change of course from one tack to another **4** : a zigzag movement or course **5** : a course of action **6** : a temporary stitch used in sewing

²tack *vb* **1** : to fasten with tacks **2** : to attach or join loosely **3** : to change from one course to another in sailing **4** : to follow a zigzag course

¹tack·le *n* **1** : a set of special equipment **2** : an arrangement of ropes and wheels for hoisting or pulling something heavy **3** : an act of tackling

²tackle *vb* **tack·led; tack·ling** **1** : to seize and throw (a person) to the ground **2** : to begin working on

ta·co *n, pl* **tacos** : a corn tortilla usually folded and fried and filled with a spicy mixture (as of ground meat and cheese)

tact *n* : a keen understanding of how to get along with other people

tact·ful *adj* : having or showing tact — **tact·ful·ly** *adv* — **tact·ful·ness** *n*

tac·tic *n* : a planned action for some purpose

tac·tics *n sing or pl* **1** : the science and art of arranging and moving troops or warships for best use **2** : a system or method for reaching a goal

tac·tile *adj* : of or relating to the sense of touch

tact·less *adj* : having or showing no tact — **tact·less·ly** *adv* — **tact·less·ness** *n*

tad·pole *n* : the larva of a frog or toad that has a long tail, breathes with gills, and lives in water

taf·fy *n, pl* **taffies** : a candy made usually of molasses or brown sugar boiled and pulled until soft

¹tag *n* **1** : a small flap or tab fixed or hanging on something **2** : an often quoted saying

²tag *vb* **tagged; tag·ging** **1** : to put a tag on **2** : to follow closely and continually

³tag *n* : a game in which one player who is it chases the others and tries to touch one of them to make that person it

⁴tag *vb* **tagged; tag·ging** **1** : to touch in or as if in a game of tag **2** : to touch a runner in baseball with the ball and cause the runner to be out

¹tail *n* **1** : the rear part of an animal or a usually slender flexible extension of this part **2** : something that in shape, appearance, or position is like an animal's tail **3** : the back, last, or lower part of something **4** : the side or end opposite the head — **tailed** *adj* — **tail·less** *adj* — **tail·like** *adj*

²tail *vb* : to follow closely to keep watch on

tail·gate *n* : a panel at the back end of a vehicle that can be let down for loading and unloading

tail·light *n* : a red warning light at the rear of a vehicle

¹tai·lor *n* : a person whose business is making or making adjustments in men's or women's clothes

²tailor *vb* **1** : to make or make adjustments in (clothes) **2** : to change to fit a special need

tail·pipe *n* : the pipe carrying off the exhaust gases from the muffler of an engine in a car or truck

tail·spin *n* : a dive by an airplane turning in a circle

¹taint *vb* **1** : to affect slightly with something bad **2** : to rot slightly

²taint *n* : a trace of decay

¹take *vb* **took; tak·en; tak·ing** **1** : to get control of : CAPTURE **2** : ¹GRASP 1 **3** : to come upon **4** : CAPTIVATE **5** : to receive into the body **6** : to get possession or use of **7** : ASSUME 1 **8** : to be formed or used with **9** : to adopt as one's own or for oneself **10** : WIN 3 **11** : CHOOSE 1, SELECT **12** : to sit in or on **13** : to use as a way of going from one place to another **14** : REQUIRE **15** : to find out by special methods **16** : to save in some permanent form **17** : to put up with : ENDURE **18** : BELIEVE 2 3 **19** : to be guided by : FOLLOW **20** : to become affected suddenly **21** : UNDERSTAND 4, INTERPRET **22** : to react in a certain way **23** : to carry or go with from one place to another **24** : REMOVE 3, SUBTRACT **25** : to do the action of **26** : to have effect : be successful — **tak·er** *n* — **take advantage of** **1** : to make good use of **2** : to treat (someone) unfairly — **take after** : RESEMBLE — **take care** : to be careful — **take care of** : to do what is needed : look after — **take effect** **1** : to go into effect **2** : to have an in-

tended or expected effect — **take hold** : to become attached or established — **take part** : to do or join in something together with others — **take place** : to come into being and last for a time — used of events or actions

²take *n* **1** : the act of taking **2** : something that is taken **3** : a bodily reaction that shows a smallpox vaccination to be successful

take back *vb* : to try to cancel (as something said)

take in *vb* **1** : to make smaller **2** : to receive as a guest **3** : to allow to join **4** : to receive (work) to be done in one's home for pay **5** : to have within its limits **6** : to go to **7** : to get the meaning of **8** : ¹CHEAT 1

take·off *n* **1** : an imitation especially to mock the original **2** : an act or instance of taking off from the ground (as by an airplane) **3** : a spot at which one takes off

take off *vb* **1** : to take away (a covering) : REMOVE **2** : DEDUCT **3** : to leave a surface in beginning a flight or leap

take on *vb* **1** : to begin (a task) or struggle against (an opponent) **2** : to gain or show as or as if a part of oneself **3** : ¹EMPLOY 2 **4** : to make an unusual show of one's grief or anger

take over *vb* : to get control of

take up *vb* **1** : to get together from many sources **2** : to start something for the first time or after a pause **3** : to change by making tighter or shorter

tak·ing *adj* **1** : ATTRACTIVE **2** : INFECTIOUS 1

talc *n* : a soft mineral that has a soapy feel and is used in making talcum powder and for coloring

tal·cum powder *n* : a usually perfumed powder for the body made of talc

tale *n* **1** : something told **2** : a story about an imaginary event **3** : ³LIE **4** : a piece of harmful gossip

tal·ent *n* **1** : unusual natural ability **2** : a special often creative or artistic ability **3** : persons having special ability — **tal·ent·ed** *adj*

tal·is·man *n, pl* **tal·is·mans** : a ring or stone carved with symbols and believed to have magical powers : CHARM

¹talk *vb* **1** : to express in speech : SPEAK **2** : to speak about : DISCUSS **3** : to cause or influence by talking **4** : to use a certain language **5** : to exchange ideas by means of spoken words : CONVERSE **6** : to pass on information other than by speaking **7** : ²GOSSIP **8** : to reveal secret information — **talk·er** *n*

²talk *n* **1** : the act of talking : SPEECH **2** : a

way of speaking : LANGUAGE **3** : CONFER-
ENCE **4** : [1]RUMOR 2, GOSSIP **5** : the topic
of comment or gossip **6** ; an informal address

talk·a·tive *adj* : fond of talking — **talk·a·
tive·ness** *n*

talk·ing-to *n* : an often wordy scolding

[1]**tall** *adj* **1** : having unusually great height
2 : of a stated height **3** : made up — **tall·
ness** *n*

[2]**tall** *adv* : so as to be or look tall

tal·low *n* : a white solid fat obtained by heating fatty tissues of cattle and sheep

[1]**tal·ly** *n, pl* **tallies** **1** : a device for keeping
a count **2** : a recorded count **3** : a score or
point made (as in a game)

[2]**tally** *vb* **tal·lied; tal·ly·ing** **1** : to keep a
count of **2** : to make a tally : SCORE **3**
: CORRESPOND 1

tal·on *n* : the claw of a bird of prey — **tal·
oned** *adj*

ta·ma·le *n* : seasoned ground meat rolled in
cornmeal, wrapped in corn husks, and
steamed

tam·bou·rine *n* : a small shallow drum with
only one head and loose metal disks around
the rim that is played by shaking or hitting
with the hand

[1]**tame** *adj* **tam·er; tam·est** **1** : made useful
and obedient to humans : DOMESTIC 3 **2**
: not afraid of people **3** : not interesting
: DULL — **tame·ly** *adv* — **tame·ness** *n*

[2]**tame** *vb* **tamed; tam·ing** **1** : to make or
become gentle or obedient **2** : [2]HUMBLE —
tam·able *or* **tame·able** *adj* — **tam·er** *n*

tamp *vb* : to drive down or in with several
light blows

tam·per *vb* : to interfere in a secret or incorrect way

[1]**tan** *vb* **tanned; tan·ning** **1** : to change
hide into leather by soaking in a tannin solution **2** : to make or become brown or tan
in color **3** : [1]BEAT 1, THRASH

[2]**tan** *adj* **tan·ner; tan·nest** : of a light yellowish brown color

[3]**tan** *n* **1** : a brown color given to the skin by
the sun or wind **2** : a light yellowish brown
color

tan·a·ger *n* : a very brightly colored bird related to the finches

[1]**tan·dem** *n* **1** : a carriage pulled by horses
hitched one behind the other **2** : TANDEM
BICYCLE

[2]**tandem** *adv* : one behind another

tandem bicycle *n* : a bicycle for two people
sitting one behind the other

tang *n* : a sharp flavor or smell

tan·ger·ine *n* : a Chinese orange with a loose
skin and sweet pulp

tan·gi·ble *adj* **1** : possible to touch or han-

dle **2** : actually real : MATERIAL — **tan·gi·
bly** *adv*

[1]**tan·gle** *vb* **tan·gled; tan·gling** : to twist or
become twisted together into a mass hard to
straighten out again

[2]**tangle** *n* **1** : a tangled twisted mass (as of
yarn) **2** : a complicated or confused state

[1]**tank** *n* **1** : an often large container for a liquid **2** : an enclosed combat vehicle that has
heavy armor and guns and a tread which is
an endless belt

[2]**tank** *vb* : to put, keep, or treat in a tank

tan·kard *n* : a tall cup with one handle and
often a lid

tank·er *n* : a vehicle or ship with tanks for
carrying a liquid

tan·ner *n* : a person who tans hides into
leather

tan·nery *n, pl* **tan·ner·ies** : a place where
hides are tanned

tan·nin *n* : a substance often made from oak
bark or sumac and used in tanning, dyeing,
and making ink

tan·ta·lize *vb* **tan·ta·lized; tan·ta·liz·ing** : to
make miserable by or as if by showing
something desirable but keeping it out of
reach — **tan·ta·liz·er** *n*

tan·trum *n* : an outburst of bad temper

[1]**tap** *n* : FAUCET, SPIGOT — **on tap** : on hand
: AVAILABLE

[2]**tap** *vb* **tapped; tap·ping** **1** : to let out or
cause to flow by making a hole or by
pulling out a plug **2** : to make a hole in to
draw off a liquid **3** : to draw from or upon
4 : to connect into (a telephone wire) to listen secretly — **tap·per** *n*

[3]**tap** *vb* **tapped; tap·ping** **1** : to hit lightly
2 : to make by striking something lightly
again and again — **tap·per** *n*

[4]**tap** *n* : a light blow or its sound

[1]**tape** *n* **1** : a narrow band of cloth **2** : a
narrow strip or band of material (as paper,
steel, or plastic) **3** : MAGNETIC TAPE **4**
: TAPE RECORDING

[2]**tape** *vb* **taped; tap·ing** **1** : to fasten, cover,
or hold up with tape **2** : to make a record of
on tape

tape deck *n* : a device used to play back and
often to record on magnetic tapes

tape measure *n* : a tape marked off for
measuring

[1]**ta·per** *n* **1** : a slender candle **2** : a gradual
lessening in thickness or width in a long ob-
ject

[2]**taper** *vb* **1** : to make or become gradually
smaller toward one end **2** : to grow gradually less and less

tape recorder *n* : a device for recording on
and playing back magnetic tapes

tape recording *n* : a recording made on magnetic tape

tap·es·try *n, pl* **tap·es·tries** : a heavy cloth that has designs or pictures woven into it and is used especially as a wall hanging — **tap·es·tried** *adj*

tape·worm *n* : a worm with a long flat body that lives in human or animal intestines

tap·i·o·ca *n* : small pieces of starch from roots of a tropical plant used especially in puddings

ta·pir *n* : a large hoofed mammal of tropical America, Malaya, and Sumatra that has thick legs, a short tail, and a long flexible snout

tap·root *n* : a main root of a plant that grows straight down and gives off smaller side roots

taps *n sing or pl* : the last bugle call at night blown as a signal to put out the lights

¹tar *n* : a thick dark sticky liquid made from wood, coal, or peat

²tar *vb* **tarred; tar·ring** : to cover with or as if with tar

³tar *n* : SAILOR

ta·ran·tu·la *n* **1** : a large European spider whose bite was once believed to cause a wild desire to dance **2** : any of a group of large hairy spiders of warm regions of North and South America whose bite is sharp but not serious except for some South American species

tar·dy *adj* **tar·di·er; tar·di·est** : not on time : LATE — **tar·di·ly** *adv* — **tar·di·ness** *n*

tar·get *n* **1** : a mark or object to shoot at **2** : a person or thing that is talked about, criticized, or laughed at **3** : a goal to be reached

tar·iff *n* **1** : a list of taxes placed by a government on goods coming into a country **2** : the tax or the rate of taxation set up in a tariff list

¹tar·nish *vb* : to make or become dull, dim, or discolored

²tarnish *n* : a surface coating formed during tarnishing

tar·pau·lin *n* : a sheet of waterproof canvas

¹tar·ry *vb* **tar·ried; tar·ry·ing** **1** : to be slow in coming or going **2** : to stay in or at a place

²tar·ry *adj* : of, like, or covered with tar

¹tart *adj* **1** : pleasantly sharp to the taste **2** : BITING — **tart·ly** *adv* — **tart·ness** *n*

²tart *n* : a small pie often with no top crust

tar·tan *n* : a woolen cloth with a plaid design first made in Scotland

tar·tar *n* **1** : a substance found in the juices of grapes that forms a reddish crust on the inside of wine barrels **2** : a crust that forms on the teeth made up of deposits of saliva, food, and calcium

task *n* : a piece of assigned work

tas·sel *n* **1** : a hanging ornament made of a bunch of cords of the same length fastened at one end **2** : something like a tassel

¹taste *vb* **tast·ed; tast·ing** **1** : ²EXPERIENCE **2** : to find out the flavor of something by taking a little into the mouth **3** : to eat or drink usually in small amounts **4** : to recognize by the sense of taste **5** : to have a certain flavor — **tast·er** *n*

²taste *n* **1** : a small amount tasted **2** : the one of the special senses that recognizes sweet, sour, bitter, or salty flavors and that acts through sense organs (**taste buds**) in the tongue **3** : the quality of something recognized by the sense of taste or by this together with smell and touch : FLAVOR **4** : a personal liking **5** : the ability to choose and enjoy what is good or beautiful

taste·ful *adj* : having or showing good taste — **taste·ful·ly** *adv* — **taste·ful·ness** *n*

taste·less *adj* **1** : having little flavor **2** : not having or showing good taste — **taste·less·ly** *adv* — **taste·less·ness** *n*

tasty *adj* **tast·i·er; tast·i·est** : pleasing to the taste — **tast·i·ness** *n*

tat·ter *n* **1** : a part torn and left hanging : SHRED **2 tatters** *pl* : ragged clothing

tat·tered *adj* **1** : torn in or worn to shreds **2** : dressed in ragged clothes

tat·tle *vb* **tat·tled; tat·tling** **1** : PRATTLE **2** : to give away secrets : tell on someone — **tat·tler** *n*

tat·tle·tale *n* : a person who lets secrets out

¹tat·too *vb* **tat·tooed; tat·too·ing** : to mark the body with a picture or pattern by using a needle to put color under the skin — **tat·too·er** *n*

²tattoo *n, pl* **tat·toos** : a picture or design made by tattooing

taught *past of* TEACH

¹taunt *n* : a mean insulting remark

²taunt *vb* : to make fun of or say mean insulting things to

Tau·rus *n* **1** : a constellation between Aries and Gemini imagined as a bull **2** : the second sign of the zodiac or a person born under this sign

taut *adj* **1** : tightly stretched **2** : HIGH-STRUNG, TENSE **3** : kept in good order — **taut·ly** *adv* — **taut·ness** *n*

tav·ern *n* **1** : a place where beer and liquor are sold and drunk **2** : INN

taw·ny *adj* **taw·ni·er; taw·ni·est** : of a brownish orange color

¹tax *vb* **1** : to require to pay a tax **2** : to accuse of something **3** : to cause a strain on — **tax·er** *n*

²tax *n* **1** : money collected by the government from people or businesses for public use **2** : a difficult task

tax·a·ble *adj* : subject to tax

tax·a·tion *n* **1** : the action of taxing **2** : money gotten from taxes

¹taxi *n, pl* **tax·is** : TAXICAB

²taxi *vb* **tax·ied; taxi·ing** *or* **taxy·ing** **1** : to go by taxicab **2** : to run an airplane slowly along the ground under its own power

taxi·cab *n* : an automobile that carries passengers for a fare usually determined by the distance traveled

taxi·der·my *n* : the art of stuffing and mounting the skins of animals

tax·on·o·my *n* **1** : the study of classification **2** : a classification (as of animals) using a system that is usually based on relationship

tax·pay·er *n* : a person who pays or is responsible for paying a tax

TB *n* : TUBERCULOSIS

tea *n* **1** : the dried leaves and leaf buds of a shrub widely grown in eastern and southern Asia **2** : a drink made by soaking tea in boiling water **3** : a drink or medicine made by soaking plant parts (as dried roots) **4** : refreshments often including tea served in late afternoon **5** : a party at which tea is served

teach *vb* **taught; teach·ing** **1** : to show how **2** : to guide the studies of **3** : to cause to know the unpleasant results of something **4** : to give lessons in

teach·er *n* : a person who teaches

teaching *n* **1** : the duties or profession of a teacher **2** : something taught

tea·cup *n* : a cup used with a saucer for hot drinks

teak *n* : the hard wood of a tall tree which grows in the East Indies and resists decay

tea·ket·tle *n* : a covered kettle that is used for boiling water and has a handle and spout

teal *n* : a small wild duck that is very swift in flight

¹team *n* **1** : two or more animals used to pull the same vehicle or piece of machinery **2** : a group of persons who work or play together

²team *vb* **1** : to haul with or drive a team **2** : to form a team

team·mate *n* : a person who belongs to the same team as someone else

team·ster *n* : a worker who drives a team or a truck

team·work *n* : the work of a group of persons acting together

tea·pot *n* : a pot for making and serving tea

¹tear *n* : a drop of the salty liquid that keeps the eyeballs and inside of the eyelids moist

²tear *vb* **tore; torn; tear·ing** **1** : to pull into

two or more pieces by force **2** : LACERATE **3** : to remove by force **4** : to move powerfully or swiftly

³tear *n* **1** : the act of tearing **2** : damage from being torn

tear·drop *n* : ¹TEAR

tear·ful *adj* : flowing with, accompanied by, or causing tears — **tear·ful·ly** *adv*

¹tease *vb* **teased; teas·ing** : to annoy again and again — **teas·er** *n*

²tease *n* **1** : the act of teasing : the state of being teased **2** : a person who teases

tea·spoon *n* **1** : a small spoon used especially for stirring drinks **2** : TEASPOONFUL

tea·spoon·ful *n, pl* **teaspoonfuls** *or* **tea·spoons·ful** **1** : as much as a teaspoon can hold **2** : a unit of measure used especially in cooking and pharmacy equal to about five milliliters

teat *n* : NIPPLE 1 — used mostly of domestic animals

tech·ni·cal *adj* **1** : having special knowledge especially of a mechanical or scientific subject **2** : of or relating to a single and especially a practical or scientific subject **3** : according to a strict explanation of the rules — **tech·ni·cal·ly** *adv*

tech·ni·cal·i·ty *n, pl* **tech·ni·cal·i·ties** : something having meaning only to a person with special training

technical sergeant *n* : a noncommissioned officer in the Air Force ranking above a staff sergeant

tech·ni·cian *n* : a person skilled in the details or techniques of a subject, art, or job

tech·nique *n* **1** : the manner in which technical details are used in reaching a goal **2** : technical methods

tech·no·log·i·cal *adj* : of or relating to technology

tech·nol·o·gist *n* : a specialist in technology

tech·nol·o·gy *n, pl* **tech·nol·o·gies** **1** : the use of science in solving problems (as in industry or engineering) **2** : a technical method of doing something

ted·dy bear *n* : a stuffed toy bear

te·dious *adj* : tiring because of length or dullness — **te·dious·ly** *adv* — **te·dious·ness** *n*

tee *n* : a peg on which a golf ball is placed to be hit

teem *vb* : to be full of something

teen·age *or* **teen·aged** *adj* : of, being, or relating to teenagers

teen·ag·er *n* : a person in his or her teens

teens *n pl* : the years thirteen through nineteen in a person's life

tee·ny *adj* **tee·ni·er; tee·ni·est** : TINY

tee shirt *variant of* T-SHIRT

tee·ter *vb* **1** : to move unsteadily **2** : ²SEE-SAW

tee·ter–tot·ter *n* : ¹SEESAW

teeth *pl of* TOOTH

teethe *vb* **teethed; teeth·ing** : to cut one's teeth : grow teeth

tele- *or* **tel-** *prefix* **1** : at a distance **2** : television

¹tele·cast *n* : a program broadcast by television

²telecast *vb* **telecast** *also* **tele·cast·ed; tele·cast·ing** : to broadcast by television — **tele·cast·er** *n*

tele·gram *n* : a message sent by telegraph

¹tele·graph *n* : an electric device or system for sending messages by a code over connecting wires

²telegraph *vb* **1** : to send by telegraph **2** : to send a telegram to

te·leg·ra·phy *n* : the use of a telegraph

te·lep·a·thy *n* : communication which appears to take place from one mind to another without speech or signs

¹tele·phone *n* : an instrument for transmitting and receiving sounds over long distances by electricity

²telephone *vb* **tele·phoned; tele·phon·ing** : to speak to by telephone

¹tele·scope *n* : an instrument shaped like a long tube that has lenses for viewing objects at a distance and especially for observing objects in outer space

²telescope *vb* **tele·scoped; tele·scop·ing** : to slide or force one part into another like the sections of a small telescope

tele·vise *vb* **tele·vised; tele·vis·ing** : to send (a program) by television

tele·vi·sion *n* **1** : an electronic system of sending images together with sound over a wire or through space by devices that change light and sound into electrical waves and then change these back into light and sound **2** : a television receiving set **3** : television as a way of communicating

tell *vb* **told; tell·ing** **1** : ¹COUNT 1 **2** : to describe item by item **3** : ¹SAY 1 **4** : to make known **5** : to let a person know something : to give information to **6** : ¹ORDER 2 **7** : to find out by observing **8** : to act as a tattletale **9** : to have a noticeable result **10** : to act as evidence

tell·er *n* **1** : NARRATOR **2** : a person who counts votes **3** : a bank employee who receives and pays out money

¹tem·per *vb* **1** : SOFTEN **2** : to make a substance as thick, firm, or tough as is wanted **3** : to heat and cool a substance (as steel) until it is as hard, tough, or flexible as is wanted

²temper *n* **1** : the hardness or toughness of a substance (as metal) **2** : characteristic state of feeling **3** : calmness of mind **4** : an angry mood

tem·per·a·ment *n* : a person's attitude as it affects what he or she says or does

tem·per·a·men·tal *adj* : having or showing a nervous sensitive temperament — **tem·per·a·men·tal·ly** *adv*

tem·per·ance *n* **1** : control over one's actions, thoughts, or feelings **2** : the use of little or no alcoholic drink

tem·per·ate *adj* **1** : keeping or held within limits : MILD **2** : not drinking much liquor **3** : showing self-control **4** : not too hot or too cold

tem·per·a·ture *n* **1** : degree of hotness or coldness as shown by a thermometer **2** : level of heat above what is normal for the human body : FEVER

tem·pest *n* **1** : a strong wind often accompanied by rain, hail, or snow **2** : UPROAR

tem·pes·tu·ous *adj* : very stormy — **tem·pes·tu·ous·ly** *adv*

¹tem·ple *n* : a building for worship

²temple *n* : the space between the eye and forehead and the upper part of the ear

tem·po *n, pl* **tem·pi** *or* **tempos** : the rate of speed at which a musical composition is played or sung

tem·po·ral *adj* : of, relating to, or limited by time

tem·po·rary *adj* : not permanent — **tem·po·rar·i·ly** *adv*

tempt *vb* **1** : to make someone think of doing wrong (as by promise of gain) **2** : to risk the dangers of — **tempt·er** *n*

temp·ta·tion *n* **1** : the act of tempting or the state of being tempted **2** : something that tempts

¹ten *adj* : being one more than nine

²ten *n* : one more than nine : two times five : 10

te·na·cious *adj* **1** : not easily pulled apart **2** : PERSISTENT

te·nac·i·ty *n* : the quality or state of being tenacious

¹ten·ant *n* **1** : a person who rents property (as a house) from the owner **2** : OCCUPANT, DWELLER

²tenant *vb* : to hold or live in as a tenant

¹tend *vb* **1** : to pay attention **2** : to take care of **3** : to manage the operation of

²tend *vb* **1** : to move or turn in a certain direction : LEAD **2** : to be likely

ten·den·cy *n, pl* **ten·den·cies** **1** : the direction or course toward something **2** : a leaning toward a particular kind of thought or action

¹ten·der *adj* **1** : not tough **2** : DELICATE 4 **3** : YOUTHFUL 1 **4** : feeling or showing love **5** : very easily hurt — **ten·der·ly** *adv* — **ten·der·ness** *n*

²tender *vb* **1** : to offer in payment **2** : to present for acceptance

³tender *n* **1** : ²OFFER **2** : something (as money) that may be offered in payment

⁴tend·er *n* **1** : a ship used to attend other ships (as to supply food) **2** : a boat that carries passengers or freight to a larger ship **3** : a car attached to a locomotive for carrying fuel or water

ten·der·foot *n, pl* **ten·der·feet** *also* **ten·der·foots** : a person who is not used to a rough outdoor life

ten·der·heart·ed *adj* : easily affected with feelings of love, pity, or sorrow

ten·don *n* : a strip or band of tough white fiber connecting a muscle to another part (as a bone)

ten·dril *n* **1** : a slender leafless winding stem by which some climbing plants fasten themselves to a support **2** : something that winds like a plant's tendril

ten·e·ment *n* **1** : a house used as a dwelling **2** : APARTMENT 1 **3** : a building divided into separate apartments for rent

ten·nis *n* : a game played on a level court by two or four players who use rackets to hit a ball back and forth across a low net dividing the court

ten·or *n* **1** : the next to the lowest part in harmony having four parts **2** : the highest male singing voice **3** : a singer or an instrument having a tenor range or part

ten·pins *n* : a bowling game played with ten pins

¹tense *n* : a form of a verb used to show the time of the action or state

²tense *adj* **tens·er; tens·est 1** : stretched tight **2** : feeling or showing nervous tension **3** : marked by strain or uncertainty — **tense·ly** *adv* — **tense·ness** *n*

³tense *vb* **tensed; tens·ing** : to make or become tense

ten·sion *n* **1** : the act of straining or stretching : the condition of being strained or stretched **2** : a state of mental unrest **3** : a state of unfriendliness

¹tent *n* : a portable shelter (as of canvas) stretched and supported by poles

²tent *vb* : to live in a tent — **ten·ter** *n*

ten·ta·cle *n* : one of the long thin flexible structures that stick out about the head or the mouth of an animal (as an insect or fish) and are used especially for feeling or grasping

ten·ta·tive *adj* : not final — **ten·ta·tive·ly** *adv*

tent caterpillar *n* : any of several caterpillars that spin tent-like webs in which they live in groups

¹tenth *adj* : coming right after ninth

²tenth *n* **1** : number ten in a series **2** : one of ten equal parts

te·pee *n* : a tent shaped like a cone and used as a home by some American Indians

tep·id *adj* : LUKEWARM 1

¹term *n* **1** : a period of time fixed especially by law or custom **2** **terms** *pl* : conditions that limit the nature and scope of something (as a treaty or a will) **3** : a word or expression that has an exact meaning in some uses or is limited to a subject or field **4** : the numerator or denominator of a fraction **5** : any one of the numbers in a series **6** **terms** *pl* : relationship between people

²term *vb* : to apply a term to

¹ter·mi·nal *adj* : of, relating to, or forming an end

²terminal *n* **1** : a part that forms the end : EXTREMITY **2** : a device at the end of a wire or on a machine for making an electrical connection **3** : either end of a transportation line or a passenger or freight station located at it **4** : a device (as in a computer system) used to put in, receive, and display information

ter·mi·nate *vb* **ter·mi·nat·ed; ter·mi·nat·ing** : END, CLOSE

ter·mi·na·tion *n* **1** : the end of something **2** : the act of ending something

ter·mi·nus *n, pl* **ter·mi·ni** *or* **ter·mi·nus·es 1** : final goal : END **2** : either end of a transportation line or travel route

ter·mite *n* : a chewing antlike insect of a light color that lives in large colonies and feeds on wood

tern *n* : any of numerous small slender sea gulls with black cap, white body, and narrow wings

¹ter·race *n* **1** : a flat roof or open platform **2** : a level area next to a building **3** : a raised piece of land with the top leveled **4** : a row of houses on raised ground or a slope

²terrace *vb* **ter·raced; ter·rac·ing** : to form into a terrace or supply with terraces

ter·rain *n* : the features of the surface of a piece of land

ter·ra·pin *n* : a North American turtle that eats flesh and lives in water

ter·rar·i·um *n, pl* **ter·rar·ia** *or* **ter·rar·i·ums** : a box usually made of glass that is used for keeping and observing small animals or plants

ter·res·tri·al *adj* **1** : of or relating to the earth or its people **2** : living or growing on land

ter·ri·ble *adj* **1** : causing great fear **2** : very great in degree : INTENSE **3** : very bad — **ter·ri·bly** *adv*

ter·ri·er *n* : any of various usually small dogs

originally used by hunters to drive animals from their holes

ter·rif·ic *adj* **1** : causing terror : TERRIBLE **2** : very unusual : EXTRAORDINARY **3** : very good : EXCELLENT — **ter·rif·i·cal·ly** *adv*

ter·ri·fy *vb* **ter·ri·fied; ter·ri·fy·ing** : to frighten greatly

ter·ri·to·ri·al *adj* : of or relating to a territory

ter·ri·to·ry *n, pl* **ter·ri·to·ries** **1** : a geographical area belonging to or under the rule of a government **2** : a part of the United States not included within any state but organized with a separate governing body **3** : REGION 1, DISTRICT

ter·ror *n* **1** : a state of great fear **2** : a cause of great fear

ter·ror·ism *n* : the use of threat or violence especially as a means of forcing others to do what one wishes

ter·ror·ize *vb* **ter·ror·ized; ter·ror·iz·ing** **1** : to fill with terror **2** : to use terrorism against

terse *adj* **ters·er; ters·est** : being brief and to the point : CONCISE — **terse·ly** *adv* — **terse·ness** *n*

¹test *n* **1** : a means of finding out the nature, quality, or value of something **2** : a set of questions or problems by which a person's knowledge, intelligence, or skills are measured

²test *vb* : to put to a test : EXAMINE

tes·ta·ment *n* **1** : either of two main parts (**Old Testament** and **New Testament**) of the Bible **2** : ²WILL 3

tes·ti·fy *vb* **tes·ti·fied; tes·ti·fy·ing** : to make a formal statement of what one swears is true

tes·ti·mo·ny *n, pl* **tes·ti·mo·nies** : a statement made by a witness under oath especially in a court

tes·tis *n, pl* **tes·tes** : a male reproductive gland

test tube *n* : a plain tube of thin glass closed at one end

tet·a·nus *n* : a dangerous disease in which spasms of the muscles occur often with locking of the jaws and which is caused by poison from a germ that enters wounds and grows in damaged tissue

¹teth·er *n* : a line by which an animal is fastened so as to limit where it can go

²tether *vb* : to fasten by a tether

text *n* **1** : the actual words of an author's work **2** : the main body of printed or written matter on a page **3** : a passage from the Bible chosen as the subject of a sermon **4** : TEXTBOOK

text·book *n* : a book that presents the important information about a subject and is used as a basis of instruction

tex·tile *n* : a woven or knit cloth

tex·ture *n* : the structure, feel, and appearance of something (as cloth)

-th *or* **-eth** *adj suffix* — used to form numbers that show the place of something in a series

than *conj* : when compared to the way in which, the extent to which, or the degree to which

thank *vb* **1** : to express gratitude to **2** : to hold responsible

thank·ful *adj* : feeling or showing thanks : GRATEFUL — **thank·ful·ly** *adv* — **thank·ful·ness** *n*

thank·less *adj* **1** : UNGRATEFUL **2** : not appreciated

thanks *n pl* **1** : GRATITUDE **2** : an expression of gratitude (as for something received) — **thanks to** **1** : with the help of **2** : BECAUSE OF

thanks·giv·ing *n* **1** : the act of giving thanks **2** : a prayer expressing gratitude **3** *cap* : THANKSGIVING DAY

Thanksgiving Day *n* : the fourth Thursday in November observed as a legal holiday for public thanksgiving to God

¹that *pron, pl* **those** **1** : the one seen, mentioned, or understood **2** : the one farther away **3** : the one : the kind

²that *conj* **1** : the following, namely **2** : which is, namely **3** : ²SO 1 **4** : as to result in the following, namely **5** : BECAUSE

³that *adj, pl* **those** **1** : being the one mentioned, indicated, or understood **2** : being the one farther away

⁴that *pron* **1** : WHO 3, WHOM, ²WHICH 2 **2** : in, on, or at which

⁵that *adv* : to such an extent or degree

¹thatch *vb* : to cover with thatch

²thatch *n* : a plant material (as straw) for use as roofing

¹thaw *vb* **1** : to melt or cause to melt **2** : to grow less unfriendly or quiet in manner

²thaw *n* **1** : the action, fact, or process of thawing **2** : a period of weather warm enough to thaw ice and snow

¹the *definite article* **1** : that or those mentioned, seen, or clearly understood **2** : that or those near in space, time, or thought **3** : ¹EACH **4** : that or those considered best, most typical, or most worth singling out **5** : any one typical of or standing for the entire class named **6** : all those that are

²the *adv* **1** : than before **2** : to what extent **3** : to that extent

the·ater *or* **the·atre** *n* **1** : a building in which plays or motion pictures are presented **2** : a place like a theater in form or use **3** : a place or area where some important action is carried on **4** : plays or the performance of plays

the·at·ri·cal *adj* : of or relating to the theater or the presentation of plays

thee *pron, archaic objective case of* THOU

theft *n* : the act of stealing

their *adj* : of or relating to them or themselves especially as owners or as agents or objects of an action

theirs *pron* : that which belongs to them

them *pron objective case of* THEY

theme *n* **1** : a subject on which one writes or speaks **2** : a written exercise **3** : a main melody in a piece of music

them·selves *pron* : their own selves

¹**then** *adv* **1** : at that time **2** : soon after that : NEXT **3** : in addition : BESIDES **4** : in that case **5** : as an expected result

²**then** *n* : that time

³**then** *adj* : existing or acting at that time

thence *adv* **1** : from that place **2** : from that fact

thence·forth *adv* : from that time on

thence·for·ward *adv* : onward from that place or time

the·ol·o·gy *n, pl* **the·ol·o·gies** : the study and explanation of religious faith, practice, and experience

the·o·ry *n, pl* **the·o·ries** **1** : the general rules followed in a science or an art **2** : a general rule offered to explain experiences or facts **3** : an idea used for discussion or as a starting point for an investigation

ther·a·peu·tic *adj* : MEDICINAL

ther·a·pist *n* : a specialist in therapy and especially in methods of treatment other than drugs and surgery

ther·a·py *n, pl* **ther·a·pies** : treatment of an abnormal state in the body or mind

¹**there** *adv* **1** : in or at that place **2** : to or into that place **3** : in that situation or way

²**there** *pron* — used to introduce a sentence in which the subject comes after the verb

³**there** *n* : that place

there·abouts *or* **there·about** *adv* **1** : near that place or time **2** : near that number, degree, or amount

there·af·ter *adv* : after that

there·at *adv* **1** : at that place **2** : because of that

there·by *adv* **1** : by that **2** : related to that

there·fore *adv* : for that reason

there·in *adv* : in or into that place, time, or thing

there·of *adv* **1** : of that or it **2** : from that cause

there·on *adv* : on that

there·to *adv* : to that

there·up·on *adv* **1** : on that thing **2** : for

that reason **3** : immediately after that : at once

there·with *adv* : with that

ther·mal *adj* : of, relating to, caused by, or saving heat

ther·mom·e·ter *n* : an instrument for measuring temperature usually in the form of a glass tube with mercury or alcohol sealed inside and with a scale marked in degrees on the outside

ther·mos *n* : a container (as a bottle or jar) that has a vacuum between an inner and an outer wall and is used to keep liquids hot or cold for several hours

ther·mo·stat *n* : a device that automatically controls temperature

the·sau·rus *n, pl* **the·sau·ri** *or* **the·sau·rus·es** : a book of words and their synonyms

these *pl of* THIS

the·sis *n, pl* **the·ses** **1** : a statement that a person wants to discuss or prove **2** : an essay presenting results of original research

they *pron* : those individuals : those ones

they'd : they had : they would

they'll : they shall : they will

they're : they are

they've : they have

thi·a·min *n* : a member of the vitamin B complex whose lack causes beriberi

¹**thick** *adj* **1** : having great size from one surface to its opposite **2** : heavily built **3** : closely packed together **4** : occurring in large numbers : NUMEROUS **5** : not flowing easily **6** : having haze, fog, or mist **7** : measuring a certain amount in the smallest of three dimensions **8** : not clearly spoken **9** : STUPID 1 — **thick·ly** *adv*

²**thick** *n* **1** : the most crowded or active part **2** : the part of greatest thickness

thick·en *vb* : to make or become thick — **thick·en·er** *n*

thick·et *n* : a thick usually small patch of bushes or low trees

thick·ness *n* **1** : the quality or state of being thick **2** : the smallest of three dimensions

thick·set *adj* **1** : closely placed or planted **2** : STOCKY

thief *n, pl* **thieves** : a person who steals : ROBBER

thieve *vb* **thieved; thiev·ing** : ¹STEAL 2, ROB

thiev·ery *n, pl* **thiev·er·ies** : THEFT

thiev·ish *adj* **1** : likely to steal **2** : of, relating to, or like a thief

thigh *n* : the part of a leg between the knee and the main part of the body

thim·ble *n* : a cap or cover used in sewing to protect the finger that pushes the needle

¹**thin** *adj* **thin·ner; thin·nest** **1** : having little size from one surface to its opposite : not thick **2** : having the parts not close to-

gether **3** : having little body fat **4** : having less than the usual number **5** : not very convincing **6** : somewhat weak or shrill — **thin·ly** adv — **thin·ness** n

²thin vb **thinned; thin·ning** : to make or become thin

thine pron, singular, archaic : YOURS

thing n **1** : AFFAIR 2, MATTER **2 things** pl : state of affairs **3** : EVENT 1 **4** : ¹DEED 1, ACHIEVEMENT **5** : something that exists and can be talked about **6 things** pl : personal possessions **7** : a piece of clothing **8** : ¹DETAIL 2 **9** : what is needed or wanted **10** : an action or interest that one very much enjoys

think vb **thought; think·ing 1** : to form or have in the mind **2** : to have as an opinion or belief **3** : REMEMBER 1 **4** : to use the power of reason **5** : to invent something by thinking **6** : to hold a strong feeling **7** : to care about — **think·er** n

thin·ner n : a liquid used to thin paint

¹third adj : coming right after second

²third n **1** : number three in a series **2** : one of three equal parts

¹thirst n **1** : a feeling of dryness in the mouth and throat that accompanies a need for liquids **2** : the bodily condition that produces thirst **3** : a strong desire

²thirst vb **1** : to feel thirsty **2** : to have a strong desire

thirsty adj **thirst·i·er; thirst·i·est 1** : feeling thirst **2** : needing moisture **3** : having a strong desire : EAGER — **thirst·i·ly** adv

¹thir·teen adj : being one more than twelve

²thirteen n : one more than twelve : 13

¹thir·teenth adj : coming right after twelfth

²thirteenth n : number thirteen in a series

¹thir·ti·eth adj : coming right after twenty-ninth

²thirtieth n : number thirty in a series

¹thir·ty adj : being three times ten

²thirty n : three times ten : 30

¹this pron, pl **these 1** : the one close or closest in time or space **2** : what is in the present or is being seen or talked about

²this adj, pl **these 1** : being the one present, near, or just mentioned **2** : being the one nearer or last mentioned

³this adv : to the degree suggested by something in the present situation

this·tle n : a prickly plant related to the daisies that has usually purplish often showy heads of mostly tubular flowers

thith·er adv : to that place : THERE

thong n : a strip of leather used especially for fastening something

tho·rax n, pl **tho·rax·es** or **tho·ra·ces 1** : the part of the body of a mammal that lies between the neck and the abdomen and con-

tains the heart and lungs **2** : the middle of the three main divisions of the body of an insect

thorn n **1** : a woody plant (as hawthorn) with sharp briers, prickles, or spines **2** : a short hard sharp-pointed leafless branch on a woody plant

thorny adj **thorn·i·er; thorn·i·est 1** : full of or covered with thorns **2** : full of difficulties

thor·ough adj **1** : being such to the fullest degree : COMPLETE **2** : careful about little things — **thor·ough·ly** adv — **thor·ough·ness** n

¹thor·ough·bred adj **1** : bred from the best blood through a long line **2** cap : of, relating to, or being a member of the Thoroughbred breed of horses

²thoroughbred n **1** cap : any of an English breed of light speedy horses kept mainly for racing **2** : a purebred or pedigreed animal **3** : a very fine person

thor·ough·fare n **1** : a street or road open at both ends **2** : a main road

thor·ough·go·ing adj : THOROUGH 1

those pl of THAT

thou pron, singular, archaic : YOU

¹though conj : ALTHOUGH

²though adv : HOWEVER 3, NEVERTHELESS

¹thought past of THINK

²thought n **1** : the act or process of thinking and especially of trying to decide about something **2** : power of reasoning and judging **3** : power of imagining **4** : something (as an idea or fancy) formed in the mind

thought·ful adj **1** : deep in thought **2** : showing careful thinking **3** : considerate of others — **thought·ful·ly** adv — **thought·ful·ness** n

thought·less adj **1** : not careful and alert **2** : NEGLIGENT **3** : not considerate of others — **thought·less·ly** adv — **thought·less·ness** n

¹thou·sand n **1** : ten times one hundred : 1000 **2** : a very large number

²thousand adj : being 1000

¹thou·sandth adj : coming right after 999th

²thousandth n : number 1000 in a series

thrash vb **1** : THRESH 1 **2** : to beat very hard **3** : to move about violently

¹thrash·er n : one that thrashes

²thrasher n : an American bird (as the common reddish brown **brown thrasher**) related to the thrushes and noted for its song

¹thread n **1** : a thin fine cord formed by spinning and twisting short fibers into a continuous strand **2** : something suggesting a thread **3** : the ridge or groove that winds around a screw **4** : a line of reasoning or train of thought that connects the parts of an argument or story — **thread·like** *adj*

²thread *vb* **1 :** to put a thread in working position (as in a needle) **2 :** to pass through like a thread **3 :** to make one's way through or between **4 :** to put together on a thread **:** STRING

thread·bare *adj* **1 :** worn so much that the thread shows : SHABBY **2 :** TRITE

threat *n* **1 :** a showing of an intention to do harm **2 :** something that threatens

threat·en *vb* **1 :** to make threats against **2 :** to give warning of by a threat or sign — **threat·en·ing·ly** *adv*

¹three *adj* : being one more than two

²three *n* **1 :** one more than two : 3 **2 :** the third in a set or series

3–D *adj* : THREE-DIMENSIONAL 2

three–dimensional *adj* **1 :** of, relating to, or having the three dimensions of length, width, and height **2 :** giving the appearance of depth or varying distances

three·fold *adj* : being three times as great or as many

three·score *adj* : SIXTY

thresh *vb* **1 :** to separate (as grain from straw) by beating **2 :** THRASH 3

thresh·er *n* : THRESHING MACHINE

threshing machine *n* : a machine used in harvesting to separate grain from straw

thresh·old *n* **1 :** the sill of a door **2 :** a point or place of beginning or entering

threw *past of* THROW

thrice *adv* : three times

thrift *n* : careful management especially of money

thrifty *adj* **thrift·i·er; thrift·i·est** **1 :** tending to save money **2 :** doing well in health and growth

¹thrill *vb* **1 :** to have or cause to have a sudden feeling of excitement or pleasure **2 :** ¹TREMBLE 2, VIBRATE — **thrill·er** *n*

²thrill *n* **1 :** a feeling of being thrilled **2 :** VIBRATION 3

thrive *vb* **throve** *or* **thrived; thriv·en** *also* **thrived; thriv·ing** **1 :** to grow very well : FLOURISH **2 :** to gain in wealth or possessions

throat *n* **1 :** the part of the neck in front of the backbone **2 :** the passage from the mouth to the stomach and lungs **3 :** something like the throat especially in being an entrance or a narrowed part

¹throb *vb* **throbbed; throb·bing** **1 :** to beat hard or fast **2 :** to beat or rotate in a normal way

²throb *n* : ²BEAT 2, PULSE

throne *n* **1 :** the chair of state especially of a monarch or bishop **2 :** royal power and dignity

¹throng *n* : a large group of assembled persons : CROWD

²throng *vb* : ¹CROWD 4

¹throt·tle *vb* **throt·tled; throt·tling** **1 :** STRANGLE 1, CHOKE **2 :** to reduce the speed of (an engine) by closing the throttle

²throttle *n* **1 :** a valve for regulating the flow of steam or fuel in an engine **2 :** a lever that controls the throttle valve

¹through *prep* **1 :** into at one side and out at the other side of **2 :** by way of **3 :** AMONG 1 **4 :** by means of **5 :** over the whole of **6 :** during the whole of

²through *adv* **1 :** from one end or side to the other **2 :** from beginning to end **3 :** to completion **4 :** in or to every part **5 :** into the open

³through *adj* **1 :** allowing free or continuous passage : DIRECT **2 :** going from point of origin to destination without changes or transfers **3 :** coming from and going to points outside a local zone **4 :** having reached an end

¹through·out *adv* **1 :** EVERYWHERE **2 :** from beginning to end

²throughout *prep* **1 :** in or to every part of **2 :** during the whole period of

throughway *variant of* THRUWAY

throve *past of* THRIVE

¹throw *vb* **threw; thrown; throw·ing** **1 :** to send through the air with a quick forward motion of the arm **2 :** to send through the air in any way **3 :** to cause to fall **4 :** to put suddenly in a certain position or condition **5 :** to put on or take off in a hurry **6 :** to move quickly **7 :** to move (as a switch) to an open or closed position **8 :** to give by way of entertainment — **throw·er** *n*

²throw *n* **1 :** an act of throwing **2 :** the distance something is or may be thrown

throw up *vb* : ²VOMIT

thrum *vb* **thrummed; thrum·ming** : to play a stringed instrument idly : STRUM

thrush *n* : any of numerous songbirds that eat insects and are usually of a plain color but sometimes spotted below

¹thrust *vb* **thrust; thrust·ing** **1 :** to push or drive with force : SHOVE **2 :** PIERCE 1, STAB **3 :** to push forth : EXTEND **4 :** to press the acceptance of on someone

²thrust *n* **1 :** a lunge with a pointed weapon **2 :** a military attack **3 :** a forward or upward push

thru·way *or* **through·way** *n* : EXPRESSWAY

¹thud *n* : a dull sound : THUMP

²thud *vb* **thud·ded; thud·ding** : to move or strike so as to make a dull sound

thug *n* : RUFFIAN

¹thumb *n* **1 :** the short thick finger next to

the forefinger **2** : the part of a glove covering the thumb

²thumb *vb* **1** : to turn the pages of quickly with the thumb **2** : to seek or get (a ride) in a passing automobile by signaling with the thumb

thumb·tack *n* : a tack with a broad flat head for pressing into a board or wall with the thumb

¹thump *vb* **1** : to strike or beat with something thick or heavy so as to cause a dull sound **2** : ³POUND 2, KNOCK

²thump *n* **1** : a blow with something blunt or heavy **2** : the sound made by a thump

¹thun·der *n* **1** : the loud sound that follows a flash of lightning **2** : a noise like thunder

²thunder *vb* **1** : to produce thunder **2** : to make a sound like thunder **3** : ¹ROAR 1, SHOUT

thun·der·bolt *n* : a flash of lightning and the thunder that follows it

thun·der·cloud *n* : a dark storm cloud that produces lightning and thunder

thun·der·head *n* : a rounded mass of dark cloud with white edges often appearing before a thunderstorm

thun·der·show·er *n* : a shower with thunder and lightning

thun·der·storm *n* : a storm with thunder and lightning

thun·der·struck *adj* : stunned as if struck by a thunderbolt

Thurs·day *n* : the fifth day of the week

thus *adv* **1** : in this or that way **2** : to this degree or extent : SO **3** : because of this or that : THEREFORE

thwart *vb* : to oppose successfully

thy *adj, singular, archaic* : YOUR

thyme *n* : a mint with tiny fragrant leaves used to season foods or formerly in medicine

thy·roid *n* : an endocrine gland at the base of the neck that produces a secretion which affects growth, development, and metabolism

thy·self *pron, archaic* : YOURSELF

ti *n* : the seventh note of the musical scale

¹tick *n* **1** : an animal with eight legs that is related to the spiders and attaches itself to humans and animals from which it sucks blood **2** : a wingless fly that sucks blood from sheep

²tick *n* **1** : a light rhythmic tap or beat (as of a clock) **2** : a small mark used chiefly to draw attention to something or to check an item on a list

³tick *vb* **1** : to make a tick or a series of ticks **2** : to mark, count, or announce by or as if by ticks **3** : OPERATE 1, RUN **4** : ²CHECK 4

¹tick·et *n* **1** : a summons or warning issued to a person who breaks a traffic law **2** : a

document or token showing that a fare or an admission fee has been paid **3** : a list of candidates for nomination or election **4** : a slip or card recording a sale or giving information

²ticket *vb* **1** : to attach a ticket to : LABEL **2** : to give a traffic ticket to

ticket office *n* : an office (as of a transportation company or a theater) where tickets are sold and reservations made

¹tick·le *vb* **tick·led; tick·ling** **1** : to have a tingling or prickling sensation **2** : to excite or stir up agreeably **3** : AMUSE 2 **4** : to touch (a body part) lightly so as to excite the surface nerves and cause uneasiness, laughter, or jerky movements

²tickle *n* : a tickling sensation

tick·lish *adj* **1** : sensitive to tickling **2** : calling for careful handling

tid·al *adj* : of or relating to tides : flowing and ebbing like tides

tidal wave *n* **1** : a great wave of the sea that sometimes follows an earthquake **2** : an unusual rise of water along a shore due to strong winds

tid·bit *n* **1** : a small tasty piece of food **2** : a pleasing bit (as of news)

¹tide *n* **1** : the rising and falling of the surface of the ocean caused twice daily by the attraction of the sun and the moon **2** : something that rises and falls like the tides of the sea

²tide *vb* **tid·ed; tid·ing** : to help to overcome or put up with a difficulty

tid·ings *n pl* : NEWS 3

¹ti·dy *adj* **ti·di·er; ti·di·est** **1** : well ordered and cared for : NEAT **2** : LARGE, SUBSTANTIAL — **ti·di·ness** *n*

²tidy *vb* **ti·died; ti·dy·ing** **1** : to put in order **2** : to make things tidy

¹tie *n* **1** : a line, ribbon, or cord used for fastening, joining, or closing **2** : a part (as a beam or rod) holding two pieces together **3** : one of the cross supports to which railroad rails are fastened **4** : a connecting link : BOND **5** : an equality in number (as of votes or scores) **6** : a contest that ends with an equal score **7** : NECKTIE

²tie *vb* **tied; ty·ing** *or* **tie·ing** **1** : to fasten, attach, or close by means of a tie **2** : to form a knot or bow in **3** : to bring together firmly : UNITE **4** : to hold back from freedom of action **5** : to make or have an equal score with in a contest

tier *n* : a row, rank, or layer usually arranged in a series one above the other

ti·ger *n* : a large Asian flesh-eating animal of the cat family that is light brown with black stripes

¹tight *adj* **1** : so close in structure as not to

allow a liquid or gas to pass through **2** : fixed or held very firmly in place **3** : firmly stretched or drawn : TAUT **4** : fitting too closely **5** : difficult to get through or out of **6** : firm in control **7** : STINGY 1 **8** : very closely packed or compressed **9** : low in supply : SCARCE — **tight·ly** adv — **tight·ness** n

²tight adv **1** : in a firm, secure, or close manner **2** : in a deep and uninterrupted manner : SOUNDLY

tight·en vb : to make or become tight

tight·rope n : a rope or wire stretched tight on which an acrobat performs

tights n pl : a garment closely fitted to the body and covering it usually from the waist down

tight squeeze n : a difficult situation that one can barely get through

tight·wad n : a stingy person

ti·gress n : a female tiger

til·de n : a mark ~ placed especially over the letter n (as in Spanish señor) to indicate a sound that is approximately \nyə\

¹tile n **1** : a thin piece of material (as plastic, stone, concrete, or rubber) used especially for roofs, walls, floors, or drains **2** : a pipe of earthenware used for a drain

²tile vb **tiled; til·ing** : to cover with tiles

¹till prep or conj : UNTIL

²till vb : to work by plowing, sowing, and raising crops on

³till n : a drawer for money

till·age n : cultivated land

til·ler n : a lever used to turn the rudder of a boat from side to side

¹tilt n **1** : a contest on horseback in which two opponents charging with lances try to unhorse one another : ²JOUST **2** : ¹SPEED 2 **3** : ¹SLANT

²tilt vb **1** : to move or shift so as to slant or tip **2** : to take part in a contest with lances : ¹JOUST

tim·ber n **1** : wood suitable for building or for carpentry **2** : a large squared piece of wood ready for use or forming part of a structure

tim·ber·land n : wooded land especially as a source of timber

tim·ber·line n : the upper limit beyond which trees do not grow (as on mountains)

¹time n **1** : a period during which an action, process, or condition exists or continues **2** : part of the day when one is free to do as one pleases **3** : a point or period when something occurs : OCCASION **4** : a set or usual moment or hour for something to occur **5** : an historical period : AGE **6** : conditions of a period — usually used in pl. **7** : rate of speed : TEMPO **8** : RHYTHM 2 **9** : a mo-

ment, hour, day, or year as shown by a clock or calendar **10** : a system of determining time **11** : one of a series of repeated instances or actions **12 times** pl : multiplied intances **13** : a person's experience during a certain period — **at times** : SOMETIMES — **for the time being** : for the present — **from time to time** : once in a while — **in time 1** : soon enough **2** : as time goes by **3** : at the correct speed in music — **time after time** : over and over again — **time and again** : over and over again

²time vb **timed; tim·ing 1** : to arrange or set the time or rate at which something happens **2** : to measure or record the time, length of time, or rate of — **tim·er** n

time·keep·er n **1** : a clerk who keeps records of the time worked by employees **2** : an official who keeps track of the playing time in a sports contest

time·ly adj **time·li·er; time·li·est 1** : coming early or at the right time **2** : especially suitable to the time

time·piece n : a device (as a clock or watch) to measure the passing of time

times prep : multiplied by

time·ta·ble n : a table telling when something (as a bus or train) leaves or arrives

tim·id adj : feeling or showing a lack of courage or self-confidence : SHY — **tim·id·ly** adv — **tim·id·ness** n

tim·o·rous adj : easily frightened : FEARFUL — **tim·o·rous·ly** adv

tin n **1** : a soft bluish white metallic chemical element used chiefly in combination with other metals or as a coating to protect other metals **2** : something (as a can or sheet) made from tinplate

tin·der n : material that burns easily and can be used as kindling

tin·foil n : a thin metal sheeting usually of aluminum or an alloy of tin and lead

¹tin·gle vb **tin·gled; tin·gling** : to feel or cause a prickling or thrilling sensation

²tingle n : a tingling sensation or condition

tin·ker vb : to repair or adjust something in an unskilled or experimental manner

¹tin·kle vb **tin·kled; tin·kling** : to make or cause to make a series of short high ringing or clinking sounds

²tinkle n : a sound of tinkling

tin·plate n : thin steel sheets covered with tin

tin·sel n **1** : a thread, strip, or sheet of metal, paper, or plastic used to produce a glittering effect **2** : something that seems attractive but is of little worth

tin·smith n : a worker in tin or sometimes other metals

¹tint n **1** : a slight or pale coloring **2** : a shade of a color

2tint vb : to give a tint to : COLOR

tin·ware n : objects made of tinplate

ti·ny adj **ti·ni·er; ti·ni·est** : very small

1tip vb **tipped; tip·ping** **1** : to turn over **2** : to bend from a straight position : SLANT **3** : to raise and tilt forward

2tip vb **tipped; tip·ping** **1** : to attach an end or point to **2** : to cover or decorate the tip of

3tip n **1** : the usually pointed end of something **2** : a small piece or part serving as an end, cap, or point

4tip n : a piece of useful or secret information

5tip vb **tipped; tip·ping** : to give a small sum of money for a service

6tip n : a small sum of money given for a service

1tip·toe n : the position of being balanced on the balls of the feet and toes with the heels raised — usually used with *on*

2tiptoe adv or adj : on or as if on tiptoe

3tiptoe vb **tip·toed; tip·toe·ing** : to walk tiptoe

1tip·top n : the highest point

2tiptop adj : EXCELLENT, FIRST-RATE

1tire vb **tired; tir·ing** **1** : to make or become weary **2** : to wear out the patience or attention of : BORE

2tire n **1** : a metal band that forms the tread of a wheel **2** : a rubber cushion that usually contains compressed air and fits around a wheel (as of an automobile)

tired adj : 1WEARY 1

tire·less adj : able to work a long time without becoming tired — **tire·less·ly** adv — **tire·less·ness** n

tire·some adj : likely to tire one because of length or dullness : BORING — **tire·some·ly** adv

'tis : it is

tis·sue n **1** : a fine lightweight fabric **2** : a piece of soft absorbent paper **3** : a mass or layer of cells usually of one kind that together with their supporting structures form a basic structural material of an animal or plant body

tit n : NIPPLE 1, TEAT

ti·tan·ic adj : enormous in size, force, or power : GIGANTIC

ti·tle n **1** : a legal right to the ownership of property **2** : the name given to something (as a book, song, or job) to identify or describe it **3** : a word or group of words attached to a person's name to show an honor, rank, or office **4** : CHAMPIONSHIP

tit·mouse n, pl **tit·mice** : any of several small birds that have long tails and are related to the nuthatches

TNT n : an explosive used in artillery shells and bombs and in blasting

1to prep **1** : in the direction of **2** : AGAINST **3**, ON **3** : as far as **4** : so as to become or bring about **5** : 2BEFORE 3 **6** : 1UNTIL **7** : fitting or being a part of **8** : along with **9** : in relation to or comparison with **10** : in agreement with **11** : within the limits of **12** : contained, occurring, or included in **13** : TOWARD 3 **14** — used to show the one or ones that an action is directed toward **15** : for no one except **16** : into the action of **17** — used to mark an infinitive

2to adv **1** : in a direction toward **2** : to a conscious state

toad n : a tailless leaping amphibian that has rough skin and usually lives on land

toad·stool n : a mushroom especially when poisonous or unfit for food

1toast vb **1** : to make (as bread) crisp, hot, and brown by heat **2** : to warm completely

2toast n **1** : sliced toasted bread **2** : a person in whose honor other people drink **3** : a highly admired person **4** : an act of drinking in honor of a person

3toast vb : to suggest or drink to as a toast

toast·er n : an electrical appliance for toasting

to·bac·co n, pl **to·bac·cos** : a tall plant related to the tomato and potato that has pink or white flowers and broad sticky leaves which are dried and prepared for use in smoking or chewing or as snuff

1to·bog·gan n : a long light sled made without runners and curved up at the front

2toboggan vb : to slide on a toboggan

1to·day adv **1** : on or for this day **2** : at the present time

2today n : the present day, time, or age

tod·dler n : a small child

1toe n **1** : one of the separate parts of the front end of a foot **2** : the front end or part of a foot or hoof — **toed** adj

2toe vb **toed; toe·ing** : to touch, reach, or kick with the toes

toe·nail n : the hard covering at the end of a toe

to·ga n : the loose outer garment worn in public by citizens of ancient Rome

to·geth·er adv **1** : in or into one group, body, or place **2** : in touch or in partnership with **3** : at one time **4** : one after the other : in order **5** : in or by combined effort **6** : in or into agreement **7** : considered as a whole

1toil n : long hard labor

2toil vb **1** : to work hard and long **2** : to go on with effort

toi·let n **1** : the act or process of dressing and making oneself neat **2** : BATHROOM **3** : a device for removing body wastes consisting essentially of a bowl that is flushed with water

to·ken *n* **1** : an outer sign : PROOF **2** : an object used to suggest something that cannot be pictured **3** : SOUVENIR **4** : INDICATION 2 **5** : a piece like a coin that has a special use

told *past of* TELL

tol·er·a·ble *adj* **1** : capable of being put up with **2** : fairly good — **tol·er·a·bly** *adv*

tol·er·ance *n* **1** : ability to put up with something harmful or bad **2** : sympathy for or acceptance of feelings or habits which are different from one's own

tol·er·ant *adj* : showing tolerance — **tol·er·ant·ly** *adv*

tol·er·ate *vb* **tol·er·at·ed; tol·er·at·ing** **1** : to allow something to be or to be done without making a move to stop it **2** : to stand the action of

¹toll *n* **1** : a tax paid for a privilege (as the use of a highway or bridge) **2** : a charge paid for a service **3** : the cost in life or health

²toll *vb* **1** : to announce or call by the sounding of a bell **2** : to sound with slow strokes

³toll *n* : the sound of a bell ringing slowly

¹tom·a·hawk *n* : a light ax used as a weapon by North American Indians

²tomahawk *vb* : to cut, strike, or kill with a tomahawk

to·ma·to *n, pl* **to·ma·toes** : a red or yellow juicy fruit that is used as a vegetable or in salads and is produced by a hairy plant related to the potato

tomb *n* **1** : ¹GRAVE **2** : a house or burial chamber for dead people

tom·boy *n* : a girl who enjoys things that some people think are more suited to boys

tomb·stone *n* : GRAVESTONE

tom·cat *n* : a male cat

¹to·mor·row *adv* : on or for the day after today

²tomorrow *n* : the day after today

tom–tom *n* **1** : a drum (as a traditional Asian, African, or American Indian drum) that is beaten with the hands **2** : a deep drum with a low hollow tone that is usually played with soft mallets or drumsticks and is often part of a drum set in a band

ton *n* : a measure of weight equal either to 2000 pounds (about 907 kilograms) **(short ton)** or 2240 pounds (about 1016 kilograms) **(long ton)** with the short ton being more frequently used in the United States and Canada

¹tone *n* **1** : quality of spoken or musical sound **2** : a sound on one pitch **3** : an individual way of speaking or writing **4** : a shade of color **5** : a color that changes another **6** : a healthy state of the body or any of its parts **7** : common character or quality

²tone *vb* **toned; ton·ing** **1** : to give tone to : STRENGTHEN **2** : to soften or blend in color, appearance, or sound

tongs *n pl* : a device for taking hold of something that consists usually of two movable pieces joined at one end

tongue *n* **1** : an organ of the mouth used in tasting, in taking and swallowing food, and by human beings in speaking **2** : the power of communication : SPEECH **3** : LANGUAGE 1 **4** : something like an animal's tongue in being long and fastened at one end

tongue–tied *adj* : unable to speak clearly or freely (as from shyness)

¹ton·ic *adj* : making (as the mind or body) stronger or healthier

²tonic *n* **1** : a tonic medicine **2** : the first note of a scale

¹to·night *adv* : on this present night or the night following this present day

²tonight *n* : the present or the coming night

ton·nage *n* **1** : a tax on ships based on tons carried **2** : ships in terms of the total number of tons that are or can be carried **3** : total weight in tons shipped, carried, or mined

ton·sil *n* : either of a pair of masses of spongy tissue at the back of the mouth

ton·sil·li·tis *n* : a sore reddened state of the tonsils

too *adv* **1** : in addition : ALSO **2** : to a greater than wanted or needed degree **3** : ²VERY 1

took *past of* TAKE

¹tool *n* **1** : an instrument (as a saw, file, knife, or wrench) used or worked by hand or machine **2** : something that helps to gain an end **3** : a person used by another : DUPE

²tool *vb* **1** : to shape, form, or finish with a tool **2** : to equip a plant or industry with machines and tools for production

tool·box *n* : a box for storing or carrying tools

tool·shed *n* : a small building for storing tools

¹toot *vb* **1** : to sound a short blast **2** : to blow or sound an instrument (as a horn) especially in short blasts

²toot *n* : a short blast (as on a horn)

tooth *n, pl* **teeth** **1** : one of the hard bony structures set in sockets on the jaws of most vertebrates and used in taking hold of and chewing food and in fighting **2** : something like or suggesting an animal's tooth in shape, arrangement, or action **3** : one of the projections around the rim of a wheel that fit between the projections on another part causing the wheel or the other part to move along — **tooth·less** *adj*

tooth·ache *n* : pain in or near a tooth

tooth·brush *n* : a brush for cleaning the teeth — **tooth·brush·ing** *n*

toothed *adj* **1** : having teeth or such or so many teeth **2** : JAGGED

tooth·paste *n* : a paste for cleaning the teeth

tooth·pick *n* : a pointed instrument for removing substances caught between the teeth

¹**top** *n* **1** : the highest point, level, or part of something **2** : the upper end, edge, or surface **3** : the stalk and leaves of a plant and especially of one with roots that are used for food **4** : an upper piece, lid, or covering **5** : the highest position

²**top** *vb* **topped; top·ping 1** : to remove or cut the top of **2** : to cover with a top or on the top **3** : to be better than **4** : to go over the top of

³**top** *adj* : of, relating to, or at the top

⁴**top** *n* : a child's toy with a tapering point on which it can be made to spin

to·paz *n* : a mineral that when occurring as perfect yellow crystals is valued as a gem

top·coat *n* : a lightweight overcoat

top·ic *n* **1** : a heading in an outline of a subject or explanation **2** : the subject or a section of the subject of a speech or writing

topic sentence *n* : a sentence that states the main thought of a paragraph

top·knot *n* : a tuft of feathers or hair on the top of the head

top·mast *n* : the second mast above a ship's deck

top·most *adj* : highest of all

top·ple *vb* **top·pled; top·pling 1** : to fall from being too heavy at the top **2** : to push over

top·sail *n* **1** : the sail next above the lowest sail on a mast in a square-rigged ship **2** : the sail above the large sail on a mast in a ship with a fore-and-aft rig

top·soil *n* : the rich upper layer of soil in which plants have most of their roots

top·sy–tur·vy *adv or adj* **1** : upside down **2** : in complete disorder

torch *n* **1** : a flaming light that is made of something which burns brightly and that is usually carried in the hand **2** : something that guides or gives light or heat like a torch **3** : a portable device for producing a hot flame

tore *past of* TEAR

¹**tor·ment** *n* **1** : extreme pain or distress of body or mind **2** : a cause of suffering in mind or body

²**tor·ment** *vb* **1** : to cause severe suffering of body or mind to **2** : VEX 1, HARASS

torn *past participle of* TEAR

tor·na·do *n, pl* **tor·na·does** *or* **tor·na·dos** : a violent whirling wind accompanied by a cloud that is shaped like a funnel and moves overland in a narrow path

¹**tor·pe·do** *n, pl* **tor·pe·does** : a self-propelled underwater weapon shaped like a cigar that is used for blowing up ships

²**torpedo** *vb* **tor·pe·doed; tor·pe·do·ing** : to hit with or destroy by a torpedo

tor·pid *adj* **1** : having lost motion or the power of exertion or feeling **2** : having too little energy or strength : DULL

tor·rent *n* **1** : a rushing stream of liquid **2** : ³RUSH 1 2

tor·rid *adj* : very hot and usually dry

tor·so *n* : the human body except for the head, arms, and legs

tor·ti·lla *n* : a round flat bread made of corn or wheat flour and usually rolled with a filling and eaten hot

tor·toise *n* **1** : any of a family of turtles that live on land **2** : TURTLE

tor·toise·shell *n* **1** : the hornlike covering of the shell of a sea tortoise that is mottled brown and yellow and is used for ornamental objects **2** : any of several brightly colored butterflies

tor·tu·ous *adj* : having many twists and turns

¹**tor·ture** *n* **1** : the causing of great pain especially to punish or to obtain a confession **2** : distress of body or mind

²**torture** *vb* **tor·tured; tor·tur·ing 1** : to punish or force someone to do or say something by causing great pain **2** : to cause great suffering to — **tor·tur·er** *n*

¹**toss** *vb* **1** : to throw or swing to and fro or up and down **2** : to throw with a quick light motion **3** : to lift with a sudden motion **4** : to be thrown about rapidly **5** : to move about restlessly **6** : to stir or mix lightly

²**toss** *n* : an act or instance of tossing

tot *n* : a young child

¹**to·tal** *adj* **1** : of or relating to the whole of something **2** : making up the whole **3** : being such to the fullest degree **4** : making use of every means to do something — **to·tal·ly** *adv*

²**total** *n* **1** : a result of addition : SUM **2** : an entire amount

³**total** *vb* **to·taled** *or* **to·talled; to·tal·ing** *or* **to·tal·ling 1** : to add up **2** : to amount to : NUMBER

tote *vb* **tot·ed; tot·ing** : CARRY 1, HAUL

to·tem *n* **1** : an object (as an animal or plant) serving as the emblem of a family or clan **2** : a carving or picture representing such an object

totem pole *n* : a pole or pillar carved and painted with totems and placed before the houses of Indian tribes of the northwest coast of North America

tot·ter *vb* **1** : to sway or rock as if about to fall **2** : to move unsteadily : STAGGER

tou·can *n* : a brightly colored tropical bird that has a very large beak and feeds on fruit

¹**touch** *vb* **1** : to feel or handle (as with the fingers) especially so as to be aware of with the sense of touch **2** : to be or cause to be in contact with something **3** : to be or come next to **4** : to hit lightly **5** : ²HARM **6** : to make use of **7** : to refer to in passing **8** : to affect the interest of **9** : to move emotionally

²**touch** *n* **1** : a light stroke or tap **2** : the act or fact of touching or being touched **3** : the special sense by which one is aware of light pressure **4** : an impression gotten through the sense of touch **5** : a state of contact or communication **6** : a small amount : TRACE

touch·down *n* : a score made in football by carrying or catching the ball over the opponent's goal line

touch·ing *adj* : causing a feeling of tenderness or pity

touch pad *n* : a flat surface on an electronic device (as a microwave oven) divided into several differently marked areas that are touched to make choices in controlling the device

touch up *vb* : to improve by or as if by small changes

touchy *adj* **touch·i·er; touch·i·est 1** : easily hurt or insulted **2** : calling for tact or careful handling

¹**tough** *adj* **1** : strong or firm but flexible and not brittle **2** : not easily chewed **3** : able to put up with strain or hardship **4** : STUBBORN 1 **5** : very difficult **6** : LAWLESS 2 — **tough·ness** *n*

²**tough** *n* : ²ROWDY, RUFFIAN

tough·en *vb* : to make or become tough

¹**tour** *n* **1** : a fixed period of duty **2** : a trip usually ending at the point where it started

²**tour** *vb* : to make a tour of : travel as a tourist

tour·ist *n* : a person who travels for pleasure

tour·na·ment *n* **1** : a contest of skill and courage between knights wearing armor and fighting with blunted lances or swords **2** : a series of contests played for a championship

tour·ni·quet *n* : a device (as a bandage twisted tight) for stopping bleeding or blood flow

tou·sle *vb* **tou·sled; tou·sling** : to put into disorder by rough handling

¹**tow** *vb* : to draw or pull along behind

²**tow** *n* **1** : a rope or chain for towing **2** : an act or instance of towing : the fact or state of being towed **3** : something (as a barge) that is towed

³**tow** *n* : short broken fiber of flax, hemp, or jute used for yarn, twine, or stuffing

to·ward *or* **to·wards** *prep* **1** : in the direction of **2** : along a course leading to **3** : in regard to **4** : so as to face **5** : ²NEAR **6** : as part of the payment for

tow·el *n* : a cloth or piece of absorbent paper for wiping or drying

¹**tow·er** *n* **1** : a building or structure that is higher than its length or width, is high with respect to its surroundings, and may stand by itself or be attached to a larger structure **2** : CITADEL 1

²**tower** *vb* : to reach or rise to a great height

tow·er·ing *adj* **1** : rising high : TALL **2** : reaching a high point of strength or force **3** : going beyond proper bounds

tow·head *n* : a person having soft whitish hair

town *n* **1** : a compactly settled area that is usually larger than a village but smaller than a city **2** : CITY 1 **3** : the people of a town

town·ship *n* **1** : a unit of local government in some northeastern and north central states **2** : a division of territory in surveys of United States public lands containing thirty-six square miles (about ninety-three square kilometers)

tow·path *n* : a path traveled by people or animals towing boats

tox·ic *adj* : of, relating to, or caused by a poison

tox·in *n* : a poison produced by an animal, a plant, or germs

¹**toy** *n* **1** : something of little or no value **2** : something for a child to play with **3** : something small of its kind

²**toy** *vb* : to amuse oneself as if with a toy

¹**trace** *n* **1** : a mark left by something that has passed or is past **2** : a very small amount

²**trace** *vb* **traced; trac·ing 1** : ²SKETCH 1 **2** : to form (as letters) carefully **3** : to copy (as a drawing) by following the lines or letters as seen through a transparent sheet placed over the thing copied **4** : to follow the footprints, track, or trail of **5** : to study or follow the development and progress of in detail — **trac·er** *n*

³**trace** *n* : either of the two straps, chains, or ropes of a harness that fasten a horse to a vehicle

trace·able *adj* : capable of being traced

tra·chea *n, pl* **tra·che·ae 1** : WINDPIPE **2** : a breathing tube of an insect

trac·ing *n* **1** : the act of a person that traces **2** : something that is traced

¹**track** *n* **1** : a mark left by something that

has gone by **2** : PATH 1, TRAIL **3** : a course laid out for racing **4** : a way for a vehicle with wheels **5** : awareness of things or of the order in which things happen or ideas come **6** : either of two endless metal belts on which a vehicle (as a tank) travels **7** : track-and-field sports

²track vb **1** : to follow the tracks or traces of **2** : to make tracks on or with

track–and–field adj : relating to or being sports events (as racing, throwing, and jumping contests) held on an oval running track and on an enclosed field

¹tract n : a pamphlet of political or religious ideas and beliefs

²tract n **1** : an indefinite stretch of land **2** : a defined area of land **3** : a system of body parts or organs that serve some special purpose

trac·tor n **1** : a vehicle that has large rear wheels or moves on endless belts and is used especially for pulling farm implements **2** : a short truck for hauling a trailer

¹trade n **1** : the business or work in which a person takes part regularly : OCCUPATION **2** : an occupation requiring manual or mechanical skill : CRAFT **3** : the persons working in a business or industry **4** : the business of buying and selling items : COMMERCE **5** : an act of trading : TRANSACTION **6** : a firm's customers

²trade vb **trad·ed; trad·ing 1** : to give in exchange for something else **2** : to take part in the exchange, purchase, or sale of goods **3** : to deal regularly as a customer

trade·mark n : a device (as a word) that points clearly to the origin or ownership of merchandise to which it is applied and that is legally reserved for use only by the owner

trad·er n **1** : a person who trades **2** : a ship engaged in trade

trades·man n, pl **trades·men 1** : a person who runs a retail store **2** : CRAFTSMAN 1

trades·peo·ple n pl : people engaged in trade

trade wind n : a wind blowing steadily toward the equator from an easterly direction

trad·ing post n : a station or store of a trader or trading company set up in a thinly settled region

tra·di·tion n **1** : the handing down of information, beliefs, or customs from one generation to another **2** : a belief or custom handed down by tradition

tra·di·tion·al adj **1** : handed down from age to age **2** : based on custom : CONVENTIONAL — **tra·di·tion·al·ly** adv

¹traf·fic n **1** : the business of carrying passengers or goods **2** : the business of buying and selling : COMMERCE **3** : exchange of information **4** : the persons or goods carried by train, boat, or airplane or passing along a road, river, or air route **5** : the movement (as of vehicles) along a route

²traffic vb **traf·ficked; traf·fick·ing** : ²TRADE 2

trag·e·dy n, pl **trag·e·dies 1** : a serious play that has a sorrowful or disastrous ending **2** : a disastrous event

trag·ic adj **1** : of or relating to tragedy **2** : very unfortunate

¹trail vb **1** : to drag or draw along behind **2** : to lag behind **3** : to follow in the tracks of : PURSUE **4** : to hang or let hang so as to touch the ground or float out behind **5** : to become weak, soft, or less

²trail n **1** : something that trails or is trailed **2** : a trace or mark left by something that has passed or been drawn along **3** : a beaten path **4** : a path marked through a forest or mountainous region

trail·er n **1** : a vehicle designed to be hauled (as by a tractor) **2** : a vehicle designed to serve wherever parked as a dwelling or a place of business

¹train n **1** : a part of a gown that trails behind the wearer **2** : the followers of an important person **3** : a moving line of persons, vehicles, or animals **4** : a connected series **5** : a connected series of railway cars usually hauled by a locomotive

²train vb **1** : to direct the growth of (a plant) usually by bending, pruning, and tying **2** : to give or receive instruction, discipline, or drill **3** : to teach in an art, profession, or trade **4** : to make ready (as by exercise) for a sport or test of skill **5** : to aim (as a gun) at a target — **train·er** n

train·ing n **1** : the course followed by one who trains or is being trained **2** : the condition of one who has trained for a test or contest

trait n : a quality that sets one person or thing off from another

trai·tor n **1** : a person who betrays another's trust or is false to a personal duty **2** : a person who commits treason

trai·tor·ous adj **1** : guilty or capable of treason **2** : amounting to treason — **trai·tor·ous·ly** adv

¹tramp vb **1** : to walk heavily **2** : to tread on forcibly and repeatedly **3** : to travel or wander through on foot

²tramp n **1** : a person who wanders from place to place, has no home or job, and often lives by begging or stealing **2** : ²HIKE **3** : the sounds made by the beat of marching feet

tram·ple vb **tram·pled; tram·pling 1** : to tramp or tread heavily so as to bruise, crush, or injure something   **2** : to crush under the feet   **3** : to injure or harm by treating harshly and without mercy

tram·po·line *n* : a canvas sheet or web supported by springs in a metal frame used for springing and landing in acrobatic tumbling

trance *n*   **1** : STUPOR   **2** : a condition like sleep (as deep hypnosis)   **3** : a state of being so deeply absorbed in something as not to be aware of one's surroundings

tran·quil *adj* : very calm and quiet : PEACEFUL

tran·quil·iz·er *n* : a drug used to ease worry and nervous tension

tran·quil·li·ty *or* **tran·quil·i·ty** *n* : the state of being calm : QUIET

trans- *prefix*   **1** : on or to the other side of : across : beyond   **2** : so as to change or transfer

trans·act *vb* : to carry on : MANAGE, CONDUCT

trans·ac·tion *n*   **1** : a business deal   **2   transactions** *pl* : the record of the meeting of a club or organization

trans·at·lan·tic *adj* : crossing or being beyond the Atlantic ocean

tran·scend *vb*   **1** : to rise above the limits of   **2** : to do better or more than

trans·con·ti·nen·tal *adj* : crossing, extending across, or being on the farther side of a continent

tran·scribe *vb* **tran·scribed; tran·scrib·ing** : to make a copy of

tran·script *n*   **1** : ¹COPY 1   **2** : an official copy of a student's school record

¹trans·fer *vb* **trans·ferred; trans·fer·ring**   **1** : to pass or cause to pass from one person, place, or condition to another   **2** : to give over the possession or ownership of   **3** : to copy (as by printing) from one surface to another by contact   **4** : to move to a different place, region, or job   **5** : to change from one vehicle or transportation line to another

²trans·fer *n*   **1** : a giving over of right, title, or interest in property by one person to another   **2** : an act or process of transferring   **3** : someone or something that transfers or is transferred   **4** : a ticket allowing a passenger on a bus or train to continue the journey on another route without paying more fare

trans·fix *vb* : to pierce through with or as if with a pointed weapon

trans·form *vb* : to change completely — **trans·form·er** *n*

trans·for·ma·tion *n* : the act or process of transforming : a complete change

trans·fu·sion *n*   **1** : a passing of one thing into another   **2** : a transferring (as of blood

or salt solution) into a vein of a person or animal

¹tran·sient *adj* : not lasting or staying long

²transient *n* : a person who is not staying long in a place

tran·sis·tor *n* : a small solid electronic device used especially in radios for controlling the flow of electricity

tran·sit *n*   **1** : a passing through or across   **2** : the act or method of carrying things from one place to another   **3** : local transportation of people in public vehicles   **4** : a surveyor's instrument for measuring angles

tran·si·tion *n* : a passing from one state, stage, place, or subject to another : CHANGE

tran·si·tive *adj* : having or containing a direct object

trans·late *vb* **trans·lat·ed; trans·lat·ing**   **1** : to change from one state or form to another   **2** : to turn from one language into another

trans·la·tion *n* : the act, process, or result of translating

trans·lu·cent *adj* : not transparent but clear enough to allow rays of light to pass through — **trans·lu·cent·ly** *adv*

trans·mis·sion *n*   **1** : an act or process of transmitting   **2** : the gears by which the power is transmitted from the engine to the axle that gives motion to a motor vehicle

trans·mit *vb* **trans·mit·ted; trans·mit·ting**   **1** : to transfer from one person or place to another   **2** : to pass on by or as if by inheritance   **3** : to pass or cause to pass through space or through a material   **4** : to send out by means of radio waves

trans·mit·ter *n*   **1** : one that transmits   **2** : the instrument in a telegraph system that sends out messages   **3** : the part of a telephone that includes the mouthpiece and a device that picks up sound waves and sends them over the wire   **4** : the device that sends out radio or television signals

tran·som *n*   **1** : a piece that lies crosswise in a structure (as in the frame of a window or of a door that has a window above it)   **2** : a window above a door or another window

trans·par·en·cy *n* : the quality or state of being transparent

trans·par·ent *adj*   **1** : clear enough or thin enough to be seen through   **2** : easily detected — **trans·par·ent·ly** *adv*

trans·pi·ra·tion *n* : an act or instance of transpiring

trans·pire *vb* **trans·pired; trans·pir·ing**   **1** : to give off or pass off in the form of a vapor usually through pores   **2** : to become known or apparent   **3** : to come to pass : HAPPEN

¹trans·plant *vb*   **1** : to dig up and plant again

in another soil or location **2** : to remove from one place and settle or introduce elsewhere

²trans·plant n **1** : something transplanted **2** : the process of transplanting

¹trans·port vb **1** : to carry from one place to another **2** : to fill with delight

²trans·port n **1** : the act of transporting : TRANSPORTATION **2** : a state of great joy or pleasure **3** : a ship for carrying soldiers or military equipment **4** : a vehicle used to transport persons or goods

trans·por·ta·tion n **1** : an act, instance, or means of transporting or being transported **2** : public transporting of passengers or goods especially as a business

trans·pose vb **trans·posed; trans·pos·ing** **1** : to change the position or order of **2** : to write or perform in a different musical key

trans·verse adj : lying or being across : placed crosswise — **trans·verse·ly** adv

¹trap n **1** : a device for catching animals **2** : something by which one is caught or stopped unawares **3** : a light one-horse carriage with springs **4** : a device that allows something to pass through but keeps other things out

²trap vb **trapped; trap·ping** **1** : to catch in a trap **2** : to provide (a place) with traps **3** : to set traps for animals especially as a business — **trap·per** n

trap·door n : a lifting or sliding door covering an opening in a floor or roof

tra·peze n : a short horizontal bar hung from two parallel ropes and used by acrobats

trap·e·zoid n : a figure with four sides but with only two sides parallel

trap·pings n pl **1** : ornamental covering especially for a horse **2** : outward decoration or dress

trash n **1** : something of little or no worth **2** : low worthless persons

¹trav·el vb **trav·eled** or **trav·elled; trav·el·ing** or **trav·el·ling** **1** : to journey from place to place or to a distant place **2** : to get around : pass from one place to another **3** : to journey through or over — **trav·el·er** or **trav·el·ler** n

²travel n **1** : the act or a means of traveling **2** : ¹JOURNEY, TRIP — often used in pl. **3** : the number traveling : TRAFFIC

traveling bag n : a bag carried by hand and designed to hold a traveler's clothing and personal articles

tra·verse vb **tra·versed; tra·vers·ing** : to pass through, across, or over

¹trawl vb : to fish or catch with a trawl

²trawl n : a large net in the shape of a cone dragged along the sea bottom in fishing

trawl·er n : a boat used for trawling

tray n : an open container with a flat bottom and low rim for holding, carrying, or showing articles

treach·er·ous adj **1** : guilty of or likely to commit treachery **2** : not to be trusted **3** : not safe because of hidden dangers — **treach·er·ous·ly** adv

treach·ery n, pl **treach·er·ies** **1** : a betraying of trust or faith **2** : an act or instance of betraying trust

¹tread vb **trod; trod·den** or **trod; tread·ing** **1** : to step or walk on or over **2** : to move on foot : WALK **3** : to beat or press with the feet — **tread water** : to keep the body in an up and down position in the water and the head above water by a walking or running motion of the legs helped by moving the hands

²tread n **1** : a mark made by or as if by treading **2** : the action, manner, or sound of treading **3** : the part of something (as a shoe or tire) that touches a surface **4** : the horizontal part of a step

trea·dle n : a device worked by the foot to drive a machine

tread·mill n **1** : a device moved by persons treading on steps around the rim of a wheel or by animals walking on an endless belt **2** : a device having an endless belt on which an individual walks or runs in place for exercise **3** : a tiresome routine

trea·son n **1** : the betraying of a trust **2** : the crime of trying or helping to overthrow the government of one's country or cause its defeat in war

¹trea·sure n **1** : wealth (as money or jewels) stored up or held in reserve **2** : something of great value

²treasure vb **trea·sured; trea·sur·ing** : to treat as precious : value highly : CHERISH

trea·sur·er n : a person (as an officer of a club) who has charge of the money

trea·sury n, pl **trea·sur·ies** **1** : a place in which stores of wealth are kept **2** : a place where money collected is kept and paid out **3** cap : a government department in charge of finances

¹treat vb **1** : to have as a subject especially in writing **2** : to handle, use, or act toward in a usually stated way **3** : to pay for the food or entertainment of **4** : to give medical or surgical care to : to use a certain medical care on **5** : to expose to some action (as of a chemical)

²treat n **1** : an entertainment given without expense to those invited **2** : an often unexpected or unusual source of pleasure or amusement

treat·ment n **1** : the act or manner of treating someone or something **2** : a substance or method used in treating

trea·ty *n, pl* **trea·ties** : an agreement between two or more states or sovereigns

¹tre·ble *n* **1** : the highest part in harmony having four parts : SOPRANO 1 **2** : an instrument having the highest range or part **3** : a voice or sound that has a high pitch **4** : the upper half of the musical pitch range

²treble *adj* **1** : being three times the number or amount **2** : relating to or having the range of a musical treble

³treble *vb* **tre·bled; tre·bling** : to make or become three times as much

¹tree *n* **1** : a woody plant that lives for years and has a single usually tall main stem with few or no branches on its lower part **2** : a plant of treelike form **3** : something suggesting a tree — **tree·less** *adj* — **tree·like** *adj*

²tree *vb* **treed; tree·ing** : to drive to or up a tree

tree fern *n* : a tropical fern with a tall woody stalk and a crown of often feathery leaves

tre·foil *n* **1** : a clover or related plant having leaves with three leaflets **2** : a fancy design with three leaflike parts

¹trek *vb* **trekked; trek·king** : to make one's way with difficulty

²trek *n* : a slow or difficult journey

trel·lis *n* : a frame of lattice used especially as a screen or a support for climbing plants

¹trem·ble *vb* **trem·bled; trem·bling** **1** : to shake without control (as from fear or cold) : SHIVER **2** : to move, sound, or happen as if shaken **3** : to have strong fear or doubt

²tremble *n* : the act or a period of trembling

tre·men·dous *adj* **1** : causing fear or terror : DREADFUL **2** : astonishingly large, strong, or great — **tre·men·dous·ly** *adv*

trem·or *n* **1** : a trembling or shaking especially from weakness or disease **2** : a shaking motion of the earth (as during an earthquake)

trem·u·lous *adj* **1** : marked by trembling or shaking **2** : FEARFUL 2, TIMID

trench *n* : a long narrow ditch

¹trend *vb* : to have or take a general direction

²trend *n* : general direction taken in movement or change

¹tres·pass *n* **1** : ¹SIN, OFFENSE **2** : unlawful entry upon someone's land

²trespass *vb* **1** : to do wrong : SIN **2** : to enter upon someone's land unlawfully — **tres·pass·er** *n*

tress *n* : a long lock of hair

tres·tle *n* **1** : a braced frame consisting usually of a horizontal piece with spreading legs at each end that supports something (as the top of a table) **2** : a structure of timbers or steel for supporting a road or railroad over a low place

T. rex *n* : TYRANNOSAUR

tri- *prefix* : three

tri·ad *n* : a chord made up usually of the first, third, and fifth notes of a scale

tri·al *n* **1** : the action or process of trying or testing **2** : the hearing and judgment of something in court **3** : a test of faith or of one's ability to continue or stick with something **4** : an experiment to test quality, value, or usefulness **5** : ²ATTEMPT

tri·an·gle *n* **1** : a figure that has three sides and three angles **2** : an object that has three sides and three angles **3** : a musical instrument made of a steel rod bent in the shape of a triangle with one open angle

tri·an·gu·lar *adj* **1** : of, relating to, or having the form of a triangle **2** : having three angles, sides, or corners **3** : of, relating to, or involving three parts or persons

trib·al *adj* : of, relating to, or like that of a tribe

tribe *n* **1** : a group of people including many families, clans, or generations **2** : a group of people who are of the same kind or have the same occupation or interest **3** : a group of related plants or animals

tribes·man *n, pl* **tribes·men** : a member of a tribe

trib·u·la·tion *n* **1** : distress or suffering resulting from cruel and unjust rule of a leader, persecution, or misfortune **2** : an experience that is hard to bear

tri·bu·nal *n* : a court of justice

¹trib·u·tary *adj* : flowing into a larger stream or a lake

²tributary *n, pl* **trib·u·tar·ies** : a stream flowing into a larger stream or a lake

trib·ute *n* **1** : a payment made by one ruler or state to another especially to gain peace **2** : a tax put on the people to raise money for tribute **3** : something given to show respect, gratitude, or affection

tri·cer·a·tops *n, pl* **triceratops** : a large plant-eating dinosaur with three horns, a large bony crest around the neck, and hoofed toes

tri·chi·na *n, pl* **tri·chi·nae** : a small roundworm which enters the body when infected meat is eaten and whose larvae form cysts in the muscles and cause a painful and dangerous disease (**trichinosis**)

¹trick *n* **1** : an action intended to deceive or cheat **2** : a mischievous act : PRANK **3** : an unwise or childish action **4** : an action designed to puzzle or amuse **5** : a quick or clever way of doing something **6** : the cards played in one round of a game

²trick *vb* : to deceive with tricks : CHEAT

trick·ery *n, pl* **trick·er·ies** : the use of tricks to deceive or cheat

¹trick·le *vb* **trick·led; trick·ling** **1** : to run or fall in drops **2** : to flow in a thin slow stream

²trickle *n* : a thin slow stream

trick or treat *n* : a children's Halloween practice of asking for treats from door to door and threatening to play tricks on those who refuse

trick·ster *n* : a person who uses tricks

tricky *adj* **trick·i·er; trick·i·est** **1** : likely to use tricks **2** : requiring special care and skill

tri·cy·cle *n* : a vehicle with three wheels that is moved usually by pedals

tri·dent *n* : a spear with three prongs

¹tried *past of* TRY

²tried *adj* : found good or trustworthy through experience or testing

¹tri·fle *n* **1** : something of little importance **2** : a small amount (as of money)

²trifle *vb* **tri·fled; tri·fling** **1** : to talk in a joking way **2** : to act in a playful way **3** : to handle something in an absentminded way : TOY

tri·fling *adj* **1** : not serious : FRIVOLOUS **2** : of little value

trig·ger *n* : the part of the lock of a gun that is pressed to release the hammer so that it will fire

¹trill *n* **1** : a quick movement back and forth between two musical tones one step apart **2** : ¹WARBLE 1 **3** : the rapid vibration of one speech organ against another

²trill *vb* : to utter as or with a trill

tril·lion *n* : a thousand billions

tril·li·um *n* : a plant related to the lilies that has three leaves and a single flower with three petals and that blooms in the spring

¹trim *vb* **trimmed; trim·ming** **1** : to put ornaments on : ADORN **2** : to make neat especially by cutting or clipping **3** : to free of unnecessary matter **4** : to cause (as a ship) to take the right position in the water by balancing the load carried **5** : to adjust (as an airplane or submarine) for horizontal movement or for motion upward or downward **6** : to adjust (as a sail) to a desired position — **trim·mer** *n*

²trim *adj* **trim·mer; trim·mest** : neat and compact in line or structure — **trim·ly** *adv*

³trim *n* **1** : the state of a ship as being ready for sailing **2** : good condition : FITNESS **3** : material used for ornament or trimming **4** : the woodwork in the finish of a building especially around doors and windows

trim·ming *n* **1** : the action of one that trims **2** : something that trims, ornaments, or completes **3 trimmings** *pl* : parts removed by trimming

trin·ket *n* : a small ornament (as a jewel)

trio *n*, *pl* **tri·os** **1** : a musical composition for three instruments or voices **2** : a group or set of three

¹trip *vb* **tripped; trip·ping** **1** : to move (as in dancing) with light quick steps **2** : to catch the foot against something so as to stumble : cause to stumble **3** : to make or cause to make a mistake **4** : to release (as a spring) by moving a catch

²trip *n* **1** : a traveling from one place to another : VOYAGE **2** : a brief errand having a certain aim or being more or less regular **3** : the action of releasing something mechanically **4** : a device for releasing something by tripping a mechanism

tripe *n* : a part of the stomach of a cow used for food

¹tri·ple *vb* **tri·pled; tri·pling** : to make or become three times as great or as many

²triple *n* **1** : a sum, amount, or number that is three times as great **2** : a combination, group, or series of three **3** : a hit in baseball that lets the batter reach third base

³triple *adj* **1** : having three units or parts **2** : being three times as great or as many **3** : repeated three times

trip·let *n* **1** : a combination, set, or group of three **2** : one of three offspring born at one birth

tri·pod *n* **1** : something (as a container or stool) resting on three legs **2** : a stand (as for a camera) having three legs

trite *adj* **trit·er; trit·est** : so common that the newness and cleverness have worn off : STALE — **trite·ness** *n*

¹tri·umph *n* **1** : the joy of victory or success **2** : an outstanding victory

²triumph *vb* **1** : to celebrate victory or success in high spirits and often with boasting **2** : to gain victory : WIN

tri·um·phal *adj* : of or relating to a triumph

tri·um·phant *adj* **1** : VICTORIOUS, SUCCESSFUL **2** : rejoicing for or celebrating victory — **tri·um·phant·ly** *adv*

triv·i·al *adj* : of little worth or importance

trod *past of* TREAD

trodden *past participle of* TREAD

¹troll *vb* **1** : to sing the parts of (a song) in succession **2** : to fish with a hook and line drawn through the water

²troll *n* : a lure or a line with its lure and hook used in trolling

³troll *n* : a dwarf or giant of folklore living in caves or hills

trol·ley *n*, *pl* **trolleys** **1** : a device (as a grooved wheel on the end of a pole) that carries current from a wire to an electrically driven vehicle **2** : a passenger car that runs on tracks and gets its power through a trol-ley **3** : a wheeled carriage running on an overhead track

trom·bone *n* : a brass musical instrument made of a long bent tube that has a wide opening at one end and one section that slides in and out to make different tones

¹troop *n* **1** : a cavalry unit **2 troops** *pl* : armed forces : MILITARY **3** : a group of beings or things **4** : a unit of boy or girl scouts under a leader

²troop *vb* : to move or gather in groups

troop·er *n* **1** : a soldier in a cavalry unit **2** : a mounted police officer **3** : a state police officer

tro·phy *n, pl* **trophies 1** : something taken in battle or conquest especially as a memorial **2** : something given to celebrate a victory or as an award for achievement

trop·ic *n* **1** : either of two parallels of the earth's latitude of which one is about 23¹/₂ degrees north of the equator and the other about 23¹/₂ degrees south of the equator **2 tropics** *pl, often cap* : the region lying between the two tropics

trop·i·cal *adj* : of, relating to, or occurring in the tropics

tropical fish *n* : any of various small often brightly colored fishes kept in aquariums

¹trot *n* **1** : a moderately fast gait of an animal with four feet in which a front foot and the opposite hind foot move as a pair **2** : a human jogging pace between a walk and a run

²trot *vb* **trot·ted; trot·ting 1** : to ride, drive, or go at a trot **2** : to cause to go at a trot **3** : to go along quickly : HURRY

¹trou·ble *vb* **trou·bled; trou·bling 1** : to disturb or become disturbed mentally or spiritually : WORRY **2** : to produce physical disorder in : AFFLICT **3** : to put to inconvenience **4** : to make an effort

²trouble *n* **1** : the quality or state of being troubled : MISFORTUNE **2** : an instance of distress or disturbance **3** : a cause of disturbance or distress **4** : extra work or effort **5** : ill health : AILMENT **6** : failure to work normally

trou·ble·some *adj* **1** : giving trouble or anxiety **2** : difficult to deal with — **trou·ble·some·ly** *adv* — **trou·ble·some·ness** *n*

trough *n* **1** : a long shallow open container especially for water or feed for livestock **2** : a channel for water : GUTTER **3** : a long channel or hollow

trounce *vb* **trounced; trounc·ing 1** : to beat severely : FLOG **2** : to defeat thoroughly

troupe *n* : a group especially of performers on the stage

trou·sers *n pl* : PANTS — used chiefly of such a garment for men and boys

trout *n, pl* **trout** : a freshwater fish related to the salmon and valued for food and sport

trow·el *n* **1** : a small hand tool with a flat blade used for spreading and smoothing mortar or plaster **2** : a small hand tool with a curved blade used by gardeners

tru·ant *n* **1** : a person who neglects his or her duty **2** : a student who stays out of school without permission

truce *n* **1** : ARMISTICE **2** : a short rest especially from something unpleasant

¹truck *n* **1** : ²BARTER **2** : goods for barter or for small trade **3** : close association

²truck *n* : a vehicle (as a strong heavy wagon or motor vehicle) for carrying heavy articles or hauling a trailer

³truck *vb* : to transport on a truck

trudge *vb* **trudged; trudg·ing** : to walk or march steadily and usually with much effort

¹true *adj* **tru·er; tru·est 1** : completely loyal : FAITHFUL **2** : that can be relied on : CERTAIN **3** : agreeing with the facts : ACCURATE **4** : HONEST 1, SINCERE **5** : properly so called : GENUINE **6** : placed or formed accurately : EXACT **7** : being or holding by right : LEGITIMATE

²true *adv* **1** : in agreement with fact : TRUTHFULLY **2** : in an accurate manner : ACCURATELY **3** : without variation from type

³true *n* : the quality or state of being accurate (as in alignment)

⁴true *vb* **trued; tru·ing** *also* **tru·ing** : to bring to exactly correct condition as to place, position, or shape

true–blue *adj* : very faithful

truf·fle *n* : the edible usually dark and wrinkled fruiting body of a European fungus that grows in the ground

tru·ly *adv* : in a true manner

¹trum·pet *n* **1** : a brass musical instrument that consists of a tube formed into a long loop with a wide opening at one end and that has valves by which different tones are produced **2** : something that is shaped like a trumpet **3** : a sound like that of a trumpet

²trumpet *vb* **1** : to blow a trumpet **2** : to make a sound like that of a trumpet — **trum·pet·er** *n*

trumpet creeper *n* : a North American woody vine having red flowers shaped like trumpets

trumpet vine *n* : TRUMPET CREEPER

¹trun·dle *vb* **trun·dled; trun·dling** : to roll along : WHEEL

²trundle *n* **1** : a small wheel or roller **2** : a cart or truck with low wheels

trundle bed *n* : a low bed on small wheels that can be rolled under a higher bed

trunk *n* **1** : the main stem of a tree apart from branches and roots **2** : the body of a person or animal apart from the head, arms, and legs **3** : a box or chest for holding clothes or other articles especially for traveling **4** : the enclosed space usually in the rear of an automobile for carrying articles **5** : the long round muscular nose of an elephant **6** **trunks** *pl* : men's shorts worn chiefly for sports

¹**truss** *vb* **1** : to bind or tie firmly **2** : to support, strengthen, or stiffen by a truss

²**truss** *n* **1** : a framework of beams or bars used in building and engineering **2** : a device worn to hold a ruptured body part in place

¹**trust** *n* **1** : firm belief in the character, strength, or truth of someone or something **2** : a person or thing in which confidence is placed **3** : confident hope **4** : financial credit **5** : a property interest held by one person or organization (as a bank) for the benefit of another **6** : a combination of firms or corporations formed by a legal agreement and often held to reduce competition **7** : something (as a public office) held or managed by someone for the benefit of another **8** : responsibility for safety and well-being

²**trust** *vb* **1** : to place confidence : DEPEND **2** : to be confident : HOPE **3** : to place in one's care or keeping : ENTRUST **4** : to rely on or on the truth of : BELIEVE **5** : to give financial credit to

trust·ee *n* : a person who has been given legal responsibility for someone else's property

trust·ful *adj* : full of trust — **trust·ful·ly** *adv* — **trust·ful·ness** *n*

trust·ing *adj* : having trust, faith, or confidence

trust·wor·thy *adj* : deserving trust and confidence — **trust·wor·thi·ness** *n*

¹**trusty** *adj* **trust·i·er; trust·i·est** : TRUSTWORTHY, RELIABLE

²**trusty** *n, pl* **trust·ies** : a convict considered trustworthy and allowed special privileges

truth *n, pl* **truths** **1** : the quality or state of being true **2** : the body of real events or facts **3** : a true or accepted statement **4** : agreement with fact or reality

truth·ful *adj* : telling or being in the habit of telling the truth — **truth·ful·ly** *adv* — **truth·ful·ness** *n*

¹**try** *vb* **tried; try·ing** **1** : to examine or investigate in a court of law **2** : to conduct the trial of **3** : to put to a test **4** : to test to the limit **5** : to melt down (as tallow) and obtain in a pure state **6** : to make an effort to do

²**try** *n, pl* **tries** : an effort to do something : ATTEMPT

try·ing *adj* : hard to bear or put up with

try on *vb* : to put on (a garment) in order to test the fit

try·out *n* : a test of the ability (as of an athlete or an actor) to fill a part or meet standards

T–shirt *also* **tee shirt** *n* **1** : a cotton undershirt with short sleeves and no collar **2** : a cotton or wool jersey outer shirt designed like a T-shirt

¹**tub** *n* **1** : a wide low container **2** : an old or slow boat **3** : BATHTUB **4** : BATH 1 **5** : the amount that a tub will hold

²**tub** *vb* **tubbed; tub·bing** : to wash or bathe in a tub

tu·ba *n* : a brass musical instrument of lowest pitch with an oval shape and valves for producing different tones

tube *n* **1** : a long hollow cylinder used especially to carry fluids **2** : a slender channel within a plant or animal body : DUCT **3** : a soft container shaped something like a tube whose contents (as toothpaste or glue) can be removed by squeezing **4** : a hollow cylinder of rubber inside a tire to hold air **5** : ELECTRONIC TUBE **6** : TELEVISION — always used with *the* — **tubed** *adj* — **tube·less** *adj* — **tube·like** *adj*

tu·ber *n* : a short fleshy usually underground stem (as of a potato plant) bearing tiny leaves like scales each with a bud at its base

tu·ber·cu·lo·sis *n* : a disease (as of humans or cattle) which is caused by a bacillus and in which fever, wasting, and formation of cheesy nodules especially in the lungs occur

tu·ber·ous *adj* : of, relating to, or like a tuber

tu·bu·lar *adj* **1** : having the form of or made up of a tube **2** : made with tubes

¹**tuck** *vb* **1** : to pull up into a fold **2** : to make stitched folds in **3** : to put or fit into a snug or safe place **4** : to push in the edges of **5** : to cover by tucking in bedclothes

²**tuck** *n* : a fold stitched into cloth usually to alter it

Tues·day *n* : the third day of the week

¹**tuft** *n* **1** : a small bunch of long flexible things (as hairs) growing out **2** : a bunch of soft fluffy threads used for ornament **3** : ¹CLUMP 1, CLUSTER

²**tuft** *vb* **1** : to provide or decorate with a tuft **2** : to grow in tufts **3** : to make (as upholstery) firm by stitching through the stuffing here and there

¹**tug** *vb* **tugged; tug·ging** **1** : to pull hard **2** : to move by pulling hard : DRAG **3** : to tow with a tugboat

²tug n **1** : an act of tugging : PULL **2** : a strong pulling force **3** : a struggle between two people or forces **4** : TUGBOAT

tug·boat n : a small powerful boat used for towing ships

tug–of–war n, pl **tugs–of–war 1** : a struggle to win **2** : a contest in which two teams pull against each other at opposite ends of a rope

tu·ition n : money paid for instruction (as at a college)

tu·lip n : a plant related to the lilies that grows from a bulb and has a large cup-shaped flower in early spring

¹tum·ble vb **tum·bled; tum·bling 1** : to perform gymnastic feats of rolling and turning **2** : to fall suddenly and helplessly **3** : to suffer a sudden downward turn or defeat **4** : to move or go in a hurried or confused way **5** : to come to understand **6** : to toss together into a confused mass

²tumble n **1** : a messy state or collection **2** : an act or instance of tumbling and especially of falling down

tum·ble·down adj : DILAPIDATED

tum·bler n **1** : a person (as an acrobat) who tumbles **2** : a drinking glass **3** : a movable part of a lock that must be adjusted (as by a key) before the lock will open

tum·ble·weed n : a plant that breaks away from its roots in autumn and is tumbled about by the wind

tum·my n, pl **tummies** : ¹STOMACH 1, 2

tu·mor n : an abnormal growth of body tissue

tu·mult n **1** : UPROAR **2** : great confusion of mind

tu·mul·tu·ous adj : being or suggesting tumult

tu·na n, pl **tuna** or **tunas** : a large sea fish valued for food and sport

tun·dra n : a treeless plain of arctic regions

¹tune n **1** : a series of pleasing musical tones : MELODY **2** : the main melody of a song **3** : correct musical pitch or key **4** : AGREEMENT 1, HARMONY **5** : general attitude — **tune·ful** adj

²tune vb **tuned; tun·ing 1** : to adjust in musical pitch **2** : to come or bring into harmony **3** : to adjust a radio or television set so that it receives clearly — often used with in **4** : to put (as an engine) in good working order — often used with up — **tun·er** n

tung·sten n : a grayish-white hard metallic chemical element used especially for electrical purposes (as for the fine wire in an electric light bulb) and to make alloys (as steel) harder

tu·nic n **1** : a usually knee-length belted garment worn by ancient Greeks and Ro-

mans **2** : a shirt or jacket reaching to or just below the hips

tuning fork n : a metal instrument that gives a fixed tone when struck and is useful for tuning musical instruments

¹tun·nel n : a passage under the ground

²tunnel vb **tun·neled** or **tun·nelled; tun·nel·ing** or **tun·nel·ling** : to make a tunnel

tun·ny n, pl **tun·nies** : TUNA

tur·ban n **1** : a head covering worn especially by Muslims and made of a long cloth wrapped around the head or around a cap **2** : a woman's small soft hat with no brim

tur·bid adj : dark or discolored with sediment

tur·bine n : an engine whose central driving shaft is fitted with a series of winglike parts that are whirled around by the pressure of water, steam, or gas

tur·bot n, pl **turbot** : a large brownish flatfish

tur·bu·lent adj : causing or being in a state of unrest, violence, or disturbance

tu·reen n : a deep bowl from which food (as soup) is served

turf n : the upper layer of soil bound into a thick mat by roots of grass and other plants

Turk n : a person born or living in Turkey

tur·key n, pl **turkeys** : a large American bird related to the chicken and widely raised for food

¹Turk·ish adj : of or relating to Turkey, the Turks, or Turkish

²Turkish n : the language of the Turks

tur·moil n : a very confused or disturbed state or condition

¹turn vb **1** : to move or cause to move around a center : ROTATE **2** : to twist so as to bring about a desired end **3** : ¹WRENCH 2 **4** : to change in position usually by moving through an arc of a circle **5** : to think over : PONDER **6** : to become dizzy : REEL **7** : ¹UPSET 3 **8** : to set in another and especially an opposite direction **9** : to change course or direction **10** : to go around **11** : to reach or pass beyond **12** : to move or direct toward or away from something **13** : to make an appeal **14** : to become or make very unfriendly **15** : to make or become spoiled **16** : to cause to be or look a certain way **17** : to pass from one state to another **18** : ¹CHANGE 1, TRANSFORM **19** : TRANSLATE 2 **20** : to give a rounded form to (as on a lathe) — **turn a hair** : to be or become upset or frightened — **turn tail** : to turn so as to run away — **turn the trick** : to bring about the desired result — **turn turtle** : OVERTURN 1

²turn n **1** : a turning about a center **2** : a change or changing of direction, course, or position **3** : a change or changing of the general state or condition **4** : a place at which something turns **5** : a short walk or ride **6** : an act affecting another **7** : proper place in a waiting line or time in a schedule **8** : a period of action or activity : SPELL **9** : a special purpose or need **10** : special quality **11** : the shape or form in which something is molded : CAST **12** : a single circle or loop (as of rope passed around an object) **13** : natural or special skill — **at every turn** : all the time : CONSTANTLY, CONTINUOUSLY — **to a turn** : precisely right

turn·about *n* : a change from one direction or one way of thinking or acting to the opposite

turn down *vb* **1** : to fold back or down **2** : to lower by using a control **3** : ¹REFUSE 1, REJECT

tur·nip *n* : the thick white or yellow edible root of a plant related to the cabbage

turn off *vb* **1** : to turn aside **2** : to stop by using a control

turn on *vb* : to make work by using a control

turn·out *n* : a gathering of people for a special reason

turn out *vb* **1** : TURN OFF 2 **2** : to prove to be

turn·pike *n* **1** : a road that one must pay to use **2** : a main road

turn·stile *n* : a post having arms that turn around set in an entrance or exit so that persons can pass through only on foot one by one

turn·ta·ble *n* : a round flat plate that turns a phonograph record

tur·pen·tine *n* **1** : a mixture of oil and resin obtained mostly from pine trees **2** : an oil made from turpentine and used as a solvent and as a paint thinner

tur·quoise *n* : a blue to greenish gray mineral used in jewelry

tur·ret *n* **1** : a little tower often at a corner of a building **2** : a low usually rotating structure (as in a tank, warship, or airplane) in which guns are mounted

tur·tle *n* : any of a large group of reptiles living on land, in water, or both and having a toothless horny beak and a shell of bony plates which covers the body and into which the head, legs, and tail can usually be drawn

tur·tle·dove *n* : any of several small wild pigeons

tur·tle·neck *n* : a high turned-over collar (as of a sweater)

tusk *n* : a very long large tooth (as of an elephant) usually growing in pairs and used in digging and fighting — **tusked** *adj*

¹tus·sle *n* **1** : a physical contest or struggle **2** : a rough argument or a struggle against difficult odds

²tussle *vb* **tus·sled; tus·sling** : to struggle roughly : SCUFFLE

tus·sock *n* : a compact tuft or clump (as of grass)

¹tu·tor *n* : a person who has the responsibility of instructing and guiding another

²tutor *vb* : to teach usually individually

TV *n* : TELEVISION

twad·dle *n* : silly idle talk

twain *n* : ²TWO 1

¹twang *n* **1** : a harsh quick ringing sound **2** : nasal speech

²twang *vb* **1** : to sound or cause to sound with a twang **2** : to speak with a nasal twang

'twas : it was

¹tweak *vb* : to pinch and pull with a sudden jerk and twist

²tweak *n* : an act of tweaking

tweed *n* **1** : a rough woolen cloth **2** **tweeds** *pl* : tweed clothing (as a suit)

¹tweet *n* : a chirping sound

²tweet *vb* : ²CHIRP

tweez·ers *n pl* : a small instrument that is used like pincers in grasping or pulling something

¹twelfth *adj* : coming right after eleventh

²twelfth *n* : number twelve in a series

¹twelve *adj* : being one more than eleven

²twelve *n* : one more than eleven : three times four : 12

twelve·month *n* : YEAR

¹twen·ti·eth *adj* : coming right after nineteenth

²twentieth *n* : number twenty in a series

¹twen·ty *adj* : being one more than nineteen

²twenty *n* : one more than nineteen : four times five : 20

twen·ty–first *adj* : coming right after twentieth

¹twen·ty–one *adj* : being one more than twenty

²twenty–one *n* : one more than twenty : 21

twice *adv* : two times

twid·dle *vb* **twid·dled; twid·dling** : ¹TWIRL

twig *n* : a small shoot or branch

twi·light *n* : the period or the light from the sky between full night and sunrise or between sunset and full night

twill *n* : a way of weaving cloth that produces a pattern of diagonal lines

¹twin *n* **1** : either of two offspring produced at one birth **2** : one of two persons or things closely related to or very like each other

²twin *adj* **1** : born with one other or as a pair at one birth **2** : made up of two similar, related, or connected members or parts **3** : being one of a pair

¹twine *n* : a strong string of two or more strands twisted together

²twine *vb* **twined; twin·ing 1** : to twist together **2** : to coil around a support

¹twinge *vb* **twinged; twing·ing** *or* **twingeing** : to affect with or feel a sudden sharp pain

²twinge *n* : a sudden sharp stab (as of pain)

¹twin·kle *vb* **twin·kled; twin·kling 1** : to shine or cause to shine with a flickering or sparkling light **2** : to appear bright with amusement **3** : to move or flutter rapidly

²twinkle *n* **1** : a very short time **2** : ²SPARKLE 1, FLICKER

twin·kling *n* : ²TWINKLE 1

¹twirl *vb* : to turn or cause to turn rapidly — **twirl·er** *n*

²twirl *n* : an act of twirling

¹twist *vb* **1** : to unite by winding one thread, strand, or wire around another **2** : ²TWINE 2 **3** : to turn so as to sprain or hurt **4** : to change the meaning of **5** : to pull off, rotate, or break by a turning force **6** : to follow a winding course

²twist *n* **1** : something that is twisted **2** : an act of twisting : the state of being twisted **3** : a spiral turn or curve **4** : a strong personal tendency : BENT **5** : a changing of meaning **6** : something (as a plan of action) that is both surprising and strange **7** : a lively dance in which the hips are twisted

twist·er *n* **1** : TORNADO **2** : WATERSPOUT 2

¹twitch *vb* **1** : to move or pull with a sudden motion : JERK **2** : ¹PLUCK 1 **3** : ²QUIVER

²twitch *n* **1** : an act of twitching **2** : a short sharp contracting of muscle fibers

¹twit·ter *vb* **1** : to make a series of chirping noises **2** : to talk in a chattering fashion **3** : to make or become very nervous and upset

²twitter *n* **1** : a nervous upset state **2** : the chirping of birds **3** : a light chattering

¹two *adj* : being one more than one

²two *n* **1** : one more than one : 2 **2** : the second in a set or series

two–dimensional *adj* : having the two dimensions of length and width

two·fold *adj* : being twice as great or as many

two–way *adj* **1** : moving or acting or allowing movement or action in either direction **2** : involving two persons or groups **3** : made to send and receive messages

two–winged fly *n* : an insect belonging to the same group as the housefly

ty·coon *n* : a very powerful and wealthy business person

tying *present participle of* TIE

¹type *n* **1** : a set of letters or figures that are used for printing or the letters or figures printed by them **2** : the special things by which members of a group are set apart from other groups **3** : VARIETY 3

²type *vb* **typed; typ·ing 1** : TYPEWRITE **2** : to identify as belonging to a type

type·write *vb* **type·wrote; type·writ·ten; type·writ·ing** : to write with a typewriter

type·writ·er *n* : a machine that prints letters or figures when a person pushes its keys down

type·writ·ing *n* **1** : the use of a typewriter **2** : writing done with a typewriter

¹ty·phoid *adj* **1** : of, relating to, or like typhus **2** : of, relating to, or being typhoid

²typhoid *n* : a disease in which a person has fever, diarrhea, an inflamed intestine, and great weakness and which is caused by a bacterium (**typhoid bacillus**) that passes from one person to another in dirty food or water

ty·phoon *n* : a tropical cyclone in the region of the Philippines or the China Sea

ty·phus *n* : a disease carried to people especially by body lice and marked by high fever, stupor and delirium, severe headache, and a dark red rash

typ·i·cal *adj* : combining or showing the special characteristics of a group or kind — **typ·i·cal·ly** *adv*

typ·i·fy *vb* **typ·i·fied; typ·i·fy·ing 1** : REPRESENT 2 **2** : to have or include the special or main characteristics of

typ·ist *n* : a person who uses a typewriter

ty·ran·ni·cal *adj* : of, relating to, or like that of tyranny or a tyrant

ty·ran·no·saur *n* : a huge North American flesh-eating dinosaur that had small forelegs and walked on its hind legs

ty·ran·no·sau·rus *n* : TYRANNOSAUR

tyr·an·ny *n, pl* **tyr·an·nies 1** : a government in which all power is in the hands of a single ruler **2** : harsh, cruel, and severe government or conduct **3** : a tyrannical act

ty·rant *n* **1** : a ruler who has no legal limits on his or her power **2** : a ruler who exercises total power harshly and cruelly **3** : a person who uses authority or power harshly

U

u *n, pl* **u's** *or* **us** *often cap* **1** : the twenty-first letter of the English alphabet **2** : a grade rating a student's work as unsatisfactory

ud·der *n* : an organ (as of a cow) made up of two or more milk glands enclosed in a common pouch but opening by separate nipples

ugh *interj* — used to indicate the sound of a cough or to express disgust or horror

ug·ly *adj* **ug·li·er; ug·li·est** **1** : unpleasant to look at : not attractive **2** : ¹OFFENSIVE 3 **3** : not pleasant : TROUBLESOME **4** : showing a mean or quarrelsome disposition — **ug·li·ness** *n*

uku·le·le *n* : a musical instrument like a small guitar with four strings

ul·cer *n* : an open sore in which tissue is eaten away and which may discharge pus

ul·cer·ate *vb* **ul·cer·at·ed; ul·cer·at·ing** : to cause or have an ulcer

ul·cer·a·tion *n* **1** : the process of forming or state of having an ulcer **2** : ULCER

ul·cer·ous *adj* : being or accompanied by ulceration

ul·na *n, pl* **ul·nas** *or* **ul·nae** : the bone on the side of the forearm opposite the thumb

ul·te·ri·or *adj* : not seen or made known

ul·ti·mate *adj* **1** : last in a series : FINAL **2** : ¹EXTREME 1 **3** : FUNDAMENTAL, ABSOLUTE — **ul·ti·mate·ly** *adv*

ul·ti·ma·tum *n, pl* **ul·ti·ma·tums** *or* **ul·ti·ma·ta** : a final condition or demand that if rejected could end peaceful talks and lead to forceful action

ul·tra *adj* : ¹EXTREME 1, EXCESSIVE

ultra- *prefix* **1** : beyond in space : on the other side **2** : beyond the limits of : SUPER- **3** : beyond what is ordinary or proper : too

ul·tra·vi·o·let *adj* : relating to or producing ultraviolet light

ultraviolet light *n* : waves that are like light but cannot be seen, that lie beyond the violet end of the spectrum, and that are found especially along with light from the sun

um·bil·i·cal cord *n* : a cord joining a fetus to its placenta

um·brel·la *n* : a fabric covering stretched over folding ribs attached to a rod or pole and used as a protection against rain or sun

umi·ak *n* : an open Eskimo boat made of a wooden frame covered with hide

um·pire *n* : a sports official who rules on plays

¹un- *prefix* : not : IN-, NON-

²un- *prefix* **1** : do the opposite of : DE- 1, DIS- 1 **2** : deprive of, remove a specified thing from, or free or release from **3** : completely

un·able *adj* : not able

un·ac·count·able *adj* : not accountable : not to be explained : STRANGE — **un·ac·count·ably** *adv*

un·ac·cus·tomed *adj* : not accustomed : not customary

un·af·fect·ed *adj* **1** : not influenced or changed **2** : free from false behavior intended to impress others : GENUINE — **un·af·fect·ed·ly** *adv*

un·afraid *adj* : not afraid

un·aid·ed *adj* : not aided

un·al·loyed *adj* : PURE 1 3

unan·i·mous *adj* **1** : having the same opinion **2** : showing total agreement

un·armed *adj* : having no weapons or armor

un·asked *adj* : not asked or asked for

un·as·sum·ing *adj* : MODEST 1

un·at·trac·tive *adj* : not attractive : ¹PLAIN 7

un·avoid·able *adj* : INEVITABLE — **un·avoid·ably** *adv*

¹un·aware *adv* : UNAWARES

²unaware *adj* : not aware : IGNORANT — **un·aware·ness** *n*

un·awares *adv* **1** : without knowing : UNINTENTIONALLY **2** : without warning : by surprise

un·bal·anced *adj* **1** : not balanced **2** : not completely sane

un·bear·able *adj* : seeming too great or too bad to put up with — **un·bear·ably** *adv*

un·be·com·ing *adj* : not becoming : not suitable or proper — **un·be·com·ing·ly** *adv*

un·be·lief *n* : lack of belief

un·be·liev·able *adj* : too unlikely to be believed — **un·be·liev·ably** *adv*

un·be·liev·er *n* **1** : a person who doubts what is said **2** : a person who has no religious beliefs

un·bend *vb* **un·bent; un·bend·ing** : RELAX 3

un·bend·ing *adj* : not relaxed and easy in manner

un·bi·ased *adj* : free from bias

un·bind *vb* **un·bound; un·bind·ing** **1** : to remove a band from : UNTIE **2** : to set free

un·born *adj* : not yet born

un·bos·om *vb* : to tell someone one's own thoughts or feelings

un·bound·ed *adj* : having no limits

un·break·able *adj* : not easily broken

un·bro·ken *adj* **1** : not damaged : WHOLE **2** : not tamed for use **3** : not interrupted

un·buck·le *vb* **un·buck·led; un·buck·ling** : to unfasten the buckle of (as a belt)

un·bur·den *vb* **1 :** to free from a burden **2 :** to free oneself from (as cares)

un·but·ton *vb* **:** to unfasten the buttons of (as a garment)

un·called–for *adj* **:** not needed or wanted **:** not proper

un·can·ny *adj* **1 :** MYSTERIOUS, EERIE **2 :** suggesting powers or abilities greater than normal for humans — **un·can·ni·ly** *adv*

un·ceas·ing *adj* **:** never stopping **:** CONTINUOUS — **un·ceas·ing·ly** *adv*

un·cer·tain *adj* **1 :** not exactly known or decided on **2 :** not known for sure **3 :** not sure **4 :** likely to change **:** not dependable — **un·cer·tain·ly** *adv*

un·cer·tain·ty *n, pl* **un·cer·tain·ties 1 :** lack of certainty **:** DOUBT **2 :** something uncertain

un·change·able *adj* **:** not changing or capable of being changed

un·changed *adj* **:** not changed

un·chang·ing *adj* **:** not changing or able to change

un·charged *adj* **:** having no electric charge

un·civ·il *adj* **:** IMPOLITE — **un·civ·il·ly** *adv*

un·civ·i·lized *adj* **1 :** not civilized **:** BARBAROUS **2 :** far away from civilization **:** WILD

un·cle *n* **1 :** the brother of one's father or mother **2 :** the husband of one's aunt

un·clean *adj* **1 :** not pure and innocent **:** WICKED **2 :** not allowed for use by religious law **3 :** DIRTY 1, FILTHY — **un·clean·ness** *n*

¹un·clean·ly *adj* **:** UNCLEAN 1, 3 — **un·clean·li·ness** *n*

²un·clean·ly *adv* **:** in an unclean manner

un·cleared *adj* **:** not cleared especially of trees or brush

Un·cle Sam *n* **:** the American government, nation, or people pictured or thought of as a person

un·clothed *adj* **:** NAKED 1, 2

un·com·fort·able *adj* **1 :** causing discomfort **2 :** feeling discomfort **:** UNEASY — **un·com·fort·ably** *adv*

un·com·mon *adj* **1 :** not often found or seen **:** UNUSUAL **2 :** not ordinary **:** REMARKABLE — **un·com·mon·ly** *adv* — **un·com·mon·ness** *n*

un·com·pro·mis·ing *adj* **:** not willing to give in even a little — **un·com·pro·mis·ing·ly** *adv*

un·con·cern *n* **:** lack of care or interest **:** INDIFFERENCE

un·con·cerned *adj* **1 :** not involved or interested **2 :** free of worry — **un·con·cern·ed·ly** *adv*

un·con·di·tion·al *adj* **:** without any special exceptions — **un·con·di·tion·al·ly** *adv*

un·con·quer·able *adj* **:** not capable of being beaten or overcome

un·con·scious *adj* **1 :** not aware **2 :** having lost consciousness **3 :** not intentional or planned — **un·con·scious·ly** *adv* — **un·con·scious·ness** *n*

un·con·sti·tu·tion·al *adj* **:** not according to the constitution (as of a government)

un·con·trol·la·ble *adj* **:** hard or impossible to control — **un·con·trol·la·bly** *adv*

un·con·trolled *adj* **:** not being controlled

un·couth *adj* **:** vulgar in conduct or speech **:** CRUDE — **un·couth·ly** *adv*

un·cov·er *vb* **1 :** to make known **2 :** to make visible by removing some covering

un·cul·ti·vat·ed *adj* **:** not cultivated

un·curl *vb* **:** to make or become straightened out from a curled position

un·cut *adj* **1 :** not cut down or cut into **2 :** not shaped by cutting

un·daunt·ed *adj* **:** not discouraged or frightened **:** FEARLESS

un·de·cid·ed *adj* **1 :** not settled **2 :** not having decided

un·de·clared *adj* **:** not announced or openly confessed

un·de·fined *adj* **:** not defined

un·de·ni·able *adj* **:** plainly true — **un·de·ni·ably** *adv*

¹un·der *adv* **1 :** in or into a position below or beneath something **2 :** below some quantity or level **3 :** so as to be covered or hidden

²under *prep* **1 :** lower than and topped or sheltered by **2 :** below the surface of **3 :** in or into such a position as to be covered or hidden by **4 :** commanded or guided by **5 :** controlled or limited by **6 :** affected or influenced by the action or effect of **7 :** within the division or grouping of **8 :** less or lower than (as in size, amount, or rank)

³under *adj* **1 :** lying or placed below or beneath **2 :** ¹SUBORDINATE 1

un·der·brush *n* **:** shrubs and small trees growing among large trees

un·der·clothes *n pl* **:** UNDERWEAR

un·der·cloth·ing *n* **:** UNDERWEAR

un·der·dog *n* **:** a person or team thought to have little chance of winning (as an election or a game)

un·der·foot *adv* **1 :** under the feet **2 :** close about one's feet **:** in one's way

un·der·gar·ment *n* **:** a garment to be worn under another

un·der·go *vb* **un·der·went; un·der·gone; un·der·go·ing :** to have (something) done or happen to oneself **:** EXPERIENCE

¹un·der·ground *adv* **1 :** beneath the surface of the earth **2 :** in or into hiding or secret operation

²un·der·ground *n*   1 : SUBWAY 2   2 : a secret political movement or group

³un·der·ground *adj*   1 : being or growing under the surface of the ground   2 : done or happening secretly

un·der·growth *n* : UNDERBRUSH

¹un·der·hand *adv* : in a secret or dishonest manner

²underhand *adj*   1 : done in secret or so as to deceive   2 : made with an upward movement of the hand or arm

un·der·hand·ed *adj* : ²UNDERHAND 1 — un·der·hand·ed·ly *adv* — un·der·hand·ed·ness *n*

un·der·lie *vb* un·der·lay; un·der·lain; un·der·ly·ing   1 : to be under   2 : to form the foundation of : SUPPORT

un·der·line *vb* un·der·lined; un·der·lin·ing   1 : to draw a line under   2 : EMPHASIZE

un·der·lip *n* : the lower lip

un·der·mine *vb* un·der·mined; un·der·min·ing   1 : to dig out or wear away the supporting earth beneath   2 : to weaken secretly or little by little

¹un·der·neath *prep* : directly under

²underneath *adv*   1 : below a surface or object : BENEATH   2 : on the lower side

un·der·nour·ished *adj* : given too little nourishment — un·der·nour·ish·ment *n*

un·der·pants *n pl* : pants worn under an outer garment

un·der·part *n* : a part lying on the lower side especially of a bird or mammal

un·der·pass *n* : a passage underneath something (as for a road passing under a railroad or another road)

un·der·priv·i·leged *adj* : having fewer advantages than others especially because of being poor

un·der·rate *vb* un·der·rat·ed; un·der·rat·ing : to rate too low : UNDERVALUE

un·der·score *vb* un·der·scored; un·der·scor·ing : UNDERLINE

¹un·der·sea *adj*   1 : being or done under the sea or under the surface of the sea   2 : used under the surface of the sea

²un·der·sea *or* un·der·seas *adv* : under the surface of the sea

un·der·sell *vb* un·der·sold; un·der·sell·ing : to sell articles cheaper than

un·der·shirt *n* : a collarless garment with or without sleeves that is worn next to the body

un·der·side *n* : the side or surface lying underneath

un·der·skirt *n* : PETTICOAT

un·der·stand *vb* un·der·stood; un·der·stand·ing   1 : to get the meaning of   2 : to know thoroughly   3 : to have reason to believe   4 : to take as meaning something not openly made known   5 : to have a sympathetic attitude   6 : to accept as settled

un·der·stand·able *adj* : possible or easy to understand — un·der·stand·ably *adv*

¹un·der·stand·ing *n*   1 : ability to get the meaning of and judge   2 : AGREEMENT 2

²understanding *adj* : having or showing kind or favorable feelings toward others : SYMPATHETIC

un·der·study *n, pl* un·der·stud·ies : an actor who is prepared to take over another actor's part if necessary

un·der·take *vb* un·der·took; un·der·tak·en; un·der·tak·ing   1 : to plan or try to accomplish   2 : to take on as a duty : AGREE

un·der·tak·er *n* : a person whose business is to prepare the dead for burial and to take charge of funerals

un·der·tak·ing *n*   1 : the act of a person who undertakes something   2 : the business of an undertaker   3 : something undertaken

un·der·tone *n*   1 : a low or quiet tone   2 : a partly hidden feeling

un·der·tow *n* : a current beneath the surface of the water that moves away from or along the shore while the surface water above it moves toward the shore

un·der·val·ue *vb* un·der·val·ued; un·der·valu·ing : to value below the real worth

¹un·der·wa·ter *adj* : lying, growing, worn, or operating below the surface of the water

²un·der·wa·ter *adv* : under the surface of the water

un·der·wear *n* : clothing worn next to the skin and under other clothing

un·der·weight *adj* : weighing less than what is normal, average, or necessary

underwent *past of* UNDERGO

un·der·world *n* : the world of organized crime

¹un·de·sir·able *adj* : not desirable — un·de·sir·ably *adv*

²undesirable *n* : an undesirable person

un·de·vel·oped *adj* : not developed

un·di·gest·ed *adj* : not digested

un·dig·ni·fied *adj* : not dignified

un·dis·cov·ered *adj* : not discovered

un·dis·put·ed *adj* : not disputed : UNQUESTIONABLE

un·dis·turbed *adj* : not disturbed

un·do *vb* un·did; un·done; un·do·ing; un·does   1 : UNTIE, UNFASTEN   2 : UNWRAP, OPEN   3 : to destroy the effect of   4 : to cause the ruin of

un·do·ing *n*   1 : an act or instance of unfastening   2 : a cause of ruin or destruction

un·done *adj* : not done or finished

un·doubt·ed *adj* : not doubted

un·doubt·ed·ly *adv* : without doubt : SURELY

un·dress *vb* : to remove the clothes or covering of

un·dy·ing *adj* : living or lasting forever : IMMORTAL

un·earth *vb* **1** : to drive or draw from the earth : dig up **2** : to bring to light : UNCOVER

un·easy *adj* **un·eas·i·er; un·eas·i·est 1** : not easy in manner : AWKWARD **2** : disturbed by pain or worry : RESTLESS — **un·eas·i·ly** *adv* — **un·eas·i·ness** *n*

un·ed·u·cat·ed *adj* : not educated

un·em·ployed *adj* : not employed : having no job

un·em·ploy·ment *n* : the state of being unemployed

un·end·ing *adj* : having no ending : ENDLESS — **un·end·ing·ly** *adv*

un·equal *adj* **1** : not alike (as in size or value) **2** : badly balanced or matched **3** : not having the needed abilities — **un·equal·ly** *adv*

un·equaled *adj* : not equaled

un·even *adj* **1** : ODD 2 **2** : not level or smooth **3** : IRREGULAR 3 **4** : varying in quality **5** : UNEQUAL 2 — **un·even·ly** *adv* — **un·even·ness** *n*

un·event·ful *adj* : not eventful : including no interesting or important happenings — **un·event·ful·ly** *adv*

un·ex·pect·ed *adj* : not expected — **un·ex·pect·ed·ly** *adv* — **un·ex·pect·ed·ness** *n*

un·fail·ing *adj* : not failing or likely to fail — **un·fail·ing·ly** *adv*

un·fair *adj* : not fair, honest, or just — **un·fair·ly** *adv* — **un·fair·ness** *n*

un·faith·ful *adj* : not faithful : DISLOYAL — **un·faith·ful·ly** *adv* — **un·faith·ful·ness** *n*

un·fa·mil·iar *adj* **1** : not well known : STRANGE **2** : not well acquainted

un·fa·mil·iar·i·ty *n* : the quality or state of being unfamiliar

un·fas·ten *vb* : to make or become loose : UNDO

un·fa·vor·able *adj* **1** : not approving **2** : likely to make difficult or unpleasant — **un·fa·vor·ably** *adv*

un·feel·ing *adj* **1** : not able to feel **2** : having no kindness or sympathy : CRUEL — **un·feel·ing·ly** *adv*

un·fin·ished *adj* : not finished

un·fit *adj* **1** : not suitable **2** : not qualified **3** : UNSOUND 1 2 — **un·fit·ness** *n*

un·fledged *adj* : not feathered or ready for flight

un·fold *vb* **1** : to open the folds of : open up **2** : to lay open to view : REVEAL **3** : to develop gradually

un·fore·seen *adj* : not known beforehand

un·for·get·ta·ble *adj* : not likely to be forgotten — **un·for·get·ta·bly** *adv*

un·for·giv·able *adj* : not to be forgiven or pardoned — **un·for·giv·ably** *adv*

1un·for·tu·nate *adj* **1** : not fortunate : UNLUCKY **2** : not proper or suitable — **un·for·tu·nate·ly** *adv*

2unfortunate *n* : an unfortunate person

un·found·ed *adj* : being without a sound basis

un·friend·ly *adj* **un·friend·li·er; un·friend·li·est** : not friendly or favorable : HOSTILE — **un·friend·li·ness** *n*

un·fruit·ful *adj* **1** : not bearing fruit or offspring **2** : not producing a desired result

un·furl *vb* : to open out from a rolled or folded state

un·fur·nished *adj* : not supplied with furniture

un·gain·ly *adj* **un·gain·li·er; un·gain·li·est** : CLUMSY 1, AWKWARD — **un·gain·li·ness** *n*

un·god·ly *adj* **un·god·li·er; un·god·li·est 1** : disobedient to or denying God : IMPIOUS **2** : SINFUL, WICKED **3** : not normal or bearable

un·gra·cious *adj* : not gracious or polite — **un·gra·cious·ly** *adv*

un·grate·ful *adj* : not grateful — **un·grate·ful·ly** *adv* — **un·grate·ful·ness** *n*

1un·gu·late *adj* : having hooves

2ungulate *n* : a hoofed animal

un·hand *vb* : to remove the hand from : let go

un·hap·py *adj* **un·hap·pi·er; un·hap·pi·est 1** : not fortunate : UNLUCKY **2** : not cheerful : SAD **3** : not suitable — **un·hap·pi·ly** *adv* — **un·hap·pi·ness** *n*

un·health·ful *adj* : not healthful

un·healthy *adj* **un·health·i·er; un·health·i·est 1** : not good for one's health **2** : not in good health : SICKLY **3** : HARMFUL, BAD — **un·health·i·ly** *adv*

un·heard *adj* : not heard

un·heard–of *adj* : not known before

un·hin·dered *adj* : not hindered : not kept back

un·hitch *vb* : to free from being hitched

un·ho·ly *adj* **un·ho·li·er; un·ho·li·est 1** : not holy : WICKED **2** : UNGODLY 3 — **un·ho·li·ness** *n*

un·hook *vb* **1** : to remove from a hook **2** : to unfasten the hooks of

un·horse *vb* **un·horsed; un·hors·ing** : to cause to fall from or as if from a horse

un·hur·ried *adj* : not hurried

uni- *prefix* : one : single

uni·corn *n* : an imaginary animal that looks like a horse with one horn in the middle of the forehead

un·iden·ti·fied *adj* : not identified

uni·fi·ca·tion *n* : the act, process, or result of unifying : the state of being unified

¹uni·form *adj* **1** : having always the same form, manner, or degree : not changing **2** : of the same form with others — **uni·form·ly** *adv*

²uniform *n* : special clothing worn by members of a particular group (as an army)

uni·formed *adj* : dressed in uniform

uni·for·mi·ty *n*, *pl* **uni·for·mi·ties** : the quality or state or an instance of being uniform

uniform resource lo·ca·tor *n* : URL

uni·fy *vb* **uni·fied; uni·fy·ing** : to make into or become a unit : UNITE

un·im·por·tant *adj* : not important

un·in·hab·it·ed *adj* : not lived in or on

un·in·tel·li·gi·ble *adj* : impossible to understand

un·in·ten·tion·al *adj* : not intentional — **un·in·ten·tion·al·ly** *adv*

un·in·ter·est·ed *adj* : not interested

un·in·ter·est·ing *adj* : not attracting interest or attention

un·in·ter·rupt·ed *adj* : not interrupted : CONTINUOUS

union *n* **1** : an act or instance of uniting two or more things into one **2** : something (as a nation) formed by a combining of parts or members **3** : a device for connecting parts (as of a machine) **4** : LABOR UNION

Union *adj* : of or relating to the side favoring the federal union in the American Civil War

unique *adj* **1** : being the only one of its kind **2** : very unusual — **unique·ly** *adv* — **unique·ness** *n*

uni·son *n* **1** : sameness of musical pitch **2** : the state of being tuned or sounded at the same pitch or at an octave **3** : exact agreement

unit *n* **1** : the least whole number : ONE **2** : a fixed quantity (as of length, time, or value) used as a standard of measurement **3** : a single thing, person, or group forming part of a whole **4** : a part of a school course with a central theme

unite *vb* **unit·ed; unit·ing** **1** : to put or come together to form a single unit **2** : to bind by legal or moral ties **3** : to join in action

unit·ed *adj* **1** : made one **2** : being in agreement

uni·ty *n* **1** : the quality or state of being one **2** : the state of those who are in full agreement : HARMONY

uni·ver·sal *adj* **1** : including, covering, or taking in all or everything **2** : present or happening everywhere — **uni·ver·sal·ly** *adv*

universal resource lo·ca·tor *n* : URL

uni·verse *n* : all created things including the earth and celestial bodies viewed as making up one system

uni·ver·si·ty *n*, *pl* **uni·ver·si·ties** : an institution of higher learning that gives degrees in special fields (as law and medicine) as well as in the arts and sciences

un·just *adj* : not just : UNFAIR — **un·just·ly** *adv*

un·kempt *adj* **1** : not combed **2** : not neat and orderly : UNTIDY

un·kind *adj* : not kind or sympathetic — **un·kind·ly** *adv* — **un·kind·ness** *n*

¹un·known *adj* : not known

²unknown *n* : one (as a quantity) that is unknown

un·lace *vb* **un·laced; un·lac·ing** : to untie the laces of

un·latch *vb* : to open by lifting a latch

un·law·ful *adj* : not lawful : ILLEGAL — **un·law·ful·ly** *adv*

un·learned *adj* **1** : not educated **2** : not based on experience : INSTINCTIVE

un·leash *vb* : to free from or as if from a leash

un·less *conj* : except on the condition that

¹un·like *adj* : DIFFERENT, UNEQUAL — **un·like·ness** *n*

²unlike *prep* **1** : different from **2** : unusual for **3** : differently from

un·like·ly *adj* **un·like·li·er; un·like·li·est** **1** : not likely **2** : not promising — **un·like·li·ness** *n*

un·lim·it·ed *adj* **1** : having no restrictions or controls **2** : BOUNDLESS, INFINITE

un·load *vb* **1** : to take away or off : REMOVE **2** : to take a load from **3** : to get rid of or be freed from a load or burden

un·lock *vb* **1** : to unfasten the lock of **2** : to make known

un·looked–for *adj* : not expected

un·loose *vb* **un·loosed; un·loos·ing** **1** : to make looser : RELAX **2** : to set free

un·lucky *adj* **un·luck·i·er; un·luck·i·est** **1** : not fortunate **2** : likely to bring misfortune **3** : causing distress or regret — **un·luck·i·ly** *adv* — **un·luck·i·ness** *n*

un·man·age·able *adj* : hard or impossible to manage

un·man·ner·ly *adj* : not having or showing good manners

un·mar·ried *adj* : not married

un·mis·tak·able *adj* : impossible to mistake for anything else — **un·mis·tak·ably** *adv*

un·moved *adj* **1** : not moved by deep feelings or excitement : CALM **2** : staying in the same place or position

un·nat·u·ral *adj* **1** : not natural or normal **2** : ARTIFICIAL **3** : causing distress or regret — **un·nat·u·ral·ly** *adv* — **un·nat·u·ral·ness** *n*

un·nec·es·sary *adj* : not necessary — **un·nec·es·sar·i·ly** *adv*

un·nerve *vb* **un·nerved; un·nerv·ing** : to

cause to lose confidence, courage, or self-control

un·no·tice·able *adj* : not easily noticed

un·num·bered *adj* **1** : not numbered **2** : INNUMERABLE

un·ob·served *adj* : not observed

un·oc·cu·pied *adj* **1** : not busy **2** : not occupied : EMPTY

un·of·fi·cial *adj* : not official — **un·of·fi·cial·ly** *adv*

un·pack *vb* **1** : to separate and remove things that are packed **2** : to open and remove the contents of

un·paid *adj* : not paid

un·paint·ed *adj* : not painted

un·par·al·leled *adj* : having no parallel or equal

un·pleas·ant *adj* : not pleasant — **un·pleas·ant·ly** *adv* — **un·pleas·ant·ness** *n*

un·pop·u·lar *adj* : not popular

un·pre·dict·able *adj* : impossible to predict

un·prej·u·diced *adj* : not prejudiced

un·pre·pared *adj* : not prepared

un·prin·ci·pled *adj* : not having or showing high moral principles

un·ques·tion·able *adj* : being beyond question or doubt — **un·ques·tion·ably** *adv*

un·rav·el *vb* **un·rav·eled** *or* **un·rav·elled**; **un·rav·el·ing** *or* **un·rav·el·ling** **1** : to separate the threads of : UNTANGLE **2** : SOLVE

un·re·al *adj* : not real

un·rea·son·able *adj* : not reasonable — **un·rea·son·able·ness** *n* — **un·rea·son·ably** *adv*

un·re·lent·ing *adj* **1** : not giving in or softening in determination : STERN **2** : not letting up or weakening in energy or pace — **un·re·lent·ing·ly** *adv*

un·re·li·able *adj* : not reliable

un·rest *n* : a disturbed or uneasy state

un·righ·teous *adj* : not righteous — **un·righ·teous·ly** *adv* — **un·righ·teous·ness** *n*

un·ripe *adj* : not ripe or mature

un·ri·valed *or* **un·ri·valled** *adj* : having no rival

un·roll *vb* **1** : to unwind a roll of **2** : to become unrolled

un·ruf·fled *adj* **1** : not upset or disturbed **2** : ¹SMOOTH 4

un·ruly *adj* **un·rul·i·er**; **un·rul·i·est** : not yielding easily to rule or restriction — **un·rul·i·ness** *n*

un·safe *adj* : exposed or exposing to danger

un·san·i·tary *adj* : not sanitary

un·sat·is·fac·to·ry *adj* : not satisfactory — **un·sat·is·fac·to·ri·ly** *adv*

un·sat·is·fied *adj* : not satisfied

un·say *vb* **un·said**; **un·say·ing** : to take back (something said)

un·schooled *adj* : not trained or taught

un·sci·en·tif·ic *adj* : not scientific — **un·sci·en·tif·i·cal·ly** *adv*

un·scram·ble *vb* **un·scram·bled**; **un·scram·bling** : to make orderly or clear again

un·screw *vb* **1** : to remove the screws from **2** : to loosen or withdraw by turning

un·scru·pu·lous *adj* : not scrupulous — **un·scru·pu·lous·ly** *adv*

un·seal *vb* : to break or remove the seal of : OPEN

un·sea·son·able *adj* : happening or coming at the wrong time — **un·sea·son·ably** *adv*

un·sea·soned *adj* : not made ready or fit for use (as by the passage of time)

un·seat *vb* **1** : to throw from one's seat **2** : to remove from a position of authority

un·seem·ly *adj* **un·seem·li·er**; **un·seem·li·est** : not polite or proper

un·seen *adj* : not seen : INVISIBLE

un·self·ish *adj* : not selfish — **un·self·ish·ly** *adv* — **un·self·ish·ness** *n*

un·set·tle *vb* **un·set·tled**; **un·set·tling** : to disturb the quiet or order of : UPSET

un·set·tled *adj* **1** : not staying the same **2** : not calm **3** : not able to make up one's mind : DOUBTFUL **4** : not paid **5** : not taken over and lived in by settlers

un·shaped *adj* : imperfect especially in form

un·sheathe *vb* **un·sheathed**; **un·sheath·ing** : to draw from or as if from a sheath

un·sight·ly *adj* : not pleasant to look at : UGLY — **un·sight·li·ness** *n*

un·skilled *adj* **1** : not skilled **2** : not needing skill

un·skill·ful *adj* : not skillful : not having skill — **un·skill·ful·ly** *adv*

un·sound *adj* **1** : not healthy or in good condition **2** : being or having a mind that is not normal **3** : not firmly made or placed **4** : not fitting or true — **un·sound·ly** *adv* — **un·sound·ness** *n*

un·speak·able *adj* **1** : impossible to express in words **2** : extremely bad — **un·speak·ably** *adv*

un·spec·i·fied *adj* : not specified

un·spoiled *adj* : not spoiled

un·sta·ble *adj* : not stable

un·steady *adj* **un·stead·i·er**; **un·stead·i·est** : not steady : UNSTABLE — **un·stead·i·ly** *adv*

un·stressed *adj* : not stressed

un·suc·cess·ful *adj* : not successful — **un·suc·cess·ful·ly** *adv*

un·sup·port·ed *adj* **1** : not supported or proved **2** : not held up

un·sur·passed *adj* : not surpassed (as in excellence)

un·sus·pect·ing *adj* : having no suspicion : TRUSTING

un·tan·gle *vb* **un·tan·gled; un·tan·gling 1** : to remove a tangle from **2** : to straighten out

un·tanned *adj* : not put through a tanning process

un·think·able *adj* : not to be thought of or considered as possible

un·think·ing *adj* : not taking thought : HEEDLESS

un·ti·dy *adj* **un·ti·di·er; un·ti·di·est** : not neat — **un·ti·di·ly** *adv* — **un·ti·di·ness** *n*

un·tie *vb* **un·tied; un·ty·ing** *or* **un·tie·ing** : to free from something that ties, fastens, or holds back

¹un·til *prep* : up to the time of

²until *conj* : up to the time that

¹un·time·ly *adv* : before a good or proper time

²untimely *adj* **1** : happening or done before the expected, natural, or proper time **2** : coming at the wrong time — **un·time·li·ness** *n*

un·tir·ing *adj* : not making or becoming tired : TIRELESS — **un·tir·ing·ly** *adv*

un·to *prep* : ¹TO

un·told *adj* **1** : not told or made public **2** : not counted : VAST

un·to·ward *adj* : causing trouble or unhappiness : UNLUCKY

un·trou·bled *adj* : not troubled : free from worry

un·true *adj* **1** : not faithful : DISLOYAL **2** : not correct : FALSE — **un·tru·ly** *adv*

un·truth *n* **1** : the state of being false **2** : ³LIE

un·truth·ful *adj* : not containing or telling the truth : FALSE — **un·truth·ful·ly** *adv* — **un·truth·ful·ness** *n*

un·used *adj* **1** : not accustomed **2** : not having been used before **3** : not being used

un·usu·al *adj* : not usual — **un·usu·al·ly** *adv*

un·ut·ter·able *adj* : being beyond one's powers of description

un·veil *vb* : to show or make known to the public for the first time

un·voiced *adj* : VOICELESS

un·want·ed *adj* : not wanted

un·wary *adj* **un·war·i·er; un·war·i·est** : easily fooled or surprised — **un·war·i·ness** *n*

un·washed *adj* : not having been washed : DIRTY

un·wea·ried *adj* : not tired

un·well *adj* : being in poor health

un·whole·some *adj* : not good for bodily, mental, or moral health

un·wieldy *adj* : hard to handle or control because of size or weight — **un·wield·i·ness** *n*

un·will·ing *adj* : not willing — **un·will·ing·ly** *adv* — **un·will·ing·ness** *n*

un·wind *vb* **un·wound; un·wind·ing 1** : UNROLL **2** : RELAX 3

un·wise *adj* : not wise : FOOLISH — **un·wise·ly** *adv*

un·wor·thy *adj* **un·wor·thi·er; un·wor·thi·est** : not worthy — **un·wor·thi·ly** *adv* — **un·wor·thi·ness** *n*

un·wrap *vb* **un·wrapped; un·wrap·ping** : to remove the wrapping from

un·writ·ten *adj* : not in writing : followed by custom

un·yield·ing *adj* **1** : not soft or flexible : HARD **2** : showing or having firmness or determination

¹up *adv* **1** : in or to a higher position : away from the center of the earth **2** : from beneath a surface (as ground or water) **3** : from below the horizon **4** : in or into a vertical position **5** : out of bed **6** : with greater force **7** : in or into a better or more advanced state **8** : so as to make more active **9** : into being or knowledge **10** : for discussion **11** : into the hands of another **12** : COMPLETELY **13** — used to show completeness **14** : into storage **15** : so as to be closed **16** : so as to approach or arrive **17** : in or into pieces **18** : to a stop

²up *adj* **1** : risen above the horizon or ground **2** : being out of bed **3** : unusually high **4** : having been raised or built **5** : moving or going upward **6** : being on one's feet and busy **7** : well prepared **8** : going on **9** : at an end **10** : well informed

³up *prep* **1** : to, toward, or at a higher point of **2** : to or toward the beginning of **3** : ¹ALONG 1

⁴up *n* : a period or state of doing well

⁵up *vb* **upped; up·ping 1** : to act suddenly or surprisingly **2** : to make or become higher

up·beat *n* : a beat in music that is not accented and especially one just before a downbeat

up·braid *vb* : to criticize or scold severely

up·bring·ing *n* : the process of raising and training

up·com·ing *adj* : coming soon

up·draft *n* : an upward movement of gas (as air)

up·end *vb* : to set, stand, or rise on end

up·grade *vb* **up·grad·ed; up·grad·ing** : to raise to a higher grade or position

up·heav·al *n* : a period of great change or violent disorder

¹up·hill *adv* **1** : in an upward direction **2** : against difficulties

²up·hill *adj* **1** : going up **2** : DIFFICULT 1

up·hold *vb* **up·held; up·hold·ing 1 :** to give support to **2 :** to lift up

up·hol·ster *vb* **:** to provide with or as if with upholstery — **up·hol·ster·er** *n*

up·hol·stery *n*, *pl* **up·hol·ster·ies :** materials used to make a soft covering for a seat

up·keep *n* **:** the act or cost of keeping something in good condition

up·land *n* **:** high land usually far from a coast or sea

¹up·lift *vb* **1 :** to lift up **2 :** to improve the moral, mental, or bodily condition of

²up·lift *n* **:** an act, process, or result of uplifting

up·on *prep* **:** ¹ON 1, 2, 3, 4, 8

¹up·per *adj* **1 :** higher in position or rank **2 :** farther inland

²upper *n* **:** something (as the parts of a shoe above the sole) that is upper

upper hand *n* **:** ADVANTAGE 1

up·per·most *adj* **1 :** farthest up **2 :** being in the most important position

up·raise *vb* **up·raised; up·rais·ing :** to raise or lift up

¹up·right *adj* **1 :** VERTICAL 2 **2 :** straight in posture **3 :** having or showing high moral standards — **up·right·ly** *adv* — **up·right·ness** *n*

²upright *n* **1 :** the state of being upright **2 :** something that is upright

up·rise *vb* **up·rose; up·ris·en; up·ris·ing :** ¹RISE 1, 2a, 7

up·ris·ing *n* **:** REBELLION

up·roar *n* **:** a state of commotion, excitement, or violent disturbance

up·root *vb* **1 :** to take out by or as if by pulling up by the roots **2 :** to take, send, or force away from a country or a traditional home

¹up·set *vb* **up·set; up·set·ting 1 :** to force or be forced out of the usual position **:** OVERTURN **2 :** to worry or make unhappy **3 :** to make somewhat ill **4 :** to cause confusion in **5 :** to defeat unexpectedly

²up·set *n* **:** an act or result of upsetting **:** a state of being upset

up·shot *n* **:** the final result

up·side *n* **:** the upper side or part

up·side down *adv* **1 :** in such a way that the upper part is underneath and the lower part is on top **2 :** in or into great confusion

upside–down *adj* **1 :** having the upper part underneath and the lower part on top **2 :** showing great confusion

¹up·stairs *adv* **:** up the stairs **:** on or to an upper floor

²up·stairs *adj* **:** being on or relating to an upper floor

³up·stairs *n* **:** the part of a building above the ground floor

up·stand·ing *adj* **:** HONEST 2

up·start *n* **:** a person who gains quick or unexpected success and who makes a great show of pride in that success

up·stream *adv* **:** at or toward the beginning of a stream

up·swing *n* **:** a great increase or rise

up to *prep* **1 :** as far as **2 :** in accordance with **3 :** to the limit of

up–to–date *adj* **1 :** lasting up to the present time **2 :** knowing, being, or making use of what is new or recent

up·town *adv* **:** to, toward, or in what is thought of as the upper part of a town or city

¹up·turn *vb* **:** to turn upward or up or over

²up·turn *n* **:** an upward turning

¹up·ward *or* **up·wards** *adv* **1 :** in a direction from lower to higher **2 :** toward a higher or better state **3 :** toward a greater amount or a higher number or rate

²upward *adj* **:** turned toward or being in a higher place or level — **up·ward·ly** *adv*

up·wind *adv or adj* **:** in the direction from which the wind is blowing

ura·ni·um *n* **:** a radioactive metallic chemical element used as a source of atomic energy

Ura·nus *n* **:** the planet that is seventh in order of distance from the sun and has a diameter of about 47,000 kilometers

ur·ban *adj* **:** of, relating to, or being a city

ur·chin *n* **1 :** a mischievous or disrespectful youngster **2 :** SEA URCHIN

-ure *suffix* **1 :** act **:** process **2 :** office **:** duty **3 :** body performing an office or duty

urea *n* **:** a compound of nitrogen that is the chief solid substance dissolved in the urine of a mammal and is formed by the breaking down of protein

¹urge *vb* **urged; urg·ing 1 :** to try to get (something) accepted **:** argue in favor of **2 :** to try to convince **3 :** ²FORCE 1, DRIVE

²urge *n* **:** a strong desire

ur·gen·cy *n* **:** the quality or state of being urgent

ur·gent *adj* **1 :** calling for immediate action **2 :** having or showing a sense of urgency — **ur·gent·ly** *adv*

uri·nal *n* **1 :** a container for urine **2 :** a place for urinating

uri·nary *adj* **:** of or relating to urine or the organs producing it

uri·nate *vb* **uri·nat·ed; uri·nat·ing :** to discharge urine

uri·na·tion *n* **:** the act of urinating

urine *n* **:** the yellowish liquid produced by the kidneys and given off from the body as waste

URL *n* **:** the address of a computer or a document on the Internet

urn *n* **1** : a container usually in the form of a vase resting on a stand **2** : a closed container with a faucet used for serving a hot beverage

us *pron objective case of* WE

us·able *adj* : suitable or fit for use

us·age *n* **1** : usual way of doing things **2** : the way in which words and phrases are actually used **3** : the action of using : USE

¹use *n* **1** : the act of using something **2** : the fact or state of being used **3** : way of using **4** : the ability or power to use something **5** : the quality or state of being useful **6** : a reason or need to use **7** : LIKING

²use *vb* **used; us·ing** **1** : to put into action or service : make use of **2** : to take into the body **3** : to do something by means of **4** : to behave toward : TREAT **5** — used with *to* to show a former custom, fact, or state — **us·er** *n*

used *adj* **1** : SECONDHAND 1 **2** : having the habit of doing or putting up with something

use·ful *adj* : that can be put to use : USABLE — **use·ful·ly** *adv* — **use·ful·ness** *n*

use·less *adj* : being of or having no use — **use·less·ly** *adv* — **use·less·ness** *n*

us·er–friend·ly *adj* : easy to learn, use, understand, or deal with — **user–friendli·ness** *n*

¹ush·er *n* : a person who shows people to seats (as in a theater)

²usher *vb* **1** : to show to a place as an usher **2** : to come before as if to lead in or announce

usu·al *adj* : done, found, used or existing most of the time — **usu·al·ly** *adv*

usurp *vb* : to take and hold unfairly or by force — **usurp·er** *n*

uten·sil *n* **1** : a tool or container used in a home and especially a kitchen **2** : a useful tool

uter·us *n, pl* **uteri** : the organ of a female mammal in which the young develop before birth

util·i·ty *n, pl* **util·i·ties** **1** : the quality or state of being useful **2** : a business that supplies a public service (as electricity or gas) under special regulation by the government

uti·li·za·tion *n* : the action of utilizing : the state of being utilized

uti·lize *vb* **uti·lized; uti·liz·ing** : to make use of especially for a certain job

¹ut·most *adj* : of the greatest or highest degree or amount

²utmost *n* : the most possible

¹ut·ter *adj* : in every way : TOTAL — **ut·ter·ly** *adv*

²utter *vb* **1** : to send forth as a sound **2** : to express in usually spoken words

ut·ter·ance *n* : something uttered

V

v *n, pl* **v's** *or* **vs** *often cap* **1** : the twenty-second letter of the English alphabet **2** : five in Roman numerals

va·can·cy *n, pl* **va·can·cies** **1** : something (as an office or hotel room) that is vacant **2** : empty space **3** : the state of being vacant

va·cant *adj* **1** : not filled, used, or lived in **2** : free from duties or care **3** : showing a lack of thought : FOOLISH

va·cate *vb* **va·cat·ed; va·cat·ing** : to leave vacant

¹va·ca·tion *n* **1** : a period during which activity (as of a school) is stopped for a time **2** : a period spent away from home or business in travel or amusement

²vacation *vb* : to take or spend a vacation — **va·ca·tion·er** *n*

vac·ci·nate *vb* **vac·ci·nat·ed; vac·ci·nat·ing** : to inoculate with weak germs in order to protect against a disease

vac·ci·na·tion *n* **1** : the act of vaccinating **2** : the scar left by vaccinating

vac·cine *n* : a material (as one containing killed or weakened bacteria or virus) used in vaccinating

vac·il·late *vb* **vac·il·lat·ed; vac·il·lat·ing** : to hesitate between courses or opinions : be unable to choose

¹vac·u·um *n, pl* **vac·u·ums** *or* **vac·ua** **1** : a space completely empty of matter **2** : a space from which most of the air has been removed (as by a pump) **3** : VACUUM CLEANER

²vacuum *adj* : of, containing, producing, or using a partial vacuum

³vacuum *vb* : to use a vacuum cleaner on

vacuum bottle *n* : THERMOS

vacuum cleaner *n* : an electrical appliance for cleaning (as floors or rugs) by suction

vacuum tube *n* : an electron tube having a high vacuum

¹vag·a·bond *adj* : moving from place to place without a fixed home

²vagabond *n* : a person who leads a vagabond life

va·gi·na *n* : a canal leading out from the uterus

¹**va·grant** *n* : a person who has no steady job and wanders from place to place

²**vagrant** *adj* **1** : wandering about from place to place **2** : having no fixed course

vague *adj* **vagu·er; vagu·est 1** : not clearly expressed **2** : not clearly understood **3** : not clearly outlined : SHADOWY — **vague·ly** *adv* — **vague·ness** *n*

vain *adj* **1** : having no success **2** : proud of one's looks or abilities — **vain·ly** *adv* — **in vain 1** : without success **2** : in an unholy way

vain·glo·ri·ous *adj* : being vain and boastful — **vain·glo·ri·ous·ly** *adv* — **vain·glo·ri·ous·ness** *n*

vain·glo·ry *n* : too much pride especially in what one has done

vale *n* : VALLEY

val·e·dic·to·ri·an *n* : a student usually of the highest standing in a class who gives the farewell speech at the graduation ceremonies

val·en·tine *n* **1** : a sweetheart given something as a sign of affection on Saint Valentine's Day **2** : a greeting card or gift sent or given on Saint Valentine's Day

va·let *n* : a male servant or hotel employee who takes care of a man's clothes and does personal services

val·iant *adj* **1** : boldly brave **2** : done with courage : HEROIC — **val·iant·ly** *adv*

val·id *adj* **1** : legally binding **2** : based on truth or fact — **val·id·ly** *adv*

val·i·date *vb* **val·i·dat·ed; val·i·dat·ing** : to make valid

va·lid·i·ty *n* : the quality or state of being valid

va·lise *n* : TRAVELING BAG

val·ley *n, pl* **valleys** : an area of lowland between ranges of hills or mountains

val·or *n* : COURAGE

val·or·ous *adj* : having or showing valor : BRAVE — **val·or·ous·ly** *adv*

¹**valu·able** *adj* **1** : worth a large amount of money **2** : of great use or service

²**valuable** *n* : a personal possession (as a jewel) of great value

¹**val·ue** *n* **1** : a fair return in goods, services, or money for something exchanged **2** : worth in money **3** : worth, usefulness, or importance in comparison with something else **4** : a principle or quality that is valuable or desirable — **val·ue·less** *adj*

²**value** *vb* **val·ued; val·u·ing 1** : to estimate the worth of **2** : to think highly of

valve *n* **1** : a structure in a tube of the body (as a vein) that closes temporarily to prevent passage of material or allows movement of a fluid in one direction only **2** : a mechanical device by which the flow of liquid, gas, or loose material may be controlled by a movable part **3** : a device on a brass musical instrument that changes the pitch of the tone **4** : one of the separate pieces that make up the shell of some animals (as clams) and are often hinged — **valve·less** *adj*

vam·pire *n* : the body of a dead person believed to come from the grave at night and suck the blood of sleeping persons

vampire bat *n* : a bat of tropical America that feeds on the blood of birds and mammals often including domestic animals

¹**van** *n* : VANGUARD

²**van** *n* : a usually closed wagon or truck for moving goods or animals

va·na·di·um *n* : a metallic chemical element used in making a strong alloy of steel

van·dal *n* : a person who destroys or damages property on purpose

van·dal·ism *n* : intentional destruction of or damage to property

vane *n* **1** : WEATHER VANE **2** : a flat or curved surface that turns around a center when moved by wind or water

van·guard *n* **1** : the troops moving at the front of an army **2** : FOREFRONT

va·nil·la *n* : a substance extracted from vanilla beans and used as a flavoring for sweet foods and beverages

vanilla bean *n* : the long pod of a tropical American climbing orchid from which vanilla is extracted

van·ish *vb* : to pass from sight or existence : DISAPPEAR

van·i·ty *n, pl* **van·i·ties 1** : something that is vain **2** : the quality or fact of being vain **3** : a small box for cosmetics

van·quish *vb* : OVERCOME 1

va·por *n* **1** : fine bits (as of fog or smoke) floating in the air and clouding it **2** : a substance in the form of a gas

va·por·ize *vb* **va·por·ized; va·por·iz·ing** : to turn from a liquid or solid into vapor — **va·por·iz·er** *n*

¹**var·i·able** *adj* **1** : able to change : likely to be changed : CHANGEABLE **2** : having differences **3** : not true to type — **var·i·able·ness** *n* — **var·i·ably** *adv*

²**variable** *n* **1** : something that is variable **2** : PLACEHOLDER

var·i·ant *n* **1** : an individual that shows variation from a type **2** : one of two or more different spellings or pronunciations of a word

var·i·a·tion *n* **1** : a change in form, position, or condition **2** : amount of change or difference **3** : departure from what is usual to a group

var·ied *adj* **1** : having many forms or types **2** : VARIEGATED 2

var·ie·gat·ed *adj* **1** : having patches, stripes, or marks of different colors **2** : full of variety

va·ri·ety *n, pl* **va·ri·et·ies** **1** : the quality or state of having different forms or types **2** : a collection of different things : ASSORTMENT **3** : something differing from others of the class to which it belongs **4** : entertainment made up of performances (as dances and songs) that follow one another and are not related

var·i·ous *adj* **1** : of different kinds **2** : different one from another : UNLIKE **3** : made up of an indefinite number greater than one

¹var·nish *n* : a liquid that is spread on a surface and dries into a hard coating

²varnish *vb* : to cover with or as if with varnish

var·si·ty *n, pl* **var·si·ties** : the main team that represents a college, school, or club in contests

vary *vb* **var·ied; vary·ing** **1** : to make a partial change in **2** : to make or be of different kinds **3** : DEVIATE **4** : to differ from the usual members of a group

vas·cu·lar *adj* : of, relating to, containing, or being bodily vessels

vase *n* : an often round container of greater depth than width used chiefly for ornament or for flowers

vas·sal *n* : a person in the Middle Ages who received protection and land from a lord in return for loyalty and service

vast *adj* : very great in size or amount — **vast·ly** *adv* — **vast·ness** *n*

vat *n* : a large container (as a tub) especially for holding liquids in manufacturing processes

vaude·ville *n* : theatrical entertainment made up of songs, dances, and comic acts

¹vault *n* **1** : an arched structure of stone or concrete forming a ceiling or roof **2** : an arch suggesting a vault **3** : a room or compartment for storage or safekeeping **4** : a burial chamber

²vault *vb* : to leap with the aid of the hands or a pole

³vault *n* : ²LEAP

VCR *n* : a device for recording (as television programs) on videocassettes and playing them back

veal *n* : a young calf or its flesh for use as meat

vec·tor *n* : a creature (as a fly) that carries disease germs

vee·jay *n* : an announcer of a program (as on television) that features music videos

veer *vb* : to change direction or course

vee·ry *n, pl* **veeries** : a common brownish woodland thrush of the eastern United States

¹veg·e·ta·ble *adj* **1** : of, relating to, or made up of plants **2** : gotten from plants

²vegetable *n* **1** : ²PLANT 1 **2** : a plant or plant part grown for use as human food and usually eaten with the main part of a meal

veg·e·tar·i·an *n* : a person who lives on plants and their products

veg·e·ta·tion *n* : plant life or cover (as of an area)

veg·e·ta·tive *adj* **1** : of, relating to, or functioning in nutrition and growth rather than reproduction **2** : of, relating to, or involving reproduction by other than sexual means

ve·he·mence *n* : the quality or state of being vehement

ve·he·ment *adj* **1** : showing great force or energy **2** : highly emotional — **ve·he·ment·ly** *adv*

ve·hi·cle *n* **1** : a means by which something is expressed, achieved, or shown **2** : something used to transport persons or goods

¹veil *n* **1** : a piece of cloth or net worn usually by women over the head and shoulders and sometimes over the face **2** : something that covers or hides like a veil

²veil *vb* : to cover or provide with a veil

vein *n* **1** : a long narrow opening in rock filled with mineral matter **2** : one of the blood vessels that carry the blood back to the heart **3** : one of the bundles of fine tubes that make up the framework of a leaf and carry food, water, and nutrients in the plant **4** : one of the thickened parts that support the wing of an insect **5** : a streak of different color or texture (as in marble) **6** : a style of expression — **veined** *adj*

veld *or* **veldt** *n* : an area of grassy land especially in southern Africa

ve·loc·i·ty *n, pl* **ve·loc·i·ties** : quickness of motion : SPEED

¹vel·vet *n* : a fabric with short soft raised fibers

²velvet *adj* **1** : made of or covered with velvet **2** : VELVETY

vel·vety *adj* : soft and smooth like velvet

ve·na·tion *n* : an arrangement or system of veins

vend *vb* : to sell or offer for sale — **vend·er** *or* **ven·dor** *n*

vending machine *n* : a machine for selling merchandise operated by putting a coin or coins into a slot

¹ve·neer *n* **1** : a thin layer of wood bonded to other wood usually to provide a finer surface or a stronger structure **2** : a protective or ornamental facing (as of brick)

²veneer *vb* : to cover with a veneer

ven·er·a·ble *adj* **1** : deserving to be venerated — often used as a religious title **2** : deserving honor or respect

ven·er·ate *vb* **ven·er·at·ed; ven·er·at·ing** : to show deep respect for

ven·er·a·tion *n* **1** : the act of venerating : the state of being venerated **2** : a feeling of deep respect

ve·ne·re·al *adj* : of or relating to sexual intercourse or to diseases that pass from person to person by it

ve·ne·tian blind *n* : a blind having thin horizontal slats that can be adjusted to keep out light or to let light come in between them

ven·geance *n* : punishment given in return for an injury or offense

ven·i·son *n* : the flesh of a deer used as food

ven·om *n* : poisonous matter produced by an animal (as a snake) and passed to a victim usually by a bite or sting

ven·om·ous *adj* : having or producing venom : POISONOUS

ve·nous *adj* : of, relating to, or full of veins

¹vent *vb* **1** : to provide with an outlet **2** : to serve as an outlet for **3** : ³EXPRESS 1

²vent *n* **1** : OUTLET 1, 2 **2** : an opening for the escape of a gas or liquid

ven·ti·late *vb* **ven·ti·lat·ed; ven·ti·lat·ing 1** : to discuss freely and openly **2** : to let in air and especially a current of fresh air **3** : to provide with ventilation

ven·ti·la·tion *n* **1** : the act or process of ventilating **2** : a system or means of providing fresh air

ven·ti·la·tor *n* : a device for letting in fresh air or driving out bad or stale air

ven·tral *adj* : of, relating to, or being on or near the surface of the body that in man is the front but in most animals is the lower surface

ven·tri·cle *n* : the part of the heart from which blood passes into the arteries

ven·tril·o·quist *n* : a person skilled in speaking in such a way that the voice seems to come from a source other than the speaker

¹ven·ture *vb* **ven·tured; ven·tur·ing 1** : to expose to risk **2** : to face the risks and dangers of **3** : to offer at the risk of being criticized **4** : to go ahead in spite of danger

²venture *n* : a task or an act involving chance, risk, or danger

ven·ture·some *adj* **1** : tending to take risks **2** : involving risk — **ven·ture·some·ly** *adv* — **ven·ture·some·ness** *n*

ven·tur·ous *adj* : VENTURESOME — **ven·tur·ous·ly** *adv* — **ven·tur·ous·ness** *n*

Ve·nus *n* : the planet that is second in order of distance from the sun and has a diameter of about 12,200 kilometers

ve·ran·da *or* **ve·ran·dah** *n* : a long porch extending along one or more sides of a building

verb *n* : a word that expresses an act, occurrence, or state of being

¹ver·bal *adj* **1** : of, relating to, or consisting of words **2** : of, relating to, or formed from a verb **3** : spoken rather than written — **ver·bal·ly** *adv*

²verbal *n* : a word that combines characteristics of a verb with those of a noun or adjective

ver·be·na *n* : a garden plant with fragrant leaves and heads of white, pink, red, blue, or purple flowers with five petals

ver·dant *adj* : green with growing plants — **ver·dant·ly** *adv*

ver·dict *n* **1** : the decision reached by a jury **2** : JUDGMENT 2, OPINION

ver·dure *n* : green vegetation

¹verge *n* **1** : something that borders, limits, or bounds : EDGE **2** : THRESHOLD 2, BRINK

²verge *vb* **verged; verg·ing** : to come near to being

ver·i·fi·ca·tion *n* : the act or process of verifying : the state of being verified

ver·i·fy *vb* **ver·i·fied; ver·i·fy·ing 1** : to prove to be true or correct : CONFIRM **2** : to check or test the accuracy of

ver·mi·cel·li *n* : a food similar to but thinner than spaghetti

ver·min *n, pl* **vermin** : small common harmful or objectionable animals (as fleas or mice) that are difficult to get rid of

ver·sa·tile *adj* **1** : able to do many different kinds of things **2** : having many uses

ver·sa·til·i·ty *n* : the quality or state of being versatile

verse *n* **1** : a line of writing in which words are arranged in a rhythmic pattern **2** : writing in which words are arranged in a rhythmic pattern **3** : STANZA **4** : one of the short parts of a chapter in the Bible

versed *adj* : having knowledge or skill as a result of experience, study, or practice

ver·sion *n* **1** : a translation especially of the Bible **2** : an account or description from a certain point of view

ver·sus *prep* : AGAINST 1

ver·te·bra *n, pl* **ver·te·brae** : one of the bony sections making up the backbone

¹ver·te·brate *adj* **1** : having vertebrae or a backbone **2** : of or relating to the vertebrates

²vertebrate *n* : any of a large group of animals that includes the fishes, amphibians, reptiles, birds, and mammals all of which have a backbone extending down the back of the body

ver·tex *n, pl* **ver·ti·ces** *or* **ver·tex·es 1** : the point opposite to and farthest from the base of a geometrical figure **2** : the common endpoint of the sides of an angle

1ver·ti·cal *adj* **1** : directly overhead **2** : rising straight up and down from a level surface — **ver·ti·cal·ly** *adv*

2vertical *n* : something (as a line or plane) that is vertical

ver·ti·go *n, pl* **ver·ti·goes** *or* **ver·ti·gos** : a dizzy state

1very *adj* **1** : 2EXACT, PRECISE **2** : exactly suitable or necessary **3** : MERE, BARE **4** : exactly the same

2very *adv* **1** : to a great degree : EXTREMELY **2** : in actual fact : TRULY

ves·pers *n pl, often cap* : a late afternoon or evening church service

ves·sel *n* **1** : a hollow utensil (as a cup or bowl) for holding something **2** : a craft larger than a rowboat for navigation of the water **3** : a tube (as an artery) in which a body fluid is contained and carried or circulated

1vest *vb* **1** : to place or give into the possession or control of some person or authority **2** : to clothe in vestments

2vest *n* : a sleeveless garment usually worn under a suit coat

ves·ti·bule *n* : a hall or room between the outer door and the inside part of a building

ves·tige *n* : a tiny amount or visible sign of something lost or vanished : TRACE

ves·ti·gial *adj* : of, relating to, or being a vestige

vest·ment *n* : an outer garment especially for wear during ceremonies or by an official

1vet *n* : VETERINARIAN

2vet *n* : 1VETERAN 2

1vet·er·an *n* **1** : a person who has had long experience **2** : a former member of the armed forces especially in war

2veteran *adj* : having gained skill through experience

vet·er·i·nar·i·an *n* : a doctor who treats diseases and injuries of animals

1vet·er·i·nary *adj* : of, relating to, or being the medical care of animals and especially domestic animals

2veterinary *n, pl* **vet·er·i·nar·ies** : VETERINARIAN

1ve·to *n, pl* **vetoes** **1** : a forbidding of something by a person in authority **2** : the power of a president, governor, or mayor to prevent something from becoming law

2veto *vb* **1** : FORBID, PROHIBIT **2** : to prevent from becoming law by use of a veto

vex *vb* **1** : to bring trouble, distress, or worry to **2** : to annoy by small irritations

vex·a·tion *n* **1** : the quality or state of being

vexed **2** : the act of vexing **3** : a cause of trouble or worry

via *prep* : by way of

vi·a·ble *adj* **1** : capable of living or growing **2** : possible to use or apply

via·duct *n* : a bridge for carrying a road or railroad over something (as a gorge or highway)

vi·al *n* : a small container (as for medicines) that is usually made of glass or plastic

vi·brant *adj* : having or giving the sense of life, vigor, or action — **vi·brant·ly** *adv*

vi·brate *vb* **vi·brat·ed; vi·brat·ing** : to swing or cause to swing back and forth

vi·bra·tion *n* **1** : a rapid motion (as of a stretched cord) back and forth **2** : the action of vibrating : the state of being vibrated **3** : a trembling motion

vi·bur·num *n* : any of a group of shrubs often grown for their broad clusters of usually white flowers

vic·ar *n* **1** : a minister in charge of a church who serves under the authority of another minister **2** : a church official who takes the place of or represents a higher official

vi·car·i·ous *adj* : experienced or understood as if happening to oneself — **vi·car·i·ous·ly** *adv* — **vi·car·i·ous·ness** *n*

vice *n* **1** : evil conduct or habits **2** : a moral fault or weakness

vice- *prefix* : one that takes the place of

vice admiral *n* : a commissioned officer in the Navy or Coast Guard ranking above a rear admiral

vice pres·i·dent *n* : an official (as of a government) whose rank is next below that of the president and who takes the place of the president when necessary

vice·roy *n* : the governor of a country who rules as the representative of a king or queen

vice ver·sa *adv* : with the order turned around

vi·cin·i·ty *n, pl* **vi·cin·i·ties** **1** : the state of being close **2** : a surrounding area : NEIGHBORHOOD

vi·cious *adj* **1** : doing evil things : WICKED **2** : very dangerous **3** : filled with or showing unkind feelings — **vi·cious·ly** *adv* — **vi·cious·ness** *n*

vic·tim *n* **1** : a living being offered as a religious sacrifice **2** : an individual injured or killed (as by disease) **3** : a person who is cheated, fooled, or hurt by another

vic·tim·ize *vb* **vic·tim·ized; vic·tim·iz·ing** : to make a victim of

vic·tor *n* : WINNER, CONQUEROR

vic·to·ri·ous *adj* : having won a victory — **vic·to·ri·ous·ly** *adv*

vic·to·ry *n, pl* **vic·to·ries** **1** : the defeating of an enemy or opponent **2** : success in a struggle against difficulties

vict·ual n **1** : food fit for humans **2 vict·uals** pl : supplies of food

vi·cu·ña or **vi·cu·na** n : a wild animal of the Andes that is related to the llama and produces a fine wool

¹vid·eo n **1** : TELEVISION **2** : the visual part of television **3** : ¹VIDEOTAPE 1 **4** : a videotaped performance of a song

²video adj **1** : relating to or used in the sending or receiving of television images **2** : being, relating to, or involving images on a television screen or computer display

vid·eo·cas·sette n **1** : a case containing videotape for use with a VCR **2** : a recording (as of a movie) on a videocassette

videocassette recorder n : VCR

video game n : a game played with images on a video screen

¹vid·eo·tape n **1** : a recording of visual images and sound (as of a television production) made on magnetic tape **2** : the magnetic tape used for such a recording

²videotape vb : to make a videotape of

vie vb **vied; vy·ing** : COMPETE

¹view n **1** : the act of seeing or examining **2** : an opinion or judgment influenced by personal feeling **3** : all that can be seen from a certain place : SCENE **4** : range of vision **5** : ¹PURPOSE **6** : a picture that represents something that can be seen

²view vb **1** : to look at carefully **2** : ¹SEE 1 — **view·er** n

view·point n : the angle from which something is considered

vig·il n **1** : the day before a religious feast **2** : a staying awake to keep watch when one normally would be sleeping

vig·i·lance n : a staying alert especially to possible danger

vig·i·lant adj : alert especially to avoid danger — **vig·i·lant·ly** adv

vig·i·lan·te n : a member of a group of volunteers organized to stop crime and punish criminals especially when the proper officials are not doing so

vig·or n **1** : strength or energy of body or mind **2** : active strength or force

vig·or·ous adj **1** : having vigor **2** : done with vigor — **vig·or·ous·ly** adv

Vi·king n : a member of the Scandinavian invaders of the coasts of Europe in the eighth to tenth centuries

vile adj **vil·er; vil·est 1** : of little worth **2** : WICKED 1 **3** : very objectionable — **vile·ly** adv — **vile·ness** n

vil·i·fy vb **vil·i·fied; vil·i·fy·ing** : to speak of as worthless or wicked

vil·la n **1** : an estate in the country **2** : a large expensive home especially in the country or suburbs

vil·lage n : a place where people live that is usually smaller than a town

vil·lag·er n : a person who lives in a village

vil·lain n : a wicked person

vil·lainy n, pl **vil·lain·ies** : conduct or actions of or like those of a villain

vil·lus n, pl **vil·li** : one of the tiny extensions that are shaped like fingers, line the small intestine, and are active in absorbing nutrients

vim n : ENERGY 1, VIGOR

vin·di·cate vb **vin·di·cat·ed; vin·di·cat·ing 1** : to free from blame or guilt **2** : to show to be true or correct : JUSTIFY

vin·dic·tive adj **1** : likely to seek revenge : meant to be harmful

vine n : a plant whose stem requires support and which climbs by tendrils or twining or creeps along the ground — **vine·like** adj

vin·e·gar n : a sour liquid made from cider, wine, or malt and used to flavor or preserve foods

vin·e·gary adj : like vinegar

vine·yard n : a field of grapevines

vin·tage n **1** : the grapes grown or wine made during one season **2** : a usually excellent wine of a certain type, region, and year **3** : the time when something started or was made

¹vi·o·la n : a hybrid garden flower that looks like but is smaller than a pansy

²vi·o·la n : an instrument of the violin family slightly larger and having a lower pitch than a violin

vi·o·late vb **vi·o·lat·ed; vi·o·lat·ing 1** : to fail to keep : BREAK **2** : to do harm or damage to **3** : to treat in a very disrespectful way **4** : DISTURB 1 — **vi·o·la·tor** n

vi·o·la·tion n : an act or instance of violating : the state of being violated

vi·o·lence n **1** : the use of force to harm a person or damage property **2** : great force or strength

vi·o·lent adj **1** : showing very strong force **2** : ¹EXTREME 1, INTENSE **3** : caused by force — **vi·o·lent·ly** adv

vi·o·let n **1** : a wild or garden plant related to the pansies that has small often fragrant white, blue, purple, or yellow flowers **2** : a reddish blue

vi·o·lin n : a stringed musical instrument with four strings that is usually held against the shoulder under the chin and played with a bow

vi·o·lon·cel·lo n, pl **vi·o·lon·cel·los** : CELLO

vi·per n : a snake that is or is believed to be poisonous

vir·eo n, pl **vir·e·os** : a small songbird that

eats insects and is olive-green or grayish in color

¹vir·gin *n* **1** : an unmarried woman devoted to religion **2** : a girl or woman who has not had sexual intercourse

²virgin *adj* **1** : not soiled **2** : being a virgin **3** : not changed by human actions

Vir·go *n* **1** : a constellation between Leo and Libra imagined as a woman **2** : the sixth sign of the zodiac or a person born under this sign

vir·ile *adj* **1** : having qualities generally associated with a man **2** : ENERGETIC, VIGOROUS

vir·tu·al *adj* : being almost but not quite complete — **vir·tu·al·ly** *adv*

virtual reality *n* : an artificial environment which is experienced through sights and sounds provided by a computer and in which one's actions partly decide what happens in the environment

vir·tue *n* **1** : moral excellence : knowing what is right and acting in a right way **2** : a desirable quality

vir·tu·o·so *n, pl* **vir·tu·o·sos** *or* **vir·tu·o·si** : a person who is an outstanding performer especially in music

vir·tu·ous *adj* : having or showing virtue — **vir·tu·ous·ly** *adv*

vir·u·lent *adj* : very infectious or poisonous : DEADLY

vi·rus *n* **1** : an agent too tiny to be seen by the ordinary microscope that causes disease and that may be a living organism or may be a very special kind of protein molecule **2** : a disease caused by a virus **3** : a usually hidden computer program that causes harm by making copies of itself and inserting them into other programs

vis·count *n* : a British nobleman ranking below an earl and above a baron

vis·count·ess *n* **1** : the wife or widow of a viscount **2** : a woman who holds the rank of a viscount in her own right

vise *n* : a device with two jaws that works by a screw or lever for holding or clamping work

vis·i·bil·i·ty *n* **1** : the quality or state of being visible **2** : the degree of clearness of the atmosphere

vis·i·ble *adj* **1** : capable of being seen **2** : easily seen or understood : OBVIOUS — **vis·i·bly** *adv*

vi·sion *n* **1** : something seen in the mind (as in a dream) **2** : a vivid picture created by the imagination **3** : the act or power of imagination **4** : unusual ability to think or plan ahead **5** : the act or power of seeing : SIGHT **6** : the special sense by which the qualities of an object (as color) that make up its appearance are perceived

vi·sion·ary *n, pl* **vi·sion·ar·ies** : a person whose ideas or plans are impractical

¹vis·it *vb* **1** : to go to see in order to comfort or help **2** : to call on as an act of friendship or courtesy or as or for a professional service **3** : to stay with for a time as a guest **4** : to go to for pleasure **5** : to come to or upon

²visit *n* **1** : a brief stay : CALL **2** : a stay as a guest **3** : a professional call

vis·i·tor *n* : a person who visits

vi·sor *n* **1** : the movable front upper piece of a helmet **2** : a part that sticks out to protect or shade the eyes

vis·ta *n* : a distant view through an opening or along an avenue

vi·su·al *adj* **1** : of, relating to, or used in vision **2** : obtained by the use of sight **3** : appealing to the sense of sight — **vi·su·al·ly** *adv*

vi·su·al·ize *vb* **vi·su·al·ized; vi·su·al·iz·ing** : to see or form a mental image

vi·tal *adj* **1** : of or relating to life **2** : concerned with or necessary to the continuation of life **3** : full of life and energy **4** : very important — **vi·tal·ly** *adv*

vi·tal·i·ty *n, pl* **vi·tal·i·ties** **1** : capacity to live and develop **2** : ENERGY 1

vi·tals *n pl* : the vital organs (as heart, lungs, and liver) of the body

vi·ta·min *n* : any of a group of organic substances that are found in natural foods, are necessary in small quantities to health, and include one (**vitamin A**) found mostly in animal products and needed for good vision, several (**vitamin B complex**) found in many foods and needed especially for growth, one (**vitamin C**) found in fruits and leafy vegetables and used as an enzyme and to prevent scurvy, and another (**vitamin D**) found in fish-liver oils, eggs, and milk and needed for healthy bone development

vi·va·cious *adj* : full of life : LIVELY — **vi·va·cious·ly** *adv*

vi·vac·i·ty *n* : the quality or state of being vivacious

vi·var·i·um *n, pl* **vi·var·ia** *or* **vi·var·i·ums** : an enclosure for keeping or studying plants or animals indoors

viv·id *adj* **1** : seeming full of life and freshness **2** : very strong or bright **3** : producing strong mental images **4** : acting clearly and powerfully — **viv·id·ly** *adv* — **viv·id·ness** *n*

vi·vip·a·rous *adj* : giving birth to living young rather than laying eggs

viv·i·sec·tion *n* : the operating or experimenting on a living animal usually for scientific study

vix·en *n* : a female fox

vo·cab·u·lary *n, pl* **vo·cab·u·lar·ies** **1** : a

list or collection of words defined or explained **2** : a stock of words used in a language, by a group or individual, or in relation to a subject

vo·cal *adj* **1** : uttered by the voice : ORAL **2** : composed or arranged for or sung by the human voice **3** : of, relating to, or having the power of producing voice — **vo·cal·ly** *adv*

vocal cords *n pl* : membranes at the top of the windpipe that produce vocal sounds when drawn tight and vibrated by the outgoing breath

vo·cal·ist *n* : SINGER

vo·ca·tion *n* **1** : a strong desire for a certain career or course of action **2** : the work in which a person is regularly employed : OCCUPATION

vo·ca·tion·al *adj* **1** : of, relating to, or concerned with a vocation **2** : concerned with choice of or training in a vocation — **vo·ca·tion·al·ly** *adv*

vod·ka *n* : a colorless alcoholic liquor

vogue *n* **1** : the quality or state of being popular at a certain time **2** : a period in which something is in fashion **3** : something that is in fashion at a certain time

¹voice *n* **1** : sound produced through the mouth by vertebrates and especially by human beings in speaking or shouting **2** : musical sound produced by the vocal cords **3** : SPEECH 5 **4** : a sound similar to vocal sound **5** : a means of expression **6** : the right to express a wish, choice, or opinion

²voice *vb* **voiced; voic·ing** : to express in words

voice box *n* : LARYNX

voiced *adj* : spoken with vibration of the vocal cords

voice·less *adj* : spoken without vibration of the vocal cords

voice mail *n* : an electronic communication system in which spoken messages are recorded to be played back later

¹void *adj* : containing nothing : EMPTY

²void *n* : empty space

vol·a·tile *adj* **1** : easily becoming a vapor at a fairly low temperature **2** : likely to change suddenly

vol·ca·nic *adj* **1** : of or relating to a volcano **2** : likely to explode

vol·ca·no *n, pl* **vol·ca·noes** *or* **vol·ca·nos** **1** : an opening in the earth's crust from which hot or melted rock and steam come **2** : a hill or mountain composed of material thrown out in a volcanic eruption

vole *n* : any of various small rodents that look like fat mice or rats with short tails and are sometimes harmful to crops

vo·li·tion *n* : the act or power of making one's own choices or decisions : WILL

¹vol·ley *n, pl* **volleys** **1** : a group of missiles (as arrows or bullets) passing through the air **2** : a firing of a number of weapons (as rifles) at the same time **3** : a bursting forth of many things at once **4** : the act of volleying

²volley *vb* **vol·leyed; vol·ley·ing** **1** : to shoot in a volley **2** : to hit an object (as a ball) while it is in the air before it touches the ground

vol·ley·ball *n* : a game played by volleying a large ball filled with air across a net

volt *n* : a unit for measuring the force that moves an electric current

volt·age *n* : electric force measured in volts

vol·u·ble *adj* : having a smooth and fast flow of words in speaking — **vol·u·bly** *adv*

vol·ume *n* **1** : ¹BOOK 1 **2** : any one of a series of books that together form a complete work or collection **3** : space included within limits as measured in cubic units **4** : ²AMOUNT **5** : the degree of loudness of a sound

vo·lu·mi·nous *adj* **1** : of great volume or bulk **2** : filling or capable of filling a large volume or several volumes

vol·un·tary *adj* **1** : done, given, or made of one's own free will or choice **2** : not accidental : INTENTIONAL **3** : of, relating to, or controlled by the will — **vol·un·tar·i·ly** *adv*

¹vol·un·teer *n* **1** : a person who volunteers for a service **2** : a plant growing without direct human care especially from seeds lost from a previous crop

²volunteer *adj* : of, relating to, or done by volunteers

³volunteer *vb* **1** : to offer or give without being asked **2** : to offer oneself for a service of one's own free will

¹vom·it *n* : material from the stomach gotten rid of through the mouth

²vomit *vb* : to rid oneself of the contents of the stomach through the mouth

vo·ra·cious *adj* **1** : greedy in eating **2** : very eager — **vo·ra·cious·ly** *adv*

¹vote *n* **1** : a formal expression of opinion or will (as by ballot) **2** : the decision reached by voting **3** : the right to vote **4** : the act or process of voting **5** : a group of voters with some common interest or quality

²vote *vb* **vot·ed; vot·ing** **1** : to express one's wish or choice by or as if by a vote **2** : to elect, decide, pass, defeat, grant, or make legal by a vote **3** : to declare by general agreement

vot·er *n* : a person who votes or who has the legal right to vote

vouch *vb* : to give a guarantee

vouch·safe *vb* **vouch·safed; vouch·saf·ing** : to grant as a special favor

¹**vow** *n* : a solemn promise or statement

²**vow** *vb* : to make a vow : SWEAR

vow·el *n* **1** : a speech sound (as \ə\, \ā\, or \ȯ\) produced without obstruction or audible friction in the mouth **2** : a letter (as *a, e, i, o, u*) representing a vowel

¹**voy·age** *n* : a journey especially by water from one place or country to another

²**voyage** *vb* **voy·aged; voy·ag·ing** : to take a trip — **voy·ag·er** *n*

vul·ca·nize *vb* **vul·ca·nized; vul·ca·niz·ing** : to treat rubber with chemicals in order to give it useful properties (as strength)

vul·gar *adj* **1** : of or relating to the common people **2** : having poor taste or manners : COARSE **3** : offensive in language

vul·gar·i·ty *n, pl* **vul·gar·i·ties 1** : the quality or state of being vulgar **2** : a vulgar expression or action

vul·ner·a·ble *adj* **1** : possible to wound or hurt **2** : open to attack or damage — **vul·ner·a·bly** *adv*

vul·ture *n* : a large bird related to the hawks and eagles that has a naked head and feeds mostly on animals found dead

vying *present participle of* VIE

W

w *n, pl* **w's** *or* **ws** *often cap* : the twenty-third letter of the English alphabet

wacky *or* **whacky** *adj* **wack·i·er** *or* **whack·i·er; wack·i·est** *or* **whack·i·est** : CRAZY 2, INSANE

¹**wad** *n* **1** : a small mass or lump **2** : a soft plug or stopper to hold a charge of powder (as in cartridges) **3** : a soft mass of cotton, cloth, or fibers used as a plug or pad

²**wad** *vb* **wad·ded; wad·ding** : to form into a wad

¹**wad·dle** *vb* **wad·dled; wad·dling** : to walk with short steps swaying like a duck

²**waddle** *n* : a waddling walk

wade *vb* **wad·ed; wad·ing 1** : to walk through something (as water or snow) that makes it hard to move **2** : to proceed with difficulty **3** : to pass or cross by stepping through water

wading bird *n* : a shorebird or waterbird with long legs that wades in water in search of food

wa·fer *n* : a thin crisp cake or cracker

waf·fle *n* : a crisp cake of batter baked in a waffle iron

waffle iron *n* : a cooking utensil with two hinged metal parts that come together for making waffles

waft *vb* : to move or be moved lightly by or as if by the action of waves or wind

¹**wag** *vb* **wagged; wag·ging** : to swing to and fro or from side to side

²**wag** *n* **1** : a wagging movement **2** : a person full of jokes and humor

¹**wage** *n* **1** : payment for work done especially when figured by the hour or day **2 wages** *sing or pl* : something given or received in return : REWARD

²**wage** *vb* **waged; wag·ing** : to engage in : CARRY ON

¹**wa·ger** *n* **1** : ¹BET 1 **2** : the act of betting

²**wager** *vb* : to bet on the result of a contest or question — **wa·ger·er** *n*

wag·gish *adj* : showing or done in a spirit of harmless mischief

wag·gle *vb* **wag·gled; wag·gling** : to move backward and forward or from side to side

wag·on *n* : a vehicle having four wheels and used for carrying goods

waif *n* : a stray person or animal

¹**wail** *vb* : to utter a mournful cry

²**wail** *n* : a long cry of grief or pain

wain·scot *n* : the bottom part of an inside wall especially when made of material different from the rest

wain·scot·ing *or* **wain·scot·ting** *n* : WAINSCOT

waist *n* **1** : the part of the body between the chest and the hips **2** : the central part of a thing when it is narrower or thinner than the rest **3** : a garment or part of a garment covering the body from the neck to the waist

¹**wait** *vb* **1** : to stay in a place looking forward to something that is expected to happen **2** : to serve food as a waiter or waitress **3** : ²DELAY 1

²**wait** *n* **1** : ²AMBUSH — used chiefly in the expression *lie in wait* **2** : an act or period of waiting

wait·er *n* : a man who serves food to people at tables (as in a restaurant)

waiting room *n* : a room for the use of persons waiting (as for a train)

wait·ress *n* : a girl or woman who serves food to people at tables

waive *vb* **waived; waiv·ing** : to give up claim to

¹**wake** *vb* **waked** *or* **woke; waked** *or* **woken; wak·ing 1** : to be or stay awake **2** : to stay awake on watch especially over a corpse **3** : ¹AWAKE 1

²**wake** *n* : a watch held over the body of a dead person before burial

³**wake** *n* : a track or mark left by something moving especially in the water

wake·ful adj 1 : VIGILANT 2 : not sleeping or able to sleep — **wake·ful·ness** n

wak·en vb : [1]AWAKE 1

[1]**walk** vb 1 : to move or cause to move along on foot at a natural slow pace 2 : to cover or pass over at a walk 3 : to go or cause to go to first base after four balls in baseball — **walk·er** n

[2]**walk** n 1 : a going on foot 2 : a place or path for walking 3 : distance to be walked often measured in time required by a walker to cover 4 : position in life or the community 5 : way of walking 6 : an opportunity to go to first base after four balls in baseball

walking stick n 1 : a stick used in walking 2 : a sticklike insect with a long round body and long thin legs

walk·out n 1 : a labor strike 2 : the leaving of a meeting or organization as a way of showing disapproval

walk·over n : an easy victory

[1]**wall** n 1 : a solid structure (as of stone) built to enclose or shut off a space 2 : something like a wall that separates one thing from another 3 : a layer of material enclosing space — **walled** adj

[2]**wall** vb : to build a wall in or around

wall·board n : a building material (as of wood pulp) made in large stiff sheets and used especially for inside walls and ceilings

wal·let n : a small flat case for carrying paper money and personal papers

wall·eye n : a large strong American freshwater sport and food fish that is related to the perches but looks like a pike

[1]**wal·lop** vb : to hit hard

[2]**wallop** n : a hard blow

[1]**wal·low** vb 1 : to roll about in or as if in deep mud 2 : to be too much interested or concerned with

[2]**wallow** n : a muddy or dust-filled hollow where animals wallow

wall·pa·per n : decorative paper for covering the walls of a room

wal·nut n : the edible nut (as the American **black walnut** with a rough shell or the Old World **English walnut** with a smoother shell) that comes from trees related to the hickories and including some valued also for their wood

wal·rus n : a large animal of northern seas related to the seals and hunted for its hide, for the ivory tusks of the males, and for oil

[1]**waltz** n : a dance in which couples glide to music having three beats to a measure

[2]**waltz** vb : to dance a waltz — **waltz·er** n

wam·pum n : beads made of shells and once used for money or ornament by North American Indians

wan adj **wan·ner; wan·nest** : having a pale or sickly color — **wan·ly** adv — **wan·ness** n

wand n : a slender rod (as one carried by a fairy or one used by a magician in doing tricks)

wan·der vb 1 : to move about without a goal or purpose : RAMBLE 2 : to follow a winding course 3 : to get off the right path : STRAY — **wan·der·er** n

wan·der·lust n : a strong wish or urge to travel

wane vb **waned; wan·ing** 1 : to grow smaller or less 2 : to lose power or importance : DECLINE

[1]**want** vb 1 : to be without : LACK 2 : to feel or suffer the need of something 3 : to desire, wish, or long for something

[2]**want** n 1 : [2]LACK 2, SHORTAGE 2 : the state of being very poor 3 : a wish for something : DESIRE

want·ing adj : falling below a standard, hope, or need

wan·ton adj 1 : PLAYFUL 1 2 : not modest or proper : INDECENT 3 : showing no thought or care for the rights, feelings, or safety of others — **wan·ton·ly** adv — **wan·ton·ness** n

[1]**war** n 1 : a state or period of fighting between states or nations 2 : the art or science of warfare 3 : a struggle between opposing forces

[2]**war** vb **warred; war·ring** : to make war : FIGHT

[1]**war·ble** n 1 : low pleasing sounds that form a melody (as of a bird) 2 : the action of warbling

[2]**warble** vb **war·bled; war·bling** : to sing with a warble

war·bler n 1 : any of a group of Old World birds related to the thrushes and noted for their musical song 2 : any of a group of brightly colored American migratory songbirds that eat insects and have a weak call

[1]**ward** n 1 : a part of a hospital 2 : one of the parts into which a town or city is divided for management 3 : a person under the protection of a guardian

[2]**ward** vb 1 : to keep watch over : GUARD 2 : to turn aside

[1]**-ward** also **-wards** adj suffix 1 : that moves, faces, or is pointed toward 2 : that is found in the direction of

[2]**-ward** or **-wards** adv suffix 1 : in a specified direction 2 : toward a specified place

war·den n 1 : a person who sees that certain laws are followed 2 : the chief official of a prison

ward·robe n 1 : a room or closet where clothes are kept 2 : the clothes a person owns

ware *n* **1** : manufactured articles or products of art or craft **2** : items (as dishes) of baked clay : POTTERY

ware·house *n, pl* **ware·hous·es** : a building for storing goods and merchandise

war·fare *n* **1** : military fighting between enemies **2** : strong continued effort : STRUGGLE

war·like *adj* **1** : fond of war **2** : of or relating to war **3** : threatening war

¹warm *adj* **1** : somewhat hot **2** : giving off heat **3** : making a person feel heat or experience no loss of bodily heat **4** : having a feeling of warmth **5** : showing strong feeling **6** : newly made : FRESH **7** : near the object sought **8** : of a color in the range yellow through orange to red — **warm·ly** *adv*

²warm *vb* **1** : to make or become warm **2** : to give a feeling of warmth **3** : to become more interested than at first

warm–blood·ed *adj* **1** : able to keep up a body temperature that is independent of that of the surroundings **2** : warm in feeling — **warm–blood·ed·ness** *n*

warmth *n* **1** : gentle heat **2** : strong feeling

warm–up *n* : the act or an instance of warming up

warm up *vb* **1** : to exercise or practice lightly in preparation for more strenuous activity or a performance **2** : to run (as a motor) at slow speed before using

warn *vb* **1** : to put on guard : CAUTION **2** : to notify especially in advance

warn·ing *n* : something that warns

¹warp *n* **1** : the threads that go lengthwise in a loom and are crossed by the woof **2** : a twist or curve that has developed in something once flat or straight

²warp *vb* **1** : to curve or twist out of shape **2** : to cause to judge, choose, or act wrongly

war·path *n* : the route taken by a group of American Indians going off to fight — **on the warpath** : ready to fight or argue

war·plane *n* : a military or naval airplane

¹war·rant *n* **1** : a reason or cause for an opinion or action **2** : a document giving legal power

²warrant *vb* **1** : to be sure of or that **2** : ²GUARANTEE 2 **3** : to call for : JUSTIFY

warrant officer *n* **1** : an officer in the armed forces in one of the grades between commissioned officers and enlisted persons **2** : a warrant officer of the lowest rank

war·ren *n* : a place for keeping or raising small game (as rabbits)

war·rior *n* : a person who is or has been in warfare

war·ship *n* : a ship armed for combat

wart *n* : a small hard lump of thickened skin

warty *adj* **wart·i·er; wart·i·est** **1** : covered with or as if with warts **2** : like a wart

wary *adj* **war·i·er; war·i·est** : very cautious — **war·i·ly** *adv* — **war·i·ness** *n*

was *past 1st & 3d sing of* BE

¹wash *vb* **1** : to cleanse with water and usually a cleaning agent (as soap) **2** : to wet completely with liquid **3** : to flow along or overflow against **4** : to remove by the action of water **5** : to stand washing without injury

²wash *n* **1** : articles (as of clothing) in the laundry **2** : the flow, sound, or action of water **3** : a backward flow of water (as made by the motion of a boat) **4** : material carried or set down by water

wash·able *adj* : capable of being washed without damage

wash·board *n* : a grooved board to scrub clothes on

wash·bowl *n* : a large bowl for water to wash one's hands and face

wash·er *n* **1** : WASHING MACHINE **2** : a ring (as of metal) used to make something fit tightly or to prevent rubbing

wash·ing *n* : ²WASH 1

washing machine *n* : a machine used especially for washing clothes and household linen

wash·out *n* **1** : the washing away of earth (as from a road) **2** : a place where earth is washed away **3** : a complete failure

wash·tub *n* : a tub for washing clothes or for soaking them before washing

wasn't : was not

wasp *n* : a winged insect related to the bees and ants that has a slender body with the abdomen attached by a narrow stalk and that in females and workers is capable of giving a very painful sting

wasp·ish *adj* : ³CROSS 3, IRRITABLE — **wasp·ish·ly** *adv* — **wasp·ish·ness** *n*

¹waste *n* **1** : ¹DESERT, WILDERNESS **2** : WASTELAND **3** : the action of wasting : the state of being wasted **4** : material left over or thrown away **5** : material produced in and of no further use to the living body

²waste *vb* **wast·ed; wast·ing** **1** : to bring to ruin **2** : to spend or use carelessly or uselessly **3** : to lose or cause to lose weight, strength, or energy

³waste *adj* **1** : being wild and not lived in or planted to crops : BARREN **2** : of no further use

waste·bas·ket *n* : an open container for odds and ends to be thrown away

waste·ful *adj* **1** : wasting or causing waste **2** : spending or using in a careless or foolish way — **waste·ful·ly** *adv* — **waste·ful·ness** *n*

waste·land *n* : land that is barren or not fit for crops

¹watch *vb* **1** : to stay awake **2** : to be on one's guard **3** : to take care of : TEND **4** : to be on the lookout **5** : to keep one's eyes on — **watch·er** *n*

²watch *n* **1** : an act of keeping awake to guard or protect **2** : close observation **3** : ¹GUARD 2 **4** : the time during which one is on duty to watch **5** : a small timepiece to be worn or carried

watch·dog *n* : a dog kept to watch and guard property

watch·ful *adj* : ATTENTIVE 1, VIGILANT — **watch·ful·ly** *adv* — **watch·ful·ness** *n*

watch·man *n, pl* **watch·men** : a person whose job is to watch and guard property at night or when the owners are away

watch·tow·er *n* : a tower on which a guard or watchman is placed

watch·word *n* : PASSWORD

¹wa·ter *n* **1** : the liquid that comes from the clouds as rain and forms streams, lakes, and seas **2** : a liquid that contains or is like water **3** : a body of water or a part of a body of water

²water *vb* **1** : to wet or supply with water **2** : to add water to **3** : to fill with liquid (as tears)

wa·ter·bird *n* : a swimming or wading bird

water buffalo *n* : a common oxlike work animal of Asia

water clock *n* : a device or machine for measuring time by the fall or flow of water

wa·ter·col·or *n* **1** : a paint whose liquid part is water **2** : a picture painted with watercolor **3** : the art of painting with watercolor

wa·ter·course *n* **1** : a channel in which water flows **2** : a stream of water (as a river or brook)

wa·ter·cress *n* : a plant related to the mustards that grows in cold flowing waters and is used especially in salads

wa·ter·fall *n* : a fall of water from a height

water flea *n* : a small active often brightly colored freshwater animal related to the crabs and lobsters

wa·ter·fowl *n* **1** : a bird that is found in or near water **2** **waterfowl** *pl* : swimming birds (as wild ducks and geese) hunted as game

wa·ter·front *n* : land or a section of a town that borders on a body of water

water hyacinth *n* : a floating water plant that often blocks streams in the southern United States

water lily *n* : any of a group of water plants with rounded floating leaves and showy often fragrant flowers with many petals

wa·ter·line *n* : any of several lines marked on the outside of a ship that match the surface of the water when the ship floats evenly

wa·ter·logged *adj* : so filled or soaked with water as to be heavy or hard to manage

wa·ter·mark *n* **1** : a mark that shows a level to which water has risen **2** : a mark made in paper during manufacture and visible when the paper is held up to the light

wa·ter·mel·on *n* : a large edible fruit with a hard outer layer and a sweet red juicy pulp

water moccasin *n* : MOCCASIN 2

water polo *n* : a ball game played in water by teams of swimmers

wa·ter·pow·er *n* : the power of moving water used to run machinery

¹wa·ter·proof *adj* : not letting water through

²waterproof *vb* : to make waterproof

wa·ter·shed *n* **1** : a dividing ridge (as a mountain range) separating one drainage area from others **2** : the whole area that drains into a lake or river

wa·ter·spout *n* **1** : a pipe for carrying off water from a roof **2** : a slender cloud that is shaped like a funnel and extends down to a cloud of spray torn up from the surface of a body of water by a whirlwind

water strid·er *n* : a bug with long legs that skims over the surface of water

wa·ter·tight *adj* : so tight as to be waterproof

wa·ter·way *n* : a channel or a body of water by which ships can travel

wa·ter·wheel *n* : a wheel turned by a flow of water against it

wa·ter·works *n pl* : a system of dams, reservoirs, pumps, and pipes for supplying water (as to a city)

wa·tery *adj* **1** : of or relating to water **2** : full of or giving out liquid **3** : being like water **4** : being soft and soggy

watt *n* : a unit for measuring electric power

wat·tle *n* : a fleshy flap of skin that hangs from the throat (as of a bird)

¹wave *vb* **waved; wav·ing** **1** : to move like a wave **2** : to move (as one's hand) to and fro as a signal or in greeting **3** : to curve like a wave or series of waves

²wave *n* **1** : a moving ridge on the surface of water **2** : a shape like a wave or series of waves **3** : something that swells and dies away **4** : a waving motion **5** : a rolling movement passing along a surface or through the air **6** : a motion that is somewhat like a wave in water and transfers energy from point to point

wave·length *n* : the distance in the line of advance of a wave from any one point to the next similar point

wave·let *n* : a little wave

wa·ver *vb* **1** : to sway one way and the other

2 : to be uncertain in opinion 3 : to move unsteadily

wavy *adj* **wav·i·er; wav·i·est** : like, having, or moving in waves — **wav·i·ness** *n*

¹wax *n* 1 : a dull yellow sticky substance made by bees and used in building honeycomb : BEESWAX 2 : a substance like beeswax

²wax *vb* : to treat with wax

³wax *vb* 1 : to grow larger or stronger 2 : BECOME 1, GROW

wax bean *n* : a string bean with yellow waxy pods

wax·en *adj* : of or like wax

wax myrtle *n* : the bayberry shrub

wax·wing *n* : a crested mostly brown bird having smooth feathers (as the American cedar waxwing with yellowish belly)

waxy *adj* **wax·i·er; wax·i·est** 1 : being like wax 2 : made of or covered with wax

¹way *n* 1 : a track for travel : PATH, STREET 2 : the course traveled from one place to another : ROUTE 3 : a course of action 4 : personal choice as to situation or behavior : WISH 5 : the manner in which something is done or happens 6 : a noticeable point 7 : ¹STATE 1 8 : ¹DISTANCE 1 9 : progress along a course 10 : a special or personal manner of behaving 11 : NEIGHBORHOOD 1, DISTRICT 12 : room to advance or pass 13 : CATEGORY, KIND

²way *adv* : ¹FAR 1

way·far·er *n* : a traveler especially on foot

way·lay *vb* **way·laid; way·lay·ing** : to attack from hiding

-ways *adv suffix* : in such a way, direction, or manner

way·side *n* : the edge of a road

way·ward *adj* 1 : DISOBEDIENT 2 : opposite to what is wished or hoped for

we *pron* : I and at least one other

weak *adj* 1 : lacking strength of body, mind, or spirit 2 : not able to stand much strain or force 3 : easily overcome 4 : not able to function well 5 : not rich in some usual or important element 6 : lacking experience or skill 7 : of, relating to, or being the lightest of three levels of stress in pronunciation

weak·en *vb* : to make or become weak or weaker

weak·fish *n* : any of several sea fishes related to the perches (as a common sport and market fish of the eastern coast of the United States)

weak·ling *n* : a person or animal that is weak

¹weak·ly *adv* : in a weak manner

²weakly *adj* **weak·li·er; weak·li·est** : not strong or healthy

weak·ness *n* 1 : lack of strength 2 : a weak point : FLAW

wealth *n* 1 : a large amount of money or possessions 2 : a great amount or number

wealthy *adj* **wealth·i·er; wealth·i·est** : having wealth : RICH

wean *vb* 1 : to get a child or young animal used to food other than its mother's milk 2 : to turn one away from desiring a thing one has been fond of

weap·on *n* : something (as a gun, knife, or club) to fight with

¹wear *vb* **wore; worn; wear·ing** 1 : to use as an article of clothing or decoration 2 : to carry on the body 3 : ¹SHOW 1 4 : to damage, waste, or make less by use or by scraping or rubbing 5 : to make tired 6 : to cause or make by rubbing 7 : to last through long use — **wear·er** *n*

²wear *n* 1 : the act of wearing : the state of being worn 2 : things worn or meant to be worn 3 : the result of wearing or use

wea·ri·some *adj* : TEDIOUS, DULL

wear out *vb* 1 : to make useless by long or hard use 2 : ¹TIRE 1

¹wea·ry *adj* **wea·ri·er; wea·ri·est** 1 : made tired usually from work 2 : having one's patience, pleasure, or interest worn out 3 : causing a loss of strength or interest — **wea·ri·ly** *adv* — **wea·ri·ness** *n*

²weary *vb* **wea·ried; wea·ry·ing** : to make or become weary

wea·sel *n* : a small slender active animal related to the minks that feeds on small birds and animals (as mice)

¹weath·er *n* : the state of the air and atmosphere in regard to how warm or cold, wet or dry, or clear or stormy it is

²weather *vb* 1 : to expose to the weather 2 : to change (as in color or structure) by the action of the weather 3 : to be able to last or come safely through

³weather *adj* : ¹WINDWARD

weath·er·cock *n* : a weather vane shaped like a rooster

weath·er·man *n, pl* **weath·er·men** : a person who reports and forecasts the weather

weather vane *n* : a movable device attached to something high (as a roof or spire) to show which way the wind is blowing

¹weave *vb* **wove; wo·ven; weav·ing** 1 : to form (as cloth) by lacing together strands of material 2 : ¹SPIN 3 3 : to make by or as if by lacing parts together 4 : to move back and forth, up and down, or in and out — **weav·er** *n*

²weave *n* : a method or pattern of weaving

¹web *n* 1 : a woven fabric on a loom or coming from a loom : COBWEB 1 3 : something like a cobweb 4 : a membrane especially when joining toes (as of a duck) 5 *cap* : WORLD WIDE WEB

2web *vb* **webbed; web·bing** : to join or surround with a web

web·foot *n, pl* **web·feet** : a foot (as of a duck) having the toes joined by webs — **web–foot·ed** *adj*

wed *vb* **wed·ded** *also* **wed; wed·ding** 1 : MARRY 2 : to attach firmly

we'd : we had : we should : we would

wed·ding *n* : a marriage ceremony

1wedge *n* 1 : a piece of wood or metal that tapers to a thin edge and is used for splitting (as logs) or for raising something heavy 2 : something (as a piece of cake or a formation of wild geese flying) with a triangular shape

2wedge *vb* **wedged; wedg·ing** 1 : to fasten or tighten with a wedge 2 : to crowd or squeeze·in tight

wed·lock *n* : MARRIAGE 1

Wednes·day *n* : the fourth day of the week

wee *adj* : very small : TINY

1weed *n* : a plant that tends to grow thickly where not wanted and to choke out more desirable plants

2weed *vb* 1 : to remove weeds from 2 : to get rid of what is not wanted

weedy *adj* **weed·i·er; weed·i·est** 1 : full of or consisting of weeds 2 : like a weed especially in coarse strong rapid growth 3 : very skinny

week *n* 1 : seven days in a row especially beginning with Sunday and ending with Saturday 2 : the working or school days that come between Sunday and Saturday

week·day *n* : a day of the week except Sunday or sometimes except Saturday and Sunday

week·end *n* : the period between the close of one work or school week and the beginning of the next

1week·ly *adj* 1 : happening, done, produced, or published every week 2 : figured by the week

2weekly *n, pl* **weeklies** : a newspaper or magazine published every week

weep *vb* **wept; weep·ing** : to shed tears : CRY

weep·ing *adj* : having slender drooping branches

weep·ing willow *n* : a willow originally from Asia that has slender drooping branches

wee·vil *n* : any of various small beetles with a hard shell and a long snout many of which are harmful to fruits, nuts, grain, or trees

weigh *vb* 1 : to find the weight of 2 : to think about as if weighing 3 : to measure out on or as if on scales 4 : to lift an anchor before sailing 5 : to have weight or a specified weight

weigh down *vb* : to cause to bend down

1weight *n* 1 : the amount that something weighs 2 : the force with which a body is pulled toward the earth 3 : a unit (as a kilogram) for measuring weight 4 : an object (as a piece of metal) of known weight for balancing a scale in weighing other objects 5 : a heavy object used to hold or press down something 6 : 1BURDEN 2 7 : strong influence : IMPORTANCE

2weight *vb* 1 : to load or make heavy with a weight 2 : to trouble with a burden

weighty *adj* **weight·i·er; weight·i·est** 1 : having much weight : HEAVY 2 : very important

weird *adj* 1 : of or relating to witchcraft or magic 2 : very unusual : STRANGE, FANTASTIC

weirdo *n, pl* **weird·os** : a very strange person

1wel·come *vb* **wel·comed; wel·com·ing** 1 : to greet with friendship or courtesy 2 : to receive or accept with pleasure

2welcome *adj* 1 : greeted or received gladly 2 : giving pleasure : PLEASING 3 : willingly permitted to do, have, or enjoy something 4 — used in the phrase "You're welcome" as a reply to an expression of thanks

3welcome *n* : a friendly greeting

1weld *vb* 1 : to join two pieces of metal or plastic by heating and allowing the edges to flow together 2 : to join closely 3 : to become or be capable of being welded — **weld·er** *n*

2weld *n* : a welded joint

wel·fare *n* 1 : the state of being or doing well 2 : aid in the form of money or necessities for people who are poor, aged, or disabled

1well *n* 1 : a source of supply 2 : a hole made in the earth to reach a natural deposit (as of water, oil, or gas) 3 : something suggesting a well

2well *vb* : to rise to the surface and flow out

3well *adv* **bet·ter; best** 1 : so as to be right : in a satisfactory way 2 : in a good-hearted or generous way 3 : in a skillful or expert manner 4 : by as much as possible : COMPLETELY 5 : with reason or courtesy 6 : in such a way as to be pleasing : as one would wish 7 : without trouble 8 : in a thorough manner 9 : in a familiar manner 10 : by quite a lot

4well *interj* 1 — used to express surprise or doubt 2 — used to begin a conversation or to continue one that was interrupted

5well *adj* 1 : being in a satisfactory or good state 2 : free or recovered from ill health : HEALTHY 3 : FORTUNATE 1

we'll : we shall : we will

well–be·ing *n* : WELFARE 1

well–bred *adj* : having or showing good manners : POLITE

well–known *adj* : known by many people

well–nigh *adv* : ALMOST

well–to–do *adj* : having plenty of money and possessions

1Welsh *adj* : of or relating to Wales or the people of Wales

2Welsh *n* : the people of Wales

welt *n* : a ridge raised on the skin by a blow

1wel·ter *vb* **1** : to twist or roll one's body about **2** : to rise and fall or toss about in or with waves

2welter *n* : a confused jumble

wend *vb* : to go one's way : PROCEED

went *past of* GO

wept *past of* WEEP

were *past 2d sing, past pl, or past subjunctive of* BE

we're : we are

weren't : were not

were·wolf *n, pl* **were·wolves** : a person in folklore who is changed or is able to change into a wolf

1west *adv* : to or toward the west

2west *adj* : placed toward, facing, or coming from the west

3west *n* **1** : the direction of sunset : the compass point opposite to east **2** *cap* : regions or countries west of a point that is mentioned or understood

west·bound *adj* : going west

west·er·ly *adj or adv* **1** : toward the west **2** : from the west

1west·ern *adj* **1** *often cap* : of, relating to, or like that of the West **2** : lying toward or coming from the west

2western *n, often cap* : a story, film, or radio or television show about life in the western United States especially in the last part of the nineteenth century

west·ward *adv or adj* : toward the west

1wet *adj* **wet·ter; wet·test 1** : containing, covered with, or soaked with liquid (as water) **2** : RAINY **3** : not yet dry — **wet·ness** *n*

2wet *n* **1** : 1WATER **2** : MOISTURE **3** : rainy weather : RAIN

3wet *vb* **wet** *or* **wet·ted; wet·ting** : to make wet

we've : we have

1whack *vb* : to hit with a hard noisy blow

2whack *n* **1** : a hard noisy blow **2** : the sound of a whack

whacky *variant of* WACKY

1whale *n* : a warm-blooded sea animal that looks like a huge fish but breathes air and feeds its young with its milk

2whale *vb* **whaled; whal·ing** : to hunt whales

whale·boat *n* : a long rowboat once used by whalers

whale·bone *n* : a substance like horn from the upper jaw of some whales

whal·er *n* : a person or ship that hunts whales

wharf *n, pl* **wharves** *or* **wharfs** : a structure built on the shore for loading and unloading ships

1what *pron* **1** : which thing or things **2** : which sort of thing or person **3** : that which — **what for** : 1WHY — **what if 1** : what would happen if **2** : what does it matter if

2what *adv* **1** : in what way : HOW **2** — used before one or more phrases that tell a cause

3what *adj* **1** — used to ask about the identity of a person, object, or matter **2** : how remarkable or surprising **3** : 2WHATEVER 1

1what·ev·er *pron* **1** : anything that **2** : no matter what **3** : what in the world

2whatever *adj* **1** : any and all : any . . . that **2** : of any kind at all

wheat *n* : a cereal grain that grows in tight clusters on the tall stalks of a widely cultivated grass, yields a fine white flour, is the chief source of bread in temperate regions, and is also important in animal feeds

wheat·en *adj* : containing or made from wheat

whee·dle *vb* **whee·dled; whee·dling 1** : to get (someone) to think or act a certain way by flattering : COAX **2** : to gain or get by coaxing or flattering

1wheel *n* **1** : a disk or circular frame that can turn on a central point **2** : something like a wheel (as in being round or in turning) **3** : something having a wheel as its main part **4** **wheels** *pl* : moving power : necessary parts — **wheeled** *adj*

2wheel *vb* **1** : to carry or move on wheels or in a vehicle with wheels **2** : ROTATE 1 **3** : to change direction as if turning on a central point

wheel·bar·row *n* : a small vehicle with two handles and usually one wheel for carrying small loads

wheel·chair *n* : a chair with wheels in which a disabled or sick person can get about

wheel·house *n, pl* **wheel·hous·es** : a small house containing a ship's steering wheel that is built on or above the top deck

1wheeze *vb* **wheezed; wheez·ing 1** : to breathe with difficulty and usually with a whistling sound **2** : to make a sound like wheezing

2wheeze *n* : a wheezing sound

whelk *n* : a large sea snail that has a spiral shell and is used in Europe for food

¹whelp *n* : one of the young of an animal that eats flesh and especially of a dog

²whelp *vb* : to give birth to whelps

¹when *adv* **1** : at what time **2** : the time at which **3** : at, in, or during which

²when *conj* **1** : at, during, or just after the time that **2** : in the event that : IF **3** : ALTHOUGH

³when *pron* : what or which time

whence *adv* **1** : from what place, source, or cause **2** : from or out of which

when·ev·er *conj or adv* : at whatever time

¹where *adv* **1** : at, in, or to what place **2** : at or in what way or direction

²where *conj* **1** : at, in, or to the place indicated **2** : every place that

³where *n* : what place, source, or cause

¹where·abouts *adv* : near what place

²whereabouts *n sing or pl* : the place where someone or something is

where·as *conj* **1** : since it is true that **2** : while just the opposite

where·by *adv* : by or through which

where·fore *adv* : ¹WHY

where·in *adv* **1** : in what way **2** : in which

where·of *conj* : of what : that of which

where·on *adv* : on which

where·up·on *conj* : and then : at which time

¹wher·ev·er *adv* : where in the world

²wherever *conj* **1** : at, in, or to whatever place **2** : in any situation in which : at any time that

whet *vb* **whet·ted; whet·ting 1** : to sharpen the edge of by rubbing on or with a stone **2** : to make (as the appetite) stronger

wheth·er *conj* **1** : if it is or was true that **2** : if it is or was better **3** — used to introduce two or more situations of which only one can occur

whet·stone *n* : a stone on which blades are sharpened

whew *n* : a sound almost like a whistle made as an exclamation chiefly to show amazement, discomfort, or relief

whey *n* : the watery part of milk that separates after the milk sours and thickens

¹which *adj* : what certain one or ones

²which *pron* **1** : which one or ones **2** — used in place of the name of something other than people at the beginning of a clause

¹which·ev·er *adj* : being whatever one or ones : no matter which

²whichever *pron* : whatever one or ones

¹whiff *n* **1** : a small gust **2** : a small amount (as of a scent or a gas) that is breathed in **3** : a very small amount : HINT

²whiff *vb* : to puff, blow out, or blow away in very small amounts

¹while *n* **1** : a period of time **2** : time and effort used in doing something

²while *conj* **1** : during the time that **2** : ALTHOUGH

³while *vb* **whiled; whil·ing** : to cause to pass especially in a pleasant way

whim *n* : a sudden wish or desire : a sudden change of mind

¹whim·per *vb* : to cry in low broken sounds : WHINE

²whimper *n* : a whining cry

whim·si·cal *adj* **1** : full of whims **2** : DROLL

¹whine *vb* **whined; whin·ing 1** : to make a shrill troubled cry or a similar sound **2** : to complain by or as if by whining

²whine *n* : a whining cry or sound

¹whin·ny *vb* **whin·nied; whin·ny·ing** : to neigh usually in a low gentle way

²whinny *n, pl* **whinnies** : a low gentle neigh

¹whip *vb* **whipped; whip·ping 1** : to move, snatch, or jerk quickly or with force **2** : to hit with something slender and flexible : LASH **3** : to punish with blows **4** : to beat into foam **5** : to move back and forth in a lively way

²whip *n* **1** : something used in whipping **2** : a light dessert made with whipped cream or whipped whites of eggs

whip·pet *n* : a small swift dog that is like a greyhound and is often used for racing

whip·poor·will *n* : a bird of eastern North America that flies at night and eats insects and is named from its peculiar call

¹whir *vb* **whirred; whir·ring** : to fly, move, or turn rapidly with a buzzing sound

²whir *n* : a whirring sound

¹whirl *vb* **1** : to turn or move in circles rapidly **2** : to feel dizzy **3** : to move or carry around or about very rapidly

²whirl *n* **1** : a whirling movement **2** : something that is or seems to be whirling **3** : a state of busy movement : BUSTLE

whirl·pool *n* : a rapid swirl of water with a low place in the center into which floating objects are drawn

whirl·wind *n* : a small windstorm in which the air turns rapidly in circles

¹whisk *n* **1** : a quick sweeping or brushing motion **2** : a kitchen utensil of wire used for whipping eggs or cream

²whisk *vb* **1** : to move suddenly and quickly **2** : to beat into foam **3** : to brush with or as if with a whisk broom

whisk broom *n* : a small broom with a short handle used especially as a clothes brush

whis·ker *n* **1** **whiskers** *pl* : the part of the beard that grows on the sides of the face and on the chin **2** : one hair of the beard **3** : a long bristle or hair growing near the mouth of an animal

whis·key *or* **whis·ky** *n, pl* **whis·keys** *or*

whis·kies : a strong drink containing alcohol and usually made from grain

¹whis·per *vb* **1** : to speak very low **2** : to tell by whispering **3** : to make a low rustling sound

²whisper *n* **1** : a low soft way of speaking that can be heard only by persons who are near **2** : the act of whispering **3** : something said in a whisper **4** : ¹HINT 1

¹whis·tle *n* **1** : a device by which a shrill sound is produced **2** : a shrill sound of or like whistling

²whistle *vb* **whis·tled; whis·tling 1** : to make a shrill sound by forcing the breath through the teeth or lips **2** : to move, pass, or go with a shrill sound **3** : to sound a whistle **4** : to express by whistling

whit *n* : a very small amount

¹white *adj* **whit·er; whit·est 1** : of the color white **2** : light or pale in color **3** : pale gray : SILVERY **4** : having a light skin **5** : ¹BLANK 2 **6** : not intended to cause harm **7** : SNOWY 1 — **white·ness** *n*

²white *n* **1** : the color of fresh snow : the opposite of black **2** : the white part of something (as an egg) **3** : white clothing **4** : a person belonging to a white race

white blood cell *n* : one of the tiny whitish cells of the blood that help fight infection

white·cap *n* : the top of a wave breaking into foam

white cell *n* : WHITE BLOOD CELL

white·fish *n* : a freshwater fish related to the trouts that is greenish above and silvery below and is used for food

white flag *n* : a flag of plain white raised in asking for a truce or as a sign of surrender

whit·en *vb* : to make or become white : BLEACH

white oak *n* : a large oak tree known for its hard strong wood that lasts well and is not easily rotted by water

white–tailed deer *n* : the common deer of eastern North America with the underside of the tail white

¹white·wash *vb* **1** : to cover with whitewash **2** : to try to hide the wrongdoing of

²whitewash *n* : a mixture (as of lime and water) for making a surface (as a wall) white

whith·er *adv* **1** : to what place **2** : to which place

whit·ish *adj* : somewhat white

whit·tle *vb* **whit·tled; whit·tling 1** : to cut or shave off chips from wood : shape by such cutting or shaving **2** : to reduce little by little

¹whiz *or* **whizz** *vb* **whizzed; whiz·zing** : to move, pass, or fly rapidly with a buzzing sound

²whiz *n* : a buzzing sound

who *pron* **1** : what person or people **2** : the person or people that **3** — used to stand for a person or people at the beginning of a clause

whoa *vb* — used as a command to an animal pulling a load to stop

who·ev·er *pron* : whatever person

¹whole *adj* **1** : completely healthy or sound in condition **2** : not cut up or ground **3** : keeping all its necessary elements in being made ready for the market **4** : made up of all its parts : TOTAL **5** : not scattered or divided **6** : each one of the — **whole·ness** *n*

²whole *n* **1** : something that is whole **2** : a sum of all the parts and elements — **on the whole 1** : all things considered **2** : in most cases

whole·heart·ed *adj* : not holding back

whole number *n* : a number that is zero or any of the natural numbers

¹whole·sale *n* : the sale of goods in large quantities to dealers

²wholesale *adj* **1** : of, relating to, or working at wholesaling **2** : done on a large scale

³wholesale *vb* **whole·saled; whole·sal·ing** : to sell to dealers usually in large lots — **whole·sal·er** *n*

whole·some *adj* **1** : helping to improve or keep the body, mind, or spirit in good condition **2** : sound in body, mind, or morals — **whole·some·ness** *n*

whol·ly *adv* : to the limit : COMPLETELY

whom *pron objective case of* WHO

whom·ev·er *pron objective case of* WHOEVER

¹whoop *vb* **1** : to shout or cheer loudly and strongly **2** : to make the shrill gasping sound that follows a coughing attack in whooping cough

²whoop *n* : a whooping sound

whooping cough *n* : a bacterial disease especially of children in which severe attacks of coughing are often followed by a shrill gasping intake of breath

whooping crane *n* : a large white nearly extinct North American crane that has a loud whooping call

whop·per 1 : something huge of its kind **2** : a monstrous lie

whorl *n* **1** : a row of parts (as leaves or petals) encircling a stem **2** : something that whirls or winds

¹whose *adj* : of or relating to whom or which

²whose *pron* : whose one : whose ones

¹why *adv* : for what cause or reason

²why *conj* **1** : the cause or reason for which **2** : for which

³why *n, pl* **whys** : the cause of or reason for something

[4]**why** *interj* — used to express surprise, uncertainty, approval, disapproval, or impatience

wick *n* : a cord, strip, or ring of loosely woven material through which a liquid (as oil) is drawn to the top in a candle, lamp, or oil stove for burning

wick·ed *adj* **1** : bad in behavior, moral state, or effect : EVIL **2** : DANGEROUS 2 — **wick·ed·ly** *adv* — **wick·ed·ness** *n*

[1]**wick·er** *n* **1** : a flexible twig (as of willow) used in basketry **2** : WICKERWORK

[2]**wicker** *adj* : made of wicker

wick·er·work *n* : basketry made of wicker

wick·et *n* **1** : a small gate or door in or near a larger gate or door **2** : a small window (as in a bank or ticket office) through which business is conducted **3** : either of the two sets of three rods topped by two crosspieces at which the ball is bowled in cricket **4** : an arch (as of wire) through which the ball is hit in the game of croquet

[1]**wide** *adj* **wid·er; wid·est** **1** : covering a very large area **2** : measured across or at right angles to length **3** : having a large measure across : BROAD **4** : opened as far as possible **5** : not limited **6** : far from the goal or truth — **wide·ly** *adv* — **wide·ness** *n*

[2]**wide** *adv* **wid·er; wid·est** **1** : over a wide area **2** : to the limit : COMPLETELY

wide–awake *adj* : not sleepy, dull, or without energy : ALERT

wid·en *vb* : to make or become wide or wider

wide·spread *adj* **1** : widely stretched out **2** : widely scattered

[1]**wid·ow** *n* : a woman who has lost her husband by death

[2]**widow** *vb* : to make a widow or widower of

wid·ow·er *n* : a man who has lost his wife by death

width *n* **1** : the shortest or shorter side of an object **2** : BREADTH 1

wield *vb* **1** : to use (as a tool) in an effective way **2** : [2]EXERCISE 1

wie·ner *n* : FRANKFURTER

wife *n, pl* **wives** : a married woman — **wife·ly** *adj*

wig *n* : a manufactured covering of natural or artificial hair for the head

[1]**wig·gle** *vb* **wig·gled; wig·gling** **1** : to move to and fro in a jerky way **2** : to proceed with twisting and turning movements

[2]**wiggle** *n* : a wiggling motion

wig·gler *n* : WRIGGLER

wig·gly *adj* **wig·gli·er; wig·gli·est** **1** : given to wiggling **2** : WAVY

wig·wag *vb* **wig·wagged; wig·wag·ging** : to signal by movement of a flag or light

wig·wam *n* : an Indian hut made of poles spread over with bark, rush mats, or hides

[1]**wild** *adj* **1** : living in a state of nature and not under human control and care : not tame **2** : growing or produced in nature : not cultivated by people **3** : not civilized : SAVAGE **4** : not kept under control **5** : wide of the intended goal or course — **wild·ly** *adv* — **wild·ness** *n*

[2]**wild** *n* : WILDERNESS

wild boar *n* : an Old World wild hog from which most domestic swine derive

wild·cat *n* : any of various cats (as an ocelot or bobcat) of small or medium size

wil·der·ness *n* : a wild region which is not used for farming and in which few people live

wild·fire *n* : a fire that destroys a wide area

wild·flower *n* : the flower of a wild plant or the plant bearing it

wild·fowl *n, pl* **wildfowl** : a bird and especially a waterfowl hunted as game

wild·life *n* : creatures that are neither human nor domesticated : the wild animals of field and forest

[1]**wile** *n* : a trick meant to trap or deceive

[2]**wile** *vb* **wiled; wil·ing** : [2]LURE

[1]**will** *helping verb, past* **would;** *present sing & pl* **will** **1** : wish to **2** : am, is, or are willing to **3** : am, is, or are determined to **4** : am, is, or are going to **5** : is or are commanded to

[2]**will** *n* **1** : a firm wish or desire **2** : the power to decide or control what one will do or how one will act **3** : a legal paper in which a person states to whom the things which he or she owns are to be given after death

[3]**will** *vb* **1** : [1]ORDER 2, DECREE **2** : to bring to a certain condition by the power of the will **3** : to leave by will

will·ful *or* **wil·ful** *adj* **1** : STUBBORN 1 **2** : INTENTIONAL — **will·ful·ly** *adv* — **will·ful·ness** *n*

will·ing *adj* **1** : feeling no objection **2** : not slow or lazy **3** : made, done, or given of one's own choice : VOLUNTARY — **will·ing·ly** *adv* — **will·ing·ness** *n*

wil·low *n* **1** : a tree or bush with narrow leaves, catkins for flowers, and tough flexible stems used in making baskets **2** : the wood of the willow tree

[1]**wilt** *vb* **1** : to lose freshness and become limp **2** : to lose strength

[2]**wilt** *n* : a plant disease (as of tomatoes) in which wilting and browning of leaves leads to death of the plant

wily *adj* **wil·i·er; wil·i·est** : full of tricks : CRAFTY

win *vb* **won; win·ning** **1** : to achieve the victory in a contest **2** : to get by effort or skill : GAIN **3** : to obtain by victory **4** : to be the victor in   **5** : to ask and get the favor of

wince *vb* **winced; winc·ing** : to draw back (as from pain)

winch *n* : a machine that has a roller on which rope is wound for pulling or lifting

¹**wind** *n*   **1** : a movement of the air : BREEZE   **2** : power to breathe   **3** : air carrying a scent (as of game)   **4** : limited knowledge especially about something secret : HINT   **5 winds** *pl* : wind instruments of a band or orchestra

²**wind** *vb*   **1** : to get a scent of   **2** : to cause to be out of breath

³**wind** *vb* **wound; wind·ing** : to sound by blowing

⁴**wind** *vb* **wound; wind·ing**   **1** : to twist around   **2** : to cover with something twisted around : WRAP   **3** : to make the spring of tight   **4** : to move in a series of twists and turns

⁵**wind** *n* : ²BEND

wind·break *n* : something (as a growth of trees and shrubs) that breaks the force of the wind

wind·fall *n*   **1** : something (as fruit from a tree) blown down by the wind   **2** : an unexpected gift or gain

wind instrument *n* : a musical instrument (as a clarinet, harmonica, or trumpet) sounded by the vibration of a stream of air and especially by the player's breath

wind·lass *n* : a winch used especially on ships for pulling and lifting

wind·mill *n* : a mill or a machine (as for pumping water) worked by the wind turning sails or vanes at the top of a tower

win·dow *n*   **1** : an opening in a wall to admit light and air   **2** : the glass and frame that fill a window opening   **3** : any of the areas into which a computer display may be divided and on which different types of information may be shown

window box *n* : a box for growing plants in or by a window

win·dow·pane *n* : a pane in a window

wind·pipe *n* : a tube with a firm wall that connects the pharynx with the lungs and is used in breathing

wind·proof *adj* : protecting from the wind

wind·shield *n* : a clear screen (as of glass) attached to the body of a vehicle (as a car) in front of the riders to protect them from the wind

wind·storm *n* : a storm with strong wind and little or no rain

wind·up *n*   **1** : the last part of something : FINISH   **2** : a swing of a baseball pitcher's arm before the pitch is thrown

wind up *vb*   **1** : to bring to an end : CON-

CLUDE   **2** : to swing the arm before pitching a baseball

¹**wind·ward** *adj* : moving or placed toward the direction from which the wind is blowing

²**windward** *n* : the side or direction from which the wind is blowing

windy *adj* **wind·i·er; wind·i·est** : having much wind

wine *n*   **1** : fermented grape juice containing various amounts of alcohol   **2** : the usually fermented juice of a plant product (as a fruit) used as a drink

win·ery *n, pl* **win·er·ies** : a place where wine is made

¹**wing** *n*   **1** : one of the paired limbs or limb-like parts with which a bird, bat, or insect flies   **2** : something like a wing in appearance, use, or motion   **3** : a part (as of a building) that sticks out from the main part   **4** : a division of an organization   **5 wings** *pl* : an area just off the stage of a theater — **wing·like** *adj* — **on the wing** : in flight

²**wing** *vb* : to go with wings : FLY

winged *adj* : having wings or winglike parts

wing·less *adj* : having no wings

wing·spread *n* : the distance between the tips of the spread wings

¹**wink** *vb*   **1** : to close and open the eyelids quickly   **2** : to close and open one eye quickly as a signal or hint

²**wink** *n*   **1** : a brief period of sleep   **2** : a hint or sign given by winking   **3** : an act of winking   **4** : a very short time

win·ner *n* : one that wins

¹**win·ning** *n*   **1** : the act of one that wins   **2** : something won especially in gambling — often used in pl.

²**winning** *adj*   **1** : being one that wins   **2** : tending to please or delight

win·now *vb* : to remove (as waste from grain) by a current of air

win·some *adj* : ²WINNING 2

¹**win·ter** *n*   **1** : the season between autumn and spring (as the months of December, January, and February in the northern half of the earth)   **2** : YEAR 2

²**winter** *vb*   **1** : to pass the winter   **2** : to keep, feed, or manage during the winter

win·ter·green *n* : a low evergreen plant with white flowers that look like little bells and are followed by red berries which produce an oil (**oil of wintergreen**) used in medicine and flavoring

win·ter·time *n* : the winter season

win·try *adj* **win·tri·er; win·tri·est**   **1** : of, relating to, or characteristic of winter   **2** : not friendly : COLD

¹**wipe** *vb* **wiped; wip·ing**   **1** : to clean or dry

by rubbing **2** : to remove by or as if by rubbing — **wip·er** n

²wipe n : an act of wiping : RUB

wipe out vb : to destroy completely

¹wire n **1** : metal in the form of a thread or slender rod **2** : a telephone or telegraph wire or system **3** : TELEGRAM, CABLEGRAM

²wire vb **wired; wir·ing 1** : to provide or equip with wire **2** : to bind, string, or mount with wire **3** : to send or send word to by telegraph

¹wire·less adj **1** : having no wire **2** : relating to communication by electric waves but without connecting wires : RADIO 2

²wireless n **1** : wireless telegraphy **2** : ²RADIO

wiry adj **wir·i·er; wir·i·est 1** : of or like wire **2** : being slender yet strong and active

wis·dom n : knowledge and the ability to use it to help oneself or others

wisdom tooth n : the last tooth of the full set on each half of each jaw of an adult

¹wise n : MANNER 2, WAY — used in such phrases as *in any wise, in no wise, in this wise*

²wise adj **wis·er; wis·est 1** : having or showing good sense or good judgment : SENSIBLE **2** : having knowledge or information — **wise·ly** adv

-wise adv suffix **1** : in the manner of **2** : in the position or direction of **3** : with regard to

wise·crack n : a clever and often insulting statement usually made in joking

¹wish vb **1** : to have a desire for : WANT **2** : to form or express a desire concerning

²wish n **1** : an act or instance of wishing **2** : something wished **3** : a desire for happiness or good fortune

wish·bone n : a bone in front of a bird's breastbone that is shaped like a V

wish·ful adj : having, showing, or based on a wish

wishy–washy adj : lacking spirit, courage, or determination : WEAK

wisp n **1** : a small bunch of hay or straw **2** : a thin piece or strand **3** : a thin streak

wispy adj **wisp·i·er; wisp·i·est** : being thin and flimsy

wis·tar·ia n : WISTERIA

wis·te·ria n : a woody vine related to the beans that is grown for its long clusters of violet, white, or pink flowers

wist·ful adj : feeling or showing a timid longing — **wist·ful·ly** adv — **wist·ful·ness** n

wit n **1** : power to think, reason, or decide **2** : normal mental state — usually used in pl. **3** : cleverness in making sharp and usually amusing comments **4** : witty comments, expressions, or talk **5** : a witty person

witch n **1** : a woman believed to have magic powers **2** : an ugly or mean old woman

witch·craft n : the power or doings of a witch

witch doctor n : a person who uses magic to cure illness and fight off evil spirits

witch·ery n, pl **witch·er·ies 1** : WITCHCRAFT **2** : power to charm or fascinate

witch ha·zel n **1** : a shrub with small yellow flowers in late fall or very early spring **2** : a soothing alcoholic lotion made from witch hazel bark

with prep **1** : AGAINST 2 **2** : in shared relation to **3** : having in or as part of it **4** : in regard to **5** : compared to **6** : in the opinion or judgment of **7** : by the use of **8** : so as to show **9** : in the company of **10** : in possession of **11** : as well as **12** : FROM 2 **13** : BECAUSE OF **14** : DESPITE **15** : if given **16** : at the time of or shortly after **17** : in support of **18** : in the direction of

with·draw vb **with·drew; with·drawn; with·draw·ing 1** : to draw back : take away **2** : to take back (as something said or suggested) **3** : to go away especially for privacy or safety

with·draw·al n : an act or instance of withdrawing

with·er vb : to shrink up from or as if from loss of natural body moisture : WILT

with·ers n pl : the ridge between the shoulder bones of a horse

with·hold vb **with·held; with·hold·ing** : to refuse to give, grant, or allow

¹with·in adv : ²INSIDE

²within prep **1** : ⁴INSIDE 1 **2** : not beyond the limits of

¹with·out prep **1** : ⁴OUTSIDE **2** : completely lacking **3** : not accompanied by or showing

²without adv : ³OUTSIDE

with·stand vb **with·stood; with·stand·ing 1** : to hold out against **2** : to oppose (as an attack) successfully

wit·less adj : lacking in wit or intelligence : FOOLISH

¹wit·ness n **1** : TESTIMONY **2** : a person who sees or otherwise has personal knowledge of something **3** : a person who gives testimony in court **4** : a person who is present at an action (as the signing of a will) so as to be able to say who did it

²witness vb **1** : to be a witness to **2** : to give testimony to : testify as a witness **3** : to be or give proof of

wit·ted adj : having wit or understanding — used in combination

wit·ty adj **wit·ti·er; wit·ti·est** : having or showing wit

wives pl of WIFE

wiz·ard *n* 1 : SORCERER, MAGICIAN 2 : a very clever or skillful person

¹wob·ble *vb* **wob·bled; wob·bling** : to move from side to side in a shaky manner — **wob·bly** *adj*

²wobble *n* : a rocking motion from side to side

woe *n* : great sorrow, grief, or misfortune : TROUBLE

woe·ful *adj* 1 : full of grief or misery 2 : bringing woe or misery

woke *past of* WAKE

woken *past participle of* WAKE

¹wolf *n*, *pl* **wolves** 1 : a large intelligent doglike wild animal that eats flesh and has ears which stand up and a bushy tail 2 : a person felt to resemble a wolf (as in craftiness or fierceness) — **wolf·ish** *adj*

²wolf *vb* : to eat greedily

wolf dog *n* 1 : WOLFHOUND 2 : the hybrid offspring of a wolf and a domestic dog 3 : a dog that looks like a wolf

wolf·hound *n* : any of several large dogs used in hunting large animals

wol·fram *n* : TUNGSTEN

wol·ver·ine *n* : a blackish wild animal with shaggy fur that is related to the martens and sables, eats flesh, and is found chiefly in the northern parts of North America

wolves *pl of* WOLF

wom·an *n*, *pl* **wom·en** 1 : an adult female person 2 : women considered as a group

wom·an·hood *n* 1 : the state of being a woman 2 : womanly characteristics 3 : WOMAN 2

wom·an·kind *n* : WOMAN 2

wom·an·ly *adj* : having the characteristics of a woman

womb *n* : UTERUS

wom·en·folk *or* **wom·en·folks** *n pl* : women especially of one family or group

won *past of* WIN

¹won·der *n* 1 : something extraordinary : MARVEL 2 : a feeling (as of astonishment) caused by something extraordinary

²wonder *vb* 1 : to feel surprise or amazement 2 : to be curious or have doubt

won·der·ful *adj* 1 : causing wonder : MARVELOUS 2 : very good or fine — **won·der·ful·ly** *adv*

won·der·ing·ly *adv* : in or as if in wonder

won·der·land *n* : a place of wonders or surprises

won·der·ment *n* : AMAZEMENT

won·drous *adj* : WONDERFUL 1

¹wont *adj* : being in the habit of doing

²wont *n* : usual custom : HABIT

won't : will not

woo *vb* **wooed; woo·ing** 1 : to try to gain the love of 2 : to try to gain

¹wood *n* 1 : a thick growth of trees : a small forest — often used in pl. 2 : a hard fibrous material that makes up most of the substance of a tree or shrub within the bark and is often used as a building material or fuel

²wood *adj* 1 : WOODEN 1 2 : used for or on wood 3 *or* **woods** : living or growing in woodland

wood·bine *n* : any of several climbing vines of Europe and America (as honeysuckle)

wood·carv·er *n* : a person who carves useful or ornamental things from wood

wood·chuck *n* : a reddish brown rodent that hibernates : GROUNDHOG

wood·cock *n* : a brown game bird that has a long bill and is related to the snipe

wood·craft *n* : knowledge about the woods and how to take care of oneself in them

wood·cut·ter *n* : a person who cuts wood especially as an occupation

wood·ed *adj* : covered with trees

wood·en *adj* 1 : made of wood 2 : stiff like wood : AWKWARD 3 : lacking spirit, ease, or charm

wood·land *n* : land covered with trees and shrubs : FOREST

wood·lot *n* : a small wooded section (as of a farm) kept to meet fuel and timber needs

wood louse *n* : a small flat gray crustacean that lives usually under stones or bark

wood·peck·er *n* : a bird that climbs trees and drills holes in them with its bill in search of insects

wood·pile *n* : a pile of wood especially for use as fuel

wood·shed *n* : a shed for storing wood and especially firewood

woods·man *n*, *pl* **woods·men** 1 : a person who cuts down trees as an occupation 2 : a person skilled in woodcraft

woodsy *adj* : of, relating to, or suggestive of woodland

wood thrush *n* : a large thrush of eastern North America noted for its loud clear song

wood·wind *n* : one of the group of wind instruments consisting of the flutes, oboes, clarinets, bassoons, and sometimes saxophones

wood·work *n* : work (as the edge around doorways) made of wood

wood·work·ing *n* : the art or process of shaping or working with wood

woody *adj* **wood·i·er; wood·i·est** 1 : being mostly woods 2 : of or containing wood or wood fibers 3 : very much like wood

woof *n* 1 : the threads that cross the warp in weaving a fabric 2 : a woven fabric or its texture

wool *n* 1 : soft heavy wavy or curly hair especially of the sheep 2 : a substance that looks like a mass of wool   **3** : a material (as yarn) made from wool

wool·en or **wool·len** adj   **1** : made of wool **2** : of or relating to wool or cloth made of wool

wool·ly adj **wool·li·er; wool·li·est** : made of or like wool

1word n   **1** : a sound or combination of sounds that has meaning and is spoken by a human being   **2** : a written or printed letter or letters standing for a spoken word   **3** : a brief remark or conversation   **4** : 2COMMAND 2, ORDER   **5** : NEWS   **6** : 1PROMISE 1 **7 words** pl : remarks said in anger or in a quarrel

2word vb : to express in words : PHRASE

word·ing n : the way something is put into words

word processing n : the production of typewritten documents (as business letters) with automated and usually computerized equipment

word processor n   **1** : a terminal operated by a keyboard for use in word processing usually having a video display and a magnetic storage device   **2** : software (as for a computer) to perform word processing

wordy adj **word·i·er; word·i·est** : using or containing many words or more words than are needed — **word·i·ness** n

wore past of WEAR

1work n   **1** : the use of a person's strength or ability in order to get something done or get some desired result : LABOR   **2** : OCCUPATION 1, EMPLOYMENT   **3** : something that needs to be done : TASK, JOB   **4** : DEED 1, ACHIEVEMENT   **5** : something produced by effort or hard work   **6 works** pl : a place where industrial labor is done : PLANT, FACTORY   **7 works** pl : the working or moving parts of a mechanical device   **8** : the way one works : WORKMANSHIP

2work vb **worked** or **wrought; work·ing**   **1** : to do work especially for money or because of a need instead of for pleasure : labor or cause to labor   **2** : to perform or act or to cause to act as planned : OPERATE **3** : to move or cause to move slowly or with effort   **4** : to cause to happen   **5** : 1MAKE 2, SHAPE   **6** : to carry on one's occupation in, through, or along   **7** : EXCITE 2, PROVOKE

work·able adj : capable of being worked or done

work·bench n : a bench on which work is done (as by mechanics)

work·book n : a book made up of a series of problems or practice examples for a student to use as part of a course of study

work·er n   **1** : a person who works   **2** : one of the members of a colony of bees, ants, wasps, or termites that are only partially developed sexually and that do most of the labor and protective work of the colony

work·ing adj   **1** : doing work especially for a living   **2** : relating to work   **3** : good enough to allow work or further work to be done

work·ing·man n, pl **work·ing·men** : a person who works for wages usually at common labor or in industry : a member of the working class

work·man n, pl **work·men**   **1** : WORKINGMAN   **2** : a skilled worker (as an electrician or carpenter)

work·man·ship n   **1** : the art or skill of a workman   **2** : the quality of a piece of work

work·out n : an exercise or practice to test or increase ability or performance

work out vb : to invent or solve by effort

work·shop n : a shop where work and especially skilled work is carried on

work·sta·tion n   **1** : an area with equipment for the performance of a particular task usually by one person   **2** : a computer usually connected to a computer network

world n   **1** : EARTH 3   **2** : people in general : HUMANITY   **3** : a state of existence   **4** : a great number or amount   **5** : a part or section of the earth and the people living there

world·ly adj **world·li·er; world·li·est** : of or relating to this world

World Wide Web n : a part of the Internet designed to allow easier navigation of the network through the use of text and graphics that link to other documents

1worm n   **1** : any of various long creeping or crawling animals that usually have soft bodies   **2** : a person hated or pitied   **3 worms** pl : the presence of or disease caused by worms living in the body

2worm vb   **1** : to move slowly by creeping or wriggling   **2** : to get hold of or escape from by trickery   **3** : to free from worms

wormy adj **worm·i·er; worm·i·est** : containing worms

worn past participle of WEAR

worn–out adj   **1** : useless from long or hard wear   **2** : very weary

wor·ri·some adj   **1** : given to worrying   **2** : causing worry

1wor·ry vb **wor·ried; wor·ry·ing**   **1** : to shake and tear or mangle with the teeth   **2** : to make anxious or upset : DISTURB   **3** : to feel or express great concern

2worry n, pl **worries**   **1** : ANXIETY   **2** : a cause of great concern

1worse adj comparative of BAD or of ILL   **1** : more bad or evil : poorer in quality or worth   **2** : being in poorer health

2worse n : something worse

³worse *adv comparative of* BADLY *or of* ILL : not as well : in a worse way

wors·en *vb* : to get worse

¹wor·ship *n* **1** : deep respect toward God, a god, or a sacred object **2** : too much respect or admiration

²worship *vb* **wor·shiped** *or* **wor·shipped; wor·ship·ing** *or* **wor·ship·ping 1** : to honor or respect as a divine being **2** : to regard with respect, honor, or devotion **3** : to take part in worship or an act of worship — **wor·ship·er** *or* **wor·ship·per** *n*

¹worst *adj superlative of* BAD *or of* ILL : most bad, ill or evil

²worst *adv superlative of* ILL *or of* BADLY : in the worst way possible

³worst *n* : a person or thing that is worst

⁴worst *vb* : to get the better of : DEFEAT

wor·sted *n* **1** : a smooth yarn spun from pure wool **2** : a fabric woven from a worsted yarn

¹worth *n* **1** : the quality or qualities of a thing making it valuable or useful **2** : value as expressed in money **3** : EXCELLENCE 1

²worth *prep* **1** : equal in value to **2** : having possessions or income equal to **3** : deserving of **4** : capable of

worth·less *adj* **1** : lacking worth **2** : USELESS

worth·while *adj* : being worth the time spent or effort used

wor·thy *adj* **wor·thi·er; wor·thi·est 1** : having worth or excellence **2** : having enough value or excellence — **wor·thi·ness** *n*

would *past of* WILL **1** : strongly desire : WISH **2** — used as a helping verb to show that something might be likely or meant to happen under certain conditions **3** : prefers or prefer to **4** : was or were going to **5** : is or are able to : COULD **6** — used as a politer form of *will*

wouldn't : would not

¹wound *n* **1** : an injury that involves cutting or breaking of bodily tissue (as by violence, accident, or surgery) **2** : an injury or hurt to a person's feelings or reputation

²wound *vb* **1** : to hurt by cutting or breaking tissue **2** : to hurt the feelings or pride of

³wound *past of* WIND

wove *past of* WEAVE

woven *past participle of* WEAVE

¹wran·gle *vb* **wran·gled; wran·gling 1** : to have an angry quarrel : BICKER **2** : ARGUE 2, DEBATE

²wrangle *n* : ¹QUARREL 2

wran·gler *n* **1** : a person who wrangles **2** : a worker on a ranch who tends the saddle horses

¹wrap *vb* **wrapped; wrap·ping 1** : to cover by winding or folding **2** : to enclose in a package **3** : to wind or roll together : FOLD **4** : to involve completely

²wrap *n* : a warm loose outer garment (as a shawl, cape, or coat)

wrap·per *n* **1** : what something is wrapped in **2** : a person who wraps merchandise **3** : a garment that is worn wrapped about the body

wrap·ping *n* : something used to wrap something else : WRAPPER

wrap up *vb* **1** : to bring to an end **2** : to put on warm clothing

wrath *n* : violent anger : RAGE

wrath·ful *adj* **1** : full of wrath **2** : showing wrath

wreak *vb* : to bring down as or as if punishment

wreath *n, pl* **wreaths** : something twisted or woven into a circular shape

wreathe *vb* **wreathed; wreath·ing 1** : to form into wreaths **2** : to crown, decorate, or cover with or as if with a wreath

¹wreck *n* **1** : the remains (as of a ship or vehicle) after heavy damage usually by storm, collision, or fire **2** : a person or animal in poor health or without strength **3** : the action of breaking up or destroying something

²wreck *vb* **1** : ²SHIPWRECK 2 **2** : to damage or destroy by breaking up **3** : to bring to ruin or an end

wreck·age *n* **1** : a wrecking or being wrecked **2** : the remains of a wreck

wreck·er *n* **1** : a person who wrecks something or deals in wreckage **2** : a ship used in salvaging wrecks **3** : a truck for removing wrecked or broken-down cars

wren *n* : any of a group of small brown songbirds (as the **house wren**) with short rounded wings and short erect tail

¹wrench *vb* **1** : to pull or twist with sudden sharp force **2** : to injure or cripple by a sudden sharp twisting or straining

²wrench *n* **1** : a violent twist to one side or out of shape **2** : an injury caused by twisting or straining : SPRAIN **3** : a tool used in turning nuts or bolts

wrest *vb* **1** : to pull away by twisting or wringing **2** : to obtain only by great and steady effort

¹wres·tle *vb* **wres·tled; wres·tling 1** : to grasp and attempt to turn, trip, or throw down an opponent or to prevent the opponent from being able to move **2** : to struggle to deal with

²wrestle *n* : ²STRUGGLE 1

wres·tling *n* : a sport in which two opponents wrestle each other

wretch *n* **1** : a miserable unhappy person **2** : a very bad person : WRONGDOER

wretch·ed *adj* **1** : very unhappy or unfortunate : suffering greatly **2** : causing misery or distress **3** : of very poor quality : INFERIOR

wrig·gle *vb* **wrig·gled; wrig·gling 1** : to twist or move like a worm : SQUIRM, WIGGLE **2** : to advance by twisting and turning

wrig·gler *n* **1** : one that wriggles **2** : a mosquito larva or pupa

wring *vb* **wrung; wring·ing 1** : to twist or press so as to squeeze out moisture **2** : to get by or as if by twisting or pressing **3** : to twist so as to strangle **4** : to affect as if by wringing

wring·er *n* : a machine or device for squeezing liquid out of something (as laundry)

¹wrin·kle *n* **1** : a crease or small fold (as in the skin or in cloth) **2** : a clever notion or trick

²wrinkle *vb* **wrin·kled; wrin·kling** : to mark or become marked with wrinkles

wrist *n* : the joint or the region of the joint between the hand and arm

wrist·band *n* **1** : the part of a sleeve that goes around the wrist **2** : a band that goes around the wrist (as for support or warmth)

wrist·watch *n* : a watch attached to a bracelet or strap and worn on the wrist

writ *n* : an order in writing signed by an officer of a court ordering someone to do or not to do something

write *vb* **wrote; writ·ten; writ·ing 1** : to form letters or words with pen or pencil **2** : to form the letters or the words of (as on paper) **3** : to put down on paper **4** : to make up and set down for others to read **5** : to write a letter to

writ·er *n* : a person who writes especially as a business or occupation

writhe *vb* **writhed; writh·ing 1** : to twist and turn this way and that **2** : to suffer from shame or confusion : SQUIRM

writ·ing *n* **1** : the act of a person who writes **2** : HANDWRITING **3** : something (as a letter or book) that is written

¹wrong *n* : something (as an idea, rule, or action) that is wrong

²wrong *adj* **1** : not right : SINFUL, EVIL **2** : not correct or true : FALSE **3** : not the one wanted or intended **4** : not suitable **5** : made so as to be placed down or under and not to be seen **6** : not proper — **wrong·ly** *adv* — **wrong·ness** *n*

³wrong *adv* : in the wrong direction, manner, or way

⁴wrong *vb* : to do wrong to

wrong·do·er *n* : a person who does wrong and especially a moral wrong

wrong·do·ing *n* : bad behavior or action

wrong·ful *adj* **1** : ²WRONG 1, UNJUST **2** : UNLAWFUL

wrote *past of* WRITE

¹wrought *past of* WORK

²wrought *adj* **1** : beaten into shape by tools **2** : much too excited

wrung *past of* WRING

wry *adj* **wry·er; wry·est 1** : turned abnormally to one side **2** : made by twisting the features

X

x *n, pl* **x's** *or* **xs** *often cap* **1** : the twenty-fourth letter of the English alphabet **2** : ten in Roman numerals **3** : an unknown quantity

Xmas *n* : CHRISTMAS

x–ray *vb, often cap* X : to examine, treat, or photograph with X rays

X ray *n* **1** : a powerful invisible ray made up of very short waves that is somewhat similar to light and that is able to pass through various thicknesses of solids and act on photographic film like light **2** : a photograph taken by the use of X rays

xy·lo·phone *n* : a musical instrument consisting of a series of wooden bars of different lengths made to sound the musical scale and played with two wooden hammers

Y

y *n, pl* **y's** *or* **ys** *often cap* : the twenty-fifth letter of the English alphabet

¹-y *also* **-ey** *adj suffix* **-i·er; -i·est 1** : showing, full of, or made of **2** : like **3** : devoted to : enthusiastic about **4** : tending to **5** : somewhat : rather

²-y *n suffix, pl* **-ies 1** : state : condition : quality **2** : occupation, place of business, or goods dealt with **3** : whole body or group

³-y *n suffix, pl* **-ies** : occasion or example of a specified action

⁴-y — see -IE

¹yacht *n* : a small ship used for pleasure cruising or racing

²yacht *vb* : to race or cruise in a yacht

yacht·ing *n* : the action, fact, or recreation of racing or cruising in a yacht

yachts·man *n, pl* **yachts·men** : a person who owns or sails a yacht

yak *n* : a wild or domestic ox of the uplands of Asia that has very long hair

yam *n* **1** : the starchy root of a plant related to the lilies that is an important food in much of the tropics **2** : a sweet potato with a moist and usually orange flesh

¹yank *n* : a strong sudden pull : JERK

²yank *vb* : ²JERK 1

Yan·kee *n* **1** : a person born or living in New England **2** : a person born or living in the northern United States **3** : a person born or living in the United States

¹yap *vb* **yapped; yap·ping 1** : to bark in yaps **2** : ²SCOLD, CHATTER

²yap *n* : a quick shrill bark

¹yard *n* **1** : a small and often fenced area open to the sky and next to a building **2** : the grounds of a building **3** : a fenced area for livestock **4** : an area set aside for a business or activity **5** : a system of railroad tracks especially for keeping and repairing cars

²yard *n* **1** : a measure of length equal to three feet or thirty-six inches (about .91 meter) **2** : a long pole pointed toward the ends that holds up and spreads the top of a sail

yard·age *n* **1** : a total number of yards **2** : the length or size of something measured in yards

yard·arm *n* : either end of the yard of a square-rigged ship

yard·mas·ter *n* : the person in charge of operations in a railroad yard

yard·stick *n* **1** : a measuring stick a yard long **2** : a rule or standard by which something is measured or judged

¹yarn *n* **1** : natural or manufactured fiber (as cotton, wool, or rayon) formed as a continuous thread for use in knitting or weaving **2** : an interesting or exciting story

²yarn *vb* : to tell a yarn

yawl *n* : a sailboat having two masts with the shorter one behind the point where the stern enters the water

¹yawn *vb* **1** : to open wide **2** : to open the mouth wide usually as a reaction to being tired or bored

²yawn *n* : a deep drawing in of breath through the wide-open mouth

ye *pron, archaic* : YOU 1

¹yea *adv* : ¹YES 1 — used in spoken voting

²yea *n* **1** : a vote in favor of something **2** : a person casting a yea vote

year *n* **1** : the period of about 365¼ days required for the earth to make one complete trip around the sun **2** : a period of 365 days or in leap year 366 days beginning January 1 **3** : a fixed period of time

year·book *n* **1** : a book published yearly especially as a report **2** : a school publication recording the history and activities of a graduating class

year·ling *n* : a person or animal that is or is treated as if a year old

year·ly *adj* : ¹ANNUAL 1

yearn *vb* : to feel an eager desire

yearn·ing *n* : an eager desire

year–round *adj* : being in operation for the full year

yeast *n* **1** : material that may be found on the surface or at the bottom of sweet liquids, is made up mostly of the cells of a tiny fungus, and causes a reaction in which alcohol is produced **2** : a commercial product containing living yeast plants and used especially to make bread dough rise **3** : any of the group of tiny fungi that form alcohol or raise bread dough

¹yell *vb* : to cry or scream loudly

²yell *n* **1** : ²SCREAM, SHOUT **2** : a cheer used especially in schools or colleges to encourage athletic teams

¹yel·low *adj* **1** : of the color yellow **2** : COWARDLY

²yellow *n* **1** : the color in the rainbow between green and orange **2** : something yellow in color

³yellow *vb* : to turn yellow

yellow fever *n* : a disease carried by mosquitoes in hot countries

yel·low·ish *adj* : somewhat yellow

yellow jacket *n* : a small wasp with yellow markings that usually nests in colonies in the ground

¹yelp *n* : a quick shrill bark or cry

²yelp *vb* : to make a quick shrill bark or cry

yen *n* : a strong desire : LONGING

yeo·man *n, pl* **yeo·men 1** : a naval petty officer who works as a clerk **2** : a small farmer who cultivates his or her own land

-yer — see ²-ER

¹yes *adv* **1** — used to express agreement **2** — used to introduce a phrase with greater emphasis or clearness **3** — used to show interest or attention

²yes *n* : a positive reply

¹yes·ter·day *adv* : on the day next before today

²yesterday *n* **1** : the day next before this day **2** : time not long past

yes·ter·year *n* : the recent past

¹yet *adv* **1** : ²BESIDES **2** : ²EVEN **4** : **3** : up to now : so far **4** : at this or that time **5** : up to the present **6** : at some later time **7** : NEVERTHELESS

²yet *conj* : but nevertheless

yew *n* : a tree or shrub with stiff poisonous evergreen leaves, a fleshy fruit, and tough wood used especially for bows and small articles

Yid·dish *n* : a language that comes from German and is used by some Jews

¹yield *vb* **1** : to give up possession of on claim or demand **2** : to give (oneself) up to a liking, temptation, or habit **3** : to bear as a natural product **4** : to return as income or profit **5** : to be productive : bring good results **6** : to stop opposing or objecting to something **7** : to give way under physical force so as to bend, stretch, or break **8** : to admit that someone else is better

²yield *n* : the amount produced or returned

¹yip *vb* **yipped; yip·ping** : ²YELP — used chiefly of a dog

²yip *n* : a noise made by or as if by yelping

¹yo·del *vb* **yo·deled** *or* **yo·delled; yo·del·ing** *or* **yo·del·ling 1** : to sing with frequent sudden changes from the natural voice range to a higher range and back **2** : to call or shout in the manner of yodeling — **yo·del·er** *n*

²yodel *n* : a yodeled shout

¹yoke *n* **1** : a wooden bar or frame by which two work animals (as oxen) are harnessed at the heads or necks for drawing a plow or load **2** : a frame fitted to a person's shoulders to carry a load in two equal parts **3** : a clamp that joins two parts to hold or connect them in position **4** *pl usually* **yoke** : two animals yoked together **5** : something that brings to a state of hardship, humiliation, or slavery **6** : SLAVERY 2 **7** : ¹TIE 4, BOND **8** : a fitted or shaped piece at the shoulder of a garment or at the top of a skirt

²yoke *vb* **yoked; yok·ing 1** : to put a yoke on **2** : to attach a work animal to

yo·kel *n* : a country person with little education or experience

yolk *n* : the yellow inner part of the egg of a bird or reptile containing stored food material for the developing young — **yolked** *adj*

Yom Kip·pur *n* : a Jewish holiday observed in September or October with fasting and prayer

¹yon *adj* : ²YONDER 2

²yon *adv* **1** : ¹YONDER **2** : THITHER

¹yon·der *adv* : at or in that place

²yonder *adj* **1** : more distant **2** : being at a distance within view

yore *n* : time long past

you *pron* **1** : the one or ones these words are spoken or written to **2** : ³ONE 2

you'd : you had : you would

you'll : you shall : you will

¹young *adj* **youn·ger; youn·gest 1** : being in the first or an early stage of life or growth **2** : INEXPERIENCED **3** : recently come into being : NEW **4** : YOUTHFUL 1

²young *n, pl* **young 1** *young pl* : young persons **2** *young pl* : immature offspring **3** : a single recently born or hatched animal

youn·gest *n, pl* **youngest** : one that is the least old especially of a family

young·ster *n* **1** : a young person : YOUTH **2** : CHILD

your *adj* **1** : of or belonging to you **2** : by or from you **3** : affecting you **4** : of or relating to one **5** — used before a title of honor in addressing a person

you're : you are

yours *pron* : that which belongs to you

your·self *pron, pl* **your·selves** : your own self

youth *n, pl* **youths 1** : the period of life between being a child and an adult **2** : a young man **3** : young people **4** : the quality or state of being young

youth·ful *adj* **1** : of or relating to youth **2** : being young and not yet fully grown **3** : having the freshness of youth — **youth·ful·ly** *adv* — **youth·ful·ness** *n*

you've : you have

¹yowl *vb* : ¹WAIL

²yowl *n* : a loud long moaning cry (as of a cat)

yo—yo *n, pl* **yo—yos** *also* **yo—yoes** : a thick divided disk that is made to fall and rise to the hand by unwinding and winding again on a string

yuc·ca *n* : a plant related to the lilies that grows in dry regions and has stiff pointed leaves at the base of a tall stiff stalk of usually whitish flowers

yule *n, often cap* : CHRISTMAS

yule log *n, often cap Y* : a large log once put in the fireplace on Christmas Eve as the foundation of the fire

yule·tide *n, often cap* : the Christmas season

Z

z *n, pl* **z's** *or* **zs** *often cap* : the twenty-sixth letter of the English alphabet

¹**za·ny** *n, pl* **zanies** **1** : ¹CLOWN **2** **2** : a silly or foolish person

²**zany** *adj* **za·ni·er; za·ni·est** **1** : being or like a zany **2** : FOOLISH, SILLY

zeal *n* : eager desire to get something done or see something succeed

zeal·ous *adj* : filled with or showing zeal — **zeal·ous·ly** *adv* — **zeal·ous·ness** *n*

ze·bra *n* : an African wild animal related to the horses that has a hide striped in black and white or black and buff

ze·bu *n* : an Asian domestic ox that differs from the related European cattle in having a large hump over the shoulders and a loose skin with hanging folds

ze·nith *n* **1** : the point in the heavens directly overhead **2** : the highest point

zeph·yr *n* **1** : a breeze from the west **2** : a gentle breeze

zep·pe·lin *n* : a huge long balloon that has a metal frame and is driven through the air by engines carried on its underside

ze·ro *n, pl* **zeros** *or* **zeroes** **1** : the numerical symbol 0 meaning the absence of all size or quantity **2** : the point on a scale (as on a thermometer) from which measurements are made **3** : the temperature shown by the zero mark on a thermometer **4** : a total lack of anything : NOTHING **5** : the lowest point

zest *n* **1** : an enjoyable or exciting quality **2** : keen enjoyment — **zest·ful** *adj* — **zest·ful·ly** *adv* — **zest·ful·ness** *n*

¹**zig·zag** *n* **1** : one of a series of short sharp turns or angles in a course **2** : a line, path, or pattern that bends sharply this way and that

²**zigzag** *adv* : in or by a zigzag path or course

³**zigzag** *adj* : having short sharp turns or angles

⁴**zigzag** *vb* **zig·zagged; zig·zag·ging** : to form into or move along a zigzag

zinc *n* : a bluish white metal that tarnishes only slightly in moist air and is used mostly to make alloys and to give iron a protective coating

zing *n* **1** : a shrill humming sound **2** : a lively or energetic quality

zin·nia *n* : a tropical American herb related to the daisies that is widely grown for its bright flower heads that last a long time

¹**zip** *vb* **zipped; zip·ping** **1** : to move or act with speed and force **2** : to move or pass with a shrill hissing or humming sound

²**zip** *n* **1** : a sudden shrill hissing sound **2**

³**zip** *vb* **zipped; zip·ping** : to close or open with a zipper

zip code *or* **ZIP Code** *n* : a number consisting of five digits that identifies each postal area in the United States

zip·per *n* : a fastener (as for a jacket) consisting of two rows of metal or plastic teeth on strips of tape and a sliding piece that closes an opening by drawing the teeth together — **zip·pered** *adj*

zip·py *adj* **zip·pi·er; zip·pi·est** : full of energy : LIVELY

zith·er *n* : a stringed instrument with usually thirty to forty strings that are plucked with the fingers or with a pick

zo·di·ac *n* : an imaginary belt in the heavens that includes the paths of most of the planets and is divided into twelve constellations or signs

zom·bie *or* **zom·bi** *n* : a person who is believed to have died and been brought back to life

¹**zone** *n* **1** : any of the five great parts that the earth's surface is divided into according to latitude and temperature **2** : a band or belt that surrounds **3** : a section set off or marked as different in some way

²**zone** *vb* **zoned; zon·ing** : to divide into zones for different uses

zoo *n, pl* **zoos** : a collection of living animals for display

zoo·log·i·cal *adj* : of or relating to zoology

zoological garden *n* : a garden or park where wild animals are kept for exhibition

zo·ol·o·gist *n* : a specialist in zoology

zo·ol·o·gy *n* **1** : a branch of biology dealing with animals and animal life **2** : animal life (as of a region)

¹**zoom** *vb* **1** : to speed along with a loud hum or buzz **2** : to move upward quickly at a sharp angle

²**zoom** *n* **1** : an act or process of zooming **2** : a zooming sound

zwie·back *n* : a usually sweetened bread made with eggs that is baked and then sliced and toasted until dry and crisp

zy·gote *n* : the new cell produced when a sperm cell joins with an egg

Confused, Misused, or Misspelled Words

a/an 'A' is used before a word beginning with a consonant or consonant sound ("a door", "a one-time deal"). 'An' is usually used before a word beginning with a vowel or vowel sound ("an operation"). 'A' is used before 'h' when the 'h' is pronounced ("a headache"); 'an' is used if the 'h' is not pronounced ("an honor").

accept/except The verb 'accept' means "to agree to, receive" ("accept a gift"). 'Except' most often means "not including" ("will visit all national parks except the Grand Canyon").

adapt/adopt The verb 'adapt' means "to change or modify" ("adapt to the warmer climate"); the verb 'adopt' means "to take as one's own" ("adopt a child").

affect/effect The verb 'affect' means to "cause a change in something" ("rain affects plant growth"); the noun 'effect' means "the result" ("the effect of rain on plant growth").

ain't 'Ain't' is used by some people in informal speech to mean "are not," "is not," or "am not," among other things. Because "ain't" is considered very informal, it is not generally used in schoolwork, or in formal speech and writing.

aisle/isle 'Aisle' means "a walkway between seats"; 'isle' is a poetic word meaning "island".

a lot, allot 'A lot', meaning "a great number", is spelled as two words; it is sometimes written incorrectly as 'alot'. 'Allot' is a verb meaning "to give out in portions" ("alloted one hour for homework").

an See 'a/an'.

apt See 'liable/likely/apt'.

as . . . as Is it more correct to say "she is as smart as I" or "she is as smart as me"? Actually, both ways are correct. In comparisons with "as . . . as", it's okay to use either subject pronouns (like "I", "you", "he", "she", "it", "we", and "they") or object pronouns (like "me", "you", "him", "her", "it", "us", and "them") after the second 'as'. However, subject pronouns sound more formal. So you may want to use subject pronouns in your comparisons when you are doing schoolwork, or anytime you are writing or speaking formally.

as/like Sometimes 'as' is used with the same meaning as 'like' ("do as I do"), ("do like I do"). At other times, 'as' means "in the role of" ("acted as a substitute teacher").

as well as When 'as well as' is used in a comparison, the pronoun following the second 'as' is usually in the subject form ("she can spell as well as I [can]", not "she can spell as well as me"). (For a list of subject pronouns, see 'as . . . as'.)

aural/oral 'Aural' and 'oral' are sometimes pronounced the same, but they have different meanings. 'Aural' means "of or relating to the ear or sense of hearing." It comes from the Latin word for "ear"; 'Oral' means "of, relating to, given by, or near the mouth," and comes from a Latin word for "mouth". (See also 'verbal/oral'.)

bare/bear 'Bare' means "without clothes or a covering" ("bare feet"); 'bear' means "to carry".

bazaar/bizarre 'Bazaar' is a fair; 'bizarre' means 'weird'.

beside/besides 'Beside' generally means "next to or at the side of" something; 'besides' means "in addition to".

born/borne 'Born' is having come into life; 'borne' means "carried".

bring/take 'Bring' usually means "to carry to a closer place"; 'take', "to carry to a farther place".

can/may 'Can' usually means "to be able to or know how to" ("they can read and write"); 'may' means "to have permission to" ("may I go?"). In casual conversation, 'can' also means "to have permission to" ("can I go?"), but 'may' is used instead in more formal speech or in writing.

canvas/canvass 'Canvas' is a cloth; 'canvass' means to ask people's opinions.

capital/capitol 'Capital' is the place or city of government; 'capitol' is the building of government.

cereal/serial 'Cereal' is a breakfast food; 'serial' is a story presented in parts.

colonel/kernal 'Colonel' is a military rank; 'kernel' is a part of a seed.

compliment/complement A 'compliment' is a nice thing to say; a 'complement' is something that completes.

council/counsel A 'council' is a group of people meeting; 'counsel' is advice.

country/county 'Country' is a nation; 'county' is a small, local government area.

data This was originally a plural form, but today it is used as both a singular and a plural noun.

desert/dessert 'Desert' (with one 's') is a dry, barren place; 'dessert' (with two 's's) is a sweet eaten after a meal.

die/dye To 'die' is to cease to live; to 'dye' is to change the color of something.

dived/dove Both spellings are common as a past tense of the verb 'dive' ("she dived into the pool", "she dove into the pool").

effect See 'affect/effect'.

except See 'accept/except'.

farther/further 'Farther' usually refers to distance ("he ran farther than I did"). 'Further' refers to degree or extent ("she further explained the situation")

flammable/inflammable Both words mean "capable of catching fire", but 'inflammable' is also sometimes used to mean "excitable",

forth/fourth 'Forth' means "forward"; 'fourth' means "number four in a sequence".

further See 'farther/further'.

good/well 'To feel good' generally means "to be in good health and good spirits." 'To feel well' usually means "to be healthy".

half/half a/a half a The 'l' in 'half' is silent; it is used in writing, but it is not pronounced. 'Half' is often used with the word 'a', which can either come before 'half' or after it ("ate a half sandwich", "ate half a sandwich"). In casual speech, 'a half a' is sometimes used ("ate a half a sandwich"), but it is avoided in more formal speech and in writing.

hanged/hung Both 'hanged' and 'hung' are used as the past tense of the verb 'to hang'. 'Hanged' is used when referring to execution by hanging; 'hung' is used in all other senses.

hardy/hearty 'Hardy' (suggestive of 'hard') means "strong"; 'hearty' (suggestive of 'heart') means "friendly, enthusiastic".

isle See 'aisle/isle'.

its/it's 'Its' means "of or relating to it or itself" ("the dog wagged its tail"). 'It's' is a contraction of 'it is' ("it's polite to say 'thank you' ").

kernel See 'colonel/kernel'.

later/latter 'Later' is the comparative form of 'late'; it means "after a given time" ("they started later than they had intended"). 'Latter' is an adjective that refers to the second of two

things mentioned, or the last one of a sequence ("of the two choices, the latter is preferred").

lay/lie 'Lay' means "to put (something) down"; 'lie' means "to put one's body in a flat position",

lead/led These two words are pronounced the same, but have different meanings. 'Lead' is a metal; 'led' is the past tense of the verb 'to lead'.

less/fewer 'Less' is usually used with things that cannot be counted ("there is less sunshine today") and 'fewer' with things that can be counted ("there are fewer people today").

liable/likely/apt All three words mean the same thing, but 'likely' and 'apt' are more often used in situations that could have a positive or neutral outcome ("she's apt to burst out laughing", "they'll likely visit today"). 'Liable' is usually used where there is a possibility of a negative outcome ("you're liable to get hurt").

lie See 'lay/lie'.

like See 'as/like'.

liter/litter A 'liter' is a unit of measurement; 'litter' is a messy collection of things.

loose/lose 'Loose' means "not tight"; 'lose' means "to misplace or fail to win".

marital/martial 'Marital' has to do with marriage; 'martial' has to do with the military.

may See 'can/may'.

moral/morale 'Moral' has to do with high ideals; 'morale' is the state of feelings of a person or group ("after the victory, morale was high").

naval/navel 'Naval' has to do with the Navy; a 'navel' is a belly button.

no way 'No way' is an expression meaning "no" or "not at all." It is used in everyday speech, but is usually considered too casual for formal speech and writing.

oral See 'verbal/oral' and 'aural/oral'.

peace See 'piece/peace'.

pedal/peddle 'Pedal' means "to use or work the pedals of something" ("pedal a bicycle"). 'Peddle' means "to sell from house to house".

piece/peace A 'piece' is a portion of something ("a piece of cake"); 'peace' is the freedom from war or fighting.

precede/proceed 'Precede' means "to go ahead of or come before"; 'proceed' means "to start or move forward".

principal/principle A 'principal' is the head of a school; a 'principle' is a rule or guiding truth. It may help you to remember that 'principal' ends with the word 'pal', and that 'principle' and 'rule' end with the same two letters.

serial See 'cereal/serial'.

set/sit The verb 'set' means "to place (something) down or to arrange or make settled" ("set the date"); 'sit' means "to rest on the part of the body where the hips and legs join".

stationary/stationery Something that is stationary stands still; 'stationery' is paper that is used for writing letters. It's easy to tell these two words apart if you remember that 'stationery' and 'letter' both contain 'er'.

take See 'bring/take'.

than/then 'Than' is a conjunction used to indicate a comparison ("better than that"); 'then' means "at that time" ("then we went home").

there/their 'There' points to a place ("there it is"); 'their' refers to "what belongs to them" ("that is their house").

to/too/two 'To' implies a direction ("went to the store"). 'Too' means "also", "very", or "excessively" ("brought a pen and pencil too", "not too difficult", "too much"). 'Two' is the number 2.

used to/use to The phrases 'used to' and 'use to' are often confused since they have the same pronunciation. 'Used to' is correct in most instances ("we used to go to the lake every summer", "I used to know that"). But when it follows 'did' or 'didn't', the correct spelling is 'use to' ("that didn't use to be a problem").

verbal/oral Both 'verbal' and 'oral' are sometimes used to mean "spoken rather than written" ("a verbal agreement", "an oral agreement"). 'Verbal' can also mean "of, relating to, or formed by a verb," or "of, relating to, or consisting of words." (For more about 'oral,' see 'aural/oral'.)

want See 'won't/want'.

were/we're 'Were' is a past tense verb form of 'be' ("they were very young"); 'we're' is a contraction of 'we are' ("we're glad to see you").

who's/whose The word 'who's' is a contraction of 'who is' ("who's there?"); 'whose' is an adjective indicating ownership or quality ("whose book is this?")

who/whom 'Who' is used as the subject of a clause (where one would use 'he', 'she', or 'they'). 'Whom' is used as the object of a clause (where one would use 'him', 'her', or 'them'), and often follows prepositions like 'to', 'for', 'from', or 'with'. Subject: "Who is coming to the party?" "He is coming to the party." Object: "John is coming with whom?" "John is coming with them."

won't/want 'Won't is a contraction of 'will not' ("I won't go"); 'want' is a verb meaning "to need or desire" ("do you want some milk?").

Xmas 'Xmas' is a shortened form of the word 'Christmas'; the 'X' comes a Greek letter which is the first letter of the Greek word for 'Christ'. 'Xmas' is used in very casual writing, but is inappropriate for formal writing or schoolwork.

your/you're 'Your' is an adjective meaning "that which belongs to you" ("is that your sister?"). 'You're' is a contraction of 'you are' ("you're going, aren't you?").

Ten General Spelling Rules

1) In general, 'i' comes before 'e' except after 'c' or in words like 'neighbor' and 'weigh'.

2) Words that end in a /seed/ sound: 'supersede' is the only word ending in 'sede'; 'exceed', 'proceed', and 'succeed' are the only three words ending in 'ceed'; all others end in 'cede'.

3) Words ending in a hard 'c' sound usually change to 'ck' before adding 'e', 'i', or 'y': picnic → picnicked, picnicking but picnics.

4) Words ending in a stressed single vowel + single consonant usually double the consonant before a suffix: abet → abetted, abetting; begin → beginner.

5) Words ending in silent 'e' usually drop the 'e' before a suffix that begins with a vowel but not before a suffix beginning with a consonant: bone → boned, boning but boneless.

6) Words ending in stressed 'ie' usually change to 'y' before a suffixal 'i': die → dying.

7) Words ending in a double vowel usually remain unchanged before a suffix: agree → agreeable; blue → blueness; coo → cooing. In forming plurals, words ending in 'ss' usually add 'es'

8) Words ending in a consonant plus 'y' usually change the 'y' to 'i' before a suffix: beauty → beautiful; happy → happiness.

9) Words ending in a vowel plus 'y' usually do not change before a suffix: boy → boys; enjoy → enjoying.

10) Words ending in 'll' usually drop one 'l' when adding another word to form a compound: all + ready → already; full + fill → fulfill; hate + full → hateful.

Ten Rules for Forming Plurals

1) Most nouns form the plural by adding 's'. bag → bags.

2) Words that end in silent 'e' usually just add 's': college → colleges.

3) Nouns ending in 's', 'x', 'z', 'ch', and 'sh' usually add 'es': hush → hushes; church → churches; buzz → buzzes.

4) Words ending in a consonant + 'y' usually change the 'y' to 'i' and add 'es': army → armies; sky → skies.

5) Words ending in a vowel + 'y' usually add 's' with no change: bay → bays; boy → boys; key → keys.

6) Words ending in a vowel + 'o' usually add 's' with no change: duo → duos; studio → studios.

7) Words ending in a consonant + 'o': some add 's' and some add 'es': ego → egos; piano → pianos; echo → echoes; tomato → tomatoes.

8) Words ending in 'f' usually change the 'f' to 'v' and add 'es': leaf → leaves; self → selves; thief → thieves.

9) Words ending in 'fe' usually change the 'fe' to 'v' and add 'es': knife → knives; life → lives.

10) Words that are the names of fishes, birds, and mammals usually have an unchanging form for the plural or have the unchanging form and an 's' plural, depending on meaning.

Frequently Misspelled Words

about	brought	develop	good-bye
accept	build	diction	government
accidental	built	dictionary	grammar
accidentally	bureau	didn't	guess
accommodate	business	die	half
ache	busy	different	handkerchiefs
acquire	buy	dived	hanged
across	calendar	divine	hardy
adapt	can	doctor	haven't
address	cannot	does	having
adopt	can't	done	hear
affect	canvas	don't	heard
afternoon	canvass	dove	hearty
again	capital	down	height
aisle	capitol	dye	hello
all right	ceiling	early	hoarse
along	cellar	easily	hospital
already	cemetery	easy	hour
always	cereal	effect	house
among	changeable	eight	how's
answer	chief	eighth	hung
antarctic	children	eligible	hygiene
anything	choose	embarrass	illegal
anyway	chose	encyclopedia	imagine
apparent	close	enough	independence
appear	cocoa	envelop (verb)	inflammable
appearance	colonel	envelope (noun)	instead
April	column	environment	isle
apt	coming	every	isn't
arctic	commit	everybody	its
attendance	commitment	everything	January
aunt	committee	exceed	judgment
awhile	complement	except	kernal
balloon	compliment	existence	knew
bare	concede	familiar	know
bargain	conceive	farther	knowledge
bazaar	conscience	father	laboratory
bear	conscious	February	laid
because	cough	fewer	later
before	could	fine	latter
beginning	couldn't	first	laugh
believable	council	flammable	lay
believe	counsel	foreign	lead
beside	country	forth	league
besides	county	forty	led
between	cousin	fourth	leisure
bicycle	cylinder	freight	less
birthday	data	Friday	letter
bizarre	debt	friend	liable
born	definite	fulfill	library
borne	dependent	further	license
bought	describe	getting	lie
boys	description	goes	like
bring	desert	going	likely
brother	dessert	good-by	liter

litter
little
loose
lose
lovely
loving
lying
maintenance
management
manual
marital
marshal
martial
mathematics
may
maybe
meant
minute
mischief
misspell
moral
morale
morning
mosquito
mosquitoes
mother
movable
naval
navel
neighbor
nice
nickel
niece
ninety
ninth
none
noticeable
nowadays
occur
occurrence
o'clock
offense
often
once
oral

ought
parallel
parliament
peace
pedal
peddle
people
piece
please
pneumonia
prairie
precede
principal
principle
probably
proceed
quiet
quit
quite
raise
raspberry
ready
receipt
receive
recommend
remember
rhyme
rhythm
right
said
sandwich
satellite
Saturday
says
schedule
school
scissors
secretary
separate
serial
set
sheriff
sincerely
sit
somebody

something
sometime
speech
squirrel
stationary
stationery
straight
strength
studying
succeed
sugar
superindentent
supersede
suppose
sure
surely
surprise
synagogue
take
tear
than
their
them
then
there
though
thought
thoughtful
through
Thursday
to
together
tomorrow
tonight
too
trouble
truly
Tuesday
two
tying
unique
until
usable
used to
use to

usual
usually
vacation
vacuum
vegetable
verbal
villain
visible
volume
want
weak
wear
weather
Wednesday
week
weird
were
when
whether
which
who
whole
wholly
whom
who's
whose
witch
women
won't
would
wouldn't
write
writing
wrote
Xmas
X-ray
yacht
yeast
yield
your
you're
youthful
zenith
zodiac